Balkan Economic
History, 1550–1950

LEARNED SOCIETIES ·

the Joint
Committee
on Eastern
Europe
Publication
Series

Number 10

THE AMERICAN COUNCIL OF

SCIENCE RESEARCH COUNCIL

THE SOCIAL

Balkan Economic History, 1550–1950

From Imperial Borderlands to Developing Nations

JOHN R. LAMPE

and

MARVIN R. JACKSON

INDIANA UNIVERSITY PRESS

Bloomington

Manufactured in the United States of America

Library of Congress Cataloging in Publication Data

Lampe, John R.
    Balkan economic history, 1550–1950.

(The Joint Committee on Eastern Europe
    publication series ; 10)
    Bibliography: p.
    Includes index.
1. Balkan Peninsula—Economic conditions. 2. Balkan
Peninsula—History. I. Jackson, Marvin R., 1932-
II. Title. III. Series: Joint Committee on Eastern
Europe publication series ; 10.
HC401.L35   330.9496   80-8844
ISBN 0-253-30368-0   AACR2
1 2 3 4 5 86 85 84 83 82

For my father and his ideas
—John R. Lampe

For Rodica and her inspiration
—Marvin R. Jackson

Contents

List of Maps

List of Tables

Acknowledgments

The extended preparation of this volume began in 1976 with the selection of Professor Lampe's prospectus for support by the East European Committee of the American Council of Learned Societies (ACLS) and its East European History Project, under the chairmanship of Michael B. Petrovich. ACLS awarded write-up grants to both authors. Professor Petrovich coordinated readings of the first chapters of the manuscript by Professors Peter F. Sugar, Keith Hitchins, and Dimitrije Djordjević. ACLS Vice-President Gordon B. Turner joined Professor Petrovich in arranging for publication. The East European Committee, with Jason H. Parker succeeding Gordon Turner, subsequently furnished a subvention that permitted the full publication of statistical tables more extensive than originally expected. The ACLS logo on this volume is well deserved.

Other readers of the full manuscript were Professors Charles and Barbara Jelavich, Alan S. Milward, Franklin Mendels, and Paul Gregory. They all have our thanks. Responsibility for the entire written text, and for the statistical tables in Part I and most of Part II, however, rests with Professor Lampe. Professor Jackson is responsible for a majority of the analysis in Part III, for all the tables in Part III and in the Conclusion, as well as for designated tables in Part II.

Facilitating the prolonged research conducted by both authors in Yugoslavia, Romania, and Bulgaria were grants from the Foreign Area Fellowship Program, the International Research and Exchanges Board (IREX), and ACLS for Professor Lampe and from IREX, the Council for International Exchange of Scholars, and the National Science Foundation for Professor Jackson from 1969 forward. The cooperation of institutes, libraries, and archives in those countries, as well as in Greece and Austria, made worthwhile these four years of combined research in Southeastern Europe. Of particular assistance were the Serbian and Bulgarian Academies of Sciences and Arts, the Romanian Academy Library in Bucharest, and the Gennadius Library in Athens. Among the American libraries whose resources we consulted, the Library of Congress in Washington, D.C., and the libraries of the University of Illinois and Arizona State University deserve special mention. Valuable dialogues with many American and Southeastern European scholars also aided preparation of the manuscript, although scarcely resulting in conclusions with which all of us could agree.

Publication of this book owes a variety of debts to the University of Maryland, whose Graduate Research Board furnished a subsidy matching the ACLS subvention. The Board also awarded Professor Lampe two summer grants, one for research and one for writing. The Department of History, under the chairmanship of Walter Rundell, Jr., and then Emory G. Evans, extended continued financial and secretarial assistance. Statistical tables were scrupulously reproduced for publication by Carol Warrington and William A. Gray on equipment of the university's Computer Science Center.

Acknowledgment is also owed to Arizona State University for a subsidy assisting in the preparation of maps and tables, and for secretarial assistance from the Department of Economics. In addition, the university provided Professor Jackson with a sabbatical leave and other leaves from normal faculty duties for extended periods of research in Southeastern Europe.

The largest part of the manuscript was typed by Leslie May, Marita Boam, and the Professional Typing Service of Columbia, Maryland.

Maps were prepared by Larry A. Bowring of Bowring Cartographic Research and Design, Arlington, Virginia.

Professor Lampe owes a final debt to Professor Anita B. Baker-Lampe who tendered both spiritual support and scholarly assistance in editing, proofreading, and organization.

John R. Lampe
Marvin R. Jackson

Balkan Economic
History, 1550–1950

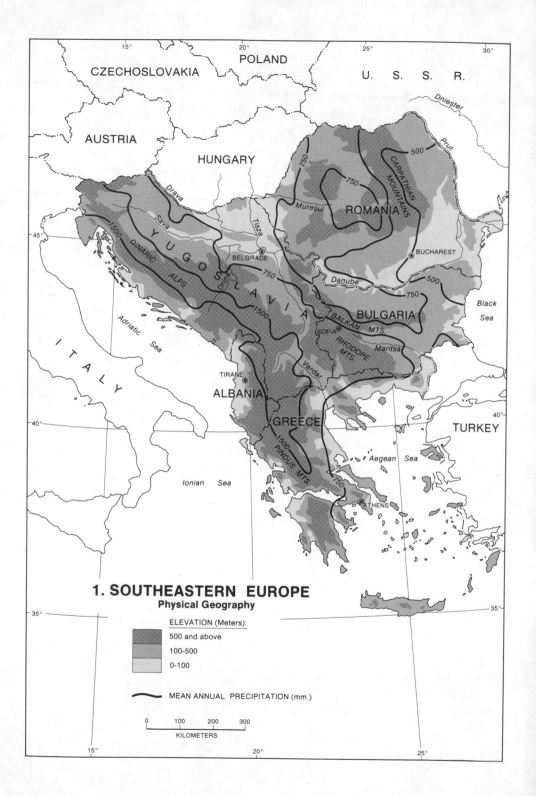

1. SOUTHEASTERN EUROPE
Physical Geography

ELEVATION (Meters):

500 and above

100-500

0-100

—— MEAN ANNUAL PRECIPITATION (mm.)

0   100   200   300
KILOMETERS

Introduction:
Issues in Balkan Economic History

Less than two hundred years ago, the area now covered from east to west by the modern states of Romania, Bulgaria, Greece, Yugoslavia, and Albania was populated by about six million people, largely peasants who knew only primitive agricultural techniques. Disorder and disease threatened the future prospects of the few commercial centers. Now the area supports a population of sixty million, primarily engaged in modern manufacture. Technical specialists from these countries now assist less advanced non-European nations in their efforts to industrialize. This remarkable transformation appears at first glance to be the result of progress since the Second World War, at least according to the testimony of the available statistical record. Yet postwar industrial growth and attendant changes in the structure of investment and employment, however striking, have not been sufficient to move any of these countries into the category of the so-called developed economies in northern Europe, North America, and Japan. Per capita production and income plus the extent of manufactured exports remain significantly lower than in the latter group.[1]

This book will examine the curious intermediate position shared by the aggregate achievements of the private market economy of Greece, the planned market economy of Yugoslavia, and the centrally planned economies of the others. It will argue as its principal hypothesis that crucial preconditions to both the extent and the limitations of rapid postwar growth must be traced from the early modern period forward. The first responsibility of the economist is to analyze significant change. That of the modern historian is to identify and explain continuity. Both will be served in this volume.

1

What follows is necessarily a pioneering work. Economic historians have traditionally concentrated their efforts on the success stories of the major developed economies. Development economists, on the other hand, have devoted most of their attention to the severe underdevelopment and overpopulation that plague much of the Third World. The intermediate cases have been neglected. These countries with a century or more of existence as separate national entities are concentrated in southern Europe and in South America. Their long and varied historical experience argues against any attempt to consider them as a single group. Fernand Braudel's famous effort to focus the economic history of southern Europe, France included, on Mediterranean interrelations stops short of the modern period and the mainsprings of modern economic development,[2] and his tendency to generalize about the entire area only follows a long-established precedent among Western European economic historians. Eastern European scholars, by contrast, rarely venture beyond the boundaries of their own national histories.

Our own intention is to construct a comparative history of the region's several empires and succeeding nation-states in order to connect the turning points in their economic development from the sixteenth century to the present one. A surprising variety of experience will emerge in the process. At the same time, the shared origins and common subsequent experience remain sufficient to justify treating the area as an economic unit. Marc Bloch, the most renowned student of the elusive discipline of comparative economic history, favored such geographic neighbors and historical contemporaries as the best subjects for comparison. Even the chances for identifying crucial differences were enhanced, he argued, because neighbors faced "the same overall causes, just because they are so close together in time and space. Moreover they have at least in part, a common origin. . . ."[3]

Important elements of geographic and political unity in this area best known as the Balkans have long been recognized. Let us briefly review them before discussing past approaches to the area's economic history and defining our own.

The Geographic Unity of Southeastern Europe

We have delayed the very mention of the word "Balkan" until now because its use must be defended and carefully defined. Its persisting appearance as a synonym for political unrest and fragmentation derives from the area's pre-1914 reputation as the "powderkeg of Europe." Native scholars rightly resent this connotation. Balkan nationalism was no better or worse than its counterparts elsewhere in Europe before the First World War. In addition, modern geographers seem agreed in rejecting the old idea of a Balkan Peninsula.[4] Only modern Greece is surrounded by water on three sides. In terms of location even Greece seems best regarded as part of a single European Peninsula, distinguished from continental land masses like Russia by a long coastline favoring trade and a temperate climate favoring agriculture.

But what of Braudel's idea that water unifies more readily than land? His impressive treatment of the Mediterranean as a unified area seeks to include most of Southeastern Europe. The effort founders on his insistence that a line dividing zones of Mediterranean and Central European influence can be drawn through the area. Eminent geographers have drawn too many different lines to mark the northern extent of "Mediterranean influence." They form a confusing mosaic that leaves us with the impression of Southeastern Europe as no more than an intermediate zone of mixed influences from the two larger areas, rather than the Ottoman part of the Mediterranean that Braudel finds it to be.[5]

To reconcile these outside influences with some concept of Balkan geographic unity, we begin with Braudel's own dictum for much of the Mediterranean hinterland: "Mountains come first."[6] The first justification for calling this area the Balkans is that the word means wooded mountains in Turkish. They are the "vertical north" that separates most of Southeastern Europe from the milder Mediterranean climate. It is their predominance across a majority of the area's terrain that sharply distinguishes Southeastern from Central Europe. Their generally modest height and scattered distribution fail to afford the Balkans the natural barrier against European penetration provided the Italian Peninsula by the Alps and the Iberian by the Pyrenees. As described by George W. Hoffman, the preeminent American geographer of Southeastern Europe, a number of "corridor-valleys" through these mountains have historically afforded easy access for people and ideas from east and west,[7] making the Balkan lands a commercial and cultural crossroads. At the same time, he goes on, these mountains have been formidable enough to preserve native particularism and to prevent widespread diffusion of the competing foreign influences. Enough separate ethnic identities have survived to discourage the emergence of one dominant native state, of the sort that has burdened the history of the unbroken plains of northeastern Europe.

To understand the long-term economic implications of this Balkan configuration, we must consider the specific characteristics of the three major mountain ranges: the Dinaric, beginning in Yugoslavia;

the Carpathians in Romania; and the Macedonian-Thracian Massif in Bulgaria. Instructively, as may be seen in Map 1, none of the three is confined to its country of origin.

The Dinaric mountains run from the Julian Alps in Slovenia down the Adriatic coastline, permitting only the narrowest of littorals, to the present-day Yugoslav border with Albania. Their branches turn inland toward the Morava-Vardar basin of Macedonia and also through Albania to continue as the Pindus mountains down the center of the Greek Peninsula.[8] The Greek range is high enough at over 6,000 feet to keep rainfall from the Mediterranean to the west from reaching the otherwise fertile basin of Thessaly to the east. The Pindus section is also distinguished by a nearly complete lack of mineral deposits. The Yugoslav ranges at least contain limited nonferrous metals in Bosnia and Hercegovina and some iron ore and coal in northern Bosnia and Slovenia.

The Carpathian chain begins its famous reverse-s just north of present-day Romania and winds southward to divide the rich, largely blacksoil plains of Wallachia and Moldavia from the less fertile upland basin of Transylvania to the west. The lower half of the reverse-s turns southward across the Danube. There it restricts river passage at the canyon known as the Iron Gates before turning eastward across Bulgaria as the Stara Planina or Balkan range.[9] The Carpathians proper also have the unfortunate effect of blocking off the fertile Wallachian and Moldavian plains from part of the rainfall that the earth's rotation brings in from the west and the Atlantic.

The Macedonian-Thracian Massif reaches southward with several fingers from southeastern Yugoslavia and southwestern Bulgaria into northern Greece. The range known as the Rhodopes is distinguished from the Dinaric in several ways. There are more traversable passes, and more rainfall. The valleys run from north to south with direct access to the Aegean Sea. The valley climate is also mild enough in winter to permit the cultivation of cotton and tobacco.[10]

What general consequences derive for the economic geography of southeastern Europe from this mountainous configuration? We find four.

(1) Annual rainfall in continental Eastern Europe is limited to thirty inches at best. North-south mountain barriers reduce rainfall by a further ten inches in the otherwise adequately endowed agricultural lowlands of eastern Greece, Bulgaria, and Romania. For these areas, recurring droughts are therefore assured.

(2) The relatively poor soil of the mountains and their foothills that cover a majority of the Balkan landscape explains the frequent predominance of livestock over field crops in wide regions. Also to be anticipated are permanent migration into the relatively limited

lowlands and seasonal migration by livestock raisers moving between upland and lowland locations.

(3) The extensive mineral deposits that might normally be associated with so much mountainous terrain turn out to be too widely scattered to afford any of the Balkan states a comparative advantage in developing heavy industry of the sort that huge, neighboring iron ore and coal deposits gave the German Ruhr basin or the Czech lands' Silesian Triangle. Of three smaller proximate deposits of iron and coal, the two in Bosnia and Transylvania were outside the border of any Balkan state until 1918. For the third, the quantity of Bulgarian iron ore and the quality of its coal have offered only a limited base for heavy industry.

(4) The low elevation of most Balkan mountains did provide two advantages over the lands bordering the Mediterranean Sea: abundant forests, with acorns and undergrowth that facilitated the feeding of livestock, and a supply of timber that encouraged coastal construction of ships before the age of steam-powered vessels. But they may also have delayed the age of steam-powered machinery, for the rapid mountain streams provided sufficient water power to inhibit the introduction of steam engines, and enough forest survived to prolong the smelting of iron with charcoal rather than coke.[11]

If mountains come first in our argument for the geographic unity of Southeastern Europe, water comes second. But it is the Danube and not Braudel's Mediterranean that seems most important. Here is the only continuously navigable waterway passing through the area. The river is surely a unifying link between the Romanian Principalities to the north and the other lands to the south, not the northern border of the Balkans as several leading geographers once argued.[12] The Danube connects the eastern Balkan lands with the Black Sea and from there through the Dardanelles with the Mediterranean. Its origin north of Budapest and Vienna automatically ties those two Central European capitals to Balkan commercial development. The river's course from west to east into the Black Sea also serves to connect the Balkan lands with early modern Polish and Russian trade routes to Central Europe.[13]

Looking southward from the banks of the Danube toward the Mediterranean we must agree with David Mitrany that this is "a continental waterway . . . more cut off from sea outlets by mountain barriers than any other of the great rivers."[14] Only the Greek lands were not bordered by the river, and only they had direct access to the Mediterranean. The failure of the Ottoman Empire to impose a compact, unitary administration on a territory so open to the north and a population so scattered along the long west to east course of the Danube can thus be understood more easily. So too, perhaps, can the failure of any single Balkan state to dominate the entire region. All the Balkan capital cities except Athens were either exposed to European penetration from the Danube or isolated in mountainous terrain inland.

Patterns of Political Development

Whatever its failings as a unitary state, and partly because of them, the Ottoman Empire provides the first justification for positing a common pattern of political development throughout these "wooded mountains"—the Balkans. The Turkish word seems an appropriate political as well as geographic description for a region under the hegemony of an essentially Turkish empire based in Istanbul from 1453, a hegemony more comprehensive than the preceding Byzantine one since it held most of Southeastern Europe, save the western Yugoslav lands, under its direct or indirect control from the sixteenth until the eighteenth century. The Empire's growing military weakness merely allowed another imperial power, the Habsburg monarchy, to extend its territorial limits to the Sava River in the south and to the Carpathian mountains in the east after 1800.

This long period of imperial domination separated Southeastern Europe from the western half of the Mediterranean, but did not place it in the political position of Asian and African colonies emerging from European domination in more recent times. Ottoman institutions were after all Islamic, Turkish, and Byzantine, not Western European. The Ottoman military presence was in the end less efficient and widespread than that, say, of the British in India. Finally, the Balkan peoples were themselves Europeans. They could honestly look forward to rejoining a cultural heritage, at least its Byzantine variant, from which Ottoman domination had cut them off for several centuries. As we shall see in Part I, important connections to the European economy were already established during the long imperial period.

Serbia, Greece, and Romania had achieved largely autonomous governments by the early 1860s. They were accorded formal independence in 1878, when northern Bulgaria won substantial autonomy. All four endured with unchanged borders and largely homogeneous ethnic populations from 1886 until the First World War. These new nation states provide the framework for Part II. Their growing political independence and modern, national ambitions, accompanied by underdeveloped economies based on peasant agriculture and yet tied to the wider European market, make them the first "developing nations." Like their many counterparts since the

Second World War, they are distinguished as much by aspirations to move rapidly toward the standards of the developed economies as by their distance from them.[15] Unlike their more recent counterparts, however, the new Balkan states were located on the immediate periphery of the European market. They faced cultural agonies but not ones equal to those of the Third World in borrowing European practices and knowledge. They never matched the record of the Scandinavian countries on the northern periphery. The Balkan states nonetheless achieved their intermediate position between the developed and underdeveloped economies by the start of the First World War.

The term "modernization" seems best suited to encompass the rapid institutional growth experienced by the four Balkan states between 1860 and 1914. This American term captures the important political and economic changes that can precede and indeed set the stage for modern industrial development.[16] We do not shrink from grappling with the implied interrelation between political and economic patterns. We do, however, regard them as simultaneous and partly independent processes. We reject their oversimplified arrangement into a stage theory in which one moves the other and the rest of society through a fixed set of predictable phases.

An enlarged Romania and Greece, a slightly smaller Bulgaria, and the new states of Yugoslavia and Albania emerged in the wake of the First World War. They provide the political focus for Part III of this volume. Their borders have remained largely unchanged to the present. Their ethnic and religious composition now becomes more mixed, their definition of a single national purpose thus more difficult. The disappearance of the Ottoman and Habsburg Empires has left the redefined Balkan states to confront the more powerful political influence and more developed economies of Germany and, since 1945, the Soviet Union. Internally, the political centralization and state-sponsored industrial growth which Marxist-Leninist regimes brought to all the Balkan states save Greece have been anticipated in the interwar period far more than is generally recognized. Part III undertakes the overdue assignment of treating the economic history of the interwar and two wartime eras as related preludes to the present postwar period, instead of separating them as Western and Eastern scholars have typically done.

Past Approaches to Balkan Economic History

Most scholarship dealing specifically with Balkan economic history has been written since the Second World War. Well aware of the need to explain the origins of modernization, the Marxist bulk of this work rejects the primacy of political leaders or institutions. The native Marxist scholars of postwar Bulgaria, Romania, and Yugoslavia have emphasized instead the primacy of economic institutions and class interests. Economic history has enjoyed pride of place in the academic communities of all Balkan countries except Greece for more than thirty years. This generally younger group of scholars has written more on this subject than all foreign observers and the previous native generations combined.[17] In doing so, they have displayed the devotion to extensive use of primary sources and to careful footnoting that has always marked the best Marxist scholarship. We welcome the recent tendency at least for the pre-1914 period to include all available data, regardless of whether they conform to the ideological interpretation provided by the introductory or concluding chapters. Without this body of conscientious endeavor, we would not feel it possible to write this book. Indeed, one purpose of the present volume is to draw Western attention to this recent research. It would otherwise remain inaccessible except for its rare translation into a Western language.

At the same time, we cannot honestly proceed without facing a less comfortable question. What assumptions lie behind this Marxist interpretation? We cannot share them when stated in their most rigorous terms. Running through the following list of unacceptable assumptions is one overriding premise: the dialectical struggle between the technical mode of production and property relations that pits capital against labor and creates the correspondingly antagonistic classes of bourgeoisie and proletariat. The inevitable victory of the mode of production makes technology the determining or independent variable. It draws the bourgeoisie ahead to its initial triumph over the previously feudal, landlord-dominated society. New factories hire the industrial proletariat that will eventually grow too numerous and too desperate for the new bourgeois society to contain.

Four more specific assumptions have been applied by dogmatic Marxist analysis to Balkan economic history:

(1) The Eurocentric view that the conditions for Balkan economic development began from the lowest possible level because the Ottoman state was a barbaric Oriental despotism, denying the existence of private property and thus precluding any capitalist tendencies before that state's dissolution.

(2) The assumption that the one essential prerequisite to capitalist development is the primitive accumulation and concentration of capital for future industrial investment in the hands of the rising bourgeoisie through the transfer of existing artisan or peasant assets. Most typically this transfer occurs as in the English enclosure

movement through the speculative purchase of peasant land on unfair terms.

(3)   The idea that subsequent modernization is essentially the history of private capitalist manufacturing as it grows according to the
labor theory of value, that is through the exploitation of workers paid
subsistence wages to produce goods sold for their substantially
higher market value. The same labor theory of value dooms the system to inevitable collapse, as the rate of labor exploitation must be
increased beyond the workers' endurance to compensate for the
growing "organic," i.e., non-labor and therefore non-exploitable,
composition of capital. Excluded from this assumption is any independent role for the state. It and all other institutions are mere
"committees for managing bourgeois affairs."[18]

(4)   The view that no comparative study of modernization need be
undertaken because the English case affords a universal model.[19]
Only a series of artificial barriers has kept the Balkans from undertaking the primitive accumulation of capital that began in Western
Europe during the early modern period. Preventing the otherwise
inevitable advance into full-scale industrialization were despotic Ottoman, feudal Habsburg, and imperialistic European restrictions.[20]

The Marxist historians of Southeastern Europe have in recent
years recognized that the first three of these four assumptions can be
relaxed without leaving the Marxist mainstream. This relaxation in
turn makes it possible for non-Marxist economic historians to learn
much more from their work than from the schematic orthodoxy of the
immediate postwar period. Let us review these relaxed assumptions:

(1)   The more complex and commercial nature of the Ottoman
Empire, even its modernizing aspects, is now acknowledged, including the extensive primary research by Turkish scholars.[21] The Ottoman Empire is now identified as a variety of disintegrating feudal
state, at least an improvement over Marx's original idea of an un-
changing Oriental despotism.

(2)   The means of primitive capital accumulation are recognized to
include not only the direct transfer of property but also the profits of
commercial exchange or lending and the state's borrowing on tax
revenues. This broader view may be found in Marx's own writings
and the best Soviet scholarship.[22] It also coexists much more com-
fortably, as we shall see, with the absence of significant land transfers from peasantry to bourgeoisie in most of the Ottoman Balkans
and at least two of the new nation states, Serbia and Bulgaria.

(3)   The emergence of independent Balkan states and subsequent
modernization to 1945 are no longer explained solely in terms of
capitalist manufacturing and the resulting bourgeois institutions. Although never explicitly admitted, this recognition of separate impor-

tance for the new national governments and for an emerging national consciousness may be seen in their dominant place and positive treatment in recent Balkan economic historiography.[23]

The most conspicuous shortcoming of this recent work is not methodological. It is the avoidance of a wider regional approach. Like most of their European colleagues, native Balkan scholars have concentrated on their own national experience within limited periods of time. Diplomatic considerations, even among neighboring Communist states, doubtless bear some responsibility. In addition, the agenda of unfinished archival research in all Balkan countries is large enough, especially in non-Communist Greece, and work done in the last thirty years impressive enough, especially in the Communist states, to justify some of the narrowness to date.

American economists are the one body of scholars outside of Southeastern Europe to have shown a continuing postwar interest in the area. Yet they have rarely gone beyond the narrow national focus of native scholarship in treating the area's economic history. Most work deals only with the period since the First World War and concentrates on a single country.[24]

Two major exceptions to this tendency deserve mention. One seeks to relate the aggregate record of pre-1914 Bulgarian industry to at least the interwar period. The other compares the industrial development of all four pre-1914 Balkan states. Both reject classic industrial capitalism, that is, the English model of the decentralized rise of private manufacturing, as a necessary first stage. Their alternatives rely on a largely institutional theory of economic change.

Alexander Gerschenkron, the late dean of American economic historians of Eastern Europe, is perhaps best known for his argument that substitutes are required for Marx's spontaneous processes of primitive and industrial accumulation of capital, if any backward economy is to overcome the obstacles to industrialization. To telescope these processes into the same period and to launch an industrial spurt big enough to sustain itself, Gerschenkron argues, a relatively backward economy such as mid-nineteenth-century Germany had to rely on new and aggressive investment banks. A more backward economy, as possessed by late nineteenth-century Russia, had to rely on government investment and initiative. Gerschenkron applies this approach to a chapter-length study of Bulgarian economic development from 1878 to 1939. He identifies and seeks to explain the slow growth of industrial output and productivity between 1909 and 1939.[25] Whatever the limitations of its conclusions, his study nonetheless remains valuable for examining the available quantitative evidence on Bulgarian industry and for emphasizing the extraordinary effort that would have been required to industrialize more rapidly.

In *The State and Economic Development in Eastern Europe,* Nicholas Spulber has given us the one comparative study of the pre-1914 Balkan states by a Western economist. It is unfortunately confined to a single chapter, accompanied but not integrated with others on the interwar and postwar periods. The postwar analysis is, not surprisingly, pessimistic about the prospects for economic development under socialism. It draws on data from no later than 1957. Like Gerschenkron, Spulber uses only aggregate data from 1910–1913 to analyze industrial development over the entire period from 1878 to 1914.[26] His stress on the state's role still performs the same service as does Gerschenkron, however, in pulling Western economic historians away from their own dogmatic tradition. Their emphasis on private, spontaneous growth as the only path to successful industrialization had been reinforced by the interwar problems of the Soviet economy and Nazi Germany's wartime failures. The more recent economic history of Eastern Europe furnishes massive evidence of centrally planned growth.

A Comparative Focus: Modern Economic Development

Our own intention is to expand Spulber's comparative focus beyond industry and back before the twentieth century. Yet we do not feel the need to prepare the several volumes it would take to describe and analyze every aspect of Balkan economic history from the sixteenth century to the present. We concentrate instead on the mainsprings of the modern development that make Balkan economic history relevant to the aspirations of today's non-European nations.

Development is usually defined as a sustained increase in real per capita income accompanied by the structural changes needed to make such growth self-sustaining. Simon Kuznets draws on his unparalleled research into the measurement of economic growth to offer a broader definition: "a long-run rise in capacity to supply increasingly diverse economic goods to [the] population . . . based on advancing technology and the institutional and ideological adjustments that it demands."[27] This rendering can accommodate the several centuries of commercial growth and institutional change that preceded and indeed preconditioned the last decades of rapid growth in total output per capita and productivity per input. Coming long before these hallmarks of modern economic growth and attendant structural changes like urbanization were less quantifiable but important changes in goods marketed and occupations pursued. Parts I and II will attempt to identify important changes and explain their interaction with first the imperial and then the national institutions affecting the Balkan economies.

We find no present basis in available and reliable data for pushing back the tenuous estimates of total production and income from the early twentieth century even into the nineteenth.[28] The familiar aggregates of national income and product are therefore left principally to Part III and its evaluation of the post-1914 period. For the pre-1914 period, the first two parts nonetheless quantify enough of the institutional growth and enough of the market relations shaping the factors of production to provide a more precise notion of overall economic change than any previous study.

Among the factors of production, our emphasis will rest on capital and entrepreneurship as the cutting edge of commercial and then industrial growth. Land and other natural resources seem better understood as parameters determining the limits within which growth may or may not take place. The size and skills of the labor force appear to be similarly passive, growing in response to some combination of already advancing industrialization and of improving public services for health and education. The traditional Marxist stress on a reserve supply of surplus labor to depress wages and inflate profits is thereby rejected, along with its recent non-Marxist restatement by Sir Arthur Lewis for largely agricultural economies. The number of workers actually transferred from agriculture in the early stages of industrialization remains too small historically to bear the weight of this approach.[29] We also reject the immediate postwar emphasis of American economists on the quantity of capital investment alone. Subsequent research with such capital/output ratios has questioned their usefulness in explaining the English Industrial Revolution. Injections of investment have in more recent Western experience played a smaller part in rapid growth than the increasing productivity of both capital and labor.[30] Hence our inclusion of entrepreneurship with capital in order to capture the crucial contribution to productivity of aggressive and efficient management, whether public or private.

Three more conceptual emphases further narrow the scope of the chapters that follow. The resulting focus will, it is hoped, be sharp enough to permit meaningful comparisons between the various experiences of a number of eventually national economies across several centuries. For the pre-1914 chapters in particular, comparisons using similarities to identify general trends and differences to isolate exceptional cases can serve as a substitute for missing statistical aggregates.

The first of these emphases is institutional continuity. For Part I, we resist the Marxist tendency to describe Ottoman and Habsburg institutions as simply "pre-capitalist" or "feudal." Nor is their subsequent change only "dissolution in the face of capitalist forces." The original Ottoman system of land tenure does not lend itself to designation as feudal. The Western phrase "command economy," with its connotation of centralized government control of production and full access to any surplus for supporting the state, seems to fit far better. Only in the subsequent decay of this Ottoman system did feudal features appear, and then *alongside* an emerging market economy and the survival of customary peasant agriculture.

For Parts II and III, we stop short of rejecting all distinction between "capitalist" institutions until the Second World War and "socialist" ones except in Greece afterwards. Some important differences obviously exist. At the same time, too strict a dichotomy between Balkan capitalism and socialism obscures the continuity across the last century of powerful government institutions and nationalistic ideologies. Bourgeois influence before 1945 and the dominance of Marxist-Leninist principles since then limit but hardly destroy this continuity. A preference for economic self-sufficiency, experience with state-owned or regulated enterprises, and restrictions on foreign capital and entrepreneurship had all appeared in the Balkan states by the early twentieth century. Thus did the command economy re-emerge under the auspices of the modernizing nation-state rather than of the military empire. The mixed record of these more recent public policies and institutions, both in promoting and in hindering modern economic development, needs to be sorted out with as few preconceptions as possible.

Our second emphasis derives from the absence of any Balkan state large enough to approach economic self-sufficiency on the Russian pattern. From the early modern period of Ottoman domination forward, European markets and influence set further boundaries within which the Balkan economies were obliged to operate. We are dealing, in short, with open rather than closed economies, with market traditions that date back as far as those of command and custom. Part I examines the nature of the shift from Ottoman to Central European markets. Parts II and III go on to consider the Balkan record and potential for growth led by rising grain exports and an increasing peasant population.

International influences should not be exaggerated. The Western neoclassical approach to primary exports as an "engine of growth" will be found wanting as a blueprint for Balkan development. So will the concept of colonialism, broadly defined by Wallerstein and others to include any enclave economy entirely dependent on the European core-states, as a blueprint for underdevelopment.[31] We join our Marxist colleagues in Southeastern Europe to stress the internal responses to relatively strong but not always irresistible external pressures. We differ with them most prominently on the extent of foreign penetration. Balkan primary exports to European markets admittedly boomed before 1914. Yet the amount of European capital investment and entrepreneurial interest they generated was too small and its distribution too skewed toward state loans to generate the aggregate foreign profits that the Leninist argument assumes. On the other hand, these exports also failed to promote the native economic growth that the neoclassical argument posits.

Our final conceptual emphasis deserves special stress. It is to shift the focus of the book from trade and agriculture to industry by the start of the twentieth century, well in advance of the rapid industrialization and structural change since 1950. According to Simon Kuznets' comprehensive calculations, such rapid growth may have been encouraged but has never been historically sustained by primary production. Even such noted agricultural economies as Denmark and New Zealand have generated less than 15 percent of their national product as unprocessed goods during the postwar period. We join Kuznets, moreover, in arguing that modern technology is simply "not compatible with the rural mode of life."[32]

PART I.

New Markets in the Old Empires, from the Sixteenth to the Nineteenth Centuries

John R. Lampe

The Ottoman and Habsburg states were large, overland empires which managed, by means of military force and enlightened despotism, to hold together their diverse nationalities well into the modern era of the nation-state, beginning with the French Revolution. Yet the middle of the nineteenth century found over half of Southeastern Europe still divided between the two empires, as it had been for three hundred years. Imperial orbits also pulled on the rest of the area, with the possible exception of Greece.

What preconditions to national economic development appeared in these imperial borderlands? "None" is not a correct answer, despite the absence of industrialization or even of sustained demographic and agricultural growth. Significant, widespread increases in population and in cultivated area admittedly occurred only at the beginning and at the end of this period spanning three centuries. In between, however, rural and urban settlement shifted geographically, albeit without greatly expanding. Peasants and artisans migrated in response to wartime pressures and peacetime opportunities. Labor and entrepreneurship, minus much capital, thus shifted laterally and existing commercial skills spread more widely. Trade outside the local market grew repeatedly if not continuously or quantifiably.

The influences of the two neighboring empires largely determined the dynamics of this growing trade and shifting population. The intersection and overlapping of their orbits shaped most of the commercial growth and structural change surveyed in Part I. The simple model of capitalistic "core-states" rising through commercial exploitation of peripheral areas, recently posited by Immanuel Wallerstein as the basis for pre-industrial growth in Western Europe, will not help us here.[1] The presence of Western European interests in the Balkans is simply too small in this period, again excepting Greece. The Ottoman and Habsburg empires are instead the decisive "core-states." The borderlands that lay between them became a periphery for both empires.

The rising trade and migration within or between the empires provided the commercial nexus around which the modern nation-states of Southeastern Europe would emerge in the nineteenth and twentieth centuries. At the same time, the institutional framework bequeathed to the region by Ottoman and Habsburg authorities can hardly be called capitalistic or, as we shall see, even mercantilistic. Both empires left their borderlands a mixture of military and feudal institutions that sought to create a command economy, whether for central or local use. Also prominent was the chance to play one commercial orbit off against the other. People and goods developed the contrary habit of free movement. Peacetime periods along the borderlands witnessed a kind of compartmentalized coexistence between market forces and imperial framework, even when the latter began to weaken, rather than the clear domination of one by the other that has been the more common pattern in European economic history. War interrupted too often for the market to prevail, as in the Western experience. Native peasants, traders, and artisans maintained too much economic leverage, if only their ability to move elsewhere, for the state to take control in Russian fashion.

The imperial Ottoman framework began the sixteenth century at the height of its strength in the Balkan lands. By 1529, its military forces had subdued all of Greece save some islands, moved west to Croatia, and crossed the Hungarian lands to besiege the Habsburg capital of Vienna. Within these wide European borders, its most illustrious Sultan, Suleiman the Magnificent, enforced a system of justice and land tenure that most European states might envy. Trade flourished. Rural and urban populations were growing.

The Sultan's initial concession of cultural and some local political autonomy to each major non-Moslem religious group was based on this confidence and strength. The famous *millet* system extended such privileges to Jews and to several varieties of Christians, including the Orthodox majority. Yet it was only as imperial authority weakened in later centuries that the concessions expanded to economic and wider political areas. Increasing power for town traders and village elders or priests combined with declining central control from Istanbul to prepare some of the way for the early nineteenth-century emergence of an autonomous Serbia and an independent Greece.[2] In the Bulgarian and Romanian lands, native populations found that less Ottoman control initially meant more power for local Turks or Albanians in the countryside and more for Greeks and others in the towns.

Of more uniform influence were the repeated efforts of the Ottoman Empire to defend itself from this decline. Ottoman efforts bore a surprising resemblance to the policies pursued by the national monarchies of Western Europe during the so-called early modern period from 1600 to 1750. Even there, representative institutions and popular participation deserve far less attention than the efforts of the central government to consolidate executive powers.

Recent research by Charles Tilly and others suggests that the national monarchies of France and England undertook such consolidation in order to build up the apparatus of government. Royal interest concentrated on creating a large standing army, based on infantry and artillery. Musketry and cannon had made feudal cavalry and medieval fortresses obsolete by the start of the early modern period. To feed growing armies and capital cities, made possible by the sixteenth-century surge in European population, these governments had to extend their powers for taxing the agricultural production of the peasant majority. The need to manufacture artillery and to pay troops set the pattern for taxation in coin rather than in kind.[3]

The Ottoman government in Istanbul had to concern itself not only with collecting such taxes but also with importing a majority of necessary manufactures. It is within the parameters of these wider imperial interests that Chapter 1 examines the patterns of trade, migration, and settlement along the long, shifting, sometimes violent Ottoman border with the Habsburg Empire from the sixteenth century forward. Chapter 2 then treats the somewhat different patterns that imperial Habsburg institutions set for the western borderlands of Southeastern Europe.

Chapters 3, 4, and 5 separate the Romanian, Serbian, and Bulgarian experiences in the later stages of the struggle along the borderlands. From the eighteenth to the mid-nineteenth century, both the national experiences and the intersection of imperial orbits varied too much for a single chapter to summarize. None of the three achieved the independence of the small Greek state (its economic history after 1830 is reserved for Part II), but each was emerging in its own way from Ottoman domination.

The Romanian and Serbian principalities used the Russo-Ottoman war of 1828–29 to win virtual autonomy. Wallachia and Moldavia shook off a corrupt system of Phanariot Greek rule, operated under Ottoman auspices, only to be marked immediately by the Russian military occupation of 1829–34. Its influences would last longer than Habsburg economic penetration. The Principalities' economic relations with Habsburg Transylvania ironically laid groundwork for eventual union with the Romanian majority there. The smaller Serbian economy had escaped either Phanariot or Russian influence. Its stronger commercial ties to the neighboring Habsburg lands offered a convenient way to begin escaping Ottoman influence before autonomy was achieved in 1830. Afterwards these northern ties became dangerously powerful in themselves.

Of the three, only the Bulgarian lands remained entirely under Ottoman control well into the nineteenth century. Partial independence followed quickly after an abortive revolt in 1876 because of the Tsarist victory in another Russo-Ottoman war. Before the century's mid-point, however, the Porte's grudging concession of local and native representation to improve tax collection accelerated the rise of Bulgarian resentment against Ottoman rule and fueled demands for full independence. At the heart of this movement were not only Russian-trained school teachers but also town merchants and village artisans. The latters' connection to the wider Ottoman market was ironically stronger and more profitable by this time than that of any native group elsewhere in the Balkans, the seafaring Greeks included. Attention must therefore be paid to ways in which the Ottoman economic order came to burden even those Balkan commercial interests that took advantage of the size of the imperial market.

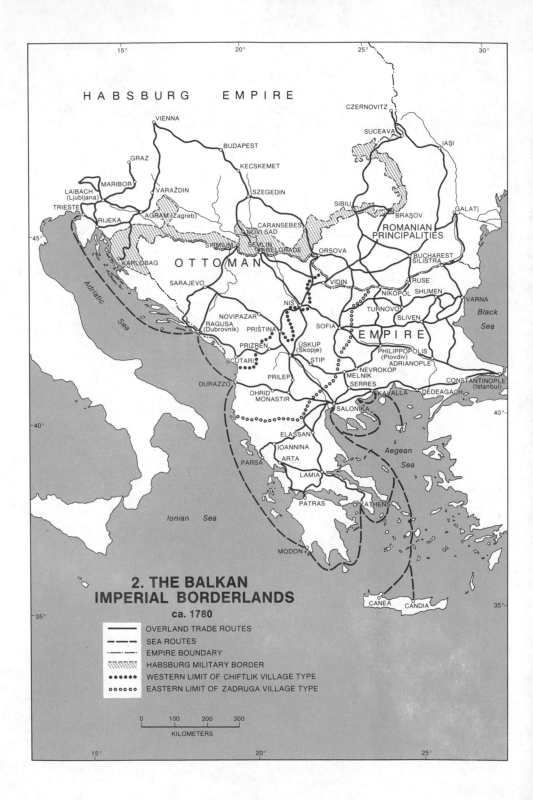

**2. THE BALKAN
IMPERIAL BORDERLANDS**

ca. 1780

	OVERLAND TRADE ROUTES
	SEA ROUTES
	EMPIRE BOUNDARY
	HABSBURG MILITARY BORDER
••••••	WESTERN LIMIT OF CHIFTLIK VILLAGE TYPE
∘∘∘∘∘∘	EASTERN LIMIT OF ZADRUGA VILLAGE TYPE

0   100   200   300

KILOMETERS

HABSBURG   EMPIRE

CZERNOVITZ

VIENNA

SUCEAVA

IAŞI

BUDAPEST

GRAZ

KECSKEMET

MARIBOR

LAIBACH
(Ljubljana)

VARAŽDIN

SZEGEDIN

GALAŢI

TRIESTE

SIBIU

RIJEKA

AGRAM (Zagreb)

CARANSEBES

BRAŞOV

ROMANIAN
PRINCIPALITIES

NOVI SAD

KARLOBAG

SIRMIUM

SEMLIN

BELGRADE

ORSOVA

BUCHAREST

SILISTRA

OTTOMAN

SARAJEVO

VIDIN

RUSE

NIKOPOL

SHUMEN

VARNA

NIS

TURNOVO

SLIVEN

Black
Sea

NOVIPAZAR

SOFIA

EMPIRE

RAGUSA
(Dubrovnik)

PRIŠTINA

PRIZREN

ÜSKUP
(Skopje)

PHILIPPOPOLIS
(Plovdiv)

ADRIANOPLE

SCUTARI

STIP

NEVROKOP

MELNIK

CONSTANTINOPLE
(Istanbul)

PRILEP

SERRES

DURAZZO

OHRID
MONASTIR

KAVALLA

DEDEAGACH

SALONIKA

Adriatic
Sea

ELASSAN

IOANNINA

ARTA

Aegean
Sea

PARSA

LAMIA

PATRAS

ATHENS

Ionian   Sea

MODON

CANEA

CANDIA

1.

The Economic Legacy of
Ottoman Domination

Most of Southeastern Europe began the second half of the sixteenth century as part of a single Ottoman economy. For little more than a century after this high point of Ottoman domination, we find enough uniformity to generalize about the empire's Balkan borderlands. Had this uniform regime lasted longer, we would need a separate chapter on the background to the modern period only for the Romanian lands, not for Serbian and Bulgarian territory as well. Had the regime reached further west, a chapter on the Habsburg legacy to Southeastern Europe might not be necessary.

The centralized Ottoman system that reached the peak of its powers around 1550 had not, let it be emphasized, been responsible for the bulk of imperial expansion. Its mainsprings came from pressures at the periphery rather than direction from the center.

The Osmanli Turks had risen from obscure tribal origins on the Anatolian border of the Byzantine Empire several hundred years earlier to seize the imperial capital of Constantinople by 1453. That fateful year marked the mid-point of a 150-year campaign to conquer most of Southeastern Europe. By the end of the fourteenth century the initial Byzantine use of Ottoman mercenaries against native Balkan princes had already allowed these Turkish agents to become the independent masters of a wide band of territory from Istanbul as far west as Bosnia. By 1521, the European realm of the Ottoman Sultan reached beyond Belgrade in the north and down across the Greek Peninsula in the south.

The exact mixture of motives that drove the Osmanli so rapidly forward remains unsettled among Ottoman scholars. The main religious, economic, and military motives had one thing in common: a frontier mentality, hostile to central control and ready to migrate in search of new opportunities. The religious impulse to advance the borders of Islam derived from no overarching plan by its clergy's established hierarchy. What occurred instead was a fundamentalist merging of Moslem and ethnic values among the Turkic tribes crowding into Anatolia. The faith that emerged was mystic and individualistic. War epics and other heroic tales supported this faith more than orthodox theology. The main economic motive in this Ottoman advance was pressure from a Turkic population that the Mongol invasion had pushed out of Central Asia to the southwest from the twelfth century forward. The rocky uplands that cover most of Anatolia encouraged further movement toward relatively better Balkan land. Military motivation came from *gazi* bands of frontier horsemen. They drew on their Central Asian cavalry skills to pursue the booty and extra land that lay across the Byzantine border.[1]

During the course of the fifteenth century, the Ottoman Sultan found that the frontier leaders of the *gazi* cavalry bands, whose feudal allegiance had been crucial to the first Balkan campaigns, were no longer so reliable. From 1453 he and his advisors were able to use the huge capital city of Istanbul as a base from which to impose a new imperial order on their increasingly large territory. A centralized system emerged by 1500 to administer already occupied land and to mobilize a predictable number of troops for new campaigns. In Istanbul a civilian center to order this military empire had also begun to assert itself. The Sultan's Imperial Council, widely known as the Porte after the place where it met with the Sultan, drew heavily on Islamic and also Byzantine precedents for arranging the new hierarchy. This bureaucratically structured but still military empire provided the economic framework with which its Balkan provinces would enter the early modern era during the sixteenth century.

The most obvious obstacle to economic growth in this early modern empire was the diversion of resources to the army. The agricultural surplus over subsistence needs that is the first prerequisite of modern growth was mortgaged to maintaining the large military establishment needed to expand the empire.

The greatest source of potential growth was the large imperial market. By the sixteenth century the Ottoman regime afforded unprecedented security for travel across the Balkan lands. Unlike the equally large Habsburg market considered in the next chapter, however, the Ottoman Balkans experienced enough political and military turmoil from the seventeenth century forward to dissipate this earlier advantage. The borderlands began to turn elsewhere for trade.

In the midst of such turmoil some change in socioeconomic structure must be anticipated. This change would not follow Marx's
scenario for early modern England and concentrate rural power and
property (and hence control of any agricultural surplus) in the hands
of a rising commercial class. A growing number of Balkan merchants
nonetheless expanded long-distance trade and took economic advantage of the migrations prompted by war and increasing disorder.
Their activities were centrifugal forces, in Oskar Jaszi's famous
phrase, that pulled at the economic unity of the Ottoman Empire
from the periphery.

In order to weigh their significance for subsequent Balkan development, we must first examine the forces that held the Ottoman
economy together when the political authority of the empire was at
its fullest. The internal market aside, these centripetal forces ironically held less promise for future growth than the centrifugal ones
that followed.

The Economics of the Ottoman System, 1500–1700

The military strength that was the cutting edge of Ottoman
authority reached its apex in 1529. Its conquests now included a
majority of Hungarian territory. That year the advance reached the
gates of Vienna, where Habsburg armies were barely able to save the
city. Until the threat to their imperial capital, the disjointed
Habsburg forces found it difficult to resist the Sultan's more integrated army. The Ottoman state was now centrally organized around
the support of its most impressive Sultan, Suleiman the Magnificent,
and his army. Here was a feudal system only in the loose sense that
the government had yet to make the transition outside the major
cities from military to civilian rule. Otherwise, the Ottoman central
government controlled a system of recruitment from outside and
promotion from within that was sufficiently comprehensive to make
the empire at its apex basically bureaucratic rather than feudal. The
decay of central authority, one generally agreed starting point for
European feudalism in the early medieval period, cannot be con-
jured up for the regime at Suleiman's command. In the economy as
elsewhere in the system, the force and extent of command from
above was too powerful during the sixteenth century to permit local
notables to carve out feudal and other customary rights for themselves.

Pushing forward the cutting edge of the army were two economic
institutions designed to maintain military supremacy. The *timar* system of land granted for military occupation and tax collection con-

trolled rural agriculture. A network of guilds regulated urban manufacture. Their two regimes applied to virtually all of Southeastern Europe, save the western Yugoslav lands and the Romanian Principalities. The former were still under Habsburg control; the latter retained autonomy in return for annual tribute to the Sultan (see, respectively, Chapters 2 and 3).

The Land Tenure and Artisan Systems

The Ottoman system of rural administration rested on the state's ownership of almost all land and on the Sultan's grants of responsibility for *timar*-sized sections thereof to selected *sipahi*, or cavalry officers, who had been instrumental in the expansion of the empire. They made up about two thirds of the 30,000 Ottoman troops stationed in Rumelia, that is the Balkan provinces, as late as 1550. Most of the grantees were initially freeborn Turkish descendants of an Anatolian *gazi*, rather than the children taken as *devshirme* slaves from Balkan Christian families and trained for service in the Sultan's standing army, the *kapikulu* or "slaves of the Porte." According to Halil Inalcik, though, the slave-recruits grew in importance during the fifteenth century. By the sixteenth their best officers provided a large fraction of *timar* holders.[2]

Even the freeborn grantees could be removed from their holdings at any time and faced a growing provincial bureaucracy. In Istanbul, the Sultan's Imperial Council came to be headed by a Grand Vizier and supported by a civilian staff. It recruited candidates from the ablest slaves. The Sultan and his Council increased the number of Balkan provincial administrations to sixteen by the end of Suleiman's reign in 1566. The district governors and their military and fiscal staffs had typically worked their way up through slave ranks. An additional branch of provincial government developed around courts run by judges, or *kadi*, who were trained in the increasingly influential Islamic system of religious education. All this put in place a considerable apparatus to hold the *timar* grantees to the terms of their tenure.[3]

From the start, the terms were strict and specific. The *sipahi* had no claim to the land itself; it remained part of the 87 percent of Ottoman territory in the 1528 census that was state land. His sons could inherit no more than a fraction of his income, not necessarily from the same *timar* and only if they too served the Sultan. The father received a small fraction of the land, or better, income grant in return for his personal support and three days of peasant labor a year (native Balkan lords had demanded two or three days of labor a week during the late medieval period). Otherwise, the peasants owed the *sipahi* no personal services. He collected prescribed amounts of their annual harvest, roughly 10 to 20 percent. He typically used this tithe to maintain the several horses and horsemen that his grant obliged him to bring to the summer campaigns. Rather than risk the use of forced labor outside the Sultan's direct control, the grant also directed the *sipahi* to collect certain money taxes from the peasants. By far the largest of these levies was a head tax for the exemption of all adult, non-Moslem males from military service. Finally, peasants might pass on the right to use their part of the *timar* holding to their sons. They could obtain an Ottoman document attesting to that right.

What we find, in other words, is a system of land tenure far removed from the conditions of peasant serfdom, enforced according to the custom of the local lord, that fit the classic Marxist definition of the feudal mode of production. This was instead a system of military occupation, staffed and controlled by the central government. Its closest parallel, and perhaps its inspiration along with Islamic precedent, was the *pronoia* regime with which tenth-century Byzantium sought to secure much of the same territory.[4]

In the towns, all residents except clergy and state officials were obliged to belong to one of a long list of *esnafi*, i.e., guilds or "corporations." A Bulgarian scholar has rightly called these guilds the most widespread social and economic organization in the Empire.[5] Their origins lay in some combination of Byzantine precedent and the Islamic ethics of *futuuwa* that made guild apprenticeship a period of obedience and disdain for wealth. The sixteenth-century Porte organized them into a comprehensive system to control nonagricultural production and to keep the urban population in place. Two means served this end: (1) state leases for all guild shops that prevented private ownership and unauthorized changes in the goods produced, and (2) the *nart* list of maximum prices for artisan guild wares, based on the Islamic code of commercial conduct and generally fixing the rate of profit at 10 percent.[6] Provincial judges and inspectors enforced these regulations. As *timar* agriculture supplied food, the urban economy was thus intended to supply the army with weapons, uniforms, and other equipment for pressing forward on the frontier. Both the rural and urban regimes were also designed to maintain civil order in the interior with a minimum of military forces.

Later Pressures on the Timar and Guilds

As the sixteenth century drew to a close. the Empire's rural and urban economies faced pressures that stretched the *timar* and guild systems beyond the limits that either could accommodate. It would be going too far to suggest that a Commercial Revolution ensued;

that phrase now seems exaggerated even for Western Europe. Yet some of the same phenomena associated with the century's several-fold increase in European trade also manifested themselves in the Ottoman economy. The absence of a comparable commercial or banking tradition, barred by an Islamic legal code increasingly isolated from secular influences, lessened their impact. Missing as well was the increased central power that the English and French monarchies could claim by 1600.[7] A progressive decline in the Sultan's authority is generally dated from Suleiman's death in 1566.

Before then the necessity of fighting European opponents had already obliged the Ottoman government to adopt the same reliance on firearms and especially salaried infantry that helped boost the annual budgets of the Western European monarchies tenfold during the sixteenth century. Improved artillery made existing defensive fortifications vulnerable. Smaller firearms then transferred the offensive advantage from cavalry to infantry.

This last change could not fail to undermine the position of the *sipahi*. Their ranks were already thinning as wars on the European and Persian fronts took a heavy toll. From a total of 63,000 officers holding *timar* throughout Southeastern Europe and perhaps 200,000 all together in 1475, the number of *sipahi* began to decline in the second half of the sixteenth century. By 1630 the total had fallen to 40,000 and those on Balkan *timar* to 8,000.[8] The decline of the *timar* system and the several sorts of land holding that replaced it will concern us below.

For now, we focus on the corresponding rise in infantry to nearly 100,000. Moslems entered the Sultan's expanded *kapikulu* standing army as salaried adults and replaced the diminishing slave-levies of non-Moslem youth. By the end of the sixteenth century, the *kapikulu* infantry were recognized as the best fighting units in Ottoman service. Their salaries and uniforms added more than the cost of new firearms to the Ottoman budget.

The Janissary corps of slave-recruits that had originally constituted the infantry were busy elsewhere by this time. First assigned to provincial towns as bodyguards for local governors, they were sent in sizable numbers to ensure public order after the Anatolian revolts began toward 1600. Once in Balkan towns, Janissaries sought to supplement their meager income by the skills which their military training had also provided. They entered and often took over existing artisan guilds, swelling the ranks illegally with their sons. They also took over the collection of increasingly regular money surtaxes, which were now levied on every district household to cover extra military expenses. Fed by these surtaxes, the military share of the central government's expenses rose from 10 to 50 percent in a total budget that was larger than its French counterpart by 1600.[9]

The revised structure of the Ottoman army was not the only source of new strain on a system of manufacturing principally intended to supply cavalry in the field. As in Europe, rural and especially urban population grew rapidly in the Ottoman Empire during the sixteenth century. A minimum increment of 40 percent seems agreed, although some Turkish scholars argue for a near-doubling.[10] The increase from an uncertain base brought the total population of the Empire to 22,000,000 and pushed that of its Balkan territories beyond 8,000,000. Urban population throughout the Empire is reckoned from the same estimates to have doubled to more than 10 percent of the total. The resulting increase in urban demand surely put pressure on an agricultural system that offered the peasantry no incentive or means to raise its production for the market place. Such demand affected the artisan guilds only by attracting more Janissaries to share in the monopolistic rights and rigid practices that discouraged new techniques of manufacturing.

The introduction of European goods to compete with the limited and expensive production of the artisan monopolies was facilitated by a fateful opening in the Islamic code of ethics. The code did not apply to non-guild merchants engaged in interregional or international trade. Islamic inhibitions did not prevent Turks and other Moslems from playing a more active part in Ottoman trade, especially overland traffic in grain, than once was thought.[11] Moneylending between individual traders added to growing commercial opportunities but, whether for religious or other reasons, did not include the spread of the bills of exchange in which European banking had its medieval Italian origins. The principal source of profit continued to be trade between the commercial centers of the newly enlarged Empire. At opposite ends of its Balkan territory, Sarajevo and Edirne grew rapidly to approach 50,000 inhabitants by 1600. Their merchants were largely Moslem.[12]

In other Balkan towns the Christian and Jewish population, typically a minority, also turned to trade. Their exclusion from the Moslem ruling class and exemption from Islamic ethics pushed them in this direction. Ottoman expulsion of European traders by 1500 created openings for them to fill. The cloth manufacturers of Thessaloniki, Plovdiv, and Edirne sent their wares to Istanbul for sale there or further shipment to the Near East. Returning imports made trade centers of towns with no manufactures to export. Among the latter were Ottoman garrison towns like Vidin in northwest and Shumen in northeast Bulgaria. The future Serbian capital of Belgrade had grown past 50,000 inhabitants by 1600 on this basis.[13]

Ottoman Commercial Policy

We can only measure the growth of Ottoman commerce across the sixteenth century indirectly. Levies on trade contributed a consistently large share of state money revenues that themselves rose perhaps threefold during this period. Among 177 Rumelian, that is Balkan, towns whose revenue was reserved for the central budget, the 45 biggest provided 48 percent of all imperial revenues from Rumelia in 1527-28.[14] An assortment of tariffs on exports and imports plus sales and other indirect taxes on all goods and shops generated about half of the revenue from these largest towns, which were considered the Sultan's personal property.

We may wonder how much tariffs and taxes not only reflected growing state demand for revenues but also restricted the potential volume of trade. The question evades any precise answer in the absence of ad valorem rates for tariffs on local trade and taxes on retail transactions. We may infer that the duties paid exclusively on imports fell well short of modern protectionist rates of 30 to 40 percent ad valorem. Most commercial taxation fell equally on imported and domestic goods. From the mid-sixteenth century forward, Ottoman concessions to France and then the other European powers kept import tariffs from exceeding 5 percent ad valorem in theory and 10 to 15 percent in practice.[15] By contrast, every 100 miles of the overland transport that was inescapable on a majority of Balkan trade routes added 50 to 100 percent to the sales price of all but the most precious imports.

In addition to the burden of longer, overland transport, Ottoman manufacturers faced guild restrictions on cheaper or more modern production.[16] Exhaustive Bulgarian research directed by Liuben Berov shows that prices in silver grams for the principal Ottoman manufactures (textiles and iron or copperware) responded to the increased demand by climbing from parity to double the prevailing European levels between 1560 and 1620.[17] Lagging local production also encouraged competing imports well beyond the power of existing tariffs to deter them. By the time that Janissaries had swollen the artisan ranks sufficiently to bring down the price of Ottoman manufactures during the second half of the seventeenth century, English and French industry was already beginning to adopt the more efficient and versatile techniques that would lead to the Industrial Revolution.

Istanbul and the Ottoman Export Surplus

Despite its relative disadvantage in manufacturing, the Ottoman Empire established an overall trade surplus with Western Europe on the strength of grain exports. This often neglected export surplus had the curious effect of opening the Greek lands to the Mediterranean market while closing off the rest of the Ottoman Balkans.

To understand this first in a series of events that divided the commercial development of the Greek Peninsula from that of its northern neighbors, we must remember the importance to the Ottoman government of supplying its huge imperial capital with food. After a great reduction during the fifteenth century, the population of Istanbul climbed back to half a million by the 1520s and approached 800,000 by 1600. This metropolis, two thirds of the Empire's urban total, would remain larger than any European city for another 100 years.[18] Its demand for grain had soon reached the Greek Peninsula, on whose harvests Dubrovnik (then Ragusa) and Venice had previously relied to help supply themselves and the other Italian city-states. Ottoman grain prices rose with internal and Italian demand to occasion the Sultan's first ban on wheat export in 1555. Then a long series of crop failures around the western Mediterranean pushed French and Italian wheat prices to several times the Ottoman level during the period 1580–1610. First Ragusan and now Greek traders could not resist the temptation of smuggling wheat westward from Crete and Thessaly. Their success was sufficient to cause shortages in Istanbul for half of the years between 1564 and 1590.[19]

The Mediterranean drain on the capital's food supply had two effects. First, it created an Ottoman export surplus with Western Europe that was big enough to start American silver from Seville flowing into the Empire to pay for it. Coins came most often from the French or Italian economies, where silver had been sent to pay for the supplies that Imperial Spain needed for its military forces and overseas colonies. Ottoman wheat prices rose two to threefold over the last half of the sixteenth century, although still lagging well behind the French, Italian, and Spanish increases. More important for our purposes, money to pay for imported European manufactures flooded into the Empire. Its own artisan sector was able to respond to rising public and private demand only by boosting prices, not by increasing production. The greater imports cut into the Ottoman export surplus.

The second effect of the Western demand for grain was to change Ottoman policy. The Porte shifted the supplying of the capital from the Mediterranean to the more easily policed Black Sea. Robert Mantran's exhaustive study of seventeenth century Istanbul reveals that the Porte now assigned areas annually from which the city's grain supplies were to come. The Romanian and Bulgarian lands were consistently put at the top of the list.[20] Only if their harvests were insufficient would grain from Anatolia or the Greek lands be imported. By the second half of the century, state farms had been established not far from Istanbul to provide for the city's royal and military needs. Ottoman authorities allowed private wholesale merchants to fill the far larger requirements remaining. Both the purchase of wheat in the Balkan hinterland and its shipment back to Istanbul became the business of largely Greek and Turkish traders.[21]

Although the Romanian and Bulgarian lands afforded Istanbul a grain supply secure from European demand, they were hardly major producers of artisan manufactures at this early date. During the course of the seventeenth century, the aforementioned limitations of the capital's own artisan sector left Istanbul dependent for the first time on European imports of cheaper woolen cloth and assorted metals, mainly bar iron and copper. The century's several Anatolian revolts had cut off the city from the more distant Arab lands and from India. Istanbul developed an import surplus over exports of perhaps two to one. The deficit could not be met by exporting Ottoman coin. The Sultan had stripped the Serbian gold mines long ago. By 1600 his Treasury's main silver mines, in Bosnia, were nearing exhaustion. Meanwhile, the state budget continued to rise. Expenditures that had tripled during the sixteenth century tripled again between 1630 and 1691, led by a military budget that accounted for half the total. Revenues only doubled during the later period.[22] The resulting deficits added to the city's money shortage.

Under these circumstances, the Porte had little choice. It tried to ban the export of all silver from Istanbul as early as 1584. Failing this, it was obliged to permit the export of sufficient grain and other staples like cotton and silk from the Greek and Arab lands in order to maintain the Empire's overall export surplus with Western Europe. Such exports served to continue the inflow of foreign coinage that relatively lower prices for Greek grain had initiated in the late sixteenth century. After 1620 Greek grain rose too much in price to hang onto the Italian markets that were its main European outlets.[23] Silk and cotton shipped from Thessaloniki, Aleppo, Bursa, and Smyrna to Marseilles sustained the Ottoman export surplus with Western Europe through the seventeenth century.

This French connection was mainly responsible for continuing the flow of foreign silver coins into the Ottoman lands and hence for monetizing their economy beyond the government's desire or capacity to do so.[24] The size of this Western European trade that generated an overall surplus and the capital's deficit is hard to measure before the eighteenth century. Yet the great predominance of French coin and ships over English, Dutch, and Spanish in Istanbul suggests that trade with France was the largest. However successful English exports of the so-called new draperies (cheaper, colored woolen cloth) were in undercutting Venetian sales to other Mediterranean markets, their sales to Istanbul and Smyrna overcame French competition only for the brief period between 1660 and 1680.[25] Thus the general tendency of English commercial interests in the Balkans to lag behind those of the other European powers had already appeared by the seventeenth century.

Ottoman Hostility to European Merchants and the Greek Ascendancy

Ottoman hostility toward all European merchants overshadowed the importance of this French victory over English interests. Again, general Islamic reservations about commercial activity do not appear to have been decisive. What did clearly emerge was a special Ottoman reluctance to deal with infidel European traders in the imperial capital. Internal revolt and the first defeats by European forces had by this time shaken the sense of confident superiority with which the Ottoman Empire had entered the sixteenth century. European traders reported increasing signs of resentment after 1600. Istanbul had never known a sense of colonial submissiveness. The offended pride of its Moslem ruling class was instead that of a Tsarist Russia in the face of similar European penetration during the nineteenth century. Exceeding the later Russian hostility were armed attacks on foreign traders who dared venture into the streets of Istanbul without armed escort. City officials sanctioned excess tariff charges and confiscation of goods. They even threatened protesting traders with imprisonment, despite its ban by the capitulations.[26]

This pattern of hostility encouraged European traders to take a portentous step. They began recruiting assistants for their agents in Istanbul from the non-Moslem, non-Turkish elements that made up 40 percent of the city's population. Facilitating this recruitment were the berât, or exemptions from Ottoman taxation and legal jurisdiction originally granted to individuals by the Sultan. Corrupt seventeenth-century practice placed 50 of them in the hands of each new European consul to distribute as he saw fit to local residents.[27] Consuls had commercial relations as their principal duty and often private interest. The English consul, for instance, was simply the head of the Levant Company's agency. Together these foreigners had come to control most of the Empire's Mediterranean trade. Not surprisingly, they issued their protective patents to groups already set partly aside from Ottoman jurisdiction by the millet system for non-Moslems described earlier.

The Armenians, with their eastern connections and homeland, were the least likely of the three millet communities to attract European attention. The Jews, with their European connections and Mediterranean homeland, were the most likely. Mostly Sephardic Jews exiled from Spain or Portugal, the Istanbul community had quickly established itself in several exclusively Jewish guilds for fruit and drink distribution. They used literacy and linguistic skills to win the position of semiofficial middlemen in the sixteenth-century dealings between the Ottoman government and the European monarchies. By 1600 Jewish private bankers, especially the Marrano family of Mendes, and several arms manufacturers were also prominent in Istanbul. From that time forward, however, the Jewish commercial position in Istanbul began to decline.[28]

Ethnic Greeks most often stepped into the openings first made by these Sephardic families. Although a smaller community in Istanbul than the Jewish one, Greeks had captured a majority of the protected *berât* positions as assistants to European traders by the second half of the seventeenth century. Many had long since established a foothold in the capital as boatmen, ship captains, and even pirates. Their promotion to official positions as *dragomen*, or secretary/translators for European negotiators, began after the success of Panegioti Kikosios in negotiating the Venetian surrender of Crete in 1669 and his subsequent appointment as Grand Dragoman.[29] No messianic movement arose as in the Jewish case to shake the political loyalty of the Orthodox community. Its absence facilitated Greek appointment to positions previously held by Jews. To these official connections we must add private ones with the largely Greek population of the Aegean islands recaptured from Venice. All these ties made the Greeks of Istanbul ideal assistants for Western European traders.

Greeks enjoyed an even better position for bringing Central European goods to Istanbul once a diplomatic agreement was signed in 1665 to permit Habsburg merchants down the Danube as far as Ruse, on the Bulgarian side due south of Bucharest. From there, Greek vessels and a few Turkish ones constituted the most reliable means for delivering such goods to Istanbul.

Subsequent patterns of eighteenth-century commerce would permit the Greeks and other Balkan peoples as well to turn to the overland trade that shifted their international connections away from the Ottoman capital and inevitably away from its influence. Before examining this shift and several related migrations, we must disect the much-discussed decay of the Ottoman agrarian order. Its decline created much of the rural disorder and depopulation that, together with new trade patterns, started the Balkan economies on their separate, national ways, operating in the imperial Ottoman framework, by the end of the early modern period.

The Decay of the Ottoman Agrarian Order

While the main sources of economic opportunity under Ottoman rule were urban, the native Balkan population suffered its greatest exploitation in the countryside. That exploitation had begun with Ottoman conquest itself. Unlike previous medieval struggles between the Byzantine Empire and the Bulgarian or Serbian Kingdoms, the Ottoman onslaught from the late fourteenth century forward destroyed peasant villages and generally disrupted settlement in the grain-growing lowlands.[30] Surviving peasants often fled to higher, safer ground where they supported themselves by raising livestock.

Many returned, how many we cannot say, during the generally peaceful sixteenth century. The above-mentioned restraints on the *sipahi* cavalry officers who administered imperial land and collected taxes under the *timar* system undoubtedly added to the attraction. The system left the Balkan peasant almost a century to cultivate grain in the lowlands on better terms, if not with more modern methods or even greater commercial incentive, than the shifting balance of feudal power between native lords had afforded them in the late medieval period. Then the decline of the cavalry's contribution to the Ottoman army and the end of territorial expansion began to replace this tightly controlled system of military occupation and tax collection with a different, more complex rural regime.

Economic Limitations of the New Chiflik System

The new *chiflik* system of land tenure, if we can call it a system, now emerged from eminently feudal origins: local notables imposed themselves or their agents on peasant villages in return for protection. In the absence of freshly conquered lands for their sons to occupy, the *sipahi* cavalry had begun to defy imperial regulations by the last quarter of the sixteenth century. Their sons joined a variety of Ottoman representatives (mercenaries, Janissaries, provincial officials, and tax collectors, mainly) to create a new rural regime far less amenable to central control than the *timar* system. Although usually based in towns, these Turks and Albanians began to lay hereditary claim to land surrounding peasant villages. The Porte was obliged to recognize their claims. By the eighteenth century some notables, or *ayan*, among this group became powerful enough to usurp all local authority from the Ottoman government and become virtual warlords. This process, if not its exact origins and cast of characters, is well known.[31]

Less well known but more important for our purposes is the limited profitability and extent of these new private holdings, or *chiflik*. Previous scholarship has made the accumulation of capital from these holdings seem so large and the distribution of *chiflik* so widespread that we might mistakenly anticipate the development of capitalistic agriculture. What might be appearing here specifically, so the argument went, was the Prussian and Polish pattern of *Gutsherrschaft*, or direct landlord control of large estates whose grain production for export grew from the late sixteenth century. These northern lords forced peasants to work on their reserves several days a week.[32]

The Bulgarian and Macedonian lands provide the best place to test this parallel for the Ottoman Balkans (hence our Bulgarian spelling of *chiflik*, rather than the Turkish *çiftlik*). These lands were the most secure and best endowed for grain cultivation under direct Ottoman rule. Yet Bulgarian Marxist scholars, from their founding father Dimitur Blagoev forward, have generally stopped short of finding a Prussian parallel to their own experience. Blagoev himself saw the *chiflik* only as a sign of growing "money-goods relationship," i.e., monetization that was spreading the exchange of agricultural for finished goods or money. Subsequest Marxist scholarship has passed from stressing the holding's capitalistic aspects to its feudal ones. Khristo Khristov has rightly called the *chiflik* one of the most complicated and difficult to explain phenomena in Ottoman economic history. He goes on in his most recent work to characterize the typical *chiflik* as accumulating too little capital and using too little wage labor or modern practice to make it a transitional institution to commercial grain cultivation and large-scale export.[33]

The most capitalistic aspect of the *chiflik* was their location. They were almost always clustered around, or on the same river as, a Balkan commercial center. The cultivated valleys near Thessaloniki, Seres, Skopje, Plovdiv, and several river ports were precisely the areas which have been recognized as *chiflik* ever since the pioneering work of the Serbian geographer Jovan Cvijić.[34] They were concentrated, in other words, in the main grain, cotton, and tobacco growing areas of Macedonia, northern Greece, and southern Bulgaria. Only a few were found in Serbia proper, where heavy forest still covered most of the terrain between Belgrade and Niš. By the late eighteenth century, groupings appeared in northern Bulgaria along the Danube, principally around the large ports of Vidin and Ruse. (See Map 2 for a line of *chiflik* demarcation.)

Yet their owners were rarely the native Bulgarian or Greek traders whose occupation and European connections were so clearly capitalistic. The larger *chiflik* in particular remained the property of the *ayan* and other Turks or Albanians who had the military means to protect such holdings from the disorder that had become the rule in the Balkan countryside after 1700.[35]

The commercial attraction of the *chiflik* must be further questioned on grounds other than security. Most holdings were so small in size that they could hardly have yielded a large marketable surplus, let alone afforded significant economies of scale. The original definition of the holding was after all the amount of land that a *chift*, or team of oxen, could plow in a single day. By the eighteenth century the typical *chiflik* in the Bulgarian, Greek, and Macedonian lands appears to have been little more than the 60–120 *dönöm*, or 15–30 acres, that the ten to twenty families in a small village could cultivate by this initial standard. The only holdings large enough to bear some comparison with contemporary Prussian or Polish estates of several thousand acres were collections of 100–200 separate and unconsolidated *chiflik* villages held by a handful of the most powerful *ayan* in the eastern Macedonian and western Bulgarian lands.[36]

Nor was the *chiflik* village itself usually organized in a fashion that promoted the rise of commercial agriculture. In the lowland areas surrounding Plovdiv and Thessaloniki, peasant families were at least attracted from the uplands to work and live on part of the holding in return for money rent, or *naem*, paid once or twice a year. The sum was sufficient to oblige the family to sell the produce from this rented land in the market place, while feeding itself from a small plot provided by the owner. The need to pay money rents helps explain the rapid spread of cotton cultivation north from Thessaloniki to Seres. The fiber earned twice the market price of wheat for the same acreage harvested, once the French and German textile industries began booming in the eighteenth century.[37] This sort of rental nonetheless fell short of the English system of leases, signed as binding contracts with the tenant. *Chiflik* owners were also unwilling to furnish any but the most rudimentary equipment or consolidate cultivation, let alone introduce crop rotation and other improved methods as English and some Prussian landlords had done. Village fields were still divided into family strips; half were left fallow every year and the other half tilled with primitive wooden plows.

The *naem* arrangements were not even the most common form of *chiflik*. They characterized perhaps half of the holdings in these two areas. The other half found itself under the more primitive sharecropping arrangement that predominated on *chiflik* elsewhere in the Bulgarian and Macedonian lands. The owner kept the peasant family from migrating to the uplands and forced it to turn over half or more of its crops on his part of the *chiflik* in return for allowing the family to keep its own house and land, tax obligations included, on the other part. Only in exceptional cases did this arrangement also include landless migrants from the uplands. As in the *naem* villages, they were housed in huts that the owner had built around his residence. Here even the simplest agricultural implements were not furnished. The generally small size of the harvest that the peasant divided with the owner may be judged from the latter's frequent reliance on seizure and sale of peasant livestock in the nearest town for a majority of his income from the *chiflik*.[38]

Crucial to any potential transition from this regime, based on feudal force, to capitalistic agriculture on the early modern pattern would be increasing commercial traffic in land itself, removing more and more from the hands of its original peasant occupants and placing it in the hands of profit-maximizing capitalists. Such was scarcely the case. For the Macedonian lands, it must be admitted, judicial records show some cases of former state land now in commercial circulation. For all the *chiflik* area, however, the same registers show that the monetary fraction of townspeoples' inheritances rose from one fifth to one half over the eighteenth century. Although peasant debts ran as high as half the debts owed to these rising inheritances, traffic in transferring rural land stayed steady and small.[39] Foreclosure on peasant debts continued to be the least common way of acquiring new *chiflik* land.

What were the most common ways? Non-Moslem merchants still obtained their minority of smaller holdings by purchase from Moslem owners of existing *chiflik*. The Turkish and Albanian assortment of soldiers and local officials remained the owners of a large majority of *chiflik* through the first half of the nineteenth century. They themselves acquired new land in ways unconnected with commerce. Khristo Gandev's exhaustive research on the Vidin area of northwestern Bulgaria reveals that new *chiflik* came overwhelmingly from three sources: (1) abandoned state land usually located near a passable road or waterway and formerly the Sultan's personal property, (2) state land bordering established agricultural villages and seized by force from the local peasants cultivating it, and (3) the occupation of empty and unregistered land, often with the need to clear it for cultivation.[40]

The foregoing supports the judgment of leading Bulgarian scholars like Strashimir Dimitrov and Khristo Khristov that the *chiflik* lacked even the potential to become a "typical capitalist enterprise." The very reimposition of rural order that normally stimulates commercial activity checked the spread of *chiflik* across the Bulgarian countryside during the first half of the nineteenth century. Even at its peak around 1800, Dimitrov reckons that the regime covered just 20 percent of the cultivated land in the regions where it was most widespread and as little as 5 percent elsewhere in the Bulgarian lands. No

more than 10 percent of the ethnic Bulgarian peasantry, he concludes, faced *chiflik* obligations.[41]

Predominant Rural Patterns

The absence of any sort of *chiflik* cultivation from so much of the
Ottoman Balkans obliges us to look for other rural patterns that predominated late in the early modern period. There appear to have
been two: lowland and upland peasant smallholdings.

The lowland peasant was less likely to come in economic contact
with a private *chiflik* owner than with a state-appointed tax collector.
As we have seen, the Porte could not rely on the *sipahi* to collect the
Treasury's tithe, the head tax on non-Moslem males and other rural
levies, as early as the seventeenth century. Collection was therefore
farmed out to the highest bidder, under a new arrangement called
mültezim. The winner paid cash in Istanbul for the privilege and
also committed himself to paying an annual amount to the Treasury.
In order to recoup more than his initial payment and later obligation,
the tax farmer came to demand 30 to 50 percent of the peasant's annual harvest instead of the prescribed 10 to 20 percent, hoping to sell
it and keep the surplus. Direct money collections like the head tax
also suffered the same abuse, again without the necessity of a *chiflik*
holding.

The *mültezim* collectors were admittedly the same Turkish
officials who later joined assorted Janissaries, mercenaries, and rene-
gades in carving out private *chiflik* holdings for themselves. It was,
however, the officials' power to collect taxes that provided the vast
majority with their largest source of income. As already noted, local
Moslem notables had begun by 1700 to set themselves up as autonomous *ayan* who bargained as equals with the Porte. Such *ayan* and
also the tax farmers in neighboring districts tended to withhold the
greater part of their revenue from the central government. By the
second half of the eighteenth century the state Treasury in Istanbul
complained that only half of the revenues it was owed from the provinces ever arrived.

Sultan Selim III (1789–1807) and his Imperial Council responded
to such disturbing reports by introducing yet another way of collecting taxes: the *maktu* system so long neglected by Western scholars.[42]
The new system was designed to exclude the existing *mültezim* collectors. All of a village's individual taxes were combined into one
lump sum. The village's native, typically Christian, elders then became responsible for its collection, following a precedent long established in a few isolated border areas as exceptions to the previous
rule. The demand for cash payment pushed monetization further into

the countryside. More immediately, the *maktu* system provided the first rural basis for native autonomy.[43]

The most common peasant response to these burdens of taxation and *chiflik* obligation was to leave the crop-growing lowland village and disperse into upland hamlets. Such hill or mountain hamlets might contain several hundred people, the same number commonly collected in a valley settlement, but its rude houses were stretched out for miles along ridges that were difficult to reach from below.[44] They supported themselves by raising livestock, subject to lower Ottoman taxes and easier to hide even if tax collectors managed to reach the remote locations. Herding was organized around the extended family commune, or *zadruga*, from the Yugoslav lands east to a line running from the Danube to the Adriatic and passing just east of Sofia and Bitola (see Map 2). Patrilocal structure (immediate families of the father and his sons) had limited its size and hence its economic potential from pre-Ottoman times. The unit did provide a force capable of protecting a hamlet from roving bandits and Ottoman mercenaries. This defensive function appears to have been the decisive one in preserving the *zadruga* with little change in size or structure through the eighteenth century.[45]

Their upland location confined most *zadruga* to far less fertile soil than the lowland villages. They could not therefore support the same number of families. This limitation plus growing disorder in the lowlands precipitated a sharp decline in overall Balkan population. From the sixteenth-century peak of at least 8,000,000, the total declined to less than 3,000,000 by the middle of the eighteenth century.[46] Only in southern Macedonia and the northern Greek lands did the urban fraction go up. There it climbed to one third mainly because of peasants fleeing the threat of *chiflik* obligations in the surrounding countryside.[47]

Elsewhere we find population declining even in the towns. The depredations of urban Janissaries and rural warlords were not the only cause. Outbreaks of bubonic plague followed Ottoman troops, largely mercenaries by this time, on their undisciplined way between campaigns against Habsburg or Russian forces. Plague during the 1716–18 campaign decimated the Turkish majorities of the northern Bulgarian towns. Near majorities of ethnic Bulgarians moved in afterwards to take their place.[48]

In the countryside, the impact of the plague on the rate of natural increase was predictably smaller, but the inhibitions to birth from fear and violence greater. Order would not be restored sufficiently to permit a massive return to the lowlands and a sustained rise in rural population until the nineteenth century. The economic consequences of this prolonged disorder went beyond the uncultivated fields and uncleared forests. There resettlement after 1800 would insulate a rapidly rising population from declining per capita returns to peasant agriculture until the end of the century (see Chapter 6). The earlier turmoil also prompted several long-distance migrations northward from the Ottoman Balkans. These movements broadened the increasing flow of Balkan trade away from Istanbul and toward Central Europe.

Eighteenth-Century Trade and Migration in the Ottoman Balkans

The general shift of Balkan trade away from the Ottoman orbit became significant only toward the end of the eighteenth century. Its diversion in several new directions had however originated earlier in the century. The divergent attractions of the Western Mediterranean and Central European markets emerge most clearly from their bifurcation of the Greek commercial network. Its outgrowth from seventeenth-century Istanbul we have already seen. Other native Balkan groups would have to await movements of population to share in and eventually take over exports and imports to Central Europe. This northern trade could begin to grow only after the Habsburg monarchy had driven the Ottoman Empire from the Hungarian lands and pushed their common frontier to the Danube and Sava Rivers in the 1690s.

Thessaloniki and the Greek Commercial Network

Despite the far greater size of Istanbul, the two most important commercial centers in the Ottoman Empire were Smyrna and Thessaloniki. Respectively, they were by this time the premier ports on the Anatolian and Balkan sides of the Aegean Sea. Greek trading colonies came to dominate them both. Smyrna's external trade was twice the value of Thessaloniki's through the eighteenth century. Yet this leading port does not concern us because its huge silk and cotton traffic was centered in Anatolia and the Near East.

Thessaloniki was the largest Balkan commercial center and city of the period. Its trade was perhaps half again the value of Istanbul's; its population approached 70,000; its mainly merchant rather than artisan shops numbered 4,400.[49] The same estimates admittedly find no Greek majority in the city. Sephardic Jews numbered about 25,000 and Turks or Albanians, typically artisans, over 20,000. Then came the Greeks with less than 20,000. This Jewish plurality had nonetheless lost its earlier commercial predominance, like their fellows in Istanbul.[50]

Greeks controlled most of the trade between Thessaloniki and the rest of the Ottoman Empire as early as the seventeenth century. They shipped grain, wool, wine, and tobacco mainly to Istanbul, although many had gotten their start smuggling wheat to Düres (then Durazzo) on the Albanian coast and then to Italy.[51] Helping Greek traders to expand from these uncertain beginnings were the familial ethics of what Traian Stoianovich has called a typically Mediterranean economic brotherhood. Its rules sanctioned the pursuit of profit at any expense to outsiders, even fellow Greeks, but insisted on full loyalty from and assistance to family members. We may speculate that this sort of tight family firm perpetuated the peculiar Byzantine aversion to credit instruments or institutions open to all comers that also characterized Ottoman economic history.[52] With these inner dynamics in mind, let us follow the subsequent expansion of Greek commercial interests.

Connections with family members in Istanbul and points east allowed the Greek traders of Thessaloniki to link up with southern Russian markets. The growing Greek merchant fleet on the Black Sea had seized the Russo-Ottoman war of 1768–74 as an occasion to revolt and demand better access to these markets. By 1783, Catherine the Great had forced the Sultan to relax his ban on Russian-based Greek ships passing through the Straits at Istanbul into the Mediterranean. Vessels bearing the Russian flag were also granted the "capitulation" of 3-percent ad valorem tariffs on exports from and imports to the Ottoman lands. These several privileges had been revoked for the Western European powers in the Black Sea since 1592 and were not restored until after the French Revolution.

Probably more important for the growth of the Greek trading network was the winning in 1774, as part of the Russo-Ottoman peace treaty, of exemption for their Russian vessels from the Ottoman *bid'at*. Ottoman authorities had imposed these extra tariffs on major unprocessed exports from the 1730s forward in a vain effort to promote processed exports. The exemption allowed wine and wool exports from Thessaloniki to the Black Sea ports to increase. In return, Russian furs and iron moved back into Mediterranean markets, where their lower price undercut the Levant Company's sales of Canadian furs and English iron for the rest of the century.[53]

The Greek merchants of Thessaloniki provided the Aegean focus for this expanded commercial network. Yet its connections through Istanbul to the Black Sea explain only part of the port's expanded trade during the eighteenth century. Exports from the Macedonian hinterland also became important. Western European markets were the initial attraction. Although two thirds of the Macedonian tobacco crop was still sent to Ottoman destinations, a majority of the remaining third went to Italy by 1750. Greek agents in Durës on the Albanian coast just across from Italy helped smuggle tobacco and also wheat from Thessaloniki to nearby markets like Venice.

French demand for Macedonian cotton drew the port's traders further west to the booming entrepôt of Marseilles. With wool and tobacco, raw cotton became one of Thessaloniki's three leading exports in the decades after 1750. Cotton from the American colonies fell far short of meeting demand for a French industry that was expanding more rapidly, by some accounts, than English textiles up to the French Revolution. By 1789, raw cotton had risen to about 70 percent of French imports from the Levant, replacing raw silk and the lesser finished amounts from Bursa that had been the Ottoman Empire's one major processed export.[54]

Greek enterprises in Thessaloniki had never dominated the cotton trade with Marseilles, however, and increasingly left it to local Jewish agents of French firms. The latter had in any case developed larger sources of supply at Smyrna, Acre, and Cyprus. Table 1.1 reveals that French trade with Thessaloniki did rise sharply during the third quarter of the eighteenth century but ceased to grow absolutely thereafter and lost its relative predominance by the end of the century. Rising exports of raw cotton, according to the same sources, appear responsible for repairing the port's chronic import surplus in its French trade for at least the 1770s. Even then, as indicated in Table 1.2, Thessaloniki did not account for a major share of French trade in the Levant, let alone of its overall total.

From 1789 to 1815 the long Revolutionary and Napoleonic Wars damaged French interests throughout the Ottoman Empire. First regular trade with Marseilles was interrupted. Then Napoleon's invasion of Egypt soured official relations with the Ottoman Empire. After 1800 the British blockade of continental Europe made the overland routes from Thessaloniki prime avenues for smuggling English goods, now better and cheaper anyway as the Industrial Revolution accelerated, into Central Europe. When hostilities disrupted the land route, as during the Serbian uprising of 1804–12 against the Ottoman Empire, ship traffic from Thessaloniki moved around the Greek Peninsula and up the Adriatic to the growing Habsburg port of Trieste (see Chapter 2). According to Svoronos, French commercial operations suffered permanent losses that transferred three quarters of the foreign trade in the eastern Mediterranean to Greek hands by 1815.[55]

TABLE 1.1
FRENCH SHARE OF THESSALONIKI'S FOREIGN TRADE, 1700-98

Annual average	France (in mil.	Others Ottoman	Total piastres)	France (in mil.	Others French	Total livres)[a]
1700-18	.3	.6	.9	1.2	2.4	3.6
1722-33	.55	.55	1.1	1.9	1.9	3.8
1733-43	.8	.8	1.6	2.6	2.6	5.2
1744-49	.45	.75	1.2	1.4	2.4	4.8
1750-70	1.3	1.4	2.7	3.9	4.2	8.1
1771-77	2.8	1.5	4.3	8.4	4.4	12.8
1778-86	2.2	1.5	3.7	6.0	4.8	10.8
1798	2.5	10.3	12.8			

Notes: (a)Converted from Ottoman silver piastres by multiplying Svoronos' calculation of their real value in Ottoman sequins (to account for the several reductions in the piastre's silver content) times 12, the constant value of the sequin in French silver livres until 1789.

Sources: Nicholas Svoronos, *Le commerce de Salonique en XVIIIe siècle* (Paris, 1956), pp. 107, 319, 387; Felix Boujour, *A View of the Commerce of Greece, 1787-1797*, trans. by Thomas H. Howe (London, 1800), p. 343.

TABLE 1.2
THESSALONIKI'S SHARE OF FRENCH FOREIGN TRADE, 1720-80
(in mil. French livres)

	Thess.	Levant	Total Fr. for. trade	Thess. % of Levant	Thess. % of Total	Levant % of Total
1720		12.1	263.1			4.6
1730	1.4	14.4	207	9.7	.07	6.4
1740	2.6	41.0	362.8	6.3	.07	11.3
1750	2.9	51.3	451.1	5.6	.06	11.4
1760		30.8	291			8.7
1770	6.4	54.3	623	11.8	.10	10.6
1780	5.8	34.4	452	16.9	.13	7.6

Sources: Svoronos, *Le commerce de Salonique*, pp. 306, 313; Vuk Vinaver, *Pregled istorije novca u jugoslovenskim zemljama, XVI-XVIII vek* (Belgrade, 1970), pp. 256, 280; Ernest Labrousse *et al.*, *Histoire économique et sociale de la France*, II, 1660-1789, (Paris, 1970), p. 502.

Macedonia and the Morea:
The Bifurcation of Greek Commerce

The accompanying bifurcation of the Greek commercial network in the Aegean overshadowed the importance for Balkan economic history of this general increase in Greek influence. Earlier in the eighteenth century Greek traders had already begun to turn Thessaloniki away from its French connection toward overland trade to

the north. Before considering this shift in detail, we must note the
separate development in the south of the commercial nucleus for
modern Greece.

The virtual Morean island now known as the Peloponnesus and
also the western coast of the mainland began to break their past connections with Istanbul, Thessaloniki, and Marseilles in favor of Italian and English markets. The majority of French purchases from the
Peloponnesus had been illegal wheat exports until Albanian mercenaries brutally suppressed the Greek revolt there in 1770. Afterwards, stricter Ottoman controls discouraged such smuggling. Up the
western coast to the narrow plains surrounding the ports of Arta in
Epirus and Düres in Albania, the local response was to raise corn for
export to the nearby Italian market.[56] The banditry of rebel Albanian
ayan continued to disrupt the traditional overland routes to Thessaloniki. In the Peloponnesus, similar disorders drove the peasantry
into the coastal hills. There they cultivated vineyards and dried the
grapes into easily transportable raisins. By the 1790s their annual
sale to fruit-starved England, and also Holland and Denmark, accounted for a majority of Morean export earnings. These destinations
recorded about three times the average value of the area's exports to
France even before the outbreak of the Revolution in 1789.[57]

New centers for the overland trade from Thessaloniki north to the
Habsburg border had also appeared before 1789. The Ottoman-
Habsburg treaty of 1718 inaugurated a period of generally safer
travel over these northern caravan routes. Although the same treaty
had accorded Habsburg merchants the right to do business on Ottoman territory, they made little use of the advantage (again, see
Chapter 2). Greek traders moving north from the disorder in the
Macedonian lands took their own advantage. Encouraging them was
Ottoman taxation on overland trade that was less than half the tariff
on goods leaving Thessaloniki by sea.[58] French agents based there
did not dare join the weekly caravans to inland towns. Their fears of
local hostility en route and in provincial marketplaces were apparently justified. Greeks and less importantly Jews and native groups
were thus free of European rivals in nearby Seres, Skopje, and
Prilep, as well as further north in Niš and Belgrade or further east in
Sofia. These towns all became transit points between Central Europe
and Thessaloniki. Their long-distance and especially their transit
trade was most often tied to a Greek family enterprise and always
conducted in the Greek language and according to Greek commercial
custom.[59] (See Map 2 for main trade routes.)

This same Greek predominance also appears to have been the rule
at the fairs that drew outside traders to Macedonian towns several
times a year. The transactions that sent raw cotton by caravan from

Seres to Vienna or Leipzig were usually conducted at such a fair, rather than in a town shop.

One place where native manufacture made noteworthy progress during this period was the Bulgarian town of Plovdiv, south of the Balkan mountains and north of the Rhodopes in the Thracian plain. There, in the usual Greek commercial milieu to be sure, Bulgarian as well as Greek and a few Turkish guild shops wove woolen yarn, spun by Bulgarian peasant households in the neighboring Rhodopes, into the rough cloth known as *aba*.[60] These artisans did their own selling and often traveled along with the caravans. But their destination, as we shall consider further in Chapter 5, was Istanbul and their major market, Anatolia. Hence they played no part in the shift of Balkan trade, southern Greece excepted, toward Central Europe.

This the Greek commercial network radiating north from Thessaloniki had accomplished in large measure. Their families were responsible for conducting almost all of the greatly increased non-French share of the port's foreign trade, as noted in Table 1.1 for 1798, with the Habsburg lands. Central European demand for Macedonian cotton and wool had already gathered momentum when the American Revolution kept the French economy from making its normal deliveries in the late 1770s. By the time that the French Revolution cut such supplies more sharply, Central European textile manufacturers were buying about three quarters of the Macedonian cotton crop and probably wool marketings too.[61]

Major Long-Distance Migrations

Several mass migrations to the north permitted other native Balkan peoples to join the Greeks in creating a growing commercial network on the periphery of Ottoman territory and influence. Their new locations became the base for secure urban prosperity and trade with the Ottoman Balkans. Lowland chaos and upland subsistence were left behind. In addition, the Serbian and Bulgarian migrations established centers, in Novi Sad and Bucharest respectively, that would contribute cultural and financial support to the movements for national liberation in the nineteenth century.

The first Balkan migration to help create the commercial network on the northern Ottoman border started not surprisingly with an established urban center. Neither the Serbian or Bulgarian populations enjoyed exclusive control over a sizable trading town. In Moskopol on the present Greek-Albanian border, the Vlach Tsintsars did. They were descended from pre-Slavic ancestors of modern Romanians. The Vlachs acquired their name from the same root as the word *Welsh*, also meaning "foreigners," when pushed into upland areas by the South Slavs and their medieval empires. As those empires crumbled before the Ottoman advance, some Vlachs still clung to the stock-herding that had been sustaining them in the hills. They returned to the valleys only for winter pasture. Others used their experience in trading livestock to settle permanently in lowland towns. The largest of these towns by far was Moskopol. Its population had grown past 40,000 by the mid-eighteenth century. Its merchants sent agents as far away as Venice and Vienna. Then disaster struck. Albanian mercenaries heard rumors that the town and its Orthodox population of Tsintsars had supported the Russian Tsar's ill-fated Orlov expedition to the southern Adriatic. They sacked the town in 1769 and returned again in 1788. Later the famous Albanian *ayan*, Ali Pasha of Ioannina, finished the job of reducing the town to a pastoral village.[62]

The merchants of Moskopol first moved their operations to Macedonian towns like Veles and Bitola. Many were drawn northward from there. Perhaps 6,000 stopped in Belgrade and other Serbian towns. A larger number continued to follow in the footsteps of Greek merchants north to the Habsburg border town of Zemun, just across the Sava River from Belgrade. They found a few of their fellows already there, sharing the grain and tobacco trade with Greeks. The new arrivals built on this foundation, supported in turn by the special privileges that Habsburg authorities had granted Tsintsar merchants since 1658. They soon dominated trade and especially money exchange and lending in Zemun.[63] With their connections deep in the Ottoman Balkans, the Tsintsars thus provided part of the entrepreneurial impetus for shifting Balkan foreign trade from the Mediterranean toward Central Europe by the end of the early modern period. Eastward Albanian migration contributed further to the transition by cutting into these traders' connections with their original focal point in Thessaloniki. Tsintsars thus joined Greeks in concentrating their activities further north.

In the Bulgarian lands, the origins of eighteenth century migration were mainly rural. Some peasants headed west to Serbia. Most moved north across the Danube to the Romanian Principality of Wallachia. Renegade Ottoman mercenaries and Janissaries made banditry widespread south of the Balkan range by the end of the seventeenth century. Then the Bulgarian lands to the north, more distant from Istanbul and separated by mountains, became the more dangerous for trade caravans and lowland peasantry. Toward the end of the eighteenth century, Ottoman authority had become so weak that the Turkish or Albanian *ayan* were able to seize control of the most active ports on the Bulgarian side of the Danube. Ruse, the Ottoman naval base on the river, was itself attacked in 1785. By 1797 the notorious Pasvanoglu of the Vidin area had taken every major port from there east to Ruse. Bulgarian peasants from these riverside regions faced the threat of *chiflik* obligations as well as violence. They began joining their brethren from the interior in fleeing to Wallachia.[64] Their numbers were relatively small, less than 10,000, especially when compared to the major Bulgarian migrations that later totalled 100,000 during the Russo-Ottoman wars of 1806–12 and 1828–29 (see Chapter 5). These initial migrations nonetheless provided an artisan labor force for the Bulgarian cloth merchants who had come earlier for economic reasons. Together they created Bulgarian commercial enclaves in Bucharest and later Giurgiu, the main Wallachian port on the Danube. These enclaves attracted the later immigrants and built a material basis for cultural revival close to native soil.[65]

The northward Serbian migration of the eighteenth century achieved similar but more rapid results. Movements into the Habsburg Vojvodina had of course assumed major proportions much earlier than the Bulgarian migration to Wallachia. Nearly 40,000 Serbian families, or several hundred thousand persons, accompanied the Serbian Orthodox Patriarch north to the Vojvodina during the 1690s. They fled Ottoman reprisals in the wake of the Archbishop's pledge of Serbian support for an ill-fated campaign against Ottoman forces. These departures plus those of the 1716–18 war were sufficient to leave almost half of all Serbian peasant villages deserted when victorious Habsburg troops began two decades of occupation in 1718. According to the most recent Yugoslav research, the forty years following the return of Ottoman rule in 1739 were marked by an even greater Serbian migration to the Vojvodina.[66] Then the Habsburg-Ottoman war of 1788–91 repeated the cycle of damage to Belgrade and rural violence that had prompted previous migrations. Only now did Habsburg willingness to remove most barriers to immigration facilitate the movement.

These latest departures prompted Ottoman authorities to seek a more secure grip on the Serbian countryside and its potential revenues by introducing the *maktu* system of tax collection by Serbian village elders, or *knezovi*, as noted above. Ottoman success in stemming the northward migration was short-lived. By 1797 territory ruled by the *ayan* Pasvanoglu of Vidin impinged on Serbia proper and attracted Janissaries expelled from Istanbul. The latter soon reached Belgrade. Their effort to destroy the *maktu* system and take over tax collection for themselves was only the last in a series of events that had removed all past benefits of Ottoman rule from the Serbian population by the end of the eighteenth century.

The first of two Serbian uprisings began in 1804, initially with the sole intent of restoring the *maktu* system. In the meantime Serbian migrants to the Vojvodina had established a position in the wholesale livestock trade with the Habsburg lands just across the border in Zemun.[67] The trade permitted support for the uprisings and also offered Serbs on both sides of the river a viable alternative to the Ottoman economy. Just how these *prečani* (Serbs who had moved north of the Sava or Danube rivers) had established their commercial foothold in the Vojvodina will be explained in Chapter 2, which explores the Habsburg economic legacy in the early modern Balkans.

The Economic Legacy of Ottoman Weakness

The sum of the Ottoman economic legacy may be seen as agricultural stagnation and increasing rural exploitation throughout the Empire's Balkan lands, mitigated by commercial opportunity on their periphery. Both bad and good derived from the failure of the Ottoman command economy to keep central control from Istanbul of imperial lands and markets past the sixteenth century. This was more than a military failure. It also reflected deficiencies in the two economic institutions that stood behind the army: the *timar* system of temporary tenure for *sipahi* cavalry officers on state land and a restrictive guild system of artisan manufacture.

The fair collection of agricultural taxes and the maintenance of rural order in the provinces eventually ran afoul of the very representatives dispatched from Istanbul to take over these responsibilities from the militarily obsolete cavalry. Areas far from Istanbul like Macedonia were precisely the ones in which the rights of private property essential to economic development according to the original English model had appeared most prominently. The owners of these private *chiflik* holdings, moreover, owed their property rights far more to armed force and official status than to commercial leverage like debt collection. The very limited sales of *chiflik* land testified to that, as did the absence of any formal code to define property rights for the marketplace.

Such holdings did spread widely, it is true, around large trading towns like Thessaloniki and Plovdiv. But the access of the local merchant community to these holdings remained restricted. Only Plovdiv was close enough to Istanbul to conduct the bulk of its trade with the Ottoman capital. Elsewhere, the strengthening of Ottoman central authority that was needed for greater trade with Istanbul would also have spelled an end to the autonomy that allowed the *chiflik* system to exist.

Peasant smallholdings were in any case more widespread in the rural Balkans. By 1600 an assortment of Moslem tax farmers were replacing the *sipahi* cavalry officers who for almost a century had collected moderate rural taxes and passed authorized amounts along to the Sultan. These tax farmers paid the Porte in advance and found themselves free to collect more than the authorized amounts. This they did with no more means or thought to improve the backward techniques of peasant cultivation than had the *sipahi*. The preference of the former for taxes paid in coin rather than in kind did monetize the peasant economy, especially in the Bulgarian lands, more than once was thought.

Yet such obligations also discouraged peasant settlement in the grain-growing lowlands. Recurring war and disease had the same effect. To avoid the exploitation that characterized their countryside after the sixteenth century, Balkan peasants most often retreated to livestock-raising communes in the abundant uplands or migrated outside the Empire to Habsburg or Romanian territory. In economists' terms, Ottoman military and political weakness at the center kept the Empire from paying the high transaction costs that would have been required to set the rural land and tax regimes in order.[68] Perhaps the greatest cost would have been the destruction not just of local autonomy but specifically of the private *chiflik* holdings that had become the Empire's main source of Mediterranean exports.

In order to restore rural order, however, the Porte would have had to rely still more heavily on imported manufactures. Balkan and overall Ottoman population had grown rapidly during the sixteenth century. So had Ottoman revenues to support the huge state apparatus and toward 1600 to pay the new salaried infantry. Such rising private and public demand had proved incapable of stimulating the artisan guilds to break free from a combination of Islamic ethics and state leasing and price regulations. Domestic production quickly became too small and too inflexible to meet this demand. Imports were needed. Merchant activities that lay largely outside Islamic ethics and Ottoman regulations became much more important than the imperial command economy had ever intended them to be.

Exports of Greek grain to the western Mediterranean generated a sufficient trade surplus to pay for these imports and to start the famous flow of American silver eastward. French, Italian, and Spanish demand for grain prompted the Porte to forsake its reliance on Aegean supplies. It began to bring Romanian and Bulgarian grain across the Black Sea in order to provision Istanbul, a city that was larger than London or Paris in 1600. The Balkan turn away from Mediterranean markets had thus begun under active Ottoman auspices. The city itself required a massive surplus of imports that included Western European manufactures but also Balkan fibers and tobacco that would soon be delivered more safely to Central Europe.

Ottoman weakness after 1600 made the turn sharper. Declining population reduced the attractiveness of the imperial market to the merchant class that was based in Istanbul or Thessaloniki. Ottoman hostility did keep Western European interests from using the foothold of the capitulations to gain direct commercial dominance, let alone the colonial empires that they created in Asia and the Americas. The Ottoman Empire's military orientation nonetheless kept the favored Moslems from entering commerce in a major way and left the role of intermediary in foreign trade to their subordinate Balkan subjects. All merchants faced mounting disorder, from the Albanian lands to Greek and Bulgarian territory. From Thessaloniki northward, Greeks, Jews, and other native traders sought connections with the Danube and Central Europe. To the south, the relative security of Morean and island ports created the commercial nucleus for modern Greece there, rather than around the much larger port of Thessaloniki. In the absence of any credit mechanism or even stable coinage from the Ottoman capital, traders had little hesitation in moving to new markets.

In all the Balkan lands, wheat had been the original connection with the Istanbul market. Its cultivation now gave way to raising livestock (especially hogs) and crops like cotton, tobacco, corn, and grapes (the latter for raisins and wine). Hogs and wine were in smaller demand in the Ottoman capital for religious reasons. In the provinces livestock and all these crops attracted less attention than wheat from soldiers or tax collectors. As the Ottoman borderlands became more and more disorderly during the eighteenth century, native Balkan traders sought more predictable profits by moving northward along with some of the peasantry. In doing so, both groups revived the tradition of migration beyond the frontier that had characterized the initial growth of the Ottoman Empire. This new and essentially economic expansion hastened the final weakening of Ottoman authority and the emergence of independent Balkan states.

2.

The Economic Legacy of
Habsburg Domination

The northward movement of Balkan trade and settlement up to and across the Habsburg border by the eighteenth century brings us to a second, sometimes overlapping, set of imperial legacies. The last buffer states between the Ottoman Balkans and the Habsburg lands had been swept aside long ago. Once the Ottoman siege of Vienna had been repulsed in 1529, the Croatian lands came under Habsburg rather than Hungarian control and became imperial borderlands.

To the west of the frontier, the Habsburg advance initiated the shift of the Croatian and other western Yugoslav lands out of the Italian, and hence the Mediterranean, commercial orbit into the Central European orbit. This shift, not to be undone until after the formation of Yugoslavia, was the first of three legacies of Habsburg domination to be discussed in this chapter.

To the east, growing economic interrelation between the Habsburg and Ottoman Empires constituted a second legacy from the late seventeenth century forward. Trade with the Ottoman Balkans and the migration that brought a Balkan commercial class to the Habsburg lands became significant only when the latter's territory expanded south and east across Hungary to include Slavonia, the Vojvodina, and Transylvania after 1690. The Banat between the latter two was added in 1718.

A final inheritance came from the failure of Habsburg authorities to make much conscious use of these growing trade relations to dominate the borderland and neighboring Balkan economies. The principal economic institutions and policies that the monarchy applied to its southern and eastern borderlands did not even attempt to build such a bridgehead. By the nineteenth century, the borderlands' access to the monarchy's large internal market remained no more than a promise. Military and feudal institutions combined curiously with policies promoting free trade to deny all the borderlands except Slovenia a comparative advantage in agriculture, industry, or any intermediate activities. The one-sided integration of the borderlands as markets but not producers would make them poor bases from which to stage further economic penetration to the southeast. For Transylvania, a special case in several respects, the inadvertent result was to push the province even at this early date toward economic integration with the Romanian Principalities on a basis entirely separate from Habsburg control.

Dubrovnik and the Fading Italian Legacy

The most impressive Habsburg endeavor in its western Yugoslav lands was the overturning of Italian hegemony from the Adriatic inland. The growth of Trieste and Rijeka as cornerstones of Habsburg commercial ascendancy must not, however, be anticipated; they became major ports only in the late eighteenth century. Until then, the early modern economic history of the Dalmatian coast and hinterland revolved around the decline of Italian influence. By Italian influence, we mean essentially the city-states of Venice and Dubrovnik on opposite sides of the Adriatic. The more important of the two was Dubrovnik, not only for its Yugoslav location and population but also for its crucial role in the demise of Venetian commercial influence.

The Decline of Venice

First, the lengthy Venetian presence on the Slovenian coast and as far inland as Ljubljana needs to be explained. Habsburg occupation from 1338 forward of what the monarchy called Carniola, the heart of modern Slovenia, cut short growing penetration by Venetian commerce and culture. Habsburg authorities simply banned the import of Venetian goods to the monarchy through Ljubljana, previously the major point of inland transit. Yet the western coast of the Istrian Peninsula remained outside Habsburg territory and tied commercially to Venice. The population of its ports from Pula northward, moreover, was largely Italian. They were able to maintain their trade with rural areas and even their ownership of agricultural land.

In the late sixteenth century Italian merchants were able to move inland again. They came to fill the gap left in the Slovenian economy

by ethnic German nobles and burghers. These German families had
at first prospered under the Habsburg rule that brought them to
Slovenia. Then their Protestant sympathies forced many of them to
move to Lutheran German lands to escape the rigors of the
Counter-Reformation. Habsburg authorities helped encourage the return of Venetian influence by favoring attendance at Italian univer-
sities. The heavy financial strain of the Thirty Years War (1618–1648)
prompted the monarchy to grant several Slovenian export
monopolies to Italian firms. Some of these enterprises were soon
buying rural land. On the long-standing Italian pattern, they employed peasants in sharecropping arrangements or in a putting-out
system for wool spinning. Thus the Habsburg monarchy actually
helped support a continued Italian presence in Slovenian territory, at
least until the eighteenth century.[1]

Similarly, no hostile Habsburg policy can explain why Venetian
traders failed to make the basic accommodation that would have
permitted them to retain commercial dominance down the Adriatic
through the early modern period. Venice neglected crucial accommodation with the Ottoman Empire. Once made, Venice could have
used it to continue acting as the principal European intermediary in
trade with the eastern Mediterranean. The Venetians had won and
held this position during the decline of the Byzantine Empire mainly
by military force. The Ottoman leadership was determined long before the capture of Istanbul not to let the same thing happen to them.
Venice persisted in aggressively pursuing a military advantage. It
held onto Corfu, Crete, and the Peloponnesus as long as possible.
This doomed its traders to unremitting Ottoman opposition during
the eighteenth century only to face growing French and then English
competition.[2]

The Rise of Dubrovnik

In the Adriatic, the Venetian position worsened with the rise of
Dubrovnik, then the city-state of Ragusa. It became the principal
entrepôt for trade with the Ottoman Balkans during the sixteenth
century. Ragusan representatives were dispatching overland caravans back from Belgrade and Sofia by the fourteenth century. Venice's European opponents encouraged Ragusan growth by permitting
the Synod of Basle in 1433 to grant the Republic the exclusive right
to trade with infidels, i.e., the advancing Ottoman Empire. The Venetians responded by trying to force other Italian city-states to forsake
all trade with their rival across the Adriatic. Dubrovnik's commerce
had initially been regarded as no more than an annoyance.[3] The
boycott had two effects. It forced the Ragusan city-state to abandon

its reliance on Italian grain imports and to search out Balkan sources of supply. (The Republic's coastal hinterland of some four hundred square miles could produce only one third of Dubrovnik's needs.) It also prompted the rise of local cloth production as an export to pay for grain imports. Doubtless easing the turn toward Balkan markets was the growing synthesis of Croat and Serb immigrants, eventually becoming a majority, with the city's originally Italian population.[4]

This was the background to the sixteenth-century heyday of the Ragusan Republic. Its fortunes rose after 1500 with the repeated wars between Venice and the Ottoman Empire. This warfare allowed it to play the role of neutral trade center for the eastern Mediterranean, like Amsterdam for northwestern Europe during the eighteenth century.[5] Ottoman authorities agreed to admit the city's woolen cloth to their territory without duty, while their European competition paid 3 to 5 percent ad valorem. More important, the decline of the Florentine trade network and then of its textile industry eliminated the main source of non-Venetian competition from Italy. Manufacturers in Dubrovnik were even able to persuade some skilled Florentine weavers to immigrate. The demand for cloth climbed in the Ottoman Balkans as urban population grew an above-mentioned 80 percent over the century. With the decline of mineral and slave exports after the Ottoman conquest, the Balkan economy found the export of Bulgarian and Serbian wool to Dubrovnik a tidy way to pay for textile imports, since Ottoman regulations (as noted in Chapter 1) made wheat exports difficult. Soon the city-state had established a network of agencies, staffed by some two hundred of its own merchants, across the Balkan lands to Istanbul.

Along the way, they were able to make further connections with the Near East. They also moved northward to the Polish lands, drawn by their reputation for minimal tariffs and tolls. This upsurge of caravan trade coincided with the general European revival of overland commerce that was characteristic of the sixteenth century. Pervasive Mediterannean piracy was responsible for this shift away from sea routes. Dubrovnik was nonetheless able to maintain the largest fleet in the Adriatic throughout the century.[6] Its merchant ships reportedly outnumbered the English total as late as 1574.

The Decline of Dubrovnik

Then began the long, uneven decline that would remove Dubrovnik and its Italian merchants from the mainstream of Balkan commerce by the eighteenth century. Victory over the Ottoman navy at Lepanto (across the Gulf of Corinth from Patras) in 1570 helped restore Venetian prominence in the declining Near Eastern spice trade.

Dubrovnik's access to it was thereby diminished. The city's traders turned west toward the Atlantic. Ragusan shipping suffered there less from piracy than from the city-state's political connection with Habsburg Spain. The latter was now a separate state from the Austrian monarchy but still a major foe of Venice. By this time, English, Dutch, and French shipping posed a far greater threat to Spanish commercial interests. Much of Dubrovnik's fleet was drawn into the losing struggle that Spain waged with privateers from the ascendant Atlantic states. These losses plus the growing competitive advantage of Western Europe in the Mediterranean textile trade left Dubrovnik to rely principally on its overland trade with the Balkans.[7]

Venice had tried and failed to divert this overland traffic from Dubrovnik by building port facilities at Split, a better and more secure Adriatic harbor about one hundred miles further north. Split did provide easier access to Bosnia and the large town of Sarajevo, the major center of Moslem trade in the Ottoman Balkans. Sarajevo's population of nearly 50,000 dwarfed the maximum of 7,000 in the port of Dubrovnik.[8] Yet the Ragusan Republic was able to attract several times as many ships as Split to its harbor during the seventeenth century by cultivating its overland trade network throughout the Serbian and Bulgarian lands. Some seven hundred representatives were dispatched between 1600 and 1650. The disintegration of this network toward the end of the century marked the final blow to the leading position of Dubrovnik in Balkan trade.

Although mystifying to Fernand Braudel, the reasons for the disintegration emerge clearly from subsequent Yugoslav research.[9] The earthquake of 1667 in Dubrovnik itself may well have dealt a psychological shock to the confidence of the commercial community. More certainly, the warfare that the city-state had used to its advantage on the Mediterranean permitted no such profitable neutrality inland. Commercial centers like Belgrade, even their foreign quarters, were sacked in the wake of internal unrest in the Ottoman Empire and then the Habsburg invasion of 1687–90. The quartering of Ottoman troops could bring the plague or cholera. Ottoman authorities sometimes banned trade when the mere threat of war prevailed. Bandits and local warlords threatened more and more trade routes. The Ragusan merchants in such towns could only record futile complaints. By 1700, few remained in Belgrade or Sofia, where agencies of more than a hundred members had previously made these locations their largest concentrations in the Balkans. Greeks and Tsintsars began taking their place in Belgrade and Sephardic Jews in Sofia. Ragusan colonies at Ruse and Vidin revived later in the eighteenth century but ran afoul of war and plague once more. They also faced growing competition from a variety of native traders and a few central Europeans too.[10]

Dubrovnik's colonies nonetheless left behind them a valuable legacy of Italian commercial practice. It was through them that Balkan commerce came to know bills of exchange and double-entry bookkeeping, otherwise little used in the Ottoman economy. This opened the way to widespread monetization and predictable profits from long-distance trade by the end of the early modern period. The Balkan ability to assimilate European banking techniques rapidly during the nineteenth century (see Chapter 7) had its earliest origins in the Ragusan presence, in turn the product of a synthesis of South Slav and Italian populations in Dubrovnik.

The city-state survived until the Napoleonic Wars. Afterwards it was absorbed into the Habsburg monarchy. Brief periods of prosperity accompanied the Mediterranean wars of the eighteenth century, especially when Venice was at a disadvantage as in 1797. Otherwise undermining Dubrovnik's neutral role on the Adriatic was the growth of direct trade between the Ottoman and Habsburg lands. Trieste and Rijeka, on either side of the Istrian Peninsula, were the principal Habsburg enclaves. They linked up with a growing number of Ottoman ports between Split and Dubrovnik.[11] Since 1518, a Venetian oversight had exempted the Peninsula from the requirement that all its Adriatic traffic bring goods for further shipment to Venice first. Istria became a center for smuggling and piracy, mainly by the Croat and Slovene *uskoci* (pirates) at the expense of both Venice and Dubrovnik. When the Habsburg monarchy began to take an active interest in tying this Istrian outlet to its own trade, the commercial focus of the Yugoslav Adriatic shifted up the coast from Dubrovnik to Trieste.

Habsburg Trade with the Ottoman Empire

Early modern Habsburg commercial policy in Southeastern Europe would seem to have lived up to its persisting mercantilist reputation among Eastern European scholars if eighteenth-century promotion of Trieste and Rijeka were the only criterion. The official decisions to build up the two ports' harbor facilities and to construct roads connecting them to Vienna and Budapest (Buda and Pest at this time) admittedly came late in the century. But this construction followed in the wake of several joint-stock companies set up with official blessing to expand Habsburg exports of manufactured goods to Ottoman and other Mediterranean markets.

The Austrian Oriental Trade Company and Others

As early as 1667, the Austrian mercantilist writer Joachim Becher had obtained an official charter for an Oriental Trade Company, patterned after joint-stock enterprises like the English and Dutch East India Companies. His venture was designed to develop the export of manufactured silk in return for livestock imports to supply the Habsburg army. It folded within a few years because of renewed Habsburg hostilities with the Ottoman Empire. Emperor Charles VI revived the idea in 1719, however. He chartered a similar Oriental Trade Company, attracting Italian capital from the Belgian port of Ostend. Branches opened there as well as in Trieste, Rijeka, and Belgrade. English objections to the Belgian base of operations forced the withdrawal of the charter of 1731. Thus ended any possibility of Habsburg colonies overseas. In return England recognized the Pragmatic Sanction for Maria Theresa's impending succession to the Habsburg throne. The company survived as a private joint-stock enterprise on a smaller scale.

From the start Trieste was the center for its Near Eastern operations. This town at the northern head of the Adriatic was officially designated as a free port in 1719, with the aim of promoting ship construction and other manufacture as well as the export trade. The company's Trieste branch enjoyed exclusive rights to represent the monarchy in the Levant trade. It helped open a state school for training navigators in the port. The branch attracted little capital, however, and collapsed later in the 1730s after the failure of a lottery loan.[12] In 1750 the Trieste-Fiume (Rijeka) Company established itself with one million florins capital (equal to about 1.2 million Ottoman piastres or 3.6 million French livres). This paid-in capital came from stockholders in the Low Countries as well as the Habsburg lands. Its charter provided a twenty-five-year monopoly to refine sugar from abroad and the Habsburg lands. The company was to supply as much of the monarchy's needs as possible. By 1755 Maria Theresa had signed a ban on the import of refined sugar. The Rijeka refinery became the largest manufacturing enterprise in the Yugoslav lands during the eighteenth century. Its seven hundred employees included fifty skilled foreigners. Although Rijeka became a free port too in 1776, it dispatched most of its sugar and other goods to Trieste for further shipment. By the census of 1786, Trieste had some fifty manufacturing enterprises, mainly tied to shipbuilding, with about a thousand employees. The port's population had grown threefold during this decade to exceed 20,000. Dubrovnik, Split, and Rijeka combined could not match that total.[13]

The several companies founded in Trieste to develop trade beyond the Mediterranean lasted only a few years each and showed meager results. The most promising of these enterprises, the Trieste-India Company, brought back Italian capital from Ostend again but did not last a decade. All the same, the scattered figures available for total trade indicate that by 1783 Trieste's surplus of export over import value, supposedly the hallmark of successful mercantilist policy, had grown to two to one. Its total value of 11,000,000 florins accounted for one third of all Habsburg exports.[14] The port's major function, however, was to give the growing textile industry of Central Europe access to Mediterranean markets. The latter included Istanbul and parts south but rarely the limited Balkan market.

Habsburg Promotion of Overland Trade

The western Yugoslav hinterland did not much join in this wider Ottoman trade. Overland routes well to the east of Istria, through Belgrade in particular, became the bearer of the bulk of Habsburg imports from the Ottoman lands. Habsburg policy permitted these overland imports to more than match Habsburg exports through Trieste for most of the eighteenth century (see Table 2.1). The net effect was more consistent with free trade than mercantilist protection. The monarchy cut internal tariff barriers between its provinces. A series of Habsburg-Ottoman agreements provided low tariffs along their common border. Thus it makes no sense to speak of an official Habsburg effort to penetrate the Ottoman Balkans for mercantilist purposes; nor should it. Balkan markets lacked the purchasing power to buy any great amount of the manufactured luxury goods that Austrian, German, and Czech industries were producing, much less the capacity to generate any competitive exports of similar goods.

From the start of Maria Theresa's reign in 1740, her advisors worked to reduce the already moderate tariffs within the monarchy. They had been set since the thirteenth century at 3-1/3 percent, then 5 percent since 1718, for trade with the hereditary Austrian lands. Croatia and Slavonia as well as Transylvania were now included in the Hungarian zone for duty-free trade. Another edict of 1754 ended guild restrictions on the manufacture of goods to be sold outside the local market. Further plans to eliminate all internal trade barriers within the monarchy failed to materialize.[15] The reductions achieved seem significant enough. They were of course consistent with the mercantilist policy of strengthening the entire state's potential for competitive export. So were edicts between 1746 and 1754 banning some manufactured imports (sugar for one, as we have seen) and enacting a tariff wall against the others that has been reckoned at 20 to 30 percent ad valorem.[16] Similar rates on imported raw materials

were also enacted to discourage their use. Only nominal, 1 to 3 percent rates remained on exports.

What was at first glance not consistent with mercantilist principle
was Habsburg insistence on concluding its victorious advance into
Ottoman Serbia in 1718 with a commercial agreement obliging the
Sultan to lower the tariff on goods exchanged between the two Empires from 5 to 3 percent ad valorem. The treaty's navigation clauses
allowed Habsburg vessels to trade down the Danube as far as Ruse.
Although the markets they might reach with Habsburg manufactures
were small, they at least offered no great danger of bringing back
competing manufactures. Then Ottoman victory in the war of 1736–
39 saw the 5 percent rate restored. More important, Habsburg fear of
offending the Porte prevented any effective opposition to the
thousands of Ottoman subjects, mainly Greeks, now trading freely in
the Hungarian lands. Over a hundred did business in Vienna. Their
advantage over native traders lacking Levant connections became a
cause for official concern after their exemption as foreigners from the
new higher tariffs of 1746–54. Throughout the 1750s and 1760s, the
new *Kommerzienrat*, or Commercial Council, in Vienna tried a variety of registration, route, and residence requirements to reduce this
influx of non-Catholics whose profits in Habsburg coin were presumably remitted back to the Ottoman lands. The Council admitted defeat in 1771. It extended the minimal tariff for Ottoman traders, again
reduced to 3 percent ad valorem, to Habsburg subjects as well.[17]
Their subjects' response to the opportunity appears to have been
negligible.

Spotty figures available for aggregate Habsburg trade show no
post-1771 increase in the overland imports that principally occupied
the Ottoman traders. As indicated in Table 2.1, it was the export trade
through Trieste and Rijeka that accounted for the doubling of
Ottoman-Habsburg trade between 1771 and 1788. Even then, the latter total fell short of one fifth of aggregate Habsburg foreign trade.
That sum in turn was barely the same small fraction of aggregate
French trade over the same period (see Table 1.2). In other words,
despite an internal market whose population nearly matched
France's 25,000,000 on the eve of the Revolution, the Habsburg
monarchy had failed to develop anything approaching the French
connection with foreign markets. It remained a largely landlocked
economy without the overseas empire or major seaports that might
have called forth a larger commercial class among its own subjects.

The Dominant Role of Balkan Traders

Returning to the Levant market, it does not seem likely that there
was any great transfer of the existing overland trade out of the hands

TABLE 2.1
THE DISTRIBUTION OF HABSBURG TRADE, 1747-1807
(in millions of Austrian florins)[a]

			EXPORTS			
Annual average	Austrian Lands	Hungarian Lands	Habsburg Total Of which:	Levant Overseas	Levant Overland	Levant Total
1747-71	10-15	5-10	15-25	1.5		1.5
1782-88	18	14	32	4.5	.5	5.0
1797-98	21	10	31	4.5	.5	5.0
1799-1805	20	11	31	2.5	.5	3.0
1807			27	1.0		1.0

			IMPORTS[b]			
Annual average	Austrian Lands	Hungarian Lands	Habsburg Total Of which:	Levant Overseas	Levant Overland	Levant Total
1747-71	10-15	5-10	15-25	.5	2.5	3.0
1782-88	18	9	27	1.5	2.5	4.0
1797-98	24	10	34	1.5	4.5	6.0
1807			44	1.5	4.5	6.0

Notes: (a)One Austrian florin, or gulden, was worth between 1 and 1.2 Ottoman piastres for most of the eighteenth century. Hence the two denominations are roughly comparable. See Vuk Vinaver, *Pregled istorije novca u jugoslovenskim zemljama* (Belgrade, 1970), pp. 305-19. (b)Transit goods included. Leipzig was the principal destination of imports forwarded through the Habsburg lands.

Sources: M. von Herzfield, "Zur Orienthandelspolitik unter Maria Theresa," *Archiv für Österreichische Geschichte*, 108 (Vienna, 1919) pp. 274, 289-90, 309; Herbert Hassinger, "Der Aussenhandel der Habsburgermonarchie in der zweiten Hälfte der 18. Jahrhunderte," *Die wirtschaftliche Situation in Deutschland und Österreich um die Wende vom 18. zum 19. Jahrhundert* (Stuttgart, 1964), pp. 51, 79, 95; Sl. Gavrilović, *Prilog istoriji trgovine i migracije Balkan-podunavlju* (Belgrade, 1969), pp. 11-12; Felix Boujour, *A View of the Commerce of Greece, 1787-1797* (London, 1800), pp. 343-44; Vinaver, *Pregled istorije novca*, p. 297.

of Ottoman subjects. Ethnic German and Jewish traders from the Habsburg lands had begun to appear in Belgrade, Sofia, and some of the Bulgarian ports along the Danube as early as the second half of the seventeenth century.[18] But their numbers were small. They came privately, with no official backing from a mercantilist enterprise. As already demonstrated in Chapter 1, the great majority of all commerce on the Ottoman side of the border was in the hands of native Balkan merchants. Now their dominant role on the Habsburg side, in the face of official opposition, must be defined.

Serbian migrants appeared as livestock traders in the Hungarian lands from 1660 forward. Rather than encouraging them, Habsburg authorities issued three separate edicts banning the Serbs from Viennese markets.[19] Thus the first Austro-Serbian trade dispute, the result of complaints from the city's German merchant guild, predated the famous tariff war of 1906–11 (see Chapter 6) by some two hundred fifty years. By the middle of the eighteenth century, the total number of Serbian, Greek, Tsintsar, and other Balkan merchants based on Habsburg territory, mainly along the Ottoman border, was estimated at roughly 18,000.[20]

The Habsburg occupation of Serbia between 1718 and 1739 gives us an indication of the subordinate role that Vienna might have liked to impose on these Balkan traders in the best of all mercantilist worlds. For political and military reasons, the new Serbian-Ottoman border was closed to trade. For fiscal reasons, all commercial transactions were subject to taxes that traders had never been forced to pay under Ottoman rule. Total commercial revenues matched the amount collected from harvest tithes, the principal source of Ottoman revenue. Serbian livestock traders were furthermore obliged to work through the branch of the Oriental Trade Company in Belgrade if they wished to continue doing business with the Habsburg lands. Little wonder that the value of Serbian exports apparently declined during this period.[21] The Serbian economy did emerge from the occupation more monetized than when it had entered. The impetus came not from export earnings but from the requirement for peasants to pay the harvest tithe in coin and the increased availability of grain for import from the Habsburg Banat, just to the north and newly annexed in 1718. Ottoman successes in the 1736–39 war shattered the Habsburg illusion of a secure southeastern border. Serbia was lost and the Banat barely retained. From Vienna's viewpoint, the borderlands would remain threatened for the rest of the century. Their integration into the Habsburg economy, or more precisely from the state's cameralist viewpoint, into the Habsburg fiscal system, was thereby delayed.[22] The gist of official policy toward Balkan traders was sporadic restriction, tempered by a reluctance to alienate them or the Ottoman Empire from which they came. A series of regulations from 1718 to 1772 tried to confine them to wholesale trade (except for fairs) but without sufficient penalties to achieve much success. The Hungarian Diet reluctantly defeated a proposal to tax traders who were still Ottoman subjects. There were simply too few native traders to take their place should they go back across the border. Bans in 1759 on Ottoman subjects shipping Habsburg coin across the border or extending credit to Habsburg subjects were equally ineffective. Finally, in the 1770s, Habsburg officials mounted a campaign to oblige all Balkan traders to become Habsburg subjects.

Only the Tsintsars responded in any great numbers. Half-hearted enforcement does not by itself explain the general failure of these official harassments. Trade on the Habsburg side of the border was more secure from banditry and several times more profitable.[23] Access to it was worth the effort of evading assorted Austrian restrictions on traders coming from the Ottoman side.

The crowning irony of this commerce, from a mercantilist point of view, was that it generated neither an export surplus nor the flow of many manufactured goods into the Ottoman market. The import of rough *aba* cloth for peasant consumption on the Habsburg side probably accounted for a larger annual value than the sale of Central European luxury fabrics. The overland import surplus over exports reached five to one in 1779. Main imports were livestock, cotton, wool, and tobacco.[24] The main Habsburg exports were timber and especially grain. The unimportance of such an unprocessed export in the mercantilist framework of Habsburg trade policy may be seen in Vienna's willingness to shut off the sale of grain to Serbia several times during the First Serbian Uprising. This was purely a political concession to the Porte, apparently involving no great economic sacrifice.[25]

Colonizing the Borderlands, 1699–1799

As Charles Wilson has reminded us, even for the English case, early modern mercantilism was more than commercial policy.[26] Its underlying impulse was the extension of the central government's power. Successful extensions of power constituted the principal events of political history in early modern England and France. The Prussian and Austrian monarchies concentrated on improving tax collection through their own corps of state officials. Thus their own brand of mercantilism was called cameralism, after taxes levied for an extraordinary purpose. Like the Ottoman *avariz*, that purpose was usually military. The separate Austrian monarchy that emerged from the break with Habsburg Spain in the 1520s organized itself around a small Secret Council, or *Geheimer Rat*, with supreme power in foreign and military affairs. The Council soon spawned finance and defense ministries (*Hofkammer* and *Hofkriegsrat*) but failed to bring the Hungarian nobility under the effective control of either body. The Habsburg government in Vienna was left to find other means of defending and taxing the newly acquired Eastern Crown Lands. By the eighteenth century, the Habsburg solution had taken on theoretical trappings under the title of "populationism."[27] The spreading of skilled labor across the new southeastern territory was seen as the best way of adding to the government's taxable wealth.

Populationism and the Military Border

Although a logical corollary to mercantilist theory, the idea of populationism also grew out of the practical military problem of defending the monarchy's southeastern border from the Ottoman threat. The Habsburg solution to this military problem began with the organization of the Croatian Military Border in the sixteenth century. The *Hofkriegsrat* then extended that regime to Slavonia, the Vojvodina, and part of Transylvania during the eighteenth century. Taking up where the defeated Hungarian kingdom had left off, the Habsburg military command had integrated largely Serb refugees from Ottoman territory into its ranks by 1553. In 1630 the Habsburg Emperor signed the *Statuta Valachorum*, or Vlach Statutes (Serbs and other Balkan Orthodox peoples were often called Vlachs). They recognized formally the growing practice of awarding such refugee families a free grant of crown land to farm communally as their *zadruga*. In return all male members over sixteen were obliged to do military service. The further guarantees of religious freedom and of no feudal obligations made the Orthodox Serbs valuable allies for the monarchy in its seventeenth-century struggle against the Catholic Croatian nobility. When the Military Border was extended eastward after the Treaty of Karlowitz in 1699, the Serb *graničari* (border guards) plus some Croats too played a similar part for the monarchy against the Hungarian nobility.[28] The Transylvanian section of the Military Border did not come into being until 1762. As we shall see at the close of this chapter, it was intended during its shorter, unhappier life to create Romanian and non-noble Hungarian border regiments for the same purpose. Throughout the early modern period, the military prowess of all these border regiments allowed the Habsburg monarchy to maintain a relatively small standing army (less than 10,000 before 1700) and still hold onto the southeastern frontier. Despite intermittent revolts, usually to preserve religious freedom to practice Orthodoxy, the loyalty of the *graničari* to the Habsburg Emperor was far more consistent than that of the Ottoman Janissaries to the Sultan.

In return, Habsburg policy can hardly be said to have assisted the spread of a skilled labor force or promoted economic development in the original Croatian border areas. Their generally mountainous and karst-covered terrain was, as already noted, inhospitable ground for any attempt to promote agricultural prosperity. Crop yields, mainly in corn and later, potatoes, were barely half those on the gentler landscape of so-called Civil Croatia adjoining to the north, even after the Military Border was dissolved and merged with Civil Croatia later in the nineteenth century. Until then, however, Habsburg promotion of isolated hamlets strung out along the Ottoman border discouraged the development of agriculture or market relations still further. So did guard duty that typically took the able-bodied men of the settlement away for several weeks during every growing season. Wars took them away for years at a time.

The *zadruga* system of wider family holdings held back what possibilities there were for more efficient cultivation. Their size was limited (18 *joch* or 26 acres of arable land maximum) and their sale or transfer impossible.[29] Joseph II initiated some promising plans for the introduction of agrarian reforms and the promotion of Jewish immigration, heretofore prohibited, as a stimulus to commerce, but they died with him during the Habsburg-Ottoman war of 1788–91.

Hindering the growth of wider, interregional trade, in any event, were the northern and southern frontiers of the Croatian Military Border. The northern border with Civil Croatia required goods from the frontier to pass from the Austrian to the Hungarian customs zones and hence to pay the appropriate tariff. Imports across the southern border faced the several weeks delay that the anti-plague precautions of the Habsburg *Sanitäts Kordon* established in 1770 along the entire Military Frontier including the Transylvanian portion treated below. To the east, however, the *Kordon's* effects were less severe. The predominant Greek, Tsintsar, Serbian, or Romanian traders there had representatives on both sides of the border. They were able to escape any delay in negotiating the sale of their merchandise, if not a delay in its delivery.

Slavonia, to the northeast of Croatia between the Sava and Drava Rivers, fared somewhat better under the Military Border. Most of its land lay at the southern edge of the Pannonian Plain. Its fertility surpassed Croatia's for grain cultivation. Although the northern half of Slavonia was supposedly outside the Military Border in the fashion of Civil Croatia, this area was in fact under joint civil-military administration from its acquisition in 1699 until 1745. The Croatian, really a mixed Croatian-Hungarian, nobility to the west, therefore, had no opportunity to establish themselves as they had in Civil Croatia. Instead, agricultural land was awarded to a few thousand German colonists, and to tens of thousands of Croats mixed with Serb migrants from the Military Border or the Ottoman lands. Little land was left for nobles to occupy following the merger with Civil Croatia in 1745. Afterwards, a peasant population only half the size of Civil Croatia's and prone to revolt or emigrate to the nearby Ottoman lands kept the manorial reserves under half the Croatian figures.[30] Primitive agricultural techniques persisted. Yet both parts of Slavonia had begun to export grain and grow potatoes, well suited to its sandy soil and a supplement to the local food supply, before the end of the eighteenth century.[31]

By far the greatest Habsburg success in pursuing populationism on its southeastern border was won in the Vojvodina. Serb, Croat, Romanian, German, Hungarian, and even Slovak immigrants assembled there to live in essential harmony until the monarchy's demise in the First World War. Their new home was a rich agricultural plain from Belgrade north to the present Hungarian border, which the Ottoman-Habsburg war of 1683–99 had left largely deserted. This vast territory has been historically divided into the Srem (between the Sava and Danube Rivers), the Bačka (between the Danube and Tisza Rivers) and the Banat (east from the Tisza to the Carpathian mountains).

The Coming of German Colonists

The Banat was furthest east. Once acquired in 1718, it naturally was the first part of the Vojvodina that the *Hofkriegsrat* in Vienna tried to repopulate for military security. While Serbian refugees were being incorporated into regiments on the Military Border to the south, German colonists were lured with free land and three-year tax exemptions to the north of the Banat. The same sort of joint civil-military administration that prevailed in northern Slavonia was enforced here until 1739. It served to keep Hungarian nobles or peasants to a minimum. Most of the nearly 25,000 Germans in this first wave came gladly from the Rhineland area so devastated in the long War of the Spanish Succession, only to encounter pioneer hardships to match anything seen in the American West. Bandits, bad roads, and dangerous river crossings hindered the growth of trade. Summer heat and winter cold were extreme. Disease unchecked by sanitary facilities or medical services and lack of reserve food supplies gave the Banat the reputation of a German graveyard.[32] Perhaps 5,000 settlers survived the ordeal.

This fraction that did were able to introduce the three field system, with its advantage of reduced fallow and two plantings of grain a year. They also began cultivating hops as a basis for brewing beer. Tobacco was grown and successfully exported. But efforts to raise a wheat surplus to sell to the Habsburg army failed.[33] Then the disorder and disease of the Ottoman war of 1736–39 swept away most of the progress that had been made.

Rebuilding from these first foundations, a larger German immigration after 1740 totalled 43,000 by 1770. Habsburg authorities lured them with free houses and a six-year tax exemption, as well as free land. Catholics and war veterans from the overpopulated south German lands were favored at first. By the 1760s the growing demand for grain to support the Habsburg army, ready to march at any opportunity to recapture Silesia from Prussia, made colonists with agricul-

tural skills the most sought after. Indeed, the army received the first
big export of wheat in 1758. Such deliveries grew steadily, although
aforementioned exports to the Ottoman lands took the majority of
surplus wheat.[34] Hemp, flax, and some mulberry trees were now
planted as well. Serbian and Romanian immigrants were officially
admitted once more to the Banat and began to forsake livestock-
raising for grain cultivation with the more advanced German techniques. Officially sanctioned migration into the neighboring Bačka
had begun in 1749 and proceeded rapidly. It attracted Germans,
Serbs, and Croats. Hungarian peasants fled their nobles' estates to
come. Slovak Protestants left behind religious persecution and barren Tatra uplands.

The reforming Habsburg Emperor Joseph II then used his brief
reign (1780–90) to launch a new wave of northern immigration to the
Banat, Bačka, and Srem. Nearly 40,000 more had come by 1787. A
significant fraction were Protestant Germans, Hungarians, and
Slovaks attracted by the promise of the same religious freedom
enjoyed by the Orthodox settlers.[35] Joseph instructed the colonization agency in Vienna to lay special emphasis on selecting immigrants who were skilled in farming or some craft and were also liter-
ate. The latter qualification favored the Protestants and provided a
pool from which local officials could be drawn. The small Jewish
immigration also increased somewhat, at the Emperor's specific urging. They remained concentrated in the few towns over 5,000 in
population: Timişoara and Pančevo in the Banat, Subotica and Novi
Sad in the Bačka, and Zemun in the Srem. By the census of 1786–87,
the total population of the Bačka and Srem each exceeded 20,000 and
that of the larger Banat approached 300,000, all tenfold increases
since the start of the century.

These figures permit no precise ethnic breakdown for the Vojvodina or its several regions. All indications point, however, to a
Romanian majority in the Banat and a Serbian plurality, if not a
majority, elsewhere.[36] Most of the initial immigration of 1690 had
come from Serbia to the Srem. This remained the area of heaviest
Serbian concentration. Little can be said about their distribution, although there was a tendency to stay as close as possible to the border
of Serbia proper. More important for our purposes is their struggle to
overcome the hardships of these early years. They lived in earthen
dugouts, used the most primitive agricultural techniques, and built
their villages as far as possible from the main towns and trade routes
to avoid Habsburg officials, especially tax collectors. Yet over the
course of the eighteenth century they began to prosper, at least in
relation to their fellows in Serbia. The spread of public order helped.
So did the Serbs' adoption of German techniques of sowing several

crops and using an iron plow.[37] But new commercial opportunities in
the towns of Zemun, Novi Sad, and Pančevo to sell such produce to
the Ottoman market were largely of their own making, in the face of
passive Habsburg commercial policy. This is the place to recognize,
however, that their agricultural accomplishments owed a great debt
to the active Habsburg policies of promoting German colonization
and of keeping the Hungarian nobility from moving in to make serfs
of the assorted immigrants. When the monarchy was obliged in 1799
to transfer all the Banat and Bačka save the Military Border to Hungarian jurisdiction, we therefore enter a new era in the economic
history of the Vojvodina.

Failure to Integrate the Borderlands, 1799–1867

The growing Hungarian assertiveness that led to revolt in 1848 and
virtual autonomy within the Habsburg monarchy by the 1867 *Ausgleich* left its marks on the Croatian lands as well as the Vojvodina.
Hungarian pressure to dissolve the Croatian Military Border was
eventually successful but did not stimulate the area's agricultural
economy any more than had restrictive Austrian policy. Nor did the
spread of the Hungarian system of large land holdings to the Vojvodina allow that area any more access to the huge imperial market
than the already existing estates in Civil Croatia or Slavonia would
enjoy. Nearer than all of them and the Habsburg market were the
grain-growing estates of Inner Hungary, still larger and on the verge
of an Agricultural Revolution.[38] Only mining and manufacturing in
the Slovenian uplands would achieve substantial integration with the
wider Habsburg economy during the first two thirds of the
nineteenth century, and then because of their nonagricultural resources rather than their long-standing location in the Austrian half
of the monarchy.

Nineteenth-Century Migration to the Vojvodina

The immigration of Germans to the Banat and Bačka resumed after
1790. Many of them were from the group of over a million Germans
scattered across Hungary proper. These new settlers took the lead in
introducing preventive measures to cut down the high incidence of
tuberculosis and other diseases. They also pioneered in the use of
artesian wells, which allowed grain cultivation to move to the richer
clay soil of the previously forested plains from the poorer alluvial soil
along the river banks. Germans consolidated scattered holdings and
cultivated four and five field systems to eliminate fallow land. All

this helped to boost wheat yields by the mid-nineteenth century. By this time, the German immigrants owned more land in the Banat than any other group.[39]

The Hungarian migration was part of a general southward movement of Germans and Hungarians from the northwest counties that characterized the first half of the nineteenth century. Hungarian peasants moved principally into the Bačka but also spilled over into the northern Banat. By the 1830s some increase in the Hungarian population was making its presence felt through the growing cultivation of grain in the Bačka and tobacco in the Banat. A colonization office in Budapest was also recruiting Slovak peasants from the poverty-stricken foothills of the Tatra Mountains, on the mistaken theory that these *aćalfi* or "little brothers" were sufficiently Magyarized to represent Hungarian interests.[40] Then the failure of the Hungarian revolt of 1848–49 allowed Vienna to reassert its interests and bar all migration from the Hungarian lands until after 1867.

During this first half of the nineteenth century, however, the Hungarian presence and legal authority had been sufficient to transfer to the Vojvodina the land tenure system of the Magyar nobility, if not much of their own presence. Ironically, that transfer had begun in the 1780s under quite different management. The reforming Austrian Emperor Joseph II first permitted the sale of agricultural land in the Vojvodina, including the right of resale. Austrian officials and the more successful German colonists appear to have been the major purchasers. In the wake of Joseph's death, the Hungarian nobility sought to acquire new land and used this commercial opportunity to reassert their old feudal rights throughout the reconquered south. Some of their number bought or seized land in the Bačka. More important, owners of more than one section of land began to oblige resident peasants to meet the *robot* labor and tithe requirements in force elsewhere in the Hungarian lands. Initially, owners accepted the commutation of these obligations in cash and used the proceeds to expand grain exports to booming European markets during the Napoleonic Wars. But uncontrolled Habsburg inflation of paper money and the devaluation of coinage (1811–16) was followed by the collapse of grain prices in peacetime. Owners now demanded their 104 or 52 days *robot* in physical labor, instead of depreciated Habsburg denominations. Extra days were often imposed for trifling wages in the same currency. By the 1840s, peasant efforts to obtain cash for state taxes and to reduce their *robot* obligations (set according to the size of their holding) by selling some of their land had rendered half of them landless.[41]

There is no record of how much land the nobility came to occupy. What we do know suggests a smaller physical presence than in Inner

Hungary. The noble proportion of the population only rose to two percent in some districts and much less in others. This contrasts with an average of nearly 5 percent for all of the Hungarian lands, even including those of the northwest where a few nobles owned immense estates.[42]

Holding Back the Military Border

Along the Military Border of the Croatian lands through the Vojvodina, Austrian authorities kept control until the Border itself was dissolved in 1881 after Hungarian pressure through the 1870s. Vienna made almost no effort to improve the Border's backward agriculture. In the Banat section at least, we may point to the still easy admission of German immigrants up to 1829. Then a property requirement of 300 florins per family reduced the flow.[43] Serfdom was still not permitted, but the state imposed heavy indirect taxes that applied to all residents once their initial three-year exemption had run out. Nearly half the still heavy forests of the Croatian Military Border, a good potential source of peasant income to pay their taxes, remained in state hands. Over half of all peasant households lacked even an iron plow. Three quarters of the adult population were illiterate. Croatian crop yields not surprisingly continued to lag well behind those for Civil Croatia.[44]

The small communal *zadruga* survived as the main form of land tenure and would have made any agricultural reform difficult. Habsburg legislation in 1850 did make the *zadruga* hereditary but failed to permit its dissolution.[45] This was the crucial change that would have permitted concentration into larger, more efficient units. The original Austrian interest in promoting border agriculture to ensure the army a food supply had long since vanished even for the Vojvodina. The likelihood of another Ottoman campaign was remote. The fertile Hungarian plains produced ample grain to feed the Habsburg army.

The Hungarians took every opportunity to undermine the economic viability of the Military Border. Their 1848–49 revolt had been defeated in large measure because of the actions of General Jelačić's Croatian border regiments. Budapest fought the distribution of state forest lands and the development of timber exports through the ports of Civil Croatia under Hungarian control. In the absence of large or efficient agricultural units, timber cutting on the 20 to 40 percent of the Border that was still forest provided peasants their best chance for commercial profit. Sales remained pathetically small. Finally, Hungarian representatives opposed the 1869 plan of the *Hofkriegsrat* to use state timber for railway construction in the Military Border. This marked the start of their eventually successful campaign to secure the Border's dissolution.[46]

Hungarian Landlords and Croatian Agriculture

In Civil Croatia and Slavonia, the nobility was predominantly Hungarian in consciousness if not ethnic purity. These nobles must be credited with importing merino sheep from Spain in 1773 and establishing the monarchy's first breeding station on Croatian territory. European demand for this high-quality wool grew first with the English blockade of Napoleonic Europe and then with the rapidly expanding English textile industry. The merino spread over most of Hungary during the reformist period of the 1820s. Magnates owning the larger estates began to enclose the land of neighboring noble smallholders for larger pastures. This profitable rise in sheepraising, usually at the expense of grain cultivation, continued until the arrival of cheaper Australian and Argentine wool on the European market after 1850.[47]

Little of this more efficient animal husbandry had spread through Civil Croatia and Slavonia, however. Noble estates were found in great numbers, it may be recalled, only in Civil Croatia. Even there, although three quarters of all arable land was held under feudal title, a majority of that feudal fraction was urbarial. This was crown land temporarily granted, along with the services of its peasants, to nobles. It was not their allodial, i.e., private, property. The urbarial holdings were typically medium-sized or small (roughly 20 to 200 acres) and belonged to the gentry, i.e., lesser or "sandal" nobility.[48] They lived on their own estates and helped the peasantry farm them, rather than using the income from several large estates to finance a life in Budapest or Vienna as did the magnates, or highest-ranking nobles.

Until the formal abolition of serfdom in 1848, the gentry were generally tied to income from natural rents or heavy *robot* obligations (up to 104 days a year) from their serfs. Such peasants could cut these obligations only by reducing their own holdings to half their normal size or less. The gentry resisted supplying any modern equipment. Peasant resistance to any extra, unrewarded labor further hindered the emergence of efficient agricultural labor. Only the so-called impoverished gentry, distinguished by holdings of thirty acres or less, were obliged to pay taxes. Their preferred collection in money was the one official stimulus to more commercial cultivation. Half of the cultivated area was still left fallow regularly. Crop rotation was unknown. Roads were so bad that a third of some crops were left in the fields to rot for want of transport.[49]

The fewer Slavonian estates tended to be larger. There, however, the peasantry's persisting division of village land into scattered strips rather than consolidated fields hampered grain growing.

Magnates in either territory whose holdings were large enough to permit much improvement in marketable cultivation found themselves hamstrung by growing indebtedness from maintaining their residences in Budapest or Vienna. In addition, the nearly complete lack of credit outside the family made it difficult even for the solvent to finance consolidation of their scattered reserve lands or the purchase of new equipment. An agricultural mortgage bank would doubtless have helped matters, but this was blocked by the noble estate's medieval privilege of *Aviticität,* or the inalienability of land, which meant that it could not be used as security in case of default. What credit there was came from lottery loans arranged individually by the most prestigious magnates, those with the largest estates and the best connections in Budapest.[50] Few of the nobles in the Croatian or Slavonian lands were so well placed.

By the 1830s, the largest magnates of Inner Hungary were able to increase their surplus of exportable grain while still concentrating on sheepraising. It was at just this time, when the European grain market was beginning to recover from the collapse following the Napoleonic Wars, that Russian and Romanian grain began arriving on both sides of the Adriatic in sizable quantities. As yet unable to undercut this competition with higher quality or a lower price, Hungarian grain traders turned inland to Croatia and Slavonia.[51] This turn undoubtedly discouraged the development of native cultivation. This was especially true on the smaller Croatian estates, which could least afford the high cost of overland transport. Bad roads made 20 to 30 miles of shipment by caravan equal to the cost of a 300-mile shipment from southern Hungary to Budapest by steamship on the Danube.[52] Railway construction was beyond Hungarian resources during the first half of the nineteenth century. Recent Croatian scholarship has rightly criticized the Austrian lines built during this period for ignoring existing east-west trade routes, thereby foregoing a link with the Danube at Zemun, in favor of a connection between Vienna and the Adriatic at Trieste.[53] Thus the northern Habsburg markets and those of Istria and Dalmatia as well remained closed to Croatian grain and timber. Meanwhile, the principal Croatian towns found themselves integrated into the Hungarian agricultural market at the expense of local production.

The larger Slavonian estates were cut off from the Croatian market by the difficult east-west roads and customs formalities of the intervening Military Border (see Map 2).

The emancipation of all the Habsburg peasantries from the *robot* and most other feudal obligations in 1849 had no immediate impact on the agriculture of these Hungarian and Yugoslav lands. True, tariff barriers to the hereditary Austrian lands fell the following year. Yet the consolidation of scattered estate holdings, their access to rail transport and credit, and their adoption of more efficient techniques and wage labor still did not gather momentum until after the 1867 *Ausgleich*.[54] Only then, for instance, could Hungarian migration to the Vojvodina resume. The general growth and modernization of Hungarian agriculture were, moreover, a phenomenon of the last fifty-five years before the First World War. Its treatment therefore belongs in Chapter 9, which will return to the remaining Habsburg and Ottoman territories in Southeastern Europe to measure their pre-1914 progress against that of the independent Balkan states.

Limits on Croatian Industry

The development of manufacturing in the Croatian lands moved even more slowly than that of agriculture. In an integrated Habsburg economy, some relative lag would be expected in view of the Czech lands' superior mineral resources and long manufacturing tradition. The prolonged Habsburg maintenance of the Military Border and the growing rivalry between Austrian and Hungarian interests in railway construction nonetheless restricted the Croatian capacity to make any contribution whatsoever to the monarchy's industrial production.

As already noted, the unit of settlement encouraged by Habsburg regulations for the Military Border was the isolated and largely self-sufficient *zadruga*. The near-complete lack of Imperial investment in the border's infrastructure also helped make the development of even the smallest manufacturing sector impossible. During the eighteenth century, the rising *robot* obligations in Civil Croatia did prompt peasant migration to the relative freedom of the Military Border, but no town in either area exceeded 5,000 population. The few attempts at manufacturing cloth, iron, and glass in Civil Croatia collected fewer than two hundred workers combined and no financial backing beyond their noble family founders. All but an iron works on the large estate of the most powerful family failed within a few years.[55]

Scant improvement followed for most of the nineteenth century. The founding in Budapest of five large flour mills severely limited the potential for milling the Croatian and Slavonian grain crops. By the 1860s these mills processed enough Hungarian grain to meet the limited urban needs of Civil and Military Croatia, except for the local markets of the Adriatic coast and the free Imperial town of Karlovac between there and Zagreb.[56] The profitability of selling a bulky good

such as flour over this wide territory doubtless derived from the Zagreb railway's connection to Budapest, completed in 1862. The link
to the Hungarian market finally allowed Croatian manufacture of
rough woolen cloth to make a modest beginning, after a century of
total failure against English and Czech competition in the Habsburg
lands. A factory founded in Osijek to make silk from the worms of the
mulberry trees increasingly grown in Slavonia did not survive the
1860s, in the absence of a similar rail link.[57]

The Effort to Develop Rijeka

The one area where these mid-century attempts to establish industrial enterprises attracted more funds from urban merchants than
rural nobles was the so-called Hungarian Littoral, centered on
Rijeka, a free port for the Hungarian lands since 1776. The town's
Croatian and Italian traders had continued to support the state sugar
refinery until its demise in 1828. They backed several private ventures for processing imported sugar. The refinery could not hope to
compete successfully against locally grown sugar beets that spread
across all the northern Habsburg lands after 1850. Much more promising in an integrated Habsburg economy would have been the processing of timber, the Littoral's principal natural resource. Indeed,
Rijeka's merchants attracted some French and English capital to
open the first Croatian paper mill in 1828. Sawmills and ship construction followed. The average size of the twenty-odd ships built
each year doubled between the 1830s and the 1860s.[58]

By 1870 the era of ironclad ships had begun. Rijeka's promise as a
construction center ended until the twentieth century. In order to
make the transition before then, Rijeka would have had to obtain the
same access to Slovenian iron and the Austrian markets for its timber
products enjoyed by Trieste, on the other side of the Istrian Peninsula. This the *Ausgleich* of 1867 specifically prevented. The southern
tip of the monarchy-wide border between Austrian and Hungarian
territory (Cisleithania and Transleithania) passed ten miles to the
west of Rijeka. By 1890, the Austrian state railway had built a
narrow-gauge spur from the main Trieste-Vienna line to the border.
Hungarian authorities grudgingly laid connecting track to Rijeka. In
the meantime, they had taken special pains to connect Rijeka to Zagreb and Budapest. The line completed in 1873 offered Rijeka no
nearby supply of iron and a smaller set of urban markets than Cisleithania. This routing seems to have been a heavier blow to the
port's prospects than the Hungarian failure to connect it with the
largely rural economy of eastern Slavonia that is emphasized by
Croatian scholars.[59] Those eastern territories suffered instead from

the lack of a direct railway to Cisleithanian Austria. They might have sold their grain or livestock much more easily there than in the Hungarian economy with its rapidly expanding agricultural sector.

Trieste and the Slovenian Economy

The potential for successful integration with the Austrian half of the monarchy may be gauged only from the successful Slovenian experience. Slovenia's territory except for Istria had been a hereditary Habsburg land since the fourteenth century. Tariff barriers separating it from the large Viennese market had been lifted, in other words, centuries before those dividing the Austrian and the Czech lands. Even more than the Czech lands, Slovenia was so mountainous that agriculture alone could not easily support its population. This was especially true before the abolition of serfdom in 1848. Peasants used their own land for grazing livestock rather than for raising crops in order to avoid the tithe obligations to the feudal landlord. That left only inefficient *robot* cultivation of the nobles' demesne to generate a grain crop. Fast-flowing streams and widespread sheepraising encouraged the expansion of household textile manufacture into the sort of "protoindustrial" development found in the Belgian and Czech uplands during the early modern period.[60] So did the continued growth of Trieste: its population doubled during the first half of the nineteenth century to exceed 60,000. Using Egyptian cotton imported to Trieste, mechanical spinning of cotton thread had begun in Slovenia by 1828. A modern mill opened in Ljubljana with English backing in 1837. The owners and employees of subsequent firms were typically Slovenian traders from rural areas who had begun by selling their own household production. Thus a growing Slovenian element joined the mainly German urban population. Although exact numbers of workers are not known, the number of mechanically powered spindles on Slovenian territory had climbed to 3 percent of the Habsburg total by the 1840s. The percentage matched the Slovenian share of the monarchy's population.[61]

All this occurred before the construction of the Vienna-Trieste railway. Its completion in 1854 had the apparent disadvantage of opening up even the Trieste market to higher-quality and lower-cost textiles from the now sophisticated production in the Czech lands. The same fate befell Slovenian glass manufacture, which dated from 1824.[62] The few early glass works also faced the rising price of wood, their main fuel, in the face of railway construction. Sawmills that sprung up during this mid-century period turned to supplying the construction trades in Trieste after the railway boom subsided. Several paper-making plants around Ljubljana were profitable enough by 1870 to attract Austrian capital in order to consolidate and modernize their operations. The coming of the Vienna-Trieste railway and its feeder network even afforded the sort of backward linkage to heavy industry that Alexander Gerschenkron has found decisive for the industrializing spurt of Tsarist Russia.[63] Significant Slovenian deposits of iron ore and coal were of course prerequisites for heavy industry not found elsewhere in the Yugoslav lands. From 1847 railway construction was sufficient to prompt the opening of several ironworks. Smelters in Trieste were soon turning this pig iron into rail and ship parts. By 1869, the Jesenice iron works, an immense complex today, had begun to manufacture such parts on its own premises. The Zagorje coal mines expanded in the 1860s, also in order to meet the rising needs of Slovenian railway traffic.[64]

Transylvania as a Special Case

If the geographic location of Slovenia within the Habsburg economy was the most fortunate among the lands of Southeastern Europe, that of Transylvania was the least. Here was the most landlocked of all the southern Habsburg territories, with no navigable outlet to the sea or to the Danube. A prohibitively long overland route barred the way to Vienna for Transylvanian agricultural goods. The area enjoyed relatively abundant rainfall, but it fell on a hilly upland plateau between the Carpathians. Just to the west, the Hungarian plain, one of the best grain-growing areas in Europe, straddled the route to Vienna. Throughout the eighteenth century, this overwhelmingly rural and agricultural economy was recording import surpluses over exports of nearly two to one, if we include its trade with the other Habsburg lands, the primary source of the imbalance.[65] From the start Transylvania was hardly a showcase for Habsburg mercantilist policy.

Perpetuating this trade deficit for longer than in the neighboring Banat was the first of two fundamental differences that set Transylvania apart from the rest of the lands on the southeastern Habsburg border. This was not an unsettled "steppe frontier," in William McNeill's phrase.[66] It could not attract and absorb belated Habsburg colonization as the Vojvodina did once the threat of recurring warfare had been removed. With the formidable Carpathian mountains ringing its territory on three sides, Transylvania had been a natural sanctuary for immigrants from Central Europe since the thirteenth century. German Saxons and Hungarian Szeklers began their medieval migration to escape feudal disorder. Persecuted Protestants continued to come in the early modern period. The native Romanian population had drawn added numbers from the Principalities of Wallachia and Moldavia. By the early eighteenth century total population approached 900,000. This was more than triple the probable figure for all Croatia, Slavonia, and the Vojvodina, together roughly comparable in size.[67] The totals for the two areas had drawn even at 1.4 million by 1787, reflecting the impact of the assorted migrations that covered the territories to the west.

A second distinguishing feature made sure that relatively few immigrants would be attracted to Transylvania during the eighteenth century. Hungarian nobles maintained sufficient authority to continue their control of the land tenure system.[68] From the reconquest in 1691 forward, they were strong enough to resist Vienna's efforts to incorporate Transylvania with the other Habsburg lands and thus bring the local nobility under urbarial obligation to limit their *robot* requirements on the peasantry. Instead of the 52 to 104 days demanded in Inner Hungary, the Romanian and Hungarian peasants of Transylvania faced obligations nearly twice as large. They were forced to work the lord's land for three or four days a week and still give him one ninth of the produce from their own land.[69] In the absence of consolidated cultivation or fertile lands, the large noble estates had little grain to export. The peasantry chose to concentrate on using their own land to raise livestock. The marketable surplus of grain thus remained minimal.

The Problems of the Transylvanian Military Border

The dominance of the Hungarian nobility dissuaded Austrian authorities from extending the Military Border along the Transylvanian frontier, a formidable physical barrier anyway, until 1762. The revolt of the Szekler peasantry against both Hungarian noble and Habsburg authority along the border with Moldavia, always in the path of a Russian advance southward, prompted Vienna to act. General Buccow was dispatched to pacify the area and to implement his plan for establishing the Military Border there with a reformed system of land tenure. Although failing to install reforms, he did set up a Romanian regiment on the eastern border that had witnessed the Szekler's unrest. By 1764, a second regiment drawn from the Romanian peasantry was in place on the southern border, to be followed by two Hungarian regiments and a mixed one twenty years later. Their total strength was small, under 15,000 men, until the Napoleonic Wars swelled them to 130,000.[70] By 1800 the Military Border contained fewer than 700,000 people, not even half the total population of Transylvania. Military service therefore put a tremendous wartime strain on the Border's agricultural economy.

That economy also recorded little peacetime progress before or after the Napoleonic Wars. The land provided free of feudal obligation to the peasant *Grenzer*, or border guard, was typically a dwarf-holding of an acre or two. The local gentry got grants of 50 to 75 acres. Growing population forced the subdivision of these dwarf-holdings into still more inefficient units. Grain shortages became a fact of border life. The *Grenzer* found relief only if they could arrange to buy grain from the Romanian Principalities.[71] But money was hard to come by. The lack of roads denied the *Grenzer* access to enough of the area's abundant timber even for their own needs. The lack of nearby urban markets limited the sale of their household textile production. They bore the added burden of continuing to pay all taxes in coin. The Hungarian nobility still paid none and retained what lands they had held before the Military Border was established.

Migration to the Romanian Principalities

The Romanian peasantry had been virtually drafted into the two border regiments. They hardly considered their new circumstances to be the improvement that Serbs fleeing Ottoman depredations to the Croatian Military Border had initially regarded service there. Chances for promotion to officer rarely came. The threat of prolonged service prompted Romanian emigration to Wallachia and Moldavia. Assorted Habsburg measures tried to stem the flow and to bring back forcibly those who had left. Yet a total of 12,000 *Grenzers* are reckoned to have deserted to the Romanian Principalities by 1784.[72] A more marked departure from the Habsburg policy of populationism, pursued with such success in the Vojvodina, could not be imagined.

The migration also included merchants. They were the largest single group leaving Braşov and Sibiu, the two long-established centers of border commerce. German immigrants from Saxony had founded these towns in the thirteenth century as Kronstadt and Hermannstadt. Armed with privileges of immunity from Hungarian customs, the towns' German merchants began to trade precious metals and locally produced cloth to Wallachia for foodstuffs. By the seventeenth century, Greeks and Macedo-Romanians, the latter known as *mocanii*, had migrated there from the Romanian Principalities. They formed trading companies whose connections throughout the Ottoman lands facilitated their rapid rise to preeminence in commerce across the border.[73] By the eighteenth century they were forced to pay higher taxes, in order to help support the Military Border, so that the two towns would not lose their status as royal free cities. From 1770 the Border's quarantine regulations, the *Sanitäts Kordon*, hindered trade. These impositions plus the heavy strain imposed on the entire border economy by military service during the Napoleonic Wars apparently explain the increase in merchant migration to Wallachia, mainly to Bucharest, at the start of the nineteenth century.[74] Border trade did not decline during this migration, nor during the repeated movement back and forth of peasants from both sides practicing transhumance or seeking to escape the impositions of their noble landlords, Hungarian in Transylvania and Romanian or Greek in Wallachia. Trade actually increased, albeit with the same import surplus into the 1820s that still characterized Transylvanian trade with the rest of the Habsburg lands.[75] The same low tariffs, about 3 percent ad valorem, that the monarchy had negotiated with the Porte in the eighteenth century continued to apply to produce from the Principalities, in contrast to the protectionist rates levied on European goods.

Now, that trade, like Ottoman commerce to the west, had shifted outside the original imperial boundaries in search of better markets than its point of origin could provide. The center of Transylvanian border trade had now moved to Bucharest. With it a sizable foundation was laid for the future union of Transylvania with the Romanian Principalities. To understand the commercial attraction of these Principalities, we must turn to the general course of economic events in this one region of the early modern Balkans which was outside the direct control of both the Habsburg and Ottoman Empires.

Habsburg Economic Institutions in the Early Modern Borderlands

To the north, the monarchy's internal market had bound its component parts more closely together by the end of the early modern period. Most of the southern borderlands, however, did not see their productive capacity integrated into the wider imperial economy. Nor can the demand that their limited growth generated have been crucial to the long-run prospects of either Czech industry or Hungarian agriculture.

Only the Slovenian economy had received and responded to a conscious Habsburg effort to promote commercial development. Ironically, the state's investment in the largely Italian port of Trieste encouraged protoindustrialization in a Slovenian hinterland that post-1918 boundaries would separate from this initial source of stimulation. Similar Habsburg investment in Rijeka, on the other side of the Istrian Peninsula and part of modern Yugoslavia rather than Italy, would not help the Croatian hinterland until the railway connections to Budapest had been completed later in the nineteenth century. As we shall see in Chapter 9, the networks of Austrian and Hungarian railways across the borderlands would come to constitute the state's main contribution to their pre-1914 development, despite the lack of coordination between the two sets of lines.

Before the mid-nineteenth century, the principal economic institutions sent south from the imperial center were much less modern: the regime of the Military Border, feudal regulations governing noble estates, and the rural settlement of German colonists. Habsburg authorities supported all three but more to secure the borderlands against Ottoman attack than to create a viable agricultural economy. In the latter task, the first two institutions failed miserably. The Military Border purposely scattered its upland settlements. It diverted peasant labor to military duties and kept families on small, nontransferable communal land holdings. All this discouraged crop cultivation. Hungarian objections to peasant use of state lands held back the timber cutting that would become so profitable to most of the borderlands by the end of the century (again, see Chapter 9). North of the Military Border, the largely Hungarian nobles resident on the smaller estates were tied by urbarial regulations to an inefficient supply of serf labor. Absentee owners of the larger estates found their capital diverted to maintaining villas in Budapest. The feudal inalienability of their land kept access to mortgage credit minimal. Bad roads and the more affluent estates of Inner Hungary barred the way to the growing markets of Budapest and Vienna.

The German colonists brought by imperial "populationism" from Swabia to the Vojvodina did spread the consolidation of separate strips, the use of iron plows, and other progressive practices so lacking on the noble estates and native smallholdings to the west and east. But official permission for commercial sale of land in the Vojvodina by the end of the eighteenth century opened the way for Hungarian estate owners. Their purchases plus those of the German colonists started the growth of a largely Yugoslav landless peasantry that continued to increase even after the formal abolition of serfdom in 1849. Otherwise, the German colonists received no further assistance from Habsburg authorities.

As a general rule, what capital accumulated and what entrepreneurial energy was expended in the early modern borderlands came from migrant or native groups. Officials or commercial interests from Vienna were typically not involved. Actual Habsburg policy toward the Ottoman Balkans permitted relatively free trade and population movement. Political and military motives rather than economic ones explain this policy. It allowed Balkan traders to join German farmers and Italian bankers in carving out modernizing enclaves (sectors seems too strong a word) in the economy of the imperial borderlands. Traders ignored the stated Habsburg intention to create a mercantilistic export surplus with relative ease. They spent most of their energy furnishing the Habsburg frontier with supplies imported from their Balkan homelands. Their commerce across the Habsburg-Ottoman border created an important if nonindustrial base around which the national economies of Yugoslavia and Romania could eventually take shape.

3.

The Romanian Principalities

between Three Empires,

1711–1859

This is the first of two chapters describing the intermediate condition of internal autonomy, short of full independence from Ottoman control, that provides a common focus for the economic history of the Romanian and Serbian lands for the greater part of the nineteenth century. Greece in the 1830s and Bulgaria in the 1880s would make the transition from an imperial to a national economic framework abruptly. Serbian autonomy had been established by 1830, almost half a century before political independence. The still longer economic transition had already begun, as we have seen in Chapter 1, by the end of the eighteenth century.

The Romanian Principalities of Wallachia and Moldavia had known only an intermediate status since the Ottoman conquest. Never an integral part of the Ottoman Empire, their native princes had contributed annual tribute and cooperated with the Porte's foreign policy. In return, these princes were permitted to continue ruling on Ottoman sufferance until several acts of Romanian defiance saw them deposed at the start of the eighteenth century. Even then, the Ottoman response did not revise the system of indirect suzerainty beyond replacing the native princes with Phanariot Greeks. The Phanariots' purchase of the office in Istanbul and their frequent replacement were the principal sources of Ottoman political leverage.

During this so-called Phanariot period, 1711–1821, the course of Romanian economic development was permanently marked not only by the dynamics of native-Greek-Ottoman relations but also by the proximity of two European empires. A Russian presence unique in

the history of Southeastern Europe began with the arrival of the
Russian army on the Dniester River, bordering Bessarabia, in 1792.
Tsarist colonization of Bessarabia proceeded from 1806, at the start of
a six-year military occupation of Wallachia and Moldavia as well.
Another occupation during 1828–34 brought the Principalities under
the Russian-designed Règlement Organique. It ratified the restoration of native nobles to the leadership of the two Principalities. This
restoration had been the principal Ottoman response to the abortive
peasant revolt of 1821. In addition to ensuring the end of Greek
Phanariot influence, the Règlement Organique also provided a pattern for administrative centralization that has marked all subsequent
modernization under Romanian governments.

The Habsburg role dated from the reconquest of Transylvania in
1691. The continuing dominance there of the Hungarian nobility
frustrated real Habsburg hegemony, while also oppressing the
Romanian peasant majority of the population. Only one sustained
Austrian effort to undo this local Hungarian dominance was relevant
to Romanian economic history. This was the extension of the Military
Border to eastern Transylvania between 1762 and 1780 (see Chapter
2).

Austrian occupation of western Wallachia (Oltenia) between 1718
and 1739 carried the Habsburg fiscal and land tenure systems into
the Principalities. More important was the increasing import of
Habsburg manufactures and migration from the Transylvanian towns,
mainly to Bucharest, that provided one of several economic bases for
the nineteenth-century Romanian independence movement. Without
question the movement drew heavily on Western European ideas of
national identity and equality.[1] But its first fruition, with the union of
the two Principalities in 1859 under a single native ruler, preceded
rather than followed any decisive increase in Romanian relations
with the industrially developed economies of Western Europe.

The Phanariot Principalities and the Ottoman Economy

Unlike the native nobility of the Ottoman Balkans, the Romanian
boyars had survived the late medieval and early modern periods with
their positions intact. Despite sizable loss of political power in 1711,
they maintained their landed estates and seigneurial rights over the
peasantry. How tempting then to assume that they used this remaining power base to take advantage of the growing European demand
for grain. Did they not expand their seigneurial reserves and bind
increasing numbers of peasants to cultivate these domainal lands?
Such a process had after all begun in the Polish and eastern German

lands during the general growth of European population and com-merce during the sixteenth century. It had culminated in a kind of "second serfdom" when the Thirty Years War reduced market de-mand and the attractiveness of money payment from the peasantry.[2] Armed with Lenin's frequent references to this "Prussian model" of *Gutsherrschaft,* Romanian Marxist scholars writing in the immediate postwar period embraced this scenario of larger, more consolidated noble estates to explain growing grain export. More recently, com-prehensive research in the available estate records has led them away from asserting this neat symmetry. What appears instead is a noticeably slow growth of grain exports, especially to Western Europe, and the equally slow rise of a second serfdom, at least one tying the peasant to an annual total of days of estate work that even approached those in the Habsburg, Prussian, or Polish lands.

The reasons for this departure from the experience of northeastern Europe derive in part from the more difficult access, especially by sea, to western markets. Yet they also derive from a familiar element of the Ottoman economic legacy to much of Southeastern Europe. War, disorder, and disease had limited the total population of the two Principalities to perhaps one million around 1700 and reduced it to not much over 500,000 by mid-century.[3] The assorted Russian and Austrian advances into the Principalities and the failure of the Phanariot rulers to keep rural order even in peacetime discouraged the Romanian boyars from expanding their estates' reserves. Some from Wallachia moved to Bucharest. Part of the surviving peasantry responded to threats of new unrest by migrating to Transylvania. Ac-cording to one rough estimate, two thirds of the peasant families in several Wallachian districts fled during the period 1753–63.[4] Habsburg border guards and Phanariot regulations turned back an unknown number. Those staying behind maintained a seminomadic way of life. They relied on livestock herding and slash-and-burn cul-tivation on the generally accurate premise that there was little chance of safe, permanent settlement.

The Ottoman Wheat Monopoly

Combining with this limited supply of labor to hold back grain cultivation was the general Ottoman policy of controlling trade in daily necessities. The ban on European ships in the Black Sea since 1592 insulated the Principalities. So did the requirement that all Ot-toman ships coming from Black Sea destinations to Istanbul offload their goods for taxation before proceeding. Thus the Mediterranean grain shortages that recurred until the nineteenth century could not be relieved by purchases from the lands bordering the Black Sea.

Perhaps more important, given the several wheat-growing areas closer to the Mediterranean market than the Principalities, were Ottoman efforts to assure the food supply of its army and Istanbul at low prices fixed by the *nart* system described in Chapter 1. The increasing insecurity of the Ottoman lands in southern Russia throughout the eighteenth century culminated in their complete loss by 1783. This focused Ottoman attention on the Principalities. An increasing number of Greek merchants were officially dispatched from Istanbul to Bucharest to collect compulsory deliveries, or *zaharea*, of wheat, livestock, and other foodstuffs from both Wallachia and Moldavia. The relatively low, fixed prices paid for these deliveries naturally discouraged wheat-growing. Marketed wheat in the two Principalities amounted to perhaps 100,000 quintals a year by the 1750s, just 15 percent of the figure 100 years later.[5] As late as 1833, wheat made up less than one fifth of the total value of the Principalities' exports. Its cultivation had spread significantly only in the neighborhood of Bucharest and the other larger towns.[6] These limits prevailed despite Ottoman efforts to expand wheat exports by lifting peacetime restrictions on maximum prices following the 1768–74 war with Russia. The prospect of renewed warfare and continuing limits on the amount of wheat that could be sold in Istanbul, beyond the prescribed deliveries two or three times a year, simply left Romanian peasants and boyars little incentive to expand their cultivation of wheat.[7]

The peasantry for its part turned to raising corn, which had first been introduced to the Principalities only at the end of the seventeenth century. The crop had several advantages, not the least of which was its exemption from Ottoman *zaharea* or any other form of taxation. It also furnished higher yields than wheat and more calories than millet. It allowed vegetables to be planted between rows and provided better feed for the livestock raising that remained the major agricultural activity of the Romanian peasant. By the end of the eighteenth century, corn had by all accounts replaced wheat and millet as the main grain crop.[8]

Agriculture on the Boyar Estates

The native and Phanariot boyars apparently added precious little to the limited amount of wheat grown by the peasantry. The smaller boyars who controlled only one village, as well as the officeholders who controlled dozens of villages and had moved to Bucharest, cultivated the minimal seigneurial reserves from holdings that were otherwise left open to peasant occupation. Only those estates drawing on large numbers of gypsy slaves deviated from this norm. The

records of monastery estates, which controlled about one third of all
cultivated land by 1800, are our principal primary source for the
eighteenth century. They indicate that barely 5 percent of all grain
output came from reserves. A survey in 1838 of all boyar and other
estates, covering three quarters of Wallachian territory, revealed reserves that accounted for under 5 percent of cultivated land.[9]

Recent Romanian research among some six hundred monastery
registers and also among the Habsburg inventories of western Wallachian estates, taken during the occupation of 1718–39, makes it
clear that such properties supported themselves largely by safer
means. They tended vineyards on their reserves and used seigneurial monopolies to charge peasants for milling grain into flour or dis-
tilling plums into brandy. They exported livestock to Transylvania.
The assorted records reflect days of peasant labor on the estate reserves for vineyards that were ten times the number for other crops
and estate expenses. Income totals showed spirits and livestock both
bringing in three or four times the 5 to 10 percent proportion for
cereals.[10] By the early nineteenth century, a fivefold increase in the
price of cattle and horses in Central Europe from the start of the
Napoleonic wars made their duty-free export to Transylvania and the
Polish lands the largest single source of income for the Moldavian
boyars. In Wallachia, cattle faced an Ottoman export tariff of about 50
percent ad valorem. Pigs were exempt from any taxation, as
elsewhere in an empire whose Moslem majority was enjoined from
eating pork for religious reasons. For the period 1812–1819, the
value of their export from Wallachia to Transylvania matched that of
the Principality's entire cereal export, a combination of wheat exported to Istanbul and corn to Transylvania.[11]

Sharecropping and the Land Tenure System

The dominant system of peasant land tenure had discouraged the
extensive cultivation of grain since the eighteenth century. The same
boyar and church estate records indicate that the boyars' exaction
from the peasantry principally took the form of a tithe, or *dijma*, of
the crops grown by the peasant family on the estate land it occupied,
rather than in labor days, or *clacă*, on the estate's reserve. Beyond
the small fraction of most estates' land in such reserves, as already
noted, the number of days required for *clacă* labor remained small,
especially when compared to the 50 to 150 days of annual *robot* seen
in Chapter 2 to be typical of the Habsburg lands. The Romanian requirement was formally fixed at twelve days a year with another
twelve days convertible to cash payment added, in Phanariot decrees
of 1746 for Wallachia and 1749 for Moldavia.

The decrees were designed to put a formal end to serfdom and stem the flow of peasant emigration to Transylvania and the Banat. Previous boyar exactions had not inspired that emigration. Instead the peasantry was fleeing the Habsburg-Ottoman wars of 1736–39 and subsequent Phanariot taxation. The decrees promised an end to such impositions. The limit on *clacă* days was intended as a guarantee that boyars would not attempt to compensate for lost rights of taxation by boosting the number of days.[12] The effect was indeed to attract enough peasants from the free upland villages, beyond the boundaries of most estates, so as to make some dent in the lowland shortage of labor, if not to lure back many emigrés.

Prince Alexander Ypsilantis of Wallachia issued his *Pravilnicească Condică* decree of 1780 to reaffirm the maximum requirement of twelve days *clacă* plus twelve more convertible by cash payment. Several surveys taken at the time revealed that the typical number of days exacted from the peasantry was still only six to eight a year.[13] Then the price of grain rose in Ottoman markets as wartime conditions returned in 1788. The accelerating depreciation in the value of Ottoman coin also prompted enforcement of the full number of days and sometimes more without rights of cash conversion. In Wallachia the attendant wartime unrest prompted still more buyers to leave the estates for Bucharest. For the first time, they began to lease their property to local traders, instead of leaving it in the care of relatives. The new Greek or Romanian lessees anticipated the behavior of Jewish merchants in the late nineteenth century. They paid more attention to commercial profit than had the boyar owners. The so-called Caragea Legislation of 1818 recognized the estates' growing interest in controlling peasant labor. It made the settlement on estate land a privilege, not a right, and increased the charge for cash conversion of *clacă* days tenfold.[14]

More important, the 1818 legislation ratified the growing estate practice of collecting up to one fifth rather than one tenth of the peasants' own produce in *dijma*. The collection of grain had exceeded the amount cultivated by *clacă* labor by three or five to one throughout the eighteenth century. From 1774 forward, it had included a fixed amount in corn, the peasants' largest single crop by the end of the century. In Moldavia, where most boyars had remained to manage their own estates, the *dijma* collection included not only corn but also the wheat delivered to meet the Ottoman *zaharea*. Even after the start of the nineteenth century, in other words, the *dijma* remained the boyars' major means of payment exploitation. Its dominance launched the growing commercial development of Romanian agriculture in the direction of sharecropping on small plots rather than consolidated cultivation on large plantations.

Its dominance should not be used, however, to downgrade the extent of peasant exploitation. Romanian Marxist scholarship can point to widespread peasant participation in a revolt against this emerging land tenure system as early as 1821.[15] Tudor Vladimirescu drew on his peasant origins as well as his experience in the Russian army to launch a Romanian peasant revolt just before the ill-fated invasion of Alexander Ypsilantis. A Phanariot himself but based in Russia, Ypsilantis sought to overthrow the Phanariot regime as the signal for a revolt against Ottoman rule on the Greek mainland. Vladimirescu decided to fight on for some sort of Romanian autonomy even after the Tsar had repudiated Ypsilantis' cause. Significantly, Vladimirescu's defeat followed on the heels of a call to his peasant power base to set aside their economic grievances and accept a native boyar government. The peasants refused. The boyars accepted the return to Ottoman hegemony rather than negotiate with peasant representatives over any change in the tax or *dijma* systems.

The Role of Bucharest, the Biggest Balkan Capital

Before turning to the Russian and Habsburg roles in the rise of Romanian agricultural exports during the post-Phanariot period of limited autonomy (1821–1859), we must remind ourselves of Bucharest's special position in Balkan economic history. By 1859, the population of the Wallachian capital had grown to 120,000, about twice the size of Thessaloniki or Iaşi, the Moldavian capital, and about four times the size of any other Balkan town, including Belgrade and Sofia.[16] From the eighteenth century until the Second World War, moreover, the city was unique not only for its size but also for its wealth and ethnic diversity.

Geographic Advantages

The location of Bucharest favored this preeminent position. Although not on the Danube like Belgrade or on the Mediterranean like Athens/Piraeus, the townsite had other advantages. Bucharest grew up at a convenient midpoint between the flood-prone Wallachian plain north of the Danube and the forested foothills south of the Carpathians. The very spot was on the unnavigable but fast-flowing Dîmboviţa River at a place where it narrowed and several islands made crossing still easier. First mentioned historically as a fortress for the famous Vlad Ţepes in the fifteenth century, Bucharest became the capital of Wallachia in 1659. Ottoman authorities were concerned about losing their suzerainty over the Principality and decided to move the capital southeast from Tîrgoviște, which was considered too close for comfort to the sanctuary of the Carpathians and Transylvania.[17] Thus, like Sofia, Bucharest was from the seventeenth century an administrative center.

Yet unlike Sofia, it was not surrounded by mountains. It was instead an easily accessible commercial crossroads, only sixty miles from the Danube over flat countryside and about the same distance from an easily traversed pass through the Carpathians. The route from Bucharest led directly to the major Transylvanian commercial center of Brașov, then Kronstadt. From there, established trade routes dating from medieval times went to Vienna and on to Leipzig. The latter's fairs were the principal entrepôt for early modern Central Europe. This connection supplied exports such as wine, wax, and salt to Leipzig in return for manufactured imports. Bucharest thus became the commercial center of Wallachia by the late seventeenth century. The city was also the first major transit point within Ottoman jurisdiction for Central European goods bound overland or by the Black Sea for the metropolis of Istanbul. A growing commerce, plus six decades' freedom from foreign occupation or plunder from 1659 until 1716, helps explain population estimates for Bucharest by 1700 that all exceed 60,000.[18]

The Wealth of Bucharest

The city's continued prosperity during the eighteenth century did not depend on the growth of Istanbul and Ottoman urban demand, at least before the last two decades. Nor did the population of Bucharest exhibit any permanent increase during the century. In fact, several cycles of war, occupation, and plague reduced its size to perhaps 30,000 before growth resumed in the last quarter of the century.[19] Until that time, however, more wealthy residents had settled there than any other Balkan town would ever attract. Only the richest of Phanariot Greek families from Istanbul could afford the prices that the Porte openly charged for the major official positions in the Principalities. This regime followed the end of administration by native Princes in 1711. Relatives flocked in to take lesser positions or to buy up titles and estates from needy boyar families. Rights to tax revenues from throughout the Principalities tempted them to stay. They invariably built their impressive residences in Bucharest. With them came a life style organized around imported luxuries. Native Wallachian boyars, feeling increasingly threatened in the countryside by war and unrest, also began to build villas within the city limits as the eighteenth century progressed.[20]

There is no way of measuring the aggregate income or expenses of this sizable privileged class. We do find several indirect indications of the commercial demand that it must have generated. New jobs were generated by the construction and furnishing of large villas and of equally elaborate churches and monasteries. The growth of a commercial quarter to support these workers can be gauged from the fact that one third of the merchants and artisans in all Wallachia resided in the city by the early nineteenth century. Roughly 3,000 inns or restaurants had accumulated in this quarter to serve the flow of commercial, official, and clerical visitors to the city. We cannot be certain of the exact number of artisan manufacturers, but it is known that their guilds increased from a handful to about fifty during the course of the eighteenth century, and that the great majority were in crafts that helped build or furnish boyar villas and churches.[21] The Central European origin of the building materials and luxury manufactures (mainly high quality cloth and paper) that could not be produced locally is attested to by the main street for import merchants. It had been renamed Lipsca (or Leipzig) by the middle of the century.

Ethnic Diversity and Trade

The merchant and artisan quarters of which this street was the central artery also accounted for the city's great ethnic diversity. As noted in Chapter 1, such communities in Istanbul and elsewhere in the Ottoman lands included representatives of the Empire's major non-Turkish groups. Bucharest was unique for including a variety of urban immigrants from the Habsburg lands as well. Chief among them were Germans and Ashkenazi Jews.

Ethnic Germans from the Habsburg lands had been recorded in the city since the sixteenth century. This was hardly surprising, given the Saxon town of Braşov (Kronstadt) just over the Transylvanian border, which had been a magnet for German immigrants from its medieval founding. By this time it was attracting Protestants in particular. Those moving on to Bucharest were largely skilled artisans. The very word *German* became synonymous in the city with *Meister*, the German word for mastercraftsman. The several eighteenth-century boyar enterprises for cloth, paper, and glass drew most of their skilled labor from this pool. They sometimes sought recruits in Transylvania, including enough weavers to prompt a Habsburg ban on their departure by 1793.[22] The baking and leatherworking guilds were also largely German. The first breakdown of the city's ethnic composition, in 1824, revealed some 4,000 Germans in a total of 60,000 to 70,000.[23]

According to the same estimate, the Jewish community was not much larger, some 4,000 to 6,000 persons. Unlike Jewish communities of similar size in many of the other large Balkan towns, however, this had a near majority that were not Sephardic or Spanish Jews from the Mediterranean, but rather Ashkenazim from Central and Eastern Europe. Sephardic immigration dated back to the sixteenth century. Ashkenazi families had been recorded in Principalities as early as 1700. Only after the Habsburg annexation of Galicia in 1772 did significant numbers spill over into Moldavia, whose population was 5 to 10 percent Jewish by 1818.[24] Excluded from owning land anyway and sometimes bringing along commercial connections to Central Europe, the more affluent began to pay for the right to join the merchant community in Bucharest, usually as moneylenders or silversmiths. A few even found their way into the list of the top twenty four merchant families. Such status entitled them to administer their own taxation under the Phanariot regime.

The Bulgarian and Serbian colonies in Bucharest also began during the eighteenth century. Bulgarians came first from Gabrovo, a center for household manufacture in the Balkan foothills, to sell their rough woolen cloth in the city's markets. Some stayed permanently as cloth merchants. Others began producing their native cloth in small shops. Bulgarian gardeners also began to show up on the staffs of boyar villas. The Serbian colony came by way of the Habsburg Vojvodina (see Chapter 2 on their substantial numbers there). They typically raised livestock and dominated the selling of meat and dairy products. The Greek and Armenian communities were mainly engaged in the grain trade and food processing. The former was probably the largest of these minority groups in the city. If we add the Phanariot officialdom, their numbers approached ten thousand by the early nineteenth century. The next largest, if least fortunate, group were the gypsies. At best they were independent ironmongers. Usually they were slaves in the boyar households.[25] Despite this ethnic diversity, the majority of the city's population appears to have been Romanian by the early nineteenth century. Yet even among their numbers, as noted in Chapter 2, the merchants and artisans were typically immigrants from the long-established Transylvanian commercial centers of Braşov and Sibiu.

By 1830, the city's commercial community accounted for one third of Wallachia's nine thousand registered merchants and artisans, and fully two thirds of the almost four thousand "foreigners", i.e., non-Ottoman subjects, included in that registration. By 1860, those absolute totals had both risen five or sixfold for Wallachia but only half that much for Bucharest.[26] To understand why that increase occurred and why it spread more rapidly outside Bucharest, we must examine the economic regime that the Russian victory over the Ottoman Empire in the war of 1828–29 brought to the Principalities.

The Economics of the Russian Règlement Organique

At first glance the postwar Russian military occupation and administration of the Principalities from 1829 to 1834 was only the sixth in a series of Tsarist occupations since 1711. But this one was different. Its administration left behind a unified set of political procedures and economic regulations called the Règlement Organique, or Organic Statutes, that remained the law of the land until 1848. Lasting much longer was their legacy of political power centralized in a permanent bureaucracy of ministries in the capital city. At the same time they allowed the boyars to strengthen their local economic power over the peasantry.

This Russian legacy deserves special attention not only because of its effect on Romanian economic development but also because it is unique in Balkan history. Until 1945, Russian economic influence in Southeastern Europe was generally negligible. During the interwar period, of course, political restrictions kept trade with the young Soviet state under one percent of total Balkan turnover. But the Balkan proportion of foreign trade with Tsarist Russia before 1914 was not much larger (see Chapter 6 for a comparison). Nor did a Tsarist economy whose military demands and small but rapidly developing industrial sector made Russia a net importer of capital have the resources to invest in the economic penetration of Southeastern Europe. Witness the Russian failure, described in Chapter 7, to assemble the necessary financing to construct the Bulgarian section of the Oriental Railway to Istanbul in the early 1880s. The occupying Tsarist army and officials could surely have used such a loan to consolidate their influence in the new Balkan state.

The Regime of Count Kiselev

During its occupation of the Romanian Principalities fifty years before, Tsarist Russia still held the diplomatic prerogative of sole responsibility for representing the interests of the Balkan Christians. The Crimean War and the Congress of Paris that transferred the responsibility to all the Great Powers were yet to come. Thus the Russian authorities were not obliged to accept a foreign prince as chief executive, like Alexander of Battenburg for Bulgaria in 1879. Instead, they were free to appoint Count Pavel Kiselev, a high-ranking Tsarist official, to a comparable position for the entire five-year occupation. This very able official was intent on modernizing reform, as represented in the Règlement Organique.[27] His efforts must now be matched against several weaknesses in the contemporary Tsarist economy, including the lack of exportable capital. Only then can we draw up a satisfactory balance sheet for this earliest Russian impact on Balkan economic development.

On the evening of Count Kiselev's arrival in Bucharest to take up his duties as Plenipotentiary for both Principalities there was a slight earthquake. The Romanian population regarded the tremor as a bad omen for his tour of duty, a reaction that was evidence of the deep suspicion that previous Russian occupations had engendered. Depredations by Russian troops and the widespread requisitioning of grain and livestock were the main collective memories.[28] They only strengthened the boyars' hand in resisting any changes that would threaten their own position. At the same time, the Russian government's awareness of past sins strengthened its resolve to improve conditions in the Principalities and thereby convert this territory into a bulwark against the Ottoman Empire. The Russian desire for greater popular support can be traced back to the occupation of 1806–12. It surfaced again in the Russian proposal of a "Règlement Général" for the Principalities, in the 1826 Akkerman Convention with the Ottoman Empire. The proposal would have the added merit, as would a similar one for the Polish lands in 1826, of making it easier to bring an independent-minded native nobility under political control. Count Kiselev had been appointed Plenipotentiary of both Principalities precisely to afford a unified command against boyar objections to such regulation.

His first major action made him more aware of the need for agrarian reform while weakening his leverage to achieve any. He toured much of the Principalities in 1829–30 to assess the extent of the plague, cholera, and then famine left in the wake of wartime conditions. He sensibly decided to set up grain reserves and storage facilities for the main towns. The Russophobe boyars mistook his action for a preliminary step in requisitioning more grain for the Russian army. Their insistence on greater economic privileges only hardened in the secret negotiations that preceded the Règlement.[29]

When the regulations went into effect during 1830–31, they established six European-style ministries and a Council of Ministers. Count Kiselev rightly regarded them as his principal leverage for reform. Venal appointments to such executive office, and the right to collect the taxes to support them that had formed a large fraction of boyar income during the Phanariot period, were eliminated. Supporting this new executive branch was a single uniform head tax to be collected by the Treasury's salaried, permanent staff. Count Kiselev used the new Interior Ministry to set up the first public health facilities outside Bucharest. The ministry also introduced the cultivation of winter wheat and spring potatoes and tried to promote peasant use of the three field system and manuring.[30]

The Frustration of Agricultural Reform before 1864

Count Kiselev was powerless, however, to put into effect the basic reforms in the land tenure system that his observation of the 1826 peasant revolt in the Ukraine and his study of the legal position of the Romanian peasant had suggested. In return for abjuring venal offices and tax collections, the most powerful Romanian boyars had insisted on revoking the peasants' right to unlimited and perpetual holdings of estate land. Peasant families, regardless of size, were now confined to one of three sizes of holdings: *fruntaşi* for peasants with two or more teams of draft animals, *mijlocaşii* with one and *condaşii* with none. Although the largest allotments went to the *fruntaşi,* their existing holdings were generally reduced most sharply. Their allotment for arable and pasture was less than ten acres and that of the *condaşii* less than five acres.[31] Virtually every peasant family was thus obliged to lease more land from the estate on a short-term basis in return for a *dijma* that now consisted of a money rent. As we have seen, lessee managers, usually Greek or Romanian grain merchants, had begun to handle these arrangements in Wallachia from the eighteenth century forward. Now similar concessions for entire estates became the rule in Moldavia as well. By the middle of the nineteenth century, about half of all estate land in Moldavia and more in Wallachia would be leased out. As early as 1833, lessees fully or partly "managed" (mainly collecting rents and other dues in coin or in kind) some 725 of the over 2,000 boyar estates in Moldavia. Of the 665 lessees, the 265 Jewish traders collected more than half the annual rents. Their total exceeded the tax revenue collected for the Moldavian government budget.[32] The road to the 1907 revolt that began against Jewish estate managers was already under construction.

This road was initially paved with sharecropping and money rents rather than the feudal obligations familiar to students of the so-called second serfdom in early modern Northeastern Europe. The three to sixfold increases in corn and wheat acreage reported from districts throughout the Principalities between 1830 and 1848 derived mainly from *dijma,* or tithing arrangements under which the peasant gave the estate one tenth or more of his harvest or its cash equivalent from his own portion of estate land and from the twelve-day *clacă* for annual labor on the estate's seigneurial reserve. The Règlement had redefined the latter in terms of tasks clearly requiring more than twelve days to perform. How much more has never been accurately determined, but recent Romanian scholarship suggests twenty four to thirty six days for Wallachia and over fifty days for Moldavia. Much more important is the peasant conversion, especially in Wallachia, of most of this *clacă* obligation into cash payment, as originally argued by Radu Rosetti in 1907 and as recently seconded by Ilie Corfus' painstaking archival research.[33]

That this conversion could occur in the face of the apparent increase in reserve acreage and in the acreage for wheat, the main reserve crop, poses an analytical problem. One part of the solution is simple. These increases were not large in terms of total arable land. Only a small fraction of Romanian agricultural land was actually cultivated by boyar, lessee, or peasant at the start of the Règlement period. Barely 5 percent of Wallachian estate land was cultivated reserve as late as 1838. The peasant proportion was less than 10 percent. The former figure probably passed 15 percent and the latter approached 30 percent by the early 1860s. The Moldavian percentages were higher but probably not by much, according to the somewhat contradictory data.[34] Most of the apparent reserve increases occurred during the 1840s, when wheat production nearly doubled to push up the volume of grain harvested in the two Principalities by perhaps two thirds. Yet a majority of this new reserve cultivation, especially in Wallachia, was the result of virtual contracts under which peasants cultivated estate land beyond their Règlement allotment and used their crop sales to pay both *clacă* and *dijma* at agreed rates of conversion. This surplus land, or *prisoare*, seems to account for most of the increase in boyar cultivation that until Corfus' research had been assumed to come from the forced application of peasant labor.

Such peasant payments did not derive from any new-found lowland prosperity. The peasants' villages were isolated, impermanent clusters of a few mud-walled dugouts. They had typically come from the hill country whose population density was twice that of the lowlands before the Règlement and still 50 percent more by 1859. There artisan manufacture, on the Bulgarian pattern already noted in Chapter 1, and transhumance spread experience with money income widely. The return of law and order to the lowlands with the Règlement attracted upland peasants to the relatively better land of the plains. The boyar *clacă* and even *dijma* obligations were met with sales of corn to lessees or merchant intermediaries, often at unfair prices, for the internal market or for Habsburg distilleries. Peasants also sold wheat in growing amounts to the foreign merchants of Galați and Brăila. This could occur only if the harvest was good. If it was not, as occurred because of drought or other climatic misfortune more often than not between 1840 and 1864, the peasant either went into debt on his contract for extra land or migrated back to the hills, as had been done seasonally before the Règlement. The latter option persisted as long as the government's program to keep and concentrate the peasantry in permanent villages continued to make the little headway it did before 1850.[35]

Nor were the boyars or their estates' lessees confident enough of keeping their scarce labor supply to attempt to prevent peasant movement by any means other than the contractual conversion of labor and harvest obligations by cash payment. Peasant resistance to these obligations was simply too strong. In addition, the boyars and their lessees were reluctant to permit a government survey of their estates. Under the terms of the Règlement, their reserves might be limited permanently to one third of the estate's acreage. Property rights on these Romanian estates thus remained to be defined.

Whether the growing imposition of sharecropping on this largely impoverished peasantry could have provoked it to widespread protest during the revolutionary summer of 1848, we shall never know. The professional class who were leaders of the short-lived provisional government in Bucharest did little to mobilize peasant support. A commission called to investigate agrarian problems went no further than allowing several peasant representatives and a few sympathetic members of the provisional leadership, most prominently Nicolae Bălcescu, to speak their piece. But the rest of the leadership voted to dissolve the commission for fear of losing boyar support. Ottoman troops then arrived and broke up the provisional government. The moderate majority's idea for a contractual agreement to compensate the boyars for giving up some of their land to the peasantry and all feudal rights would surface again as the basis for the reform of 1864.[36]

The agricultural history of the period between the formal end of the Règlement regime in 1848 and the land reform of 1864 has received recent attention from Romanian scholars. Its longstanding reputation as an interregnum marked only by steadily rising exports to Great Britain and France, with little change in trends from the Règlement era, has not survived this scrutiny very well. The uneven growth of Romanian grain exports and the special role of Crimean War demand are described below.

The one striking change of direction was the reduction of money conversion for *clacă* and *dijma* obligations and the increasing use of peasant labor on the reserves of boyar estates. Boyar interests rode high during this period. They were able to manipulate the redefinition of their land rights in 1851 so as to deny the peasantry in both Principalities any formal improvement in their obligations. Estate owners and lessees then went ahead to impose actual labor obligations on an increasingly numerous lowland peasantry (over half of the perhaps four million people in the Principalities in 1860).[37] Peasants were not only less scarce but also more restricted in their movement and expectations following the failure of the 1848 revolution.

The result was a much more limited expansion of reserve acreage than had occurred in the 1840s. Faced with *clacă* obligations on estate reserves estimated at fifty days a year for Wallachia and more for Moldavia, the peasantry responded by expanding its own unauthorized cultivation of estate land as compensation. The peasant share of crop land in Moldavia had fallen behind that of the reserves by 1846, but now recovered to double its amount by 1864. Leading the roughly 20-percent rise in Moldavian grain acreage during this period was a 50-percent jump in the cultivation of corn, grown principally by the peasantry as their main bread grain. Hence the final imposition of a second serfdom in Moldavia and to a lesser extent in Wallachia was unable to prevent peasant acreage from increasing faster than that of estate reserves.

Nor was the boyars' and lessees' use of forced peasant labor associated with any significant improvements in agricultural technology.[38] Several new varieties of seed had been introduced during the 1840s, but the crucial innovation, the planting of winter wheat to provide an additional export crop less vulnerable to drought and capable of occupying peasant labor for another season, made little headway. By 1863, winter wheat still accounted for just 12 percent of the total wheat harvest in Wallachia, despite several government efforts to promote it. Total wheat harvests in turn continued to lag behind corn by a two-to-three margin. The introduction of sugar beets and rapeseed (yielding a variety of oil) on the estate reserves is noteworthy, yet made little progress. Rapeseed seemed a promising export crop, but was grown in limited quantities and then abandoned when overplanting without rotation allowed worms to attack it in the early 1860s. Manuring, crop rotation, irrigation, and the use of mechanized threshers made limited beginnings on the Moldavian estate reserves whose peasant labor was now directly supervised. On the Wallachian reserves, such changes had not even gotten underway.

Yields per hectare, not surprisingly, remained at low Russian levels during this period. Peasant labor services were given grudgingly, often inefficiently to boot. Additional wage labor was available only for the long-standing estate cultivation of vineyards. The slow growth of total harvests throughout the 1850s testifies to these limitations. It also reflects recurring drought and the irregular course of grain exports to Western Europe.

Foreign Trade under the Règlement

The commercial provisions of the Règlement Organique made a greater contribution to modernizing the Romanian economy than its agricultural measures. The former were essentially as outlined in the Treaty of Adrianople, which concluded the Russo-Ottoman war of 1828–29. True, the boyars continued to enjoy exemption from all taxes. The standard Ottoman import and export tariff of 3 percent ad valorem was unchanged. But the comprehensive fiscal regulations that went into effect in 1831 undoubtedly encouraged foreign trade in a variety of other ways.[39] Tariff collection was taken away from the venal appointees who had enriched themselves by charging several times the existing duty. Facilitating fairer collection by the new salaried employees was the adoption, at least in Wallachia, of the metric system of weights and measures, which replaced a confusing welter of Ottoman, Russian, and Austrian measures. Commercial courts were set up to resolve disputes, and the fledgling police force was urged to arrest smugglers.

Most important, both the Danube and the Dardanelles were opened to merchant shipping under all flags. Ottoman rights to requisition fixed amounts of grain from the Principalities, even at market prices, were ended. Internal trade also received encouragement. With the famine of 1829–30 in mind, Count Kiselev expanded the list of "noncommercial goods," in which the regulations permitted free trade between the two Principalities, to include livestock. The list continued to expand after his departure. By 1846, it included all sorts of grain. Helping to increase both internal and external trade was Kiselev's decision to improve the Danubian port facilities for Moldavia at Galați. Wallachia was to do the same thing up river at Giurgiu and to create virtually a new port at Brăila, not far from Galați and the mouth of the Danube. By 1840, both had been declared free ports. Their combined populations climbed toward 40,000.[40]

The Règlement Organique also promoted the rise of merchants to a predominant position in the Principalities' urban economy. Its licensing requirement for every sort of urban commerce permitted the artisan guilds that had grown up around a variety of hand manufacturing during the eighteenth century to reestablish themselves only in Bucharest and then with virtually no economic functions. Although their license fees were barely one third of those charged the foreign traders, artisans faced price and other restrictions on their own production. Import merchants had only to pay relatively low taxes and tariffs. The guilds objected to this increased competition, especially to the importers' printed advertising, but their complaints generally went unheeded. The net result of these pressures could be seen as early as 1835. In just four years, the number of general merchants registered for selling all goods had jumped from 7 to 19 percent of the reduced number of licenses, mainly at the expense of the textile and leather artisans. The trend continued until the 1850s, when the spread of village artisan shops accounted for most of the unprecedented doubling of licensees to more than 100,000 in the two Principalities by 1863.[41] These totals dwarfed the Serbian commercial sector discussed in the next chapter.

Modern industry in the Principalities proper made too little progress from the slim eighteenth-century list of boyar-backed, unmechanized textile and glass factories to constitute a significant additional pressure on the artisan sector. More mechanized manufacture seems noteworthy during the Règlement period for only one reason. The Interior Ministry encouraged its expansion with tax exemptions and monopoly privileges of just the sort that an independent Romanian government would initiate in 1886, over a decade before the other Balkan states (see Chapter 8).[42]

The Economic Role of Jewish Immigration

The Jewish immigration from the Russian and Polish lands to Moldavia was of more immediate importance. Permissive provisions of the 1829 Russo-Ottoman Treaty of Adrianople greatly accelerated it. In 1833 Count Kiselev tried to stem the flow, introducing passport restrictions on the Moldavian border; this had little effect. Still barred from owning rural land on Kiselev's explicit instructions, Jews were also denied residence in most villages. A series of Règlement obligations discouraged any trader or artisan, Jewish or not, from settling in a village. In the face of these restrictions, Jewish immigrants had no choice but to settle in the larger towns and to pursue ventures outside the existing structure of craft production. At the invitation of local boyars anxious to avoid the onus of selling wine or brandy to the peasantry, they turned first to trafficking in liquor and running local inns. The growth of foreign trade in imported manufactures and exported grain naturally attracted their attention. By the end of the Règlement period, they constituted over two thirds of all merchants in the Moldavian capital of Iași and about half in the river port of Galați. By 1840, they and the rest of the largely non-Romanian merchant community were able to buy property there. Some, usually from the more affluent families, found their way to the new Wallachian port of Brăila and to the existing Jewish commercial community in Bucharest.[43]

Their infusion into the urban economy during the Règlement

period kept the conduct of Romanian commerce largely in foreign hands. Prior to this time, it may be recalled, Greek traders had taken advantage of Phanariot connections to play the leading role. Now the Phanariot boyars had lost their official influence and were assuming a Romanian identity. Greek merchants in Bucharest and Brăila began to lose ground to Jews and assorted Habsburg immigrants, some Romanians included, as the trade around the Black Sea that had been their special province began to diminish in importance to the Principalities. Their predominance in Bucharest probably endured until mid-century but was not sufficient thereafter to preserve the animus toward Greek traders in Wallachia as much as Moldavian hostility to the more recent Jewish immigrants. The Jewish predominance in Moldavian trade and artisan crafts would become more noticeable after 1850. Their near-majority in urban numbers became a greater advantage with the decline in estate or village fairs, where Jews had rarely ventured. If we may generalize from the Wallachian experience, such fairs accounted for the bulk of internal commerce at the start of the Règlement period; perhaps one thousand were held during the 1830s. Thereafter, improved roads and the rise of town shops cut their numbers and reduced their wares to livestock, on the pattern of late medieval Western Europe.[44]

The Money Supply and Russian Assignats

Like the regulations intended to limit Jewish immigration and economic activity, the Russian financial regime had several unintended effects on Romanian commercial development. The arrival of increased amounts of Russian denominations did not replace the coinage in circulation but only added to a long list. The total exceeded 30 by 1848. The nearly fivefold depreciation in the Ottoman piastre during the thirty years preceding the Règlement Organique (see note 47 below) was of course largely responsible for the demand for non-Ottoman coins. The aforementioned dominance of Austrian imports throughout this period naturally made Habsburg denominations the most sought after. Indeed, the Règlement Organique proclaimed the Habsburg gold ducat and silver florin (*sorocovaţul* in Russian adopted into Romanian) as official coins of the Principalities. The ruble was added to the list later.

The Russian denominations posed several problems. First, there was an apparent abundance of counterfeit Russian coin, introduced to the Principalities during the 1806–12 occupation and even minted on Romanian soil during the 1830s.[45] Second, there were the so-called assignats, now named after the inflationary notes of the French Revolution but issued by Russia to meet state obligations abroad from the time of Catherine the Great. The inflationary growth of their issues had ended shortly after the Napoleonic Wars. Their exchange rate for silver rubles still continued to fluctuate sufficiently to make their use in trade risky. A merchant buying goods at one exchange rate of assignats to foreign coin might find himself forced to sell them only a short time later at a less favorable one. In addition, there were fluctuations in the "popular rates," or informal premiums on the going exchange rate for the assignat, that were usually charged if it were to be accepted in place of a metallic ruble.[46] During his regime in the Principalities, Count Kiselev sought vainly to use his influence in Russia to prevent a depreciation of the assignat/ruble rate. Surely this uncertainty deterred the growth of internal and external Romanian trade to some extent, discouraging the holding of assignats as liquid asset of stable value. Yet it must also be remembered that the near-doubling of prices during the period of the Règlement greatly outweighed the 20-percent fluctuation in assignat exchange values or the even smaller depreciation in the Ottoman piastre.[47] Exports' growing attractiveness had the principal effect of drawing merchants in the Principalities still more to trade conducted in Habsburg denominations. So did the failure of the underdeveloped Tsarist economy to furnish the imported manufactures or capital that might also have helped place the Romanian Principalities in the Russian economic orbit by the Crimean War.

Foreign Trade in the Habsburg Orbit

The failure of the Règlement Organique to place the Principalities in the Russian orbit cannot be separated, however, from Habsburg commercial penetration during the same period. This success was based not only on a relatively stronger currency and manufacturing sector but also on superior access to Wallachian, if not Moldavian, markets. Ongoing overland trade through the Carpathian passes, particularly from Braşov to Bucharest, joined with the start of steamship traffic on the Danube from Vienna to Giurgiu, south of Bucharest, and beyond. Bucharest was closer to the mountain passes and such river ports than to the Black Sea.

In the absence of any Romanian rail transport before 1860, this geographic advantage is worth emphasizing. Nevertheless, the greater proximity of Bucharest to the Habsburg lands might not have been so important during the post-Phanariot period had it not been for the Russian failure to dredge the mouth of the Danube for steam-powered navigation.

Opening the Mouth of the Danube

The Danube turns north to circumvent the Dobrogean plateau before turning east to empty into the Black Sea. Thus the overland route from the city to Constanța on the Black Sea is barely half as long as the river route from Giurgiu downstream. But the former Roman port of Constanța suffered from an exposed position on the coastline that only an expensive breakwater, finally to be constructed toward the end of the century, would correct. More important, the high cost of overland transport, at least twenty times that on any ship, prompted talk from 1837 forward that only a canal from the Danube to the Black Sea could make the Bucharest-Constanța route profitable.[48] Several such projects were discussed, but failed to materialize. The Danube remained the principal Wallachian route to the Black Sea. For Moldavia, there was no possible alternative. The Danube's last eastward jog to the Black Sea formed its southern border.

The mouth of the Danube is not a single, wide channel but rather a vast delta, crossed by three separate channels some miles apart, and subject to silting up at its confluence with the Black Sea. The first Russian rights in these channels dated from 1812. The Treaty of Bucharest that concluded the Russo-Ottoman war of 1806–12 ceded the Tsarist regime authority to control navigation in the northernmost channel of Chilia. The least changeable channel is, however, the middle one, emptying at Sulina. By 1817, the Russian government had negotiated similar rights over the Sulina channel. The Akkerman Convention with the Ottoman Empire confirmed them in 1826. The rights would remain exclusively Russian until overturned in 1856 by the other Great Powers at the Congress of Paris.[49] The main navigational problem with the Sulina channel lay at its mouth. At the end of the spring rainy season its depth could only accommodate ships with an 11 to 13-foot draft. By the late summer and fall, at the height of the season for grain exports, the maximum draft had dropped to 6 to 8 feet. At that point, all steamships (about half the traffic on the lower Danube by 1850) and some sailing vessels over two hundred tons were obliged either to take the risk of running aground or to transfer their cargoes to light barges, or "lighters," owned and operated by Greek boatmen. The offloading and reloading was by all accounts expensive and invited further loss from mishandling or outright theft.[50]

The Russian refusal to dredge and thus remove this obstacle to the growth of Romanian grain exports had at least two origins. First, Tsarist officials undoubtedly wanted to promote the expansion of Russian grain exports. The southern location of their richest wheat lands made the Black Sea port of Odessa the nearest outlet to the Mediterranean and European markets for this chief Russian export.[51] It would hardly have made economic sense to encourage a rival outlet to the Black Sea some one hundred miles to the south. The Russian quarantine regulations and their harsh enforcement for ships entering or leaving the delta must be seen in this light.[52]

Second, however, the Tsarist failure to improve the Sulina channel in the face of repeated urgings by English and Austrian diplomats reflected the inability of the Russian economy to afford the export of capital for any sort of foreign investment. On the eve of the unwelcome Habsburg decision to abandon the Holy Alliance with Russia and to remain neutral during the Crimean War, the Russian government lost a chance to maintain Habsburg goodwill by neglecting a signed commitment to make the Sulina channel more passable. Article 5 of the 1840 Austro-Russian Convention on Danube traffic had so provided; its breach prompted the Ballhausplatz to refuse the Convention's renewal in 1850.[53] In the absence of the needed monograph treating the evolution of Russian policy toward the Danube, we may assume that lack of investment capital played some role in the Russian decision to forego this opportunity to improve relations with its most likely European ally.

Whatever the case may be, Article XVI of the 1856 Treaty of Paris created a European technical commission whose task it was to clear the Sulina channel. Led by an English engineer and well financed by several English bankers and a guarantee from the Ottoman government, the commission nonetheless suffered from international rivalries and was slow to start its work. By 1860 it had built two jetties into the Black Sea. Sheer water pressure soon increased the maximum draft to 17 feet during the driest possible fall. Accompanying that improvement was an immediate jump in the number of steamships annually crossing the channel from under 10 to over 200. By 1864 total tonnage for all ships had doubled.[54] Most steamships belonged to the English and Italian companies (see Table 3.1) that were responsible for finally opening up Western European markets to regular shipments of Romanian grain during the 1860s.

The Slow Growth of Exports to Western Europe

Prior to that time, according to the spotty figures in Table 3.2, the annual value of exports from the two Romanian Principalities had more than doubled between 1832–37 and 1843. This increase did slightly exceed the exact doubling between 1850–54 and 1860–64 that was their next major increment.[55] The breakdown of Moldavian exports in Table 3.3 further reveals that grain assumed its predomi-

TABLE 3.1

DISTRIBUTION OF DANUBIAN MOUTH SHIP TRAFFIC, 1847-70

	HABSBURG EMPIRE		OTTOMAN EMPIRE		GREEK ORIGIN		GREAT BRITAIN		ITALY	
	Ships[a]	Th. Tons	Ships	Th. Tons	Ships	Th. Tons	Ships	Th. Tons	Ships	Th. Tons
1847	144	29	663	76.5	630	94.5	151	22.6		
1850	96	19.5	174	29.4	860	154.8	108	17.7		
1853	111	19.5	406	56.3	1049	1993.1	205	35.2		
1856	239	46.0	125	13.6	996	1578.2	161	32.1	99	13.1
1860	186	46.5	703	70.1	1354	1637.6	374	96.7	237	39.9
1870	223	86.4	549	42.4	724	1104.7	366	1364.7	374	159.1

Notes: (a)Defined as the number of ships passing in or out of the Sulina channel from or to the Black Sea.

Source: Henry Hajnal, *The Danube* (The Hague, 1920), pp. 156-57, 164.

TABLE 3.2
FOREIGN TRADE OF THE ROMANIAN PRINCIPALITIES, 1818-1900
(in millions of post-1867 lei)[a]

	EXPORTS	% + or -	IMPORTS	% + or -
1818	ca 20 mil.		ca 20 mil.	
1832-37 av.	23	+ 15	22	+ 10
1840	35	+ 52	20	- 9
1843	50	+ 43		
1850	47	- 6	28	+ 40
1850-54 av.	60	+ 28	32	+ 14
1855-59 av.	89	+ 48	54	+ 68
1860-64 av.	120	+ 35	69	+ 28
1865-69 av.	134	+ 12	75	+ 9
1871-75 av.	156	+ 17	101	+ 34
1876-80 av.	210	+ 35	267	+162
1881-90 av.	243	+ 16	312	+ 17
1891-1900 av.	275	+ 13	361	+ 16

Notes: (a)Calculated by dividing pre-1867 totals by 2.7 to reflect 1867 revaluation of lei to equal that of French franc and by adjusting the pre-1855 figures to reflect the lei's depreciation in terms of Habsburg gold ducats, as reckoned in G. Zane, *Economica de schimb în principatele române* (Bucharest, 1930), p. 224.

Sources: G. Christodorescu, *Comerţul Romániei* (Bucharest, 1902), pp. 9, 13, 15, 17; Georgeta Penela, "Relaţul economice dintre Ţara Româneasca şi Transilvania în epoca regulamentară," in N. Adaniloaie and Dan Berendei, *Studii şi Material: de Istoria Modernă*, IV (Bucharest, 1973), p. 37; *Istoria Rominiei* (Bucharest, 1965), III, pp. 667-68; IV, pp. 209-11; *Enciclopedia Rominiei* (Bucharest, 1943), IV, p. 463.

TABLE 3.3
VALUE AND VOLUME OF MOLDAVIAN GRAIN EXPORTS, 1837-63
(in millions of current lei and thousands of hectoliters)

	Total Export Value	Grain Export Value	Grain Export Vol. (th. hec.)	Implicit Price Increases (%)[a]
1837	ca 30	12	691	
1843		30	1118	+57
1847	52	45	1591	- 8
1857	58	40	1527	- 7
1859	72	59	1728	+33
1863	134	120	3409	+ 9

Note: (a)Data available on the composition of Moldavian grain exports indicates that while the proportion of corn versus wheat, overwhelmingly the two major export crops, climbed from 1/1 to 2/1 between 1847 and 1863, their prices rose in close tandem to give the above aggregates of total grain exports validity as indicators of the general price level rather than the changing composition of exports.

Sources: Constantin Buşe, "Le commerce extérieur de la Moldavia par le port du Galati, 1837-1847," *Revue romaine d'histoire* XII, 2 (1973), pp. 302-7 V Popovici, *Dezvoltarea economiei Moldovei, 1848-1864* (Bucharest, 1963), pp. 342-52, 380.

nant share of the total during this earlier period. Aiding the advance, however, was an implicit price increase that far surpassed the inflation in the later.

Most important for our purposes, the greater volume of Moldavian grain exports by the 1840s continued to move largely in Greek and Austrian bottoms (see Table 3.1) to traditional Ottoman and Habsburg destinations. The erratic, generally limited access of Romanian grain to Western European markets before 1860 may help to explain the slow growth of grain cultivation on the seigneurial reserves of the boyar estates. Earlier scholarship has typically made the false assumption of their rapid rise after 1830 and cited as proof the equally inaccurate premise of booming grain exports to Great Britain and France. Even on the Moldavian estates, where the expansion of boyar reserves was proceeding faster than in Wallachia, the reserves' cultivated area only just surpassed the total for peasant smallholdings by the mid-1840s. Before 1850, Moldavian grain exports continued to be channeled to Istanbul for consumption or reexported to the eastern Mediterranean except for one exceptional year, 1847. Then the disastrous harvest in France and England (plus Ireland) prompted the combined purchase, as noted in Table 3.4, of 56 percent of Moldavian exports. Although exact figures are lacking on most other years, British purchases probably did not constitute more than 5 percent of Moldavian grain exports until 1852. French imports exceeded that small proportion only in 1843, when an Algerian shortage attracted about 10 percent to Marseilles. Throughout most of the 1830s and 1840s, about 90 percent of Moldavian grain exports appear to have been equally divided between Ottoman, Habsburg, and Italian destinations.[56]

Only with the coming of special conditions during the Crimean War did the British and French shares of Romanian grain exports recapture the heights of 1847. Demand revived for 1853–56 largely to replace previous imports of Russian grain or to feed their armies at the nearby Russian front. Restrained in part by a series of bad harvests, the volume, in contrast to the value, of Romanian grain exports did not show a consistent advance until 1861–64. The combined English and French share now went as high as one third, largely at Italian expense (see Table 3.4). Then the arrival of cheap American and Canadian grain in iron steamships by 1870 closed out this brief Romanian access to the English market. Further growth in Romanian wheat exports to other European markets would have to await not only the deepening of the Sulina channel but also railway construction and the land reform of 1864 (see Chapter 6).

TABLE 3.4
THE DISTRIBUTION OF ROMANIAN EXPORTS, 1843-68 (%)

Moldavia	OTTOMAN EMPIRE	HABSBURG EMPIRE	GREAT BRITAIN	FRANCE	ITALY
1843	60	5	4	10	
1845	43	32	3	8	
1847	17	9	28	28	10
1853	28	29	36	4	3
1863	41	14	21	11	
Moldavia and Wallachia					
1863	42	17	12	17	6
1864	46	16	8	15	9
1865	78	18		1	
1866	71	24	1	1	
1868	40	22	6	18	6
1869	69	16	4	7	

Sources: Same as Table 3.3; *Buletinul statistic al României*, XII, 40 (Bucharest, 1915), pp. 757, 760; The. Lefebre, *Études diplomatiques et économiques sur la Valachie* (Paris, n.d.), pp. 292-93.

The Shift toward Habsburg Markets

The several decades preceding the Crimean War were a period when Wallachian trade outside the Ottoman Empire was drawn closer not to Western but rather to Central Europe. This tendency of more than a century's standing in the Ottoman Balkans thus continued here as well. The one difference was that this Principality had never achieved the access to Mediterranean markets that the Greek coast and now Moldavia enjoyed. Wallachia's traditional ties were instead with Transylvania. Wallachia exported mainly its own grain and Levant cotton there. The total to Transylvania maintained about the same absolute value from 1829 to 1859, although dropping as a proportion of overall Romanian exports from one half to one quarter during the last decade.

More important, Wallachian imports from Transylvania showed a surplus over exports of 10 to 30 percent of the latter's value.[57] This new import surplus reflected Wallachia's growing population and expanding urban economy. Between 1833 and 1840, the Transylvanian share of Wallachian imports admittedly declined from over two thirds to one half. Yet by 1844 the former fraction again prevailed and continued through the Crimean War. During the 1860s, over half of the imports for both Principalities still came from Habsburg territory, versus just one fifth for Great Britain and its supposedly all-conquering textiles.[58] For Wallachia alone, the imbalance was presumably greater.

Although disguised in the aggregate data, the one permanent change in Romanian imports during the Règlement period appears to have been a shift away from the Leipzig fairs to goods produced in the Habsburg lands themselves.[59] This was to be expected once Saxony had decided to join the Prussian *Zollverein* in 1834 and Habsburg authorities chose to ignore this customs union in favor of strengthening their own protectionist policies.

The theoretically pro-Russian Règlement regime facilitated this Transylvanian trade, from whatever source, by making an investment in improved transport of the sort that the Tsarist government itself had been unwilling to make at the Sulina channel. European engineers were hired to widen and improve the Bucharest-Braşov road in 1838. It took two years to complete the badly needed project. Habsburg authorities in Transylvania also did their part to promote overland traffic during the early 1840s. They expanded the number of border crossing points and reduced the delay attached to quarantine procedures. What precise effect these several measures had on Wallachian imports we cannot say, but some encouragement to the revived flow from Transylvania in 1844 seems likely.

Appraising Habsburg Policy toward Danubian Trade

Habsburg policy toward the Danube appears more hesitant. Austrian rights to navigate on the river dated back over a century. The 1718 Treaty of Passarowitz (Požarevac) had authorized Habsburg consular posts and free commercial navigation up to the mouth of the Danube. An Ottoman concession in 1784 granted Black Sea access. Joseph II ended illegal local fees for passage through Hungarian territory and started a program of tariff rebates and exemptions. Regular commercial traffic to several Wallachian and Bulgarian river ports was operating by the end of the century. This traffic began to challenge overland trade, however, only after the *Erste österreichische Donau Dampfschiffahrts Gesellschaft* began regular service downriver in 1831. The company increased its fleet by 1856 to nearly one hundred, with a total horsepower of 10,000. From 1840 the firm enjoyed a monopoly on Habsburg steamship service, in return for reducing freight rates and carrying the mails free. It carried perhaps one half of the total traffic between Vienna and Brăila.[60] Efforts to maintain service in the Black Sea were abandoned by 1845 but left to the Austrian Lloyd Company of Trieste. As reflected in Table 3.1, Austrian shipping generally carried more Black Sea cargo than the English did through the Crimean War.

Yet the Habsburg development of lower Danubian trade was hardly as large as it might have been if more Austrian capital had been attracted to it. Some abortive blasting in 1847 and 1854 at the Iron Gates narrows between far western Wallachia and eastern Serbia did deepen the sections that took only a 3 to 4 foot draft during the fall. But sufficient deepening and widening of the channel to relieve any steamship of the need to offload and reload its cargo there would not be completed until Hungarian state subsidies provided the necessary funding in 1896–97.[61]

Beyond this failure to finance needed infrastructure, the monarchy was also unable to provide Wallachia with the credit demanded to meet its newly persisting surplus of Habsburg imports. True, Romanian bills of exchange had been accepted on the Vienna money market since the late eighteenth century. Despite the fact that thirty nine private bankers were operating in Bucharest by 1859, the several Austrian attempts to found a joint-stock bank all ended in failure.[62] The first railway construction in the Principalities, linking the Danube with Constanța and Bucharest with Giurgiu during the 1860s would be left to English investors.[63] Vienna thus failed to take full advantage of the opportunity to penetrate the Romanian economy afforded by Russian financial weakness during the Règlement period. This failure would return to haunt Habsburg efforts to dominate the new Romanian state later in the nineteenth century.

Comparing Ottoman and Russian Influence

Across a century and a half of mixed dependence and autonomy, Ottoman and Russian influences had done more to shape the emerging Romanian economy than any conscious Habsburg effort. The condition in which the still distinct economies of Wallachia and Moldavia found themselves when first united under a Romanian Prince in 1859 was largely the result of relations between these influences and the only native nobility to survive the Ottoman conquest. The major Habsburg contribution to this condition, as was noted at the end of Chapter 2, had been the inadvertent promotion of economic ties between the two Principalities and the Romanian majority in neighboring Transylvania.

Several strands of the Ottoman economic legacy intertwined to make Bucharest at one and the same time a center both for foreign commercial interests and for the most powerful boyar families from

Wallachia. The city's position outside the territory controlled by the complete Ottoman system made it the principal point of transit for imperial trade with central Europe by the start of the eighteenth century. This intermediary's role attracted traders and artisans from both the Habsburg and Ottoman lands. Bucharest became the wealthiest as well as the largest Balkan city by the end of that century. The new Phanariot rulers came from Istanbul with the resources and taste to demand luxurious housing, goods, and services. The growing rural disorder familiar across the Ottoman Balkans and an Ottoman wheat monopoly whose operation discouraged grain cultivation on estate reserves combined to push boyar landowners into Bucharest as well. Phanariot and boyar demand attracted still more immigrants to provision them. The largest non-native and non-Turkish presence in any major Balkan city thus emerged before 1800 and added a major dimension to the persisting Romanian sensitivity to foreign penetration.

As for the Russian legacy, the Règlement Organique that the Tsarist occupation of 1829–34 imposed on both Principalities had no more impact on the evolving Romanian system of peasant sharecropping on unconsolidated boyar estates than had the Ottoman or Habsburg systems of land tenure. This Napoleonic system of executive, rather than legislative, government made its main impact elsewhere. The six European-style ministries in Bucharest excluded venal appointments as a means of supporting boyar families at the same time that they reached out to bring Moldavia under joint administration with Wallachia. The Règlement also stimulated foreign trade by reforming tax and tariff collection, improving commercial courts, restraining artisan guild monopolies and building new port facilities. Yet these modernizing reforms left too little room for immediate Romanian participation, whether boyar or peasant, for the nation-state to emerge as an economic unit. More than in any other Balkan state, powerful state ministries in the capital city would become the chief agents seeking that unification before and after the First World War, let alone under more recent Communist government.

4.

The Serbian National Economy
and Habsburg Hegemony,
1815–1878

The continuing Habsburg desire to dominate the new Serbian state made a well-known contribution to the outbreak of the First World War. Austria-Hungary's final resort to military force would have some of its roots in the lesser-known failure to retain sufficient economic leverage over its nearest Balkan neighbor during the last prewar decades. Before Serbia achieved full independence in 1878, however, Habsburg hegemony over the Serbian economy had become greater than it ever was in the more complex Romanian case. Both the extent and the definite limits of this early economic dominance help the historian understand the long background of the tensions that later led to war. Prominent in that background were Serbian fears that their commercial and financial dependence on the monarchy before 1878 might be revived. These fears conflicted with Austrian hopes for finally overcoming all limits on official Habsburg leverage in the Serbian national economy, a conflict whose resolution must await discussion in Chapters 6, 7, and 8.

The present chapter concentrates on the virtual free trade that mushroomed between the two territories in the second quarter of the nineteenth century and the variety of financial instruments and institutions that appeared in the third quarter to facilitate that trade. Total rural population and the urban presence of ethnic Serbs also increased in response to these commercial opportunities. The improved security provided by the autonomous Serbian government helped as well. The institutional framework erected by that government and native commercial interests nonetheless centered on meeting an increasingly sophisticated set of financial needs without a national money supply. Even joint-stock banking, in contrast to the Romanian and Bulgarian experiences, would appear before independence, although continued Serbian reliance on Habsburg coinage and credit kept the scale of operations small.

The close connection between the Serbian and Habsburg lands dated from the eighteenth century. The two shared a common border from 1699 forward. Belgrade quickly became a principal point of transit for growing Ottoman-Habsburg trade. Serbian livestock joined the list of Habsburg imports by the end of the century. As indicated in Chapters 1 and 2, the repeated warfare on Serbian soil between the two empires may have interrupted this trade seriously but at the same time prompted sizable Serbian migration to the Habsburg Vojvodina. Some Serbs became middlemen facilitating trade with their native land to the south.

These origins alone do not explain the dangerous Serbian dependence on the Habsburg economy by the third quarter of the nineteenth century. That dependence also derived from Serbian suffering and success in winning substantial autonomy from Ottoman control by 1830.

Unlike the Romanian Principalities, Serbia had been an integral part of the Ottoman Empire since the sixteenth century. It had benefited as a border province from occasional Ottoman leniency in enforcing imperial taxation. As noted in Chapter 1, however, the Porte periodically sought to increase the revenues reaching Istanbul. To this end, it installed the *maktu* system of native Serbian tax collectors, in the aftermath of the 1788–91 war with the Habsburg monarchy. Then rebellious Janissaries precipitated the First Serbian Uprising in 1804 by forcibly taking over the province's fiscal regime. Both the Porte and the native population objected. Serbian defense of the Sultan quickly turned into defiance. Until it was finally crushed in 1813, the revolt managed to keep some part of Serbian territory independent.

The economic price of this transitory independence was almost as heavy as the human price. We have no reliable estimates of how many Serbs were killed in the fighting, were massacred by Ottoman troops, or died of disease. We do know that total Serbian population remained under half a million until 1820, still at the mid-eighteenth century nadir from which the other Balkan populations were rapidly recovering by the early nineteenth century.[1] Recurring emigration to the Habsburg Vojvodina, a clear economic burden given this scarcity of population, followed every Serbian setback during the First Uprising. Although many of those who had left in 1804 and 1806 had returned by 1808, another 10,000 fled in 1809. Perhaps 100,000 went in the final debacle of 1813. Some three quarters of them had returned from the Vojvodina by 1817.[2]

Habsburg authorities in the Vojvodina made little use of the opportunity that these refugees and their needs afforded for long-run penetration of the Serbian economy. The chance to train soldiers or otherwise support the Serbian cause was completely foregone. The masses of Serbian emigrants were treated suspiciously on landing. Only other Serbs helped them survive once they had been allowed to leave the banks of the Sava and the Danube. The arrival of erstwhile Belgrade traders in Zemun, just across the Sava, prompted tighter Habsburg controls against smuggling and efforts by the local merchant community to keep these newcomers from entering trade.[3] As noted in Chapter 2, the Habsburg high command in Vienna did not hesitate to cut off badly needed grain exports from the Vojvodina to Serbia proper when asked to do so by the Porte.

The principal commercial consequence of the First Serbian Uprising was not therefore to draw the rebellious province closer to the Habsburg economy. It was rather to sever ties with the Ottoman Empire that the Romanian and Bulgarian lands would maintain for another half century or more. The Ottoman-Habsburg transit trade through Belgrade had collapsed with the Serbian siege of Belgrade during 1804–06. It never fully recovered. Ottoman inability to check *ayan* banditry and illegal collections of local tariffs southward into Macedonia cut permanently into the volume of trade between Belgrade and Thessaloniki. The departure of many of the city's Greek and Hellenized Tsintsar merchants by 1806 also disrupted this southern trade.[4] Native Serbian traders took advantage of the openings. Both these merchant positions and the *sipahi* land holdings taken over after 1806 were, however, lost with the complete Ottoman victory in 1813.[5] Rampaging Albanian and Bosnian troops sacked Belgrade, adding many civilian deaths to the Serbian battle casualties. Then the plague and disease that had followed the Ottoman army in all its eighteenth century campaigns exacted a final price. The Serbian economy entered the post-Napoleonic era newly crippled and isolated.

Prince Miloš and the Engine of Habsburg Trade

The reduction of that weakness and isolation began in 1815 with another unsuccessful Serbian uprising. This time, however, the Porte's representative had better control of Ottoman troops in the field. He was also more disposed to compromise. So was the new Serbian leader. Karadjordje, the head of the Serbian notables or *knezovi* during the first uprising, had fled after its defeat in 1813 to Habsburg territory. Miloš Obrenović now emerged to lead the second. He made greater use of his background as a peasant livestock trader to strike a bargain with the new Ottoman Vezir for Serbia. Their unwritten agreement ended the revolt in November, 1815.

The main economic provision was the restoration of the *maktu* system of tax collection by the native *knezovi*. Miloš used this fiscal base and his political position as the sole Serbian representative to higher Ottoman authority to carve out considerable autonomy for the so-called *paşaluk* of Belgrade. Then formal Ottoman decrees of 1830 and 1833 provided for a self-administered Serbian Principality.

During the period 1815–30, Miloš proved himself the master of salami tactics. Always giving the outward appearance of firm support for the Ottoman regime, he steadily sliced away at its authority.[6] His political leverage came mainly from control of the court system, including the right to impose the death sentence on Christian citizens after 1818, and from power to appoint his own men as the twelve regional "captains," i.e., *ober-knezovi* in the terminology of the Habsburg occupation of 1718–39. Miloš used tax revenues to pay these appointees salaries for the first time, rather than leaving them to take their own share of taxes as in Ottoman practice. Their loyalty allowed him to use local courts systematically to keep tithes, actually rents authorized for the surviving Moslem *sipahi*, to a minimum. After 1821 he denied *sipahi* the right to use the peasantry for *kuluk*, or forced labor. Under these conditions a sizable if undetermined number gladly sold their claims to Miloš's agents, who were empowered to use state revenues for the purpose.

Miloš Obrenović used outright bribery to gain the support of the Ottoman officialdom that still remained in Serbia. They were few in number and vulnerable to corruption for having purchased their positions from the Ottoman governor of the *paşaluk*. In order to compensate for their initial investment, most of them and the governor as well borrowed heavily from Miloš and his agents. Miloš regularly agreed to cancel such debts in return for political concessions. Higher Ottoman officials from Istanbul also received Serbian sweeteners. In 1830 Miloš used tax revenues to bribe the Ottoman commissioner who negotiated the formal grant of Serbian autonomy. As a result, they recognized him as hereditary prince and cancelled existing Serbian debts to the Ottoman Treasury. To clinch the deal, Miloš added a gift of 300,000 piastres to the Sultan. In 1833 a similar payment to Ottoman officials saw all compensation for past Ottoman holdings of Serbian land included in the fixed annual tribute of 2.3 million piastres instead of being added to it as originally specified. More bribery in 1835 frustrated the Porte's efforts to raise the amount of annual tribute. It also exempted the Serbian government from the obligation to repair Ottoman fortresses on its territory.

The Growth of Livestock Exports

The political corruption of local Ottoman authorities during this era holds an essentially economic meaning for Serbian history. The record above reflects nothing so much as the growing commercial activity on Serbian territory after 1815. How else are we to explain the rising revenues, largely consisting of tariffs and indirect taxes on trade, and the private income for loans on which Miloš was able to draw so readily?

This income came from the rapid growth of Serbian livestock exports to the Habsburg lands. Although even roughly accurate tariff records of trade totals are not available before 1843, earlier evidence suggests that Austrian buyers imported more Serbian than Hungarian hogs. The total value of Serbian exports rose at least threefold during the 1820s.[7] Miloš Obrenović artfully used limited administrative powers granted him by the Porte before 1830 to take the largest share of this trade for himself. It made him the wealthiest man in Serbia. Much of the rest he shared with his appointed partners, who numbered fewer than sixty in 1820. To ration out the best opportunities to himself and his friends, Miloš kept a close rein on the Ottoman-style trading passports required to travel outside Serbian borders on business. Austrian manufactures were yet to replace salt as the biggest Serbian import. All available indicators point to exports whose total value was double that of exports from the early 1820s through the 1830s. Capital for private or public purposes was thus accumulating.

The granting of formal autonomy to Serbia, forced on the Porte after its Russian defeats in 1828–29, pushed the new Principality several steps further in the direction of a market economy.

The now Prince Miloš used the Ottoman abdication of most authority over Serbian trade to consolidate his commercial position and that of his partners. The Sultan's decrees, or *firman,* of 1830 and 1833 gave Serbian officials control of collecting tariffs and of issuing passports for internal as well as external trade. The Prince pushed through other regulations that were used blatantly to his own advantage: minimum prices for livestock, a tax on market use, stipulations on the quality of goods, the forbidding of credit arrangements outside partnerships with Miloš, and a monopoly on the ferryboats available for crossing to Habsburg territory.[8] Traders also faced direct intimidation.

But rising prices on the Viennese market for hogs, still the largest Serbian export by far, encouraged peasants to enter this trade. Scattered evidence indicates that price increases explain virtually all of the threefold rise in the value of Serbian hog exports between 1828 and 1837.[9] Lucrative price differentials had opened up to spur such trade. Serbian hogs were sold to Austrian or Serbian middlemen across the Danube or Sava from Belgrade at two or three times their original price in the Serbian interior. Middlemen might then anticipate twice this second price once the animals had been transferred to Vienna, one of the most rapidly expanding urban markets in Europe by the 1830s.[10] Increasing numbers of stock-raising Serbian peasants therefore struggled to enter the potentially lucrative export trade, despite the obstacles that Prince Miloš had placed in their path and despite the absence of serviceable roads over which their animals could be driven to Belgrade.

Several policies of the new Serbian government did help pull or push them to the marketplace. True, the levies of forced labor that the Prince placed on the peasantry did not significantly improve the primitive network of unpaved roads. The 100-mile trip from Belgrade to Kragujevac required a full week's journey until real improvements were made in 1845. But security to travel free from bandit attacks and other civil disorder was greatly increased.[11] More importantly, the Serbian government converted completely to money taxation from the payment in kind that had predominated under Ottoman rule. The costs of running its own bureaucracy and of paying the annual Ottoman tribute of nearly half a million francs equivalent left Miloš no choice. A head tax substantially higher than the Ottoman levy and payable twice a year in coin was assessed in 1830 and doubled in 1835. During the latter year, the land tax on households, previously one tenth of the year's produce, was changed to apply to individuals and to vary with the nature of the holding. Like indirect taxes on market and pasture use, it was now made payable only in coin, preferably of Habsburg denomination. The average amount of taxation remains unclear. Yugoslav scholars of the period nonetheless agree that the burden of money payment was significantly higher than under Ottoman rule and did push peasants into the export trade.[12] Once there Serbian peasants earned Habsburg coin and found that rising livestock prices kept pace with increasing taxes. (The import trade remained in a few foreign hands, mainly Tsintsars'.)

Although the peasantry plainly did not move en masse into the export of livestock at this time, over 1,000 were participating by the late 1830s, according to the passport permissions given for internal and foreign trade.[13] The net effect of Prince Miloš's monopolistic practices may therefore be best seen as having prevented still more peasants from engaging in this trade.

The Changing Structure of Peasant Landholding

The sum of market attractions and tax pressure also changed the basic unit of organization in Serbian agriculture. By the end of Miloš's reign in 1839, the long-predominant *zadruga,* a communal unit of ten to twenty members based on the extended family, had largely given way to the individual smallholding, or more precisely a scattering of five to ten small plots held by the head of the immediate family.[14] These individual holdings were less self-sufficient. Their limited manpower produced a lesser variety of goods. Such units were drawn toward market production if only to earn the means for buying other essentials. We may infer that foreign trade served as the main impetus for the more rapid spread of individual holdings and market agriculture in the northern border areas. They were the centers for livestock-raising and exports.[15]

Other factors also contributed to the decline of the communal *zadruga.* The conversion of the land tax from imposition on households to individual units in 1835 removed the tax incentive for the largest possible household. In addition, the end of warfare and most civil disorder during the period of autonomy deprived the *zadruga* of its function as a unit of self-defense. Then a law in 1844 guaranteeing rights of private rural property created a market in which *zadruga* members could sell their share of its land.[16]

Increased security of life and property in autonomous Serbia encouraged two further, interrelated changes in agricultural structure. The cultivation of grain spread as population began a sustained increase. Peasants moved down from the hills. They felt safe enough to plant their crops in lowlands free of Turkish or Albanian attacks and most bandit intimidations.

Secondary accounts agree that corn acreage exceeded that of wheat and other grains by several fold.[17] A rising population required not only wheat and corn to feed itself but also corn to feed the livestock that could be exported for cash. The acorns previously used for feed began to disappear with the clearing of the vast forests that had covered Serbia as late as 1830.[18]

Techniques of cultivation nonetheless remained more primitive than those used in Western Europe during its major period of land-clearing in the twelfth and thirteenth centuries. Serbian transition to the three field system was far from complete. Plows were still entirely wooden, and pulled by oxen or even by the peasants themselves instead of horses. Seed was of poor quality. No large estates existed to demonstrate more advanced techniques. State regulations that set village standards for improved cultivation were soon abandoned because of local indifference or opposition.[19] Such pervasively backward methods helped to limit the size of individual holdings. Productivity per hectare did not rise.

The rapid increase in rural population that began in the 1830s can be traced instead to increased security. Estimates of Serbian population before the first official census in 1834 are too rough to permit earlier estimates of the rate of growth. Table 4.1 indicates that thereafter total population increased by 2.4 percent a year from 1834 to 1854, half again its rate of advance for 1854–74 and, as noted in Table 6.3, for the period 1880–1910 as well.

The rate of natural increase before 1854 most likely fell short of the annual average of 1.7 percent achieved thereafter. In any case it largely derived from the end of the warfare and chaos that had made settlement of cleared, grain-growing lowlands unsafe and from quarantine measures that successfully prevented the plague from re-entering Serbia across the Ottoman border. Immigration accounted for the rest of the overall increase, about one third of the 666,000 added between 1834 and 1874 but probably over half of the 320,000 already added by 1854.[20] These immigrants were mainly Serbs drawn from Bosnia-Hercegovina, Montenegro, Macedonia, and the Kosovo region bordering modern Albania. Some returned from the Habsburg Vojvodina. They came to settle on the rolling plain south of Belgrade and in the Timok and Morava River valleys to the east and south respectively. As already noted, much wooded land remained for clearing. In 1840, after sizable numbers had already come, only 17 percent of the arable land was reckoned to be under the plow and another 25 percent in meadows, pastures, and vineyards.[21] The immigrants were also attracted to the newly autonomous status of their ethnic homeland. Prince Miloš encouraged them to migrate by borrowing some incentives from aforementioned Habsburg practice in the Vojvodina (see Chapter 2). His plan gave peasants a free homestead of three hectares (about seven and a half acres) and exemption from all taxes for three years.

This last policy helped to prevent his commercial rivals from accumulating large holdings of available land. In some cases his lieutenants forcibly took land from the larger owners to provide immigrants with homesteads. Miloš also excluded leading traders from the redistribution of Ottoman *sipahi* lands that began in 1830. Another law in 1836 guaranteed peasants a certain minimum holding as immune from confiscation for nonpayment of debts. It did attract Serbs from Bosnia and other Ottoman lands.[22] Once used, however, this law denied peasants access to future borrowing to expand or improve their holding in better times. Such measures plus the limitations on scale imposed by primitive techniques made smallholding, even where market-oriented, the overwhelming rule in the Serbian countryside by 1878.

TABLE 4.1
THE POPULATION OF AUTONOMOUS SERBIA, 1834-74

	Total Population	Town[a] Population	Belgrade Population	% in Towns	% in Belgrade
1834	678,192	41,347	8,450	6.5	1.3
1841	828,895	—	—	—	—
1846	915,080	—	14,386	—	1.6
1854	998,919	—	16,733	—	1.7
1859	1,078,281	86,841	18,890	8.0	1.8
1866	1,216,348	116,007	24,612	9.5	2.0
1874	1,353,890	138,710	27,605	10.2	2.0

Notes: (a)Towns were defined to include any nuclear village over 500 persons.

Sources: *Statistički godišnjak Kr. Srbije, 1907-08*, XII (Belgrade, 1913), p. 31; Vl. Milenković, *Ekonomska istorija Beograda* (Belgrade, 1932), pp. 15, 70.

The vast majority of the Serbian population still lived in villages of a hundred or less such smallholders. These peasant settlements multiplied most rapidly during the 1830s. Their number increased by about one half to over 2,000 during the decade. Two compelling reasons keep us from according this rural growth the predominant place that we might otherwise accord it in this chapter. First, the virtual absence of statistical records for almost all villages limits our knowledge to unquantified impressions that are more useful as social anthropology than economic history. Second, the available evidence suggests that rural change occurred only in response to the urban impulses of export markets and tax obligations. That response did not include the greater capital and efficiency that could in turn leave their own mark on the urban economy.[23]

Serbian Ascendancy in the Towns and Rural Trade

At first glance, urban population fell far short of providing the focal point for the expansion of a market economy in nineteenth century Serbia. Total urban numbers, even including towns of less than a thousand, have been reckoned at barely 50,000 in 1834. Sizable concentrations existed only in Belgrade with 18,000 and in Užice on the Bosnian border with 12,000. Only half a dozen other towns (Šabac, Požarevac, Valjevo, Jagodina, and Kragujevac) had even a few thousand inhabitants at this later date. As noted in Table 4.1, the urban proportion of the total had only advanced to 10 percent by 1874. Belgrade did not reach 20,000 before 1865, partly because of the inhibiting presence of an Ottoman garrison. No other town save Užice had as many as 10,000.[24]

The lack of striking aggregate growth in the towns, particularly during the first ten years of formal autonomy, should not obscure two important shifts that did occur in the structure of Serbian commerce. First, the growing departure of Turks and other Moslems camouflaged the migration to the towns of a significant number of Serbs. They were mainly the peasant livestock traders who had first achieved political predominance in the two uprisings against the Turks. Belgrade is the best case in point. Its Serbian and other Christian population in 1820 was around 2,500, in contrast to nearly 20,000 Turks and other Moslems, troops not included. In 1834, Serbs numbered 10,000 and Moslems about the same, with Tsintsars and other Christian groups totalling 2,000. By 1844, only 4,000 to 6,000 nonmilitary Moslems remained in Belgrade and perhaps 10,000 to 12,000 in all of Serbia.[25] After little more than a decade of autonomy, Serbs constituted a clear majority in Belgrade and the handful of other towns of over 5,000 population that the small Principality possessed.

Serbian dominance of urban commerce was slower in coming. The export trade, based on livestock and not confined to Belgrade, had of course been theirs since the start of the century. Belgrade's import and transit trade was still the almost exclusive province of Greek, Tsintsars, and Jews as late as 1830. By all reports the city's market-place and nearby inns, or *kafane*, continued to have a Hellenic appearance, with Greek commercial practice and language prevailing. Prince Miloš was able to affect this situation only by favoring the Vlach Tsintsars and the largely Sephardic Jews over Greeks in the granting of trade passports and state orders.[26] His regulation of 1836 requiring Serbian citizenship of all foreign traders was also aimed at excluding the Greeks. They had long controlled a majority of the trade between Serbia and the Macedonian lands. Capitalizing on their capacity to adopt a foreign culture, as noted in Chapter 1, the Tsintsars began to move from the complete Hellenization that had served them in their northern Greek homeland and in Macedonia toward comprehensive assimilation of Serbian language and customs. During the 1840s, while Jews were temporarily barred from Serbian citizenship or permanent residence in Belgrade, a number of Tsintsar and also Macedonian merchants expanded their enterprises by readily accepting Serbian partners. Thus the Serbianization of urban commerce had gone farther by 1862 than the half of Belgrade's import business still in non-Serbian hands would suggest.[27]

Rural shops and inns spread widely enough during the first thirty years of formal autonomy to account for another basic change in Serbian commercial structure. Here ethnic Serbs predominated from the start. A more mixed group of itinerant peddlers had preceded these village shops as the first rural link with the sale of manufactured goods. Miloš Obrenović tried to deny peddlers access to trade passports and rural shops permits to operate, in hopes of keeping the rural market for himself and favored merchants in Belgrade. Only during the 1840s, after the end of Miloš's privileges, did the number of rural shops grow sufficiently to limit the position of the Belgrade merchants and to end the era of wandering peddlers. Once Prince Miloš's annual taxes on village shops had been removed, the cost of going into business was cut in half. Most peasants simply used their own houses. The number of rural inns, or *kafane,* had already surpassed 1,000 by 1840. They spread the chances for exchanging commercial or political news, as well as the undesirable habits of drinking and gambling. The number of shops approached 1,000 soon thereafter, as did the number of fairs. The latter had totalled just 100 in 1833 but for 1845 reached half again the number held in Wallachia during the entire period 1830–45 (see Chapter 3).[28] This gave Serbia an average of one shop or fair for every village by 1850, despite the continuing opposition of Belgrade importers to such competition.

The volume of rural sales nonetheless remained low. A shop's annual inventory would typically constitute a few days' sales for a Belgrade merchant. European textiles and other imports were in fact rarely stocked at these village outlets. Their principal wares were agricultural tools and salt. All the same, they had helped spread some experience with money and commercial practice across most of the Serbian countryside by mid-century.

Cutthroat Competition under the State Council

Political and business rivals were able to force Prince Miloš to abdicate in 1839. He left the Principality and his partial trade monopoly behind for Austrian exile. His deposers earned their name "defenders of the constitution," or *ustavobranitelji,* by using their influence in the National Assembly to put into effect a constitution already promulgated in 1838. The return of a Karadjordjević Prince to the throne in 1842 solidified their political position. They remained in power until Miloš's return in 1858.

The period of their oligarchic rule has rarely been viewed with much favor in Serbian historiography. True, no strong Prince emerged. Informal Ottoman influence revived, as the *ustavobranitelji* resisted the Russian presence that was its only realistic alternative before the Crimean War. Ironically, Russian pressure had shaped the constitution of 1838 in the mold of the Romanian Règlement Organique so as to favor a strong executive branch and limit parliamentary initiative. The Prince's powers were shared only with a seventeen-man State Council, composed not surprisingly of *usta-vobranitelji*. The State Council used its considerable powers to begin building a permanent bureaucracy on the European pattern. Whatever other charges against the Council and its bureaucracy may be justified, two common indictments of their role in Serbian economic development are not. They did not favor education for state service over that for the private economy. Nor did they use their political power to take over the assorted privileges of Miloš's trade monopoly for themselves.

Higher Education and the Economy

Illiterate himself, Prince Miloš never saw the need for higher education in the emerging Serbian state. The first high school, or *gimnazija*, did not open in Belgrade until after his abdication. By then the several Greek schools that had provided the closest thing to a commercial education there had gone into permanent decline. Although the State Council set about expanding the system of primary education, it did not see fit to expand the number of students of all sorts in secondary schools much past 500.[29] The best of these institutions was the state artillery school. The Czech specialist Zach, who had first come to Serbia on a political mission, opened this future military academy in 1850 with state support and scholarships. Soon Serbian graduates of European military schools returned to help him with instruction. Academy graduates received substantial training in engineering but all forsook the private economy for army careers until the end of the century.

Yet state support had also helped a commercial high school to open in Belgrade in 1844. Trained teachers were nowhere to be found, even among *prečani* Serbs from the Habsburg lands, and the school attracted few pupils until after 1858. From that time forward an experienced Viennese director stiffened entrance requirements and modernized the curriculum, even dropping Greek in favor of Italian. The ill-fated agricultural school that operated between 1853 and 1859 graduated just 300 students during its brief existence. Despite state scholarships, students balked at coming to Belgrade only to be trained under a rural regimen. Most graduates chose government jobs in the capital rather than return home to less pay and prestige. The State Council opened no professional school for government service, as it had for commerce and agriculture. The state employees that had already become the largest occupational group in Belgrade by the 1860s thus lacked formal training beyond rough clerical skills.

The Coming of Free Trade

The 1838 constitution included provisions that established virtual free trade. Above all the *ustavobranitelji* must be credited with implementing them fully, thus resisting the temptation to take over Miloš's monopoly privileges. They abolished all minimum and maximum price controls. Passports for internal and external trade became an easy formality until they were abolished entirely in 1848. Peasants were freed of governmental intimidation in choosing merchants with which to deal. Several petitions to the 1848 *Skupština*, one of two National Assemblies that the Council allowed to convene between 1839 and 1858, complained that export traders who also held positions in the government were paying peasants lower prices for their livestock than other merchants.[30] The Council thereupon banned all officials from taking part in foreign trade. Guild regulations that the State Council had passed the previous year left anyone not employed by the state free to trade in "natural products" without the need to join a guild.

This lack of regulation unfortunately resulted in a comparable lack of historical records. Agricultural traders and their enterprises were not registered anywhere. Thus reliable evidence of even their approximate numbers does not exist. The one detailed Yugoslav study of this period still concludes that free entry brought literally thousands of new participants into the export trade.[31]

In any case, the value of total exports tripled between the late 1830s and the late 1840s, largely on the strength of an increase in the quantity of hogs and cattle sold to the Habsburg lands. Table 4.2 reflects the early overall increase and the relatively constant level of Serbian exports from 1846–50 through 1861–65. Then a booming Austrian economy raised Habsburg prices for livestock sharply. This combined with the first appearance of Serbian exports to double the annual value of total exports by 1871–75, as noted in Tables 4.2 and 4.3.

The absolute value of imports grew roughly in tandem with exports, leaving a trade surplus that was an increasingly small percentage of total turnover. The variety of imports now expanded. Under Prince Miloš, only salt and a few manufactures had been brought into the country. The controversy generated by his investments in Romanian salt mines and estate land discouraged future investments outside of Serbia.[32] Internally, the minimum homestead law and the scarcity of hired labor discouraged the investment of trade profits in agricultural land. Buying and selling imports posed no such problems.

The demand for imports broadened for other reasons too. Serbian

TABLE 4.2
SERBIAN FOREIGN TRADE, 1835-75
(million post-1873 dinars)

Annual average	Exports	Habsburg %	Imports	Habsburg %
1835-38	4.8		2.4	
1843-45	6.9	84.3	7.2	59.4
1846-50	12.7	78.7	8.7	50.0
1851-55	13.6	83.1	10.6	46.2
1856-60	14.3	70.0	13.0	59.7
1861-65	16.4	80.4	15.7	69.7
1866-70	29.2	80.2	26.6	79.3
1871-75	32.5	85.8	29.4	78.1

Sources: Vl. Milenković, *Ekonomska istorija Beograda* (Belgrade, 1932), p. 47; S. B. Milošević, *Spoljna trgovina Srbije, 1843-1875* (Belgrade, 1902), pp. 34-35, 38-39, 46-47.

TABLE 4.3
COMPOSITION OF SERBIAN EXPORTS, 1843-75
(% of total value)

Annual average	Pigs	Cattle	Sheep	Grain	Leather	Other[a]
1832-45	63.3	12.2	3.6	.1	11.7	9.0
1846-50	59.3	7.9	3.1	1.1	7.3	21.4
1851-55	49.2	18.3	5.9		7.5	19.6
1856-60	28.2	19.5	2.9	1.4	12.7	34.8
1861-65	42.0	9.4	1.6	.6	13.2	32.2
1866-70	52.1	15.1	1.2	7.2	6.3	17.9
1871-75	49.0	13.5	1.8	8.9	6.6	20.3

Note: (a)The bulk of these other exports was apparently dried nuts until after 1870, when dried plums made up almost half the total.

Source: S. B. Milošević, *Spoljna trgovina Srbije, 1843-1875* (Belgrade, 1902), p. 8.

duties did not much deviate from the low Ottoman tariff on imports of 3 percent ad valorem and encouraged the inflow of foreign goods. The sizable merchant class now rising from peasant ranks was turning to European dress and ways of living by the 1850s. They were eager to exchange the old Ottoman conventions for what seemed most modern. By this time manufactured goods, mainly glass and ironware, pottery, sugar, and an assortment of textiles from the

Habsburg lands, had replaced salt as the largest import. To this must be added the state's purchases of arms and other military equipment, which comprised 5 to 10 percent of annual imports during the 1860s.[33]

Belgrade's expanding network of retail outlets helped to broaden the base of Serbian demand for imported manufactures. The capital city since 1841, it was the center for retail as well as import trade. The town counted ninety five retail shops by 1850. Almost half of them had opened during the preceding decade.[34]

The rising demand for machine-made goods prompted the "creative destruction" of a large segment of the traditional Serbian craft shops. Along with household production, they had previously furnished all manufactures. The number of craft guilds declaring bankruptcy from 1842 to 1862 was no less than seventy. The craftsmen whose names dominated lists of those purchasing property in Belgrade during the first half of the nineteenth century gave way to traders and state officials by the 1850s.[35]

Doubtless the accumulation of trading capital broadened with the number of participants during the freewheeling decades following the departure of Prince Miloš. Yet the question of precisely how these profits were made remains unresolved. Postwar Yugoslav historiography, arguing from Marxist first principles, has maintained that a large fraction came from usurious loans to lesser traders and the nontrading peasantry rather than from commerce directly.[36] The already noted absence of official or merchant records for the period makes this contention difficult to prove or disprove. What evidence there is tends to show that indeed, in the absence of organized credit, those borrowing from the larger traders were often badly treated. But proof that such gains were a major part of the earnings of those traders does not emerge from this evidence.

Serbian credit conditions during the period of autonomy did work a variety of hardships on peasants trying to enter the export trade. The commercial atmosphere can be better described as cutthroat competition, rather than "free trade" as idyllically defined by contemporary English economists. Reliable secondary sources, writing from non-Marxist as well as Marxist points of view, agree that established traders charged at least 10 to 20 percent a month for short-term private loans to the struggling newcomers.[37] This was a rate of interest far in excess of the annual maximum of 12 percent prescribed by legislation dating back to Prince Miloš. In addition, the borrower could be subjected to outright deception. Usually illiterate, he might be lent less than the sum recorded as due in the loan agreement. If he failed to make repayment on time, the borrower might find himself obligated to repay the principal sum a second time over. Under the best of loan agreements the returns from small-scale livestock trading were often less than the interest charged.[38]

The rapid spread of capitalist principles in a business world that was regulated before 1860 by no more than a general civil code of laws accounts in part for the low level of commercial honesty. It should also be remembered that these Serbian merchants were the descendants of peasants accustomed to take what advantage they could in the disorder of the decaying Ottoman Empire. Slobodan Jovanović, Serbia's most eminent prewar historian and hardly renowned as a critic of social conditions, has pointed out that such peasant-traders "accepted their new profession as a mixture of good luck and cheating." He also estimated that fifty peasants failed for every one who successfully entered the export trade. According to Jovanović, most of the indebted peasants of the 1850s were those who had not survived the dangers of "speculating," as the peasantry called export transactions.[39]

Successful traders still did not draw a large part of their earnings from making such loans, according to the several pieces of indirect evidence. One is the large body of lawsuits initiated in Serbian courts by merchants seeking recovery of unpaid debts.[40] A good many borrowers admittedly suffered confiscation or sale of property up to the minimum homestead as a result. At the same time, the courts worked very slowly. No legal provision for bankruptcy existed before 1853. Most important, courts could rarely find enough of commercial value in the borrower's assets to compensate the lender. The volume of such lawsuits reached a sizable several hundred a year by the late 1850s. The suits were surely a testimony to the risks of lending as much as to those of borrowing.

The larger Serbian merchants' agitation for a French-style commercial code and court reflected their greater concern with profits from regular trade than from private loans. These reforms might have accelerated handling of their lawsuits for unpaid debts but would also have deterred excessive interest rates and corrupt lending practices. The main Belgrade merchants nonetheless began to seek such reform as early as the 1840s. The State Council refused. The Council feared that such regulations might be used to restore monopolistic trading practices of the sort used by Prince Miloš. Then the Congress of Paris opened the Danube to international traffic in 1856. Belgrade merchants convinced the government that the newly increased opportunities for trade would act to prevent any such monopoly. The State Council thereupon appointed an advisory committee of merchants to begin work on a commercial code. Their draft was closely patterned on the French model. It included provisions to refund interest in excess of the legal 12 percent a year. The draft became law in 1860 and dealt a blow to outright deception. Whether the code trimmed high interest rates during the subsequent decades before full independence in 1878 is, however, doubtful.[41]

The Demand for Commercial Banking

The absence of an organized Serbian system of short-term credit at reasonable rates limited the growth of a market economy. Such a deficiency restricted the number of participants and probably the volume of trade as well. Prince Miloš himself had begun the practice of private lending in 1817, soon collecting a wide range of debtors. Although the terms of his loans were apparently less onerous than those described above, he generally limited them to those few traders who were in partnership with him. He also required that all livestock trade be conducted in hard cash. This rule suppressed the bartering of livestock as partial downpayment on agricultural supplies. These arrangements had begun to spring up as a substitute for instruments of credit.

Bills of exchange were rarely used in Serbia for at least the first half of the nineteenth century. The few written credit instruments of the period that were not secured by immovable property were those based on partnership arrangements. Prince Miloš's was only the first. These partnerships provided the principal access to short-term credit before 1870.[42]

In Lieu of Mortgage Lending

The decades after the departure of Prince Miloš witnessed the appearance of a limited amount of long-term credit secured by property guarantees. Loans were drawn mainly on the mounting surplus in the state treasury. They had already begun, on an ad hoc basis, during his last years in power. Political pressure mounted for the Prince to separate his own commercial dealings from state finance and generally to cut them down. The reduction in Miloš's lending left a large gap in available credit. To fill it, the Serbian treasury began to grant a number of loans from its own reserves. By 1839 the treasury published formal regulations for such loans. They stipulated repayment at a rate of only 6 percent per annum but were to be guaranteed by immovable property half again the value of the loan. The Prince's former partners and other large traders made up the great majority of the customers for the hundred-odd loans granted each year. This limited distribution was narrowed further in 1841. The minimum loan was raised from 50 to 300 Austrian gold ducats, the equivalent of

an increase from 600 to 3,600 francs. While the minimum was reduced to the equivalent of 1,200 francs by 1858, proposals for unsecured loans of much lower amounts were defeated. Subsequent lists
of treasury debtors continued to show high government officials and
the larger Belgrade merchants taking the majority of these loans. The
number of loans remained under 200 a year for an aggregate outstanding of 250,000 francs equivalent at most.[43]

Town and village governing bodies, or *opštine*, as well as church,
educational, and private trust funds also gave long-term loans at 6 to
12 percent interest a year when secured by immovable property. But
their total number was no larger than that of the treasury loans. The
high cost of assessing property value helped confine such credits to
the same small circle of borrowers.

Limitations on the Money Supply

Adding to the shortage of credit that accompanied the increasing
monetization of the Serbian economy was the absence of a domestic
money supply. Goods were exchanged in the midst of what one
French visitor called "a terrible money anarchy." Over forty varieties
of gold, silver and copper coin circulated in autonomous Serbia,
mostly of Ottoman or Habsburg origin.[44]

Such a situation would not necessarily have restricted commerce
had a consistent rate of exchange among the various denominations
been maintained over time. The practice of an imaginary unit of account, on the pattern of medieval "ghost money," had in fact been
introduced during the Austrian occupation of 1718–1739. Afterwards
an informal exchange rate continued to mediate between the existing
Ottoman and Habsburg denominations that the transit trade and later
livestock exports brought into Belgrade. The last and most rapid
phase of the centuries-long devaluation of Ottoman coinage began
after 1800, in the face of an increasing imbalance of trade with
Europe. The *groš*, an informal unit of account (not to be confused
with the Ottoman copper coin of the same name), was the value of an
Austrian gold ducat in terms of Ottoman silver piastres. This rate rose
from 7 to 14 between 1800 and 1819.[45] Miloš Obrenović thereupon
fixed a formal rate of exchange to help himself and other Serbian
traders avoid disputes with Austrian middlemen about the current
rate. In line with the further weakening of the piastre, Miloš had
boosted the *groš* to 24 for an Austrian ducat by 1826.

With the coming of autonomy in 1833, the Serbian ruler seized on
the Ottoman insistence at being paid the annual tribute at a rate
based on Austrian ducats to set a "market rate" for the *groš* of 48
piastres to the ducat. A "tax rate" for the tribute was left unchanged

at 24. The Prince's procedure was to collect the tribute at the market rate and pay it at the tax rate. This helped accumulate a surplus in the state treasury and halved the effective burden of the tribute. It also contributed to further decline in the value of Ottoman coin. By 1839, the market value of the piastre had already fallen by one half from 1833. Thereafter its decline accelerated. Yet the formal units of account were not changed again until 1856 and then only slightly.[46]

These developments made Austrian coin, which was relatively much more stable in value, the only one generally accepted in Serbian trade. By the 1830s the Serbian government stipulated that no Ottoman coin could be accepted in return for livestock exports to the Habsburg lands. The device did no more than formalize what was fast becoming accepted practice.[47] Traders incapable of obtaining Austrian coin or credit, i.e., interior traders selling stock to Belgrade exporters and lesser importers, incurred the most obvious disadvantage. They were reluctant to hold Ottoman coin for any length of time in fear of further depreciation. Barter arrangements often resulted.

The unsettled exchange rates also inhibited transactions of the larger livestock exporters. Because personal loans were virtually the only source of short-term credit, ready agreement on debt repayment was essential to expanding the scope of the market economy. The practice of repaying a debt in a denomination other than the one in which it was incurred led to frequent disputes about the correct rate of exchange. Each party naturally sought the rate most favorable to himself. From the time of Prince Miloš, Serbia's slow and loosely organized judicial process was the only recourse to resolving such differences. Similar disputes often developed when a trading partnership, the vehicle for most short-term loans, broke up and accounts in assorted denominations had to be settled.[48]

The First Serbian Banks

Growing dependence on Austrian coin and credit, not disputes over rates of exchange, first roused the larger Serbian traders to show interest in founding a domestic bank of issue. The occasion was, not surprisingly, the spread of the European monetary crisis of 1845 to Vienna and from there to Belgrade. Access to Austrian credit dried up in the Serbian capital. Soon after the crisis broke, influential Belgrade merchants placed a series of articles in the official newspaper, *Srpske novine*, urging the creation under state control of a private joint-stock bank with powers of minting its own coin.[49] Failing to win state participation in the ownership of stock, the project collapsed. It surfaced again briefly in 1852, sponsored by some eighty Belgrade merchants. The Serbian Ministry of Finance now approved of government support, but the State Council again used its legislative prerogatives to reject any official role. The Council argued that it could not balance any direct advantage to the government against the risk of having to make good on liabilities outstanding if the bank failed. Since 1833, banking services for the government had been performed both in and out of the country by a state banker, or *praviteljstveni bankar,* appointed from among the main Belgrade merchants. There was, moreover, no foreign debt to repay and thus no official enthusiasm for a bank that might lend funds to meet such obligations. As already noted, the state treasury was itself accumulating a surplus of loanable funds.

The next private initiative for a bank of issue grew out of the commercial optimism generated in 1856 by the opening of the entire Danube to international traffic, under the terms of the Treaty of Paris.[50] A professor of the newly opened commercial high school and a number of Belgrade merchants organized a meeting attended by over two hundred interested parties. Among the proposals suggested in order to take advantage of the expected increase in Danube traffic was the entirely private subscription of stock for a bank of issue. Some merchants argued that Belgrade's commercial community now commanded sufficient resources to forego any state subscription. The meeting's final memorandum led only to the creation of an official committee to study the founding of such an institution. The committee's proposal reopened the possibility of government support. It sought to use the surplus from the state treasury to set up the bank. The bank would then issue the equivalent of 2.4 million francs in paper currency that would circulate in and out of Serbia.[51]

The European financial crisis of 1857 gave the project added impetus. A general commercial recession after the end of the Crimean War put pressure on Serbian exporters through the contraction of the Vienna money market, just as it had in 1845. The concurrent founding of a limited German-Austrian Customs Union and the resulting adjustments in the market value of Habsburg coins further disrupted that market.[52] The state treasury was able to assist Belgrade merchants with emergency credits totalling only the equivalent of 50,000 francs. The Serbian Chamber of Commerce, formed the same year, cited such trifling state support to bolster the argument for founding a domestic bank. The State Council nonetheless turned aside the project and a subsequent scheme put forward by the Ministry of Finance. The Council cited the decline in the Treasury surplus that was to furnish the state's contribution.[53]

From this time forward there would be no question of state financial help for this kind of undertaking. The Chamber of Commerce immediately adopted the policy of urging an entirely private subscription among Belgrade merchants. Yet the actual collection of such funds was not undertaken until 1864. Then the assembling of only half a million francs equivalent took several years. The proposed bank failed to materialize. The Chamber was simply unable to agree on a set of statutes. This lack of urgency can be traced in part to generally favorable conditions in the European money market during the 1860s and to the continued absence of a Serbian trade deficit, as noted in Table 4.2. In addition, the Ministry of Finance established an agency in 1862 to make mortgage loans from the various trust funds maintained in the state treasury. The new Administration of Funds, or *Uprava Fondova,* expanded the amount without improving the terms of the secured loans on immovable property that had been granted regularly from the treasury surplus since 1839.[54] This money continued to flow predominantly to Belgrade traders, along with state officials, so there was at least an increased supply of long-term loanable funds for many Chamber members.

Whatever the exact play of forces dulling these purely domestic initiatives, the founding of the so-called First Serbian Bank, or *Prva Srpska Banka,* was left partly to foreign capital. It was left entirely to the extravagantly ambitious aims of Western European banking practice during this boom period. A series of foreign efforts to set up a Serbian bank had begun as early as 1856, when the Romanian founder of a Bucharest bank offered to establish one in Belgrade.[55] The State Council refused. In 1861 an obscure French speculator, Constant de Vaux, suggested forming a Franco-Serbian Bank, based on capital stock of 4 to 5 million francs and enjoying correspondent relations with the Banque de Commerce of Paris. On the recommendation of the Chamber of Commerce, however, the Serbian Ministry of Finance turned down the offer in anticipation of the domestic bank that the Chamber was trying to promote.[56] The proposal of a Brussels concern in 1865 was rejected on similar grounds. Two years before, a London financial house had sought to set up an agrarian bank. The project had been refused for overlapping with the mortgage loans that the Administration of Funds was supposed to provide. Serbian reluctance to admit foreign financial interest was thus evident from the start.

The continued failure of the Serbian Chamber of Commerce to form a domestic bank led a number of Belgrade merchants to turn abroad anyway. In 1869 they joined the Franco-Hungarian Bank of Budapest as equal stockholders in forming a joint-stock bank in Belgrade.

The brief history of this First Serbian Bank hardly assuaged Serbian suspicions of foreign financial activities. Founded with a paid-in capital equivalent to 2.4 million francs, the bank operated under a set of statutes permitting the widest possible range of activities, excepting currency issue, on the model of the French Credit Mobilier.[57] The first two years of operations did bring acceptable dividends of 6 to 7 percent of paid-in capital. Total turnover increased nearly threefold. Yet this was income earned mainly from interest on short-term credit to Belgrade traders. At the same time the bank's director, a Viennese who spoke no Serbian, had agreed to undertake large-scale speculative investments outside of Serbia. Half of the bank's paid-in capital had been sunk into a consortium to construct a railway from south of Zagreb to Rijeka in the Dual Monarchy's Croatian lands. Another one sixth was invested in a shipping partnership with a Budapest merchant. This last scheme was a misadventure from the outset. The European economic crash of 1873 took the railway project with it. The bank's Serbian stockholders declared bankruptcy in 1875, after the refusal of their Budapest partner or any other foreign bank to make up the losses. In the process, a severe blow was dealt to Serbian confidence in financial institutions, particularly those inclined to operations other than cautious, short-term lending.

The commercial optimism of the early 1870s had also witnessed the founding of three other Serbian banks. Each was based entirely on domestic capital. They were able to survive the collapse of the First Serbian Bank only through the small-scale and very conservative nature of their operations.

The Beogradski Kreditni Zavod, established in 1871, was the only one of the three located in Belgrade. Its paid-in capital was 50,000 Austrian gold ducats, equivalent to 600,000 francs or one quarter of the amount held by the First Serbian Bank. Although discounting a few of the bills of exchange that had begun to appear in Serbia during the 1860s, the bank concentrated its activities on small secured loans to artisans and petty traders.[58]

There was a similar bank in Smederevo, a trading town down the Danube from Belgrade. It used more of its assets to discount bills of exchange for exporters and expedited livestock shipments for a commission, but its paid-in capital and scale of operations remained still smaller than those of the Beogradski Kreditni Zavod.[59]

The third bank was modeled on the Schulze-Delitzsch sort of savings bank, with paid-in capital built up gradually from many tiny deposits, which had spread from Germany in the 1860s and would become common in Serbia by the 1880s. This was the Valjevska Stedionica, set up in the prosperous interior town of Valjevo in 1871. During a business trip to the Habsburg lands, its artisan-merchant founder had accidentally become acquainted with this type of bank and decided to follow suit.[60] The initial paid-in capital, i.e., total savings deposits, was only 1,000 Austrian gold ducats but grew quickly to match the 50,000 ducats or 600,000 francs equivalent of the Beogradski Kreditni Zavod by 1875. Such progress was made in the face of opposition from local traders frightened by the failure of the First Serbian Bank. The Valjevo savings bank granted a certain amount of short-term credit, but generally to artisans rather than to agricultural traders.

Most Serbian traders seeking short-term credit were still forced to turn either to local money lenders charging upwards of 12 percent a month for discounting bills of exchange or, for more reasonable discount rates of 8 to 9 percent a year, to Austrian banks or merchants in border towns like Zemun and Pančevo. According to a thorough survey of the country a few years later by the Belgian Ambassador, larger Serbian merchants continued to find the Habsburg lands the main source of short-term credit for foreign trade through 1878.[61] Thus the severe economic recession and money shortage that seized the Habsburg lands in 1873, after the collapse of the Vienna stock market, unavoidably caused a serious contraction in the money and credit available to Serbian commerce.

Serbian Monetization and Habsburg Economic Leverage

On the eve of full political independence, therefore, some serious limitations confined the Serbian commercial sector that had been largely responsible for the spread of monetization since 1815. Independence from the Ottoman market had been won. But Serbian traders gained access to the Habsburg market only at a price: heavy dependence on Austrian coin and credit. The European monetary crises of 1845 and 1847 had revealed Serbian vulnerability under this arrangement. These disorders were at least short-lived. The general contraction following the crash of 1873 did not promise to be brief. Belgrade faced the further danger that economic dependence on Austria-Hungary might turn into political subjugation now that Serbia's last ties to the Ottoman Empire were being cut.

Yet the preceding half century of autonomy also laid valuable groundwork for successful Serbian resistance to that danger during the last decade before the First World War. The official Habsburg penetration or institutional influence that we found missing in the Romanian Principalities was missing here as well. No Viennese ministry showed an interest in extending the railway construction in the Croatian and Hungarian lands during the 1860s even as far as Belgrade. Private Austrian interests put forward no serious rail scheme and opened few commercial offices in the Serbian capital.

The *prečani* Serbs returning from several generations of residence in the Vojvodina did bring back clerical skills from the Habsburg educational system that were otherwise scarce in the newly autonomous Principality. Their assistance was needed to create a separate national economy, especially to take over the export trade from Greek and other Ottoman merchants. It was also indispensable in providing the great majority of the staff for the fledgling state bureaucracy and school system. The bureaucracy was modeled, although less directly than in the Romanian case, on a Russian transposition of the Napoleonic ministries. The schools grew without much state supervision or reference to any model during these first years. In all of the above cases, the *prečani* Serbs did not return to represent Habsburg interests or institutions. They wore no political strings that Vienna could conceivably pull at a later date.

An emerging class of native Serbian exporters had been able under these circumstances to move originally rural operations to Belgrade. Their profits from livestock export, not Austrian loans, paid the bribes that removed a variety of Ottoman controls even before formal autonomy was granted in 1830. The native Prince Miloš helped keep this new merchant class in Belgrade by denying them the chance to assemble large landholdings in the interior. Rural labor and cleared land were in any case scarce. The spread of feudal estates from the neighboring Habsburg lands was never a possibility. Nor were there German colonists to contest for smallholdings as in the Vojvodina and Slovonia. Even the native communal *zadruge* broke up more quickly than in the Habsburg lands, where they were officially supported. Their dissolution aided the growth of individual property and access to commercial profit.

The resulting distribution of income in the rapidly monetizing Serbian economy was undoubtedly skewed. This very inequality encouraged a concentration of successful native exporters in Belgrade that soon exerted a powerful influence in the Serbian government. By 1839, they were strong enough to oust Prince Miloš. For all their mid-century dependence on Austrian trade or credit, they and their government were already in a position that otherwise owed little to the Habsburg monarchy. From this perspective a native system of money and banking was not the first prerequisite for the emergence of the small nation-state that successfully challenged Austria-Hungary during the last prewar decade. It was one of the last.

5.

The Bulgarian Lands in a
Declining Ottoman Economy

The period of Ottoman history between the Russian wars of 1828–29
and 1877–78 is remembered above all as the so-called Tanzimat era
of unsuccessful reform. Distinguishing the period were two defensive decrees intended to ward off European interference. The Sultan's Gulhane decree of 1839 and his Hatti Hümayun decrees of 1856
both promised political reform in general and greater representation
for the Empire's non-Moslem subjects in particular. Their failure
only invited further European interference and assured the debacle
surrounding the abortive constitution of 1876. The repressive reign
of Abulhamid followed immediately. Roderic Davidson has analyzed
the political anatomy of these failures at length.[1] He stresses a lack of
administrative will at the center and a shortage of able officials
throughout the system.

At least for the Bulgarian lands, the failure of the Tanzimat reforms
is better understood in economic terms. (European Turkey, roughly
the area between Istanbul and Edirne, is outside the scope of this
study.) Renewed depreciation of Ottoman coinage, the decline of
processed exports, and for the first time a growing European debt all
testify to the ebbing strength and self-sufficiency of the imperial
economy.[2] The Sultan's decrees of 1839 and 1856 carried with them
provisions to increase the import of European manufactures and the
agricultural exports to help pay for them. Payment of the European
debt was a more immediate need. The resulting Ottoman effort to
reform the Bulgarian system of land tenure and to improve tax collection placed more land and local authority in native hands by the
1860s. Buttressing this growing autonomy was the survival, more

than previously believed, of Bulgarian artisan manufacture for local and Ottoman markets. The reaction of these Bulgarian interests to tighter Ottoman tax collection constituted an indispensable part of the several-sided independence movement of the 1870s.

In the Macedonian and northern Greek lands, on the other hand, relative stagnation of agricultural exports and of artisan manufacture settled over this once-prosperous hub of the Ottoman Balkans. The accompanying limits on capital accumulation and entrepreneurial energy helped to delay even partial political independence for most of the area until the twentieth century. The Greek independence movement in this territory would of course remain largely unrealized until the First Balkan War in 1912. Only Thessaly, the grain-growing plain south of Macedonia, had been transferred to the Greek state in 1881. Data on Macedonia and these northern Greek lands before then are sketchy. Their experience can best be described in this chapter as background to the more dynamic course of Bulgarian economic history during the nineteenth century.

Rising Exports under a Shrinking *Chiflik* System

Agricultural exports from the Ottoman Balkans might well be expected to increase during the middle decades of the nineteenth century. World trade began two decades of unpredecented growth after European grain prices turned upward around 1850. The end of the Napoleonic wars and then the disbanding of the unruly Janissaries in 1826 had allowed relative order to return to the Balkan countryside. The English experience of the early modern period would lead us to expect that this later rise in Balkan grain exports came from a growing number of large, private estates. The appearance of *chiflik* estates may indeed be recalled from Chapter 1. It only remained for these holdings to spread in size and distribution, for their ownership to change hands from Ottoman officers and officials to native merchants, and for their labor force to shift from sharecropping smallholders to landless wage earners. The last two of these classic capitalist tendencies did finally appear in the Macedonian and northern Greek lands but without noticeable stimulus to exports.

The Lack of Bulgarian Chiflik Estates

In the Bulgarian lands, where a much greater expansion of grain exports occurred, the limited if indefinite number of Bulgarian *chiflik* at the start of the period plainly decreased after 1850. Officials of the Russian occupation arrived to survey land holdings in 1878–79 before the mass flight of Turks from newly independent Bulgaria. As noted in Table 5.1, they found barely 200 *chiflik* both north and south of the Balkan mountains. Almost half of the 108 whose size they recorded amounted to less than 15 acres. The general smallness of these estates across the mid-century period is confirmed by Bulgarian research in Ottoman sources.[3] The estimate of a Bulgarian scholar that the early nineteenth century *chiflik* occupied no more than 20 percent of cultivated Bulgarian land and employed less than 10 percent of the peasant labor force, already cited in Chapter 1, seems too high for the 1860s and 1870s. By contrast, Table 5.2 suggests a still dominant role for the Macedonian *chiflik* during the same decades, albeit from a skimpier statistical record. And if we can generalize for the north from the situation of the southern Greek peasants in the 1820s and of those in Thessaly around 1800, the *chiflik* in northern Greece occupied at least half of the arable land and most of the better lowland locations.[4]

In order to understand the decline in the already limited extent of the Bulgarian *chiflik*, we must look away from the growing European grain market. Ottoman efforts to reform agricultural taxation were more important. The *chiflik* had emerged by the Napoleonic wars as an obstacle to such reform. A local official's letter from Turnovo in 1816 shows imperial dissatisfaction with the amount of tithe, or *detsetak*, collected. The Porte's concern had already prompted it to consider sending agents from Istanbul to do the job more efficiently.[5] The greatest offenders in the existing system were identified as *sipahi* cavalry officers who had used their official position to establish *chiflik* holdings and to withhold state taxes.

By 1832 the Porte moved to displace the *sipahi*, long devoid of military importance since the decline of cavalry described in Chapter 1. A plan to pension off the remaining *sipahi* holders of tax-collecting rights proceeded in three stages between 1838 and 1844. New tax farmers, although as yet not agents from Istanbul, now replaced *sipahi*. New regulations reiterating the old 10 percent maximum on crop tithes and barring the use of forced labor were widely publicized.[6] The existing *chiflik* initially survived these reforms. Then Turkish owners began to leave. The lost possibility of supplementing their income as agricultural tax collectors forced them to rely on the profits of their generally small holdings. The few available estate records show these profits to have been generally low.[7]

The Nature of Peasant Agriculture

The *chiflik* owners continued to rely on peasant sharecropping of strips of land, scattered inefficiently across several fields, in all but

TABLE 5.1
TYPE, SIZE, AND OWNERSHIP OF BULGARIAN CHIFLIK ESTATES, 1877-79

Region	Total Chiflik, of which:	Hired Labor	Leased	Mixed System	Forced Labor	Unknown
Plovdiv	60	27	42			21
Sofia	41		26			15
Ruse	12	1		2		9
Vidin	7	1	4			2
Turnovo	2	1	1			
Sliven	85	6	8	5	19	47
	207	36	51	7	19	94

Size in Hectares	Under 10	10-20	20-50	50-100	Over 100	Unknown
	50	9	18	16	15	99

Ownership	Turkish	Greek	Bulgarian	State	Monastery	Unknown
Plovdiv area	19	18	7	2	1	4
Rest of Bulgarian lands	104	22	17	1	1	64
	123	40	24	3	2	68

Source: N. G. Levintov, "Agrarnii perevorot v Bolgarii 1877-1879 gg.," in *Osvobozhdenie Bolgarii ot turetskogo iga, 1878-1953* (Moscow, 1953), pp. 158-60.

TABLE 5.2
CHIFLIK PROPORTION OF MACEDONIAN VILLAGES, 1853 and 1876

1853	Area	Total Villages	Chiflik Villages	% of Chiflik Villages
	Bitola	165	87	52.7
	Skopje	150	78	52.0
	Prilep	131	61	46.6
	Kumanovo	165	63	32.2
	Shehipski	119	46	38.7
	Debar	73	8	11.0
1876	Thessaloniki	48	20	41.7
	Melnik	72	53	74.0
	Demirkhisarska	52	32	61.5
	Petrich	40	31	77.5

Source: Khristo Khristov, *Agrarnite otnoshenie v Makedoniia prez XIX v. i v nachaloto XX v.* (Sofia, 1964), pp. 86-87.

the Plovdiv area. Nor were these leasing arrangements any more conducive to the adoption of more modern equipment than they were in the Romanian Principalities. Use of a Roman-style wooden plow pulled slowly by several oxen remained the rule. The deeper furrowing iron plow, pulled several times more rapidly by horses, was the rare exception.[8] Planting and threshing techniques remained equally backward. Despite an abundance of manure, from livestock that still outnumbered the peasantry, the use of fertilizer was virtually unknown. What little irrigation there was reportedly relied on using roads as ditches, thereby damaging the already inadequate access to wider markets.[9] Although data on productivity are entirely lacking, it seems likely that only the fruit or vegetable gardens around Plovdiv and large Ottoman garrison towns like Sliven were cultivated more efficiently during this period.

Otherwise, the third quarter of the nineteenth century was distinguished mainly by the transfer of *chiflik* land from Turkish officials to Bulgarian peasants. The slump in grain exports and prices immediately after the Crimean War, plus the series of bad harvests plaguing the eastern Balkans during the 1850s, encouraged Turkish owners to sell out.[10] The new Ottoman land code of 1858 helped them to do so. Although the code fell short of fully and formally recognizing the existence of private rural property, it spelled out safeguards for the holder's interests, including his right to future sale, regardless of ethnic origin or religious denomination. It also eliminated the rights of local landholders to collect agricultural taxes. They were finally replaced with agents of the central government. This last provision sent still more Turkish *chiflik* holders back to Istanbul in search of profitable positions elsewhere in the Empire.[11] In the Macedonian and northern Greek lands, transfers more frequently took the form of rentals, usually to Greek merchants. These *chiflik* holdings thus were more apt to remain intact than their Bulgarian counterparts.

Growing peasant unrest marked these several decades in the western Ottoman Balkans. Their protest should not be regarded, however, as evidence of discontent with the survival of the *chiflik* system. Bulgarian scholars explain the scattered local revolts as primarily a reaction against a boost in the state's harvest tithe from 10 to 12.5 percent in 1858. Also resented were recurring demands from Istanbul that the local peasantry be obliged to perform corvée labor without compensation. The projects for railway construction that began in the 1860s accounted for new demand for forced labor.[12]

Varying Ties to the European Market

The absence of peasant agitation against the Greek and Macedonian *chiflik* system may also have been a function of the system's failure to respond to the growing mid-century demand for grain from the European market. Judging by the Romanian experience throughout the nineteenth century, rising exports could consistently expand the area and amount of cultivation and lead in turn to increased exploitation of a sharecropping peasantry. A variety of qualitative evidence suggests that grain exports through Thessaloniki were relatively stagnant during this period and hence reflected no such expansion.[13] Some of the port's Greek merchants appear to have left for the new Greek state to the south or for Marseilles as the post-Napoleonic slump in European grain prices persisted into the 1830s. The heavy loss of Greek shipping during the Revolution took its toll. Direct access to French and especially Belgian cloth imports also reduced the Turkish and Jewish artisan communities that had flourished toward the end of the eighteenth century.

It was instead the Bulgarian lands that responded to growing European demand. As promised in the 1838 Ottoman trade agreements with Britain and France, the Sultan's reform decree of 1839 lifted all vestiges of the Ottoman grain monopoly from native Bulgarian traders by 1842. The first Bulgarian wheat exports to reach Western Europe arrived that fall. They came in sufficient quantity to increase the tonnage of total Bulgarian grain exports severalfold. More wheat and barley exports maintained this higher new total through the 1840s and then doubled it by the 1860s. The trade turnover of Varna, the principal Bulgarian port on the Black Sea, moved ahead of Thessaloniki's on the strength of these grain exports as early as 1845–48, to be succeeded by Burgas in the 1860s. At least one Bulgarian scholar has called these two decades of expanding grain exports and cultivation crucial to the shrinking of the *chiflik* system.[14] Without such growing demand in the 1840s, Bulgarian peasants and merchants would have lacked a profit motive to buy up these estates when bad harvests and lost privileges of tax collection brought them onto the market in the 1850s. Where Bulgarian grain exports might go when American and Canadian shipments took up most of the British market after the 1870s poses a problem to be considered in Chapter 6.

For now, it is important to understand that English manufactures never made the inroads into the Bulgarian market that the reverse flow of exports to Great Britain might lead us to expect. Great Britain accounted for less than 25 percent of Bulgarian imports from outside the Ottoman Empire for 1857–77 versus half of exports. Purchases from France and Austria-Hungary were responsible for the overall Bulgarian import surplus during this period. Each of these countries supplied 30 to 40 percent of non-Ottoman imports, in return buying just 10 to 20 percent of Bulgarian exports.[15] Sugar and coffee were the major imports from France. Left to sell themselves without any local agents or promotion, French textiles and other manufactures hardly sold at all in the Bulgarian market.

French success at Thessaloniki derived from active local agents as well as easy access to the Mediterranean. Revived in the process were northern Greek ties to the maritime market that had been broken during the Napoleonic wars. These ties formed a commercial basis for the eventual absorption of the north into a Greek state whose southern nucleus had always been attached to the Mediterranean orbit (see Chapter 1).

Habsburg traders were at least able to offer Viennese credit and to discount prices for the Czech and Austrian manufactured goods that they shipped down the Danube to the Bulgarian river ports. In 1870 the French and British warehouse at Istanbul burned down at the same time that the Franco-Prussian war disrupted the French economy. Austrian producers took over the Bulgarian sugar market. According to contemporary reports, however, the Austrian potential to penetrate this new Balkan market was also limited.[16] A lack of local agents and an inability to alter production for local needs and tastes consistently held back the advance of Habsburg interests.

Bulgarian Proto-Industrialization for the Ottoman Market

Although its penetration by the more developed European economies fell short of what some Marxist scholarship has suggested, the Ottoman market for Bulgarian goods nonetheless expanded during this period. The Bulgarian response largely corresponds to the model for "proto-industrialization" posited for parts of eighteenth century Western Europe by Franklin Mendels.[17] The scenario calls not only for rising artisan manufacture from seasonally unemployed agricultural labor to serve more than the local market but also for a resultant rise in population to expand the commercial cultivation of grain by adding to the supply of seasonal labor. Experiences around Western Europe suggest that population pressure may continue to build beyond the absorptive capacity of agriculture, thus actually discouraging the introduction of labor-saving machinery into manufacturing. Growing labor-intensity had appeared in the artisan industries of the Bulgarian lands by the mid-nineteenth century. The large exports of livestock and then also plums that provided more continuous agricultural employment in northern Serbia (see Chapters 4 and 6) would not materialize here, so far from Central European markets.

Bulgarian population grew steadily after 1830. The restoration of relative order after the several Russo-Turkish wars and the demise of *ayan* warlords like Pazvanoglu encouraged emigrants to return from Serbia and the Romanian Principalities. Rough estimates suggest that total population of the territory that became the pre-1914 state climbed from 1½ to 3 million during the two middle quarters of the nineteenth century. Despite repeated epidemics of cholera and the plague, town population matched this rate of increase and held its one-fifth share of the total. Unlike their autonomous or independent Balkan neighbors, moreover, the Bulgarian lands did not concentrate their urban growth in a single capital city. By mid-century there were over twenty Bulgarian towns whose population exceeded 5,000 and half a dozen ranging from 15,000 to 30,000. Their widely scattered locations encouraged the growth of a national commercial network.[18]

The Bulgarian Trading Network

Also encouraging commerce beyond the local marketplace was the presence by mid-century of over half a million Bulgarians living outside the broadest definition of the Bulgarian lands. About 25,000 lived on Habsburg territory, 50,000 in Istanbul, and 100,000 in Bessarabia and the Ukraine. The several hundred thousand in Wallachia were by far the largest contingent. As noted in Chapter 1, they had come largely to escape the consequences of the Russo-Turkish war of 1828–29. Others such as the Georgiev family came to Bucharest specifically to take advantage of the business opportunities in the large Wallachian capital. Starting in 1839, the two Georgiev brothers shifted from trading livestock to selling other goods and extending credit. By the 1860s they had accumulated sufficient capital to lease several boyar estates.[19] The Bulgarian trading and artisan community in Bucharest now numbered over 10,000.[20]

With the first Tanzimat decrees of 1839 Bulgarian merchants based on Ottoman territory obtained legal rights to trade freely throughout the Empire. These rights undoubtedly facilitated contacts with their fellows across the border. We lack even the roughest figures for this intra-Balkan trade during the last Ottoman decades, but several indirect indicators point to steadily growing commercial activity. Annual fairs spread to more towns; the larger towns held as many as a half dozen a year. Following the pattern of medieval Western Europe, their increase forced down the number of itinerant merchants. The added Ottoman and even European military demands of the Crimean

War prompted a number of town- or fair-based merchants to begin specializing in one good only.[21]

Another specialty that had emerged by mid-century was money lending. Merchants typically began by exchanging the wide variety of coins circulating in the Ottoman Empire. They went on to extend short-term credit to other traders directly or by accepting their bills of exchange. Interest rates were generally high, over 12 percent a year, and only increased with the Crimean War. At the same time, the trade in bills of exchange, first introduced during the seventeenth century by Ragusan merchants (see Chapter 2), revived and spread. These bills augmented the existing, largely Ottoman supply of money and aided the general monetization of the economy.

Most money lenders still operated on a very small scale. Accountants or other staff were as a rule employed only in Gabrovo.[22] The more sophisticated money market there served a chiefly artisan clientele. Gabrovo, situated high in the foothills north of the Balkan Mountains, was not much involved in the rising export of grain that was so prominent in the Bulgarian lowlands, but significant livestock trade did exist. Agents for the Ottoman army were the biggest buyers. As much as half of the annual value of meat purchased there for the army had already been killed and preserved in one of the town's three slaughterhouses. Army purchases of shoes made from the skins accounted for four fifths of the leather trade.[23] This and textile production gave the town its commercial focus. Such artisan manufacture gave the Bulgarian lands an economic and perhaps a political advantage over the Macedonian and northern Greek lands several decades before the creation of a Bulgarian state in 1878.

Bulgarian Proto-Industrialization

For Gabrovo, the principal artisan crafts were unquestionably wool spinning and the weaving of the rough wool *aba* cloth and *gaitan* braid. The widely scattered households that produced them had kept Gabrovo from formally qualifying as a town until 1860. By that time it had some 20,000 inhabitants. Over a thousand looms produced perhaps 10,000 pieces of cloth a year.[24] Supplementing army orders were sales to local, primarily peasant, markets as far away as Bosnia and Anatolia.

The experience of a *gaitan* artisan named Ivan Kalpazanov illustrates the entrepreneurial avenues that were open.[25] Born in Gabrovo in 1835, Ivan's artisan father died when he was seventeen. He was forced to support his eight brothers and sisters in some fashion. Two years later he began to sell *gaitan* made in the households of several relatives. By 1860 he had bought three looms of his own. The dowry from marrying a merchant's daughter afforded him capital to assemble twenty looms and to operate his own dyeing shop by 1870. He used profits from the Russo-Ottoman War of 1877–78 to buy German mechnical looms, 240 spindles, and the steam engines to run them. It took Kalpazanov a full year to construct Bulgaria's first fully mechanized textile factory. All of Gabrovo turned out to celebrate its opening in 1882. On that day the plant produced only cloth in the Bulgarian national colors of red, white, and green. The subsequent and less happy fortunes of modern textile manufacture in the pre-1914 Bulgarian state is a matter for Chapter 8 to appraise.

Our present concern is the bridge that these artisan antecedents built between Bulgarian agriculture and commerce before 1878. Over a century in the building, this bridge appears to have been completed only in the last decades before 1878. By then the household manufacture of textiles, leather, and ironware had probably started to supplement the peasantry's insufficient money income from agriculture, in a fashion similar to the experience of the Belgian peasantry in the early modern period.[26] Not yet faced with rural overpopulation as in the Low Countries, the eighteenth-century Bulgarian peasantry had nevertheless been pushed into less fertile uplands by disorder and Ottoman taxes. Then the doubling of Bulgarian population in the half century before 1878 made non-agricultural income still more essential for the growing numbers in the uplands. Seasonal harvest labor in the grain-growing lowlands was on the rise but offered only partial relief.

At least until the 1850s, wider Ottoman demand for Bulgarian artisan manufacture luckily grew in tandem. Total population was rising at the Bulgarian rate throughout the Ottoman Empire, in the outlying provinces as well as Istanbul. In the Ottoman capital there was also the need from 1826 forward to supply the new and sizable standing army. Nor did the Crimean War deal the fatal blow to the sum of these Bulgarian markets that scholars once believed. The postwar flood of European manufactures entering Istanbul left the military market and those in the outlying provinces largely intact, for textiles and leather if not for ironware.[27] Only with the loss of the wider Ottoman market and the arrival of German and Austrian textiles in the new Bulgarian state after 1878 did the number of artisans decline noticeably.[28]

As late as 1866, artisans in towns totalled over 60,000. They were the largest occupational group by far in the forty five Bulgarian towns for which we have detailed records. Within this urban population of nearly 200,000, artisans outnumbered merchants three to one. Their numbers had reportedly grown during the post-Crimean period. Immigrant Bulgarian artisans came from the Ottoman cities hit hard-

est by European competition, Istanbul and Thessaloniki. Average
artisan income for hired labor, apprentices, or even masters now lagged badly behind that of the merchants. Grain traders' earnings were
typically four to seven times greater.[29] This discrepancy doubtless
explains why the majority of merchants came from an artisan background but only rarely reinvested their new wealth in any sort of
manufacture. How frequently they made the plainly more promising
investment of buying up *chiflik* land from departing Turkish officials
awaits further investigation.

Case Studies of Six Bulgarian Towns

Again, aggregate figures for manufactured output, investment, or
exports are nowhere to be found. The best substitute available would
seem to be brief case studies of a half dozen of the twelve to fourteen
towns over 5,000 in population. The leading artisan and other firms
emerge as not very different from those in Gabrovo. Together their
experiences may therefore be taken as representative of the restricted potential of artisan manufacture for sustained growth in the
Ottoman market.

Karlovo got its start as the site of a major Ottoman *vakf*, or Moslem
endowment, opposite Gabrovo on the southern side of the Balkan
range. During the half century preceding 1878 its population
climbed from 5,000 to 10,000, while its Bulgarian minority of twenty
five to thirty percent became a majority approaching seventy-five
percent. Household weaving of *gaitan* braid was mainly responsible
for the Bulgarian ascendancy. This presumably included some of the
artisan migration from Macedonia and the northern Greek lands. The
dominant textile sector was less diversified than Gabrovo's but included even more looms, upwards of 4,000. The larger Gabrovo
manufacturers had apparently introduced foot-powered German
looms to Karlovo early in the century, importing them from Braşov in
Transylvania. Gabrovo continued to provide them to many of the
town's artisans into the 1860s. This connection failed, however, to
create in Karlovo any larger artisan/merchant enterprises of the sort
appearing in Gabrovo at this time.[30]

To the west of Karlovo on the Balkans's southern flank was Koprivshtitsa, a town of some 6,000 to 8,000. It is preserved today in its
entirety as a historical monument to this period. The Koprivshtitsa
Garment Company calls our further attention to the division of labor
among Bulgarian towns, already noted for Gabrovo *aba* and Karlovo
gaitan. Drawing on the *aba* production of nearby Pazardzhik, the
firm's artisan founder had ten to fifteen employees sewing finished
garments there by the Crimean War. He himself spent half the year

in Istanbul, cultivating mainly the private Egyptian market. In the decade following the war the enterprise hired representatives and even some local labor at Alexandria and several other locations in the Ottoman lands, all to increase Egyptian sales. Total employees now reached 100. Several difficulties then combined to stunt the firm's growth permanently by the 1870s. The opening of the Suez Canal in 1869 added British-controlled Indian competition to that of Western Europe. Also debilitating was the firm's failure to generate any system of management or accounting. The still-powerful textile guild of Koprivshtitsa added to the firm's woes with repeated sanctions for violating guild rules against free competition.[31]

Since early Ottoman times, Samokov was the center of Bulgarian iron manufacture. It was a town of about 5,000 on the northern foothills of the Rhodopes just south of Sofia. Samokov was alone among the almost one hundred smelting sites across the Bulgarian lands in having as many as four furnaces operating by the start of the nineteenth century. English imports had forced many of the others, especially those to the north and east along the Danube, out of business or at least confined them to village markets by mid-century. In Samokov, however, the number of charcoal furnaces had grown to forty three by 1864. They produced agricultural implements that still undersold English imports, once overland transport costs from Ruse on the Danube had been added.[32] Included in this regional market were several large garrisons of Ottoman troops that remained steady customers.

The Jewish family of Arie had smelted and traded iron in Samokov from the eighteenth century. Its activities during the 1850s and 1860s are instructive in two respects. First, the family failed in its efforts to introduce a more efficient coke-smelting furnace from Vienna, largely because of the opposition of local Turkish ironmongers, and lost some 300,000 piastres (25,000 francs) in the process.[33] Second, the family had by this time diversified its activities. They included banking in Istanbul, general trade in Plovdiv, Ottoman tax collection in the Sofia area, and the operation of several *chiflik* holdings purchased around Samokov. Each of these activities had apparently become more profitable than the original craft of iron-making.

Away from the mountain foothills, the role of the Ottoman state in sustaining profitable enterprises became still more important. To the northeast, in addition to the Danubian ports discussed in Chapter 1, lay Sliven, a town of over 20,000 that contained the main Ottoman garrison for the southern Dobrudja. The wool-weaving enterprise that opened there in 1834 is usually considered Bulgaria's first partly mechanized textile factory.[34] Its Bulgarian founder, Dobri Zheliazikov, had learned modern methods in Russia after his flight there during the Russo-Ottoman War of 1828–29. He returned to Sliven with water-powered machinery. By the 1840s he had imported upwards of twenty steam engines from England and Belgium for wool spinning. The number of employees approached 500. More important for our purposes than Zheliazikov's Russian training or his Western European machinery was the source of his capital. It came from the Ottoman military budget. Since the 1820s, the Porte had complained that cloth purchases for army uniforms in Thessaloniki and Plovdiv were insufficient. Zheliazikov's enterprise was specially chosen to meet that demand. From the start, he saw none of the firm's profits and received instead the salary of an upper-middle Ottoman official. He pleaded in vain to modernize the firm's weaving operations, still scattered through artisan households in the town. Ottoman authorities took over the entire operation from him when the Crimean War suddenly boosted demand.

Located south of the Balkan Mountains, Plovdiv had been a main commercial crossroads since Roman times. It was probably the largest Bulgarian town of the mid-nineteenth century, close to 30,000. Its leading merchant families were Greek, reflecting the town's position on the main overland route between Thessaloniki and Istanbul. The Giumiushgerdan family was most prominent.[35] They had started in Plovdiv as *aba* masters almost a hundred years earlier. By 1840 they employed fifteen agents to purchase wool *aba* from the household production of more than twenty neighboring villages. Their manufacture of finished garments in Plovdiv included the use of Austrian spinning machinery from 1847 forward. But the bulk of their output continued to come from town artisans.

The Ottoman army and government were continually their principal customers. The army contracted for one quarter of the firm's annual output and was identified in company records as the justification for trying to mechanize production. Profits even in a banner year like 1853 nonetheless remained below those available in agricultural trade. Annual gifts to Ottoman officials assured state contracts but cut into profits. So did concessions to local guilds that restricted the mechanization of production.

Both bribes and guild concessions would have continued to hold back the modernization of Bulgarian manufacture had an independent state not emerged in 1878. Their burden probably outweighed the limited advantages of Ottoman military purchases and some state investment in any counterfactual accounting of the economic costs and benefits of imperial dependence vs. national independence. Chapters 8 and 9 attempt to draw up an industrial balance sheet for the various Balkan territories during the period 1878–1914.

Belated Ottoman Reform vs.
the Bulgarian Renascence, 1835–1878

To stress the question of industrial potential for the period preceding 1878 is, however, misleading. It does not lead us to the mainsprings of the Bulgarian movement for political independence that is the most fateful feature of these mid-century decades in the Ottoman Balkans. The Bulgarian Renascence of 1835–78 gathered momentum in large measure because of the relative prosperity of the artisan and merchant communities. Without their resources to draw upon, the movement could never have created bases of national consciousness in the school system and of potential autonomy in local government. Neither did growing artisan and merchant dissatisfaction with Ottoman rule have its main roots in the lack of economic opportunity within the Empire. Instead, it was a series of Ottoman fiscal reforms that fed Bulgarian resentment.

Ottoman Municipal Reform and the Bulgarian Chorbadzhiia

These reforms began with the aforementioned Ottoman decision of 1830 to replace the local *sipahi* cavalry officers or whoever had purchased their rights to collect taxes with designated representatives of the Bulgarian community. This was essentially the *maktu* system of non-Moslem tax collectors for a mainly non-Moslem population that we saw in Chapter 1 being extended to Serbia during the late eighteenth century. Turkish and Albanian Janissaries had tried to overturn the new system. They undermined the Serbian population's continued tolerance of Ottoman rule. For the Bulgarians, it was rather the very Christians selected to represent their fellows who undermined it.

The Porte understandably picked the local *chorbadzhiia*. These were town or village elders whose families had performed administrative functions for Ottoman authorities in the Orthodox *millet* in return for special privileges since the seventeenth century. Taxfarming or money lending had allowed many of them to accumulate agricultural land by foreclosing on peasants in arrears. By the nineteenth century, they had emerged as a separate élite, rarely marrying outside their group. In the phrase of an eminent Bulgarian scholar, they are best understood as a "stratum" distinguished by their administrative role, rather than as a classic Marxist economic class of "big bourgeoisie."[36]

The rest of the Bulgarian population resented their wealth all the more for having been accumulated through administrative privilege. Their installation as local Bulgarian representatives in the 1830 reform too often constituted formal recognition of rights to tax collection that they already held. What now changed was new accountability of the *chorbadzhiia* for the performance of such duties. For allies they could turn only to the local Orthodox bishops, whom they had long supported with the collection of the diocesan tithe for the *millet*. This hierarchy was not Bulgarian but Phanariot Greek. Since the eighteenth century even the parish priest was sometimes ethnically Greek. Together they preserved Hellenic domination of the Orthodox faith. Their religious denial of Bulgarian linguistic and cultural identity had prompted Father Paisii to assert the need for reawakening Bulgarian consciousness as early as 1762.[37]

Had the Ottoman reform stopped with appointing an Orthodox mayor and tax collector (often the same *chorbadzhi*) in each town, there might have been no immediate repercussions. It did not. There was also a council of five to ten members to be nominated by the major interest groups in the town's economy. Artisans and merchants predominated here. These councils had no power as yet to deal with the higher Ottoman authorities. But they were able to do battle with the *chorbadzhiia* over the disposition of those tax revenues earmarked for local use. Two issues came up most often.

First, artisan guilds led the fight to establish primary schools offering a secular, nationalistic, and vocational education in the Bulgarian language. When the first of these schools opened its doors in 1835, not accidentally in the artisan stronghold of Gabrovo, the era of the active Bulgarian Renascence is generally agreed to have begun. The *chorbadzhiia* and their Phanariot allies usually lost the struggle to keep the schools from opening. They were more successful in keeping under their conservative control the curriculum and the young teachers, typically one to a school.

This the other council members resented but not as much apparently as the general refusal of the *chorbadzhiia* mayors to account for tax revenues and their expenditure.[38] The artisan and merchant guilds were especially sensitive on this issue. Members rarely missed a chance to point out how carefully they attended to their own fiscal accountability. Their complaints helped push the Porte into putting tax collection in the hands of its own direct agents in 1842. By 1850, however, the function had largely returned to the hands of local *chorbadzhii*, who paid the central government for the right every five years. The councils could hardly find much hope for the future in this sequence of events. From the 1850s forward a so-called Young political faction emerged in the councils and in popular literature. Its members began to reject continued allegiance to the existing Ottoman framework, as urged by the "Old" faction that centered around the *chorbadzhiia*.

A more radical faction that rejected any accommodation with the

Ottoman Empire, however reformed, had appeared on the Bulgarian political scene by the 1860s. These were the revolutionaries whose heroic although futile struggle for national liberation had cost several their lives before the uprising of 1876. Thomas Meininger's pioneering study of their background reveals them to be typically neither peasant, artisan, nor merchant.[39] They were most often teachers, hired to staff the evergrowing system of locally supported Bulgarian schools. Half of them had now been educated abroad, and half of those in Russia. They returned, full of modernizing zeal and revolutionary ideas, to teach for low, irregular salaries under the constant harassment of the local *chorbadzhiia* and parish priest. They were often fired or forced to move. These discontented intellectuals took the lead in organizing the revolutionary committees to which Marxist scholars rightly point as the forerunners of the biggest socialist movement anywhere in the pre-1914 Balkans. Disaffected schoolteachers appear equally prominent in the founding of the Narrow Socialist movement (see Chapter 8), which became the only Leninist party outside of Russia and the Polish lands before the Bolshevik Revolution.[40]

For the period preceding 1878, however, these genuinely revolutionary stirrings appear less important than the three-cornered struggle between the *chorbadzhiia,* the artisan/merchant class, and the Ottoman administration. The latter had promised the *millet* representatives of Bulgarian local government a place on the new provincial councils, or *meclis,* set up in 1840 as part of the Tanzimat reform. But Moslem representatives, seconded by a few token *chorbadzhiia* and Phanariot clergy, completely controlled the new councils and little changed. The Hatti-Hümayun decrees of 1856 renewed the promise. It stayed an empty promise until 1864. Only then were non-Moslem seats specifically designated on advisory councils for the provincial government. At least some of those seats were filled from the local Bulgarian *obshtina* councils. By the early 1860s artisan and merchant representatives had incorporated formal controls that spelled out members' duties and discouraged financial abuses. Imagine their dismay on finding that the 1864 reform, although giving them leverage over the *chorbadzhiia,* increased their fiscal obligation to the Ottoman state.

The Danubian Vilayet under Midhat Pasha

The 1864 reform also included a comprehensive plan to centralize and to tighten provincial government throughout the Ottoman Empire. Imperial territory was redivided into a reduced number of provinces. As a trial run for the rest, the plan was immediately introduced into the new Danubian *vilayet,* essentially northern Bulgaria and the

Niš triangle. One reason for choosing the area was to put an end to the disruption caused there by the massive Circassian migration from the Crimea. Unaccumstomed to settled agriculture, the unfortunate 100,000 that were forced to leave during 1862–63 arrived starving and sick. In the absence of any organized effort to resettle them, they soon fell back on their equestrian skills to practice banditry across the Bulgarian countryside.[41]

The prosperity of the northern Bulgarian lands, greater than that of any other Ottoman territory by mid-century, offers another clue to their selection for this trial run. Their tax revenues would be the most promising if the efficiency of collection could be improved. The urgency of better collection dated from a judgment in 1861 by the British Board of Trade that this was indeed possible. Twenty years before the actual fact, the British government was already considering whether direct European control of the Ottoman budget would be necessary to assure repayment of the growing state debt to British, French, and German lenders. The Porte did not want the Board of Trade to reconsider the latter's decision that the Ottoman debt did not yet require foreign control. The Ottoman government therefore made its first effort to draw up a precise annual budget on the European pattern in 1862.[42] From 1863 forward, there was a concerted Ottoman effort to show their European creditors an annual increase in total budget revenue. The Porte counted on the new Danubian *vilayet* to lead the way in these increases.

No explanation of this provincial reorganization could proceed further without mentioning the Danubian *vilayet's* first governor, Midhat Pasha. He was after all one of the chief authors of the plan for the Empire as a whole. He was also born of Pomok (Bulgarian Moslem) parents and spent much of his childhood in the northern Bulgarian lands. He returned there several times as an Ottoman official to tackle difficult assignments before his tour as governor.[43] There was perhaps no abler administrator anywhere in the Sultan's service. He was, in other words, the best man that the Ottoman Empire could hope to select as a reforming governor for the Bulgarian lands. The shortcomings of his economic policies therefore stand as an indictment of the best that Ottoman rule could have hoped to accomplish in the Bulgarian lands had their independence not been achieved.

Midhat achieved the principal economic goal that the Porte had assigned him in the Danubian *vilayet*. During his years as governor, from 1864 to 1867, tax revenues increased by about one third (see Table 5.3). This was only slightly better than the gains achieved elsewhere in the Empire. Yet total Danubian revenues reflected a more comprehensive registration of agricultural land and a larger percentage of revenue from agricultural taxes than elsewhere.

These sharply increased agricultural taxes made continued Otto-

TABLE 5.3
OTTOMAN REVENUES IN THE DANUBIAN VILAYET, 1864-67
(in million piastres)[a]

	Total Revenues	Of which:	Harvest Tithes	Tax on Livestock
1864	113		ca 40	16
1865	117			
1866	132		53	
1867	151		68	28

Note: (a)12 Ottoman piastres generally equalled one French franc during the 1860s.

Sources: Zhak Natan, *Stopanska Istoriia na Bulgariia* (Sofia, 1957), p. 195; Bulgarska Akademiia na Naukite, *Istoriia na Bulgariia*, I (Sofia, 1961), p. 396.

man rule more of a burden to the peasantry. Their imposition also alienated the artisans or merchants who had bought up former *chiflik* land as a supposedly profitable investment. If Midhat's administration had used these revenues well enough to compensate landowners by greatly increasing the region's potential for agricultural exports, the prospects for continued Ottoman rule in the Bulgarian lands might have been brighter, its reputation in standard scholarship to the contrary.[44] Midhat Pasha cannot be credited with using these revenues for significant modernization. In the first place, three quarters of the total was transferred outside the *vilayet* to the Treasury in Istanbul.[45]

The remaining one quarter was not well used. Agricultural machinery imported for the several model *chiflik* that Midhat had established with great fanfare usually lay idle for lack of skilled operators or repair facilities. Private landowners imported a few mechanical threshers, but their use was also limited. The diffusion of mechanized techniques to Bulgarian agriculture appears to have been negligible before 1878.[46] Nor does an English engineer's devastating appraisal of Midhat's extensive program of road building lead us to expect that access to markets was much improved thereby.[47]

Midhat's renowned network of agricultural savings banks, although setting a valuable precedent, as noted in Chapter 6, found it difficult to collect large deposits. In the absence of state deposits, they confined themselves to small loans given mainly to peasants in dire circumstances and then only after a complicated process of application. Modernizing investment could not flow from such a restricted line of credit. Regular short-term lending based on bills of exchange, in the fashion of Serbian commercial banks or the private banks of

Vienna and Bucharest which dealt in Balkan trade, was not permitted. Private banks in Istanbul were not able to take up the slack, and the Anglo-French Banque Ottomane Imperiale was uninterested before the 1880s.[48]

These failings in the face of a rising tax burden make it easier to understand the readiness of broad sections of the Bulgarian population to give open support to the growing national revival by the 1870s. The relative prosperity of the Bulgarian lands by mid-century doubtless generated rising native expectations. Ottoman authorities met them only with the obligation to contribute more to the economic well-being of the rest of the Empire. The example of neighboring Serbia, whose annual tribute to the Ottoman authorities had become a fixed, now insignificant, amount added to Bulgarian discontent.

Mid-Nineteenth-Century Prospects for Ottoman Bulgaria

Here, then, as elsewhere in Southeastern Europe, the opportunities for economic growth inherent in the large markets of the Ottoman and Habsburg Empires had gone unfulfilled. Long-distance trade was too difficult to control from the imperial centers. Unlike the Yugoslavs and the Romanians, the Bulgarians did not even occupy an Ottoman-Habsburg borderland that would attract immigrants from both sides and would shift the majority of Balkan trade toward Central Europe under the control of native traders. Bulgarian trade remained tied to nearby Istanbul, Thessaloniki, and the Romanian Principalities. This traffic had nonetheless grown up under native commercial interests, similar to those in the Greek and Serbian lands, only far more dependent on the major Ottoman markets. All such interests had received little support from imperial authorities. Monetization and Mediterranean, essentially Italian, commercial practice still spread to many Balkan towns under their auspices. European merchants or even investors were rarely involved.

Then Ottoman fiscal impositions and renewed monetary depreciation began to discourage Bulgarian trade by the mid-nineteenth century. After being spared the warfare previously associated with the borderlands in earlier centuries, Bulgarian territory suffered under the decay of public order within the Ottoman Empire after 1800. Even the imperial routes to Istanbul and Thessaloniki became unsafe. By 1860, significant numbers of Bulgarian traders and artisans had concluded that a national system of law, property rights, money, taxes, and tariffs would offer them a better chance for commercial growth than would the imperial Ottoman framework. The Tsarist victory in the Russo-Ottoman War of 1877–78 gave them that chance.

Ironically, the principal Ottoman legacies to the new Bulgarian state came from the last decades of imperial reform rather than from the previous centuries of pre-modern subjugation. During these first 400 years the Bulgarians like the other Balkan peoples had survived, although probably not growing much in numbers or otherwise progressing, as a result of the initial equanimity of the Ottoman system and the long-term resilience of their own religious and ethnic ties. The political weakness of the Empire was sufficiently pervasive by the eighteenth century to permit disorder that depopulated the grain-growing lowlands and prompted migration throughout the Balkans.

For the Bulgarian lands, however, the disorder and disease also opened the way for the native population to return in large numbers to the upland towns. Along with emigrants now returning with commercial experience from Istanbul and Thessaloniki, they formed the nucleus for the artisan and trader class which prospered during the first half of the nineteenth century. They supplied Istanbul and manufactured equipment for the Ottoman army whose modernization was the first step toward imperial reform. The centuries-old structure of Ottoman guilds would provide a poor basis from which to modernize Bulgarian manufacturing later in the century but nicely served the political apprenticeship of this growing commercial class. The municipal councils included enough guild representatives to allow them to begin the best system of primary education in any Balkan state. Ottoman favoritism for their local Bulgarian *chorbadzhii* gave these tax collectors an equally strong position on the councils. After 1878 their conservative influence would play into the hands of the ruling German Prince in denying the native commercial class the predominant position in governing the independent state that their Serbian fellows enjoyed over the more pliant *prečani* returning from the Habsburg Vojvodina.

Before 1878 the savings of both artisans and *chorbadzhii* had few chances for modernizing investment in the Bulgarian economy. A majority of the increased tax revenues were diverted elsewhere in the Ottoman Empire. Further Ottoman reform provided one major opportunity by recognizing the ownership of private property and allowing Bulgarians to buy or to finance the sale of agricultural land from departing Turkish officials and officers. Thus the rural system of native-owned smallholdings and indebted peasants with which the Bulgarian economy would begin its national existence also took shape under the auspices of imperial reform during the final Ottoman decades.

The combination of Ottoman reforms that had created both the commercial base and the fiscal grievances to support a Bulgarian independence movement contrasts sharply with passive Habsburg policies toward autonomous Serbia. The Bulgarian experience was similar to the Romanian one with the Russian Règlement Organique. Both made state action the agency for economic change. Yet all three experiences deepened native nationalist resentment of imperial domination. It now remained for the independent nation-states so plainly desired as a political alternative by all the Balkan peoples to begin their search for effecting desirable economic change during the last half century before the First World War.

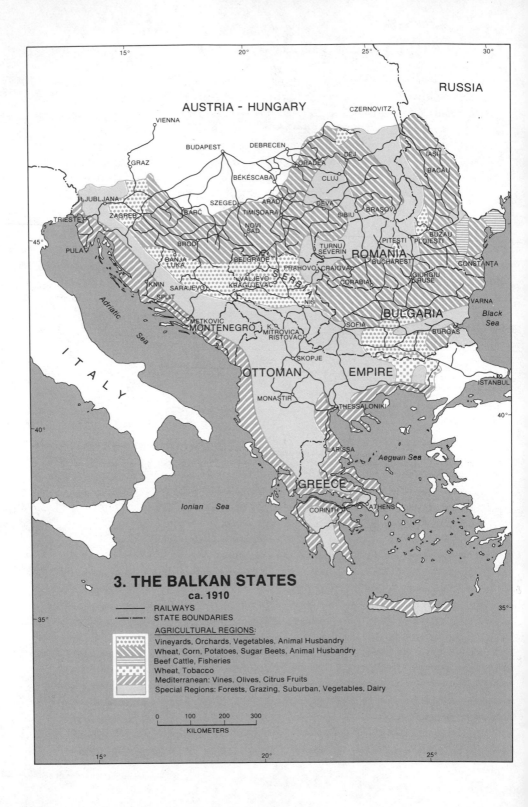

RUSSIA

AUSTRIA - HUNGARY

CZERNOVITZ

VIENNA

BUDAPEST   DEBRECEN

GRAZ

DEJ   IASI
ORADEA   BACĂU

BÉKÉSCABA   CLUJ

LJUBLJANA   ARAD
                 SZEGED   DEVA
ZAGREB   BARĆ TIMIŞOARA   SIBIU BRAŞOV
TRIESTE   NOVI
                       SAD
PULA   BUZĂU
              BRODI   TURNU/ PITEŞTI PLOIEŞTI
                                   SEVERIN   ROMANIA
              BANJA   BELGRADE   CRAIOVA BUCHAREST   CONSTANŢA
KNIN   LUKA   VALJEVO SERBIA
SARAJEVO   KRAGUJEVAC   CORABIA GIURGIU
SPLIT   RUSE
                                        NIŠ   VARNA
              METKOVIC   BULGARIA   Black
Adriatic   K.   Sea
              MONTENEGRO MITROVICA SOFIA
Sea   RISTOVACA   BURGAS

                           SKOPJE
                 OTTOMAN   EMPIRE   ISTANBUL

              MONASTIR
ITALY   THESSALONIKI
                                                              40°

                           LARISSA   Aegean Sea

                           GREECE

Ionian   Sea   CORINTH   ATHENS

3. THE BALKAN STATES
ca. 1910

—————— RAILWAYS
— · — · — STATE BOUNDARIES
AGRICULTURAL REGIONS:
Vineyards, Orchards, Vegetables, Animal Husbandry
Wheat, Corn, Potatoes, Sugar Beets, Animal Husbandry
Beef Cattle, Fisheries
Wheat, Tobacco
Mediterranean: Vines, Olives, Citrus Fruits
Special Regions: Forests, Grazing, Suburban, Vegetables, Dairy

0   100   200   300
KILOMETERS

PART II.

Modernization in the
New Nation-States, 1860–1914

John R. Lampe

The national independence of the four Balkan states is generally dated from 1878. In that year the Great Powers had gathered at the Congress of Berlin to cut the last Ottoman controls over the foreign relations of Serbia and Romania. They also sanctioned the immediate addition of the Niš triangle to southern Serbia and the Greek annexation by 1881 of Thessaly and Arta. Greece in particular became a more viable economic entity. Even in their creation of a small but separate Bulgarian state, however, the Great Powers' seemingly decisive role would have been unthinkable, except under the exclusively Russian auspices that the Congress was convened to reject, without the native independence movement of the 1860s and growing demand for economic autonomy within the Ottoman Empire.

The other three Balkan states had used European reaction to the Russo-Turkish War of 1828–29 and the Crimean War of 1853–56 to carve out autonomy or independence by the 1860s. They also used it to begin constructing the apparatus of a modern nation-state. Prince Mihailo Obrenović, autonomous Serbia's first European-educated ruler, added Ministries of Education, Construction, and War to the four created in the 1840s and completed staffing them with a trained bureaucracy. A Constitution ratified in 1869 after Mihailo's death gave the elected Assembly (Skupština) limited legislative authority over this growing executive branch. Once Russian influence waned after the Crimean War, the Greek monarchy underwent a similar transformation following the ascension of the British-backed King George I in 1863. The Danish ruler received only the powers specifically voted him by the Parliament. The previous era of political parties and ministry officials tied to the British, French, or Russian embassies came to an end.

For Romania, the unification in 1859 of the two Principalities of Wallachia and Moldavia under a single native Prince was the decisive event. The two separate legislative bodies, judicial systems, and the powerful ministries established in the 1830s on the Russo-French model all gained greater power by their consolidation into a single set of institutions in Bucharest. By 1866, the struggle between the native Prince Cuza and the boyar-controlled Chamber of Deputies ended in his replacement by the Hohenzollern Prince Carol and a Constitution. It gave the Interior Ministry powers to appoint chief officials for the 32 prefects (județ) into which the unified state was divided. As a check to the boyar landowners, it allocated almost 40 percent of the seats in the bicameral legislature to urban representatives.

Although no other Balkan state would give its towns such formal representation, all of their capital cities became the focus sometime during the 1870s for fledgling political parties. The parties' cohesion and conduct were often questionable, their influence over the state apparatus still limited. Yet their efforts to combine class and national interest according to the contemporary Western European model gave further impetus to the idea of modernizing the entire country. At least the Romanian Liberals and the Serbian Radicals, and less directly the Bulgarian Agrarian Union, would leave their mark on the essentially native governments that were the principal modernizing agent with which the Balkan national economies entered the last prewar decades.

The following four chapters revolve around the efforts of these newly independent states, and of their governments in particular, to "modernize" their national economies within the fixed borders that prevailed from 1886 (when Ottoman Eastern Rumelia became southern Bulgaria) until the First Balkan War in 1912. Cyril Black's term, as noted in the Introduction, is consciously chosen for several reasons. Modernization escapes the bounds of the Marxist phrase, "industrial capitalism," with attention narrowed to the growth of factory industry in the private sector. It also avoids the bias of the Western phrase, "economic growth," against treating noneconomic influences and slow aggregate growth if agriculture is included. For either schematic approach, pre-1914 Balkan economic history displayed too little industrialization and too much state initiative. More than once that initiative fit contemporary European criteria for what was "modern" and yet derived from noneconomic motives and discouraged growth.

Such inconsistencies in public economic policy run like a thread through Chapters 7 and 8. They deal respectively with the rapid emergence of a European-style financial structure and the mini-spurt of modern industry during the final prewar decade. Another thread connecting finance and industry is the complex role of Balkan relations with the developed European economies, more passive than Marxist scholarship has assumed but less constructive than Western economists might hope. Chapter 9 will then compare economic change in the Habsburg and Ottoman borderlands of Southeastern Europe with that in the independent Balkan states. Although limited by the lack of independence in several ways, the economies of the Habsburg borderlands were ironically able to use the wider imperial market to develop along lines that would ease their absorption into the enlarged Balkan states that emerged from the First World War.

Before these areas of economic modernization that accompanied political independence can be understood, however, Chapter 6 must outline the framework of expanding agricultural exports and an increasing peasant population within which any pre-1914 structural change had to occur. To follow the account, the reader had best be forewarned that the largely unquantified notions of changing markets and the missing measures of land, labor, and capital in Part I no longer hamper us nearly so much, especially after 1900. Part II thus concentrates on statistical turning points. It is hoped that the more rigorous analysis that can now be applied to a far larger number of time series and other tables remains free enough of technical terms to be readily understandable to the student of history as well as of economics.

6.

The Export Boom
and Peasant Agriculture

Rapidly growing agricultural exports hold out promises to small states that have long been heralded among Western economists. Adam Smith and David Ricardo identified the gains from specializing in a large international market. As noted in the Introduction, primary exports promise a developing economy the further advantages of increasing domestic savings to reinvest in the economy, of earning foreign exchange to pay for manufactured imports, and of attracting foreign investment to build infrastructure, all prior to industrialization. These advantages seem to make foreign trade, especially for the period 1850–1914, what Sir Dennis Robertson has called "an engine of growth." Canadian scholars have retitled this approach the staple theory and apply it to their country's experience before the First World War.[1] Balkan income data will scarcely bear the weight of Canadian calculations. The impressive jumps in export value for all four states from 1879 to 1912 still cry out for some connection with aggregate growth. Chapters 7 and 8 will weigh the effect of this dynamic export sector on domestic savings, foreign investment, and native industry.

Primary exports can also bring potential problems to a developing economy.[2] Overdependence on a particular foreign market carries political and economic risks that have troubled a majority of non-European nations at some time during the twentieth century. Foreign demand, whether its vagaries are real or imagined, remains outside a small economy's control by definition. A less obvious problem awaits any country on the side of domestic supply. Exports must continue to grow once population begins rising at a high, modern

rate and available reserves of land have been put to work. One un-
satisfactory way to increase export is to reduce the domestic food
supply. Clearly preferable would be an increase in the productivity
of labor through the spread of more intensive methods. Yet neither of
the two predominant systems of land tenure in the pre-1914 Balkan
states augured well for the introduction of modern techniques. With
their increasing subdivision as rural population increased, peasant
smallholdings offered limited prospects. The large Romanian and
Greek estates offered more, but at the expense of increased exploitation for peasant sharecroppers. Only the Romanian experience provoked open revolt. By the turn of the century, however, the conditions of both smallholding and estate tenure in all the Balkan states
were generating some variety of peasant discontent. Its extent calls
into question the ability of international demand and internal demographic pressure to have sustained continued agricultural growth on
socially tolerable terms. However limited the future prospects, we
must first recognize the sizable growth, or, more precisely, the extensive growth already achieved. (See Map 3 for crop distribution.)

Indicators of Aggregate Growth

The best indicator of aggregate growth is of course an annually
increasing sum of all goods and services produced in the economy.
For pre-1914 Serbia, Romania, and Bulgaria, we have only the notion
of this sum for the last peacetime year afforded by the calculations in
Table 6.1. They record gross output, without removing the double-
counting between sectors that the national accounts, assembled in
more recent times, eliminate from the familiar Gross National Product. Agricultural activities accounted for over 75 percent of gross
output recorded for the three countries. Serbia and Bulgaria approached 80 percent. Romania exceeded 75 percent if the obvious
double-counting of grain and forest inputs is removed from the milling, brewing, and lumbering industries. Without removing *all* the
double-counting between sectors and then deducting another 10 to
20 percent for indirect taxes and depreciation, we dare not add up
the sectoral totals to obtain a precise measure of national incomes per
capita. Yet the rough reduction of the sums of all sectors by one third
still leaves us with benchmark approximations for Serbia and
Romania by the end of the prewar period that approach 250 francs if
we adjust them down another 10 to 20 percent for wartime inflation
that their 1912–13 data include and the 1911 Bulgarian figures do
not. The Bulgarian approximation exceeds 200 francs. These averages compare favorably with national income per capita of perhaps

400 francs equivalent for the Hungarian economy in 1911–13, less than 700 to 800 for the largely industrialized Czech lands, and nearly 1,000 for Germany, by then the leading industrial nation in Europe.[3] Consider the current ten- to fiftyfold gaps between European income per capita and the least developed non-European states. By contrast, the pre–1914 Balkan economies appear to have reached levels close to those of the developed nations of their day. The limitations of the late Ottoman period, emphasized in Part I, suggest that the Balkan economies must have grown in the late nineteenth and early twentieth centuries to stay so close to European levels of income per capita that were themselves increasing severalfold.

Foreign Trade and Population Growth

One more indicator of Balkan economic growth before 1914 is foreign trade. It is one of the two most accurately recorded statistics, along with population, from 1860 to the start of the Balkan Wars. Aggregate values of exports and imports, subject to marginal inaccuracies because of some uncertainty in exchange rates before 1900, are complete for all the Balkan states except Bulgaria from the 1860s forward. The five-year averages in Table 6.2 suggest that autonomous or independent regimes enjoyed increasing access to European markets. Romanian, Serbian and Greek export values all tripled during the first two decades after 1860. Until the depression of 1873–79, this period following the Crimean War had witnessed the most rapid growth in the modern history of international trade.[4] The opening created for Balkan agricultural exports was obvious. Bulgaria took its turn in the first two decades after the long-awaited independence of 1879. Export values tripled from what rough estimates we have for its Ottoman trade of the 1870s. Table 6.10 reflects a Bulgarian reliance on European markets that quickly became comparable to that of the other Balkan states.

The relatively modest increases in Romanian and Serbian export value between 1880 and 1900 were followed by another doubling over the last prewar decade. Bulgarian exports matched these post-1900 growth rates, over 10 percent a year. The boom was sufficient in all three cases to eliminate the large trade deficits that European manufactures had created well before 1900. Only Greece failed to end the import surpluses that had characterized its trade balances since before 1860. After increasing exports at an annual rate of 10 percent from 1860 to 1880, the average Greek increment fell off to one percent for 1881–1911. By recapturing 10 to 12 percent growth rates of the 1860–80 period after 1900, Romania and Serbia were able to achieve rates of 4 and 5 percent respectively for these three

TABLE 6.1
GROSS OUTPUT OF SELECTED ECONOMIC SECTORS, 1911-13
(in lei, leva and dinars)

SECTOR	TOTAL IN MILLIONS			PER CAPITA		
	Romania (1912-13)	Bulgaria (1911)	Serbia (1911, 1913)[a]	Romania (1912-13)	Bulgaria (1911-13)	Serbia (1911, 1913)
Large-scale private industry[b]	519	112	95	71	26	33
Small-scale private industry[c]	185	78	46	25	18	15
Agriculture	1,501	611	490	206	139	163
Forestry	206	97	95	28	22	32
Livestock products[e]	292	217	273	40	48	91
Mining, oil	106	1	16	15	.3	5
Other	493	310	206	68	71	69

Notes: (a)The figures for large-scale industry and mining are for 1911. The others are for 1913, after Serbia had been at war for two years and had experienced a marked but not runaway inflation of 10 to 20 percent. (b)Generally defined as an enterprise using some mechanical horsepower and employing at least 20 workers and 20,000 lei, leva or dinars in capital. (c)Generally defined as artisan shops. (d)Hay and straw excluded. (e)Serbian data probably exaggerated by gross annual addition to livestock.

Source: John R. Lampe and Marvin R. Jackson, "The Genesis of the State Sector in the Balkans," *Faculty Working Papers in Economics*, 74–38 (Tempe, Arizona: College of Business Adminstration, Arizona State University, 1974), Table I, with revisions and discussion of data problems in Marvin R. Jackson and John R. Lampe, "Survey of the Evidence of Industrialization in Southeastern Europe, 1900–1950". *East European Quarterly*, XVI (1982), in press.

TABLE 6.2
COMPARATIVE REAL GROWTH RATES, 1901-15
(annual average rate by geometric method)

Sector	ROMANIA Gross Per Output Capita	BULGARIA Gross Per Output Capita	SERBIA Gross Per Output Capita
Large-scale private industry	(1901/02--1915) 7.0% 5.3%	(1904-1911) 14.7% 13.0%	(1901-1911) 11.6% 10.0%
Grain crops	(1901/05--1911/15) 1.7% 0.0%	(1894/1904--1909/12) 2.3% 0.5%	
Mining and oil	(1901/02--1912/13) 13.4% 12.0%		(1901-1911) 21.5% 19.3%
Population (1901-1911)	1.6%	1.5%	1.5%

Source: Same as Table 6.1, as calculated by Marvin R. Jackson.

later decades. By the last prewar years, Romanian export value approached one quarter of our rough notion of national income. Bulgarian exports exceeded one fifth, the typical proportion for all the developed European economies save France. The Serbian ratio, like the French, fell just short of 15 percent.[5]

The Balkan pattern of population growth casts immediate doubt on what sort of long-run contribution to national income and economic development these large export sectors might have made had war not intervened. The calculations in Table 6.4 reveal rates of natural population increase that are too low before 1880 to suggest a rapid response to the initial export boom. Afterwards, natural increase accelerated but for more complex reasons. First the Romanian and then the Bulgarian birthrates turned upward to levels past 40 per thousand that only Russia and Italy exceeded in prewar Europe. The Serbian birthrate turned downward slightly after 1880, but still hovered around 40. After 1900, the deathrates of all three states started to decline. The growth of their populations during the last prewar decade, essentially unaffected by urban or external migration, proceeded in near uniformity at a rate of about 1½ percent a year. This rate does more than set their populations apart from the Greek experience. Although falling short of the annual rates of over 2 percent that plague non-European developing nations in the present era, 1½ percent was double the rate for Austria-Hungary, as well as for Greece, and half again the one percent recorded by Germany and Great Britain after 1870.[6]

Prospects for maintaining per capita growth in the export or other sectors were thereby limited, especially for Romania and Bulgaria where diverging birth and deathrates promised a still faster rise in population. The nearly 50-percent rise in grain and livestock prices during the last fifteen prewar years wiped out the rest of the post-1900 jump in export values, when converted from money to real per capita terms in Table 6.5. For Serbia, the one state for which we have a comprehensive estimate of export value in constant prices from 1862 forward, the major per capita gains were made in the 1860s and the 1880s. Like Bulgaria, its per-capita peak during 1891–95 is surpassed only for 1901–05, with significantly lower averages on either side. Romanian data available only for grain exports shows an upward trend after the bad harvests of 1897–1900 but not one sufficient to equal the level of 1891–95. Table 6.6 spells out the decisive importance of grain for both Romanian and Bulgarian exports during these last prewar decades. Wheat and some corn and other cereals consistently accounted for more than 70 percent of export value. The absence of Greek grain exports and the smaller share recorded for Serbia will help explain a somewhat different relationship between their foreign trade and population growth.

TABLE 6.3
EXPORT VALUE AND TRADE BALANCES, 1861-1911
(million lei, leva, dinars, or drachmae)

Annual Average	ROMANIA		BULGARIA		SERBIA		GREECE	
	Exports	(Surplus or Def.)	Exports	(Surplus or Def.)	Exports	(Surplus or Def.)	Exports	(Surplus or Def.)
1861-65					16	(+1)	26	(-24)
1866-70					29	(+2)	38	(-33)
1871-75	150	(+52)			32	(+3)	58	(-31)
1876-80	210	(-53)					57	(-38)
1881-85	221	(-73)	38	(-11)	40	(-6)	76	(-46)
1886-90	266	(-65)	63	(-8)	40	(+1)	96	(-26)
1891-95	298	(-97)	78	(-6)	47	(+11)	85	(-29)
1896-1900	251	(-75)	69	(+1)	60	(+16)	88	(-39)
1901-05	361	(+62)	120	(+25)	66	(+14)	87	(-52)
1906-10	499	(+90)	119	(-22)	85	(+14)	120	(-30)
1911	692	(+122)	185	(-15)	117	(+2)	141	(-33)

Sources: B. R. Mitchell, *European Historical Statistics, 1750-1970* (New York: Columbia University Press, 1975), pp. 489-97; John R. Lampe, "Varieties of Unsuccessful Industrialization: The Balkan States Before 1914," *Journal of Economic History,* XXXV, 1 (March, 1975), table 4, p. 63.

The Spread of Grain Cultivation

The rapid spread of grain cultivation across the Balkan countryside could not begin while the insecure travel and unpredictable tax collection of the late Ottoman period continued. Hence the leap forward in Bulgarian grain cultivation and export was delayed until after independence in 1879. The sequence of events was nonetheless similar to those in autonomous Serbia and Romania earlier in the century, as described in Chapters 3 and 4. New native governments restored public order and began to make the rule of law regular practice. They levied predictable and relatively high money taxes that pushed the peasantry into producing a marketable surplus, more quickly and cheaply earned with crops than livestock. Security pulled and taxes pushed peasants back into the long underpopulated lowlands, whose soil was not only more fertile than the highlands but so long uncultivated that it gave initially large yields however primitive the methods.[7] The pre-1914 illusion of "peasant prosperity" on a largely fertile Balkan landscape had its origins in this experience. The rapidly growing rural population that the profits of the initial export boom engendered unfortunately continued to grow long after the land's initial fertility had given way before the geological and climatic limitations emphasized in the Introduction.

TABLE 6.4
GROWTH OF BALKAN POPULATION, 1859-1912

Census date	ROMANIA	BULGARIA	SERBIA	GREECE
		(in thousands)		
1859	3,865	—	1,078	—
1861				1,097
1866	—	—	1,216	
1870	—	—	—	1,458[c]
1874		—	1,354	—
1878-79	4,486	—	—	1,679
1880	—	2,823[a]	—	—
1884	—	—	1,902[b]	—
1887	—	3,154	—	—
1889-90	5,038	—	2,162	2,187[d]
1892	—	3,311	—	—
1894	5,406	—	—	—
1895-96	—	—	2,312	2,434
1899-1900	5,957	3,744	2,494	—
1905	—	4,036	2,689	—
1907	—	—	—	2,632[e]
1910	—	4,338	2,912	—
1912	7,235	—	—	—

Notes: (a)Includes imprecise census for Eastern Rumelia, part of Bulgarian state after 1885. (b)Includes 330,000 in Niš triangle added by Treaty of Berlin in 1878. (c)Includes addition of Ionian Islands in 1863, otherwise 1,394 thousand. (d)Includes addition of Thessaly in 1881 according to Treaty of Berlin, otherwise 1,893 thousand. (e)Includes loss of part of Thessaly in 1897 after Ottoman war, otherwise 2,648 thousand.

TABLE 6.4 (continued)

Birth rate (per thousand)	ROMANIA	BULGARIA	SERBIA	GREECE
1860-1911	38.1	—	42.0	—
1881-1911	40.8	39.2	41.7	—
1860-1878	33.3	—	42.7	28.9
1895-1911	40.6	41.2	39.5	—
Death rate (per thousand)				
1860-1911	27.5	—	27.9	—
1881-1891	27.1	23.4	25.1	—
1860-1878	27.3	—	32.7	21.5
1895-1911	25.9	22.4	24.0	—
Natural increase (per thousand)				
1860-1911	10.7	—	14.1	—
1881-1911	13.9	16.8	16.6	—
1860-1878	6.0	—	10.0	8.0
1895-1911	14.7	17.8	15.5	—
Growth rate (annual percentage by geometric method)				
Population (1859-1912)	1.19	—	2.07	1.92
Natural increase	1.07	—	1.41	—
Population (1859-1878)	.75	—	—	2.39
Natural increase	.60	—	1.00	—
Population (1880-1900)	1.36	1.42	1.71	—
Population (1899-1912)	1.51	1.48	1.56	.71[a]
Natural increase				
Population (1881-1912)	1.43	1.44	1.65	—
Natural increase	1.07	1.68	1.66	—

Note: (a)Extrapolated from 1896 and 1907 census.

Sources: B. R. Mitchell, *European Historical Statistics, 1750-1970* (New York: Columbia University Press, 1975), pp. 19-21, 26, 84-94, 108-118: *Anuarul statistic al României, 1915-1916* (Bucharest, 1919), p. 15: *Anuarul statistic al României, 1934* (Bucharest, 1935), p. 27: *Statisticheski godishnik na Bulgarskoto Tsarstvo, 1912* (Sofia, 1913), pp. 21-23: *Greek Statistical Yearbook, 1971* (Athens, 1972), p. 18, as calculated by Marvin R. Jackson.

Greece faced the severest natural limitations; its grain cultivation suffered accordingly. Not even 20 percent of Greek territory was arable, versus over 40 percent for the rest of Southeastern Europe.[8] The addition in 1881 of Thessaly with its broad if arid plains did permit grain acreage to rise from 7 percent to two thirds of the total under cultivation for 1880–1911. Per capita output rose well above the pitiable level of 1860 (see Table 6.8). This was mainly wheat; too little moisture crossed the Pindus range into eastern Thessaly to permit much corn cultivation. With little corn for fodder, Greek cattle and hog totals were less than one third those of the other Balkan states (see Table 9.6). Nor was wheat, always earning a greater cash

TABLE 6.5
PER CAPITA EXPORTS, 1886-1911, IN CONSTANT 1906-11 PRICES
(in lei, leva, dinars and drachmae = francs)

Annual Average	Total		Per Capita Value		Real Per Capita Value	
	ROMANIA	BULGARIA	ROMANIA	BULGARIA	ROMANIA	BULGARIA
1886-90	266 mil.	62 mil.	51.2	19.7		28.4
1891-95	298	78	54.2	23.2		31.6
1896-1900	251	69	42.8	19.0		24.5
1901-05	360	120	57.7	30.8		40.3
1906-10	531	130	77.8	30.9		30.9
	SERBIA	GREECE	SERBIA	GREECE	SERBIA	
1861-65	17 mil.		14.0		24.0	
1866-70	28		21.5		30.7	
1881-85	40		20.7		31.4	
1886-90	40	96 mil.	19.7	46.7	33.6	
1891-95	47	85	21.0	36.8	35.6	
1896-1900	60	88	25.0	35.6	34.3	
1901-05	66	87	25.5	34.0	37.0	
1906-10	90	123	32.0	46.0	33.9	

ROMANIA

	Grain Value	Grain Value In Constant Prices	Real Per Capita Grain Value
1886-90	220	265	51.1
1891-95	263	344	62.6
1896-1900	201	265	45.1
1901-05	259	328	54.9
1906-10	399	399	59.2

Sources: Table 6.3 above on population; B. R. Mitchell, *European Historical Statistics, 1750-1970* (New York: Columbia University Press, 1975), pp. 245-66, 340, 342, 489-97; I. Adam and N. Marcu, *Studii despre dezvoltarea capitalismului în agricultura Rominiei,* II (Bucharest, 1965), pp. 268, 274; C. I. Băicoianu, *Istoria politicei noastre vamale şi comerciale,* Vol. I, Part I (Bucharest, 1906), pp. 356-57; *Bulatinul statistic al Rominiei,* XII, 38-39 (1915), p. 593; I. Mollev and A. Iu. Totev, *Tseni na zemedelskite produkti u nas, 1881-1934* (Sofia, 1935), pp. 90-92; Kiril Popoff, *La Bulgarie économique, 1879-1911* (Paris, 1920), pp. 169, 402; Michael R. Palairet, "The Influence of Commerce on the Changing Structure of Serbia's Peasant Economy, 1860-1912" (Ph.D. Dissertation, Edinburgh University, 1976), pp. 37-38; Douglas Dakin, *The Unification of Greece, 1770-1923* (London: Ernest Benn, 1972), pp. 320-21.

yield per acre than corn, sufficient to meet domestic needs, let alone generate export earnings. Grain climbed from 13 to 26 percent of total import value from 1863 to 1893 and stayed there until the First World War.[9] Limited Greek cultivation goes a long way toward explaining the lowest rate of population growth and the highest emigration among any of the Balkan states.

The Bulgarian experience underlines the difficulties of overdependence on wheat cultivation where a domestic surplus for export did exist. The country's grain area doubled during the last twenty years of the ninteenth century to reach 26 percent of total arable and

TABLE 6.6
PERCENTAGE VALUE OF PRINCIPAL EXPORTS, 1886-1911

Annual Average	ROMANIA		BULGARIA	SERBIA		GREECE
	Cereals	Oil	Cereals	Cereals	Livestock & Proc. Meat[a]	Currants[b]
1886-90	76.8		72.2	17.8	38.0	54.7
1891-95	79.5		78.0	30.4	42.0	45.2
1896-00	74.2	.8	72.7	27.7	29.9	42.0
1901-05	75.1	2.2	68.8	20.5	44.6	34.5
1906-10	79.7	7.3	64.4	43.5	11.8	30.8
1911	71.4	11.8	70.1	31.7	19.8	33.1

Notes: (a)Processed meat exceeds 1 percent of total export value only after 1895 and averages 4 to 8 percent until rising to 17 percent in 1911. (b)Essentially raisins.

Source: John R. Lampe, "Varieties of Unsuccessful Industrialization: The Balkan States Before 1914," *Journal of Economic History*, XXXV, 1 (March, 1975), Table 5, p. 64.

87 percent of cultivated land.[10] Only Romania employed a higher proportion of total arable. Yet Bulgaria's real per capita export value by the end of the prewar period fell short of the Serbian as well as the Romanian average (see Table 6.8).

This failure derived principally from a greater dependence on wheat. Corn had been the principal hog feed in Serbia since the 1830s. Its cultivation could not be expected to spread widely in the Bulgarian lands. Their closer geographic and political relationship to the Ottoman Empire had made Islamic restrictions on consuming pork more effective. Indeed, scarcely any hogs were raised or corn grown south of the Balkan range in the Bulgarian lands bordering directly on what became European Turkey after 1886. Corn grown principally in the moister northeast never accounted for much more than half the value of Bulgarian wheat harvests and exports.[11] With the same high percentage of corn as wheat exported, no base for livestock exports came into being. Their value remained minuscule. Further advantages foregone were crop rotation between corn and wheat to renew the soil and a somewhat hardier summer crop like corn to take the pressure off the general grain supply if rain or hail damaged the winter wheat crop. Bad weather ruined several crops in succession between 1897 and 1900. Bulgaria then suffered the worst agricultural depression of any Balkan state in the prewar period. Grain production declined by 20 percent. Wheat harvests were cut by perhaps one half. Overall exports fell by one third.[12] The Balkan dangers of drought, flood, and hail made overdependence on a single season's grain crop risky business, however promising the rise in international prices between 1896–1914. For Romania and Serbia, corn acreage and output exceeded those for wheat throughout the prewar period. Neither country suffered more than a year's serious reduction in its harvests and exports during the repeated climatic reverses of 1897–1900.

The Romanian advance for all grains was the most impressive among all the Balkan states. Starting from a base that was undoubtedly larger than the Serbian, Bulgarian, and Greek totals combined in the early 1860s, the Romanian cultivated area for the five principal grains doubled by 1890. Grain covered 39 percent of total arable land by 1910, and 86 percent of cultivated area. Even on the per capita basis calculated in Table 6.7, its total area for 1901–10 averaged 40 percent more than Bulgaria and still more than Serbia or Greece. Only the United States, Canada, and Argentina surpassed the Romanian average for per capita acreage.

By 1910, the value of the biggest Balkan country's wheat exports had passed those of the United States to place it fourth in the world just behind Canada. At the same time, it is essential for the discussion of Romanian agricultural productivity that follows to remember that rising population and prices were sufficient to reduce the real growth rate per capita for grain output between 1901 and 1915 literally to nil.[13] Prices aside, Tables 6.7 and 6.8 reflect pressure from rising rural population over the same period that reduced Romanian grain acreage per capita and did not permit the volume of production any per capita increase.

As elsewhere in the Balkans, wheat and corn made up over 80 percent of the Romanian grain totals. Half of the huge wheat harvest was exported, versus barely 30 percent for Bulgaria. The other Romanian half was mainly sold to the urban market, the largest among the Balkan states. Yet wheat, the quintessential commercial crop, was unable to record any consistent rise in per capita production over the last two prewar decades (see Table 6.8). Only 40 percent of the corn production was exported. The rest went mainly to feed the rural peasantry that still comprised just over 80 percent of overall population. Typically grown on peasant plots rather than leased estates, its per capita volume made a steadier advance than wheat. Oats replaced rye as the leading secondary crop by 1905: Romania had to feed the largest Balkan population of horses.[14] Otherwise, Romanian livestock per capita lagged behind the other Balkan states, let alone the Habsburg lands, as noted in Table 9.6. By 1910, grazing area for livestock had dropped to under 11 percent of arable land, versus about 20 percent for the other Balkan states.

The slower Serbian transition to grain cultivation in general and wheat in particular had its roots in the nearby Habsburg market for

TABLE 6.7
CULTIVATION PER CAPITA OF MAJOR GRAINS, 1862-1915

Wheat (5 year av.)	ROMANIA thousand hectares	ROMANIA per cap. rural pop.	BULGARIA thousand hectares	BULGARIA per cap. rural pop.	SERBIA thousand hectares	SERBIA per cap. rural pop.	GREECE thousand hectares	GREECE per cap. rural pop.
1862-66	697	.19				.08		
1886-90	1,282	.30						
1891-95	1,435	.31			317	.16		
1896-1900	1,561	.33	823	.28	319	.14		
1901-05	1,681	.33	865	.28	343	.15		
1906-10	1,835	.33	1,019	.30	377	.15	351	.13
1911-15	1,922	.32	1,143	.32	387	.15		.16
Corn								
1862-66	980	.27				.14		
1886-90	1,766	.41						
1891-95	1,796	.39			532	.26		
1896-1900	1,993	.42	447	.15	489	.22		
1901-05	2,090	.41	477	.15	532	.23		
1906-10	1,828	.33	559	.17	567	.23	110	.05
1911-15	2,097	.32	638	.18	585	.23		.05
Major Grains[a]								
1862-66	2,084	.58						
1886-90	4,020	.94						
1891-95	4,181	.92						
1896-1900	4,649	.98	1,763	.60	1,107	.57		
1901-05	4,822	.94	1,962	.62	1,043	.50		
1906-10	4,809	.87	2,216	.66	1,114	.50	575	.18
1911-15	4,987	.82	2,428	.68	1,202	.51		.27

Note: (a)Defined as wheat, corn, rye, barley, and oats.

Sources: B. R. Mitchell, *European Historical Statistics, 1750-1970* (New York: Columbia University Press, 1975), pp. 212-26, 250-66; *Amarul statistic al Romîniei, 1915-1916* (Bucharest, 1919); I. Adam and N. Marcu, *Studii despre dezvoltarea capitalismului in agricultura Romîniei*, II (Bucharest, 1965), pp. 202-05; Michael R. Palairet, "The Influence of Commerce on the Changing Structure of Serbia's Peasant Economy, 1860-1912" (Ph.D. Dissertation, Edinburgh University, 1976), pp. 8-9, 215-16; E. J. Tsouderos, *Le relèvment économique de la Grèce* (Paris-Nancy, 1919), pp. 132-33.

TABLE 6.8
PER CAPITA OUTPUT OF MAJOR GRAINS, 1862-1915

Wheat (5 year av.)	ROMANIA thousand tons	ROMANIA per cap. rural pop.	BULGARIA thousand tons	BULGARIA per cap. rural pop.	SERBIA thousand tons	SERBIA per cap. rural pop.	GREECE thousand tons	GREECE per cap. rural pop.
1862-66	672	.19						
1886-90	1,329	.31						
1891-95	1,596	.35						
1896-1900	1,386	.29	647	.22	293	.14		
1901-05	2,086	.41	1,023	.33	292	.13	344	.16
1906-10	2,080	.37	944	.28	337	.14		
1911-15	2,223	.36	1,266	.35	417	.17		
Corn								
1862-66	912	.25						
1886-90	1,616	.38						
1891-95	1,678	.37						
1896-1900	1,852	.39	508	.17	678	.32		
1901-05	1,773	.35	455	.14	444	.20	151	.07
1906-10	2,267	.41	566	.17	660	.28		
1911-15	2,666	.44	750	.21	674	.28		
Major Grains[a]								
1896-1900	ca. 3,800	.80	1,579	.54	1,171	.56		
1901-05	ca. 4,950	.98	2,903	.68	888	.39		
1906-10	ca. 5,350	.96	2,057	.62	1,185	.50	613	.28
1911-15	ca. 6,000	.98	2,637	.75	1,307	.54		

Note: (a)Defined as wheat, corn, rye, barley, and oats.

Sources: Same as for Table 6.7.

livestock and in the growing German market for plums. The large Hungarian estates between Belgrade and the major centers of Habsburg consumption cut off Serbian grain from its closest big market. As with Romania and Bulgaria, land under grain cultivation had doubled from the 1860s to the 1890s and then increased only slightly to the First World War. But by 1897, the year of Serbia's first comprehensive survey of agricultural production, the exported share of total harvest was just 12.5 percent, versus 27 percent for Bulgaria and 46 percent for Romania with its sharecropping estates.[15] The domestic urban market, less than one fifth of the total population, accounted for a faster rising share of grain sales than did exports.[16] Before 1905, the cereal share of Serbian export value had never exceeded 30 percent (see Table 6.6). We may speculate that the Serbian birthrate owned its decline from the 1880s forward to the relative unimportance of a labor-intensive activity like grain cultivation.

The Serbian potential for sustained growth of agricultural exports appeared to lie elsewhere. Per capita grain output for Serbia actually dropped between 1886–1900 and 1901–05. During the later period Romanian and Bulgarian agriculture responded to rising export prices and much better weather with marked increases (see Tables 6.5 and 6.8). Chapter 4 has explained the predominant role of Serbian livestock exports to the Habsburg lands from 1815 to 1878. The further evolution of this dependence on a single major market must now be examined.

Central vs. Western European Demand

More than any other Balkan state during the pre-1914 period, Serbia found the pattern of its export growth shaped by dependence on a single foreign market. The conscious effort to shake free of Austro-Hungarian demand for livestock and grain was only partly successful. Table 6.9 indicates that the overall percentage of Serbian export value shipped to Austria-Hungary was still high enough by 1911 to contrast sharply with the more balanced distribution of exports from the other Balkan states. At the same time, the processing of Serbian plums into prunes had come to rely heavily on the German market. Their limited prospects for future growth may perhaps be judged from the longer experience of Greek raisins with the English market.

TABLE 6.9
DIRECTION OF BALKAN EXPORTS, 1871-1911

	Average Exports	% to AUSTRIA-HUNGARY	% to GERMANY	% to FRANCE	% to U. K.	% to BELGIUM	% to OTTOMAN EMPIRE
Romania	(mil.lei)						
1871-75	147	27	1	12	12		
1876-80	210	37	1	10	18		
1881-85	221	34	1	9	38	1	
1886-90	265	7	4	7	54	1	
1891-95	298	12	19	3	33	20	
1896-1900	252	20	5	3	19	29	
1901-05	361	13	7	3	9	29	
1906-10	501	10	6	7	10	30	
1911	692	9	5	7	8	38	
Bulgaria	(mil. leva)						
1886-90	62	5		22	16		44
1891-95	78	4	14	21	17		29
1896-1900	69	9	13	12	22	9	26
1901-05	120	10	9	6	16		19
1906-10	119	8	12	6	12	18	27
1911	185	6	12	6	13	29	16
Serbia	(mil. dinars)						
1871-75	33	86					
1876-85							
1886-90	40	87	2				10
1891-95	47	89	3				7
1896-1900	60	86	6				6
1901-05	66	86	5	------- 1 --------			6
1906-10	84	28	25	------- 1 --------			10
1911	117	41	25	------- 1 --------			8
Greece	(mil. drachmae)						
1874	68	12		4	68		12
1887-90	101	9	3	24	39		10
1891-95	85	8	5	12	37		7
1896-1900	88	9	7	10	32		7
1901-05	87	14	8	10	27		6
1906-10	120	10	10	8	26		11
1911	141	10	11	10	24		4

Sources: B. R. Mitchell, *European Historical Statistics, 1750-1970* (New York: Columbia University Press, 1975), pp. 510-559; *Statisticheski godishnik na Bulgarskoto Tsarstvo, 1912* (Sofia, 1915), p. 252; Kiril Popoff, *La Bulgarie économique, 1879-1911* (Paris, 1920), p. 407.

Serbian Livestock Exports and
the Tariff War with Austria-Hungary

Livestock exports from autonomous Serbia to Habsburg markets had largely consisted of lean hogs raised on acorns in the interior and then collected along the Sava River between Belgrade and Šabac to the west. Serbian peasant traders and Habsburg middlemen then ferried them across the river and drove them overland to Budapest or Vienna or farther. The virtual Hungarian Agricultural Revolution over the last third of the nineteenth century doomed this initial Serbian trade to extinction.[17] The improved feeding and then breeding of lean hogs on the large Hungarian estates forced Serbian exporters to switch to fattening their hogs for a bacon and lard market in which Hungarian smallholders were their only competition. The agricultural land west of Belgrade was too well endowed in soil and annual rainfall to divert a majority of its cultivation to the corn fodder needed to fatten hogs. Smederevo on the Danube east of Belgrade briefly became the new center of Serbian hog exports. By the 1890s, the completion of the Orient Express line through the interior to Belgrade moved the fattening process inland. There the Morava River valley admittedly provided better corn-growing land. It even yielded a surplus for export through this period. Yet the relatively narrow lowlands of the valley limited the amount of pasture that could be profitably spared from cultivation during the fattening process.[18]

The main pressures constraining the further growth of Serbian hog exports came in any case from the demand rather than the supply side. Hungarian hog population nearly doubled from 1870 to 1895 and made the Dual Monarchy a net exporter of hogs by the later date.[19] The prohibitive Habsburg tariff on Romanian hogs from 1882 forward had given Serbian traders a respite from the political pressures of Hungarian smallholders for similar actions against them. With the fixing of a higher German tariff on Austro-Hungarian hogs in 1885, however, the Hungarian concern for securing the internal Habsburg market intensified. By 1895–96, Budapest had obliged Habsburg authorities in Vienna to bar Serbian hogs from entering the monarchy on a veterinary pretext. The ban cut the value of live hog exports to half their 1890–94 average by 1895.[20]

That same year, further German restriction virtually closed this huge northern market to Hungarian cattle raisers. They added their voices to the clamor for the same sort of protective tariffs against Serbian livestock. The minimal level of existing Habsburg tariffs on Serbian exports came with a commercial treaty essentially imposed by Vienna on the newly independent Belgrade government (and its badly indebted Prince Milan). It assured nearly duty-free access for Austrian and Czech manufactures. But Hungarian interests had the power to call such a foreign agreement into question. Their customs union with the Austrian half of the monarchy came up for renewal every ten years, according to the terms of the 1867 *Ausgleich*. Austrian and Czech dependence on Hungarian food supplies required that some attention be paid to demands from Budapest. It was no accident that the Habsburg tariff war with Romania, treated in Chapter 8, began in the renewal year of 1886. Similarly, the initial closing of the Habsburg border to Serbian hogs occurred during 1895-96. It was another veterinary ban on all Serbian livestock exports in 1906 that precipitated a five-year tariff war. Popularly known as the Pig War, the dispute turned on Budapest's protectionist pressures as much as on Vienna's political anxiety over increased Serbian independence since the deposing of the Austrophile Obrenović dynasty in 1903.[21]

Serbian cattle exports actually fared worse than hogs in the generally favorable final settlement. Smaller and not cross-bred, these cattle were inferior to the Hungarian estate herds. They had to share the Habsburg market for low quality beef with Romania until the tariff war. Then efforts to move cattle live or slaughtered by rail to Thessaloniki and from there by ship to Mediterranean markets essentially failed. As described in Chapter 8, it was the successful processing of slaughtered hogs for Central European markets that helped Serbia to conclude the tariff war by 1911 largely on its own terms.

Livestock exports did not recapture more than half of their former market in the last peacetime year after the dispute. A majority of hogs were slaughtered, now for the Habsburg market. The Serbian potential for continued expansion of cattle exports was in any event limited. Their steady growth since the 1860s had taken place solely at the expense of domestic consumption. Total numbers of cattle had not increased significantly, not at all after 1900. Hog numbers declined by 10 percent from 1901 to 1910, as much before as during the tariff war.[22] Chapter 9 will examine and Table 9.6 quantify the growing Croatian numbers of cattle and hogs, both significantly larger than the Serbian totals by 1910. Future prospects for expanded Serbian sales of livestock to Habsburg markets closer to and politically integrated with Croatia/Slavonia must therefore be minimized.

The overall rise in Serbian export value throughout the tariff war must be further discounted against price and population increases. They were sufficient to drive real per capita exports downward (see Table 6.6). Heavy wheat sales during the first half of the dispute and the large corn export during the second half did not quite make up for reduced livestock exports in real per capita terms. The grain sales are still worth noting. They confirm Vienna's limited power to impose economic hegemony on Serbia. A majority of the wheat went to Germany, the monarchy's closest ally, and the corn to Hungarian stock-raisers in the monarchy itself. The next two chapters will fill in the financial and industrial aspects of the Habsburg failure to win the Serbian tariff war. The monarchy's inability to maintain a monolithic single market even for Serbian exports surely set the stage for that failure.

Serbian Prunes vs. Greek Raisins

For Serbia, the promise of processing agricultural exports derived not only from livestock but also from plums. Their yields per hectare were half again those for wheat or corn. (Plum yields were in turn only one third those of tobacco, sugar beets, cotton, or hemp. The usually machine-powered factory manufacturing required to process those latter four dictates that we postpone our consideration of them until Chapter 8 on industrial stirrings.) By the mid-nineteenth century, millions of plum trees blanketed northern Serbia. Yet the difficulty of transporting fresh fruit kept exports to a minimum. Peasants probably distilled a majority of the annual crop into plum brandy or *šlivovica*, prospects for export of which were equally limited. Market demand for *šlivovica* did not extend far beyond the Balkans. In 1880 revised Ottoman and Habsburg tariffs closed off the brandy markets on either side of the Serbian border. The resulting surplus of plums available for prune exports attracted a number of immigrant entrepreneurs from Ottoman Bosnia, most particularly the partnership Krsmanović-Paranos.[23] They brought with them wholesaling experience and a Bosnian technique for drying plums into prunes in a mud-brick stove, or *pušnica*, that peasants could easily operate. After dominating the import trade for salt by the 1860s, the partnership turned to bringing in migrant Bosnian builders to construct stoves in villages throughout northwest Serbia. The partnership's network of rural agents and credit agreements then drew about half of the region's peasant families into devoting some of their land and labor to producing prunes for export.

The efforts of these and other firms quickly expanded prunes' export value to one quarter of the Serbian total by 1886. Yet that share had shrunk to barely 10 percent by the 1890s. It did not revive noticeably before the First World War. Erratic export variations confirm the special vulnerability of plum trees to drought and hail. Beyond the danger of a bad crop, the predominantly German market remained limited unless Serbian prunes could be consistently delivered in better condition.[24] The American market had not been so discriminating, but it was lost to both Serbian and Bosnian producers with the high McKinley tariff of 1890. The resulting dependence on sales to Berlin and other German towns left Serbian exporters to face growing complaints about the poor condition in which their produce arrived. Prunes were after all no necessity of life, but rather one of those little luxuries bought by the growing middle classes. Complaints could cost customers. They could be silenced only by redrying the prunes according to modern French technology before they began their long rail journey northward. As we shall see in Chapter 8, such an improvement in the quality of production was beyond Serbian means.

Had that barrier been overcome, the thousands of Serbian producers would most probably have faced the problem of limiting their output so as not to flood the German market and drive prices down to an unprofitable level. Such was surely the experience of the many small Greek vineyards with the British raisin market. Both products were too trivial a luxury in the average European diet for their demand to respond elastically to lower prices, as for instance meat's would, with increased sales volume and total value.

By the last decades of the nineteenth century, according to Table 6.6, raisins accounted for nearly 50 percent of Greek export value, almost twice the share that prunes ever achieved for Serbia. Greek potential for grain exports had remained minimal even after the annexation of Thessaly in 1881. Grape and olive vineyards suited the climate and hilly terrain far better. They had spread steadily around the Peloponnesus and up the southwestern coast since the 1830s. Urged on by the extensive Greek commercial network between major European ports, southern peasants planted more and more vineyards in hopes of supplying European wineries with grapes if not the finished product. The greatest expansion took place during the 1870s, at the time that the Mediterranean phylloxera epidemic struck, even reaching the fledgling vineyards in southern Serbia. Inexplicably, Greece was left untouched. When French cultivation recovered by the early 1890s, the numerous Greek vineyards expanded the drying of their grapes into raisins. The process posed no technological problems, took only ten to twelve days, and required skilled labor but no machinery.

On the demand side, Greek representatives persuaded the British government to cut its duty on raisins (identified as "currants" by British documents) in 1890, just as the French market for grapes was about to close and the Russian government was preparing a new tariff law that would eventually exclude Greek raisins. The British market alone, with some transshipment to the United States and Canada, was left to absorb over half the value of Greek raisin exports for the rest of the prewar period. The rest were mainly shipped to Germany and Austria-Hungary through Trieste.[25]

The erratic annual pattern of raisin export value and its declining annual share of total Greek exports after 1900 (again, see Table 6.6) did not result from disease, climatic reverses, or the Serbian sort of problem with quality control. Instead they testify to overproduction for apparently inelastic British and Central European markets. A series of government policies tried unsuccessfully to cut back production.[26] By the late 1890s the promise of foreign sales had boosted production enough to leave an unsold surplus half again estimated world demand. Prices fell drastically. The Retention Law of 1899 established the general direction of Greek government policy by holding back 20 percent of annual grape output for local wine distillers. Higher raisin prices resulted but only brought in new vineyards on inferior land, a classic response in a purely competitive market. The government then established the so-called Currant Bank to pay fixed prices and collect all revenues from raisin sales, while holding 15 percent of production off the market. The Bank's negligible effect on world prices brought a proposal into the Greek parliament by 1903 for a European consortium that would manage distribution. A legislature already uneasy with Great Power supervision of foreign debt repayment (see Chapter 7) rejected the proposal in an uproar. Yet the 15 percent export tariff for raisins that was slapped onto a renewed requirement for retaining annual output still left sizable unsold surpluses in 1904–05. European participation became unavoidable. English and French bankers put up half the 40 million francs capital needed in 1906 to establish a new Privileged Company. These funds allowed it to bear the risk of buying the vineyards' entire output, retaining 35 percent (with 20 percent for its own winery) and selling the rest on the international market. The government belatedly gave it the authority to ban new plantings. Despite this power and an advertising campaign in Britain and North America stressing raisins' healthfulness and cheapness, more raisin surpluses appeared in 1908–09. Only a 25-million-franc loan from one of the London bankers allowed the company to begin paying peasants to destroy their own vines. As the war approached, in other words, prospects for controlling domestic supply or increasing British demand (by making it either price or income elastic to raisins) were not encouraging. The Privileged Company earned only one year's respectable dividends and, in the words of a contemporary English observer, "may be regarded in the light of a philanthropic rather than a profitmaking institution."[27]

Origins of the Balkan Import Surplus with Central Europe

Whatever the limitations of the export markets for Serbian prunes and Greek raisins, their export was at least free of the spectre confronting the grain exports that were so important for Romania and Bulgaria. Prunes and raisins did not face the prospect of competing in a Central European region where proximity to markets, consolidated estate agriculure, and state policy gave an edge to Hungarian grain in the Habsburg lands and to German, Polish, and, until 1902, Russian grain in Imperial Germany. Romania and Bulgaria paid a potentially high price for having little except grain to sell to the breadbasket of Europe. In contrast to the relatively even export/import ratios of Serbia and Greece with that region, the other two Balkan states had seen sizable import surpluses open up in their trade with both Austria-Hungary and Germany by the last prewar decade. These surpluses could have been reduced only slightly by the undetermined amount of Romanian and Bulgarian grain funneled through the port of Antwerp for wider distribution, thus accounting for the surprisingly large Belgian share of their exports. The wider distribution went mainly to the United Kingdom and Western Europe, with little to Germany and virtually none to Austria-Hungary.[28]

This foretaste of German commercial leverage during the 1930s appeared in the structure of Balkan imports as well as exports. The presumed dominance of British and French manufactures in peripheral nineteenth-century markets like the Balkans had in fact given way to the expanding industries of Central Europe by 1900. Even for Greece, long believed to be an enclave for British manufacturers, the figures in Table 6.10 reveal that German and Austro-Hungarian imports combined to exceed the total for the United Kingdom from 1904 forward. British imports into Greece, moreover, divided themselves almost entirely between textiles and coal. The key producers' goods of metals and machinery were largely left to German, Austrian, and Czech manufacturers.[29] Elsewhere, Central European imports easily exceeded the combined British and French amounts and by 1911-12 comprised 45 to 55 percent of total import value. As Table 6.11 makes plain, substantial import surpluses, or trade deficits, characterized the growing commerce of all the Balkan states except Serbia with Germany and Austria-Hungary.

British imports had never been important for Serbia. They had lost out in Romania by the 1860s (see Chapter 3). The frittering away of their initial lead in newly independent Bulgaria by the late 1880s is also instructive. Contemporary British consular reports tell the familiar Eastern European story of German and Czech machinery, Austrian and Italian textiles winning markets away from Manchester and

TABLE 6.10
ORIGINS OF BALKAN IMPORTS, 1871-1911

	Average Imports	% from AUSTRIA-HUNGARY	% from GERMANY	% from FRANCE	% from U.K.	% from OTTOMAN EMPIRE
Romania	(mil. lei)					
1871-75	102	37	7	13	24	
1876-80	264	51	9	9	17	
1881-85	294	46	13	8	19	
1886-90	330	18	28	9	27	
1891-95	395	24	29	9	22	
1896-1900	327	28	22	7	20	
1901-05	299	27	28	6	17	
1906-10	409	25	34	5	15	
1911	570	24	32	6	15	
Bulgaria	(mil. leva)					
1886-90	71	30	4	6	28	14
1891-95	84	36	11	5	21	12
1896-1900	68	28	13	4	22	10
1901-05	95	27	15	6	17	14
1906-10	140	27	17	6	16	14
1911	199	24	20	13	15	8
Serbia	(mil. dinars)					
1871-75	29	78				
1881-85						
1886-90	39	69	5		10	
1891-95	37	59	9		11	
1896-1900	44	55	15		11	
1901-05	53	58	13		9	
1906-10	70	33	33		12	
1911	115	41	27		8	
Greece	(mil. drachmae)					
1874	88	18		20	44	24
1887-90	122	13	4	9	20	14
1891-95	114	13	7	8	28	14
1896-1900	126	12	8	9	24	10
1901-05	140	14	9	8	21	10
1906-10	149	12	9	7	22	9
1911	174	17	9	8	24	5

Sources: Same as for Table 6.9.

the Midlands. Means to this end were discounts and delayed payment, complete catalogues of products, and traveling salesmen that British manufacturers disdained.[30]

During the last prewar decade largely industrial German goods cut heavily into the Austro-Hungarian leads in Serbian and Bulgarian

TABLE 6.11
DISTRIBUTION OF BALKAN TRADE BALANCES, 1886-1911

Romania

	AVERAGE X – M	AUSTRIA-HUNGARY	GERMANY	FRANCE	BELGIUM and U. K.	OTTOMAN EMPIRE
1871-75	147-102 (+45)	39-38 (+1)	2-7 (-5)	18-14 (+4)	17-25 (-8)	
1876-80	210-264 (-54)	77-135 (-58)	1-24 (-23)	21-23 (-2)	37-45 (-8)	
1881-85	221-294 (-73)	75-135 (-60)	3-38 (-35)	19-24 (-5)	83-57 (+26)	
1886-90	265-330 (+65)	19-60 (-41)	10-93 (-83)	20-28 (-8)	43-89 (+54)	
1891-95	298-395 (-97)	36-94 (-58)	51-114 (-57)	9-34 (-25)	98-87 (+11)	
1896-1900	252-327 (-75)	50-93 (-42)	13-71 (-58)	7-23 (-16)	48-64 (-16)	
1901-05	361-299 (+62)	47-81 (-34)	25-85 (+60)	12-17 (-5)	32-50 (-18)	
1906-10	499-409 (+90)	50-101 (-51)	30-139(-109)	35-22 (+13)	50-63 (-13)	
1911	692-570(+122)	63-137 (-74)	33-184(-151)	49-35 (+14)	56-86 (-30)	

Bulgaria

	AVERAGE X – M	AUSTRIA-HUNGARY	GERMANY	FRANCE	BELGIUM and U. K.	OTTOMAN EMPIRE
1886-90	62-71 (-9)	4-21 (-17)	0-3 (-3)	13-4 (+9)	10-20 (-10)	27-10 (+17)
1891-95	78-84 (-6)	3-30 (-27)	9-9 (0)	16-4 (+12)	13-18 (-5)	23-10 (+13)
1896-1900	69-68 (+1)	5-19 (-14)	9-9 (0)	8-3 (+5)	15-16 (-1)	18-7 (+11)
1901-05	120-95 (+25)	12-26 (-14)	11-14 (-3)	8-6 (+2)	20-17 (+3)	23-13 (+10)
1906-10	119-140 (-21)	8-37 (-29)	14-24 (-10)	7-9 (-2)	14-23 (-9)	33-19 (+14)
1911	185-199 (-14)	11-48 (-37)	23-40 (-17)	11-25 (-14)	24-30 (-6)	29-16 (+13)

Serbia

	AVERAGE X – M	AUSTRIA-HUNGARY	GERMANY	FRANCE	BELGIUM and U. K.	OTTOMAN EMPIRE
1871-75	33-29 (+4)	28-23 (+5)	1-2 (-1)		0-4 (-4)	
1886-90	40-39 (-1)	35-27 (+8)	1-3 (-2)		0-4 (-4)	
1891-95	48-37 (+11)	42-22 (+20)	4-7 (-3)		0-5 (-5)	
1896-1900	60-44 (+16)	51-24 (+27)	3-7 (-4)		0-5 (-5)	
1901-05	66-53 (+13)	57-31 (+26)	24-23 (+1)		1-9 (-8)	
1906-10	84-70 (+14)	24-23 (+1)	29-31 (-2)		0-9 (-8)	
1911	117-115 (+2)	48-47 (+1)				

Greece

	AVERAGE X – M	AUSTRIA-HUNGARY	GERMANY	FRANCE	BELGIUM and U. K.	OTTOMAN EMPIRE
1874	58-88 (-30)	8-16 (-8)	3-5 (-2)	3-18 (-15)	46-39 (-7)	8-21 (-13)
1887-90	101-128 (-27)	9-17 (-8)	4-8 (-4)	24-11 (+13)	39-26 (+13)	10-19 (-9)
1891-95	85-114 (-29)	7-15 (-8)	6-10 (-4)	10-9 (+1)	32-32 (0)	6-15 (-9)
1896-1900	88-127 (-39)	8-15 (-7)	7-12 (-5)	9-11 (-2)	28-31 (-3)	6-13 (-7)
1901-05	87-139 (-52)	9-19 (-10)	11-14 (-3)	9-11 (-2)	23-26 (-6)	6-14 (-8)
1906-10	120-149 (-29)	11-18 (-7)	13-16 (-3)	10-10 (0)	31-32 (-1)	6-13 (-7)
1911-13	141-174 (-33)	14-24 (-10)		10-14 (-4)	34-41 (-7)	5-9 (-4)

imports. Germany had moved past the Dual Monarchy in its Romanian sales by 1906. The most obvious casualty here was the often proclaimed Habsburg intention to penetrate Balkan markets as compensation for the growing difficulties in selling their manufactures to Germany. Aggregate Balkan sales accounted for barely 10 percent of total Austro-Hungarian export value by 1911. The rising German shares of Balkan imports noted in Tables 6.10 and 6.11 hardly promised a higher Habsburg percentage.

Parenthetically, it should be recorded that the importation of predominantly Central European manufactures before or after 1900 was not forcing the Balkan economies to pay rising prices for finished goods with exports of primary products whose prices were declining. Recent research persuasively shows that the worsening terms of trade for unprocessed goods, so long assumed as an article of faith for the course of international trade over the past century, were in fact based on League of Nations' data biased by reliance on British prices. This data also failed to remove falling transport costs that loomed larger for bulkier primary products. Corrected estimates for continental Europe reflect no significant change in the terms of trading agricultural for manufactured goods during 1872–1913, 1896–1913, or even 1872–1929.[31]

The Dynamics of Land Distribution and Agricultural Productivity

Had the First World War not intervened, the Central European powers were not likely to have coordinated their trade relations to gain decisive political leverage over the Balkan states. Austria-Hungary was the traditional adversary of Serbia and Romania. Yet the Dual Monarchy received no assistance from Germany in the tariff wars it waged and lost against its two immediate Balkan neighbors. The separate Habsburg share of Balkan imports only declined after 1900. Finally, as Chapter 7 will demonstrate, Balkan governments came in the last prewar decades to rely principally on the Paris capital market to the near-exclusion of Vienna and Berlin.

The far greater threat to the continued growth of Balkan agricultural exports—if the war had not cut back European population and prices, eliminated one of the two Central powers, and sapped French resources for foreign lending—would probably not have come from foreign political pressure to limit demand. The weakness of domestic supply was more ominous. The intensive crop cultivation and stock-raising that might have added value to agricultural exports and freed labor for industrial employment, as occurred in Dualist Hungary, failed to materialize in any of the prewar Balkan states. Neither the two predominant systems of land tenure, peasant smallholding and estate sharecropping, nor the agricultural policies of the Balkan governments allowed any significant, sustained advance in agricultural productivity. All three are better thought of as constraints.

Smallholdings in Serbia and Bulgaria

The family-owned peasant smallholding had become almost the only form of land tenure in Serbia by the early nineteenth century. Chapter 4 has described the absence of native noble or Ottoman *chiflik* estates that allowed the lowland valleys to begin filling up with family-size individual holdings throughout the rest of the country. According to Table 6.12, properties of less than 20 hectares accounted for 84 percent of private rural land and 98 percent of landowners in Serbia.

The one calculation of peasant money income according to size of holding does reveal a surplus of crop income over expenses for Serbian holdings over 2 hectares (about 5 acres).[32] The resultant savings appear to have been invested less in modern agricultural equipment than in buying more land for heirs to the family property. That property was still divided into 6 to 8 unconsolidated strips. Without primogeniture, all sons had the right to inherit an equal share of the father's holding once the communal *zadruge* had dissolved over the nineteenth century (see Chapter 4). The considerable land purchases made to prevent these inheritances from shrinking may be judged from the increased population and yet essentially constant percentage of properties in each size category between 1897 and 1908. The number of iron plows, reapers, and other agricultural tools per capita did not increase from 1863 to 1893. By 1900, it is true, iron plows were in a two to one majority across the main grain-growing areas along the Sava and Morava rivers. After 1900, the scattering of available evidence suggests that they and other imported iron implements spread even more widely in these northern regions.[33] At the same time, much of this equipment went without horses to draw it. Other livestock was still not kept or fed in stalls, and their fertilizer was not systematically used. Crop rotation was inconsistent. Irrigation was rare. Elementary steam-powered threshers and reapers began to be imported, but their total was minuscule when compared to the Romanian figures. Peasants reportedly harvested more grain bent over with a sickle than standing with a scythe.[34]

The sharp increase in iron equipment on smallholdings whose methods and equipment otherwise remained the same produced understandably meager results. Using crop data per hectare for 1891-1900 as a base, corn yields for the period 1900-12 showed

TABLE 6.12
STRUCTURE OF BALKAN LANDOWNERSHIP, 1905-08

Size of property (hectares)	ROMANIA (ca 1907)[a]		BULGARIA (1908)[b]		SERBIA (1905)[c]	
	% of owners	% of land	% of owners	% of land	% of owners	% of land
Up to 2	30.2	4.1	32.8	5.5	27	7
2-5	46.9	21.5	30.0	18.3	38	33
5-10	18.2	14.5	23.1	29.4	24	1
10-20	} 3.7	} 8.9	11.0	26.6	9	31
20-50			2.7	13.4	2	15
50-100		2.1	.3	3.0	0.3	1
100-500	}	10.4	}	3.1	}	}
500-1,000		10.3				
1,000-3,000	} .6	15.8	} .1	} .7	} .3	} .1
3,000-5,000		5.6				
Over 5,000	}	6.7	}	}	}	}

Notes: (a)All arable, meadow and pasture land. (b)All private arable land. (c)All private rural land.

Sources: Henry L. Roberts, *Rumania: Political Problems of an Agrarian State* (New Haven,Conn.: Yale University Press, 1951), p. 362; *Statisticheski godishnik na Bulgarskoto Tsarstvo, 1913-22* (Sofia, 1924), pp. B10; Michael R. Palairet, "The Influence of Commerce on the Changing Structure of Serbia's Peasant Economy, 1860-1912" (Ph.D. Dissertation, Edinburgh University, 1976), p. 42-43.

great variations and wheat no significant increases except for 1909–12 (see Table 6.13). Total wheat acreage remained just over half that for corn throughout the period.[35] In sum, the corner toward intensive cultivation does not appear to have been turned.

Bulgarian smallholders had a similar experience. Iron plows and other small implements multiplied almost tenfold from 1893 to 1910. Although just 18 percent of all peasant households had even an iron plow by then, the proportion was reportedly much higher in the main grain-growing areas. The number of horses per capita doubled the Serbian average to nearly match the Romanian, but the importation of machine-powered equipment moved no faster than for Serbia.[36] Most important, yields per hectare for corn achieved literally no increase over the period 1896–1910. Wheat yields advanced during 1911–12 but still fell short of the level reached in 1901–05 (see Table 6.13).

A British consular report explained the lack of increased productivity in terms of smallholdings, peasant illiteracy, and resistance to new tools or techniques.[37] But the ready adoption of iron plows undercuts this line of reasoning as the sole explanation. So do the unfavorable circumstances under which most Bulgarian smallholders acquired at least part of their land. As pointed out in Chapter 5, northern peasant proprietors effectively owned the great majority of the land under cultivation by the 1860s but had gone into debt to do so. In the wake of the Russian army's liberation of the Bulgarian lands from Ottoman rule in 1878, native peasants seized up to 40 percent of the cultivated land south of the Balkan range and smaller, more scattered sections in the northeast.[38] The Congress of Berlin, beyond returning the south to Ottoman custody until 1885, revoked these seizures, north and south, unless the Bulgarian peasant could pay the former Turkish owner. Pay they did, 40 to 80 million leva (or francs) worth for some half million hectares by the mid-1880s. Up to three fourths of the purchasers held less than 20 hectares. These smallholders were typically obligated to borrow money at high interest rates from the native *chorbadzhii* officials or town merchants in order to keep such land. They therefore began these last prewar decades with future savings already mortgaged to repay past debts.

The relatively few large landowners among the *chorbadzhii* and others chose to rent out most of their holdings to sharecroppers with no equipment furnished. Wage labor was on the rise but never exceeded 10 percent of the rural work force in prewar Bulgaria. Profits from the larger northeastern and southern holdings where it was used reportedly lagged behind those available in commerce or industry.[39] Hence, the incentive to invest in intensive agriculture remained low. As with pre-1914 Serbia, rapidly rising prices for rural land must be taken as a sign of population pressure rather than increasing profitability.

Sharecropping in Greece and Romania

The predominant pattern of peasant smallholding extended into the other two Balkan states as well. Even in rural Romania, dominated by boyar estates, 72 percent of the peasantry owned some land.[40] What distinguished Romania and northern Greece was the unusually small size—one or two hectares—of the majority of peasants' holdings and their recourse to estate sharecropping in order to survive. Southern Greece lacked such estates but suffered from the greatest shortage of arable land for any major Balkan region, well under the low 20 percent average for all Greek territory, 1881–1912. Witness the minuscule grain yields recorded within the small southern state in 1860 (Table 6.13). Although no census was taken, other sources indicate a growing subdivision of holdings already under 5 hectares in the face of increasing population and no primogeniture. The uncontrollable tendency of southern Greek smallholders to convert as much of their land as possible to vineyards for the raisin market can easily be understood: their plots would not yield enough grain or support enough livestock for subsistence anyway.

In the wheat-growing plains of Thessaly to the north, Greek merchants had taken over some of the larger estates composed of *chiflik* villages (see Chapter 1) prior to annexation in 1881. Among the 658 villages of Thessaly that year, fully 446 or over two thirds were somehow working for a *chiflik* estate. The latter figure had declined to 264 by 1907, concentrated in western estates averaging 750 hectares. A British consular report estimated that half of this northern peasantry, including smallholders, still worked for estates that could exceed 2,000 hectares under some kind of sharecropping agreement.[41] Unwritten contracts not only left the peasant open to exploitation but also made no attempt to overcome his inability to afford iron tools or to end excessive religious holidays. The estates notwithstanding, only half the peasant households even had iron plows after 1900, versus two thirds for the Serbian grain belt. The one major European investment in prewar Balkan agriculture, the English-backed and managed Lake Copais Company, was obliged to confine its introduction of threshing machines, fertilizer, drainage and irrigation, and new high-yield crops like cotton and barley to the quarter of its holdings farmed directly by wage labor. For lack of wage labor, the other three quarters operated under the standard sharecropping arrangement and maintained past methods of cultivation. When total Greek wheat cultivation expanded to meet wartime demand from 1911 to 1916, yields dropped by one-third, admittedly with manpower reduced by military mobilization.[42]

The large Romanian estates were more numerous and their experience better recorded statistically. Designating estates roughly as those properties over 100 hectares, they accounted for 55 percent of Romanian agricultural land. Table 6.12 above makes clear the contrast with the Serbian and Bulgarian landholding structures, where holdings over 100 hectares made up less than 5 percent of the total. Recent Romanian and American research, moreover, confirms the decisive role of the large estates in doubling an already large area of grain cultivation between 1862 and 1890.[43] The 20-percent advantage in wheat and corn yields per hectare that the large estates achieved over smaller Romanian holdings was, however, insufficient to push the national average past those for Bulgaria and Serbia during the last prewar decades. Table 6.13 records no significant Romanian advantage for either grain. Per capita output declined for wheat, the principal estate crop, and rose for the corn that covered most peasant plots. (The failure of corn exports to keep up with the increase in its production recorded in Table 6.8 argues against any great increase in estate cultivation of corn after 1900.)

The reasons for higher estate yields still deserve careful analysis. In the absence of badly needed research on the actual operation of the Romanian estates at the microeconomic level, the following appraisal can still be offered. The boyar estates had access to better

TABLE 6.13
BALKAN GRAIN YIELDS, 1862-1912
(quintals per hectare)

Wheat	ROMANIA	BULGARIA	SERBIA	GREECE
1862-66	9.6		9.5	
1886-90	10.4			
1891-95	11.1		8.7	
1896-1900	8.9	7.9	9.4	
1901-05	12.4	11.8	8.4	
1906-10	11.3	9.3	9.3	
1911-15	11.6	11.1	11.1	9.8
Corn				
1862-66	9.3		11.8	
1886-90	9.2			
1891-95	9.3		7.5	
1896-1900	10.3	11.4	14.0	
1901-05	8.5	9.5	8.4	
1906-10	12.4	10.1	12.0	
1911-15	12.7	11.8	10.7	13.7

Sources: Tables 6.7 and 6.8 above; Jack Tucker, "The Rumanian Peasant Revolt of 1907: Three Regional Studies" (Ph.D. Dissertation, University of Chicago, 1972), p. 73; Michael R. Palairet, "The Influence of Commerce on the Changing Structure of Serbia's Peasant Economy, 1860-1912" (Ph.D. Dissertation, Edinburgh University, 1976), p. 214.

land that was closer to the main rivers not only by dint of centuries of local power but also because of the new unified central government's land reform in 1864. Although resisted by the boyars, Prince Cuza's reform gave them final legal right to two thirds of all estate land, assorted advantages in making sure it was the best two thirds, and further access to state land.[44] Their holdings continued to grow until 1890, as already noted. Afterwards, the estates were the principal purchasers of a far greater influx of iron tools and steam-powered agricultural equipment than either Serbia or Bulgaria received. Romanian numbers of threshers and harvesters were perhaps twenty times greater and approached the sizable Hungarian totals.

Some estates' practice of crop rotation, seed selection, flood control, and irrigation also emulated the modern standards being set in Dualist Hungary. All this was apparently not enough to initiate the Agricultural Revolution that rising labor productivity and more intensive cultivation precipitated in prewar Hungary proper. Together the two sources accounted for over half the increase in Hungarian grain output from 1867 to 1913. Jack Tucker's calculation of labor productivity in Romanian grain cultivation shows no increase after the early 1890s.[45] As for intensiveness, recall that neither the value of Romanian exports, about 80 percent cereals, or the volume of grain production increased on a per capita basis after 1900 (see Tables 6.5 and 6.8).

The explanation of these Romanian shortcomings surely lies in the sharecropping system whose eighteenth-century origins were examined in Chapter 3. The 1864 reform only strengthened that system. Peasants now lost all rights to increase (and possibly consolidate) their scattered holdings other than by inheritance. This limited avenue increased aggregate peasant holdings by only 10 percent from 1864 to 1906. Another 20 percent added from state lands could not prevent the size of the average holding from declining after 1896.[46] With the reform's new taxes and the fifteen-year redemption owed the state for final title to the peasants' third of estate lands, the Romanian peasant was pushed further into sharecropping in order to keep his own land.

The ground rules for sharecropping were undergoing a fundamental change. The money rents that peasants had paid to Wallachian and even Moldavian estate owners for use of their land earlier in the century (see Chapter 3) could not survive the export boom of the 1850s and 1860s. Boyars and their agents increasingly obliged tenants to sign labor contracts to work one section of estate land in return for a year's lease on another section. Already squeezed for cash, the peasants at least escaped one monetary obligation. By 1866, these contracts were placed outside the government's legal jurisdiction and in the hands of the boyars and local authorities. Their terms forced the peasant to work the owner's section before the one leased, and to give the landlord a share of the latter's crop as well. The legalistic, essentially English conception of property rights based on written documents was new to the Romanian countryside, if *dijma* sharecropping was not (see Chapter 3). The abrupt introduction of contracts and leases during the second half of the nineteenth century clashed with peasant notions of customary rights, however exploitative. Persisting peasant illiteracy multiplied misunderstandings. The resulting ill will undoubtedly contributed to outright revolt in 1907, as will be discussed below.

The decline in world grain prices after 1873 probably delayed the estates' shift away from fixed money rents, worth more in a deflationary period. The boyars' legal leverage did allow them to expand wheat cultivation and exports by increasing the size of their own section that peasants worked in return for a given amount of leased land. When prices turned upward after 1896, more owners abandoned money rents, albeit informally in Moldavia. They tried to increase crop and labor requirements still further despite the near exhaustion of new land to divide with the peasantry. The owners' share of crops on leased land rose instead most sharply where peasant holdings were smallest. The estates' combined share of peasant cultivation, from leased land or from labor elsewhere on the estate, rose from 20 percent during the 1870s to 50 to 60 percent after 1900. This increase, rather than greater productivity, explains the post-1900 jump in Romanian grain exports even when adjusted for price changes. As also recorded in Table 6, above, the failure of real per capita exports to rise over the same period must therefore have meant a *decline* in per capita peasant earnings from the export trade. Peasants had largely exhausted their capacity to increase export earnings from their own small holdings by converting pasture land to cultivation. Many households also found themselves obliged to pay a rising annual rent for access to estate pasture in order to maintain any livestock at all. The dependence on grain grew accordingly. Their only compensation was a one-quarter increase in the domestic, largely rural, consumption of corn, probably at the expense of meat and vegetables, if the spread of pellagra is any indication.[47]

The boyar owners themselves favored grain cultivation over live-stock raising. Always requiring less long-term investment, grain also promised quicker returns once international prices turned up after 1896. Owners' negotiation of management leases with Jewish or other merchant agents became more frequent for each lease, often yearly after 1900, as well as more widespread. By 1907, 57 percent of all cultivated estate land was leased to outside managers. They sought to recapture their escalating bids for leases with ever-higher terms for the combined sharecropping and labor contracts offered to the peasantry. The inefficiency of this system may be seen in the owner's preference for cultivating wheat, more widely marketable internationally than corn, on land farmed with modern machinery and wage labor that included only one seventh of the native rural labor force and over 50,000 seasonal migrants from Bulgaria, Macedonia, Serbia, or Ruthenia.[48] (See Chapters 10 and 12 on the way in which smaller-scale renting replaced the sharecropping system in the interwar period.)

The Absence of State Aid to Agriculture

Before turning to the economic and social repercussions of the increasing impasse facing the prewar Balkan peasantry, some comment on state aid to agriculture must be made. It can be brief, because none of the four pre-1914 Balkan governments made any significant contribution to tearing down the barriers that we have noted to higher agricultural productivity. No Balkan state even aspired to the active role in agriculture that they at least attempted to play in other economic regards like monetary regulation and tariff protection (see Chapters 7 and 8).

Aggregate state expenditures on agriculture were small. Of the impressive budget totals set down in Chapter 7, more than matching export earnings stride for stride, no Balkan government spent as much as 5 percent on agricultural improvements. None had a separate Ministry of Agriculture until Greece formed one in 1910; the others had divisions for agriculture in the Ministries of National Economy or State Domains that were established during the 1890s. They were in every case the most poorly funded division in the ministry.[49]

Extension services of the sort so successfully run by the U.S. Department of Agriculture were perhaps the most glaring omission. Romania made a good start with an agricultural school and model farm proposed under the 1864 land reform. A small one actually opened in 1871 on the estate of the boyar reformer and agronomist, Ion Ionescu de la Brad. Only three more were set up before 1900, however. The 1901 law prescribing one for each of Romania's several hundred subdistricts, or communes, never came close to being carried out.[50] Bulgaria could claim the best Balkan system of rural primary education (see Chapter 8) but like Serbia and Greece had placed only several hundred students in a handful of agricultural schools or model farms by 1910. Serbian legislation of 1897 had mandated appointment of a resident agricultural agent in each of seventeen districts across the country. Only eight were ever filled. Even in Romania, graduates were given little support in spreading their knowledge among the mass of peasants.

Serbian and Greek state nurseries sought to improve viticulture but proved unable to disseminate techniques for effective control of disease. In any case they served a sector that declined steadily after 1890. The Serbian Ministry of National Economy did make a major effort to modernize the growing prune trade by selling at half price multiuser drying stoves that saved increasingly scarce firewood. No more than 10 percent of peasant producers bought them. The ministry's inspectorate for quality control of prune exports, set up in 1895, became so powerless and open to corruption as to be judged primarily a "nuisance."[51]

Agricultural infrastructure was also neglected, with one Romanian exception. Flood control and irrigation projects were rare and skimpily funded in all the Balkan states. Until 1900 Serbian railway lines were laid out with the strategic aims in mind of the European powers whose loans largely paid for them. The line south from Belgrade to Niš and then dividing to reach both the Bulgarian and Ottoman Macedonian frontiers helped to fill out the route of the Orient Express from Central Europe. The east-west lines across the northern region where most grain was grown were not built until after 1900 and even then were narrow gauge (see Map 3 for lines in service). Railway use for grain export appears to have been limited largely to the less heavily cultivated southern areas. They accounted for almost one half of grain tonnage carried in 1908 as rail freight. That total in turn amounted to only 41 percent of the Serbian grain tonnage exported that year.[52] Serbia's proximity to the Danube and the state railway's refusal to cut rates below the cost of road transport were apparently responsible for the network's carrying a lower percentage of the grain trade than less satisfactory data suggest for Bulgaria and especially Romania. The Bulgarian network, because of problems with European financing discussed in Chapter 7, did not connect the major grain-growing areas with the Danubian ports of Ruse and Svishtov or the Black Sea outlets at Varna and Burgas until after 1900. By 1909–11 the cereal tonnage carried by the state railway doubled as a proportion of grain exports to approach 70 percent.

By contrast, the Romanian network had linked Brăila, Galaţi, and lesser Danubian ports with the Wallachian and Moldavian grain belts by the 1880s. Its share of the grain tonnage carried to all Romanian ports actually reached 98 percent in 1911. During the last decades before the turn of the century, moreover, the state railway had cut freight rates by more than two thirds. This reduction was comparable to those in the other major grain-producing countries, rather than the one third by which Serbian and Bulgarian rates were lowered from about the same initial level during the 1890s.[53]

For those two states, their principal aid to agriculture appears to have been a system of taxation that was much less oppressive for the peasantry than previously assumed. Both their regimes and also the Romanian chose not to increase the basic land tax in the post-1895 era of rising grain prices and money incomes. Instead, as noted in Chapter 7, they boosted indirect taxes on a variety of necessities, which peasants either produced for themselves or were in a good position to obtain illegally. If the Serbian experience is any guide, the tax burden of most Balkan peasants declined by over one half between 1880 and 1910.[54]

Patterns of Peasant Discontent

Whatever the lessening of their tax burden, the Balkan peasantry's response to their overall economic circumstances during the last prewar decades offers cold comfort to the theory that growing agricultural exports were leading the way to sustained internal development. What emerged instead was a varied pattern of peasant discontent. In the grain-deficit areas of Greece and southern Serbia, smallholders voted with their feet. They migrated in search of seasonal or longer-term wage labor, usually outside the country. Peasants in the grain-surplus area of northern Serbia could supplement their income with livestock or prune exports. The Bulgarian peasantry could not. Following the series of bad harvests during 1897–1900, they began to join the new Bulgarian Agrarian National Union that Alexander Stamboliski would briefly lead to power after the First World War. The common dissatisfaction of Bulgarian, Serbian, and Greek peasants appears to have been a shortage of money rather than food or other necessities, money not to pay taxes but to buy more manufactures and especially to buy more land as a rational response to population pressure. The actions of the Balkan governments in the face of the resulting credit shortage, far from aiding agriculture, were part of the problem.

Spontaneous Violence in Romania: The 1907 Peasant Revolt

Only in Romania, significantly the pre-1914 Balkan country with the largest and fastest-growing agricultural exports, did peasant discontent spill over into widespread revolt and bloodshed. The long-term background to the 1907 revolt is well known.[55] In addition to the general Balkan problem of access to money and credit, peasants faced a land shortage in the midst of the region's richest soil. The competitive bidding for leases to run the sharecropping of boyar-owned estates had forced the Romanian peasantry, as we have seen, to accept increasingly exploitative contracts after 1895. In northern Moldavia, where the revolt originated, peasant resentment focused on the Jewish merchants who were most often the lessees, or aren-daşi. Typically nineteenth-century immigrants from the Russian or Habsburg lands, they were barred from owning land under Romanian law. Thus they saw their leases as short-term ventures and tended to pursue the maximum short-term profit.

Throughout all Romania, however, the greater incidence of alcoholism, an increasingly meatless diet, illness, and higher infant mortality marked the peasantry off from their Serbian or Bulgarian fellows. These social conditions suggest a wider problem, both economic and legal as we have seen, than the behavior of Jewish lessees. The state's distribution of some of its land to the peasantry during 1888–89 had come to pass only after several local revolts brought in a new Conservative government, dominated by Moldavian estate owners. To spare themselves further violence, they pushed the sale, on long-term credit, of 5-hectare plots to the land-hungry peasant smallholders.[56]

The short-term causes of the subsequent 1907 uprising were also important, although less well known until recently. They revolved around two interlocking schemes by the essentially Wallachian Liberals to strengthen the peasants' position without radically changing the regime for land tenure.

The first was a system of communal banks that were set up on the Schulze-Delitzsch model to attract savings from the more prosperous peasants and then extend them credit to buy more land or better equipment. A few of these Popular Banks had actually been initiated under private merchant auspices during the 1890s, but it took the reforming minister, Spiru Haret, and a new Liberal government to boost their numbers from a handful to 88 by 1901. They mushroomed to nearly 3,000 by 1913. Like other Schulze-Delitzsch banks, they failed to serve the wider peasant community, except perhaps in western Wallachia which already had the most prosperous peasantry. Deposits were concentrated in too few hands. The principles of commercial profit kept loans too small and their duration too short to pay for land purchases.[57]

The Liberals went ahead in 1904 with a law sanctioning village cooperatives. The associations were intended to replace the merchant lessee as the party contracting for sharecropping with boyar estate owners. Popular Banks were designed to give the cooperatives credit in bidding for these contracts. In the northern Moldavia area of overwhelmingly Jewish *arendaşi*, however, the largely Conservative boyars opposed the scheme. Even after the cooperatives acquired a legal personality, owners were reluctant to deal with them because they offered lower payments for managing estate sharecropping. During the following decade, the cooperatives were able to acquire only 10 percent of leased estate land. The *arendaşi* still managed over 60 percent. Early peasant hopes for their widespread displacement were thus dashed.

By early 1907, the Conservatives' return to power brought peasant discontent to a boil. The government's 1906 surtax of 5 lei (or francs) per capita, rationally intended to buy up a reserve of corn in case of a bad harvest, exempted among others the village schoolteachers who had frequently become managers of the local Popular Bank as well. The scattered revolts against the new tax in late 1906 thus included resentment against some bank officials. Then in January 1907, the Popular Bank in the Botoşani prefect in northern Moldavia proved unable to extend enough credit for the local cooperative to win the region's major sharecropping contract. Two Jewish *arendaşi* families were left to outbid each other in promising to extract more of next year's crop from the peasantry. The winning Fischer family's agents confronted one estate's sharecroppers with the new contract in February. The peasants beat them badly. Rioting spread spontaneously from village to village. It moved south into Wallachia and out of the area of exclusive Jewish leasing before a new liberal government used the army to suppress it. Perhaps 10,000 were killed. This repression and some minor concessions pacified the peasantry until the First World War. The sharecropping system remained intact. Still, the Liberal leadership turned from the ruins of previous agricultural policies to begin discussing the massive redistribution of estate land that they would put into effect between 1918 and 1921.[58]

Peasant Migration from Greece and Serbia

Faced with shrinking holdings of generally poorer land, Greek peasants chose to leave their native villages and look elsewhere for work rather than revolt. Some from the northeastern area came to Athens, where they typically worked for several years as bakers, construction laborers, or craftsmen and then returned.[59] But more of this migrant labor probably came from north of the pre-1912 border, further into Epirus. The great majority of the migration starting within the Greek state went outside its borders, although on the same temporary basis. Greek emigration to the United States, according to Table 6.14 below, was responsible for almost all of the overseas movement. It gathered momentum after 1900. The gross total passed 250,000 by 1912 to approach 10 percent of the population. This was the largest proportion for any European state after 1900 and was half again the combined emigration from the other Balkan states.[60]

For the Greek economy, the frequently cited gain from this emigration was a flow of remittances that from 1903 forward cancelled out the sizable import surplus (see Table 6.3) in the balance of payments. Yet British consular reports reckon that several losses probably combined to outweigh this addition to domestic savings and purchasing power.[61] First, this foreign source of domestic income was fragile and unpredictable. The American recession of 1908–09 cut the number of Greek emigrants in half and forced others to return. They joined those returning after a few years as planned to cut the net emigration for 1906–10 to two thirds of the gross figure. This anticipated the greater problem of Greek labor returning en masse from temporary French employment at the start of the 1930s depression. The emigration was also sufficient to force industrial wages up in some of the country's struggling factories (see Chapter 8). Finally, as the departures spread northward from the fragmented holdings of the Peloponnesus to the grain-growing plains of Thessaly, it created a sufficient labor shortage to drive up by one half the wages to agricultural labor. Such hired labor will be remembered from the preceding section as the only efficient alternative to the backward system of sharecropping that dominated Greek estate agriculture.

For Serbia, with over twice the arable land per capita, the fragmen-

TABLE 6.14
BALKAN OVERSEAS MIGRATION, 1876-1915

To areas outside EUROPE[a]	ROMANIA Gross	BULGARIA Gross	SERBIA Gross	GREECE Gross
1876-85	1,224			530
1886-90	5,224			1,881
1891-95	2,211			4,790
1896-1900	10,541	160		11,189
1901-05	37,225	6,661	42	51,479
1906-10	20,707	37,643	228	122,275
1911-15	15,295	35,836	1,117	127,811

To the U.S.A. only	ROMANIA Gross	ROMANIA Net[c]	BULGARIA Gross	BULGARIA Net[c]	SERBIA[b] Gross	GREECE Gross	GREECE Net[c]
1876-85	1,224					530	
1886-90	5,135					1,881	
1891-95	2,209					4,790	
1896-1900	10,541		160			11,189	
1901-05	35,185		6,662		42	49,962	
1906-10	17,823	14,239	32,643	21,889	228	117,557	84,355
1911-15	11,187	9,057	21,487	1,575	1,052	118,916	46,577

Notes: (a)Includes Canada, Australia, New Zealand, Argentina and Brazil as well as the United States. (b)Serbia and Montenegro combined. (c)Extrapolated on basis of 1908-10 data.

Sources: Imre Ferenzi, *International Migrations*, I, *Statistics* (New York: Arno Press, 1970, reprint of National Bureau of Economic Research Study, 1929), pp. 261-71, 472; *Statistical Yearbook of Greece, 1975* (Athens, 1976), p. 46.

tation of peasant holdings had probably not gone as far. Lacking any Greek figures for comparison, we may still note that the one careful census of prewar Serbian land distribution indicates that 70 percent of the heads of peasant households owned more than the two hectares of land whose cultivation was previously identified as the Serbian peasant's necessary minimum for breaking even with crops for the money economy.[62] True, the fraction of literally landless peasants among the remaining 30 percent was undoubtedly much lower than the 11 percent of the overall total long cited by Yugoslav scholars. Yet the proportion of the 100,000 peasant households with an average holding of one hectare that raised enough plums or livestock to break even has been estimated at little more than half. The remaining 10 to 15 percent of all Serbian peasant households, perhaps 50,000 of 380,000 total, were obliged to find income away from their land or retreat from the money economy.

Such a retreat into premodern poverty and banditry appears to have occurred only in certain sections of southwest Serbia. Poor soil gave them the country's largest grain deficits to begin with.[63] For the rest of the country, seasonal migration to neighboring countries in search of construction or agricultural wage labor constituted the principal peasant recourse. It brought them extra cash income from outside their own holding. Exact numbers are uncertain; the movement's seasonal nature excluded it from official emigration data. After 1900 a few thousand went annually both to Bulgaria and to Dualist Hungary, while about 15,000 sought work on the large Romanian estates.[64] Only Bulgaria attracted skilled labor, mainly peasants from the Pirot region with construction skills learned from their close proximity to Macedonia with its long tradition of *pečalbarstvo*, or rural labor migrating in search of money wages. *Pečalbari* from both Macedonia and the Pirot region furnished skilled labor to construction projects in Belgrade and Sofia, as well as to larger peasant smallholdings in both countries.

The bulk of the seasonal migration was unskilled labor drawn by higher wages than any Serbian employer could pay to the large estates of Wallachia and southern Hungary. Unskilled *pečalbarstvo* began among southern peasants who had lost not their land but rather their main source of cash income when the wine trade failed to recover from the phylloxera epidemic of the 1880s. Men even came from southern households with profitable 10 to 20-hectare properties in order to expand them, sometimes hiring harvest labor while absent earning much higher wages. The migrants earned the same disposable income as northern peasants on the best grain and plum-growing land.

After 1900 the departures spread steadily northward as word spread of higher wages outside the country. Migration from the northern areas was different. Families trying to hang onto one-hectare holdings were more typical. Many soon found themselves drawn into debt by Romanian estate managers and forced to return every summer until it was repaid.

The main *pečalbar* areas of southern Serbia earned enough income from working outside the country to keep their tax arrears down to half the national average. Yet the extra income was not used to intensify local cultivation or to invest otherwise in Serbian economic development. Nor was this body of probably surplus, clearly energetic, labor available to the Serbian industrial stirrings discussed in Chapter 8.

Organized Protest in Bulgaria: Stamboliski's Agrarian Union

A similar if unquantifiable flow of Bulgarian peasant *pečalbari* made the seasonable migration to Romanian and Hungarian estates. As with Serbia, the movement originated in the southern territory closest to Macedonia (indeed, the Pirin region of Bulgaria was one of the Macedonian lands). How much it spread to the north and east, we do not know. At least we should not confuse this migration with the appearance of a large landless rural proletariat in either country. A majority of the growing number of agricultural wage laborers were still smallholders themselves.

What put the Bulgarian peasantry at a disadvantage compared to their Serbian counterparts was conditions in the main grain-growing area of the northeast. The former had few opportunities for extra cash income through livestock or prune exports that sustained the northern Serbian peasant through climatically inevitable failures of the wheat or corn harvests. The artisan manufacture noted in Chapter 5.6 as a basis for peasant proto-industrialization in central Bulgaria became less attractive after 1878, when access to the large Ottoman market became more difficult and more expensive. The resulting dependence on grain prices and exports left the Bulgarian smallholder more exposed. So did annual rainfall a third lower than in Serbia, as noted in the Introduction. The low prices and bad harvest of 1907 even prompted emigration to the United States on the Greek scale, according to Table 6.14 above, albeit for that year only.[65]

A more constant problem was the lack of agricultural credit. The demand for cash income pushed the northeastern fraction of peasant labor working for wages on someone else's holding, usually in addition to their own, to two or three times the national average of 9 percent.[66] But with no Serbian export alternatives and no large Romanian estates, the Bulgarian peasant had little extra income with which to finance the next year's seeding of his smallholding or to buy the extra land needed to keep inheritance from making it smaller. When local money lenders behaved as elsewhere in the Balkans, charging high interest rates and imposing exorbitant penalties for late payment, the results were therefore more onerous. Falling grain prices during the last decades of the nineteenth century had persuaded many peasants to agree to repayment in kind rather than cash.[67] Imagine their anger at the close of the century, when the Bulgarian government belatedly proposed to collect the tithe on annual harvests in kind just when international grain prices were turning up again and a series of bad harvests boosted the domestic price as well.

The uproar over the proposed change in tithe collection brought a group of local schoolteachers and peasants together in 1899. They formed the *Bulgarski Zemedelska Naroden Soiuz* (BZNS) or Bulgarian Agrarian National Union early the following year. Its power lay precisely in the northeastern grain belt. The one organized movement of genuinely populist origins in prewar Eastern Europe started slowly. Its petitions and sometimes violent demonstrations did help

to defeat the change in tithe collection. At the same time, its 400
hastily organized producers cooperatives, or *druzhbi,* soon dwindled
to 40. Of the 23 delegates elected to the 1901 *Subranie* (of 156 total),
16 defected to other parties. Indeed, the Union did not decide to
break with the utopian Russian populism that was its philosophical
inspiration and pursue national power as a political party until its
decline had continued into 1903.

The organization's revival from that low point must clearly be
credited to Alexander Stamboliski. He emerged from the schoolteachers heading the organization to edit its newspaper by 1904 and
soon afterwards assume its leadership. Stamboliski gave the Agrarian
Union its distinctive ideology as a political party organized entirely
from a single occupational group, the peasantry.[68] Their great majority in the Bulgarian population would bring them to power when the
Subranie was reorganized to represent the major Bulgarian occupational groups, or estates. Stamboliski turned the party away from
sponsoring specific legislation in the *Subranie* to advocating a reordering of society. He wanted to restrict the essentially urban
influence of the other estates. His greatest fear was not the continued
growth of industry, but rather that the army would emerge as a separate estate and make any future reordering impossible. In elections
largely rigged by the King and the party in power, the Agrarian
Union was unable to win even 15 percent of the delegates in any
pre-1914 election.[69] Stamboliski's opposition to Bulgarian participation in both the Balkan Wars and the First World War completed the
heritage of radical protest that would bring his party to power in the
postwar wake of Bulgarian defeat.

Unable to do more than stage protests in the prewar *Subranie,* the
Agrarian Union made its principal impact on the Bulgarian economy
through a revived network of producers and credit cooperatives.
Their numbers multiplied rapidly, from 68 in 1904 to 1,123 by 1908,
and about 1,400 by 1911, the largest number for any Balkan state.
Their functions expanded to include life and hail insurance funds, a
number of cooperative stores and warehouses, and a limited amount
of agricultural extension service to peasant members.[70]

Most important was the access to agricultural credit furnished
through the Bulgarska Zemedelska Banka, the Bulgarian Agricultural
Bank, which was the country's second largest after the note-issuing
Narodna Banka (see Chapter 7). The relationship between the
cooperatives and the bank's eighty-five local branches deserves a
separate monograph. In its absence, we offer the following brief account.

The bank's origins lay with the rural savings banks, or *zemedelske
kase,* organized by Midhat Pasha in the 1860s (see Chapter 5). They

were revived by the new national government in 1880 but attracted few peasant deposits and favored local merchant borrowers. Their organization into a single bank with its headquarters in Sofia began in 1894 but was not complete until 1903. Only then could the bank begin to provide the mortgage loans that were the most badly needed form of long-term agricultural credit. Their amount tripled by 1911 to approach 15 percent of bank assets. Nearly 90 percent of their loans were given to peasants, in average amounts of 5,000 leva, as was a variety of short-term credit in amounts of 500 to 1,000 leva (recall the Romanian Popular Banks' insufficient average of only 100 lei). Agricultural equipment and fertilizer were offered to peasants on easy terms in the years just before the war. Lines of current credit were extended to half the Agrarian Union's cooperatives, allowing them to function in turn as small credit associations on the mass-based Raiffeisen model. In 1910, the Zemedelska Banka helped these associations form their own Central Cooperative Bank. The 576 local credit cooperatives had almost 40,000 members by 1911.

The net result of these efforts fell short of furnishing sufficient agricultural credit. They did succeed, even according to Bulgarian Marxist scholarship, in forcing interest rates down to the 6 to 8 percent charged by the Zemedelska Banka.[71] Some noticeable intensification of cultivation and increase in yields might have occurred, and rural discontent would surely have been less, had the rest of the Bulgarian financial structure favored peasant agriculture in the same way. How and why it did not, in any of the pre-1914 Balkan states, will concern us in the next chapter.

For now, the first decades of political independence appear to have had the following consequences for peasant agriculture. Safer rural conditions and new money taxes brought peasants back into lowlands where grain cultivation could spread rapidly. Improved access to European markets also came with formal Balkan independence from Ottoman restrictions. At about the same time steamships were cutting the cost of bulk transport drastically. First Romanian and then Bulgarian grain exports boomed despite the downturn in international prices after 1873. The movement to new land, with the money income and debts it entailed, unfortunately prompted peasant birthrates to rise. By the last prewar decade, the increase was sufficient when combined with rising grain prices to reduce the growth of real per capita exports to nil.

Neither Bulgarian smallholdings nor Romanian sharecropping promised much improvement in future prospects. More efficient Hungarian and German agriculture already dominated the Central European markets which provided the Balkan economies most of their manufactured imports.

Only Serbian livestock enjoyed enough access to these markets to prevent the appearance of a significant import surplus without relying on wheat sales to Western Europe. The Serbian tariff war with neighboring Austria-Hungary nonetheless brought the small state face to face with the sort of political pressure under which dependence on Central European imports placed all the Balkan economies. The successful Serbian resistance did not derive from grain sales to Western Europe, open to the dangers of North American competition in the short run and of unstable prices in the long run. Rather, it came from French state loans and a native transition to processed meat-packing. Why the loans did not pay for this transition the next two chapters will make clear.

7.

Financial Consequences of
Political Independence

While peasant agriculture was little modernized during the first decades of national independence, the financial structure of the four
pre-1914 Balkan states made rapid strides toward Western European
standards. Central banks were founded and issued national currencies whose circulation soon displaced foreign denominations; Balkan
governments could thenceforth tax and spend their own monies.
State budgets grew accordingly. The practice of modern commercial
banking spread widely. Joint-stock and savings banks appeared.
Their numbers per 10,000 population matched British levels late in
the first Industrial Revolution. The potential to create credit, to
mobilize savings, and even to direct their investment thus came into
being. By 1911, Balkan ratios of total bank assets to national product
were without exception approaching 80 percent. This proportion exceeded the average for other less developed European countries by
over one half. It equalled the 1880 level for the more developed
economies and amounted to 60 percent of their 1911 ratios.[1] The
financial modernization of these first developing nations thus deserves a separate chapter.

Both this chapter and the next will explore the consequences that
this relatively sophisticated financial structure held for Balkan economic development during the last prewar decades. Our inquiry
does not rest on any universal theory of such an interrelation. The
Leninist intuition that the European Great Banks created Balkan
financial institutions and through them controlled the Balkan
economies will be found wanting. So will the tendency of Western
economists to join Marx himself in dismissing financial and other in-

stitutions as a façade behind which the real factors of production—
the supply of capital and labor, perhaps entrepreneurship and
technology, plus the demand for goods—operate decisively.

Few economists dealing with the experience of developing nations
since 1945 would still join Joseph Schumpeter in ranking the banking system along with entrepreneurship as one of two agencies most
crucial to rapid growth. Yet the eminent Austrian economist drew
most of his world view from the same pre-1914 period that concerns
Part II. As noted in the Introduction, Alexander Gerschenkron has
suggested that financial institutions played a decisive part in
nineteenth-century German industrialization. That they did not in
Tsarist Russia or pre-1914 Bulgaria, he goes on, makes them unlikely
to initiate growth in less developed economies. Recent examinations
of this generalized Gerschenkron hypothesis have found it wanting.
Two volumes of comparative nineteenth-century case studies suggest
instead a more varied European experience with money and banking.[2] They show national sets of institutional traditions helping to
determine when and where that country's financial structure initiated, followed, or hindered economic growth. The several Balkan
experiences also display enough variety to demand a comparative
approach of this sort. One common denominator that emerges from
them and Western European case studies is the state's repeated restriction of bank potential for initiating economic growth. This restriction and the state's growing budgetary resources demand that
fiscal policy be given fair weight in the analysis of financial structure
that follows.

Founding Central Banks and National Currencies

Without the emergence of independent Balkan states, however,
the central banks and national currencies that are the cornerstones of
a modern money economy could not have been established. Together
they gave these Balkan economies the capacity to regulate their own
money supply and to create domestic credit, free of the chaotic legacy of the Ottoman monetary orbit. By the mid-nineteenth century,
repeated devaluations of Ottoman coinage and the failure of paper
money to establish itself left the Ottoman economy dependent on
European denominations for a stable standard of value and an acceptable means of international payment.

By 1885, all four Balkan states had successfully established national banks with exclusive powers of note issue. None were primarily in the hands of European investors. All had been consciously
copied from European models. They offered at least the potential for

financial independence from European lenders and, to the extent that their sizable commercial lending promoted it, national economic development. By the last prewar decade, the four banks had sought to enlarge that potential by establishing their note issues as internationally acceptable currencies convertible at par with the French gold franc. They succeeded, without forsaking their own commercial operations. In so doing, however, they served the political independence that had created them more than the pace of economic development.

The National Bank of Greece

Almost forty years ahead of the rest, the National Bank of Greece was able to open its doors in 1842.[3] Romanian and Serbian autonomy from 1830 to 1878 proved too limited to permit similar banks of issue to survive the planning stage.

After futile attempts to attract enough English and French capital to found a Greek bank of issue in 1828 and again in 1836, the Swiss Philhellene Eynard took over the project. Enough overseas Greeks joined him to permit the private joint-stock bank to open in Athens in 1842 with 3.75 of its 5 million drachmas of nominal capital already paid in. English and French shareholders were in a minority. The state held only 20 percent of its capital. More important than Eynard in these first years of the National Bank of Greece was George Stavrou, one of many Greeks returning from successful business activities in Western Europe. Such returnees gave Greek finance and commerce an early advantage over their Balkan counterparts. Stavrou became the bank's director and kept that position until 1868. In a country where individuals would dominate political as well as financial life, he was the first in a series of directors who ran the bank on his own terms rather than on those of its private shareholders.

By 1846, the bank's note issue had proved acceptable to peasants dealing with the provincial offices of the state treasury. A branch had been opened in the port of Patras. The National Bank survived the European panic of 1848 only to face the start of a half century of currency issues "forced" by and for the Greek government without metallic reserves. Repeated issues would bar the way to an internationally convertible drachma and to an active role for the National Bank in Greek economic development until after 1900. To understand the removal of this obstacle, we must first trace the changing relations of the Balkan central banks to their own governments and the tempting lines of European credit that soon entangled those governments.

The Romanian and Serbian Banks

By the 1860s a growing Romanian and Serbian desire for economic self-assertion focused on efforts to issue separate national currencies. The political symbolism of minting coins bearing their own rulers' visages and the national language was hardly lost on the autonomous regimes in Bucharest and Belgrade.[4] Nor was nationalism the only incentive. Ottoman denominations continued their destabilizing depreciation. The Porte's borrowing from the buoyant European capital market carried it closer to the virtual bankruptcy of 1881.[5]

As it turned out, little could be officially done to escape the Ottoman orbit before full independence in 1878–79. During 1866–67 both governments were able to update the exchange rates expressed in Romanian lei and Serbian groši for the welter of forty to eighty European and Ottoman denominations in circulation.[6] Only the Romanian reorganization adjusted rates to reflect a decline by over half in Ottoman coin values since the 1830s. It also went one step further than the Serbian effort by setting its unit of account equal to the French franc. As early as 1859, the French consul in Iaşi had aroused official Romanian enthusiasm for adopting his country's entire monetary system in return for a large loan to start printing notes. This project collapsed. Louis Napoleon's creation of the Latin Monetary Union a few years later revived the idea. The Sultan's *firman* to recognize the united Principalities' constitution of 1866 included a provision authorizing a separate Romanian monetary system. The new Liberal regime went ahead in 1867 with the actual printing of 4 million gold lei, pegged to the French franc. At the insistence of Liberal leaders still imbued with the spirit of the abortive 1848 revolution, the authorizing legislation called money "a part of the nation's arms." It also tied this gold coinage to the fixed silver exchange ratio of the Latin Monetary Union at just the moment when that ratio began a rise of several decades' duration on world markets.[7] By the European financial crash of 1873, all of this issue had disappeared from circulation because of the profits to be gained from selling it for metallic content. That year the Treasury minted a 25-million-lei silver issue to compete with numerous foreign denominations still comprising the bulk of the Romanian money supply.

The Serbian government of Prince Milan Obrenović made less progress. There was a token issue of copper coins in 1869. The minting of the first dinars accompanied Serbian accession to the Latin Monetary Union in 1873. These 6 million silver dinars, also pegged to the French franc, made up only a small fraction of the foreign coinage, mainly Habsburg and Ottoman, remaining in circulation. The Ministry of Finance entertained suggestions about the paper note issue essential for credit creation and the easy transfer of large sums, but rejected them for fear that the Serbian peasantry would refuse them as had their Anatolian counterparts.[8] Meanwhile, the nearly complete Serbian dependence on Habsburg bank notes and bills of exchange, noted in Chapter 4, spelled serious trouble when the Vienna stock market crash of 1873 reduced the overall supply of Austro-Hungarian credit. The Romanian economy was similarly although not as severely affected. Three post-1873 attempts to found a bank of issue in Bucharest all fell through.

The coming of full independence in the late 1870s broadened the political options for Romania and Serbia to found such banks. It also heightened the economic pressures to do so. About 35 million lei worth of Russian silver rubles remained in circulation after Bucharest had been obliged to accept the injection of 40 million during the passage of the Tsarist army through the Principalities in 1877–78.[9] Their value declined and fluctuated in the destabilizing fashion of the Russian assignats of the 1830s, described in Chapter 3, until their demonetization began in 1880. By then, a flood of largely Austrian imports for textiles, railway materials, and military equipment had wiped out the export surplus that had allowed the Romanian government to begin European borrowing in the 1860s without its own currency.

The new Serbian state also lost its export surplus during the first years (see Table 6.3), and for the same reasons. Then came the government's ill-fated decision in 1881 to accept the first large European loan for railway construction, 90 million francs, under the auspices of the famous or infamous French financier, Eugene Bontoux. He promised as part of the deal to found a bank of issue in Belgrade.[10] The spectacular collapse of his empire the following year left Serbia without a bank and without further access to the European capital market until 1884.

Beyond long-standing patriotic ambitions, the shortage of private and public credit constituted the short-run cause for the founding of the Banca Naţională a României in 1881 and the Narodna Banka Kr. Srbije in 1883. Both were set up explicitly to conform with the Belgian model. The Romanian bank was much bigger. Its initial paid-in capital amounted to 12 million lei, versus just 2.5 million dinars in the Serbian one. This difference in part reflected the wealthy boyar aristocracy, the larger population and export sector of the Romanian Principalities.

It also reflected the success of the Romanian Liberals in getting the state to contribute one third of the bank's capital and in buying up a majority of the remaining shares within a few hours of their going on sale.[11] For these reasons the Romanian bank would, at least until 1900, be more of a state bank than its Serbian counterpart, especially when the Liberals were in power. None of the latter's shares went to the state. No private buyer could buy more than 600 dinars worth, and the majority went to Belgrade importers whose political allegiance generally lay with the Progressives. This was a small austrophile party that would never challenge the ruling Radicals for control of the Skupština after 1885. Habsburg investors missed a golden opportunity to acquire de facto control of the bank by failing to buy even 5 percent of its shares.[12]

With the technical assistance of the head accountant of the Belgian Banque Nationale during 1884–85, the new bank attempted to introduce 2.5 million worth of 100-dinar gold notes, printed in Brussels, as the only legal paper currency. The issue foundered on the continued rise of gold prices in silver terms that led to its notes' conversion for gold coin or metal. But the suspicion of one French diplomat that the Serbian population would, like the Anatolian Turks, prove "not civilized enough" to accept paper money was soon belied.[13] Almost 2 millions in smaller 10-dinar silver-backed notes were introduced in 1885 and made legal tender for all transactions. Some 4 million were added annually to the money supply over the next six years (see Table 7.4). All foreign bank notes had disappeared by the late 1800s.

The Reorganized Bulgarian National Bank

The Bulgarian central bank got off to a slower start. It relied more heavily than any of the others on state support. Under Ottoman rule a bank issuing exclusively Bulgarian currency could not even be discussed. The initial Bulgarska Narodna Banka opened in the first flush of independence in 1879 but hardly as a joint-stock institution, let alone a central bank. Its original statutes provided 2 million gold leva, pegged to the franc, in paid-in capital from state funds. The right of note issue was specifically denied the bank on the grounds that there was too much Ottoman currency, worth less than 10 percent of its face value, already in the country. No mortgage or any other sort of long-term credit was to be granted, despite peasant demands in the *Subranie* (National Assembly). Finally, the bank's location in Sofia, a commercial backwater compared to half a dozen other Bulgarian towns, made it so hard to place assets profitably that the Bulgarska Narodna Banka suspended acceptance of interest-bearing deposits for several months just three days after opening its doors.[14]

The badly needed restructuring of the bank was not completed until 1886. The St. Petersburg banking house of Poliakov and Ginsburg tried to found a joint-stock bank of issue in 1880. Their connection with the unlikely Russian project to finance the Sofia-Ruse railway caused the surprisingly independent Bulgarian government to veto the project.[15] It also refused a succession of Austrian, German, and French offers to contribute the needed capital on the grounds that no foreign stockholders were desired. The government itself reorganized the institution in 1885 as a joint-stock bank, drawing on the Greek, Swiss, and Belgian models. All 10 million leva of paid-in capital came from the Bulgarian state treasury. Prince Ferdinand's right to appoint the entire Administrative Council reinforced the government's dominant role in bank activities. The new statutes also provided exclusive rights of note issue and allowed short-term mortgage lending.[16]

Shortly after reopening for business in 1886, the Bulgarian bank affectively doubled its working capital. The government arranged a 10-million-leva loan for it from the Deutsche Bank, with eventual repayment through an equivalent amount of the bank's mortgage preference shares. The two thirds of the loan earmarked for long-term credit helped the bank's silver-backed notes become acceptable in commercial transactions throughout the newly enlarged country.[17] Once again, however, the long monetization process described in Part I had apparently laid the groundwork for rapid local acceptance of national bank notes.

Building State Railways and the First Foreign Loans, 1864-1900

The Deutsche Bank's 1886 loan to the Bulgarska Narodna Banka was not typical of Balkan borrowing on the European capital market during the last decades of the nineteenth century. The representative loans of this period were at least intended for the railway construction that economic historians have until recently regarded as indispensable to pre-1914 economic development.[18] Although the railways probably varied in their effect on Balkan agriculture (see Chapter 6), the financing of their construction had more uniform consequences. The European Great Banks lent Balkan governments the funds to develop their own state railways. The loans served not so much to introduce direct Euorpean influence as to push Balkan state budgets into permanent reliance on further loans in order to continue the rapid growth in state expenses begun during these decades. Whenever the European capital market did not oblige, the new national banks would face initially irresistible demands to furnish funds.

The immediate impetus for this railway construction in Bulgaria and Serbia was the European powers' Treaty of Berlin in 1878. It provided for the extension of existing track from Paris, Berlin, and Vienna across the two Balkan states to Istanbul by 1888. In the course of completing this route for the Orient Express, the two governments' sensitivity about preserving newly won independence discouraged the granting of direct concessions to European contractors. Bulgarian legislation of 1885 forbade the granting of any foreign ownership in return for constructing the Orient Express line. Its first large European loan of 46 million leva in 1888 went to permit the purchase of the existing Ruse-Varna line from English interests.[19] Proceeds from a 90-million-dinar Serbian loan of 1890 were similarly used to buy out all existing European owners of the country's railways, thereupon taken over entirely by the state.

The Romanian Experience before 1878

The era of direct European investment in Balkan railways had, in any case, already passed its heyday after the general economic and speculative boom of the 1860s. This period had coincided with the brief Ottoman experiment in granting European investors liberal concessions. Lingering in the Balkans were English and French civil engineers, originally drawn to the area by Allied projects during the Crimean War.[20]

Even then, the decade accounted for less than 50 miles of the 600 miles of track laid in the Romanian Principalities before 1878. The only construction elsewhere in the future Balkan states consisted of a token two miles in Greece and the English line from Ruse to Varna built under the Ottoman administration of Midhat Pasha in the northern Bulgarian lands (see Chapter 5). The far more extensive construction in pre-1878 Romania established instead the eventual Balkan pattern: state-owned railways built with long-term loans from the European capital market.

The one exception to this pattern was the first railway built anywhere in the Balkans, the line from Cernavoda on the Danube to Constanţa on the Black Sea. English engineers and investors had begun the project in 1857 to try to lure Danube river traffic away from the delays of the delta to the north. The unexpected expenses of constructing the line and building port facilities at Constanţa, plus the improvement of Sulina channel through the delta, combined to make the company a losing proposition throughout the 1860s. When in 1866 the English engineering partnership of Barklay and Staniforth turned from the Ruse-Varna project to Wallachia, they found the Romanian government unprepared to accept private ownership of a proposed line from Bucharest to Giurgiu on the Danube.

Their original proposal emerged from the legislature as an offer to work for the Romanian government. The 140-mile line opened to traffic in 1869 as the first section of the newly formed state railway (CFR).[21]

Most of the remaining 420 miles of pre-1878 Romanian railway construction proceeded under loans from major German banking houses to the Romanian government or its new Hohenzollern Prince, Carol I. His personal agreement with a Prussian financial consortium undertook an obligation of 247 million lei to finance 560 miles of track lines from Bucharest west to Turnu-Severin far up the Danube and north through the Danubian port of Galaţi. Three state loans whose obligations totalled 154 million lei nominal were obtained from the houses of Oppenheim and Bleichröder between 1868 and 1875 to complete the links to Bucharest and the Danube northeast to the Moldavian capital of Iaşi and finally in 1879 northwest 100 miles to the Habsburg border and rail network at Predeal.[22] Table 7.1 indicates the long headstart in total trackage that Romania enjoyed over the other Balkan states.

The young Romanian state paid two prices for the privilege of connecting its capital and major commercial centers with each other and with Central Europe several decades ahead of its neighbors. First, the absence of any profitable lines already operating in Southeastern Europe meant that bonds for these loans could not be sold to European investors, especially after the Central European crash of 1873, at much over 70 percent of their nominal or par value. The effective interest rate on the sum actually realized for the three aforementioned state loans approached 12 percent. By 1879, the repayment annuity on these loans exceeded 20 percent of state budget expenses.[23] Second, and in spite of their burden on the budget, the availability of such funds for railway construction drew the government into seeking more loans for military and administrative expenses. From 1880 to 1914, the Romanian government would borrow some 1.5 billion lei mainly for those purposes plus debt repayment.[24] By 1875, budget expenses had more than doubled those of 1863, only to rise another 50 percent after the War on Independence in 1877–78. They almost doubled again by the end of the century (see Table 7.2). Influential boyars in both parties imposed political limits on direct taxation. A small urban sector set economic limits on indirect taxation. Such large budget increases would thus have been impossible without repeated access to the European capital market.

The Balkan Experience after 1878

The unfortunate fiscal record of the other Balkan states during the first twenty years of full political independence is well known.[25] All

TABLE 7.1
BALKAN RAILWAY LINES IN SERVICE, 1862-1912
(in kilometers)

	ROMANIA	BULGARIA	SERBIA	GREECE
1870	248	221	0	12
1880	921	224	0	12
1885	1,359	224	253	222
1890	2,424	803	540	697
1895	2,534	861	540	916
1900	3,100	1,566	571	1,033
1905	3,179	1,567	707	1,351
1910	3,437	1,897	892	1,573
1912	3,532	2,109	976	1,584

Source: B. R. Mitchell, *European Historical Statistics, 1750-1970* (New York: Columbia University Press, 1975), pp. 581-85.

were drawn into the Romanian pattern of escalating budget expenses and European loans. None were able to avoid the large deficits of budget expenses over receipts, as the Romanian state did successfully for all but a few of these pre-1900 years. By the mid-1890s recurring budget deficits brought the Greek, Serbian, and Bulgarian governments face to face with bankruptcy because of their inability to repay European creditors. Greece acquired almost 500 million drachmas of new debt from 1881 to 1893. Only the last loans were even intended for railways. Then the disastrous war of 1897 with the Ottoman Empire forced more borrowing and the Greek acceptance of a European Financial Commission with access to budget revenues to assure repayment of all past debts.[26] Serbia and Bulgaria started on this slippery path with loans actually applied to railway construction.

Serbia started fast. Loans to build the Serbian section of the Orient Express line to Istanbul piled up a majority of the 265 million dinars of European debts between 1881 and 1885. The state budget had doubled in the meantime. Debt repayment reached one third of total expenses by 1887, when only 4 percent of Bulgarian budget expenses were so allocated. By 1898 Serbia's annual budget expenses had doubled again. Total European debt passed 400 million dinars, according to Table 7.7. Yet not one kilometer of additional railway track had been financed with foreign loans during this last decade. The additional loans were largely directed toward covering budget deficits and meeting existing long or short-term repayment obligations.[27]

Bulgaria followed suit during the 1890s. Obligations for its three railway loans between 1888 and 1892 amounted to 180 million leva. State budget expenses jumped from 42 million leva in 1887 to 93 million by 1896. Debt repayment approached 20 percent of the total.

An ordering of Balkan state finances after 1900 ended these

TABLE 7.2
BALKAN STATE BUDGETS, 1864-98
(in millions of lei, leva, dinars, and drachmae)[a]

	ROMANIA			BULGARIA			SERBIA			GREECE		
	Rev.	Exp.	R-E	Rev.	Exp.	R-E	Rev.	Exp.	R-E	Rev.	Exp.	R-E
1864	60	62	- 2									
1870	62	72	-10									
1875	98	99	- 1									
1880	152	141	+11	33	25	+ 8		20		45	89	- 44
1881	123	131	- 8	23	24	- 1	23	26	- 3	107	103	+ 4
1882	142	137	- 5	27	29	- 2	26	33	- 7	72	64	+ 8
1883	135	136	- 1	31	30	+ 1	28	34	- 6	59	68	- 9
1884	116	130	-14	29	31	- 2	32	37	- 5	107	93	+ 14
1885	125	130	- 5	27	34	- 7	39	46	- 7	61	123	- 62
1886	141	129	+12	49	39	+12	32	46	-14	96	130	- 34
1887	143	140	+ 3	55	42	+13	38	44	- 6	176	107	+ 69
1888	162	161	+ 1	56	55	+ 1	36	45	- 9	94	108	- 14
1889	160	159	+ 1	70	65	+ 5	38	52	-14	183	169	+ 14
1890	170	162	+ 8	69	70	- 1	42	46	- 4	123	142	- 19
1891	180	168	+12	81	71	+10	53	56	- 3	106	123	- 17
1892	182	179	+ 3	77	81	- 4	55	60	- 5	107	108	- 1
1893	220	199	+21	79	84	- 5	55	60	- 5	97	92	+ 5
1894	200	210	-10	83	84	- 1	59	64	- 5	103	85	+ 18
1895	198	215	-17	77	84	- 7	59	64	- 7	95	92	+ 3
1896	213	210	+ 3	82	93	-11	60	66	- 6	97	91	+ 6
1897	211	217	- 6	86	92	- 6	62	72	- 6	92	137	- 45
1898	237	225	+12	89	91	- 2	66	81	-15	105	312	-207

Note: (a)Equivalent in nominal value to the French gold franc.

Sources: *Anuarul statistic al României, 1915-1916* (Bucharest, 1919). p. 248: Kiril Popoff, *La Bulgarie économique, 1879-1911* (Paris, 1920). p. 285; John R. Lampe, "Financial Structure and the Economic Development of Serbia, 1878-1912" (Ph.D. Dissertation, University of Wisconsin, 1971). pp. 140, 184; Douglas Dakin, *The Unification of Greece, 1770-1923* (London: Ernest Benn, 1972). p. 320.

chronic deficits. Therefore, it does not seem fair to judge the pattern of state expenses for its contribution to economic development until the last prewar decade. Their division into productive and non-productive investment deserves to be examined then, rather than in this early, transitional period.

Balkan Bimetallism in the Shadow of the Gold Standard

To the considerable extent after 1890 that Balkan state budgets were mortgaged to European loan repayment, the respective national banks could not make up state deficits simply by issuing additional currency. These loans were repayable only in the gold denominations on which the major European currencies were all based by the

1890s. The Balkan economies continued to accept, however, the bimetallic system of silver and gold-backed denominations that their adherence to the Latin Monetary Union in the 1860s and 1870s had initiated. The 1872 break in the world silver price in gold terms had yet to reverse itself during the 1890s.[28] The Alaskan and South African gold discoveries lay ahead. France, Austria-Hungary, and Russia had already followed Germany's conversion to the Gold Standard. The Balkan central banks also aspired to it. Only the Romanian economy had enjoyed the long-standing access to the European capital market, and hence to gold-backed denominations, to make the transition. The rest remained tied to silver-backed notes as their only means of increasing the money supply. Limiting such issues throughout the 1890s were the premiums, or *agio*, over the franc's exchange rate that the free market charged for a silver note's conversion to a gold denomination. To make matters worse, native and European efforts to eliminate the *agio* and thus pave the way for adopting the Gold Standard also held back silver issues. Within this general pattern, moreover, the impact of the Gold Standard reflected the particular vulnerabilities that each Balkan economy had developed in its relation with industrialized Europe.

Restricting Serbian and Greek Note Issue

Serbia was especially vulnerable to changes in Habsburg demand. Hungarian livestock interests, as noted in Chapter 6, used Austrian fears that Budapest might not renew the imperial customs union in 1896 to close Habsburg borders to Serbian hog and cattle exports several times during 1895–96. Their success, plus the continuing slump in international grain prices, meant that Serbia still had no chance of reestablishing its sizable export surpluses of the 1860s and 1870s.

Adding to the pressure on the Serbian economy at the start of the 1890s was the Habsburg conversion to the Gold Standard, completed in 1892 after a four-year transition.[29] Belgrade importers thus lost their ability to pay for their purchases in the Dual Monarchy, still the source of 60 percent of Serbian imports, directly in silver dinar notes. The dearth of new long-term Euorpean loans after 1890 further heightened the demand for gold at the expense of silver denominations. The premium on any gold or currency in terms of silver dinars climbed from 3.1 percent in 1887 to 7.2 percent in 1892.[30]

Both the Belgrade importers and the Serbian Ministry of National Economy made elimination of the premium their highest monetary priority. They sought to limit National Bank issues of silver notes to 2-1/2 times the amount of silver reserves only. This 40-percent reserve ratio had previously been calculated on the basis of combined reserves of gold and silver. Given the bank's successful accumulation of gold reserves at the close of the 1880s to twice the value of its silver reserves, such a restriction would have forced the Narodna Banka to reduce its outstanding silver notes from 29 to 10 million dinars.[31] In late 1893, these interests pushed through legislation giving the bank just four years to do so. Other than cuts in discounting exporters' bills of exchange, the bank could reduce its notes substantially only if the state paid back some of its outstanding loans. By 1893, the latter totalled almost one third of all debts owed the bank.[32] The credit-starved Serbian government refused to make any repayment. The bank thereupon cut its discounting by 20 percent, driving the gold premium to a record 15.9 percent during 1894. The Ministry of National Economy had to back down and eventually repealed the law in 1896. The net result, however, was to reduce the Serbian money supply by 3 million dinars during these difficult years and then to freeze further issue, except for new government borrowing, until after 1900.[33] This maximum silver note issue of 25 million dinars regularly cut short a reviving export trade by forcing the bank to interrupt its discounting every fall until 1904, for fear of going over the maximum.

The National Bank of Greece faced a more prolonged restriction of its note issue at just the time that the Serbian central bank was beginning to reassert its independence. By 1898 the Greek bank had succeeded in finally freeing itself from repeated government demands for loans in unsecured note issue. From 1868 to 1895 these loans had climbed past half of the bank's total assets and actually exceeded its outstanding note issue.[34] But the occasion for ending this drain was the government's acceptance of a European Financial Commission to monitor its budget. Regular repayment of 580 million drachmas in European debts contracted since 1881 might then resume. Heavy borrowing of gold-backed European denominations and unrelieved trade and budget deficits had prompted the silver-backed drachma to slip so badly by the 1890s that it could be exchanged for gold only at a huge premium. The European commission obliged the National Bank to do its share in reducing a premium that peaked at 68 percent in 1898. The explicit goal was par value for the silver-backed drachma and then Greek adoption of the Gold Standard. To this end the commission imposed a moratorium on new note issue and mandated the withdrawal of 2 million drachmas a year from circulation until par was achieved. Although this last stipulation was dropped after 1900, the bank's note issue did not rise significantly until 1910, several years after virtual par had been achieved.[35]

In the meantime, the enterprises founded in the 1890s to take advantage of the de facto import tariff and export subsidy (furnished by the domestic premium payable for European currencies and goods) had been badly squeezed. The gradual reduction of the premium had eliminated its hidden import tariff and export subsidy at the same time that the limit on note issue restricted domestic credit. Ironically, a British consular report suggests that the principal reason for the paper drachma's rising exchange rate was not the bank's restricted note issue, but rather the government's success, as noted in Table 7.8 in eliminating large budget deficits and recording slight surpluses in all but four years from 1899 to 1912.[36]

Romanian and Bulgarian Aspirations to the Gold Standard

Even without pressure from European creditors or their own government, Balkan central banks were sufficiently wedded to orthodox European monetary thinking to pursue the Gold Standard on their own. The Bulgarian National Bank tried to adopt it and the Romanian bank succeeded.

Bulgarian suspicion of silver-backed lev notes had its origins in the Ottoman and Russian monetary legacies of the 1880s. The Bulgarian desire to adopt the Gold Standard immediately after gaining partial independence in 1879 had foundered on the outflow of gold to the Ottoman lands during the 1880s. The outflow was payment of tribute and especially compensation to former Turkish owners for Bulgarian land bought or seized from them. While these gold and largely European denominations earned in foreign trade were leaving, a flood of Russian silver rubles was coming in with the Tsarist occupation of 1879–85.[37] Russian authorities prevented the new Bulgarian government from reducing the exchange rate for these rubles as rapidly as in Serbia and Romania, thus attracting more. The Ottoman decision to demonetize all foreign silver money in 1883 brought in still more.

When the Bulgarian government finally demonetized the ruble in 1886, a significant number remained in private circulation. The chief offender here was apparently the still Austrian-financed construction of the Oriental Railway line across Bulgaria to Istanbul. Its construction sites often used rubles and old Ottoman silver coin to meet their payrolls.[38] The result was a gold premium until 1888 of about 9 percent on the 20 million leva in silver coin issued by the Bulgarian National Bank in an effort to establish a national money supply.

Suspicion of any silver money carried over into the bank's own issuing policy during the 1890s. Its directors endorsed a government commission's report of 1890 calling for adoption of the Gold Standard as soon as possible. An 1891 obligation to lend the government most of its gold reserves forced the bank to continue the virtual silver standard on which it had operated since its founding. Three silver note issues between 1891 and 1893 added 25 million leva to the 20 million in coin already circulating. But the bank's 1894 report feared the return of *agio* against silver. A government decree of 1897 re-affirmed the Bulgarian commitment to the Gold Standard "as soon as conditions permit."[39] Significantly, the gold premium rose just slightly to 2 to 6 percent with these silver issues. It climbed to 10 to 15 percent during 1899-1902 only in the face of the severe trade and budget deficits, explained respectively by a series of bad harvests and the government's continuing dearth of European credit.[40]

Always in front of the Bulgarian bank, according to its annual reports, was the Romanian example. A new Conservative government, eager to attract more foreign and especially German capital late in Romania's 1886-91 tariff war with Austria-Hungary, opted for the Gold Standard in 1890. Minimal trade and budget deficits made the conversion possible. Forty million lei of small silver notes were demonetized and 110 million larger ones converted to gold backing. Forty million lei of silver coins were left in circulation.

From the start, however, this was what one Romanian observer rightly called a Cereal Standard.[41] The Banca Naţională a României was never prepared to export its gold reserves to support the leu internationally and would exchange only small amounts of currency for gold in Bucharest. Large export surpluses were counted on to keep the leu at par. In their frequent absence, the bank did export foreign exchange reserves but was unable to prevent an average annual premium of 2½ percent on francs bought with lei. This premium actually passed the gold export point only once (in 1899, the year of Romania's worst prewar harvest). The recurring threat of higher premiums was nonetheless sufficient to restrain the bank's note issue, even after the reserve requirement was reduced from 40 to 33 percent in 1901. As noted in Table 7.3, that issue's rate of increase never exceeded those for the mainly silver-backed notes of the Serbian and Bulgarian central banks until the huge Romanian export surpluses of the last prewar decade. In addition, the attempt to adhere to the Gold Standard repeatedly frustrated the Romanian bank's announced intention of aiding the private sector by adjusting its rates countercyclically. Discount rates shot up from 5 to 7 or 8 percent during the monetary crises of 1894, 1899-1900, 1904, and 1907. The bank's preoccupation with protecting its reserves won out every time.

Variations on a European Financial Structure, 1898–1912

In spite of their difficult experience with or against the Gold Standard, the Balkan central banks had by the last prewar decade become the cornerstones of the European-style financial structures that had emerged in all four states. The banks' pattern of note issue followed accepted European practice in controlling a national money supply. Their credit policies as lenders of last resort permitted a variety of savings deposit and joint-stock banks to operate as well. These savings institutions were the principal weak point, according to contemporary European standards, of the individual financial structures of Romania, Serbia, Greece, and Bulgaria. Private joint-stock banks were the strong point.

The Independence of the Central Banks

The most striking feature common to all the Balkan central banks save the Bulgarian was their eventual independence. European financial circles had missed the opportunity, as noted above, to buy controlling interests in these banks during their early, difficult years. In the Serbian case, Austrian interests rejected a specific invitation. After the turn of the century the central banks began to establish their independence from their national governments as well.

The Romanian experience is instructive. During 1900–01, the Banca Naţională freed itself not only from the drain of further state borrowing, but also from state ownership of one third of its paid-in capital.[42] Nor did this last change leave the bank's administration to be manipulated at will by the Liberal party members who, it will be recalled, were its majority shareholders. The board of directors enjoyed a strong enough position by now to maintain the bank's adherence to the Gold Standard throughout the rest of the prewar period. Liberal party leaders had opposed the standard's adoption in 1890 and continued to do so, on the grounds that its supposed attraction for European capital was not the best way to develop Romanian industry.

The Narodna Banka Kr. Srbije was slower to achieve its freedom from state borrowing. The bank's leadership continued to be drawn largely from the reputedly austrophile Belgrade importers. The Radical-led regime installed after the assassination of the last Obrenović King in 1903 drew its strength from provincial export merchants and widespread anti-Austrian sentiment. Thus, the bank was able to extract the repayment of only one third of the state's outstanding debt to it from the new French loan of 1903.[43] Its board of direc-

tors did, however, negotiate an agreement for access to the sizable
revenue from the turnover tax as a guarantee for future repayment of
all state borrowing. The total outstanding was cut in half by 1905 and
eliminated by 1906. A significant debt reappeared again in 1909,
after the partial mobilization prompted by the Dual Monarchy's annexation of Bosnia-Hercegovina, but was quickly reduced.

The parliamentary regimes that the new Karadjordjević King, Peter
I, had allowed to govern after 1903 must also be credited with the
centralizing of budgetary accounting and the tightening of tax collection. The ensuing end to unpredictable state deficits virtually
eliminated the gold premium on silver dinar notes. It also helped the
government meet its obligations to the Narodna Banka.[44]

Radical reluctance to cooperate with the Narodna Banka surfaced
again but did not prevail when the bank's original 25-year charter
came up for renewal in 1908. Only a few weeks before the charter
was to expire, a Radical government hard pressed by the 1906–11
tariff war with Austria-Hungary agreed to a compromise generally
favoring the bank. In return for an immediate increase in its capital
from 5 to 7.5 million dinars and the promise of another like increase
by 1912, the Narodna Banka won the right to replace the inflexible
30-million-dinar limit on its silver note issue by a ratio of 5 to 1 between the note issue and paid-in capital. An additional 10 percent
over that amount might be authorized by the National Assembly in
exceptional circumstances. The government could also exchange its
own gold reserves temporarily for an issue of the bank's gold notes.
These crucial changes plus the bank's accumulation of some gold
reserves of its own since 1900 allowed the Serbian supply of paper
money to double during the last years of the tariff war with Austria-
Hungary. Despite a near doubling of exports, the bank was able to
continue its discount services during the fall season, rather than suspending them as it had every year from 1896 to 1904. As indicated in
Table 7.3, this increase took place with no reduction in the high reserve ratio common to other European and Balkan central banks of
the pre-1914 period. By this time, moreover, the Serbian note issue
surpassed outstanding coinage by a 5 to 1 ratio. It became the decisive element, like the other Balkan paper currencies, in determining
the total stock of money.[45]

The National Bank of Greece won a lesser victory in 1910 from the
European Financial Commission. Its ban on new note issue, dating
from 1898, was finally overturned with the passage twelve years later
of the so-called GXMA law. The legislation allowed the bank to increase its note issue by 25 million drachmas from the maximum of
140 million at which it had effectively been frozen for the past 12
years.[46] The Commission could hardly object. The near 70-percent

TABLE 7.3
NOTE ISSUE AND RESERVE RATIOS FOR BALKAN CENTRAL BANKS, 1886-1912
(in millions of leva, dinars, lei and drachmae)

	BULGARIA		SERBIA		ROMANIA		GREECE
	N.I.	(R.R.%)	N.I.	(R.R.%)	N.I.	(R.R.%)	N.I.
1880					10	(60)	67.8
1886	.1	(984)	5.1	(53)	116	(61)	90.0
1890	2.0	(509)	23.5	(54)	135	(53)	120.8
1895	19.4	(97)	24.6	(48)	157	(63)	
1897	19.0	(219)	23.7	(60)	175	(59)	140.7
1900	18.2	(58)	35.9	(46)	157	(59)	
1901	17.9	(58)	35.0	(49)	176	(60)	150.4
1905	37.2	(83)	37.1	(70)	274	(53)	141.3
1906	44.6	(58)	30.2	(74)	292	(55)	138.3
1910	81.6	(96)	49.8	(74)	399	(57)	133.3
1911	110.8	(70)	65.8	(77)	410	(56)	158.7
1912	164.4		93.6	(86)	425	(60)	227.8

Sources: *Iubileen sbornik na Bulgarska Narodna Banka, 1879-1929* (Sofia, 1929), pp. 63, 192-94; Kiril Nedelchev, *Parichnoto delo v Bulgariia, 1879-1940* (Sofia, 1940), pp. 70-73; John R. Lampe, "Financial Structure and the Economic Development of Serbia, 1878-1912" (Ph.D. Dissertation, University of Wisconsin, 1971), pp. 124, 199; C. C. Kirițescu, *Sistemul banesc al leului și precursorii lui*, II (Bucharest, 1965), pp. 553-54; M. S. Eulambio, *The National Bank of Greece* (Athens, 1924), p. 28.

premium paid for exchanging silver-backed or uncovered drachma notes that occasioned the restriction in the first place had fallen to below 10 percent by 1906 and to nothing by 1910. Stephen Streit, the bank's governor from 1900 to 1910, had used his previous tour as Finance Minister to begin reducing the budget deficits that were largely responsible for the gold premium. It was this Leipzig-trained lawyer, the son of a Hungarian immigrant, who had initiated the reordering of state finances that made revenues predictable and expenses restrainable.

The influx of new currency during 1910–12 allowed the bank to avoid suspending its discounting during the fall season for current exports. It was too small a sum to stimulate the Greek economy further. Past government debts were an added limitation on potential bank activity in the private sector. They still constituted about one quarter of the bank's total assets during the period 1910–12. They had at least been reduced from one half since 1898, under Streit's strong urging.

The Bulgarian National Bank had no hope of achieving even the Greek bank's limited independence from the state. Its directors remained frequently replaced royal appointees rather than powerful figures in their own right like Stephen Streit. The state's debt to the bank continued to increase until 1911, rather than declining or disappearing. Advances to the state treasury doubled between 1905 and

1907 and doubled again by 1909.[47] Yet the total debt of 45 million leva only amounted to one quarter of the bank's assets in this peak year of 1909. The relatively light Bulgarian burden derived from the smallest amount of pre-1900 European borrowing undertaken by any of the Balkan states. Much less Greek-style pressure developed to turn the central bank into the government's lender of last resort in aiding its European debt repayment. By 1911, moreover, the Bulgarian National Bank was able to negotiate an increase in its paid-in capital from 10 to 20 million leva. This doubling permitted roughly the same infusion of new silver-backed notes as the Greek bank had been permitted the year before. The same legislation put a limit of twice the bank's capital, or 40 million leva, on total state borrowing.[48]

State borrowing to this limit might still have been enough, had war not intervened in 1912, to continue biasing the bank's distribution of long-term credit toward government needs and away from the private sector. A general shift to short-term assets had begun among all the Balkan central banks during the 1890s and continued past 1900. This was best practice among contemporary European central banks. For the Bulgarian National Bank, the proportion of total assets in long-term loans had dropped steadily from a peak of 44.1 percent in 1891 to 20.4 percent by 1905.[49] (On the side of liabilities, the bank began a similar process after 1900 that reduced time deposits through lower interest rates and prompted a fivefold rise in current account deposits by 1911. They became the largest single liability. This rise in what were effectively demand deposits probably added as much to the Bulgarian money supply from 1905 to 1911 as did increased note issue. [50]) State-owed debts, even when fixed at the 1911 maximum, accounted for virtually all of the long-term assets in the bank's portfolio. The private sector would have to make do with the limited short-term credit described in Chapter 8. Here was one restriction under which the rest of the Balkan economies did not have to operate.

Otherwise, the Bulgarian National Bank achieved the same major success as the other Balkan central banks: par value with the French gold franc for their largely silver-backed paper currencies despite large new issues during the last prewar years and equivalent additions to the money supply from current account liabilities that were essentially demand deposits. What limited use this achievement was to industrial development can be judged from the subsequent chapter.

Weak Savings and Mortgage Banks

The growing withdrawal of the central banks from long-term lending made the general weakness of savings and mortgate banking in all four Balkan economies especially harmful. Most obviously, limits on land mortgages restricted the long-term credit that the solid small-holders (typical everywhere but Romania) needed to finance any investment in modern machinery or improved techniques. As seen in the previous chapter, only the branches of the Bulgarian Agricultural Bank and to a much lesser extent the Romanian Popular Banks achieved some success in advancing such productive, long-term investment. Both institutions were in any case outside the existing structure of commercial banks. Aside from these two special institutions, the Bulgarian and Romanian National Banks were the principal sources of mortgage lending. Accompanying the steadily smaller share of such loans in their assets was a tendency, ratified in Bulgaria by a new mortgage law of 1907, to grant them only to municipalities or urban properties.[51]

For Serbia, the rapid growth of a network of small provincial savings banks accounted for all 54 of the financial institutions formed during the first decade of the Narodna Banka's existence, 1884–1893. They were generally administered by untrained stockholders and held less than 100,000 dinars paid-in capital. They sprang up partly because of the central bank's successful issue of a national currency and its willingness to extend them current account credit if secured by their major asset, discounted bills of exchange for the export trade. Yet they also appeared because of the central bank's reluctance, understandable with a board of directors drawn largely from Belgrade importers, to risk opening branches outside the capital city. The local savings banks that flourished in their place nonetheless remained too small and too much tied to short-term discounting to afford any potential for long-term agricultural credit. By 1910, only a half dozen of those interior savings banks were able to offer agricultural mortgages. Their total amounted to a meager one million dinars.[52]

The semiofficial mortgage bank, or Hipotekarna Banka, was created from the state treasury's Uprava Fondova in 1898, on the model of the French Credit Foncier. The so-called Administration of Funds had been granting a small number of mortgage loans from treasury funds since 1862. The new bank was expected to expand the volume of mortgages greatly, once given the power to collect its own debts. It was not to be. Soon the largest Serbian bank save the Narodna Banka, the Hipotekarna was unable to place much over half of its assets in the long-term mortgages for which it had been designed. Its liabilities simply contained too few savings deposits or long-term bonds. Public buildings and urban residences received preference for mortgage loans anyway, over industry as well as agriculture. Then the withdrawal of half the bank's private savings deposits during the 1908 crisis over Habsburg annexation of Bosnia-

Hercegovina left the Hipotekarna Banka crippled for the rest of the prewar period.[53]

For Greece, its National Bank had begun to grant mortgage loans in 1891 on agricultural land as well as commercial or state property. Yet a plan the same year to found a separate agricultural bank would remain unrealized until 1928. Initially the National Bank of Greece had been a promising source of mortgage credit. Five years prior to 1891, the bank had 57 million drachmas of mortgate loans outstanding, or about one fourth of total assets. A majority of this sum already consisted, however, of state obligations drawn on public works projects. The overall total declined from 1886 forward, in line with the general tendency of European central banks to reduce their long-term lines of credit. The declining amounts were increasingly channeled to Athens and the other major municipalities.[54]

The Varying Strength of Private Commercial Banking

The great bulk of Balkan bank assets were concentrated elsewhere, in the short-term commercial lending of the National Banks and of the private joint-stock banks that grew up in the last two prewar decades. According to the pattern of nineteenth-century Europe, the greatest potential for a modern financial structure to promote industry-led growth lay within such joint-stock commercial banks. Chapter 8 will judge just how well they initiated or followed, ignored or hindered the mini-spurts of industrial growth in all four Balkan states during the last prewar decade. For now, it will suffice to set down the share of these banks in total financial assets.

Table 7.4 indicates that Romania and Serbia occupied the middle ground in total assets per capita. Yet for native assets apart from the central banks they both move to the forefront. The overall Greek lead may be traced to the massive contributions of the National Bank of Greece and two European banks.[55] The Bulgarian disadvantage may also be traced to the still more preponderant role of the National and Agricultural banks. As we have already seen, the central bank's network of branches throughout Bulgaria (and Romania and Greece as well) discouraged the rise of rival banks in provincial towns. But in Sofia, unlike the other Balkan capitals, the central bank was so powerful that no rival bank was successfully found there until 1906, and then it was a small German-backed institution.[56] Ferdinand's aforementioned success in fragmenting the Bulgarian political spectrum by 1900 prevented the emergence of two or three major parties that might draw on national resources to establish their own banks in the capital city, independent of whatever government was in power.

Political rivalry goes a long way toward explaining the presence of

TABLE 7.4
DISTRIBUTION OF BANK ASSETS IN 1911
(in lei, leva, dinars and drachmae)

Aggregate (in millions)	Central Bank	Other State Banks (N)	Private Native Banks (N)	Foreign Banks (N)	Total[a]
Romania	760	463 (2)	512 (144)	295 (4)	2,030
Bulgaria	310	235 (1)	100 (53)	90 (5)	735
Serbia	210	164 (1)	320 (172)	70 (3)	764
Greece	494	0 (0)	125 (2)	375 (2)	994
Per capita					
Romania	109	66	73	42	290
Bulgaria	71	54	23	21	167
Serbia	72	57	110	24	263
Greece	176	0	45	134	355

Note: (a)These totals should be reduced by about 5 percent for layering of interbank transactions, if the Serbian situation is any guide.

Source: John R. Lampe, "Varieties of Unsuccessful Industrialization: The Balkan States Before 1914," *Journal of Economic History,* XXXV, 1 (March, 1975), Table 9, p. 74.

large native joint-stock banks in Bucharest and Belgrade by the first decade of the twentieth century. The Romanian Liberal and Conservative parties each established their own banks. The largest of these was the Banca Românească, set up in Bucharest in 1910 by Liberal interests as counterweight to the four large European banks that provided most of the foreign assets listed for Romania in Table 7.4. This largest native bank reflected the Liberals' inability to control the central bank sufficiently after 1900, although still holding a majority of its stock.[57] Its influence and that of the eight other large Bucharest banks exceeded their joint 500-million-lei assets. A majority of the numerous provincial banks that sprang up during the last prewar decade owed their existence to informal status as branches of the Bucharest banks.[58] Lines of credit from the Banca Națională were essential to the operations of the large Bucharest banks, who in turn extended credit to the lesser ones outside the capital.

This access to central bank credit loomed even larger in the Serbian case. Credit to other banks consistently took over 80 percent of the current account loans that were the principal credit instrument of the Narodna Banka Kr. Srbije after 1905. Neither the Romanian nor the Bulgarian central bank directed as much as 20 percent of their current account credit to other banks during the prewar period.[59]

At the same time, these other Serbian banks were not just more numerous than their counterparts elsewhere in the Balkan states. They were also significantly more independent. We have already seen how the absence of central bank branches in the Serbian interior encouraged the founding of provincial savings banks during the 1880s. Then in the decade surrounding the turn of the century a dozen large Belgrade banks, each with joint-stock capital exceeding one million dinars, came into being. The first were formed to alleviate a mid-90s credit shortage caused by the above-mentioned restrictions on the note issue of the Narodna Banka. Almost all of these banks represented one of the several major political parties. By this time the list did not include the Progressive Party of the Belgrade importers who controlled the Narodna Banka. The export merchants who dominated the ruling Radical Party led the way in a second wave of Belgrade bank foundings, during the 1906–11 tariff war with Austria-Hungary. They hoped to put their funds from the hard-hit livestock trade to some profitable use.

By 1911 the number of Belgrade joint-stock banks with paid-in capital over one million dinars and assets over 10 million had jumped to 36. The more flexible current account loan had at the same time replaced discounted bills of exchange from foreign trade as their principal source of earnings.[60] Unlike the interior banks, moreover, they employed full-time staffs with formal training in double-entry bookkeeping. Their management began to enjoy a reputation for competence and commercial honesty among Western European observers. Their performance reinforces the reputation of commercial banking techniques for transferring more easily than industrial technology to an underdeveloped country.[61]

The new Belgrade banks were responsible for giving Serbia the most competitive banking system among all the Balkan states. Table 7.5 records net profit as a percentage of total assets, a better indicator of overall bank operations than paid-in capital. The percentage is in turn the best available surrogate for the relative level and movement of interest rates.

A halving of the Serbian percentage between 1895 and 1905 admittedly reflects the switch to shorter-term assets and the ordering of state finances. Similar tendencies, plus a slight general decline in European interest rates, may well have prompted the similar declines in the Bulgarian, Romanian, and Greek ratios to 1905. We do not know. What emerges from Table 7.5 is that the Serbian ratio, after the further 40-percent decline of 1906–11, was just over one third the Bulgarian ratio and just over half the Romanian and Greek ones for 1911. The increasingly competitive and interrelated makeup of the Serbian financial structure seems the best explanation for this

TABLE 7.5

NET PROFIT AS A PERCENTAGE OF BALKAN BANK ASSETS, 1895-1912

	SERBIA		BULGARIA		ROMANIA		GREECE	
	all banks	(private) (banks)	all banks	(private) (banks)	all banks	(private) (banks)	all banks	(private) (banks)
1895	2.15	(1.27)						
1903	1.63	(.70)						
1905	1.06	(.66)						
1906			1.75	(2.90)				
1907			1.21	(2.60)				
1908	1.05	(.60)	1.60	(2.20)				
1909	.76	(.70)	1.91	(2.15)				
1910	.76	(.59)	1.52	(2.18)			1.36	(1.03)
1911	.67	(.49)	1.84	(2.00)	1.40	(.88)	1.13	(.85)
1912					1.36	(.77)	1.02	(.72)

Sources: John R. Lampe, "Financial Structure and the Economic Development of Serbia, 1878-1912" (Ph.D. Dissertation, University of Wisconsin, 1971), p. 256; S. Bobchev, *Bulgarski aktsii i oblagatsii* (Sofia, 1910), *passim.*; *Iubileen sbornik na Bulgarska Narodna Banka, 1879-1929* (Sofia, 1929), p. 194; V. Slavescu, *Istoricul Băncii Naționale a României, 1880-1924* (Bucharest, 1924), p. 201; P. M. Sitescu, *Die Kreditbanken Rumänien* (Bucharest, 1915), pp. 62-63; British Parliamentary Papers, *Sessional Papers,* 92 (1914), no. 5224; K. und K. Österreichische Handelsmuseum, *Griechenland: Wirtschaftsverhältnisse, 1911* (Vienna, 1912), Table III.

continued decline. Free competition would also account for the narrowing of the gap between the Serbian central and other bank ratios. The dominance in Serbia of private joint-stock banks seems all the more significant when we consider the European level of total bank assets as a percentage of national income that was noted at the start of this chapter. The falling and increasingly uniform cost of credit from such a large commercial banking sector ranks as a major feat of modernization by pre-1914 standards.

The Reluctant Imperialism of the European Great Banks

This feat takes on added significance when we consider the relatively weak penetration of European financial institutions into the Balkan economies. These last prewar decades were after all the widely celebrated heyday of Finance Capitalism, a concept originating with the Austrian Marxist Rudolph Hilferding. He explained the prolonged survival of European capitalism in terms of powerful investment banks that could still earn large profits by encouraging industrial concentration at home and manipulating government policy abroad. Lenin quickly adopted the concept. Several generations of European Marxist scholars have embellished it with their research. The debate over the internal dynamics of industrial concentration continues to prompt some of the best historical research from Eastern

Europe. Yet the slim evidence for bank control of European foreign policy makes Finance Capitalism hard to defend as a theory of international behavior before the First World War.[62]

By the 1890s, as we have seen, native central banks had denied the so-called Great Banks of England, France, Germany, and Austria-Hungary the highest ground in the financial structure of all the Balkan states. But why did the subsequent Balkan activities of the Great Banks include no direct branches? Why did their affiliates only assemble assets which fell short of 15 percent of the total for all banks in Romania, Serbia, and Bulgaria by 1913? (See Table 7.4.) Answers emerge from more specific questions. Why did the European power with the greatest economic interest in Balkan penetration, Austria-Hungary, do so little? How did France, with the least interest, do so much? The reluctant role of banks from the two most developed industrial economies, the British and the German, is also instructive.

The Absence of English Influence

The British presence in Balkan financial institutions was clearly the smallest of all the Great Powers. There had been aggressive beginnings earlier in the century.[63] The Ionian Bank, established in 1839 when the islands were under British rule, became their bank of issue after incorporation into the Greek state in 1863. During the same year English engineers constructing the Bucharest-Giurgiu railway were able to organize the Bank of Romania Ltd. to help finance the project. Thereafter, neither bank grew much or expanded its operations at all.

At least they did not close, as did the branches that the Banque Imperiale Ottomane opened in several Bulgarian towns. English and French interests had founded this huge bank in Istanbul in 1863, using their connections with the Porte to make it the most powerful financial institution in the Ottoman Empire, virtually its central bank. Branches in Plovdiv and Ruse had been forced to close briefly in the mid-1880s but opened again in 1889. They soon cornered most of the international sales of grain, Bulgaria's principal export. In the process they inhibited the founding of native banks and cut into the commercial operations of the central bank. Then in 1895, as another branch was opening in Sofia, the parent bank in Istanbul permanently closed all its Bulgarian branches without warning. The decision had nothing to do with the condition of the Bulgarian economy. The closings stemmed from a run on reserves of its Anatolian branches and some losses in South African gold speculation.[64] The Bulgarian central bank had to divert the bulk of its loanable funds to former branch customers. The Narodna Banka and several fledgling native banks were left with few resources to cushion the impact of the bad harvests and agricultural depression of 1897–1900.

German Great Banks in Bulgaria

When Sofia saw its first foreign bank some years later in 1905, the Berliner Disconto-Gesellschaft and several other German Great Banks were the founders. No British rival ever appeared. Yet the German-backed Kreditna Banka did not play an important part in Bulgaria's financial history until the First World War. Before then it could not fulfill its promise of securing arms deliveries for the Krupp complex. Industrial promotions, as noted in Chapter 8, were trifling. Its origins lay partly in repairing the lack of a German commercial agency in Bulgaria. Still, the selection of Sofia as the site, rather than Plovdiv or a Black Sea port, and the bank's subsequent tendency to appoint prominent Bulgarian politicians to its administrative board, point to the prominence of purely political motives. Unwilling to arrange a large state loan even to finance the purchase of German artillery and munitions, the bank's prewar assets grew slowly. They never reached half the respective totals of the native Bulgarska Trgovska Banka in Ruse or the subsequent French and Austro-Hungarian affiliates in Sofia.[65]

The reputation of the Kreditna Banka for cautious entry into relatively risk-free ventures is consistent, but not with the theory of Finance Capitalism. Rather, it matches the actual behavior of other German banks in prewar Balkan and Ottoman ventures. The largest of them, Berlin's Deutsche Bank, is a case in point. The bank proceeded with the construction of the Berlin to Bagdad railway east from Istanbul only reluctantly in response to pressure from the Foreign Office.[66] Equally cautious was the bank's handling of the Bulgarian section of that route that came into its hands in 1896. It did not use this new leverage to penetrate the Bulgarian economy with a large state loan or a branch bank. On the contrary, the Deutsche Bank chose to pursue the short-run profitability of its Oriental Railway Company, which used delayed rebates to undercut freight traffic on the Bulgarian state railway. Its tactics prompted the latter to try buying out the former. Failing this because of the Porte's right to veto the sale, the state railway tried to assemble funds for constructing a parallel line in southeastern Bulgaria that would connect with the Black Sea port of Burgas. The Deutsche Bank thereupon used its influence to help deny the Bulgarian government access to European capital until 1902.[67]

German bank behavior in Bulgaria set the pattern throughout the Balkans. The investments in Romanian oil described in Chapter 8 must be regarded as the one major exception to the rule. In Serbia, the Great Banks confined their influence to buying minority interests in several existing institutions. The Berliner Handelgesellschaft undertook the largest of these purchases in 1909 rather than go ahead with founding its own branch bank as the Foreign Office had been urging. It bought into a Hungarian bank whose assets and activities, as we shall see, had not grown since the 1890s. In Greece, German financial penetration was unable to secure more than an estimated 2 percent of total European investment by the start of the First World War. Greek affiliates consisted of one small "second-class bank," founded in Athens in 1904.[68]

Missed Opportunities for Austria-Hungary

For Austria-Hungary, the logic of Balkan economic penetration was obviously more compelling than for Germany. The Dual Monarchy had been losing its market for processed exports to its rapidly industrializing northern neighbor during the late nineteenth century. Why not turn to the less developed Balkan economies for new markets and investment opportunities, with the added promise of political leverage over its smaller southern neighbors? Habsburg interests missed this several-sided opportunity for two fundamental reasons. First, the combined population of the four Balkan states in 1910 was only one third of the Habsburg total: 17 million versus 51 million. In the absence of significant foreign investment, sustained industrial spurts in the Czech and Hungarian lands were by the 1890s attracting most of the monarchy's relatively limited supply of capital. Second, the Viennese Great Banks stayed shy of investing in new private enterprises after their losses in the stock market crash of 1873. Their preference for state bonds and well-established firms continued with minor exceptions to the First World War.[69] All of this left little room for Balkan assets.

The record of the Viennese Great Banks in the Balkan capitals shows only scattered pursuit of new export markets or manufacturing investment and then by institutions established in cooperation with Paris banks. The Leninist explanation of the First World War— growing national rivalry because of conflicts generated by Finance Capitalism—thus receives scant support.

Several large new banks opened in Bucharest and Sofia after 1905. They received Austrian support only because French participation divided the risk and added to reserves available in case of trouble.[70] The Banque Commerciale Roumaine used its sizable capital of 12 million lei to pursue oil, metallurgy, and timber investments, as well as building new facilities for wheat storage on the Danube. Yet it did not open until 1907 and remained the only Romanian bank with major Viennese participation. The two new Sofia banks were smaller and showed less interest in long-term investment. The Generalna Banka began operations in 1905. One million of its four million leva in founding capital was contributed by the Pester Ungarische Komercialbank of Budapest (itself partly supported by French funds). Two million came from the Paris-Bas bank. Once its initial purpose of checking the influence of the German-backed Kreditna Banka had been accomplished, the Generalna confined its long-term activities to municipal loans and to support for the state tobacco and match monopolies described in Chapter 8.

For founding capital in 1906, the Balkanska Banka drew about half of its 3 million leva from Vienna's Wienerbankverein and most of the rest from French investors. The Balkanska joined with the Generalna in supporting the consolidation of the state tobacco monopoly but otherwise concentrated its commercial operations on short-term credit to foreign trade that the Neufield firm of Vienna had previously provided. The Habsburg Foreign Office was dissatisfied with the modest activities and French connections of these two banks. The Ballhausplatz repeatedly pressured the Länderbank to open a branch in Sofia. The supposedly wide-ranging Viennese bank never did.

The Länderbank had not even seen fit to establish a branch in Belgrade, the Balkan capital of greatest concern to Habsburg interests. As noted earlier, the parent institution had declined Serbian offers to found their central bank during the early 1880s. Instead the Länderbank had confined its Belgrade interests to the small Srpska Kreditna Banka. From its opening in 1883, paid-in capital remained less than half that of the central bank or, from the 1890s, the native Belgrade banks. Its assets were placed almost exclusively in short-term credit to foreign trade. They stayed there throughout the 1906–11 tariff war with the Dual Monarchy, despite suggestions from the Austrian consul that they be withdrawn.

The only other Habsburg representative among the Belgrade banks was the small Andrejević and Company. The Pester Ungarische Komercialbank had taken it over in 1889 but never expanded its assets to equal even those of the Srpska Kreditna Banka. The bank contented itself with small forward loans to the Serbian government and short-term credit to foreign traders. Its hasty withdrawal of reserves to Habsburg territory in 1908, following the Austro-Hungarian annexation of Bosnia-Hercegovina, provoked a hostile Serbian reaction that hindered the restoration of even its modest position on returning to Belgrade.[71]

Paris Banks and Les Affaires Plus Grandes

The deserved reputation of Paris as the major capital market of pre-1914 Europe has given its major banks a generally undeserved reputation as aggressive entrepreneurs seeking new investments outside France in the fashion of the Périere brothers and their mid-nineteenth-century Credit Mobilier. French and American scholarship make it clear that the principal foreign promotions of these later banks were state loans, typically undertaken at the urgings of the Foreign Ministry for diplomatic advantage rather than on their own initiative for maximum profit.[72] The massive Russian loans were only the best known example. The majority of post-1900 bond issues for the Balkan states were handled by major Paris houses. They underwrote nearly two thirds of the 461 million francs effectively borrowed by Bulgaria and virtually all of the 312 million by Serbia between 1902 and 1912. This surge during the last prewar decade allowed French sources of state loans to increase their large lead over other European leaders in Serbia, to surpass the Central Powers in Bulgaria, and to cut into the large Austro-German lead in Romania and the British predominance in Greece. Table 7.6 reflects the foreign sources of Balkan state debt incurred up to the First World War.

The impressive French percentage did not prompt a single Paris bank to pursue the avenues thus opened for further economic penetration by establishing its own branch in a Balkan capital. In Bulgaria and Romania, only combinations of several French banks joined with Viennese and Budapest institutions to set up the three aforementioned foreign banks between 1905 and 1907. Typical of the French interest in these banks was the first president of the Generalna Banka in Sofia. He was the official French delegate to the international commission for the repayment of Bulgarian state loans.

The one exception to this overriding concern for debt repayment was the Bank of Athens. Constructed from a similar combination of French and other European interests in 1894, the bank's capital had grown to 60 million drachma by 1911, five times the totals for the next largest Balkan banks in which there were French interests. The French held a majority share of 35 million and pushed the bank to credit trade in Egypt and the Ottoman Near East, until losses in the former curtailed these operations in 1912.[73] How much the Bank of Athens was able to stimulate Greek exports, in addition to serving the traditional French interest in the Levant trade, remains a subject for further study.

The one Balkan bank combining only French funds bears little resemblance to the active Bank of Athens. Despite the 240 million

TABLE 7.6
SOURCES OF LONG-TERM EUROPEAN LOANS, 1867-1912 (%)

	SERBIA	ROMANIA	GREECE	BULGARIA
France	79	32	28	45
Great Britain			49	6
Germany	} 21	} 52	7	} 39
Austria-Hungary				
Native		11	16	
Belgium		5		
Russia				10

Sources: Herbert Feis, *Europe: The World's Banker, 1870-1914* (New York: W. W. Norton, 1965 reprint), pp. 269, 287; L. Aleksić-Pejković, *Odnosi Srbije ca Francuskom i Engleskom, 1903-1914* (Belgrade, 1965), pp. 806-12; William H. Wynne, *State Insolvency and Foreign Bond Holders*, II (New Haven: Yale University Press, 1951), pp. 531-43.

francs of new Serbian state bond issues placed by the Paris banks among French investors in 1906 and 1909, the Banque Franco-Serbe did not open its doors in Belgrade until mid-1910. Its consortium of four Paris banks excluded the most active of foreign investments, the Banque de Paris et des Pays-Bas, better known as Paris-Bas. Those participating had in any case been recruited by the several Serbian political parties, rather than the reverse. The occasion was a new municipal loan for Belgrade which could not otherwise be arranged on the Paris capital market. By 1911, the bank had assets of 41 million dinars, enough to make it larger than any of the native Belgrade banks.

The Banque Franco-Serbe used these assets largely to pursue what one French diplomat called "les affaires plus grandes": further state loans and the political aid needed to secure them.[74] Only the original loan of 30 million dinars to complete the Belgrade water system was ever placed on the Paris capital market. The bank made its principal mark by undercutting the operations of the Hungarian-backed Andrejević and Company. Already facing strong criticism from the Serbian government and public for its removal of reserves to Habsburg territory in 1908, the Andrejević bank saw the Banque Franco-Serbe open its offices in the same building literally across the hall. It actively pursued Andrejević customers with offers of higher interest on deposits and lower interest on loans if they would switch their accounts. Many did. What positive effect they may have had on Serbian economic development remains doubtful. Its commercial operations concentrated on short-term credit to members of the Radical Party. The limited contribution that the Banque Franco-Serbe and other foreign banks made to the sources of industrial growth surveyed in the next chapter may thus be anticipated.

European Loans and the Balkan State Budgets

Even the state loans generated by these European banks and encouraged by native aspirations to the Gold Standard did not make the contribution to railway construction and other infrastructure that apostles of the pre-1914 monetary system might expect. The Romanian financial structure included far more foreign assets on a per capita basis than that of Bulgaria or Serbia (see Table 7.4). It was also the only one among all the Balkan states based directly on the European Gold Standard. Yet the European capital that the Romanian government borrowed from the standard's adoption in 1890 through the last peacetime year of 1911 was barely cheaper and hardly better used than the totals borrowed by Serbia and Bulgaria. By the last prewar decade, according to Table 7.7, the latter two states were able to contract European loans at virtually the same effective rate of interest as Romania: 5½ percent. Despite incomplete data on the balance of payments, the trade balances in Table 6.3 suggest that Romania was the only Balkan state to have achieved export surpluses by that time which matched the annual outflow of capital for debt repayment. Perhaps the need of the other two for capital inflow explains why, with these presumed advantages, Romanian borrowing over the last two decades fell short of Serbia's per capita total and just exceeded Bulgaria's.

Whether any Balkan government would have even tried to promote greater economic development with more European loans is doubtful. The Romanian fraction of effective borrowing after 1900 spent on infrastructure, as opposed to nonproductive military and administrative expenses or debt service, fell somewhere between the 20 percent allocated by the Bulgarian government and the Serbian 30 percent.[75] This is the same fraction that emerges from the rapidly growing budgets of the Balkan governments. No major reallocation of state spending accompanied the tighter accounting and rising indirect taxation that permitted the reduced budget deficits noted in Table 7.2. True, the burden of foreign debt still surpassed 30 percent only for Greece. Yet its per capita sum if added to military expenditures exceeded the total in every Balkan state budget for the three economically productive expenses: infrastructure, education, and direct investment in agriculture or industry. The three together barely reached 40 percent of the Bulgarian budget and less than 30 percent elsewhere.

While debt service took the biggest part of the large Greek total for all expenses and the rest is unknown, the breakdown of the still larger Romanian aggregate suggests a clearer lesson. Economic and military expenses plus debt service accounted for little more in per capita terms (see Table 7.9) than they did in Serbia and Bulgaria. Explaining the far larger Romanian aggregate were a variety of administrative expenses for maintaining the state and the royal apparatus that amounted to fully half the total, versus less than one quarter for Serbia and Bulgaria. These extra expenditures, sufficient to push the Romanian per capita total past that of industrial Germany if not that of France's huge central government, were never intended to serve economic development.

The Balkan governments' weight in their respective economies was potentially far heavier than that of their Western and Central European counterparts. Balkan per capita incomes, reckoned roughly from the estimates of social product in Chapter 6, reached 200 to 250 francs equivalent a year by 1911, in contrast with figures at least three or four times greater in the developed economies. Bulgaria, with the smallest state budget per capita, still extracted for state use over 20 percent of income averaging about 200 francs. Romania had

TABLE 7.7
LONG-TERM EUROPEAN LOANS TO BALKAN GOVERNMENTS, 1864-1911
(in millions of francs)

	Nominal Amount	Effective Amount	% Nominal Interest	% Effective Interest
1864-1889				
Romania[a]	722.7	518.9	5.6	7.8
Bulgaria[b]	76.8	71.4	6.0	6.5
Serbia[c]	63.5	46.6	3.8	5.2
Greece[d]	690.9	514.0	4.8	6.1
1890-1900				
Romania	1,009.4	779.2	4.4	5.7
Bulgaria	150.0	131.2	5.8	6.6
Serbia	367.8	258.1	4.0	5.7
Greece				
1901-1911				
Romania	951.8	880.0	4.9	5.3
Bulgaria	522.0	464.0	4.7	5.5
Serbia	555.0	476.0	4.8	5.6
Greece	55.3	44.2	4.0	5.0

Notes: (a)From 1864. (b)From 1888. (c)From 1876. (d)From 1833.

Sources: I. Tutuc, *Studiul valorilor mobilare* (Bucharest, 1927), pp. 34-35; Kiril Popoff, *La Bulgarie économique, 1879-1911* (Paris, 1920), p. 285; L. Aleksić-Pejković, *Odnosi Srbije ca Francuskom i Engleskom, 1903-1914* (Belgrade, 1965), p. 808; William H. Wynne, *State Insolvency and Foreign Bondholders*, II (New Haven: Yale University Press, 1951), pp. 283-337.

TABLE 7.8
BALKAN STATE BUDGETS, 1898-1912
(in millions of lei, leva, dinars, and drachmae)[a]

	ROMANIA Rev.	Exp.	R-E	BULGARIA Rev.	Exp.	R-E	SERBIA Rev.	Exp.	R-E	GREECE Rev.	Exp.	R-E
1898	237	225	+ 12	89	91	- 2	66	81	- 15	105	312	-207
1899	200	235	- 35	78	90	- 12	72	85	- 13	111	105	+ 6
1900	210	237	- 27	81	96	- 15	75	84	- 9	120	109	+ 11
1901	239	218	+ 21	90	91	- 1	69	84	- 15	168	114	+ 54
1902	250	218	+ 32	96	95	+ 1	74	78	- 4	139	125	+ 14
1903	258	230	+ 28	98	109	- 11	78	88	- 10	116	116	0
1904	259	252	+ 7	114	113	+ 1	92	87	+ 5	134	116	+ 18
1905	308	263	+ 45	128	125	+ 3	95	87	+ 8	130	116	+ 14
1906	318	265	+ 53	136	137	- 1	96	85	+ 11	133	122	+ 11
1907	332	269	+ 63	149	147	+ 2	100	87	+ 13	137	132	+ 5
1908	469	417	+ 52	151	154	- 3	101	125	- 14	126	134	- 8
1909	523	482	+ 41	167	159	+ 8	116	134	- 18	125	137	- 12
1910	583	525	+ 58	181	198	- 17	126	128	- 2	175	141	+ 34
1911[a]	644	533	+111	199	181	+ 18	140	125	+ 15	240	181	+ 59
1912[a]	621	522	+ 89	170						255	208	+ 17

Note: (a)Discrepancy with figures in Table 11.1 because prewar data used here for continuity with earlier years.

Source: Same as for Table 7.2.

TABLE 7.9
STRUCTURE OF STATE EXPENSES PER CAPITA IN 1911
(in franc equivalents)

1911 Expenses	Public Debt	Military	Infra-structure	Public Education	Agriculture and Industry	Total
Romania	13	12	13	7	1	75
Serbia	12	10	5	3	1	43
Bulgaria	9	9	10	5	2	42
Greece	28	11		2		67
Austria-Hungary	10			2		62
Germany	5	16				55
France	32	25		8		114
Great Britain		19		11	1	126

Sources: Tables 7.2 and 7.3; Kiril Popoff, *La Bulgarie économique, 1879-1911* (Paris, 1920), pp. 484-89; B. R. Mitchell, *European Historical Statistics, 1750-1970* (New York: Columbia University Press, 1975), pp. 709-726.

the largest budget. It approached 30 percent of the country's 250-franc average income. The limited direction of those revenues toward economic development constituted a major opportunity foregone. We may expect to find some inverse relations, in other words, between the small size of the modern factory labor force examined in the next chapter (45,000 for Romania and 16,000 for Bulgaria and Serbia with wages averaging 1,000 lei, leva, or francs a year) and state bureaucracies whose number and payroll were much larger. By 1910 Bulgaria's central government paid over 47,000 employees, most of the army excluded, salaries totalling 78 million leva, out of a budget of 198 million. Serbian state employees numbered at least 25,000 and Greece's over 50,000. The Romanian government paid 87,000 employees 121 million lei in salaries out of a budget of 482 million. In every case these employment figures exceed the 5 percent of the labor force in the French state bureaucracy, generally considered the largest proportion in prewar Europe.[76]

The financial structure of prewar Europe provided the Balkan economies with just two realistic ways to make use of such imposing government sectors. The first was to attract private European capital to state loans. This the Balkan governments did only to squander a majority of the proceeds. European lenders gave their blessings as long as the earnings of the state monopolies and indirect tax revenues continued to guarantee repayment on schedule. The second way was for the European Great Banks to invest in the private sector because the Balkan governments had improved budgetary management and their central banks achieved par between the national currency and the French gold franc. Yet these achievements occasioned little European response.

The successful ordering of state finances had allowed the independent central banks to increase their note issue during the last prewar decade and thus add some native impetus to economic growth. As we have seen, however, the new issues were limited in view of the long-standing restriction. They did not promote any adjustment of discount rates counter-cyclically, e.g., downward in time of recession. They did not interrupt the central banks' increasing reliance, in line with European best practice, on short-term credit. The allocation of that credit continued to favor the same borrowers, the state in Bulgaria and the traditional trading interests in Serbia and Romania.

In the absence of strong mortgage or savings banks to take up the slack left by the central banks, the provision of long-term credit fell to private commercial banks. They were able to flourish in Romania and especially in Serbia, where easy access to central bank credit and the dynamics of political rivalry contributed to the emergence of a competitive system. Yet the inferred decline in their interest rates hardly encouraged a shift into long-term assets. Only within the structure of short-term lending was there movement from bills of exchange to the more flexible overdrafts on current account so predominant in German banking.

The more powerful European banks, whose liabilities were increasingly long-term savings deposits, failed to found branches in the Balkan capitals. Their affiliates generally neglected the supply of long-term, private credit that remained the one striking deficiency in the otherwise complete and modern financial structures of the pre-1914 Balkan states. Chapter 8 now considers the best that native industry could make of its bad bargain with the European monetary system.

8.

Industrial Stirrings and the
Sources of Growth

By any acceptable definition of that much-abused phrase, no Industrial Revolution occurred in any of the Balkan states before 1914. Mechanical power had only begun to replace human labor. Manufacturing sectors, as noted in Table 8.3 used trivial amounts of mechanical horsepower, the best single indicator of modern technology. Neither had those sectors recorded enough decades of sustained growth in real per capita terms even to approach employing the majority of Balkan land, labor, and capital in manufacturing or mining. Such a majority affords the best brief definition of an industrialized economy.[1] We have no notion of industrial output for Greece before 1917 and must largely exclude its probably similar experience from this chapter. During the last prewar years, the value-added industrial output of the other three Balkan states did not amount to 10 percent of the total gross output for their economies recorded earlier in Table 6.1. That proportion has passed 50 percent only in the last twenty years (see Chapter 10).

At the same time, the progress made before 1914 deserves our attention for several reasons. Balkan manufacturing faced difficulties in organizing enterprises, finding sufficient markets, and obtaining the necessary capital and labor. Such difficulties continue to make industrial development something less than the automatic process that many Marxists assume it to be. Perhaps more important for our purposes, foreign and native entrepreneurs, Balkan banks and governments strove to overcome these formidable obstacles in ways that have marked the area's economic history ever since. All of these stimuli, some positive and some negative, were at work in the mini-

spurts of industrial activity that characterized the final fifteen years
before the First World War.

Mini-Spurts after 1900

The manufacturing and mining sectors of the Romanian, Serbian,
and Bulgarian economies all recorded rates of aggregate growth after
1900 (see Table 6.2) that were high enough to arouse suspicion that
they might have become self-sustaining and begun to absorb the
surplus agricultural population had war not intervened. The present
chapter spends much of its space laying that suspicion to rest for
industry as a whole. Closer examination of several prominent
branches nonetheless reveals potential for further growth in the
enlarged interwar economies.

Our second task is to address the principal questions for comparative industrial history that emerged from Table 6.1. Why did Romanian industry start from a far higher base in 1900 than the Serbian or
the Bulgarian? Its per capita industrial output by the start of the war
more than doubled that of the other two despite half the growth rate
over the intervening years. Why couldn't Bulgarian industrial output
exceed or even match the Serbian figure in view of the former's
mid-nineteenth-century head start over the latter as described in
Chapters 4 and 5?[2]

Concentrated Demand in the Capital Cities

The first obstacle facing pre-1914 Balkan manufacturing was the
lack of sufficient demand. Export opportunities were obviously limited in an era that saw sophisticated German and other European
manufactures join English goods in competing for most international
markets. Bulgarian textiles, as we shall see, were able to hang onto a
shrinking share of the Ottoman market, large in numbers if low in
per capita income. Romanian and Serbian manufactures made little
headway there and virtually none in the neighboring Habsburg market of 51 million.[3] The great majority of the native Balkan population
were rural peasants whose tastes, again save textiles, and incomes,
save possibly in Serbia, did not afford a major market for modern
manufactures. The principal market was instead urban population,
less than 20 percent of the total for Romania, Bulgaria, and Serbia
and less than 30 percent for Greece.

One part of the Romanian advantage in urban demand emerges
from the figures in Table 8.1. The largest pre-1914 Balkan state was
more populous than Serbia and Greece combined and half again the

size of Bulgaria. Its capital city of Bucharest approached 350,000 by 1914 to equal the combined total for the other three capitals. Given the poor quality of prewar Balkan roads, concentration of over half of Romania's urban numbers in Bucharest, the Moldavian capital of Iași, and the Danubian ports of Brăila and Galați probably counted for more than total urban numbers. Together these towns offered Romanian industrial enterprises a market that promised to justify the larger scale generally required to make mechanized production profitable. The other Balkan states would not approach these urban numbers until the unprecedented growth of their capital cities during the 1920s (see Chapter 10).

Bucharest had the further, unquantifiable advantage of a higher concentration of private income and hence purchasing power than any other Balkan capital. Chapter 3 has already identified its source. The movement of wealthy boyar landowners and Phanariot officials into the city began during the eighteenth century and continued into the nineteenth. It created a tradition of constructing sumptuous residences and otherwise vying to meet European standards of conspicuous consumption. Indeed, the villas of pre-1914 Bucharest bear comparison to the most lavish private homes built during that era in Chicago and other American cities. To the growing construction of public buildings and other state expenses that also characterized the other Balkan capitals, we must add the greater royal expenditure symbolized by an immense palace in the center of Bucharest. The other three royal residences, in Belgrade, Sofia, Athens, would easily fit inside. Thus the concentration in the capital city of over half of Romanian industrial enterprises, a higher proportion than for Serbia or Bulgaria, appears to be a response to greater demand.[4]

The collection of even one third of Bulgarian manufactures in the capital of Sofia was neither a reflection of broad-based demand nor a stimulus to further industrialization. The solution to this paradox begins with the city's small size and poor commercial location at the time it became the capital in 1879. Its population of 20,000 was only two thirds that of Ruse or Plovdiv and was matched by three or four other Bulgarian towns, all of which were on the Danube, the Black Sea, or in the center of a major agricultural area. Sofia's upland location, largely surrounded by mountains, offered a commercial advantage only if access to the neighboring Serbian and Macedonian markets were assured. In 1879, the first Bulgarian Minister of Education had successfully petitioned the occupying Russian army to make Sofia the capital. He doubtless assumed that such access would follow when the smaller Bulgarian state sanctioned by the Treaty of Berlin was eventually replaced by the far larger territory authorized by the original Russo-Ottoman Treaty of San Stefano. Those borders

TABLE 8.1
POPULATION OF TOWNS[a] AND CAPITAL CITIES, 1860-1910
(thousands)

	ROMANIA		BULGARIA		SERBIA		GREECE	
	Total Pop.	Urban %	Total Pop.	Urban %	Total Pop.	Urban %	Total Pop.	Urban %
1860-61	3,918	12	—	—	—	—	—	—
1874	—	—	—	—	1,354	11	—	—
1877-79	4,486	—	—	—	1,700	—	1,654	18
1884	4,862	—	3,024	18	1,902	12	—	—
1889-90	5,318	17	3,232	19	2,162	13	2,187	—
1895-96	5,710	—	3,441	—	2,312	14	2,434	—
1899-1900	5,957	19	3,716	19	2,493	14	—	—
1907	6,684	—	—	—	—	—	2,632	24
1910	6,996	18	4,306	19	2,912	14	—	—

	Urban Pop.	Bucharest	Urban Pop.	Sofia	Urban Pop.	Belgrade	Urban Pop.	Athens
1860-61	313	122	—	—	—	—	—	41
1874	—	—	—	—	174	27	—	—
1877-79	—	177	543	20	—	—	293	63
1884	—	—	—	—	236	35	—	—
1889-90	—	220	610	45	286	54	465	108
1895-96	—	—	—	—	319	59	526	—
1899-1900	1,120	276	700	67	351	70	—	111
1907	—	—	—	—	—	—	628	167
1910	1,195	341	829	103	483	90	—	—

Note: (a)Minimum of 2,000 people.

Sources: B. R. Mitchell, *European Historical Statistics, 1750-1970* (New York: Columbia University Press, 1975), pp. 76, 78; John R. Lampe, "Varieties of Unsuccessful Industrialization: The Balkan States Before 1914," *Journal of Economic History,* XXXV, 1 (March, 1975), Table 8, p. 72.

had included all of Macedonia and reached south almost to Thessaloniki. The restoration never came, thereby poisoning the Bulgarian body politic for generations. The young state was left to develop its economy from an unfortunately chosen center.

As was the case with early modern Madrid, an increasingly centralized government soon created the country's largest city in a relatively isolated upland location.[5] The city's growing bureaucracy and King Ferdinand's control of patronage eventually made it Bulgaria's commercial and industrial center by the last prewar decade. Sofia reached 100,000 by 1912. Even then it took little part in trading grain, the principal export. Sofia owed the survival of most of its struggling factories to government contracts and credit. These enterprises used a third of the industrial labor force to produce a fourth of total output. Their profit for 1902 amounted to only 4 percent of paid-in capital, versus a national average of over 8 percent.[6] Meanwhile previous economic centers suffered, as we shall see, for being far from the seat of political power. The river town of Ruse, in particular, saw its population decline and its economy stagnate, and, as noted in Chapter 6, became the center for Bulgaria's briefly heavy emigration to the United States during 1907–08.

Industrial Structure and Labor Supply

One consequence of the wider and deeper Romanian market for manufactures may be inferred from the distribution of industrial output at the end of the prewar period for all four Balkan countries. Table 8.2 reflects the Romanian manufacturing sector's ability to add 39 percent to the value of its total output, versus only 30 percent for the Bulgarian. The lower use of fuel by Bulgarian industry also suggests that its manufactures operated on a smaller scale and were unable to add as much value to the raw materials from which their goods were processed.

True, Bulgarian horsepower per industrial worker by 1910 averaged only about 15 percent less than the Romanian, according to Table 8.3. But the average number of workers and value of fixed capital for Bulgarian (and Serbian) firms amount to no more than half of the Romanian figures. Employment in Romanian manufacturing reached 45,000 by 1910, while totals for the other two were 16,000 apiece. A still greater concentration of fixed capital in Romanian industry emerges when we turn to its distribution between firms. The 53 enterprises with over one million lei of paid-in capital in 1902 and the 83 in 1913 contrast with three for Bulgaria and a half dozen for Serbia in 1904–05. In other words, although Romanian industry was hardly passing through a technological revolution, it did achieve sufficiently greater firm size and capital intensity to presume a relative advantage in economies of scale. Data from 472 "larger" Romanian firms in 1910 also suggest a rate of profit that was generally twice the 8 percent of fixed capital recorded by Bulgarian manufactures in 1904.[7] This higher rate, if verified by needed archival research, would place Romanian industrial investment on a par with or ahead of private banking in its expected rate of return. The same could not be said, as we shall see, for investment in Bulgarian or Serbian industry.

The dependence of Balkan industrial stirrings on capital and entrepreneurship emerges from the shortage not only of modern machinery but also of skilled labor. Unskilled, often illiterate labor from the Serbian and Bulgarian countryside, as well as the larger Greek emigration described in Chapter 6, tended to leave the country in search of seasonal or permanent employment. Small numbers of Macedonian construction workers came to Sofia and Belgrade. They were joined by assorted Serbian and Bulgarian artisans who contin-

TABLE 8.2
COMPOSITION OF ROMANIAN AND BULGARIAN MANUFACTURING
(in millions of lei or leva = francs)

Branch	ROMANIA (1915)				BULGARIA (1911)	
	Gross Output	Net Output	Price Index[a]	Gross Real % Growth Rate[b]	Gross Output	Net Output
Textiles	45.8	20.9	151	7.1	21.4	9.5
Flour	115.5	17.2	117	2.3	46.3	5.0
Other Foodstuffs[c]	99.6	49.9	187	6.3	18.6	10.6
Leather	24.6	3.5	98	9.0	5.5	.9
Chemicals	13.4	4.3			4.2	2.5
Paper	20.9	9.5	73	8.4	.9	.4
Wood Processing	56.7	26.3	177	4.4	2.7	1.2
Metal Processing	42.2	14.6	102	11.0	3.0	1.5
Construction Mat'ls	21.4	13.3	89	10.6	4.7	2.9
Subtotal	413.4	161.5	129	6.2	107.3	34.5
Petroleum	141.3	48.7	243	14.9		
Total	584.1	210.2	145	7.0		

Notes: (a)Index of gross output based on 1901/02 prices. (b)Average annual real growth of gross output for 1901/02-1915, computed by geometric method. (c)Of which Romanian sugar accounted for 37.8 million lei gross and 20.3 net, with a 6.6 percent real growth rate from 1901/02 based on price index of 143 by 1915.

Sources: Marvin R. Jackson, "Quantitative Economic History in the Balkans: Observations on the Period Before 1914," *Faculty Working Papers in Economics*, 74-39 (Tempe, Arizona: College of Business Administration, Arizona State University, 1974); *Statisticheski godishnik na Bulgarskoto Tsarstvo, 1912* (Sofia, 1915), pp. 192-93.

ued to collect in Bucharest, as had been customary since the late eighteenth century (see Chapter 3). The movement of such Balkan labor to the Romanian capital appears to have slackened by 1900. Whatever the case, skilled labor in most branches of manufacturing required some acquaintance with modern machinery. These jobs were typically filled by Czechs or Austrian Germans who migrated only in return for wages that were above the going rate in their native lands, let alone their new location.[8]

The going rates for Balkan industrial labor, unskilled and skilled, climbed during the mini-spurt after 1900. The start of large-scale emigration between 1903 and 1907 had prompted a one third rise in Greek urban wages. Similar increases occurred in the other Balkan economies, in the absence of comparable emigration but in the presence of better documented industrial growth. Also pushing up industrial wages during this last prewar decade was the jump in world grain prices that kept Balkan export values climbing. Had this trend continued, and the European losses in population during the First World War made sure that it did not, Balkan industrial enterprises

TABLE 8.3
INDUSTRIAL CAPITAL, FIRM SIZE AND HORSEPOWER FOR ROMANIA, BULGARIA AND SERBIA

	Fixed Capital		
	(million lei, leva or dinars)		
	ROMANIA (1915)	BULGARIA (1911)	SERBIA (1910)
Textiles	26.2	15.9	4.6
Flour	41.0	15.9	9.8
Other foodstuffs	69.6	18.5	14.9
Leather	2.5	2.8	.6
Chemicals	11.0	3.3	2.9
Oil	49.6		
Paper	31.4	1.6	.3
Wood processing	45.4	3.3	3.7
Metal processing	31.3	3.3	6.3
State monopolies		5.0	
Construction materials	39.3	6.4	4.0
Other	17.8	6.1	2.6
Total	369.1	82.1	49.7

	Average Workers Per Firm		Average Horsepower Per Worker	
	ROMANIA	BULGARIA	ROMANIA	BULGARIA
Textiles	105.8	66.6	1.26	.92
Flour	30.4	10.6	7.57	5.64
Other foodstuffs	70.0	23.6	2.26	2.32
Leather	49.1	18.1	1.22	1.27
Chemicals	44.9	17.3	3.00	1.05
Paper	109.3	50.7	1.74	1.53
Wood processing	89.4	62.8	1.43	.61
Metal processing	105.2	55.7	1.08	.42
Construction materials	60.4	115.8	1.32	.57
Other				
Total	71.6	39.0	2.08	1.72

Sources: N. P. Arcadian. *Industrializarea României* (Bucharest, 1936). p. 130; *Anuarul statistic al României. 1915-1916* (Bucharest, 1919). pp. 192-95; *Statisticheski godishnik na Bulgarskoto Tsarstvo. 1912* (Sofia, 1915). pp. 188-193; Industrijska Komora Kr. Srbije *Izveštaj. 1910* (Belgrade, 1911). Table 4.

would have been obliged to keep operating under the handicap of rising domestic food prices.

Prewar employers were forced to increase the wages of unskilled workers enough to match rising food prices and of skilled labor by more than that amount. According to Table 8.4, bread prices in Serbia and Bulgaria and pork and bean prices in grain-rich Romania increased by over 30 percent during the period after 1900. The response of both construction and day labor wages suggests that pre-

1914 Balkan industry could not draw on an unlimited supply of rural labor to increase production without adding to unit costs.[9] Judging by a detailed study of Belgrade and general indications for the other Balkan capitals, these cities had not only become the center of national industry. They were also the most expensive place to live and hence to pay wages in the entire country.[10]

Immigrant and Native Entrepreneurship

What Western European entrepreneur, let alone a major company, would be attracted to investing in the sort of manufacturing sector growing up in the pre-1914 Balkan states? Precious few, as the record shows. The capital cities afforded the best domestic market but allowed no usable access to the supply of unskilled peasant labor in the hinterland and no cheap access to skilled labor.

Only native entrepreneurs and Central European immigrants were likely to begin with the modest expectations for early profit and the intimate knowledge of local conditions that would make such an investment economically rational. With the ethnic Czechs and Germans came the added possibility of bringing their fellows along as skilled labor. With the Ashkenazi Jews that appeared during the nineteenth century came connections to Central European capital markets.

Not surprisingly, this limited flow of immigrant entrepreneurship, basically from the Habsburg lands, settled most often in neighboring Serbian and Romanian territory. The attendant advantage to their pre-1914 industrial development over the more isolated Bulgarian economy must be borne in mind throughout this section. Its division into subsections on textiles, food processing, construction materials, and heavy industry calls attention to further Romanian and Serbian advantages. The wool textiles that were the biggest part of Bulgarian industrial production remained burdened with imported raw materials and an artisan sector that used its political influence to inhibit modern manufacture. The livestock processing that dominated Serbian production by 1911 used strictly domestic raw materials, except for fuel, and faced no craft competition. The construction materials, metallurgy, and oil extraction that dominated Romanian industry had the same advantages.

Textile Manufacture

Gabrovo and several other upland towns on either side of the central Balkan range had become the center of Bulgarian textile man-

TABLE 8.4
INDEX OF URBAN FOOD PRICES AND DAILY WAGES, 1900-11

1900=100	ROMANIA[a]			BULGARIA[b]			SERBIA[b]		
	Bread	Pork	Beans	Bread	Pork	Beans	Bread	Pork	Beans
1901	104	100	122	96	102	92	105	97	110
1902	96	100	117	94	106	95	111	103	130
1903	100	106	130	89	123	95	105	117	155
1904	108	113	152	88	108	107	95	118	184
1905	108	115	156	94	117	121	95	130	251
1906	104	130	130	91	123	116	105	116	203
1907	117	136	139	115	129	132	125	106	163
1908	133	140	113	130	148	149	140	115	155
1909	133	149	135	135	160	121			
1910	121	164	152	119	158	106	136	132	246
1911	113	166	152	110	154	133	136	146	299

	ROMANIA	BULGARIA		SERBIA	
	1905=100	1891-1900=100		1892-1902=100	
	Railway Worker	Day Laborer[b]	Brick-layer[c]	Day Laborer	Brick-layer[d]
1900		86	84	104	100
1901		85			100
1902		85		102	100
1903		88		103	104
1904		90	87	106	104
1905	100	98	96	105	109
1906	104	106	107	110	113
1907	124	111	118	111	118
1908	128	112	121	114	121
1909	135	118	124		
1910	128	124	131		
1911	134	129	138		

Notes: (a)Bucharest only. (b)All towns. (c)Sofia only. (d)Belgrade only.

Sources: John R. Lampe, "Varieties of Unsuccessful Industrialization: The Balkan States Before 1914," *Journal of Economic History*, XXXV. 1 (March, 1975), Table 7, p. 67: *Statisticheski godishnik na Bulgarskoto Tsarstvo, 1912* (Sofia, 1915), p. 264.

ufacture by the start of the nineteenth century. As explained in Chapter 5, such manufacture of braid and rough woolen cloth had already moved from artisan shops to partly mechanized factories by the first years of Bulgarian independence in the 1880s. Following the example of eighteenth-century England, the typical pattern for the half dozen factories operating by 1887 was for a group of native artisan weavers to set up a mechanized mill to spin wool yarn and then add a shop for power looms some time later. Peasant women made up about 80 percent of the work force in the Gabrovo region. The pro-

portion was less in other textile towns, where a majority of employees lived in the factory on the Russian pattern but still more than in
any other Balkan industry.[11] With women's wages less than 40 percent of the male average, Bulgarian textiles thus made connections
with the cheap supply of rural labor that largely eluded manufacturers in Balkan capitals. After 1900, previously insignificant cotton
goods rose to one third of annual textile output. The combined total
doubled in value from 1904 to 1911, according to Table 8.5. This rate
of growth nearly kept pace with the mini-spurt in total Bulgarian industrial production.

Yet the most important textile industry in any Balkan economy
faced serious limitations on both the demand and supply sides. Artisan output was cut only in half between 1878 and 1888. The new
factories thus faced domestic as well as English and Austrian competition for the home market. This competition kept textile prices
from rising when the general level jumped by perhaps 40 percent in
the 1880s, as connections with the Ottoman market began to be sev-
ered.[12] Textile exports to the Ottoman market suffered from the
enforcement of the general 8-percent Ottoman tariff. Increased Austrian attention to Eastern markets that accompanied recovery from
the 1873–79 depression also hurt. By 1886, Bulgarian textile exports
to the Ottoman Empire and elsewhere shrank from the probable
pre-independence figure of between 20 and 30 percent to 5 percent
of total export value. The proportion had dropped to 3 percent by
1911. The Sofia area imported a majority of its textiles. It was not
until 1906 that a Bulgarian entrepreneur and a Czech technician
opened a small woolen factory in the city to begin cutting into the
sales of Central European goods.[13]

On the supply side, Table 8.5 tells us that the 72 firms operating by
1911 had made little advance in mechanical horsepower per worker
over the 51 firms of 1904 or in average fixed capital over the 30 of
1894. And, as Alexander Gerschenkron has pointed out, the coarse-
ness of Bulgarian wool and the slow spread of cotton cultivation
meant that a majority of the industry's raw materials had to be imported. Any backward linkage from textiles to agriculture was
thereby thwarted.

Fixed capital remained over 90 percent native Bulgarian on the
eve of the First World War.[14] Foreign investment in major firms consisted of one English cotton-spinning enterprise.

The other Balkan textile industries were based in the capital cities.
There they gained minor savings in transporting a light product at
the cost of paying higher wages. None generated increasing exports.
They also lost touch with the tastes of a peasant market that, in Serbia at least, held untapped promise after 1900.[15] No European manu-

TABLE 8.5
BULGARIAN TEXTILE PRODUCTION, 1894-1911
(in millions of leva)

	Number of Firms	Output	Capital	Labor	Horsepower
1894	30		4.9	2,019	
1900	34		6.2	2,544	
1904	51	10.7	8.2	2,743	1,075
1907	57	9.2	12.5	3,063	
1909	61	17.5	12.6	3,971	4,481
1911	72	21.4	15.9	4,257	5,069

Source: Kiril Popoff. *La Bulgarie économique. 1879-1911* (Paris, 1920). p. 351.

facturer appears to have exported to the Balkan states the rough and durable cloth that peasant families growing grain as a cash crop no longer had the time to weave for themselves, much less spin the yarn for.

The hinterlands of the other three pre-1914 states did not include the territory needed for textile manufacture to develop even to the Bulgarian standard. The major Greek cotton-growing area was north of Thessaloniki on Ottoman territory. Efforts to introduce its cultivation in the south went slowly despite good climatic conditions.[16] The major Romanian cloth-producing area with ties to upland household artisans was the Transylvanian town Brașov, just inside Habsburg territory. For Serbia, the southern triangle around Niš and Leskovac that had been annexed in 1878 brought with it a long-established tradition of wool cloth, braid, and hemp rope manufacture in town shops, unmechanized but otherwise run like factories. The area was, however, too dependent on neighboring Bulgarian industry for its rude machinery and on duty-free access to Bulgarian markets. The brief Serbo-Bulgarian war of 1885–86 closed traffic in both directions. The Bulgarian government imposed a ban on exporting such machinery and a tariff that exceeded the authorized 8 percent on all Serbian imports.

In the Leskovac region, rope production became mainly a small-scale rural operation. The export of raw hemp rose. Skilled male labor left for Bulgaria in search of higher wages. A projected Belgian investment in rope production quickly fell through. The successful enterprise of a German immigrant only prevailed after prolonged opposition to modern machinery from the remaining town artisans. The poor quality of local wool discouraged the introduction of steam-powered machinery to textile manufacture. Several native entrepreneurs with artisan backgrounds made the transition but soon transferred most of their resources to cloth production in Belgrade.[17]

Food Processing

The most rapidly growing agricultural industry throughout Central and Eastern Europe during the nineteenth century was the refining of beet sugar. The extent and relative capital intensity of the process in Austria-Hungary and Russia denied any Balkan economy the realistic prospect of an export market there.[18] French and Austrian sugar exports had taken over the Ottoman market. All that Balkan refiners of home-grown sugar beets could therefore hope to do was to capture their own domestic, essentially urban markets from Habsburg imports.

This they did with the exception of Greece, where the one major project for growing and processing sugar beets on a Thessalian estate was sold off to the state and ended by 1909.[19] Elsewhere, several refineries were founded in each country and enough sugar beet cultivation was introduced on the larger peasant holdings to eliminate competing imports by 1911. Yet as subsequent sections will demonstrate, neither European capital or state policy took full advantage of the existing domestic market.

The market itself was more of a problem to the milling and brewing industries. Czech and Austrian German immigrants had opened mechanized and relatively modern flour mills and breweries in Belgrade and Bucharest during the mid-nineteenth century and in Sofia toward its end. Despite a few efforts to organize distribution in the hinterlands, their production remained largely bound to the capital cities.[20] Beer was of course foreign to the taste of the Balkan peasant, who preferred wine or plum brandy. The spring barley and hops needed to produce beer had to be imported.

By 1900, the big flour mills had introduced the European machinery needed to make fine white flour. Yet the Serbian and Bulgarian flour industries as a whole grew during the last two prewar decades through the easy entry into the provincial market of enough small, barely mechanized mills to make the average number of employees, fixed capital, and horsepower the lowest of any branch of Balkan manufacturing (see Table 8.3). The main Bucharest mills, the largest and longest in operation throughout the Balkans, complained of overcapacity for the city's market and an inability to export more than a small fraction of their output from the late nineteenth century forward. Their declining numbers and fixed capital during the last prewar decade translated into stagnating production not only for flour but also for the food processing sector of industry that they dominated.[21] The bigger Bulgarian mills in Ruse and other Danubian ports did export enough of their output to the Ottoman Empire to account for almost half of the industry's annual production. At the same time, delays in shipping the easily perishable product down the Danube through Romanian ports to the Black Sea (railway transport was too expensive) made native mill owners despair of earning acceptable profits once the price of wheat began rising during the last prewar decade.[22]

Meat-packing lacked much domestic potential but was by far the best Balkan prospect for a processed food export to a rapidly growing European market. A mechanized English enterprise at the Danubian port of Galați had attempted to begin exporting processed Romanian beef during the 1860s but failed to last out the decade. The Romanian (and Bulgarian) capacity for meat export, processed or live, declined thereafter. Grain cultivation grew at the expense of pasturage, except in Serbia. Table 8.6 spells out the tremendous advantage in rate of growth that meat-packing had achieved over other sectors of Serbian industry by 1911.

Serbian livestock exporters had first developed widespread interest in slaughtering and processing their own hogs a decade before the 1906–11 tariff war with Austria-Hungary disrupted livestock exports. Hungarian pressure, it may be recalled, had closed the Habsburg border to Serbian livestock for much of 1895–96. Up to this time, the great majority of Serbian hogs and cattle had been slaughtered after the overland drive or rail shipment to the huge Steinbruck stockyards south of Budapest. Among a series of ventures by Austrian or German immigrants dating back to the 1850s, only the small interior partnership of Kleefisch and Scheuss had survived more than a few years.[23]

Only after the prolonged border closure in 1895–96 did the Serbian merchant community show enough financial enthusiasm to launch the state's long-standing plan for a Belgrade stockyards and slaughterhouse. Even then, private investors purchased no more than 20 percent of the projected 1.25-million-dinar stock issue for the *Klanično društvo*. The state had to buy up the rest.

The German-educated Serbian engineer, Miloš Savčić, was able to construct a plant meeting European sanitary specifications by 1897. Yet it had little capacity to produce the sausage and other seasoned produce that offered the best prospects for selling the relatively lower quality meat of Serbian hogs on a European market which, outside of Austria-Hungary, offered less and less of a market for salted pork. After increasing its annual volume steadily to 1902, the Belgrade *klanica* (meat-packing plant) allowed the greater mix of pork products plus eggs and poultry from the several Kleefisch and Scheuss enterprises to overtake its total sales for 1903–05 and again during 1909–10.

The Belgrade plant's sale of salted pork to the British and French

TABLE 8.6
GROSS REAL OUTPUT OF SERBIAN INDUSTRY, 1898-1911
(million dinars in 1898 prices)

BRANCHES	1898	1900	1902	1904	1906	1908	1910	1911
Tobacco and matches[a]	10.0	11.0	11.0	11.0	11.0	12.0	12.0	13.0
Flour	8.0	10.0	11.0	14.0	16.0	20.0	18.0	20.0
Brewing	3.0	3.0	3.0	3.0	4.0	5.0	6.0	7.0
Meatpacking	.3	2.5	6.3	3.5	3.2	5.8	4.6	21.0
Textiles	1.7	4.1	2.2	1.8	1.9	3.0	4.0	5.0
Sugar		1.1			1.5	3.1	4.0	5.0
Leather	.5	.7	.6	.4	.9	1.5	.9	
Chemicals			.1	.1	.1	.2	.2	
Wood Processing	.1	.1	.3	.8	.9	.7	1.5	2.0
Metal Processing		.1		.2	.4	1.0	1.4	
Construction mat'ls	.1	.1	.5	.5	.5	.4	.4	5.2
	25	34	39	37	45	60	61	

Note: (a)State monopolies.

Source: John R. Lampe. "Serbia. 1878-1912." in Rondo Cameron. ed., *Banking and Economic Development: Some Lessons of History* (New York: Oxford University Press. 1972). pp. 125-27.

military early in the tariff war proved to be a one-time boost. All slaughterhouse sales combined were only sufficient to make up a third of the loss in live hog exports to Austria-Hungary that Serbia sustained for 1906–10.[24]

The *Klanično društvo*'s great boom of 1911 must be viewed against this rather unpromising background. Its sales that year accounted for 17 percent of Serbia's total export value and 23 percent of real industrial output (see Tables 6.2 and 8.6). Its advantage over Kleefisch and several other smaller interior concerns rested entirely on the official agreement signed with Austria-Hungary to end the tariff war. The agreement permitted sales to Habsburg territory only from Belgrade slaughterhouses, thus giving the *društvo* a virtual monopoly. The huge markets of Vienna and Budapest, totalling more than the entire Serbian population, were attractive enough to allow the *društvo* to pay prices for live hogs that interior packers could not match. At the same time, another part of the agreement stipulated a minimum weight for slaughtered hogs that excluded lighter bacon animals. Such stock had been instrumental in the widely admired growth of Danish meat exports. Until then Serbia's interior packers had been encouraging peasants to begin breeding them.[25] Political necessity thus confined the prewar horizons for Serbia's infant meat-packing industry to the Belgrade plants and to the Habsburg market. Hungarian protectionist pressure would doubtless have made the latter less accessible the next time the customs union between the two halves of the Dual Monarchy came up for renewal in 1916.

Construction Materials

Far less promising for export, because of their bulk or relative fragility, were construction materials. Their manufacture was encouraged instead by the growth of the Balkan capital cities. Cement, glass, and lumber were essential to the extensive public works undertaken during the 1880s, in the flush of national self-assertion following the Congress of Berlin, and again after 1900. With their high transport costs, these goods appeared to offer native industry, already concentrating in the capital cities anyway, the best prospects for import substitution. Their local production, especially of cement and glass, nonetheless demanded a greater investment in fixed capital and more sophisticated machinery than either textiles or food processing. Essential European technology came most prominently from Habsburg immigrants and not at all from established European enterprises. Multinational European construction companies or even projects would have to await the period since 1950.

The greater size and levels of private or royal wealth already ascribed to Bucharest make the city the logical place to concentrate our attention. Bucharest's production of these materials amounted to ten times the value of comparable output in Belgrade or Sofia on the eve of the First World War.[26] At the same time, Romanian production minus lumber was able to advance its share of real industrial output, as recorded in Table 8.2, only from 7.4 to 10 percent between 1901 and 1915. Lumber's share grew more slowly but did exceed 10 percent of total output by 1915. As early as 1902, when the city's population like that of the other Balkan capitals was still growing rapidly, the organizer of Romania's first and foremost cement plant thought little of the market's prospects for further growth. I. A. Cantacuzino actually took the lead in organizing a cartel to divide up sales at existing levels. Either the biggest Balkan capital city was not big enough, or the tendency to imitate current European practice blinded Romanian producers to the prospects for further growth that the German and Austrian cartel movements, born in the wake of the 1873–79 depression, tended to overlook in their own economies.

Balkan makers of construction materials also had to struggle for access to modern technology and sufficient funding. Romanian access to boyar accumulation of landed wealth helped here. Cantacuzino used his family's huge resources to spend two years studying engineering and cement production in France and Germany. He returned to convert the aforementioned cement plant, founded in Brăila in 1890 also with family funds. It manufactured the Portland cement needed for multi-story, high-stress construction by 1893.

A small firm also launched the second great technical innovation for pre-1914 Romanian cement. Its boyar owner, Prince Bibescu, used the family fortune to introduce the rotating oven in 1908. Never a cartel member, the firm cut prices by 15 percent and improved quality with the new process. In the ensuing scramble to catch up, cartel members violated their association's rules by also cutting prices. The value of the industry's production by 1912 was almost 10 times the figure for 1902, although still constituting less than 2 percent of total industrial output.[27] Real output of these and other construction materials had grown faster between 1901 and 1915 than any other sectors save metal processing and petroleum. According to Table 8.2, their price level actually declined.

The Slovenian director of Serbia's only cement plant until the 1906–11 tariff war, at Ripanj near Belgrade, tried to raise the capital to adopt Portland production in 1902–03. His joint-stock issue found few takers. He managed a partial transition, and took some illicit profits for himself, only by draining the firm's working capital. He finally sold off four fifths of its fixed assets in 1905–06. The value of its output never exceeded 10 percent of the amount imported from the modern Beočin plant in nearby Habsburg Slavonia.[28]

The Romanian lumber and paper industries had an equally large lead over their Serbian and Bulgarian counterparts. Their forest lands were not proportionately greater but, unlike the others, were located along the Habsburg border of Transylvania. Rather than facing competition from just across the border, like Serbian cement manufacturers, Romanian sawmills were able to draw on Austrian capital and immigrant entrepreneurs from Vienna, again with bank assistance. The paper plants used similar German resources from the nearby Carpathian city of Braşov, long the best connecting link on Habsburg territory available to any Balkan economy. These connections, rather than any ties to major European enterprises, were largely responsible for the foreign share of 70 percent in the fixed capital of the Romanian timber-processing industry and 46 percent share for paper.[29] Most of the management and at least one third of the labor force were also foreign.

What growth Serbian cement, lumber, and glass production was finally able to achieve, rising to just 4 percent of real industrial output according to Table 8.6, occurred during the 1906–11 tariff war. It was so closely tied to the support of private Belgrade banks that its treatment belongs in the next section. For now, let us note that the same civil engineer who set up the Belgrade meat-packing plant in 1898 was able to construct a conveyor system for bringing timber down from the remote, rugged uplands of southwestern Serbia to the Drina River for shipment to the main Belgrade sawmill by 1904. Almost ten years earlier, the first native glass factory had been able to open at Paraćin because the Serbian glass importers organizing the venture dispatched the one architectural drafting professor from the Velika Škola in Belgrade (later Belgrade University) to Prague. Posing as a wholesale glass merchant, he visited the most advanced Czech producers and memorized his observations, recording enough of them at night in his hotel room to provide the complete layout and technical procedure for the new Paraćin plant. Such were the variety of indirect ways in which Balkan manufacturers might import contemporary European technology. In this pre-1914 world, a few well-trained specialists could go a long way.[30] The experience of the Serbian glass plant was unusual only because of the willingness of native merchants to invest in such new industrial technology.

The Limited Role of Native Banks

The best practice of European banking, as we have seen in Chapter 7, was transferred more quickly and comprehensively than industrial technology to the Balkan capital cities. Included were several ways to convert merchant savings into industrial investment. An impressive structure of central and private joint-stock banks was already in place by the start of the mini-spurts around 1900. Hence the question of what part this financial structure played in leading, supporting, or discouraging industrial growth.

The attitude of major European banks toward supporting, let alone undertaking, new and therefore risky industrial ventures had changed over the last half of the nineteenth century. The aggressive policies of the Périere and Rothschild brothers, joined by several other French and German banks during the 1850s and 1860s, had largely vanished since the depression of 1873–79. With few exceptions, most notably the French Banque de Paris et des Pays-Bas, the major continental and English banks of the last prewar decades conducted their operations to maximize short-term profits and to minimize the risk from any long-term investments.[31] They had ceased to be the centers of entrepreneurial activity that Alexander Gerschenkron and others have found them to be for mid-nineteenth-century Germany. This was especially true of the Viennese Great Banks that were the closest European models for the Balkan economies. Yet these institutions were also well versed in a variety of special services to industrial enterprises, new and established. Before examining the extent that these services spread to the southeast, we must assess the more conventional bank activities, the flow of short and long-term credit and the entrepreneurial content thereof.

The High Cost of Short-Term Credit

The general increase in total assets after 1900 cut the overall level of central bank interest rates from 8 to about 6 percent. No special reductions, however, were extended to industrial borrowers.

The large Romanian Banca Naţională does not appear to have used its assets, nearly half again those of the Serbian or the Bulgarian banks in per capita terms, to afford industry more than one fifth of the total. This fraction did not exceed the Serbian proportion for 1908–11, despite the fact that the Liberal party leadership of the Romanian bank often spoke of encouraging industrial development. The Serbian bank's management was drawn largely from Belgrade import merchants who had a vested interest in opposing native industry and import substitution.[32]

The significant contrast among central bank policies for short-term industrial lending appears instead from the behavior of the Bulgarska Narodna Banka. During the last prewar decade, while the Serbian central bank was shifting its short-term lending on discounted bills of exchange and current account overdrafts up from 10 to 20 percent of the total, the Bulgarian bank was reducing its industrial proportion from 20 to 10 percent. Annual reports from the Narodna Banka Kr. Srbije suggest that some effort to promote import substitution during the tariff war with Austria-Hungary was responsible for its increasing industrial lending. Bulgarian bank reports are silent on why its fraction fell. One likely reason was that the overwhelming proportion of loans granted to Sofia firms, ten times the value of those granted elsewhere in Bulgaria, ran into the lower profits earned by those enterprises, and became too risky for the bank to continue at their previous volume. The new European banks in Sofia after 1905 also drained credit from the Narodna Banka. Enterprises in Gabrovo, Ruse, and other provincial towns repeatedly complained of their neglect by the Bulgarska Narodna Banka in favor of these banks and the commercially isolated Bulgarian capital.[33]

The general rule among native joint-stock banks was to extend significant short-term credit only to those industrial enterprises in which they held stock or had otherwise contributed to fixed capital. The Serbian banks, especially the large joint-stock institutions in Belgrade, were the exception. They had greater access to short-term credit from the central bank, it will be recalled from Chapter 7, than their counterparts in the other Balkan capitals. A sampling of balance sheets suggests that the proportion of this short-term credit devoted to industry did not even reach the 20 percent granted by the central bank during the 1906–11 tariff war. In addition, these Belgrade banks, typically charged industrial firms an interest rate on either discounted bills or the increasingly dominant current account over-drafts that were 2 to 4 percent above their normal level of 6 or 8 percent.[34] None of this suggests a leading bank role in the creation of short-term credit for the industrial advance after 1900.

Native Long-Term Investment

Better than short-term credit, long-term bank commitments served the relatively larger sectors of modern industry with which Serbia and Romania ended the prewar period. Bulgarian private banks, for their part, made no significant industrial investment.

As also noted in Chapter 7, the Bulgarska Narodna Banka's net-work of branches served to discourage the growth of provincial joint-stock banks. At the start of the industrial mini-spurt in 1895, two of Bulgaria's three large private banks, i.e., ones with paid-in capital of 1 million leva or more, were located in Ruse. The lower Danubian port had been the commercial center for northern Bulgaria before independence made Sofia the political capital. The behavior of both institutions during the last prewar decades is instructive. They were the only two Bulgarian banks to show a consistent entrepreneurial interest in long-term assistance to modern industry. Neither the Gir-dap nor the Bulgarska Turgovska Banka could make a significant con-tribution. By the last prewar years, both had cut the percentage of their assets invested in industrial enterprises from over 10 to 5 per-cent of the total. Given profit rates for these enterprises that never matched the bank's overall percentage, this was not surprising. For all of Bulgaria in 1911, native banks earned an average dividend of 10 percent, while joint-stock industrial enterprises achieved 8 per-cent.[35]

Native Serbian banks did much better. True, they did not provide more mortgage loans to industrial enterprises than had the state-dominated financial structure of Bulgaria.[36] Yet they did furnish two thirds of the 15 million dinars in new long-term investment for native industry during 1906–10. Table 8.7 below indicates the major addi-tion to existing fixed capital that this sum constituted. It included virtually all of the investment in the manufacture of construction ma-terials. To this long-term commitment must be added an undeter-mined amount of short-term credit, principally renewable, hence

potentially long-term overdrafts on current account from the investing bank. These banks were concentrated in Belgrade. Roughly a
dozen accounted for ten times the long-term credit or joint-stock purchases by five interior banks, mainly from two in Niš.

Although exact figures are lacking, the contribution of existing industrial enterprises was not much greater than that of the interior
banks. The Czech or German immigrant families who had owned
respectively the largest flour mill, brewery, and textile factory in
Serbia for a generation or more all made no new commitments during the last prewar decade other than to place investments in a variety of European-backed mining ventures, typically copper, for which
native industry had little use.[37]

At the same time, only two of the investing Belgrade banks took
the entrepreneurial risk of backing new firms during the early years
of the tariff war with Austria-Hungary. The rest aided existing
enterprises. Most were not yet well established but commanded
higher prices for import substitutes once the tariff war began in 1906.
At that time, all of these banks had found themselves with a flood of
new savings deposits from livestock exporters who wanted to earn
interest on funds otherwise idled by the suspension of sales to
Habsburg markets. Balance sheets of the larger Belgrade banks indicate that they were the major recipients of long-term deposits that
more than doubled for all Serbian private banks between 1905 and
1911.[38] For several years prior, moreover, the Belgrade banks had
been searching for new kinds of assets to complement the discounting of bills of exchange on which they had concentrated. Even before
the tariff war cut into the volume of such bills, bank managements
had complained of discounting defaults. More importantly, they
faced declining profit margins as the growing number of banks forced
down short-term rates of interest (see Chapter 7).

The two biggest private banks turned not to industry but to merchant banking. The Izvozna Banka, founded in 1902 by Radical party
interests as a rival to the central bank, opened trade agencies in
Budapest and Berlin two years later, by which time it was also drying
a million dinars worth of prune exports in its own ovens. At the start
of the tariff war, the Izvozna expedited the shipment of three quarters of the Serbian grain exports through Black Sea ports and of all
livestock exports through Thessaloniki. Debts for undelivered livestock to an English middleman named Johnson forced the Izvozna to
withdraw in 1908. Then the next largest Belgrade bank, the Beogradska Zadruga, stepped in. It was unable to do any better than
break even on these shipping commissions for the rest of the tariff
war. Several unprofitable years in Thessaloniki had already passed
when the Zadruga finally turned to an industrial project in 1910, pur-

TABLE 8.7
SERBIAN BANK AND TOTAL INVESTMENT IN INDUSTRY, 1906 AND 1910
(in millions of dinars)

Fixed Investment	1906			1910		
	Native	Foreign	Total	Native	Foreign	Total
Milling	9.5		9.5	15.5		15.5
Brewing	4.0		4.0	3.5		3.5
Other private industry	8.5	4.3	12.8	24.0	6.0	30.0
Mining		11.2	11.2		17.0	17.0
Total	22.0	15.5	37.5	43.0	23.0	66.0

Fixed Investments by Native Banks in 1910

Beogradska Trgovačka Banka	Cement, meat-packing	2.9
Prometna Banka	Sawmill, windowglass	2.5
Beogradska Zadruga	Glass	1.4
Opšta Privredna Banka	Meat-packing	.7
Zemaljska Banka	Hemp, silk	.7
Beogradski Kreditni Zavod	Construction materials	.6
Other Belgrade banks	Miscellaneous	5.4
Niška Trgovačka Banka	Leather, bricks	.7
Niška Akcionarska Štedionica	Cotton spinning	.6
Other Interior banks	Miscellaneous	.2
Total		15.8

Sources: John R. Lampe, "Serbia, 1878-1912," in Rondo Cameron, ed., *Banking and Economic Development: Some Lessons of History* (New York: Oxford University Press, 1972), p. 146; Lampe, "Financial Structure and the Economic Development of Serbia, 1878-1912" (Ph.D. Dissertation, University of Wisconsin, 1971), pp. 306-07.

chasing three quarters of the joint-stock shares in the struggling Paraćin glass factory. Merchant backers had been trying for two years to sell them. The accompanying injection of current account credit allowed the firm to buy badly needed equipment and boost its sales in 1911 at the expense of Habsburg imports.[39]

The Beogradska Trgovačka Banka was the largest single beneficiary of the new deposits occasioned by the tariff war. Its liabilities doubled by 1908 to surpass those of either the Izvozna Banka or the Beogradska Zadruga. By that time, however, the latter two banks had a virtual monopoly on expediting the new southern export trade. Only this preemption led the Trgovačka to found Serbia's fourth cement plant the same year.[40] Its million-dinar investment, plus several hundred thousand in current account credit, made the plant the country's largest. The plant's production for 1908 exceeded the value of imported cement. Profits were nonetheless minimal. The bank did not commit its funds to another industrial venture until 1911. It placed nearly two million dinars in a new Belgrade enterprise for the processing into sausage of meat slaughtered by the *Klanično društvo*. The belated investment, after the slaughterhouse won a monopoly on sales to the Habsburg market, appears to have been the only bank promotion of what we have already seen to be Serbia's best hope for a processed agricultural export.

The other entrepreneurial bank began its activities well before the tariff war but only to shore up sagging profits. The Prometna Banka had been founded in 1896 with the specific purpose of granting secured loans. In the absence of the widespread joint-stock issues that were the common collateral for secured loans in European banking practice, the Prometna had suffered several substantial losses on sales of merchandise received in lieu of defaulted loan repayments by 1901. That year the aforementioned Miloš Savčić, perhaps the only Serbian civil engineer not to use his European training by returning to an army commission, joined the bank's administrative board. He was able to persuade the board to back his project for constructing Belgrade's first steam-powered sawmill with 100,000 dinars only if he accepted personal responsibility for any losses.

Opening in 1903, the sawmill soon accounted for half of Serbian lumber production. Annual profits did not pass 10 percent of paid-in capital, however, until the tariff war permitted a 50-percent rise in prices. Real output doubled between 1906 and 1910, helping to cut the share of imported Austrian timber in domestic sales from two thirds to one quarter. Yet, because of its relatively small size, the Prometna Banka lacked the resources to begin another major industrial enterprise during these last prewar years.

One Balkan bank did possess both the capital and the entrepreneurial initiative needed to promote a broad range of industrial ventures. Bucharest's Banca Marmorosch-Blank dated its founding from 1848. The Marmarosch family of Habsburg Jewish immigrants turned from the Leipzig wholesale trade to merchant banking.[41] Although unincorporated until 1905, the bank joined with a Viennese private bank in 1883 to convert the Austrian Götz sawmill (see above) into a joint-stock company based in Bucharest. In the process, it sold half the shares to Romanian buyers. Yet its use of connections to the Jewish banking community in Central Europe would leave the bank open to unfounded charges of foreign control in future years. By 1890 the bank's director, young Maurice Blank, had joined with the engineer I. A. Cantacuzino to back the conversion of an existing plant to Romania's first production of Portland cement. Yet, like the Prometna Banka's Savčić with his sawmill, the two Romanian entrepreneurs could not initially arrange long-term financing without guaranteeing to make good any losses personally.

Over the next two decades the assets of the Bucharest bank grew steadily. The total was more than 10 times that of the Prometna. Its support for industrial enterprises, new and old, grew apace to include flour mills, breweries, textile plants, sugar and oil refineries, and metal-working shops, over a dozen in all. The annual sum of its long-term industrial investments admittedly never exceeded 5 percent of total assets. But the lines of current account credit to these firms, often long-term in fact and at lower than regular rates of interests, were sufficient to push the bank's aggregate commitment to industry past 25 percent of its assets before war broke out.[42]

Special Services to Industry on the Austrian Model

If the industrial promotions of the large Banca Marmorosch-Blank and the several smaller Belgrade banks appear to have been roughly equal, the overall impact of private banking on Romanian and Serbian industry probably was not. A Romanian advantage that helps to explain that country's larger industrial sector derives from bank underwriting and sale of joint-stock issues accorded manufacturing and mining enterprises. Four native and four European banks in Bucharest held assets that matched or exceeded those of the Banca Marmorosch-Blank. They joined it in rendering this essential, although typically passive, special service in the collection of investment capital. A scattering of indirect evidence suggests that these banks were principally responsible for turning almost one third of Romanian industrial enterprises into joint-stock firms by 1913. This third accounted for over 60 percent of total production.[43] The joint-stock proportion of Serbian enterprises barely exceeded 10 percent, and the share of output just 30 percent.

The Romanian enterprises' access to joint-stock capital and the investors' access to an asset liquid enough to be sold off on short notice constituted an advantage not fully captured by the above figures. A comparison of the fledgling Romanian and Serbian stock exchanges (Bulgaria had none) suggests a far greater disparity. The Bucharest Bourse had admittedly not gone beyond listing stocks for the central bank, a few insurance firms plus state bonds between its founding in 1881 and 1904. Then the last prewar decade witnessed rapid growth. Only the general European crisis of 1907 interrupted it. Both total issues traded and the value of industrial stocks increased. Total value almost doubled between 1908 and 1912, with industrial stocks generally above par and accounting for perhaps 10 percent of the value traded. (Boyar capital might thus be directly tapped for industry without the need to found a family firm like the Cantacuzino or Bibescu cement plants.) While modest in themselves, the Bucharest total and low industrial fraction were fully twenty times the comparable figures for the small Belgrade *Berza*, which had opened in 1894 but scarcely expanded its activity after 1897.[44]

Underwriting of industrial stock issues was undoubtedly the most important of the special services that were offered enterprises in the fashion of the Viennese Great Banks. The larger Belgrade banks concentrated on other services, mainly arranging export sales on commission. They took the lead in setting up insurance offices and separate technical departments to import modern machinery and instruct in its use. They also carried out an assortment of municipal construction projects. As might be imagined, the Prometna Banka's technical department operated under the personal direction of Miloš Savčić. It was active in river dredging, the completion of the Belgrade water system, and several other projects. The department never afforded the bank more than a small fraction of its annual income, however. The small Srpska Banka was the single bank to earn the majority of its profit in this fashion. A shortage of technically trained employees hampered its several construction projects. Among the large Bucharest banks, only the Banka Marmorosch-Blank set up the equivalent of a technical department. The rest did not go beyond hiring agents to collect general business information for their clients.[45]

Limited Penetration by the European Great Banks

The industrial role of the Banca Marmorosch-Blank and the Belgrade banks becomes more impressive when we weigh the smaller contribution of European affiliates in the Balkan capitals. As outlined in Chapter 7, English banks were virtually absent from Romania, Serbia, and Bulgaria after 1900. The several French institutions concentrated their considerable resources on negotiating state loans used largely for armaments and debt repayment.

The French banks participated in industrial activity only to the extent of investment in the processing plants for the state tobacco and match monopolies in Serbia and Bulgaria. Their revenues were in turn pledged to the repayment of French state loans. With the maximization of short-term revenue rather than long-term growth in mind, the Banque Franco-Serbe in Belgrade and the Generalna Banka in Sofia urged the respective state monopolies to go ahead with 40 to 50 percent price increases that effectively closed off a promising export market until the interwar period. As for private industry, the two banks engaged only in a few token ventures.[46] By 1912 the Serbian Finance Minister was expressing his chagrin at the lack of industrial activity from the Banque Franco-Serbe. Nor did these French affiliates favor industry with short-term credit. They generally charged manufacturers 2 to 4 percent above the normal 6 to 7 percent rate.

In Romania, the most active Balkan field for the European Great Banks, French financial institutions played their smallest part. With only a minority interest in the Banca Marmorosch-Blank, they barely held 10 percent of the assets in the big Bucharest banks. The lesser role of French capital in Romanian state loans was doubtless responsible. Similarly, the French proportion of joint-stock capital in Romanian industry was less than 5 percent of the total, ranking sixth behind Belgium among the European shareholders.[47]

The Czech Exception to the Austro-Hungarian Rule

The Austro-Hungarian banks with greatest proximity and the most to gain politically for their government from widespread economic penetration of the Balkan states did even less than their supposed French rivals. In Bulgaria, as Chapter 7 has demonstrated, the major Viennese commitments were made to joint Austro-French banks set up in Sofia. Their purpose was to check a growing German presence. They tendered limited support for several smaller, established industrial enterprises. Austro-Hungarian citizens ranked just behind Germans as joint-stock shareholders in Romanian industry not because of bank penetration but because of a wide scattering of smaller, individual investors.[48] In Serbia, the two separate Austrian and Hungarian banks founded in Belgrade during the 1880s literally ignored industry. Both were rebuked by the Austrian consul general during the tariff war for failing to afford the Dual Monarchy any control over the Serbian capacity to produce import substitutes.[49]

The Balkan activities of several Prague banks show us what opportunities their counterparts in Vienna and Budapest were missing. For Serbia, Czech banks were responsible for about two thirds of the long-term industrial investment undertaken by foreign banks. A spirit of Slavic solidarity may have impelled them to choose Belgrade. Yet we must join Richard Rudolph in wondering whether any of their Balkan affiliates and investments would have materialized had there not been available interest rates several points higher than prevailed in the Habsburg lands and freedom from the long-entrenched interests of the Viennese Great Banks.[50] Whatever the mix of their motives, the Czech banks were in any event outside the circle of Great Power institutions that the Lenin-Hobson thesis of imperialist expansion had argued were busy penetrating less developed economies for national aggrandizement.[51] As we have seen, French and Austrian banks with close ties to their governments may be criticized instead for slighting Balkan economic development to assure themselves of debt repayment and political favor.

The Czech branch banks that opened in Belgrade, Sofia, and Bucharest after 1908 turned most prominently, moreover, to the branch of industry least suited to serve the general Habsburg interest in penetrating Balkan markets. The refining of domestic sugar beets could only discourage sales for what had become the Dual Monarchy's leading export industry. Between 1910 and 1912, the Uverena Banka Branch in Belgrade and the Praeger Kreditbank branch in Sofia sank between 2 and 3 million dinars and leva respectively (half the foreign bank investment in prewar industry) into sugar refineries. Austrian consular reports regarded them as aimed specifically at reducing Habsburg imports.[52] Both succeeded. Similar plans in Romania were frustrated by the First World War. In 1910, the Prague Sporobanka lent the Beogradska Trgovačka Banka the million dinars it needed to avoid liquidating its aforementioned industrial investments. The Belgrade bank also reopened its technical department with a fresh stock of machinery and several Czech technicians to demonstrate its proper use. During 1911–12 the Sporobanka extended the Trgovačka two 600,000-dinar mortgage loans to buy new equipment for its cement plant and to build a railway spur linking the plant to the state line running into Belgrade. Unless the Ballhausplatz could expect to control continued Czech support for these enterprises, the Prague banks had only strengthened the Serbian capacity to resist any future interruption of trade with Austria-Hungary.

The German Great Banks in Romanian Oil

With the one exception of its Romanian oil investments, the participation of the German Great Banks in prewar Balkan industry was much closer to the minute Austrian and Hungarian efforts than to the aggressive Czech activity. The Kreditna Banka founded in Sofia in 1905 by several German banks fulfilled its promise to promote industry only to the extent of supporting a small cement plant in 1912. Like its futile urgings to speed up bank financing for the eastern sections of the Berlin to Bagdad railway, repeated efforts of the German Foreign Office did not succeed in persuading any of the Great Banks to found a branch in Belgrade. The efforts are significant only because they continued into the Serbian tariff war with Austria-Hungary, further reflecting the lack of commercial support that the Dual Monarchy received in the Balkans from its major diplomatic ally.[53]

The prewar petroleum industry was well suited to overcome the banks' reluctance to participate. The European origin of most demand and capital plus the lack of major deposits in Western Europe made foreign, even multinational, investment a necessity.

Attracting several German Great Banks to play a more aggressive role were the Romanian oil fields north of Bucharest around Ploeşti

and Prahova.[54] Petroleum deposits had been discovered during the
1860s but were little exploited until the last decade of the century.
Then American advances in drilling techniques combined with the
Conservative government's permissive mining law of 1895 to throw
open these fields to foreign investors. A high paraffin content hampered distillation into kerosine, still the principal petroleum product.
The Romanian deposits were nonetheless closer to the major European markets than either of the existing sources of supply in Russia
and the United States.

As soon as the new mining law went into effect, the Berliner
Disconto-Gesellschaft and the Bleichröder bank, also of Berlin,
founded the only large foreign bank anywhere in the Balkans that
was specifically intended to promote a new industry. The Banque
Generale Roumaine opened in 1895 with 5 million lei of capital. It
thus became the country's largest financial institution outside of the
central bank. Capital had grown to 15 million by 1913, after the bank
had merged its oil interests with some French capital and the English Telega Company in 1903 to form the Concordia corporation. Its
support for this multinational enterprise and several related ventures
typically took the form of underwriting stock issues and of providing
lines of overdraft credit on current account, rather than direct long-
term investment.[55]

The most powerful single German bank, the Deutsche Bank, took
over the largest Romanian producer, the Steaua Română S.A, in 1902.
The resources of Budapest's Pester Ungarische Komercialbank and
then the Viennese Wienerbankverein (both were supported by
French capital plus some English investment) had proved unable to
overcome technical difficulties in obtaining electric power. They also
lacked access to the huge German market. Smoothing the Deutsche
Bank's way was the furious reaction of the Romanian Liberal party to
the efforts of Standard Oil to apply the price-cutting techniques that
it had used so successfully against American competitors. The powerful Dresdener and Schaffhausen banks formed their own petroleum company in 1904.

All this brought total German investment by 1906 to 74 million
francs worth of the 185 million in fixed capital. Their French and
Dutch rivals were left far behind. Standard Oil was confined to 12.5
million, even less than the native Romanian share of 16 million.[56]
Actual German control of the industry was still greater. Their Great
Banks had taken the leading role in organizing the management of all
the major enterprises save the American and Dutch companies.

At the same time, the technical level of the prewar Romanian oil
industry hardly made extraordinary advances because of German
management. The Great Banks were unwilling to finance the badly

needed pipeline to the Black Sea port of Constanţa unless it could be
tied to a safe loan to the Romanian government. The government
finally completed the pipeline itself by 1915. In addition, the crucial
innovation for processing high paraffin Romanian crude into even-
burning kerosine came from the native chemist Edeleanu. His innovation permitted petroleum products to jump from a few percentage
points to 12 percent of total Romanian export value by 1911 (see
Table 6.6).

The Role of Native Governments

Oil aside, the rest of Romanian industry did not derive its preëmi-
nent position among the pre-1914 Balkan economies from direct
European penetration. Foreign entrepreneurs were crucial to the
Romanian advantage but were typically resident Jews or ethnic
Germans who sought out Central European capital, rather than the
reverse. This active assortment of resident entrepreneurs has already
been identified above as one important Romanian advantage over
other Balkan industrial sectors.

Another appears to have been state support for industry. The
Romanian government afforded manufacturing greater tariff protection, earlier industrial legislation, larger facilities for technical education, and more actual state ownership of enterprises than either
Bulgaria or Serbia, let alone Greece. The relative importance of
these several facets needs to be defined, not only to understand the
Romanian industrial advantage but also to help explain the Bulgarian
disadvantage even compared to Serbia.

Unprotective Tariffs for Infant Industry

For as long as a free international trade has seemed a short-cut to a
small country's rapid economic growth through expanded agricultural exports, tariff protection against imported manufactures has
been held up as a short-cut to the same goal through developing native industry. The pre-1914 Balkan states proved unable, as noted in
Chapter 6, to expand real per capita exports much beyond the levels
reached by the early 1890s. Part of the reason for this failure lay with
the revival of European protectionism from the 1870s forward. By
1879, Germany had taken the lead in imposing duties designed to
limit agricultural imports from Russia and the rest of Eastern Europe.
All the developed economies except Great Britain used tariffs to protect native industry. How irresistible must have been the temptation
for the Balkan states to follow suit for their fledgling manufacturers.

They seemed to fit perfectly List's original definition of infant industries.[57]

Romania made the turn about twenty years ahead of the other Balkan states. The Romanian Liberals had become the one ruling Balkan party to make a strong commitment to industrialization. Rather than rising native bourgeoisie or small estate owners forced out of agriculture by the depression after 1873, their leadership consisted essentially of Francophile families of wealthy Wallachian boyars. The abortive revolt of 1848 first brought them together, in opposition to Habsburg rule of Transylvania. They were generally educated in Paris and based in Bucharest, unlike the Moldavian boyars who tended to stay on their estates and ally their Conservative party with Austrian or German interests. In Bucharest, the Liberals were more conscious of the non-Romanian groups that Chapter 3 recorded as dominating the local commerce and foreign trade of the capital. Unlike the Jewish merchants controlling trade in Moldavian towns, this more mixed group seemed connected to Habsburg rather than Russian interests. The Liberals fastened on industrial development as a means of reducing this non-Romanian influence and the dependence on Habsburg imports at the same time. Some invested personally in manufacturing. Most were determined to break Romania free of the German financiers and pro-Austrian commercial interests who had supported the Hohenzollern King Carol I since his accession to the throne in 1866.

The start of a six-year tariff war with Austria-Hungary prompted the Liberal regime to revise import duties sharply upward in 1886. Further legislation increased some rates in 1891 and, on the occasion of a new commercial treaty with Germany, lowered others in 1893. Major new increases were not forthcoming until the Costinescu tariff of 1906.

That same year Serbia took the occasion of its own tariff war with Austria-Hungary to impose the full terms of its first protectionist legislation on Habsburg imports. Just a few months earlier, however, a new Serbian commercial agreement with Germany gave the latter's goods major exemptions from these 1904 duties. Bulgaria overcame the lack of full independence from the Ottoman Empire to enact a similarly comprehensive tariff by 1906. In the preceding parliamentary debate in the Subranie, the only delegate to speak against the bill asked merely that it be extended to crafts. The rest supported it strongly. Many delegates praised France's highly protective Méline tariff of 1893 and the Romanian measures.[58] The Greek government enacted no comprehensive legislation until 1910, nearly a decade after the disappearance of the high domestic premiums for European currencies that had acted like a tariff (see Chapter 7).

The structure of Romanian tariffs on finished and semifinished imports probably averaged, if conversions from specific rates are correct, over 20 percent ad valorem between 1886 and 1906.[59] Serbian and Bulgarian rates were generally 8–14 percent over this period. Significantly, the Serbian duties on Habsburg manufactures reduced to a few percentage points under the special border rates of the 1881 convention assuring Serbian livestock exports similar treatment. Habsburg imposition of similar border rates on the Romanian Principalities in 1876 had led to a flood of imported Austrian manufactures. Romanian reaction to their attempted renewal in 1886 occasioned the 1886–92 tariff war. A summary of the League of Nations' survey of potential European tariffs in 1913 gives harder evidence of another rise in Romanian duties from the 1906 tariff forward. With higher rates for agricultural as well as finished and semifinished manufactures, the overall Romanian maximum was 33 percent, versus 25 percent for Bulgaria and Serbia. Table 8.8 records these calculations in greater detail. The significantly higher rates on

TABLE 8.8
BALKAN IMPORT TARIFFS IN 1913
(in *ad valorem* percentages)

GROUP OF GOODS	ROMANIA		BULGARIA		SERBIA	
	Minimum	Maximum	Minimum	Maximum	Minimum	Maximum
A. Foodstuffs						
Cereals and flour[a]	39.0	39.0	9.7	9.7	25.7	25.7
livestock	6.6	11.1	2.5	9.7	4.0	20.0
Animal foodstuffs	47.3	47.3	24.0	30.5	23.6	24.7
Fruit and vegetables	19.0	19.0	25.0	25.0	20.8	35.0
Other foodstuffs	59.0	60.0	55.0	56.0	71.0	71.0
Alcoholic drinks and						
tobacco	72.0	72.0	94.5	117.0	25.8	31.0
Average of A	40.5	41.4	36.4	41.3	28.5	34.6
B. Semi-Manufactured Goods						
Textiles	10.0	22.8	18.2	23.0	9.4	20.0
Timber, paper, co	61.0	61.0	16.4	16.4	16.5	20.7
Metals	12.1	15.4	19.7	20.4	17.0	17.8
Chemicals	22.0	35.2	30.0	49.0	17.8	18.3
Mineral oils	27.3	27.3	28.5	32.5	9.5	76.0
Average of B	26.5	32.3	22.6	28.3	14.0	30.6

TABLE 8.8 (continued)

GROUP OF GOODS	ROMANIA		BULGARIA		SERBIA	
	Minimum	Maximum	Minimum	Maximum	Minimum	Maximum
C. Manufactured Goods						
Textiles	18.3	27.0	19.2	22.2	16.8	21.8
Paper	61.3	61.3	31.3	31.3	20.3	32.3
Glass, cement	25.0	31.0	21.0	22.4	30.0	37.0
Metal goods	22.7	45.2	10.7	19.5	14.0	26.8
Machines	5.7	8.0	3.8	3.8	3.9	6.0
Vehicles	18.8	27.0	8.6	8.6	7.3	7.3
Apparatuses	8.3	8.3	12.4	12.4	6.8	6.8
Average of C	22.5	28.5	18.7	20.3	15.0	21.5
Average of A,B,C	27.7	33.0	21.0	24.6	19.4	25.0

Maximum Potential Level	Foodstuffs	Semi-Manufactures	Manufactures	General[b]
Romania	41.4	32.3	28.5	33.0
Bulgaria	41.3	28.3	20.3	24.6
Serbia	34.6	30.6	21.5	25.0
Germany	29.3	19.7	11.7	17.2
France	31.3	66.0	19.7	28.4
Austria-Hungary	36.7	30.6	24.0	25.7
Italy	40.0	43.4	16.7	28.4
Spain	46.0	53.0	49.5	42.0

Notes: (a)Flour only. (b)Excludes alcohol, tobacco and mineral oil.

Source: H. Liepmann, *Tariff Levels and the Economic Unity of Europe* (New York: Macmillan, 1938), pp. 383-400. See pp. 22-27 for a description of the League of Nations list of 140 commodities, their prices and *ad valorem* tariffs, converted from specific duties where necessary, on which these potential rates are based, plus a justification of their unweighted averaging.

semifinished than on finished manufactured goods strongly imply the absence of any coherent policy to favor native industry by easing its access to partly processed inputs like yarn, pig iron, or soda.

The actual ratio of tariff revenue collected to total import values suggests that the Romanian rates were now high enough to deter the import of some European manufactures. Finished and semifinished goods still comprised over four fifths of the country's total imports, as was the case with the other Balkan states save Greece, with its massive wheat purchases. The actual Romanian ratio of 11.4 percent for 1907–11 is well under half the several potential rates just cited. This contrasts with 20.8 percent for Bulgaria and 15.4 percent for Serbia, figures only a few points under the potenti; l rates.[60] The inference is plain. Romanian protection was effective and the others' was not.

Yet when we turn to the particular branches of Romanian industry which faced European competition, we find little evidence that tariff levels played a decisive role in the import substitution that did or did not occur. Wool and cotton textiles received rates approximating 50 percent ad valorem. Romanian producers were still not able to make much headway against English and especially Central European imports. Economists may rightly wonder how much lower the real rate of such a tariff was for a country like Romania or any other Balkan state whose central bank insisted, with increasing influence and independence, on maintaining parity with the French gold franc throughout this period. The result, as we saw in Chapter 7, was undoubtedly to overvalue the Balkan currencies in the face of recurring trade deficits. The implicit import subsidy of some 15 to 20 percent ad valorem, if we can judge Romania by the 1890s *agio* that Bulgaria and Serbia overcame to achieve parity with the franc after 1900, thus reduced the nominal tariff of 50 percent to a more moderate level.

Nor did the branches of Romanian industry that successfully excluded European competition make their major advances in response to higher import duties. Cement tonnage had already increased fourfold from its low point in 1901 to the passage of the 1906 tariff. The duty on cement more than doubled to 48 percent ad valorem only at that time. This rate nonetheless fell short of the Serbian level of 61 percent levied in 1906.[61] As we have seen in the previous section, Serbian cement plants were able to expand production but could not use the higher rate to cut substantially into the imported majority of domestic consumption. The further fourfold increase in the volume of Romanian cement production over the 1906–12 period has already been attributed to the introduction of the rotating oven.

Paper and sugar manufacture were the other two big branches of Romanian industry to succeed at import substitution. During the late 1890s both progressively expanded their share of a domestic market previously dominated by Habsburg imports.[62] By 1901, Romanian paper accounted for over 85 percent of domestic sales and sugar over 95 percent, proportions that were maintained until the First World War. Protective tariffs cannot explain their advances between 1896 and 1911. The 1893 tariff had increased their accorded specific duties under the 1891 tariff several fold to 30 to 40 percent ad valorem. There they stayed despite a 5 to 10 percent price increase until the 1906 tariff. Refined sugar stayed the same in 1906, while the levy on some varieties of paper import did more than double to 80 to 90 percent. Yet this boost is best explained as compensation to domestic manufacturers forced to raise prices following the 1906 doubling of tariffs on wood pulp and cellulose to 100 percent. These essential inputs for paper production were still largely imported from Austria-Hungary, even after 1906. Their prices plus the new tariff were still less than the cost of local pulp and cellulose. In economists' terms, the effective tariff on the value added to paper by Romanian producers was simply restored to its previous level. Assuming that these inputs were half of paper production costs, the effective tariff on Romanian value added remained under 50 percent ad valorem.[63] This attempt to coordinate protection of the timber and paper industries simply passed the resulting price increase for paper along to a domestic market already limited by size. Why higher prices did not prevent the doubling of paper tonnage sold between 1906 and 1912 will concern us next.

Industrial Legislation

However unimpressive their actual reduction of imported manufactures, the Romanian tariffs of 1886 and 1891 helped create a climate in which entrepreneurs could believe investment in domestic industry would yield at least long-term prospects for satisfactory profit. Two pieces of industrial legislation passed at the same time probably did more to promote this climate than the prospect of tariff protection.

In 1886, the Liberal government revised the commercial code of 1840. The new version drew freely on provisions of the recent Italian code, thereby facilitating joint-stock incorporation rather than hindering it as the old, French-style code's favoritism for partnerships had done. Bulgaria and Serbia did not pass similar commercial codes until 1896, and pre-1914 Greece not at all.[64] The incorporated proportion of Romanian industrial enterprises clearly surpassed those of the other Balkan states by the last prewar years, as noted in the preceding section. The only branches of Romanian industry other than oil in which joint-stock enterprises greatly predominated were sugar, paper, and lumber. Their greater access to long-term capital through incorporation was facilitated by a second piece of legislation.

In 1887, the Liberal government gave most Romanian industry direct encouragement, a decade ahead of similar measures in Bulgaria and Serbia. Firms with at least twenty five employees and some modern machinery and minimum capital received exemptions from import tariffs and state taxes, plus free access to state land. Railway rebates up to half the cost of freight were added later, and the number of employees cut to twenty. Preceding this comprehensive legislation, however, had been bills in 1881 and 1882 that had granted such concessions for fifteen years to paper and sugar manufacturers.[65] They included special privileges not accorded other branches in 1887. The state agreed to furnish the few paper manufacturers low-priced timber from its land and to buy all of its production. The latter provision persisted until the First World War, thus explaining why total sales continued to grow rapidly even after the 1906 tariff forced up the price of imported inputs and hence output. Sugar production received a flat subsidy per kilogram that approached 15 percent of the retail price. Hungarian legislation from 1881 had begun this practice as compensation for having no import tariffs, in the Dual Monarchy's customs union, against Austrian and Czech manufactures. Here the subsidy supplemented the tariff. We can gauge the subsidy's greater importance from the upsurge in paper and sugar production that displaced Habsburg imports. This upsurge occurred immediately after the renewal of all privileges to those branches for another fifteen years in 1896.[66]

Benefits to the rest of Romanian industry always lagged behind the 6 to 15 percent of paid-in capital granted consistently to paper, sugar, and metallurgy. The overall proportion amounted to only 4.1 percent in 1904 and probably declined thereafter. High profits exceeding 15 percent in the few branches with extra privileges and among the European oil companies contrasted with rates of 8 to 10 percent in other areas. They were responsible for giving Romanian industry the highest Balkan rate of aggregate profits, roughly 10 to 15 percent of paid-in capital during the last prewar decade versus 5 to 10 percent for Serbia and Bulgaria.[67]

The experience of Bulgarian industry from 1897 forward reinforces our impression that the modest privileges of such blanket tax and tariff exemptions could not achieve a decisive turn toward import substitution. Combined Bulgarian exemptions exceeded 4 percent of industrial capital in 1912. Yet they had failed to raise the recipients' average profits past the 8 percent available as a mimimum for investment in banking or commerce, let alone displace the European imports that exceeded even the domestic sales of the Balkans' biggest textile industury. The one noticeable effect of these exemptions was to favor firms in Sofia. The concentration of low-profit industry in an isolated capital, with poor trade connections even to the rest of Bulgaria, only increased.[68]

Bulgarian industrial legislation elicited a weaker response than the Romanian not just because it came later, at the start of the agricultural depression during the late 1890s, and because it failed to concentrate on a few branches. It also lacked the support of a powerful political party like the Romanian Liberals. In the absence of a native class as wealthy and influential as the Romanian boyars, Prince Ferdinand had used patronage in Sofia's ruling bureaucracy to divide both the emerging Liberal and Conservative parties into several factions before 1900. Only one faction had direct ties to the academic economists who favored unlimited aid to manufacturing in the so-called Industrialization Debate of the last two prewar decades. Their statements are almost identical to those of the Romanian Liberals. They lack only the emphasis on economic independence from Austria-Hungary.[69] The Bulgarian speakers differ principally in the far smaller weight that they carried in national politics. In addition, several factions of academic economists and of the fragmented political parties favored amending the 1890s legislation to favor craft production as much as modern industry. So did the artisan majority of the socialist movement. Their combined weight was sufficient to prevent the granting of special, Romanian-style privileges to certain industries and to amend the 1890s legislation to include artisan manufacture by 1909. In Romania, where over half the artisans were not ethnic Romanians, a similar campaign had no success, and the socialist movement was slower to develop.[70]

However much the Romanian Liberals may have encouraged private investors by their repeated endorsement of native industry, their repeated periods in power hardly produced a systematic, centralized program for coordinating tariff and industrial legislation in order to achieve aggregate goals for native industry. No European government, we must emphasize, had such a program before the First World War. Protective tariffs were assembled piecemeal in response to the sometimes conflicting demands of separate enterprises and cartels. Romanian legislation was no different. Recall the need to boost the duty on paper because of increased protection for native wood pulp and cellulose. Readiness to resolve such conflicts at the consumer's expense were not confined to the private sector. In 1899, the Liberal Finance Minister and noted Romanian industrialist, I. A. Cantacuzino, did not hesitate to help repair his government's budget deficit with a 30-percent excise tax on sugar. There it stayed until the war, at double the subsidy to the branch of Romanian industry most favored by state support. Little wonder that the five sugar refineries, despite their largely Western European ownership and hence their access to outside investment capital, felt price competition so unpromising that they had formed a sales cartel by 1902.[71] State sanction of this defensive arrangement followed a few years later. Legislation simply banned any new producers.

The still more limited effect of the Serbian law for industrial encouragement suggests what fate would have awaited both the Bulgarian and the Romanian legislation had their national assemblies been more powerful and more representative. The overwhelming majority of peasant delegates in the Serbian Skupština had little taste for raising the prices they paid for manufactures. Then the tariff war of 1906–11 made greater independence from Habsburg markets and goods imperative. The higher general tariff of 1906 still left Serbia with the lowest duties among the Balkan states. During the National Assembly's debate of the tariff in 1904, no delegate opposing or favoring the measure raised the issue of industrial protection. The higher new duties were approved solely on the fiscal grounds of adding revenue to assure European debt repayment. The industrial encouragement law of 1898 offered the familiar tax and tariff exemptions, but only a fifth of the eligible enterprises were ever accorded these privileges.[72] Parliamentary infighting between two factions of ruling Radicals produced a virtual two-party system by 1903. Both parties opposed projects sponsored by rival members. Their gains in partisan political advantage and peasant support apparently outweighed any commitment to industrial development even for the younger Belgrade-based Independents.

State Enterprise and Technical Education

None of the ruling Balkan parties thought in terms of using tax revenues to found state factories or to compensate existing owners and nationalize their enterprises. The governments' European creditors would scarcely have approved either initiative, especially where their own firms were concerned. As it was, neither of the two approaches came within the ideological spectrum or the practical competence of prewar Europe. The total mobilization of the First World War was needed to force governments into their first experiences with national planning. Even the Romanian Liberals, the ruling party most inclined to resist foreign enterprises, stopped short of demanding that the state seize or buy out the European oil companies. These bank-sponsored firms had moved in to take advantage of the 1895 law permitting easy exploitation of state lands. Liberal leaders contented themselves with blocking the intrusion of American Standard Oil after 1900 by granting further concessions to the very German banking interests that the rival Conservatives had intended to favor with the 1895 law in the first place.[73]

Two interrelated state activities nonetheless contributed directly to industrial growth in the pre-1914 Balkans and laid some groundwork for the appearance of dominant public sectors in socialist economies since 1945. These were the state railways and facilities for technical education. The railways appear to have determined the list of state industrial enterprises, arsenals excepted, and stimulated related private production. They also pushed the secondary school system toward vocational or scientific training. Hence one further explana-

tion of prewar Romania's greater industrial stirrings may be anticipated. Its more extensive railway network, with a majority in place
before 1890, should have generated more related enterprises and
trained more employees than its Serbian or Bulgarian counterparts.

The state-owned enterprises created to finance the CFR, the
Romanian state railways, were not the source of this greater
encouragement. As with Serbia and Bulgaria, state monopolies for
tobacco, matches, salt, and vegetable oil had been established by the
early 1880s for the purpose of collecting predictable revenue that
would aid in repaying the European loans initiated by Balkan railway construction. By 1902 the Serbian and Bulgarian monopolies
had incorporated representatives of the major European lenders and
explicitly mortgaged earnings to assure repayment of foreign borrowing that had gone well beyond the needs of railway construction (see
Chapter 7). The tobacco monopolies were by far the largest and most
likely to export a significant share of their production. Yet from the
start these regimes sought only to maximize tax revenues on domestic sales, at the expense of expanding cultivation or exports. Once
their revenues covered the foreign debt annuity, the monopolies saw
no reason to expand further. The European representatives went
along with the established policy of paying low prices to peasant
growers and charging all customers 40 percent above cost. Production grew, but very slowly. Serbia's cultivated area did not increase
at all during the period 1899–1912, and that of the other two only
during the last few prewar years. Bulgarian tobacco exports barely
amounted to one percent of total value, versus about 15 percent during the interwar period. A fourfold jump in cultivated area had followed greater access to the German market during the First World
War.[74]

The coal mines that were the other state enterprise spawned by
railway construction confronted limited deposits. The reserves that
have made present-day Yugoslavia, Bulgaria, and Romania largely
self-sufficient in coal lay in territories added since 1912. The state
mines that provided over 90 percent of pre-1914 tonnage for Bulgaria
and over half for Serbia and Romania had virtually nothing left, after
supplying the railways, for the rest of the economy. Prewar industrial
stirrings were largely fueled with the English imports that furnished
40 percent of the coal consumed in Bulgaria and over half in Serbia
and Romania. Had war not intervened, those imported proportions
would have had to rise still further if the threefold rise in Balkan coal
consumption in the first decade of the twentieth century were to be
repeated in the second.[75]

Maintaining and repairing the railway network itself was instead
the source of the last advantage enjoyed by Romanian industry over

its neighbors. The longer trackage, more bridges, larger rolling stock, and more extensive connections to port facilities gave the Romanian network the largest operating expenses of any enterprise in the pre-war Balkan states. Table 8.9 reflects its disproportionately greater revenues and expenses than other state railways or enterprises. All of these railways were obviously profitable. Less obviously, the shops at their railheads worked on a greater quantity of machines and metals than any other in the country, although producing little.

Their connection to overall industrial growth derives from goods produced elsewhere in the economy for their use in repair and maintenance. Only the Romanian railways recorded significant linkage. In the absence of any iron ore and precious little coal, such backward linkage could not include the manufacture of locomotives, rolling stock, and rails on the pattern that Alexander Gerschenkron found so decisive for the impressive industrial growth of late Tsarist Russia.[76] Enough smaller parts and other ironware were nonetheless produced to make the metal-processing sector of private Romanian industry much larger than the comparable sectors in Serbia and Bulgaria. According to Table 8.2 and 8.6 above, the value of private Romanian metal production in 1915 was over ten times the Bulgarian and thirty times the Serbian figure for 1911. While the latter two accounted for only 1 to 2 percent of manufactured output, Romanian metallurgy was responsible for 10 percent. Its real rate of growth since 1900 was, moreover, the highest among all branches of Romanian industry save petroleum. Its price level was virtually unchanged. Activity in the oil fields undoubtedly contributed something to this growth. But the continuing location of almost all metallurgical enterprises in the railheads of Bucharest, Brăila, Galaţi, and Craiova plus some notion of exactly what they produced suggest that the railway and related infrastructure absorbed a majority of their production.[77]

Public vs. Private Sources of Pre-1914 Growth

Few owners of the dozen enterprises just discussed were ethnic Romanians. Of these, the Costinescu nail factory was the one large concern. Its founder too came from a wealthy Wallachian boyar family. All the same, scattered Austrian investors provided half of its 3 million lei in paid-in capital and non-Romanian Habsburg immigrants one third of its labor force. Even counting Costinescu's firm as entirely Romanian, three quarters of the joint-stock capital in metal production was foreign-owned. Like the timber-processing and paper manufacture described above, these owners were typically small German or Jewish investors from Austria-Hungary, rather than the Great Banks or big Western European companies. Most had immigrated permanently to Romania.

TABLE 8.9
RAILWAYS AND OTHER STATE ENTERPRISES, 1895-1912
(in millions of lei, leva and dinars = francs)

	ROMANIA		BULGARIA		SERBIA	Surplus or Deficit
	Revenues	Surplus	Revenues	Surplus	Revenues	
Railways						
1895	43.0	+11.1	4.1	+ .7	5.8	+2.1
1900	50.2	+14.5	6.?	+ 2.3	6.9	+2.7
1905	70.9	+32.4	11.2	+ 3.8	8.3	+4.0
1910	97.3	+36.9	22.6	+ 7.5	12.3	
1911	110.9	+45.8	27.7	+10.2	15.5	
1912	111.8	+39.7	24.8	+ 5.5		
Tobacco Monopoly						
1895	36.1	+25.8			9.3	-3.7
1900	37.3	+28.0			12.2	-4.0
1905	40.4	+30.5	17.3		14.6	-4.2
1910	51.4	+36.4	20.8			
1911	56.7	+40.0	21.1			
1912	60.9	+44.1				
Other State Monopolies						
1895					5.6	
1900	2.7	+1.7			7.3	
1905	3.1	+2.1			9.1	
1910	3.5	+1.9	8.8			
1911	3.9	+2.1	9.5			
1912	4.1	+2.1	9.8			
Coal and Other Mines						
1895					2.0	
1900					2.3	
1905	.2					
1910	.2		2.6			
1911	.3		3.1			
1912	.3		3.5			

Sources: *Anuarul statistic al României, 1915-1916* (Bucharest, 1919), pp. 117-30, 201, 211-12, 252-53; *Statisticheski godishnik na Bulgarskoto Tsarstvo, 1912* (Sofia, 1915), pp. 200-02, 312-13, 352-57; *Statistički godišnjak Kr. Srbije, 1905* (Belgrade, 1906), pp. 339, 349, 355, 388-99.

Their foreign origins did not hold much promise, however, for the continued growth of these several branches, whose production combined with the Western European sugar refineries to account for half of the value of Romanian manufacturing in 1915. Liberal antipathy to foreign interests extended from the Western European sugar companies to these immigrants whose entrepreneurship was one of the major advantages enjoyed by Romanian industry over that of the other Balkan states before 1914. Indeed, the party's famous slogan of the 1920s—*prin noi înşine* (through ourselves alone)—which led to the national if not state takeover of Austrian firms and sustained pressure on Jewish interests, had already appeared in a prewar pamphlet.[78]

We must await the account of interwar industry in Chapters 11 and 12 to judge whether the new native management of such enterprises performed more or less efficiently and whether their relations with the government ministries who installed them prepared the way for state control after 1945. For now, we can condemn the non-Romanian firms dominating these most rapidly growing sectors only for a failing that was common to the rest of private industry. Like the Liberal Costinescu's nail factory, they tended to rely on immigrant management and skilled labor, with little or no effort to train ethnic Romanians for these positions.

The railway administration itself made noteworthy progress along these lines. It consistently employed civil engineers who were ethnically Romanian and, unlike the other Balkan state railways, relied on a state school for their training. The National School of Bridges and Roads dated from 1864. Several reorganizations were needed before it could produce graduates comparable to those of its famous French namesake. By the 1890s, a former instructor at the school, now Chief Engineer of the CFR, was recruiting its civil engineers. Their first great project was to build the bridge across the Danube at Cernavoda, needed to connect the Black Sea port of Constanţa with Bucharest and the Wallachian grain trade. Using students currently at the National School to assist them, they completed the modern iron bridge by 1896. They began the further task of tunneling through coastal bluffs down to the docks in collaboration with several European firms but were able to finish the project on their own by 1899. In subsequent years the National School continued to send the state railway a majority of its graduates and performed other services like chemical testing for the CFR.[79]

Remaining to be answered with badly needed research is the question of how the activities of this largest prewar state enterprise may have stimulated the growth of more technical and vocational training than any other Balkan system of public education provided.

Such an inquiry might answer the wider question of whether this training was more result or cause of the larger Romanian industrial stirrings. More certain at this writing is the absence of such a technical emphasis in the Serbian or even in the broader and better funded Bulgarian system of primary and secondary education.[80] The latter's achievement of the highest literacy rate in the pre-1914 Balkans rested on instruction in native and European culture. However great its significance for the future of Bulgarian nationalism and socialism, this emphasis denied Bulgarian industry, the relative laggard among the three surveyed in this chapter, one of the few direct stimuli that a pre-1914 state could offer.

Meanwhile, Balkan state revenues continued to rise at one or two points faster than the roughly 10 percent annual increase in nominal export values after 1900. State expenditures clearly failed to promote some alternative to the unprocessed agricultural products upon whose sharply, if temporarily, rising prices this export boom and the growing state budgets were based.

The prewar industrial stirrings drew most of their capital and entrepreneurship from other sources. The native bankers of Serbia and the immigrant entrepreneurs of Romania proved the most effective, the existing class of import merchants and the founders of pre-1900 factories the least. Yet even the former were unable to do more than modernize sectors that remained relatively small in the national aggregates of industrial production. Serbian meat-packing and Romanian oil refining involved more initial risk and investment than they cared to undertake. Limited domestic demand and rising wages in the wake of scarce urban labor and increasing food prices were serious constraints. The restricted money supply and overvalued currency, enforced by the state's desire to ensure access to European loans, also worked against the possibility of their doing better, especially in international markets.

At the same time, the per capita production of Serbian and Romanian industry by 1911 amounted to over 75 percent of corresponding averages both for nominal export value and government revenues. The Bulgarian proportion approached 60 percent.

Bulgarian and Serbian industrial production was growing more rapidly during the last prewar decade than either exports or revenues. Given the rather gloomy prospects for the continued growth of unprocessed agricultural exports on a real per capita basis as described in Chapter 6, all three industrial sectors had laid at least the groundwork for an alternative approach to economic growth later in the twentieth century.

9.
Economic Development in the
Imperial Borderlands to 1914

The four independent, modernizing Balkan states entered the last prewar years with roughly half the territory of their postwar successors still under Habsburg or Ottoman control. This chapter confronts some obvious yet neglected questions about how these assorted borderlands fared in a wider imperial economy. How well were Slovenia, Croatia-Slavonia, Dalmatia, the Vojvodina, Transylvania, and Bosnia-Hercegovina integrated with Austria-Hungary, and Macedonia and northern Greece with the Ottoman Empire? How did the course of their economic development compare with and affect that of their independent neighbors? Their positive and negative experiences as imperial provinces constitute the economic legacy that they brought with them into the successor states after the First World War. Part III of this volume, dealing with that subsequent period, cannot properly begin without such a balance sheet.

Preconceived notions of what the balance might be are difficult to avoid. Western economic theory suggests that the relatively greater industrial development in the northern Habsburg regions would push ahead agricultural production in these southern and eastern borderlands. Conversely, the absence of modern industry elsewhere in the Ottoman Empire should have opened the way for manufacturing in Thessaloniki on the Aegean Sea and perhaps in Skopje as well. Two large imperial markets beckoned. The Habsburg population exceeded 50 million and the Ottoman 20 million by 1910, in contrast to a combined total of less than 20 million for the Balkan states. Marxist economics emphasizes supply rather than demand, alerting us to the role of European governments and the Great Banks in mobilizing the

278

necessary capital and labor to exploit new sources of expanding profit. Interwar Austrian and Hungarian studies have argued, without enough disaggregation, that the Habsburg market and investment therein significantly raised the level of development and income of all component parts; scholars from Southeastern Europe generally disagree, without extending the analysis beyond their particular ethnic area.[1]

Our inquiry draws on both sets of scholarship and scattered statistical data to reach some rather surprising conclusions. With the important exception of livestock, the agricultural development of the Habsburg borderlands did not much respond to the imperial market, nor did public or private investment promise better days. Grain output during the last prewar decades lagged well behind that of independent Romania and was not much better than that of Ottoman Macedonia. Industry, on the other hand, made important progress in Austrian Slovenia and Hungarian Croatia/Slavonia and Transylvania. It scarcely stirred in Ottoman Greece and Macedonia, where the Great Banks were better represented by their own branches than in the Habsburg borderlands.

In order to understand these apparent paradoxes, we must do more than examine the general trend toward agricultural stagnation and industrial development. The fiscal and monetary conditions that divided investment among agriculture, industry, and other uses again deserve the separate treatment that they received in Chapter 7. As we have seen there for the Balkan states, a restrictive monetary policy supported by European lenders worked against tariffs and other fiscal measures that encouraged industry. For the Habsburg borderlands, foreign loans and tariffs were impossible in the absence of independence. Only railway construction afforded state policy the occasion to make a positive contribution to economic development. It remained for native banks and capital from the Great Banks of Vienna, Budapest, and Prague to promote specific industries. Still, no comprehensive plan emerged for the development or exploitation of any borderland as a whole.

Imperial Markets and Estate Agriculture

The potential advantage of the large imperial marketplace emerges clearly from a calculation of per capita exports in the borderlands. The population of the various Habsburg territories and Ottoman Macedonia, according to Table 9.1, was generally somewhat smaller than that of the independent Balkan states and rose less rapidly after 1900 because of emigration. Yet even relatively backward Bosnia-

Hercegovina, as reflected in Table 9.2, exported more per capita than all the Balkan states save Romania. Slovenia with 121 francs (115 Kr.) in 1913, surpassed the Romanian average of 98 francs per capita. (Ottoman Albania, like Montenegro among the independent states, generated such a negligible amount of exports and experienced so little other interaction with its neighbors and the rest of Europe that its stagnant rural economy is excluded from the present analysis.)[2]

At the same time, the borderlands did not develop the same export surpluses that were appearing after 1900 for all the Balkan states save Greece. The sources for Table 9.2 suggest slight trade deficits for Slovenia and Croatia. The Bosnian deficit doubled from 13 to 26 percent of export value during the period 1903–11. The financing of capital imports by means of export surpluses was thus frustrated. Not much wheat or corn, presumably the largest potential exports, were moving to imperial markets. Nor did the systems of land tenure appear any more promising for the future growth of agricultural exports than the peasant smallholding and sharecropping that characterized the independent states (see Chapter 6). The large estates of the Ottoman and Habsburg borderlands did not respond to their export opportunities with major efforts to modernize crop cultivation.

Thessaloniki and the Macedonian Chiflik Estates

The focus for agricultural exports to Ottoman markets from northern Greece and Macedonia should have been Thessaloniki. The port's sizable trade with Istanbul and Anatolia by the eighteenth century may be recalled from Chapter 1. The provisioning of Ottoman-based British and French troops during the Crimean War and then the opening of the Suez Canal in 1868 provided further stimuli to trade within the Ottoman Empire. The city itself grew from 50,000 to 120,000 between 1865 and 1895, making it a major urban market in its own right.[3]

The Aegean port virtually ceased growing during the last two prewar decades, however. World grain prices rose and the Balkan states' exports boomed with them. Thessaloniki (and nearby Kavalla) all the same developed a chronic import surplus that was half again export value. Grain imports came mainly from the Balkan states. They grew to exceed purchases from the Macedonian hinterland after 1900. Wheat, the principal grain in international trade and long the staple for Istanbul, had become the largest Macedonian crop by far since the Crimean War. Yields were respectable even without modern methods. The soil and climate favored wheat and discouraged corn cultivation. Yet Macedonian wheat acreage did not even match the Serbian total by 1910, despite twice the total area.[4] The relatively

TABLE 9.1
POPULATION OF IMPERIAL BORDERLANDS AND BALKAN STATES, 1890-1910
(in thousands)

Imperial Borderlands	1890	1900	1910	Annual % Growth rate 1890-1900	Annual % Growth rate 1900-1910	Pop.per sq. km.
Croatia/Slavonia	2,202	2,416	2,622	.99	.82	61.7
Slovenia	1,234	1,268	1,321	.18	.35	51.3
Transylvania	3,615	3,942	4,226	.87	.70	37.1
Bosnia-Hercegovina	1,402	1,678	1,898	1.81	1.24	35.8
Macedonia (Ottoman)	ca 2,000	2,248	ca 2,400			
Balkan States						
Romania	5,318[b]	5,957[c]	6,966	1.69	1.51	55.2
Bulgaria	3,311[b]	3,744	4,338	1.44	1.48	45.0
Serbia	2,162[d]	2,494[d]	2,911[d]	1.44	1.56	60.3
Greece	2,187[d]	2,434[d]	2,631[d]	1.54	.71	41.6

Notes: (a)Within borders as narrowly defined by the Hungarian statistical yearbook. (b)1892 census. (c)1899 census. (d)1889, 1896 and 1907 censuses respectively.

Sources: *Annuaire statistique hongroise, 1910* (Budapest, 1912), p. 12; Toussaint Hočevar, *The Structure of the Slovenian Economy, 1848-1963* (New York: Studia Slovenica, 1965), pp. 81-83; Nikolai Jarak, *Poljoprivredna politika Austro-Ugarske u Bosni i Hercegovni i zemljoradničke zadruge* (Sarajevo, 1956), p. 312; L. Sokolov, *Industrijata vo NR Makedonija* (Skopje, 1961), p.5: Table 6.1 above.

TABLE 9.2
PER CAPITA EXPORTS OF IMPERIAL BORDERLANDS AND BALKAN STATES,
1903-1911
(in millions of franc equivalents)

Imperial Borderlands	Average Exports 1903-05	Average Exports 1908-10	Exports 1911	Exports Per Capita 1911
Croatia/Slavonia			152^a	56^a
Slovenia			163^b	121^b
Transylvania				
Bosnia-Hercegovina	95	126	128	67_c
Macedonia (Ottoman)		28		31^c
Balkan States				
Romania	358	487	692	98
Bulgaria	138	117	185	42
Serbia	65	90	117	40
Greece	87	119	141	46

Notes: (a)Manufactured exports for 1912 from firms employing over 20 workers and using some mechanical horsepower, plus livestock and related exports. (b)All exports for 1913. (c)All exports for 1910.

Sources: Rudolf Signjar, *Statistički atlas Kr. Hrvatske i Slavonije, 1875-1915* (Zagreb, 1915), p. 49; Toussaint Hočevar, *The Structure of the Slovenian Economy, 1848-1963* (New York: Studia Slovenica, 1965), pp. 116-17; Ferdinand Schmid, *Bosnien und die Herzegovinien* (Leipzig, 1914), p. 550; Great Britain Diplomatic and Consular Reports, *Annual Series* (1911), no. 4797; M. Dimitrijević, *Privreda i trgovina u novoj Srbije* (Belgrade, 1913), p. 123; Rudolph Bićanić, "Ekonomske promene u Hrvatskoj izazvane stvaranjem Jugoslavije, 1918," *Prilozi za ekonomsku projijest Hrvatske* (Zagreb, 1967), pp. 86-87.

constant cultivation of tobacco in Seres and other areas accounted for less than 10 percent of total crop acreage but nearly 10 times the export value of wheat and wheat flour, if we include the bulk of tobacco exports leaving from Kavalla.[5] Tobacco amounted to over half of total Aegean exports but went largely to the Italian and Austro-Hungarian tobacco monopolies through Trieste. Other major exports (sheep and goat skins, silkworm cocoons, and opium) also went outside imperial territory. Only wheat flour (to Istanbul) and the still smaller value of livestock (to Egypt) stayed within Ottoman boundaries. Thessaloniki even became a net importer of flour by 1910.

The port's failure to develop a larger flour industry or to export more to grain-hungry Ottoman cities did not lie within itself. As we shall see in the next section, capital from Greek merchants and European banks was not in short supply. Instead, the semifeudal and ill-defined system of land tenure in the Macedonian hinterland bore the basic responsibility. It restricted grain cultivation. Independent peasant smallholdings were rare, accounting for less than 10 percent of agricultural land. They were essentially properties of the Turkish peasant minority. The Macedonian and Greek majority of the peasantry remained largely in the *chiflik*, or privately owned villages, described in Chapter 1. Their agricultural land was 60 percent of the Macedonian total. From their origins in the weakening of Ottoman central control over state agricultural land in the eighteenth century until final dissolution in the First Balkan War in 1912, their ownership was concentrated in the hands of Ottoman officers and officials, typically Turks or Albanians. Bulgarian surveys undertaken in 1908 and after the First Balkan War indicate that such individuals still controlled over 90 percent of the *chiflik* villages of the Skopje, Bitola, and Thessaloniki districts that comprised Ottoman Macedonia. Even at this late date, a Bulgarian scholar recently concluded, merchant or foreign capital was making no greater inroads into the ownership of these estates than it had´ during the early nineteenth century.[6]

The primitive and exploitative methods of cultivation had also stayed the same. The *chiflik* holdings were not large to begin with. In the representative region of Prilep, two thirds of these "estates" were a string of several villages with less than 50 hectares of arable land combined; almost all were less than 200 hectares. They were further divided into a series of unconsolidated plots of 5–10 hectares. To the plots groups of peasants, sometimes an entire village, brought their own oxen and primitive wooden plows. The peasants owed half of their crop, usually wheat, to the *chiflik* owner under verbal agreements that were subject to abuse. Another quarter belonged to the local Ottoman tax collector, often the same owner. In addition, the Macedonian peasant had to perform at least ten days of forced labor, or *angariia,* at the owner's behest.

In order to enforce this harsh regime, especially in the wake of the nationalist uprising against Ottoman rule in 1903, owners turned to roving bands of Albanians and a growing number of Turkish and Albanian immigrants from Bosnia-Hercegovina. Ottoman authorities tended to overlook the resulting violence and intimidation. The Macedonian and Greek peasantry had little incentive to expand the cultivated area around their villages. Instead they began to emigrate, principally to the United States or, as noted in Chapter 6, to the rest of the Balkans. Roughly 100,000 had already come in the decade preceding the 1903 uprising. Perhaps twice that number came afterwards. The total from 1890 forward exceeded 10 percent of the population remaining by 1912. What remittances they sent back from these three or four-year expeditions in search of day labor, called *pečalbarstvo,* we do not know. More clearly, their departure was sufficient after 1903 to leave the fields of some *chiflik* uncultivated for several years at a time and to drive up wages for day labor in Thessaloniki.[7]

Bosnia-Hercegovina and the Ottoman Legacy

The Habsburg occupation of Bosnia-Hercegovina from 1878 forward did little to change a similar system of backward, exploitative sharecropping left behind as the principal Ottoman legacy to the province. Here the counterpart of the Macedonian *chiflik* owner was less often Turkish or Albanian than a native Bosniak, or South Slav Moslem, descended from converts at the time of the Ottoman conquest. They were entrusted with maintaining local security in return for land rights limited to tax collection, in the fashion of Ottoman *sipahi* or cavalry noted in Chapter 1. As is well known, these Bosniak "captains" and other officers took advantage of declining Ottoman central authority during the eighteenth century to turn their authorized holdings into virtual *chiflik* or private property and to seize new land from which they were able to evict recalcitrant peasants. By the nineteenth century they were typically extracting up to one third of peasant harvests, plus some days of *corvée* or forced labor. Less well known is the same Ottoman effort noted in Chapter 5 for the Bulgarian lands during the 1860s and 1870s to reform a system of tax collection by which too little revenue reached Istanbul. The decade following the general Tanzimat reform of 1839 had seen the Porte struggle to eliminate the Bosniak nobles from local military positions. Partial success permitted stricter fiscal regulations after 1859 to raise the state's direct tax collection from 10 to 20–30 percent of peasant income. In return, requirements for forced labor were eliminated, and the owner-tenant relationship was codified.[8] Taxes and sharecroppers' rent took over half of peasant income by the 1870s.

The arriving Habsburg authorities chose to keep both burdens essentially in place. For reasons of military security, the army's Geographic Institute hurriedly performed a cadastral survey of land holdings. The subsequent tax on all produce from these holdings was cut back to 10 percent but was now collected every year without fail and in cash. Habsburg tax assessors continued the Ottoman requirement that peasants keep their crops in the field, often damaging the harvest, until it had been appraised.[9] The end of this practice in 1907 and a more careful cadastral survey did not reduce the agricultural tax. It still constituted over half of Habsburg revenue in the province. As we shall see, maximizing tax revenue to defray the costs of military occupation was always the major Habsburg motive in Bosnia-Hercegovina, along with maintaining military security.

The latter concern prompted the new *Landesregierung* to drop plans for reforming the system of land tenure. Bosniak officers continued collecting sharecropping rents from peasants on their land. Three quarters of these so-called *kmet* peasants were Serbs, adding fuel to the political fire burning in Serbia ever since the young Balkan state had failed to take the province for itself in 1876. This ethnic difference between owner and sharecropper tended to obscure the fact that free smallholding households slightly outnumbered landless *kmet* peasants in 1895 and were almost double their numbers by 1910.[10] These smallholders, over half of them Bosniaks, generally occupied tiny plots. Three quarters of their acreage comprised unconsolidated series of plots totalling under 5 hectares. We simply cannot conclude that the increasing numbers of Serbs and Croats joining them during the last prewar decades did much to encourage efficient farming. Such new smallholders had usually spent any cash reserves on indemnifying the Bosniak owner for *kmet* land converted to peasant property, under the provisions of an Ottoman law of 1876. Table 9.3 spells out the ethnic divisions, especially between Bosniaks, and Serbs, that characterized the province's property in 1910.

The crops and livestock market from such a rural economy, even in the northern 30 percent of the province where the soil and terrain were comparable to the flatlands or arable hill country of Croatia or Serbia, could not be expected to take much advantage of the wider Austro-Hungarian market. Total trade turnover for Bosnia-Hercegovina had increased more than threefold, as noted in Table 9.2, after three decades of Habsburg occupation. But by 1905 an import surplus of 10 percent over export value had opened up. It reached 30 percent if only trade within the monarchy is considered. Within the export total, moreover, agricultural products accounted for less than half the value.[11] Timber and minerals comprised over half. Cultivated exports were about evenly divided between dried plums and grain, each averaging about 10 percent of export value. The grain that had become the main export of the pre-1914 Balkan states, despite an assortment of tariff barriers, was of negligible importance to Bosnia-Hercegovina who faced no tariffs in the huge Dual Monarchy. Corn cultivation grew more rapidly than wheat, the principal export grain, and doubled its acreage if 1903-12 is compared to 1882. Population growth of 50 percent and increased numbers of smallholdings absorbed almost all the added production of the peasants' chief staple. Total grain output per capita was less than two thirds of the Romanian figure.[12] Plum production per capita doubled for 1882–98 but then fluctuated erratically around a stagnant average because of the same sensitivity to weather that we saw restraining Serbian plums in Chapter 6.[13]

TABLE 9.3
STRUCTURE OF LANDHOLDING IN BOSNIA-HERCEGOVINA IN 1910

Properties with Kmets	Adult male peasants	% of subtotal	Peasants with families
Moslem	9,537	91.2	35,719
Orthodox (Serb)	633	6.1	3,227
Catholic (Croat)	267	2.6	1,399
Other	26	.1	115
Subtotal	10,463		40,460
Free Peasants			
Moslem	77,518	56.7	334,811
Orthodox (Serb)	35,414	25.9	111,905
Catholic (Croat)	22,916	16.7	183,268
Other	1,006	.7	4,805
Subtotal	136,857		634,789
Kmets			
Moslem	3,653	4.5	16,127
Orthodox (Serb)	58,895	73.9	333,739
Catholic (Croat)	17,116	21.5	94,992
Other	13	.1	62
Subtotal	79,677		444,920

Size of Properties in 1906	% Free Peasants	% Kmets
under 2 hectares	51.3	20.0
2-5 "	25.5	28.1
5-10 "	13.8	28.4
over 10 "	9.4	23.5

Sources: M. Erić. *Agrarna reforma u Jugoslaviji, 1918-1941* (Sarajevo, 1958), pp. 72, 75.

As for modernizing the processing of plums into prunes, the Habsburg *Landesregierung* for Bosnia-Hercegovina had no more success in introducing the new double-drying French ovens to the peasantry than did Serbian authorities.[14] A system of licensing oven masters found few takers. Several state plum orchards and fourteen marketing stations made no noticeable impact on the irregular quality of prunes actually exported.

State efforts to improve grain production were even more meager.[15] Four stations for agricultural extension services were set up after 1900, but their traveling agents and the several "master farmers" selected to introduce new techniques in the area of each station made no noticeable impact on the practice of cultivation. A staggering illiteracy rate of over 90 percent in the countryside made it difficult to organize instruction for significant numbers. In addition, the marketable surplus for either *kmet* or smallholder families was simply too small to compel any change in traditional ways. Only the few thousand colonists' households that remained from the Austrian and Polish peasants brought to Bosnia-Hercegovina in the 1880s were consistently using horses, iron plows, and some mechanical threshers by 1910. They had received free 11–12-hectare holdings and initial tax exemptions. Almost 30,000 native colonists had received plots by 1910, but they averaged only 1.2 hectares. Wooden plows pulled by oxen or by hand were still overwhelmingly the implements of this native peasantry, placing them well behind their fellows in the independent Balkan states (see Chapter 6).

The one rational economic recourse was to emigrate. Exact figures do not exist, but perhaps 100,000 Croats and especially Serbs had left by 1914, over 5 percent of the population at that fateful date. Table 9.1 reflects a one third reduction in the rate of population increase after 1900. Most emigrants went for stays of several years in the United States. Some sought seasonal labor in the Hungarian lands, Romania, or Serbia. One Serbian youth, Gavrilo Princip, left his impoverished *kmet* family for brief schooling in Sarajevo, then walked several times to Serbia and back. He returned the last time to assassinate the heir to the Habsburg throne.[16]

Estate Agriculture in the Austro-Hungarian Borderlands

The dissatisfactions of the Croat, Serb, and Romanian majorities in the south and east of Dualist Hungary grew after 1880. Cultural Magyarization now joined political control from Budapest. Prospects for the rural economy might at first glance be excluded from the list of national grievances. Surely the Agricultural Revolution that was the Hungarian response to the opportunities of the huge Habsburg customs union should have spread to neighboring Croatia/Slavonia, Transylvania, and the Vojvodina.[17] Rather than spreading, however, it acted to choke off the borderlands from principal Habsburg markets.

The notion that it spread rests largely on the long-standing assumption that here, unlike Ottoman Macedonia, genuinely large estates of 1,000 hectares or more and large smallholdings of 50 hectares or more at least controlled a significant fraction of agricultural land. Table 9.4 indicates that for Transylvania, this fraction is cut by more than half (to 12 percent) when we consider only cultivated land on estates over 1,000 hectares and by one third on holdings over 50. The 22.5 percent of exploited land in large estates in Croatia/Slavonia probably falls by a similar amount when pasture and forest land are subtracted. For Slovenia and Dalmatia, the drop is even more drastic.

At the turn of the century, exploitations over 50 hectares in mountainous Slovenia and Dalmatia accounted for 25 and 14 percent of
respective rural acreage and just 3 percent of cultivated land. The
predominance of large estates in the Vojvodina was just as high as for
Croatia-Slavonia within the 35 percent of all agricultural property
that Table 9.4 identifies in holdings over 50 hectares. Here percentage of cultivated land in larger holdings was not much lower, in the
absence of the extensive forests that accounted for a majority of estate property in other Habsburg borderlands. For Transylvania, large
estates comprised two thirds of the holdings over 50 hectares. The
latter were 48 percent of all holdings, but less than one third of cultivated land. Even the Vojvodina could not match the figures for Hungary proper and its equally unforested plain. Some 55 percent of
Hungarian exploitations were 50 hectares or more and 38 percent
exceeded 500.[18]

The smaller arable proportion of borderland belonging to the large
estates also generated a lesser impetus toward modern, mechanized
agriculture. Official data from 1896 indicate that only the Vojvodina
could come close to matching Hungary proper in numbers of
threshers, harvesters, and other mechanized equipment on a per
capita basis. Transylvania had half as many and Croatia/Slavonia only
one quarter. The same statistics show a greater concentration of this
equipment on the large Hungarian-owned estates.[19]

The division of cultivation between crops in Croatia/Slavonia, the
only borderland for which we have a comprehensive record of agricultural production, also suggests that the large estates were not
moving into production for distant markets, even within the Dual
Monarchy. As in Bosnia-Hercegovina, the predominant crop continued to be corn. The peasant staple still amounted to 42 percent of
grain acreage between 1911 and 1913 for Croatia/Slavonia. More
marketable wheat covered just 33 percent of that acreage. For Hungary proper, the proportions were neatly reversed.[20] The failure of
wheat cultivation to make much headway is more striking in terms of
tonnage per head of rural population. Croatia/Slavonia averaged only
two fifths of the per capita wheat production recorded by Hungary
proper or the independent Balkan state of Romania. According to
Table 9.5, lower wheat and corn production combined to keep the
province's total grain output per capita under the Serbian and less
than half the Romanian totals.

Brightening this unpromising picture was a sharp increase in the
raising and export of livestock. The value of livestock sold jumped
47.5 percent for 1885–1914, compared to 19.8 percent for crops. Its
share of all agricultural output climbed from 41 to 46 percent over
the same period. Exports of hogs and especially cattle to the rest of

TABLE 9.4
STRUCTURE OF LANDHOLDING IN HABSBURG BORDERLANDS

Size of Exploitation[a]		CROATIA/SLAVONIA (1895)[c]		TRANSYLVANIA (1895)		
		% of all landowners	% of all holdings	% of all landowners[c]	% of all holdings[c]	% of cult. holdings
under 5	joch[b]	44.2	8.5	49.6	6.5	9.1
5-20	"	47.3	41.5	39.8	29.0	37.8
20-50	"	7.5	18.4	8.9	18.4	22.0
50-200	"	.8	5.5	1.6	9.6	10.5
200-1,000	"	.1	3.7	.3	11.1	8.8
over 1,000	"	.05	22.5	.1	26.5	11.9

Grouped subtotals (braces):
- CROATIA/SLAVONIA landowners: 99% / 1%; holdings: 68.4% / 31.7%
- TRANSYLVANIA landowners: 98% / 2%; holdings: 52.9% / 47.2%; cult. holdings: 68.9% / 31.1%

Size of Exploitation[a]		SLOVENIA (1902)[c]		VOJVODINA (1900)[c]		DALMATIA (1900)[c]	
		landowners	% of all holdings	landowners	holdings	landowners	holdings
under 2	hectares	31.3					
2-5	"	19.5					
5-20	"	39.2					
20-50	"	8.6					
50-100	"	1.0					
100-1,000	"	.3					
over 1,000	"	.1					

Grouped subtotals (braces):
- SLOVENIA holdings: 74.8% / 25.2%
- VOJVODINA landowners: 98.8% / 1.2%; holdings: 65% / 35%
- DALMATIA landowners: 99.6% / .4%; holdings: 85.5% / 14.5%

Notes: (a)Rural property operated as a single farm, even if not a consolidated holding. (b)One cadastral joch equals .576 hectares. (c)All cultivated, pasture and forest land.

Sources: Ştefan Pascu et al., *Die Agrarfrage in der österreichische-ungarische Monarchie* (Bucharest, 1965), pp. 9, 16, 19; M. Erić, *Agrarna reforma u Jugoslaviji, 1918-1941* (Sarajevo, 1958), pp. 23, 40; Iosif Kovacs, *Desfiinţarea relaţiilor feudale in Transilvania* (Cluj, 1973), p. 165.

TABLE 9.5
CROATIAN, SERBIAN AND ROMANIAN GRAIN AREA AND OUTPUT, 1891-1915

	CROATIA/SLAVONIA		SERBIA		ROMANIA	
	1,000s hects.	per capita	1,000s hects.	per capita	1,000s hects.	per capita
Wheat Area						
1891-95	215	.11	317	.16	1,435	.31
1896-1900	248	.13	319	.14	1,561	.33
1901-05	288	.11	343	.15	1,681	.33
1906-10	304	.14	377[b]	.15	1,835	.33
1911-15	334	.15	387[b]	.15	1,922	.32
Corn Area						
1891-95	357	.19	532	.26	1,796	.39
1896-1900	371	.19	489	.22	1,993	.42
1901-05	391	.19	532	.23	2,090	.41
1906-110	404	.19	567[b]	.23	1,828	.33
1911-15	427	.19	585[b]	.23	2,097	.32
Major Grain Area						
1891-95	1,059	.56	1,107	.57	4,181	.92
1896-1900	1,111	.56	1,043	.50	4,649	.98
1901-05	979	.47	1,114	.50	4,822	.94
1906-10	978	.45			4,809	.87
1911-15	1,015	.45	1,202	.51	4,987	.82
Wheat Output						
1891-95	216	.11	293	.14	1,596	.35
1895-1900	257	.13	292	.13	1,386	.29
1901-05	328	.16	337	.14	2,086	.41
1906-10	309	.14	417	.17	2,080	.37
1911-15	348	.15			2,223	.36

TABLE 9.5 (continued)

Wheat Area	CROATIA/S_AVONIA		SERBIA		ROMANIA	
	1,000s hects.	per capita	1,000s hects.	per capita	1,000s hects.	per capita
Corn Output						
1891-95	412	.22			1,678	.37
1896-1900	442	.22	678	.32	1,852	.39
1901-05	454	.22	444	.20	1,773	.35
1906-10	540	.25	660	.28	2,267	.41
1911-15	501	.22	674	.28	2,666	.44
Major Grains[a]						
1891-95	360	.46	1,171	.56	ca. 3,800	.80
1896-1900	970	.49	888	.39	ca. 4,950	.98
1901-05	1,061	.51	1,185	.50	ca. 5,350	.96
1906-10	1,060	.49	1,307[b]	.54	ca. 6,000	.98
1911-15	1,074	.48				

Notes: (a)Defined as wheat, corn, rye, barley and oats.   (b)1911-1912 only.

Sources: B. R. Mitchell. *European Historical Statistics, 1750-1970* (New York: Columbia University Press, 1975). pp. 216, 256; Tables 6.7 and 6.8 above

the Monarchy led the way. The number of head exported precisely doubled between 1896–99 and 1910–13. Head exported from independent Serbia increased only slightly. By the latter dates, Croatian livestock exports averaged 65 million Kr. a year, or almost three times the amount exported by Serbia in the banner years before the 1906–11 tariff war with Austria-Hungary.[21] Most of these livestock came from the larger Croatian estates near Zagreb or the rail line leading north from it. Their access to mortgage lending from the large Zagreb banks, to be discussed in the next section, allowed many to introduce the superior Central European breeds of cattle and the stall-feeding of hogs with corn that smaller Hungarian estates began to adopt before 1900. The larger Hungarian estates continued to concentrate on growing wheat for the wider Habsburg market. They thus left an opening for stockraising that the Croatian estates joined the smaller Hungarian ones in filling. The unfortunate consequences for an interwar Yugoslavia composed of too many regions, Croatia and Serbia most prominently, that previously relied on livestock exports are discussed in Chapter 10.

A prewar Croatian advantage over all the independent Balkan states and the other Hungarian lands as well emerges from Table 9.6. Only Croatian herds of hogs and cattle increased significantly, by 31 and 25 percent respectively, during the last two prewar decades. Balkan totals held constant or declined. In terms of animals per square kilometer, the two Croatian figures surpassed even the Hungarian ones. In terms of animals per 1,000 inhabitants, the number of Croatian hogs increased by 10.9 percent from 1895 to 1911, and cattle by 5.3 percent. With the exception of Greek and Bulgarian hogs rising from a small base, all other per capita figures declined. Serbia and Romania experienced sharp drops. Combined hogs and cattle for Croatia totalled 842 per 1,000 inhabitants by 1911, clearly ahead of 694 for Hungary and of 626 for Serbia, the Balkan leader. In addition, the sheep and goat herds that in Europe are usually associated with a backward pastoral economy were far smaller for Croatia than for the independent Balkan states.

Prewar demand for livestock fodder from the large Croatian estates must be part of the explanation for the continued concentration of corn-growing in the area around Zagreb. To what extent this demand reached peasant smallholders, who typically consumed their corn, we cannot say.

Planting crops for local or self-consumption was responsible for the relatively rapid rate of long-run growth in the constant price value of grain production for Croatia/Slavonia. An average annual rate of 2.1 percent between 1869 and 1900 falls short of the Hungarian rates of 2.3 percent, but not by much. Hidden in this long-term rate, moreover, is the fact that the Croatian rate slowed down drastically after 1900. The five-year average centered on 1910 showed only a 3-percent increase over the same average centered on 1900, just as the value of Hungarian grain made its greatest advance, 16 percent. Even after emigration has been subtracted, the Croatian rural population was growing almost three times as fast as grain value over this decade.[22]

The great obstacle barring grain grown in Croatia/Slavonia and the Vojvodina and Transylvania as well from the wider Habsburg market was of course Hungary proper. Its largely fertile plain lay astride the

TABLE 9.6
HABSBURG AND BALKAN LIVESTOCK HERDS, 1895-1912

Country or Area	Year	Horses	Cattle	Pigs	Sheep	Goats
			(in thousands)			
Croatia-Slavonia	1895	311	909	883	596	22
	1911	350	1135	1164	850	96
Other Hungary	1895	1997	5830	6447	7527	
	1911	2001	6184	6416	7698	
Bulgaria	1901	495	2027	368	7015	1580
	1905	538	2173	465	8131	1691
	1910	478	2019	527	8669	1412
Greece	1899	159	417	80	4568	3339
	1912	149	304	227	3545	2638
Romania (Old Kingdom)	1900	864	2589	1709	5656	232
	1910	825	2667	1022	5270	187
Serbia	1901	185	957	960	3062	432
	1906	174	963	908	3160	510
	1910	153	957	866	3819	631

		Animals per Square Kilometer				
Croatia-Slavonia	1911	7.98	25.86	26.53	2.19	2.19
Other Hungary	1911	7.24	22.36	23.20		
Bulgaria	1910	4.96	20.96	5.47	14.66	14.66
Greece	1912	2.30	4.69	3.50	40.72	40.72
Romania	1910	6.34	20.49	7.85	1.44	1.44
Serbia	1910	3.06	19.16	17.34	12.63	12.63

TABLE 9.6 (continued)

Country or Area	Year	Horses	Cattle	Pigs	Sheep	Goats
			(in thousands)			
	Animals per 1000 Inhabitants					
Croatia-Slavonia	1895	135	395	384	255	10
	1911	128	416	426	311	35
Other Hungary	1895					
	1911	110	341	353	424	
Bulgaria	1901	132	541	98	1874	422
	1905	133	538	115	2015	419
	1910	110	488	121	1998	325
Greece	1899[a]	65	171	33	1877	1372
	1912	57	116	86	1347	1002
Romania	1900	145	435	287	949	39
	1910	114	369	141	728	26
Serbia	1901	24	384	385	1228	173
	1906	65	358	338	1175	190
	1910	53	329	297	1311	217

Note: (a)Population of 1896.

Sources: B. R. Mitchell. *European Historical Statistics. 1750-1970* (New York: Columbia University Press. 1975). pp. 297-302. 321. as extrapolated by Marvin R. Jackson.

route to the Austrian and Czech urban centers. As already mentioned in Chapter 2, whatever outlet the Adriatic and the Mediterranean markets might have provided for Hungarian grain was largely closed off in the 1830s. Russian competition was quick to appear once the Treaty of Adrianople had opened the Black Sea to European shipping. The Habsburg monarchy, borderlands included, became the major Hungarian outlet. From this time forward, some Croatian and more Slavonian estate owners interested in profitable use of their land turned to exploiting their abundant forests. (They matched estate arable in size.) So at some later date did the Transylvanian estate owners. In contrast to the Slavonian ethnic mixture, they were over 80 percent ethnic Hungarians and presumably had better access to investment capital in Budapest. By 1895, however, they still held only 31 percent of the province's arable total but retained 85 percent of the forest area.[23] We may thus anticipate timber's decisive role in the Transylvanian industrial stirrings to be discussed in the chapter's final section.

The Land Shortage and Peasant Emigration

For now, the peasantry's place in the largely agricultural economy of these Hungarian borderlands needs to be defined. It could hardly be expected to be a favorable one, even if estate cultivation was growing and modernizing as in Hungary proper. The profits from that expansion went to the larger landowners and eventually into the bona fide beginning of sustained industrial growth that, along with its Agricultural Revolution, distinguished the pre-1914 Hungarian economy from all of Southeastern Europe. Estate wages responded to the boom by rising only where increased emigration cut the numbers of workers available more than the mechanization of harvesting reduced the demand.

The limits to such a rise may be seen on those Transylvanian estates where crop cultivation was a large-scale operation. By 1900, over 400,000 day laborers were working on Transylvanian holdings, mainly on large estates over 500 hectares. Another 100,000 were permanently hired hands or *argaţii*, generally on middle-sized properties. Together they comprised 31 percent of the active agricultural population. An increase of one third in their wages during the last prewar decade only matched the same increase in the general price level. According to the calculations of a Transylvanian scholar, these wages left the average day laborer and his family enough to subsist but on a bad diet.[24] The hired hand fared slightly better because he typically received a small plot from the landowner on which to grow some of his own food supply.

Indeed, the shortage of land for his own smallholding was the peasant's heaviest burden throughout Dualist Hungary and its borderlands. By 1900 the landless proportion among them reached 36 percent for Transylvania and 38 for the Vojvodina. This was far beyond the Serbian or Bulgarian figures of less than 10 percent, well ahead even of Romania's 28 percent.[25] Although difficult to measure, the Croatian percentage was surely much lower. More than the other borderlands, however, the recurring division of Croatian peasant property in the absence of primogeniture reduced the majority of their holdings below the 5 hectares generally needed for subsistence. Table 9.4 has already suggested the striking imbalance between the borderlands' great number of peasant holdings and their small average size by 1900.

The sale of estate lands after 1880 offered some slight relief to the Transylvanian process of subdivision. Such sales reflected the aforementioned reluctance of many Transylvanian estates to concentrate on field crops against competition from Hungary proper. The Romanian peasant majority had purchased more than 100,000 hectares by 1895. As we shall see in the next section, several Transylvanian banks bought up a majority of this land and then mortgaged it to the largely Romanian peasantry. Yet this total would barely have added 5 percent to the largely Romanian acreage under 5 hectares, had none been sold to larger ones (little was). The division of even 100,000 hectares among over 400,000 Romanian peasant households, two thirds of whom held plots under 5 hectares, cannot have afforded much relief. Neither could the land's distribution in narrow strips often unconnected to the peasants' other holdings. (Only the large estates would begin consolidation before the war.) Roughly another 300,000 hectares of estate land had been sold between 1880 and 1895. Buyers were small estate owners, town merchants and bankers who generally leased it back to the peasantry under sharecropping or the aforementioned arrangements for *argaţi* labor.[26]

New Hungarian legislation in 1896 did attempt to codify the procedures for estate sales. The law gave peasant smallholders twenty years to reimburse their estate for land purchased. Even under these terms, the steadily growing Transylvanian peasantry was unable to buy enough land to support their families with some margin for bad harvests. Most were forced to continue using estate land under neo-feudal contracts for fifty days of annual labor elsewhere on the estate. They had few other recourses. They could join the day laborers and hired hands whose ranks swelled after 1880. They could also emigrate. Between 1889 and 1913, over 220,000 left for the United States or other distant points. About 100,000 went to Romania permanently and another 30,000 seasonally.[27] The total emigration approached 8 percent of the prewar population. It was the largest among the Habsburg borderlands, exceeding the levels of 6 percent in Croatia/Slavonia and largely mountainous Slovenia. As noted in Table 9.1, population growth thereby slowed to half the annual rates of the Balkan states.

Heavier emigration from the more fertile eastern areas, especially in the rich Banat plain, stands in contrast to the relatively small outflow of 4–5 percent from the Vojvodina west of the Banat and from Slavonia. This discrepancy would seem to have at least two explanations: the somewhat lower density of rural population in these western plains and the absence in neighboring Serbia of even Romanian-style estate agriculture to attract landless peasants for seasonal employment. For the Vojvodina at least, the *prečani* or Habsburg Serbs were a majority of the landless. There, the German colonists whose arrival was described in Chapter 2 took advantage of the post-1848 dissolution of the Military Border to buy more land from the Serbs who had predominated in the guard regiments. The so-called Swabians established the only sizable block of mid-sized free holdings, 50–200 hectares apiece and accounting for a fifth of the agricultural land, anywhere in the borderlands.

The bulk of the Croatian emigration came from Croatia proper, to the west and south of the fertile Slavonian plain. Nearly 7 percent of the mean population for 1901–10 emigrated, mainly to the United States, pulling the average for Croatia/Slavonia up to 6 percent. Despite a rate of natural increase that rose to 12.8 per thousand and approached Serbia's 15.5, net population growth for the decade declined to .82 percent a year, versus 1.56 for Serbia (see Tables 6.4 and 9.1). Slovenian growth, although considerably lower at .35 percent a year, had at least turned upward after 1900. Its slightly lower overall emigration was moreover accompanied by much smaller departures from the industrial areas discussed in the chapter's last section. It was here that urban migration had reduced the rural proportion for all Slovenia from 81 to 67 percent between 1880 and 1910.[28]

The Croatian rural proportion declined only slightly from 84 to 79 percent, as more migrants went overseas than into towns. They left most heavily from the areas dominated by the *zadruge* rather than the great estates. These communal landholdings were concentrated in the southwestern section of the Military Border and in the heavily populated Zagorje region north of Zagreb. Zagorje's population had twice the density of the rest of Croatia/Slavonia. The *zadruge* accounted for 40–70 percent of the agricultural land there, versus less than 20 percent for the entire province by 1895. About two thirds of *zadruge* land had been secretly divided to accommodate growing family size and monetization. Secrecy avoided the higher taxes, the expense of formal dissolution, and the risk of individual loss for failure to pay debts accumulating since the abolition of serfdom in 1848.[29] Pressures for formal division rose during the last prewar decades. These covert arrangements spread still further. Their principal economic effects were to discourage the consolidation of scattered strip holdings and yet to keep a significant landless class from appearing. What did appear offered no prospect for modernizing production and little advantage to the peasants' living standard. The mean smallholding for these regions dropped below 5 hectares by 1900 and continued to fall, dragging the overall figure for Croatia/Slavonia with it to less than 7 hectares.[30] The rising tide of emigrants from these two regions testified to the distress that dwarf-holdings, more extensive than elsewhere in the Hungarian borderlands, brought with them.

Financial Consequences of Political Dependence

Official support for agriculture is hardly fair ground on which to assess the impact of the Habsburg and Ottoman financial structures within which the borderlands found themselves before 1914. Noncommercial castes of noble or military landowners lay too close to the center of political power, especially in the Habsburg case, to permit serious land or tax reform, let alone state investment to aid the mass of peasants. At the same time, only Romania among the independent Balkan states possessed a similar class of rich and powerful landowners. None of these states devoted significant expenses in the government budget to the agricultural sector that provided the great majority of its tax revenues (see Chapter 6). In fact, active promotion of modern farming lay beyond the capacity as well as the vision of pre-1914 European governments.

The borderland's financial structure is better judged by fiscal and monetary standards of the time. The smaller size of budget revenues, and thus a lesser tax burden in the borderlands than the Balkan states must be balanced against the proportion of imperial taxation spent outside the province where it was collected. The division of imperial expenditures within the borderlands merits comparison with the expenses of the Balkan states to finance railway construction and to educate their populations.

The monetary issues related mainly to the Habsburg borderlands. They enjoyed access to a major European currency, based since 1892 on the Gold Standard that had eluded all the Balkan states except Romania. Did this not mean that the Viennese Great Banks would rush to penetrate the borderlands' economies, seeking new markets and sources of supply for the Austrian and Czech industrial enterprises whose stock they often owned? Chapters 7 and 8 have demonstrated their failure to do so in the Balkan states. Here, the record does less violence to the traditional Marxist canons of aggressive Finance Capitalism only when we include the activities of the nationalistic new banks of Budapest and Prague.

Imperial Motives for Railway Construction

Official Habsburg policy toward achieving the economic integration of the borderlands with the more developed northern regions of the monarchy does not, however, fit the Marxist or the Western models. The litmus test for state economic policy before 1914 was of course railway construction. After 1873, Habsburg authorities in Vienna and Budapest did not leave railway building to private enterprise as Adam Smith would have wished. Neither did they push construction ahead to serve Austrian and Czech industry in the fashion that Karl Marx might have predicted. Instead a mixture of political, military, and fiscal motives revolved around the growing struggle for dominance between Austrian and Hungarian authorities. At least for Bosnia-Hercegovina, the dominant motives were the same military ones for which Ottoman authorities tried to push the course of Macedonian railway construction away from its greatest commercial potential. (In Ottoman Macedonia, these more commercial routes must have been obvious to the European Great Banks who assembled the necessary funding for the financially sick man of Europe. They evidently could not prevail over the Porte, as noted below, in determining the routes.)

The three major lines from Vienna and Budapest to the Balkan borderlands were completed, through Slovenia to Trieste and through Hungary into Transylvania and Croatia, before the Austrian stock market crash of 1873. The crash ended the era of enterprising private banks that had built and owned the majority of existing European railways over the previous twenty years. State ownership resumed thereafter. The Rothschilds' Creditanstalt of Vienna arranged the connection of their *Nordbahn* (from Vienna to the Czech and Silesian metallurgical centers) with a line running east through Budapest to Arad and Alba Julia into the western Carpathian foothills, where the main Transylvanian deposits of coal and iron were located. By the time this line had reached Alba Julia in 1857, the same interests had won out from the Périere brothers' model investment bank, the Credit Mobilier of Paris, for the rights to complete the *Südbahn* from Vienna.[31] It had reached the Slovenian capital of Ljubljana in 1849 and was not extended, as noted in Chapter 2, to Trieste at the head of the Adriatic. This chapter's final section will explore the decisive importance of these early lines for the pre-1914 development of Transylvanian and Slovenian industry.

The 1867 *Ausgleich*, with its limited autonomy for the Hungarian half of the monarchy, occurred before the same Austrian banking interests could construct a direct connection from Vienna to Croatia/ Slavonia. Instead, the newly powerful authorities in Budapest were able to draw on rival French financing to complete lines from their capital to Zagreb in 1870 and Rijeka on the Adriatic by 1873, the year of the crash. The subsequent effect of this exclusive connection on Croatian economic development was more favorable than the assessment of its initial impact in Chapter 2 might suggest. Slavonian grain exports suffered, it is true, from the repeated Hungarian veto of a railway from Osijek in the east to Rijeka.[32] This trade had previously moved along the Sava River. High freight rates to and cheap rates from Budapest now made it impossible to compete with Hungarian grain or flour. But after the Hungarian government took full control of this network in 1891, freight rates on the Budapest-Rijeka line had been reduced to the Austrian level. The latter were less than half the fees on the far smaller Serbian network.[33] Rijeka found itself becoming a major Adriatic port because of the official Hungar-

ian desire to avoid Trieste as the outlet for its flour and sugar production. High Austrian rates on the short line finally built to connect
Rijeka with the *Südbahn* to Trieste also discouraged use of the latter
port, destined to become part of Italy since 1918. It seems doubtful
that Rijeka's export tonnage could have multiplied tenfold from 1870
to 1910 or the building of steamships (today its major industry) gotten
under way had the attraction of Trieste not been checked by
Austro-Hungarian rivalry.[34]

The overall Croatian advantage from the Budapest-Zagreb-Rijeka
line and the secondary lines is nonetheless reduced when we weigh
the expenses and revenues associated with it. Unlike the Balkan
states whose railway and other foreign loans demanded debt service
that became 20 to 30 percent of budget expenses, the Habsburg borderlands bore no direct burden. For Croatia/Slavonia, the form if not
the substance of its own administration since the 1868 compromise,
or *Nagodba,* with Budapest generated a separate budget. Total state
revenues had reached only an average of 45 million Kr. for 1900–
1905. The independent Serbian government collected an annual average of 81 million dinars, or 31 francs per capita, versus 19 francs
worth for its Croatian counterpart. Yet, while Serbia was able to
spend slightly more than 81 million a year because of deficit financing early in the period, Croatia/Slavonia was entitled to retain less
than half of 47.5 million in revenues (19.8 million) for its own expenses. Over half went to Budapest, a proportion that exceeded the
share of debt service and military expenses combined in the Serbian
budget.

In addition, the Serbian budget could draw revenues from the
railways and other state monopolies, as well as tariffs. Croatia/
Slavonia collected none but spent half its retained revenues on maintaining the railways and roads. Three quarters of its total revenue,
versus barely one quarter for Serbia, continued to come from a land
tax based on the size of peasant harvest.[35] Croatian national spokes-
men did not fail to note that railway profits had become the largest
item in overall Hungarian revenues by the late 1890s. The growing
state bureaucracy in Zagreb, although less than one fifth of the Serbian total, was too heavily Hungarian for its smaller numbers to offer
Croatian interests much consolation.

Despite the above limit on retained revenues, the educational
facilities that constituted the prewar state's other principal means of
promoting economic development were not neglected. Croatian
budgetary expenditure for education, it is true, averaged only 4.4
million Kr. a year during 1904–13. The per capita amount was four
fifths of the Serbian average. But the number of students in higher
education was slightly greater; the access to further training in

Budapest or Vienna was presumably better. The Croatian educational system spent a full quarter of the far smaller total for state expenses. It therefore operated at no significant disadvantage compared to that of Serbia, especially in the absence of the Magyarization that plagued the Romanian majority in Transylvania. The literacy rate by 1912 was 54 percent for ages 7 and over, well ahead of the probable Serbian rate of less than half that figure.[36]

For Bosnia-Hercegovina, the problem of unretained tax revenues did not blunt the advantages of Habsburg railway construction. All revenues were spent in the province. They averaged 50 million Kr. for 1900–15, or 50 percent more than for Croatia/Slavonia on a per capita basis, by drawing on income from the railways and especially, as we shall see, other state enterprises. Almost half of the railway network of Table 9.7 had been constructed between 1881 and 1895. So-called Common Credits drawn from joint Austro-Hungarian funds in the hands of the Finance Ministry, responsible for administering Bosnia-Hercegovina, provided a majority of the capital. The War Ministry supported their award to the occupied province as "profitable" and therefore nonrepayable investments.

The Bosnian railways suffered, all the same, from the military and fiscal motives that had determined how the lines were built and then operated. Army engineers had actually constructed the first section of the line from Brod on the Croatian border to Sarajevo with Occupation Credits in 1879. Concerned only with moving troops, they built a narrow-gauge line, which followed the hilly terrain so consistently that speeds could rarely exceed fifteen miles per hour. This line set the pattern for most of the nearly 1,000 miles built in Bosnia-Hercegovina before the First World War. All but 71 were narrow gauge. Average speed increased but was still under thirty miles an hour. Moreover, the Austro-Hungarian administration of the *Bosnabahn* set bulk freight rates proportionally higher than small shipments in order to maximize revenue for the provincial budget. These rates stayed 50–100 percent higher than those of the adjoining Hungarian network, actually *increasing* with the distance traveled.[37] As a result, railway income did show a 5 percent surplus over expenses from 1897. It is hard to imagine a more shortsighted use of rail transport to discourage economic development. In the long run lower rates might have increased rail revenues with greater freight volume.

The three Macedonian railways radiating out from Thessaloniki (see Map 3 above) owed their existence to similarly noneconomic motives. The Austrian financier Baron Hirsch admittedly won the concession for the first line, directly north to Skopje. He completed it just before the stock market crash of 1873. His motive may well have been to take advantage of the growing commerce that more secure

TABLE 9.7
BORDERLAND AND BALKAN RAILWAY LINES IN SERVICE BY 1910
(in kilometers)

Imperial Borderlands	Total of All Gauges	Kilometers per 100 th. pop.
Croatia/Slavonia (Habsburg)	2,139	82
Slovenia "	1,150	82
Transylvania "	4,018	96
Bosnia-Hercegovina "	1,478	74
Macedonia (Ottoman)	450	19
Balkan States		
Romania	3,437	49
Bulgaria	1,897	43
Serbia	892	31
Greece	1,573	56

Sources: *Annuaire statistique hongroise, 1910* (Budapest, 1912), p. 213; Toussaint Hočevar, *The Structure of the Slovenian Economy, 1848-1963* (New York: Studia Slovenica, 1965), pp. 22-23; Peter Sugar, *The Industrialization of Bosnia-Hercegovina, 1878-1918* (Seattle: University of Washington Press, 1963), p. 233; Krste Bitoski, ed., *Istorija na železnicite vo Makedonija, 1873-1973* (Skopje, 1973), p. 41; Tables 6.4, 7.1 and 9.1 above.

Serbian roads and the Crimean War boom had engendered. The Porte, however, granted the concession only with the thought of moving troops to quell internal disorder or potential invasion from Serbia to Greece. The Ottoman General Staff was sufficiently powerful to divert the original extension of the line to the Serbian border west of the railway coming south from Belgrade and away from open country. Instead, the Ottoman line passed through a narrow canyon where its northern section might easily be cut. A separate line met the Serbian railway by 1888, but political and military reluctance kept other commercially logical lines from Skopje to Sofia and from Thessaloniki to the Greek border from ever being built under Ottoman auspices. The Porte agreed to concessions for lines from Thessaloniki west to Bitola and east to Istanbul in the 1890s, again in order to move troops more easily. The Istanbul line through Dedeagach stayed away from the coast to avoid naval bombardment, thereby pushing it through difficult and less settled terrain.[38]

Although regular gauge, this and the other Macedonian lines were built over rough, easily defended terrain that limited average speeds to fifteen miles per hour. High initial freight rates were set slightly below the cost of caravans. Manufactured imports to Skopje and grain export from the Prilep area undoubtedly grew with their increased rail ties to Thessaloniki. Elsewhere, the survival of horse and mule caravans testifies to the limited impact of these several lines on the Macedonian economy. The failure of railway freight earnings to surpass passenger (read troop) revenue as it soon did in the Habsburg borderlands or the Balkan states is also damning.[39]

Native Banking and Foreign Capital

The canons of Finance Capitalism would not lead us to expect any state, Balkan or Central European, to play the decisive role in tying peripheral areas to the more developed economy of the Austrian and Czech lands. Once the Viennese Great Banks had revived following the 1873 crash and received a completely stable currency with the 1888–92 transition to the Gold Standard, they would surely orchestrate the economic integration of the Habsburg borderlands. This they generally did for mining and metallurgy, as the next section will demonstrate. Yet these were separate investments in individual projects. No comprehensive plan for developing or exploiting the borderlands ever emerged, as none had for the independent Balkan states (see Chapters 7 and 8). The rush of Viennese Great Banks to set up branches or affiliates in the borderlands that would have accompanied such a plan never occurred. A spate of recent scholarship agrees that these banks were busy elsewhere in the monarchy with less risky ventures.[40] This neglect proved benign for the financial structure of Croatia/Slavonia, Slovenia, and Transylvania. Native institutions were able to grow to an extent to which, say, Bulgarian commercial banks had been unable because of the overpowering position of the state's central bank and its branches. Table 9.8 indicates that the number and assets of borderland banks, Bosnia-Hercegovina and Macedonia emphatically excepted, compared favorably with the Serbian and Romanian figures celebrated in Chapter 7. Where Great Banks contributed capital to Croatian or Slovenian banks, they were likely to be Czech, rather than Austrian or Hungarian, institutions.

The Croatian practice of commercial banking had mid-nineteenth-century origins. Largely native merchants and artisans in Zagreb, acting through a newly formed Chamber of Commerce, had formed two joint-stock banks during the 1860s. The impending railway connection with Budapest and the general European boom created high expectations. Though these institutions and most of the thirty two savings banks opened at the time vanished with the 1873 crash, they still provided valuable experience for the far greater upsurge after 1895. The most important commercial bank in Slavonia, where twenty five of the Croatian joint-stock total of sixty one were located by 1913, was the Hrvatska Zemaljska Banka. The Croatian president of the local Chamber of Commerce had founded it in Osijek in 1909. The bank used Czech capital and assistance from the

TABLE 9.8
IMPERIAL BORDERLAND AND BALKAN BANKS IN 1910-11
(in millions of franc equivalents)

Imperial Borderlands (1910)	Number of Commercial Banks	Assets	Assets Per Capita
Croatia/Slavonia	189	580	223
Slovenia			
Transylvania	430	ca 1,400	331
Bosnia-Hercegovina	38	ca 70	37
Macedonia (Ottoman)	7	ca 100	42
Balkan States (1911)			
Romania	151	2,030	290
Serbia	177	764	263
Bulgaria	60	735	167
Greece	5	999	355

Sources: *Annuaire statistique hongroise. 1910* (Budapest. 1912). pp. 273-79: Nikolae Jarak. *Poljoprivredna politika Austro-Ugarske u Bosni i Hercegovini i zemljoradničke zadruge* (Sarajevo. 1956). p. 16; M. Dimitrijević. *Privreda i trgovina u novoj Srbiji* (Belgrade. 1913). p. 138; Table 7.4 above.

Živnostenska Banka of Prague to boost its capital to 5 million Kr. by the following year. Its domination of the Slavonian flour trade and milling industry provoked complaints in the Budapest press. Yet no Hungarian bank or the branch of the Habsburg central bank in Osijek had taken the earlier initiative that might have prevented it.

In Croatia proper, the dominant joint-stock institutions were savings banks that shied away from any industrial investment and from some other normal commercial operations as well. The largest of these were located in Zagreb and assembled savings deposits of 71 million Kr. by 1905 and 171 million by 1913, well ahead the 39 and 70 million equivalent that was the sum total of savings in all Serbian banks in 1905 and 1911 respectively. Accompanying these large amounts for the Zagreb banks were bonds, totalling 125 million Kr. by 1913, that paid 4 to 6 percent interest for the duration of the 5–20-year mortgages that typically secured them. These so-called mortgage bonds were a more reliable long-term liability than savings deposits on which to expand the mortgage loans to Croatian agricultural properties that were the Zagreb banks' unique contribution to the area's economic development before 1914. Outstanding mortgages totalled 150 million Kr. by 1913, more than 10 times the Serbian aggregate.[41] Mortgage bonds were initially the exclusive province of Hrvatska-Slavonska Zemaljska Hipotekarna Banka, founded in Zagreb in 1892 with the backing of the Wienerbankverein and several Hungarian concerns. The value of bonds and mortgage loans stayed small, however, until the largest of the half-dozen big Zagreb savings banks (and the one most nearly under native control) was able to force Hungarian authorities to relax the Hipotekarna's monopoly on bond issue. The Prva Hrvatska Štedionica, the First Croatian Savings Bank in fact (founded 1846) as well as name, held paid-in capital of 25 million Kr. Its savings deposits were 30 million in 1900 and 89 million by 1913. It took the lead in using expanded mortgage lending facilitated by bond issues totalling 36 million Kr. in 1913 to favor estates that borrowed to modernize their raising of livestock. The foreign-backed Hipotekarna Banka turned instead, as did most of its European counterparts in the independent Balkan states, to municipal loans under official auspices. Such loans absorbed the great majority of the proceeds from the bank's 60 million Kr. in outstanding bond issues by 1913.

The one bank with noteworthy ties to Serbia was, not surprisingly, the Sprska Banka u Zagrebu. From its founding in 1882, this institution had grown from a small savings bank for the Serb community near the Bosnian border to attract capital and savings combined that surpassed those of any Belgrade bank. Never able to secure official permission for issuing mortgage bonds, its extensive commercial operations included several direct investments in Serbia's grain trade and textile industry. The investments totalled only a few million dinars, but their placement at the height of the Serbian tariff war with Austria-Hungary hardly served Habsburg interests.[42]

The impact inside Croatia/Slavonia of some 145 smaller savings banks and 800 cooperative savings associations operating by 1913 awaits further exploration. The absence of significant modernization on smallholdings suggests that it may not have been much. Nor did the banks' division into separate sets of Serb and Croatian institutions create the framework for a single, unified financial structure in interwar Yugoslavia.

The supposed potential of peasant cooperatives for collecting sufficient savings and then distributing loans broadly enough to raise the technical level of agriculture helped them spread through Central Europe, up to the Scandinavian countries, and down to Italy during the second half of the nineteenth century.[43] Although most successful in Danish dairying, they had at least begun to relieve the shortage of rural credit in Bulgaria (see Chapter 6). Slovenia was the scene of their greatest success in Southeastern Europe. There, as elsewhere in the Habsburg borderlands, the new repayment requirements for noble land and increased money taxes that accompanied the end of serfdom in 1848 forced most peasants to borrow money at high interest rates to meet their needs. Austrian and Italian merchant lenders charged the high rates typical of small-scale operations but aroused extra resentment because they were not ethnically Slovenian. The only Slovenian representative to the Prague Slavic Congress of 1868 returned with the same tales of Czech savings cooperatives that would prompt the founding of the first Serbian savings bank a few years earlier (see Chapter 7). His first efforts failed. No real start was made until his brother, a civil engineer, organized a federation office at Celje in 1883 to assist new cooperatives, promote uniform balance sheets, and supervise their auditing. Such professional management was typically a critical ingredient in effective cooperative savings.

The other was a broad base of savers and borrowers. This base continued to elude the growing numbers of cooperatives (eighty one by 1894) as long as they set up the Schulze-Delitzsch sort of association, which denied voting rights and limited borrowing for small depositors. By 1895, a rival Catholic federation had begun to organize its own cooperatives under the Raiffeisen principle that avoided these restrictions in order to achieve nearly complete membership in a small area. It opened a central reserve bank in Ljubljana to lend reserves to new cooperatives. By 1905, the Catholic federation's 224 cooperatives almost doubled the numbers of its rival, which now switched to Raiffeisen practice if not principle. Combined membership swelled to 165,000 by 1910, or more than 10 percent of the population. Total savings deposits of 212 million Kr. were more than 6 times the Serbian total on a per capita basis. Most important, cooperative credit did more than allow members to avoid selling their land. It also financed the spread of steam-powered equipment and of modern techniques for cattle-breeding and dairy farming. Slovenian milk served a market of several hundred thousand people living in and around Trieste. A literacy rate of 85 percent over age 7, one positive Habsburg legacy to Slovenia, doubtless aided the cooperatives in disseminating the necessary techniques.[44]

Two Slovenian financial institutions deserve separate mention because of the role played by Czech and Austrian banks in their creation. The Ljubljanska Kreditna Banka was established in 1900 as the province's first commercial bank with a combination of support. Slovenian merchants, the same National Liberal party that sponsored the Schulze-Delitzsch cooperative federation, and Prague's Živnostenska Banka all joined in. The Ljubljanska's capital approached 9 million Kr. by 1913. Its investment in light industry was very limited. More important was the use of its central office and five branches to break the previous dependence of southern Slovenian trade and industry on Trieste and Italian short-term credit. Slovenian capital also drew on the Živnostenska to found the large Jadranska Banka in Trieste itself in 1905. Two other Prague banks soon opened their own

branches there. Also boosting the development of the Slovenian hinterland at the expense of the largely Italian industry of Trieste was
the Wienerbankverein's purchase of the larger of the two principal
Italian banks in the port the year before. The Vienna bank cut away
much of its new affiliate's remaining business with Italy. It assembled 50 million Kr. to complete badly needed new port facilities.[45]
These facilities favored the growth of Trieste as a port, but easier
imports hurt its potential as an industrial center. Slovenian industry
was thus better able to develop in the interior on its own terms.

The one new Habsburg borderland, Bosnia-Hercegovina, was presumably the most vulnerable to colonial exploitation because of its
backwardness and ethnic divisions. Yet it received even less attention from the monarchy's Great Banks. The Czech Živnostenska
Banka made inquiries in 1910 about establishing a Sarajevo branch
but decided against it. Only its partner, the Ljubljanska Kreditna
Banka, opened a small branch there the following year. A French
scholar finds no mention of Bosnian ventures in Viennese bank reports before the province's formal annexation in 1908 and few afterwards. Little wonder, with a Habsburg Finance Minister from 1882
to 1903 who he describes as "totally foreign to the capitalist spirit."[46]
The Hungarian noble and career official Benjamin Kallay actively
opposed any penetration by the Viennese banks. He favored German
investment only as a lesser political threat to his independent administration of the province. Several German Great Banks provided almost 90 percent of the 100 million Kr. of foreign investment in
Bosnia-Hercegovina, mainly in railroad bonds. Kallay did invite the
Wienerbankverein to take over the founding of an official Länderbank in 1883. The Budapest Hitelbank had refused to add the undertaking to its concession for the salt and tobacco monopoly. The
Hitelbank lost the concession in the process to the Wienerbankverein, from whom the provincial government reclaimed it in 1895 because of the bank's commercial reluctance to place railway bonds. In
addition, Kallay left this major Viennese bank little say in running
the new Landesbank. The Wienerbankverein finally opened its own
branch in Sarajevo to seek, with small success, better access to
financing government projects.

Meanwhile the financial structure of Bosnia-Hercegovina remained stillborn outside of these narrow official circles. According to
Table 9.7, assets of the thirty eight banks operating in 1910 were
even smaller than the total for Ottoman Macedonia. The provincial
economy was left with limited access to short-term, let alone long-
term, credit. Rural areas experienced the greatest shortage. Short-
term loans to meet tax obligations were in constant demand, as were
mortgages to allow more of the *kmet* peasantry to buy the land they

sharecropped for Bosniak owners. A mortgage bank assembled from
fourteen local institutions in 1904 never got off the ground. The
Länderbank continued to provide almost half the 17 million Kr. in
mortgage loans granted in 1909.[47] The prestigious Pester Ungarische
Komercialbank had bought monopoly rights to the issuing of *kmet*
mortgages in 1908. Austrian objections over undue Hungarian
influence plus the bank's own hesitation quickly brought the project
down. The cooperative movement and its savings associations also
made little headway against official opposition to granting them unlimited liability or the right to organize along ethnic lines. Both these
restrictions had been lifted by 1908, but the Länderbank used complicated credit regulations to keep the majority of rural lending in its
own hands.[48]

Austrian and other European Great Banks paid more attention to
Ottoman Thessaloniki than to Habsburg Sarajevo. The Viennese
Länderbank had joined French and local interests in founding the
Banque de Salonique in 1888. Its large initial capital of 10 million
francs had doubled by 1909. Yet its management had become
sufficiently independent by then to come into serious conflict with
the Länderbank. The Viennese bank used the occasion of some ill-
fated livestock sales in Egypt to withdraw its financial support, but
the institution survived until Greek owners took over after the First
Balkan War.[49] The other foreign banks also worked to expand the
port's Mediterranean commerce. They afforded scant stimulus to the
Macedonian hinterland.

Macedonian agriculture lacked the short overland connection to
the developed economy of Central Europe and the burgeoning native cooperatives that benefited the Slovenian hinterland north of
Trieste. It could not hope to attract capital to modernize *chiflik* cultivation or to allow peasant sharecroppers to buy adequate smallholdings. Credit still consisted of what small sums church and guild
funds could provide, plus what bills of exchange or usurious loans
individuals could agree on.[50] Belgrade's Beogradska Zadruga, as
noted in Chapter 7, had established its branch in Thessaloniki in
1908 only to export Serbian livestock to Mediterranean markets. The
French Banque d'Athens and the German Orientbank of Athens
opened branches there in anticipation of a railway connection to
southern Greece. Ottoman authorities denied permission for this line
until they lost the entire province in 1912. At least the banks' neglect
of Macedonia made it less dependent on a port from which new
Greek frontiers with Bulgaria and the future Yugoslavia would separate it permanently.

Industrial Stirrings in the Habsburg Borderlands

Industrial stirrings comparable to those in the independent Balkan states did not occur in all the imperial borderlands. Ottoman Macedonia and Habsburg Bosnia-Hercegovina no more generated the wide range of industrial activity with several rapidly growing branches that Chapter 8 recorded than did the growth of commercial banking fill out their financial structure. In the absence of widespread activity in either industry or banking, we will never know whether one might have stimulated or retarded the other.

As with commercial banking, the Macedonian record was the most meager. In Skopje, whose population barely exceeded 30,000 by 1910, enterprises using mechanical power and employing more than twenty workers consisted essentially of four small flour mills. Orders from the Ottoman army supported three of them. About a dozen textile weaving mills were concentrated in several small towns. In Thessaloniki, the Alatini brothers used their contribution to the founding of the Banque de Salonique to push the capital of their flour mill and brewery past two million francs and to incorporate the latter by 1911. A British cotton spinning mill founded in 1879 grew to 8,000 spindles and 550 employees. Most of its sales were made to the Macedonian interior. Beyond the above enterprises, however, this port city of 130,000 contained only twenty two other firms meeting our minimal definition of a factory. There were fifty two more for the rest of Ottoman Macedonia, most of them flour mills with few employees or largely unmechanized tobacco plants that employed half of the province's industrial labor force of perhaps 10,000.[51]

Bosnia-Hercegovina did slightly better. Unlike Macedonia, the state offered at least limited encouragement to industry. Yet Finance Minister Kallay's concept of industrial development was as uncapitalistic as his attitude toward the Viennese banks. Kallay promoted only industrial enterprises under direct state control and typically appointed noble acquaintances to manage them. His purpose was not to encourage industry per se but rather to increase provincial tax revenues, thereby reducing his reliance on the joint Occupation Credits agreed to by Vienna and Budapest essentially for military security.[52] The Great Banks were typically reluctant to invest in projects over which they had little control. Witness the withdrawal of Rothschild interests from ventures in both coal and nonferrous mining. The state-controlled coal monopoly eventually earned high profits by charging all users, including Bosnian industrial firms, exorbitant prices. Iron mining was confined to the worked-out Vares area because Austrian and Hungarian officials could not agree on the division of richer reserves elsewhere.

For light industry, sugar cultivation and refining affords a revealing case study of Kallay's policy. The provincial government introduced the cultivation of sugar beets and opened a refinery in 1890. Kallay's intention was to reduce imports from the rest of the monarchy in favor of locally produced and therefore taxable goods. Any losses to Czech sugar manufactures were immaterial. Tax concessions to *kmet* sharecroppers cut their obligations to the state and the landowner in return for planting sugar beets but they were soon trimmed. The objections of Bosniak owners convinced Kallay that the sizable tax revenue that their holdings collected might be placed in jeopardy. Given the reduced concessions and the low prices paid to the peasant cultivators, sugar beet harvests made early advances only by dint of police coercion. They dropped back to half of the initial peak after 1900. The state's Usori refinery made no profits until 1910. Indirect taxes on the sale of sugar rose more than twice as fast as production and kept profit margins down.[53]

Kallay's successor Count Burian shared his noncommercial background. He refused to license or encourage any new industrial enterprises. Hence the 114 manufacturing firms with over 20 workers in 1910, totalling 13,300 workers, represented little growth during the last prewar decade. Nor did the 91 joint-stock companies in industry and commerce reflect any significant response by Austrian or Hungarian private capital to taxation that was just 30 percent of the normally high rate for corporations in the monarchy. Perhaps two thirds of Bosnian corporations were state owned in one form or another.[54]

The rest of this chapter therefore turns to the industrial stirrings elsewhere in the Habsburg borderlands. They were comparable to, indeed, statistically more impressive than, those of the independent Balkan states. Table 9.9 reflects the relatively higher standing of Slovenia, Transylvania, and Croatia/Slavonia in terms of industrial firms, workers, capital, and output, if not horsepower. The first two borderlands clearly derived their advantage from a combination of mining, metallurgy, and timber cutting. Croatian growth relied first on timber and then other branches of light industry. The following examination of these sectors emphasizes the Habsburg markets and sources of capital that supported them.

Mining and Metallurgy

The flow of Austrian and Hungarian capital into the coal mines and ironworks of Slovenia and especially Transylvania did not generate profits that afforded any Viennese or Budapest Great Bank a major source of new earnings. Yet, as with most British and French invest-

TABLE 9.9
IMPERIAL BORDERLANDS VS. BALKAN INDUSTRIAL INDICATORS IN 1910

Imperial Borderlands	Number of Firms [a]	Workers per firm	Horsepower Per worker [b]	Paid-in Capital (mil. franc equivalents)	Mil. Output [b]	Output per capita [b]
Croatia/Slavonia	271	87	1.71	—	177	67
Slovenia (1912)	441	82	—	—	126[c]	94
Transylvania	692	98	—	270[d]	500	118
Bosnia-Hercegovina	145	158	—	—	—	—
Macedonia (Ottoman)	74	ca 135	—	—	—	—
Balkan States						
Romania (1915)	837	72	2.08	329	584	80
Bulgaria (1911)	345	39	1.72	82	112	25
Serbia	464	54	1.56	50	71	24

Notes: (a)Manufacturing and mining enterprises employing 20 or more workers with some use of mechanical horsepower. (b)1912 horsepower and output data. (c)1913 output data. (d)1911 capital and output data.

Sources: I. Karman, "Osnovna obilježa razvitke industrijske privede u sjevernoj Hrvatskoj do prvog svetskog rata," Acta historico-oeconomica iugoslaviae, I (Zagreb, 1974), pp. 48-52; Toussaint Hočevar, The Structure of the Slovenian Economy, 1848-1963 (New York: Studia Slovenica, 1965), pp. 44-47, 116; L. Vajda, "Despre situaţia economica şi social-politica a Transilvaniei in primii ani al sec. XX-lea," Studii şi materiale de istoria modernă, I (Bucharest, 1957), pp. 300-05; Frederick von Fellner, "Die Verteilung des Volksvermögens und Volkseinkommens der Länder der ungarischen Krone," Metron, III, 2 (Rome, 1922), pp. 267, 283; Ferdinand Schmid, Bosnien und die Herzegovinien (Leipzig, 1914), p. 541; L. Sokolov, Industrijata vo NR Makedonija (Skopje, 1961), p. 25; Annuaire statistique hongroise, 1910 (Budapest, 1912), pp. 182-85; Tables 8.2 and 8.3 above.

ment in their colonial empires, this did not mean that the flow was also insignificant for the receiving economy. Such investment was decisive in creating mining and metallurgical sectors that by 1910 accounted for one third of the capital and labor in the industrial enterprises of the two Habsburg provinces. Located at opposite ends of the southern borderlands, they share the richest mineral deposits in Southeastern Europe. They had a ruling nobility and urban bourgeoisie, Austrian for Slovenia and Hungarian for Transylvania, that were able to attract capital and entrepreneurs from the most developed areas of the monarchy. Like independent Romania, the two provinces also possessed industrial sectors that responded to railway construction.[55]

The main Slovenian coal mines, located in the Trbovolje area, traced their origins to the mid-eighteenth century; sugar refiners in Trieste and Rijeka apparently opened them in order to assure their own supply of fuel. When the refineries declined in the face of Czech competition, so did the mines. From 1857 the completed Süd-bahn from Vienna to Trieste passed through the Trbovolje area and made the huge Austro-Hungarian railway system the mines' best customer. The local and Ljubljana owners proved unable to expand and modernize the existing shafts enough to take advantage of this opportunity. In 1873, with the assistance of the Wienerbankverein, a group of Viennese investors bought the mines and formed a joint-stock company. Despite the crash on the Vienna stock market that year, the new capital allowed the firm's output to triple by 1874. Its ownership passed in 1880 to a French consortium backed by the Credit Foncier. The new ownership reportedly introduced modern techniques that quadrupled annual output by 1912.[56]

The availability of nearby coal permitted glassblowing the transition from traditional potash to gas only in the Trbovolje area. The ironworks that had long operated in the well-forested highlands were not so fortunate: Slovenian coal was chemically unsuited to coking.

Thus the Krainische Industrie Gesellschaft, incorporated in Ljubljana in 1869, faced supply as well as demand problems if it were to open an integrated steel works that might survive Czech and Austrian competition. Capital from a leading noble family of local Austrian landowners allowed the enterprise to survive the 1873 crash, but its plants remained small and scattered. The famous integrated steel works at Jesenice, still Yugoslavia's largest, was completed in 1891 at a cost of 2 million Kr. To do so, however, the enterprise's local Austrian manager had to recruit new investors. The capital stock now climbed to 5.4 million. Significantly, one new owner was a Viennese arms firm that brought with it access to extensive military orders and to a variety of German investors. The largest was a Prussian noble who purchased forested estate land in Slovenia as part of the deal. The Great Banks were not involved. From this date forward the enterprise went on to adopt the latest Siemens-Martin technology. It built a separate smelting plant near Trieste, from which came the necessary imports of British coking coal.[57]

Austrian Great Banks were very much involved in the rapid rise of Transylvanian coal mining and ferrous metallurgy over the last third of the nineteenth century. Railway construction first brought them to the area and then made further investment attractive. The Rothschilds' Creditanstalt of Vienna and its STEG railway enterprise had built the line from Budapest southeast through Arad to Alba Jiuliu in central Transylvania by 1857. Using locally mined iron ore, the STEG accounted for 60 percent of the pig iron and half of the twenty four furnaces operated by the four European firms in the area ten years later. Well-known coal reserves in the nearly Carpathian foothills prompted the same Rothschild interests to complete secondary lines to reach newly purchased concessions in 1870. The quantity of coal mined from this Valea Jiuliu area jumped fiftyfold during the first two years after the railway arrived. Iron ore mining around the major Hunedoara and Reşiţa metallurgical centers in present-day Romania also responded. In contrast to Macedonia, freight for these and other enterprises soon provided 75 percent of railway income. By 1900 the original STEG mines and ironworks, now state-owned along with the railways, still turned out 20 percent of the largest coal and iron production anywhere in Southeastern Europe. About 95 percent of aggregate coal production and 60 percent of the pig iron was in European hands. Of these holdings, the Viennese Great Banks controlled upwards of one third, the Budapest banks one fifth, and German and French institutions another fifth.[58]

The Habsburg market furnished an ever larger share of the demand for this production. Relatively little was exported to Romania. Although not yet suitable for coking, some coal went to the nearby Reşiţa or Hunedoara iron mining and smelting centers. The rest was delivered to the state railway or to the growing population and industry of Budapest. Transylvanian mines furnished 26 percent of Hungarian coal by 1900. The share for iron ore reached 45 percent.[59]

The development of Transylvanian mining and metallurgy after 1900 does not suggest, however, that the Great Banks and other private interests were responding aggressively to the increasing European income and industrial production that distinguished the last decade and a half before the First World War. True, the volume of coal mined nearly tripled and the production of pig iron almost doubled during the period 1898–1910. Yet these increases were not as promising for continued growth as they seem at first glance. No in-

vestments were made to modernize coal mining techniques dating
from the 1870s, in contrast to the Slovenian experience. The private
companies relied on high prices rather than finding new markets to
assure their profits. The situation in ferrous metallurgy was still more
serious: its total fixed capital actually declined from 1901 to 1910.
The state ironworks at Hunedoara became the largest producer of pig
iron, with 38 percent of total output and over half the branch's labor
force. Private production probably went down. Little new technology
was introduced once the STEG works at Reşiţa had adopted
Siemens-Martin furnaces in the 1890s.

What was missing after 1900 was the next step in developing any
metallurgical complex: machine production. The Viennese and
Budapest Great Banks evidently preferred to promote such development closer to home. Transylvanian machine works remained essentially repair shops, typically serving the railway or some other
state enterprise. The area continued to import up to 80 percent of its
machinery from the Dual Monarchy or elsewhere in Europe until the
First World War.[60]

Timber and Other Light Industry

Although richer in mineral resources, the Habsburg borderlands
shared comparably extensive stands of upland timber with the independent Balkan states. The borderlands' closer proximity and location inside the monarchy's customs union gave them the obvious advantage in timber processing for the plains of Hungary proper and
the world cities of Budapest and Vienna, grown to a combined population of 3 million by 1910. Although exact figures are lacking, timber
production undoubtedly dominated the light industry of all the borderlands, Bosnia-Hercegovina included. Timber explained up to half
of the advantage in total output the other three enjoyed over Serbian
and Bulgarian industry. At the same time, the borderlands' most
prominent light industry showed few signs before 1914 of developing the sophisticated processing, including paper manufacture, that
allowed Swedish producers to survive the inevitable depletion of
timber reserves.[61]

For Transylvania, timber cutting or processing firms more than
doubled for 1890-1900 to 98 of the 310 industrial enterprises with
over twenty employees. The number nearly doubled again for
1900-10. Fixed capital climbed more than threefold to account for
almost one quarter of the industrial total. These 48 million Krs.
nearly matched the 55 million invested in metallurgy, down from 59
million in 1900.[62] Timber had attracted primarily Viennese capital
until 1890. Then the 1881 Hungarian law for industrial encourage-

ment was revised in order to check rising emigration. It prompted a
number of Budapest banks to begin investing in Transylvanian light
and heavy industry. As with metallurgy, however, the combined flow
of Austrian and Hungarian capital did not see fit to develop the
further processing of timber. Most enterprises remained rudimentary
sawmills. A majority of the seventeen paper mills founded during the
1890s soon collapsed for lack of the sophisticated machinery needed
to compete with firms in the upper Austrian and Slovakian areas. The
eight cellulose plants survived, but combined investment in paper
and cellulose enterprises dropped from 10 to 5 percent of the industrial total between 1900 and 1910.[63]

For Slovenia, timber-cutting so close to the wood-poor Mediterranean grew with the rise of Trieste as a city and as a port during the
second half of the nineteenth century. Railway construction and a
variety of overhead conveyors expanded the area for exploitation far
beyond that served by mountain streams. Investors like the main
steel manufacturer, the Krainische Industrie Gesellschaft, joined the
Viennese Great Banks in crediting local Austrian estate owners and
financing the modernization of some of their sawmills with high-
speed machinery. By 1913, the production of lumber, charcoal, and
firewood amounted to 104 million Kr., or almost half of total industrial output.[64] Yet the great majority of sawmills remained small-
scale, barely mechanized operations. Paper production, moreover,
had failed to spread much beyond the pioneering Tespinc enterprise.
This ethnically Slovenian undertaking used capital from the Wienerbankverein to make the firm's own wood pulp and cellulose for use
in the latest pressing machinery. Fixed investment reached 20 million Kr. by 1913. Other paper manufacturers trailed far behind, however, and the sector never produced more than 2 percent of the industrial total.

For Slavonia, center of the Croatian timber industry, the prospects
for modernization were even more limited. Sawmills were mainly
located on the estates of Austrian or Hungarian nobles. They attracted scant outside capital, partly because of less accessible rail
connections than Slovenia and partly because of the opposition of the
Hungarian governors to transferring such operations into towns. The
few French investments lasted no longer than the several years
needed to cut a particular stand of timber. They were rarely incorporated as joint-stock companies and little mechanized. Sawmill numbers and their labor force in 1900, over 40 percent of the respective
totals for Croatian industrial firms over twenty workers, exaggerate
their importance. When reserves began to run low and the German
tariff rose after 1900, their relative share of Croatian industry began
to decline. Then the world depression of 1907 delivered a further

blow by sharply reducing prices. During the decade ending in 1910, the number of timber-processing firms fell from 113 to 101 and their employment from 9,800 to 8,600.[65]

The rest of Croatian light industry more than took up the slack. The number of other firms over twenty workers rose from 100 to 170 for 1900–10 with employment up from 9,000 to 15,000. Virtually all were in light industry. Between 1906 and 1912, the value of joint-stock capital and the mechanical horsepower in Croatian industry doubled to move past the Serbian totals. Table 9.10 reflects percentages of value added that exceed the Bulgarian and even the Romanian levels. Cement, glass, and other construction materials except wood led the way, rising to 19 million Kr. and recording the highest value added of all industrial sectors by 1912. These enterprises, also according to Table 9.10, achieved an average horsepower per worker which was double that of the sawmills. Flour milling and other food processing remained the largest single branch of Croatian industry but appears to have grown less rapidly. In addition, its value added to output was one third that of construction materials. Smaller firm size negated any significance for the higher horsepower per worker recorded by food processors. Light industry accounted for almost the entire 168 million Kr., more than double the 1911 Serbian figure in per capita terms. Timber-processing totalled just 32 million Kr. The 136 million in other light industry in Croatia/Slavonia relied on sales to the rest of the Habsburg monarchy for 60 percent of its export value (versus less than 20 percent for Slovenia) and for 40 percent of total industrial production (versus about 10 percent for Slovenia). Table 9.11 indicates that, like Slovenia, total Croatian export value for all industry was about half of total output. Hungarian markets alone absorbed 34.7 million Kr. of the 60.2 million sent by all Croatian industry to the Habsburg lands. Cement sales, largely from the Beočin works near Osijek, represented almost one quarter of the Hungarian imports and over one third of Croatian production of construction materials.

By contrast, timber exports to the Hungarian lands were now below cement and not much ahead of textiles or chemicals, mainly soda. Sales of processed fats and oils as well as leather surpassed their export to the Austrian lands. Total export of animal fat and vegetable oil nearly matched the 1911 Serbian sale of processed meat to the Dual Monarchy celebrated in the previous chapter. Unlike Serbia, however, these food products accounted for one fifth, not four fifths, of manufactured exports. Timber remained 27 percent of Croatian industrial export value only because sales outside the monarchy accounted for over one half. (Processed wood and charcoal were still more than 40 percent of Slovenian industrial exports. Mining and

TABLE 9.10
COMPOSITION OF CROATIAN, ROMANIAN AND BULGARIAN MANUFACTURING
(in millions of franc equivalents)

BRANCH	CROATIA/SLAVONIA (1912)		ROMANIA (1915)		BULGARIA (1911)	
	Gross Output	Net Output	Gross Output	Net Output	Gross Output	Net Output
Textiles	15.3	5.7	45.8	20.9	21.4	9.5
Flour and other foodstuffs	73.3	22.3	215.1	67.1	64.9	15.6
Leather	12.4	4.1	24.6	3.5	5.5	.9
Chemicals	13.6	9.1	13.4	4.3	4.2	2.5
Paper	4.1	2.4	20.9	9.5	.9	.4
Wood Processing	33.5	16.2	56.7	26.3	2.7	1.2
Metal Processing	4.1	2.2	42.4	14.6	3.0	1.5
Construction Mat'ls	20.3	15.8	21.4	13.3	4.7	2.9
Total	176.7	74.2	413.4	161.5	107.3	34.5

BRANCH	Average Workers per Firm			Average Horsepower per Worker		
	CROATIA/SL.	ROMANIA	BULGARIA	CROATIA/SL.	ROMANIA	BULGARIA
Textiles	40	106	67	2.20	1.26	.92
Flour and other	18	30	11	2.94	7.57	5.64
foodstuffs		70	24		2.26	2.32
Leather	134	49	18	.73	1.22	1.27
Chemicals	21	45	17	1.49	3.00	1.05
Paper	26	109	51	1.53	1.74	1.53
Wood Processing	61	89	63	.67	1.43	.61
Metal Processing	61	105	56	8.56	1.08	.42
Construction Mat'ls	46	60	116	1.74	1.32	.57
Total	34	72	39	1.71	2.08	1.72

Sources: Rudolf Signjar. *Statistički atlas Kr. Hrvatske i Slavonije. 1875-1915* (Zagreb, 1915). pp. 48-49; Tables 8.2 and 8.3 above.

metallurgy added another 35 percent.) Croatian light industry was therefore unique among the Habsburg borderlands. It alone overcame the decline of timber processing during the last prewar decade and exploited openings in the wider Habsburg market with a variety of more sophisticated production.

Only the Beočin works represented a major commitment of bank capital from Budapest. No Viennese bank made a comparable Croatian investment. Thus the principal Habsburg stimulus to Croatian light industry probably lay on the side of demand rather than supply. In the absence of a detailed survey of ownership and investment in existing Croatian industry, the question cannot be answered definitively. Nor do we know how much further these largely local

TABLE 9.11
CROATIAN AND SLOVENIAN MANUFACTURED[a] EXPORTS IN 1912-13
(in millions of franc equivalents)

PRODUCT	CROATIA/SLAVONIA (1912)			SLOVENIA (1913)		
	Exports in mil. crowns	Exports in mil. francs	% of total manufacture	Exports in mil. crowns	Exports in mil. francs	% of total manufacture
Textiles	8.6	9.0	59	6	6.3	40
Animal fat, etc.	17.6	18.5	25	7	7.4	33
Leather	10.3	10.8	87	2.9	3.0	74
Chemicals	2.0	2.1	15	1.8	1.9	36
Paper	2.1	2.2	54			
Wood Processing	19.4	20.4	61	50	55	48
Cement and glass	9.1	9.6	47	1.9	2.0	100
Mining and metallurgy				42.5	44.6	67
Others	8.1	8.5		7.4	7.8	35
Total	77.2	81.1	46	119.5	125.5	51

DESTINATION	Exports in mil. crowns	Exports in mil. francs
Austria	25.5	26.8
Hungary	34.7	36.4
Bosnia-Hercegovina	4.4	4.6
Serbia	.3	.3
Bulgaria	.6	.6
Germany	5.3	5.7
Great Britain	1.5	1.6
France	1.2	1.3
Belgium	.4	.4
Switzerland	.3	.3
Italy	3.0	3.2
Total	77.2	81.2
(of which, through Rijeka)	(5.8)	

Note: (a)Produced by enterprises with at least 20 employees and some mechanical power.

Sources: Rudolf Signjar, *Statistički atlas Kr. Hrvatske i Slavonije, 1875-1915* (Zagreb, 1915), p. 49; Toussaint Hočevar, *The Structure of the Slovene Economy, 1848-1963* (New York: Studia Slovenica, 1965), p. 114.

enterprises, resident Austrian where not ethnically Croatian, might have moved into the openings left by the rapid but incomplete industrial development under way in Hungary proper had the First World War not intervened. Much more certain is the barrier that these Croatian enterprises would have placed in the path of Serbian or other Balkan light industries had they tried to expand beyond their limited domestic markets into neighboring Austria-Hungary. The Croatian lands were even closer than Transylvania or Slovenia to the rapidly growing, partly industrialized area around Budapest that was the monarchy's most dynamic internal market.

In the event, the breakup of the huge Habsburg customs union after the First World War allowed the Croatian economy to integrate itself within the new Yugoslav state. In addition to Serbia, Yugoslavia's large market included all the other borderlands we have just discussed, save Transylvania, which joined the enlarged Romanian state, and northern Greece. Part III now turns to their transition from participation in an imperial to a national economy. Chapters 11 and 12 will consider the experience that awaited Croatian, Slovenian, and Transylvanian industry within the smaller national markets of interwar Yugoslavia and Romania.

The Imperial Borderlands versus the Independent Balkan States

A balance sheet of the borderlands' prewar development shows several important similarities to the experience of the independent Balkan states. The narrow national boundaries that seemed to confine Bulgaria, Romania, Serbia, and Greece within smaller economic units than the Habsburg or Ottoman borderlands had not prevented these states from being drawn into the wider dynamics of Western and especially Central European industrialization. Industrial and urban growth demanded more food, more raw materials. New rail lines allowed both the borderlands and the independent states of Southeastern Europe to respond to this demand. Both earned capital that European-style financial institutions were soon distributing and absorbed growing imports that European manufacturers supplied. Neither the flow of funds or industrial goods was actually of great importance to the developed economies; this fact hardly lessened the modernizing impact of such a flow into most of Southeastern Europe.

The agricultural exports that started this reverse flow and its irreversible impact did not display characteristics by the last prewar decade that promised continued growth. Leading that growth had been rising rural population and land usage. Grain was generally the main source of an exportable surplus. By the turn of the century, however, the output of grain per capita and even per hectare in the Habsburg borderlands had begun to turn slightly down, as in the Balkan states. Extensive agricultural growth was thus coming to an end.

Nor was the way open to more intensive grain cultivation by modern methods. On the side of domestic supply, private banks and state ministries typically paid little attention to the long-term credit needed for newer equipment. The greater Habsburg reliance on direct taxation of the peasantry and less local retention of revenues cancelled the apparent advantage of the lower general level of borderland taxation than in the Balkan states.

On the side of international demand, growing protectionism in Central Europe had served to reduce the German and Austro-Hungarian share of Balkan grain exports after 1900. It did not limit them as severely as Hungarian primacy had limited the borderlands within the Habsburg customs union. That constraint had already appeared by the 1830s (see Chapter 2).

Livestock exports to the large urban markets of the customs union more than compensated the Croatian lands and the Vojvodina for the Hungarian advantage in grain. The larger local banks of the former drew on capital from Vienna and Budapest to issue mortgage bonds that financed the expansion and improved breeding of estate cattle. But peasant smallholders had little access to long-term credit except from the Raiffeisen cooperatives in Slovenia, better financed and more concerned with modernization than their Bulgarian counterparts. Slovenian land less suited to raising livestock or crops limited their impact. In any case, the much less intensive use of labor in raising livestock than for crops left the rural sector little chance to absorb a peasant population whose rate of natural increase matched the high Balkan levels. The result was a rate of overseas migration from Croatia and Slovenia that, like the other borderlands, matched that of Greece, the one Balkan state to experience any significant emigration (see Chapter 6).

The success of Croatian cattle exports to the rest of the Dual Monarchy cast a long shadow over Serbian prospects to go much further with its own livestock exports, unless scientific hog-breeding or modern meat-packing could be greatly expanded. Hungarian protectionism had nearly ended existing Serbian exports, under half the Croatian average to begin with, during the 1906–11 tariff war. Such an end had in fact been written to Romanian livestock exports to the Habsburg lands following an 1886–91 tariff war.

The only other forms of intensive agriculture open to the prewar independent Balkan states were grape cultivation, and the processing of Serbian prunes, Greek raisins, and Bulgarian tobacco. Native

governments and financial institutions again made no real contribution to improving the methods of processing. Probably more important than quality in the European markets for prunes and raisins
during the pre-1914 period was the limited demand. These were
considered luxuries, not necessities. Hence the need for state intervention in Greece, to limit production of raisins, and the likelihood
of its necessity in Serbia as well, had the plum crop not been so
vulnerable to bad harvests every few years. Bosnian plums faced the
same limitation, while the more predictable harvests of Dalmatian
vineyards would remain little used for exportable wine until after the
Second World War.

Turning to industry, more differences appear between the experience of the Balkan states and at least the Habsburg borderlands.
Official Habsburg policy offered industry little direct encouragement
except where railways were concerned. Balkan-style tax exemptions
and Hungarian-style subsidies were never extended to the borderlands. Part of the Habsburg customs union, they had no protection
against Czech or Austrian manufacturers. They did attract more investment capital, largely to heavy industry, from the Great Banks of
Vienna and Budapest than did the Balkan states from all of Europe
combined.

As we have seen in Chapter 7, the Great Banks devoted most of
their efforts in Bulgaria, Romania, Serbia, and Greece to underwriting state loans. Here was the first large-scale infusion of European
capital into the Balkan economies. Yet the resulting diversion of
scarce long-term funds to state budgets saw less and less devoted to
economic purposes. The general availability of credit was also constrained. Balkan governments joined central banks in restraining
note issue to protect the par value of the respective currencies. They
thereby assured access to further foreign loans and generally maintained stable exchange rates, pegged to the French gold franc, after
1900. The Balkan Wars of 1912–13 and the large new loans that they
engendered would have tightened available credit still more, even if
the First World War had not intervened.

Such constraints did not apply in the borderlands. From 1892 forward the Austro-Hungarian crown maintained a stable relationship to
gold without recourse to such severe credit restraints. In Slovenia,
Croatia, and Transylvania, the Great Banks that had made the initial
railway investments before 1890 continued afterwards with the
development of mining and, especially for Transylvania, metallurgy
along the new state-owned lines. The pace of construction, as noted
in Table 9.7, surpassed that of all the Balkan states except Romania.
Native or resident banks, of comparable size to their Balkan counterparts as noted in Table 9.8, also contributed. Private European in-

vestment stopped short of manufacturing machinery and increasingly deferred to the Austro-Hungarian state railway in metallurgy. All the same, only Romanian oil could attract as much foreign capital in the Balkan states. In Bosnia-Hercegovina, where Habsburg state policy held greatest sway, industrial growth was pursued only through a few scattered projects and private investment was officially discouraged.

Croatian light industry developed more broadly than in the other borderlands, where lumbering predominated and prospects faded after 1900. It also did better than in the neighboring Balkan states where food processing was the main manufacture. As the previous section has demonstrated, this advantage was not the result of any sizable movement of capital, labor, or entrepreneurship from the more developed northern regions southward. Rail access to the huge Habsburg market created the opportunity. Native or immigrant financial institutions rather than the European Great Banks provided local industry with short term credit. Management was of mixed ethnic background but drawn from resident immigrants. In other words, the Croatian borderland could not draw on the free movement of factors of production that elevate a customs union to a full economic union on the American or German model. Under such a union the largely backward rural regions of all the Habsburg borderlands would have attracted capital and sent their surplus peasant population northward to work in Hungarian agriculture or Czech industry, rather than overseas to emigrate. The odyssey of the young Josip Broz, later Tito, to Vienna and then to Prague before 1914, was an exception to the rule.

The Habsburg borderlands, like the Balkan states, thus found themselves on the war's eve with a set of modern financial and industrial sectors.[66] They approached European best practice and had recorded rapid rates of growth since 1900. Despite differences between them, both sets were less dependent on foreign capital and management than colonial counterparts in, say, British India or French Indochina. Both had grown remarkably in the last prewar decades but had failed to effect structural change within their respective economies that encompassed anything like a majority of the factors of production. These essentially native enclaves awaited some positive connection with the rural sector and the governments of the enlarged Balkan states before broadly based development could occur.

PART III.

War and Economic Development, 1912–1950

Marvin R. Jackson and John R. Lampe

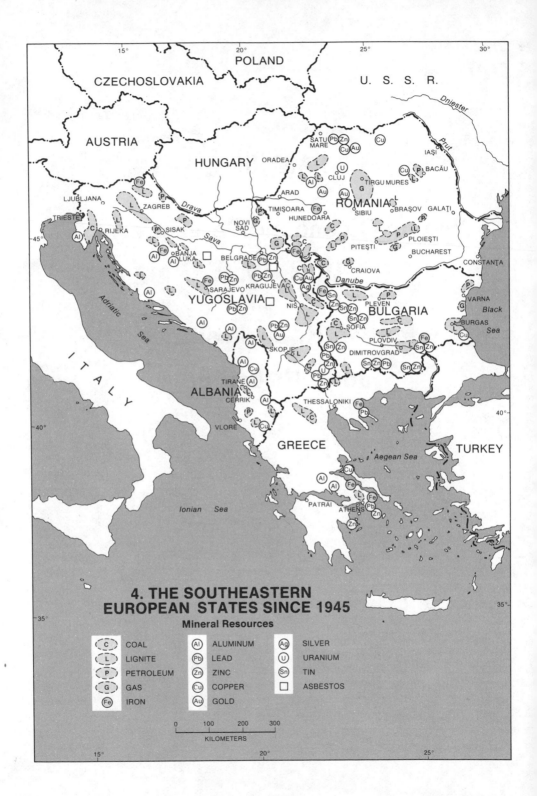

4. THE SOUTHEASTERN
EUROPEAN STATES SINCE 1945

Mineral Resources

(C) COAL	(Al) ALUMINUM	(Ag) SILVER
(L) LIGNITE	(Pb) LEAD	(U) URANIUM
(P) PETROLEUM	(Zn) ZINC	(Sn) TIN
(G) GAS	(Cu) COPPER	☐ ASBESTOS
(Fe) IRON	(Au) GOLD	

0   100   200   300
KILOMETERS

Part III begins with the disruptive consequences of one world war and ends with those from another. Yet during the two interwar decades Southeastern Europe made significant strides beyond the disjointed effort in the nineteenth century to copy whatever seemed modern in Central Europe; the region began to pursue and achieve, however imperfectly, national economic development. The quest for national economic development was continued, more consciously and successfully, in the three decades following World War II.

The year 1912 initiated a decade of warfare, beginning with the two Balkan Wars: that between the Balkan states and the Ottoman Empire and that between Bulgaria and the other Balkan states. Serbia suffered grievous losses throughout the First World War. The other Yugoslav lands, Bulgaria, Romania, and Greece experienced their trials toward the end of or after the 1914–1918 war. All the independent states had fought in the Balkan Wars. They gained new territory and population (precious little in Bulgaria's case) but sacrificed educated young men and borrowed heavily abroad. Military mobilization cut into the agricultural exports whose surplus over imports would be counted on to repay these unprecedented loans. This pattern persisted through the First World War. European military occupation or presence brought little new investment, and it accelerated inflation and depressed foreign trade. The chance to use the military emergency to rationalize the state's role in the national economy was largely foregone, although belatedly recognized. Postwar governments were thrust into conditions of economic disorder and financial uncertainty reminiscent of those that characterized the period of imperial domination treated in Part I. Peasant smallholders were discouraged, in the same way as they had been before the mid-nineteenth century, from selling grain for the export market and from buying manufactured goods.

Uncertainty and the threat of more disorder continued throughout the interwar period. The prewar Balkan states were nonetheless compensated. Their frontiers expanded to incorporate permanently the imperial borderlands. Native governments, including an independent Albania from 1912, now represented the entire population of Southeastern Europe. Their designation as Balkan states became geographically obsolete. Larger internal markets, bigger tax and resource bases, more financial and human capital were obvious economic advantages. There would be no such compensations after the Second World War.

Despite the economic importance of the two world wars for the region, especially in discouraging the close ties with the Central European economies that had begun to be formed before the nineteenth century, the focus of Part III belongs on the interwar period. Native Marxist scholars have not struck a satisfactory balance in assessing both the increasing development and the mass poverty of those years. While Western scholars have paid considerably more attention to this period than to any of the earlier eras, they still have not given it the credit it deserves. The statistical evidence that follows, though uneven in quality, and insufficient for comparable estimates of national product, suggests a more positive record. Agricultural production became more intensive, at least at the margin. Industrial output grew rapidly. Altered patterns of investment and employment constituted the start of the structural change needed for self-sustained growth. (Albania's premodern economy shared so little in the advance prior to 1945 that it will be mentioned only in passing.)

The sweeping impact of the Great Depression and the newly aggressive domination by the state of other economic institutions nonetheless distinguished the second half of the interwar period from the first. The 1920s were essentially a postwar decade. The enlarged states of Romania and Yugoslavia unified the legal and fiscal structures of their new component parts in 1923 and 1929, respectively. Bulgaria and especially Greece were grappling with the absorption of a large influx of refugees. All governments relied on prewar institutions and practices until the Depression struck.

Within the interwar period, the political leadership of the 1920s, and to a lesser extent the political institutions, must be distinguished from those of the 1930s. Prewar politicians dominated the first postwar decade. The Brătianu brothers in Romania found the rival Conservative Party virtually destroyed by its wartime support of the Central Powers; the brothers and their National Liberal Party ruled from the wings until 1922. They then won a series of corrupt elections to hold power until a year after the elder Ionel's death in 1927. In Yugoslavia Nikola Pašić led his Serbian Radical Party to power and to increasing pluralities in a series of less corrupt elections until his death in 1926. The old man had been a far more practical politician than his principal rival, Stjepan Radić, the erratic leader of the Croatian Peasant Party until his assassination in 1928. Neither dominant party, however, was able to establish a constituency in the new territories, to prevent massive opposition in Transylvania and Croatia, or even to preserve a unified party in Wallachia and Serbia, once their great leaders had died.

Bulgaria's loss of the war and Macedonia brought the foremost of the prewar opposition, Alexander Stamboliski and his Agrarian Union, to power from 1919 to 1923. Following them closely in prewar strength and in voting for the first, relatively free postwar elections, were Dimitur Blagoev and the Bulgarian Communist Party.

(The rival Social Democrats lost their pre-1914 parity with these "Narrows" after supporting the ill-fated war effort.) The two parties failed to pool the nationwide bases of rural and urban support that they enjoyed respectively. Both were brutally expelled from national political life in 1923. Macedonian irredentists murdered Stamboliski, and the prewar establishment (royal, bureaucratic, military and commercial interests combined) reassumed power.

Only Greece entered the 1930s with a prewar political leader still heading its government. Eleutherios Venizelos and his republican, so-called Liberal, followers had divided power since 1924 with monarchist interests. Some of the latter did survive the disastrous national defeat in Anatolia in 1922–23, and the departure of the King and the restaffing of the army's officer corps with republicans that followed. But five years of coalition governments and military coups created enough public dissatisfaction to give Venizelos a sweeping victory in the 1928 elections. He and his essentially personal party would remain in office until his attempt to force monarchist elements from public life misfired in 1935. The King soon returned. By the next year the royalist officer Metaxas had formed an authoritarian military government.

Elsewhere in Southeastern Europe, royal and military influence also grew after 1930. With the exception of the illegal Communists, existing political parties splintered beyond recognition, and elections gave way to perfunctory plebiscites. It is ironic that Romania and Bulgaria began the decade with reformist regimes led by parliamentary parties. Despite a number of promising reforms (see Chapter 11), Maniu's National-Peasant regime in Romania and then Malinov's Democratic coalition with the remnants of Stamboliski's Agrarians in Bulgaria were forced aside. By 1933 Romania's royal dictatorship under Carol II was well established. Military officers replaced civilian prefects under the new 1938 constitution. In Bulgaria, the Zveno group of military reformers seized power briefly during 1934–35, and subjected the ministerial bureaucracy to an overdue housecleaning and consolidation. King Boris, backed by more senior army officers, took personal control for the remaining prewar years, pursuing perhaps the most enlightened economic policy of the four monarchs (five, if we include King Zog of Albania). Boris favored light industry as well as the rearmament that all supported.

Royal dominance was unclear only in Yugoslavia and then because of King Alexander's assassination in 1934. Six years before, he had imposed the first of the so-called royal dictatorships in Southeastern Europe. The Prime Minister under the regency that followed the assassination, Milan Stojadinović, was a Serb like all but one of his interwar counterparts. Although he was a trained economist, Stojadinović, in office until 1938, made no more noticeable headway against the international depression than did any of his counterparts. Nor was his halfhearted resort to fascist trappings any more successful in creating a new mass party in Serbia, let alone in the resentful Croatian lands, than such devices had been in Greece and Romania.

Two separate chapters explore the economic development that did manage to take place during the 1920s under each of these political settings. Chapter 10 treats the flawed efforts of prewar leadership and practice to maintain agricultural and overall growth through the difficult years from 1912 to 1930. Chapter 11 treats finance and industry during the same period. The role of the state increased in all three sectors during the 1930s. This greater role of the state, set against a background of worldwide depression and rising Nazi ambitions, provides the focus for Chapter 12. Chapter 13 ends Part III by examining the consequences of the Second World War for the state sector, whose expansion immediately afterwards is attributable more to the economic consequences of the war itself, beyond the obvious political consequences of Soviet domination, than has previously been acknowledged.

10.

The Disruption of Prewar
Patterns: Agriculture and
Aggregate Growth

The prewar pattern of economic growth in Southeastern Europe had depended on increasing agricultural production and exports. Grain provided most of the export earnings. Greek raisins and Yugoslav prunes and livestock also contributed a share. Rising peasant population in the independent Balkan states, as we have seen in Chapter 6, checked the growth in real per capita production and exports after 1900. Steady or slightly declining export levels sufficed, under restricted credit regimes, to keep the national currencies at par with the French gold franc and to maintain access to the European capital market. Balkan state revenues had continued to command an increasing share of national income. They surpassed both the per capita value of exports and European levels of taxation by the last prewar decade (see Chapter 7). Small industrial sectors faced competing imports made cheaper by overvalued domestic currency. They received little compensation from foreign capital or state expenditures. Several branches of native industry nonetheless grew rapidly to reach the limits of relatively small domestic markets (see Chapter 8).

The territorial settlements that followed the Balkan Wars and the First World War obviously increased the size of those domestic markets, although not greatly for Bulgaria. At the same time the wider European market for Balkan agricultural exports was disrupted. Sales to Western Europe, as we shall see, never really returned to the prewar level. Standard Western accounts of Southeastern Europe during the 1920s have paid attention mainly to the disruption of the former Habsburg market and to the efforts of the new regimes at land reform and industrial promotion. Smaller land holdings and higher import tariffs are both claimed to have cut into the peasant majority's disposable income. Little wonder, we are told with scant statistical support, that agriculture and industry made so little progress even before the depression of the 1930s.[1]

The more statistical account that follows will suggest some significant areas of agricultural and industrial advance, in marginal if not aggregate terms. Access to markets and capital will emerge as the most serious obstacles to further growth. Admitted failures of state policy will appear more the result of applying the monetary and fiscal imperatives of prewar financial orthodoxy than of misdirected land reforms or of any systematic effort to favor industry over agriculture.

The Agricultural Impact of the First World War

More important to agriculture than land reform or industrial tariffs was the massive impact of the First World War. Its course and immediate aftermath fell most heavily on the predominant agricultural sector, with the possible exception of Serbia where every sector was devastated. Battle damage, contrary to popular assumption, was not the main cause of dislocation. Western Europe's more intensive cultivation suffered greater losses in this regard.[2] It was a series of nonmilitary disruptions that continued to plague the agricultural sectors of Southeastern Europe well into the 1920s.

War-related changes in national boundaries pose serious problems in connecting statistical records from before 1912 to those after 1920. But, once untangled, aggregate changes in population, production, and foreign trade within new boundaries make clear the weight of the wartime decade. Portentous differences among the national experiences also emerge.

Land, Population, and Aggregate Growth

The territorial gains and population changes set down in Table 10.1 point toward these varied national experiences. The parameters of Bulgarian land and population were relatively undisturbed by wars and peace settlements. Within the greatly expanded postwar boundaries of Greece, Romania, and Yugoslavia, these populations found their rapid prewar growth interrupted, although for different reasons. Romania and Yugoslavia suffered the war's highest casualty rates; Greece appears to have experienced an abrupt decline in birth rates,[3] although Greek data on vital statistics, especially birth records, are incomplete or inconsistent until 1926. This much is clear:

any small propensity for greater natural growth for 1921–25 was swamped by a reversal of the large prewar emigration. Largely responsible was the disastrous military campaign in Asia Minor in 1922–23. Over one million Greek refugees from Anatolia streamed in to more than replace the departure of at least 350,000 Turks and Albanians. By 1926–30 lower birth and death rates combined with virtually no net emigration to produce a "normal" population growth rate only slightly lower than the 1½ percent prevailing elsewhere in Southeastern Europe. Down from the abnormal 2½ percent recorded for 1921–25, this overall rate was still about twice Greece's prewar increment.[4]

Romania and Yugoslavia recorded lower crude birthrates for 1921–30 than did the prewar Old Kingdom and Serbia. Table 10.2 makes this clear but does not resolve the question of whether birthrates in Transylvania and the western Yugoslav lands, lower before 1914, were responsible. Better statistical evidence for Bulgaria suggests that after the postwar baby boom its rate of reproduction began a long-term downturn.[5] Generally, however, lower postwar death rates and sharply reduced overseas emigration, especially from the former Habsburg territories in western Romania and Yugoslavia, brought overall population growth back to prewar levels of roughly 1½ percent.

Rapid population growth renewed pressure on the predominantly agricultural resources of the region. It is this pressure on the land, and not the absolute increases in population density recorded in Table 10.1, that gives economic significance to population growth in the 1920s. Population density in Southeastern Europe was and remains the lowest in Europe, but so is the arable proportion of the area's territory, so there is continued pressure on available land, as we can see from Table 10.3. Even the modest increases in shares of agricultural dependency that took place in the 1920s yield large absolute increases in persons depending on the land for their livelihood when multiplied by the growth of total population. It would be incorrect to overlook increasing man/land ratios. Larger proportions of those people born between 1910 and 1920 nonetheless came to depend on nonagricultural occupations. Some marginal movement from agriculture was thus underway. Whether from push or by pull, younger people were shifting occupational dependence and location. Increases in urban population shares between 1910 and 1930 were moderate in all countries but Greece. The share of population in towns over 20,000 rose markedly in Bulgaria and spectacularly in Greece. In addition, nearly half a million, or 11 percent, of Bulgaria's rural population drew their livelihood from nonagricultural occupations.

TABLE 10.1
TERRITORIAL AND POPULATION CHANGES, 1910-30

	ALBANIA	BULGARIA	GREECE	ROMANIA	YUGOSLAVIA
Territory (sq. km.)					
Prewar		96346	63211[b]	130177[a]	59618[a]
Postwar	28748	103146	129281[b]	295049	247542
Population (1000 persons)[c]					
1910					
Prewar territory		4338	2684	7026	3162
Postwar territory		4363	4924	15805	12241
1920	803	4847	5017	15635	11985
1930	1003	5696	6415	18057	13883
Density (persons per sq. km.)					
1910					
Prewar territory		45.0	42.5	54.0	53.0
Postwar territory		42.3	38.1	53.6	49.5
1920	27.9	47.0	38.8	53.0	48.4
1930	34.9	55.2	49.6	61.2	56.1
Population growth					
A. Percentage					
1910 to 1920					
Prewar to postwar territory		11.7	86.9	122.5	279.0
On postwar territory		11.1	1.9	(-)1.1	(-)2.1
1920 to 1930	24.9	17.5	27.9	15.5	15.8
1910 to 1930					
Prewar to postwar territory		31.3	139.0	157.0	339.1
On postwar territory		30.6	30.3	14.2	13.4
B. Average annual percentage					
1910 to 1920					
On postwar territory		1.06	0.19	nil	nil
1920 to 1930	2.25	1.63	2.46	1.45	1.48
1910 to 1930					
On postwar territory		1.34	1.33	0.67	0.63

Notes: (a)Prewar Romania is Old Kingdom only; prewar Yugoslavia is Serbia and Montenegro. (b)Greece's interwar territory was given in interwar sources as 127,000 sq. km. Its area was not accurately surveyed until 1963. The figure in the Table is the result of a 1971 revision of the survey estimates. (c)Population figures are year-end estimates.

Sources: Marvin R. Jackson, "Comparing the Balkan Demographic Experience, 1860 to 1950," *Faculty Working Papers in Economics*, No. 79-86 (Tempe, Arizona: College of Business Administration, Arizona State University, 1979), Tables B-1 and B-3.

TABLE 10.2
SOURCES OF POPULATION CHANGE, 1910-30
(annual average per 1000 population)

Area and Year	Actual Increase	Births	Deaths	Natural Increase	Implied Net Migration[a]
Bulgaria					
1910-15	15.0	40.6	22.4	18.1	- 3.2
1906-10[d]	14.4	42.1	24.0	18.1	- 3.6
1911-20[d]	10.5			9.1	+ 1.4
1921-25[d]	20.4	39.0	20.8	18.2	+ 2.2
1926-30[d]	14.5	33.0	17.9	15.3	- 0.8
Greece					
1897-07[d]	7.8				
1911-20[d]	1.9			3.5[b]	- 1.6[b]
1921-25[d]	35.5	(21.5)[c]	(15.4)[c]	(6.1)[c]	+(18-27)[c]
1926-30[d]	13.4	29.9	16.4	13.5	- 0.1
Romania					
1900-12[e]	14.9	40.1	25.5	14.6	+ 0.3
1911-20[d]	-1.1			0.2	- 1.3
1921-25[d]	14.5	36.7	22.3	14.4	+ 0.1
1926-30[d]	14.3	34.5	20.8	13.7	- 0.6
Yugoslavia					
1901-10[f]	15.4	39.2	23.5	15.7	- 0.3
1901-10[g]	8.2	39.7	26.8	12.9	- 4.7
1901-10[h]	4.1			10.7	- 6.3
1911-20[d]	-2.1			-0.7	- 1.4
1921-25[d]	14.8	35.0	20.2	14.8	nil
1926-30[d]	14.8	34.2	20.0	14.2	+ 0.6

Notes: (a)Except for Greece in 1911-20 and 1921-25, calculated as the difference in actual increase and natural increase implied by vital statistics. (b)Natural increase estimated by subtracting from actual increase; net migration estimated directly. (c)Until 1926, Greek vital statistics are clearly defective; net migration rates are estimated directly. (d)Postwar territory. (e)Old Kingdom. (f)Serbia. (g)Croatia. (h)Slovenia.

Sources: Marvin R. Jackson. "Comparing the Balkan Demographic Experience, 1860 to 1950," *Faculty Working Papers in Economics*, No. 79-86 (Tempe, Arizona: College of Business Administration, Arizona State University, 1979), Tables A-5, B-3, and C-2.

Changes in occupational structure, estimated in Table 10.4, were not connected in any simple fashion to changing urban shares or agricultural dependency. The potential growth of Greek, Romanian, and Yugoslav labor forces was more rapid than their overall population growth; their proportions of population of employable age (15 to 64 years) increased at a faster rate. Bulgaria's less difficult demographic experience during the war reduced the weight of its working-age population and potential growth in the labor force. In all four countries rates of participation in the labor force moved up.

Changes in the structure of the labor force are probably more accurately revealed, as in Table 10.4, by the male proportions. Female proportions, especially in agriculture, were subject to such a variety of changing statistical practices that real changes in occupation could easily be obscured.

The large increase in shares of Greek males occupied in agriculture from 1904 to 1920 must be attributed to new northern territories with higher proportions of agricultural employment rather than any overall reversion to agriculture. Interestingly, the share of industrial labor force still increased by 1920. Over the next decade industrial shares were boosted again by the Anatolian immigrants, 25 percent of whom were so occupied in the 1928 census.[6] Bulgaria and

TABLE 10.3
URBAN POPULATION AND POPULATION
DEPENDENT ON AGRICULTURE, 1910-30

Area	Year	Percentage of Urban Population			Population Dependent on Agriculture[c]	
		National Definition[a]	Places over 2,000	Places over 20,000	(1000)	(% of total)
Albania	1930				800[d]	80.0
Bulgaria	1910	19.1	36.4	7.4	3266	75.3
	1920	29.9	42.8	9.0	3689	76.1
	1930[b]	21.0	46.8	12.0	4268	73.9
Greece	1907-11[b]	24.0	33.0	12.6	1790	66.3
	1920	27.0	37.0	17.0	3555	70.9
	1928-30[b]	33.0	42.0	27.0	4380	68.3
Romania	1910-12	15.5				
	1920	22.2			11500[d]	74.0
	1930	20.2	23.6	13.2	13063	72.3
Old Kingdom	1912	17.2		10.7	4990[d]	69.0
S. Dobrogea	1910	18.2				
Translyvania	1910	12.9				
Bessarabia	1911	13.9				
Bucovina	1910	21.9				
Old Kingdom	1930	23.8	20.2	12.0	6241	71.0
Transylvania	1930	17.4				69.7
Bessarabia	1930	13.0				82.5
Bucovina	1930	26.7				69.6

TABLE 10.3 (continued)

Area	Year	Percentage of Urban Population			Population Dependent on Agriculture[c]	
		National Definition[a]	Places over 2,000	Places over 20,000	(1000)	(% of total)
Yugoslavia	1910				10282[d]	80.0
	1920[b]			7.8	9456	78.9
	1930[b]	18.7		9.3	10771	76.5
Slovenia	1910		26.7			
Serbia	1910	14.0				
Croatia	1910				2719	78.6
Macedonia	1900	31.4				
Slovenia	1920[b]					63.1
Croatia	1920[b]				2487	72.6
Macedonia	1920[b]	27.4				74.3
Slovenia	1930[b]					60.5
Croatia	1930[b]				2635	69.5
Macedonia	1930[b]	28.3				74.4

Notes: (a)The national definition of urban population for Greece and Yugoslavia was the population of places with 5,000 or more persons. Bulgaria and Romania defined an urban place qualitatively. (b)Bulgarian data for 1930 are averages of data from year-end censuses in 1926 and 1934. Greek data for 1907-11 and 1928-30 refer to percentages from the population censuses of 1907 and 1928 while the number of agriculturally dependent persons is derived by applying those percentages to estimated total populations of 1911 and 1930. Yugoslav data for 1920 and 1930 refer to the censuses of January 1921 and March 1931. (c)Agriculture includes related occupations of forestry, fishing and hunting. (d)Albania's population dependent on agriculture is estimated by Kirk as the same as the neighboring Yugoslav *banovina* of Zetska and Vardar. Population dependent on agriculture (Y) in Romania's Old Kingdom for 1912 is estimated on the basis of the percentage of males occupied in agriculture (X) and Kirk's regression equation, $Y = 0.6 + 0.808927X + 0.0021238X^2$ (see Kirk, pp. 62-63). Romania's population dependent on agriculture is Tomasevich's estimate (p. 317). Yugoslavia's population dependent on agriculture in 1910 is a percentage estimate for population on post World War II territory applied to the estimated 1910 population on interwar territory (see Vinski, p. 211).

Sources: Table 8.1; Dudley Kirk, *Europe's Population in the Interwar Years* (Princeton, 1946), pp. 262-75; P. Bairoch *et al.*, *The Working Population and Its Structure* (Brussels, 1968), pp. 89, 101, 113, 120; United Nations, Department of Economic and Social Affairs, *Growth of the World's Urban and Rural Population, 1920-2000*, Population Studies, No. 44 (New York, 1969), pp. 104-06; *Statisticheski godishnik na Bulgarskoto Tsarstvo, 1912* (Sofia, 1915), p. 28; *1934* (Sofia, 1935), pp. 13, 17; *1938* (Sofia, 1939), pp. 24, 38-39, 40-41; *Statistikē epetēris tēs Ellados, 1930* (Athens, 1931), pp. 23, 28-29, 34, 75; Ch. Evelpidi, *Theoria kai praxis agrotikēs politikēs kai oikonomias*, Vol. A (Athens, 1939), p. 86; *Anuarul statistic al României, 1915-16* (Bucharest, 1919), pp. 15, 18; *1939-40* (Bucharest, 1940), pp. 44, 142; Louis B. Michael, *Agricultural Survey of Europe: The Danube Basin—Part 2. Rumania, Bulgaria, and Yugoslavia*, Technical Bulletin No. 126, United States Department of Agriculture (Washington, October 1929), p. 15; Institutul Central de Statistica, *Recensământul general al populaţiei României din 29 decemvrie 1930*, Vol. IX (Bucharest, 1 pp. 747-841; Ivo Vinski, "National Product and Fixed Assets in the Territory of Yugoslavia, 1909-1959," in International Association for Research in Income and Wealth, *Income and Wealth*, Series IX, *Studies in Social and Financial Accounting* (London: Bowes and Bowes, 1961), p. 211; Vladimir Stipetić, *Kretanje i tendencije u razvitku poljoprivredne proizvodnje na području NR Hrvatske* (Zagreb, 1959), p. 105; Jozo Tomasevich, *Peasants, Politics, and Economic Change in Yugoslavia* (Stanford, 1955), pp. 303, 317; L. Sokolov, *Promene u strukturi stanovništva na teritoriji NR Makedonije 1921-1953 godine kao odraz ekonomskog razvoja* (Skopje, 1962), pp. 63, 74, 90-95; Toussaint Hočevar, *The Structure of the Slovenian Economy, 1848-1963* (New York: Studia Slovenica, 1965), p. 91.

TABLE 10.4
WORK PARTICIPATION AND OCCUPIED LABOR FORCE, 1910-30

Country	Year	Active Population as percentage of Population 15-64[a]		Agriculture[b]		Occupied Labor Force					
						Industry			Other		
		Males	Females	Males (1000)	(%)	Total (1000)	Males (1000)	(%)	Total (1000)	Males (1000)	(%)
Bulgaria	1910	92.5	65.7	929	72.4	180	160	12.5	223	194	15.1
	1920	103.5	81.8	1035	72.6	211	182	12.8	247	209	14.7
	1930[d]	103.6	83.4	1258	71.2	279	235	13.3	325	273	15.5
Greece	1907[e]	89.5	7.6	(331)	49.3	(128)	(108)	16.1	(262)	(231)	34.6
	1920	104.5	22.2	817	58.7	304	243	17.4	640	454	23.9
	1928	109.0	39.4	1008	56.6	436	336	18.8	893	689	24.6
Romania											
Old Kingdom	1912[f]	104.3	83.3	1584	71.0	318	255	11.4	493	391	17.5
Old Kingdom	1930[f]	112.4	88.2	1876	68.2	449	363	13.2	718	508	18.5
Total	1930[f]	107.8	84.4	4047	70.4	963	784	13.6	1354	914	15.9
Yugoslavia	1910					491			715		
	1920	(86.1)	52.0			535			650		
	1930	109.3		3234	72.7	678	557	12.5	906	655	14.7

Notes: (a)Based on variable standards of active classification. (b)Including forestry, fishing and hunting. (c)Including mining, manufacturing, utilities and construction. (d)Average of 1926 and 1934 census data. (e)Numbers are understated by the relatively large proportions in the category "occupied-unclassified." (f)Industry total given in the 1930 census is increased by 204 thousand estimated repair and maintenance employees of the railroads, a figure estimated as the difference between total railroad employees of 284 thousand given by Madgearu and 80 thousand in transportation proper given by the Romanian enterprise census of 1930. Ten percent of the increase is assumed to have been classified as occupied in agriculture and ninety percent as occupied in other areas. Male occupation in industry and both total and male occupation in industry in Old Kingdom areas for 1930 are adjusted by the same proportions.

Sources: Same as for Table 10.3 and V. N. Madgearu, Evoluția economiei românești (Bucharest, 1940), p. 137.

Romania's Old Kingdom exhibited similar trends from 1910 to 1930. Shares of males in agriculture fell slightly and shares in industry rose by the same marginal amount. Estimates for Yugoslavia did not separate male and female active populations before 1930. Their combined share in agriculture was down nearly 4 percent by 1930 and up 2 percent in industry compared to 1910.

Occupational structure, like urban and agricultural-dependency data, shows no "revolutionary" change in any of the four economies in Table 10.4. Yet marginal changes away from agriculture and toward industry took place. Industry absorbed one quarter more of the increment in the male labor force for 1910 to 1930 than industry in 1910 employed. The Bulgarian case is particularly striking because of the slower growth of the total labor force. Given that only 160,000 were employed in Bulgarian industry in 1910 and that 483,000 males were added to its labor force by 1930, one would hardly have expected Bulgarian industry to employ 643,000 in 1930. That it did suggests that rising industrial employment completely stopped the growth of agricultural labor. We shall return in Chapter 11 to the question of what sort of industrial development prompted this small but significant shift in employment.

Before examining such structural change, we must set down the available record of economic growth during the first post-war decade. In the absence of preferred estimates of gross national product, we have assembled in Table 10.5 for Bulgaria, Greece, and Romania (a) indices of changes in real per capita gross output for leading sectors of "material" production and (b) the structure of gross and net material production for 1929 (excluding transportation and communications and for Yugoslavia, only net production) in terms of each country's own current prices. These 1929 production values cannot be compared from country to country in any meaningful way.[7] As shown by Table 11.2 below, quite different inflationary experiences destroyed any sense of the purchasing power parity among lev, drachma, leu, and dinar that the prewar Gold Standard and common membership in the Latin Currency Union had afforded. No careful study of inflation rates among the various sectors or of relative prices in 1929 has yet been done. It would therefore be unwise to derive comparisons by deflation of aggregate values with aggregate price indices to common prewar value bases, even if they were available for the same year.

Several important features are nonetheless unmistakable. Manufacturing outperformed crop production in all four countries. Manufacturing in Bulgaria and Greece, both less industrialized in 1910 and with internal economies less disturbed by the course of the war, grew much faster than manufacturing in the two larger and naturally better endowed countries.

TABLE 10.5

GROWTH AND STRUCTURE OF MATERIAL PRODUCT SECTORS, 1911-30

| Country and Sector | Growth of Gross Production Per Capita — Constant Price Indices[a] | | | | | | Structure of Per Capita Production in 1929 | | | |
| | | | | | | | Value[b] | | Percent | |
	1911	1914	1919	1922	1929	1930	Gross	Net[d]	Gross[c]	Net[d]
Bulgaria[d,f]										
Crops	100	70 (64)	71 (65)	66 (61)	91 (84)	110 (102)	3278	2923	63.6	47.6
Livestock[g]							1746	1678		26.9
Other[h]								74		1.2
Forestry	100	60	80	207	130	111	278	278		4.4
Extraction	100	139	166	187	304	288	88	58	1.7	0.9
Manufacturing	100			159	374	416	1790	512	34.7	8.2
Construction								48		0.8
Artisan	100			161	370	409		673		10.6
Sub-total							(5156)	6244	(100.0)	100.0
Total[i]	100			74	122	143				
Greece[e]										
Crops	129	100	79	73	80	83	1387	1290	53.3	37.5
Livestock[g]							760	685		20.0
Other[h]								116		3.4
Forestry								179		5.2
Extraction	180	100	48	72	100	88	181	50	2.9	1.5
Manufacturing		100		220	304	309	(76)[j] (1139)[k]	636	43.8	18.5
Construction										
Artisan				203	280	283		477		13.9
Sub-total							(2602)	3433	(100.0)	100.0
Total[i]	100			97	119	122				

TABLE 10.5 (continued)

	Constant Price Indices[a]					Value[b]		Percent	
	1913	1919	1922	1929	1930	Gross[c]	Net[d]	Gross[c]	Net[d]
Romania[e,k]									
Crops[g]	(100)	(76)[n]	71	88	84	4931	4625	52.6	44.4
Livestock[g]						2329	1953		18.8
Other[h]						49	49		0.5
Forestry						588	588		5.6
Extraction	100	52	78	142	149	665	640	7.1	6.1
Manufacturing	100	70	71	115	109	3771	1835	40.3	17.6
Construction						570	299		2.9
Artisan							422		4.1
Sub-total	100		72	118	114				
Total[i]	100		71	100	96	(9367)	10411	(100.0)	100.0

	1909–12	1920	1923	1929	1930	Gross[c]	Net[d]	Gross[c]	Net[d]
Yugoslavia[m]						(m)		(m)	
Crops	100	71	(100)[p]	(106)[p]	(104)[p]		2189		60.0
Livestock									
Other									
Forestry			(100)[p]	(109)[p]	(102)[p]		313		8.6
Sub-total			111	118	115				
Extraction			(100)[p]	(127)[p]	(127)[p]				
Manufacturing							707		19.4
Construction			(100)[p]	(104)[p]	(129)[p]		51		1.4
Artisan			(100)[p]	(112)[p]	(109)[p]		389		10.7
Sub-total			132	159	159				
Total	100		120	133	131		3649		100.0

TABLE 10.5 (continued)

Notes: (a)Indices for crops, forestry and extraction in Bulgaria, Greece and Romania are based on physical output series weighted by 1938 prices. Indices for manufacturing and for Yugoslavia are explained in sources. (b)Current prices in respective national currency units. (c)Total and percentages of gross production are only for three sectors for which growth indices are given (forestry excluded for Bulgaria). Net values are not value-added (see respective notes). Net crops are gross crops minus requirements for seeds (inputs from other sectors are not subtracted). Net livestock is gross livestock minus cereal crops used for feed. Net manufacturing is gross manufacturing minus costs for raw materials and fuels. (e)Gross crop value and indices include only fodder crops exported or delivered to non-farm sectors as reported in the respective statistical yearbooks except Bulgarian tobacco is valued according to Chakalov; values for fresh grapes and fruits other than plums have been added to Romania and Greece includes olives and olive oil (see sources below). (f)Bulgarian crop indices are in parenthesis are based on the value of production in 1911 on Bulgaria's prewar territory. (g)Gross livestock values include the same products for Bulgaria, Greece and Romania (meat, milk and milk products, eggs, poultry, hides, wool and goat hair). Bulgarian hide production has been estimated as the same percentage of meat production as in Romania. Items such as slaughter by-products, poultry feathers, animal manure and animal reproduction have not been included. (h)Includes fishing, hunting, bee-keeping and sericulture. (i)Total index is based on indices for crops, extraction and manufacturing weighted by gross production values in 1929; for Bulgaria, the crop index used is that for postwar territory. (j)Greek gross extraction is estimated as the same ratio to net as in Bulgaria. (k)Greek gross manufacturing value in 1929 is underestimated because it excludes the values of wheat flour, wine and olive oil (the latter is included in gross crop production). (l)The base for Romanian crops is the average of 1909-13. (m)Gross production values could not be found for Yugoslavia. (n)Old Kingdom only; 1911 = 100. (o)Crop index based on five main cereals, potatoes, sugar beets and tobacco; 1909-13 = 100. (p)Indices of these individual sectors given to indicate their growth in the 1920s; they are based on different prices than the subtotal and total indices.

Sources: See sources for Tables 10.7, 10.9 and 11.8; Ivo Vinski, "National Product and Fixed Assets in the Territory of Yugoslavia, 1909-1959," in International Association for Resarch in Income and Wealth, *Income and Wealth*, Series IX (London: Bowes and Bowes, 1961), pp. 221, 226-27; Stevan Stajić, *Nacionalni dohodak Jugoslavije 1923-1939 u stalnim i tekućim cenama* (Belgrade, 1959), Tables 1-3.

Both Bulgaria and Greece enjoyed considerable wartime expansion of their manufacturing sectors, Greece perhaps the most if we possessed the necessary data for 1911. Greek growth slackened after 1921. Bulgarian manufacturing actually doubled its wartime momentum during the 1920s to record a real per capita growth rate for the entire period 1911–1929 that averaged 7.8 percent a year. (Aggregate growth exceeded 9 percent a year.) Romanian industry was badly set back by the war. So, surely, despite the lack of quantification, was that of Yugoslavia. In the 1920s, both of their extractive sectors grew faster than manufacturing. Romania's industrial recovery was remarkably slow. Manufacturing barely recaptured 1913 levels by 1929. For any comparison with Bulgaria and Yugoslavia, however, the rapid Romanian expansion from 1910 to 1913 should be recalled. Its per capita manufacturing index for 1929 if based on 1910 would probably show at least 20 percent more growth, yet still not as much as in Bulgaria or Yugoslavia (see sources for Table 10.5). In sum, the early lead of the Romanian industrial sector over those of its Balkan neighbors continued to shrink during the 1920s. The tendency of the others' manufactured production, led by Bulgaria, to grow at least twice as rapidly had already appeared during the past prewar decade (see Chapters 6 and 8).

Despite the most rapid growth in the area, Bulgarian manufacturing produced less than its neighbors when compared to other sectors in 1929. According to Table 10.5, gross output of manufacturing barely exceeded half that of crops. Its net output, with a much smaller value added, was less than one fifth of the net value of crops or a little more than one tenth of that of crops and animal products.

The value of Greek manufacturing compared to crops in gross terms, or crops and animal products in net terms, reveals a relative size on a par with manufacturing (or industry) in Romania and Yugoslavia. The size of Greek manufacturing would be still larger if the missing values of wheat flour and wine production could be added.

Greek manufacturing compared to agriculture loomed so large only because, as suggested by the share of labor in Table 10.4, the latter's role even before the war was attenuated. Then followed two difficult decades for crop production. Per capita output on admittedly different territories was already down more than a fifth from 1911 to 1914. By 1919, less than two thirds of the 1911 level was produced. Almost none of the lost ground had been recovered as late as 1930.

Agriculture's performance elsewhere was better only because of mild recoveries from extraordinary lows. Bad weather and wartime dislocation pushed Bulgaria's per capita crop down a third or more by 1914. Results in 1919 and 1921 were even worse. Romanian output in 1920 was down comparably; Yugoslavia's performance was slightly better. By 1929 or 1930, only Bulgarian and Yugoslav agriculture had managed to equal prewar levels of per capita crop production on equivalent territories.

Given the weight of crop output in material production, it is not surprising that Romania, with a lackluster industrial performance as well, just equalled its 1913 level of gross material production per capita by 1929. Bulgaria and Greece did better, but their rapidly growing manufacturing sectors, which accounted for relatively small shares of net output, surely cause the index of gross output to overstate the per capita growth of net material product. Overall growth indices recalculated with net weights of 1929 show a bare 6 percent improvement per capita by 1929 in Greece (compared to 1914), a smaller 3 percent increase in Bulgaria (compared to 1911), and a 3 percent decrease in Romania (compared to 1913). Production in Romania's Old Kingdom was undoubtedly higher in 1913 than 1911. Its index of overall growth, if based on 1911, would therefore have been raised closer to that of Bulgaria. Crop production on new Greek territories in 1914 was undoubtedly lower than in 1911. If based on 1911, its rate of net economic growth would have been pushed down toward that of Bulgaria. This leaves Yugoslavia's growth index, because of a better agricultural performance, as the only one showing enough improvement over prewar levels to keep the gap between its net product and that of the developed European economies from widening.

Reduced levels of per capita crop output in all but Yugoslavia in the 1920s could hardly bode well for exports no matter what conditions might have been in Western and Central European markets. In order to trace the commercial impact of the war and its aftermath, Table 10.6 follows per capita exports and imports in values deflated to account for each country's falling exchange rate. The data bear unavoidable ambiguities because territories changed. Yugoslavia's postwar trade is paired with that for prewar Serbia, and that for Greater Romania with the prewar Old Kingdom. Also troubling is the possibility that exchange rates, under pressure from capital movements and speculation, failed to mirror actual foreign trade prices.

Several important continuities with the pattern of overall production still emerge. Yugoslavia's higher increase in net material product is matched by one quarter increases in per capita exports for both 1921–25 over Serbia's 1909–12 and for 1926–30 over 1921–25, with a negligible import surplus. Bulgarian national product and also exports, despite the loss of the Dobrudjan grain lands, stayed up surprisingly well for 1921–25. The near absence of export growth after 1925 corresponds to the insignificant advance in national product. The drop in Romanian per capita exports in 1921–25 exceeds the fall in crop production. Neither had recovered by 1926–30 to three quarters of Old Kingdom levels. Greece, having acquired wheat lands in 1912, might have been expected to reduce imports. The tide of immigrants after the war swamped the absolute advance in grain production. Per capita imports doubled. The surplus of imports over export value jumped from 25 percent before the war to nearly double exports throughout the 1920s.

Romania's total crop production, as opposed to the per capita figure, just recaptured its 1913 levels of 1929. Even this performance trailed European growth of 11 percent. Greece came closer to the European level, if its per capita crop index is multiplied by the 1929 population noted in Table 10.9. Bulgaria exceeded European growth and matched an estimated rise in world foodstuffs of 16 percent.[8] Given the confusing territorial and demographic changes already noted, it makes little sense to convert real per capita exports in Table 10.6 to total export growth indices. We may still conclude that only Romania's real export value failed to match the inconsequential European rise of 3 percent from 1913 to 1929.

This body of comparisons tells us that the prewar gaps between per capita national incomes of Europe's more developed countries and those of Bulgaria, Greece, and Romania, given similar growth rates, actually increased during the two decades from 1910 to 1930. Yet this growing disadvantage reflects neither an inability of industry to grow faster than the European average nor, Romania excepted, of exports per se to recover. Rather the difficulty lay in the small initial size of the industrial sectors and the slow recovery of agriculture. The latter's relative performance was not a poor one, with the excep-

TABLE 10.6
PER CAPITA FOREIGN TRADE IN CONSTANT PREWAR EXCHANGE VALUES, 1906-30[a]

A. National Currency Units

	ALBANIA (francs)			BULGARIA (leva)[b]			GREECE (drachmae)[b]		
	Exp.	Imp.	Bal.	Exp.	Imp.	Bal.	Exp.	Imp.	Bal.
1906-10				28.3	33.5	-5.2	45.3	56.5	-11.2
1921-25				39.2	41.3	-2.1	57.5	115.2	-57.7
1926-30	13.0	30.9	-17.9	41.5	42.6	-1.1	65.9	126.7	-60.8

	ROMANIA (lei)[b]			YUGOSLAVIA (dinars)[b]		
	Exp.	Imp.	Bal.	Exp.	Imp.	Bal.
1906-10	74.0	60.4	13.6	30.0	25.0	5.0
1921-25	38.4	38.8	-0.4	38.6	44.0	-5.4
1926-30	54.8	52.5	2.3	48.3	50.9	-2.6

B. Indices

	BULGARIA		GREECE		ROMANIA		YUGOSLAVIA	
	Exp.	Imp.	Exp.	Imp.	Exp.	Imp.	Exp.	Imp.
1906-10	100	100	100	100	100	100	100	100
1921-25	139	123	127	204	52	64	129	176
1926-30	147	127	145	224	74	87	161	204

Notes and Sources: (a)Citations in "gold" or exchange values vary depending on market used (London, Zurich, Paris, New York) and method of deflation (monthly or annual figures). Bulgarian data are figures in Swiss francs from *Statisticheski godishnik na Bulgarskoto Tsarstvo, 1940* (Sofia, 1940), p. 499. Greek data are figures in "gold drachmae" from *Statistikē epetēris tēs Ellados, 1930* (Athens, 1931), p. 201. Deflations for Romania and Yugoslavia are based on New York dollar rates from Ingvar Svennilson, *Growth and Stagnation in the European Economy* (Geneva, 1954), pp. 318-19, and trade data from: *Anuarul statistic al României, 1915-16* (Bucharest, 1919), pp. 175-77; *1939/40* (Bucharest, 1940), pp. 601-11; and B. R. Mitchell, *European Historical Statistics, 1750-1970* (New York: Columbia University Press, 1975), pp. 493, 497. (b)Bulgarian and Greek data through 1913 are for prewar territory. Romanian data through 1915 are for the Old Kingdom. Yugoslav data for 1906-10 are for Serbia.

tion, again, of Romania. The agricultural sector's heavier weight in Southeastern Europe simply pulled overall growth back down toward the overall European average. Agriculture, let it be recalled, was also the poorest performing sector in the developed European economies but was relatively smaller and thus counted for less than in Southeastern Europe.

The Wartime Agricultural Economies

The Old Kingdom of prewar Romania saw its agricultural exports suffer more from the First World War than either Bulgaria or Greece.

All three were late entering the war but the latter two escaped any extended combat or enemy occupation on their own territory. Serbia would endure one or the other throughout the war, losing at least one quarter of its population. It was not destined, however, to be the breadbasket of postwar Yugoslavia as was the Old Kingdom for Romania. We may recall from Chapter 6 that Romania had become the world's fourth largest exporter of wheat by the last prewar years. Oil exports were rising but had not yet reached 15 percent of total value. By 1915 shipping restrictions on the Black Sea and the Danube had cut oil exports to half of their 1915 level. The domestic shortage of tank cars cut them by half again in 1916. Meanwhile, grain exports had virtually ceased from the fall of 1914 to the start of 1916. During the last months of neutrality, the Liberal government was able to arrange two sales to the Central Powers and one to Great Britain. They disposed of a majority of the bumper crop from 1915.[9]

Romania delayed its entry into the war through the summer of 1916 in part to assure the collection of the harvest. Then the losing battle against the Central Powers from August to the end of the year interrupted the fall seeding. For 1917–18 German forces occupied Wallachia and southern Moldavia. The Romanian army still held the north. Cultivated crop acreage led by the major grains declined in both areas in 1917, respectively 17 and 23 percent from the 1911–15 averages. In 1918 German authorities were able to record a 7-percent increase by a combination of forced labor, somewhat higher prices, and a staff of district agronomists. Both prices and other policies favored vegetables and oil plants badly needed for the German war effort. Valuable as the virtual introduction of these crops may have been in the long run, exportable grains received no such attention. Peasants distrusted money payments in occupation currency. Bad weather and the heavy-handed German policies combined to cut the 1918 grain harvest to 22 percent of the real value of 1915 and 26 percent of 1914. Romanian authorities in northern Moldavia appear to have adopted the German system of agronomists and government incentives, if not forced labor. Yet they were unable even to prevent a further decline in crop and especially grain acreage.[10]

The end of the war made the situation worse, especially for grain exports. Whether eaten by peasants because of the bad harvests or taken along by the retreating Germans, the seed supply available for the 1919 planting was badly depleted. Wheat was the chief export crop. Its seed had always been several times more expensive than corn seed, and this disparity grew larger after the war. The planting of wheat was also neglected for two other reasons that would persist well into the 1920s.

First, the Romanian railway network that was overwhelmingly the means of moving grain exports to market was slower to recover from the war than the neighboring systems (see Table 10.15). In addition to having both Austro-Hungarian and Russian trackage to combine with its own, the Romanian network was forced to operate with far too few locomotives and even fewer freight cars than before the war.[11] Western European buyers seeking to resume prewar connections unique among the Balkan states and attracted by the large harvest of 1920 found the dispatch of rolling stock unthinkable.

Second, the Romanian government decided to deal with the threatened food shortages (and also the general shortage of revenue to be discussed in Chapter 11) by instituting first small export quotas and then export duties that fell principally on grain. The practice actually dated from 1915–16. So did a state monopoly on grain exports that returned with the government in 1918 and lasted until 1923. Requisitions until 1921 made the introduction of export levies in 1922 seem like a relief. The latter stayed in effect until 1926, collecting more revenue than import tariffs by 1923. The levies amounted to 15–25 percent of state revenue and, more important to our present purposes, the same fraction of agricultural export value.[12]

Grain production in Bulgaria and Greece underwent similar trials during the last years of the First World War. By 1914 Bulgarian grain capacity had already been reduced 9 percent because of the loss of Dobrudja during the Second Balkan War. Good weather in 1915 after a bad previous year kept the loss in output from the 1911 level close to that reduced capacity. Subsequent declines culminated with the drought of 1918. Crop production dropped to just 52 percent of 1911. Making matters worse was the army's decision in April, 1917 to take over a nascent civilian apparatus for export and price controls. The civilian agency had foundered on the failure to control black market purchases of grain and outright smuggling of exports by their German and Austrian allies.[13] Peasants now resisted army requisitions. Near-famine resulted in 1918, despite grain imports that exceeded exports, and helped force Bulgaria out of the war by October.

The Greek experience was apparently no better. The addition of the Macedonian and Thracian provinces in the First Balkan War had boosted the cultivated area for grain by almost two thirds. Previous production is not known. Unsettled conditions in this northern border area held its contribution to the country's 1914 harvest to an increment of one third, not enough to increase per capita output for the enlarged population. By 1917–18 even this increment had completely disappeared in the wake of increased fighting in the north and government efforts to prevent black market sales to their allies, the British and the French. Agricultural imports, of which two thirds was wheat, had risen in the meantime from 30 percent of import value in 1914 to an average of 52 percent for 1915–18. These goods were largely responsible for the tremendous widening of the Greek import surplus noted in Table 10.6, a potential deficit in the balance of payments that was closed until 1918 by shipping earnings and a large inflow of emigrant remittances.[14]

The Greek deficits throughout the war and the Bulgarian import surplus in 1918 would have been far worse, however, had not tobacco exports to their respective allies, Egypt included as part of the British market, risen from relative prewar obscurity. By 1918 tobacco accounted for no less than 43 percent of Greek export value and 80 percent of the Bulgarian total (Romanian land lay too far north for a similar opportunity to present itself). Indeed, the Bulgarian turn to tobacco began with the expansion of her borders southward after the First Balkan War. The physical quantity of tobacco harvested in 1914 jumped 22 percent over 1911 and tobacco's share of export value from one to 18 percent essentially because of this addition. Germany and Austria-Hungary, already Bulgaria's main customers in 1914 and cut off from other suppliers by the war, bought literally all of the country's tobacco exports during 1916–18. In physical terms these exports doubled to 116 percent of their 1911 level by 1918 and continued to rise after the war to 186 percent by 1920.[15] In 1918 alone, prices had risen almost threefold to provide peasants with their major stimulus to expanding cultivation. This tobacco boom makes sense of an interwar Bulgarian calculation that average agricultural income per hectare had risen by three quarters over the 1906–10 and 1911–15 averages even adjusting for the depreciation of the leva.[16]

Greek exports of tobacco came from the area annexed in 1912 on the Aegean, south of the new Bulgarian and Serbian territory. Physical production had doubled by 1914 but climbed only another 28 percent by 1918, given the less captive Western European market and the threat of Bulgarian advances. A price rise of 260 percent for 1918 still allowed tobacco to surpass the value of raisin exports, the long-standing leader for Greece.[17] The international prices of both commodities would not prove able, as we shall see, to sustain consistently high levels far into the 1920s.

Otherwise, tobacco and raisins did not face the marketing problems that plagued Romanian wheat. Both were less bulky to begin with. And neither Bulgaria nor Greece found its system of rail transportation in the postwar shambles of newly enlarged Romania (see Table 10.15). German authorities had controlled Bulgaria's international rail lines during the war and at least protected them and their precious rolling stock from damage. This advantage, plus the limited fighting inside Bulgaria borders, allowed tonnage of railway freight to recapture its prewar level by 1921.[18] Greece expanded its railway network during the war. British and French assistance allowed completion of the crucial line from Athens to Thessaloniki in 1916. Rolling stock admittedly remained in short supply, and the number of merchant steamers had been cut in half by 1919. The location of most large towns near the coast allowed the ample fleet of small ships to take up some of the slack for provisions, if not replace the lost foreign earnings.[19]

Greek state tobacco and raisin taxes were levied regardless of whether the commodity was exported or not. The combination of state and local taxes climbed sharply during and after the war to approach 65 percent ad valorem by 1922. Bulgarian state levies on tobacco and export tariffs on grain leveled off at a much lower rate under Stamboliski's Agrarian regime. This disparity between Bulgarian agricultural taxes and the significantly higher levels in Greece and Romania persisted well into the 1920s. Greek tobacco taxes had dropped to 22 percent ad valorem by 1925 but were still over three times the Bulgarian level.[20]

Macedonia would grow a majority of the tobacco on the territory of postwar Yugoslavia. Its wartime experience only discouraged the crop's cultivation, however, in contrast to the neighboring Bulgarian and Greek tobacco lands. The peasant smallholders who had taken over much of the Turkish chiflik land following the Balkan Wars found themselves under Bulgarian military occupation from 1915 to 1918. This regime apparently requisitioned tobacco at minimal prices, pushing peasants to expand grain cultivation for their own consumption.[21] They smuggled as much of their surplus as possible across the southern border to their traditional market of Thessaloniki, shorter than ever of grain in wartime.

Macedonia's incorporation into Yugoslavia hardly restored full access to the port that the region had served as prewar agricultural hinterland. French military authorities had begun importing more supplies than their army needed from Thessaloniki to Skopje by early 1918. These imports passed through Greek customs duty free and the proportion that found their way into the Macedonian marketplace would have stimulated local traders and peasants to pay for more with wheat and tobacco exports. It was not to be. The Greek government ended tariff exemptions for the French army by mid-March. More importantly, the Yugoslav government began limiting grain exports to Thessaloniki with an effective combination of export duties and quotas plus high freight rates. The region's postwar import surplus endured until 1922. At the Greek port, meanwhile, American and eventually Soviet grain joined Romanian and Bulgarian exports to take away most of the prewar market by the time Greece and Yugoslavia could restore normal trade relations in 1925.

Chapter 9 notes that Macedonia had already lost a majority of the port's wheat market to foreign competition after 1900. Macedonian tobacco growers were confined within a Yugoslav state monopoly that discouraged exports and refused demands even to move some of its processing plants to Skopje. Opium exports also relied on connections in Thessaloniki, and livestock on winter pastures south of the Greek border. Imports from the free port facilities finally granted Yugoslavia in Thessaloniki in 1926 went by rail directly to Belgrade. The growing frustration of the merchants who came to dominate Skopje's Chamber of Commerce and Industry may be judged from their demands for railway construction to link Macedonia with Albania and allow a privileged relationship to develop with at least that small, primitive market. Their estimate of the largest possible exports to and through Greece fell short of the modest prewar total in real terms.[22]

Bosnia-Hercegovina was also an Ottoman borderland until occupied in 1878 by Austria-Hungary. The province had recorded per capita exports that were over two times the Macedonian level by 1910 (see Table 9.2). The main commodities were timber and prunes. The postwar breakup of the Habsburg monarchy cost both their duty-free access to this huge market. Bosnian timber production, as we shall see, passed largely into the hands of the Zagreb banks. Prunes now faced Serbian competition. Bosnian exports were soon managed by Belgrade and Zagreb interests. The largest city of Sarajevo lost the need for extensive imports along with its function as provincial center for the Habsburg administrative apparatus. Like its counterpart in Skopje, the city's Chamber of Trade and Industry would spend the rest of the 1920s pleading vainly with the Serbian-dominated government in Belgrade for new railway access to the Adriatic and for a commodity exchange market that might stimulate local trade.[23]

For Bosnia and most other Yugoslav lands, the war created more uniform shortages of grain and livestock than once was thought, at least after the initial warfare on Serbian soil had ended. Serbia's suffering under Austro-Hungarian occupation from 1915 to 1918 appears to have differed only by degree from the experience of all the monarchy's borderlands except the Vojvodina and Slavonia. These two continued to export important amounts of grain northward and experienced no serious food shortage even at the war's end. Elsewhere, in Croatia, Slovenia, Bosnia, and Dalmatia, the same sort of Habsburg *centrale* as in Belgrade tried to requisition and ration grain and livestock from a headquarters in the largest provincial city. Peasants hid their goods or sold them on the black market. Cattle numbers held their own, as noted in Table 10.7. Hogs declined with their greater need for grain feed. Prices in Zagreb rose even more than in Belgrade.[24] Most towns were short of food by 1918. Habsburg authorities undertook no systematic efforts to improve cultivation in the countryside. In occupied Serbia prisoners of war manned the few isolated and ineffective agricultural stations.[25]

Postwar food shortages pushed the new Yugoslav government to take over and extend the life of the rationing *centrale* from 1918 to 1921. This policy had the unintentional but fateful effect of discouraging the necessary growth of trade between the constituent parts of the new state. Such trade had been very limited before the war; witness the Croatian export of processed goods to Serbia in 1912

TABLE 10.7
LIVESTOCK HERDS, 1910-30

Area	Year	Horses	Cattle	Pigs	Sheep	Goats
A. Total (1000 head)						
Bulgaria						
Prewar territory	1910	490	2019	527	8669	1412
Postwar territory	1910	450	2051	546	8581	1641
	1920	424	2295	1090	8923	1332
	1930[a]	539	2069	952	8790	1087
Greece						
Old Kingdom	1911	229	304	227	3545	2638
Old Kingdom	1916	291				
New Areas	1914	184	356	138	2614	1650
Total	1920	330	668	416	5811	3418
	1921	304	689	404	5789	3747
	1930	471	881	335	6799	4637
Romania						
Postwar territory	1910-11	1921	5781	3249	11133	528
Old Kingdom	1911	895	2851	1045	6073	291
	1916	1220	2938	1382	7811	301
	1919	603[b]	1991	323	3660	
	1920	681[b]	2151	1011	4189	
Total	1919	1462[b]	4772	2289	8317	
	1920	1495	4876	2514	8690	500
	1921	1698	5721	3132	11119	574
	1929	1877	4355	2300	12092	362
Yugoslavia						
	1910-11	1202	5108	3925	10499	2920
	1914	1556[c]	6277	5239	11570	2445
	1919	1009[c]	4555	2793	5250	1200
	1920	1058[c]	4752	3269	6750	
	1921	1080	5002	3350	7002	1553
	(1922)[d]	(1059)	(4090)	(2887)	(8462)	(1801)
	(1930)[d]	(1177)	(3849)	(2924)	(7953)	(1731)

TABLE 10.7 (continued)

Area	Year	Index[e]	Horses	Cattle	Pigs	Sheep	Goats

B. Value Per Capita Index and Animals Per 1000 Total Population[h]

Area	Year	Index[e]	Horses	Cattle	Pigs	Sheep	Goats
Bulgaria	1910[f]	100.0	103	470	125	1967	324
	1920	99.2	87	473	225	1841	275
	1930[a]	81.4	95	363	167	1543	191
Greece	1911	100.0	85	113	85	1321	983
	1914[g]	103.3	92	140	77	1301	919
	1920	91.3	66	133	83	1158	681
	1930	89.5	73	137	52	1060	733
Romania	1910-11	100.0	122	366	206	704	33
	1920	82.7	96	312	161	556	32
	1929	75.2	106	245	129	681	20
Yugoslavia	1910-11	100.0	98	417	321	858	239
	1920	90.0	90	396	273	563	
	(1930)	(69.7)	(85)	(277)	(211)	(573)	(125)

Notes: (a)Average of 1926 and 1934. (b)Horses and asses. (c)Horses only. (d)Farm animals only. (e)Based on total herd values in constant 1938 prices. (f)Postwar territory. (g)Herds in Old Greece territory for 1914 are estimated as the average of 1911 and 1916. (h)Year-end estimates to match normal December herd counts. (i)Includes mules.

Sources: Herd estimates for Bulgaria 1910 on postwar territory, the Romanian Old Kingdom in 1911 with Southern Dobrogea, Greater Romanian territory in 1910/11 and future Yugoslav territory 1910/11 from Louis G. Michael, *Agricultural Survey of Europe: The Danube Basin—Part 2, Rumania, Bulgaria, and Yugoslavia,* Technical Bulletin No. 126, United States Department of Agriculture (Washington, October, 1929), pp. 67-78, 121-28, 170-80; other Bulgarian data from *Statisticheski godishnik na Bulgarskoto Tsarstvo, 1912* (Sofia, 1915), pp. 166-67; *1913-22* (Sofia, 1924), pp. B72-74; *1940* (Sofia, 1940), pp. 236-37; *Statistikē epetēris tēs Ellados, 1930* (Athens, 1931), pp. 164-66; *1935* (Athens, 1936), pp. 123-25; Romanian Old Kingdom data for 1916 and Greater Romania for 1920-1929 from *Anuarul statistic al României, 1915-1916* (Bucharest, 1919), pp. 40-42; *1939-1940* (Bucharest, 1940), pp. 450-51; for 1919 and Old Kingdom for 1920 from Great Britain, Overseas Trade Department, *Economic Survey of Romania* (London, April, 1922), p. 50, and David Mitrany, *The Land and the Peasant in Rumania* (London and New Haven, 1930), p. 360; for Yugoslavia in 1914, 1919 and 1920 from V. M. Djuričić *et al., Naša narodna privreda i nacionalni prihod* (Sarajevo, 1927), p. 63, and B. Stojsavljević, *Seljaštvo Jugoslavije, 1918-1941* (Zagreb, 1952), p. 54; for Yugoslavia 1921-1930, *Statistički godišnjak Kr. Jugoslavije, 1929* (Belgrade, 1932), pp. 155-58; and *1938/39* (Belgrade, 1939), pp. 180-81.

that was well under one percent of total value. Unlike prewar Romania and Transylvania, Serbia's huge trade with Austria-Hungary and Germany did not pass through Croatia/Slavonia or Slovenia. Now the *centrale* and a series of trade regulations requiring special permission to move foodstuffs from one region to another made it almost impossible for surplus grain from the neighboring Vojvodina to be sent to Serbia in exchange for other badly needed supplies.[26] The movement of all goods in or out of Serbia to the west was held back until its badly damaged rail lines could be repaired and the vital railway bridge across the Sava River into Belgrade rebuilt.[27]

In the western Yugoslav lands, Croatian agriculture found that the new borders separated it from duty-free access to nearby urban markets in Graz, now in Austria, and in Rijeka, no longer a Habsburg naval base and shortly to be absorbed into interwar Italy. Slovenian agriculture lost similar access to its even more important prewar market in Trieste (see Chapter 9), now permanently a part of Italy.[28] Rather than turning toward the enlarged Yugoslav market, however, agricultural interests in both provinces appeared to prefer getting permission to export or smuggling their surplus into the desperately pressed economies of Austria and Hungary. Why not, when the same administrative permissions had to be obtained for shipping grain to other parts of Yugoslavia?[29] Once these restrictions were removed in 1923, continued exports from these western lands to Central Europe largely explain Yugoslav increases in real per capita exports for 1921–25 and 1926–30 that surpassed those of Bulgaria, Romania, and even Greece (see Table 10.6). This increase now loses much of its luster by the large if uncalculated measure to which the Yugoslav-wide market failed to integrate sufficiently following the discouraging start made under the restrictions of 1918–23.

Reappraising Peasant Agriculture under the Reforms

Before considering the crucial problems of external marketing and internal credit in the postwar decade, we owe the reader a more precise notion of how land was distributed and what was produced in the agricultural sector. Previous accounts have typically concentrated on tenure and neglected production. The exaggerated hopes and subsequent disappointments surrounding the postwar land reforms are responsible for this emphasis. No one can deny that this mass redistribution of large into smaller units of ownership was essentially a political act, undertaken in response to rural unrest imminent in all four countries except Bulgaria. Careful preparations to improve economic efficiency were generally not part of the legislative process. All the same, it will not do to jump from the reforms' political origins to the easy presumption that the scale of farming was drastically reduced and that more smallholdings meant less efficiency. Recall the impressive growth of agricultural output and productivity in Japan during the half century preceding the First World War. The Japanese Agricultural Revolution, like most others, drew more on the application of better seeds, fertilizer, and crop rotation than on expensive mechanization. It occurred almost entirely within the existing system of small-scale peasant farming, where the productivity of both land and labor increased significantly.[30]

Land Reform and Redistribution of Ownership

After the war Southeastern Europe essentially expanded an existing system of smallholdings. The reform changed land ownership but altered the size of farming units hardly at all. Some financial burdens, marketing responsibilities, and crop decisions were shifted from former land renters to new peasant owners, but the resulting changes in farming were marginal. An unfortunate limitation of the reforms was that relatively little consolidation of holdings was undertaken. In comparative perspective, land fragmentation in Southeastern Europe was not so great as, sometimes much less than it was in the more advanced economies of Europe.[31] A graver limitation of the reforms derived from the delayed and uncertain settlement of ownership rights. This discouraged not only investment but also the transfer of land by market sales to more efficient farmers. Such was certainly the case for the two reforms that have received the greatest scholarly attention, those of Romania and Yugoslavia.[32] Both began in response to political pressure. When the pressure subsided, their implementation slowed.

The Romanian Liberal government had begun to consider land reform after the 1907 peasant revolt (see Chapter 6) but made no specific promises until pushed into northern Moldavia by the Central Powers in 1916. To assure the loyalty of largely peasant soldiers, the same government passed a decree in December 1918, expropriating all holdings of foreign and absentee owners or institutions and other private holdings over 250 hectares in grain-growing plains. Later exceptions were provided for exceptionally well managed farms. Landless or smallholding peasants were to receive 5-hectare plots in return for twenty years of payment to the state, but eventual assignments of ownership averaged 2.8 hectares per household. Of 5.8 million hectares, or one fifth of all agricultural land, 67.5 percent was distributed to individual peasants.

The reform assigned them the cost of surveying the property. Many could not or would not pay. State payments to former owners went slowly, and slower still the peasants' establishment of clear, credit-worthy title to their new holdings.[33] Uncertain ownership plus the danger that former owners who were dissatisfied with slow compensation would somehow reestablish their titles might have discouraged any new holder from investing in intensive cultivation.

The Yugoslav reform may be dated from Serbian promises after the First Balkan War in 1912, when the largely non-Serbian peasants of Macedonia were told that Turkish *chiflik* estates (see Chapter 9) would be distributed to them. It remained for representatives from the western Yugoslav lands to renew the promise in November 1918.

The war was ending. Slavonian peasants in particular began seizing estate land until stopped by Serbian troops. Rents went unpaid. The Zagreb-based National Council (*Narodno Vijeće*) soon gave way to the new Yugoslav government in Belgrade. Its Serbian Radical leadership passed an interim decree cancelling rent payments and committing the state to redistribution of "large estates" in all the new lands. Actual assignment of titles went more slowly than in Romania, except for Bosnia-Hercegovina, where the Radicals came quickly to financial terms with the mainly Moslem owners in return for their political support. Title to some 2.5 million hectares, or about one tenth of Yugoslavia's agricultural land, was eventually parcelled out in all the new territories.[34] The definition of a "large estate" and the many Austrian and Hungarian claims for compensation remained in legal limbo until 1930–31. Pending this settlement, and in contrast to the Romanian use of village associations, the government was obliged to *lease* redistributed land to the peasants under ten- to forty-year contracts which forbade them to sell or mortgage their new holdings. Uncertainty again discouraged investment. Mortgages became almost impossible.

The Greek land reform had its origin in the same pressure from the Macedonia peasantry that had initiated the Yugoslav measure. Promises first made in Thessaloniki in May, 1916 became a decree in Athens by December, 1917. Distribution was limited until the aforementioned influx of one million refugees in 1923–24. Terms were then hardened to expropriate all holdings over 10 hectares in Macedonia, where most refugees were sent, and over 30 in the south. Refugees received more than four fifths of the land reallocated. The autonomous Refugee Settlement Commission (two state-appointed Greeks, a League representative, and an American) took the lead in accelerating distribution, although lack of registry offices in the north slowed the granting of clear titles. This second wind made the final redistribution of ownership proportionally the largest in Southeastern Europe, some 600,000 hectares. This was over 40 percent of agricultural land versus 20 percent in Romania and 17 percent in Yugoslavia.[35]

Postwar Bulgaria underwent the smallest redistribution of ownership, about 330,000 hectares or 6 percent of interwar agricultural land. Most came from state holdings. Large private holdings were relatively rare even before the war. Only 13 percent of private arable land was in units of 20 to 50 hectares and another 5 percent exceeded 50 hectares. Great pressure for land reform did not develop from below, from the peasants; it came from above, in the person of Alexander Stamboliski and his Agrarian Union. The Agrarians swept into power on the strength of their continuous opposition to a war now disastrously concluded. They proclaimed a maximum holding of 30 hectares to bolster the small family farm. Thus their reform served a political purpose as well. The maximum has long been regarded as yet another of Stamboliski's irresponsible and irrational policies. However, recent American research on his regime refutes this reputation generally and shows in particular that the land reform was the result of at least 10 months of detailed preparations in 1920.[36] Exemptions to the 30-hectare maximum for one household were already granted to holdings promising conversion to fruits and vegetables or to some form of manufacture. The urban and military interests that overthrew Stamboliski in 1923 did not invent these prudent exemptions but only elaborated on them. Moreover, the branch of the Ministry of Agriculture created to administer the reform paid former owners their promised, partial compensation and surveyed the holdings of new owners.

The Growth of Agricultural Production

The record of these reformed holdings does not submit to easy analysis. Contemporary scholars have mistakenly compared ownership distributions such as those in Table 6.12 with land-use distributions such as those in Tables 9.4 or 10.8 and made the erroneous assumption that large prewar ownership units were generally managed as large-scale farms.[37] This approach contends that the reforms resulted in massive increases in the numbers of "uneconomical" smallholdings (generally those under 5 hectares). Quite aside from how "uneconomical" farms under 5 hectares might have been, massive increase in their numbers generally did not take place. For example, comparable Bulgarian data on rural properties over a 37-year period show only a slow increase in the percentage under 5 hectares, from 50.6 percent in 1897 to 58.9 percent in 1934. More relevant to the reforms' impact is that farms (exploitations or land-use units) under 5 hectares in Croatia-Slavonia only increased from 71.5 percent in 1895 to 73.5 percent in 1931; from 1902 to 1931, those shares increased in Dalmatia from 87.3 percent to 89.6 percent and in Slovenia from 51.0 to 57.5 percent.[38]

Interwar data on property distribution appear to be entirely lacking for Greece and Yugoslavia and deficient in the Bulgarian and Romanian cases. Distributions of land as used, not always in comparable categories, are presented in Table 10.8. The reforms' influences on property distribution are seen only indirectly. Complicating any direct relationship between the reforms and the data are two other avenues for changing ownership: inheritance and land sales. Despite some efforts to restrict the prevailing practice, equal division of inheritances may be faulted along with high birthrates as a more likely source of fragmentation than the reforms. Restrictions on land sales (and mortgaging) were also part of all the reform laws. The unintended barriers arose from the delayed settlement of reform-obtained titles. We know that in Romania, at least, restrictions on land sales were violated or evaded. How much land changed hands through sale is known only for Bulgaria, where reforms had the least impact on ownership. By 1926, 15 percent of privately owned land had been acquired by purchase, 84 percent came by inheritance, and only 1 percent by other means (including reforms).[39]

Rentals were another influence on the distribution of land recorded in Table 10.8. They accounted for 6.1 percent of private agricultural land used in Bulgaria in 1926 and increased to 10.1 percent in 1934 under policies that encouraged the provision of state land through renting. Yugoslav data for 1931 probably understated renting because they excluded lands under state control. They show rented land as only 4 to 6 percent of the total used. Romanian data are not comparable with the above figures. They show the portion of owned, not used, land rented out to others. The share of owned land rented out fell from about 19–20 percent in 1922 to only 6 percent in 1927 and 4.4 percent in 1928. The latter figure corresponds to a comparable Bulgarian share in 1934 of 4.5 percent.[40] These low average shares are less important than how renting redistributed land within certain categories of holdings.[41]

According to the 1934 record of net renting in Bulgaria, both very small and very large land holders rented out more land than they rented for use. They were net suppliers of rented land to holders of from 2 to 40 hectares. Romania's data from its 1941 census show a similar pattern. Farms of less than 3 hectares and more than 10 hectares supplied rented land to middle-sized farms; those of 5–10 hectares farmed 13.5 percent more land than they owned.[42]

Land transactions were not the only "factor markets" in the area's interwar agriculture. Labor was also drawn into the marketplace. Bulgarian and Yugoslav census data show that, as the size of holding decreased, the percentages of land holders having nonagricultural occupations, primary and secondary, increased.[43] Romanian data indicate that the share of income from sources other than farm operations increased as farm size decreased.[44]

As might be expected, land and labor markets were more intense near urban areas. Nearly 10 percent of Bulgarian farms in 1934 were found in urban areas, accounting for a much larger 35.3 percent of all farms using 0–1 hectares and 13.1 percent of those using 1–2 hectares. Their uncommonly small size and large share of the total numbers of smallholdings follow from nearby markets that promoted a much higher than average intensity of cultivation. Farms in the Belgrade prefectures in 1931 were also smaller and more intensively cultivated than average Yugoslav farms. These tendencies recurred in and around all large urban areas of Southeastern Europe. As in Bulgaria's case, these farms used greater proportions of rented land, rented out greater proportions of owned land, and more often supplied labor off the farm.[45]

Neither the reforms nor the operation of "factor markets" eliminated the possibility of a reasonably efficient agricultural base in Southeastern Europe. Net rental patterns added to the share of land cultivated in middle-sized farms, verifying their relative efficiency in the context of the interwar economic environment. Yet large holdings were not eliminated by the reforms or land markets. As many as 1,800 holdings of 100 hectares or more remained in Yugoslavia in 1931. Romania's fiscal census in 1927 counted nearly 2,500 properties over 250 hectares.[46] There is all the same the suspicion that most large properties in both countries exploited forest or pastures and rented crop land for others to use. Bulgarian data in part B of Table 10.8 provide a reason, familiar from the prewar period, why larger farms might not possess greater efficiency: in general, they were not consolidated holdings but simply greater numbers of scattered parcels.

At the other end of the spectrum were certain holdings *under* 5 hectares whose small size alone would not prevent viable operation. After all, prosperous Swiss farms averaged only 5.9 hectares of arable land in 1930, and those in Belgium a tiny 1.7 hectares.[47] In Southeastern Europe, potentially efficient holdings under 5 hectares would have included those near urban areas or generally those with a few hectares of vineyards, orchards, or industrial crops that were more easily marketed in any case. Greece, with the smallest average holdings of cultivated or arable land, also had a greater proportion of this cultivation and a higher urban percentage. In the remaining three countries, Table 10.8 shows an ample core about which a progressive agricultural sector could emerge. As many as 35 percent of Bulgarian farms and nearly 70 percent of its arable land were in holdings over 5 hectares. In Romania and Yugoslavia, where distributions based on exploitations included nonagricultural land and thus exaggerated both numbers of farms and farmland in holdings over 5 hectares, possibly 20–25 percent of farms and 65 percent of arable land were in holdings over 5 hectares.

Agricultural Production and the Market Mechanism

Land and labor markets played no less a role than the reforms in determining how these factors of production were used following the

TABLE 10.8
SIZE DISTRIBUTION OF FARMS AROUND 1930[a]

A.

	Type of Land[b]	Year	Percent of Farms			Farms[a] (1000)	Percent of Land			Land 1000 ha
			0-5 ha	5-10 ha	over 10 ha		0-5 ha	5-10 ha	over 10 ha	
Bulgaria[c]	exploited	1926	57.0	23.0	15.0	750.6	23.6	34.5	41.9	4,291
	exploited	1934	63.1	26.2	10.7	884.9	30.0	36.9	33.1	4,363
	arable	1926		f			23.9	35.2	40.9	3,286
	arable	1934	61.3	27.5	11.2	839.8	29.8	37.5	32.7	3,464
Greece[d]		1929	87.1	8.9	4.0	953.4				
Romania[e]	exploited	1930	75.0	17.1	7.9	3280.7	28.0	20.0	52.0	19,750
	arable	1930		f			35.8	24.2	40.0	12,850
Yugoslavia[e]	exploited[h]	1931	67.9	29.2	2.9	1985.7	28.0	27.0	44.0	10,646

B.

	Type of Land	Year	Parcels per Holding				Hectares per Holding			
			0-5 ha	5-10 ha	over 10 ha	Total	0-5 ha	5-10 ha	over 10 ha	Total
Bulgaria[c]	exploited	1926	9.7	20.3	27.0	15.3	2.37	7.04	15.95	5.72
	exploited	1934	9.3	18.6	24.9	13.4	2.35	6.93	15.42	4.94
	cultivated	1926	8.6	17.5	23.1	13.3	2.12	6.18	13.44	4.95
	cultivated	1934	8.2	16.4	21.9	11.8	2.13	6.24	13.37	4.40
	arable	1926	6.7	13.9	18.4	10.5	1.84	5.49	11.92	4.38
	arable	1934	6.7	12.9	17.5	9.7	2.00	5.61	12.14	4.13
Greece	exploited	1929				5.6				6.30
	cultivated	1929								2.78
	arable	1929								2.10
Romania	exploited	1930				(5)[g]	2.25	7.06	39.5	6.02
	cultivated	1930								4.51
	arable	1930					1.87	5.55	19.8	3.92
Yugoslavia	exploited	1931								5.36
	cultivated	1931								3.86
	arable	1931								2.94

First World War. Markets for foodstuffs themselves probably exerted a stronger influence on the subsequent growth and structure of agricultural production than did the reforms.

Table 10.9 summarizes the growth of production in constant prices and its changing structure from 1911 to 1930.

The figures for total cultivation suggest a significantly better postwar performance than does the cereal index alone. Only Bulgarian and Greek crops grew past prewar levels during the 1920s. Their respective indices of 108 and 120 for 1926–30 stemmed from severalfold increases in fruit and tobacco output, enough to show up in comparable jumps in their share of the total. Similar increments in Romania joined the spread of potato cultivation. Together they overcame the far better performances of Yugoslav cereals, which returned to prewar levels, to record total growth during the 1920s that went faster and higher, from 74 to 95 percent of the 1911 aggregate versus a Yugoslav rise from 81 to 90. The poor performance of Romanian cereals may thus be explained in part by the diversion of land to other cultivation. It reduced the share of cereals in total crop production from 83 to 64 percent.

Romanian wheat yields in the 1920s undoubtedly declined from their immediate prewar level, as noted in Table 10.10. This drop constitutes the centerpiece of the standard argument agianst the Balkan land reforms. Because it corresponds roughly to prewar yields from peasant smallholdings, the postwar level has often been ascribed to the spread of smallholdings (see the works cited in note 37 above). Postwar data on yields by size of holdings are lacking, but other evidence casts doubt on this argument. Unlike the area under corn, wheat acreage declined between the two periods by 10–15 percent and may have represented the transfer out of better land. Rainfall, so crucial on the rich soil of the Old Kingdom, decreased by

---

Notes: (a)A farm means a land exploitation unit, not a property unit. (b)"Exploited" land includes land exploited for crops, husbandry, forestry, fishing, hunting and other economic uses. "Cultivated" land includes arable (cropland-seeded and fallow), land with tree crops and vineyards, and natural grasslands from which hay is harvested. (c)Bulgarian farms and land includes only privately owned land. (d)The land base used for Greek distribution is unclear. Farm units include all types—individual, religious, communal, state and other social forms. (e)The basis of farms and land ownership or operation is uncertain in Romania and Yugoslavia. (f)The distribution of arable land in Bulgaria (1926) and Romania (1930) is according to farm units whose size classification is based on exploited land. Thus, for example, a proper interpretation of the 0-5 hectare figure for Bulgaria in 1926 is that farms with 0-5 hectares of exploited land used 23.9 percent of the arable land. In 1934, a separate distribution of farms having arable land is given for Bulgaria. (g)As of 1941. (h)The amount of land included in the Yugoslav distribution is significantly less than the amount of land estimated to be exploited in 1931.

Sources: Statisticheski godishnik na Bulgarskoto Tsarstvo, 1933 (Sofia, 19 pp. 110-15; 1940 (Sofia, 1940), pp. 183-87, 266; Statistikē epetēris tēs Ellados, 1938 (Athens, 1939), p. 115; A. A. Pepelasis, "The Legal System and Economic Development of Greece," The Journal of Economic History, XIX, 2 (June, 1959), p. 13; Henry L. Roberts, Rumania: Political Problems of an Agrarian State (Palo Alto, Calif.: Stanford University Press, 1955), p. 366; Anuarul statistic al Romîniei, 1939-1940 (Bucharest, 1940), p. 403; Jozo Tomasevich, Peasants, Politics and Economic Change in Yugoslavia (Palo Alto, Calif.: Stanford University Press, 1955), p. 384; Statistički godišnjak Kr. Jugoslavije, 1936 (Belgrade, 1937), pp. 86-89.

5 percent during the 1920s versus 1909–1913 and by 30 percent during the fall season in which winter wheat got started.[48] Wheat yields fell precisely in the Old Kingdom, and not in Transylvania, where prewar estates were more consolidated and postwar holdings smaller. (The same was true for Croatia/Slavonia compared to Macedonia according to Tables 10.8 and 10.10). That tendency, it should be added, had its origins in prewar practice on the sharecropping estates of the Old Kingdom. Peasants were obliged to plant and harvest a

TABLE 10.9
GROWTH[a] AND STRUCTURE[b] OF GROSS CROP OUTPUT, 1911-30

	Cereals		Vegetables		Industrial		Vine & Tree		Total	

Bulgaria

A. Growth (Index)

	1911	1921	1911	1921	1911	1921	1911	1921	1911	1921
1911[c]	100		100		100		100		100	
1914[c]	68		78		119		84		72	
1921	61	100	80	100	132	100	119	100	68	100
1925	86	141	119	149	294	223	233	197	106	155
1930	116	191	144	180	269	204	284	240	134	195
1911-15[c]	87		89		90		102			
1916-20	58		57		152		115			
1921-25	68	112	99	125	282	214	159	134	86	125
1926-30	92	151	104	131	235	178	276	232	108	158

B. Structure (Percent)

	Cereals	Vegetables	Industrial	Vine & Tree	Total
1909-12[c]	77.4	6.7	3.3	12.6	100.0
1921-25	70.5	5.7	15.0	8.7	100.0
1926-30	74.1	5.7	11.9	8.3	100.0

Greece

A. Growth (Index)

	1911	1921	1911	1921	1911	1921	1911	1921	1911	1921
1911[d]	100		100		100		100		100	
1914[e]	130		242		204				139	
1921[e]	107	100	139	100	163	100	95	100	84	100
1925	116	108	119	85	421	259	119	125	115	137
1930	112	104	167	120	459	283	141	148	125	149
1926-30	117	109	151	109	440	271	131	138	120	143

B. Structure (Percent)

	Cereals	Vegetables	Industrial	Vine & Tree	Total
1911[d,f]	51.9	5.4	6.3	36.4[i]	100.0
1914[e,f]	52.6	8.2	14.3	24.8[i]	100.0
1920-22[e,f]	47.4	7.6	13.5	31.4[i]	100.0

TABLE 10.9 (continued)

	Cereals		Vegetables		Industrial		Vine & Tree		Total	

Romania

A. Growth (Index)

	1909-13	1921	1909-13	1921	1909-13	1921	1909-13	1921	1909-13[h]	1921
1909-13[h]	100		100		100				(100)	
1921	51	100	119	100	51	100	100		(61)	100
1925	66	130	190	160	95	185	126		(83)	136
1930	87	172	220	185	126	246	118		(104)	170
1921-25	59	117	173	145	76	255	104		(74)	121
1926-30	77	153	223	187	131	255	100		(95)	155

B. Structure (Percent)

Old Kingdom 1914	83.0		9.2		2.8		5.0		100.0	
1921-25	67.8		13.9		6.3		12.0		100.0	
1926-30	64.1		15.6		6.1		14.2		100.0	

Yugoslavia

A. Growth (Index)

	1909-13	1921	1909-13	1921	1909-13	1921	1909-13	1921	1909-13[h]	1921
1909-13[h]	100		100		100				(100)	
1921	66	100	56	100	67	100	100		(65)	100
1925	110	167	192	164	86	128	122		(99)	153
1930	107	162	112	201	122	182	98		(98)	151
1921-25	83	126	74	132	96	144	112		(81)	124
1926-30	100	152	87	155	97	145	100		(90)	139

B. Structure (Percent)

1911[d,g]	44.9		4.7		5.4		44.9		100.0	
1920-22[e]	36.2		5.8		10.2		47.9		100.0	
1923-25	29.3		4.1		26.2		40.3		100.0	
1926-30	32.9		4.1		23.2		39.6		100.0	

Notes: (a)Based on values in constant prices of 1938 except Romania for 1909-13 to 1921 which is based on constant 1914 prices. (b)Based on current prices and percentage shares in current prices averaged for given periods. (c)Based on production on prewar territory through 1912, territory without gains and with losses in 1913 and postwar territory after 1913. (d)Based on production on 1911 territory. (e)Based on production on postwar territory without Western Thrace. (f)Without table grapes, olives and olive oil and fruit. (g)Production of olives and olive oil and fruit in 1911 estimated on basis of number of trees. (h)Postwar territory of Romania and Yugoslavia. Indices from 1909-13 to 1921 based on five major cereals, only potatoes (vegetables) and only tobacco and sugar beets (industrial). Total index from 1909-13 to 1921 includes only these crops and no vine or fruit crops. (i)Vines only

Sources: Table 10.12 and Marvin R. Jackson. "Agricultural Output in Southeastern Europe. 1910-1938," ACES Bulletin, vol. 14, no. 2 (1982), in press

corn crop on leased land to prepare the soil for winter wheat that they also planted, thus delaying these duties on their own smallholdings. After the war, peasants, now freed of sharecropping obligations, and with little financial incentive to plant winter wheat, used the fall to cart harvests to market rather than to plant wheat.

Romania was the only one of our four states where hectares per capita declined for the agricultural population during the 1920s.

YIELDS OF SELECTED CROPS, 1910-30
(quintals per hectare)

Country and Year	Wheat	Corn	Barley	Potatoes	Cabbage	Tobacco[a]	Sugar Beets	Must[b]	Raisins
Bulgaria									
1908-12	10.3	10.7	10.3	38.8	145.2	7.6	176.3	13.1	
1921-25	8.8	9.1	13.5	36.1	163.6	8.5	145.0	14.8	
1926-30	10.7	10.1	12.5	38.4	200.6	8.4	145.0	19.8	
Greece									
1911	9.7	13.6	10.1			8.2		33.4[h]	25.8
1914	8.1	12.2	9.8			7.7		28.2[h]	27.5
1921-25	5.9	9.1	8.0	36.7[d]		7.8		16.2[h]	22.8
1926-30	6.2	7.8	7.9	33.0[e]		6.9		22.4[h]	25.4
Romania									
1909-13	11.4	12.5	9.9	80.1	165.2	9.9	221.4		
1921-25	8.6	9.9	6.9	85.6	143.4	5.7	158.6		
1926-30	9.8	10.6	10.4	100.4		6.6	171.7	27.6[c]	
a. Old Kingdom									
1909-13	12.7	12.2	10.0	87.5	147.9	7.7	210.1	17.5	
1926-30	9.4	9.8	10.8	90.1		6.1	162.9	(39.2)[c]	
b. Transylvania									
1909-13	11.1	14.2	12.3	69.5	131.1	13.5	255.2		
1926-30	11.3	13.1	12.3	92.9		8.3	174.9	(44.6)[c]	
c. Bucovina									
1909-13	12.8	11.0	14.0	105.3	191.0	10.9	207.3		
1926-30	12.5	11.9	11.8	139.3			210.5		
d. Bessarabia									
1909-13	8.1	11.1	9.1	68.3	148.5	8.3	79.1		
1926-30	7.8	11.3	9.5	67.0		5.1	135.2	(26.9)[c]	
Yugoslavia									
1909-13	10.7	14.0	9.8	69.0	54.2	9.8	244.2	22.6	
1921-25	11.6	13.8	8.4	45.6	59.5	8.4	157.6	19.0	
1926-30	11.2	12.9	9.6	51.1		7.9	162.9		
a. Yugoslavia									
1921-23	9.1	10.6	7.6	42.6	46.4	7.9	137.8	24.1	
1929-30	11.1	15.7	9.4	60.1	65.7	9.1	165.6	19.0	
b. Croatia									
1909-13	10.4	13.7	8.2	77.6	60.2	17.2	149.3	17.5	
1921-23	10.6	11.1	7.6	42.2	35.1	9.5	96.0		
1929-30	12.5	18.1	10.6	64.2	58.7	9.2	159.4		
c. Macedonia									
1903	3.3	9.9	3.3	91.5		5.8			
1921-23	8.4	9.8	7.9	72.6		9.4			
1929-30	6.1	8.1	6.6	79.4[g]		7.8			

Given basically equal rates of population growth, the Bulgarian and Yugoslav increases call attention to the absolute increases in cultivated area also noted in Table 10.11. These increases together with the rise past the prewar level in animals per hectare suggest a reduction in fallow land rather than pasture.

Anything beyond a temporary connection between the reforms and the postwar decline in cultivated area cannot be supported here. Owners facing expropriation avoided the cost and trouble of planting. Market incentives for wheat export had also been dulled.

Generally, however, peasants used their land to respond to market conditions as soon as seed and weather permitted. Data for Bulgaria, Romania, and Yugoslavia all show a similar profile. The smaller the holding, the more land was cultivated; the larger the holding, the more land was in forests, natural pastures, and other noncultivated uses. The turn from cereals, less pronounced in Yugoslavia according to Table 10.9, corresponds to Romanian and more clear-cut Bulgarian data, which show that the areas cultivated in vineyards, fruit tree, vegetable and garden crops tended to increase as farm size decreased. The only more labor-intensive crops whose shares did not increase were those in the industrial category. Even the peasants' choice of corn over wheat can be considered a case of opting for the more labor-intensive alternative.[49] The tendency, already noted, for greater shares of labor on smallholdings to be occupied elsewhere than on that unit's operations did not keep the labor available per unit from rising as farms became smaller. We should not therefore be surprised if smallholders turned to crops requiring more labor. Market responses probably explain why Bulgarian, Romanian, and Yugoslav smallholdings also used more capital per hectare than larger ones, in buildings especially, but also in livestock and land improvements.[50]

Greece was an exception to patterns in the other three countries. Its smaller average holdings partially reflect the greater concentration of vine, tree, and tobacco crops. The first two had characterized the country's pre-1912 territory. The acquisition of new northern land for field crops and the conscious effort to move refugees onto it was sufficient to increase the cultivated area by one half and cereal output by one third, if not to prevent a fall in per capita output, between 1924 and 1929.[51]

Notes: (a)Tobacco quality and consequently value per hectare varied widely; therefore, yields are a poor indicator of productivity. (b)In hectoliters per hectare. (c)Romanian data consider yields only on the basis of productive vines; it might not be comparable to other data. In addition, yields for regions in 1926-30 were taken from data which was subsequently revised downward. (d)1922-25. (e)1926-28. (f)1921-24. (g)1925-28.

Sources: See Tables 10.9 and 10.12.

TABLE 10.11
SEEDED AND VINEYARD AREAS, 1910-30

| Country and Year | Total[a] (1000 ha.) | Hectares per Capita[b] | | Hectares per Large Animal[c] |
		Dependent on Agriculture	Total Population	
Bulgaria[d]				
1909-12[e]	2845	0.87	0.66	1.13
1920-21	2418	0.66	0.50	0.89
1929-30	3222	0.75	0.57	1.24
Greece				
1911[e]	865	0.48	0.32	1.62
1914[f]	1336		0.28	1.26
1920-21[f]	1276	0.36	0.25	1.28
1929-30	1663	0.38	0.26	1.23
Romania				
1909-13[g]	5892	1.18	0.80	1.57
1920-21[g]	4587			1.62
1909-13	11847		0.75	1.54
1921[h]	10243	1.02	0.65	1.38
1929-30	11053	0.84	0.62	1.77
Yugoslavia				
1909-13	6047	0.59	0.47	0.96
1920-21	3754	0.40	0.31	0.63
1929-30	6794	0.63	0.50	1.35

Notes: (a)Excludes fallow and includes only seeded fodder crops. (b)Based on mid-year population estimates. (c)Includes horses, mules and cattle. (d)Bulgarian area also includes rose gardens. (e)Pre-Balkan War territories. (f)Not including Western Thrace. (g)Old Kingdom and Southern Dobrogea. (h)Area in 1920 not available.

Sources: Total and agriculturally dependent populations from Tables 10.1 and 10.3; land areas same as sources for Tables 10.9 and 10.12.

Market influences stand out most clearly from the data available on Bulgaria's "urban" farms, patterns presumably repeated on farms near urban areas elsewhere. They show even greater shares of crops requiring large inputs per hectare of labor and reproducible capital like vineyards than were cultivated on equal-sized rural farms. That postwar markets, under the not always enlightened influences of state policies, failed to lift more than a small part of the region's growing rural population off the borderline of subsistence is not in question. But markets were at work. Equity, in any event, was not the standard to which postwar institutions had to respond if economic development were to take place after the First or the Second World War.

The main criterion by which to judge such smallholdings' potential for modernizing the economy is the marketable or investible surplus created for use in other sectors, especially the urban economy and the state budget, or for sale as exports. These money earnings or tax payments also represent rural demand for manufactures or state services. It is this "instrumental value of agriculture," in Gerald Meier's phrase, that deserves our attention, rather than the levels of disguised rural unemployment which interwar statistics from the League of Nations chose to emphasize.[52]

A marketed share of agricultural production that reached 35–40 percent for Bulgaria and Yugoslavia by the late 1920s may be taken as a roughly representative figure for Romania and Greece as well.[53] A higher share of grain production probably lowers the marketed Romanian proportion; higher raisin and tobacco shares raise the Greek one. We have no reliable notion of whether this proportion, hard to calculate without precise records on the distribution of domestic consumption, rose or by how much before major improvements in statistical measurements by the 1930s. The Bulgarian figure reportedly dropped, and rural consumption of manufactures with it, when a bad local harvest and falling world prices cut the volume of tobacco sales in 1925–26.[54] What we also know is that by the early 1920s consumption of grain per capita was not much below the prewar level and by the late 1920s had surpassed it everywhere but Greece, with its needs as a net importer of grain. Wholesale crop prices for urban markets in Romania and Yugoslavia actually turned downward after 1924–25. They fell, when allowance is made for postwar inflation of gold exchange rates, to or below prewar levels for the rest of the decade, 1928 excepted.[55] The basic postwar disparity in per capita terms is therefore between domestic consumption and foreign sales. The decline in exports is almost as striking for Yugoslavia in Table 10.12 as for Romania or Bulgaria.

Trade Patterns and Marketing Problems

The contours of agricultural performance during the 1920s are now clear. Grain production recovered but its export did not. Other crops were left to take up the slack in the absence of sufficient mineral or manufactured exports. Any explanation of agricultural performance must therefore treat sources of international demand as well as factors of domestic supply.

Romania's unique postwar decline in per capita exports (see Table 10.6) does not derive simply from grain's preponderance over other cultivation. The share of Bulgarian grain in crop output was larger and growing, its per capita exports compared to the prewar period smaller and shrinking. Yet Bulgarian per capita export totals managed to recover (see Tables 10.9 and 10.12 above). Bulgarian tobacco, as is well known, made up the difference. The reason for falling

TABLE 10.12
INDICES OF CEREAL AREA, PRODUCTION, YIELDS, NET EXPORTS
AND CONSUMPTION FOR 1921-25 AND 1926-30
(1901-13 = 100)[a]

	BULGARIA[b]	GREECE[c]	ROMANIA	YUGOSLAVIA
Area				
1921-25	97.3	102.3	91.8	94.7
1926-30	110.5	125.7	101.4	108.9
Total production				
1921-25	84.3	75.1	69.0	77.7
1926-30	114.4	89.2	90.8	99.9
Yields per hectare				
1921-25	86.6	73.4	75.2	82.1
1926-30	103.6	71.0	89.6	91.8
Per capita production				
1921-25	72.1	64.2	67.6	80.4
1926-30	89.4	69.2	82.9	96.0
Per capita net exports				
1921-25	36.9	(176.0)[d]	23.0	58.0
1926-30	32.8	(202.4)[d]	40.5	63.5
Per capita consumption				
1921-25	80.4	85.5	103.2	84.6
1926-30	102.8	94.4	116.7	102.1

Notes: (a)Wheat, corn, rye, barley and oats. (b)Bulgaria's base is postwar territory for 1909-12. (c)Greece's base is postwar territory without Western Thrace for 1914. (d)Net imports.

Sources: Estimates of production and trade on postwar territory for Bulgaria (1909-12), Romania (1909-13) and Yugoslavia (1909-13) are calculated from Louis B. Michael. *Agricultural Survey of Europe: The Danube Basin—Part 2, Rumania, Bulgaria, and Yugoslavia,* Technical Bulletin No. 126, United States Department of Agriculture (Washington, October, 1929), pp. 8, 103-07, 148-66; Greek sources: *Statistikē epetēris tēs Ellados, 1930* (Athens, 1931), pp. 148-51; *1935* (Athens, 1936), pp. 109-12; Alexandre J. Boyazoglu. *Contribution a l'étude de l'économie rurale de la Grèce d'apres guerre* (Paris, 1931). pp. 168-69; Ch. Evelpidi, *E georgia tēs Ellados* (Athens, 1944), p. 45; Other sources for Bulgaria, Romania and Yugoslavia: *Statisticheski godishnik na Bulgarskoto Tsarstvo, 1912* (Sofia, 1915), pp. 154-63; *1925* (Sofia, 1926). pp. 156-58; *1926* (Sofia, 1927), pp. 134-36; *1931* (Sofia, 1932), pp. 165-67; *1940* (Sofia, 1940), pp. 268-73; *Anuarul statistic al României, 1939/40* (Bucharest, 1940), pp. 411, 579-89, 628-29; *Statistički godišnjak Kr. Jugoslavije, 1929* (Belgrade, 1932), pp. 138-52; *1930* (Belgrade, 1933), p. 99; *1936* (Belgrade, 1937), pp. 284-85; Jozo Tomasevich, "Foreign Economic Relations, 1918-41," in Robert J. Kerner (ed.), *Yugoslavia* (Berkeley and Los Angeles: University of California Press, 1949), pp. 173, 178.

grain exports is less well known. Table 10.14 reveals that the decline of Bulgarian grain as a proportion of total exports was even more precipitous than for Romania. As noted in Table 10.13, postwar exports to Western Europe dropped off sharply for both countries, reflecting the latter's failure to resume grain purchases.

Some loss of the British market was inevitable once the war had increased its dependence on expanding American and Canadian wheat exports. But prewar exports of Romanian and Bulgarian wheat

TABLE 10.13
DIRECTIONS OF FOREIGN TRADE, 1906-30
(average annual percent in current prices)

Percentage of Trade with:

Country and year	Northwestern Europe Export	Import	Germany Export	Import	Eastern Europe Export	Import	Italy Export	Import	Southeast Eur. + Turkey Export	Import	Other Export	Import
Albania												
1921-25	0.8	2.1		0.1		1.5	56.6	72.1	23.6	22.3	19.3	4.0
1926-30	0.9	8.9		3.5		8.0	56.7	54.9	25.1	12.2	17.3	12.1
Bulgaria												
1906-10	36.6	28.5	12.1	17.1	7.3	30.3	2.6	4.0	35.0	18.8	6.4	1.3
1911-14	42.2	25.8	14.9	20.6	9.8	33.4	3.9	5.2	18.9	12.2	10.3	2.8
1915-18	2.8	9.4	41.5	32.4	37.1	33.4	1.0	3.0	9.0	18.6	8.5	3.2
1921-25	19.9	29.3	14.4	19.4	17.3	15.2	12.9	15.6	25.9	14.7	9.6	5.8
1926-30	17.9	26.1	25.3	21.9	25.3	20.2	9.8	13.6	14.3	11.2	7.4	7.0
Greece												
1906-11	34.3	28.5	9.5	9.4	11.8	30.5	7.0	4.3	5.0	8.6	32.4	18.7
1911-13	49.3	33.5	10.6	7.8	12.8	34.1	4.9	3.9	10.3	4.9	12.3	15.8
1921-25	31.5	28.4	19.8	5.9	1.1	4.1	12.1	9.2	5.7	12.7	29.8	39.7
1926-30	20.9	27.1	23.1	8.6	3.4	7.7	18.0	6.2	2.3	17.8	32.3	32.6
Romania												
1906-10[d]	61.1	26.8	6.2	33.9	10.7	27.3	11.0	4.9	5.9	4.4	10.0	2.7
1911-14[d]	48.7	24.0	7.1	36.7	16.6	26.1	11.2	4.9	6.4	3.3	14.4	5.0
1921-25	26.5	25.0	6.3	17.4	33.8	39.4	6.6	10.4	12.4	4.2	13.6	3.6
1926-30	17.8	21.5	19.1	23.7	31.9	36.7	8.9	8.1	8.7	1.7		8.3
Yugoslavia												
1906-10[e]	9,0[c]	14.4[c]	23.6	30.3	25.4	32.9	3.4	3.0	16.9	5.5	5.0	1.5
1912[e]			21.7	29.3	42.9	46.1	4.5	3.2	8.4	6.7	6.0	5.5
1921-25	11.1	14.5	8.0	7.7	39.1	46.9	27.4	18.7	9.0	5.1	9.3	11.1
1926-30	9.6	13.5	10.4	14.2	35.9	43.9	25.8	12.2				

had gone more to the Low Countries and western Germany via the Belgian ports, all closed to North American trade from 1914 to 1918. When they reopened in 1919, their purchasing agents apparently returned to the Romanian and Bulgarian ports. Their shipping distances to Antwerp were shorter than from the United States and Canada. What these agents found to discourage them were, first, the chaotic conditions of internal transport noted above, especially the shortage of railway rolling stock. They would persist in Romania well into the 1920s, compounded by a failure to add to existing lines apparent from Table 10.15. Single tracks were still the only access to the main grain outlets of Galaţi and Brăila.

The better Bulgarian record of railway construction and additions to rolling stock during the 1920s allowed its network to narrow the Romanian lead during the decade. These gains and faster rising freight tonnage per capita must, however, be balanced against the sharp drop in exports through Varna, down from a prewar one third to one fifth of total value, that followed the loss of the Dobrudja and its larger grain growing properties. Varna's good facilities for grain storage and railway loading were thus underutilized. Western European agents had typically relied on bulk shipments from the larger Dobrudjan properties through Varna, where their offices were located. The high prices set by Stamboliski's State Grain Commission until its demise in 1921 may also have put them off. The spread of smallholdings in both countries meant that the full freight car shipments from a single supplier which they had purchased before the war were now a series of small lots from many suppliers, cleaned and carried to the rail station under far less uniform conditions. A total lack of provincial elevators meant that some lots began to spoil while waiting for enough others to fill a freight car. Only Austrian and Hungarian buyers in prewar Serbia had been willing to go into the interior to price such shipments more accurately and to assemble them more quickly for rail or river transport to their destinations. Western European agents arranged shipment by sea and were not prepared to deal with problems inland.[56]

Notes: (a)France, Holland, Belgium, Britain and Switzerland.   (b)Austria, Hungary, Czechoslovakia, Poland and Russia (USSR). (c)Includes only France and Britain.   (d)Data for the Old Kingdom in 1906-10 and 1911-14.   (e)Data for Serbia in 1906-10 and 1912.

Sources: *Statisticheski godishnik na Bulgarskoto Tsarstvo, 1912* (Sofia, 1915), pp. 206-07; *1913-1922* (Sofia, 1924), pp. B130-131; *1925* (Sofia, 1926), pp. 192-93; *1929-1930* (Sofia, 1930), pp. B200-210; *Anuarul statistic al României, 1915-1916* (Bucharest, 1919), pp. 175-77; *1931-1932* (Bucharest, 1932), pp. 280-87; B. R. Mitchell, *European Historical Statistics, 1750-1970* (New York: Columbia University Press, 1975), pp. 531, 559; League of Nations, *Memorandum on Balance of Payments and Foreign Trade Balances, 1911-1925*, Vol. II (Geneva, 1926), pp. 21, 158-59, 310-11; League of Nations, *International Trade Statistics, 1931/1932* (Geneva, 1933), pp. 8, 309, 331, 336; League of Nations, *Memorandum on International Trade and Balance of Payments, 1913-1927*, Vol. I (Geneva, 1928), pp. 271, 275, 293, 297.

A further turn of Balkan foreign trade toward Central Europe, already underway before the war as recorded in Chapter 6, thus occurred in the 1920s, long before the celebrated Nazi *Drang nach Südosten* to be discussed in Chapter 12. The area's large demand for Balkan tobacco made this postwar turn all the easier. Only Greece stayed outside the Central European orbit, by substituting the American market for the Western European one.

TABLE 10.14
COMPOSITION OF EXPORTS, 1907-30
(average annual percent of current export values)

Albania		1921-25	1926-30
Olives and olive oil		21.1	9.6
Corn		2.3	2.6
Cheese and butter		16.6	18.7
Eggs		7.4	11.6
Livestock		12.8	11.1
Crude wool		8.1	7.0
Crude hides		12.7	14.8
Wood and charcoal		3.3	7.7
Other		15.7	16.9
Bulgaria	1907-11	1921-25	1926-30
Crude cereals	55.7	23.4	14.5
Cereal products	7.5	4.1	3.0
Other unprocessed crops	17.2	5.6	6.4
Tobacco	1.3	26.5	38.5
Rose essence	4.1	1.4	3.5
Eggs	7.6	8.1	12.4
Livestock	5.6	3.1	4.4
Crude hides	2.2	2.0	4.4
Other		25.8	12.9
Greece	1914	1921-25	1926-30
Tobacco	14.6	44.6	55.8
Currants and raisins	29.5	26.2	16.0
Wine	14.5	3.9	7.5
Olives and olive oil	7.0	8.4	3.8
Other fruit	4.5	2.0	2.0
Crude hides	1.4	1.6	2.5
Ores and metals	16.2	0.4	2.2
Other	12.3	13.9	10.2
Romania	1913	1921-25	1926-30
Five main cereals	60.2	37.9	32.8
Cereal products	5.3	2.7	2.3
Other crops and derivatives	4.2	7.9	7.1
Eggs	1.2	1.4	1.7
Livestock	2.0	10.7	7.2
Other animal products		2.4	3.4
Forest products	3.4	17.6	14.9
Petroleum products	19.5	18.5	29.6
Other	4.2	0.9	1.0

TABLE 10.14 (continued)

Yugoslavia	1912	1921-25	1926-30
Cereals	33.1	17.0	16.8
Flour	2.1	3.9	0.8
Plums and prunes	2.1	3.5	2.4
Other crops		4.6	6.8
Other processed crops	1.3	1.2	1.8
Livestock	5.6	15.3	12.6
Meat	18.1	6.2	3.9
Crude hides	5.9	2.3	1.8
Eggs	4.7	6.8	7.2
Other animal products		4.0	2.5
Forest products	0.8	17.2	20.0
Ores and metals	11.2	5.0	7.5
Other	11.5	13.0	15.9

Sources: See Table 10.13; Kenneth S. Patton, *Kingdom of Serbs, Croats and Slovenes (Yugoslavia)—A Commercial and Industrial Handbook*, U.S. Department of Commerce, Bureau of Foreign and Domestic Commerce, Trade Promotion Series, No. 61 (Washington, D.C.: U.S. Government Printing Office, 1928), p. 226; Jozo Tomasevich, "Foreign Economic Relations, 1918-1941," *Yugoslavia*, Robert J. Kerner, ed. (Berkeley and Los Angeles: University of California Press, 1949), pp. 172-78.

Encouragement for Old and New Exports

Tobacco and other exports needed to ease the loss of the Western European market for Balkan grain received effective public promotion in Bulgaria. Elsewhere the Ministries of Agriculture and the growing cooperative movement devoted most of their efforts to promoting grain production.

The Bulgarian Ministry of Agriculture appears to have placed greatest emphasis on better breeding and use of livestock. Stall-raising and systematic use of manure had not been practiced before the war. The three prewar stations for agricultural experiment, joined now by Stamboliski's Agricultural Faculty at the state university in Sofia, worked to introduce new seeds for fodder crops and to set up village funds for cattle breeding and care. Fodder acreage and output did not move much past prewar levels, however. Supplies stayed at half of estimated needs and caused the number of cattle to decline from their peak in 1920.[57] The capacity for meat exports was a long way off.

Bulgarian credit facilities did better by cultivated exports. The state Bulgarian Agricultural Bank (Bulgarska Zemedelska Banka) plus the rural credit societies and other cooperative organizations so dear to Stamboliski's heart survived his fall in 1923. Their creation had of course predated his rise to power (see Chapter 6). Their number multiplied most rapidly in the mid-1920s. This padded the Bulgarian lead over its neighbors in real assets from agricultural

TABLE 10.15
RAILROADS, 1910-30

Indicator	Years	BULGARIA	GREECE	ROMANIA[a]	YUGOSLAVIA[a]
Total line–kilometers	1910-11	1,897	1,573	3,347	976
	1920-21	2,589	2,463	10,578	(9,340)[b]
	1930	3,041	2,678	11,133	10,041
Line per 1000 persons	1910-11	0.44	0.59	0.48	0.34
	1920-21	0.53	0.49	0.67	(0.77)[b]
	1930	0.55	0.42	0.62	0.73
Ton/km of freight per capita	1910-11	70.7	18.2	196.0	(126.7)[b,c]
	1920-21	97.6		(184.2)[c]	
	1929	155.4	29.0	262.5	316.6
	1930	148.9	31.1	244.5	279.3
Locomotives per million persons	1910	37.6	70.3	99.2	
	1930	77.3	64.9	121.1	204.8[b]
Freight cars per million persons	1910	881.3	679.7	2490.3	
	1930	1738.9	1010.4	3066.1	4,293.2[b]

Notes: (a)1910-11 refers to the Romanian Old Kingdom and Serbia.   (b)Data for state-operated lines only.   (c)Romania for 1923 and Yugoslavia for 1922.

Sources: *Statisticheski godishnik na Bulgarskoto Tsarstvo, 1932* (Sofia, 1933), pp. 305-10: *Statistikē epetēris tēs Ellados, 1935* (Athens, 1936), pp. 247-50; *Anuarul statistic al României, 1915-1916* (Bucharest, 1919), pp. 120-27; *1930* (Bucharest, 1931), pp. 140, 146-47; *Statistički godišnjak Kr. Jugoslavije, 1920* (Belgrade, 1933), pp. 142-51, 163; B. R. Mitchell, *European Historical Statistics, 1750-1970* (New York: Columbia University Press, 1975), pp. 584, 587.

credit institutions if we add the Zemedelska Banka's total to the cooperatives assets per member recorded in Table 10.16 and subtract for double-counting. Most cooperative members owned just 3–5 hectares. A few banded together to form "rings" for the purchase of tractors and other steam-powered equipment for grain cultivation, but the pace of mechanization remained slow. Joint irrigation or electricity projects were far more common. The number of plows grew threefold in the 1920s, but 60 percent were still of the traditional wooden variety. Tobacco growing depended more on plant selection, irrigation, and artificial fertilizer. Loans constituting 40 percent of the Zemedelska Banka's credit to cooperatives helped facilitate the first two and introduce the latter.[58]

All this was not enough for tobacco to play the same dynamic role as prewar grain exports. The long-term credit need for major investments was admittedly hard to find. Mortgages made up no more than 6 percent of the Zemedelska's assets. Short term credit, as noted in Chapter 11, remained expensive at an 8–9 percent rate of interest in order to stabilize the currency's rate of international exchange. More important for tobacco exports was peasant reaction to the unstable behavior of international prices. Their sharp decline from 1925 coincided with a bad Bulgarian harvest that same year. By 1926 peasants had withdrawn over half of 1923's tobacco acreage from cultivation.[59] Its partial restoration during 1926–30 permitted tobacco's share of export value to rise to a predominant 38.5 percent from 26.5 percent for 1921–25 (see Table 10.14). World tobacco prices recovered by the next year, but acreage cultivated did not and kept export value from recording more than a 5-percent increase. The constant price index of industrial crop production, overwhelmingly tobacco, declined by one fifth (see Tables 10.6 and 10.9).

The Greek experience with tobacco exports was also initially promising. Cultivation recovered from the 1925–26 recession to push the volume of production up by 30 percent over its 1925 peak by 1929. Tobacco jumped to 55 percent of export value for 1926–30 and its absolute increase accounted for most of the one-fifth rise in the real value of per capita exports over the same period from 1921–25 (see Tables 10.14 and 10.6). Refugees from Asia Minor were responsible for perhaps half of this production, concentrated as they were in the tobacco-growing areas of Macedonia and western Thrace.[60]

Other than the financial aid given these immigrants by the Refugee Settlement Commission, public policy did not afford tobacco (or raisins, Greece's other major export) much support. Agricultural credits were available only from the Commission or from the National Bank of Greece through the growing network of cooperatives. They tended to favor grain cultivation.[61] A state-sponsored associa-

TABLE 10.16
AGRICULTURAL COOPERATIVES IN 1930

Country and Type	Cooperatives[a]		Members (1000)		Total Assets Current Prices (million local currency units)		Assets/Member Gold Values[b] (units)	
	Total	Rural	Total	Rural	Total	Rural	Total	Rural
Bulgaria								
Credit[c]	1783	1714	333.1	304.5	6269	5550	706	684
Consumer	138		77.6		198		308	
Marketing/Purchase	286	234	65.8	61.7	982	789	616	
Production	237		61.5		1012		630	
Other	1015		191.6		3226			
Total	3459	1944	729.6	366.2	11687	6339	601	649
Greece[d] (1928)								
Credit	3801	3740						
Consumer		115						
Marketing/Purchase	690	526						
Production	866	250						
Other	886	296						
Total	6243	4927	226.3		1233		367	

Romania				
Credit	5225	1129.3	8877	244
Consumer and Marketing/Purchase	1602	237.8	846	111
Production	368	50.3	807	498
Other	241	27.1	701	803
Total	7436 6879	1444.5	11231	241
Yugoslavia				
Credit	3851	500.1	9651	1767
Consumer and Marketing/Purchase	900	184.7	1362	675
Production and Other	1045	99.3	1285	1185
Total	5796	784.1	12298	1436

Notes: (a)Cooperative centrals and unions are excluded where data are known. (b)Current values are deflated by rates of exchange depreciation from prewar rates, as given in Table 11.1 below. (c)Agricultural credit unions include popular banks; Bulgarian data are designated by function and not location (that is, some agricultural credit unions were located in urban areas). (d)Greek and Romanian data exclude associations set up expressly as part of the land reforms. (e)Production cooperatives include those for forestry. (f)In 1931, Romanian urban credit cooperatives (popular banks) included 434 organizations, 147,393 members and total assets of 1,595 million lei.

Sources: Statisticheski godishnik na Bulgarskoto Tsarstvo, 1934 (Sofia, 1935), pp. 261-63; Statistikē epetēris tēs Ellados, 1930 (Athens, 1931), p. 286; 1935, p. 304; Anuarul statistic al României, 1939-1940 (Bucharest, 1940), pp. 700-03; Gr. Mladenatz et al., "Întreprinderile cooperative," Enciclopedia României, Vol. IV (Bucharest, 1943), pp. 638, 643; Statistički godišnjak Kr. Jugoslavije, 1930 (Belgrade, 1933), pp. 294-301. On problems of comparing cooperative statistics, see: "An Attempt to Compile International Statistics of Cooperative Societies," International Labor Review, XXIX: 5 (May 1934), pp. 866-86.

tion was set up to control the growing and marketing of tobacco but failed to coordinate the volume exported. Hurting the competitiveness of Greek tobacco in world markets were high rates for railway shipment, a recurring ban on the export of unmanufactured tobacco, and most of all the aforementioned export taxation. Levies came down by two thirds from the early 1920s but were still 22 percent ad valorem for all but the smallest shipments.[62]

For raisins, the government established an autonomous Central Currant Office in 1925 to replace the prewar Privileged Company of native and foreign interests (see Chapter 6) and also postwar control directly by the state ministries. The new office was able to raise the amount of annual output whose disposal was at its discretion from 35 to 50 percent once a new treaty for easy access to Great Britain, long the major market, had been negotiated in 1926. The share of raisins in Greek export value still fell sharply between 1921–25 and 1926–30, from 26 to 16 percent as noted in Table 10.14. A series of taxes designed in part to discourage excess production added 70–90 percent to export prices that American and Australian competition began to undercut by the late 1920s.[63]

Like Greece, Romania and Yugoslavia would not establish state agricultural banks until the ill-fated year 1929. Their other sources of agricultural credit and assistance were even skimpier than the Greek ones. No influx of refugees gave special impetus to the cooperative movement, nor attracted state and foreign funding to a Refugee Settlement Commission. Both found that post-reform uncertainty over land titles and postwar inflation combined to wipe out the mortgage bonds in which prewar private banks had done extensive business in the Croatian and Romanian lands. Regular mortgages, with the banks rather than the bondholder assuming all risks, were still few in number, and they were available only at an interest rate of 12 percent or more.[64]

The potential for short-term credit inherent in the cooperative movement also remained untapped for Romania and Yugoslavia. The Liberal regime in Romania had initially tried to revive its prewar plans for *obşti sateşti*, or communal associations, and their popular banks. The party had tried to make them the middlemen in negotiating sharecropping contracts with the large estates before the 1907 peasant revolt (see chapter 6). During the postwar reform, the Liberals had attempted to place expropriated estate land under the control of the revived associations, as recorded in note 33. Peasant demands for full possession forced the government to abandon this plan, however. The subsequent growth of cooperatives turned toward consuming and marketing. Credit facilities and land purchase were deemphasized. The Serbian Radical regime in Yugoslavia hastily set up its own network of largely Serbian cooperatives after the war largely to rival the established prewar networks in Croatia and Slovenia. The separate networks never pooled their resources, let alone integrated their organizations. Only the Slovenian system, already strong before the war as noted in Chapter 9, made a major contribution to the availability of short-term credit. Its cooperatives accounted for one third of outstanding peasant debt by the early 1930s versus 15 percent for Croatia/Slavonia and 5–10 percent for the other parts of Yugoslavia.[65]

We must therefore turn to the rest of the financial structure in Yugoslavia and elsewhere if we are to understand the more general nature of credit restrictions on postwar agriculture. Cooperative credit offered public policy perhaps its greatest opportunity to assist the rural sector. Sufficient funds for such credit could come only from the central and commercial banks which dominated the financial structure. Funds for railway construction and other infrastructure essential to the improvement of agricultural marketing also had to come from these banks or from the state budgets.

11.

The Disruption of Prewar
Patterns: Finance and Industry

Restrictions on postwar credit for agriculture were not the result of any systematic state policy in favor of industry, but part of a wider shortage of short- and long-term capital that constrained all sectors of the economy. Only those industrial regions and branches that could overcome the constraint could hope to grow during the 1920s.

Postwar Problems with a Prewar Financial Structure

This section traces the shortage to the failure of the European-style financial structure of the prewar Balkan states to cope with the war and its consequences without contracting the supply of credit. First, wartime borrowing unbalanced state budgets. The influx of foreign denominations and the need to reestablish national currencies immediately after the war added to the inflationary pressure created by budgetary disorder, a confusion of state debts, and a collapsing capacity for exports. Second, postwar governments reacted to the resulting trade and balance of payment deficits by trying to reduce expenditures and to rebalance their budgets. They hoped thereby to reopen the flow of long-term European credit. The central banks also pursued this goal. They cut back note issue and attempted to adopt the prewar Gold Standard to which, it may be recalled from Chapter 7, they had all aspired. Finally, the networks of commercial banks drew on their prewar experience with sophisticated financial practice to confront these assorted restrictions. High rates of interest and reduced lines of credit were the unsurprising results. Each of these three tendencies merits a separate subsection.

Inflation and the National Currencies

Monetary and fiscal policy in the prewar Balkan states had been based on two cornerstones. Currencies were exchanged at par with the French gold franc to attract European loans. State revenues were based on indirect taxation supplemented by such loans. The success of these policies during the last prewar decade, supported by large export surpluses, had promised governments further access to foreign funds. Such was their experience during the Balkan Wars of 1912 and 1913: the Great Powers provided large long-term loans that kept the huge deficits that military expenditures opened up in the state budgets from starting serious inflation. Only Bulgaria's loss of the Second Balkan War prompted its currency to depreciate against the gold franc. It quickly returned almost to par in 1914.[1]

The First World War was a different matter. Like Greece, Bulgaria had the advantage of maintaining its own government, national bank, and currency across almost all of its territory throughout the war. For 1915–18, however, the double expenses of fighting on the Salonika front and of occupying Macedonia created unprecedented deficits in the Bulgarian state budget. As budget deficits rose (see Table 11.1), so did note issues and prices. The lev's exchange value slipped to 75 percent by 1916 and 50 percent by 1918. Official note issues expanded more each year than budget deficits recorded from 1915 to 1918. Prices increased less than note issues, more because of peasant hoarding of notes when goods were scarce than because of attempted price controls. Real note circulation was actually larger by significant amounts of illegal German marks and Austrian crowns. The excess of new currency over budget deficits had two sources. A variety of payment orders and requisition documents that were not recognized in the budget covered up to one billion leva in state expenditures with promises to pay later. Bank notes came to be issued against them. The second source consisted of German and Austro-Hungarian war credits. Most of them accumulated as foreign reserves in the Bulgarian National Bank. They became legal cover for note issues to finance the state's swollen domestic debt, rather than financing Bulgarian imports as intended. Bulgaria's deficit in combined German and Austro-Hungarian trade of over 86 million leva in 1914 had turned into an export surplus of nearly 25 million leva by 1915. Bulgaria exported a third more than she imported from her two allies in 1916 and over twice more in 1917. The imports needed to relieve domestic shortages and inflationary pressures were increasingly unavailable.

Much worse was to come. Harvests failed in 1918, and record trade deficits were recorded in 1918 and 1919. After the war's loss came the spectre of paying reparations to the Allies. From 1918 to 1922, the lev declined from 50 to 5 percent of its prewar value. Its exchange rate fell nearly three times more than domestic prices increased.[2]

The Greek government had been slower to commit its forces to the fighting, but as noted in Table 11.1 was incurring large deficits by 1917–18. The Allied blockade of 1916 had already upset monetary stability. Then the Salonika front and continued mobilization in 1919 ran up massive military debts. To cover them, the National Bank of Greece issued new notes against temporary credit lines opened by the British and French. Given the Allied victory, this strategy seemed to promise a smoother financial transition to the post-war period than Bulgaria was experiencing. Then King Constantine returned in 1920. The Allies, who considered him a German sympathizer, cut off further credits just as the ill-fated campaign in Asia Minor was getting under way. By the campaign's collapse in 1923 the National Bank had been obliged to triple its note issue. The exchange value of the drachma plummeted from 58 percent of prewar value to 9 percent during 1920–23.[3]

The similar postwar behavior of the Yugoslav and Romanian state budgets and currencies noted in Table 11.1 had different origins than the Bulgarian and Greek inflations. The latter two derived from military defeat, on the Salonika front and in Asia Minor respectively, the former two from victory. The enlarged states of Yugoslavia and Romania faced the potentially inflationary task of absorbing rapidly depreciating imperial currencies in their new lands and also in prewar territories that had endured Austro-Hungarian occupation. Serbia's military expenses during the First World War had begun in 1914. Resulting budget deficits were sufficient to push the dinar's exchange rate down to 60 percent of the gold franc by 1915. Then the Austro-Hungarian occupation drove the dinar out of circulation until the end of the war. The artificial Habsburg exchange rate of first 2 and then 4 dinars for one crown prompted Serbian peasants to hoard any dinars they had. The dinar eventually slipped to 25 percent of its prewar rate on the Geneva exchange. Yet the National Bank of Serbia, exiled in Marseilles, was able to draw on Allied credits without the formal need of note issue.[4] This was a more favorable arrangement than any enjoyed by the other Balkan states.

There remained in 1919, however, a sum of Austro-Hungarian crowns in Serbia alone that was half again the outstanding issue of all dinars and in both Croatia/Slavonia and the Vojvodina sums that were twice that value. More flowed in from Austria and Hungary as long as Serbian authorities converted them to dinars at a 2/1 rate, well over what crowns would fetch on Vienna and Budapest exchanges. Croatian and Slovenian complaints over an inconsistent system for rubber-stamping crowns into dinars were not stilled by a single set of adhesive postage-style stamps initiated from Belgrade in September, 1919. This more efficient *markiranje* also made 4 crowns equal to one dinar, actually a 5/1 rate once a 20-percent tax refundable only in ten year bonds had been added. Some Serbian leaders had wanted a 10/1 or 20/1 ratio, on the unfounded assumption that the bulk of crown holders in the western Yugoslav lands had profited from the Habsburg war effort against Serbia. Croatian and Slovenian interests did not think even a 4/1 ratio fair to their financial institutions, although this was roughly the current rate in Vienna. The compromise at 5/1 left both sides dissatisfied. It constituted the first of several misunderstandings that would hinder the economic integration of the first Yugoslavia.[5]

Whether the existing exchange rate of 5/1 was itself inflationary or deflationary could only be judged if we could compare crowns and dinars at purchasing power parity. Lacking such sophisticated data, we cannot say whether this rate held back or accelerated an inflation fed by wartime and postwar deficits in the various state budgets. One point remains clear: the old 2/1 rate would have added to existing inflation.

That seems the lesson of the lower Romanian rate of exchange.[6] The country's wartime inflation had been modest until mid–1916. Then entrance on the Entente side quickly brought Wallachia and southern Moldavia under German occupation. The German-backed Banca Generală Româna moved into the building of the former National Bank of Romania, now evacuated to Iaşi, and began to issue its own notes. Occupation authorities broke their promise to confine this issue to military payments. Its total ballooned to 2 billion lei by October, 1918. Meanwhile in Iaşi, the Banca Naţională a României was forced to finance the war for a government cut off from the majority of its tax base and from foreign loans. As noted in Table 11.1 above, the resulting deficits pushed up the combined total of Banca Generală and Banca Naţională issues from 3 billion lei to 4.6 billion by the war's end. Then came the task of absorbing crowns in Transylvania and rubles in Bessarabia. Crowns posed the greatest problem. Fearing the reaction of the Hungarian minority, the government in Bucharest turned down the request of the new Romanian leadership in Transylvania to issue Romanian crowns as the only legal tender. The initial stamping of Austro-Hungarian crowns was delayed until August, 1919, and not systematically done. The 4 million crowns stamped were less than half the 8.5 million in circulation. The Liberal government's belated decision to convert completely to lei in August 1920 exchanged crowns for lei at 2/1. This generous rate served the designs of Liberal banks on crown deposits and helped to

TABLE 11.1
STATE BUDGETS AND FINANCIAL INDICATORS, 1911-23[a]
(million national currency units or indices)

Country and Fiscal Year[b]	Budgets[c]			Trade Balances[i]		Note Issues		Exchange Rates[d]	Prices[g]	
	Rev.	Exp.	Bal.			Value	Index		Retail	Wh.
Bulgaria										
1911	199	203	-4	-15	-15	111	100	100	100	100
1912	170	302	-132	-57	-57	164	148	100	126	125
1913	169	359	-191	-96	-93	187	168	103	130	129
1914	224	304	-80	-87	-79	227	205	128	146	(177)
1915	195	323	-129	+36	+28	370	333	108	230	(346)
1916	193	491	-299	+6	+5	834	751	137	412	(860)
1917	338	973	-635	+120	+69	1,493	1,345	174	799	(1,070)
1918	567	1,294	-727	-152	-91	2,299	2,071	167	1,504	(1,504)
1919-20	844	1,313	-469	-412	-111	2,858	2,575	434	2,819	(3,086)
1920-21	2,006	2,022	-14	-199	-15	3,354	3,022	1,175	2,603	(2,780)
1921-22	2,844	3,889	-1,044	-174	-23	3,615	3,257	1,892	3,157	
1922-23	4,422	4,512	-90	+1,860	+65	3,886	3,501	2,797		
Greece										
1911	136	181	-145	-30	-30	159		100	100	
1912	131	208	-77	-12	-12	228		100	119	
1913	174	262	-88	-59	-59	245		100	159	
1914	218	486	-268	-140	-140	265	100	100	266	
1915	222	386	-164	-71	-69	392	148	103	372	
1916	226	238	-12	-244	-242	569	215	101	322	
1917	234	317	-83	-110	-110	865	326	100	351	
1918	516	1,446	-930	-437	-437	1,274	481	100	393	
1919	286	1,354	-768	-758	-708	1,382	522	107	632	
1920	725	1,683	-958	-1,495	-864	1,508	569	173	1,213	
1921	978	2,476	-1,498	-820	-248	2,161	815	331		
1922	1,895	3,460	-1,565	-681	-117	3,149	1,188	581		
1923	3,712	5,000	-1,288	-3,532	-313	4,681	1,766	1,129		

Country and Fiscal Year[b]	Budgets[c] Rev.	Exp.	Bal.	Trade Balances[i]		Note Issues Value	Index	Exchange Rates	Prices[g] Retail	Wh.
Romania										
1911–12	575	465	110	122	122	443		100		
1912–13	578	488	99	4	4	425		99		
1913–14	609	512	97	81	83	437		98		
1914–15	568	540	28	−52	−53	437	100	99		
1915–16	662	543	120	237		578	132			
1916–17	364	831	−468			1,452[f]	332	200	100	
1917–18	105	821	−716			4,110[f]	941	280		
1918–19	421	1,694	−1,273			4,638[f]	1,061	355		
1919–20	2,003	5,205	−3,203	−3,656	−1,007	6,364	1,456	363		
1920–21	4,100	7,406	−3,307	−3,532	−360	10,455	2,392	980		
1921–22	8,081	10,008	−1,927	−3,882	−247	13,722	3,140	1,569	1,249	
1922–23	14,904	10,468	−4,436	1,714	62	15,162	3,470	2,757	1,708	
1923[b]	18,792	13,639	5,153	5,061	128	17,917	4,100	3,939	2,500	
Yugoslavia[e]										
1911	120	120				66				
1912	128	118	10			94				
1913	131	131		2		114	100	100	100	100
1914	214	214		−22		198			94	
1915						484				
1916						597				
1917						617				
1918						617				
1919–20	861	2,013	−1,152			773[h]	678[h]	317	523	541
1920–21	1,643	1,957	−314			3,349		526	976	948
1921–22	747	806	−59			4,688		814	875	857
1922–23	6,484	6,125	359			5,040		1,428	1,415	1,344

conciliate the new territory. The conversion, even excluding Banca Generală lei, had by 1921 accounted for two thirds of state debt added since the end of the war and a large fraction of the doubled note issues. As Table 11.1 shows, the leu's international value fell from roughly a third of its prewar level at the end of the war to 3½ percent by 1923. The strongest Balkan currency before 1914, and the only one that formally adhered to the Gold Standard, had now become the weakest.

Less Money, Smaller Budgets, and the Role of the Central Banks

Prewar financial practice provided only one solution to such inflation: the money supply and state expenditures must be reduced in order to restore or at least stabilize the currency's exchange rate. The high nominal level reached by postwar note issue and budgets has long obscured the actual contractions that took place. Table 11.2 records per capita note circulation, deflated to prewar exchange values, which were higher in all four countries in 1920. They had, however, fallen by 1926–30 to nearly half prewar levels in Romania and to just below prewar levels in Bulgaria and Greece. They re-

---

Notes: (a)Dating of magnitudes presents some ambiguity. Years indicated and budgets are for each country's fiscal year. All other data refer to the first year indicated in the fiscal year. Note issues are for each December 31 since annual average issues were not usually available. Exchange rate and price indices are annual, except for Bulgarian wholesale prices which are for December 31. (b)Bulgaria's budget data for 1919/20 covers 15 months when the fiscal year was changed from December 31 to March 31; Romania's data for 1923 covers only 9 months when the fiscal year was changed from December 31 to March 31; Yugoslavia's data for 1919 covers only 3 months when the fiscal year was changed to March 31. (c)Budget revenues, as nearly as can be determined, show only ordinary revenues, including those of state railroads, but exclude borrowing; expenditures cover all expenditures, and state railroad expenditures. (d)Exchange rate indices show the local currency costs of buying stable currencies, either the U.S. dollar in New York or the Swiss franc in Zurich; rate citations vary somewhat depending on reference currencies, market place and method of annual average calculation. (e)Budget figures for Serbia and Yugoslavia are highly uncertain. Those given for 1919-1922/23 are from Mihailovitch; Mitchell gives no expenditure data, but revenue figures of 3,884 for 1920/21, 6,258 for 1921/22 and 8,135 for 1922/23 (see sources). (f)Including Banca Generala lei issues. (g)Retail and wholesale prices. Indices have differing qualities and are based on linking together available series. (h)From 1911 to 1919, only Serbian dinars. (i)Under trade balances, the first column is in current prices, while the second column estimates values in terms of prewar gold parity of foreign exchange.

Sources: (a) (Budgets)—*Statisticheski godishnik na Bulgarskoto Tsarstvo, 1926* (Sofia, 1927), pp. 369-70; *1931* (Sofia, 1932), p. 423; *Statistikè epetèris tès Ellados, 1930* (Athens, 1931), pp. 371-74; *1935* (Athens, 1936), pp. 474-75; *Anuarul statistic al României, 1915-1916* (Bucharest, 1919), p. 248; *1933* (Bucharest, 1934), p. 283; *1934* (Bucharest, 1935), p. 375; M. Gh. Dobrovici and V. I. Feraru, "Finanţele statului," *Enciclopedia României,* Vol. IV (Bucharest, 1943), pp. 769, 775, 778; M. Maievschi, *Contribuţii la istoria finanţelor publice ale României,* (Bucharest, 1957), pp. 196, 214, 217, 249-53, 271, annex I, annex II; D. P. Mihailovitch, *Le problème monétaire en Yougoslavie* (Strasbourg, 1929), p. 38; *Statistički godišnjak Kr. Jugoslavije, 1929* (Belgrade, 1932), pp. 486-88; *1930,* p. 457; B. R. Mitchell, *European Historical Statistics, 1750-1970* (New York: Columbia University Press, 1975), pp. 701-02, 720, 726. (b) (Trade balances)—See sources to Table 10.6. (c) (Note issues)—See sources to Table 10.2; Mihailovitch, p. 44 (cited above); Table 7.3 (for Serbia and Greece in 1911 and 1912). (d) (Exchange rates)—*Statisticheski godishnik na Bulgarskoto Tsarstvo, 1940* (Sofia, 1940), p. 499 (calculated from exports in leva and Swiss francs); *Statistikè epetèris tès Ellados, 1930,* p. 285 (London quotations on the pound); A. M. Andreades, *Les effets économiques et sociaux de la guerre en Grèce* (Paris, 1928), p. 285 (New York dollar quotations from 1914 to 1920); C. C. Kiriţescu, *Sistemul bănesc al leului şi presursorii lui,* Vol. II (Bucharest, 1967), p. 554 (Paris quotations from 1911 to 1914); I. Mincu, *Politica noastră monetară, 1914-1931* (Rome, 1933), p. 72; Ljubomir Dukanac, *Indeksi konjunkturog razvoja Jugoslavije, 1919-1941* (Belgrade, 1946), p. 61; Ingvar Svennilson, *Growth and Stagnation in the European Economy* (Geneva, 1954), pp. 318-19. (e) (Prices)—*Statisticheski godishnik na Bulgarskoto Tsarstvo, 1912* (Sofia, 1915), p. 264; *1913-1922* (Sofia, 1924), p. 394; *1933* (Sofia, 1934), p. 281; J. P. Kozul, *La restauration financière de la Bulgarie (1922-1931)* (Paris, 1932), pp. 172, 372; Andreades, p. 285; *Statistikè epetèris tès Ellados. 1938* (Athens, 1939), pp. 232, 468-70; *1935* (Athens, 1936), pp. 238, 511; *Buletinul statistic al României,* Ser. IV, Vol. XVI: 6-7 (Bucharest, 1921), pp. 196-97; N. N. Constantinescu (ed.), *Situaţia clasei muncitoare din România, 1914-1944* (Bucharest, 1966), pp. 129, 211; *Anuarul statistic al României, 1922* (Bucharest, 1923), p. 159; Kiriţescu, p. 559; V. Madgearu, *Evoluţia economiei româneşti* (Bucharest, 1940), p. 78; Mihailovitch, p. 62; Dukanac, p. 14; League of Nations, *Memorandum on Currency, 1913-1921* (Geneva, 1922), p. 102.

mained above that benchmark only in Yugoslavia.[7] Real per capita state budgets were lower in 1920 than in 1911 for Bulgaria and Romania. They bounced back in both countries during the 1920s, slightly exceeding prewar levels in Bulgaria but reaching only 70–88 percent for Romania. In other words, the Romanian government did not even recover prewar financial leverage. Romania's economy suffered, like Greece's, from a growing contraction in its real money supply and in its ability to provide investment credit.

Relief from this restriction might have come from foreign loans, if prewar capital markets were still in working order. They were not, as is well known.[8] Record trade deficits and disordered state finance sharply reduced the borrowing ability of the successor states in Southeastern Europe immediately following the war. Their position as potential borrowers was further confused by massive debt obligations from the war or the peace settlement. Table 11.3 untangles the several layers that made up the respective state debts for 1920 and 1930. Prewar debts were carried over. They brought along numerous disputes with foreign creditors, chiefly whether annuities would be resumed in gold values or in now-depreciated French francs or in local currencies. Prior to settlement of such questions, new loans were nearly impossible. By 1930, despite renegotiation and some payment resumption, prewar loans still accounted for about 38 percent of Bulgarian and Greek total state debts, 23 percent of Yugoslavia's, and only 15 percent for Romania.

Bulgaria was the area's only state on the losing side at the Paris peace conference and therefore faced the added burden of impossibly heavy reparations. As originally announced in 1920, these levies raised Bulgaria's per capita debt obligation in real terms to over five times the 1911 level. In the event, Bulgaria's actual reparations burden was hardly more than the amounts paid by victorious Romania and Yugoslavia on a variety of war, relief, and "liberation" debts, including a share of Austro-Hungarian obligations. By 1930, Bulgarian reparations had been more negotiated than paid down to about 18 percent of the state's total debt, versus war-related proportions that amounted to almost half of the total Yugoslav debt and just over half for Romania.

A third and more disparate group of debts derived from wartime internal borrowing, special sources such as Romania's land reforms and Yugoslavia's internal war indemnities, and the governments' floating debts, mostly to their central banks. The floating debts represented budget deficits before 1925 that were not settled by currency stabilization loans. Little room remained, and here is the principal consequence for postwar economic development, for new debt that improved infrastructure and thus might be called productive. Internal borrowing to such purposes was on a small scale. The "productive" new foreign borrowing noted in Table 11.3, even when augmented by the obligations incurred for acquisition of existing, principally Austro-Hungarian, railway lines, accounted for only 22–29 percent of 1930 debt balances for Bulgaria, Greece, and Romania, just 14 percent for Yugoslavia. These ratios represented no improvement on the low share of productive investment that came from the foreign borrowings of the prewar Balkan states (see Chapter 7).

The apparent burden of recorded debts in Romania in 1920 rose much less than in Bulgaria or Greece. Including war and relief debts,

TABLE 11.2
PER CAPITA STATE BUDGETS AND NOTE ISSUES IN
CONSTANT PREWAR FOREIGN EXCHANGE VALUES
(national currency units)

Period	BULGARIA		GREECE		ROMANIA		YUGOSLAVIA	

Per Capita State Budgets (Revenues-Expenditures)

In Current Prices

1911[a]	45.5	46.5	50.5	67.2	81.1	65.6	40.7	40.7
1920	415.8	419.1	144.8	336.1	263.8	476.5	(390.5)[d]	(465.1)[d]
1926-30	1251.8	1518.7	1589.9	1786.5	1921.6	1977.4	910.3	867.1

In Constant Foreign Exchange Values

1911[a]	45.5	46.5	50.5	67.2	81.1	65.6	40.7	40.7
1920	35.4	35.7	83.8	194.6	26.9	48.6	(74.2)[d]	(88.4)[d]
1926-30	46.7	56.6	107.6	120.9	56.4	58.0	83.0	79.0

Per Capita Note Issue

In Current Prices

1911[a]	25.4	59.4	62.5	22.4
1920	695.1	301.1	672.7	281.4
1926-30	657.3	822.3	1194.8	423.0

In Constant Foreign Exchange Values

1911[a]	25.4	59.4	62.5	22.4
1920	59.2	174.3	68.6	53.5
1926-30	24.5	55.7	35.0	38.5

Notes: (a)Prewar territories, including Romania's Old Kingdom and Serbia. (b)Budgets based on fiscal year 1920/21 where applicable. (c)Budgets based on fiscal years 1926/27 through 1930/31 where applicable. (d)Budget figures increased by 25 percent to correct for presumed exclusion of state enterprise revenues and expenditures.

Sources: Calculated from data in Tables 10.1, 11.1, 12.11 and 12.13.

real per capita debt was 75–80 over 1911 levels in 1920 and 1930. Without them, it was 15 percent less in 1930.

In addition to the general limitations on the European capital markets in London and Paris, the Romanian government faced Allied claims for a variety of unsettled prewar and war debts. They effectively closed the American market to Romania. The ruling Liberals were in any case opposed to the resumption of repeated foreign borrowing. As we shall see in our discussion of the 1924 Mining Law, they were also hostile to foreign investment. One sizable loan of £30 million (or about 28 billion lei) was floated in London and Paris in 1922 for the conversion of treasury bonds. This sum only refinanced external floating debt, at the cost of first call on Romania's customs revenues. Then from 1923 to 1928 Liberal reluctance to settle wartime debts essentially closed off all European capital markets except the small Italian one.[9]

Yugoslavia's per capita debts increased the least, rising 40 percent in 1920 roughly to equal Serbia's prewar burden when war and relief debts were included. Without them, Yugoslavia's real per capita burden in both 1920 and 1930 was 40–45 percent less than the old Serbian average.

The first Yugoslavia was left to stabilize its currency by 1925 with almost no foreign assistance. Such was also the desire of Milan Stojadinović, the Radical regime's Finance Minister from 1923. An expensive American loan of $45 million, only one third of which could be floated initially, had been contracted for construction of the Adriatic railway line connecting Zagreb with Split. The similar sized French loan of 1924 was floated at a better interest rate, at 5 rather than 8 percent, but the great majority of its proceeds were tied to armaments. A large one billion franc loan to allow Yugoslavia to adopt the Gold Standard formally was not forthcoming until 1931, exactly when Great Britain abandoned gold under pressure from the Depression.[10]

King Constantine's departure in 1922 removed one obstacle to Greek access to foreign capital. From then until 1927, however, internal political chaos left it no better off than its neighbors. Only Canada's relief loans were settled promptly in 1923. Greek counterclaims helped delay the settlement of British and French war debts until 1927 and 1930 respectively. American war debts were settled in the course of arranging for the 1928 stabilization loan. Relations with private foreign capital were hardly better. Conflict with the International Control Commission, which had represented foreign bondholders since 1898 (see Chapter 7), broke out in 1922. The Greek government's forced loan of that year and excessive note issues violated the basic control agreement. Conflict was renewed in

1926–1928 over how many gold francs were due foreign bond-holders. Only international arbitration settled the issue. Under these circumstances it was understandable that the Refugee loan of £12.5 million negotiated from late 1923 to 1924 was only available under the sponsorship of the League of Nations. Its dispensation was controlled by a Leage-appointed Refugee Commission and its repayment by the International Controı Commission. So was a majority of the billion gold francs' worth borrowed between 1924 and 1930.[11]

TABLE 11.3
STATE DEBT, 1911-30

Per Capita State Debts	1911[a]	1920[b]	1930[c]
1. In Current Values			
Bulgaria (leva)	137.0	7,913.0	4,732.8
(without reparations)	137.0	2,451.5	3,927.4
Greece (drachmae)	319.4	2,498.6	6,056.1
(without war debts)	319.4	1,919.7	5,582.1
Romania (lei)	225.7	4,270.8	9,827.2
(without war and relief debts)	225.7	3,379.7	5,142.4
Yugoslavia (dinars)	233.2	1,647.6	2,616.3
(without war and relief debts)	233.2	678.0	1,425.4
2. In Constant Foreign Exchange Values[d]	1911	1920	1930
Bulgaria (leva)	137.0	750.4	176.6
(without reparations)	137.0	231.5	146.7
Greece (drachmae)	319.4	978.7	406.9
(without war debts)	319.4	751.7	375.0
Romania (lei)	225.7	403.6	304.6
(without war and relief debts)	225.7	319.4	159.4
Yugoslavia (dinars)	233.2	326.2	239.6
(without war and relief debts)	233.2	134.3	130.5
3. Indices of (2)			
Bulgaria	100.0	547.7	128.9
(without reparations)	100.0	169.0	107.1
Greece	100.0	178.8	135.0
(without war debts)	100.0	141.5	70.6
Romania	100.0	178.8	135.0
(without war and relief debts)	100.0	141.5	70.6
Yugoslavia	100.0	139.9	102.8
(without war and relief debts)	100.0	57.6	56.0

Bulgaria's apparent reparations burden in 1920 pushed its per capita debt far beyond those of its neighbors at that time. As we have seen, however, these reparations had been largely written off by 1930. Bulgaria's total per capita debt at that later date stood nearly 30 percent over its prewar level. The increment was similar to Greece's but less than Romania's. Bulgarian reparations payments nonetheless proved harder to evade than the war-related debts of Romania and Yugoslavia, since they were not compensated for by reparations paid in return. From 1923 to 1930 Bulgarian reparations and related levies did account for 5.5 percent of state expenditures. Until prewar debt annuities were renegotiated, the government could obtain no foreign

TABLE 11.3 (continued)

Foreign Debt as % of Total Debt.	1920	1930
Bulgaria	97.6	80.2
(without reparations)	92.2	76.2
Greece	85.5	79.5
(without war debts)	81.1	77.5
Romania	88.0	90.5
(without war and relief debts)	84.9	81.9
Yugoslavia	82.0	74.0
(without war and relief debts)	56.2	57.7

Notes: (a)The Romanian Old Kingdom and Serbia. (b)Includes debts in dispute for which service was unpaid or disrupted. (c)Does not include Romanian internal indemnities for war damages. Does not include Yugoslav "Liberation" debts which were settled in April, 1930, or claims of the Czech Savings Bank, Hungarian companies for local railroad nationalization or the Danube-Sava-Adriatic Southern Railway Company. (d)Currency conversions: *Romania*—The conversion of 1920 foreign debts to current leu values is made by the average monthly depreciation from gold parity for 1920 given in Table 11.1. This conversion exaggerates the resulting current leu equivalents because (1)depreciation by April 1, 1920, was probably less than the yearly average and (2)some foreign debts were due in depreciated currencies. The conversion of 1930 foreign debts is made in the Romanian sources according to the parity value of the stabilized leu. *Yugoslavia*—The conversion of 1920 foreign debts to current dinars is made by the December, 1920, quotation for dinars in New York. The resulting dinar balances are exaggerated because some debts were due in depreciated currencies. The conversion of 1930 foreign debts to current dinars is made according to the rates of individual currencies of each debt item and of dinar rates as quoted in New York (average monthly for 1930). *Bulgaria*—The conversion of 1920 foreign debts to current leva is made by December, 1920, quotations in New York except debts in francs or gold leva are converted by the depreciation of the lev from its gold parity. The conversions of 1930 foreign debts are those in Bulgarian sources. *Greece*—Method of conversion is the same as for the lev.

Sources: Calculations from the following sources: Kiril Popoff, *La Bulgarie économique, 1879-1911* (Paris, 1920), pp. 497-98; Harold G. Moulton and Leo Pasvolsky, *War Debts and World Prosperity* (New York: The Brookings Institution, 1932), pp. 82, 98, 101, 116, 123-36, 234, 243-45; William H. Wynne, *State Insolvency and Foreign Bondholders*, Vol. II (New Haven: Yale University Press, 1951), pp. 347-51, 544-60; Royal Institute of International Affairs, *The Balkan States*, Vol. I—Economic (London, 1936), pp. 142-45; League of Nations, *Memorandum on Currency and Central Banks, 1913-25*, Vol. II (Geneva, 1926), pp. 138-39, 154-55, 172-73, 176-77; *Statisticheski godishnik na Bulgarskoto Tsarstvo, 1913-22* (Sofia, 1924), pp. C36-38; *1928* (Sofia, 1929), pp. 346-63; *1929-1930* (Sofia, 1930), pp. 348-51; Overseas Trade Department, *Economic Conditions in Greece* (London, 1921), p. 8; A. Andreades (ed.), *Les effets économiques et sociaux de la guerre en Grèce* (Paris, 1928), pp. 8, 13, 15, 30, 40, 44-48, 50, 53-54, 76; *Statistikē epetēris tēs Ellados, 1930* (Athens, 1931), pp. 380-82; *Anuarul statistic al României, 1915-1916* (Bucharest, 1919), pp. 258-61; *1922* (Bucharest, 1922), pp. 268-69; *1930* (Bucharest, 1932), pp. 304-06; *Enciclopedia României*, Vol. IV (Bucharest, 1943), pp. 775, 801-10; Gh. M. Dobrovici, *Istoricul datoriei publice a României* (Bucharest, 1913), pp. 433, 477; Overseas Trade Department, *Economic Conditions in Romania* (London, 1931), p. 19; Overseas Trade Department, *Economic Conditions in Yugoslavia* (London, 1921), pp. 10-12; (London, 1928), pp. 12-14; (London, 1924), pp. 13-14; *Statistički godišnjak Kr. Jugoslavije, 1929* (Belgrade, 1932), pp. 498-99; *1930* (Belgrade, 1933), pp. 468-69.

capital. Then in 1926, a small League-supervised loan of $16 million was obtained for refugee settlement. Just over half of a similar loan realized in 1928 at $24 million finally went to cover state advances from the National Bank and budgetary arrears. These new loans left Bulgarian per capita debt, without reparations, just 7 percent higher than prewar levels.[12]

Albania was the single state in Southeastern Europe to attract foreign funding throughout the 1920s that permitted large budget deficits and also growing note issue by the central bank. But this was done at the onerous price of sacrificing national independence. Italian loans covered 50 percent of deficits. A National Bank of Albania was established in Rome in 1925 under virtually complete Italian control.[13]

The real per capita growth of state debt recorded in the other four countries for 1920 can hardly be attributed to the propensity of their governments for living beyond available financial means. For Yugoslavia, the share of total debt service in ordinary government revenues stayed well below half of the 21 percent recorded for Serbia in 1914. The relative burden on Romania's state resources did not rise to levels faced by the prewar Old Kingdom until 1928. Then annuities on its large stabilization loan and other suspended obligations began to be paid. The ratio of debt service to revenues in Bulgaria from 1919 to 1923 stayed at about the 1911 level, after 1923 fell below it for three years, and did not exceed it until payments were required on new international loans. Only the Greek debt service burden on government revenues never fell below prewar levels in the 1920s. But the ratio of foreign debt service to Greek exports did fall from 23 percent in 1914 to less than 4 percent for 1920–23 and 11 percent for 1924–26. Payments on the stabilization loan pushed the percentage over that for 1914 only if one includes roughly one third of the foreign debt held by Greeks themselves.

The drain of foreign debt service on export earnings generally followed the Greek pattern. In every case, it was not until the late 1920s that settlements on suspended prewar or war debts and then new loans brought debt service drains on state revenues and export earnings back to prewar levels. The burdens were all the same heavy ones. Until annuities on previous debts were resumed, private capital remained very expensive. The possibility of having to pay full reparations and war debts drove down external values of national currencies and further raised the cost of any available capital. The greatest burden fell on native banks and governments, not on foreign capital. Fear of having to pay foreign debts in the badly depreciated currencies of the first postwar years is the best single explanation for conscious governmental efforts to reduce state debts at the central banks and for the bank's own restrictive credit policies. Both led to the reductions in real per capita note issues shown in Table 11.2. This last limitation did more to cause a capital shortage and high interest rates than reductions either in foreign lending or in the population's propensity to save.

In Romania, where there was least initial success in controlling inflation rates or currency issue, the National Bank came to carry larger reserve ratios by the mid-1920s than central banks in either Bulgaria or Yugoslavia. The National Bank, moreover, had actually proposed a deflationary strategy to the government as early as 1920. None other than Aristide Blank, a governor of the National Bank from the famous family of Jewish bankers, argued that the leu should be deflated immediately by 15 percent a year until it reached prewar parity. Romania's most prominent postwar monetary historian suggests that the bank's position represented interests of the bourgeoisie who had little to gain in speculation, in contrast to government officials.[14]

The issue hardly seems so clear. We may note, for example, the government's need to relieve extra scarcities of credit in the Banat and Transylvania, where significant funds had been lost or frozen in Austro-Hungarian bonds and Budapest banks. The Banca Naţională a României set up branches in all the new territories just after the war. It faced serious commercial competition only from the private Liberal banks of Bucharest which had beaten the central bank to establishing branches there. Partly to offset this competition and partly for political reasons, the National Bank branches boosted discount credits to Transylvania tenfold by 1923 to double the province's proportion of the national total to 20 percent. Credit from the bank's headquarters in Bucharest to Transylvania probably doubled that percentage again to bring its aggregate close to that accorded the Old Kingdom per se.[15]

Romanian state debt had reached a peak of 12.4 billion lei at the end of 1921. Deflationary policies were incorporated in the first unified Romanian budget, submitted by Titulescu for 1921–22. It included his proposals for increased direct taxation. Although this budget was not balanced, the Bratianu government that assumed power in January 1922 succeeded in recording official surpluses whose exaggeration at least concealed no more deficits.[16]

The National Bank did not treat the private sector with similar restraint at that time. Its credit increases averaged 46 percent a year for 1921–24 but did not satisfy a seemingly insatiable demand. Prime interest rates for commercial banks rose from 13.5 percent in 1922 to over 19 percent in 1925. Buoyed by export surpluses, the leu did not depreciate after 1922. Mild exchange controls by the National Bank did not prevent the leu's rate from fluctuating widely during these next three years.[17]

The Bratianu brothers' deliberate delay in settling Romania's prewar and war-related debts rested in part on the hope that the leu would be revalued first. Vintîlă Bratianu incorporated a plan to this end in the government's convention with the National Bank in May 1925. One provision placed a statutory limit on note issues at the level of December 1924. The eventual aim was to restore the leu's prewar gold value by confining private credit from the National Bank to 25 percent of gold reserves (recall the similar Serbian measure in the 1890s, as noted in Chapter 7). Based on Romania's gold holdings in 1925, note issue for the private sector would have to be reduced 77 percent over 15–20 years, at an average annual rate of 3–5 percent.[18]

The National Peasant party and advocates of industrialization like Mihail Manoilescu bitterly opposed this deflationary provision. That it failed to affect the leu seems more a result of 1925's poor harvest and import surplus than of such opposition. Better harvests and export surpluses in 1926 and 1927 did permit the Liberal government and the National Bank to stabilize the leu but at an overvalued rate. Reserves of foreign exchange had to be sold and more borrowed in order to defend this rate on the eve of "official" stabilization in 1928. The statutory limit on note issues remained in force until July 1928, when the stabilization law replaced it. During the three years of its duration, the limit served more to restrict the supply of private credit than to stabilize the currency's rate of exchange.[19]

In Yugoslavia, the new National Bank of Serbs, Croats, and Slovenes was not owned by the ruling Serbian Radicals. Its distribution of credit, all the same, was biased toward Serbia more than that of the Liberals' Banca Naţionala was toward the Old Kingdom. Created from the existing Narodna Banka Kr. Srbije, the new Yugoslav central banks was to be based like its predecessor on private emission of joint stock. First efforts in 1920 to raise the 40 million dinars deemed necessary for addition to the Serbian bank's capital of 10 million dinars admittedly gave an option to the holders of existing shares, all Serbians, to buy three new for every old one they held. They did not exercise that right, buying barely 500,000 dinars' worth of the 20 millions offered in October 1920. But the powerful Croatian financial interests to be discussed in the next subsection bought even less at that time, and again during a second sale in May 1921 that required only partial payment in gold. Not until a third sale entirely for delayed payment in banknotes was the entire issue taken up, three quarters of it by Serbian, largely non-Radical banks. Short-term profits kept Croatian and Slovenian investors who were earning

13–21 percent dividends for 1920–21 in their own private banks away from the new National Bank with its 8 percent limit.[20] This was unfortunately forgotten in the western Yugoslav lands, along with relatively low interest rates, when the National Bank increasingly favored Serbian borrowers, more than 2/1 over Croatian and 4/1 over Slovenian ones by 1927.[21] The resulting acrimony compounded the misunderstanding over the conversion of Habsburg currency. Together they helped make the difficulties of integrating the first Yugoslavia seem to be Serbia's fault to the western lands and vice versa.

Greater regional acrimony than in Romania proved no barrier to better Yugoslav management of monetary stabilization and deflation. The distribution of the National Bank's assets in Table 11.4 reflect a steady decline in state debt and a nearly constant supply of private credit. Note issues had increased about 8 percent in 1922 and 14 percent in 1923. They slowed to 4 percent in 1924 and remained constant thereafter. As Finance Minister, Milan Stojadinović discontinued tight exchange controls in 1923. The dinar began to appreciate. The National Bank's successful intervention in the exchange market helped here and also made dinars more stable internationally than lei, leva, or drachmae. The resulting deflation was not without its price. Credit restrictions fell with particular severity on agricultural and timber exports in 1924 and were just partly relaxed thereafter. The National Bank did manage to reduce real note circulation less, according to Table 11.4, than any of the other central banks. Yugoslav industrial interests were noticeably unhappy with both the lack of easy credit and the reduced protection afforded by the dinar's higher international value. When discussion of formal stabilization started in 1928, they favored some devaluation but were unable to prevail.[22]

The Bulgarian National Bank turned more resolutely toward the Gold Exchange Standard than any of the others. Under prodding from the Allied Commission for extracting reparations, the Bulgarian government passed legislation in 1926 and 1928 that made the lev formally convertible to gold and ended the long dependence of the National Bank on the state. The bank's prewar and immediate postwar problem with heavy state borrowing, apparent from Table 11.4, was finally ended. The price exacted was, however, high for the Bulgarian economy. The bank lost all rights of direct commercial lending; its interest rate for discounting and current accounts was set at a high 10 percent and confined to three-month obligations. Note issue was tied to a reserve ratio of 33⅓ percent on gold.[23] By 1928 the Narodna Banka's reduced capacity for short-term credit left mainly the smaller commercial banks to benefit from the discounts on bills of exchange and current account overdrafts that it could ex-

TABLE 11.4
CENTRAL BANK BALANCES, 1913-30
(end of year)

Country and Year	Total Assets^c	Reserve Assets	Credit Assets		Government Credit to Total Assets (%)	Bank Notes to Total Assets (%)	Reserve Assets to Bank Notes (%)
			Governments	Other			
	(million national currency units)						
Bulgaria							
1913	463	68	152	187	32.8	39.9	35.6
1918	3410	262	1757	172	51.5	67.4	13.4
1920	6037	1047	3532	175	58.5	55.6	31.3
1923	7903	1855	5108	661	64.6	52.4	44.8
1925	8777	1574	5462	1337	62.2	41.6	43.3
1927	8527	1631	(4505)^f	(1791)^f	52.8	43.6	43.8
1928^a	10393	4109	3766	1626	37.5	41.6	98.5
1929	8386	2547	3470	1693	41.4	43.0	70.6
1930	7154	2248	3319	948	46.4	46.1	68.2
Greece							
1913	676	252	196	205	28.9	34.7	107.5
1918	2357	1602	384	305	16.3	53.4	127.3
1920	3620	399	2421	547	66.9	41.4	26.4
1923	9644	1486	5948	1173	61.7	48.5	31.7
1925	12380	2187	5915	2701	48.1	43.1	41.1
1927		2500					50.3
1928^a	9418	4241	3790	111	40.2	60.4	74.5
1929	9130	3117	3597	380	39.4	56.9	60.0
1930	8412	3012	3389	407	40.3	57.1	62.7

Country and Year	Total Assets[c]	Reserve Assets	Credit Assets Government[c]	Credit Assets Other	Government Credit to Total Assets (%)	Bank Notes to Total Assets (%)	Reserve Assets to Bank Notes (%)
	(million national currency units)						
Romania							
1913	593	208	46	256	7.8	73.7	47.8
1918	3813	988	1776	112	46.6	65.3	39.7
1920	14392	3120	8325	860	57.8	65.9	32.9
1922	28689	9774	11154	6295	38.8	62.5	54.6
1925	33897	11371	10933	9099	32.3	59.4	56.5
1927		11097	13479	9794			52.7
1928		8328	13089	10555			39.3
1929[a]	34903		5469	10415	15.7	60.6	
1930	28373	11097[g]	3617	8917	12.7	59.1	56.6
Yugoslavia							
1913[b]	181	74	58	39	32.0	50.4	81.1
1918	872	533	276	43	31.7	39.0	156.5
1920	4537	952[h]	3282	268	72.3	73.7	28.4
1923	8623	2297[h]	4518	1533	52.3	67.1	39.7
1925	8688	2002[h]	4407	1383	50.7	69.8	33.0
1927	9461	2395	4338	1723	45.8	60.7	41.7
1928	8704	1869	4202	1777	48.3	63.5	33.7
1929	9958	2549	4154	1583	41.7	58.4	43.8
1930	8145	1752	4021	1726	49.9	65.3	32.5

tend. The National Bank therefore ceased to be the dominant institution it had been in prewar Bulgarian finance. Its assets had been 43 percent of the national total for banks in 1911; they had shrunk to 27 percent by the late 1920s.[24]

New Contours of Commercial Banking

The prewar commercial and central banking had already favored short-term instruments. This had become best practice in the most sophisticated European banks. The growth of savings deposits had facilitated the spread of one new long-term instrument, the mortgage bond. As may be recalled from Chapter 9, these bonds and the attendant bulk of savings deposits needed to permit long-term assets became significant only for several Zagreb banks in Croatia/ Slavonia. In the independent Balkan states, the central and commercial banks shifted their assets away from mortgages and within the short-term spectrum from discounting bills of exchange to current account overdrafts. This flexible and potentially long-term instrument had replaced direct joint-stock investment as the main form of industrial credit even among the leading German banks before the turn of the century. Only a few Belgrade and Bucharest banks held noteworthy amounts of stock before the war, respectively for Serbian light industry and Romanian oil. The postwar rise in stockholding, to be considered below, only contracted the supply of short-term credit still further. Yet this change and others in the contours of commercial banking after the war were more than anything short-term responses to the general monetary and fiscal restriction.

The Bulgarian banking system alleviated its credit shortage, especially for imports, and at the same time covered 80 percent of the

TABLE 11.4 (continued)

Notes: (a)First year of stabilization; for Greece, balances are for the National Bank up to 1927 and for the Bank of Greece after 1927. (b)June, 1914; the Serbian National Bank   (c)Total assets are adjusted two ways from those that appear in official reports: (2) accounts are adjusted to eliminate certain items such as paper held in mortgages or security, according to a methodology used in League of Nations, *Memorandum on Currency and Central Banks, 1913-25*, Vol. II (Geneva, 1926), pp. 138-39, 154-55, 172-73, 176-77; (2) gold and, in the case of Yugoslavia, certain foreign assets carried at the old prewar parity are revalued according to end of year exchange values of paper currency. (d)Reserve assets include gold (excluding that of Romania in Russia carried on the books until 1928 at value) and legitimate foreign claims, but not silver, token money or domestic gold treasury bonds (as in Romania's case). (e)Includes the official debt accounts and, whenever they can be identified, government securities, temporary advances, discounts by the treasury of treasury bonds, etc. (f)The "other" account may include some government debt. (g)Foreign claims may yet include some "gold" treasury bonds. (h)The larger sum for 1923 reflects a more depreciated dinar than in 1925; nominal (old gold parity) values of gold and foreign claims were higher in 1925 than in 1923

Sources: League of Nations, *Memorandum on Currency, 1913-1921* (Geneva, 1922), p. 36; League of Nations, *Memorandum on Currency and Central Banks, 1913-25*, Vol. II (Geneva, 1926), pp. 5-9, 38-39, 54-55, 138-39, 154-55, 172-73, 176-77; League of Nations, *Commercial Banks, 1929-1934* (Geneva, 1935), pp. XXI-XXIV; League of Nations, *Money and Banking, 1937/38* (Geneva, 1938), pp. 43, 105, 129, 213; League of Nations, *Statistical Yearbook, 1932/33* (Geneva, 1933), pp. 221-23, 262; *Statisticheski godishnik na Bulgarskoto Tsarstvo, 1913-22* (Sofia, 1924), pp. B408-409; *1928* (Sofia, 1929), pp. 286-87; *1931* (Sofia, 1932), pp. 366, 370-72; *Statistikē epetēris Ellados, 1930* (Athens, 1931), p. 270; *1938* (Athens, 1939), p. 490; *Anuarul statistic al României, 1915-1916* (Bucharest, 1919), pp. 272-75; *1922* (Bucharest, 1922), pp. 278-83; *1930* (Bucharest, 1932), pp. 322-23; Florin Oromolu, "Institutul de emisiune," in *Enciclopedia României*, Vol. IV (Bucharest, 1943), pp. 719, 721, 725; *Statistički godišnjak Kr. Jugoslavije, 1930* (Belgrade, 1933), pp. 240-41.

economy's huge trade deficit for 1924–28 with short-term credit from new European banks in Sofia. These five large banks, with only the German Kreditna surviving from before the war, filled the gap left by the National Bank's declining real assets. Private native banks did not repair the prewar weakness noted in Chapter 7. Interest rates of 20 percent or more for short-term loans on current account attracted this first serious European attention to Bulgarian banking. By 1927 the five big foreign banks in Sofia commanded paid-in capital that was nearly twice that of the four largest native banks.[25] By 1929 the former had doubled their capital from 1923. They drew on extensive lines of credit from their parent European banks to multiply their assets severalfold as well, to reach 2½ times the total of the native four and to exceed those of the National Bank. We may recall foreign banks' prewar tendency to obtain much of their credit by siphoning it from the National Bank at the expense of native institutions. Table 11.5 confirms the judgment of a contemporary Bulgarian economist that "the most independent state in the Balkans economically before the war had become the most dependent afterwards."[26]

Yugoslav commercial banks were accorded less attention from European financial interests during the 1920s. The foreign share of Yugoslav bank capital amounted to just 14 percent by the following decade, versus 31 percent for Bulgaria.[27] This disparity derived from the concentration of European funds in the large Zagreb banks. The former Serbian and new Yugoslav capital city of Belgrade had not attracted any large foreign affiliates before the war except the Banque Franco-Serbe. It and the important native Belgrade banks described in Chapter 7 found their immediate postwar operations stymied by the moratorium on payment of state, essentially Serbian, debts to them until 1920. Several large Western European banks made inquiries about opening affiliates or branches in Belgrade during this period but backed away because of the prevailing uncertainty and lack of information. The Banque Franco-Serbe never regained its prewar importance. The three foreign banks that eventually opened were smaller still. During the rest of the 1920s the native Belgrade banks compensated themselves for minimal access to foreign credit by taking the lion's share of the Bank's extensive lending in Serbia. The Narodna Banka specifically denied credit to the smaller provincial banks. Also caught in this bind were the fledgling financial institutions of other regional capitals. In Sarajevo, for instance, these credit restrictions were instrumental in reducing the number of banks in the largest Bosnian city from twenty in 1923 to nine by 1927.[28]

The only Croatian or Slovenian bank under direct foreign control was the Jugoslovenska Banka of Prague's Živnostenska Banka. The

TABLE 11.5
POSTWAR STRUCTURE OF BULGARIAN COMMERCIAL BANKING

Private Commercial Banks

Year	Number of Banks	Total Assets	Capital and Reserves (million leva)	Loans[a]	Total Assets	Capital and Reserves	Loans (index-per capita prewar foreign exchange values)
1912	42	165.3	41.5	147.8	100.0	100.0	100.0
1920	117		425.6	1,696.9	57.9	80.1	89.7
1924	117	4,311.9	654.7	3,452.9		35.0	51.9
1928	128	7,837.1	1,007.1	6,448.1	97.2	49.8	89.4

Nine Largest Sofia Private Commercial Banks

Year	Total Assets	Capital and Reserves (million leva)	Loans[a]	Total Assets	Capital and Reserves (percent of total)	Loans
1924	2,921.0	271.7	2,345	67.7	41.5	67.9
1928	5,026.1	425.7	4,597	64.1	42.3	71.3

Agricultural and Cooperative Banks

Year	Total Assets	Capital and Reserves (million leva)	Loans[a]	Total Assets	Capital and Reserves	Loans (index-per capita prewar foreign exchange values)
1912	236.6	65.6	135.8	100.0	100.0	100.0
1920	673.5	154.1	650.8	22.2	18.4	37.4
1924	3,050.2	196.3	2,715.5	28.6	6.6	44.4
1928	5,641.1	652.8	3,860.7	48.9	20.4	58.3

Prva Hrvatska Štedionica remained the largest Zagreb bank, with a majority of its stock in native hands. But individual investors as well as surviving banks from Vienna and Budapest soon discovered the high interest rates, exceeding 20 percent in the early 1920s, that awaited assets financing Yugoslav trade with Austria and Hungary or import substitution. Prewar mortgage bonds at a fixed 4–6 percent interest gave way to short-term or dividend paying instruments. The resultant growth made Zagreb bank assets about half of the Yugoslav total for 1920–24. Despite a fourfold rise in this total for 1920–29, the Croatian share still approached 40 percent, one third again the Serbian proportion by the late 1920s.[29] Table 11.6 reveals that in 1927 the structure of Croatian bank assets remained heavily weighted toward enterprise credits that were partly long-term. Four fifths of Serbian assets were divided between short-term bills of exchange and current account credits. Such instruments preserved their prewar dependence on the National Bank's discounting and acceptances, in the absence of any substantial flow of credit from the new Belgrade branches of several Croatian and Slovenian banks. The continuing Serbian shortage of credit emerges from a 1927 rate of profit that exceeded 13 percent, higher than the Croatian rate, despite a far greater reliance on short-term, normally lower-interest, assets.

The only nation-wide system of branch banking in postwar South-

TABLE 11.5 (continued)

Volume of Loans by Type of Bank (mil. leva)

Banks	1911	1926	1927	1928
Private commercial banks	125	4,307	4,983	6,446
National bank	126	885	902	1,288
(to private banks)		(131)	(259)	(447)
Agricultural bank	113	2,448	2,654	3,207
Central cooperative bank	2	284	289	372
Popular banks		829	1,044	1,429
Agricultural credit cooperatives		353	405	487
Total	366	9,105	10,177	13,229

Notes: (a)Loans include portfolio and current accounts.

Sources: Banque Nationale de Bulgarie, *Comptes rendus de la B.N.B.*, *1925* (Sofia, 1926), p. 54; *1926* (Sofia, 1927), p. 56; *1927* (Sofia, 1928), p. 58; *1928* (Sofia, 1929), p. 56; Asen Chakalov, *Formi, razmer i deinost na chuzhdiia kapital v 1878-1944* (Sofia, 1962), p. 129; *Izvestiia na Bulgarskata narodna banka*, October, 1926 (Sofia), pp. 240-41; J. P. Kozul, *La restauration financière de la Bulgarie (1922-1931)* (Paris, 1932), p. 155; G. T. Danailov, *Les effets de la guerre en Bulgarie* (Paris, 1932), pp. 439-40; *Statisticheski godishnik na Bulgarskoto Tsarstvo, 1912* (Sofia, 1915), pp. 289, 301; *1913-1922* (Sofia, 1924), pp. 425, 433; *1923-1924* (Sofia, 1925), pp. B244-251; *1929-1930* (Sofia, 1930). pp. 293-96, 300; Great Britain Overseas Trade Department, *Economic Situation In Bulgaria* (London: July, 1930), p. 13.

TABLE 11.6
POSTWAR STRUCTURE OF YUGOSLAV COMMERCIAL BANKING

Commercial Bank Assets[a]

	Current Dinars	In Constant Prewar Exchange Values[b]		
Year	(mil.)	Amount (mil.)	Per Capita (dinars)	Index[c] (1911 = 100)
1921	6,056	744.0	61.7	31
1923	9,906	550.3	44.3	22
1925	13,286	1,173.6	91.7	46
1928	15,627	1,424.5	106.5	54
1930	19,879	1,820.4	132.1	66

Regional Structures

1. Prewar	Banks (No.)	Assets[d] (mil. francs)		Assets per Bank (mil. francs)
Serbia	177	764		4.32
Croatia/Slavonia	189	580		3.07
Bosnia-Hercegovina	38	70		1.84

2. 1927	Banks (No.)	Assets[d] (mil. francs)	(%)	Assets per Bank (mil. francs)
Serbia and Montenegro	307	371.3	28.0	1.21
Croatia/Slavonia	142	500.2	37.7	3.52
Bosnia-Hercegovina	71	117.9	8.9	1.66
Slovenia	11	141.1	10.6	12.83
Dalmatia	13	24.4	1.8	1.88
Voivodina	127	172.8	13.0	0.73
Total	672	1,327.6	100.0	1.98

Structure of Bank Assets and Loans in 1930

Bank	Assets (mil. dinars)	(%)	Loans (mil. dinars)	(%)
National Bank	8,145[e]	20.4	5,746	18.4
Postal and Mortgage Banks	5,151	12.9	3,965	12.7
649 Commercial Banks[f]	19,879	49.9	16,792	53.7
56 Savings Banks	2,634	6.6	1,684	5.4
Cooperative Credit	4,042	10.1	3,087	9.9
	39,851	100.0	31,274	100.0

Notes: (a)Asset basis with statistical accounts eliminated for international comparability. (b)Exchange values cited in Table 11.1. (c)Based on a prewar average of 199 dinars (or francs) for Serbia, Croatia/Slavonia and Bosnia-Hercegovina derived from Table 9.8. (d)Francs or prewar gold dinars; asset values have not been corrected for overstatement from statistical accounts. (e)National Bank assets have statistical accounts eliminated and foreign assets and gold valued at 1930 exchange rates. (f)Includes the Agricultural Bank and the Artisan Bank.

Sources: Table 9.8; N. Popović and P. Mišić. *Naša domaća privreda* (Belgrade, 1929). p. 55; Ch. Evelpidi, *Les états balkaniques* (Paris, 1930). pp. 329-30; League of Nations, *Commercial Banks, 1919-1929* (Geneva, 1929). pp. 304-05; *1929-1934* (Geneva, 1935). pp. 134-36; *Statistički godišnjak Kr. Jugoslavije, 1929* (Belgrade, 1932). p. 285; *1930* (Belgrade, 1933). pp. 235, 244-45, 249-51, 294-99.

eastern Europe grew up in Greece. The National Bank of Greece maintained its dominant commercial role through a network of some eighty branches. Its preeminance, even after giving up the right of note issue to the new Bank of Greece in 1928, did, however, discourage the growth of private commercial banks. The two main foreign banks were French. The Bank of Athens and the formerly German Orient Bank had a combined total in 1928 that was just under 30 percent of all bank assets versus the National Bank's share of just under 40 percent. Another ten larger banks and twenty to thirty smaller ones were mainly native institutions set up in the early 1920s for currency speculation. Only one held even 10 percent of total assets. They did not provide enough loanable funds to take pressure off the National Banks' supply of commercial credit. The latter's interest rate typically exceeded 10 percent and sometimes approached 15 percent even after the drachma's exchange rate had stabilized.[30]

Evidence of the Romanian credit shortage does not come from the interest rates of the Banca Naţională a României. They were low and well below the market rate, as already noted. Barely one quarter of the bank's impressive total assets were economically active. Both the Jewish Banca Marmorosch-Blank and the Liberals' Banca Românească had greater active assets. Each had a network of branches, fifteen and twenty respectively. The clearest indication that these and the other large Bucharest banks failed to furnish an adequate supply of short-term credit may be found in the more rapid growth of smaller banks after 1924. Their share of total assets rose at the expense of the large Bucharest banks from two thirds to over three quarters between 1924 and 1929. They specialized in short-term credit. The large Bucharest banks had diverted loanable funds to long-term export credit and, as we shall see, to industrial investment in order to earn the 20–30 percent dividends necessary to keep up with inflation in the early 1920s. The Banca Marmorosch-Blank in particular also maintained a high liquidity ratio, further reducing the supply of loanable funds. The Jewish bank's steady loss of superiority in assets to its arch-rival, the government-backed Banca Românească, nonetheless prompted its native directors to reduce that liquidity from roughly 30 to 10 percent of assets and to borrow from European banks to restore its position. Marmorosch-Blank's vulnerability to the collapse of the Viennese Credit-Anstalt in 1931, quickly forcing its own demise, was of ironically recent origin.

Taken as a whole, moreover, the assets of the nine large Bucharest banks did not recapture their prewar level in real per capita terms at any time during the 1920s. In contrast, the eight large, also mainly European, financial institutions in Sofia boosted this level by almost

TABLE 11.7
POSTWAR STRUCTURE OF ROMANIAN COMMERCIAL BANKING

Commercial Bank Assets[a]

Year	Current Lei (mil.)	In Constant Prewar Exchange Values[b]		
		Amount (mil.)	Per Capita (lei)	Index[c] (1911=100)
1920	11,753	1,199	77.2	27
1921	19,123	1,219	77.5	27
1923	31,688	804	49.6	17
1925	47,789	1,189	71.3	25
1928	78,933	2,495	143.5	49
1930	83,782	2,646	147.9	51

Regional Structure of Joint Stock Banks and Capital

Region	1920			1929			Indices 1929/1930	
	Banks	Percent of Capital	Capital per Bank	Banks	Percent of Capital	Capital per Bank	Banks	Capital per Bank
Muntenia	106	63.5	11,780	260	54.8	23,564	245	200
Oltenia	34	5.3	3,087	106	5.4	5,674	312	184
Moldova	55	6.2	2,209	154	8.8	6,379	280	289
Dobrogea	16	0.7	872	27	1.6	6,596	169	756
Bessarabia	2	0.6	5,500	46	2.5	6,113	2,300	111
Bucovina	3	1.0	6,800	34	2.0	6,682	1,133	98
Transylvania	185	16.0	1,703	248	14.7	6,626	134	389
Banat	113	3.7	643	137	4.1	3,324	121	517
Crisana-Maramures	29	3.0	2,013	85	6.1	8,059	293	400
Total	543	100.0	3,622	1,097	100.0	10,192	202	281

TABLE 11.7 (continued)

Large Bucharest Commercial Banks

Year	Banks	Assets per Banks[d]	Percent of All Banks	Percent of All Assets	Assets per Bank Bucharest/All	Indices of assets Bucharest	Indices of assets All
1919	8	380 mil.	1.6	54.6	33.1	100	100
1924	10	1,472 mil.	1.2	33.2	28.0	484	798
1929	9	2,770 mil.	0.8	24.0	29.3	820	1,864

Structure of Bank Assets and Loans in 1930

Banks	Assets (mil. lei)	(%)	Loans (mil. lei)	(%)
National Bank	28,373	22.6	12,534	
Savings Banks	(4,384)[e]	3.5		
Commercial Banks	83,782	66.7	71,657	
Cooperative Credit	9,045	7.2	8,066	
Total	125,584	100.0		

Notes: (a)Asset basis with statistical accounts eliminated for international comparability. (b)Exchange values cited in Table 11.1. (c)Based on prewar assets of 290 lei cited for the Old Kingdom in Table 9.8. (c)Declines in asset values are overstated because statistical accounts were not eliminated in Table 9.8. (d)Statistical accounts included in assets of Bucharest and all banks. (e)Deposits only.

Sources: Table 9.8; League of Nations, *Commercial Banks, 1913-1929* (Geneva, 1931), pp. 238-39; *1929-1934* (Geneva, 1935), pp. 96-97; *Enciclopedia României*, Vol. IV (Bucharest, 1943), pp. 568, 591; *Anuarul statistic al României, 1939-1940* (Bucharest, 1940), pp. 700-02; Institutul central de statistică, *Statistica societăţilor anonime din România*, Vol. XXII-1940 (Bucharest, 1942), pp. 4-5.

one third. Their 1929 figure of 36 gold leva per capita nearly matched the Bucharest bank's 43 lei per capita. The prewar imbalance had been about three to one for Bucharest over Sofia.[31]

Regional Industrialization for National Markets

The foregoing financial restraints make the industrial growth actually recorded during the 1920s all the more striking. Bulgarian production's rate of increase deserves special attention, being the most rapid, according to Table 11.8, despite the sharpest reduction in the leverage of its central bank. The Romanian growth rate is noteworthy for lagging behind the others, despite the Liberal regime's reputation for favoring industry through protective import tariffs. The larger initial size of the Romanian industrial sector is at best a partial explanation for the lower rate.

On the demand side, the size of national markets for domestic manufacture and minerals seems crucial. We have already seen two serious limitations placed on those postwar markets. Levels of per capita income, according to Chapter 10, had probably fallen below prewar levels by 1920 and took the rest of the decade to surpass them. Slow agricultural growth was largely responsible, slow enough to hold Romania's 1929 level to that of 1913. The postwar reduction in the state's real per capita expenditures, again most severe for Romania, was a second sort of limitation (see above). Tariff protection for the existing domestic market constituted the main response by public policy. The varying structure and effect of these tariffs deserve attention.

On the supply side, sources of capital and entrepreneurship need to be spelled out. The balance between private, incorporated, and public initiatives now proves more important than the earlier distinction between native, immigrant, and European entrepreneurs. The postwar pattern of industrial production must also be examined for signs of concentration and reduced competition among enterprises.

Sectoral Growth for Protected Markets

The temptation to generalize about the overall performance of a country's industry can overlook significant variations between branches and between regions. Hence the effort to map at least the sectoral distribution of industrial production in Tables 11.8 and 11.9.

The record of the wartime decade reveals an overall Romanian increase only to 1916. Petroleum production had declined with its export since 1914. Then war damage to the fields, pipelines, and railway facilities during 1916 coincided with the virtual end of trade with Western Europe. Little new German trade or investment took its place in the occupied area, other than processing plants for the aforementioned export of vegetables and oil seeds. Transylvanian metallurgy, two thirds of it concentrated in the iron ore mining and smelting complexes at Reşiţa and Hunedoara, benefited from the construction of five new steel furnaces in 1915. Several other facilities there were dismantled and moved to Hungarian territory as the war was ending. Coking coal also became scarce. Total output from the two complexes dropped to one quarter of its prewar level by 1918 and had only recovered to half by 1920.[32] Aggregate manufactured production in Romania and its new territories suffered, as did western Yugoslav industry, from the dislocation of foreign occupation and changing borders more than from battle damage. Table 11.8 identifies a number of branches whose output dropped precipitously. Romanian industry grew at a real rate of under .8 percent a year between 1913 and 1922.

Greek manufactures advanced at far greater rates during this period. Greece's index (1914=100) had stood, as already noted in Table 10.5, at 220 by 1921. Romania recorded 70 for 1919 and 71 for 1922. Bulgaria's wartime record was closer to that of Romania than Greece for state-encouraged manufactures. By 1917 military authorities had taken over about two thirds of prewar capacity in the encouraged firms. Civilian resistance to military control plus a shortage of supplies kept output under half of prewar levels. Coal mined mainly from the state mines at Pernik nonetheless began a wartime advance that continued afterwards. Cement plants and non-encouraged enterprises for sugar and tobacco manufacture also grew impressively between 1911 and 1921. Cement production was responsible for non-wood building materials recording the only positive rate of growth for any branch of encouraged industry during that decade. Increased sugar refining was a function of four large new plants opened in 1912–13, by French and Czech interests near Sofia and by Belgian interests in Plovdiv and Ruse. Their output plus that of an existing refinery pushed up the 1911 volume of production by 1914. It stayed above the earlier level for all the war years except 1918. Tobacco processing accounted for the largest wartime growth. From less than 10 percent before the war its value climbed to 22 percent of the total for all manufacturing by 1921.[33] Growth in these several branches explains the overall increase of 59 percent in real industrial production between 1911 and 1921 recorded in Table 10.5.

TABLE 11.8
INDUSTRIAL GROWTH, 1911-30

Indices of Real Output

Branch	BULGARIA 1911	1921	1930	ROMANIA 1913	1919	1920	1929	YUGOSLAVIA 1913	1920-22	1929
Metals and machinery	100	69	702							
Smelting				100	26	43	192			
Fabrication				100	19	26	112			
Iron and steel	100	57	514	100	42	50	226	100	8	36
Chemicals				100	52		165			
Petroleum refining				100	40		259			
Other				100	90		95			
Non-wood building materials	100	134	601	100		58	58	100	28	119
Cement	100	160	1,160							
Wood processing	100	62	239	100	50		167			
Paper	100	62	172	100	30		62	100		160
Textiles	100	44	297	100			152			
Cotton	100	107	226	100	50[c]		346			
Wool				100	26[c]		95			
Leather				100	25		64			
Foodstuffs				100	57-65					
Flour milling	100	83	166	100	68		31			
Other	100	95	308	100	55-63		14			
Sugar	100	236	961	100	11-21		122	100	30	101

Average Annual Growth of Output (percent)

TABLE 11.8 (continued)

Branch	BULGARIA		GREECE		ROMANIA		YUGOSLAVIA	
	1911-30	1921-30	1911-30	1921-30	1913-29	1919/20-29	1913-29	1920-29
Metals and machinery	10.8	29.4		21.9	4.2	19.8		
Smelting					0.7	18.4		
Fabrication								
Iron and steel					5.2	18.2	(-)	18.0
Chemicals	9.0	27.9		6.6	3.2	12.2		
Petroleum refining					6.1	20.5		
Other					(-)	0.5		
Non-wood building materials	9.9	18.2		11.6				
Cement	13.8	24.6			3.3	12.5	1.1	17.4
Wood processing	4.7	16.2			(-)	2.2	3.0	
Paper	2.9	12.1		32.4	2.7	17.6		
Textiles	5.9	23.5		12.6	2.5	22.6		
Cotton					8.1	14.6		
Wool					(-)	9.9		
Leather	1.5	10.8		1.2	(-)			
Foodstuffs								
Flour milling	2.7	7.8			(-)	(-)		
Other	6.1	14.0		3.1	(-)	(-)		
Sugar	9.0	12.6			(-)	23.8	(-)	14.4

TABLE 11.8 (continued)

Average Annual Growth of Inputs, 1920-1929 (percent)[a]

Branch	Labor			Horsepower			Combined[b]		
	BUL.	ROM.	YUG.	BUL.	ROM.	YUG.	BUL.	ROM.	YUG.
Metals and machinery	19.702	0.878	5.794	25.407	4.009	2.210	22.55	2.44	4.00
Chemicals	14.843	8.260	4.801	19.339	2.062	1.255	17.09	5.16	3.03
Petroleum refining		6.857			4.200			1.33	
Other		9.044			1.034			5.04	
Building materials	5.597	0.271	1.883	14.000	3.510	0.547	9.80	1.89	1.22
Wood processing	4.228	-0.002	3.541	4.877	3.510	1.669	4.55	1.75	2.61
Paper	-2.908	7.299	4.566	16.357	6.642	0.056	6.72	6.97	2.31
Printing		-0.006	4.201		2.322	1.923		1.56	3.06
Textiles	20.794	14.530	8.739	15.119	10.270	3.892	17.96	12.40	6.32
Leather	10.714	2.341	6.663	10.349	6.910	1.423	10.26	4.63	4.04
Foodstuffs	0.608	-0.158	2.707	8.029	2.511	1.075	4.32	1.18	1.89
Flour mills	10.299	-2.955		9.599	1.214		9.95	-0.87	
Other food	-0.438	0.854		6.687	3.794		3.12	2.32	
Total	11.597	2.683	4.812	11.205	3.781	1.521	11.40	3.23	3.17

Notes: (a)Bulgaria, 1921-29; Romania. 1919-29; Yugoslavia. 1918-28. (b)Simple average of labor and horsepower growth rates. (c)Average, 1919-20.

Sources: Marvin R. Jackson, "Survey of Evidence of Industrialization in Southe.stern Europe. 1900-1950: The Cases of Bulgaria and Romania." *East European Quarterly.* XVI. 2 (1982), in press; Stevan Kukoleča, *Industrija Jugoslavije. 1918-193°* (Belgrade, 1941), pp. 110, 112. 141, 150; Ingvar Svennilson, *Growth and Stagnation in the European Economy* (Geneva, 1954). pp. 258-59, 283-85; Louis G. Michael. *Agricultural Survey of Europe: The Danube Basin—Part 2, Rumania, Bulgaria, and Yugoslavia,* Technical Bulletin No. 126, United States Department of Agriculture (Washington. D.C.: Government Printing Office, 1929). p. 163; League of Nations, *Statistical Yearbook, 1928* (Geneva, 1929), pp. 69. 91. 100-01.

The Yugoslav experience during this wartime decade remains the most elusive. Postwar industrial production was not recorded until 1923, after substantial recovery had already occurred. Table 10.5 noted a real per capita index (100=1909–12) of 130 for manufactures and mining combined. This figure probably masks great regional disparities. Serbian industry, after all, had lost over half of its equipment and one third of its plants during the war. With its own small mines badly damaged, Serbia suffered the worst of the postwar coal crises.[34] Macedonian industry had been small before the war and did not prosper during or afterwards. In the western Yugoslav lands, we need to know much more about the Croatian experience before any statements can be made about the net effect of the Austro-Hungarian war effort on industrial capacity there.

For the 1920s, Tables 11.8 and 11.9 afford a somewhat better notion of the sectoral variations in industrial recovery and growth. The record for light industry resists generalization, but one common tendency stands out. The processed exports of agricultural products, especially to Austrian and Hungarian markets, fell significantly. The export losses for flour-milling, meat-packing, and leather-processing helped to reduce output from prewar levels for Yugoslavia, Romania, and Bulgaria. The latter's lost foreign market was of course the Ottoman Empire, a major prewar consumer of woolen textiles as well as flour. Bulgaria's rising output of cotton textiles compensated for the wool loss. This new textile production served the domestic market as elsewhere in the region. So did the general boost in construction materials. These above-average increases extended to timber-processing in Yugoslavia but not in Romania, where the loss of the former Habsburg markets hurt too much. Sugar refining increased everywhere and promoted the cultivation of sugar beets, the one case of widespread backward linkage. The export of chemical fertilizers from both of these countries did not match the prewar level from their respective Habsburg borderlands, even though domestic demand from the agricultural sector remained minimal.[35] Heavy industry behaved more consistently. Above-average growth was the rule in machinery, metallurgy, and mining. Only Albania still lacked any semblance of heavy industry.

Patterns of geographic concentration became more prominent in postwar manufacturing. The prewar tendency of industrial enterprises to collect in the Balkan capital cities has already been discussed in Chapter 8. For Romania, a wider set of regional concentrations now emerged. Recent research by a British geographer finds that large-scale industrial employment along the Bucharest-Braşov axis, led by textiles and chemicals, was at least double that of other regions in all major branches as a percentage of total population by

TABLE 11.9
SHARES OF GROSS AND NET OUTPUT BY BRANCHES
OF MANUFACTURING, 1911-30
(current price shares)

Gross Output	BULGARIA			GREECE[a]		ROMANIA		
	1911	1921	1930	1921	1930	1913	1919	1930
Metals and machinery	2.97	2.90	5.93	5.94	5.33	6.46	11.60	16.17
Chemicals	3.98	3.33	8.16	19.02	15.52	15.62	10.62	18.62
Building materials	4.51	4.13	5.11	7.09	6.74	5.94	3.72	7.66
Paper	0.89	0.77	0.76	0.71	3.62	10.53	14.19	2.69
Printing						1.23	1.51	1.92
Textiles	20.46	13.40	23.08	22.34	31.83	5.11	8.79	15.52
Leather	5.27	3.89	3.08	19.49	10.15	4.25	8.05	4.32
Foodstuffs[a]	62.05	69.71	51.72	28.95	21.27	47.23	38.52	29.23
Flour	(44.23)	(46.55)	(28.36)	(a)	(a)	(31.98)	(22.31)	(8.57)
Total	100.0	100.0	100.0	100.0	100.0	100.0	100.0	100.0

Net Output[b]	BULGARIA			ROMANIA		
	1911	1921	1930	1913	1919	1930
Metals and machinery	5.04	3.56	8.16	7.52	19.65	17.36
Chemicals	4.53	3.98	10.46	21.38	15.68	15.36
Building materials	7.29	7.96	9.13	6.31	3.00	5.87
Wood processing	3.87	1.58	2.54	11.68	5.94	6.82
Paper	1.12	1.03	1.24	1.97	1.72	3.12
Printing				1.83	1.91	2.82
Textiles	29.41	16.57	22.28	6.77	11.15	13.66
Leather	2.56	3.07	2.34	5.11	10.70	3.61
Foodstuffs	46.18	62.25	43.84	37.42	32.94	31.24
Flour	(14.75)	(20.36)	(9.72)	(19.92)	(13.68)	(3.05)
Total	100.0	100.0	100.0	100.0	100.0	100.0

Notes: (a)Greek output does not include the values of wine, olive oil and wheat flour. (b)Net output equals gross output minus fuels and materials.

Sources: Table 11.12: *Statistikē epetēris tēs Ellados, 1939* (Athens, 1940), p. 454.

the 1930s.[36] Any increment from the prewar period can be measured only for the Bucharest area. Most had already occurred by 1920. Between 1902 and 1930 its *judeţ*, or county, increased its share of the Old Kingdom's population from 14.3 to 17.6 percent but its share of employment in large-scale industry from 46.6 to 54.9 percent and in all industry from 31.6 to 44.8. Several major firms in Transylvania opened plants in Bucharest. Yet metallurgy in Transylvania and wood and food processing in the Banat formed their own concentrations. The new territories' share of incorporated industrial enterprises rose from 33 to 40 percent during the 1920s. In postwar Bulgaria, however, Sofia's primacy over other industrial regions grew more pronounced. The capital city and its environs accounted for 54 percent of all industrial employment by the 1930s. The city's postwar advances followed the decline of Grabovo and Sliven as textile centers. Foreign trade through Sofia rose as result of the new railway line to Thessaloniki and of Varna's loss of Dobrudjan grain exports after Romania annexed the province. The Athens-Piraeus area accounted for a larger share of Greece's population and was better situated for foreign trade. It contained about half of the Greek force of large-scale industrial labor in 1930.[37] Both capitals shared access to electric power and a relatively abundant labor supply.

Hampering the further development of these geographic concentrations was the inability of leading enterprises in one center to spread their production facilities to the others. This was a special handicap in Yugoslavia, less so in Romania. Neither of the two main concentrations, Zagreb and the Slovenian uplands, contained the capital city. Zagreb's immediate postwar advantages, as the nexus for foreign trade with Central Europe and as a labor market for Croatian troops quickly demobilized from the disbanded Habsburg army, had largely been lost by the mid-1920s. Only its financial advantage over Belgrade remained. Yet the Croatian capital's leading firms made no noticeable effort to shift their operations to the national capital in Belgrade. The Croatian and Slovenian share of total employment in manufacturing climbed from 40 to 45 percent between 1918 and 1923, staying there for the rest of the decade. The Belgrade area could advance only from 7.5 to 9.5 percent. The fractions for numbers of joint-stock enterprises were about the same. Belgrade's industrial horsepower was just 5.4 percent of the 1923 total, versus 22.5 percent for Croatia, 18.4 percent for Slovenia, and 20 percent for Dalmatia.[38] This concentration of 60 percent in western lands that made up under one third of Yugoslavia's territory contrasts with about 5 percent for the southeastern third.

If balanced regional growth eluded postwar Balkan industry, the creation of national markets generally did not. The small amounts of industrial exports, as we have seen, confined manufactured goods to domestic sales. The one consistent state policy to promote access to this market during the 1920s was the protective tariff. By 1926 all the states of Southeastern Europe had revised their prewar rates upward, first informally and then with formal legislation. In 1926 the Bulgarian government imposed what Table 11.10 below records as the highest duties on industrial imports of any state in the area. The prewar maximum for semi-manufactures was doubled to an average of 50 percent ad valorem and that on finished goods almost quadrupled to 75 percent. This was half again Romanian rates that the Liberal regime liked to tout as the area's highest and almost three times the Yugoslav level.

The obvious question for economic analysis is how much credit these Bulgarian duties deserve for what we have already seen to be the most rapid rate of industrial growth in postwar Southeastern Europe. The following doubts may be cast on such a simple correlation. Other than cement, an unlikely import anyway because of its weight/value ratio, and textiles, the most rapidly growing branches of production in Bulgaria and the other states (see Tables 11.8 and 11.9) do not match up consistently with the highest rates of ad valorem incidence noted in Table 11.10. Bulgarian sugar production responded after 1926, but the size of the domestic market and heavy indirect taxation confined sales to about two thirds of output. Chemicals and metals were the two fastest growing sectors for Bulgaria. The former was favored with a 50-percent rate but also did well in Romania and Yugoslavia at under half of that rate. The latter was relatively less protected everywhere.

In addition, the Bulgarian advance for 1921–25 was achieved within the framework of the relatively low prewar tariffs that Stamboliski had simply reimposed in 1919. Exchange controls were added, but inflation reduced the ad valorem impact of the specific rates. League restrictions, imposed on Bulgaria as a defeated state owing reparations, prevented any new legislation until 1926.

Tariffs aside, the Bulgarska Zemedelska Banka started a project that succeeded by the 1930s in raising the long-deficient standard of Bulgarian cotton cultivation to a level permitting its use in modern textile manufacture. More generally, a sweeping reduction in railway freight rates in 1928 has been credited with facilitating industrial sales and supplies more than the combined effect of import tariffs and their waiver for industrial firms bringing in machinery or materials for use in domestic production.[39] Whatever the mix of incentives to produce for the national market, the value of Bulgarian industrial

TABLE 11.10
IMPORT TARIFF LEVELS AND CHANGES, 1913-31
(percentage ad valorem levels[a] or change in levels[b])

COMMODITIES	BULGARIA Level 1927	Level 1931	Change 1927/13	Change 1927/31	ROMANIA Level 1927	Level 1931	Change 1927/13	Change 1927/31	YUGOSLAVIA Level 1927	Level 1931	Change 1927/13	Change 1931/27
Foodstuffs												
Cereals and flour	18.0	66.0	185.6	366.7	13.8	36.4	35.4	263.8	9.2	80.0	36.2	869.6
Livestock	15.7	26.8	257.4	170.7	6.3	7.4	70.8	117.5	21.2	30.3	176.7	142.9
Animal foodstuffs	103.8	169.0	376.6	164.4	48.0	87.0	101.4	181.3	60.0	101.5	247.9	169.2
Fruit & vegetables	102.3	138.5	409.2	135.4	83.0	156.5	436.8	188.6	22.9	35.5	82.1	155.0
Other foodstuffs	154.4	267.0	278.4	172.8	77.5	151.5	99.2	195.5	66.3	120.5	93.4	181.7
Alcohol and tobacco	329.0	373.0	311.0	113.4	118.0	136.0	163.9	115.3	82.5	80.5	290.5	97.6
Semi-manufactures												
Textiles	87.5	123.5	424.8	141.1	24.0	29.7	146.3	165.4	12.2	18.0	83.0	147.5
Timber, paper	26.2	44.0	159.8	167.9	52.5	39.3	86.1	74.9	24.3	24.3	130.6	104.1
Metals	33.8	35.7	168.2	105.6	28.2	39.8	204.3	141.1	34.1	39.4	196.0	115.5
Chemicals	49.7	55.8	125.8	112.3	26.0	66.5	110.0	255.8	28.5	40.0	157.5	140.4
Mineral oils	102.2	245.4	335.1	240.1	18.3	41.5	67.0	226.8	66.7	190.0	155.8	284.9
Manufactures												
Textiles	143.5	174.5	693.2	121.6	125.0	171.0	550.7	136.8	33.1	33.9	171.5	102.4
Paper	45.9	57.9	146.6	126.1	49.7	80.9	81.1	162.8	24.8	37.0	94.3	149.2
Glass, china, cement	77.0	66.0	354.8	85.7	65.1	45.7	232.5	70.2	36.8	34.5	109.9	93.8
Metal goods	46.0	54.5	304.6	118.5	39.9	44.7	117.4	112.0	34.2	47.1	167.4	137.7
Machinery	7.8	6.6	205.3	84.6	10.5	9.9	152.2	94.3	11.3	12.0	226.0	106.2
Vehicles	13.3	13.3	154.7	100.0	20.2	24.5	113.4	121.3	16.8	16.3	230.1	97.0
Appliances	47.0	51.5	279.0	322.3	37.4	24.7	450.1	66.0	21.0	21.0	208.9	112.9

TABLE 11.10 (continued)

	Foodstuffs				Semi-manufactures				Manufactures			
	Level		Change		Level		Change		Level		Change	
	1927	1931	1927/13	1931/27	1927	1931	1927/13	1931/27	1927	1931	1927/13	1931/27
Average levels[c]												
Bulgaria	79.0	133.0	319.8	168.4	49.5	65.0	204.5	131.3	75.0	90.0	384.6	120.0
Romania	45.6	87.5	131.4	191.8	32.6	46.3	108.7	142.0	48.5	55.0	190.2	113.4
Yugoslavia	43.7	75.0	138.3	171.6	24.7	30.5	143.6	123.5	28.0	32.8	155.6	117.1
Austria	16.5	59.5	56.7	360.6	15.2	20.7	76.0	136.2	21.0	27.7	108.8	131.9
Czechoslovakia	36.3	84.0	124.7	231.4	21.7	29.5	108.5	135.9	35.8	36.5	185.5	102.0
Hungary	31.5	60.0	108.2	190.5	26.5	32.5	132.5	122.6	31.8	42.6	164.8	134.0
Poland	72.0	110.0	103.7	152.8	33.2	40.0	52.3	120.5	55.6	52.0	65.4	93.5
Spain	45.2	80.5	108.9	178.9	39.2	49.5	150.8	126.3	62.7	75.5	147.5	120.4
Germany	27.4	82.5	125.7	301.1	14.5	23.4	94.8	161.4	19.0	18.3	190.0	96.3
France	19.1	53.0	65.4	277.5	24.3	31.8	96.0	130.9	25.8	29.0	158.3	112.4
Italy	24.5	66.0	111.4	259.4	28.6	49.5	114.0	173.1	28.3	41.8	193.8	147.7
Belgium	11.8	23.7	46.3	200.8	1C.5	15.5	138.2	147.6	11.6	13.0	122.1	112.1
Switzerland	21.5	42.2	146.3	196.3	11.5	15.2	157.5	132.2	17.6	22.0	189.2	125.0

Notes: (a)Tariff levels are defined as "potential" levels and measured by country's import duty as a percentage of the f.o.b. unit export value of Europe's leading exporter. Figures in the table are the average of lowest and highest rates within each commodity group. (b)See Table 8.8 for 1913 levels. (c)Average levels do not include alcohol and tobacco in foodstuffs and mineral oils in semi-manufactures.

Source: Calculated from H. Liepmann, *Tariff Levels and the Economic Unity of Europe* (New York, 1938), pp. 396-98 and 413.

output rose 45 percent for 1925–29. Total industrial consumption including imports advanced only 17 percent. During the decade domestic output had in fact grown impressively from 38 to 62 percent of domestic consumption.[40]

Yugoslavia's 1924 tariff legislation set the region's lowest rates, as noted in Table 11.10. They also coincided with the general stabilization of the dinar's exchange rate and specific increases in a number of industrial prices. The major interwar study of Yugoslav industry finds the latter two stimuli to be more important than the new tariff in the growth that followed until the Depression's onset.[41] Textile production, as elsewhere in Southeastern Europe, responded to rates exceeding 50 percent ad valorem. Output nearly doubled its share of domestic consumption to 61 percent by 1929. Northern food processing and particularly flour milling would have had the national market to themselves had they supplied the southern hinterlands. Yet Dalmatia sometimes imported more flour than the Vojvodina and Croatia exported. Mills continued to operate well under capacity. So did meat-packing. By 1928 three quarters of the country's modern plants had stopped working. Sugar refineries met all domestic needs but worked at less than full capacity as in Romania and Bulgaria. Paper and metal-processing, the manufacture of replacement parts aside, faced European imports that overcame tariffs exceeding 50 percent to keep a majority of the small domestic market. There was no manufacture of heavy machinery, in the absence of the sort of demand generated by the Romanian oil fields. Far lower rates on most industrial inputs served the same purpose as exemptions under industrial laws elsewhere. Interwar Yugoslavia lacked the industrial legislation providing the familiar tariff and tax exemptions which even Greece had finally adopted in 1922.

The less developed regions like Macedonia were already complaining that lower rates on inputs gave a cost advantage to modern manufacturers in Slovenia and Croatia/Slavonia that forced artisan wares out of local markets. Regional impulses to create a series of separate economies formed a barrier to the integration of the Yugoslav market. Belgrade's political power was unaccompanied by the economic leverage to overcome these impulses that was concentrated in the other Balkan capital cities. How higher tariffs on industrial inputs might have helped less developed regions is unclear in any case. The respective 98 and 180 percent tariffs on cement in Yugoslavia and Romania permitted high prices that when coupled with transport costs for a heavy cargo kept the two main centers of domestically used production (Beočin and the Bucharest area) working at only 80 and 50 percent of capacity respectively even in the late 1920s.[42]

The domestic shares of industrial inputs in Table 11.11 reflect the low percentages that Alexander Gerschenkron has emphasized for Bulgaria, foodstuffs excepted. They extended to Yugoslavia and Greece but not so much to Romania, if textile yarn is excepted. Romania's overall share of 71 percent domestic inputs versus 60 percent for Bulgaria by 1929–30 suggests that the latter's more rapid industrial growth during the decade may have benefited from greater recourse to imports. They were often free from the high post-1925 tariffs under the terms of prewar industrial legislation (see Chapter 8). Its tariff and tax exemptions were broadened in 1928 from firms with twenty to those with ten employees.

Bulgaria's imported fraction of industrial raw materials doubled during 1921–30, led by textile yarn, mainly cotton, and inputs for non-wood construction and the rapidly growing chemical and metal sectors. In Romania only textiles displayed a correspondingly high share and recorded not incidentally the sharpest rise in share of manufactured output for 1919–30 of any major branch in Table 11.9 from 11.6 to 13.7 percent. Romania's imports of finished textiles did decline from 72 to 54 percent of domestic consumption over this same period.

Here is a classic dilemma that continues to plague developing economies: rising production of finished manufactures, while desirable in itself, brings with it the need for semifinished inputs that limited industrial and agricultural capacity cannot easily provide but whose import strains the trade or payments balance. To concentrate on producing the inputs risks either dependence on importing more finished goods or, as with Bulgaria and Romania after the Second World War, severe restrictions on consumption.

Sources of Capital and Entrepreneurship

On the supply side, capital generally proved to be a more flexible factor of production than entrepreneurship. Industrial labor, as we have seen, was available. The huge rural majorities, about 80 percent of the Yugoslav, Romanian, and Bulgarian populations, came down only slightly during the 1920s but enough to add a relatively large increment to the small totals of urban labor (see Tables 10.3 and 10.4). Entrepreneurial risk-taking in postwar Southeastern Europe remained bound, however, to the prewar pattern: private investors sought out short-term profit and governments relied either on direct investment for strictly fiscal purposes or on indirect encouragement.

Greek entrepreneurship provided one exception to this general rule. Urban population had already reached 24 percent of the Greek total before the war. Now the influx of refugees made it 33 percent.

TABLE 11.11
IMPORT SHARES IN INDUSTRY

Import Percentage of Domestic Consumption of Industrial Products

Country	1909	1915	1921	1925	1927	1928	1929
Bulgaria[a]	70.3		62.2				38.5
Greece				36.7			
Romania[b]		81.8[c]		49.6	36.5[c]	34.2	34.8

Import Percentage of Domestic Consumption by Branch of Industry

Branch	BULGARIA	GREECE	ROMANIA			YUGOSLAVIA
	1927	1925	1915[b]	1925	1929[b]	1927
Metals and machinery	86.0	69.4	85.9	61.9	56.9	75.0
Chemicals		37.6	94.0	46.6	41.0	
Non-wood building materials		12.2		40.9		
Cement	0.0	60.0		0.0	0.0	(d)
Wood processing		5.7		(d)		
Paper		74.7		22.5		50.0
Textiles	65.0	62.3	80.5	71.5	54.4	55.0
Leather		15.0	45.7	24.8	18.7	
Foodstuffs .		25.1		2.8		

Import Percentage of Manufacturing Inputs (raw mat'l and fuels) by Branch

Branch	BULGARIA				ROMANIA		
	1909	1921[e]	1921[f]	1930	1902	1915	1929
Metals and machinery	93.1	93.0	92.2	86.9	85.0	82.5	39.1
Chemicals	76.0	43.1	36.2	46.3	39.6	5.2	6.6
Non-wood building materials	40.9	30.0	29.6	59.0		27.4	28.3
Wood processing	31.8	8.0	8.9	6.7	8.7	10.0	2.6
Paper	85.7	71.6	70.4	64.2		22.9	
					39.2		12.8
Printing						21.0	
Textiles	60.5	42.8	41.7	80.1	51.0	72.6	85.1
Leather	67.2	72.2	76.2	75.8	33.0	42.6	21.5
Foodstuffs		36.4	21.0		5.3	6.1	7.8
Total	26.6	15.5	17.0	40.1	20.6	19.6	28.8

Notes: (a)For 165 industrial products. (b)Product inclusion for Romania in 1915 and 1929 is unclear. (c)Only four branches (metals and machinery, chemicals, textiles and leather) included. (d)Large net exports. (e)Encouraged establishments. (f)All factory industry.

Sources: L. Berov, "Kum vuprosa za tempovete na kapitalisticheskata industrializatsiia na Bulgariia," *Izvestiia na ikonomicheski institut*, 1954:3-4 (Sofia), p. 134; Demetre Tsamis, *L'évolution monétaire en Grèce, 1928-1930* (Nancy, 1939), pp. 14-15; T. S. Kapsalis, *La balance des comptes de la Grèce* (Lausanne, 1927), pp. 4, 14; N. Arcadian, *Industrializarea României* (Bucharest, 1936), pp. 130, 212, 226; V. Madgearu, *Evoluția economiei românești* (Bucharest, 1940), pp. 122, 256-57; M. Lupu, "Studii privind dezvoltarea economiei României în perioada capitalismului," *Studii și cercetări economice*, 1967 (Bucharest), pp. 282-83; Ch. Evelpidi, *Les états balkaniques* (Paris, 1930), pp. 278, 282, 285; *Statisticheski godishnik na Bulgarskoto Tsarstvo, 1911* (Sofia, 1912), pp. 239, 242-43; *1923-1924* (Sofia, 1924), pp. B84-37; *1940* (Sofia, 1940), pp. 379-83, 387-91.

Four fifths lived in towns over 20,000. More importantly, both the refugees themselves and the state-sponsored if autonomous Refugee Settlement Commission injected fresh entrepreneurial energy. Refugees were reportedly responsible for a majority of the new textile firms, woolen and silk as well as cotton, and for virtually all of the carpet factories founded from 1923 to 1930. Textile totals for firms, looms, and employment doubled during this period. Aided by state purchases, the real value of production tripled. The share of textiles in overall industrial output climbed to over 20 percent, making it the largest single branch. Carpet production rose from nothing to 15 percent of industrial export value by 1929. The Refugee Commission provided long-term loans for the buildings and equipment needed to start many enterprises. They were typically small, in keeping with the more rapid growth of firm numbers than size elsewhere in Southeastern Europe.[43]

Offering some relief to these small firms, with more than 25 but typically fewer than 100 employees, was the long-overdue end to Greek restrictions on joint-stock incorporation and even partnerships (see Chapter 8). New commercial legislation in 1920 and 1923 cleared the way for the incorporation of 265 new industrial firms between 1921 and 1930, almost exactly one half the total manufacturing enterprises founded. For textiles, joint-stock enterprises also comprised half of the additions. Access to joint-stock funding did not extend to the northern areas where most refugees had been sent, however. Thessaloniki accounted for only 6 percent of the decade's incorporations. Most occurred in the Athens/Piraeus area (58 percent for Athens and 14 percent for Piraeus).[44]

This further stimulus to concentration in the capital city was more pronounced in the Bulgarian case. Sofia strengthened its position as the country's predominant industrial center by virtue of the far easier access to joint-stock capital there than elsewhere. The relative lack of joint-stock enterprises before the war gave way to a rash of incorporations, perhaps encouraged by the prospect of German or government purchases of shares during 1917–18. By 1926 Sofia firms had issued 62 percent of Bulgarian industrial shares. A majority were incorporated, versus a declining minority in the rest of the country. Industrial incorporations per capita were just two thirds of Yugoslav and Romanian averages, liquidations twice as frequent. It also proved difficult to combine large Sofia firms and smaller provincial ones in the cartel arrangements that threatened soon after the war to dominate virtually all branches of Bulgarian industry. For this reason and because high tariffs eased entry for new firms, most of the 40-odd cartels formed during the 1920s lasted only one or two years. The decline in the proportion of joint-stock firms in the total for encouraged industry, from 23 to 21 percent for 1921–30 according to Table 11.13, may also have derived from these circumstances.[45]

Scholars from Eastern Europe have consistently assumed that industrial concentration, in the classic Marxist sense of fewer and fewer firms producing more and more, must have been growing throughout the decade. The numbers of enterprises, employees, horsepower per enterprise listed in Table 11.12 suggest a different story. Immune from the problem that inflation poses for calculations of capital and output, these figures are the best available indicators of the extent of concentration.

The number of large-scale firms did increase more rapidly during the 1920s than that of the smaller ones under 20 employees. But numbers of larger firms also grew faster than their own labor force, and employment in turn more rapidly than horsepower. In Romania, horsepower and especially workers per enterprise continued to decline from the prewar levels noted in Table 9.7 above. All the same, the number of "large" enterprises over 20 employees rose in every country. The average number of employees per firm remained relatively high by European standards.[46]

A noticeably faster growth of employment and horsepower than enterprises occurred only in extraction. This sector's share of total employment nonetheless stayed under .5 percent for both Bulgaria and Greece. It did not employ much over one percent for Romania, slightly less for Yugoslavia. Romanian extraction consisted mainly of oil from the Old Kingdom, unique in Southeastern Europe, and coal and iron ore from Transylvania, rivaled only in the western Yugoslav lands. The two sets of coal mines boosted the output of prewar Serbia and Romania tenfold. By 1930 combined Romanian extraction accounted for 8.6 percent of total industrial employment and 18.1 percent of horsepower but only 3.8 percent of enterprises. The number of Transylvanian firms dropped by one half during the 1920s to provide the only unmistakable evidence of growing concentration in any of the major industrial branches. Yet the Transylvanian mines did not respond to the presumed advantages of concentration with increased output. The production predominantly of coal never regained its prewar level. After rising to 80 percent of that level during 1921–1927, its real value fell back to 70 percent by 1929. Here domestic competition from the rapidly growing oil industry cut into lignite coal's share of the fuel and heating markets (see sources for Table 11.12).

Yugoslav and Romanian incorporation derived less from concentration than from investment assembled through the large private banks in Zagreb and Bucharest. Outside of shares underwritten or bought by banks, joint-stock enterprises did not mobilize much new

TABLE 11.12
EMPLOYMENT AND HORSEPOWER IN MANUFACTURING, 1920-30[a]

Country and Branch[b]	Establishments		Workers per Establishment		Horsepower per Establishment		Horsepower per Worker	
	1921	1929[c]	1921	1929	1921	1929	1921	1929
Bulgaria								
Metals and machinery	43	136 (127)	30.4	43.3	28.7	59.4	0.94	1.37
Chemicals	34	104 (86)	17.2	20.5	26.6	43.2	1.55	2.10
Non-wood building materials	44	101 (83)	56.4	43.6	105.6	150.7	1.87	3.46
Wood processing	24	48 (29)	32.1	40.2	52.3	63.9	1.64	1.59
Paper	8	4 (4)	53.5	84.5	56.3	378.0	1.05	4.47
Printing								
Textiles	66	198 (171)	54.7	55.7	87.8	104.6	1.61	1.09
Leather	27	54 (46)	17.6	22.4	51.5	66.4	2.93	2.96
Foodstuffs	181	468 (355)	31.9	20.0	138.5	131.0	4.34	6.55
Flour milling	121	313 (235)	10.4	11.7	90.6	97.1	8.71	8.30
Other foods	60	155 (120)	75.4	36.7	235.1	197.3	3.12	5.42
Total	427	113 (906)	36.1	41.1	95.5	105.2	2.64	2.56

Country and Branch	Establishments With Over 25 Employees		Establishments With Motors			
	Number 1930	Employees per Establishment 1930	Number		HP per Establishment	
			1920	1930	1920	1930
Greece						
Metals and machinery	56	73.2	229	566	9.09	24.33
Chemicals	24	132.9	147	111	35.31	110.64
Textiles	226	100.0	311	349	32.37	95.26
Non-wood building materials	119	177.1		133		32.69
Other	218	68.1	7,066	7,889	3.86	15.54
Paper and printing	49	66.1		238		32.60
Wood processing	27	57.3		41		98.80
Leather	5	443.6		474		15.84
Food and tobacco	137	64.1		7,227		14.51
Total	689	101.3	7,753	9,139	5.90	20.91

TABLE 11.12 (continued)

Country and Branch	Establishments		Employees per Establishment		Horsepower per Establishment		Horsepower per Employee	
	1919	1929	1919	1929	1919	1929	1919	1929
Romania								
Metals and machinery	305	460	123.4	89.3	192.1	188.7	1.56	2.11
Chemicals	187	248	47.5	53.9	302.3	133.3	6.47	2.47
Petroleum refining	69	36	48.1	178.9	191.9	239.1	3.99	1.34
Other	118	212	45.9	60.4	366.8	286.4	7.99	4.74
Non-wood building materials	216	363	67.1	52.4	184.2	154.7	2.75	2.95
Wood processing	490	787	86.4	52.9	135.9	93.8	1.57	1.77
Paper	12	19	212.0	270.9	1,191.0	1,430.9	5.62	5.28
Printing	134	128	43.8	43.1	16.6	21.8	0.38	0.50
Textiles	156	516	66.7	69.7	86.7	78.3	1.30	1.12
Leather	133	211	47.3	37.6	58.3	71.6	1.22	1.90
Foodstuffs	977	1,004	26.7	25.5	100.9	125.8	3.76	4.93
Flour milling	395	266	19.8	21.8	131.1	219.7	6.62	10.08
Other food	582	738	31.3	26.9	80.4	92.0	2.57	3.41
Total	2,610	3,736	59.2	53.9	131.7	133.3	2.22	2.47
	1918	1928	1918	1928	1918	1928	1918	1928
Yugoslavia								
Metals and machinery	93	193	297.6	251.9	381.1	228.5	1.28	0.91
Chemicals	77	157	152.9	119.8	334.5	185.9	2.19	1.55
Non-wood building materials	187	251	125.9	113.1	178.3	140.3	1.42	1.24
Wood processing	265	452	130.1	108.0	144.1	99.7	1.11	0.92
Paper	20	37	136.8	115.6	602.7	327.6	4.41	2.83
Printing	30	51	131.0	116.3	67.8	48.3	0.51	0.42
Textiles	120	269	214.3	221.0	186.3	121.7	0.87	0.55
Leather	40	87	170.6	149.5	181.4	96.0	1.06	0.64
Food	724	1,061	40.4	36.0	112.5	85.4	2.79	2.37
Total	1,565	2,558	104.9	104.0	356.2	282.6	3.40	2.72

capital, at least in manufacturing. Underwritten shares were typically sold in small lots, at least to native investors. A number of Austrian, Hungarian, and other Yugoslav firms had incorporated themselves in Zagreb until official permission was required in 1922. Yet the city's stock exchange continued to trade more foreign notes than stock shares throughout the 1920s. Belgrade's *berza* was instead the center for the limited stock market that came into being.[47] The incorporation of the most prominent of the prewar Belgrade manufacturers did not produce impressive results. The Vajfert brewery successfully expanded in this fashion, but the Ilić textile mill, the Čukarica sugar refinery, and even the meat-packing plant of the Klanično drustvo, each dominating enterprises in prewar Serbia as described in Chapter 8, sold few shares. The Ilić brothers had to rely on army purchases to stay open. The state was forced to buy up the Čukarica refinery by 1926. Belgrade's municipal government had to take over the Klanično društvo a few years later. Newly incorporated manufacturers in Sarajevo and Skopje struggled to survive the decade.[48]

In Romania, Jewish merchants or moneylenders had accounted for over half of what was the most extensive prewar issue of industrial stock. During the 1920s the large Bucharest banks undoubtedly helped to diversify ownership of an increased amount of industrial stock. Beyond their important if undocumented role in underwriting stock sales, these banks also kept shares in some enterprises for themselves. "Nationalized" firms, i.e., ones obliged to accord ethnic Romanians a majority interest, located in the new territories were favored. The acquisition of the Reşiţa metallurgical complex in 1923 was the largest case in point, although English investment was also included.

As the decade wore on, moreover, the waves of Romanian incorporation and bank participation both receded. The proportion of joint-stock firms in the total of "large" industrial enterprises had risen from 24.6 percent in 1922 to 32.3 percent in 1925, well past the Bulgarian peak of 23 percent noted above, but then slipped back to 29

TABLE 11.12 (continued)

Notes: (a)Bulgarian employment includes only workers; other countries include proprietors and all employees. Bulgarian horsepower in 1921 and after is reported as "effective" horsepower while in earlier years it is reported as "nominal" horsepower. In 1909, both figures were reported with "effective" horsepower 81.1 percent of "nominal" horsepower (*Statisticheski godishnik, 1912*, pp. 251-77). The basis for horsepower reports in other countries is unknown. (b)In all cases "establishment" refers to an independent technical unit, not an ownership unit. Electric power generation and tobacco processing excluded in all countries. State manufacturing establishments are excluded for Bulgaria and Romania. Bulgarian data covers "private encouraged" establishments; in 1921, cooperatives are excluded, but some are included in 1929. The Bulgarian industrial encouragement law of June 14, 1928 applied to establishments in defined branches having at least 10 horsepower and 10 workers while "encouragement" in earlier years might have been more restrictive. Romanian data includes so-called "large" (*mare*) establishments with over 20 horsepower or 10 workers. The basis of Yugoslav data is unclear. (c)The number of establishments in parentheses are those reporting (as opposed to those in existence); averages are based on numbers reporting.

Sources: *Statisticheski godishnik na Bulgarskoto Tsarstvo, 1923-1924* (Sofia, 1925), pp. B65-79; *1940* (Sofia, 1940), pp. 376-83; *Statistikė epetėris tēs Ellados, 1930* (Athens, 1931), p. 177; *1935* (Athens, 1936), pp. 137-40; *Anuarul statistic al României, 1922* (Bucharest, 1923), pp. 200-07; *1930* (Bucharest, 1932), pp. 184-97; Stevan Kukoleća, *Industrija Jugoslavije, 1918-1938* (Belgrade, 1941), pp. 110, 113, 150.

TABLE 11.13
LIMITED OR JOINT STOCK COMPANIES[a], 1920-30

Number (yearend)	1921	1922	1923	1924	1925	1926	1927	1928	1929	1930	1931
Bulgaria											
Industrial[b]	204	219	233	247	268	274	289	301	328	353	397
Banking	138	138	136	129	131	137	145	151	172	164	154
Insurance	15	17	16	19	19	19	18	18	17	16	16
Commerce[b]	120	138	138	142	151	156	165	182	210	238	283
Other[b]	21	19	16	14	10	12	11	12	12	14	16
Total	498	531	539	551	579	598	628	664	739	785	866
Romania											
Industrial[b]	529	720	874	1014	1108	1171	1168	1123	1078	1063	1054
Banking	556	683	756	844	928	1029	1054	1122	1097	1102	1037
Insurance[b]	9	15	17	20	21	24	24	30	31	25	27
Commerce[b]	159	218	277	293	352	368	414	415	418	448	463
Other[b]	13	14	18	17	31	30	34	39	38	44	39
Total	1266	1650	1942	2188	2440	2622	2694	2729	2662	2682	2620
Yugoslavia											
Industrial[b]											667
Banking									637	659	639
Insurance[b]											
Commerce[b]											186
Other[b]											52
Total											1544

TABLE 11.13 (continued)

Formations

Year	New Formations								Liquidations		Number Yearend[c]
	Mining, Manufacturing, Construction, Utilities		Banking[c] Insurance		Other		Total				
	BULGARIA	GREECE	BULGARIA	GREECE	BULGARIA	GREECE	BULGARIA	GREECE	BULGARIA	GREECE	BULGARIA
1921	26	7	6	3	31	3	63	13	30	3	498
1922	19	12	3	1	14	3	34	16	26	0	531
1923		20		4		8		32	33	1	539
1924		31		10		13	45	54	19	5	551
1925	28	43	5	7	14	38	47	83	18	1	579
1926	14	64	11	10	12	34	37	108	24	7	598
1927	26	45	11	2	17	30	54	77	11	14	628
1928	16	46	8	6	23	33	47	87	27	19	664
1929	39	41	28	2	35	42	102	85	38	30	739
1930	37	34	5	2	42	31	84	83		23	785
Total	(205)[d]	(305)[d]	(77)[d]	(34)[d]	(187)[d]	(219)[d]	513	630	226	100	

Notes: Romanian and Greek data are for limited companies; Bulgarian and Yugoslav data are for stock companies. (b)"Industry" includes mining, manufacturing, construction and public utilities; "commerce" includes trade, hotels, theaters and hospitals; "other" includes transportation, communications and those not otherwise identified. (c)Classifications in banking may not be the same. (d)Excluding 1921. (e)Not available for Greece.

Sources: *Statisticheski godishnik na Bulgarskoto Tsarstvo* annually 1913-22 through 1932; *Statistikē epetēris tēs Ellados, 1930* (Athens, 1931), p. 287; *1935* (Athens, 1936), p. 304; Institul cenral de statisticǎ, *Statistica societǎṭilor anonime din România*, Vol. XII-1940 (Bucharest, 1942), pp. 2-3; *Statistički godišnjak Kr. Jugoslavije, 1931* (Belgrade, 1933), pp. 222, 228-29.

percent by 1929. The maximum share of bank ownership in industrial stock dropped more significantly from 15.8 percent in 1923 to 8
percent in 1927. The borrowed portion of total assets in incorporated
industrial enterprises fell from 52.4 percent in 1925 to 43.6 percent
in 1930. Many examples could be cited of individual firms that grew
into large-scale enterprises without benefit of incorporation or bank
participation. Most obvious is the huge Malaxa machine works in
Bucharest, which began by repairing locomotives and was building a
variety of heavy machinery by 1929. The Rizescu partnership for
producing cotton textiles and the metallurgical firm of Goldenberg
and Son also expanded their operations and installed the most modern equipment.[49]

Bank investment or credit for industry generally favored mining or
other raw materials over manufacturing in postwar Southeastern
Europe. This tendency was most clear in the Greek and Bulgarian
cases. Among the eight largest institutions whose assets made up
about 90 percent of the total for Greek banks, only the National Bank
of Greece appears to have made joint-stock investments in manufacturing firms. From 1927 the National Bank cut back such investments
from about 20 to less than 10 percent of its assets, as part of the
drachma's stabilization. The two small banks which devoted a
significantly larger share of their assets to investments in manufacturing never accounted for more than 5 percent of total bank assets.[50]
Other Greek banks, including the large French Bank of Athens, concentrated on short-term advances and discounts for foreign trade.
The substantial French and British investments in Greek mines recorded in Tables 11.14 and 11.15 came directly from overseas consor-
tiums of banking interests.

European bank investment also concentrated on Bulgarian mining.
They did so directly without recourse to the large foreign institutions
that had grown up in Sofia after the war. French and Belgian ownership of the Plakalnitsa copper mine followed its German exploitation during the war. Several Italian banks joined in the purchase of
the Rusalka coal mine. The Belgian Société Generale and a number
of Swiss banks accounted for over half the foreign ownership of 48
percent of all Bulgarian joint-stock emissions by 1930. Czech banks
led by the Živnostenska Banka, Prague's largest, made the only
noteworthy investments in manufacturing. They brought majority
shares in Bulgarian sugar and glass firms and a minority in textile
production. The one major project of resident banks was the export of
tobacco. The Franco-Belgiska Banka of Sofia assembled a cartel that
controlled about 85 percent of manufactured tobacco. The small
German Kreditna Banka of Sofia invested in cigarette manufacture.
The native Zemedelska Banka made a greater contribution by decen-

tralizing the basic drying process from Plovdiv to a long list of smaller towns. The central bank also did its part. Although confined to short-term credit, the Narodna Banka reversed its prewar policy in 1924 and began to accord industry more discounting and other commercial credit. Industry's share reached 40 percent by 1925. This preeminence lasted until 1928. Credits to smaller native banks pushed down the share given industry to 32 percent, then to 21 percent the following year.[51]

For Yugoslavia, we must distinguish between the activities of three separate banking centers, in Belgrade, Zagreb, and Ljubljana, plus the mining investments of European financial interests. The Narodna Banka in Belgrade continued its prewar policy of favoring credits to other banks over industry, roughly 2/1 for 1924–27. Serbian, mainly Belgrade, banks were also favored with more credits than for Croatian and Slovenian banks combined. Industry suffered in the process. Most of the Belgrade banks whose prewar commitments had been crucial to Serbian industrial growth during the 1906–11 tariff war with Austria-Hungary now backed away. Only the small Prometna Banka continued its several ventures, still under the prompting of its engineer-director, Miloš Savčić. The main foreign bank, the Banque Franco-Serbe, confined its long-term industrial investment to one cement plant.[52]

Before the war several Zagreb banks had already assembled the large savings deposits needed to expand long-term assets. Then the postwar inflation and land reform combined to undermine fixed interest mortgage bonds on agricultural land. Prewar banks had relied on them for long-term investment. Only joint-stock dividends promised rates of return that would be high enough to keep up with inflation and pay out the high interest needed to maintain savings deposits. This short-term strategy pushed the essentially native Prva Hrvatska Štedionica, still the largest Zagreb bank, into joint-stock investment in fifty one industrial enterprises by 1924. The new Czech Jugoslovenska Bank and the Austrian Jugoslovenska Udružena Banka each had over twenty such ventures. Individual Austrian investors trying to escape the postwar trials of the Viennese Great Banks and at the same time get around Yugoslav restrictions on foreign ownership thereby accounted for roughly 30 percent of the industrial capital in Croatia during the period 1923–25.[53] The flow of Croatian and foreign capital through these banks tended to favor timber-processing and made Zagreb the center of one of the most rapidly expanding branches in postwar Yugoslav industry. In Slavonia, Hungarian investors put together a Swiss consortium and hired a Yugoslav director to keep control of the Beočin cement plant, the largest even in the prewar Yugoslav lands.

TABLE 11.14
JOINT-STOCK COMPANIES IN INDUSTRY

Organizational forms of manufacturing enterprises in censuses

	BULGARIA (1934)		ROMANIA (1930)	
	No.	%	No.	%
Individual proprietorship	27,138	89.9	133,621	97.1
Partnership	2,173a	7.2	2,552	1.9
Cooperative	234	0.8	215	0.2
Joint stock	319	1.1	1,376	1.0
Public	308	1.0	407	0.3
Total	30,172	100.0	137,577b	100.0

Organizational forms of Bulgarian "encouraged" manufacturing establishment

	Number			Percentage		
	1909	1921	1930	1909	1921	1930
Individual proprietorship	93	134	281	39.9	24.4	22.3
Partnership a	121	192	618	45.4	35.0	49.0
Cooperative	0	95	89	0.0	17.3	7.1
Joint stock	37	128	263	13.9	23.3	20.9
Public	5	9		1.9	0.7	
Total	266	549	1,260	100.0	100.0	100.0

Manufacturing joint stock companies by branch in 1931

	Number			Percentage		
	BULGARIA	ROMANIA	YUGOSLAVIA	BULGARIA	ROMANIA	YUGOSLAVIA
Metals and machinery	25	171	59[e]	7.3	16.3	11.6
Chemicals	41	95	58	11.9	9.1	11.4
Building materials (non-wood)	10	141	63	2.9	13.5	12.4
Wood processing	11	183	93	3.2	17.5	18.3
Paper	10	54	4	2.9	5.2	0.8
Printing	27		41	7.8		8.1
Textiles	69	131	68	20.1	12.5	13.4
Leather	35[c]	34	12	10.2	3.2	2.4
Food	113[d]	238	111[f]	32.8	22.7	21.8
Total	344	1,047	509[f]	100.0	100.0	100.0

Notes: (a)Includes limited and "en commandite" partnerships. (b)Excludes branches and "other and not declared." (c)Includes 17 companies in "clothing and shoes." (d)Includes 11 companies in "tobacco products." (e)Includes repair companies in transportation and communications. (f)Excludes 33 companies in "agricultural industries" and 9 in "other industry."

Sources: Statisticheski godishnik na Bulgarskoto Tsarstvo, 1911 (Sofia, 1914), p. 212: 1931 (Sofia, 1932), pp. 240-45; 1932 (Sofia, 1933), p. 303: 1940 (Sofia, 1940), pp. 374, 380, 384; Recensământul general al populaţiei României, 1930, Vol. X (Bucharest, 1938), pp. LXIV, 2; N. Arcadian, Industrializarea României (Bucharest, 1936), p. 250; Statistički godišnjak Kr. Jugoslavije, 1931 (Belgrade, 1933), pp. 220-23.

TABLE 11.15
INDICATORS OF FOREIGN CAPITAL INVESTMENTS

Comparative Levels and Distribution around 1928

	ALBANIA	BULGARIA	GREECE	ROMANIA	YUGOSLAVIA
1. Per capita in gold francs	97	122	293	123	105

2. Distribution (%)

Public Finance		82.6	70.7	74.6	67.7
Trade		2.0	7.7	0.8	3.3
Banking		2.8	7.1	1.8	6.4
Industry		12.2	3.5	22.1	20.2
Transport and					
Communications			7.3	0.8	1.9
Insurance		0.1			0.1
Other		0.3	3.5	0.2	0.4

3. Source (%)

French		11.2	9.0	16.4	20.5
English		1.4	53.0	20.6	19.8
Belgian		28.5	5.0	10.8	4.4
Italian		9.8	4.5	7.4	4.9
German		5.3	5.0	2.0	6.6
Czech		6.3		5.6	13.3
Swiss		23.4	2.0	1.6	10.3
American		8.4	8.0	5.8	5.2
Austrian/Hungarian		4.2		4.5	1.6

Romania[d]

Sector	Percent of Foreign Capital	
	1912-13	1929
Total	52	36
Banking	43.5	65
Commerce--Large scale	40	
Small scale	5.7	50
Industry--Large scale	80	70
All	56	
Industry--Joint stock		75
Mining		80
Metal and Machinery		70
Forestry		42
Chemicals		75
Paper		25
Textiles		60
Leather		50
Glass and ceramic		60
Electric power		25

TABLE 11.15 (continued)

Bulgaria

1. Joint Stock Companies with Foreign Capital[a]

	1911				1929			
Sector	Companies	Capital (mil. leva)	Percent of Companies	Capital[b]	Companies	Capital (mil.-leva)	Percent of Companies	Capital[b]
Banking	4	15.0	7.5	35.3	13	422.9	7.6	37.6
Industry	11	15.2	15.2	39.6	50	625.9	15.2[c]	45.2[c]
Transport	1	1.0	20.0	337.4	5	6.1	c	c
Trade	1	0.4	50.0	80.0	36	131.3	c	c
Insurance					10	8.5	58.8[c]	11.5[c]
Total	17	31.5	12.7	36.1	114	1,194.2	18.8[c]	31.5[c]

2. Percent of Foreign Capital by Branch of Industry

Branch	1921		1921
Mining and quarries	47.3	Textiles	4.4
Metal and machinery	13.5	Woodworking	6.5
Non-wood building materials	10.6	Leather	16.3
Chemicals	19.3	Paper	35.9
Foodstuffs	37.0	Printing	5.6
Tobacco	33.5	Electric Power	
		All Branches	26.8

Notes: (a)It is unclear if the data mean companies with only some foreign capital or companies with controlling foreign capital. (b)Not to be taken as the percent of foreign capital. (c)Totals are calculated on the basis of only part of all joint-stock companies; figures for total companies in transport and trade corresponding to Chakalov's figures for companies with foreign capital could not be identified. (d)Romanian data are educated guesses; percentages for industry branches include some companies with foreign capital shares as low as 30 percent.

Sources: L. Berov, "Le capital financier occidental et les pays balkaniques dans les années vingt," Études balkaniques, 1965:2-3 (Sofia), pp. 141-45; Izvestiia na Bulgarskoto narodna banka, May, 1926 (Sofia), p. 134; 1930:1 (Sofia), p. 24; Statisticheski godishnik na Bulgarskoto Tsarstvo, 1931 (Sofia, 1932), p. 387; Asen Chakalov, Formi, razmer i deinost na chuzhdiia kapitai v 1873-1944 (Sofia, 1962), p. 62; M. Lupu, "Studii privind dezvoltarea economiei româniei în perioada capitalismului," Studii și cercetări economice, 1967 (Bucharest), pp. 291, 293; C. Murgescu and N. N. Constantinescu (eds.), Contribuții la istoria capitalului strain în România (Bucharest, 1960), pp. 140-71, 238-39.

Slovenian industry saw less foreign capital, perhaps half the Croatian proportion for industry and far less for banking. The northwestern region's network of peasant cooperatives and savings banks weathered the early 1920s to retain more assets than all the Ljubljana commercial banks combined. The largest of these, the Ljubljanska Kreditna Banka, did nonetheless turn to direct stock investment in a number of paper, chemical, and machinery plants. This investment persisted to the end of the decade.

By then the foreign-backed Zagreb banks had begun to shift away from long-term assets and savings deposits to 6–9 month credits and sight deposits. Foreign support for long-term bank investment was set further back by the collapse of the Viennese Creditanstalt in 1931. By the 1930s European holdings of Yugoslav bank stock dropped from a peak of 35–40 percent in 1926 to 10–15 percent versus over 30 percent for Bulgaria.[54]

Direct investment in mining allowed European financial interests to own nearly half of Yugoslav industrial stock by the Depression. English holdings in a variety of nonferrous mines accounted for 48 percent of this fraction, French investment for 41 percent, mainly in Slovenian coal and the large Bor copper mines. The famous Paris-Bas investment bank limited itself to two smaller Serbian mines.[55]

The large French and Italian banks in postwar Bucharest approached long-term industrial investment with similar restraint. Leading the Romanian turn in this direction were instead the largest ethnic Romanian and Jewish banks, the Banca Românească and the Banca Marmorosch-Blank. Their prewar rivalry now intensified. The Banca Românească used its close ties to the Liberal regime to set up a network of branches in the new territories and to triple its capital in 1920. From that point the two banks began a competition that pushed both of them into more sectors of industry and into a larger entrepreneurial role than any other Balkan bank would ever venture. By 1928 the Banca Românească held stock or exercised some managerial authority in forty enterprises, led by ten in metallurgy and timber, and Marmorosch-Blank in forty five, with twelve in food processing, eleven in metallurgy and 9 in timber. Together they totalled just over half of the 162 firms under at least partial bank control and explain the surprisingly even distribution of bank capital among the separate branches of Romanian manufacturing. Only metallurgy with 67 percent and leather with 22 percent bank capital diverged by more than a dozen points from the overall average of 47 percent.[56] Both banks tried to maintain these commitments beyond the early inflationary years of the decade by means of separate industrial institutes. These agencies provided technical assistance in management that doubled the number of encouraged firms beyond the total from stock ownership alone. From the start the Banca Românească relied for leverage on its institute and on current account credits whose total was twice that of the Banca Marmorosch-Blank. The latter leaned more toward direct ownership. It held almost four times the Românească's value of joint-stock by 1926, amounting to one quarter of its own assets. Then the reduced liquidity noted earlier and the tighter European capital market of the late 1920s pushed the bank to begin retreating from long-term assets. The steady decline of profits on industrial stock doubtless made itself felt as well. Net bank profits minus losses as a proportion of joint-stock capital dropped from 20 percent for 1920–23 to 8 percent in 1925–26 to 3 percent by 1928. Marmorosch-Blank halved the absolute value of its industrial investment between 1926 and 1928.[57]

The central bank also set up a separate Societatea Naţională de Credit Industrial in 1924. Its 9–10 percent short-term loans were about half of the market rate. Their annual amount dropped off after a promising first year to less than half of the modest sum, 2–3 percent of all assets, given industry by the regular lines of short-term credit from the National Bank. The latter's limited size may be judged by its correspondence in real per capita terms to the short-term industrial credit of the far smaller Bulgarska Narodna Banka. The Societatea did make a long-term contribution unique among Balkan state banks or their agencies. It accorded manufacturers' mortgage loans that typically matched the combined sum of its short-term credit and that of the Banca Naţională. Yet the largest part of these mortgages, over one third of their value, went to food-processing, one of the least dynamic branches of interwar Romanian industry.[58]

The flow of direct foreign investment relieved some of the pressure on credit supplies elsewhere in Southeastern Europe. It did not reach its greatest potential in Romania. Petroleum production was the source of this limitation, despite the fact that oil exports climbed to 30 percent of the Romanian total by 1926–30 (see Table 10.13). This doubling of the prewar percentage was not sufficient, as we have seen, to restore the large export surplus that had permitted heavy import of capital. Hindering both capital imports and oil output during the 1920s was the struggle between the Liberal government and the main foreign oil companies. German and Austro-Hungarian ownership of the largest prewar enterprise, Steaua Română, opened the way for Romanian nationalization of 25 percent of crude oil capacity as part of the postwar settlement. The Deutsche Bank's success in selling part of its assets to the Paris-Bas bank confined the eventual Romanian share to 51 percent of share capital. The several Liberal banks and the Banca Marmorosch-Blank put up, or rather borrowed, the Romanian proportion.

The government's new Creditul Minier drew on support from the central bank and the Banca Românească to distribute concessions of state oil lands and to run the pipelines from the fields north of Bucharest to Giurgiu on the Danube and Constanţa on the Black Sea. Western European and American ownership of the fields was not eroded, however, until the Liberal's Mining Law of 1924. It required even existing companies to place 55 percent of their shares in Romanian hands and to appoint Romanians as two thirds of the Board of Directors, including the head. Only the American Rockefeller and the Anglo-Dutch Shell enterprises refused to conform. The principal English study of the subsequent infighting is right in noting the drilling and refining restrictions that noncompliance visited on these two concerns.[59]

The actions of British, French, and Belgian enterprises after accepting the new law deserve further study in Romanian sources.

These enterprises reduced the level of their activity and investment after 1925. How much this was a conscious effort to sabotage the operation of the law and how much a response to the halving of world petroleum prices between 1924 and 1928 remains to be seen.

More certain is the fact that the state's failure to improve railway facilities or build a second pipeline to Constanţa during the 1920s did not derive mainly from native incompetence or corruption, although the Liberal regime had a large share of the latter. The greater restraint was the postwar reduction in real financial resources that this chapter has repeatedly stressed. Such a reduction was the price exacted by a return, even belatedly, as with Romania, to the prewar pattern of balanced budgets and fixed exchange rates.

Why Growth Rates Differed

The relatively slower rate of Romanian industrial growth admittedly dates back to the last prewar decade. Table 6.2 recorded annual rates for Bulgaria and Serbia that were at least twice the Romanian average of 5.3 percent. Most of this disparity has been traced to the head start and hence larger base that Romanian manufacturing had already achieved by the turn of the century. The better industrial records of Romania's Balkan neighbors during the 1920s derived from more, however, than further growth from a smaller base. Greece's industry and agriculture could draw on the labor and entrepreneurial energy of the million refugees from Asia Minor. By contrast, Romania's postwar addition to its population came along with new territories previously in a peripheral, disadvantaged position in a variety of imperial economies. Yugoslavia's territory was just as new and as large. Its economy could draw on if not integrate the public resources of a Serbian-dominated government and the private resources of powerful Croatian banks and Slovenian industrial enterprises. The big Romanian banks remained in Bucharest, still the center of political power. Such a coincidence of economic and political power existed in Sofia (and Athens) as well. But the Bulgarian economy had no new territory to integrate. More important, its major banks in Sofia received a significant influx of new, albeit largely foreign and short-term, assets. These funds, together with state and cooperative credit for agriculture, allowed total bank assets to regain their prewar level in real per capita terms, unlike the Romanian and Greek totals.

Such financial distinctions must be added to the reduced Romanian capacity for grain export and the failure of Romanian oil exports to maintain their rapid growth through the 1920s. Together they provide the best available explanation of why Bulgarian industrial growth continued to exceed the Romanian rate despite the burden of reparations and far less access to long-term foreign capital. The private sector furnishes most of this explanation. Higher Bulgarian tariffs on industrial imports cannot be correlated with the domestic branches which grew most rapidly. Other relevant areas of public policy, most notably taxation, direct investment, and technical education, await Chapters 12 and 13. They assess the state's economic role as it grew from the 1930s through the Second World War to the start of central planning on the Soviet model everywhere but Greece.

12.
Structural Change and the
State Sector during the
Depression

The two decades that began with the Depression and ended with the consolidation of Communist power everywhere in Southeastern Europe except Greece served to isolate the area from European trade and finance. Its previous connection had hardly proved to be an ideal engine of economic growth. The pre-1914 pattern of agricultural exports and trade surpluses had generated a larger return flow of unproductive loans to native governments than of foreign investment into the domestic economy. Postwar recovery had witnessed a revised distribution of foreign funds more in favor of private investment. But the old export surpluses based on grain never returned save for a few, scattered years. International prices for agricultural commodities dropped so sharply by 1930 that the Balkan capacity for imports of goods, let alone capital, fell accordingly. The European financial crisis, framed by the failure of the Credit-Anstalt in Vienna and the British departure from the Gold Standard, followed the next year. Real service on outstanding debts also rose until payments began to go unmet.

Unlike the late Ottoman period, emigration offered no relief to this growing isolation. Migrant labor was in fact forced to return from France to Yugoslavia and Greece. The nineteenth-century turn toward Central European trade that started to relieve isolation from Mediterranean markets had continued into the twentieth century. Its further evolution under Nazi auspices brought only limited German investment, restrictive trade agreements, and eventual wartime occupation.

This chapter treats the period from 1929 through 1939. Western scholarship has typically organized its view of the decade around the foreign economic relations of Southeastern Europe. Its problems of debt settlement with Western Europe in the early 1930s and the dynamics of subsequent Nazi penetration have received instructive attention. The present chapter is more concerned with the internal evolution of agriculture, trade, finance, and industry. The obvious institutional question is to what extent government initiative grew in these areas and thereby facilitated the postwar transition to public ownership and Communist central planning in every state but Greece.[1]

Certainly the economic crisis of the early 1930s pushed native governments permanently away from the neoclassical devotion to expanding exports and to maintaining a convertible currency that had survived the First World War. A new if scarcely ideal set of political figures replaced the prewar leaders and parties that had dominated the 1920s. The new regimes were a curious mixture of royal and military establishments with a huge ministerial bureaucracy. The latter's typically budgetary interests put their own stamp on more state promotion of industrialization first for import substitution and then for rearmament.

Our inquiry in these two final chapters follows the institutional growth of state enterprise and initiative through the war and the initial period of postwar recovery and transition. At the same time, we draw on an extensive but uneven statistical record to identify several areas of economic growth that laid previously neglected groundwork for the Industrial Revolution which has transformed most of Southeastern Europe, including Greece, since 1950.

Agricultural Performance and Policy

The native governments' first efforts to combat the depression concerned agriculture rather than industry. In 1930 Yugoslavia and Bulgaria took the lead in establishing purchasing agencies to buy cereals at prices well above slumping international levels, hoping to sell them on the external market. Greece followed suit for tobacco in 1931 and Romania for cereals in 1932. A British scholar has aptly called these and subsequent interwar measures "the genesis of étatism" in Southeastern Europe.[2] They mark the start of policies that go beyond the passive fiscal measures and the actual ownership of certain enterprises, again for essentially fiscal reasons, that had constituted the extent of state intervention since the period before the First World War. To appraise these and other government policies properly, though, we must first record agricultural performance for the 1930s.

Indicators of Agricultural Performance

The variety within the region's experience is surprising, given the presumably uniform impact of the world depression and falling international prices on Southeastern Europe. The principles of comparative economic history noted in the Introduction should once again prove useful in explaining differences within common parameters. Table 12.2 identifies some significant variations in real agricultural output. Table 12.1 provides the population data needed to express output in per capita terms. These demographic data also reveal several common tendencies. Moderately declining death rates, except for Romania, suggest that some marginal improvement occurred in medical services or diet. (Vegetable production did rise, as we shall see.) The greater decline in birthrates, confirming a long-term trend downward in net reproduction noted in Chapter 10, was sufficient to bring down rates of natural increase. Here was testimony to the peasants' reaction to the shrinking size of average holdings. The exceptional drop in the Bulgarian birthrate, down by one third from 1926–30 to 1936–40, deserves further consideration. Even in Bulgaria, however, the movement of an overwhelmingly rural population into the towns was so slight that the rural share was still 77 percent, as in Romania and Yugoslavia. This continuing concentration left the problem of agricultural overpopulation unsolved despite declining birthrates.[3]

Only Greece recorded a noteworthy rise in price-adjusted cereal output per capita and per hectare for 1931–35 and again in 1936–38 over the 1926–30 average. This, plus still larger increases for vegetables, compensated for sagging tobacco harvests and yields (the main industrial crop) to generate a 48-percent rise in overall per capita output and a 28 percent rise in yields by 1936–38. The comparable Bulgarian increases of 22 and 16 percent overall may be traced by contrast to all sectors except cereals. The moderate Yugoslav increments of 18 percent in output and 19 percent in yield derived from cereals and industrial crops. Only for the latter sector could Romanian agricultural production record any sort of advance. They declined elsewhere and overall from Romania's 1926–1930 levels. The decline of the 1930s left the real per capita value of crop production at just 70 percent of its prewar level for the Old Kingdom, after climbing to 95 percent during the good harvests of 1929–30 (see Table 10.5). Yugoslavia and Bulgaria had recovered prewar levels during 1931–35 and exceeded them by 11–12 percent in 1936–38. Neither of these last levels, it should be added, surpassed the real per capita crop production of prewar Romania.

Greek crops for 1931–35 rose to the 1914 level, and the further

TABLE 12.1
SOURCES OF POPULATION CHANGE, 1930-40
(annual average per 1000 population)

Country and Period	Actual Increase	Births	Deaths	Natural Increase	Implied Migration[b]
Bulgaria					
1926-30	14.5	33.0	17.9	15.3	-0.8
1931-35	12.0	29.3	15.5	13.8	-1.8
1936-40	7.8	23.3	13.7	9.6	-1.8
Greece					
1926-30	13.4	29.9	16.4	13.5	-0.1
1931-35	14.2	29.4	16.5	12.9	1.3
1936-40	13.6[a]	25.8	14.0	11.8	1.8
Romania					
1926-30	14.3	34.5	20.8	13.7	-0.6
1931-35	12.3	32.9	20.6	12.3	nil
1936-40	10.5[a]	29.3	19.2	10.1	0.4
Yugoslavia					
1926-30	14.8	34.2	20.0	14.2	0.6
1931-35	13.6	31.9	18.0	13.9	-0.3
1936-40	13.9	27.4	15.7	11.7	2.2

Notes: (a)1936-39. (b)Natural increase minus actual increase.

Sources: See Table 10.2.

increase for 1936–38 matched the prewar peak of 1911. A striking advance in cereal, largely wheat production, led the way. The increment of 49 percent by 1931–35 and 93 percent by 1936–38 must be balanced against the bad harvests of 1928–30 that bias the benchmark period downward. Some advance in wheat cultivation was nonetheless taking place. Its acreage grew by one quarter between 1933 and 1935, following a 60-percent rise since 1923. A number of reclamation projects in Macedonia, including three by U.S. firms, contributed to wider cultivation. Wheat yield for 1933–35 averaged 9.7 hectoliters per hectare versus 6.1 for 1923–27 and 8.1 in 1914. These better yields continued for 1936–38, despite bad harvests in two of those years. As a result Greece was able to cover 64 percent of its own wheat requirements for 1933–37, in contrast to 40 percent in 1928 and about 25 percent before the war.[4] Sales of cereal-cultivating machinery rose significantly from 1933, mainly through imports.

TABLE 12.2
INDICES OF CROP PRODUCTION, AREAS, YIELDS AND PRICES, 1926-38

Country and Years	Cereal Crops	Vegetable Crops	Industrial Crops	Tree and Vine Crops	Total Crops
Gross Output in Constant Prices (1926-30 = 100)					
Bulgaria					
1931-5	116	154	102	133	117
1926-8	131	195	119	153	135
Greece					
1931-5	159	216	74	131	127
1936-8	219	362	119	141	168
Romania					
1931-5	92	113	83	116	100
1936-8	108	96	126	112	110
Yugoslavia					
1931-5	111	136	87	105	112
1936-8	144	147	138	95	134
Per Capita Gross Output in Constant Prices (1926-30 = 100)					
Bulgaria					
1931-5	109	144	95	124	109
1936-8	118	175	107	138	122
Greece					
1931-5	149	202	69	122	119
1936-8	193	320	105	124	148
Romania					
1931-5	86	105	77	108	93
1936-8	96	86	112	100	98
Yugoslavia					
1931-5	103	127	81	98	105
1936-8	127	129	122	84	118

TABLE 12.2 (continued)

Country and Years	Cereal Crops	Vegetable Crops	Industrial Crops	Tree and Vine Crops	Total Crops
Land in Cultivation (1926-30 = 100)					
Bulgaria					
1931-5	106	127	127	117	109
1936-8	107	154	234	150	116
Greece					
1931-5	120	150	91	123	100
1936-8	132	208	159	133	131
Romania					
1931-5	103	114	98	93	102
1936-8	106	107	126	103	107
Yugoslavia					
1931-5	110	112	88	112	109
1936-8	113.	114	113	117	113
Output per Hectare in Constant Prices (1926-30 = 100)					
Bulgaria					
1931-5	109	117	80	114	108
1936-8	123	127	51	102	116
Greece					
1931-5	133	144	67	(102)[a]	103
1936-8	166	174	75	(155)[a]	128
Romania					
1931-5	89	99	85	125	97
1936-8	102	90	100	109	102
Yugoslavia					
1931-5	101	121	99	94	103
1936-8	127	129	122	81	119

TABLE 12.2 (continued)

Country and Years	Cereal Crops	Vegetable Crops	Industrial Crops	Tree and Vine Crops	Total Crops
Changes in Producer Prices (1926-30 = 100)					
Bulgaria					
1931-5	47	47	60	63	51
1936-8	62	73	84	68	66
Greece					
1931-5	99	106	107	101	105
1936-8	112	131	156	127	127
Romania[b]					
1931-5	55	54	64	59	55
1936-8	73	91	65	66	74
Yugoslavia					
1931-5	59	52	61	55	57
1936-8	63	64	76	67	66
Composition of Output in Current Prices (percent)					
Bulgaria					
1926-30	72.3	5.6	13.0	9.1	100.0
1931-35	66.8	6.8	13.5	12.9	100.0
1936-38	66.0	8.9	14.6	10.0	100.0
Greece					
1926-30	32.9	4.2	23.0	39.8	100.0
1931-35	39.0	7.2	13.8	39.9	100.0
1936-38	37.7	9.3	19.8	33.2	100.6
Romania					
1926-30	65.2	13.1	5.9	15.8	100.0
1931-35	60.0	14.6	5.7	19.8	100.0
1936-38	64.8	15.9	4.9	14.3	100.0
Yugoslavia					
1926-30	64.4	13.5	4.6	17.5	100.0
1931-35	65.4	14.8	3.9	15.9	100.0
1936-38	67.2	14.5	5.5	12.7	100.0

TABLE 12.2 (continued)

Country and Years	Cereal Crops	Vegetable Crops	Industrial Crops	Tree and Vine Crops	Total Crops
Composition of Output in Constant Prices (percent)					
Bulgaria					
1926-30	69.4	6.9	17.1	6.9	100.0
1931-35	68.3	9.0	14.9	7.9	100.0
1936-38	67.2	9.9	15.0	7.8	100.0
Greece					
1926-30	38.5	5.3	35.4	44.1	100.0
1931-35	48.9	9.1	21.0	46.4	100.0
1936-38	49.3	11.2	24.5	36.2	100.0
Romania					
1926-30	62.3	17.9	4.8	15.0	100.0
1931-35	58.4	20.3	3.9	17.4	100:0
1936-38	62.6	17.7	4.5	15.3	100.0
Yugoslavia					
1926-30	62.0	12.7	5.8	19.5	100.0
1931-35	61.6	15.5	4.5	18.4	100.0
1936-38	66.4	13.9	5.9	13.8	100.0

Notes: (a)Vine crops only. (b)Base 1927-30 equals 100.

Sources: See Table 10.9.

Soviet efforts to enter this market were unsuccessful but indicate its reputation was growing.

Like Romania and Serbia, Bulgaria had long produced a surplus of cereals for export. Its output mainly of wheat and corn had recaptured its 1910–11 volume by 1926 and rose with several good harvests by 6 percent for 1926–30 over that level. Hence the further increment of 9 percent in output per capita and yield for 1931–35 represents a greater advance than Table 12.2 by itself suggests. The drop in international prices was sufficient to reduce the total cereal acreage by 1936. A start on consolidating separate plots and the increased import of agricultural machinery, especially from Germany, after 1928 helped to boost yields again after the slight decline of 1936–38. For 1934–39, wheat yields were 31 percent beyond the 1907–11 level.[5]

Still more striking for Bulgaria were the increases in acreage of industrial crops and in the output per hectare for vegetables. Acreage for industrial crops, principally tobacco but also now cotton, climbed by 54 percent between 1926–30 and 1936–38. They now amounted to 11 percent of cultivated acreage or about twice the fraction in neighboring states. Their increase in real output was only 7 percent for 1936–38, however, and yields went down almost as sharply. These declining yields probably represented the expansion of acreage into less favorable land more than anything else.

Table 12.3 reinforces skepticism about the relative inefficiency of smallholdings. Under the influence of the International Agricultural Institute in Rome, the governments of Bulgaria, Romania, and then Yugoslavia began about 1930 to sample the financial and economic profiles of individual holdings. Figures for gross output per hectare suggest again, but with better evidence than in Chapter 10, that production generally declined as farm size increased. Bulgarian and Yugoslav holdings of 5–10 hectares produced about 80 percent of the average per hectare for those under 5 and those over 10 from 60 to 65 percent. In terms of net output, or value added per hectare, Bulgarian farms of medium size (5–10 hectares) were slightly closer to the value added by those under 5, larger farms (over 10 hectares) slightly further away. For Romania, the net output of medium-sized farms was 4 percent more than that of smallholdings but larger farms lagged just as far behind those under 10 hectares as in Bulgaria.

The greater net and gross output of small farms resulted, if the reader is prepared to follow some factor analysis, from their application of more labor and more reproducible assets (buildings, animals, machinery, and inventories) per hectare. This fact, plus their tendency to be located closer to urban areas, explains higher land values on small farms in rational economic terms. No resort need be made to the existence of "irrational" preferences for land among the peasants. At the same time, small farms were relatively more labor than capital intensive. Bulgarian farms of less than 5 hectares used about 22 percent more labor per unit of reproducible assets than those with 5–10 hectares. Romanian small farms tended to be even more labor intensive compared to their larger counterparts.

The question remains, which farms, smaller or larger, made the most efficient use of resources? Greater output per hectare on small farms does not necessarily reflect greater efficiency. They also applied more labor and capital per hectare. Efficiency must be judged by returns per unit of factor input, i.e., net output as the sum of wages, interest, rent, and profit, divided by the value of assets used. So measured, the rates of return between categories of Bulgarian farms turn out to be remarkably similar: 10.2 percent for farms

TABLE 12.3
INCOME AND FACTOR PROPORTIONS BY SIZE OF FARM[a]

Size of Farm (ha)	Gross Income	Material Expenditures	Wages[b]	Interest and Rent	Net Profit	Value Added	Labor Units (persons/ha)	Land and Capital						
								Total	Land	Plants	Buildings	Equipment	Livestock	Working
Bulgaria (leva per ha.)														
0-5	12,530	5848	3753	2752	177	6682	1.2	65516	28056	5118	17413	7593	3469	3867
5-10	10,180	4073	3379	2545	183	6103	0.6	51599	26696	5158	10212	2615	3381	3507
over 10	8,130	4345	1930	1627	228	3785	0.2	37740	22622	2035	6167	1937	2189	2790
(Percent)														
0-5	100.0	46.7	30.0	22.0	1.4	53.3		100.0	42.8	7.8	26.6	11.6	5.3	5.9
5-10	100.0	40.0	33.2	25.0	1.8	60.0		100.0	51.7	10.0	19.8	5.1	6.6	6.8
over 10	100.0	53.4	23.7	20.0	2.8	46.6		100.0	59.9	5.4	16.3	5.1	5.8	7.4
Romania[c] (lei per ha.)														
0-5			1156		2253	3409	0.85	22629	13262		6210	990	2167	
5-10			1206		2353	3559	0.46	19405	10388		6582	873	1562	
over 10			840		1679	2319	0.13	16545	10105		4444	980	1016	
(Percent)														
0-5								100.0	58.6		27.4	4.4	9.6	
5-10								100.0	53.4		33.8	4.5	8.0	
over 10								100.0	61.1		26.9	5.9	6.1	

TABLE 12.3 (continued)

Size of Farm (ha)	Gross income	Material Expenditures	Wages[b]	Interest and Rent	Net Profit	Value Added	Labor Units (persons/ha)	Land and Capital						
								Total	Land	Plants	Buildings	Equipment	Livestock	Working
Yugoslavia (dinars per ha..) **(116 farms in Croatia-Slavonia ca 1932)**														
0-2	8,131										5784	1537	4623	
2-5	4,731										3661	859	3488	
5-10	4,146										2736	805	2964	
10-15	4,096										2535	799	2830	
over 10	3,791										2525	684	1738	
(60 farms in Croatia-Slavonia, Bosnia-Hercegovina and Dalmatia 1940)														
0-3								100.0	33.4	9.7	42.9	3.5	4.0	6.6
3-5								100.0	39.8	11.4	32.0	2.7	4.8	9.4
5-10								100.0	38.9	7.2	32.7	4.0	6.6	10.5
10-15								100.0	43.3	6.0	27.7	4.5	6.8	11.7
over 15								100.0	47.0	4.9	25.3	3.6	8.2	11.0

Notes (a)Data based on farm accountancy studies of samples of farms in the early 1930s. (b)Wages include family labor imputed at rates for hired labor. (c)Value added equals the sum of wages, interest and rent and net profit.

Sources: A. Iu. Totev, *Sravnitelno izuchavanie na Bulgarskoto i Yugoslavenskoto narodno stopanstvo* (Sofia, 1940), pp. 67-68; I. C. Vasiliu, "Structura economică al agriculturii româneşti", in *Enciclopedia României*, Vol. III (Bucharest, 1943), p. 316; N. Cornatzeano, "La situation de l'agriculture," in D. Gusti et al., *La vie rurale en Roumanie* (Bucharest, 1940), pp. 51-54; Jozo Tomasevich, *Peasants, Politics, and Economic Change in Yugoslavia* (Palo Alto, Calif.: Stanford University Press, 1955), pp. 434-36.

smaller than 5 hectares, 11.8 percent for those with 5–10 hectares, and 10.0 percent for those over 10 hectares. The slightly greater variation for Romania favored small farms, which returned 15.1 percent versus 12.1 percent for medium-sized farms and 14.0 percent for larger ones.

In both Bulgaria and Romania these rates of return contain an important distortion which, if removed, would widen the small farms' marginally greater efficiency. This distortion is the inclusion with assets of the value of farm residences. If asset values reflected only productive assets used to produce farm output, then small-farm rates of return would probably be significantly higher than those for larger farms in both countries.

This argument that small farms were more efficient units of production does not, however, suggest that they necessarily provided sufficient income for peasant families after deductions had been made for rent, interest payments, and possibly wages for hired labor.

The generally higher rates of return on Romanian farms do not tell us that they were more efficient than their Bulgarian counterparts. What is suggested instead is that Romanian farms paid relatively more for rented land, and agricultural credit. Table 12.3 clearly shows a tendency in Bulgaria to use more labor and assets per hectare, regardless of farm size, than in Romania. (Note that one Bulgarian lev was worth at least 1.2 Romanian lei during the 1930s.) Why this should be the case emerges from the much higher ratio of interest, rent, and profit to wages in Romania than in Bulgaria, nearly 2/1 versus less than 1/1. The Romanian ratio reflects higher interest rates and limited access to credit for land rental or any other purpose that continued, as we shall see in the next section, to plague the country's agriculture throughout the 1930s.

The poor Romanian record can be partly written off to a greater number of harvests damaged by climatic reverses than any other state in Southeastern Europe during the decade. Droughts held down the grain harvests for 1932, 1934–35, and 1937. Only 1936 was an unusually favorable year. We may recall from the Introduction the lower average rainfall and greater vulnerability to drought of the rich Wallachian and Moldavian plains, on the eastern side of the Carpathian mountains and thus cut off from the regular flow of wet weather from the Atlantic. This same climatic limitation had visited bad harvests on Romania in 1927 and 1928. Thus the index of 100 for 1926–30 does not represent the relatively high level of output that it does for Bulgaria.

Another part of the Romanian problem lay with continued emphasis on wheat and corn cultivation. The relative areas given to categories of crops noted in Table 12.2 reveal no significant shift away from cereals, as occurred for Bulgaria. All areas increased in absolute terms over their levels for 1926–30. Industrial crops rose to almost 5 percent of the cultivated area on the strength of greater hemp cultivation for home use. Areas for the main commercial crops, tobacco and sugar beets, declined with the restrictive policies of the state tobacco monopoly and the private sugar cartel to be considered below. Within the composition of cereal cultivation itself, however, we find a small but perhaps more significant shift. The area under wheat and corn grew at the expense of other grains. The corn area rose consistently after 1930. An expanding peasant population needed to feed itself. Wheat was still grown more on the larger holdings and was more sensitive to market conditions, which made its growth in area more sporadic. Together these increases involved some combination of moving onto less fertile land and rotating cultivation less frequently with other cereals. The increase in the two crops' share of cereal production, from 29.6 to 31.7 percent for wheat and from 44.2 to 48.6 percent for corn between 1924–28 and 1934–38, thus helps explain the relative decline in cereal output per capita and per hectare recorded in Table 12.2 for the period 1931–38.[6]

The performance of Yugoslav agriculture appears at first glance to have nicely exceeded that of Romania. After holding its own for 1931–35, real output per capita and per hectare jumped 18–19 percent for 1936–38 over 1926–30. Cereals and industrial crops led the way, according to Table 12.2, rising by twice that percentage. Imports and domestic manufacture of agricultural equipment turned up, although not enough to cover the disinvestment of the early 1930s. Numbers of hogs and cattle also multiplied by 15–20 percent. Table 12.4 records the Yugoslav lead in livestock per capita over the rest of Southeastern Europe by 1938, finally restored during the 1930s after great wartime losses.

Closer scrutiny reveals a less promising picture. Livestock exports, as we shall see in the next section, still lagged well behind their promising pre-1914 pace. Cultivated crop area per capita in 1931 was barely one acre, about half the Romanian and Bulgarian average of one hectare. The disparity with Romania widened slightly during the 1930s, despite cultivated land in Yugoslavia that grew 13 percent in area versus 6 percent for Romania. The much smaller Yugoslav average derived not from generally smaller holdings but rather from regional differences rivaled only by Greece.[7] There, however, the mountainous areas in grain-deficit had typically sent their largely surplus population as harvest hands into the grain-surplus plains or as migrant labor to Athens or overseas.[8] Rural labor in the more heavily populated Yugoslav uplands was less mobile. Exceptions were the Adriatic coast and Macedonia with its tradition of *pečal-*

TABLE 12.4
LIVESTOCK HERDS AND PRODUCTION, 1930-38

	Total Value[a]	Horses[d]	Cattle	Pigs	Sheep	Goats
Value in millions and animals in 1000's						
Bulgaria						
1930	12,277	539	2,069	952	8,790	1,087
1939	11,196	541	1,760	752	9,413	596
Greece						
1930	6,167	471	881	335	6,799	4,637
1938	7,048	546	1,034	430	8,139	4,356
Romania						
1929	40,237	1,877	4,355	2,300	12,092	362
1938	42,094	2,159	4,348	3,165	12,768	(400)[b]
Yugoslavia						
1930	12,856	1,177	3,849	2,924	7,953	1,731
1938	14,564	1,283	4,305	3,451	10,137	1,890
Value per capita and animals per 1000 total population						
Bulgaria						
1930	2,127 (100)	93	359	165	1,523	188
1939	1,772 (83)	86	279	119	1,490	94
Greece						
1930	961 (100)	73	137	52	1,060	723
1938	983 (102)	76	144	60	1,135	607
Romania						
1929	2,265 (100)	106	245	129	681	20
1938	2,121 (94)	109	219	160	643	20
Yugoslavia[c]						
1930	926 (100)	(85)	(277)	(211)	(573)	(125)
1938	940 (102)	(83)	(278)	(223)	(654)	(122)

TABLE 12.4 (continued)

Animal Products Index of Gross Output (1926-30 = 100)

| | BULGARIA | | ROMANIA | | YUGOSLAVIA | |
Year	Total	Per Capita	Total	Per Capita	Total	Per Capita
1928	99	99	103	103	97	97
1929	99	98	99	98	98	97
1930	100	97	99	96	105	102
1931	101	97	101	97	109	104
1932	102	97	97	92	104	98
1933	105	98	98	91	103	96
1934	108	100	103	95	107	98
1935	107	98	107	98	114	103
1936	122	111	106	95	117	105
1937	114	103	104	93	116	102
1938	125	112	106	93	116	101
1939	121	107			123	105

Notes: (a)National currency values are not comparable across countries. (b)1937. (c)Yugoslavia includes only farm animals. (d)Includes mules.

Sources: Marvin R. Jackson, "Agricultural Output in Southeastern Europe, 1910-1938," *ACES Bulletin*, vol. 14, no. 2 (1982), in press.

barstvo, or migration for temporary labor. This migration had in any case typically left the country, an avenue now blocked by the Depression. The rising crop yields of 1936–38 were, not surprisingly, confined to the grain-surplus plains. More favorable weather than in Romania helped these harvests. Poor facilities for storage and internal transportation plus other marketing problems severely restricted the transfer of surplus grain to the deficit areas. The result was a persistent price differential of 50 to 150 percent for corn, still the main Yugoslav grain, between the two types of areas. Some compensation for the Macedonian deficit came from that area's rising production of hemp and cotton. This advance in industrial crops was in turn restrained, like Romania's, by declining cultivation of tobacco. The state monopoly cut the number of authorized growers by three quarters between 1926 and 1934.[9]

State Agricultural Policies and Peasant Debt

The most frequently acknowledged agricultural institutions of Southeastern European governments during the early 1930s were undoubtedly the agencies set up to buy and sell grain. The state's monopoly powers were brought to bear on maintaining domestic prices well over slumping world levels and on earning such higher prices for exports where possible. The evidence suggests that these monopolies did not address the fundamental problems facing Balkan agriculture, particularly the freeing of smallholders' money income from the overpowering claims of taxation, transport costs, and existing debt. State policy toward these claims allows us a better explanation of the noteworthy variation in agricultural performance between the several states.

The first state purchasing agency for grain was actually established before the Depression. It was designed to promote greater production for Greece's domestic market, long a national grain-deficit area. The Greek government initiated a series of measures that culminated in 1928 with the formation of the Organization for the Concentration of Wheat. Its plan to expand cultivation involved paying peasants twice the price of imported wheat, mainly from the United States, Australia, and the Soviet Union. The wheat harvests for 1928–31 were so bad, however, that peasants could not even retain enough seed for the next year's crop. The Organization was left to distribute imported seed.[10] More important aid for increasing output would have to come from Agricultural Bank credits.

Yugoslav authorities were the first to respond to falling world prices in defense of grain exports. Legislation in April 1930 set up the Privileged Joint-Stock Export Company, known by the acronym PRIZAD, whose purpose was to replace foreign and domestic middlemen in wheat and corn export. The amount paid peasants would thereby rise at the expense of private middlemen but leave the basic price unchanged. After exporting about half of that year's relatively low total for the two crops, PRIZAD received monopoly privileges the following summer for the internal market as well as exports. The agency's domestic price was not set well above the low world level. Profits from high-priced internal sales were intended to cover exports sold at a loss. The bumper crop of 1931 forced the agency to rely on private merchants for a majority of its purchases. A great lack of storage facilities, unremedied until after the Second World War, forced the agency to store much of its export surplus in Austria, Hungary, and Czechoslovakia. The internal monopoly's extra expenses and corruption contributed to its abolition the following year in favor of higher taxes on bread and flour plus a bond issue. The surviving export monopoly saw poorer harvests reduce the surpluses available to it until the huge crops of 1936. By that time, export quotas to Germany and other Central European states included rebates on import tariffs and artificially high exchange rates (see below) that cushioned the cost to PRIZAD. Only a small fraction of this premium above the world price was used to improve the techniques of grain cultivation.

None was paid to the peasants directly or spent to encourage greater cultivation of industrial crops in the lowlands (a process otherwise discouraged by the agency's grain premiums) or to reduce the exorbitant retail prices for grain in the uplands even by improved storage facilties.[11]

The Bulgarian government had created Hranoiznos, the Cereal Export Agency, in 1930 with the same purpose of subsidizing wheat and rye exports. Its domestic purchases at several times the world price level ran up sizable deficits for 1931–33. The initial practice of paying peasants half of the purchase price in state bonds usable for tax obligations had to be dropped in favor of 100 percent cash. By 1934 the cost of these deficits prompted Bulgaria's last elected government, and the last one including agrarian interests, to extend the monopoly to purchases for internal consumption. Hranoiznos used its monopsony, or buyer's monopoly, to charge high prices to the flour mills and provide itself the profits provided to cover losses on low-priced exports.[12] The agency just broke even with no funds left over for agricultural investment. Cereals' small share of overall Bulgarian export value, 8–13 percent, limited the impact of such premiums in encouraging greater grain cultivation.

Romanian cereals retained the highest share of total exports in Southeastern Europe. They averaged 35 percent for 1929–31. State support for such grain exports was therefore more promising. Support began with export subsidies in 1931, replacing the postwar export tariffs that had been heavily used until 1925. The State Cereal Commission was established the following year to support prices above world levels. It essentially relied on these subsidies of about 30 percent ad valorem. By the large harvest of 1936 the size of the subsidies it paid out obliged the commission to apply a special tax to flour processed by domestic mills, in the same fashion as Bulgaria.[13]

The aforementioned doubling of Romanian wheat acreage between 1930 and 1937 must have been greatly encouraged by such subsidies. They were admittedly short of matching the proportional drop in world prices and still further below the support levels afforded by Bulgarian and Yugoslav authorities. The peasantry's desperate efforts to bring money income up to expenses took on a special urgency in Romania given the burden of peasant debt and the shortage of credit. The funding needed to switch to new crops was less accessible. Such constraints seem more important than the efforts of the National Peasant Party to "place the decisive weight on wheat production and to reestablish the unquestionable reputation which Romanian wheat had enjoyed before the war," in the words of the noted economist Virgil Madgearu when Minister of Agriculture. The party's fall from power by 1931 cut its efforts short. The Depression would in any case have reduced the tax revenues needed to continue the land reclamation, the leasing of machinery to grain cultivators and the spread of seed selection stations that the National Peasant regime had initiated in 1929.[14]

Pressuring the peasantry after 1930 to expand their cultivation of wheat, still the major cash crop, were a series of financial obligations. They were made much worse by the halving of export prices. Railway freight rates had remained high through the 1920s. They never underwent the substantial reductions noted for Bulgaria in Chapter 11. The Romanian government's failure to cut them during the early 1930s meant their virtual doubling in terms of grain sales. Higher rates for grain moved to the domestic market, now amounting to half of the sunken sales price for wheat and corn, kept Romanian cities from replacing foreign markets as magnets for the rural surplus. Direct taxes were at least halved by 1932. Unfortunately their collection continued to require that crops be kept in the fields, subject to rot and climatic reverse, until cash payment was made.[15] Levels of indirect taxation remained the same nominally and thus rose in real terms.

In addition, the Romanian peasantry had incurred the largest personal debt in Southeastern Europe. Smallholders with less than 10 hectares accounted for over 70 percent of that debt. The government's moratorium on its repayment in 1932 and the 50 percent reduction of principal owed in 1934 admittedly reduced the burden. Unfortunately, in the process the state-sponsored Popular Banks, which continued to be the peasantry's only source of credit at less than a 10 percent interest rate, lost from one to two thirds of their capital. The Popular Banks had first appeared in the last prewar decade (see Chapter 6) and at their apex in 1929, they had furnished the peasantry just one quarter of its agricultural borrowing. Commercial banks and private lenders had provided almost all the rest and at much higher interest rates. In 1929 the reorganized Central Bank of Cooperatives and the new Agricultural Mortgage Bank were left to fill the gap created by the Popular Banks' losses and the National Bank's reduction of the agricultural share of its commercial loans. That share fell from a record 38 percent in 1931 to less than 5 percent afterwards, according to Table 12.6. The drop is less severe when we subtract from the 1931 peak the "bad agricultural debts" that the bank wrote off in 1932. Both institutions failed to begin filling even this reduced gap. Not until the government set up a new National Institute of Agricultural Credit in 1937 did credit for agricultural crops, marketing, and equipment, let alone mortgages, appear in useful if still not sufficient amounts the following year.[16]

One thing that made Bulgaria's agricultural performance superior

TABLE 12.5
COOPERATIVES, 1937-38[a]

Country	Number of Cooperatives[a]	Number of Members	Trade Total	Supplies	Sales	Total Assets[b]	Total Turnover	Per Cooperative[c] Assets (Francs)	Members	Assets per Member (e)	(f)
					(1000 Swiss Francs)[b]			(Francs)		--(Francs)--	
Agricultural Co-operative Societies											
Bulgaria	2317	331452 (2317)	22014 (1522)	5276 (1522)	16739 (1522)	62651 (1393)		27040	143		
Greece	5948	250890	13512 (3651)	1309 (3651)	9647 (3651)	47413 (3651)		12986	69		
Romania	6751	1149689 (6751)				118087 (6751)		17492	170		
Yugoslavia	7899	799657 (6517)	28065 (1911)	18161 (1753)	11028 (694)	165756 (4213)		25434	123		
a. Rural Co-operative Credit Societies											
Bulgaria	1899	216538 (1899)	22014 (1522)	5276 (1522)	16739 (1522)	62651 (1393)	211394 (1,393)	27040	114	(237)	(394)
Greece	4327	193901	6308 (2977)	2840 (2977)	3468 (2977)	38454 (2977)	(2977)	12917	65	198	198
Romania	4638	905420 (4638)				89657 (4638)		19331	195	99	99
Yugoslavia	4283	414645 (270)	2840 (3495)	(148)	(148)	156830 (2011)	349603 (2431)	77986	119	(655)	(657)
B. Urban Co-operative Credit Societies											
Bulgaria	216	172559 (216)				91737 (65)	696401 (65)	1,411338	799	(1766)	(1767)
Greece											
Romania	597	197421 (597)				34739 (597)		58189	331	176	176
Yugoslavia	280	85211 (270)				15228 (270)	84194 (270)	56400	316	179	179

Notes: (a)Figures in parentheses give number of cooperatives reporting. (b)Based on Swiss franc values before devaluation in September, 1936, and official exchange rates. (c)Only for reporting cooperatives. (d)Figures in reporting cooperatives. (e)Assumes assets per member are equal for those reporting and those not reporting assets. (f)Assumes that membership per cooperative is the same for those reporting assets and those reporting members.

Source: International Labor Review, XI, 2 (August 1939), p. 254-71.

TABLE 12.6
AGRICULTURAL BANK ASSETS AND CREDIT, 1929-39

Bulgaria (million leva)

Year	Agricultural and Cooperative Bank						Coop Unions & Centrals			Credit Cooperatives				Other Coops	
	Total Assets		Loans to Farmers		Loans to Cooperatives		Debts	Own Funds	Loans	Debts	Own Funds	Credits Total[c]	Net[d]	Debts	Own Funds
	(a)	(b)	(a)	(b)	(a)	(b)									
1929	6,820	658	2,726	(485)	1,293	(25)	390	253	301	1,329	3,049	3,609	3,498	1,864	(1,251)[e]
1930	6,204	795	2,522	(267)	1,391	(42)	551	206	247	1,355	3,526	3,646	3,504	2,038	(1,414)[e]
1931	6,820	1,021	2,588	(294)	1,508	(122)	938	245	312	1,498	4,130	3,740	3,798	2,335	1,629
1932	7,533	1,038	2,602	(384)	1,665	(150)	681	276	330	1,472	4,219	4,003	3,996	2,225	1,744
1933	8,177	1,337	2,553	(497)	1,831	(84)	823	298	402	1,586	4,044	4,106	4,135	2,531	1,901
1934	7,555	1,435	2,488	(454)	1,894	(147)	982	315	438	1,636	4,412	4,233	4,169	2,827	2,009
1935	9,072	—	2,373	—	1,851	—	1,122	412	481	1,740	4,743	4,607	4,388	2,859	2,253
1936	9,589	—	1,622	—	1,849	—	1,384	591	543	1,735	5,027	4,159	4,477	3,131	2,536
1937	10,465	—	984	—	1,938	—	1,828	577	520	1,525	5,424	4,717	4,525	3,732	2,836
1938	11,017	—	982	—	2,145	—	2,354	682	829	1,676	6,064	5,019	5,008	4,390	2,943
1939	13,944	—	1,127	—	2,449	—	2,207	1,422	903	1,994	6,401	5,527	5,476	4,337	3,932

Greece (million drachmae)

Year	Agricultural Loan Balances[f]				All Loans of Agricultural Bank[f]	Annual Loans Made to Agriculture			Agricultural Cooperatives Member Deposits and Capital
	All Banks	Bank of Greece	National Agricultural Bank	Agricultural Bank		Agricultural Bank		(% to coops)	
						Long Term	Short Term		
1929	1,279	20.2	1,258.1	—	—	17	1,289	—	(153)[g]
1930	1,033	10.1	513.7	—	—	36	1,318	—	—
1931	1,253	7.4	390.8	—	—	21	1,105	65.8	—
1932	1,172	7.3	302.1	—	—	27	1,337	66.6	—
1933	1,101	6.4	235.6	851.2	1,240.4	48	1,884	74.9	375.9
1934	1,168	11.1	174.9	852.2	1,896.7	80	1,837	50.8	—
1935	1,335	18.3	164.2	1,048.4	1,798.9	148	2,737	57.7	—
1936	1,722	10.2	93.6	1,596.5	2,715.8	315	3,552	61.6	—
1937	2,095	8.3	61.0	2,080.8	2,875.3	416	3,592	—	—
1938	—	—	—	—	3,538.3	418	3,899	—	—
1939	—	—	—	4,000.0	3,999.1			—	—

TABLE 12.6 (continued)

Romania (million lei)[h]

Year	National Bank — Loans Made To Agriculture[i] Value	% of Total	Suspended Portfolio Under Moratorium[j]	Central Cooperative Bank Total Assets[k]	Loans[k]	Federal Cooperative Bank Total Assets[k]	Loans[k]	Credit Cooperatives Debts	Own Funds[k]	Total Loans[k]	Other Coops Debts[k]	Own Funds[k]
1929	15,355	34.0		2,269	1,164	1,385	1,193	2,714	3,877	6,411	1,663	910
1930		—		2,240	1,173	1,437	1,286	2,815	4,609	7,033	1,355	804
1931	15,025	38.0		2,543	1,164	1,403	1,295	3,033	5,458	8,066	1,420	852
1932	14,698	32.0	3,004	2,485	1,204	1,520	1,394	3,156	5,610	8,269	1,276	749
1933	5,203	13.0	3,166					3,119	5,463	7,955	1,219	690
1934	1,555	5.1	2,946	2,458	1,172	1,833	1,552	3,021	5,404	7,778	1,024	678
1935	1,395	5.5	2,727					1,925	5,194	6,635	897	776
1936	390	2.4	2,430	1,977	687			1,338	4,182	4,886	855	716
1937	604	3.2	1,997			2,833	2,494	1,278	3,925	4,836	935	775
1938	720	3.5	1,776					1,276	4,109	4,961	1,152	784
1939	1,584	4.9	1,221									
	1,860	3.3										

Yugoslavia (million dinars)

Year	Agricultural Bank Assets	Loans	Cooperative Unions and Centrals Debts	Own Funds	Loans	Credit Cooperatives Debts	Own Funds	Credits	Other Coops Debts	Own Funds
1929										
1930	741	600	530	489	799	424	2,555	2,288	327	460
1931	825	766	490	611	838					
1932	831	748	222	535	514					
1933	825	747	241	514	506					
1934	821	762	256	530	506					
1935	822	768	267	565	518					
1936	845	801	313	535	582	586	2,237	1,947	229	288
1937	882	775	571	611	924	514	2,250	1,884	333	324
1938	918	868[m]	570	595	808	501	2,228	1,989	434	355
1939	940	840[m]	614	740	885					

to Romania's during the 1930s was probably continuing access to agricultural credit. Cooperative credit associations were able to increase their assets by one quarter between 1932 and 1934, just when the Romanian Popular Banks were contracting theirs in the face of cancelled debts. Bulgarian legislation to reduce the principal owed on peasant debts cut those obligations by only 20–40 percent and was not passed until 1934. That year's merger of the Central Cooperative Bank with the Zemedelska Banka, the state Agricultural Bank that had become the country's largest after the war, may have reduced the credit cooperatives' independence. It also added greatly to their loanable funds. Cooperative numbers and membership continued to grow. So did loans, often large enough for investment in new equipment, crop diversification, or, from 1936, in the vital consolidation of the 10–12 separate plots that made up the typical Bulgarian smallholding. Private banks and individuals were left with less than 40 percent of the market for agricultural loans, in contrast to 75 percent shares in Romania and Yugoslavia.

The still better performance of Greek agriculture could also draw on greater access to credit despite the onset of the Depression and the accumulation of unpaid debt. Almost 80 percent of this debt, the smallest per capita average for Southeastern Europe anyway, was owed to public institutions, largely to the National Bank of Greece. By 1930, however, the new Agricultural Bank had pushed its total loans to four times the amount given agriculture by the National Bank. The good harvests of 1932–33 permitted peasants to repay at least some of their obligations. Moreover, the new bank continued the practice of granting over two thirds of its loan value to cooperatives, thus facilitating their use in improving methods of cultivation. The Agricultural Bank also established separate sections for technical assistance and cooperative relations that employed their own ag-

Notes: (a) and (b)Prior to merger in 1935, (a) is for the Agricultural Bank and (b) is for the Central Cooperative Bank. Loans of the latter are estimates based on identifiable shares of total loans made annually and yearend balances (portfolio and current account). (c)Portfolio and current account. (d)Including the unions of popular banks. (e)Comparable sums for 1929 and 1930 are estimated using the 1931 proportions. (f)Yearend balances. (g)End of 1928. (h)Other sources of agricultural credit in Romania included the Agricultural Mortgage Bank (with assets c. 1,409 million in 1931), Casa Rurală, Creditul Funciar Rural (and its county and communal credit offices) and Casele de Imprumut pe Gaj, whose total loan volume diminished in the 1930s. (i)Total loans made during the year. (j)Sums of bad loans subject to conversion in 1934. (k)Balances on December 31. (l)Changed in 1937 to the National Cooperative Institute and later to the National Agricultural Credit Bank. (m)Of which 241 million dinars in 1938 and 221 dinars in 1939 were current accounts of cooperatives and their unions under agricultural debt conversion.

Sources: *Statisticheski godishnik na Bulgarskoto Tsarstvo, 1931* (Sofia, 1931), p. 376; *1935* (Sofia, 1935), pp. 290, 298, 311-17; *1938* (Sofia, 1938), pp. 592-93, 598-99; *1940* (Sofia, 1940), pp. 578, 591, 596, 609, 614-15; *Statistikē epetēris tēs Ellados, 1930* (Athens, 1932), pp. 271-75, 286; *1935* (Athens, 1936), pp. 290-95; *1939* (Athens, 1940), pp. 282-88, 491; Ch. Evelpidi, *E georgia tēs Ellados* (Athens, 1944), p. 134; Georges Servakis and C. Pertounzi, "The Agricultural Policy of Greece," in O. S. Morgan (ed.), *Agricultural Systems of Middle Europe* (New York: AMS Edition, 1933), pp. 178, 198; Naval Intelligence Division, *Greece*, Vol. II (London, 1944), pp. 185, 189-91; *Enciclopedia României*, Vol. IV (Bucharest, 1943), pp. 599-602, 638-48, 725-29; V. N. Madgearu, *Evoluția economiei românești* (Bucharest, 1940), pp. 343-45; *Anuarul statistic al României, 1930* (Bucharest, 1932), pp. 110-11; *1934* (Bucharest, 1935), pp. 148-49, 154-55; *1939-1940* (Bucharest, 1940), pp. 690, 700-03.

ronomists. The Metaxas regime disbanded the cooperative section in 1937. The bank still favored cooperative borrowers, especially those growing grain. It now granted low-interest credit that included some for medium- and long-term loans up to twelve years. Metaxas also cancelled all private agricultural debts if the amount already paid equalled the principal without interest.[17]

The Yugoslav peasant debt reflected in Table 12.6 amounted to the lowest in per capita terms and the highest in cooperative assets. Low debt and high assets did not prompt more than moderate advances in output and yield. Blame belonged to that familiar Yugoslav feature, uneven regional distribution. Croatia/Slavonia and especially Slovenia could draw on their own extensive and well-funded network of cooperatives. Their resources were large enough to push average assets per Yugoslav cooperative well past the impressive Bulgarian figure in Table 12.4. The new Agricultural Banks in Belgrade neglected the rest of the country for Serbia and the Vojvodina. The latter's sizable German minority had its own set of heavily endowed cooperatives. As in the 1920s, however, these solid sources of agricultural credit were strictly confined to their own region. Over half of the country's total peasant debt was owed to individual lenders, often rural storekeepers, at high interest rates. It had typically been borrowed for food, more land, or debt consolidation rather than capital improvements.[18] Legislation in 1932–33 first placed a moratorium and then reduced the interest rates on this debt. Its principal was not reduced. The Debt Consolidation act of 1936 finally allowed the state to assume this debt, cut it by 25 percent, and undertake its collection as part of the bill for direct taxation.

The Gamble on the Greater German Market

The better performance of Bulgarian and also Greek agriculture during the Depression decade thus derived in part from a superior credit structure. We need to connect agriculture credit to the wider framework of public and private finance, especially if we are to grasp the serious limitations that plagued the Romanian economy in this regard. Before widening our perspective on the supply of capital, however, the reaction of Balkan agricultural exports to reduced international demand merits its own section.

The region's record was not a bad one when the Depression is placed in comparative international perspective. Exports from Southeastern Europe declined relatively less in terms of U.S. gold dollars than did the world average for primary-producing countries during 1928–33; the region's recovery from 1934 to 1938 saw its exports actually increase their modest share of the total European market.[19] Among the individual states of Southeastern Europe the Bulgarian reaction again emerges as the most successful, at least until the outbreak of the Second World War, and the Romanian the least. An earlier and easier turn to the German market distinguished the evolution of Bulgaria's foreign trade through the 1930s. Exchange controls and clearing agreements explain some but not all of this turn to Nazi Germany, which was far less uniform across Southeastern Europe than has often been assumed.

The attraction of Central European markets for Balkan exports dates back to the transit and border trade of the late Ottoman period described in Part I of this volume. Part II detailed the growth of agricultural exports in this direction from the independent Balkan states. Austro-Hungarian tariff wars with Romania in 1886–91 and Serbia in 1906–11 saw Germany soon buying a larger share of the Romanian and Serbian goods that had formerly been sold to the Habsburg monarchy than any other country. Bulgaria and even Greece, with its presumed orientation to the Mediterranean and the British orbit, shipped over one quarter of their exports to Imperial Germany by the last prewar decade. Weimar Germany, as noted in Chapter 10, did not relinquish this preeminent position except in trade with Yugoslavia.

The interwar German impulse to increase its trade with Southeastern Europe predated the Nazi period. Recent West German scholarship has called our attention to the emphasis that Chancellor Brüning's government placed on such expansion.[20] Table 12.7 indicates the considerable advances made in trade with Yugoslavia and especially Bulgaria from 1929 to 1932.

Barriers to Balkan Economic Integration

During these early years of the Depression the Balkan governments could pursue only one alternative direction, a customs union.[21] French self-sufficiency and the British adoption of imperial preference, a set of trade regulations favoring Commonwealth agriculture, closed off the two major markets of Western Europe. Trade with the revisionist states of Hungary and the Soviet Union was restricted for political reasons. Efforts to tie Balkan agricultural exports to Czech industrial imports would have been politically feasible but never went beyond the talking stage at various conferences. Several ministerial meetings in 1930 did culminate with a "First Balkan Conference" in Athens, which proposed a customs union among all the Southeastern European states. How much help such a union would have been to economies that conducted only 9 percent of their

TABLE 12.7
DIRECTIONS OF FOREIGN TRADE, 1929-39ᵃ
(percent in current prices)

Country and Year	Northwestern Europe Exp.	Imp.	Germany and Austria Exp.	Imp.	Eastern Europe Exp.	Imp.	Italy Exp.	Imp.	Southeastern Europe and Turkey Exp.	Imp.	Other Exp.	Imp.
Albania												
1929	0.4	11.4	1.0	7.7		6.7	60.4	46.2	22.0	12.1	16.2	15.9
1930	0.5	13.1		8.8		8.2	59.7	50.2	22.4	11.5	17.4	8.2
1931	2.4	10.5		4.5		6.7	66.2	46.9	20.8	13.4	10.6	18.0
1932	0.3	10.9		7.8	0.1	8.9	62.7	39.1	14.3	12.1	22.6	21.2
1933	2.2	15.6		8.8	0.1	8.5	79.6	41.9	9.0	11.4	9.1	13.8
1934	0.9	16.5		8.7	0.4	8.9	63.5	34.1	25.4	11.9	9.8	20.0
1935	1.3	16.7		11.9	0.9	9.?	61.0	28.2	21.8	8.8	14.5	25.1
1936	1.3	17.9	3.0	9.0	1.4	9.?	66.6	24.9	12.7	20.5	15.0	18.6
1937	1.1	15.8	0.1	8.0	0.9	10.1	78.6	24.0	9.8	25.9	9.5	16.2
1938	3.6	9.5	0.2	6.0	2.6	6.1	68.4	36.3	15.4	29.9	9.8	12.2
Bulgaria												
1929	15.1	27.3	42.4	29.8	16.0	12.3	10.5	10.7	10.8	14.2	5.2	5.7
1930	20.4	27.3	33.9	30.0	20.4	12.9	8.3	13.6	6.6	12.4	10.4	3.8
1931	22.3	29.6	46.3	30.5	15.9	14.6	5.8	13.7	3.3	7.9	6.4	3.7
1932	26.7	28.4	41.0	31.9	9.1	13.1	12.5	15.6	2.8	6.9	7.9	4.1
1933	23.6	24.0	45.7	44.4	6.5	7.3	9.1	12.7	1.5	7.4	13.6	4.2
1934	18.4	27.4	48.0	44.9	5.6	6.9	9.2	7.8	3.0	7.0	15.8	6.0
1935	14.9	14.5	52.6	59.9	11.5	12.9	8.8	3.2	2.5	4.6	9.7	4.9
1936	26.8	11.1	50.6	66.7	8.4	12.3	3.6	0.6	1.8	4.6	8.8	4.7
1937	25.6	17.5	47.1	58.2	11.3	10.7	4.2	5.0	1.5	4.3	10.3	4.3
1938	13.1	15.9	58.9	52.0	11.8ᵇ	14.2ᵇ	7.6	7.5	1.9	5.5	6.7	4.9
1939	9.4	7.4	67.8	65.5	5.9ᵇ	11.1ᵇ	6.1	6.9	2.2	5.5	8.6	3.6

TABLE 12.7 (continued)

Country and Year	Northwestern Europe		Germany and Austria		Eastern Europe		Italy		Southeastern Europe and Turkey		Other	
	Exp.	Imp.	Exp.	Imp.	Exp.	Imp.	Exp.	Imp.	Exp.	Imp.	Exp.	Imp.
Greece												
1929	29.1	27.4	25.7	10.5	2.4	7.6	18.3	5.7	2.7	17.5	21.8	31.3
1930	30.2	29.8	26.0	11.7	6.5	9.2	14.0	6.3	2.6	15.8	20.7	27.2
1931	33.0	28.6	19.6	13.7	4.7	11.0	16.6	6.1	3.1	17.9	23.6	22.7
1932	42.4	28.5	18.7	11.9	3.3	14.9	16.5	5.7	2.6	17.2	16.5	21.8
1933	37.8	29.7	19.7	11.5	3.0	13.1	14.0	5.7	4.3	13.1	21.2	26.9
1934	30.2	31.5	24.6	16.5	3.6	11.0	9.8	4.9	7.1	13.2	24.7	22.9
1935	25.4	24.7	31.1	20.7	4.7	9.8	6.0	3.7	7.1	14.1	25.7	27.0
1936	24.4	24.9	38.7	24.4	4.7	9.3	1.8	0.5	7.9	10.8	22.5	30.1
1937	18.9	19.4	32.7	29.7	7.7	7.3	6.3	2.9	6.4	18.9	28.0	21.8
1938	16.3	20.0	40.4	30.4	7.1	7.1	5.2	3.4	5.6	15.9	25.4	23.2
Romania												
1929	13.9	20.3	37.0	36.6	19.4	18.7	7.7	6.9	9.0	3.0	13.0	14.5
1930	27.3	22.6	27.9	36.7	16.1	13.8	12.9	7.9	6.2	2.1	9.6	11.9
1931	33.2	22.6	22.1	37.9	19.2	16.2	9.5	9.8	5.6	2.5	10.4	11.0
1932	38.1	32.1	18.7	28.6	14.0	15.0	10.6	11.3	7.0	2.5	11.6	10.5
1933	41.8	36.4	17.2	27.4	12.4	13.1	9.2	10.5	5.0	2.7	14.4	9.9
1934	29.9	40.6	25.7	25.4	12.5	14.2	7.7	7.3	6.4	2.7	17.8	9.8
1935	20.4	24.6	29.4	36.2	14.0	21.4	15.6	7.7	6.2	3.2	13.5	6.9
1936	36.0	18.2	26.4	49.5	12.9	18.6	6.1	1.5	5.3	3.5	13.3	8.7
1937	27.6	22.1	26.0	37.4	14.1	22.2	6.6	4.3	8.7	2.5	17.0	11.5
1938	22.1	27.2	26.5	36.8	16.0	17.8	6.2	5.0	10.2	2.1	19.0	11.1
1939			32.3	39.3	(a)	(a)	12.1	8.8				

TABLE 12.7 (continued)

Country and Year	Northwestern Europe Exp.	Imp.	Germany and Austria Exp.	Imp.	Eastern Europe Exp.	Imp.	Italy Exp.	Imp.	Southeastern Europe and Turkey Exp.	Imp.	Other Exp.	Imp.
Yugoslavia												
1929	9.0	13.7	24.1	33.0	13.4	26.3	24.9	10.8	22.1	3.6	6.5	12.6
1930	10.5	14.0	29.4	34.4	16.1	25.2	28.3	11.3	9.7	4.3	6.0	10.8
1931	10.5	16.8	26.5	34.5	23.2	24.9	25.0	10.3	8.0	2.8	6.8	10.7
1932	10.0	18.1	33.3	31.3	19.4	20.8	23.1	12.7	5.5	4.3	8.7	12.8
1933	12.3	19.1	34.6	29.3	15.5	17.9	21.5	15.9	5.2	3.2	10.9	14.6
1934	14.8	21.5	31.8	26.3	16.2	16.6	20.6	15.5	5.9	5.7	10.7	14.4
1935	13.3	21.1	32.4	28.1	20.0	18.9	16.7	10.0	4.6	4.2	13.0	17.7
1936	21.1	18.3	38.4	37.0	17.5	20.3	3.1	2.5	7.3	5.7	12.6	16.2
1937	26.2	14.8	35.2	42.7	11.9	15.0	9.4	8.2	4.7	4.5	12.6	14.8
1938	22.3	16.5	42.0	39.4	13.7	15.3^b	6.4	8.9	4.6	3.8	11.0	16.1
1939	21.6	11.6	31.9	47.7	20.0^b	5.7^b	10.6	11.7	4.4	4.3	11.5	19.0

Notes: (a)Data in this table and Tables 12.8 and 12.9 reflect official country data uncorrected for errors of reporting (noted in Table 12.9) or for distortions from variations in exchange rates and prices of clearing agreements. (b)Trade with Czechoslovakia in 1939 was: Bulgaria (with Bohemia-Moravia), exports 3.3 percent and imports 4.1 percent; Romania, exports 10.9 percent and imports 16.8 percent; Yugoslavia, exports 14.5 percent and imports 0.6 percent.

Sources: *Statisticheski godishnik na Bŭlgarskoto Tsarstvo, 1934* (Sofia, 1934), pp. 176-77; *1940* (Sofia, 1940), pp. 500-01; *Statistikē epetēris tēs Ellados, 1935* (Athens, 1936), p. 160; *1939* (Athens, 1939), p. 150; *Statitique du commerce de la Grèce avec les pays étrangers pendant l'année 1930* (Athens, 1933), pp. 5-7; *Anuarul statistic al României, 1939-1940* (Bucharest, 1940), pp. 600-05; I. V. Totu (ed.), *Progresul economic în România, 1877-1977* (Bucharest, 1977), p. 309; *Statistički godišnjak Kr. Jugoslavije, 1932* (Belgrade, 1936), pp. 178-79; *1940* (Belgrade, 1940), pp. 234-35; League of Nations, *International Trade Statistics, 1931 and 1932* (Geneva, 1933), pp. 306, 328; *1935* (Geneva, 1936), pp. 178-79; *1938* (Geneva, 1938), p. 8.

foreign trade with each other remains to be seen. In any event the abortive Austro-German customs union of 1931 soured general European opinion toward such projects, especially if Czechoslovakia were to be tied to Southeastern Europe. Renewed interest in such a project surfaced again in 1933, but foundered on West European objections that it would have violated the most favored nation principle. In addition, Greek authorities feared that their existing import surplus with their neighbors, especially Romania, would only increase under such an arrangement with little growth for Greek exports. The dilemma of similar exports affected Greek as well as Bulgarian and Yugoslav tobacco. The Balkan Tobacco Office opened in 1932 but could never resolve the issue of how much the member states should reduce their exports in a glutted world market whose prices had dropped precipitously. In the end, precious little was actually accomplished toward Balkan economic cooperation. There was not even a bridge across the Danube connecting Romania and Bulgaria, from Giurgiu to Ruse, until after the Second World War.

German Trade and the New Clearing Agreements

The failure of economic integration left Southeastern Europe open to continuing influence from Central Europe. The pre-Nazi expansion of German trade was not the only one. Bilateral clearing agreements increasingly replaced the use of currency converted at fixed exchange rates after Britain left the Gold Standard in 1931. The president of the Austrian National Bank first proposed bilateral clearing at the Prague conference of central bankers that same year. Exporters would now be paid with central bank deposits in their own currency and importers would pay by drawing on the same account. Only the cumulative balance need be settled in foreign exchange and then, as it turned out, at infrequent intervals. Such a system encouraged balanced, even barter trade and allowed countries with past import surpluses to delay the settling of those accounts. Austria, not incidentally, fit this description; so did the Southeastern Euorpean states in the late 1920s (see Table 12.8). To make sure that such import surpluses or payment deficits did not recur, all these states resorted to a system of import licenses for agricultural as well as industrial goods.[22] To do business with each other under these licensing and clearing arrangements, Central and Southeastern European states began to sign bilateral trade agreements for a year or less that did not differ significantly from those signed regularly between Communist governments since 1948. The preponderant share of Balkan foreign trade that clearing agreements came to provide may be seen in Table 12.8. Only the Greek share was not well over 50 percent.

TABLE 12.8

FOREIGN TRADE BALANCES AND CLEARING SHARES, 1926-39[a]

Year	BULGARIA (million leva)			GREECE (million drachmae)			ROMANIA (million lei)			YUGOSLAVIA (million dinars)		
	Imports	Exports	Balance	Imports	Exports	Balance	Imports	Exports	Balance	Imports	Exports	Balance
1926	6,246	5,617	- 629	9,967	5,439	-4,527	37,127	38,223	+ 1,095	7,623	7,817	+ 194
1927	6,128	6,627	+ 498	12,600	6,040	-6,560	33,841	38,110	+ 4,269	7,278	6,400	- 878
1928	7,039	6,231	- 808	12,416	6,330	-6,086	32,145	26,919	- 5,225	7,831	6,444	-1,387
1929	8,321	6,388	-1,932	13,275	6,960	-6,315	29,625	28,960	- 665	7,594	7,921	+ 327
1930	4,587	6,187	+1,599	10,523	5,985	-4,538	22,951	28,516	+ 5,565	6,955	6,779	- 175
1931	4,658	5,933	+1,274	8,763	4,203	-4,559	15,425	22,188	+ 6,763	4,793	4,800	+ 7
1932	3,470	3,381	- 89	7,870	4,577	-3,292	11,451	16,709	+ 5,258	2,823	3,055	+ 232
1933	2,201	2,845	+ 643	8,424	5,152	-3,272	11,738	14,165	+ 2,426	2,833	3,377	+ 544
1934	2,247	2,534	+ 287	8,790	5,472	-3,318	13,209	13,655	+ 446	3,482	3,847	+ 364
1935	3,008	3,253	+ 245	10,679	7,100	-3,579	10,847	16,756	+ 5,908	3,602	4,028	+ 426
1936	3,153	3,906	+ 756	11,962	7,378	-4,583	12,637	21,703	+ 9,065	3,984	4,376	+ 392
1937	4,661	5,019	+ 358	15,203	9,555	-5,648	20,162	31,359	+11,196	5,148	6,272	+1,124
1938	4,929	5,578	+ 648	14,760	10,149	-4,611	18,693	21,524	+ 2,830	4,948	5,047	+ 98
1939	5,197	6,065	+ 868	12,281	9,200	-3,081				4,757	5,521	+ 764

Per Capita Average in 1929 Prices[b]

	Imports	Exports			Exports		Imports	Exports		Imports	Exports	
1926-30	1,177	1,414			993		1,735	1,777		560	574	
1931-35	693	1,281					1,011	2,154		317	481	
1936-38	876	1,381			892		1,012	2,181		391	553	

Index[c]

	Imports	Exports			Exports		Imports	Exports		Imports	Exports	
1906-10	78	68			68		115	135		49	62	
1926-30	100	100			100		100	100		100	100	
1931-35	58	90					58	121		56	83	
1936-38	74	97			89		58	122		69	96	

Estimated Shares and Balances in Clearing Trade[d]

Year	BULGARIA (million leva)			GREECE (million drachmae)			ROMANIA (million lei)			YUGOSLAVIA (million dinars)		
	Imports (%)	Exports (%)	Balance (value)	Imports (%)	Exports (%)	Balance (value)	Imports (%)	Exports (%)	Balance (value)	Imports (%)	Exports (%)	Balance (value)
1929[e]		79.8			48.6			73.0			84.0	
1934		68.3			42.8			52.4			74.9	
1932[f]	70.9	75.3	+ 85.1	38.1	28.9	-1,675.8	67.2	51.3	+ 877.0	55.9	59.6	+ 243.0
1934	77.2	75.1	+ 168.8	40.8	36.7	-1,578.3	53.7	47.3	- 634.2	52.4	61.4	+ 537.3
1935	80.2	76.6	+ 76.4	37.6	41.7	-1,054.7	89.9	84.5	+4,407.1	52.8	60.3	+ 527.1
1934[g]	87.5	83.6	+152.8	70.5	59.5	-2,941.4	76.4	75.2	+3,222.0	75.0	83.5	+ 600.5
1936	90.6	76.9	+150.5	61.1	61.5	-2,770.9	83.6	68.9	+4,388.5	73.6	78.9	+ 520.5
1937	90.5	77.0	-353.7	59.5	56.8	-3,618.9	80.1	62.5	+3,449.2	76.0	78.5	+1,011.1
1938	86.7	88.0	+634.8	70.5	64.3	-3,880.3	82.5	72.9	+ 269.1	76.4	79.5	+ 75.3
1929[h]							69.3	69.6	- 368			
1930							68.2	60.5	+1,556			
1931							69.7	53.4	+ 870			
1932							60.6	46.0	+ 412			
1933							56.0	39.5	975			
1934							51.4	48.5	- 163	73.5	84.9	+ 664
1935							64.5	61.9	+3,374	71.4	82.8	+ 693
1936							84.1	56.3	+1,587	73.3	76.2	+ 346
1937							73.3	55.8	+2,743	75.7	76.2	+ 816
1938							61.7	52.0	- 386	69.5	67.0	- 75

Notes: (a)Official foreign trade data are subject to recording errors of as much as 10 percent as explained in sources to Table 12.25. In addition, values do not consider the effects of changes in clearing exchange rates and prices. (b)Bulgarian, Romanian and Yugoslav trade are deflated with foreign trade prices given in Table 12.10; Greek trade is deflated by dollar exchange rates. (c)Per capita trade levels for 1906-10 are based on constant foreign exchange values as explained in Table 10.6. (d)As illustrated in the table, estimates of clearing trade are widely different depending on whether accounts record countries with exchange controls or countries with whom clearing agreements exist, whether consideration of is given to trade shares subject to compensation, partial convertibility or trilateral clearing and whether price and exchange rate adjustments have been made. Estimates in the table are from the following sources: (e)Basch. (f)Royal Institute of International Affairs. (g)Momtchiloff and th(Georgescu-Roegen and Obradovic.

The restrictive general effects and the specific stimulus to industry from this new trade regime are treated in subsequent sections. Here we address the variety of bilateral dealings that grew up between the Southeastern European States and Nazi Germany. Hitler's interest in stimulating trade with the area dated only from 1935. By then the needs of rearmament and Schacht's fear of an inflationary import surplus that would depreciate the Reichsmark dictated a turn to clearing agreements.[23] In these agreements the Reichsmark was consistently overvalued in order to attract necessary imports without the need to pay in foreign exchange.

Bulgaria first resorted to strict exchange controls in 1931, despite a good harvest and an export surplus. Deficits in the balance of payments and also the government budget (see Tables 12.25 and 12.13) had created a "transfer problem" (earning or borrowing the foreign currency needed to service foreign debts without widening the deficit). By 1936 four separate lists of goods that could be traded only under clearing agreement had been consolidated into one. The Bulgarska Narodna Banka awarded a 35 percent premium on freely exchanged leva to exporters (equivalent to a 26.5 percent devaluation) but also retained a share of their earnings.[24] Add the lack of a heavily demanded export to the Western European countries still trading freely, and the incentives for Bulgarian interests to favor clearing agreements appear powerful. The government pushed for them even with Britain and France. German overtures were thus irresistible.

Bulgaria's road to the largest share of trade in clearing accounts and with Germany was also built by the nature of its exports. More widely marketable crops like wheat had now given way to tobacco, cotton, table grapes, and dairy products. The latter had received special encouragements from the cooperative network.

Only sales of rose oil, mainly to French perfume manufacturers, declined during the 1930s. The others continued the increase in shares of Bulgarian exports noted in Table 12.9 mainly because of German purchases under clearing agreements. The overvalued Reichsmarks, which they earned in a cumulative account at the Bulgarian National Bank, compensated for continued low prices that these differentiated luxury goods still fetched on world markets in the late 1930s. In this fashion the already large German share of Bulgarian exports—30 percent in 1929 and 36 percent in 1933—rose still more to 43 percent by 1937 and to nearly 75 percent by 1939 for economic reasons separate from any political attraction to Nazi Germany. Tobacco and table grapes had found some British markets earlier in the 1930s but would have earned little if sold for going prices by the end of the decade.[25]

Romania continued to rely on petroleum and cereals for three quarters of its export value throughout the period. The volume of both could be increased easily to compensate for falling prices. Hence the rise in its real per capita exports by the mid-1930s, noted in Table 12.8. Its neighbors were struggling to recapture their 1926–30 levels. Those levels were about half again prewar figures, while Romania's was over one quarter lower.

The Romanian government adopted exchange controls more readily than it relied on clearing agreements. By 1932 foreign exchange was receiving an 18 percent premium over its lei value. From 1935 forward the National Bank of Romania began collecting foreign exchange earned through exports. It dispensed import certificates that were soon discounted to reflect the official premium, now raised to 38 percent against the lei or higher. Until then several large grain harvests and a string of export surpluses had combined with the British loan of 1931 to delay the transfer problem.[26] By 1935 the state budget had succeeded in reducing the share paid for foreign debt by one half to 11 percent.

The British share of this debt and of arrears in import payments was large enough to encourage Romanian maintenance of its exports for freely exchanged, i.e., Western, currencies. A clearing agreement was finally signed with Germany in 1935, but exports were slow to respond. Until 1936 the royalist government in Bucharest actively discouraged the rising export of Romanian oil to Germany by the sale of clearing Reichsmarks on the open market. That year the observance of League of Nations sanctions against Mussolini because of his Ethiopian aggression closed off the Italian market for Romanian oil. Sales to Great Britain or other Western customers were hampered by an unfavorable ratio between the world price of petroleum as set on the U.S. Gulf Coast and the official rate for the leu. These pressures finally pushed up the German share of total Romanian export value from about 15 percent for 1934–36 to 19 percent for 1937. Only in the summer of 1938 did revised German military plans place Romanian oil high on the list of import priorities. Prior to that time, Romania's allegiance to the French-backed Little Entente (with Czechoslovakia and Yugoslavia) and the threat posed by Romanian grain exports to Nazi plans for agricultural self-sufficiency had held Hitler back.[27] Now the Nazi trade offensive could move ahead for Romania too, no longer limited by Hjalmar Schacht's concern for the balance of payments, since the cautious German Finance Minister had resigned in 1937.

Yugoslavia, the other Balkan member of the Little Entente, did not hold out as long against German penetration. At the outset of the Depression its royalist regime had avoided import quotas, cut the state budget more sharply, and allowed internal prices to fall more

TABLE 12.9

COMPOSITION OF EXPORTS, 1928-38

(percent of total in current prices)

Country and Year	Cereals and Derivates	Tobacco	Industrial Crops	Fruit	Live Animals	Animal Food Products	Hides and Leather	Textiles and Fibers	Forestry Products[a]	Shares of Listed Items
Bulgaria										
1928	14.7	36.0	8.2	0.6	4.2	10.4	6.8			80.9
1929	9.2	45.3	2.3	0.9	3.5	13.2	5.9			80.3
1930	15.1	42.8	2.1	1.3	3.3	16.0	4.8			85.4
1931	22.3	43.5	2.2	1.6	2.1	16.8	2.6			91.1
1932	25.6	31.9	6.4	2.1	1.7	22.2	2.8			92.7
1933	14.3	41.3	5.7	4.3	2.0	19.2	4.6			91.4
1934	10.7	38.7	6.3	8.3	3.9	18.3	5.6			91.8
1935	2.6	42.5	10.8	13.3	3.1	18.2	3.6			94.1
1936	14.8	32.3	9.6	9.5	2.2	19.5	4.4			92.3
1937	19.7	32.0	9.3	7.4	3.4	14.7	5.8			92.3
1938	10.0	42.5	4.7	17.6	3.6	13.5	3.1			95.0
1939	7.7	41.0	7.3	19.6	1.8	10.9	2.8			91.1
	(Minerals and metals)		(Raisins)	(Wine & Brandy)	(Other Fruit)	(Olives & Oil)				
Greece										
1928	6.8	51.1	17.8	8.1	2.5	4.2	3.1	1.1	1.7	96.4
1929	2.3	56.5	15.1	8.4	2.8	6.2	2.2	1.0	1.2	95.7
1930	6.7	56.5	16.2	4.4	3.2	3.8	2.4	1.6	1.2	96.0
1931	4.4	53.5	22.2	4.3	2.1	5.6	2.3	0.7	1.3	96.4
1932	6.2	38.3	27.3	3.7	3.9	12.7	1.4	0.8	1.6	95.9
1933	4.2	33.6	26.1	6.3	4.7	12.4	2.5	1.7	2.4	94.3
1934	4.8	37.0	26.0	3.6	5.2	8.6	2.6	1.7	3.4	92.3
1935	3.9	50.3	17.3	2.5	4.6	9.9	2.1	1.7	2.8	95.1
1936	4.8	40.0	17.7	2.8	3.8	8.1	4.7	2.2	2.4	87.5
1937	7.3	45.9	14.9	2.8	4.4	5.7	3.8	2.2	3.4	90.4
1938	5.4	50.4	14.4	2.7	10.0	8.9	2.6	1.4	2.5	98.3

TABLE 12.9 (continued)

Country and Year	Cereals Derivates	Vegetables	Industrial Crops[c]	Fruit	Live Animals	Animal Food Products	Hides and Leather	Forestry and Fibers	Petroleum Products[a]	Shares of Listed Items
Romania										
1928	28.2	4.2	2.4	1.9	7.8	2.7	0.8	18.0	30.0	80.9
1929	30.9	1.5	2.7	1.0	6.9	3.1	0.7	16.2	33.3	80.3
1930	35.0	1.2	1.9	1.2	6.6	3.7	0.4	10.9	36.6	85.4
1931	39.5	1.0	2.6	1.0	7.0	3.7	0.4	10.7	30.8	91.1
1932	34.3	1.2	1.2	0.7	3.8	3.4	0.4	7.4	43.1	92.7
1933	23.1	0.9	4.0	0.9	2.8	2.6	0.6	7.2	55.3	91.4
1934	17.5	1.7	4.7	1.4	4.6	2.9	0.5	10.8	52.8	91.8
1935	19.6	1.7	5.8	1.4	5.7	2.6	0.5	8.7	51.7	94.1
1936	31.5	1.7	4.2	1.8	5.0	3.1	1.4	7.8	41.3	92.3
1937	32.2	1.4	4.4	1.3	4.2	2.3	1.7	9.0	40.5	92.3
1938	24.4	1.7	5.1	1.7	5.7	3.0	0.9	11.4	43.2	95.0
Yugoslavia									_Minerals_	
1928	7.6		6.2	4.1	13.7	11.7	2.5	24.4	8.4	78.6
1929										
1930	15.7		2.8	5.1	13.3	12.1	1.6	21.8	11.7	84.1
1931	14.7		4.3	3.7	15.3	13.7	1.5	19.1	11.4	83.7
1932	10.6		9.7	7.1	15.2	12.3	1.4	16.8	11.7	84.8
1933	14.1		8.7	5.0	14.0	10.4	2.0	20.4	12.5	87.1
1934	19.7		4.9	4.4	11.6	7.2	2.4	19.8	13.9	83.9
1935	9.8[b]		13.8	5.2	12.7	11.3	2.2	21.0	12.5	88.5
1936	12.3[b]	3.2	12.0	4.6	13.9	12.7	3.4	15.0	15.3	92.4
1937	21.0[b]	2.7	9.1	1.7	11.4	8.8	2.2	18.1	18.7	93.7
1938	14.7	2.7	10.3	3.3	10.7	11.0	2.2	17.7	19.1	92.2
1939	8.9	1.1	8.0	5.6	12.9	11.7		20.3		

Notes: (a)Excluding paper; for Yugoslavia 1931-34, wood and wood products. (b)Excluding bran. (c)Includes plant seeds for Romania.

Sources: See Table 12.7.

drastically. This classic liberal prescription had not helped. Neither did exchange controls; *agio* on internationally traded dinars, in the fashion of the 1890s described in Chapter 7, appeared by 1932. The Narodna Banka was forced to begin paying a premium of 28.5 percent for foreign exchange, an effective devaluation of 22.5 percent on the dinar.[28] Exports did not respond. From late 1934 forward, Yugoslav economic policy passed into the hands of Milan Stojadinović. As Finance Minister in 1923–24 (see Chapter 11), he was a strong disciple of the liberal reliance on monetary discipline. The Depression had disillusioned him not only with this philosophy but also with dependence on Western Europe. His efforts to reflate the Yugoslav economy required the isolation from further international pressure on the dinar that the German market promised. In addition, Stojadinović wrongly anticipated political neutrality in any future European war as an added benefit from supplying Nazi Germany with what it wanted.[29]

After a brief turn away from clearing countries in 1936, Yugoslav exports in that direction again passed 80 percent of the total. Nonferrous ores, initially bauxite and chrome and eventually copper, were at the top of the Nazi shopping list in Yugoslavia. By 1937 the country was shipping 32 percent of its exports to Germany. With the absorption of Austria in 1938, four fifths of the Yugoslavian wheat and hog exports plus the majority of its hemp and plums were also sent to Germany. Timber products had been the largest interwar Yugoslav export. They accounted for over 20 percent of total value and enjoyed the best potential for sales to Western Europe. As in Romania, timber exports slumped badly with the Depression. They failed to recover later in the 1930s. Yugoslav imports from Germany had already been 16 percent of total value during 1925–32 on the strength of war reparations and the needs of a growing metallurgical sector. By 1937 Germany and Czechoslovakia combined provided 55 percent of machinery imports and 75 percent of coal. German imports alone reached 33 percent of total value, two years before the absorption of Czechoslovakia.[30]

Greece was the only net importer of cereals in Southeastern Europe. The Depression initially promised the country lower bread prices. But the British departure from the Gold Standard in 1931 hit the Greek economy harder than its neighbors. It depended more on British credit and held more British pounds. Consecutively bad raisin and tobacco harvests from 1929 to 1931 weakened Greece's capacity to ride out this reverse. The Venizelos government therefore decided to leave the Gold Standard in April 1932, the only state in the area to do so formally. The drachma was devalued to about 43 percent of the previous parity value with gold. This alone was not sufficient. Nor were several small British loans able to close the balance of payments deficit created by a huge import surplus (see Tables 12.8 and 12.25) and to meet a debt service on past foreign loans that took 40 percent of state budget expenses and amounted to 70 percent of export earnings. Exchange controls were introduced in 1932. They aimed to reduce the import surplus and to limit the transfer problem of paying for imports or debt service in foreign denominations.[31]

The value of agricultural imports dropped more than earnings from tobacco and Greece's other agricultural exports. The continuing import surplus was still big enough to draw exports steadily toward the Central European countries with which Greece signed clearing agreements from 1932. Germany was the leading purchaser. Its share of total Greek export value had, however, slipped from 36 percent in 1936 to 31 percent the next year. By 1937, League sanctions were having less success in diverting trade away from Italy. The German shares for tobacco and raisins exceeded 40 percent. Imports from Germany amounted to 27 percent of total value, led by 63 percent of machinery imports. The British loss of this market may perhaps be traced to superior German goods. Yet German provision of 50 percent of coal imports versus just 5 percent from Britain was largely the result of Greek accumulation of overvalued Reichsmarks and further exchange controls that encouraged their use.[32]

The New Balance between Public and Private Finance

Most research on the Balkan economies during the Depression has concentrated on Nazi penetration. The historian's concern with the origins of the Second World War makes this concentration understandable. For foreign trade, as we have just seen, German penetration was too important for economists to ignore.[33] Trade with Nazi Germany affected the long-term course of Balkan economic development less, however, than did a neglected shift in financial structure during the 1930s which originated, to some extent, in financial consequences of the new clearing trade. In part because of their role in managing such trade, public financial institutions grew stronger at the expense of private commercial banks. The decline in note issue from the central banks was slower than the fall in wholesale prices noted in Table 12.10 and less abrupt than the drop in short-term foreign credit to the commercial banks. At the same time the central banks lost some of the independence from the government that they had begun to carve out for themselves in the 1920s. Also lost was the access to long-term Western European finance that had been painstakingly repaired with debt settlements and new loans by the end of the first postwar decade. Financial isolation now threatened Southeastern Europe. The collapse of world prices for agricultural exports by the early 1930s doubled or tripled the volume of Balkan exports required to sustain the existing flow of public and private debt service. The region's terms of trade fell, as also recorded in Table 12.10, making foreign imports more costly. The price collapse forced the partial suspension of foreign debt service due from the Bulgarian and Greek budgets in May 1932. Romania and Yugoslavia followed suit shortly thereafter and did not resume payment until 1935. During the same period, moratoriums on peasant debt dealt another blow to private domestic creditors, banks included. Weakened commercial banks and more powerful but less independent central banks would of course ease the postwar spread of direct state controls under Communist auspices.

Public Finance and the Central Banks

The Greek experience tempts us to correlate the region's most consolidated financial structure during the 1930s with the successful growth of the one non-Communist economy in Southeastern Europe since the 1950s. Whatever the correlation, public financial institutions became more powerful but also retained more independence.

Almost entirely responsible for this consolidation were the country's two largest banks, the Bank of Greece and the National Bank of Greece. The first was the new central bank, created in 1928 with exclusive rights of note issue (see Chapter 11). In 1931 it was accorded the equally exclusive and important right to deal in foreign exchange directly or through designated commercial banks. Clearing agreements were soon channeled through the Bank of Greece as well. The outflow of gold that culminated in Greece's above-mentioned departure from the Gold Standard in 1932 also obliged the Bank of Greece to enlarge its powers. It blocked various accounts and held the drachmae usually released from the state budget to the International Financial Commission, which still oversaw the Greek foreign debt under the 1898 arrangements described in Chapter 7. This compulsory debt conversion plus the aforementioned devaluation that accompanied the break with the Gold Standard more than doubled the bank's reserves of gold and foreign exchange in 1933. When combined with the cut in reserve requirements, the Bank of Greece was able to raise its note issue by more than one third for 1933 over 1931 and by 5 percent over 1929. The Greek bank's superior record in augmenting its reserves and its note issue throughout the decade, recorded in Table 12.11, must be reduced in real terms by the greater rise in Greek wholesale prices. More important for our purposes, the end of severe exchange controls in 1936 deprived the new authoritarian regime of General Metaxas of the leverage that would have increased direct government control over the Bank of Greece. The stabilization and further devaluation of the drachma also removed the need for the regime's strictures against smuggling foreign exchange, and they were dropped a few months after their introduction in mid-1936.[34]

The National Bank of Greece had of course been an official bank of issue since its founding in 1841. The massive commercial operations noted in Chapter 7 had also continued to grow after the First World War. Legislation to establish a new strictly central bank in 1928 left the National Bank of Greece to pursue its commercial operations but at the same time preserved its semiofficial character. The government continued to appoint its governor and his two top assistants. In return for its heavy financial support for the state's new Agricultural Bank, the Trapeza Ethniki tes Ellados received the banking business

TABLE 12.10
TERMS OF TRADE AND FINANCIAL INDICATORS[a]

Year	BULGARIA Export Prices	Import Prices	E/I[b]		GREECE	ROMANIA Export Prices	Import Prices	E/I	YUGOSLAVIA Export Prices	Import Prices	E/I
1926	66.4	97.2	68.3		Not	141.4	122.0	115.9	87.5	109.4	80.0
1927	72.1	97.7	73.8		Avail-	113.2	96.7	117.2	93.7	102.1	91.8
1928	89.9	103.3	86.8		able	111.4	102.0	109.2	100.3	106.0	94.6
1929	100.0	100.0	100.0	(100.0)		100.0	100.0	100.0	100.0	100.0	100.0
1930	72.7	91.1	79.8	(83.4)		69.9	94.3	74.1	81.8	87.3	93.7
1931	61.5	77.7	79.2	(82.8)		45.6	80.2	56.9	63.7	75.4	84.5
1932	47.0	76.7	61.3	(61.6)		41.9	65.0	63.6	53.3	74.7	71.4
1933	39.2	76.4	51.2	(63.2)		38.5	64.2	60.0	51.1	81.3	52.9
1934	38.2	75.0	51.0	(52.0)		37.7	65.1	57.9	51.7	76.7	67.4
1935	43.8	70.9	61.8	(70.2)		42.6	66.9	63.7	55.6	75.8	73.4
1936	47.6	71.3	66.8	(77.7)		46.2	74.2	62.3	56.7	77.8	72.9
1937	55.6	84.2	66.1	(79.1)		69.7	91.6	76.1	63.5	81.1	78.3
1938	66.1	77.9	84.9	(82.6)		60.0	92.2	65.1	66.7	77.9	85.6
1939	73.1	78.9	92.6						67.5	87.2	77.4

Official Exchange Rates[c]

Year	BULGARIA Dollar	Gold	GREECE Dollar	Gold	ROMANIA Dollar	Gold	YUGOSLAVIA Dollar	Gold
1928	100.0		100.7		100.0		100.0	
1929	100.0	100.0	100.0	100.0	100.0	100.0	100.0	100.0
1930	100.0	99.9	100.7	100.2	100.0	99.8	100.5	100.5
1931	100.0	99.3	100.0	99.9	100.0	99.7	100.5	100.5
1932	100.0	99.7	64.3	64.3	100.0	100.1	93.2	93.3
1933	138.9	97.2	55.8	43.4	130.0	98.9	100.1	77.8
1934	179.2	96.3	72.9	43.3	166.7	97.9	129.1	77.0
1935	180.6	98.5	72.9	43.0	155.0	90.1	129.8	77.0
1936	180.6	98.9	72.1	42.5	123.3	72.6	130.5	77.1
1937	179.2	99.7	70.5	41.2	121.7	72.0	131.0	77.3
1938	172.2	99.1	69.8	40.8	121.7	72.3	131.4	77.5
1939	168,1	98.7	63.6	37.1	118.3	70.0	128.6	76.1

TABLE 12.10 (continued)

Domestic Prices (1929 = 100)

	BULGARIA		GREECE		ROMANIA		YUGOSLAVIA	
Year	Cost of Living	Wholesale Prices	Cost of Living	Wholesale Prices	Cost of Living	Wholesale Prices	Cost of Living	Wholesale Prices
1928	97.7	97.0	96.7	95.0	97.3	105.2	98.8	111.3
1929	100.0	100.0	100.0	100.0	100.0	100.0	100.0	100.0
1930	91.5	81.2	87.0	90.9	99.1	78.4	92.1	82.2
1931	79 9	66.9	86.5	81.3	70.8	60.2	84.7	76.7
1932	73.5	58.6	91.8	97.5	59.2	54.0	76.6	69.0
1933	68.2	52.4	98.5	110.3	54.6	52.3	66.2	65.7
1934	63.7	54.3	100.3	108 7	53.4	52.4	61.0	62.2
1935	59.5	55.2	101.3	110.6	55.6	60.0	60.4	65.5
1936	57.0	56.0	104.9	112.5	57.9	68.5	61.3	65.6
1937	58.1	63.2	113.1	126.0	66.1	78.2	65.1	71.4
1938	60.1	65.5	112.5	123.0	74.6	78.3	69.4	75.2
1939	61.6	66.6	112.1	122.0	83.0	87.8	70.6	77.6

Currency Issues (1929 = 100)

	BULGARIA		GREECE		ROMANIA		YUGOSLAVIA	
Year	Total	Per Capita	Total	Per Capita	Total	Per Capita	Total	Per Capita
1929	100.0	100.0	100.0	100.0	100.0	100.0	100.0	100.0
1930	91.3	90.1	92.5	91.3	92.7	91.4	92.8	91.4
1931	80.9	78.8	77.1	75.0	112.3	109.0	88.9	86.3
1932	73.0	70.2	90.8	87.2	103.1	98.7	82.0	78.5
1933	82.7	78.5	104.9	99.5	100.4	94.9	74.4	70.3
1934	67.9	63.6	109.5	102.3	105.5	98.4	75.4	70.3
1935	69.2	64.2	115.3	106.0	109.4	101.1	84.0	77.2
1936	71.4	65.7	119.4	108.3	121.4	110.9	93.0	84.3
1937	71.2	65.2	130.5	116.7	139.0	125.5	100.3	89.8
1938	77.6	70.3	139.4	122.9	165.1	147.4	119.0	105.0
1939	117.6	105.8	182.0	158.4	230.8	204.2	166.7	145.1

Notes: (a)Price indices and exchange rates are annual averages whereas currency circulations are based on issues as of December 31. (b)Data in parentheses are calculations of Berov from unit export and import values whereas the official Bulgarian data are price indices of exported and imported products. (c)Indices of dollar and gold exchange rates differ because of the dollar devaluation. Indices reflect "official" values whereas under exchange controls actual rates for dollars and convertible currencies reflected more depreciation of domestic currencies. For example, in 1937 dollar indices with premiums were 134.8 in Bulgaria, 69.9 in Greece, 89.3 in Romania and 102.3 in Yugoslavia.

Sources: Tables 11.1 and 12.11; League of Nations, *Statistical Yearbook, 1940/41* (Geneva, 1941), pp. 188-89; *Statisticheski godishnik na Bulgarskoto Tsarstvo, 1940,* pp. 567, 584; Liuben Berov, *Ikonomicheskoto razvitie na Bulgariia prez vekovete* (Sofia, 1974), p. 137; V. N. Madgearu, *Evoluţia economiei româneşti* (Bucharest, 1940), Annex III-2; *Statistički godišnjak Kr. Jugoslavije, 1940* (Belgrade, 1940), p. 297.

of all government agencies except the Treasury. It was also handed the control of the independent but semiofficial Currant Administration. The bank further augmented its resources by absorbing one of two large foreign financial institutions in Greece, the Bank of the Orient, on its liquidation in 1932. Even before legislation made it mandatory in 1931, the National Bank tended to deal largely in short-term transactions. All this allowed the bank to boost its share of total liabilities for Greek commercial banks from 47 percent in 1928 to 69 percent by 1934. The National Bank, with the region's largest network of branches, and four commercial banks accounted for 85 percent of liabilities. The other twenty to twenty five institutions were left to handle parts of local markets. Here was real concentration. Here also, supported by sizable and diverse liquid assets, was the one Balkan record of growth in commercial banking during the Depression. Total liquidity and bank deposits actually rose from 1933 forward. Only in Greece, moreover, were these commercial deposits larger than either notes in circulation or deposits in savings banks.[35] Table 12.10 makes clear the decisive part played by the National Bank of Greece in attracting these funds.

The Bulgarian National Bank had also lost its commercial functions in 1928 so it could concentrate on central banking. Before then, as we have seen, the bank had already lost its prewar position as the country's largest financial institution. Tables 12.11 and 12.12 do not reveal any return to preeminence. Nor do they indicate that the assets of Bulgarian banks as a whole made the significant advances just noted for Greece. The Bulgarska Narodna Banka nonetheless acquired new official powers during the 1930s that greatly augmented its authority. The bank set up state control, or, more accurately, state restriction, of foreign trade. Since 1930 the bank's policy had been to encourage trade relations that would protect the lev and provide foreign exchange for external obligations. Legislation on foreign exchange in January 1933 required bank authorization for all imports. By 1936 the bank was supervising a system of import quotas and licenses, paid for with export premiums that had effectively cut the level of imports in half.[36] This system also served to expand the share of foreign trade conducted under official clearing arrangements, principally with Germany.

The country's predominant financial institution since the First World War was also a state bank. The Bulgarska Zemedelska Banka (see Table 12.5) increased its proportion of total bank deposits to 38 percent by 1937. Slight slippage thereafter in favor of state and local savings banks was not sufficient to stop a rise in absolute value of 42 percent for 1931–39. The bank's amalgamation with the state's small Central Cooperative Bank in 1934 had added just 14 percent to its deposits. In the provision of new credit, the agricultural bank was still more dominant. Its share rose from one third to one half during 1931–39.[37]

Finally, the government and the central bank joined forces in 1934 to support the merger of eight, eventually twelve native joint-stock banks, with over 40 percent of all commercial bank assets, into the single Banka Bulgarski Kredit. Including its resources in our calculations for Table 12.11, state financial institutions accounted for two thirds of all deposits and three quarters of all new credit by 1936.

TABLE 12.11

CENTRAL BANK BALANCES, 1929-39

(million domestic currency units on December 31)

Country and Year	Total Assets	Reserves Gold	Reserves Other[b]	Credit Assets Government	Credit Assets Other	Bank Note Liabilities	Government Credit: Total Assets (%)	Bank Notes: Total Assets (%)	Gold: Bank Notes (%)
Bulgaria									
1929	8,386	2,300	247	3,470	1,693	3,609	41.4	43.0	70.6
1930	7,154	1,767	481	3,319	948	3,296	46.4	46.1	68.2
1931	6,838	1,653	116	3,274	896	2,919	47.9	42.7	56.6
1932	6,273	1,529	114	3,326	717	2,635	52.2	41.3	58.0
1933	6,597	1,601	85	3,631	735	2,984	55.0	45.2	53.7
1934	6,386	1,500	169	3,383	652	2,449	53.0	38.3	41.2
1935	7,271	1,503	551	3,581	879	2,497	49.3	34.3	60.2
1936	7,372	1,652	723	3,488	849	2,577	47.3	34.9	64.1
1937	8,760	1,994	584	3,880	1,402	2,569	44.3	29.3	77.7
1938	8,839	2,006	1,239	3,841	988	2,800	43.5	31.7	71.6
1939	10,530	2,010	1,749	3,793	2,335	4,245	36.0	40.3	47.3
Greece[c]									
1929	9,130	3,117		3,597	380	5,193	39.4	56.9	60.0
1930	8,412	3,012		3,389	407	4,803	40.3	57.1	62.7
1931	7,469	2,137		3,126	820	4,003	41.9	53.6	53.4
1932	9,111	1,920		5,193	1,415	4,714	57.0	51.7	40.7
1933	12,078	1,599		5,958	1,087	5,449	49.3	45.1	29.3
1934	11,659	3,954		4,714	1,440	5,686	40.4	48.8	69.5
1935	12,750	4,012		6,455	1,835	5,988	50.6	47.0	67.0
1936	13,961	3,261		7,430	1,975	6,203	53.2	44.4	52.6
1937	15,642	3,173		7,583	2,821	6,776	48.5	43.3	46.8
1938	18,651	3,469		9,919	3,332	7,239	53.2	38.8	47.9
1939	23,406	3,685		13,045	4,017	9,453	55.7	40.4	39.0

TABLE 12.11 (continued)

Country and Year	Total Assets	Reserves Gold[a]	Reserves Other[b]	Credit Assets Government	Credit Assets Other	Bank Note Liabilities	Government Credit: Total Assets (%)	Bank Notes: Total Assets (%)	Gold: Bank Notes (%)
Romania									
1929	34,903		46	5,469	10,415	21,144	15.7	60.6	
1930	28,373	11,021	77	3,617	8,917	19,605	12.7	69.1	56.2
1931	32,959	9,953	45	3,767	14,483	23,750	11.4	72.1	41.9
1932	37,492	10,022	65	5,726	11,090	21,594	15.3	56.6	56.4
1933	36,184	10,152	13	5,681	9,900	21,219	15.4	58.6	57.8
1934	38,922	10,376	1,135	5,655	7,390	22,307	14.5	57.3	45.5
1935	41,292	10,894	1,861	5,639	6,075	23,127	13.7	56.0	47.1
1936	47,684	15,568	3,585	3,624	7,162	25,663	7.6	53.8	60.7
1937	49,795	16,458	2,338	5,607	7,030	29,391	11.3	59.0	56.0
1938	59,285	18,190	1,706	5,589	15,263	34,902	9.4	58.9	52.1
1939	74,298	20,768	2,272	5,572	26,061	48,800	7.5	65.7	42.6
Yugoslavia									
1929	9,958	2,549	0	4,154	1,583	5,818	41.7	58.4	43.8
1930	8,145	1,752	0	4,021	1,726	5,397	59.9	66.3	32.5
1931	6,583	2,096	86	1,799	2,334	5,172	27.3	78.6	40.5
1932	7,233	1,968	2	2,409	2,523	4,773	33.3	66.0	41.2
1933	6,966	1,906	55	2,316	2,168	4,327	33.2	62.1	44.0
1934	6,832	1,906	104	2,300	1,882	4,384	33.7	64.2	43.4
1935	6,976	1,464	332	2,301	1,912	4,890	33.0	70.1	29.9
1936	7,736	1,626	552	2,350	1,884	5,409	30.4	69.9	30.1
1937	9,040	1,709	440	2,439	1,901	5,834	27.0	64.5	29.3
1938	9,731	1,910	644	2,464	2,028	6,921	25.3	71.1	27.6
1939	12,324	1,988	731	4,017	2,495	9,698	32.6	78.7	20.5

Notes: (a)Gold and gold or convertible currencies. (b)Other foreign exchange. (c)The division of Bank of Greece foreign assets into gold and other was not reported.

Sources: League of Nations, *Money and Banking, 1937/38* (Geneva, 1938), pp. 43, 105, 129, 213; *Money and Banking, 1940/42* (Geneva, 1942), pp. 85, 121, 159, 199.

These figures surpass the public concentration of financial power in Greece when we consider the private stockholders and the only semiofficial character of the largest Greek institution, the National Bank of Greece.

The Declining Role of Commercial Banks

Bulgarian private banks declined in numbers as well as in their share of liabilities and assets. Their total, according to Table 12.11, dropped from 140 in 1930 to 89 by 1938. Most of the loss came from the failure of provincial banks. Plans were made to expand the new

TABLE 12.12
STRUCTURE OF BANK ASSETS, 1929-39[a]
(December 31 balances)[b]

Country and Year	National Banks	State Savings Banks[c]	Mortgage Banks[d]	Commercial Banks[e] Assets	No.
Bulgaria (million leva)					
1929	8,386	748	570	8,442	135
1930	7,154	913	600	7,412	138
1931	6,838	1,325	763	6,684	131
1932	6,373	1,552	759	5,861	128
1933	6,597	2,783	769	5,072	119
1934	6,386	2,088	772	4,929	116
1935	7,271	2,334	806	4,885	97
1936	7,372	2,608	626	5,004	93
1937	8,760	2,926	608	4,998	88
1938	8,839	3,411	617	5,375	87
1939	10,530	3,702	631	6,207	87
Greece (million drachmae)					
1929	9,130	1,171	2,248	20,195	35
1930	8,412	1,572	2,614	21,642	34
1931	7,469	1,998	2,696	19,325	32
1932	9,111	2,281	2,677	20,427	26
1933	12,078	2,902	2,621	22,217	27
1934	11,659	3,422	2,574	22,011	26
1935	12,750	3,770	2,369	22,612	26
1936	13,961	4,356	2,473		26
1937	15,642	4,987	2,551		28
1938	18,651				
1939					
Romania (million lei)					
1929	34,903	4,365		84,280	1,097
1930	28,373	4,384		83,782	1,102
1931	32,459	4,615		65,459	1,037
1932	37,492	4,703		56,201	953
1933	36,184	5,392	(2,871)	53,234	893
1934	38,922	6,103	(2,695)	46,100	873
1935	41,292	6,912		44,021	920
1936	47,684	9,568		35,632	553
1937	49,795	10,403		38,240	530
1938	59,285	11,105		37,707	483
1939	74,298	11,986		39,521	451

TABLE 12.12 (continued)

Country and Year	National Banks	State Savings Banks[c]	Mortgage Banks[d]	Commercial Banks[e] Assets	Commercial Banks[e] No.
Yugoslavia (million dinars)					
1929	9,958	797	3,552	18,419	637
1930	8,145	1,331	3,820	19,879	649
1931	6,583	1,254	3,956	17,952	639
1932	7,233	1,486	4,110	15,587	632
1933	6,966	1,839	4,462	14,840	620
1934	6,832	1,988	4,621	13,333	615
1935	6,976	2,180	5,011	13,125	610
1936	7,736	2,639	5,331	13,275	610
1937	9,040	3,325	6,118	12,703	
1938	9,731	3,292	6,056	13,063	
1939	12,334	3,318	7,244		

Notes: (a)See Table 12.6 for agricultural and cooperative banks. (b)Except for the Greek savings and loan banks whose account was available for the fiscal years. (c)One institution for Bulgaria and Yugoslavia and two institutions for Greece and Romania. Yugoslav private municipal savings banks are excluded. (In 1929, 56 banks with assets of 1,927 million dinars; in 1938, 61 banks with assets of 2,872 million dinars.) Only total deposits are included for Greek postal savings and Romanian savings and loan; only total funds are given for Romanian postal savings. (d)Sums indicated for Romania are assets of the Bucharest Urban Mortgage Bank; in 1938, the Iaşi Urban Mortgage Bank had assets of 679 million lei. Both institutions were private and included in the assets of commercial banks. (e)Joint-stock banks in Romania and Yugoslavia. Romanian data covers only active banks after 1935.

Sources: *Statisticheski godishnik na Bulgarskoto Tsarstvo, 1934* (Sofia, 1934). pp. 257-58; *1935* (Sofia, 1935). pp. 290, 311-12, 316-17; *1936* (Sofia, 1936), pp. 364-65; *1937* (Sofia, 1937), pp. 458-59; *1938* (Sofia, 1938), pp. 563, 584, 592-93, 598-99; *1939* (Sofia, 1939), pp. 602-03; *1940* (Sofia, 1940), pp. 578-79, 587, 596-601, 608-09, 614-15, 868; *Statistikē epetēris tēs Ellados, 1930* (Athens, 1932), p. 272; *1935* (Athens, 1936), p. 292; *1938* (Athens, 1939), pp. 282-86, 492; *Enciclopedia României* Vol. IV (Bucharest, 1943), pp. 548, 573-74, 604; *Anuarul statistic al României, 1933* (Bucharest, 1934), p. 104; *1934* (Bucharest, 1935), p. 156; *1939-40* (Bucharest, 1940), pp. 693-95; Institutul central de statistică, *Statistica societăţilor anonime din România*, Vol. XXII-1940 (Bucharest, 1942), pp. 22-23; *Statistički godišnjak Kr. Jugoslavije, 1930* (Belgrade, 1931), pp. 235-37; *1933* (Belgrade, 1934), pp. 200-33; *1940* (Belgrade, 1940), pp. 272-81; League of Nations, *Commercial Banks, 1929-34* (Geneva, 1935), pp. 10-12, 58-61, 96-98, 134-38; League of Nations, *Money and Banking, 1937/38* (Geneva, 1938), pp. 105-07, 212-15; *1940/42* (Geneva, 1942), pp. 86, 121, 160-61, 199.

Banka Bulgarski Kredit to include virtually all provincial banks, but this never materialized. Several of the lesser Sofia banks had been included in the original merger. The large Sofia banks were affiliates of large Western European institutions, as noted in Chapter 11. Five of the six survived the decade but without much influx of new foreign funds.[38] Only the Generalna Banka merged in 1938 with the Banque Franco-Belge, to save itself after some ill-fated industrial ventures.

The transfer of private assets from commercial banks or accounts to public savings institutions represented a major change in the financial structure of all the states in Southeastern Europe during the 1930s. The movement of Bulgarian funds was proportionally the largest but may be subsumed under the continued rise of the state's agricultural and cooperative banks.

For Yugoslavia, however, this transfer assumed a more independent role. The country's large commercial banks, it may be recalled, were concentrated in Zagreb rather than the political capital of Belgrade. By 1929 the city's twenty nine joint-stock banks and their branches controlled 43 percent of the country's commercial banking assets. Most of the large Zagreb banks relied significantly on Central European stockholders or depositors. These institutions were hit hard during 1931 by the successive collapse of the huge Credit-Anstalt in Vienna, the July closing of the German Banks, and the three-day bank holiday in Hungary. Then, to make matters worse, came the British decision to go off the Gold Standard in September, just a few months after the National Bank had decided to go on it. Withdrawals from Yugoslav commercial banks, already heavy in the summer, became heavier in the fall. The top twenty had lost 41 percent of their deposits by the end of 1933. Provincial banks, mostly located in Serbia, were far more numerous. They pushed the total number of commercial banks past 600. Most provincial banks survived the Depression but typically found that half of their assets were tied up in agricultural credits, repayment of which was frozen under the government's aforementioned moratorium on peasant debts. Promised state aid in merging these banks on the Bulgarian model never arrived. The large Zagreb banks had made fewer agricultural loans, but, in addition to the loss of Central European funds, they faced the continuing favoritism of the National Bank in Belgrade for Serbian borrowers (about half of total credits). This plus higher National Bank rates for what credit was granted left the Zagreb banks with no choice but to draw on their so-called Iron Reserves for survival.[39]

The shift of bank liabilities (and thus private assets) to savings and other deposits in public institutions did not begin immediately. The state's postal savings banks attracted more deposits from 1930 forward, but sizable increases did not appear until 1935–36. Then all accounts rose by one third. The State Mortgage Bank, the Državna Hipotekarna Banka, had pursued passive prewar policies, and had hardly grown during the 1920s, but now acquired a new lease on life. Together with the postal savings banks it accounted for half of the 1936–37 increment to total Yugoslav deposits. What undoubtedly lay behind this growth was the January 1935 decision by the Stojadinović government to place the state postal savings and mortgage banks directly under the authority of the Minister of Finance. With this authority went a guarantee of solvency. The loanable funds of these institutions climbed from less than one quarter to about two thirds of the commercial bank total between 1930 and 1938.[40]

The Yugoslav government not surprisingly proved to be the best customer for this new supply of internal funds. The Državna Hipotekarna Banka in particular advanced the state budget funds for new military spending. Rearmament was largely responsible for increasing state expenditures by 27 percent from 1935 to 1940 and another 23 percent in 1941. The rising internal debt allowed the state to reduce its foreign indebtedness slightly in absolute terms and to shavé the foreign share of the state debt from 79 percent in 1932 to 71 percent by 1937 and to 52 percent by 1941.[41] Table 12.13 suggests that a similar process was underway across the area. British and French lenders had been obliged to forgive too many interest payments in the early 1930s to be much interested in new loans anyway. In short, the Southeastern European states were using the growth of public bank assets to finance greater independence from the foreign loans on which they had relied so heavily since the late nineteenth century.

Romanian budgetary expenditures and the internal state debt rose more sharply than the Yugoslav, Greek, or Bulgarian aggregates for 1934–38. Internal debts doubled for Romania. Its foreign debt dropped by one third, according to Table 12.13. Rearmament again received the bulk of this greater spending. The transfer of private assets from commercial banks to public institutions did not occur in nearly the measure recorded for Yugoslavia. Tables 11.9 and 11.10 imply a different means of covering the cost, namely the printing press of the Romanian National Bank. The bank's note issue climbed by two thirds from 1934 to 1938 and then doubled by 1940. Official statistics badly understated both the huge budget deficits implied by rising internal debt and also the advances given the government in new notes by the Banca Națională a României.[42]

Romanian banking, even its public institutions, simply did not recover from the initial shocks of the Depression. The Creditul Agricol Ipotecar, or Agricultural Mortgage Bank, did little after an initial flurry of activity. This had not prevented the National Bank from virtually deserting the rural sector after 1931. Its debts frozen under the 1932–34 moratorium comprised 30 percent of its total portfolio. Commercial bank deposits were halved by 1931 and continued to decline from then until the late 1930s. Two problems plagued the private joint-stock banks. First, there were too many small provincial banks. They swelled the national total by 1939 to almost double the large Yugoslav figure. A British advisor to the National Bank recommended that their number be cut at least in half. In 1934 the bank set up the Consiliul Superior Bancar for the government in order to coordinate commercial banking. The Council did succeed in halving the already reduced number of banks but no more. In addition, only 85 of the 545 banks affected from 1934 to 1941 merged so as to protect existing liabilities. The rest were entirely liquidated, four fifths of them after 1938, which raised the suspicion that the government's increasingly anti-Semitic policies were at least partly responsible. Council funds to liquidate frozen assets had already been doled out mainly to the big Bucharest banks.[43]

Second was a problem unique to Romania. Several major banks

TABLE 12.13
STATE BUDGETS AND THE BURDEN OF DEBT[a]

A. Per Capita State Budgets in 1926-30 Average Prices (million domestic currency units)[b]

Period	BULGARIA Rev.[c]	Exp.[c]	GREECE Rev.[c]	Exp.[c]	ROMANIA Rev.[c]	Exp.[c]	YUGOSLAVIA Rev.[c]	Exp.[c]
1936-38[d]	1949	1990	1235	1400	2127	2081	1076	1014
1926-30[d]	1252	1519	1590	1787	1922	1977	881	857
1911[e]	1220	1248	746	999	2763	2237	493	493

Indices

Period								
1936-38	160	159	166	140	77	93	218	206
1926-30	103	122	213	179	70	88	177	174
1911	100	100	100	100	100	100	100	100

B. Estimates of Debt Service

Bulgaria (million leva)

Year	Charged to Budget	Percent of Budget Revenue	Untransferred Foreign Service	Internal Service	Foreign Services Paid[h]	Percent of Exports
1926-27	1,302	20.9	—	181	302	5.4
1927-28	1,477	22.1	—	190	858	12.9
1928-29	1,746	24.3	—	330	479	7.7
1929-30	2,224	27.9	—	619	804	12.7
1930-31	2,216	32.8	—	606	792	12.8
1931-32	2,020	31.4	—	500	849	14.3
1932-33	1,891	32.2	—	692	460	13.6
1933-34	1,767	28.2	—	736	191	6.7
1934[f]	1,254	27.0	176	472	215	8.5
1935	2,089	31.6	532	580	207	6.4
1935	1,952	26.4	415	1,457	194	5.0
1937	2,105	24.7	408	801	—	—
1938	1,870	20.0	398	938	—	—
1939	1,730	17.9	367	—	—	—

Greece (million drachmae)

Year	Charged to Budget	Percent of Budget Revenue	Foreign Service Paid To Greeks	To Foreigners	Percent of Exports
1926-27	2,638	—	245	1,064	19.6
1927-28	2,671	2.83	—	—	—
1928-29	—	—	—	—	—
1929-30	—	—	489	1,241	17.9
1930-31	3,173	31.4	544	1,185	19.8
1931-32	2,968	31.2	314	1,554	37.0
1932-33	1,128	13.5	426	283	6.2
1933-34	—	—	159	532	10.3
1934-35	—	—	175	1,121	20.5
1935-36	3,045	28.6	354	301	4.2
1936-37	3,129	30.9	414	793	10.7
1937-38	3,185	—	408	404	4.2

Romania (million lei)

TABLE 12.13 (continued)

Year	Charged to Budget	Percent of Budget Revenues	Foreign Debt Service[i]	Percent of Exports
1926	4,654	14.9	3,165	8.3
1927	5,956	16.5	4,279-4,366	11.2-11.5
1928	5,816	17.7	3,784-4,012	14.1-14.9
1929	6,463	17.9	4,128-5,393	14.3-18.6
1930	6,251	20.1	5,032-5,230	17.6-18.2
1931	7,363	26.6	6,090-6,299	27.4-28.4
1932-33[g]	8,114	35.3	4,776-7,154	28.5-42.8
1933-34	4,553	24.7	3,754	26.5
1934-35	2,278	12.1	1,439	10.5
1935-36	2,954	12.7	1,896	11.3
1936-37	3,510	12.6	2,090	9.6
1937-38	3,702	11.7	2,117	6.8

Yugoslavia (million dinars)

Year	Charged to Budget	Percent of Budget Revenue	Foreign Services Paid[j]		Percent of Exports
			State	Public Institutions	
1926-27	571	4.6	987	16	15.7
1927-28	602	5.3	767	19	12.2
1928-29	868	7.6	1,208	280	18.9
1929-30	1,097	8.3	1,188	26	17.8
1930-31	1,017	8.1	1,124	49	24.4
1931-32	1,220	11.3	588	13	16.4
1932-33	1,559	16.3	234	12	7.3
1933-34	—	—	347	31	9.8
1934-35	—	—	(729)	—	17.2
1935-36	665	6.6	702	27	16.6
1936-37	691	6.5	—	—	—
1937-38	970	8.1	—	—	—

Notes: (a)Estimates of debt service are uncertain. Among their complications are the translation of domestic into foreign currencies where exchange rates are unclear, the unclear impacts of various payment suspensions and the practice of budget charges for services not actually paid. The estimates of total debt service for Yugoslavia are inconsistent with those for foreign debt service by Obradović. (b)Budgets for 1926-30 to 1936-38 are deflated by wholesale price indices; those for 1911 and 1926-30 are deflated by exchange rates. (c)Budgets cover ordinary revenues and total expenditures. (d)For fiscal years ending with these years as indicated in part B. (e)Previous territories including Romania's Old Kingdom and Serbia for 1912. (f)Nine months. (g)Fifteen months. (h)As indicated in estimates of balances of payments. (i)Where more than one estimate is given in the sources below, the low and high estimates are given in the table. It is not known if any of the Romanian estimates consider suspended debt service. (j)As indicated in note (a), estimates of Yugoslav total and foreign debt service are inconsistent.

Sources: Statisticheski godishnik na Bulgarskoto Tsarstvo, 1932 (Sofia, 1932), pp. 348-53; 1940 (Sofia, 1940), pp. 640-42, 658-61; M. Maievschi, Contribuţii istoria finanţelor publice ale României (Bucharest, 1957), p. 258; Enciclopedia României, Vol. III (Bucharest, 1943), p. 818; C. Murgescu and N. N. Constantinescu (eds.), Contribuţii la istoria capitalului strain în România (Bucharest, 1960), pp. 434-36; V. Slavescu, La situation économique de la Roumanie et sa capacité de paiement (Bucharest, 1934), p. 199; Enciclopedia României, Vol. IV (Bucharest, 1943), p. 698; Statistički godišnjak Kr. Jugoslavije, 1937 (Belgrade, 1938), pp. 401-02; 1938-1939 (Belgrade, 1939), p. 484; S. D. Obradović, La politique commerciale de la Yougoslavie (Belgrade, 1939), appendix; League of Nations, Balance of Payments, 1931 and 1933 (Geneva, 1933), p. 119; 1933 (Geneva, 1934), p. 93; 1934 (Geneva, 1935), p. 104; 1938 (Geneva, 1939), p. 77; League of Nations, Statistical Yearbook, 1928 (Geneva, 1929), pp. 180-81; 1932/33 (Geneva, 1933), pp. 203-12; 1938/39 (Geneva, 1939), pp. 283-88.

failed at the start of the Depression. These unfortunately included one of the two most prominent private institutions in the country. The Banca Marmorosch-Blank found itself saddled with a variety of bad debts by mid-1930 but did receive enough assistance from the National Bank and several others in Bucharest to tide it over. Then came the collapse of its principal foreign creditor, the Credit-Anstalt in Vienna, and the bank was forced to suspend payment. Efforts by the state and the Banca Naţională to save Marmorosch-Blank at this

later date resulted only in a limited concession from the state's tobacco monopoly and the right to continue commercial operations for
three years in order to be able to pay off its creditors without interest.
It remains unclear whether the bank's collapsing Central European
connections and its long-term placement of funds made this aid
generous or whether state and Liberal interests had generated a plan
to make the liquidation of the Jewish, albeit native, bank certain, if
painless to the rest of the economy. We may only observe here that
the bank's long-term Liberal rival, the ethnically Romanian and
state-connected Banca Românească, was asked by the Minister of Finance to join a consortium with two other banks in order to keep
Marmorosch-Blank afloat in 1931. The project collapsed when the
Liberal bank refused. It had held as many long-term investments as
Marmorosch-Blank at the start of the 1930s and yet survived. Annual
dividends reached 15 percent by 1935 and ranged from 21 to 28 percent for 1936–40.[44]

Industrial Development during the Depression

From the vantage point of the mid-1930s, an authoritative British
survey of Southeastern Europe could already conclude that the Depression's onset earlier in the decade had "profoundly altered" the
area's attitude toward rapid industrial development. The crisis had
transformed industrialization "from the political desideratum which
it had largely been in the previous period into a vital economic
necessity."[45] Falling agricultural exports limited what manufactures
might be imported in return and also invited a larger native industry
that would limit reliance on agricultural exports. More manufacturing
would also increase the potential for processed exports.

Whatever its other limitations, the industrial performance of the
Southeastern European economies overcame the general world
tendency toward stagnation or decline during the 1930s. In addition,
imports were reduced by an amount sufficient to cut back deficits in
the balance of payments. These had been met during the 1920s with
foreign loans now no longer available. (Table 12.25 makes clear to
what extent trade deficits were cut or eliminated along with large
surpluses on capital account.) At the same time this relatively successful performance could not escape the dilemma posed in Chapter
11, that increased production of finished manufactures required
greater imports of machinery and materials, especially for small
economies.

These are the boundaries within which any shift from purely private production to reliance on state supervision or investment had to

occur. The nature and extent of that shift concerns one of the subsections that follow. The other examines the continuing dominance
of Western European investment in mineral and oil extraction, despite Nazi pressures, until 1939–40.

The Record of Industrial Growth

First of all, we need to know how much growth took place and how
domestic shares of industrial outputs and inputs behaved. Tables
12.14, 12.15, and 12.16 provide the best available estimates.

Balkan rates of industrial growth slowed after 1929 but were still
high by international standards. The value of European manufacturing grew by an annual average of just 1.1 percent from 1929 to 1938.
After a slow period in the early 1930s, Greek manufacturing accelerated to record Europe's fastest rate for the decade, 5.7 percent. Bulgaria's pattern of growth was similar and placed it second, along with
Sweden and Finland, at 4.8 percent. Romanian and Yugoslav output
did fall early in the Depression. The Romanian decline had actually
begun in 1927 and lasted until 1933. Thereafter it grew by 6.2 percent a year through 1938 to record a 3.4 percent average for 1929–38.
The latter rate ranked third in Europe with Denmark.[46] Yugoslav
manufacturing managed an average rate of 2.4 percent only by growing at 10.7 percent a year for 1936–38.

National rankings for 1929–38 were largely reversed in mining.
The small Greek and Bulgarian sectors were severely depressed
until 1936. The extremely rapid growth of the larger Yugoslav sector
was probably sufficient, when contrasted with the poor performance
of Romanian mining and especially oil production, to reverse the
standing of the two countries' rates of overall industrial growth.

An important part of the growth in Romanian and Yugoslav manufacturing came from putting unused capacity back into operation. At
the bottom of its recession in 1933, Romanian manufacturers were
using only 43 percent of their theoretical capacity (from 16 percent
for soap up to 87 percent for cotton textiles). In order to use all of this
existing capacity by 1938, production would have had to increase at
18 percent a year, a rate nearly three times faster than Romania actually achieved. The existence of so much unused capacity leads us
to expect that output would grow faster than inputs. It did so in the
branches of metallurgy, cement, leather, and food processing, but not
for manufacturing as a whole.

In addition, Romanian horsepower, a surrogate for new capacity,
increased faster than labor. This suggests modernization rather than
expansion of production. The data also suggest a decline in Romanian productivity per worker, unlike Bulgarian or Yugoslav manufac-

TABLE 12.14
REAL INDUSTRIAL GROWTH, 1929-38

Indices

Country and Branch	1929	1930	1931	1932	1933	1934	1935	1936	1937	1938
Extraction										
Bulgaria	100	96	85	99	87	100	100	99	107	128
Greece	100	89	77	76	84	105	100	113	135	171
Romania	100	100	111	119	120	132	131	136	117	115
Yugoslavia	100	115	140	163	195	213	213	213	238	262
Manufacturing										
Bulgaria[a]	100	107	132	129	123	120	116	135	142	152
Greece[b]	100	103	107	101	110	125	140	139	151	165
Romania	100	97	101	84	100	123	121	129	134	135
Yugoslavia	100	109	100	79	92	93	93	104	111	126

Average Annual Growth Rates of Gross Output (percent)

Branch	BULGARIA	GREECE	ROMANIA	YUGOSLAVIA
Metals and machinery	(-) 0.7	17.1	—	—
Iron and steel	—	—	6.6	8.7
Smelting	—	–-	—	7.5
Rolled metals	—	—	4.9	—
Chemicals	5.6	4.8	—	—
Petroleum refining	—	—	3.2	—
Sulfuric acid	—	6.6	5.8	1.5
Non-wood building materials	4.4	4.0	—	—
Cement	2.8	7.9	5.9	(-) 2.2
Wood processing	2.6	—	(-) 2.6	—
Paper	16.7	4.1	3.1	0.0
Textiles	6.9	6.9	4.3	—
Leather	6.1	(-) 2.6	4.4	—
Foodstuffs	—	—	2.6	—
Flour milling	3.1	4.5	1.5	—
Otherfood	2.3	0.3	3.5	—
Tobacco	(-) 1.0	2.1	—	—
Total manufacturing	4.8	5.7	3.4	2.6
Extraction	2.8	6.1	1.6	11.3
Electric power	11.8	10.1	9.5	7.9

Notes: (a)Bulgarian manufacturing growth is based on deflated values for "encouraged" industry from 1929 to 1937 and official indices for 1937 and 1938 (1935/35 100). (b)Greek total manufacturing indices do not include flour milling. olive oil processing or wine making.

Sources: Marvin R. Jackson. "National Product and Income in Southeastern Europe before the Second World War." *ACES Bulletin*. vol. 14, nos. 3-4 (1982). in press; League of Nations. *Statistical Yearbook. 1939/40* (Geneva. 1940). pp. 171. 176; *1940/41* (Geneva. 1941). p. 163; Institutul Românesc de Conjunctură. *Bulletin trimestrial*, Vol. III. No. 1 (Bucharest. 1935). p. 61; N. P. Arcadian. *Industrializarea României* (Bucharest. 1936). p. 213; M. F. Iovanelli. *Industria românească. 1934-1938* (Bucharest. 1975). pp. 135. 144. 232; *Enciclopedia României*. Vol. IV (Bucharest. 1943). p. 447; L. Dukanac. *Indeksi konjunkturnog razvoja Jugoslavije. 1919-1940* (Belgrade. 1946). p. 34; Stevan Stajić. "Realni nacionalni dohodak Jugoslavije u periodima 1926-1939 i 1947-1956." *Ekonomski problemi: :bornik radova* (Belgrade. 1957). p. 36.

turing. For the former, output grew 80 percent faster than inputs of horsepower and labor, and for the latter, about 10 percent faster. Here we find possible support for the notion that Romania's economy was being sacrificed on a "cross of iron," that industrial capacity was being needlessly expanded beyond the ability of the Romanian market to absorb production.[47]

TABLE 12.15
GROWTH OF INPUTS TO MANUFACTURING, 1927-38
(average annual percentage)

Period and Branch	Labor	Horsepower	Combined[a]	Labor	Horsepower	Combined[a]
1928 to 1938		ROMANIA			YUGOSLAVIA	
Metals and machinery	2.90	6.35	4.63	2.27	1.40	1.84
Chemicals	3.67	10.97	7.32	-1.76	10.06	4.15
Non-wood building materials	1.71	3.92	2.82	1.53	0.78	1.16
Wood-processing	0.88	-1.11	-0.12	1.46	1.64	1.55
Paper	4.92	7.06	5.99	2.76	1.11	1.94
Printing				0.81	1.30	1.06
Textiles	7.15	7.35	7.25	2.73	2.30	2.52
Leather	3.81	-1.25	1.28	2.43	2.38	2.41
Food and tobacco	2.40	0.55	1.48	2.18	1.53	1.86
Total	3.42	4.69	4.06	1.88	2.70	2.29
1927 to 1937		ROMANIA			BULGARIA	
Metals and machinery	2.86	7.17	5.02	-2.21	2.79	0.29
Chemicals	4.56	12.82	8.70	5.04	7.42	6.23
Non-wood building materials	2.81	1.64	2.23	-0.20	1.31	0.56
Wood processing	0.73	-1.68	-0.48	-0.23	7.46	3.62
Paper	4.16	7.64	5.90	14.12	24.86	19.49
Printing						
Textiles	7.19	8.02	7.61	5.07	7.20	6.14
Leather	5.27	-1.28	1.50	-0.22	1.84	0.81
Food and tobacco	3.86	0.15	2.01	-4.05	-0.55	-2.30
Total	4.17	4.76	4.47	1.97	3.15	2.56

Note: (a)Simple average of growth rates for labor and horsepower.

Sources: See Table 12.14.

Influencing the growth of industrial output and inputs on the demand side were international as well as domestic markets. The pull of export markets remained selective and absorbed reduced shares of growing industrial production in all four countries. Greek manufactured exports were still just 3–4 percent of total export value. The dominant exports of processed food did not increase in volume during the 1930s. Sales of chemical fertilizer outside the country dropped from one third to one fifth of production. Bulgaria did better, despite the reduced export of rose essence to France's slumping perfume industry. The export of processed foods led the Bulgarian upturn. For factory enterprises, a broader category than state-encouraged industry, the exported share of all production rose by 1938 to 16–17 percent, led by foods and tobacco with 33 percent.

Romania and Yugoslavia exported other sorts of industrial goods, mainly mineral. Two thirds of Romanian petroleum value had been exported in 1929. The proportion rose to a record 78 percent in 1937 and then slipped to 73 percent the following year, as production turned down by one quarter. The exported share of Romanian timber processing had been even higher, 80 percent, in 1929, but exported

TABLE 12.16
INDICATORS OF IMPORT SUBSTITUTION, 1928-38

Import Percentage of Domestic Consumption of Industrial Products

	1928	1929	1930	1931	1932	1933	1934	1935	1936	1937	1938
Bulgaria		38.5			26.2		13.7				11.7
Greece	41.4					23.6	25.3	25.0	27.2	25.6	
Romania	34.2	34.8	31.7	32.4	26.3	25.0	24.0	19.0	19.7	26.2	21.4
Yugoslavia											18.6

Import Percentage of Domestic Consumption by Branch of Industry

BRANCH	GREECE 1937	ROMANIA 1929	ROMANIA 1938	YUGOSLAVIA 1937
Metals and machinery	78.9	56.9	45.9	38.8
Chemicals	28.0	41.0	18.4	23.5
Non-wood building materials	3.0			18.7
Wood processing	0.4			3.1
Paper	17.5			
Printing				31.8
Textiles	29.0	54.4	19.5	21.2
Leather	5.0	18.7	7.5	7.5
Foodstuffs				1.0
Total	26.2	(64.8)[a]	(29.4)[a]	18.6

Import Percentage of Manufacturing Inputs by Branch

BRANCH	BULGARIA 1930[b]	1932[b]	1937[b]	1937[c]	1938[c]	ROMANIA 1929	1932	1937
Metals and machinery	86.9	87.0	82.5	83.0	84.2	39.1	27.9	33.5
Chemicals	46.3	58.0	50.0	52.0	58.7	6.6	7.2	6.5
Non-wood building materials	59.0	48.9	38.3	48.3	22.1	28.3	22.5	20.8
Wood processing	6.7	5.1	2.8	1.5	1.8	2.6	3.0	2.4
Paper	64.2	73.9	78.9	69.1	64.4	12.8	12.6	4.8
Printing								
Textiles	80.1	87.2	56.2	56.6	52.8	85.1	88.2	67.0
Leather	75.8	72.2	75.0	69.8	68.9	21.5	27.0	16.0
Foodstuffs				3.9	4.6	7.8	7.4	8.6
Total	40.1	50.2	38.4	30.4	28.9	28.8	27.0	27.1

Notes: (a)Only four indicated branches included in total. (b)Encouraged establishments. (c)All factory industry. (d)Materials and fuels.

Sources: Table 11.11; Stevan Kukoleća, *Industrija Jugoslavije, 1918-1938* (Belgrade, 1941), pp. 402-07.

value had dropped to 60 percent of production by 1938, as Central
European markets sagged. The export share of all Romanian manufacturing had come down from 22 percent of output in 1929 to
16–17 percent by 1938, just matching the rising Bulgarian proportion. For Yugoslavia, the export share for manufacturing recorded
similar levels for both years, higher ones if we add the one third of
Yugoslav mineral production that was exported. The manufacturing
share was also more broadly distributed among branches than
Romanian exports. Leather producers exported 20 percent of their

1938 output, paper 12 percent, metal smelting 24 percent, and cement 25 percent (the last figure had exceeded 75 percent in 1935 before the start of the country's industrial upturn). Chemical exports amounted to 29 percent of 1938 output and processed timber exports at least half, although neither branch had brought production back to more than three quarters of the 1929 level.[48]

In contrast to the general decline in overall shares of manufactured exports, the domestic shares of manufactured consumption noted in Table 12.14 increased for Bulgaria, Greece, Romania, and by inference Yugoslavia between 1929 and 1938. This process of import substitution had gotten underway after 1925, with the passage of higher tariffs, and had proceeded in the early 1930s. Depreciating or controlled currencies and import quotas had by 1935 taken the process as far as it would go before the Second World War. Balkan dependence on manufactured imports was however less in the late 1930s than it would be during the supposedly autarkic period, for the Communist states at least, of the early 1950s.

How much could import substitution alone have accounted for industrial growth? In Bulgaria's case, where the data is most reliable, the increase of domestically produced shares of manufactures from over 60 percent in 1929 to nearly 90 percent by 1934 would by itself have generated an annual increase of 8 percent in annual output, if we assume a constant level of domestic consumption. The lesser increase in the Greek domestic share for 1928–33 would have generated growth of 6 percent a year, and the Romanian rise from 65 to 80 percent would have been a 3½ percent increment. That actual growth in all three countries was lower tells us that "market space," the total domestic consumption of manufactures had not been constant but fell. Under the combined financial and marketing constraints of the Depression, we could hardly expect otherwise.

The greater actual growth after 1934, we must not forget, took place without benefit of any significant increase in the domestic share of aggregate consumption of manufactures. Several important distinctions may nonetheless be made between the most rapidly growing branches of Bulgarian industry. Table 12.16 indicates that less import substitution was achieved among industrial inputs than outputs. Virtually none took place for the pulp imported to supply the paper production whose output was the fastest growing, to the growing exclusion of imported paper. Leather manufacture was also growing faster than the Bulgarian average. Yet the imported share of hides was not reduced as output rose, mainly because of the poor quality of domestic hides.[49]

Textiles deserve special emphasis because of inputs' better showing. They were also a much larger branch, accounting for 34 percent of state-encouraged manufacturing (energy excluded) by 1937. Neither paper nor leather exceeded 5 percent. Alexander Gerschenkron has dismissed rising textile output because it relied, like leather, on imported inputs.[50] His argument is called into serious question by imports' decline from 87 to 53 percent of textile inputs for 1932–38, as noted in Table 12.17. This table provides a more complete picture of what was happening. Bulgarian cotton spinning led the way with a ninefold increase in real value from 1929 to 1938. The country's imports of cotton cloth dropped from 11–14 to 4 percent in the process. Cotton yarn climbed from 9 to nearly 14 percent of total imports from 1926 to 1934 but then fell back to half that figure by 1938. Even cotton fiber imports, which had jumped from 3 to 14 percent for 1926–34, turned sharply downward thereafter.

The Greek textiles, unlike those of Romania and Yugoslavia, also achieved the same sort of substitution for imported yarn as well as cloth. (Table 12.17 unfortunately does not include secondary imports such as dyes and machinery.) Only in Greece, moreover, did textiles, most especially cotton yarn and cloth, comprise a sector almost as large as the Bulgarian one (30 percent of 1938 output). Greece enjoyed a geographic location far enough south to permit widespread cultivation of cotton. Yugoslavia had only Macedonia; Romania lacked a genuinely suitable region. Both countries' imports of cotton fiber rose throughout the decade, while Greece's held steady at a low level. Proportionally more cotton manufacture and cultivation thus seem to have been crucial to the faster rising indices of Bulgarian and Greek industrial production during the 1930s. Their domestic production furnished more than the 80 percent share of the consumption of all textiles that the Romanian and Yugoslav branches did.

Textiles' share of total imports nonetheless declined from their previously high fraction for Romania as well as Bulgaria. Both came down by half or more from 1928 to 1938. The Greek share had been low to begin with and barely decreased. Only Yugoslavia devoted a higher share of its total imports to textiles by 1938 than in 1928.

Metal and machine imports, on the other hand, placed a growing strain on the balance of trade and payments in all four countries. The share of these goods in total imports had risen roughly twice as fast for Bulgaria and Romania, where they were higher to begin with, than in Greece and Yugoslavia. Between 1928 and 1938 their import share had vaulted past that of textiles everywhere. By 1938 metals and machinery accounted for half of Bulgarian import value and over half of the Romanian.

The domestic consumption of metal products was surprisingly similar in all four countries. The per capita consumption of steel, for

TABLE 12.17

PRODUCTION AND IMPORTS OF TEXTILES[a], 1926-39

Country and Year	Cotton Cloth Supply Total (1000 tons)	Cotton Cloth Supply Domestic Percent	Imports (1000 tons) Cotton Fiber	Imports Cotton Yarn	Imports Cotton Cloth	Imports Wool Fiber	Imports Wool Yarn	Imports Wool Cloth	Production (1000 tons) Cotton Fiber	Production Cotton Yarn	Production Cotton Cloth	Production Wool Fiber	Production Wool Yarn	Production Wool Cloth
Bulgaria														
1926	4.2	36	0.8	4.9	2.8	1.2	0.2	0.3	0.5			11.5		0.4
1927			1.4	7.0	2.7	1.4	0.3	0.3	0.8		0.7			0.5
1928			1.7	7.1	2.4	1.7	0.3	0.2	0.7		1.1		0.4	0.6[b]
1929			1.9	6.6	0.6				0.9			9.6	0.9	
1930			2.7	4.2	0.5	1.2	0.3	0.1	0.8	1.3	(100)[b]	8.9	0.6	(100)[b]
1931			3.1	7.1	0.8	2.2	0.6		0.9	2.2	(94)	9.0	0.6	(95)
1932			3.8	8.1	0.8	2.4	0.7		1.3	2.7	(97)	9.4	0.5	(95)
1933			4.8	3.7	0.4	1.2	0.3		2.4	3.1	(133)	9.5	0.4	(134)
1934			7.2	2.9	0.6	1.2	0.4		4.2	4.5	(119)	9.7	0.3	(147)
1935			6.3	2.9	0.2					6.5	(115)	9.6	0.5	(124)
1936			8.3	1.9	0.4				6.7	6.2	(106)	9.3	0.6	(135)
1937			10.4	2.0	0.4				10.2	8.8	(155)	9.5		(154)
1938			12.0	1.6	0.8				6.9	10.1		9.6		
1939	5.1	82	9.6	1.1	1.0				5.7	11.5	4.1	10.0	0.8	1.5
Greece														
1926	6.4	23	2.4	0.9	4.9	1.0	1.3		3.9			7.3		0.8
1927	8.8	19	3.7	0.8	7.1	1.1	1.5		2.7	7.7	1.5	7.9		0.9
1928	7.8	26	3.4	0.7	5.8	1.3	1.4		3.3	8.1	1.7			1.1
1929									3.3	7.9	2.0	4.6		0.9
1930	7.8	35	5.9	0.7	5.1	1.3	1.3		3.5	8.2	2.3	5.2	0.5	1.2
1931	7.7	38	10.2	0.8	4.8	1.2	1.0		3.0	9.4	2.7	6.6	0.4	1.1
1932	5.9	49	7.3	0.7	3.0	1.0	0.5		4.9	10.1	2.9	6.7	0.5	1.1
1933	6.1	51	7.6	0.7	3.0	1.5	0.4		10.0	10.1	3.1	7.3	0.6	1.5
1934	6.7	52	7.3	0.7	3.2	1.5	0.5		11.3	11.1	3.5	7.6	0.7	1.6
1935	7.4	45	7.1	0.8	4.1	1.5	0.5		14.7	14.7	3.3	7.9	0.7	1.9
1936	7.6	43	4.1	0.8	4.3	1.6	0.5		15.8	13.5	3.3	8.3	1.1	2.2
1937	6.9	49	2.9	0.8	3.5	1.5	0.5		20.3	15.2	3.4	8.4	0.9	2.2
1938	6.7	49	2.5	0.7	3.4	1.6	0.4		15.7	15.8	3.3	8.0	0.8	2.0
1939			1.5						15.5	17.1	4.8	7.8	1.8	2.0

TABLE 12.17 (continued)

Country and Year	Cotton Cloth Supply Total (1000 tons)	Domestic Percent-	Imports (1000 tons) Cotton Fiber	Cotton Yarn	Cotton Cloth	Wool Fiber	Wool Yarn	Wool Cloth	Production (1000 tons) Cotton Fiber	Cotton Yarn	Cotton Cloth	Wool Fiber	Wool Yarn	Wool Cloth
Romania														
1926	22.1	19	3.3	13.0	17.9		1.7	1.4		2.6	4.2	24.1	5.8	7.3
1927										2.3	5.5	24.9	6.7	6.9
1928[c]	19.1	47	(3.3)	(14.9)	(10.2)		2.5	0.5		2.7	8.9	24.2	4.6	5.7
1929	18.6	53	3.3	24.0	8.8		2.0	0.3		3.2	9.8	23.8	3.4	5.0
1930	17.9	64	3.0	25.2	6.5		1.8	0.1		3.1	11.4	24.7	3.1	1.6
1931	15.4	69	3.7	22.4	4.7		2.0	0.1		2.9	10.7	24.6	2.1	4.1
1932	17.3	76	5.0	28.7	4.1	1.1	3.1	0.1	0.2	3.5	13.2	24.0	4.0	5.0
1933	20.8	84	5.7	30.0	3.3		3.2	0.1	0.4	3.5	17.5	24.0	4.8	6.1
1934[c]			(6.0)	28.4	2.8			0.1	0.2	4.9	19.1	24.0	5.5	5.8
1935[c]			(9.4)	(19.7)	(1.3)				0.4			23.6		
1936			16.7	22.9	1.0		2.2	0.0	1.0			23.6		
1937	19.7	92	20.3	26.9	1.5		2.6	0.2	1.3	14.5	18.2	23.6	7.4	3.6
1938				14.0	0.8		1.3	0.1	1.4	16.5		24.7	7.0	
1939										16.5		25.5		
Yugoslavia														
1926	20.4		6.9	7.6	12.8	3.8	0.7	3.0	0.1			13.0		
1927		31	7.0	10.6	14.1	3.7	1.0	2.7	0.1		6.3			2.0
1928			7.0	10.8	11.4		1.2	2.4	0.2			12.2		
1929									0.2			12.2		
1930			8.8	13.1	10.2	3.6	1.5	2.2	0.1			12.6		
1931									0.2			13.4		
1932									0.1			13.5		
1933			10.6	12.9	3.0	2.2	1.1	0.8	0.1			13.7		
1934									0.3			12.5		
1935									0.3			14.4		
1936			16.8	12.5	2.7	4.5	1.5	1.2	0.7			14.9		
1937			20.8	18.3	4.1	3.2	1.8	1.6	1.1			15.2		
1938			21.6	14.0	2.6	4.8	1.5	1.2	2.1			15.3		
1939	16.0	84	18.1	12.2	2.6	3.7	1.8	1.4	1.8	18.9	13.4		6.2	3.3

instance, was virtually the same for Bulgaria and Romania in 1938, just 4 percent less for Greece, and 13 percent less for Yugoslavia.[51] This similarity obscures the fact that in absolute terms the much larger Romanian and Yugoslav states had much larger metal and machinery sectors. They accounted not only for larger shares of manufactured output than in Bulgaria and Greece but also greater shares of domestic consumption. The Romanian sectors produced the highest shares of their own inputs and generally outperformed their Yugoslav counterparts until the late 1930s. The Romanian state's essential role on the demand side of this growth may be seen in its reported purchase of 70 percent of machinery production in 1938.[52] Its role on the supply side must now be examined.

State Supervision and Investment

A widely held assumption dating from Marx's own writings is that bad times reduce the number of private capitalist enterprises and concentrate the economic power of those remaining. The evolution of foreign investment in Southeastern Europe during the 1930s will generally bear out this assumption. Yet for commercial and central banking, as we have already seen, the noteworthy concentration that occurred took place under direct or indirect state control. For industry, native Marxist scholarship continues to assume that private concentration was the most important single tendency during this decade.[53] Table 12.18 indicates that the number of industrial enterprises did not fall except for state-encouraged Bulgarian industry. The Yugoslav number rose by one third. Joint-stock numbers grew only for Bulgaria. They nearly doubled for 1929–39 to approach the Yugoslav total. Nor did average size in terms of labor or horsepower rise significantly from 1929 to 1938, with the exception of workers per Romanian and state-encouraged Bulgarian enterprise. Evidence that the four or five largest firms accounted for large and increasing shares of total branch output and employment would of course over-

---

Notes: (a)Cotton cloth converted from square meters to metric tons at one ton equals 8,300 sq. meters; wool cloth converted at one ton equals 3,500 sq. meters. (b)Production indices. (c)Romanian cotton imports for 1928 and 1935 from Madgearu differ slightly from League of Nations' data.

Sources: Tables 12.9 and 12.14: *Statisticheski godishnik na Bulgarskoto Tsarstvo, 1933* (Sofia, 1933), pp. 254-57; *1940* (Sofia, 1940), pp. 522-25, 577; Leo Pasvolsky, *Bulgaria's Economic Position* (Washington: The Brookings Institution, 1930), p. 215; V. N. Madgearu, *Evoluția economiei românești* (Bucharest, 1940), p. 276; N. Arcadian, *Industrializarea României* (Bucharest, 1936), p. 274; *Enciclopedia României*, Vol. III (Bucharest, 1943), pp. 370, 525, 973; M. F. Iovanelli, *Industria românească, 1934-1938* (Bucharest, 1975), pp. 165-67; *Anuarul statistic al României, 1939-1940* (Bucharest, 1940), p. 413; Ch. Evelpidi, *Les états balkaniques* (Paris, 1930), pp. 277-78; B. R. Mitchell, *European Historical Statistics, 1750-1970* (New York: Columbia University Press, 1975), pp. 437-41; W. S. Woytinsky and E. S. Woytinsky, *World Population and Production* (New York: The Twentieth Century Fund, 1953), pp. 1068-70, 1084-85; *Statistikē epetēris tēs Ellados, 1954* (Athens, 1955), p. 88; League of Nations, *World Production and Prices, 1936/37* (Geneva, 1937), pp. 122-27; *Statistički godišnjak Kr. Jugoslavije, 1938-1939* (Belgrade, 1939), pp. 262-63; *1940* (Belgrade, 1940), p. 244; *1936* (Belgrade, 1937), p. 241.

turn our conclusion, but such data have yet to be collected, if they are available at all.

A series of cartels generally failed to prevent an increase in the number of enterprises or to stop the introduction of greater state supervision of industry. Since their appearance in Central Europe after the stock market crash of 1873, these "children of bad times" had typically contrived to preserve the existing number of enterprises in the particular cartel's branch of industry. They had traded political passivity toward the state for independence from economic regulation. Trusts and large corporations like the Krupp works in Germany opposed them precisely because they hindered genuine concentration.[54] The majority set up in Southeastern Europe during the interwar period were price cartels, sometimes setting other conditions of sale as well. Few attempted and fewer succeeded in fixing production quotas for their members as the German variety had come to do.

The Bulgarian list of sixty five cartels formed during the entire period 1919–1944 was shorter than either the Romanian or Yugoslav totals. A majority continued to last for no more than one or two years. At any one time, member firms probably accounted for much less than the one quarter of industrial production laid to 94 Romanian cartels and the 12 percent to 79 in Yugoslavia in 1938. The Bulgarian sugar and tobacco cartels were exceptional, as noted in Chapter 11. They had controlled a majority of production continuously since 1921. More typical were the two abortive cartels set up for cotton textiles in the mid-1930s. Both broke apart in less than a year because the largest member reserved itself too large a sales quota for the others to tolerate.[55] Smaller firms shied away from joining with larger firms for just this reason.

Table 12.17 suggests that incorporation advanced no more than cartellization. Neither process had made much progress during the late 1920s (see Chapter 11). Only the Romanian joint-stock firms among industrial enterprises rose slightly during the 1930s.

Bulgaria's Agrarian regime of 1931 introduced state supervision of cartels early. Its legislation reluctantly recognized present and future cartels in return for their registration with and control by the Ministry of Trade and Industry. By 1933 state permits were required for any new firms to operate in a "saturated industry," whether it belonged to a private cartel or not.

State price controls, and possibly incorporation, proved more instrumental than cartels in the striking growth of textile production. This was a "saturated industry" that was almost 90 percent state-encouraged. Now prices for textile products were put under virtual state control. So were prices for necessary inputs. Coal already came

TABLE 12.18
NUMBER AND SIZE OF MANUFACTURING ESTABLISHMENTS, 1929-39

Bulgaria

| | Number of Encouraged Establishments | | | | | | Number of Factory Establishments | | | | | |
| | 1929 | | 1931 | | 1937 | | 1931 | | 1937 | | 1938 | |
	(a)	(b)	(a)	(b)	(a)	(b)	(a)	(b)	(a)	(b)	(a)	(b)
Metals and machinery	136	127	122	121	103	103	132	131	131	131	144	144
Chemicals	104	86	111	105	96	96	120	114	271	264	325	323
Non-wood building materials	101	88	99	99	87	86	126	126	141	141	153	153
Wood processing	48	29	62	57	46	46	90	85	142	142	223	222
Paper	4	4	4	4	4	4	14	14	15	15	19	19
Printing							30	30				
Textiles	198	171	227	218	197	194	260	251	382	379	405	502
Leather	54	46	55	55	46	45	65	65	63	62	68	68
Food and tobacco	468	355	465	443	275	269	951	862	1,740	1,729	1,861	1,853
Flour milling	313	235	313	301	157	153					897	896
Other food	155	120	152	142	118	116					739	733
Tobacco							184	127			225	224
Total	1,113	906	1,145	1,102	854	843	1,788	1,678	2,885	2,863	3,198	3,184

TABLE 12.18 (continued)

A. Encouraged Establishments

	Workers per Establishment			Horsepower per Establishment			Horsepower per Worker		
	1929	1931	1937	1929	1931	1937	1929	1931	1937
Metals and machinery	43.3	30.7	44.7	59.4	68.8	91.3	1.37	2.24	2.04
Chemicals	20.5	23.6	27.3	43.2	47.5	68.7	2.10	2.01	2.52
Non-wood building materials	43.6	32.0	43.9	150.7	133.6	171.1	3.46	4.17	3.90
Wood processing	40.2	29.8	24.9	63.9	43.0	73.2	1.59	1.44	2.88
Paper	84.5	107.5	243.0	378.0	607.8	2,233.0	4.47	5.65	9.19
Printing									
Textiles	95.7	73.1	125.3	104.6	96.0	160.8	1.09	1.31	1.28
Leather	22.4	17.3	19.2	66.4	65.7	78.6	2.97	3.80	4.09
Food and Tobacco	20.0	14.2	19.0	131.0	120.8	165.8	6.53	8.51	8.71
Flour milling	11.7	8.5	9.4	97.1	91.7	116.3	8.30	10.83	12.34
Other food	36.4	26.4	31.6	197.3	182.4	230.3	5.41	6.92	7.28
Tobacco									
Total	41.1	31.5	51.5	105.2	100.0	144.9	2.57	3.18	2.82

B. Factory Establishments

	Workers per Establishment			Horsepower per Establishment			Horsepower per Worker		
	1931	1937	1938	1931	1937	1938	1931	1937	1938
Metals and machinery	29.2	43.4	45.1	65.2	85.7	77.6	2.24	1.97	1.72
Chemicals	23.2	15.2	14.8	46.0	31.7	31.5	1.98	2.08	2.13
Non-wood building materials	28.0	35.1	34.2	112.1	114.7	110.0	4.00	3.26	3.22
Wood processing	25.7	19.3	15.5	41.8	46.1	36.6	1.30	2.39	2.36
Paper	66.7	112.3	90.5	209.9	687.7	578.6	3.15	6.12	6.39
Printing	32.2			35.8			1.11		
Textiles	65.4	81.5	76.2	87.7	93.9	97.4	1.34	1.15	1.28
Leather	18.1	21.8	20.7	58.9	64.7	64.2	3.25	2.96	3.09
Food and Tobacco	26.6	22.1	20.2	84.2	53.0	52.6	3.17	2.40	2.60
Flour milling			6.0			67.0			11.24
Other food			8.7			49.0			5.66
Tobacco	123.8		115.0	12.9		6.5	0.10		0.06
Total	32.5	31.3	28.6	79.8	64.2	62.3	2.45	2.05	2.18

TABLE 12.18 (continued)

	Number of Establishments		Employees per Establishment		Horsepower per Establishment		Horsepower per Worker	
	1929	1938	1929	1938	1929	1938	1929	1938
Romania								
Metals and machinery	460	397	89.3	136.0	188.7	390.7	2.11	2.87
Chemicals	248	397	53.9	71.3	133.3	461.9	2.47	6.48
Petroleum refining	36		178.9		239.1		1.34	
Other	212		60.4		286.4		4.74	
Non-wood building materials	363	331	52.4	67.8	154.7	167.5	2.95	2.70
Wood processing	787	713	52.9	60.8	93.8	89.9	1.77	1.48
Paper	19		270.9		1,430.9		5.28	
Printing	128		43.1		21.8		0.50	
Textiles	516	640	69.7	115.7	78.3	124.3	1.12	1.07
Leather	211	158	37.6	84.6	71.6	84.9	1.90	1.00
Food	1,004	974	25.5	39.5	125.8	140.7	4.93	3.57
Flour milling	266		21.8		219.7		10.08	
Other	738		26.9		92.0		3.41	
Total	3,736	3,767	53.9	76.7	133.3		2.47	2.58
	1928	1938	1928	1938	1928	1938	1928	1938
Yugoslavia								
Metals and machinery	193	267	251.9	227.8	228.5	138.2	0.91	0.83
Chemicals	157	211	119.8	74.9	185.9	360.7	1.55	4.82
Non-wood building materials	251	299	113.1	110.5	140.3	127.3	1.24	1.15
Wood processing	452	570	108.0	99.1	99.7	93.0	0.92	0.94
Paper	37	51	115.6	110.1	327.6	265.4	2.83	2.41
Printing	51	66	116.3	97.3	48.3	42.5	0.42	0.44
Textiles	269	453	221.0	171.7	121.7	90.7	0.55	0.53
Leather	87	116	149.5	142.6	96.0	91.2	0.64	0.64
Food	1,061	1,320	30.0	35.9	85.4	79.9	2.37	2.23
Total	2,558	3,373	104.0	94.8	282.6	116.0	2.72	1.22

Notes: (a)Number in existence. (b)Number reporting data.

Sources: *Statisticheski godishnik na Bulgarskoto Tsarstvo, 1933* (Sofia, 1933), pp. 188-89; *1940* (Sofia, 1940), pp. 376-413; *Anuarul statistic al României, 1939-1940* (Bucharest, 1940), pp. 478-93; Stevan Kukoleča, *Industrija Jugoslavije, 1918-1938* (Belgrade, 1941), pp. 100, 112, 165.

TABLE 12.19
JOINT STOCK COMPANIES, 1929-39

Number of Limited or Joint Stock Companies (end of year)[a]

	1929	1930	1931	1932	1933	1934	1935	1936	1937	1938	1939
Bulgaria[b]											
Industrial	328	353	397	368	387	410	422	456	497	546	599
Banking	172	164	154	129	119	87	105	102	67	45	42
Insurance	17	16	16	21	21	20	19	21	24	24	23
Commerce	210	238	283	259	297	353	412	464	431	519	634
Other	12	14	16	18	22	25	29	29	30	31	37
Total	739	785	866	795	846	895	987	1,072	1,049	1,165	1,335
Romania[c]											
Industrial	1,078	1,063	1,054	1,049	1,079	1,136	1,214	1,038	1,145	1,160	(941)
Banking	1,097	1,102	1,037	953	893	873	920	823	841	753	(491)
Insurance	31	25	27	27	25	24	22	21	20	21	(19)
Commerce	418	448	463	514	548	661	831	794	934	857	(755)
Other	38	44	39	46	47	50	30	53	55	66	(55)
Total	2,662	2,682	2,620	2,589	2,582	2,744	3,017	2,729	2,995	2,857	(2,261)
Yugoslavia[d]											
Industrial	637	659	667	697	667	749	799	729	692	626	
Banking			639	632	620	615	610	610			
Insurance											
Commerce			186	195	154	227	244	237	148	176	
Other			52	58	59	69	75	67	57	61	
Total			1,544	1,582	1,500	1,660	1,728	1,643			

TABLE 12.19 (continued)

Joint Stock Company Formations

Year	Formations								Liquidations	
	Mining Manufacturing Construction Utilities		Banking Insurance		Other		Total			
	BULGARIA	GREECE	BULGARIA	GREECE	BULGARIA	GREECE	BULGARIA	GREECE	BULGARIA	GREECE
1929	39	41	28	2	35	42	102	85	27	30
1930	37	34	5	2	42	31	54	83	38	23
1931	54	26	1	0	57	42	112	68	31	22
1932	39	18	0	0	58	13	98	31	32	20
1933	33	32	0	0	54	37	87	69	36	15
1934	33	56	2	0	64	59	99	115	51	23
1935	32	59	2	2	81	84	115	143	34	19
1936	48	75	0	2	68	74	116	151	33	12
1937	45	60	1	0	87	64	133	126	47	31
1938	45	59	0		97	43	142	102	56	37
1939	51		0		98		149		34	
Total 1931–8	329	385	6	4	766	416	902	805	320	179

Notes: (a)Further definitions are given in Table 11.13. (b)Bulgarian numbers for end of years and beginning of years differ; table data are for end of years. (c)Data for 1939 includes companies in territories lost in 1940. (d)Includes companies for which balances were unreported because they were in liquidation or had not operated a full year.

Sources: Tables 11.13 and 12.24; *Statistikē epetēris tēs Ellados, 1934* (Athens, 1935), p. 130; *1939* (Athens, 1940), p. 293.

from state mines. Duty-free imports, especially of cotton yarn and
fiber, had helped swell the duty-free share of total imports from 18 to
37 percent between 1927 and 1932. New tariff regulations in 1933
introduced ad valorem rates of 10–60 percent on most industrial inputs. These new rates reportedly allowed spinning plants to operate
at a profit without feeling the need to join a cartel in search of higher
prices. Further industrial legislation presented to the Council of
Ministers that same year but not implemented until 1936 empowered
the Ministry of Trade and Industry to fix all prices of raw materials,
imported or domestic.[56] Lower domestic prices pressed domestic cotton fiber and yarn on the textile industry. The tremendous growth of
cotton spinning during the 1930s suggests but does not prove that
quality was also improving. Only a sharp upturn in textile exports
would have resolved all doubt. They remained minuscule in a bad
world market.

Textile production led by cotton yarn and woolen cloth was also
the largest branch of Greek industry. The quality of locally grown
cotton reportedly improved. Unlike Bulgaria, the production of cotton cloth grew as rapidly as that of yarn in the 1930s. Despite a certain amount of sales to its Balkan neighbors, combined textile exports
were still just 2 percent of the total exports. Joint-stock enterprises
now manufactured the great majority of both countries' cotton goods.

Cartels were generally less in evidence for Greece. No legislation
appeared to register or regulate them as elsewhere in the area. The
industrial law of 1922 (see Chapter 11) stayed on the books unchanged. Its provisions plus the growing need for urban housing of
the Anatolian refugees prompted the greater production of construction materials during the decade. By 1937 Greece had become self-
sufficient in cement. Yet all such materials accounted for just 4 percent of industrial output in 1938. Chemical production became the
other large branch of manufacturing with 24 percent. It grew largely
as a result of the aforementioned Kanelopoulos enterprise in Piraeus.
The firm's joint-stock capital now reached one billion drachmae. Its
exports of soap and fertilizer to the Near East prospered, but such
goods never passed one percent of total exports. For the domestic
market, textile production did receive the same sort of added tariff
protection as Bulgaria's for outputs and inputs in the early 1930s.
According to anti-protectionist British accounts of the period, the increased cost of raw and semi-finished materials prompted some revival of finished textile imports from Germany by 1937.[57] Yet their
purchase with overvalued Reichsmarks earned from Greek tobacco
exports calls into question the extent to which such imports were a
response to relative domestic prices.

Romanian industry seems to have been the most heavily cartellized in Southeastern Europe. State supervision had also appeared earlier. Legislation in 1918 had placed manufacturers of sugar, paper, glass, and several daily necessities into obligatory cartels. The Ministry of Industry and Commerce fixed their prices. A 1924 law established a cartel for domestic sales of oil. Further regulations in 1937 required that all cartels register with the same ministry and gave it the right to set minimum prices for their inputs and maximum ones for their outputs. The 94 cartels registered that year grew to 183 by 1939, including 49 controlling production itself. Cartels controlled 23 percent of industrial output and 46 percent of capital in 1937. They were concentrated in four branches of industry: food (35 percent of output), paper (41 percent), metallurgy (41 percent) and construction materials (47 percent).[58] The surging manufacture of cotton yarn was however not involved. The cartellized share of textile output was reckoned at just 6 percent.[59]

Metallurgy was the one branch of the four that was, like textiles, both large and rapidly growing (see Table 12.13 and 12.16). The two largest enterprises were at Reşiţa and Hunedoara in Transylvania, the latter state owned. They had combined to form the Socomet cartel in 1926. Reconstituted in 1931, this cartel controlled virtually all of the country's iron and steel manufacture. Production grew with state support for rearmament after 1936, particularly at the private works and the state-financed Concordia munitions plant between Bucharest and Braşov. Direct subsidies pushed the military share of the state budget to 32 percent by 1937 and helped introduce the most modern techniques and equipment, under a 1936 law promoting new types of production. This successful expansion of heavy industry could not prevent the rising proportions of metal and machine imports recorded in Table 12.14. From 1936 forward, imported metal tonnage almost matched the combined Bulgarian, Greek, and Yugoslav totals. A British geographer has recently echoed a notion from a German study made in 1928: the demand for such imports would have justified new smelting capacity (now in place at Galaţi) on the eastern Danube.[60] Russian ore was of course unacceptable for political reasons. Related military considerations made Galaţi a risky location before the Second World War.

Rhetoric from several Romanian leaders, most prominently the economist Mihail Manoilescu, argued that the state should now assume the direction of overall industrial development.[61] Outside of the drive for rearmament, however, this direction of production did not materialize. Luxury imports were not noticeably restricted. A separate Ministry for the National Economy did not begin operations until 1939. The Case Autonome a Monopolurilor had been set up in 1929 to administer the various state monopolies, led by tobacco, sep-

arately from the state budget. But their net revenues continued to
flow directly into state expenses, accounting for 26 percent of the
total in 1937 versus 23 percent in 1929. Investment was neglected.
Pricing policy still followed the long-standing rule of maximizing
short-term revenues at the expense of developing the long-term market. The declining returns from regular tax revenue noted in Table
12.20 pushed the Romanian government to price its tobacco and
other monopoly products by the same formula that it had imposed on
the private sugar cartel. State indirect taxes on these goods were kept
at the same specific, i.e., absolute, level despite the Depression and
general price decline. Their share of tax revenue rose but net profits
dropped to a few percent of capital and production. Domestic consumption fell to one half the 1929 level by 1934.[62] On the side of
expenditures, economic investment dropped below that of its Balkan
neighbors proportionally, if we exclude defense spending. Only the
increase in the budgetary share for education past 20 percent
emerges from Table 12.20 as a positive Romanian development.

The Yugoslav budget relied more heavily than the others on state
industries and monopolies. Together they took a larger share of expenses (16 percent) than anywhere else and provided 49 percent of
budget revenues for 1937–38. State enterprises accounted for 15 percent of the country's industrial capital in 1938. This fraction approached the 22 percent under cartels. They had come under control
of the Ministry of Commerce and Industry by late 1935. Over four
fifths of the cartels' capital and output was concentrated in metallurgical, chemical, and food production.[63] The first two were dependent
by the same fraction on foreign capital. Firms processing food and
drink grew in number but struggled through the 1930s. Table 12.16
records a decline in their average employment and mechanical
horsepower. Restricting growth more than cartel membership were
stiffer tax levels than in the Romanian case. They included more than
levies to shore up the state budget. A series of surtaxes up to 40
percent and sales taxes or *trošarina*, were added to close municipal
deficits. Sugar, beer, and flour production used about half of available capacity. British consular reports blamed these surtaxes more
than any other factor.[64] To make matters worse, the burden of local
taxes was set unevenly by the central government in Belgrade to
favor the Serbian areas in the east. The maximum rates imposed on
Zagreb, when added to the Croatian capital's high rents and wages,
were reportedly responsible for the measurable movement eastward,
although still not to Belgrade, of industrial firms in several branches
by the period 1934–38.[65]

The same fiscal motivation dominated the operation of state
enterprises and monopolies, except again where rearmament was

TABLE 12.20

DISTRIBUTION OF STATE EXPENDITURES, 1929-38[a]
(percent)

Country and Year	Economic[b]	Education[c]	Public Welfare[d]	Military[e]	Public Order[f]	Debt Service[g]	Total[a]	Labor Share	Railroads[a]	Value of Total[i]
Bulgaria[g]										
1929-30	17.9	14.1	2.1	17.3	15.0	32.9	100.0		17.0	6,719
1930-31	16.7	14.6	1.9	17.5	14.6	34.8	100.0	(39.4)	19.7	6,375
1935					18.1	30.4				
1935	10.8	14.4	2.9	23.4	10.5	38.0	100.0	43.6	22.1	5,498
1937					14.1	24.1				
1937	13.6	12.6	2.6	32.9	8.5	29.7	100.0	35.9	22.8	7,083
1938					11.4	21.2				
1938	15.4	14.0	2.9	35.0	6.2	26.4	100.0	35.9	30.2	7,073
Greece[g]										
1929-30	7.2	4.5	4.4	11.5	72.3		100.0		3.1	19,354
1930-31	12.0	8.4	5.4	15.8	31.5	26.1	100.0		5.3	12,180
1934-35	15.7	8.7	6.2	13.8	36.2	14.3	100.0		5.3	10,836
1937-38	14.5	5.9	7.0	30.5	22.7	19.5	100.0		4.3	16,375
1938-39	15.6	6.5	7.2	24.6	46.0		100.0			15,295
Romania[e]										
1929	12.2	12.4	7.0	20.1	31.6	15.5	100.0	43.7	36.0	39,085
1930	9.4	16.8	3.8	21.4	32.8	15.7	100.0	68.9	31.8	39,935
1934-35	10.1	16.9	3.7	20.3	40.0	9.0	100.0		24.6	25,447
1934-35	9.7	16.3	3.5	23.2	38.6	8.6	100.0		33.3	26,415
1937-38	7.9	21.7	3.8	22.0	31.6	12.9	100.0		39.7	28,610
1937-38	6.9	18.9	3.3	32.0	27.5	11.3	100.0		34.6	32,806
1938-39	7.1	20.8	3.2	25.4	31.0	12.4	100.0	60.0	43.4	31,637
1938-39	6.0	17.8	2.7	36.2	26.6	10.6	100.0		37.1	36,988
Yugoslavia[h]										
1929-30	17.6	10.9	2.8	28.1	30.0	10.6	100.0		32.7	8,218
1930-31	17.1	9.8	3.1	27.7	29.7	12.6	100.0		31.3	8,723
1934-35	15.0	13.4	3.1	27.4	30.0	11.0	100.0	54.8	31.9	6,206
1937-38	16.2	11.3	3.9	31.4	25.5	12.6	100.0	45.9	27.6	7,697
1938-39	(18.3)	(10.8)	(2.7)	(31.0)	(25.1)	(15.4)	100.0	42.5	(25.9)	(9,446)

concerned. No comprehensive industrial law or one simply to monitor imports was passed during the 1930s. The principal agent for state economic policy and also for management of the monopolies remained the Ministry of Finance. Its overriding aim was to maximize tax revenue, even under the Stojadinović regime of 1935–38 with all its pronouncements about balanced growth and industrial exports.[66]

The states' one clear-cut contribution to industrial development during the Depression was continuing attention to higher education and technical training. Table 12.21 points to the major interwar advances made in this regard by all the states of Southeastern Europe. Primary pupils per thousand of population made good gains everywhere by 1930. Bulgaria kept its lead in secondary pupils and also in higher education. All four countries boosted these latter averages severalfold. Nor were the majority lawyers, as is sometimes assumed. The proportion of these students engaged in some form of technical training (for engineering, commerce, agriculture, medicine, and science) rose during the 1930s to approach half for Romania and Greece and to 57 percent for Bulgaria. Yugoslavia alone lagged somewhat behind here, as it also did in primary pupils and in the share of the state budget spent for education. Those students who could manage to survive the Second World War (and again, the Yugoslav share would be the lowest) constituted valuable human capital that must have contributed to the rapid industrial growth of the 1950s, before a new generation could be trained.

The breakdown of public employment in Table 12.22 suggests that the Bulgarian educational system was still the area's largest in terms of teachers and other staff per capita. Here the Yugoslav system had at least closed the gap separating it from the Greek and Romanian

---

Notes: (a)In order to increase comparability, expenditures distributed as "total" include those for post, telegraph and telephone and exclude those for railroads. Railroad expenditures, compared with totals, include all railroad expenditures for Greece, but only expenditures for state railroads for the other countries. (b)Includes ministries of commerce, industry, labor, agriculture, public works, state domains and communications. (c)Includes religion. (d)Includes health, public assistance and pensions, but financing of the latter was often unclear. (e)In Romania, military was financed from both ordinary and special budgets in 1934/35 and after. For these years, the first line includes only ordinary military budgets, while the second line includes both ordinary and special budgets. (f)Includes ministries of interior, justice, finance (except for debt service), foreign affairs and budgets for royal courts and legislative branches. (g)From about 1932 forward not all debt service appropriations were paid. The unpaid amounts are given precisely only for Bulgaria where they were treated as budget income in the next year. The first line for Bulgaria reduces debt service by the untransferred portion. Greek debt service was not shown separately from expenditures of the ministry of finance. (h)For Yugoslavia in 1938/39 only budget commitments and not actual expenditures are given. (i)Million domestic currency units.

Sources: *Statisticheski godishnik na Bulgarskoto Tsarstvo, 1940* (Sofia, 1940), pp. 629, 640-41; *Statistikē epetēris tēs Ellados, 1930* (Athens 1932), p. 377; *1935* (Athens, 1936), p. 335; *1938* (Athens, 1939), pp. 245, 332; *1939* (Athens, 1940), pp. 239, 321, 483; M. Maievschi, *Contribuţii la istoria finanţelor publice ale României* (Bucharest, 1957), pp. 52-53, 216-19, 252-53; *Anuarul statistic al României, 1930* (Bucharest, 1932), pp. 148-49, 178; *1939-1940* (Bucharest, 1940), pp. 532, 566; *Enciclopedia României*, Vol. IV (Bucharest, 1943), p. 1002; *Statistički godišnjak Kr. Jugoslavije, 1929* (Belgrade, 1931), pp. 482-87; *1930* (Belgrade, 1932), p. 457; *1934-1935* (Belgrade, 1935), pp. 130, 465; *1937* (Belgrade, 1938), pp. 401, 453; *1938-1939* (Belgrade, 1939), p. 484; *1940* (Belgrade, 1940), pp. 200, 218.

levels during the course of the 1930s. Overall levels of public employment and the "other" category that we may take as an approximation of the state bureaucracy had continued to rise faster than population during the decade everywhere but Romania. The Romanian decline even in absolute terms must be balanced against a per capita aggregate that was initially the largest. In 1938–39, the Romanian total of 340,000 public employees was still larger than a labor force of 290,000 in manufacturing.

Foreign Investment, Rearmament, and Nazi Penetration

Southeastern Europe's experience with foreign investment during the 1930s must not be oversimplified. British and French investors

TABLE 12.21
GROWTH OF PUBLIC EDUCATION AND TECHNICAL TRAINING, 1910-38

	BULGARIA[a]	GREECE	ROMANIA[b]	YUGOSLAVIA[c]
A. Total Enrollments				
Primary (1000)				
1910-11	506	454	260	587	412
1920-21	649	560		1,516	908
1930-31	783	656	772	2,111	1,185
1937-38	956	662	985	2,491	1,393
Secondary (1000)				
1910-12[d]	36	88		31	14
1921-22	62	151		155	150
1930-31	70	197	100	190	189
1937-38	121	414	132	208	246
Higher (number)				
1911-12[e]	1,508	1,508	779	4,817	780
1923-24[f]	4,423	6,069		20,363	11,223
1930-31	6,972	8,688	8,466	30,369	14,693
1937-38	8,192	10,528	11,140	30,771	16,207
B. Percentage of Enrollments in Technical and Scientific Education[i]				
Secondary				
1910-21[d]	19.2	7.9		35.7	
1921-22	15.1	6.2		13.0	31.0
1930-31	39.9	14.2	30.4	38.5	39.9
1937-38	37.5	10.9	38.9	35.9	31.3
Higher				
1911-12[e]	15.1	15.1	37.4	33.1	
1923-24[f]	33.7	48.2		39.3	48.9
1930-31	36.3	47.0	45.3	37.4	38.4
1937-38	47.9	57.3	47.3	49.4	40.2

TABLE 12.21 (continued)

	BULGARIA[a]		GREECE		ROMANIA[b]		YUGOSLAVIA[c]	

C. Enrollments per 1000 Population

Primary	Total Pop.^{g}	Age 5-14^g	Total Pop.	Age 5-14	Total Pop.	Age 5-14	Total Pop.	Age 5-14
1910-11	105.4	415	97.2	403	84.3	356	74.4	
1920-21	116.1	447			97.5	447	76.4	311
1930-31	114.4	515	121.3	613	118.0	593	86.0	420
1937-38	106.4	448	139.2	614	126.8		91.1	

Secondary	Total Pop.^{h}	Age 10-19^h	Total Pop.	Age 10-19	Total Pop.	Age 10-19	Total Pop.	Age 10-19
1910-12^d	8.3-20.1	38.2- 92.6			4.3	20.1	2.5	
1921-22	12.9-52.9	52.9-129.2			9.9	48.4	12.6	53.4
1930-31	12.3-60.7	60.7-169.9	15.7	75.1	10.6	54.4	13.7	80.1
1937-38	19.4-66.6	101.0-346-6	18.6	89.6	10.6		16.1	

Higher

1911-12^e	0.35		0.29		0.68		0.26	
1923-24^f	0.92-1.26				1.26		0.90	
1930-31	1.22-1.52		1.33		1.70		1.07	
1937-38	1.32-1.69		1.57		1.57		1.06	

Notes: (a)Two sets of figures are given for Bulgaria. The first set of figures for primary and secondary education assumes progymnasia are primary, as was the case following the Second World War. The second set counts progymnasia as secondary education. The first set of figures for higher education excludes enrollments in the "Free University"—Balkan Institute of the Near East. (b)Romanian figures for 1910/12 are for the Old Kingdom. Only public educational enrollments are counted in 1910/12 for primary and secondary education and in 1920/21 for primary education. (c)Yugoslav figures for 1910/12 include Serbia and Croatia-Slavonia for primary and secondary education and for higher education are Serbian data for 1906. (d)Bulgaria-1911/12; Romania and Yugoslavia-1910/11. (e)Bulgaria-1911/12; Greece-1912/13; Romania-1910/11; Yugoslavia-1906/07. (f)Bulgaria and Greece-1922/23; Romania and Yugoslavia-1923/24. (g)Based on Bulgarian enrollments excluding progymnasia as primary schools. (h)The first set of figures exclude progymnasia as secondary schools while the second set includes them. (i)Technical and scientific education includes, (1) at the secondary level, schools for commerce, industry, trade, agriculture, railroads, communications, marine and pedagogy, and, (2) at the higher level, faculties in medicine, mathematics, science, technology, agronomy, commerce, economics and architecture.

Sources: *Statisticheski godishnik na Bulgarskoto Tsarstvo. 1913-1922* (Sofia, 1924), pp. C76, C80-83; *1932* (Sofia, 1932), pp. 409-15; *1940* (Sofia, 1940), pp. 702-17; *Statistikē epetēris tēs Ellados, 1933* (Athens, 1934), p. 380; *1935* (Athens, 1936), pp. 345, 439; *1939* (Athens, 1940), pp. 341, 366; *Anuarul statistic al României, 1922* (Bucharest, 1923), pp. 287-93; *1931-1932* (Bucharest, 1933), pp. 357-65; *1933* (Bucharest, 1934), pp. 340-43; *1939-40* (Bucharest, 1940), pp. 262-74, 284-90; *Statistički godišnjak Kr. Jugoslavije, 1930* (Belgrade, 1932), pp. 306-09, 328-29; *1940* (Belgrade, 1940), pp. 336-37, 352-53; B. R. Mitchell, *European Historical Statistics, 1750-1970* (New York: Columbia University Press, 1975), pp. 761-68.

did not retreat by some prearranged signal in favor of Nazi enterprises, as native scholars suspected just after the Second World War. Nor did the German share of the area's foreign investment rise rapidly like the share of foreign trade. European investment in the area generally declined across the decade and turned up toward its end largely because of the Nazis' Balkan initiatives. Two missing links made sense of these several conflicting tendencies. First was the German absorption of Austria and Czechoslovakia in 1938–39, Balkan investments included. Second was the effort of native governments to assure their own security and sovereignty in the darkening

GROWTH OF PUBLIC EMPLOYMENT, 1928-40

Bulgaria

A.

Year	Total	Positions Provided in State Budget						Other State Agencies[c]
		Railroad	PTT	Military	Religion	Education[b]	Other	
1931-32	86,611	17,535	5,718	7,469	2,397	24,259	29,233	
1932-33	87,899	17,278	5,683	7,434	2,397	26,341	28,766	
1933-34	89,650	17,263	5,696	7,383	2,396	25,653	31,269	
1934	85,567	13,999	4,974	7,488	2,414	25,851	30,841	
1935	90,694	17,286	5,045	7,625	2,415	25,432	32,391	
1936	91,878	17,385	5,119	8,176	2,419	26,608	32,171	
1937	97,784	17,639	5,314	9,565	2,429	27,219	35,618	4,478
1938	100,963	18,449	5,428	10,568	2,430	27,629	36,459	4,694
1939	101,374	19,815	6,108	11,346	2,525	27,928	33,652	4,648
1940	106,090	20,092	6,408	12,549	2,557	28,261	36,223	

B. Related Census Data

	Public Adm.	Railroad	PTT	Military	Religion	Education
1926	(34,278)[d]	11,005	5,450	(34,670)[d]	4,900	27,362
1934	49,099	(e)	5,481	29,709	5,623	35,424

Greece

A.

Year	Total (f)	Non-military Positions in State Budget					State Railroads	Total Employment		
		Titled Functionaries Only			Railroads	Other		Railroads	PTT	Education
		Total	PTT	Education						
1928	43,943	36,775	5,511	15,574		15,690	7,152	12,732	7,096	19,839
1929	45,523	38,302	5,588	15,967		16,747	7,053	12,757	7,246	20,233
1930	47,306	40,628	6,116	15,782		17,730	7,067	14,414	7,080	21,308
1931	48,180	41,282	6,086	16,913		18,283	6,663	11,622	7,053	22,571
1932	48,481	41,256	6,007	16,718		18,531	6,170	11,074	6,973	22,224
1933	48,534	41,359	5,911	16,931		18,517	5,622	10,516	6,828	21,316
1934	48,979	42,093	5,922	17,339		18,832	5,417	10,360	6,904	21,762
1935	48,502	41,692	5,835	16,726		19,131	5,413	10,334	6,947	23,219
1936	51,402	45,010	6,185	18,688		20,137	5,727	10,532	7,022	24,023
1937	52,219	45,727	6,047	18,685	(g)	20,995	5,727	10,532	7,126	24,336
1938	53,379	47,515	5,712	19,306	(141)	22,497	6,032	11,261	6,950	23,948

B. Related Census Data

	Public-Service	Transportation and Communications
1928	44,472	106,758

TABLE 12.22 (continued)

Romania

A.

Year	State Employment Total	Total Without Railroads	Railroads	PTT	Military[i]	Education, Religion, Arts Total	Religion and Arts	Education[j]	Other
1928	345,507	241,640	78,568	20,843	31,551	(88,989)[l]		66,546	125,466
1929		241,867		(k)				67,451	
1930		239,175		(k)					
1931		223,697		(k)					
1932		228,340		(k)				57,514	
1933-34		225,231		(k)				(57,759)	
1934-35	248,021	234,566	21,178	16,299	34,989	80,161		(60,583)	95,394
1935-36								(58,123)	
1936-37								(62,665)	
1937-38								(64,165)	
1938-39									
1939-40	331,915	275,354	56,561	16,170	44,543	91,322	23,013	68,309	123,319

B. Related Census Data

Year	Public Adm.	Army and Police	Religion	Education
1930	129,583	225,370	43,783	87,211

TABLE 12.22 (continued)

Yugoslavia

A. Positions Provided in the State Budget

Year	Total[m] New Series	Total[m] Old Series	Railroads[n]	PTT[n]	Military[m]	Education[o]	State Employment from Other Sources[p] Other	State Railroads	PTT	Public Education
1929-30		128,879	(32,250)[n]	11,244	3,228	33,145	49,012			35,657
1930-31		139,518			3,510	33,612		76,058		36,222
1931-32		151,471	45,704		3,038	34,413	68,316	71,453		39,536
1932-33	186,737	153,852	46,973		3,580	33,935	69,364	70,960		41,814
1933-34	207,130		42,406 / 58,726	12,737	36,465 / 34,959	33,810	79,635	71,822		44,173
1934-35	205,119		42,869 / (44,852)	11,763	34,792	33,722	79,990	70,400		45,927
1935-36	208,277		42,869 / 57,464	11,792	34,763	36,247	79,808	73,158	15,517	46,954
1936-37	212,634		(46,946)	11,160	34,832	37,555	82,141	74,158	14,881	47,561
1937-38	208,752		(47,391)	11,329	28,025	38,527	83,480	80,806	15,240	49,272
1938-39	199,206		(40,625)	11,066	28,743	39,287	79,305	86,143	15,928	50,655

B. Related Census Data

	Communications and Transport	Army and Navy	Public Service and Liberal Professions
1931 (March)	102,385 of whom "proprietors" 13,880	94,813 of whom "workers" 75,130	305,770 of whom "proprietors" 19,245

international atmosphere. The desire to rearm and, for Romania, to constrain traditional Western European investors ironically opened the way for some peacetime Nazi penetration, without any real protection once war broke out.

The share of foreign investment in joint-stock manufacturing and mining shows a sharp decline for Bulgaria and Romania, according to the benchmarks for 1929–30 and 1937–38 in Table 12.23. No data are available for Greece. Yugoslav shares for 1937–38 point to a lower proportion for manufacturing than the 40–45 percent range of the other two but a much higher one, nearly 70 percent, for mining.

Table 12.24 calls our attention to a likely source of slower industrial growth for Romania and Yugoslavia. Bank credit for industry, both short- and long-term obligations as a percentage of enterprise liabilities, came down significantly in the two countries. Most of the Yugoslav decline occurred in 1932–33, in the wake of the 1931 crisis, and most of the Romanian in 1930–31 and in 1935–36, when the state put commercial banking under the supervision of its Consiliul Superior de Bancar. The relatively lower Bulgarian fraction hardly fell at all. The Romanian decline was the most severe. The value of bank participations in other enterprises fell by one half from 1929 to 1938, with barely half of that amount remaining in industry. Bank credit as a share of incorporated industrial assets dropped from 46 to 33 percent. The comparable Yugoslav share declined from 48 to 40 percent for 1931–38 and the Bulgarian from 37 to 36 percent.

State financial institutions were the only new source of credit for Romanian industry. Two such banks founded in 1937 especially to aid industry had few funds at their disposal. The Societatea Naţionalǎ de Credit Industrial, set up in 1924, carried more weight. Its assets had grown by almost two thirds from 1928 to 1937 and now exceeded 5 billion lei. By 1937 it was granting industrial loans whose

TABLE 12.22 (continued)

Notes: (a)Only administrative personnel and permanent officer corps including the Direction of Aeronautics, but not the Obligatory Labor Service. (b)Total public educational employment, as reported in educational statistics, exceeded budget positions by about 3,000 in 1938. (c)Including the Pernik mines, the National Bank and the Agricultural-Cooperative Bank. (d)In 1926 a single figure is given for "army and police"; for comparison, in 1934 the Ministry of Interior included 6-7 thousand in "police and administration." (e)Separate railroad employment not given in yearbook data. (f)"Total" includes service employees whose distribution was available only in 1929. (g)Not available in earlier years. (h)Including private employment. (i)Excluding persons serving obligatory military duty. (j)For 1937/38, the total teaching corps in Romania numbered 72,457, of whom 64,165 or 88.6 percent were in public schools. Figures in parentheses from educational data may not include administration. (k)Larger figures are given for total PTT employees in the yearbooks for 1934 and earlier. (l)Estimated as the same ratio to education as in 1939/40. (m)Prior to 1932/33, only civilian employees of the Ministry of Army and Navy were reported. (n)Railroad and PTT employment includes different groups of higher administrative employees as administrative subordination changed through the period. (o)Including small numbers in physical education. (p)As reported under railroad, communications and educational sections of yearbooks.

Sources: *Statisticheski godishnik na Bulgarskoto Tsarstvo, 1931* (Sofia, 1931), pp. 415, 458; *1935* (Sofia, 1935), pp. 326-27; *1940* (Sofia, 1940), pp. 46-47, 52-53, 628-39, 694-95; *Statistikē epetēris tēs Ellados, 1930* (Athens, 1932), pp. 75, 297, 301, 332, 5354-?55; *1935* (Athens, 1936), pp. 250, 280, 312-15; *1938* (Athens, 1939), pp. 245, 274, 350-51, 483; *1939* (Athens, 1940), pp. 297-98, 341, 483, 492; V. N. Madgearu, *Drumul echilibrului financiar* (Bucharest, 1935), pp. B35, 232-33; M. Maievschi, *Contribuţii la istoria finanţelor publice ale României* (Bucharest, 1957), pp. 154, 218; *Anuarul statistic al României, 1934* (Bucharest, 1935), p. 227; *1939-1940* (Bucharest, 1940), pp. 28-34, 244-90, 479; *Statistički godišnjak Kr. Jugoslavije, 1929* (Belgrade, 1931), pp. 353, 483; *1930* (Belgrade, 1932), p. 312; *1934-1935* (Belgrade, 1936), pp. 285, 449, 459, 461; *1937* (Belgrade, 1938), pp. 269, 391; *1940* (Belgrade, 1940), pp. 339-41.

TABLE 12.23
INDICATORS OF FOREIGN INVESTMENT, 1928-39

A. Bulgaria--Joint-stock Companies Having Predominantly Foreign Capital

	Percent of Companies				Percent of Capital			
Year	Industry	Banking	Other	Total	Industry	Banking	Other	Total
1928	14.6	9.3	23.1	17.2	36.8	38.9	25.9	25.3
1929	15.2	7.6	20.5	18.9	45.2	37.6	24.8	31.5
1930	16.1	5.5	18.3	17.8	77.1	33.1	30.7	46.7
1931	15.1	5.8	15.6	15.6	71.4	31.6	29.2	44.5
1932	16.3	7.0	16.4	15.2	62.8	27.6	29.9	44.5
1933	14.5	7.6	14.4	13.7	53.8	35.2	39.8	46.8
1934	13.2	10.3	12.3	12.4	52.6	38.7	36.8	45.0
1935	11.6	7.6	10.0	10.4	49.3	32.1	37.3	43.9
1936	10.5	7.8	9.1	9.6	48.7	23.9	33.0	41.4
1937	9.3	7.5	10.7	9.8	48.3	17.0	37.3	40.2
1938	9.9	8.9	9.4	9.6	44.5	17.7	33.9	37.2
1939	8.7	9.5	7.8	8.2	21.6	20.5	30.7	23.3

B. Yugoslavia

(1) Ownership of Industrial Estab:ishments

		Percent of		
Category	Establishments	Capital	Horsepower	Gross Output
All Yugoslav	81.3	50.1	44.2	53.9
All Foreign	3.8	7.4	19.5	8.1
Majority Yugoslav	5.4	14.3	10.3	19.0
Majority Foreign	4.8	26.7	24.9	17.5
Half and Half	1.1	0.8	0.5	0.7
Unknown	3.5	0.7	0.6	0.8
Total	100.0	100.0	100.0	100.0

(2) Amount (million dinars) and Shares of Foreign Capital
    in Joint Stock Companies

1937	Capital (and reserves)	Credit	Total	Share
Industry	2,610.6	1,182.3	3,792.9	82.93
Banking	262.2		262.2	5.73
Trade	49.0	75.7	124.7	2.73
Transportation	318.8	31.0	349.8	7.65
Insurance	41.7		41.7	0.96
Total Foreign	3,282.3	1,289.0	4,571.3	100.0
(a)	3,282.3	2,832.8	6,115.1	
Total Capital(a)	7,441.0	11,150.0	18,591.0	
Share Foreign(a)	44.1%	25.4%	32.9%	

1936	Share of Capital	Share of Credit	Share of Total
Industry	52.8	15.8	13.9
Banking	11.1	42.3	46.5
Trade	30.2	35.9	41.1
Transportation	13.1	43.6	26.7
Insurance	51.7	17.9	38.0
All sectors	35.3	32.5	33.8

TABLE 12.23 (continued)

C.   Joint-Stock Companies with a Predominant Foreign Capital--1938

	Percent of Companies		Percent of Capital	
Branch	BULGARIA	YUGOSLAVIA	BULGARIA	YUGOSLAVIA
Food	11.54	3.80	24.43	22.33
Beverages	7.14	8.78	1.49	12.15
Tobacco	11.11		68.14	
Vegetable oil		1.89		0.16
Chemicals	8.33	10.88	31.65	52.64
Rubber				34.28
Wood		5.97		18.59
Paper	33.33	7.84	59.33	5.52
Printing	4.17	1.52	7.28	0.48
Leather	5.26	6.04	16.09	4.39
Textiles	11.48	18.52	31.32	41.56
Non-wood building materials	11.54	11.04	87.16	51.63
Metals		39.28		56.88
Metal fabrication	8.89	12.62	26.59	20.26
Machinery		24.24		54.99
Electric power	16.67	16.30	60.24	34.23
Other	5.89	25.00	9.76	57.01
All	8.86	10.65	47.37	33.12
Mining	21.95		7.0	

D.   Romania

(1)   Estimated Percentage of Foreign Capital

	1929	1938
All capital	36	21
Large-scale industry	70	40.5
Commerce (large and medium scale)	50	43.5
19 large banks	65	25

(2)   Foreign Capital by Origin--1938 (percent)

	All Joint-Stock Companies	Petroleum
English	13.59	30.73
French	9.33	16.12
American	5.88	10.51
German	0.60	0.18
Italian	3.04	3.53
Dutch		2.85
Belgian	(3.6)[b]	6.70
Czech	(1.6)[b]	
Total	37.64	70.62

(3)   Foreign Capital by Branch of Industry--1938 (percent)[c]

Food	38	Building Materials	52
Textiles	60	Glass and Ceramics	71
Metal	61	Wood	30
Electrical Eng.	53	Leather	30
Paper and Printing	42	Extraction	27
Chemicals	31	Total	40.5

Notes: (a)Data from Tomasevich; other data from Kukoleća. (b)Basic data from Totu; Belgian and Czech shares are estimated from 1937 shares given by Marguerat. (c)Estimated by Lupu using 1946 data.

Sources: Asen Chakalov, *Formi, razmer i deinost na chuzhdiia kapital v 1878-1944* (Sofia, 1962), p. 128; *Statisticheski godishnik na Bulgarskoto Tsarstvo, 1939* (Sofia, 1939), p. 609; Stevan Kukoleća, *Industrija Jugoslavije, 1918-1938* (Belgrade, 1941), pp. 196, 204; M. Filipović, *Obnova naše industrije: prvi bilans* (Belgrade, 1946), p. 8; Jozo Tomasevich, "Foreign Economic Relations, 1918-1941," in Robert J. Kerner (ed.), *Yugoslavia* (Berkeley and Los Angeles: University of California Press, 1949), p. 191; M. Lupu, "Studii privind dezvoltarea economiei Romániei in perioada capitalismului," *Studii și cercetări economice* (Bucharest, 1967), pp. 293-94, 343; I. V. Totu (ed.), *Progresul economic in România, 1877-1977* (Bucharest, 1977), pp. 307, 315; Philippe Marguerat, *Le IIIe Reich et le pétrole roumain, 1938-1940* (Geneva, 1977), pp. 29-32.

TABLE 12.24
CREDIT FINANCING OF INDUSTRIAL JOINT-STOCK COMPANIES

	BULGARIA		ROMANIA		YUGOSLAVIA	
Year	Value[a]	Asset Share[b]	Value[a]	Asset Share[b]	Value[a]	Asset Share[b]
1929			46,585	45.6		
1930			43,660	41.9		
1931			41,982	39.5	6,141	48.3
1932	2,420	37.1	39,094	39.4	6,129	47.9
1933	2,470	36.6	38,285	38.9	6,111	43.0
1934	2,674	37.9	39,668	38.7	5,914	43.0
1935	2,453	36.6	41,879	38.5	6.102	41.0
1936	2,264	35.1	35,725	33.4	6,215	41.0
1937	2,593	35.7	44,805	34.2	6,575	40.2
1938	2,634	35.6	45,877	32.7	6,904	40.2

Notes: (a)Million domestic currency units. (b)All borrowed funds as a percentage of total assets or liabilities.

Sources: *Statisticheski godishnik na Bulgarskoto Tsarstvo, 1934* (Sofia, 1934), p. 277; *1935* (Sofia, 1935), p. 323; *1936* (Sofia, 1936), p. 373; *1937* (Sofia, 1937), p. 473; *1938* (Sofia, 1938), p. 609; *1939* (Sofia, 1939), p. 613; *1940* (Sofia, 1940), p. 625; Institutul Central de Statistică, *Statistica societăților anonime din România*, Vol. XXII-1940 (Bucharest, 1942), pp. 56-57; *Statistički godišnjak Kr. Jugoslavije, 1931* (Belgrade, 1932), p. 225; *1933* (Belgrade, 1934), p. 217; *1934-1935* (Belgrade, 1936), p. 197; *1936* (Belgrade, 1937), p. 255; *1937* (Belgrade, 1938), p. 205; *1938-1939* (Belgrade, 1939), p. 289; *1940* (Belgrade, 1940), p. 267.

value was twice the combined total from the two largest commercial banks, the Banca Românească and the Banca de Credit Român.[67]

An absolute decline in specifically foreign investment cannot be demonstrated from year to year with the scattered data on individual enterprises or even with the better figures for industry as a whole. The annual balance of payments figures in Table 12.25 nonetheless help confirm our aggregate notions. The current account column for private interest and dividends and the capital account columns for private short-and long-term lending show sharply reduced, negative balances for Yugoslavia and especially Bulgaria. These declines suggest the curtailment of foreign investment's annual earnings flowing out and new commitments of funds flowing in. The reduced but positive Greek figures for interest and dividends imply that native investments outside the country were significant as nowhere else in Southeastern Europe. The diaspora still earned more than foreign investment took out of the country. Whether these Greek interests were responsible for the modest inflow of private capital remains unproven if probable. A Romanian breakdown is unfortunately not available.

Within the several branches of industry that did receive more foreign investment during the 1930s, textiles occupy an uncertain position. Both Romanian and Yugoslav cotton textiles received a certain undetermined amount of new long-term investment from British and French profits in extractive enterprises that exchange regulations kept from leaving the country by the mid-1930s. Sources for Table 12.21 tell us only that the share of foreign capital in textiles was 60 percent in 1938. Much of the spinning machinery imported with these otherwise blocked funds was unfortunately old equipment available at bargain prices.[68] This diverted foreign investment thereby failed to bring in best practice to textile industries that were already less prominent and growing less rapidly than those of Bulgaria and Greece.

Rearmament touched only isolated enterprises in light industry.[69] Metallurgy and related heavy industry received more investment from it. With relatively larger natural resources and existing capacity in this area, Yugoslavia and Romania could most easily approach rearmament with the prospect of advancing their industrial self-sufficiency at the same time.

TABLE 12.25
CURRENT AND CAPITAL ACCOUNTS IN THE BALANCE OF PAYMENTS, 1924-38

Bulgaria (million leva)

	Current Account					
	Trade		Services[a]	State Debt Service	Private Interest, Dividends	Current Balance
Year	Goods Official	Goods Corrected				
1924		+ 386	+113	-222	-228	+ 49
1925		- 160	+131	-319	-240	- 588
1926	- 629	- 193	+163	-287	-191	- 508
1927	+ 498	- 934	+169	-845	-299	- 41
1928	- 809	- 236	+276	-463	-304	- 727
1929	-1,933	-1,774	+ 88	-740	-349	-2,775
1930	+1,600	+1,208	+ 60	-702	-439	+ 127
1931	+1,275	+ 839	-107	-826	-295	- 389
1932	- 90	+ 531	- 50	-426	- 83	- 28
1933	+ 644	+ 429	-117	-179	- 14	+ 119
1934	+ 288	+ 273	- 59	-202	- 17	- 5
1935	+ 245	+ 910	+ 3	-204	- 47	+ 662
1936	+ 757	+1,134	+ 23	-181	- 33	+ 943
1937	+ 358	+ 777	-----	------(-227)-------------		+ 550
1938						

Greece (million gold Swiss francs)[c]

	Current Account				
	Trade		State Debt Service	Private Interest, Dividends	Current Balance
Year	Goods	Services			
1929	-420.8	+147.4	- 83.2	+121.5	-235.1
1930	-331.7	+123.9	- 83.8	+ 86.7	-204.9
1931	-308.4	+174.6	-104.1	+ 18.8	-219.1
1932	-157.0	+ 81.5	- 12.2	+ 31.8	- 55.9
1933	- 88.6	+124.0	- 15.5	- 6.2	+ 14.3
1934	- 95.1	+ 90.5	- 32.6	+ 5.5	- 31.7
1935	-102.3	+ 58.5	- 8.7	+ 18.6	- 35.3
1936	-127.1	+ 46.7	- 22.4	+ 14.6	- 89.4
1937	-148.4	+ 64.6	- 11.2	+ 11.4	- 84.3
1938	-122.6	+ 60.6	- 18.8	+ 18.6	- 66.3

Foreign investment in Greek industry remained as it had since before 1914 almost entirely in nonferrous mining. The native Kanelopoulos chemical enterprise mined most of the ferrous ore, iron pyrite, and shipped almost all of it abroad. Pyrite accounted for more exports in 1938 than regular iron ore, whose quantity had declined from a pre-1914 peak. The former matched the nonferrous total. A British joint-stock company accounted for about 40 percent of the manganese, and a French firm for half the bauxite and most of the zinc and lead. That firm's output had, however, slipped to 15 percent of prewar levels. The Lavrium lead mines included Greece's only smelting capacity until the German offer of one Siemens-Martin steel furnace was accepted in 1940. One native shipyard in Piraeus was capable of constructing steel-bottomed vessels by the 1930s. Their

TABLE 12.25 (continued)

| Rep. & Treaties[b] | Capital Account | | | | | Change in Central Bank Reserves | |
	State Loans	Short Term	Long Term	Gold	Capital Balance	Gold & Gold Currency	Other Currency
-280	0	+ 884	+135	- 8	- 49		
-347	0	+ 105	+ 59	- 8	+ 588		
-423	+ 47	+ 781	+125	-22	+ 508		
-435	+ 925	- 546	+124	-30	+ 41		
-210	+2,763	-2,155	+344	-15	+ 727	+2,478	
-158	+ 529	+2,147	+279	-22	+2,775	-1,562	
-246	+ 745	- 685	+ 68	-22	- 127	-533	+234
-230	+ 413	+ 73	+152	-19	+ 389	-144	-365
- 36	0	+ 64	0	0	+ 28	-124	- 2
- 21	0	- 80	- 18	0	- 119	+ 72	- 29
(b)	0	+ 6	- 1	0	+ 15	-101	+ 84
(b)	0	- 762	+100	0	- 667	+ 3	+382
(b)	0	- 544	-399	0	- 943	+149	+172
					- 550	+342	-139
						+ 12	+655

| Reparations | Capital Account | | | | Errors & Omissions | Change in Central Bank Reserves (mil drs) |
	State Loans	Long Term	Short Term	Capital Balance		
+ 3.9	-39.3		+119.4	+235.1	+151.1	-1,124
+27.3	-71.6		+248.4	+204.9	+ 0.8	- 105
+24.3	-23.1		+207.1	+219.1	+ 10.8	- 875
			+ 59.9	+ 55.9	- 4.0	- 217
+ 2.0		+59.6	+ 16.3	- 14.3	- 92.2	- 321
	- 2.5	+23.0	+ 11.2	+ 31.7	0	(+2,325)[d]
			+ 8.0	+ 35.3	+ 27.3	+ 58
			+ 6.6	+ 89.4	+ 82.8	- 751
		+45.0	+ 7.6	+ 84.3	+ 32.0	- 88
		+29.4	- 12.9	+ 66.3	+ 49.8	+ 296

TABLE 12.25 (continued)

Yugoslavia (million dinars)[e]

| | | Trade | | Current Account | | |
	Goods Official	Goods Corrected	Services[a]	Gov. Debt Service	Private Interest, Dividends	Current Balance
Year						
A. 1926	+ 186	- 163	+ 340	- 783	-570	-1,176
1927	- 886	-1,247	+ 634	-1,003	-653	-2,269
1928	-1,390	-1,784	+ 711	- 786	-631	-2,490
1929	+ 327	+ 159	+ 826	-1,488	-657	-1,160
1930	- 180	- 529	- 74	-1,204	-549	-2,356
1931	+ 1	- 627	+ 198	-1,173	-514	-2,116
1932	+ 196	- 72	+ 91	- 601	- 39	- 621
1933	+ 495	- 131	+ 52	- 246	- 50	- 374
1934	+ 305	- 205	+ 39	- 378	- 35	- 579
1935	+ 428	+ 293	+ 646	- 693	-399	- 153
1936	+ 393	+ 368	+ 623	- 729	-131	+ 131
1937						
1938						
B. 1926		- 744	+ 612	- 783	-570	-1,485
1927		-1,796	+1,042	- 991	-653	-2,398
1928		-2,180	+ 712	- 768	-631	-2,867
1929		- 531	+ 866	-1,441	-657	-1,763

ROMANIA[i]

| | | Trade | | Current Account | | |
	Goods	Goods	Service	Private Interest, Dividends	State Debt Service	Current Balance
Year						
A. 1929	- 665				-4,761	
1930	+ 5,566				-5,131	
1931	+ 6,763				-6,195	
1932	+ 5,259				-5,965	
1933	+ 2,429				-3,754	
1934	+ 447				-1,439	
1935	+ 5,909				-1,896	
1936	+ 9,066				-2,090	
1937	+11,196				-2,117	
1938	+ 2,831				-2,158	
B. 1927[j]	+ 4,261	+4,258	+2,407	-4,279	+2,386	
1928[j]	+ 4,621	-5,226	+1,861	-4,012	-7,377	
1929[j]	- 665	- 668	+ 403	-5,392	-5,657	
1930[j]	+ 5,566	+5,477	-5,009	-5,032	-4,564	
1931[j]	+ 6,763	+6,442	-7,590	-6,090	-7,238	
1932[j]	+ 5,259	+4,701	-1,926	-4,776	-2,001	
1933[j]		+2,485	- 503	-2,423	- 441	

TABLE 12.25 (continued)

| Reparations[h] | Capital Account | | | | Errors and Omissions | Change in Central Bank Reserves | |
	Gov. Loans[g]	Long Term	Gold	Short Term		Gold & Convert. Currency	Other Foreign Currency
0	+ 587	0	+ 9	+ 145	- 435		
+ 22	+1,681	+ 4	+10	+ 317	- 235		
+ 25	+1,019	- 25	+ 5	+ 425	-1,041	-526	
+ 608	+1,526	-200	+ 6	- 114	+ 666	+680	
+ 592	0	-480	+14	- 300	-2,530	-797	0
+ 293	+2,419	-100	+11	- 866	- 359	+344	+ 86
0	0		+ 2	+ 222	- 397	-128	- 84
0	0			- 154	- 528	- 62	+ 53
0	0		+92	- 237	- 724	0	+ 49
0	+ 441	+486	-97	- 34	+ 643	-442	+228
0	0		- 9	+ 21	- 143	+162	+220
						+ 83	-112
						+203	+204
+ 589	+ 587	+162	+ 8	+ 508	+ 369		
+ 579	+1,681	+276	+ 4	+1,150	+1,292		
+ 645	+1,019	+325	+ 8	+ 868	- 2		
+1,290·	+1,526	+180	+ 8	- 462	+ 779		

| Reparations | Capital Account | | | | Errors and Omissions | Change in Central Bank Reserves | |
	State Loans	Other Long Term	Capital Short Term	Capital Balance		Gold & Gold Currency	Other Currency
							+ 31
						- 1,068	- 32
						+ 69	+ 20
						+ 130	- 52
						+ 224	+1,122
						+ 518	+ 726
						(-4,674	+1,724)[d]
						+ 890	-1,247
						+ 1,732	- 632

(Gold & Gold Cur.)	(Loans & Advances)
+2,820	+ 434
-2,783	+ 4,646
+7,962	+13,617
-3,725	+ 838
-3,620	+ 3,618
- 354	+ 1,647
- 593	- 208

size was still too small for anything but the coastal trade; the huge merchant fleet still consisted of ships built abroad.[70]

Bulgaria mined mainly coal or lignite dug from state-owned pits. Sources for Table 12.23 found just 7 percent of joint-stock capital in mining to be foreign, most of that in the French copper mine at

TABLE 12.25 (continued)

Romania[i] (continued)

Year	Trade Goods	Goods	Service	Current Account Private Interest, Dividends	State Debt Service	Current Balance
C. 1926	+1,134	+1,368	+2,533	-75	-3,504	+ 322
1927	+4,261	+4,587	+2,314	-85	-4,046	+2,770
1928	-4,621	-4,841	+1,905	-35	-3,923	-6,894

Year	Goods Balance	Estimated Outflows Current Account Services	Private Interest, Dividends	State Debt Service
D. 1922	+1,714	- 600	-3,000	- 560
1923	+5,061	- 800	-4,150	-1,991
1924	+2,096	- 700	-4,750	-2,383
1925	- 786	- 800	-5,550	-2,810
1926	+1,134	-1,050	-7,150	-3,165
1927	+4,261	-1,400	-7,200	-4,366
1928	-4,621	-2,000	-7,500	-3,784

Reparations	Capital Account State Loans	Other Long Term	Capital Short Term	Capital Balance	Errors and Omissions
+340		+1,710		- 322	+2,372
+422		+ 855		-2,770	+4,048
+495		+4,630		+6,894	-1,769

Estimated Outflows Capital Account Private Debt Payment	Private Savings Abroad	Goods Balance Plus Estimated Outflows	Net Capital Imports	Balance
- 200	-180	- 2,826	+ 1,143	+1,683
- 330	-200	- 2,410		
- 800	-170	- 6,707	+ 4,400	+2,307
-2,000	-150	-12,096	+10,208	+1,888
-1,500	-150	-11,919	+10,652	+1,267
-1,800	-100	-10,597	+ 7,666	+2,931
-1,500	-100	-20,110	+18,524	+1,586

Notes: (a)Includes emigrants' remittances and railway freight on imports. (b)Reparations and treaty payments included in state debt service for these years. (c)Except, as noted, changes in central bank reserves which are in million drachmae. (d)Increase due to devaluation. (e)Part A estimates from Obradović; part B from the League of Nations. (f)Including emigrants' remittances. (g)Including service of debts of public institutions. (h)Estimates in part B include the money value of reparations in kind. (i)Part A from available data; part B from Slavescu; part C from the League; and part D from Murgescu and Constantinescu and the United Nations. (j)Eleven months.

Sources: Asen Chakalov, Formi, razmer i deinost na chuzhdiia kapital v Bulgariia. 1878-1944 (Sofia, 1962), p. 130; Victor Slavescu, La situation économique de la Roumanie et sa capacité de paiement (Bucharest, 1934), p. 199; C. Murgescu and N. N. Constantinescu (eds.), Contribuţii la istoria capitalului strain în România (Bucharest, 1960), p. 436; S. D. Obradović, La politique commerciale de la Yougoslavie (Belgrade, 1939), annex; League of Nations, Memorandum on International Trade and Balance of Payments. 1913-1927. Vol. I (Geneva, 1928), pp. 130-31; 1926-1928. Vol. II (Geneva, 1929). pp. 158-59; 1927-1929. Vol. II (Geneva, 1930). pp. 212-14; League of Nations, Balance of Payments, 1931 and 1932 (Geneva, 1933). pp. 64-66. 76-78; 1934 (Geneva, 1935). pp. 61-62; 1936 (Geneva, 1937). pp. 71-72, 123-25; 1938 (Geneva, 1939). pp. 76-78; United Nations, International Capital Movements During the Interwar Period (Lake Success. N.Y., 1949), p. 12.

Plakalnitsa. Western Europen investment was concentrated instead in the large Granitoid cement works in Sofia, the city's Belgian power company, two Italian textile mills, the largely French United Tobacco Factory, and the French and Czech sugar refineries.[71] The prewar territorial changes of 1938–39 created potential German leverage only over the latter. Even that was frustrated when Bulgarian Agrarian Bank bought out the sugar refineries in 1939. The principal change in foreign industrial investment during this last peacetime year was not the modest increase in the German share from less than 5 to 9 percent but rather the sharp drop, 42 to 22 percent, in the combined foreign proportion of the total as war approached.

Over two thirds of the Yugoslav production of cement, sugar, and electricity was like Bulgaria's in the hands of foreign stockholders. The greatest shares of Austrian and Czech investors in the Yugoslav cement and sugar industries gave Nazi interests a foothold there by 1939. Primarily responsible, however, for the rise in the German share of foreign industrial investment from .8 percent in 1936 to over 6 percent in 1939 were metallurgy and related mining operations. From less than 10 percent, German capital in metal manufacture jumped to 35 percent. The inheritance of Austrian holdings in the Trbovlje coal mines and the Jesenice steel works strengthened the German position in Slovenia. Elsewhere state projects made urgent by rearmament predominated. The largest was of course the new Yugoslav Steel Company. Jugočelik was incorporated as a state enterprise in 1938 to modernize the Zenica works near Sarajevo, with its attendant iron ore and lignite mines. The purpose of Jugočelik was to cover all military requirements. Nazi representatives subsequently arranged for the credits and equipment needed to put several Siemens-Martin blast furnaces into operation by 1939.[72]

The mining and processing of nonferrous ores remained overwhelmingly in British and French hands until after the Second World War had started. Their combined share of foreign investment in Yugoslav mining was nearly 90 percent in 1937. The controlling French interests in the Bor copper mining and smelting complex added an electrolytic converter to remove gold and silver in 1938. They continued to resist intimidating Nazi offers to buy out their stock, as did French investors in the Trbovlje coal mine, until the puppet Vichy government came to terms with the Nazis in 1940. British owners of the Trepča lead mines also in Serbia held out until the Nazi attack on Yugoslavia itself the following year.[73]

Romanian rearmament had gotten under way in 1936 with the aid of Czech investment and imported machinery. That year the country's second largest arms manufacturer, the basically state-owned

Československa Zbrojovka, brought a one fifth share in the Romanian state's principal arms factory at Copsa Mică. Shortly thereafter the Czech enterprise bought up 10 percent of the stock in Romania's biggest iron and steel works at Reşiţa. This purchase tipped the balance of control toward the British-dominated CEPI holding company over the native Malaxa machine works of Bucharest. Both purchases brought new Czech metallurgical machinery into Romania. In addition the Romanian government bought 16 million Reichsmarks' worth of sophisticated armaments from Czechoslovakia in 1936 and twice that amount in 1937 and 1938. Almost nothing came from France and Britain. German deliveries included no finished equipment until 1938 and then fell short of 10 million Reichsmarks.[74] The Nazi annexation of the Czech lands the following year thus dealt a death blow to Romanian efforts at maintaining its military forces outside the German orbit.

Meanwhile the Romanian government was continuing its long struggle with the Western European petroleum firms in a fashion that played more directly into German hands.[75] These first genuine multinational corporations can be fairly accused during the 1930s of being prepared to retreat from heavy Romanian investments in any event. New discoveries in Iraq were attracting the interest of French investors. The British were drawn to the further growth of American fields, where world prices were now set on the U.S. Gulf Coast. Romania's aforementioned difficulty in matching these prices at Constanţa and in holding its Western European markets was, however, partly of the government's making. Its aforementioned need for budget revenue had prompted a 12 percent tax on internal sales (about one fifth of the total) and exports in 1935. For the same reason the state railway kept its freight rates high and prevented the construction of a second Constanţa pipeline. When contributions to local authorities for public works in return for storage facilities are added, the oil companies are estimated to have retained only 10–30 percent of the internal sales price.[76] Clearing agreements to improve the country's terms of trade, as noted above, further inhibited oil exports by encouraging a higher official rate of exchange for the lei and thereby adding to the price disadvantage of Romanian production in the free-currency Western markets.

Oil exports to Germany, the largest of the clearing partners, were a tempting solution to the problem. Their sharp rise in 1935 created a Reichsmark surplus for Romania, however, that only widened the gap between the official and unofficial lei rates. Hjalmar Schacht, Hitler's Finance Minister, tried to trim this surplus by payment not in cash but in direct deliveries of drilling machinery to the Creditul Minier, the largest of the two native companies set up earlier by the

National Liberals. The scheme failed. It conflicted with Romanian efforts to produce such machinery (at a Malaxa plant) and with the government's wishes to use oil to earn as much convertible Western currency as possible. The increasingly nationalist orientation of the royal regime did produce a new mining law in 1937 that "destroyed the long-term basis of the 'foreign capital companies'"; the law has been correctly called "the last flourish of National-Liberal policy toward the oil industry."[77] Acquired concessions and further expansion were so tightly constrained that in fact any private enterprise would have been discouraged from continuing. Domestic and foreign opposition forced a few minor changes, but output on the existing fields declined from 1937 to 1939 under the basic legislation. That year the government finally set up its own agency, complete with technically trained staff, to conduct further explorations and to improve production techniques. The new ACEX enterprise lacked facilities to proceed immediately unless renewed German offers were accepted. For political as well as economic reasons, Western European investment was already falling.

These were the economic circumstances under which Nazi representative Wohltat was able to conclude the agreement of March 23, 1939. The Romanian government agreed to the formation of mixed, semiofficial German-Romanian companies. Their structure anticipated the postwar Soviet enterprises, for oil exploration, drilling, and refining. In return, delivery to Germany of Romanian petroleum was assured. A sizable German share of foreign investment in Romanian industry was finally in prospect. Its share had been minuscule, .4 percent as recently as 1937, and reached just 1.9 percent in 1938 before rising to over half of the reduced total for 1940.[78]

In sum, the German advance into the economies of Southeastern Europe during the 1930s was too sporadic to permit the conclusion that it was the decade's decisive event in the evolution of the state sector. The Depression itself had prompted the state agencies to control grain exports. The collapse of the Gold Standard and the subsequent decline, Greece excepted, in Western European loans and investment seems to have done more to advance the state's financial and industrial position. Hitler's political ambitions provoked the general European tensions which led to rearmament. The worldwide agricultural crisis also played its part. The German economic role in undermining private enclaves of modern financial and industrial practice in Southeastern Europe would become decisive only during the Second World War.

13.

The Economic Consequences of

the Second World War

This chapter pursues wartime connections with the immediate postwar period of uneven recovery and institutional transition. For the socialist economies and their Communist governments, the role of the state ministries is the obvious point of continuity. For Greece, several large, semiofficial banks continued to consolidate the preeminent positions that they carved out for themselves during the Depression. These connections are not always statistical. Neither the length nor the scope of the present study will permit the intricate task of reconciling the sizable but disjointed data from the 1930s and the skimpier, less reliable record of the 1940s with the surfeit of statistics since then. The record since 1950 is more comprehensive but organized for the socialist economies on a different basis.[1]

Our historical analysis has attempted to identify institutional and structural change from the Ottoman period forward. War and internal disorder provided the context within which national economies began to emerge from the imperial borderlands during the early modern period treated in Part I. The same is true of the brief but momentous period from 1940 to 1950. The burdens of the Second World War and the uncertain years of recovery immediately thereafter were also similar in some respects to the consequences of the First World War noted in Chapter 10. More portentous for the future and therefore deserving greater emphasis in this chapter were a number of neglected differences.

The first of these differences emerges from Table 13.1. Surprisingly, the Second World War set the growth of population back less than the First. If we include the Balkan Wars in the earlier period, more Bulgarians and Romanians lost their lives then than in the Second World War. No other state in either war approached the Serbian loss of more than one quarter of its population from 1912 to 1918.

Although Romania and Yugoslavia emerged with more survivors in 1945, they did not benefit from the great additions of territory that followed the First World War: Romania lost Bessarabia and the Bukovina, one fifth of its prewar territory, to the Soviet Union; Yugoslavia gained only the small Istrian Peninsula from Italy. The much larger markets, bases for taxation, and mineral resources that had accrued to them in 1918 were not part of the second postwar settlement. Nor were the administrative problems of pulling together ethnically diverse populations under a single central government posed for the first time: Greece and Bulgaria did not face the absorption of an incoming flood of native refugees from the former Ottoman lands. On balance, these differences suggest less opportunity for economic expansion but also a certain basis for stability.

Southeastern Europe also had a different set of prewar economic trends and policies to remember the second time around. Distinguishing the 1930s from the pre-1914 decade were less foreign investment and more state expenditure in industry. During the Depression, European financial institutions had less capital to lend abroad. A significant fraction of international trade was no longer conducted in convertible currencies but through bilateral exchange rates. Hence the policies of the late 1920s to restore a Gold Standard and access to private foreign capital could not, under any set of political circumstances, have looked very attractive to the governments of Southeastern Europe after 1945. Perhaps the most striking change in postwar perspective was the radical reduction in what could be expected from agricultural exports. Grain and tobacco prices in particular had failed to recover fully after 1918 and then slipped badly by the early 1930s. For Southeastern Europe, the turn away from private capital and multilateral trade toward state-supported import substitution and clearing agreements followed logically from the difficulties of trying to maintain the pre-1914 reliance on agricultural exports.

The area's new political alignment after the Second World War also made it unlikely that any successful strategy based on the old agricultural exports could have been devised for achieving rapid economic growth. The Communist governments shifted their foreign trade in varying degrees to the Soviet Union, and Greece to the United States. Both superpowers were themselves agricultural producers and potential exporters. Their need for such imports from Southeastern Europe would have to be selective, especially when compared with British or German demand. Table 13.2 reflects the major shift away from the German market that was the most obvious, if short-run, economic consequence of the Nazi defeat. Table 13.3 notes the massive reductions in the quantity of old agricultural exports from 1934–38 to 1948–52. Bulgaria's greater reliance than its neighbors on trade with a single partner continued, with the USSR replacing Nazi Germany. Romanian exports had been the least dependent on prewar Germany but shifted almost as sharply eastward after 1945, led by a heavy flow of reparations to the Soviet Union in 1946–47. One third of Greek imports had come from Germany in 1938. The U.S. and Canada furnished two thirds by 1948, although this high fraction would not last into the 1950s. Greek exports across the Atlantic never exceeded 20 percent. The postwar direction of Yugoslav trade is perhaps the most surprising. Its lesser reliance on the Soviet Union and the rest of Eastern Europe, for only half or less

TABLE 13.1
TERRITORIAL AND POPULATION CHANGES, 1939-47

	ALBANIA	BULGARIA	GREECE	ROMANIA	YUGOSLAVIA
Territory (sq km.)					
Prewar	28,748	103,146	129,281	295,049	247,542
Postwar	28,748	110,842	131,944[a]	237,500	255,804
Population (1000 persons)					
1939-Prewar territory	1,064	6,319	7,270	20,030	15,703
1939-Postwar territory	1,064	6,644	7,270[a]	15,963	16,403
1947	1,145	6,743	7,259[a]	15,871	15,790
Density (persons per sq. km)					
1939-Prewar territory	37.1	61.3	56.2	67.9	63.4
1939-Postwar territory		59.9		67.2	64.1
1947	39.8	60.8	56.1	66.8	61.7
Birth Rates (per 1000 persons)					
1936-40	(32.4)[b]	23.3	25.8	29.3	27.4
1941-45	(30.5)[c]	22.5	19.6	21.8	
1946-50	(38.8)[d]	24.8	24.2	25.2	28.7
Death Rates (per 1000 persons)					
1936-40	(16.4)[b]	13.7	14.0	19.2	15.7
1941-45	(15.7)[c]	15.8	17.1	19.3	
1946-50	(14.1)[d]	11.8	9.3	16.5	13.2
Natural Increase (per 1000 persons)					
1936-40	(14.5)[b]	9.6	11.8	10.1	11.7
1941-45	(14.8)[c]	6.7	2.5	2.5	
1946-50	(24.7)[d]	13.0	14.9	8.7	15.5

TABLE 13.1 (continued)

BULGARIA GREECE ROMANIA YUGOSLAVIA

Comparative Population Impact of Two War Periods

1. Ratio of projected postwar population (using prewar rates of natural increase) to actual postwar population:

	BULGARIA	GREECE	ROMANIA	YUGOSLAVIA
1920	106.40	113.35	114.99	116.66
1947	106.30	110.00	109.27	113.68

2. Attribution of the differences (percentage of actual postwar population)[e]:

a. To emigration (and Jewish disappearance):

	BULGARIA	GREECE	ROMANIA	YUGOSLAVIA
1910-20	(+)1.32[f]	1.63	1.30	1.24
1939-47	1.97	0.87	2.99	3.53

b. To "abnormal" birth and death rates:

	BULGARIA	GREECE	ROMANIA	YUGOSLAVIA
1910-20	7.70	11.72	13.69	15.21
1939-47	4.33	9.13	6.29	10.15

of which, estimated war deaths:

	BULGARIA	GREECE	ROMANIA	YUGOSLAVIA
1910-20	5.45	4.17	5.72	8.53
1939-47	0.52	6.20	3.15	(10.77)[g]

Notes: (a)Area of the Dodecanese Islands acquired in 1949 is included in territory, but the population (estimated in 1951 as 151.000) is not included. (b)1935-39. (c)1940-42. (d)1950. (e)The percentage of emigration plus the percentage of "abnormal" birth and death rates equal the percentage difference of actual and projected postwar populations. (f)Estimated net immigration; all other figures are net emigration. (g)Estimated war casualties higher than deviation of birth and death rates.

Sources: Marvin R. Jackson, "Comparing the Balkan Demographic Experience, 1860 to 1950," Faculty Working Papers in Economics, No. 79-86 (Tempe, Arizona: College of Business Administration, Arizona State University, 1979), Table C-1; United Nations, Demographic Yearbook, 1952 (Geneva, 1953), pp. 228, 268; 1960 (Geneva, 1961), pp. 484, 507; 1975 (Geneva, 1975), p. 163; Stavro Skendi (ed.), Albania (London: Atlantic Press, 1957), p. 49.

of its exports and imports, undoubtedly helped set the stage for economic survival after the Tito-Stalin split.

The incomplete estimates of price-adjusted values of foreign trade in Table 13.3 indicate that the real level of Yugoslav exports did slip downward after the split. Imports held up much better. In the immediate postwar period that is the limit of this chapter's scope, both Yugoslav exports and imports had come closer than Bulgaria's to recapturing their real 1938 values by 1948, despite wartime Bulgarian levels that were half again the prewar figure. This more rapid revival of Yugoslav foreign trade coincides, as it did after the First World War, with a rise in estimated national income that surpassed the other states of Southeastern Europe. The Yugoslav increment for the difficult period 1948–52 actually exceeded the one quarter increase in both exports and national income recorded in Chapter 10 for 1921–25 over 1909–12. Impetus for this greater advance came from

the capacity to push real per capita income by 1948 to 106 percent of
its 1939 level. The far slower starts by Romania and Greece did not
reach two thirds of that level. Bulgarian national income rebounded
to just 89 percent, according to Table 13.4. The Yugoslav advantage
was still more pronounced in the recovery of agricultural output per
capita.

TABLE 13.2
DIRECTIONS OF FOREIGN TRADE, 1938-50
(percent of total)

The War Years		1939	1940	1941	1942	1943	1944	
BULGARIA								
Germany	Imports	65.5	71.5	62.7	62.7	66.8	72.2	
	Exports	67.8	59.2	70.5	72.5	78.6	87.7	
Italy	Imports	6.9	6.6	4.4	15.6	8.7	0.3	
	Exports	6.1	9.0	8.5	11.1	4.1	0.0	
Other	Imports	27.6	21.9	32.9	21.7	24.5	27.5	
	Exports	26.1	31.8	21.0	16.4	17.3	12.3	
ROMANIA								
Germany	Imports	39.3	50.6	74.1	69.7	73.7	76.7	
	Exports	32.3	43.6	67.9	58.4	63.3	87.7	
Italy	Imports	8.8	9.5	16.3	21.6	15.0	9.6	
	Exports	12.1	9.4	13.7	24.4	15.8	0.0	
Other	Imports	51.9	39.9	9.6	8.7	11.3	13.7	
	Exports	55.6	47.0	18.4	17.2	20.9	12.3	
Prewar and Postwar Years		1938	1945	1946	1947	1948	1949	1950
ALBANIA								
Soviet Union	Imports	0.0						37.2
	Exports	0.0						62.7
Eastern Europe[a]	Imports	26.2						62.9
	Exports	3.3						37.3
Other	Imports	73.8						0.0
	Exports	96.7						0.0
BULGARIA								
Soviet Union	Imports	0.0	79.6	81.9	60.5	58.4		50.2
	Exports	0.0	95.1	66.0	51.9	52.0		54.5
Eastern Europe[a]	Imports	18.2	8.8	8.9	27.0	25.1		35.6
	Exports	12.5	2.2	17.0	33.9	29.2		37.1
Czechoslovakia	Imports	5.9	0.0	6.0	15.8	12.1		15.9
	Exports	4.6	0.0	10.5	18.9	10.5		14.7
Other	Imports	81.6	11.6	9.2	12.5	16.5		14.2
	Exports	87.5	2.7	17.0	14.2	18.8		8.4

TABLE 13.2 (Continued)

Prewar and Postwar Years		1938	1945	1946	1947	1948	1949	1950
ROMANIA[b]								
Soviet Union	Imports	0.1						44.4
	Exports	0.0						58.9
	Total	0.1			51.0	45.0		50.0
Eastern Europe[a]	Imports	17.4						33.7
	Exports	18.4						30.3
	Total	17.6			24.4	27.8		33.3
Other	Imports	82.5			29.9	37.0	20.0	21.0
	Exports	81.6			9.3	16.1	16.2	11.0
	Total	82.2			25.6	27.2	18.2	16.7
YUGOSLAVIA								
Soviet Union	Imports	0.1		23.0	22.6	11.1	1.3	0.0
	Exports	0.0		43.3	17.3	15.3	4.9	0.0
Eastern Europe[a]	Imports	17.7		47.2	34.5	37.2	13.0	0.0
	Exports	15.5		32.9	37.3	36.3	9.4	0.0
Czechoslovakia	Imports	10.7		17.3	18.0	17.5	6.4	0.0
	Exports	7.9		26.6	19.5	15.7	4.4	0.0
Other	Imports	82.2		29.8	42.9	51.7	85.7	100.0
	Exports	84.5		23.8	45.4	48.4	85.7	100.0
GREECE								
Germany	Imports	28.8				4.7	3.9	8.0
	Exports	34.5				3.0	10.4	19.9
Italy	Imports	3.4				4.5	4.1	6.2
	Exports	5.2				14.3	7.3	4.9
United Kingdom	Imports	13.0				7.5	9.1	12.4
	Exports	8.3				25.7	21.1	15.0
United States	Imports	7.2				47.1	41.4	32.5
	Exports	17.1				14.0	19.0	16.6
Other	Imports	47.6				36.2	41.5	40.9
	Exports	34.9				43.0	42.2	43.6

Notes: (a)Excluding Greece and Turkey and in 1938 East Germany. (b)Data for socialist countries is taken as approximating Romania's trade shares with Eastern Europe; for 1950 total trade shares (from Montias) have not been reconciled with separate import and export shares (from Vanous).

Sources: L. Berov. "Kum vuprosa za vunshnoturgovskata orientatsiia na Bulgarskiia fashizum. 1929-1944," Trudove na V.I.I. "Karl Marks", 1954: 1 (Sofia), p. 169; S. D. Zagoroff, Jeno Vegh and Alexander Bilimovich. The Agricultural Economy of the Danubian Countries, 1939-45 (Palo Alto, Calif.: Stanford University Press, 1955), p. 462; S. D. Zagoroff. The Economy of Bulgaria (Washington: Council for Economic and Industry Research, 1955), pp. 99, 102; M. Maievschi. Contribuţii la istoria finanţelor publice ale Rominiei. 1914-1944 (Bucharest, 1957), p. 269; I. V. Totu (ed.), Progresul economic in România. 1877-1977 (Bucharest, 1977), p. 309; John Michael Montias. Economic Development in Communist Romania (Cambridge, Mass.: The MIT Press, 1967), pp. 161-62; Paul Marer. Soviet and East European Trade. 1946-1969 (Bloomington: Indiana University Press, 1972), pp. 25-42; B. R. Mitchell. European Historical Statistics, 1750-1970 (New York: Columbia University Press, 1975), pp. 532-33; Jan Vanous. Project CMEA-FORTRAN Data Bank of Foreign Trade Flows and Balances of CMEA Countries (Vancouver: Department of Economics, University of British Columbia, 1977), pp. 219-27.

Agriculture and the Transition from Private Marketing

Southeastern Europe's experience under German control during the Second World War played its own part in reducing postwar expectations for agricultural exports. It also strengthened the state's role in marketing what was sold at home and abroad. The transition to collectivized agriculture, although rapidly done only in Bulgaria, thus received an important impetus. The modernization of agricultural techniques did not much advance then or immediately after the war.

In the absence of the comprehensive statistical yearbooks that had first appeared in the 1930s our analysis again calls on the comparative method. Once again significant differences emerge, this time helping the reader to understand the distinctive directions pursued since 1948 not just by Greece but also by the socialist economies of Bulgaria, Romania, and Yugoslavia. During the war itself the basic distinction in Southeastern Europe was between those states allied

TABLE 13.3
FOREIGN TRADE BALANCES AND VOLUME, 1939-50

A. Foreign Trade in Constant Prices--Indices

Country and Year	Imports		Exports		Foreign Trade Prices Imports		Exports		Terms of Trade[a]	
Greece (1938 and 1950 unit export values)[b]										
1938			100		100					
1949			54		50					
1950			53		50					
Yugoslavia (1955 Prices)[c]										
1935-39	100			100		100		100		100
1947-51	102			65		1,796				101
1946	30			11						
1947	46			54		2,381		1,802		76
1948	117			86		1,728		2,052		119
1949	111			68		1,752		1,737		99
1950	101			64		1,506		1,433		95
1951	132			55		1,917		1,931		101
Bulgaria (see note e)										
1939	100	100	100	100	100	100	100	100	100	100
1940	106	85	100	112	129	158	116	103	90	66
1941	106	85	110	123	186	239	139	124	75	54
1942	116	80	143	127	215	310	155	174	72	56
1943	115	82	150	125	254	352	179	215	70	61
1944	41	27	56	74	306	448	332	253	109	56
1948		87		66	827		913		110	
1949		118		74						
1950		97		102	(298)[f]		(211)[f]		71	

TABLE 13.3 (continued)

B. Foreign Trade In Current Prices[g]

Country and Year	Imports	Exports	Balance		Ratio of Exports to Imports
Albania	(1000 gold Albanian francs)				
1938	22,316	9,129	(-)	13,539	40.9
1939	40,601	9,467	(-)	31,134	23.3
(1939-43)	(balance with Italy)		(-)600-650,000		
	(million postwar leks)				(million postwar leks)
1938	1,004	339	(-)	665	33.8
1945	81	22	(-)	59	27.2
	(million postwar lek--revised)				
1946	123	115	(-)	8	93.5
1947	1,816	285	(-)	1,531	15.7
1948	1,091	500	(-)	591	45.8
1949	773	349	(-)	424	45.1
1950	1,324	389	(-)	935	29.4
Bulgaria	(million prewar leva)				
1938	4,930	5,576	(+)	646	113.1
1939	5,197	6,065	(+)	868	116.7
1940	7,028	7,019	(-)	10	99.9
1941	10,239	9,234	(-)	1,005	90.2
1942	12,929	13,437	(+)	1,198	103.9
1943	15,131	16,271	(+)	1,140	107.5
1944	6,478	11,357	(+)	4,879	175.3
1945	5,820	12,397	(+)	6,577	213.0
1946	17,514	14,942	(-)	2,572	85.3
1947	21,416	24,533	(+)	3,117	114.6
1948	37,741	36,351	(-)	1,390	96.3
	(million postwar leva--revised)				
1939	310	369	(-)	9	119.0
1950	910	797	(+)	104	88.5

to the Third Reich and those under German military occupation. Although German leverage in the so-called Independent State of Croatia (NDH) was more comprehensive than in Romania and Bulgaria, all three satellite states maintained enough independence to deserve separate treatment, here and in the chapter's other sections.

The Satellite States

The Romanian alliance with Nazi Germany was complete by late 1939. It did not prevent Hitler's award of a majority of Transylvania to Hungary, and the loss of Bessarabia to the Soviet Union and southern Dobrudja to Bulgaria in 1940. This debacle forced an end to King Carol II's regime, and he fled the country. Upon decision of General Antonescu's new military government to join the German invasion of the USSR the following year, Bessarabia was recovered for the rest of the war.

Too much of the considerable German technical aid to Romanian agriculture was concentrated in this ill-fated eastern province for its

TABLE 13.3 (continued)

B. Foreign Trade In Current Prices[g] (continued)

Country and Year	Imports	Exports	Balance		Ratio of Exports to Imports
Greece	(million prewar drachmae)				
1938	14,759	10,149	(-)	4,610	68.8
1939	12,281	9,200	(-)	3,081	74.9
1940	12,243	9.079	(-)	3,164	74.2
1941	4,384	3,899	(-)	485	88.9
1942	12,589	5,405	(-)	7,184	42.9
1943	28,182	10,202	(-)	17,980	36.2
1944		11,328			
1945	2,830	1,225	(-)	1,605	43.3
1946	515,000	202,000	(-)	313,000	39.2
1947	930,000	387,000	(-)	543,000	41.6
1948	1,822,000	470,000	(-)	1,352,000	25.8
1949	2,048,000	575,000	(-)	1,473,000	28.1
1950	2,141,000	452,000	(-)	1,689,000	21.1
Romania	(million prewar lei)				
1938	18,694	21,515	(+)	12,821	115.1
1939					
1940					
1941	30,579	41,286	(+)	10,707	135.0
1942	44,907	52,816	(+)	7,909	117.6
1943	89,988	71,132	(-)	18,856	79.0
1944					
1945					
1946	334,253	102,569	(-)	231,684	30.7
	(million postwar lei)				
1946	130	135	(+)	5	103.8
1947	389	252	(-)	137	64.8
1948	756	876	(+)	130	115.9
1949	1,122	1,056	(-)	66	94.1
	(million postwar lei--revised)				
1948	752	896	(+)	144	119.1
1949	1,162	1,159	(-)	3	99.7
1950	1,461	1,274	(-)	187	37.2

impact to remain significant within postwar Romanian borders, which again included all of Transylvania but forfeited Bessarabia. It was in northern Bessarabia that the private I. G. Farben company had pioneered officially sponsored German-Romanian corporations in 1934. The Soya Corporation introduced soybean cultivation to Romania. Acreage climbed past 100,000 hectares by 1939 through guaranteed purchases at fixed prices. Cultivators were trained by German agricultural instructors. Other joint corporations sprang up once the two countries had signed the 1939 economic agreement noted at the end of Chapter 11. Most important of these was Solagra, to expand the cultivation of sunflowers in similar fashion and to direct the export of their oil seeds to Germany. Acreage tripled to 567,000 hectares and output rose two thirds by 1943, but a majority of this acreage was in Bessarabia or further east in the occupied Soviet

TABLE 13.3 (continued)

B. Foreign Trade In Current Prices[g] (continued)

Country and Year	Imports	Exports		Balance	Ratio of Exports to Imports
Yugoslavia	(million prewar dinars)				
1938	4,975	5,047	(+)	72	101.4
1939	4,757	5,521	(+)	767	116.1
1946	10.574	16,232	(+)	5,658	153.5
	(million postwar dinars)				
1945	1,∩7∩	461	(-)	619	42.7
1946	1.`∺`	2,789	(+)	1,045	159.9
1946	8,∠/2	8,642	(+)	370	104.5
1948	15,783	15,112	(-)	670	95.7
	(million postwar dinars--revised)				
1946	1,760	2,705	(+)	945	153.7
1947	8,305	8,185	(-)	120	98.6
1948	15,325	14,845	(-)	480	96.9
1949	14,740	9,935	(-)	4,805	67.4
1950	11,535	7,715	(-)	3,820	66.9

Notes: (a)Index of export prices divided by index of import prices. (b)Calculated from data in Varvaressos. (c)Calculated from data in Macesicn; Savezni zavod za statistiku, *Jugoslavija, 1945-1964*. (d)Approximation based on comparing tons of imports and exports in 1946 and 1947. (e)The first of each index for 1940-44 is based on official data; the second is from Berov. (f)Current prices in postwar leva. (g)Postwar data for Albania, Bulgaria, Romania and Yugoslavia have been subject to revisions of price levels, valuation and import-export classification. In the cases of Albania, Bulgaria and Yugoslavia postwar values are given in "old" foreign currency units. In 1965, ten "old" leks were made equal to one new lek for Albania. In 1962, one "old" leva was made equal to 0.171954 new leva for Bulgaria. In 1952, four "old" dinars were made equal to one new dinar for Yugoslavia. "Revised" postwar data in each case reflect changes in import-export classification.

Sources: *Vunshna turgoviia na N.R.B., 1939-1972* (Sofia, 1973), p. 9; *Statisticheski godishnik na narodna republica Bulgariia, 1956* (Sofia, 1957), pp. 82-83; Zhak Natan, V. Khadzhinikolov and L. Berov (eds.), *Ikonomika na Bulgariia*, Vol. I (Sofia, 1969), pp. 619, 621; Stavro Skendi (ed.), *Albania* (London: Atlantic Press, 1957), pp. 225, 228; *Comerţul exterior al republicii socialiste România, 1974* (Bucharest, 1974), p. 15; John Michael Montias, *Economic Development in Communist Romania* (Cambridge, Mass.: The MIT Press, 1967), p. 137; Savezni zavod za statistiku, *Jugoslavija, 1945-1964* (Belgrade, 1965), pp. 197-98; George Macesich, *Yugoslavia* (Charlottesville: University Press of Virginia, 1964), pp. 185, 188; Robert Lee Wolff, *The Balkans in Our Time* (Cambridge, Mass.: Harvard University Press, 1974), p. 334; Paul Marer, *Soviet and East European Trade, 1946-1969* (Bloomington: Indiana University Press, 1972), pp. 25-42, 346; B. R. Mitchell, *European Historical Statistics, 1750-1970* (New York: Columbia University Press, 1975), pp. 493-501; K. Varvaressos, *Report on the Greek Economic Problem* (Washington: International Bank for Reconstruction and Development, 1952), pp. 162-63.

territory called Transnistria. Sizable exports to the German war effort never materialized. Romanian authorities in these territories could not replace the marketing network of small Jewish traders that they had abruptly abolished. Local requisitioning agents and cooperative organizations proved to be poor substitutes. Thus the increase in industrial crop acreage for 1938–43, led by sunflowers, from 7.6 to 12.7 percent of total arable, made no permanent contribution to Romanian agriculture other than to cut one sector off from the mechanism of the private market.[2]

More effective assistance tended to come directly from purely German enterprises. Südostropa promoted greater flax production with guaranteed purchases at fixed prices. It also furnished high quality seeds. Processing plants were built and equipped with German machines and staffed with German managers. Several plants were set up on a similar basis for other seeds by the Semina Corporation. Other German enterprises promoted the crossbreeding of livestock and financed the long-overdue construction of a network of grain silos. Yet the only ventures of this sort that systematically trained the Romanians themselves were the several institutes set up there and in the Reich by German manufacturers of agricultural equipment. Their technical staff trained selected Romanians, on the model of Berlin's Deulakraft school for tractor drivers.[3]

By the end of 1940 the Antonescu government had agreed to broaden the 1939 agreement with Nazi Germany. All Romanian agricultural exports would now be geared to the needs of the German market. In order to deliver specified amounts at fixed prices for the foreseeable future, the Romanian Ministry of Agriculture and State Domains drew up a ten-year plan that set production targets for the main crops. It attempted to allocate shares to the existing system of private smallholdings. German agricultural experts attached to the Embassy in Bucharest helped to draft the plan. Otherwise they confined their assistance to coordinating the activities of the aforementioned corporations and to delegating advisors to Romanian agricultural authorities in Bessarabia and the other area lost to the USSR after the war, northern Bukovina. Under a plan more ambiti-

TABLE 13.4
GROWTH AND STRUCTURE OF NATIONAL INCOME, 1938-50

A. Growth of National Income[a] in Constant Prices

	(b)	1938	1939	1945	1946	1947	1948	1949	1950
Albania	unk	100	—	—	—	—	—	—	167
Bulgaria	1957[c]	—	100	—	—	—	101	94	100
	1939[c]	—	100	—	—	—	105	—	—
	1939[d]	—	100	71	—	—	—	—	—
	1939[e]	—	100	80	88	—	—	—	—
Romania	1938[f]	100	—	61	—	—	—	—	—
	1950[c]	100	—	—	—	—	67	—	100
Yugoslavia	1938[g]	100	105	—	—	95	113	124	115
	1953[h]	100	106	—	—	93	112	124	115
Greece	1929[i]	100	102	—	66	88	97	—	—
	1938[e]	100	—	—	—	66	72	—	—
	1958[i]						100	116	118

B. Growth of Per Capita National Income

Albania	unk	100	—	—	—	—	—	—	143
Bulgaria	1957[c]	—	100	—	—	—	89	82	87
	1939[c]	—	100	—	—	—	92	—	—
	1939[d]	—	100	64	—	—	—	—	—
	1939[e]	—	100	72	79	—	—	—	—
Romania	1938[f]	100	—	61	—	—	—	—	—
	1950[c]	100	—	—	—	—	66	—	83
Yugoslavia	1938[g]	100	104	—	—	94	110	120	108
	1953[h]	100	105	—	—	93	109	120	108
Greece	1929[i]	100	101	—	—	83	88	—	—
	1958[e]	100	—	—	—	62	65	—	—
							100	115	116

TABLE 13.4 (continued)

C. Structure Of National Income (percent)

Country and Year	Industry and Construction	Agriculture and Forestry	Transport and Communications	Trade	Other
Albania (net material product--uncertain prices)					
1938	4	93	2	—	1
1950	16	76	8	—	0
Bulgaria (net material product in current prices)					
1939	18	65	2	12	3
1948	27	59	2	8	4
1949	36	49	2	8	5
1950	39	45	2	8	5
Romania (net material product in current prices)					
1938	35	38	7	—	—
1948					
1950	50	28	4	12	6
Greece (net national income at factor cost in current prices)					
1938	20	41	6	12	21
1946	25	38	5	9	23
1948	25	32	6	12	25
1950	28	28	6	13	25
Yugoslavia (net material product in 1938 prices)[g]					
1938	31	52	6		8
1939	32	51	6		9
1947	41	45	3		6
1948	40	45	4		5
1949	41	44	4		5
1950	46	38	5		6
(net material product in 1956 prices)[j]					
1939	36	49	7		3
1947	43	45	4		8
1948	44	43	5		8
1949	45	42	5		8
1950	50	35	6		9

Notes: (a)Gross national product for Greece (1958); net national product for Greece (1929) and (1938), for Bulgaria, line 3, and for Romania (1938); for all others, net material product. (b)Price base year. (c)Official estimates. (d)Kiranov. (e)United Nations citation. (f)Georgescu-Roegen estimate. (g)Stajić estimate. (h)Vinski estimate. (i)Mitchell citation. (j)Macesich citation. (k)Unknown.

Sources: *Statisticheski godishnik na narodna republika Bulgariia, 1956* (Sofia, 1956), p. 22; *1960* (Sofia, 1961), p. 88; *1977* (Sofia, 1978), p. 12; P. Kiranov, "Natsionalni dokhod na Bulgariia, 1939-1944-1945" in *Izvunredno izdanie na trimesechno spisanie na glavnata direktsiia na statistikata* (Sofia, 1946), p. 81; *Statistikē epetéris tēs Ellados, 1954* (Athens, 1955), p. 169; Stevan Stajić, "Realni nacionalni dokhod Jugoslavije u periodima 1926-1939 i 1947-1956," *Ekonomski problemi: zbornik radova* (Belgrade, 1957), pp. 45-48; Ivo Vinski, "National Product and Fixed Assets in the Territory of Yugoslavia, 1909-1959" in *Studies in Social and Financial Accounting*, Interarnational Association for Research in Income and Wealth, Income Wealth Series IX (London: Bowes and Bowes, 1961), p. 221; *Jugoslavia, 1945-1964* (Belgrade, 1965), p. 88; George Macesich, *Yugoslavia* (Charlottesville: University Press of Virginia, 1964), pp. 20-21; Hans-Joachim Pernack, *Probleme der wirtschaftlichen Entwicklung Albaniens* (Munich, 1972), p. 165; Ramadan Marmullaku, *Albania and the Albanians* (Hamden, Conn.: Archon Books, 1975), p. 165; N. Georgescu-Roegen, *Modificări structurale în venitul naționale al României în urma celui de al doilea război mondial* (Bucharest, 1947), p. 7; United Nations, *National Income Statistics of Various Countries, 1938-48* (Lake Success, 1950), pp. 84-85; B. R. Mitchell, *European Historical Statistics, 1750-1970* (New York: Columbia University Press, 1975), pp. 786, 792.

ous than the German recommendations, combined agricultural production was supposed to rise by 50 percent over the first five years.[4]

In addition, the Ministry of Agriculture began by 1942 to organize
Agricultural Associations that tried to draw peasants into joint-
production without eliminating their rights of private ownership.
The Associations were designed to end the inefficient practice of
strip farming and to promote the joint acquisition of machinery, seed,
and other products. As a condition of membership, peasants had to
agree to comply with the government's long-term plan. About two
hundred Associations had reportedly been formed by 1944 and had
been favored in deliveries of German agricultural machinery. Tractors and other equipment were distributed by the Institutul Național
al Cooperației (INCOOP). In addition to acquiring a wartime
monopoly on the acquisition and sale of cereals, this state organization had received German credits and deliveries that had doubled
Romania's supply of tractors between 1940 and 1943. INCOOP
would remain the chief state organization for agricultural marketing
after the war, one of the first to be controlled by the Communist-
inspired Ploughman's Front.[5]

Tables 13.5 and 13.6 show how far short all these efforts fell during
and after the war. Substituting the eastern territories for much of
Transylvania in 1941 admittedly left Romania with a total area for
grain cultivation that was 14 percent smaller than before the war.
The area under actual cultivation dropped by 10 percent as a result
of the army's prolonged mobilization. Poorer land was presumably
left untilled, as labor was also scarce. Grain yields, for wheat in particular, dropped well below the high 1935–39 levels for 1940–42.
For the first two of these years rainfall was above average. Drought
struck down the 1942 harvest. Only for 1943 did output and yield of
wheat per hectare slightly exceed the 1934–38 average. Export goals
for the German war effort never came close to materializing. Deliveries were discouraged by export prices in clearing Reichsmarks
that rose only 123 percent from 1939 to 1944, versus a 614 percent
rise in prices of German imports, when they were available. Even in
the peak year of 1943, the total tonnage of Romanian agricultural exports to Germany amounted to 17 percent of 1939 exports. For
1940–44, moreover, these exports accounted for just 7 percent of
Romanian cereal production over the first four years.[6]

Romania's agricultural circumstances were, all the same, not bad as
the war drew to a close. The rationing of a few foodstuffs had been
initiated in late 1941 but became broad and strict only as reserves
declined by the second half of 1944. Livestock numbers remained
about the same throughout the entire period. Two reasons suggest
themselves: no fighting had taken place within the prewar bound-

TABLE 13.5
AGRICULTURAL INDICATORS DURING THE SECOND WORLD WAR

A. Bulgaria--Indices of Production in 1939 Prices

Year	Total	Total Crop Production With Seed Deductions					Net Production		
		Cereal	Vegetable	Industrial	Fruit and Vine	Forage	Total	Crops	Animal
1939	100.0	100.0	100.0	100.0	100.0	100.0	100.0	100.0	100.0
1940	77.7	72.4	72.2	104.7	44.3	107.2	87.6	74.2	101.6
1941	84.1	69.3	107.4	104.2	64.3	104.0	103.0	78.9	128.5
1942	68.0	40.1	102.9	87.9	101.2	80.1	91.4	57.7	126.9
1943	90.9	72.6	139.7	83.5	105.8	86.8	75.7	87.3	63.4
1944	81.3	60.2	131.2	72.0	103.6	84.5	76.2	75.8	76.7
1945							58.5	39.4	78.7

Structure of Production (percent)

Year	Total	Cereal	Vegetable	Industrial	Fruit and Vine	Forage	Total	Crops	Animal
1939	100.0	48.5	18.3	14.0	9.3	9.9	100.0	51.3	48.7
1944	100.0	35.9	29.5	12.4	11.9	10.3	100.0	51.0	49.0
1945							100.0	34.5	65.5

B. Output of Selected Crops (1000 metric tons)

	Year	Wheat	Barley	Corn	Potatoes	Sugar Beets	Sunflower Seed	Soy-beans	Tobacco	Grapes
Bulgaria										
Prewar	1939	1857	362	949	127	229	158	17.1	40.7	654
	1939	2003	414	1077	136	234	171		41.1	659
	1935-39[a]	1861	361	922	108	137	149	37.3	33.0	475
Postwar	1940	1404	252	975	127	282	132	68.0	45.0	228
	1941	1225	234	923	186	337	156	18.4	39.3	362
	1942	782	143	513	172	219	91	12.6	41.7	636
	1943	1498	248	526	220	350	77	4.2	38.1	680
	1944	1581	169	758	182	328	87	1.5	32.4	639
	1945	992	98	223	44	126	33	6.4	22.8	690
	1946	1513	170	424	36	242	70	10.5	40.4	553
	1947	912	131	783	62	176	108		47.8	
	1948	1688	198	802	159	560	166		28.0	473

TABLE 13.5 (continued)

B. Output of Selected Crops (1000 metric tons) (continued)

	Year	Wheat	Barley	Corn	Potatoes	Sugar Beets	Sunflower Seed	Soy-beans	Tobacco	Grapes
Greece	1935-38[a]	768	197	116	148				61	187
	1939	903	185	127	157				97	175
	1940	766	165	131					27	
	1941	566	122	112					16	
	1942	334	58	53						
	1943	368	72	69						
	1944									
	1945	375	81	46	128				23	23
	1946	729	163	89	230					
	1947	578	129	78	301				47	102
	1948	800	215	108	320				37	100
Romania										
Prewar	1938	4912	823	5223	1889	720		52	11.7	
Postwar	1938	3625	502	4092	1547	446		9.5	8.9	
	1934-38[a]	2630	602	4056		393	48.4	11.6		1049
	1944	3290	451	4128			20.5			
	1945	1276	337	1821						
	1946	1607	233	1006	675	342				
	1947	1278	360	5280	1630	600				
	1948	2396	279	2259	717	597	306.4			447

TABLE 13.5 (continued)

Year	Wheat	Barley	Corn	Potatoes	Sugar Beets	Sunflower Seed	Soy-beans	Tobacco	Grapes
(Boundaries of 1941)									
1935-39[a]	2596	550	3902						
1940	1376	371	3742						
1941	1986	333	3348						
1942	854	337	2135						
1943	2329	453	2228						
1944	2653	350	3266						
1945	1088	233	1315						
(Boundaries of 1942)									
1935-38[a]	3140	954	4695	1570	515	166	40		
1942	1369	1120	4582	2617	671	282	36		
1943	3564	1291	3845	2605		275	31		
Yugoslavia									
Postwar									
1934-38[a]	2430	403	4691	1631	509	12	2		
1939	3910	424	4070	1546	922	27	3		888
1940	1907	377	4580	2030	783		8		
1945	890	220	2525	950	410	77	70		
1946	1930	309	2140	922	636	78	4		
1947	1660	255	4210	1190	1200	152	10		
1948	2530	353	4080	1480	1500	121	33		843

TABLE 13.5 (continued)

C. Animal Herds--1000 head

Bulgaria (farm animals)

		Cattle	Horses	Pigs	Sheep	Goats	Poultry
Prewar	1939-Aug. 1	1449	507	751	9413	581	12773
	1940-Aug. 1	1511	509	860	9182	546	
	1939-Aug. 1	1532	593	807	10262	597	
Postwar	1941-Unknown	1639	591	1095	10128	594	
	1942-Unknown	175	594	1061	8847	615	
	1943-Unknown	1492	522	498	7471	647	7661
	1944-Unknown	1390	478	675	6390	611	6979
	1945-Unknown	1351	476	836	7178	739	6649
	1946-Dec. 31	1631	509	783	8416	896	

Bulgaria (all animals)

	Cattle	Horses	Pigs	Sheep	Goats	Poultry
1946-Dec. 31	1693	549	870	8784	1005	11412
1948-Dec. 31	1783	558	1078	9265	720	11380
1949-Dec. 31	1678	516	1038	8853	648	10359
1950-Dec. 31	1664	498	818	7820	715	9703

Greece (year end)

	Cattle	Horses	Pigs	Sheep	Goats	Poultry
1938	974	363	430	8139	4356	11945
1939	1103		358	7795	3499	
1944	505	194	280	5300	2700	8200
1945	533	200	330	5830	2868	7816
1946	561	220	400	6125	3131	8377
1947	693	241	480	7116	3535	8324
1948	709	237	509	6767	3527	8516
1949	751	246	537	6785	3629	8148
1950	815	279	582	6905	3710	9050

Romania (year end)

Prewar	1937	4161	2158	3165	12768		34666
	1938	4254	2043	2926	12851		35406
Postwar	1937	3477	1581	2761	10087	364	27110
	1938	3558	1460	2529	10264		27324
	1944	(3248)b	849	1201			
	1945	3193	857	1389	6799	203	14010
	1946	2975	787	1384	7100	237	11931
	1947	(4183)b	932	1591	10634	543	15263
	1948	(4164)b	917	1967	10303		14014
	1949	(4309)b	971	2211	9834		17507
	1950	(4502)b	1002	2197	10222	498	17610

Yugoslavia (year end)

Prewar	1937	4267	1264	3451	10137		19419
	1938	(4263)b	1273	3504	10154		19221
Postwar	1945	(3494)b	766	2640	7046		
	1946	(3929)b	897	3485	9192		
	1947	(4246)b	973	3439	9970		
	1948	(5278)b	1050	4135	11654		19354
	1949	(5248)b	1097	4295	10045		20207
	1950	(4740)b	1095	3917	10276		17174

Notes: (a)Annual average. (b)Includes buffalo.

Sources: Zhak Natan, *Stopanska istoriia na Bulgarskoto Tsarstvo* (Sofia, 19 p 253; P. Kiranov, "Natsionalni dokhod na Bulgariia, 1939-1944-1945," *Izvantredno izdanie ne trimesechno spisanie na glavnata direktsiia na statistikata* (Sofia, 1946), p. 81; *Statisticheski godishrik na Bulgariia, 1941* (Sofia, 1941); *Statisticheski godishrik na Bulgariia, 1941* (Sofia, 1943), pp. 272-75; 1942 (Sofia, 1943), pp. 248-49; 1956 (Sofia, 1956), pp. 44-49; S. D. Zagoroff, *The Economy of Bulgaria* (Washington: Council for Economic and Industry Research, 1955), pp. 45-46, 64-67, 69; Gregor Lazarcik and Wayne Znayenco, *Bulgarian Agricultural Production, Output, Expenses, Gross and Net Product and Productivity, 1939 and 1948-1967*, Occasional Papers of the Research Project on National Income in East Central Europe, OP-32 (New York: Riverside Research Institute, 1969), pp. 59-60; *Statistikè epetéris tès Ellados, 1954* (Athens, 1955), pp. 39-42; Ch. Evelpidi, *E georgia tés Ellados* (Athens, 1944), pp. 9, 30, 37, 186; Wray O. Candilis, *The Economy of Greece, 1944-66* (New York: Praeger, 1968), p. 18; Lawrence H. Shaw, *Postwar Growth in Greek Agricultural Production* (Athens: Center for Planning and Economic Research, 1969), pp. 51, 64, 157, 175, 181, 209; *Anuarul statistic al României, 1939-1940* (Bucharest, 1940), pp. V411-15; 1957 (Bucharest, 1958), pp. 22, 97, 106-08, 134, 137; 1977 (Bucharest, 1978), pp. 89, 218-22, 272, 278, 319-20; Institutul de cercetări economice, *Dezvoltarea economiei R.P.R. pe drumul socialismului, 1948-1957* (Bucharest, 1958), p. 269; John Michael Montias, *The Economic Development of Communist Romania* (Cambridge, Mass.: The MIT Press, 1967), pp. 99-100; Gregor Lazarcik and George Pall, *Rumania: Agricultural Production, Output, Expenses, Gross and Net Product and Productivity, 1938, 1948, and 1950-1971*, Occasional Papers of the Research Project on National Income in East Central Europe, OP-38 (New York: Riverside Research Institute, 1973), pp. 5, 10; Savezni zavod za statistiku, *Jugoslavija, 1945-1964* (Belgrade, 1965), pp. 97-105; Vladimir Stipetić, "Poljoprivredna proizvodnja na današnjem području F.N.R. Jugoslavije, 1929-1955," *Ekonomski problemi* (Belgrade, 1957), pp. 124, 128; Stevan Stajić, "Realni nacionalni dohodak Jugoslavije u periodima 1926-1939 i 1947-1956," *Ekonomski problemi* (Belgrade, 1957), p. 45; Joseph Bombelles, *Yugoslav Agricultural Production and Productivity, Prewar and Postwar 1948-1965*, Occasional Papers of the Research Project on National Income in East Central Europe, OP-31 (New York: Riverside Research Institute, 1970), pp. 52-56; S. D. Zagoroff, Jeno Vegh and Alexander Bilimovich, *The Agricultural Economy of the Danube Countries, 1935-45* (Stanford: Stanford University Press, 1955), pp. 120-27, 252, 282; Karl Brandt, *Management of Agriculture and Food in the German-occupied and Other Areas of Fortress Europe* (Palo Alto, Calif.: Stanford University Press, 1953), pp. 203-04, 219, 234, 245; B. R. Mitchell, *European Historical Statistics, 1750-1970* (New York: Columbia University Press, 1975), pp. 255, 251, 273, 280-87, 311-22.

aries, and, more important, although individual German troops sent home many food packages, Nazi representatives chose to avoid pressure for receiving their promised deliveries at any cost. The Romanian oil exports which had always been paramount in Hitler's plans were thus better assured at projected levels.

Food prices had nonetheless risen severalfold by 1943. They jumped again in 1944. Black marketing accompanied greater rationing. Uncertainty over the future mounted. Russian occupation in August 1944, proved the anxiety well founded. The Red Army seized tractors and draft animals out of hand, remembering the Romanian

TABLE 13.6
AGRICULTURAL OUTPUT AND STRUCTURE, 1938-50

		ALBANIA	BULGARIA	GREECE	ROMANIA	YUGOSLAVIA
Horses[b]		107	78	77	69	86
Cattle[b]		105	101	82	120	112
Pigs		305	91	135	87	112
Sheep		108	73	85	100	101
Poultry		64	76	76	64	89

Commercial Fertilizer (kilograms per hectare of agricultural land)

		ALBANIA	BULGARIA	GREECE	ROMANIA	YUGOSLAVIA
Prewar[c]			0.5	7.3	0.2	0.6
1948-52 av.[d]			2.2	17.0	0.5	1.4

Tractors (number per 1000 hectares of agricultural land)

		ALBANIA	BULGARIA	GREECE	ROMANIA	YUGOSLAVIA
Prewar[c]		0.024	0.28	0.379	0.26	0.15
1948-52 av.[d]		0.236	1.6	2.2	0.9	0.5

Indices of Land Use (1938 or 1939 = 100)[a]

		ALBANIA	BULGARIA	GREECE	ROMANIA	YUGOSLAVIA
Arable	1945		96			93
	1948		109		97	
	1950	136	113	96	93	92
Cereals	1945		85	82		83
	1948		94	106	91	
	1950	124	97	118	85	82
Vegetable[f]	1945		188	58		95
	1948		139	73	122	
	1950	200	143	97	183	104
Industrial	1945		73	47		131
	1948		118	77	267	
	1950	967	143	151	336	217
Orchards	1945					95
	1948		108		89	
	1950	117	125	96	74	111
Vineyards	1945					105
	1948		109		91	
	1950	75	109	83	91	105

TABLE 13.6 (continued)

	ALBANIA	BULGARIA	GREECE	ROMANIA	YUGOSLAVIA
Indices of Gross Production (1938 or 1939 = 100)[g]					
Total					
1946			(h)		70[i]
1948		103	(h)	62	93[i]
1950	119	85	(h)	74	67[i]
Animal					
1946			61		66
1948		108	64	76	87
1950	100	86	76	94	72
Crop					
1946			88		72[i]
1948		99	95	55	97[i]
1950		83	113	65	64[i]
Cereals					
1946			85		72
1948		82	94		100
1950	108	77	97	57	67
Vegetable					
1946			109		69
1948		140	141		100
1950		112	179	151	64
Industrial					
1946			64		70
1948		151	101		149
1950	313	109	149	(j)	33
Fruit					
1946			101		(74)[k]
1948		(103)[k]	72		(82)[k]
1950	110	(77)[k]	69	28	(57)[k]
Vine					
1946			59		
1948			73		
1950			88	58	
Fodder					
1946			101		(i)
1948		155	124		(i)
1950		76	183	64	(i)

incursion into Soviet territory as far as Stalingrad. The armistice agreement with the Russians guaranteed them access to existing inventories of grain (the winter wheat crop of 1943–44 had just been harvested) and mineral oil. Both stocks were virtually gone before the end of the war in May 1945. Over four fifths of all cattle losses by March 1946 came from Soviet requisitions.[7] The railway network was also taken over, and quickly broke down under the exigencies of moving the Red Army westward and Romanian supplies eastward. Prices skyrocketed, as we shall see in the next section.

The new coalition government undertook only one real initiative toward agriculture in the immediate postwar years: a land reform that made good political capital but that added 2.7 percent, according to Table 13.7, to the number of smallholders' exploitations and cut

TABLE 13.6 (continued)

		BULGARIA	GREECE	ROMANIA	YUGOSLAVIA
Structure of Gross Production (percent)[1]					
Animal	Prewar	34.1	32.0	30.3	31.5
	1948	36.2		37.4	29.5
	1950	34.8	22.0	38.6	36.1
Crops	Prewar	65.9	68.0	69.7	68.5
	1948	63.8		62.6	70.5
	1950	65.2	78.0	61.4	63.9
Cereals[m]	Prewar	40.7	32.0		44.1
	1948	33.5			39.0
	1950	37.4	28.3		57.7
Vegetable[m]	Prewar	7.4	10.7		8.5
	1948	10.5			11.0
	1950	10.0	18.3		9.0
Industrial[m]	Prewar	10.5	13.4		3.2
	1948	12.1			4.3
	1950	13.4	9.5		3.9
Fruit & Vine[m]	Prewar	21.5	39.4		14.4
	1948	22.6			15.5
	1950	19.9	40.1		17.0
Fodder[m]	Prewar	6.7	4.5		24.5
	1948	10.5			24.5
	1950	6.1	3.8		6.1
Other[m]	Prewar	13.2			5.3
	1948	10.7			5.7
	1950	12.9			6.3

Notes: (a)Based on year-end herds and postwar territory; for Bulgaria, the base year is 1939 and herd equivalents for farm animals based on 1946 ratios. (b)Including buffalo for Greece and Romania. (c)Albania and Romania, 1938; Bulgaria, Greece and Yugoslavia, 1939. (d)Albania, 1950; Greece, 1952. (e)Based on postwar territory and 1938 for Albania and Romania; areas for Albania are incomplete, but crop coverage is the same for 1938 and 1950. (f)The 1950 vegetable crop area for Yugoslavia includes plant nurseries. (g)Base years 1938 for Albania, Greece and Romania; price weights are Albania (unknown), Bulgaria (1955), Greece (1957/59 average), Romania (1955), and Yugoslavia (1938). (h)Unavailable for a base of 1938; based on 1935-38 100, indices for gross output are 1946 (77), 1948 (85), 1950 (98). (i)Yugoslav totals are for "agricultural output" rather than "gross production"; crops fed to animals and animal products used on farms are deducted. (j)A single figure is unavailable for Romania; its 1950 indices are textile plants 195, oil plants 106 and industrial plants 135. (k)Fruit and vine crops. (l)Price weights are the same as in note (g) above except for Yugoslavia which is in 1956 price weights; product classifications differ among countries and, therefore, cross country comparisons have little meaning. (m)Percentage of total crops.

Sources: Table 13.5; Ramadan Marmullaku, *Albania and the Albanians* (Hamden, Conn.: Archon Books, 1975), pp. 168-69; Economic Research Service, United States Department of Agriculture, *Agricultural Statistics of Eastern Europe and the Soviet Union, 1950-66* (Wash., D.C.: U. S. Government Printing Office, 1969), pp. 12-19; Gregor Lazarcik, "Growth of Output, Expenses, and Gross and Net Product in East European Agriculture," in *Economic Developments in Countries of Eastern Europe*, a compendium of papers submitted to the Joint Economic Committee, Congress of the United States, 91st Congress, 2d Session (Wash., D.C.: U. S. Government Printing Office, 1970), p. 513; Ch. Evelpidi, *Agrotikēs politikēs*, Vol. B (Athens, 1942), p. 82.

those over 10 hectares by less than one percent. The much-smaller-scale Bulgarian reform added 5.4 percent to private holdings under 5 hectares and cut the acreage of those over 10 hectares by 2.8 percent. The average Romanian increment of 1.16 hectares was unaccompanied by new investment.

To make matters worse, drought cut the 1945 harvest to one third of 1944. The next year's harvest climbed to just 59 percent, but the Soviet Union still claimed its deliveries. The severe winter of 1946–47 led to actual famine in parts of Moldavia. American shipments of foodstuffs were summoned to provide some relief.[8] Little wonder that rural death and infant mortality rates rose between 1944 and 1947 and that agricultural recovery proceeded more slowly in Romania than elsewhere in Southeastern Europe.

The Bulgarian experience was similar to the Romanian one in several respects. Crop yields, especially for grain, were lower than before the war. The same drought that hit Romania in 1942 made matters worse by cutting livestock numbers about 15 percent and by forcing imports of German grain. Grain could be exported to the Reich only for 1943–44 and then at half the level for 1939–40. Rationing began after the crop failure of 1942. Black markets sprang up in the major towns and pushed food prices to five times their 1939 level by mid-1944, almost double the official rate of inflation.[9]

Several significant differences from Romania nonetheless laid the groundwork for more rapid agricultural recovery and more rapid state collectivization. First, the Bulgarian government did not bind its wartime agricultural policies so directly to German interests. Far fewer German troops were stationed there. Bulgarian agencies saw to their provisions. The best postwar study of Nazi food management across Europe finds no official enterprises or programs such as appeared in Romania.[10] The few private ventures either failed or never progressed past their small initial scale, with the exception of the same I. G. Farben project to promote soybean cultivation that was at work in Romania. The output and yield of soybeans ceased their rapid rise after 1941 and fell below prewar levels. Südostropa was unable to spread flax cultivation for its processing plants in the Dobrudja for lack of German technical experts as well as for climatic reasons. The Buschag Corporation formed by German sheep breeders to cross Bulgarian and Merino stock made little progress because of opposition from the Bulgarian Ministry of Agriculture. The Buschag effort at cattle-breeding also failed. A training program for the use of farm machinery, again on the Deulakraft pattern, was successful in two model villages with the limited number of peasants who attended.

Much more widespread were the central controls applied to agriculture by the government itself. Its principal agency was the Cereal Export Agency (Hranoiznos) that we first encountered in Chapter 12. The Agency had fallen into disuse during the period 1936–39; rising world prices for wheat obviated the need for supporting domestic prices, its original mandate in 1930. During the

TABLE 13.7
SIZE DISTRIBUTION OF FARMS, PREWAR AND POSTWAR

Country and Land Category	Year	Percent of Farms				Number of Farms (1000)
		0-2 ha.	2-5 ha.	5-10 ha.	over 10 ha.	
Bulgaria						
Private Exploitations	1934	27.1	36.1	26.2	10.7	884
Private Exploitations	1946	29.8	38.8	24.5	6.9	1,039
Greece						
Exploitations	1929	59.3	27.8	8.9	4.0	953
Exploitations	1950	59.7	28.2	9.4	2.7	1,312
Romania		(0-3 ha.)	(3-5 ha.)			
Exploitations	1930	52.1	22.9	17.1	7.9	3,280
Properties	1941	58.4	18.4	16.9	6.3	2,257
Exploitations[a]	1941	54.1	19.5	19.8	6.6	2,240
Exploitations[a]	1941	54.3	19.2	19.5	7.0	2,303
Exploitations[a]	1948	52.7	23.3	17.8	6.1	2,596
Exploitations[a]	1948	52.8	22.8	17.8	6.6	2,096
Ownership	1948	78.4	12.7	6.6	2.3	5,501
Yugoslavia						
Exploitations	1931	33.8	34.0	29.2	2.9	1,985
Exploitations	1931	34.3	33.6	20.4	11.7	2,067
Exploitations	1941	47.0	24.0	19.0	10.0	2,636
Private Holdings	1949	37.2	34.7	19.6	8.5	2,605
Private Holdings	1950	29.8	39.3	21.6	9.3	2,010

Notes: (a)Differences among sources.

Sources: Table 10.8 above; *Statistikē epetēris tēs Ellados, 1935* (Athens, 1936), p. 113; *1954* (Athens, 1955), p. 31; Nicholas Spulber, *The Economics of Communist Eastern Europe* (New York: M.I.T. and Wiley, 1957), pp. 240-41; F. E. Ian Hamilton, *Yugoslavia, Patterns of Economic Activity* (New York: Praeger, 1968), p. 171; Henry L. Roberts, *Rumania, Political Problems of an Agrarian State* (New Haven: Yale University Press, 1951), pp. 370-75.

Second World War, however, Hranoiznos expanded into a state monopoly for the export and also internal distribution of all vegetable products.[11] The initial list of wheat, rye, cotton, flax, and hemp had grown to twenty three items by 1943. Tobacco was the only significant exclusion. The Agency's delivery orders to licensed local merchants or cooperative authorities became obligatory or even forced as the war economy evolved. By 1942 state inspectors were being used to check the grain threshed per harvested hectare. Their reports formed the basis for delivery orders to middlemen. Meat, butter, and sugar were collected and rationed in similar if less coordinated fashion. Forced requisitions by army units were also carried out on a number of occasions. From mid-1943 forward the government's Civil Mobilization Directorate received expanded powers to coordinate the activities of Hranoiznos, several ad hoc agencies, and the main state ministries. Yet the annual production plan down to the unit level, first drafted by Hranoiznos and the Ministry of Agriculture for 1942, was not successful in meeting its targets. The new Directorate for the War Economy had little time to improve coordination. In September 1944, the Red Army and the Bulgarian Communist Party swept the government from power.

All the same, the wartime performance of Hranoiznos was an impressive one, for the internal market if not for exports to Germany. The price-adjusted volume of its purchases rose to just over half again the 1939 level by 1943, the last full year under the prewar government. The area sown for grain crops on prewar territory did not decline like Romania's as a percentage of the arable total. Falling acreage for soybeans, sunflowers, and other industrial crops used mainly for export was matched by comparable increases for sugar beets, beans, and potatoes, all intended for domestic consumption. After the drought of 1942, yields per hectare for 1943 and 1944 approached prewar levels. On those cooperatives for which we have data, yields exceeded prewar levels. More efficient methods, more days worked, and a threefold greater use of tractors gave cooperatives up to two thirds greater income than comparable private holdings received.[12] Here was more thorough and widespread intensification than the two hundred new Romanian Associations were able to achieve. The decline in marketed output may be traced to the army's mobilization and to the government's decision to hold down the fixed prices paid for most agricultural products, first to the middleman and then to the producer himself. Peasant smallholders responded by withholding their produce from the market. Grain exports to Germany were minimal except for 1943. The total volume of wheat exports dropped to one third of the 1937–39 average by 1940–42. Only tobacco sales, almost entirely to Germany, held up. Tobacco was not essential to the war effort, however, and fetched prices in Reichsmarks whose severalfold increase during the war fell short of even the rise in other export prices, let alone imports.[13]

Marketed shares slid still further during 1945–46 under the new Soviet-backed regime. Net real value of crop and animal production fell from the 90 percent of 1939 maintained for 1940–41 and the 75 percent for 1943–44 to 60 percent for the drought years of 1945–46.[14] The new government kept Hranoiznos in place to continue the wartime practice of calculating and collecting delivery orders, now in the form of annual contracts. Private middlemen nonetheless survived until 1947. Price controls had already squeezed their profit margins during the war, although not as much as the cooperatives. New regulations forced private enterprise out of retail and wholesale trade by 1948–49. Marketed output moved quickly upward thereafter as a command economy took hold. Half of this trade was still formally in the hands of the reconstituted cooperative organizations as late as 1953. Their officials were often appointed to administrative positions in the new Soviet-style collective farms.[15] The decision to begin collectivization in 1948 therefore stands revealed as an economic policy to control the process of production itself and a political device for undermining the potential independence of the cooperative marketing network. The agricultural production projected for the First Five Year Plan (1948–53) was of course not the first set of comprehensive targets drawn up by a Bulgarian government. That had occurred in 1942, and even earlier in Romania.

The cooperatives and the powerful Agricultural Bank may have been perceived as rivals to the new state Bulgarian apparatus in grain production but served the state well in the tobacco trade. They bought out the private, largely foreign, shares in the United Tobacco Factory by late 1944 and purchased all but 12 percent of the 1945 crop on behalf of this state. The creation of a state tobacco monopoly in 1947 therefore involved no transfer from private or foreign hands. Tobacco remained the chief Bulgarian export in this early postwar period of transition to the Soviet market, accounting for 64 percent of export value in 1946 and 80 percent in 1947.[16]

The Occupied Areas

The usual diversity of Yugoslav conditions multiplied with the breakup of the country in April 1941. The German Blitzkrieg split the first Yugoslavia into four administrative jurisdictions. Only Serbia and the Banat were placed directly under German military occupation. The puppet regime of the Croatian Ustaši extended the borders of its so-called Independent State of Croatia to include most of Bosnia-Hercegovina. Italian forces occupied the Dalmatian and Montenegrin coast. Finally, several border areas were annexed to their neighbors: Germany took northern Slovenia, and Italy southern; Hungary absorbed the Bačka (located west of the Banat) and Bulgaria the Macedonian lands of both Yugoslavia and Greece.

These annexed areas found themselves under virtual military occupation. The Macedonian area was self-supporting in wheat and other essential foodstuffs only when climatic conditions were especially favorable. When they were not, as in 1942, the already reduced reserves of the Bulgarian Hranoiznos had to make up the deficit. This they failed to do, giving the local population another reason to support Tito's Yugoslav Partisans. The rural situation in northern Slovenia was better in the beginning. The administrative apparatus of the Reich Food Estate, the Nazi Ministry of Agriculture, installed itself with promises of technical aid and even new social legislation to strengthen the peasant's economic condition. No more finally came of these promises than in Germany proper. What technical services and training materialized were in any case negated by the deportation of peasant labor to the Reich and by growing Partisan activity. Foodstuffs had to be imported from the Reich. Rationing was imposed, albeit on the relatively moderate German scale. More severe conditions in the Italian south of the province may be deduced from a significantly lower bread ration and a large black market.[17] Dalmatia and Montenegro faced food deficits that Italian authorities did not repair. Little is known of economic conditions in the Hungarian Bačka. Persecution of the sizable Serbian population did include transfer of their land to Hungarians.

The war's consequences for the Yugoslav agricultural sector and state policy may in any case be judged from the experiences of Serbia, the Banat, and the short-lived fascist regime in Croatia. Occupied Serbia suffered the most, as it did during the First World War.[18] Five separate Nazi agencies competed for the spoils within unclear lines of jurisdiction. In addition to two military and two SS offices, a Plenipotentiary for the Economy was installed to report directly to Göring's Four Year Plan. This last office became the most active, in no small measure because its director was Franz Neuhausen, the former German Consul General in Belgrade. He had done Nazi business in Belgrade as early as 1937 by representing German oil interests.

In early 1942, Göring's planning agency charged Neuhausen and his food division with stepping up Serbian agricultural exports to the Reich and also with provisioning a far larger number of German troops than were stationed in Bulgaria or Romania. For grain collection the Nazis relied on the prewar PRIZAD organization. It had been restaffed with a German supervisor and Serbian collaborators as Bulgaria's similar Hranoiznos had not. PRIZAD's estimates of crops harvested and its ability to collect projected deliveries improved markedly by 1943, especially for wheat. It and other grains constituted over two thirds of total Serbian exports to Germany. But anticipated collections were better met in 1943 than 1942 mainly because targets had been lowered, to one quarter of the wheat crop for instance. Passive peasant resistance to making deliveries and repeated guerrilla activity took their toll. A German center for requisitioning livestock on the pattern of the Austrian occupation during the First World War could assemble only insignificant numbers for export. To make matters worse for the local economy, over 40,000 able-bodied men were dispatched from Serbia to the Reich by 1943 as "contract" labor, twice the total for Bulgaria and Romania combined.[19] Belgrade and the other major towns soon faced serious food shortages. German price controls and then ration cards could not prevent the emergence of a widespread black market.

The German response to these assorted Serbian difficulties was to rely instead on the neighboring Banat for the bulk of any exportable agricultural surplus. Better agricultural land and a sizable German minority, with its efficient cooperative organizations, were available there anyway. The first step, in November 1941, was to proscribe the export of most produce from the Banat into Serbia, where the Belgrade black market alone could sell any quantity obtained. The adverse effect on the Serbian population played no noticeable part in deterring this or other Nazi decisions. Then followed the sort of German technical assistance for the Banat, largely through the German minority's cooperative network, that we observed in Romania. Credits for irrigation, silo construction, and cross-breeding of cattle were probably the most useful measures. Serbia meanwhile received little more than consignments of steel plows. This background explains the Banat's ability to provide 87 percent of the wheat and 76 percent of the corn exported to Germany from the two occupied areas together for 1942–43. Oil exports from Banat sunflowers expanded with the area cultivated. Serbian totals still lagged sufficiently to keep the two areas' combined exports of all goods to Germany from reaching the 1939 level.

The oversized Croatian state included much of Bosnia-Hercegovina and Dalmatia. The NDH thus had the misfortune to contain a majority of the food-deficit areas in the first Yugoslavia. German troops stationed in the northern half drew only on local meat supplies. Some 300,000 Italian troops in the south requisitioned all their foodstuffs locally. Shortages thus appeared at once. Price controls and rationing went into effect before the end of 1941. They could not prevent the growth of an extensive black market. Conditions grew so desperate in some Bosnian and Dalmatian deficit areas that their population reportedly clogged the roads in search of food. German imports of food offered limited relief. They covered 20–25 percent of grain consumption. The regime's Ministry of Agriculture set up a Food Economy Division, Pogod, to provision the army, the large towns and the deficit areas. It was similar to PRIZAD and Hranoiznos except that it handled no exports. Pogod failed to build up the reserves it needed to become an effective internal monopoly. The extensive network of existing agricultural cooperatives (see Chapter 10) was used to collect its delivery orders, but harvests that were half the prewar level left too little to go around.[20]

Yugoslav agriculture therefore emerged from the Second World War with the apparatus of the central government's most powerful prewar agency divided and discredited. Its Bulgarian counterpart had never come under such close German control and postwar reconstitution was therefore easier than for PRIZAD. Further distinguishing the Yugoslav experience from the Bulgarian was the amount of wartime destruction. Wheat acreage had fallen to one third of the 1934–38 average by 1945. Livestock herds were largely destroyed, down in some areas to 10 percent of their prewar numbers. Some peasants pulled their own plows to plant the 1945 crops. By the year's end horse numbers were still just 60 percent of the 1938 figure. Cattle and hogs were back to 75–80 percent. One fifth of the surviving population was reckoned to be in an area of 80 percent food deficiency, i.e., a starvation zone.[21] Railway lines were largely destroyed and rolling stock cut in half, much of that damaged.

Massive efforts by the new Communist government combined with $428 million of UNRRA relief aid to achieve the virtual recovery to prewar levels by 1948 recorded in Table 13.6. The early going was extremely difficult from the standpoint of foreign trade. For the period January–September 1945, Yugoslavia could export only 16,000 tons of goods. It imported 121,000 or $12.7 million, without counting food shipments from UNRRA that were twice the latter amount. This assistance rose for the rest of 1945 and still totalled 490,000 tons in 1946. Bad harvests and postwar dislocation made it impossible to export grain, except for small gifts to Romania and Albania. Merchandise exports were just 21 percent of import value in 1946 before rising to 60 percent in 1947 and 85 percent in 1948.[22]

One advantage over Romania, now without Bessarabia, was the retention of the agricultural land in the Banat where German-sponsored modernization had gone further. A related disadvantage was the need for training the native population to use more efficient methods. It had to be brought in from grain-deficit areas under the 1945 land reform to replace the departed Germans. Other advantages over Romania were the clearly broader base created for the new government by the massive Partisan resistance during the war and the absence of Soviet seizures and reparations afterwards. We cannot be certain how much the abortive attempt to collectivize Yugoslav agriculture that began in 1946 suffered from the wartime compromise of the state's prewar agency for grain collection and sale. PRIZAD was in any case the vehicle through which the Communist government began to nationalize wholesale trade in early 1945.[23]

Agricultural supplies and sales had posed more problems for Greece than Yugoslavia during the Second World War. Joining the burden of German and Italian occupation was the Bulgarian annexation of eastern Macedonia and Thrace. These two northern areas had provided about one fifth of the prewar wheat crop. As we have seen in Chapter 11, Greece still had to import over one third of its annual consumption of wheat during the last prewar years. Athens and Piraeus in particular were dependent on imports across a Mediterranean Sea now closed by British blockade. Their population had swollen to 1.3 million during the Italian and German campaigns of 1940–41. Actual famine threatened them by the winter of 1941–42. Wheat acreage and output on the remaining territory fell by over 40 percent. In addition, growing guerrilla activity prevented free traffic southward from the main cultivated areas in Thessaly or further north. German troops in Greece and also those in North Africa requisitioned at will among the various crops grown in the southern half of the country. The urban population survived further famine only because the British command agreed to lift its naval blockade for ships and staff of the Swedish Red Cross, whose deliveries of American and Canadian foodstuffs cut back the death rate and closed part of the black market in Athens by 1943.[24]

Tobacco and to a lesser extent raisins had afforded the bulk of prewar export earnings, as we saw in Chapters 10 and 11. A majority of the tobacco land now came under Bulgarian occupation. The German occupation made no noticeable effort to intensify raisin cultivation through technical assistance. Neither raisins nor tobacco were, after all, essential to the Nazi war effort. The German command simply used the restaffed apparatus of several Greek ministries to buy up for export to the third Reich the entire surplus of the tobacco and raisin crops. Including the Bulgarian area, both were down to small fractions of prewar production.

The war's end cut off this German market and left Greek producers heavily dependent on sales to the United States. Less American dependence on Oriental tobacco and relatively lower Turkish prices posed immediate postwar problems. Greek tobacco exports had risen by 1947 but to no more than 37 percent of their 1939 tonnage. Raisins did slightly better, but total value for all exports reached only 24 percent of the prewar level in 1947 before falling back to 19 percent in 1948. Adding urgency to the need for revived export earnings were postwar grain crops that were less than half of 1939 volume in 1945 and still fell one fifth short in 1947.[25] Modernizing investment to increase agricultural productivity generally, to expand grain production, and to diversify agricultural exports, quickly emerged as an immediate priority for postwar Greece. The provision of this investment came to depend on financial institutions. They played a decisive role in Greek economic recovery, as contrasted to their eclipse in the rest of Southeastern Europe.

Pressures on Independent Financial Institutions

The immediate consequences of the Second World War seemed to spell the end of independent financial institutions throughout the area. The pressures against private commercial banking were powerful even in Greece. Supported by Communist political power, they soon proved irresistible in Bulgaria, Romania, and Yugoslavia. For different reasons, however, the potential for an independent set of financial institutions survived the difficult years of the 1940s in Yugoslavia as well as in Greece. Both countries' institutions have been credited with crucial contributions to the rapid economic growth and structural change in their respective countries since the 1950s.[26] The story of how they weathered German occupation and in Greece a worse inflation than the one that followed the First World War merits the majority of this section.

Greece and Yugoslavia

The interwar experience of the two central banks set the stage for the more important part to be played by the Bank of Greece, postwar political changes aside. Chapters 11 and 12 have already noted how the limitations that its Serbian base put on the Narodna Banka contrasted with the rise of the Bank of Greece from its creation in 1928. The war itself exaggerated the latter's advantage.

For Greece the Second World War had begun with the abortive Italian invasion of October 1940. The Bank of Greece boosted its note issue by 72 percent between then and the German conquest of April 1941. The public's withdrawal of deposits from the central and commercial banks, under way since late 1939, nonetheless slowed velocity and internal inflation. This hoarding also allowed the drachma to maintain its rate of exchange in Western markets, as long as the British government was able to continue lending the Greek government sufficient funds for military expenses.[27]

Catastrophic inflation, the first of several waves, followed the Nazi occupation. Prices in Athens were said to have risen 13,000 percent by mid-1942. The Bank's printing press covered four fifths of the budgetary expenses for the German-held area, once the drachma was restored as the national currency in August 1941. Almost all of the inflationary note issue went to cover the costs of Nazi occupation. They included the requisitions needed to supply the several hundred thousand German personnel stationed there and in North Africa. Nazi efforts to slow down the currency's depreciation consisted mainly of selling gold coins on the internal market. This was the start of the "gold mania" that was to bedevil the Bank's effort to restore convertible paper currency even after the war.[28]

Limiting the German capacity for gold circulation was the fact that the Bank of Greece had been able to evacuate its own gold and foreign exchange reserves to Egypt and then South Africa before the occupation. The Bank's Governor plus a number of key officials and staff had gone along to Cairo. Governor Varvaressos was therefore able to represent the Bank of Greece during the main Allied meetings that drafted plans for wartime aid and postwar recovery, including the 1943 conference to set up the United Nations Relief and Rehabilitation Administration (UNRRA). Postwar access to massive Western credit, a distinguishing feature of the Greek experience after the First World War, was again assured.

Meanwhile the economy of the Greek mainland faced further strains that would delay full recovery and further growth into the 1950s. The rate of inflation had slowed slightly during 1942–43. It accelerated again in 1944. Early hopes for an Allied invasion following the victory in North Africa had now faded. German requisitions remained high despite the defeat of the Afrika Korps. British gold delivered to the resistance groups put further pressure on the drachma. Table 13.8 records the incredible volume of note issue, over 8 million times the nominal value in April 1941, by October 1944. During that period gold prices had soared by 2.3 billion percent.[29]

Liberation in October 1944, brought back not only the leadership but also the gold and foreign exchange reserves of the Bank of Greece. These were unfortunately not used to support the new drachma, issued at a rate of 1=600 old drachmae in the abortive November monetary reform. The Bank simply printed up the new currency and left the task of supporting its value in gold sovereigns to the largest commercial bank, the National Bank of Greece. These decisions, plus the political uncertainty that culminated in the Communist uprising of December 1944, triggered another round of unprecedented inflation. In 1945 the Governor of the Bank of Greece, again Professor Varvaressos after several months under Professor Zolatas, attempted to stem the tide. He banned gold exchange, introduced new and progressive direct taxes, and controlled imports and prices. UNRRA and other Anglo-American aid could cover only one third of the prewar level of domestic consumption. Agricultural and industrial production, let alone exports, could not revive to anywhere near the extent needed to make up the other two thirds. His ambitious plan therefore failed, and Varvaressos resigned again in favor of Zolatas. The Bank restored the exchange in sovereigns and began to support their rate of exchange for drachmae directly. These measures joined in 1946 with a good harvest and the further British credits of

January's London agreement to improve monetary confidence briefly.[30] The renewed civil war and the end of UNRRA aid in 1947 delayed recovery to prewar levels for agriculture and industry until 1949. The important part played therein by U.S. technical and financial assistance, especially in electrification, has received thorough treatment elsewhere.[31]

More important for our purposes is the role assumed by the Bank of Greece in the immediate postwar period. Its Governor had become the government's ranking economic official. Its credits were crucial to the recovery that was achieved. The continuing inflation kept depositors from returning their funds to commercial banks. By mid-1947 their real level still amounted to just 6 percent of the prewar amount. Credits from the Bank directly to the economy and indirectly through the Agricultural Bank and the commercial banks were virtually all that was available to industry and agriculture for 1946–47, outside of UNRRA assistance. Both sources of funds concentrated on agriculture in general and tobacco in particular.[32] Table 13.8 reflects the background of continuing inflation and unprecedented note issue. Both surpassed German figures for 1921–24. This was the context within which the Greek economy continued to operate until the civil war with Communist guerrillas entered its final stages in 1950.

The Yugoslav central bank had ceased to exist in 1941. Officials of the Narodna Banka had managed to assemble the bank's gold and other reserves in Sarajevo hours before the German attack, but were not able to carry out their plan to transport it out of the country, as the Bank of Greece had done. The country's dismemberment left the various occupying authorities to set up their own banking systems. Old notes were quickly withdrawn from circulation, first in the Hungarian Bačka, then in Croatia and in the German and Italian areas of occupation, and finally in Bulgarian-held Macedonia. The new currencies that were introduced became the only legal tender within each area. Trade between areas came to a virtual standstill. Commercial credit disappeared, with rare exceptions. The purchasing power of these assorted notes on the black market slid to 5–10 percent of their face value. Total note issue, according to Table 13.8, jumped about twentyfold in value for 1941–44.

The "kuna" issued by the new Croatian State Bank, or Hrvatska Državna Banka, was able to maintain the ratio of the prewar Yugoslav dinar to the German Reichsmark but otherwise derived little advantage from its satellite status. The Croatian government was obliged to accept German demands that it take over 45 percent of prewar Yugoslav debts, despite its plea for 5 percent. The bank's advances to the regime for the German troops for their maintenance on Croatian territory accounted for perhaps half of its assets by the end of 1943.[33]

A Serbian National Bank, or Srpska Narodna Banka, was set up in

TABLE 13.8
INDICES OF INFLATION, 1938-50[a]

	Year	BULGARIA	GREECE	ROMANIA	YUGOSLAVIA
A.	Currency in Circulation				
	1939	100[c]	100[d]	100[e]	100
	1940	142	163	132	143
	1941	276	516	198	(158)[f]
	1942	413	3,543	240	
	1943	631	33,841	328	
	1944	1,182		731	3,011[g]
	1944	100	100	100	100[h]
	1945	109	7,398	340	297
	1946	102	39,299	1,715	342
	1947	113	71,147	12,989	492
	1948		87,801		654
	1949		135,793		752
	1950		137,838		666
B.	Cost of Living				
	1939	100[i]	100	100	100
	1940	112	111	136	131
	1941	135	391	195	177
	1942	178	6,115	286	
	1943	226	25,778	386	
	1944	334	(j)	579	
	1944	100	100[k]	100	
	1945	149	339	592	
	1946	168	2,509	3,647	
	1947	186	2,983	46,718	
	1948		4,271		
	1949		4,882		
	1950		5,288		

Notes: (a)Except as noted, note circulation is for December 31, while price indices are annual averages. This difference accounts for part of the discrepancies between quantity of money and price movements. (b)Index for Romania only covers Bucharest; that for Greece only covers Athens and during the years 1941 to 1944 is based on food costs of 1,904 calories per day. Retail price indices in Romania and Bulgaria, in 1944, were slightly higher by amounts, respectively, of 7.7 and 12.1 percent, probably because of the lower inflation of housing costs in costs of living. (c)In addition to national bank notes, the Bulgarian index includes special three percent bonds issued beginning in 1942 and which circulated as a means of payment until the currency reform in 1947. Romania also circulated bonds and payment certificates which could be used to pay taxes, but evidently not as general means of payment. (d)During the war, the area of drachma circulation was reduced and during the war some unknown amounts of occupying-country currencies circulated in addition to significant quantities of gold sovreigns. After the war, from the date of liberation to May 31, 1945, British Military Authority pounds were also legal tender in Greece. (e)The Romanian index includes only national bank notes. By 1939, coin circulation was 14.6 percent of the value of notes and, in 1946, only 4.6 percent of the value of notes. (f)March. (g)The Yugoslav figure for 1944 represents the dinar equivalent (292 billion) of Serbian (Nedic) dinars, Croatian kunas, Reichsmarks, Italian lire, Albanian francs, Hungarian pengös, Bulgarian leva and, possibly, promissory notes of the Partisans, Slovenian fascists and occupying powers at the end of the war. (h)The base figure of 100 for 1944 represents the 6 billion new federal dinars issued at the time of currency conversion on April 10, 1945. (i)The Bulgarian cost-of-living index in the table is the official index reflecting legal prices; an unofficial index using estimated black-market prices showed the following movements (1939100): 151 (1941), 229 (1942), 320 (1943) and 513 (1944). (j)During 1944, the Greek index, compared to the average of 1943, increased nearly 10 times by January and on November 10, at the time of currency reform, increased about 750,000,000 times the average 1943 level. (k)The base 100 for 1944 is taken as the average level of prices in November and December after currency reform.

*Given data reflect conditions at the time of currency reforms: *Bulgaria*—On March 7, 1947, the special three percent bonds were withdrawn from circulation and old leva replaced by new leva at a ratio of 1:1 (sums above 2,000 leva per person were blocked). Some 44.4 billion leva in notes and 31.5 billion leva in bonds were replaced by 30-35 billion new leva. *Greece*—On November 10, 1944, old drachmae were converted to new drachmae at a ratio of 50,000,000,000:1; also, new drachmae were made "convertible" to British Military Authority pounds at a ratio of 600:1. At the time, some 6,279,943 trillion old drachmae were replaced by 126.6 million new drachmae. *Romania*—On August 15, 1947, old lei were converted to new lei at a ratio of 20,000:1 (with quotas and restrictions on amounts exchanged). Of some 48,451 billion old lei, 57 percent, or 27,550 billion, were replaced by 1.3 billion new lei and another 550 million new lei issued in exchange for gold and foreign currencies. *Yugoslavia*—On April 10, 1945, some 292 billion of various currencies (see note g) were converted into 6 billion new dinars.

Sources: B. R. Mitchell, *European Historical Statistics, 1750-1970* (New York: Columbia University Press, 1975), pp. 676-79, 738-39, 745-56; Nicholas Spulber, *Economics of Communist Eastern Europe* (New York: MIT Press and John Wiley, 1957), pp. 104-05, 113-17, 128; Dimitrios Delivanis and William C. Cleveland, *Greek Monetary Developments, 1939-1948* (Bloomington: Indiana University, 1949), pp. 112-13, 175-89; M. Maievschi, *Contribuţii la istoria finanţelor publice ale României* (Bucharest, 1957), Annex IX; P. Kiranov, "Natsionalni dokhod na Bulgariia, 1939-1944-1945," *Izvunredno izdanie na trimesechno spisanie na glavnata direktsiia na statistikata* (Sofia, 1946), pp. 43, 79; Zhak Natan, V. Khadzhinikolov and L. Berov (eds.), *Ikonomika na Bulgariia*, Vol. I (Sofia, 1969), pp. 625-26; Zhak Natan, *Stopanska istoriia na Bulgariia* (Sofia, 1957), p. 526; C. C. Kiriţescu, *Sistemul bănesc al leului şi precursorii lui*, Vol. II (Bucharest, 1967), pp. 522-24.

Belgrade, also in May 1941, directly by the aforementioned German Plenipotentiary for the Economy. New dinars were fixed at an exchange rate with the Reichsmark that was about one third below the prewar level. Its credit was restricted to small amounts approved by German authorities. The bank joined other official collaborators in trying to collect 40 percent of all Serbian income for occupation costs. German authorities nonetheless suspected bank officials of diverting funds to aid the Četnik forces of the controversial Serbian resistance movement under Draža Mihailović. Whatever the truth of these suspicions, the fact remains that on a per capita basis the German occupation cost the Serbian population six times the financial contributions paid by Croatia and seven times the estimates for Bulgaria and Romania made by the Bank of International Settlements.[34]

The German retreat and Soviet advance of late 1944 left all political power in the hands of Marshal Tito's Partisans. This resistance movement had spread its activities across all Yugoslav territory, thereby winning British and American support despite its Communist leadership. The practical imperatives of reunifying Yugoslavia thrust the recreation of a central bank and a single currency into the hands of the new government. A new "federal" dinar soon replaced the various wartime denominations. Only small wartime accumulations of funds could be converted from a total issue that was over forty times the prewar level. Croatian kuna were accepted at a still more unfavorable rate of exchange than Austro-Hungarian crowns had been in 1918–20. The Ustaši regime had discredited itself too thoroughly to generate the same Croatian resentment as followed the First World War. The new Narodna Banka in Belgrade could begin to build its position free from the onus of collaboration carried by its counterparts in Sofia and Bucharest.[35]

Although private institutions did not survive the first year of Communist power, commercial banking did retain the foothold from which the financial basis of decentralized market socialism would develop a decade later. The large Zagreb banks had no hope of surviving, given their ties to Central European depositors and to the Ustaši regime. Belgrade now became the financial center of Yugoslavia. Four private banks in the capital, including the pre-1914 Izvozna, Beogradska Zadruga, and Beogradska Trgovačka Banka, were allowed to survive and merge into the Export and Credit Bank, or Izvozna i Trgovačka Banka. Soon nationalized, it nonetheless joined the Investment Bank, formed from the longstanding State Mortgage Bank, or Državna Hipotekarna Banka, as one of the two powerful Belgrade institutions with commercial functions. They and a network of sixty local banks received official sanction to multiply in 1948. Stripped of private stockholders, these two sorts of financial institutions would create the Yugoslav practice of socialist commercial banking during the decade that followed.[36]

Bulgaria and Romania

Commercial banking even under state auspices has been conspicuous in Bulgaria and Romania since 1948 only by its absence.[37] Treatment of its experience during the decade that ended in 1948 can therefore be brief. The smoother Bulgarian transition away from private commercial banking and easier adjustment to the pressures of immediate postwar inflation still deserve emphasis.

The state share of Bulgarian bank capital was already the largest in Southeastern Europe before the war. It included not only the central bank and the postal savings banks but also the country's preeminent financial institution, the Agricultural and Cooperative Bank, and a 40 percent interest in the Banka Bulgarski Kredit that merged twelve private native banks in 1934. Together they accounted for two thirds of all bank deposits and three quarters of credit by 1936, as noted in Chapter 12. Their share of deposits climbed still further to 94 percent and credit to 97 percent by the end of 1944. The Agricultural and Cooperative Bank had made some of these gains later in the war. The bulk came afterwards from the expansion of the so-called state-private sector to include all foreign banks. All but one had become German or Italian during the course of the war. They were taken over by Soviet authorities during the period 1944–47. The Bulgarian government formally bought out the foreign stock of the non-Axis Banque Franco-Bulgare from the Paris-Bas bank in 1947 but had been in practical control from the war's end. By 1947, the tripling of deposits and credits in both the Agricultural Bank and Bulgarski Kredit swamped the small private sector, led by the pre-1914 Bulgarska Turgovska Banka, still further. During these few years the state's share of Bulgarski Kredit's capital had grown to 91 percent.[38] Legislation at the end of 1947 to end all private holdings of bank capital, therefore, hardly sent shock waves through Bulgaria's financial structure.

We may speculate that the state's existing leverage in central and commercial banking helped to achieve the most moderate of the postwar inflations. Whereas the note issue of the Narodna Banka and the cost of living in black market prices had risen more than fivefold for the period 1939–44, Table 13.8 indicates only a 41 percent rise in 1945 and a decline thereafter.

Romanian prices did not increase so rapidly during the war. Ordinary revenues, it is true, covered just 52 percent of the state's budgetary expenses by 1943, in contrast to 81 percent for Bulgaria.

Outweighing this greater stimulus to inflation and also the Germans' direct purchase of their own provisions, however, was the smaller size of the Romanian surplus in its clearing account for German trade. This surplus represented new currency that the central bank had to issue in order to compensate local exporters (see Chapter 10 for similarities to German practice in the First World War). The Bulgarian surplus amounted to 66 percent of new note issue from the National Bank in 1943. The Romanian figure was much lower, 23 percent, thanks in part to over one billion Reichsmarks in German credit that Bulgaria did not receive. Without this credit, the Romanian percentage could have been doubled.[39]

The Romanian rate of inflation from 1944 to 1947 was much greater than the Bulgarian. Note issue and the cost of living climbed by ever larger amounts in each of these years. Only Greece experienced a more rapid rate, as noted in Table 13.8. Romania faced participation in the rest of the war plus a series of Soviet impositions. From August 1944 until June 1945, the Romanian government could not cover more than 35 percent of its budgetary expenditures with regular revenues. Military costs accounted for almost one third of those expenses. A similar amount went to meet obligations under the armistice agreement with the Soviet Union. They were half reparations, and the rest support for the Soviet garrision in Romania and the conversion of all Red Army script into lei. Rubles were also converted for various Soviet activities, including the joint companies. All of the resulting budgetary deficit had to be covered with new note issues.[40]

No exports earning Western currency were permitted. The tonnage of paid exports barely matched the low percentages of prewar level recorded in war torn Greece. The Romanian proportion was 3 percent in 1945 and reached 25 percent in 1947. The value of exports as a fraction of imports was 31 percent in 1946, the last year before a currency revaluation, not much better than Yugoslavia's 21 percent. Unpaid deliveries to the Soviet Union were responsible for keeping the Romanian figures so low.[41]

The Soviet presence ironically weakened the state's control over the financial sector. The weakening of private, especially Jewish, commercial banks had already begun in the 1930s. The infusion of agricultural credit needed to revive the native provincial banks had not followed, even during the war years. The National Bank remained mainly in the hands of private Liberal stockholders. The large Bucharest banks were tainted in varying degrees with German stock purchases. The four foreign banks were quickly converted to joint Soviet-Romanian enterprises. Their assets and the authority of their new Russian directors allowed them to control 53 percent of the bank credit granted in 1947. By this time the first Romanian Communist appointed to the National Bank's board in 1945 had become director. The former director was the only non-Communist left on the board. By the middle of 1947, the National Bank could investigate the background of anyone borrowing from a commercial bank. Such measures and a series of mergers that cut the number of banks to 70 had effectively nationalized them by the year's end.[42] The lack of comparable control over the large Soviet-Romanian banks nonetheless denied the Communist-dominated regime the financial leverage available to the Bulgarian government. The much poorer Romanian record in controlling postwar inflation thus becomes more understandable.

Industry in the German War Effort and Afterwards

Rapid industrial and urban growth have easily been the most striking features of the Southeastern European economies since the Second World War. Almost all of the quantum statistical jumps over 1938–39 levels have taken place since 1950. The 1940s barely permitted recovery to prewar totals for Romanian and Greek industrial production. Yet Table 13.11 below calls our attention to the fact that Yugoslav and Bulgarian industry increased their real output to more than half again the 1938–39 level by 1948. This section seeks to explain that superior performance. It also deals with the varied institutional pattern set for further growth in all four economies. Albanian industrial growth before 1939 was almost nonexistent and the wartime experience poorly recorded. Its first industrial stirrings in the late 1940s therefore escape the connection to historical context that would justify inclusion in this chapter.[43]

The widespread urbanization that would reduce the rural share of population to less than half everywhere except Albania by the early 1960s made only limited progress during the 1940s. Table 13.9 reflects modest increments of 2–4 percent in urban proportions during the decade. Greece was still the most urbanized at 36 percent by 1950, with 30 percent in towns over 20,000. The Greek population dependent on agriculture was also the lowest proportion of the total, just over 50 percent, but hardly budged between 1940 and 1949. The migration from mountain villages in food-deficit areas to the plains and eventually the towns, which William McNeill has identified as the most important economic consequence of the Greek Civil War, was just beginning. Elsewhere the efforts of the new Communist governments to transfer people from rural agriculture to urban industry did not show much statistical progress by 1950.[44] Ratios of dependence on agriculture, according to Table 13.10, dropped from just

over 70 percent to just under 70 during the decade. The industrial
share of the male labor force advanced a few points to about 15 percent. For Bulgaria, the leader in industrial growth for the 1940s, that
share slipped from 14.5 back to 12.3 percent between 1946 and 1950.
In other words, rapid urbanization for whatever reason did not follow, let alone lead, the industrial recovery just after the Second
World War.

The shape of that recovery emerges from Table 13.11. Several sectors of light industry turn out to have contributed as much as the
heavy industry which the Communist governments supposedly emphasized in the transition to Soviet-style planning. The rapid postwar
advances of net industrial output in Yugoslavia until 1948 and in
Bulgaria through 1950 derive not only from high indices of growth
for metal processing and the extraction of fuels and raw materials.
The still major branches of textile, timber, and food production also
moved well past prewar levels. Romanian industry by contrast could
not even resume its 1938 output in any of these branches. Its total
net output by 1948 amounted to 94 percent of that level, then jump-
ing to 164 percent by 1950. This was the first of the intensive,
forced-draft spurts characteristic of its subsequent growth.[45] Greek
industry would make little overall progress until the Civil War ended
in 1952. Mining was especially hard hit. Only cigarette manufacture
and, as everywhere in Southeastern Europe, capacity for electric
power, jumped ahead before then.

Bulgaria and Romania

Industry made a faster postwar recovery in Bulgaria than in
Romania. This occurred partly because the former's larger Communist Party established its economic authority more quickly and
because the burden of Soviet reparations was far lighter. This much
is well if not precisely known. The relatively better Bulgarian experience during the Second World War has not received the same
recognition.

Until the turbulent, transitional year of 1944, Bulgarian industry
produced more in real terms than it had in 1939. According to Table
13.12, manufacturing output had risen 17 percent by 1941 and fell
back only to the 1939 level in 1943. Food, tobacco, and chemical
processing showed the sharpest increases. Mining, principally coal,
continued to climb to 71 percent beyond the prewar level by 1943.
Romania's gross manufacturing output, on the other hand, had already fallen by one third in 1941 from the 1938 level for comparable
territory. (Thus the loss of much of Transylvania to Hungary in 1940
does not enter into this decline.) Manufacturing recovered some lost

TABLE 13.9
URBAN SHARES OF POPULATION, 1940-50

YEAR	ALBANIA	BULGARIA	GREECE	ROMANIA	YUGOSLAVIA
A. As Nationally Defined					
1940	15.4	23.0	32.0	22.8	22.8
1946	21.3	24.7		22.8	
1947					
1948		26.4		23.6	
1949					
1950	20.5	27.5	36.3	24.7	25.9
B. In Places of 20,000 Persons or More					
1940	8.0	15.0	25.0	18.0	10.0
1950	11.3	19.3	30.3	18.2	12.6

Notes and Sources: Unless otherwise noted: United Nations, *Demographic Yearbook, 1955* (New York, 1956), p. 195; *1960*, pp. 385, 394; United Nations, Department of Economic and Social Affairs, *Growth of the World's Urban and Rural Population. 1920-2000*, Population Studies, No. 44 (New York, 1969), pp. 104-06. *Albania*: Official urban definition includes towns and other industrial centers with more than 400 inhabitants. Population of places with 20,000 or more (in 1940 and 1950 only three—Tirana, Shkoder and Korce) from Stavro Skendi (ed.), *Albania* (London: Atlantic Press, 1957), p. 53. *Bulgaria*: Official urban definition includes localities legally established as urban. Data are for postwar territory from *Statisticheski godishnik na narodna republika Bulgariia, 1976* (Sofia, 1977), p. 31. *Greece*: The official urban definition has changed. Figures in the table are from U.N. sources and include all communes of Greater Athens and other places having a population of 10,000 or more. The current and more complex definition gives slightly higher figures of 32.8 percent for 1940 and 37.7 percent for 1951 (in place of 36.8 percent). The latter figures are from: *Statistikē epetēris tēs Ellados, 1972* (Athens, 1973), p. 26. *Romania*: Official urban definition includes cities, towns and other localities having an urban socio-economic character. Data are for postwar territory from *Anuarul demografic al republice socialiste România, 1974* (Bucharest, 1975), p. 3.

ground in 1943, according to Table 13.12. Growth in metallurgy rose 19 percent past prewar output, and construction materials also exceeded that level. Chemicals, including petroleum refining, wood, and paper, had the poorest records, dropping to half of their 1938 production by 1941 and continuing to slip thereafter. Extraction fared just slightly better than manufacturing, whose gross output decreased to half of the prewar level in 1944 and to less than half in 1945.

The changing number of enterprises and their changing size and horsepower give us another basis for comparing Bulgaria to Romania. The latter's data on industrial production allow a matchup only with the Bulgarian aggregate for 1945, after the war's end but before the Soviet Union could organize industrial reparations. The Bulgarian index of 112 on a 1938 base is well ahead of the Romanian figure of 74. Our reading back of this Bulgarian advantage into the war years draws support from Table 13.13. The number of Bulgarian firms multiplied by about one third from 1939 to 1944; a similar Romanian increase curiously occurred from 1944 to 1947.

Before examining these later years, more must be said about Bulgarian industry and the Nazi war effort. Few new German or Italian

TABLE 13.10

ESTIMATES OF POPULATION DEPENDENT ON AGRICULTURE AND LABOR FORCE—BEFORE AND AFTER THE SECOND WORLD WAR

Country	Year	Population Dependent on Agriculture (1000)	(%)	Agriculture Males (1000)	(%)	Labor Force Industry Total (1000)	Males (1000)	(%)	Other Total (1000)	Males (1000)	(%)
Albania	1950	(see notes)									
Bulgaria	1934[a]	4,447	73.2	1,347.9	71.1	274.7	228.5	12.0	413.5	323.3	17.0
	1938[a]	4,560	72.7								
	1946	4,975	68.7	1,540.5	66.1	430.4	337.9	14.5	592.3	453.6	19.5
	1950			1,923	67.5	455	350	12.3	677	575	20.2
Greece	1928[a]	4,380	68.3	1,008.0	51.1	436.2	336.1	17.0	833.6	628.2	31.9
	1940[a]	3,847	52.6								
	1949	3,920	52.3								
	1951			1,152.3	49.5	550.2	426.5	18.3	922.0	750.1	32.2
Romania	1930[a]	13,063	72.3	4,054.5	71.3	755.1	614.4	10.8	1,471.4	1,013.2	17.9
	1941[b]	9,690	71.6								
	1950			4,606	68.2	1,243	953	14.1	1,553	1,190	17.6
Yugoslavia	1930[a]	10,629	76.5	3,234.3	74.5	717.0	592.7	13.7	661.9	513.1	11.8
	1938[a]	11,586	74.8								
	1948[c]	10,606	67.2	3,322.3	68.3	908.0	725.3	14.9	1,204.8	816.6	16.8
	1953[c]	10,315	64.3	3,079.2	64.7	1,192.7	978.8	20.6	977.0	703.0	14.8

firms were established in industry or commerce. Their share of the total peaked in 1942 at just 4 percent of joint-stock enterprises. State-owned coal mines, as noted earlier, dominated the fast-rising extractive sector. Sofia was the site for 90 percent of the new corporations. Its overall share rose from 27 to 42 percent. Industrial concentration in the capital city that was unique even in Southeastern Europe received another boost. Capital for joint-stock enterprises tripled in real terms during the war.[46] The volume of machinery imports by 1943 was almost twice the 1939 tonnage. Thus we further infer that the fourfold rise in horsepower per metallurgical worker and the 40 percent increments for food, tobacco, and timber processing from 1939 to 1946, recorded in Table 13.13, must largely have occurred before the end of the war.

Bulgarian industry not only came out of the war with greater momentum than in Romania but was also freer to draw upon it. State control of a majority of coal mines, including 85 percent of combined output, precluded the sort of joint German ownership that would have handed them over to Soviet administration for the first postwar years. The joint Soviet-Bulgarian mining enterprise had been left with the Plakalnitsa copper mine and a variety of smaller operations. No such companies were formed for Bulgarian manufacturing other than the two construction material and ship-building enterprises.[47]

The state sector in Bulgarian manufacturing had admittedly been much smaller than in mining. It furnished less than 5 percent of total output in 1944 and 24 percent as late as 1947. State purchases of the

---

Notes: (a)From population on prewar territory. (b)From population on postwar territory without northern Transylvania. (c)Labor force distribution based on total employed.

Sources: *Albania*—In 1950, the total Albanian labor force is estimated at 387,991 persons (out of a population of 1,218,900 of whom 589,200 were of working age). Agriculture (and forestry) employment, including state employees, numbered 295,715, or 76.2 percent; state employees in industry (including mining) numbered 39,751, or 10.2 percent of total employment (employment in manufacturing was about 20,759). A small number of additional employees were found in private and cooperative industry. Ramadan Marmullaku, *Albania and the Albanians* (Hamden, Conn.: Archon Books, 1975), pp. 159-61; Hans-Joachim Pernack, *Probleme der wirtschaftlichen Entwicklung Albaniens* (Munich, 1972), p. 163; Michael Kaiser and Adi Schnytzer, "Albania—A uniquely Socialist Economy," in *East European Economies*, A Compendium of Papers Submitted to the Joint Economic Committee, Congress of the United States, 95th Congress, 1st Session (Wash., D.C.: U. S. Government Printing Office, August 25, 1977), p. 618.

Other Countries—Jozo Tomasevich, *Peasants, Politics, and Economic Change in Yugoslavia* (Palo Alto, Calif.: Stanford University Press, 1955), p. 377 (estimates of population dependent on agriculture in 1938 for Bulgaria and Yugoslavia by projecting its growth for 1926-34 and 1921-30 respectively); Henry L. Roberts, *Rumania, Political Problems of an Agrarian State* (New Haven: Yale University Press, 1951), p. 359 (population dependent on agriculture from the Romanian agricultural census of 1941); Food and Agricultural Organization of the United Nations, *Production Yearbook, 1961* (Rome, 1962), p. 16 (population dependent on agriculture for Greece in 1940 and 1949; data in this source for Romania in 1941 and Yugoslavia in 1951 are misleading); Savezni zavod za statistiku, *Jugoslavija, 1945-1964* (Belgrade, 1965), p. 46; P. Bairoch et al, *The Working Population and its Structure*, International Historical Statistics, Vol. 1, Institut de Sociologie, Université Libre de Bruxelles (Bruxelles, 1968), pp. 89, 101, 113, 120; Andrew Elias, "Magnitude and Distribution of the Labor Force in Eastern Europe," in *Economic Developments in Countries of Eastern Europe*, A Compendium of Papers Submitted to the Joint Economic Committee, Congress of the United States, 91st Congress, 2d Session (Wash., D.C.: U. S. Government Printing Office, 1970), pp. 209-37 (data from this source were used to estimate male labor force distributions in 1950 for Romania and Bulgaria by applying the percentages of female labor in the socialized non-agricultural sectors of Bulgaria for 1952 and Romania for 1957 to total employment in "industry" and "other" for 1950; female labor in agriculture was estimated by subtracting the estimates of females in non-agricultural sectors from estimated total female employment in 1950); *Anuarul statistic al R. S. România, 1977*, p. 101 (the official estimate of the distribution of occupied persons in 1950 is not available by sex, but the totals differ from the Elias estimates with larger totals in agriculture which reflect higher levels of female participation in agriculture).

TABLE 13.11
INDUSTRIAL OUPUT, 1938-50

Country	(a)	1938	1939	1945	1946	1947	1948	1949	1950
A. Net Output									
Albania	(ukn)								
Bulgaria	(1939)		100	112^g	115^g	133^g	159	189	222
Greece^c	(1954)	100					88	113	125
Romania	(1950)	100		$(74)^e$			94		164
Yugoslavia	(1938)	92	100			120	150	166	167
B. Gross Output									
Albania	(ukn)	100_b		24_h	97_h	159	254	306	395
Bulgaria	(1939)	100^b	106	97^h	102^h				
	(1956)		100				203	268	309
Greece	(1939)	100^b	106		56	71	77	93	117
Romania	(1938)	100^e	$(102)^d$	56^e					
	(1955)	100_b							147
Yugoslavia	(1955)	100^b	106	$(32-37)^f$	84	113	159	177	182

Notes and Sources: (a)Base year of price-weights. (b)Official indices shifted from 1939 to 1938 using prewar indices in Mitchell and the League of Nations. (c)Mining excluded. (d)For manufacturing only. (e)Georgescu-Roegen estimates. (f)Tomasevich citation for December. (g)Data from Zagoroff. (h)Data from *Ikonomika na Bulgariia*, as cited in Table 13.12. Vol. II, pp. 126 *Albania*: It remains unclear if Albanian data are in constant prices or in current prices. The source implies that they are in current prices; see Stavro Skendi (ed.), *Albania* (London: Atlantic Press, 1957), pp. 192-93. However, the dimension of change to 1950 approximatels the real sectoral indices in Michael Kaser and Adi Schnytzer, "Albania—A Uniquely Socialist Economy," in *East European Economies Post-Helsinki*, A Compendium of Papers submitted to the Joint Economic Committee, Congress of the United States, 95th Congress, 1st Session (Wash., D.C.; U. S. Government Printing Office, 1977), p. 634. *Bulgaria*: Table 13.12; *Statisticheski godishnik na narodna republika Bulgariia*, *1957*, pp. 26-30; Gregor Lazarcik and Alexej Wynnczuk, *Bulgaria: Growth of Industrial Output, 1939 and 1948-1965*, Occasional Papers of the Research Project on National Income in East Central Europe, OP-27 (New York: Columbia University Press, 1968), p. 4 (the cited official gross output index in 1956 prices deviates slightly from that given in the Bulgarian yearbook). *Greece*: *Statistikē epetēris tēs Ellados, 1954*, pp. 51-52; *1957* (Athens, 1958), p. 211; George Coutsoumaris. *The Morphology of Greek Industry* (Athens, 1963), p. 372. *Romania*: *Anuarul statistic al R. P. R., 1957*, p. 79; *Anuarul statistic al republicii socialiste România, 1974*, p. 51; N. Georgescu-Roegen, *Modificări structurale în venitul nationale al României în urma celui de al doilea război mondial* (Bucharest, 1947), pp. 7, 20-21. *Yugoslavia*: Savezni zavod za statistiku, *Jugoslavija, 1945-1964*, pp. 144-45; Stevan Stajić, "Realni nacionalni dohodak Jugoslavije u periodima 1926-1939 i 1947-1956," *Ekonomski problemi zbornik radova* (Belgrade, 1957), p. 45; Jozo Tomasevich, "Postwar Foreign Economic Relations," in Joseph R. Kerner (ed.), *Yugoslavia* (Berkeley and Los Angeles: University of California Press, 1949), p. 397.

Granitoid cement works and several other large joint-stock companies accounted for the increase that had occurred by 1947. Nationalization of most industrial enterprises at year's end pushed the fraction up to 85 percent in 1948. But state participation in manufacturing went beyond these modest pre-1948 figures. From late 1944 forward private firms could not stop or even limit production without state authorization. Initial delivery orders issued to firms by the new ministerial apparatus had become part of a coordinated annual plan by 1946 and a two-year plan for 1947–48. In the rapidly recovering food industry, the state's Hranoiznos revived the old Ottoman *ishleme* system (see Chapter 5) of furnishing private firms with raw materials and assuming responsibility for the sale of flour or other finished products.[48]

TABLE 13.12

BULGARIAN AND ROMANIAN INDUSTRIAL PRODUCTION, 1938-45

Bulgaria	1938	1939	1940	1941	1942	1943	1944[f]	1945[f]
Net Output	—	100	111	118	113	110	(97)[f]	(112)[f]
Mining	—	100	120	125	160	174	134	159
Manufacturing	—	100	110	117	106	100	90	97
Gross Output	94	100	111	118	113	110	90	91
Investment Goods	89	100	99	91	102	97	97	115
Food	90	100	124	135	104	114	98	—
Other Consumer	96	100	110	118	117	114	102	—
Mining	94	100	119	126	157	171	184	201
Metals	98	100	81	99	112	89	77	60
Non-wood building materials	84	100	109	89	95	101	70	110
Chemicals	132	100	149	132	110	101	56	65
Food and tobacco	100	100	123	150	136	112	106	85
Textiles	90	100	97	92	67	66	58	72
Woodworking	100	100	115	96	128	113	93	202
Leather	76	100	81	76	63	61	89	58
Paper	95	100	109	145	161	(181)[g]	85	99
Electric power	88	100	110	113	119	(122)[g]	114	149

TABLE 13.12 (continued)

Romania	1938	1939	1940	1941	1942	1943	1944	1945
Gross Output								
Food	100	—	—	81	64	78	60	46
Metal and machinery	100	—	—	84	102	119	83	42
Chemicals	100	—	—	50	51	48	30	46
Construction materials	100	—·	—	92	116	113	67	54
Wood, paper, printing	100	—	104	42	41	35	37	33
Textiles	100	—	92	57	55	60	29	47
Leather	100	—	116	—	—	—	—	77
Total manufacturing	100	—	102	—	—	—	—	45
(excluding leather)	100	—	—	68	70	76	52	44
Extraction	100	—	—	85	89	88	63	72
Total Industry	100	—	—	—	—	—	—	56
(Excluding leather)	100	—	——	75	78	81	56	56
Net Output								
Manufacturing	100	—	—	—	—	—	—	29
Extraction	100	—	—	—	—	—	—	72
Electric power	100	—	—	—	—	—	—	118
State monopolies	100	—	—	—	—	—	—	108
Artisan	100	—	—	—	—	—	—	97
Total	100	—	—	—	—	—	—	60

Notes: (a)Without Bessarabia and Southern Dobrogea. (b)Without Northern Transylvania. (c)Excluding transportation equipment except locomotives. (d)Data from Natan. (e)Data from *Ikonomika na Bulgariia*, Vol. I. (f)Data for values and indices of total net industrial production in 1944-46 from Zagoroff; gross output indices for branches in 1944-46 from *Ikonomika na Bulgariia*, Vol. II. (g)For first half of year.

Sources: *Statisticheski godishnik na Bulgarskoto Tsarstvo, 1940*, pp. 384, 504, 622; Asen Chakalov, *Natsionalniiat dokhod na Bulgariia, 1924-45* (Sofia, 1946), pp. 66, 78, 80; Zhak Natan, *Stopanska istoriia na Bulgariia*, pp. 506, 524, 545; Zhak Natan, V. Khadzhinikolov and L. Berov (eds.), *Ikonomika na Bulgariia*, Vol. I (Sofia, 1969), pp. 615, 626; N. Popov, A. Miloshevski and I. Kostov, *Ikonomika na Bulgariia*, Vol. II (Sofia, 1972), pp. 126-27; P. Kiranov, "Natsionalni dokhod na Bulgaria, 1939-1944-1945," in *Izvunredno izdanie na trimesechno spisanie na glavnata direktsiia na statistikata* (Sofia, 1946), pp. 42, 81, 85; League of Nations, *Statistical Yearbook, 1942/44* (Geneva, 1945), p. 182; S. D. Zagoroff, *The Economy of Bulgaria* (Washington, D.C.: Council for Economic and Industry Research, 1955), p. 46; N. Georgescu-Roegen, *Modificări structurale în venitul nationale al României în urma celui de al doilea război mondial* (Bucharest, 1947), pp. 7, 18, 20-21; C. C. Kirițescu, *Sistemul bănesc al leului*, Vol. III (Bucharest, 1968), pp. 17-18, 37-40; Maria Curteanu, *Sectorul de stat în România anilor 1944-1947* (Bucharest, 1974), p. 48; League of Nations, *Statistical Yearbook, 1939/40* (Geneva, 1940), p. 176.

The slower postwar start experienced by Romanian industry also had its origins in the country's wartime experience. Largely to blame was the far greater extent to which German capital and management penetrated Romanian heavy industry. Its purpose was of course to tie Romanian metallurgy and oil refining directly to the German war effort. The same sectors were small or nonexistent in Bulgaria. Their expansion in Romania opened them up to risks of Allied bombing and eventual Soviet confiscation that Bulgarian tobacco fields hardly faced.

TABLE 13.13
CHANGES IN BULGARIAN MANUFACTURING ESTABLISHMENTS, 1939-46

Branch	Establishments[a]		Employees		Horsepower		1946/1939		
	1939	1946	1939	1946	1939	1946	Est.	Emp.	H.P.
Metals	144	210	6,661	6,325	5,515	19,503	146	95	354
Chemicals	323	372	4,585	5,697	10,764	15,512	115	124	144
Non-wood building materials	178	203	5,738	8,190	18,159	21,816	114	143	120
Wood	260	659	4,181	7,183	10,295	23,805	253	172	231
Paper and printing	19	24	1,753	2,321	11,778	15,381	126	132	131
Textiles	369	606	31,964	36,028	42,034	54,651	164	113	130
Leather	66	124	1,497	1,927	4,534	6,071	188	129	134
Food and tobacco	1,735	1,884	33,752	30,578	99,651	127,585	109	90	128
Other	10		331		408				
Total	3,104	4,082	90,502	99,152	209,326	284,324	132	110	136

Branch	Employees per Establishment[a]		Horsepower per Establishment[a]		Horsepower per Employee		1946/1936		
	1939	1946	1939	1946	1939	1946	(c)	(d)	(e)
Metals	46.3	30.1	38.3	92.9	0.83	3.08	65	243	371
Chemicals	14.3	15.4	33.5	42.0	2.35	2.72	108	125	116
Non-wood building materials	32.4	40.5	102.6	108.0	2.22	2.66	125	105	120
Wood	16.1	10.9	39.6	36.1	2.46	3.31	68	91	135
Paper and printing	92.3	96.7	619.9	640.9	6.72	6.63	105	103	99
Textiles	86.6	59.5	113.9	90.2	1.32	1.52	69	79	115
Leather	22.7	15.5	68.7	49.0	3.03	3.15	68	71	104
Food and tobacco	19.6	16.3	57.5	67.9	2.95	4.17	83	118	141
Other	33.1		40.8		1.23				
Average all branches	29.3	24.4	67.7	70.0	2.31	2.87	83	103	124

Notes: (a)With at least 10 workers and 10 horsepower. (b)Based on number of reporting establishments. (c)Employees per establishment. (d)Horsepower per establishment. (e)Horsepower per employee.

Sources: S. D. Zagoroff, The Economy of Bulgaria (Washington, D.C.: Council for Economic and Industry Research, Inc., 1955), p. 79

TABLE 13.14

CHANGES IN ROMANIAN MANUFACTURING ENTERPRISES, 1938-47

Branch	Number of Private Enterprises[a]								
	Total 1947	Formation Year of Those Existing in 1947					With Motors 1947	With 10 employees or 20 h.p.[b]	
		to 1940	1941-44	1945	1946	1947		1947	1938[b]
Metals and Machinery	2,872	1,530	390	335	352	265	2,559	714	397
Chemicals	1,445	652	227	217	203	146	873	394	397
Petroleum refining	(59)	(53)	(4)	(1)	(1)		(37)	(37)	(41)
Other	(1,386)	(599)	(223)	(216)	(202)	(146)	(836)	(357)	(356)
Non-wood building materials	1,099	612	161	115	120	91	609	591	713
Wood	4,745	4,635	20	12	17	11	4,018	1,004	331
Paper and printing	602	335	87	59	38	23	535	231	157
Textiles	4,529	2,658	526	433	460	442	3,839	882	640
Leather	999	552	161	122	81	83	627	272	158
Food and tobacco	18,127	14,065	1,529	564	941	1,028	17,494	4,774	974
Other	30	14	3	5	5	3	27	9	
Total	34,448	23,456	3,557	2,238	2,672	2,525	30,581	8,893	3,767
(percent)	100.0	68.1	15.2	5.5	7.8	7.4	88.8	25.8	

Branch	Persons Occupied				Occupied per Enterprise		Horsepower per Enterprise			
	1947	1938[c]	Index	1938[d]	1947	1938[f]	1947	1938[f]	1938[b]	1938[b]
Metals and Machinery	107,064	72,146	144	54,005	40.0	47.2	101.6	136.0	114.1	390.7
Chemicals	39,587	29,783	133	28,298	32.6	45.7	141.7	71.3	234.5	461.9
Petroleum refining	16,572	11,571	143	5,980	436.1	218.3	1,467.9	145.9	2,340.7	904.0
Other	23,015	18,212	126	22,318	19.6	30.4	85.2	62.7	141.3	411.0
Non-wood building materials	46,958	35,322	133	22,447	51.9	57.7	89.6	31.5	161.8	85.3
Wood	85,419	43,405	197	43,326	21.7	9.3	25.6	130.9	30.2	193.7
Paper and Printing	19,065	14,205	134	15,222	32.9	36.0	187.1	97.0	210.5	339.9
Textiles	78,045	63,605	123	74,077	23.4	23.8	43.2	115.7	51.0	123.5
Leather	18,519	12,367	150	13,366	21.4	22.4	24.8	84.6	39.5	84.9
Food and tobacco	62,314	49,768	135	38,376	4.6	2.1	23.9	39.4	24.8	140.7
Other	335	97	345		14.0	6.9				
Total	462,306	320,698	144	289,117	16.3	13.7	43.4	76.7	48.8	198.2

TABLE 13.14 (continued)

Branch	Horsepower		Horsepower per worker	
	1947	1938	1947	1938
Metals and machinery	291,885	155,105	2.54	2.87
Chemicals	204,695	183,393	4.35	6.48
Petroleum refining	86,607	37,063	3.37	6.20
Other	118,088	146,330	4.35	6.56
Non-wood building materials	98,522	60,810	1.73	2.71
Wood	121,286	64,121	1.18	1.48
Paper and printing	112,628	53,366	5.69	3.50
Textiles	195,867	79,018	1.85	1.61
Leather	24,752	13,415	1.16	1.00
Food and tobacco	433,674	137,018	5.20	3.57
Total	1,493,339	746,789	2.66	2.58

Notes: (a)Enterprises included were any (i) occupying over five persons, (ii) using motor power in production, (iii) producing motor power and (iv)producing chemicals, pharmaceuticals or precision and measuring instruments. (b)"Large" (*mare*) enterprises on prewar territory. (c)Of enterprises in existence in 1947 and 1938. (d)In "large" (*mare*) enterprises on prewar territory. (e)Based on numbers of active enterprises. (f)Based on enterprises existing in 1947 and formed before 1941. (g)Of "large" (*mare*) enterprises on prewar territory.

Sources: Institutul central de statistică, *Întreprinderile particulare industriale, comerciale şi de transport: rezultate provizorii ale inventarierii din octomvrie 1947,* Vol. 1 (Bucharest, 1947), pp. ix, 2-11; *Anarul statistic al României, 1939-1940* (Bucharest, 1940), pp. 478-79, 488.

The agreement providing German investment and technical assistance to the Malaxa works set the pattern for metallurgy. Signed with the Herman Göring Werke in September, 1940, it eventually furnished Malaxa with a modern rolling mill and more Siemens-Martin steel furnaces, among other items. This complex became the joint enterprise Rogifer. The Reşiţa and state-owned Hunedoara complexes received similar installations. Partial German ownership in Reşiţa and the political leverage to set production targets in both assured that German interests were served. Several armaments works in the area between Ploeşti and Braşov operated on the same basis. Perhaps more important was the increased production of pipeline and railway rolling stock needed to shift the transport of Romanian oil from the Black Sea outlet to the overland route to Germany. The resulting demand for metal production, without much of the assistance or materials promised by the Germans, reportedly overworked and ran down these expanded facilities.[49]

The Western European and American oil companies themselves did not so much come under German ownership as under direct management by the Romanian government. The German share of foreign capital in the country's petroleum enterprises had risen from almost nothing before the war but reached only 12.3 percent by its end. More important for the future was the government's new mining law of 1942. This legislation not only placed the wartime management of refining, transportation, and export entirely in state hands, but also left foreign interests little leeway for peacetime investment or expansion. These prerogatives were reserved to the new National Petroleum Institute. German authorities apparently accepted the restrictions as long as the flow of oil exports continued. German investment in new facilities was, however, confined to the Air Ministry's construction of a chemical plant near Ploeşti. State efforts did raise refining efficiency. First reduced extraction and then Allied bombing nonetheless reduced the tonnage refined steadily after 1939.[50]

The virtual nationalization of Romanian oil operations, if not ownership, from 1942 forward made it easy for Soviet authorities to create the so-called joint company Sovrompetrol in May 1945. The largest of these enterprises anywhere in Eastern Europe, it controlled 36 percent of petroleum output by 1947. Sovrompetrol began at once to export up to two thirds of total production to the USSR. This outflow covered Russian military needs and also reparations, including oil to cover shortfalls in other goods. The Western-owned oil companies could conveniently be left with the remainder for three years. They struggled to survive against severe restrictions whose circumvention required black market dealings. These violations were later to be used against them when they were formally nationalized in the first half of 1948.[51]

The rest of Romanian private industry went through a curious expansion in the number if not the size of its enterprises from 1945 to 1947. Table 13.14 reflects additions to the number of metallurgical, non-petroleum chemical, and textile firms for each of those years that matched the totals added for 1941–44. More food and tobacco enterprises appeared in these postwar years than during the war. Reduced horsepower per worker in the branches of heavy industry, also noted in Table 13.14, suggests that massive Soviet reparations from the plants of large existing firms may have opened the branches up to new smaller producers. Increased horsepower per worker for textiles and especially foodstuffs seems a response to the wartime disruption of the many Jewish enterprises and soaring postwar prices for clothing and food. How far this boom in private enterprise might have gone can never be known. Although the Communist Party had deferred its demands for immediate nationalization, any large enterprise in which the state had participated came under the new government's complete control in June 1945. Some of these plus all those previously under German or Hungarian ownership passed into the hands of Soviet authorities under the terms of the armistice agreement. A longer list of enterprises whose owners stood accused of collaboration with the German war effort, loosely defined, came under state "supervision." Actual state ownership as late as 1947 still covered only 3 percent of manufacturing enterprises, with 21 percent of the labor force.

The appointment of Gheorgiu-Dej, the leading ethnic Romanian in the Communist Party, as Minister of National Economy in December 1946 nonetheless signalled the beginning of the end for private industry. State industrial bureaus (oficii industriale) were set up for all branches by early 1947. There were originally announced as joint-stock enterprises whose management would be shared by the regime and labor representatives with the existing management. In fact, the bureaus helped coordinate the delivery of reparations to the USSR ($300 million worth were owed). They also helped prepare the way for formal nationalization of all enterprises with a minimum of ten workers and twenty horsepower, beginning in June, 1948. By October, state ownership had expanded to 13 percent of such manufacturing enterprises and 77 percent of combined employment and horsepower. That year's census of enterprises also counted 974 joint Sovroms or firms otherwise under Soviet control in all sectors, of which 228 were in manufacturing. The latter accounted for 6 percent of industrial labor and 4 percent of horsepower. The Sovroms were not finally disbanded until 1956.[52]

Yugoslavia and Greece

The postwar performance of Yugoslav industry pushed output to half again the Romanian and Greek levels for 1948, as already recorded in Table 13.11. After grievous losses during the war, Yugoslavia at least paid no reparations afterwards. Rather it received them from Germany, Italy, and Hungary along with the aforementioned UNRRA assistance. Reparations from Bulgaria were forgiven. Forces of the Serbian Četnik and the Croatian Ustaša movements commanded too little support to initiate a Greek-style civil war. Moreover, the Communist-led Partisans had fought the Germans more consistently than any other Balkan resistance movement and probably enjoyed a greater measure of popular support than any of the area's other regimes in the immediate postwar period.[53] The significance of this support grows when we juxtapose the country's record of rapid industrial recovery, at least until the Tito-Stalin split, with the destructive effects of Italian and especially German occupation. At the same time, the very thoroughness of German exploitation paved the way for postwar nationalization by taking over most enterprises under other foreign ownership and making them immediately vulnerable, unlike the Western oil companies in Romania.

In Serbia, however, the German occupation authorities acted more to destroy than to take over prewar private industry. A majority of the more than 500 industrial firms in prewar Serbia simply ceased operations. Von Neuhausen's office amalgamated the rest into just 29 enterprises, all obliged to produce strictly for the war effort. All but one metallurgical plant, including the several state armaments works, and several large firms in light industry, including the modern shoe manufacturing plant set up at Borovo by the Czech enterprise Bat'a, were dismantled and shipped to the Reich. A majority of those still operating were textile mills. Lack of raw materials and fuel kept output from meeting much more than two thirds of military orders. The coal shortage could be alleviated only by imports from Germany. Their insufficiency prompted German authorities to construct several electric generators in order to save coal. These installations and an isolated dairy and a canning plant appear to have been the only investments in Serbian industry during the war. By its end, Serbia's share of Yugoslav industrial capital had shrunk from over 30 to just 15 percent.[54]

Most of the 160,000 Serbs employed as essentially forced labor in the German occupied area were engaged in railway work or in existing mines. Extensive repairs were needed to make the Bor copper mines operational again, as the Yugoslavs had blown up much of the facility before the German army arrived in April 1941. Contrary to a postwar German account, the cost of this rebuilding did not surpass the value of production for 1942–44. The funds were in any case collected from internal Serbian sources by the puppet Nedić regime. Plans for a badly needed installation of a new smelter, an electric power plant, and a rail connection to the Danube were drawn up but never implemented.[55]

The organization of the rest of Yugoslav industry was not restructured as in Serbia. Existing enterprises producing war materials simply found their ownership taken over by German firms in Slovenia and their management seconded by Croatian officials in the NDH.[56] The Slovenian metallurgical complexes and lignite mines were largely located in the territory annexed to Germany. Almost all of their production was either exported to the Reich or delivered to German troops in Yugoslavia. Their physical plant remained intact, only the aforementioned shipment of Slovenian labor northward limited output.

Mining, especially of Bosnian coal, should have constituted the main Croatian contribution to the German war effort. Despite a variety of state controls, coal mines within the borders of the NDH produced only two thirds of the tonnage planned for 1942. A majority was intended for the German garrison. The fraction fell to one third for 1943 as Partisan sabotage took its toll. Imports of coal from Germany were needed from the start. Two thirds of the amounts ordered were never delivered. Other sectors of Croatian industry found their production slowed by the resulting shortage of fuel.

The combination of German, Italian, and fascist Croatian control over the most modern sectors of Yugoslav manufacturing and mining helped make their postwar nationalization the most rapid in Southeastern Europe. During 1945 the "sequestering" of enemy property, largely foreign and originally British or French, put 19 percent of estimated industrial capital, twice that proportion for Croatia, into the hands of the new Yugoslav government. Such sequestration was the seemingly temporary device hit upon by the Communist leadership, sincerely or not, to hold out the prospect of pending restoration of their property to prewar Western investors. These included among others the British owners of the Trepća lead mines and even the French owners who sold out the Bor copper mines to German interests after the fall of France in 1940. All these facilities, unlike their Romanian and Bulgarian counterparts, had come under the complete control of Nazi officials after April 1941. The Bor complex, despite a postwar decision by the French government to take over private French shares, found itself entirely under Yugoslav authority at the end of 1944. It was nationalized by the end of 1945. British holdings followed when the Labor government did not abandon Conservative opposition to the Yugoslav claims to Trieste. Native Yugoslav owners facing unresolved charges of collaboration or "war profiteering" in the courts also had their property sequestered. Typically, however, such charges were quickly resolved against the defendants. They joined the assorted German, Hungarian, and Italian wartime owners who had taken over native or non-Western enterprises in facing immediate seizure by the new government. Confiscations by December 1945 totalled 53 percent of industrial capital and reached a peak of 69 percent in Slovenia, where German interests has assumed ownership of metallurgy and mining. Legal and some blatantly extralegal measures taken under a decree of November 1944, permitted seizure of this property.[57] The nationalization of most industrial enterprises in December 1946, and the launching of the first Balkan five-year plan the following year could therefore proceed with private ownership in the minority and foreign investment largely eliminated.[58]

Still less need be said of the immediate postwar experience of Greek industry. This is partly because our notion of wartime production under German, Italian, and Bulgarian occupation is too sketchy to record. Just the Italian campaign of 1940 reportedly cut industrial output by 30 percent.[59] Presumably it fell much further after the German invasion of 1941. For Greek manufacturing, moreover, we have already identified the key institutional change of the 1940s in the previous section. The successful evacuation of the Bank of Greece, its leadership and its reserves, at the start of the war allowed it to return with the non-Communist government in exile as the country's most powerful economic institution during the rest of the decade. The Bank's aforementioned tendency to favor agriculture left industrial undertakings with about 5 percent of its outstanding credits at the end of 1946 and 1947. Greek manufacturing and mining received just 15 percent of investment from all sources in 1948 and 20 percent in 1951. These shares were well below the 40–55 percent accorded industry by the Communist governments of Yugoslavia, Bulgaria, and Romania. Their overall investment took in turn a proportion of national product that was half again the 17 percent achieved by Greece in 1948–49, and then only with American financial assistance.[60]

The Civil War delayed Greek recovery to prewar levels of industrial production until 1950. The war was felt most strongly in mining, followed among the major branches by metallurgy and chemicals (see Table 13.15). Lack of male labor for the largely heavy work may have been responsible for the low indices of production in the two latter sectors. The low figures for mining (24 percent of 1939 volume as late as 1950) derive from more extensive wartime damage, including the loss of over 90 percent of all railway rolling stock, than in

TABLE 13.15
CHANGES IN GREEK MANUFACTURING ESTABLISHMENTS, 1930-51
(with 25 or more employees)[a]

Branch	Establishments		Employees		Employees per Establishment		1951/1930		
	1930	1951	1930	1951	1930	1951	Est.	Emp.	Emp./Est.
Metals and machinery	56	142	4,098	16,541	73.2	116.5	254	404	159
Chemicals	24	82	3,190	13,996	132.9	170.7	342	439	128
Non-wood building materials	119	86	21,075	6,478	117.1	75.3			
Woodworking	27	35	1,548	1,622	57.3	46.3	130	105	81
Paper and printing	49	67	3,237	5,648	66.1	84.3	137	174	128
Textiles	226	391	22,608	55,826	100.0	142.8	173	247	143
Leather	5	19	2,281	6,406	443.6	337.2	380	281	76
Food and tobacco	183	177	11,736	21,189	64.1	119.7	97	181	187
Other		31		1,399		45.2			
Total	689	1,030	69,773	123,709	101.3	119.8	150	177	118

Notes: (a)1930, over 25; 1951, over 24.

Sources: Calculated from *Statistikè epeirìs tès Ellados, 1935* (Athens, 1936), pp. 137-38; *1954*, pp. 71, 74.

western Yugoslavia and from continued disruption during the Civil War. The generally slow recovery discouraged the return of Western investment to the sector where it had been concentrated before the war. Lignite was the one exception, recapturing 91 percent of the 1939 level by 1948.[61] Ferrous and nonferrous ores were previously exported. They had not been processed enough before the war for use in native industry, say shipbuilding. Their loss for export in the immediate postwar period accentuated the large import surplus that returned to characterize the Greek economy as it had earlier in the twentieth century. This disparity has continued since 1950 despite the fivefold increase in industrial production.[62]

The State Sector and the Postwar Transition

German economic penetration of Southeastern Europe finally assumed the proportions during the Second World War that it was commonly believed to have achieved in the 1930s. Its immediate effect on industry was hardly uniform. Yet the final result was everywhere to strengthen the state's hand for the postwar period. The principal commercial banks in Zagreb, Bucharest, and Sofia were hopelessly compromised for the future by German influence and stockholders. They had served as the major sources of private credit during the industrial mini-spurt of the 1920s. Such a role would now be unthinkable under any postwar regime.

Wartime contraction of the number of enterprises occurred only in Serbia and probably Greece, under the auspices of Nazi officials rather than German capitalists. Increasing concentration according to a Marxist model would be hard to find in Romania and especially Bulgaria, where the number of enterprises rose significantly. So, however, in both cases did the native governments' powers over industry, perhaps partly for Bulgaria to marshal these larger numbers for the war effort. For Romania, a combination of German aid and investment in the main metallurgical enterprises and the state's direct authority to regulate petroleum investment under the new mining law of 1942 left private interests in these two pivotal branches with no real basis to resume postwar operations.

What sort of state sector did the Communist governments inherit? The question deserves to be asked despite the political discontinuity after 1944. Obviously the new regimes brought their own theory and practice with them. Both Soviet-style planning and a new Communist set of top managers were committed to an overriding emphasis on heavy industry and balanced growth. Capital for almost all investment would come directly from the state budget. This was new. Much less ahistorical were the state's ownership of important industrial enterprises and state agencies with wide powers in agriculture, trade, and finance. This inheritance derived not only from the experiences of the Depression, rearmament and the Second World War but also from the longer-standing legacy of governments more powerful than any private sector of the economy, industry in particular. Also available, thanks to earlier state attention to higher education, were personnel already trained in technical and administrative skills.

Unlike Yugoslavia, Romania and Bulgaria have continued to adhere to central planning. This fact should not obscure some significant divergence in their experiences, even before 1950. Romania's persistent emphasis on heavy industry and balanced growth began with more initial difficulties in postwar recovery than any state in Southeastern Europe except Greece. The resulting need for a greater push to begin rapid growth has of course been followed by a political desire to avoid dependence on the Soviet Union that has ironically perpetuated Soviet growth strategy. The popular appeal of this strategy speaks less, however, to growing Marxist consciousness than to the National Liberal tradition of restricting the imported manufactures that threatened economic independence and aiding the domestic production that promoted it. Bulgarian reliance on the Soviet market, although based more on processed tobacco and foods, brings to mind similarly strong ties to the German market during the Depression. This connection appeared earlier and went farther before war broke out than elsewhere in Southeastern Europe. (Ties to a single imperial market had also characterized the Bulgarian economy more than they had its Balkan neighbors during the Ottoman period.) The Bulgarian rate of industrial growth during the 1930s was twice the Romanian and Yugoslav levels. Such an official trade connection seemed a good substitute for a private European capital market that had historically opened itself to the Bulgarian economy only during the 1920s and then on a short-term basis.

Native enclaves of private banking and manufacturing had largely accounted for industrial growth before 1930 but even then proved unable to overcome the Balkan governments' pursuit of other interests. This was true not just before the First World War, when these governments obtained massive foreign loans for their budgets at the price of overvalued currencies and restricted money supplies, and then spent them on largely noneconomic ends. The 1920s saw no new sorts of state initiative to aid these two capitalist enclaves. Credit supplies and note issue were again squeezed to return to the prewar Gold Standard and regain state access to foreign loans. Genuinely protective import tariffs for industry were augmented with a variety of revenue-raising taxes on consumer goods that reduced the already limited domestic markets. The Romanian regime in particular also relied heavily on revenues from export tariffs until the mid-1920s.

The Depression of the 1930s finally eliminated the restraints of the Western European monetary system. The governments of Southeastern Europe were still left with the legacy of manipulating the production and consumption of manufactured goods for fiscal or political purposes. Such manipulation since 1950, even in non-Communist Greece, goes to the heart of continuing difficulties with the quality of industrial production for foreign as well as domestic markets. The growth of exported manufactures that is needed to lead these economies past their present level of intermediate development awaits the demise of this longest-standing legacy.

Conclusion: Postwar
Industrialization in
Historical Perspective

This concluding chapter addresses the wider question of what legacy four hundred years of Balkan economic history left to the two decades of extensive industrialization between 1950 and 1970. A period of more intensive and slower growth, in a more intricate international environment, began about 1970. Since this most recent period has yet to run its full course, we will not attempt to assess it in historical perspective.

The abrupt postwar appearance of Communist governments in four of the five states of Southeastern Europe suggests a lack of continuity with prewar experience. Confirming such discontinuity is the initial determination of these four governments to impose Soviet-style central planning and to use it, with the state budget as the financial means for assembling savings, to distribute investment and spread technological skills. From 1950 to 1970 the record of rapid economic and especially industrial growth also appears to be unprecedented. It prompted the structural shift of a majority of labor and capital into nonagricultural activities within one generation. From a political perspective, the only connection between postwar industrialization and the past might seem to be the growth of state sectors and the compromise of private institutions and free markets from the Depression through the Second World War.

Yet the Greek economy has also achieved a similar record of rapid growth and structural change. Its response to expanding international trade and investment has been more positive than in the somewhat analogous boom before the First World War. We may infer from Greece's non-Communist government and substantial private sector that forces whose mainsprings predate at least the Second World War also facilitated modern economic development. The same inference also follows from the increasingly varied experience of the socialist economies.

The bold Yugoslav experiment with market socialism comes most quickly to mind. Since 1960, market forces, more than official agencies, have served to discipline relatively autonomous enterprises. By 1970 Yugoslav socialism had also come to rely on commercial, if now nonprivate, banks to mobilize domestic capital and emigrants' remittances to assemble private savings. These two hallmarks had already appeared in most of the Yugoslav lands before the First World War. They have also characterized the Greek experience throughout the twentieth century.

The Romanian and especially the Bulgarian economies have continued to rely on agricultural exports and foreign capital, although less than before 1914. They remain major means of financing the imports of machinery and materials needed to sustain the region's highest rates of industrial growth. Both have adhered since the war to the basic tenets of Soviet-style central planning. Their contrasting demographic profiles and agricultural patterns nonetheless combine with differing geographic distributions of foreign trade to set Bulgarian and Romanian development apart in ways suggestive of their interwar differences.

Albania remains a special case of underdevelopment. Structural change and international specialization had barely begun before the Second World War. Prolonged Ottoman domination, belated independence, and interwar Italian colonization had set the area's smallest state well behind its neighbors economically. Since 1945 its commitment to Stalinist economics and Maoist politics has continued to isolate Albania from the rest of Southeastern Europe, as well as from the international economy.[1]

More general limitations in postwar growth deserve scrutiny here. They remain sufficient to keep any of these economies from reaching Western European levels of per capita income or industrial exports. Particular problems of efficiency for public enterprises derive from the lack of market incentives and flexible interest rates. Such problems have admittedly plagued socialist economies elsewhere in Eastern Europe. Communist governments must, of course, bear the responsibility for these shortcomings. But other failings laid to Eastern European socialism by recent Western analysis—distorted price regimes, questionable agricultural performance, and insufficient variety in international specialization—have prewar as well as postwar origins, at least for Southeastern Europe.[2]

Our chief concern here is to sketch the historical dynamics behind the intermediate levels of industrial development achieved since 1950 by all the economies of Southeastern Europe except Albania. The most direct approach would be to compare the two mini-spurts of industrial growth before and after the First World War with the more recent record, but serious statistical problems stand in the way. The reliability of aggregate estimates and comparability of sectoral breakdowns simply diverge too much to permit precise comparison. Missing data during and after both wars prevent the construction of continuous time series. In addition, official postwar statistics on in-dustrial output and capital investment, while more detailed than earlier data, remain incomplete or unexplained, especially for Romania. All contain too little consistency in rates of depreciation and rates of branch growth to be combined into any rigorous sort of economic model for the region as a whole. A variety of Western esti-mates adds to the often incomparable mass of postwar data.[3] Their satisfactory reconciliation still lies in the future. Table 14.1 presents some comparable calculations of the pace of postwar industrial growth.

The previous chapters have, in any case, argued that the growth of industrial production and the mobilization of capital cannot be sepa-rated from peasant agriculture, which controlled a majority of the fac-tors of production as recently as 1950. We must therefore review the less quantifiable and longer-term history of agricultural population and performance, especially for export markets. They have remained surprisingly relevant to the period of rapid industrialization since 1950, not only for the supply of urban labor and foodstuffs but also for exports to help pay for needed imports of industrial machinery and materials. Only with these agricultural parameters in mind may we realistically compare the more direct sources of industrial growth and capital formation since 1950 with those of the mini-spurts earlier in the twentieth century.

Agricultural Population and Performance

The region's long period as common periphery to the Ottoman and Habsburg empires began in the sixteenth century. By the time that the modern Balkan states had emerged in the nineteenth century, imperial policies toward settlement and long-distance trade had in-advertently helped create a commercial nexus for each of the new states. Each network was centered around the future capital city. Rural population and grain production did not grow after the six-teenth century, and declined in the eighteenth. But mass migration and the rise of other sorts of agricultural and artisan production dis-

persed market practices and entrepreneurial skills, if not modern
technology, more widely than was once assumed. Factors of production failed to grow geometrically but did shift and spread geographically.

The imperial framework for this process was a mixture of military
and feudal institutions, not the capitalist or even mercantilist practice
that Marxist analysis might lead us to expect. In both the Ottoman
and the Habsburg cases, the military measures of each central government initially brought peasant populations back into newly won
areas to help secure the borderlands. The Ottoman *sipahi* system of

TABLE 14.1
GROWTH OF POPULATION, LABOR FORCE AND PRODUCTION, 1950-70

| | Indices | | | Average Growth Rate[a] | | |
	1950	1960	1970	1951-60	1961-70	1951-70
Population						
Albania	100	132	176	2.8	2.9	2.9
Bulgaria	100	109	117	0.8	0.8	0.8
Greece	100	110	116	1.0	0.5	0.8
Romania	100	113	124	1.2	1.0	1.1
Yugoslavia	100	114	125	1.3	1.0	1.1
Labor Force						
Bulgaria	100	100	104	0.0	0.4	0.2
Greece	100	125	116	2.3	-0.7	0.7
Romania	100	110	114	1.0	0.4	0.7
Yugoslavia	100	108	104	0.8	-0.2	0.2
GNP at constant market prices[g]						
Bulgaria	100	199	349	7.1	5.8	6.4
Greece	100	177	376	5.9	7.8	6.8
Romania	100	182	301	6.2	5.2	5.7
Yugoslavia	100	173	293	5.6	5.4	5.5
NMP at constant market prices[d,h]						
Albania	100	239	491	9.1	7.5	8.3
Bulgaria	100	282	593	10.9	7.7	9.3
Romania	100	268	599	10.3	8.3	9.4
Yugoslavia	100	198	373	7.1	6.5	6.8
Labor in agriculture[e]						
Bulgaria	100	74	50	-3.0	-3.8	-3.4
Greece[b]	100	143	97	3.6	-3.8	-0.2
Romania	100	102	79	0.2	-2.5	-1.2
Yugoslavia	100	85	71	-1.7	-1.8	-1.7

TABLE 14.1 (continued)

Indicators	Indices			Average Growth Rate[a]		
	1950	1960	1970	1951-60	1961-70	1951-70
Labor in industry[f]						
Bulgaria	100	127	286	7.0	3.9	5.4
Greece[b]	100	127	153	2.4	1.9	2.1
Romania	100	131	209	2.7	4.8	3.8
Yugoslavia	100	224	304	8.3	3.1	5.7
GDP in agriculture (constant prices)[e,i]						
Bulgaria	100	137	174	3.2	2.4	2.8
Greece	100	146	233	3.9	4.8	4.3
Romania	100	179	169	6.0	-0.6	2.7
Yugoslavia	100	154	181	4.4	1.7	3.0
NMP in agriculture (constant prices)[e,h]						
Bulgaria	100	166	175	5.2	0.5	2.8
Romania	100	169	165	5.4	-0.2	2.5
Yugoslavia	100	162	199	4.9	2.1	3.5
GDP in industry (constant prices)[f,i]						
Bulgaria	100	323	731	12.4	8.5	10.5
Greece	100	225	571	8.4	9.8	9.1
Romania	100	170	470	5.4	10.7	8.0
Yugoslavia	100	193	426	6.8	8.2	7.5
NMP in agriculture (constant prices)[e,h]						
Bulgaria	100	166	175	5.2	0.5	2.8
Romania	100	169	165	5.4	-0.2	2.5
Yugoslavia	100	162	199	4.9	2.1	3.5
GDP in industry (constant prices)[f,i]						
Bulgaria	100	323	731	12.4	8.5	10.5
Greece	100	225	571	8.4	9.8	9.1
Romania	100	170	470	5.4	10.7	8.0
Yugoslavia	100	193	426	6.8	8.2	7.5
NMP in industry (constant prices)[f,h]						
Albania	100	955	2896	25.3	11.7	18.3
Bulgaria	100	405	1123	15.0	10.7	12.9
Romania	100	327	1297	12.6	14.8	13.7
Yugoslavia	100	215	541	8.0	9.7	8.8

Notes: (a)Average growth rates are calculated as the geometric rate between the beginning and ending years, a procedure that distorts the trends (for example, both 1950 and 1970 were poor years for agriculture in Romania). (b)Greek labor growth and structure are distorted by changing census standards for occupied population. (c)Yugoslav labor growth for 1950 to 1960 is estimated by projecting growth rates from 1953 to 1961. (d)Net material product excludes, directly, values of "nonproductive" services. (e)Including forestry and fishing. (f)Including construction, mining, utilities and artisan production. (g)GNP gross national product. (h)NMP net material product. (i)GDP gross domestic product.

Sources: National statistical yearbooks, except as follows: Michael Kaser and Adi Schnytzer, "Albania—A Uniquely Socialist Economy," and Thad P. Alton, "Comparative Structure and Growth of Economic Activity in Eastern Europe," in *East European Economies Post-Helsinki*, a compendium of papers submitted to the Joint Economic Committee, Congress of the United States (Wash., D.C.: U. S. Government Printing Office 1977), pp. 229-30, 581-83, 617-19; Thad P. Alton, "Economic Growth and Resource Allocation in Eastern Europe," in *Reorientation and Commercial Relations of the Economies of Eastern Europe*, a compendium of papers submitted to the Joint Economic Committee, Congress of the United States (Wash., D.C.: U. S. Government Printing Office 1974), pp. 270-74; OECD, *National Accounts of Member Countries* (Paris) various issues.

the sixteenth century took a small fraction of the peasants' crop. In return, the system provided more land and better security than a variety of feudal regimes had been able to give peasants in the grain-growing areas of the Serbian, Bulgarian, and Greek lands. The same assessment applies to the military border that Austrian authorities extended further across upland areas of Croatia and Transylvania during the seventeenth and eighteenth centuries. By 1699, Habsburg forces had pushed the Ottoman border back to Serbia and proceeded to settle the rich plains of the Vojvodina and Slavonia with Central European migrants lured to free land on the frontier.

This eighteenth-century policy of assembling people, rather than exporting goods in mercantilist fashion, also attracted migration from the Ottoman side of the border. Habsburg concern with population coincided with the degeneration of the Ottoman agrarian regime. Disorder and exploitation spread, especially at the periphery. This degeneration reduced the local peasant populations and pushed the rest into the nearby uplands or further away, to Habsburg territory for Serbs and some Romanians or elsewhere in the Ottoman or Romanian lands for Bulgarians and Greeks. Chapter 1 has described the Greek experience with long-distance trade from Istanbul to the Black Sea and, more significantly for the future nation-state, from southern Greece into the Mediterranean. Chapter 5 records the proto-industrialization of the Bulgarian uplands for the huge Istanbul market in artisan manufacture. Chapters 2–4 examine the Habsburg role in the movement of Serbian and Romanian population. These extensive migrations permitted few Balkan peasants a taste of urban life but did involve many in market practices. Imperial regulations were more concerned with controlling and taxing crop production than with restricting trade. A surprisingly mobile peasant population used the periphery shared by the two empires to escape such restrictions. At the same time, the war and disorder that also characterized these borderlands prevented the market place from dominating economic life in Western fashion.

This coexistence between the imperial framework and market forces at least left the native Balkan states to emerge in the early nineteenth century with some commercial legacy. Their peasant populations were more familiar with market behavior than were those in many traditional rural societies. Moreover, emigrants returning from the two empires brought back the best practice from European or Mediterranean commerce.

Both returning emigrants and upland peasants joined in resettling the depopulated lowlands from about 1830 forward. Grain cultivation spread rapidly in response to improved security and to the new native governments' desire for tax revenues in cash rather than in kind. The volume of grain exports rose through the nineteenth century. The Ottoman state's wheat monopoly gave way to market demand from Central Europe. After 1870 falling food prices and transportation costs expanded that market. World grain prices turned up again after 1895. Peasant cultivators found that their tax burden, largely composed of fixed indirect taxes, declined for the first time. The overvalued exchange rates that the Balkan governments maintained to attract foreign loans probably reduced the size of the trade surpluses generated by these grain sales. They were the largest single export for all the Balkan states except Greece by 1910.

Other limitations also hemmed in Balkan agricultural exports as an engine of growth, even without the disruption unleashed by the First World War. Bulgarian smallholders and Romanian sharecroppers alike were drawn by the world market into overdependence on their wheat and corn crops. When their harvests failed, as the region's uneven rainfall caused them periodically to do, the consequences were severe. Serbian prunes and Greek raisins offered some relief from this dependence but faced a competitive world market and demand that was no more elastic than that for grain. Romanian and Serbian exports of livestock to the huge Habsburg market prompted Hungarian producers to initiate tariff wars, in 1886–91 and 1906–11, respectively. Only Serbian exports survived, largely by conversion to meat-packing. Still larger Croatian sales of livestock and meat products in the Dual Monarchy restricted the Serbian potential for further growth (see Chapters 6 and 9).

The most serious structural problem for Balkan agriculture was a peasant population growing beyond the bounds of available land and accessible markets. Urban or industrial employment did not add significantly to their small share of the total before the First World War. Perhaps the first sign that rural growth was outrunning the availability of land and the state of Balkan agricultural technology was the decline in grain area and output per capita, which began about 1895. Population figures do not suggest any downturn in birthrates before the war except for Serbia, but their precision is open to doubt. The better data afterwards reveal a consistent decline in rural births after the understandable postwar boom. From 1925 to the present these rural rates have dropped steadily, for Bulgaria in particular. The argument that birth control followed the shrinking size of holdings through the interwar period gains credibility from the attention otherwise paid to market pressures by the Bulgarian peasantry. The great majority had been smallholders since the nineteenth century. They generally operated above the subsistence level from that time forward. For the interwar period, Bulgarian land values were well ahead of the Romanian levels, due to larger inputs of both capital and labor per hectare.

Even for Bulgaria, grain exports failed to recover their prewar level during the 1920s. Romania suffered the sharpest decline, as much because of her greater previous dependence on Western European markets as from the indirect effects of the land reforms that broke up sharecropping estates. Even in prewar Romania, peasant smallholdings had occupied the largest share of cultivated land. As Chapter 10 has demonstrated, smallholdings were not inherently less efficient than the exploitative sharecropping system. Delay in establishing ownership or sale rights, also common to the Yugoslav reform, did limit Romania's marketed surplus. So did the admitted tendency of the Romanian peasantry, especially those now receiving land rents, to consume more grain than they had in their growing prewar deprivation. Probably more important in the short run were the immediate postwar difficulties of transporting bulk shipments to Western Europe, because of railway damage and also from the new need to combine smaller shipments. To make matters worse, revenue-starved governments overvalued their exchange rates, again in search of foreign loans. Now they also resorted to actual taxes on exports.

Under the best of circumstances, the greater presence of American grain on Western European markets would probably have left Southeastern Europe to continue its turn toward Central Europe. This tendency had appeared before the war, as noted in Chapter 6. It naturally grew after 1918 in the absence of Russian supplies. The severe food shortages in postwar Austria and Hungary attracted Yugoslav foodstuffs in particular.

The drop in world agricultural prices after 1929 prompted the four governments to establish state agencies for marketing grain abroad, preferably through clearing agreements that could adjust exchange rates to compensate for lower prices. Once the belated attempt to form a Balkan customs union had failed, the separate governments had little choice but to turn to Nazi Germany, the one large grain-importing economy whose leaders were prepared to sign such agreements. Bulgaria committed the greatest share of its prewar exports to the German clearing trade because tobacco was its only major alternative to grain. Romania committed the least. Its oil was in greater demand on international markets. Once war broke out in 1939, Romania could no longer resist Nazi pressures, even before Yugoslavia and Greece had been overrun. Only the Bulgarian economy appeared to derive genuine prewar benefit from this overdependence, as with its earlier ties to the Ottoman market and subsequent links to the Soviet one.

For Bulgaria and also for Romania, the postwar record of agricultural performance and exports provides partial vindication for the Communist decision to collectivize peasant smallholdings into much larger Soviet-style units. The state agencies for agricultural trade created in the 1930s had survived into the Second World War, more successfully than their counterparts in occupied Yugoslavia and Greece. Bulgaria's Hranoiznos had preserved substantial independence from Nazi influence and, along with the Bulgarian Agricultural Bank, played a significant role in the postwar transition (see Chapter 13). Under Communist management, the two institutions provided a ready-made framework for state control of agricultural marketing and credit that undoubtedly made control of production itself easier. The most rapid collectivization anywhere in Eastern Europe was largely complete by the early 1950s.

For the period 1950–66 the net agricultural output of Bulgaria more than doubled. This amounted to an average annual growth rate of 4.7 percent, versus less than 3 percent for Western Europe and the Third World. Fixed investment on enlarged collective farms, replacing labor with machinery for field crops, and maximizing the marketed surplus led the way. Agricultural investment peaked as a percentage of total investment for 1955–65, partly compensating for the peasant exodus. Higher delivery prices allowed peasant incomes to approach industrial levels. During this period, agricultural exports declined as a percentage of total exports but were still 49 percent of the total value in 1965 and 43 percent in 1970 (and 22 percent of net national product). Meanwhile, that export total was growing faster than industrial output. Exports also jumped from 15 to 23 percent of gross national product between 1960 and 1970.[4] A recent Western study compares shares of Bulgarian agricultural products in total exports to those of other Eastern European countries. It concludes that for 1960 and 1970 Bulgaria alone recorded a ratio in excess of what its size and income might lead us to expect.[5] Romania's share was, like Yugoslavia's, below the normal ratio.

Soviet purchases admittedly took more than half of Bulgarian agricultural and nonagricultural exports. On the supply side, Soviet-style collectivization does not deserve all the credit. Its techniques applied mainly to grain crops. Widespread cultivation of tobacco and new industrial crops had begun by the 1920s. A cadre of agronomists was already being trained, as noted in Chapter 10. The lowest prewar levels of livestock-raising and corn cultivation in Southeastern Europe except for Greece make the rapid postwar growth in these traditional lines of production less spectacular. Their domestic consumption continues to lag. Since 1966, admittedly a bumper harvest year, growth rates for net agricultural product have virtually stagnated. A continuing exodus from the countryside has combined with

declining rural birth rates, less than urban rates since 1965. Labor
shortages appeared on collective farms by the 1970s. An aging stock
of mechanized equipment adds to the problem. Whether the current
reorganization into agro-industrial complexes, combining collectives
with nearby towns and manufacturing, will suffice without large,
new commitments of capital remains to be seen.[6]

The history of Romanian agriculture since the Second World War
has continued to be less fortunate than that of Bulgaria. The belated
decision to begin collectivization in the late 1950s did not include
high delivery prices or large agricultural investment. Both would
have been needed to raise output at more than the 1 ½ percent a year
actually recorded for 1953–1965 (the prewar level had been reached
again by 1953). Lack of urban employment left a larger fraction of the
active Romanian labor force in the countryside (57 percent in 1965,
versus 44 percent for Bulgaria). Their numbers reduce the per capita
weight of the 4.3 percent average annual growth in net agricultural
product that Romania subsequently recorded for 1960–66, especially
when compared to the Bulgarian experience. Use of tractors and fertilizer per hectare was still, save Albania, the lowest in Eastern
Europe. After 1965 labor productivity rose with a falling rural work
force but lagged behind the Bulgarian level, which already reflected
a far greater substitution of equipment and trained personnel for raw
peasant labor.[7]

Agricultural exports have nonetheless played a surprisingly large
part in certain stages of the postwar Romanian drive for industrialization. From 1945 to 1947, all exports were held hostage to Soviet
reparations. The halving of those reparations in 1948 allowed agricultural goods to account for half of an increased export total (3 ½ times
larger than 1947). The agricultural fraction dropped to one quarter of
export value for 1953. It rose again with collectivization in the late
1950s and early 1960s. This increase coincided with a decline in the
percentage of petroleum and timber exports, although those natural
resources had not yet begun to run down. By the early 1970s, agricultural products had slipped back to one quarter of an export total increasingly composed of manufactures. They included chemicals and
furniture admittedly processed from petroleum and timber. Had total
exports grown in Bulgarian fashion as a percentage of national product, Romanian prospects for international specialization would be
greater within its already diverse markets. By 1970 exports had yet to
reach the 15 percent of GNP achieved by Bulgaria as early as 1960.[8]

The agricultural share of postwar Yugoslav exports has consistently
recorded the lowest levels in Southeastern Europe. From just 28
percent for 1952–1955, the fraction had fallen to 16 percent by
1966–1970. Falling grain exports and the failure of tobacco or indus-

trial crops to advance beyond a modest 5 percent share of cultivated output left sales of livestock or processed meats to make up 50–60 percent of agricultural exports by the late 1960s.[9] Germany and Italy have been the principal customers, as they were for pre-1914 Serbia and Habsburg Croatia. Yugoslav export totals have amounted to about 20 percent of national product, falling short of Bulgaria's 23 percent but exceeding the Romanian figure. Only the superior growth of manufactured exports, especially in the 1950s, made this possible.

The juxtaposition of such a record with the abandonment of collectivization in the early 1950s has led Eastern European economists to identify agriculture as the weak link in the postwar Yugoslav economy. The private smallholdings that make up almost 90 percent of cultivated land received little state credit or American technical aid during the 1950s. Since then the state farms that cover the rest have continued to receive over 70 percent of total investment in agriculture. For the 1960s, however, private smallholdings increased their yields for wheat and corn by one half to almost Western European levels. Access to credit allowed the numbers of tractors to jump from 1,000 to 39,000. Despite a persisting decline in average size and in total area cultivated, these holdings have increased their output, for all crops except wheat, sugar beets, and sunflowers, proportionally to the 6 percent rate of annual agricultural growth recorded for 1956–1969 (with 1951–1955 = 100). Since then Yugoslavia's agriculture has averaged the same growth rate—2 percent a year—as Bulgaria and Romania, with the same sharp swings between good and bad harvests. Progress has still been made in meeting the needs of an urban population much larger than before the shift. Agricultural production for the domestic market has further contributed to industrialization by freeing imports for machinery and raw materials. By 1970 foodstuffs had dropped to 8 percent of total imports—not far from the 5 percent needed in 1939 by a much more agricultural Yugoslav economy.[10]

As with Yugoslavia, Bulgaria, and Romania, the agricultural share of Greece's gross national product had fallen below 20 percent by 1970. In the absence of collectivization or even a Yugoslav-style state sector, Greek agricultural output had still grown at an annual rate of about 4 percent for the period 1950–1970. Its pace proceeded more steadily than in the other three countries, partly because of decreased reliance on vulnerable grain crops. Agricultural goods continued to provide over twice the proportion of total exports, still 40 percent in 1970, as for Yugoslavia and Romania. Sales of fresh and processed fruits, among which raisins were now of minor importance, had risen to compensate for the declining share of tobacco, no longer so important for American cigarette manufacturers. Food imports, always larger for Greece than its neighbors, had also fallen steadily to less than 10 percent of the total.[11] Rising domestic production of wheat was largely responsible.

Postwar American aid deserves recognition for initiating this agricultural advance. It took the form of technical assistance, land reclamation, and deliveries of modern equipment, rather than the grain shipments subsequently sent to Yugoslavia under the P.L. 480 program. For 1948–52 the Greek increment in tractors and fertilizer actually surpassed those of its collectivizing neighbors (see Table 13.6). Since then the Agricultural Bank and Greek commercial banks have maintained access to modernizing credit at low interest rates, first for short-term and since 1965 for long-term loans as well. A peasant propensity to invest savings in housing rather than in new equipment has not, however, helped to reduce excessive dependence on these lines of credit.[12]

Financing Industrial Growth

We have identified the small size of Balkan industry as the principal restraint on aggregate growth and per capita income before 1950. Peasant agriculture remained the largest sector in all the area's economies. When Balkan industry first began to stir in the late nineteenth century, the ongoing expansion of agricultural exports and rural population made the small manufacturing sector look even smaller. The latter's subsequent growth would not succeed in reducing the absolute size of agricultural employment until after 1950.

Before that, however, the Balkan states experienced two periods of rapid industrial growth, in the decade preceding the First World War and in the interwar years. Each mini-spurt left a legacy of capital formation, accumulated skills, and related institutional changes that built a foundation for postwar industrialization. These two periods of prior conditioning and the long commercial experience from which they grew seem as important to rapid Balkan growth since 1950 as do the antecedents to the English Industrial Revolution that Charles Wilson has traced back to the early seventeenth century.[13] Yet both mini-spurts were based on substituting domestic manufactures for imports within a limited national market. Both faced shortages of capital that would have held them back even without war and depression.

For agricultural exports to have become an engine of self-sustaining growth, as postulated by British economists before the Second World War and by Canadian historians afterwards, the developing nations' industrial sector would have to receive sufficient imports of capital, equipment, and raw materials in return for its exports. Capital was supposed to come from a stable currency that would attract foreign loans and a trade surplus that could service the debt from direct investment of modern technology and entrepreneurial skills by the developed Western economies.

This direct flow never developed for prewar Southeastern Europe. Like Southeast Asia before 1914, Balkan primary exports created the requisite exchange rates and private European capital failed to respond.[14] Balkan extraction grew after 1900 but was still relatively small. Only the big oil companies' interwar commitments to Romanian refining processed enough of the extraction and required enough related manufacture to escape designation as an isolated enclave, employing little local labor and dispersing less technology.[15] Local manufacture attracted almost no direct investment from the German and Austrian Great Banks in their pre-1914 heyday. Their direct interests were concentrated in their own countries or in Italy. Aggressive investment banking both in the Habsburg borderlands and in the independent Balkan states was left to several smaller Czech banks.

Balkan governments meanwhile restricted note issue by the central banks in order to maintain the stable, probably overvalued exchange rates that Western monetary wisdom assumed essential for attracting foreign capital. Large sums were indeed attracted after 1900. Unfortunately, funding came in the form of mainly French loans to the Balkan governments themselves, which spent the majority of the proceeds on the noneconomic ends of debt service, military equipment, or bureaucratic expansion. State expenditures had grown by the last prewar years to reach 20–30 percent of our rough estimates of national income, proportions higher than those for contemporary Western Europe. The bulk of the revenue to support these expenditures came not from foreign loans but from rising indirect taxes. Chapter 8 supports the argument that these levies fell most heavily on urban markets, further restricting a domestic demand for manufactures that was already small. The Habsburg borderlands paid lower taxes but also retained less revenue. Austro-Hungarian rivalry in the Habsburg ministries further limited the financing of railways and other necessary infrastructure in the western Yugoslav lands (see Chapter 9).

The First World War broke up the Habsburg monarchy. The war's aftermath cut back the capacity of Central and even Western Europe to maintain the prewar flow of capital to the Balkan governments. These cuts applied to regimes which had backed the winning Allied side as well as to Bulgaria, on the losing German side. Chapter 11 has emphasized the financial burdens that faced the supposedly triumphant new Romanian and Yugoslav governments, which had to administer greatly enlarged territories with less revenue in real per capita terms than before the war. Their efforts to squeeze the money supply again in order to reestablish overvalued exchange rates had just begun to yield British and French loans when the Depression struck in 1929. The subsequent collapse of the gold exchange standard in the early 1930s prevented any further influx of significant Western capital, public or private.

Nor was the new Nazi leadership quick to move through the door now reopened for German capital, long slammed shut since the peace settlements. Chapter 12 has traced the inconsistent course of German economic penetration during the 1930s. Aforementioned clearing agreements facilitated the growth of trade ties, especially with Bulgaria. Yet it was not until the late 1930s that the combination of Balkan rearmament and the Nazi absorption of the Czech lands finally brought sizable German investment into Southeastern Europe. Oil production for Western investors and markets allowed Romania to avoid this new Nazi leverage until 1940.

Financing for the industrial growth that did occur before both world wars derived principally from domestic sources, as it has since 1950. The mainsprings of the mini-spurt before 1914 in both the Balkan states and the Habsburg borderlands were profits reinvested by native or at least resident entrepreneurs and credit—mainly short-term loans on current account—from native commercial banks, which carried out the direct investment in manufacturing that the European Great Banks had failed to do. During the last prewar decade, all the Balkan governments also passed protective tariffs and, Greece excepted, a series of tax and tariff exemptions to promote these industrial stirrings, although there is serious doubt, as we saw in Chapter 8, whether these measures had much positive effect. Overvalued exchange rates may have aided infant industries by reducing the cost of imported machinery and materials, but also helped to restrict already small domestic markets for manufactures by passing on the high prices of agricultural exports to urban consumers. The resulting pressure to raise industrial wages, backed by an emerging socialist movement, discouraged local manufacturers still further. Little wonder that excess capacity and cartel restrictions on output began to appear after 1900.

Public policy did not make any greater contribution to the area's industrial growth during the 1920s. Its institutional framework essentially carried over from the prewar period. Central banks still struggled for independence from the central government. State revenues came mainly from the same indirect taxes, if less from foreign loans. Tariff and other trade legislation remained the major economic instruments of public policy. Private enterprises sought more secure markets through tariffs and, increasingly, cartels.

The postwar regimes met economic problems of the decade by trying to apply the best prewar practice of the developed European economies. Monetary and fiscal policy was still favored over state enterprise. All four governments soon turned to monetary restriction in order to raise and stabilize their currencies' depreciating exchange rates and to adopt a Gold Standard. They also relied on protective tariffs to promote the substitution of domestic manufactures for imports. Bulgaria gave greatest emphasis to monetary restriction, perhaps to meet the threat of unbearably large reparations that followed from being the only Balkan loser at the Paris Peace Conference. The Romanian government claimed, not always correctly, to place greatest stress on tariffs. The ruling National Liberals were aiming to intensify a prewar commitment to industrialization that already surpassed, as we have seen in Chapter 8, that of the other Balkan states.

It was, however, Bulgaria's industrial sector that made the most rapid postwar advance. As before, when its annual growth rate of 14 percent for the last prewar decade surpassed that of Serbia and especially Romania, Bulgarian industry began from the smallest base. Ouput in all branches save flour milling grew by annual averages of 10–30 percent for the period 1920–1929. Bulgarian industrial labor and horsepower rose 11.5 percent a year, in contrast to increments of 3 percent for Yugoslavia and Romania. The modern direction of Bulgarian growth emerges from an imported share of manufactured inputs that climbed from 27 percent before the war to 40 percent by 1930, the highest rate in Southeastern Europe. The temptation to link this rapid growth with the region's highest protective tariffs, at a time when all Eastern European states had passed rates two and three times the prewar level, must, however, be resisted, since the most highly protected branches of Bulgarian industry were not those growing rapidly in the 1920s.

Responsible instead was a sharp increase in the number of manufacturing enterprises late in the First World War, supported by the postwar influx of short-term credit from several European banks. Their Sofia affiliates dominated a commercial banking sector whose assets now exceeded those of the central bank. Native commercial banks were still weak; their insignificance had already separated the Bulgarian experience before 1914 from that of its Balkan neighbors. It was the influx of short-term credit that financed the growing import of industrial inputs. These Western European banks stopped short, however, of direct or long-term investment in industry. Horsepower per employee and enterprise in manufacturing did not rise noticeably. After an initial surge, joint-stock incorporation declined and was still the exception rather than the rule. Economies of scale, in other words, did not accompany the postwar Bulgarian advance.

The continued if reduced growth of Bulgarian industry through the Depression decade of the 1930s did, however, depend on public policy. More important than legislation to control restrictive cartels, according to Chapter 12, was a system of price controls. Guaranteed higher prices for textile production and lower ones for inputs accelerated import substitution and actually discouraged cartel membership. The government also expanded its role in central and commercial banking in a significant fashion for agriculture and foreign trade, as noted in the previous section. Industry's access to capital was not, however, noticeably enhanced, except where rearmament was involved.

Greek industrial growth of 5.7 percent a year for 1929–1938 surpassed the Bulgarian rate of 4.8 percent. Romania and Yugoslavia trailed further behind. Construction materials and especially metals and machinery, not important for Bulgaria until the postwar advance, were the sources of the Greek advantage. Rearmament played some part for metalworking, although probably less than repair of the growing Greek merchant fleets. The one million refugees who had arrived from Asia Minor in the early 1920s provided the principal new source of entrepreneurship and labor. Capital came from the region's most sustained rise in joint-stock formation for manufacturing through the interwar period. Industrial cartels, with the greater tendency to restrict production, were less prominent in interwar Greece than elsewhere in Southeastern Europe. Also scarce were the large enterprises that we associate with sustained industrialization.

The slower rates of industrial growth recorded by Romania and Yugoslavia for both interwar decades appear to have common origins. First, we must not underestimate the difficulties each faced in assimilating disparate economic patterns within greatly enlarged borders. Some of this task still confronts their present governments. Second, the impetus that large, essentially native, commercial banks in Bucharest and Zagreb gave, with some European assistance, to joint-stock manufacture during the 1920s proved too artificial to sustain itself. Bank support for new incorporations and stock issues did not survive the decline of the abnormally high interest rates, up to 20 percent, that asset holders had needed to hedge the postwar inflation and credit shortage. Stock shares met this need best. Problems of creating a common currency exaggerated the rise in interest rates. The stabilization of the leu and the dinar by the mid-1920s brought rates down. Stock dividends no longer looked like the only way to earn a sufficient return. Bank participation in industry was already declining before the Depression hit in 1929. The retreat continued through the next decade.

This lag in rates of overall growth should not obscure the fact that several important branches of Romanian and Yugoslav industry achieved significant interwar progress, especially during the 1930s. Like Bulgaria, their textile manufacture succeeded in substituting more domestic production for imported inputs as well as outputs. Unlike Bulgaria, both experienced an impressive rise in metal and machine production. Romanian iron and steel production grew by 6.6 percent a year from 1929–1938 and the Yugoslav branch by 8 percent. The Romanian rise probably carried the greatest significance for the industrial sector as a whole. Metal goods rose to one half of total Romanian imports. Domestic production also climbed to account for two thirds of consumption of metal outputs and for all of raw material input. Led by metallurgy and chemicals, inputs of labor and horsepower for all Romanian manufacturing grew by 4.1 percent a year during the period 1929–1938, versus 2.3 percent for Yugoslavia and 2.6 percent for Bulgaria. Rearmament clearly came to dominate Romanian metallurgical growth. By the last years of the decade, state agencies were purchasing 70 percent of Romanian machine production.

From 1940 to at least 1970, the mainsprings of Romanian industrial growth are more comparable to the Bulgarian experience, while Yugoslav sources of savings and investment have evolved to resemble those of Greece. The latter two countries began this most recent period, under German occupation. The Nazis destroyed vast amounts of financial and human capital, as described in Chapter 13, and left nothing new to take its place. The Romanian and Bulgarian economies escaped such harshness. New capital formation even occurred in some branches of their industrial sectors.

Both economies then suffered more in the immediate postwar settlement than did their Yugoslav and Greek counterparts. The balance between Soviet aid and reparations was clearly negative for Romania and not clearly positive for Bulgaria until the 1950s. Western capital was also unavailable before 1960, except for Romanian acquisition of former German assets from the Soviet Union in 1955.[16]

Since then Romania's foreign trade has shifted away from Eastern Europe. By 1970 just under half was conducted with countries of the Council for Mutual Economic Assistance (CMEA) and over 35 percent with the developed Western economies. Bulgaria's Western proportion also grew but not past 20 percent. Both countries had the capacity, unlike the advanced CMEA economies, to export surpluses of agricultural and semifinished goods that could easily be sold for hard currency in Western markets. The CMEA price structure provided economic incentives for such a shift. Its prices penalized exporters of these goods and favored finished goods, especially machinery. Why did Romania alone begin to transfer greater shares of its trade to the West after 1960? Political motives are presumed to predominate, but an economic rationale also existed. The balance between them is unclear. For 1955–59, the total value of Soviet loans committed (including the 1956 grain loan) and of aid delivered to Romania was 17 percent less than Bulgaria received, much less in per capita terms. Their total covered a smaller share of Romanian imports from the Soviet Union. Romania admittedly did not suffer less favorable terms of trade with the Soviet Union than did Bulgaria until after 1959. Both gained about 10 percent from 1955 to 1959. Romania's terms then declined 7 percent for 1959–1964, while Bulgaria's rose by 4 percent. The Soviets extended no more loans to Romania after 1958, revoking a previous pledge to help the Galati steel works. By 1963 West German, French, and British capital had stepped in. Meanwhile, the Soviet Union had given Bulgaria a loan of 610 million rubles for expanding their troubled steel facility at Kremikovtsi. For 1961–65, deliveries of Soviet aid to Romania covered just 7 percent of the latter's imports from the USSR, versus 17 percent for Bulgaria.[17]

The 1960s are in any case well known as the time when Romania turned to the Western economies for trade and credits. Its estimated net balance of debt in hard currencies rose to about $230 million in 1965 and to slightly over a billion by 1970. Romanian borrowing covered 16 percent of its increased Western imports for 1961–65 and 23 percent for 1966–70. Less well appreciated is the fact that Bulgaria began to borrow earlier, despite the absence of a similar shift in overall trade. By 1960 Bulgarian borrowing covered 30 percent of its growing Western imports. By 1965, net debts to the West climbed past $250 million and reached about $640 million by 1970. The increased debt covered 20 percent of Western imports for 1961–65 and 23 percent for 1966–70, exactly equal to the Romanian ratio. By 1970 the Bulgarian ratio of debt to exports in hard currency actually surpassed the figure for 1930, if we subtract reparations and other debts related to the First World War.[18]

By attributing Romanian and Bulgarian behavior solely to political motives, we lose sight of enduring international orientations already pursued, albeit by different means, before the war. These orientations have amounted to two different strategies for development. In economic terms, the so-called Romanian shift to the West is better described as a revival of National Liberal policy. The key ingredients remain import substitution and a diversification of trade, all to avoid dependence. From Ottoman times forward the recurring Bulgarian orientation has been toward export specialization for one major partner. The present contrast between the two emerges from their patterns of machine trade. In 1960 Romania exported 11 percent of its machinery production and just 9 percent by 1970. Bulgaria, on the other hand, exported 19 percent in 1960 and fully 31 percent in 1970. The volume if not the quality of preferred Bulgarian machine export appears to have benefited by being tied to preferred agricultural exports for which there was heavy demand in the CMEA countries. On the import side, only 23 percent of Romanian machine investment was purchased outside the country in 1960, 30 percent in 1970. For Bulgaria, this imported share was 56 percent in 1960 and still 53 percent in 1970. The much greater Bulgarian dependence on machine imports, another prewar pattern repeated, is responsible for bringing the proportion of *Western* equipment in total machine investment up to the Romanian level.[19]

The impressive industrial growth achieved by Bulgaria and Romania between 1950 and 1970 has obviously relied on Soviet-style organization. The state budgets assembled private savings through indirect taxes on consumers. Such taxes were nothing new in Balkan economic history, but their postwar purpose was to restrict demand rather than to mobilize savings for investment. The real power for Communist investment lay not in the budget but in central planners' control over the physical flow of goods. They favored investment in heavy industry over light, and capital formation over wages and services. Interestingly, their allocation of labor favored light industry. The two economies' ratios of gross fixed investment to gross national product rose from about 20 percent in the 1950s to exceed 30 percent in the 1960s. During these two decades both rates of industrial growth averaged over 10 percent a year, even by Western calculations.[20] Elsewhere only Japan could match these rates. Recall, however, that Bulgarian industry had grown at a similar pace during the last pre-1914 decade and during the 1920s. Rates of Romanian industrial growth lagged behind by then but had begun from the largest industrial sector and metallurgical branch among the Balkan states in 1900, while Bulgaria had the smallest of each. In addition, Romanian output of metals and machinery continued to grow in the interwar period by an annual average of about 14 percent. The postwar rates of growth for heavy industry were, in other words, not unprecedented.

From 1950 to 1970, the industrial share of Bulgarian national income (in current prices) climbed from 37 to 49 percent and the Romanian share from 44 to 60 percent. According to Table 14.2, however, industrial employment grew more rapidly, from 12 to 30 percent of the labor force for Bulgaria and from 10 to 23 percent for

Romania. A majority of the two populations became urban principally for this reason. This sort of structural change was, of course, something new for both economies. It was also the sort that is supposed to reinforce modern industrial growth, and not restrain it as may have been the case.

Bulgarian and Romanian reliance on massive injections of planned investment have not generated the even industrial growth that these aggregate figures and average rates might suggest. Sharp fluctuations in growth rates have characterized the annual data more consistently than most observers have acknowledged. These variations go beyond what we might expect from the reduced levels of investment dictated by the so-called New Course of the mid–1950s in order to boost consumer production, housing, and wage rates, and from the accelerated levels projected in both countries for the period 1958–1962. Periodic swings have continued since then, despite the repeated efforts of Romanian and Bulgarian policymakers to smooth them out.[21] Sharp variations in agricultural output continue to affect industrial production, if not employment. The greater Bulgarian interest in international specialization and microeconomic reform began in 1962. So did the Romanian emphasis on self-reliance and tighter central controls.

Recurring problems have not differed significantly for the two countries. Greater Romanian contact outside CMEA with international markets and prices has perhaps compensated for the relative lack of specialization. Both countries' industrial sectors still seem hampered by the lack of microefficiency that Soviet-style economies suffer without market prices for goods or factors of production. Witness the two sectors' comparable reliance on Western loans and technology. These contemporary limitations have been thoroughly treated elsewhere.[22]

It is tempting for Western observers to see problems of such socialist economies solely in terms of the Soviet legacy, just as Eastern observers see the aggregate advances in the same terms. We deny neither legacy but suggest one deeper historical difficulty that has helped prevent rapid postwar industrialization from closing the gap with the developed Western economies. The very speed of the structural change from rural to urban occupations, as recorded in Table 14.2, could not provide Bulgarian and Romanian industry the skilled middle management and labor force with which the developed economies entered the postwar period. The most rapid European growth during these years has come in international trade and specialization. Economies with less experienced labor and less well trained management were exposed to competitive disadvantages, whatever their country's social system. As a result, industrial productivity has not kept up with the pace of structural change, probably the reverse of the prewar experience.

The pattern of Yugoslav and Greek industrialization since 1950 includes the same structural transformation of employment, although it is less abrupt for Greece. A similar legacy of earlier industrial growth had also accumulated, more rapid for the Yugoslav lands before 1914 (see Chapters 8 and 9) and more rapid for Greece in the interwar period (see Chapters 11 and 12). In quantitative terms, their postwar growth has lagged only slightly behind the Romanian and Bulgarian rates in Table 14.1. In qualitative terms, their record has probably been superior. Their capital has come from more traditional sources.

Yugoslavia and Greece have made greater use of external financing than Bulgaria and Romania, especially before 1960. Both governments received grants or loans that exceeded $3 billion during the 1950s. Most of this inflow came from the United States. Since then, foreign aid has fallen off sharply. Long-term government loans have fallen to 15–20 percent of their external debt. Precious little direct investment from Western enterprises, some 10 percent of the debt of even non-Communist Greece, took its place. This had been Greece's prewar experience as well. Medium-term credits to cover imports, often given directly to the purchasing enterprise by the foreign supplier, made up the bulk of both countries' external debts by 1960. Ratios of hard currency debt to exports, as we have seen, dropped significantly below the 1930 level by 1970 for Greece but not for Yugoslavia.[23] Currency devaluations for Greece in 1953 and for Yugoslavia in the 1960s have sought to limit the resulting deficits on balance of payments. Both currencies had become basically convertible by 1970 but were still open to prewar charges of overvaluing their exchange rates to the detriment of the trade balance.

Covering at least two thirds of import surpluses since 1960 have been tremendous increments in invisible earnings. Shipping and tourism have provided one half of these earnings. Remittances from temporary emigrants working mainly in Western Europe account for the other half. The Greek flow of permanent emigration to North America gave way after 1960 to the long-standing southern pattern of temporary labor in northern Europe. Chapters 6 and 9 describe the pre-1914 antecedents of this emigration. During the 1960s about one million Greeks and one million Yugoslavs found and typically kept foreign employment. This amounted to over 20 percent of the Greek labor force and almost 10 percent of the Yugoslav.[24] Most came from rural areas, thus easing the domestic weight of urban migration. Commercial banks served to channel the massive remission of their savings back into the two domestic economies.

Such a transfer of external savings into investment has proved

TABLE 14.2
STRUCTURE OF POPULATION, LABOR FORCE AND PRODUCTION, 1950-70
(percentage)

Indicators	1950	1960	1970
Urban population			
Albania	20.5		33.7
Bulgaria	27.5	38.8 (1961)	54.7 (1971)
Greece	36.3	43.3 (1961)	53.2 (1971)
Romania	24.7	32.5 (1961)	41.1 (1971)
Yugoslavia	25.9	28.3 (1961)	35.3 (1971)
Labor in agriculture			
Albania	76.2		
Bulgaria	73.6 (1952)	55.5	35.7
Greece	48.2 (1951)	55.3 (1961)	40.5 (1971)
Romania	74.3	65.6	49.3
Yugoslavia	68.3 (1953)	56.3 (1961)	47.4 (1971)
Labor in industry			
Albania	11.0		
Bulgaria	14.0 (1952)	27.1	38.8
Greece	19.4 (1951)	19.7 (1961)	25.6 (1971)
Romania	14.2	20.0	30.8
Yugoslavia	7.5 (1953)	13.5 (1961)	18.5 (1971)
GDP in agriculture (current prices)			
Greece	31.1	24.7	18.9
Yugoslavia	30.1	24.0	17.8
NMP in agriculture (current prices)			
Albania	42.7	32.2	22.6
Bulgaria	28.0	33.1	18.9
Romania	76.3	44.4	34.5
Yugoslavia	25.9 (1952)	19.2	22.0
GDP in industry (current prices)			
Greece	21.2	26.3	30.5
Yugoslavia	41.5	45.0	44.6
NMP in industry (current prices)			
Albania	15.6	43.6	52.6
Bulgaria	43.4	52.7	57.8
Romania	50.0	53.1	68.4
Yugoslavia	59.9 (1952)	55.8	48.9

Notes: (a)For qualifications and definitions, see Table 14.1.

Sources: See Tables 13.9, 13.10 and 14.1.

possible only because by the 1960s internal financing for Yugoslav and Greek industry relied more heavily on bank financing than any other single source. Their industrial sectors have arrived at this same point, we must emphasize, by different routes. The Yugoslav retreat from central planning through the 1950s did not include any desire to abandon socialist principles in general or to allow enterprises to raise capital through stock sales in particular. The only alternative to continued reliance on budgetary dispensations proved to be a system of publicly owned but essentially commercial banks. Limited to short-term credit in theory, they were soon allocating large sums of renewable loans that became long-term in practice. The general economic reform of 1965 reduced the number of these banks from over two hundred to about fifty, but failed to encourage them sufficiently to credit enterprises outside of their own region[25] Such funding remained the province of several state investment banks and a budgetary fund for the underdeveloped southeastern area. The banks' common location in Belgrade has led to resentment from other regions. The efforts of the central bank to make all credit allocation more rational have been hampered by official reluctance to allow interest rates to rise and clear the market in capitalist fashion. Despite these difficulties, the Yugoslav banking system steadily increased its share of total industrial assets throughout the 1960s to 40 percent by 1970. Its share of fixed industrial investment, setting short-term assets aside, was still higher at 51 percent. The state's budgetary share has meanwhile fallen from 60 to 16 percent, leaving retained enterprise earnings as the only other major source of new capital.[26]

The share in Greek industrial assets of commercial banking, here private in the Western sense rather than public in the Yugoslav sense, was even higher by 1970. It touched 70 percent of total assets, well past the 40–45 percent fractions recorded in interwar Southeastern Europe. Only 22 percent of this latter total came from foreign banks and 48 percent from Greek ones. Unlike Yugoslavia, 70 percent of the total consisted of short-term assets. This high proportion points to the particular limitation of the Greek reliance on bank financing. Too little long-term capital is provided. The Greek stock market grew rapidly in the interwar period as noted in Chapters 11 and 12. It never recovered the public confidence lost in the wartime and postwar inflations. Annual transactions in the 1960s were less than 5 percent of the 1928 level.[27] Small family firms have continued to dominate Greek manufacturing. Their average size of 41 employees in 1973 is dwarfed by the Yugoslav and Bulgarian averages of over 500. Problems of labor productivity in Greek industry have been blamed on unusually small firms. The failure to grow in size has been traced in turn to private owners' desire to diversify the investment of their profits, especially into housing, and the reluctance of commercial banks to provide long-term credit.[28]

The pre-1914 reluctance of commercial banks to provide investment capital on the mid-nineteenth-century pattern of Central Europe thus continues to restrain economic development in at least one country of Southeastern Europe. Regional imbalances still hamper both Greek and Yugoslav development.[29] Elsewhere, the main obstacle to more rapid growth seems to be large, inefficient firms hampered by the problems of central planning and urban assimilation. Relatively small internal markets still restrict economies of scale and encourage the monopolistic practices already inherent in societies dominated by state institutions. Even the decentralized Yugoslav economy seems to suffer in this last regard.[30] Manufactured exports, including processed food, afford the best prospect for escaping these restraints and paying for growing oil imports as well.[31] Juxtaposition of the wider international market and state power promises, in other words, to retain its historic importance in determining the course of Balkan economic development. The remarkable period of *extensive* industrialization that began early in the twentieth century has now run its course for all the states of Southeastern Europe save Albania. The reserves of rural labor ready for transfer into urban manufacture have been largely exhausted. So have the surpluses of grain, timber, and minerals available to export unprocessed in return for needed imports.

The industrial sector now claims the largest single share of the factors of production in the Romanian, Bulgarian, Yugoslav, and Greek economies, thus placing them within the ranks of the developed nations by this criterion. But for production itself to continue to rise rapidly enough to bring national incomes to a developed level, these economies must make a successful transition to *intensive* industrialization,[32] the hallmark of which is increasing productivity per unit of resources expended. Only the better quality of production implicit in such an increase can generate the sort of manufactured exports upon which both the West and East German economies have based their recent records of intensive industrial growth. Only such improved quality can service both an impatient domestic demand for better consumer goods and an international debt that the desire for Western, export-oriented technology has pushed toward pre-1914 proportions during the past decade.

Notes

Introduction

1. See the figures on national income and production for Southeastern Europe, Western Europe, and the rest of the world in Chapter 10.

2. Fernand Braudel, *The Mediterranean and the Mediterranean World in the Age of Philip II*, vol. I (New York: Harper & Row, 1972).

3. Marc Bloch in Frederic J. Lane and J.C. Ricmersma, *Enterprise and Secular Change* (Homewood, Ill.: Richard D. Irwin, 1953), p. 498. For a more recent view of the state of comparative economic history, see Elias H. Tuma, *Economic History and the Social Sciences: Problems of Methodology* (Berkeley: Univ. of California Press, 1971), pp. 38–39.

4. George W. Hoffman, ed., *Eastern Europe: Essays in Geographic Problems* (London: Methuen, 1971), p. 21; Joseph L. Roglić, "Die Gebirge als die Wiege des geschichtlichen Geschehens in Südosteuropa," *Colloquium geographicum, Argumenta geographica*, vol. 12 (Bonn, 1970), pp. 225–30.

5. Considering climate alone, a proper line can be drawn, but far to the south of most others suggested. The East European continental climate of cold winters and humid summers reaches so far southward as to stop short only of the Greek and Adriatic coastlines. For other geographic (and nongeographic) influences, no single line seems satisfactory. For a map depicting the assortment of demarcation lines for Mediterranean influence in southeastern Europe, see Roglić, p. 227. A good recent review of this issue may be found in the editor's introduction to Francis W. Carter, ed., *An Historical Geography of the Balkans* (New York: Academic Press, 1977), pp. 6–10.

6. Braudel, vol. I. pp. 25–27.

7. George W. Hoffman, *Regional Development Strategy in Southeastern Europe* (New York: Praeger, 1972), pp. 3–5.

8. The Yugoslav sections are largely responsible for putting 45 percent of the territory in the present boundaries at an elevation of 1,500 feet or higher. Well-forested at the Slovenian end, these mountains turn to barren *karst* rock on moving southward. They remain the least-populated areas in Yugoslavia. The sometimes lengthy upland valleys form basins for enough karstic limestone deposits from the surrounding mountains to drain rainfall deep underground and impose almost the same limits on agriculture as the *karst* itself. While water-retaining crystalline rock becomes more typical of the section turning inland toward the Morava-Vardar valley, the same predominance of limestone rock and soil makes the Pindus range in Greece equally unsuited to agriculture. For a more detailed and technical description, see ibid., pp. 15–17, 22; idem, ed., *Eastern Europe: Essays*, p. 23; Roy E.H. Mellor, *Eastern Europe: A Geography of the Comecon Countries* (New York: Columbia Univ. Press, 1975), pp. 103, 174; Norman J.G. Pounds, *Eastern Europe* (Chicago: Aldine, 1969), p. 37.

9. While the Carpathians of Romania are several thousand feet higher than this lowest range in Southeastern Europe, they share with it a well-forested and long-cultivated soil and an abundance of easily crossed passes. Both ranges, as we shall see, furnished not only political refuge but also nodes of economic development from which ethnic Romanians and Bulgarians could operate. If we discount the limited amount of Bulgarian iron ore in the upland basin of Sofia, only the Carpathians possess any significant mineral deposits. These were mainly iron ore and copper on the slopes into southwestern Transylvania. Hoffman, *Regional Development Strategy*, pp. 10–12; idem, ed., *Eastern Europe: Essays*, pp. 27–30; Mellor, p. 174; Pounds, pp. 15, 28, 33–36; A. Oțetea, *The History of the Romanian People* (Bucharest, 1970), pp. 10–16.

10. They may also be grown in the wider Maritsa River basin bending around the northeastern edges of the range eastward from Plovdiv across southern Bulgaria and then southward through Edirne to the same sea. The Rhodopes themselves contain the most ample deposits of brown coal and lignite in these Balkan lands. Hoffman, *Regional Development Strategy*, pp. 13–14, 24; idem, ed., *Eastern Europe: Essays*, p. 25; Pounds, p. 17.

11. See Traian Stoianovich, *A Study in Balkan Civilization* (New York: Alfred A. Knopf, 1967), pp. 30–33, 89.

12. Roglić, p. 226, calls rivers the most important means of communication and joins the Romanian geographer Y. Chatigneau, in *Les pays Balkaniques*, *Geographie universelle*, vol. VII (Paris, 1934), in rejecting other geographers' claims that the Danube forms a "natural border."

13. Braudel, pp. 191–223, calls the Polish and Russian lands two of the four trading "isthmuses" that gave commercial unity to early modern Europe.

14. David Mitrany, *The Effect of the War in Southeastern Europe* (New Haven: Yale Univ. Press, 1936), pp. 6–14.

15. For an eminent economist's recognition of the importance of national aspirations as the driving force behind the policies of such new states, see Harry G. Johnson, ed., *Economic Nationalism in Old and New States* (Chicago: Univ. of Chicago Press, 1967), p. 126.

16. Cyril E. Black, *The Dynamics of Modernization* (New York: Harper Torchbooks, 1966), pp. 7, 46, 91, 114–16.

17. For a lengthy bibliographic survey and critical review of old and new scholarship on this subject, see John R. Lampe and Marvin R. Jackson, "An Appraisal of Recent Balkan Economic Historiography," *East European Quarterly*, IX, 2 (June, 1975), pp. 197–240.

18. For a carefully argued Marxist exposition of these assumptions, see Maurice Dobb, *Studies in the Development of Capitalism* (New York: International Publishers, 1962), pp. 178–85. For a non-Marxist exposition, see M.M. Bober, *Karl Marx's Interpretation of History*, rev. ed. (New York: Norton, 1948), pp. 128–205. Their specific application to Balkan economic history may be found concisely stated for the Romanian case in *Istoria Rominiei*, III (Bucharest, 1964), pp. 585–91.

19. English economic historians' disenchantment with the hypothesis that the eighteenth-century enclosures drove much rural labor into the new manufacturing towns, thus creating an "industrial reserve army," dates back to J.D. Chambers, "Enclosures and Labour Supply," *Economic History Review*, 2nd Series, vol. 5, no. 3 (1953), pp. 322–35. A good summary of subsequent English research may be found in Peter Mathias, *The First Industrial Nation* (New York: Scribners, 1969), pp. 60–63. The exceptional nature of the English Industrial Revolution as a whole receives recent recognition even from the English Marxist scholar Tom Kemp, in his *Industrialization in Nineteenth Century Europe* (London: Longmans, 1970), pp. 1–33.

20. The classic statement of the Leninist view is of course found in V.I. Lenin, *Imperialism: The Last Stage of Capitalism* (Moscow: 1947). Perhaps its most persuasive application to Central and Southeastern Europe during the early modern period may be found in the work of the eminent Hungarian economic historian, Zigismund S. Pach. See his "Favorable and Unfavorable Conditions for Capitalist Growth, the Shift in Trade Routes in the XVth through XVIIth Centuries," *Proceedings*, IV, Congress, International Economic History Association, Bloomington, In., 1968. For a recent Yugoslav restatement of the view that the English Industrial Revolution still constitutes the benchmark against which all subsequent industrialization must be measured, see the comment by Branko Kojić in *Acta historico-oeconomica iugoslaviae*, vol. I (Zagreb, 1974), pp. 155–61.

21. For a Balkan scholar's acknowledgement of some positive features in the sixteenth-century Ottoman economy and reliance on the painstaking research of Professor O.L. Barkan and other Turkish scholars, see Nikolai Todorov, *Balkanskiiat grad, XV–XIX vek* [The Balkan Town, 15th–19th Centuries] (Sofia, 1972), pp. 80–126.

22. Western recognition of Marx's broader view on this subject and the best brief summary of them are in Alexander Gerschenkron, *Economic Backwardness in Historical Perspective* (New York: Praeger, 1965), p. 97–98. For a similar Soviet view, see P.I. Liashchenko, *The History of the National Economy of Russia to 1917* (Moscow, 1949).

23. Evidence of this recognition is cited in Lampe and Jackson, "Recent Balkan Economic Historiography," *East European Quarterly*, pp. 209–19.

24. See, for instance, David Mitrany, *The Land and the Peasant in*

Rumania (New Haven: Yale Univ. Press, 1930), Henry L. Roberts, *Rumania: Political Problems of an Agrarian State* (New Haven: Yale Univ. Press, 1951), Jozo Tomasevich, *Peasants, Politics and Economic Change in Yugoslavia* (Palo Alto: Stanford Univ. Press, 1955), and S.D. Zagoroff, J. Vegh, and A.D. Blimovich, *The Agrarian Economy of the Danubian Countries, 1933–1945* (Palo Alto: Stanford Univ. Press, 1955).

25. He concludes that both the European investment banks and the Bulgarian government missed an opportunity about 1900 to promote widespread railway construction that would have in turn prompted the Russian-style growth of a metallurgical sector to supply rails and rolling stock. How this might have occurred in the face of the aforementioned deficiencies in the quality of Bulgarian coal and the quantity of Bulgarian iron ore is not made clear, nor is the full play of institutional forces in the pre-1914 Bulgarian economy. Alexander Gerschenkron, "Some Aspects of Industrialization in Bulgaria, 1878–1939," in his *Economic Backwardness in Historical Perspective*, pp. 198–234.

26. The relatively higher output and mechanization of Romanian industry than the Serbian or the Bulgarian by 1913 are traced back in time only to the earlier Romanian passage of legislation affording tariff rebates and other state aid to native industry. Our Chapter 8 will suggest that the greater Romanian advance had more complex origins. Nicholas Spulber, *The State and Economic Development in Eastern Europe* (New York: Random House, 1966), pp. 18–21, 64–66.

27. From Kuznets' Nobel Prize lecture in his *Population, Capital and Growth —Selected Essays* (New York: W.W. Norton, 1973), p. 165.

28. These early efforts to measure the aggregate dimensions of economic activity are used in Chapters 6 and 10. Time series for population, finance, commerce, and agriculture generally date from the second half of the nineteenth century. Although the very existence of these data is sometimes a better indicator of the nation-building process than the phenomena they purport to measure, we have used them throughout Part II to reflect relative growth.

29. The influential Lewis argument was first stated in Arthur V. Lewis, "Economic Development with Unlimited Supplies of Labor," *Manchester School of Economic and Social Studies*, XXII (May, 1954), pp. 139–91. The subsequent Western argument against the availability of an infinitely elastic supply of labor at fixed subsistance wages is summarized in Everett D. Hagen, *The Economics of Development* (Homewood, Ill.: Richard D. Irwin, Inc., 1968), pp. 306–309.

30. Evidence that English capital investment grew only from 5 to 6 percent of national product during the course of the Industrial Revolution (roughly from 1760 to 1830) may be found in Phyllis Deane and W.A. Cole, *British Economic Growth, 1688–1959* (Cambridge: Cambridge Univ. Press, 1967). On the decisive role of rising productivity in American and Western European growth during the twentieth century, see Edward H. Denison, *Why Growth Rates Differ* (Washington, D.C.: Brookings Institution, 1967).

31. A brief statement of the arguments for and against the neoclassical approach to J.C. Gould, *Economic Growth in History* (London: Methuen,

1972), pp. 240–47. The most comprehensive recent statement of the "core-state" view of European development at the expense of peripheral areas is Immanuel Wallerstein, *The Modern World-System: Capitalist Agriculture and the Origins of the European World Economy in the Sixteenth Century* (New York: Academic Press, 1974). A thought-provoking attempt to apply this view to Romanian economic history is Daniel Chirot, *Social Change in a Peripheral Society—The Creation of a Balkan Colony* (New York: Academic Press, 1976).

32. Kuznets, pp. 165–66. The limited extent of agricultural goods in twentieth-century statistics for national product is discussed in Bruce F. Johnston and Peter Kilby, *Agriculture and Structural Transformation-Economic Strategies in Late-Developing Countries* (New York: Oxford Univ. Press, 1975), p. 35.

Part I
New Markets and the Old Empires

1. Immanuel Wallerstein, *The Modern World-System: Capitalist Agriculture and the Origins of the European World Economy in the Sixteenth Century* (New York: Columbia Univ. Press, 1974).

2. For a concise description of the *millet* system and its role in Ottoman society, see H.A.R. Gibb and Harold Bowen, *Islamic Society and the West*, vol. I, part II (London: Oxford Univ. Press, 1957), pp. 212–24. On what role the institution played in Serbian and Greek society in the eighteenth century, see Michael B. Petrovich, *A History of Modern Serbia*, 1 (New York: Harcourt Brace Jovanovich, 1976), pp. 7–26, and John Petropoulos, *Politics and Statecraft in the Kingdom of Greece, 1833–1843* (Princeton, N.J.: Princeton Univ. Press, 1968), pp. 24–35.

3. The decisive role of artillery in the changing military technology of the sixteenth century is discussed in Richard Bean, "War and the Birth of the Nation-State," *Journal of Economic History*, XXXIII, 1 (March, 1973), pp. 203–21. On the wider implications of changing technology and a growing population for political institutions, see the essays in Charles Tilly, ed., *The Formation of National States in Western Europe* (Princeton, N.J.: Princeton Univ. Press, 1975).

1. The Economic Legacy of
Ottoman Domination

1. For a summary of the military and economic explanations, see Kemal H. Karpat, *Social Change and Politics in Turkey* (Leiden: E.J. Brill, 1973), pp. 29–33. The classic statement of the religious view, i.e., that *gazi* or frontier warriors driven by Moslem zeal created the Ottoman state in prolonged struggle against infidel Byzantium, is found in Paul Wittek, *The Rise of the Empire* (London: Royal Asiatic Society of Great Britain, 1938 and 1967).

2. Halil Inalcik, *The Ottoman Empire, The Classical Age, 1300–1600*

(New York: Praeger, 1973), pp. 104–16. Also see Peter Sugar, *Southeastern Europe under Ottoman Rule, 1354–1804* (Seattle: Univ. of Washington Press, 1977), pp. 14–23, 65–71.

3. The original Western definition of these military, civil, and Islamic institutions of the Ottoman government at their apex remains Alfred H. Lybyer, *The Government of the Ottoman Empire in the Time of Suleiman the Magnificent* (Cambridge, Mass.: Harvard Univ. Press, 1913), especially pp. 148–95. The most recent summary is Stanford Shaw, *History of the Ottoman Empire and Modern Turkey*, I (Cambridge: Cambridge Univ. Press, 1976), pp. 112–27. On the application of these institutions to the Balkan provinces, see Sugar, pp. 39–51.

4. For a comprehensive definition of the *timar* system of land tenure, see H.A.R. Gibb and Harold Bowen, *Islamic Society and the West*, vol. I, part 1 (London: Oxford Univ. Press, 1950), pp. 235–48. On the *pronoia* system, Angliki Laiou-Thomadakis, *Byzantine Peasant Society* (Princeton, N.J.: Princeton Univ. Press, 1977). For precise but somewhat varied definitions of European feudalism, see the French medievalist, Georges Duby, *The Early Growth of the European Economy* (Ithaca, N.Y.: Cornell Univ. Press, 1974), pp. 162–80; the English economist Sir John Hicks, *A Theory of Economic History* (London: Oxford Univ. Press, 1969), pp. 16–24; and the English Marxist, Maurice Dobb, *Studies in the Development of Capitalism* (New York: International Publishers, 1963), pp. 35–37.

5. Nikolai Todorov, *Balkanskiiat grad, XV–XIX vek* [The Balkan Town, 15th–19th Centuries] (Sofia, 1972), pp. 110, 121–23.

6. Halil Inalcik, "Capital Formation in the Ottoman Empire," *Journal of Economic History*, XIX, 1 (March, 1969), pp. 97, 106; Gibb and Bowen, pp. 281–99; Todorov, pp. 106–10.

7. On the decline of the Sultan's political power following the reign of Suleiman the Magnificent (1520–66) and on its connection to the introduction of the *kafes* system for conferring all potential successors to the harem, see A.D. Alderson, *The Structure of the Ottoman Dynasty* (Oxford: Clarendon Press, 1956), pp. 8–37.

8. Inalcik, *The Ottoman Empire*, pp. 48–51. Following their desertion of an Anatolian battlefield in 1596, some 30,000 *sipahi* were stripped of their *timar* holdings at one stroke. See Kemal H. Karpat, "The Stages of Ottoman History," paper presented to the Conference on Ottoman Studies, Univ. of Wisconsin, Madison, May 3–6, 1971.

9. Karpat, *Social Change in Turkey*, p. 35. On the generally similar spread of artillery and infantry units among sixteenth century European armies, see Carlo M. Cipolla, *Guns, Sails and Empire: Technological Innovation and the Early Phases of European Expansion, 1400–1700* (New York: Minerva Press, 1969), and Sir Charles Oman, *A History of the Art of War in the Sixteenth Century* (London: Methuen, 1937). The corresponding rise in budgets is noted in Fernand Braudel, *The Mediterranean and the Mediterranean World in the Age of Philip II*, I (New York: Harper & Row, 1972), p. 451.

10. Braudel, pp. 395–96; O.L. Barkan, "Research on the Ottoman Fiscal Surveys," in M.A. Cook, ed., *Studies in the Economic History of the Middle East* (London: Oxford Univ. Press, 1970), pp. 167–70. The overall Ottoman

population of 22,000,000 by 1580 exceeded that of France, the largest European state, by 6,000,000. The Balkan figure of over 8,000,000 matched contemporary Spain. On urban population, see Inalcik, *The Ottoman Empire*, pp. 158–59.

11. Inalcik, "Capital Formation," pp. 106–107, 138; Robert Mantran, *Istanbul dans la seconde moitié du XVIIe siècle* (Paris, 1962), p. 214.

12. Barkan, pp. 166–70. On Edirne see Inalcik, "Capital Formation," pp. 124–32, and on Sarajevo, Hamdja Kreševljanović, *Gradska privreda i esnafi u Bosni i Hercegovini*, I [The Urban Economy and Guilds in Bosnia and Hercegovina], (Sarajevo, 1949).

13. Vasa Čubrilović, ed., *Istorija Beograda* (The History of Belgrade), I (Belgrade, 1974), pp. 360, 426.

14. O.L. Barkan, "Les particularités du système financier ottoman et son evolution du XVe au XVIIe siècle," in *L'impot dans le cadre de la ville et l'etat, Collection Histoire-Historische Uitgaven*, no. 13 (Liège, 1966), pp. 267–73. Also see Todorov, pp. 81–99.

15. Felix Boujour, *A View of the Commerce of Greece, 1787–1797*, translated by Thomas H. Howe (London, 1800), p. 158.

16. Helping to enforce these restrictions was the growing influence of the Moslem religious hierarchy over Ottoman life late in the sixteenth century. Its control of the courts allowed rigid enforcement of guild regulations. Its learned elite, the *ulema*, used their control of the educational system to restrict general Ottoman access to new technology just as the Scientific Revolution began to spread across Western Europe during the seventeenth century. On the technical backwardness and conservatism of the Ottoman artisan guilds, see Mantran, pp. 416–24; G. Baer, "The Administrative, Economic and Social Functions of Guilds," *International Journal of Middle East Studies*, 1 (1970), pp. 28–50; and Inalcik, "Capital Formation," pp. 135–37.

17. Liuben Berov, "Changes in Price Conditions in Trade Between Turkey and Europe in the 16th–19th Centuries," *Études Balkaniques* no. 2–3 (Sofia, 1974), pp. 169–78. This valuable summary is based on the continuous prices of 106 items (artisan wares as well as foodstuffs) that have been assembled by Bulgarian researchers from a variety of data from Istanbul and the Ottoman Balkans. Constant values are expressed in silver grams. The full study in Liuben Berov, *Dvizhenieto na tsenite na Balkanite prez XVI–XIX v. i Evropeisakata revolutsiia na tsenite* [The Movement of Prices in the Balkans during the 16–19th Centuries and the European Price Revolution] (Sofia, 1976).

18. Inalcik, *The Ottoman Empire*, pp. 140–41, and Barkan, "Research," pp. 167–70. On the Empire's military population, see Mantran, pp. 398–416. On contemporary European cities, see Roger Mols, "Population in Europe, 1500–1700," in Carlo M. Cipolla, ed., *The Fontana Economic History of Europe—The Sixteenth and Seventeenth Centuries*, vol. 2 (London: Collins/ Fontana Books, 1974), pp. 42–43.

19. Kristof Glaman, "European Trade, 1500–1700," Cipolla, ed., pp. 438–39, 455–56; Braudel, pp. 591–93; Marcel Aumard, *Venise, Raguse et le commerce du blé dans la seconde moitié du XVIe siècle* (Paris, 1966). Once the European price of grain exceeded the Ottoman level by more than one

half, as it did by 1590, grain became profitable to ship across the Mediterranean despite the transport costs. See Berov, "Changes in Price Conditions," pp. 172–73. The documentary evidence of sizable wheat smuggling after the Ottoman ban is summarized in M.A. Cook, *Population Pressure in Rural Anatolia, 1450–1600* (London: Oxford Univ. Press, 1972), p. 3.

20. Mantran, pp. 187–92. By this time, the Romanian Principalities of Wallachia and Moldavia paid most of their tribute to the Sultan in shipments of grain, usually wheat.

21. They needed only an official document from Istanbul, cosigned by the local *kadi* at the point of export and recording the details of the shipment, to bring their purchases back to Istanbul. True, the Grand Vezir himself fixed the maximum wholesale price in the city, usually at about two thirds the level in the larger provincial towns. Grain merchants still found some leeway for price bargaining, especially on any surplus over the amount they were supposed to deliver. Ibid., pp. 398–416.

22. Ibid., pp. 235–48, 258–61, 280–85; Barkan, "Les particularités du système financier ottoman," pp. 267–73; Fernand Braudel and Frank Spooner, "Prices in Europe, 1450–1750," in *The Cambridge Economic History of Europe*, IV (Cambridge: Cambridge Univ. Press, 1967), pp. 378–486.

23. Berov, "Changes in Price Conditions," p. 174.

24. The pressure of this assortment of European coins on the basic Ottoman denomination, the silver *asper* or *akçe*, proved irresistible. Between 1585 and 1688, its silver content was reduced three times, in favor of copper, and its market value fell by more than two thirds. The advantage that this devaluation might otherwise have brought to Ottoman exports was lost because no merchant wished to conduct foreign trade unless it was for barter or European denominations. A.G. Wood, *A History of the Levant Company* (London: Barnes & Noble, 1964), pp. 100–101, and Ralph David, *Aleppo and Devonshire Square* (London: Macmillan, 1967), pp. 191–92.

25. Davis, p. 28 and idem, "English Imports from the Middle East, 1580–1780," in Cook, ed., *Studies*, 195–98, and Wood, pp. 102–108. For a demonstration of English success in undercutting Venetian textiles, see Richard T. Rapp, "The Unmaking of the Mediterranean Trade Hegemony," *Journal of Economic History*, XXXV, 3 (Sept. 1975), pp. 499–525.

26. Mantran, pp. 604–606, Wood, pp. 101–105, 228–35. On the nature of the opposition to European economic penetration in Tsarist Russia, see John P. McKay, *Pioneers for Profit: Foreign Entrepreneurship and Russian Industrialization, 1885–1913* (Chicago, Ill.: Univ. of Chicago Press, 1970), pp. 276–86.

27. Wood, p. 135; Gibb and Bowen, I, p. 310.

28. Their close connection with Venetian traders identified Ottoman Jews with the Empire's principal adversary. As Venetian power in the Eastern Mediterranean diminished after 1600 with the loss of their Greek possessions, most prominently Crete in 1669, so did Jewish opportunities in Istanbul. General Ottoman tolerance of its Jewish population declined by this time. Official suspicion was fueled not only by the long struggle with Venice but also by the Jewish messianic movement that briefly challenged the Sultan's authority in the 1650s. Mantran, pp. 448–51; Inalcik, "Capital Formation," pp. 121–24.

29. William H. McNeill, *Europe's Steppe Frontier, 1500–1800* (Chicago, Ill.: Univ. of Chicago Press, 1964), pp. 152–153, George B. Leon, "The Greek Merchant Marine, 1750–1850," in S.A. Papadapoulos, ed., *The Greek Merchant Marine, 1453–1850* (Athens: National Bank of Greece, 1972), pp. 19–26, notes that Greeks were also able to share in the large amount of European coin speculation.

30. Roy E.H. Mellor, *A Geography of the Comecon Countries* (New York: Columbia Univ. Press, 1975), p. 176. On the agricultural economies of the medieval Serbian and Bulgarian kingdoms, see Miloš Blagojević, *Zemljoradnje u srednovekovnoj Srbiji* [Agriculture in Medieval Serbia] (Belgrade, 1973); Robert Browning, *Byzantium and Bulgaria* (Berkeley, Calif.: Univ. of California Press, 1975), pp. 79–88; and D. Angelov, *Obrazuvane na bulgarskata narodnost* [The Emergence of the Bulgarian People] (Sofia, 1971).

31. See Deena R. Sadat, "Rumeli Ayanlari: The Eighteenth Century," *Journal of Modern History*, vol. 44, no. 3 (Sept., 1972), pp. 346–63, Halil Inalcik, "Land Problems in Turkey," *Muslim World*, 45 (1955), pp. 221–28, and Traian Stoianovich, "Land Tenure and Related Sectors of the Ottoman Economy," *Journal of Economic History* XIII, 4 (Fall, 1953), pp. 398–411.

32. Richard Busch-Zantner, an interwar German scholar, made the Prussian parallel to the Balkan experience explicit; see his *Agrarverfassung, Gesellschaft und Siedlung in Südosteuropa* (Leipzig, 1938). The immediate postwar generation of Marxist historians, prompted by Lenin's frequent references to *Gutswirtschaft* as a transitional phase from feudalism to capitalism, accepted Busch-Zantner's assumption. On the Polish experience, which fits the Marxist model rather nicely, see Jerzy Topolski, "Economic Decline in Poland from the Sixteenth to the Nineteenth Centuries," in Peter Earle, ed., *Essays in European Economic History, 1500–1800* (London: Oxford Univ. Press, 1974), pp. 126–42.

33. Khristo Khristov, *Agrarnite otnoshenie v Makedoniia prez XIX vek i nachalata XX v.* [Agrarian Relations in Macedonia during the 19th and at the Start of the 20th Century] (Sofia, 1964), p. 24, and his *Argarniat vupros v Bulgarskata natsionalna revolutsiia* [The Agrarian Question in the Bulgarian National Revolution] (Sofia, 1976), pp. 118–41.

34. See the map on p. 214 of Jovan Cvijić, *La Peninsule balkanique* (Paris, 1918) or on p. 352 of Sadat. For a textual treatment, see Khristov, *Agrarnite otnoshenie*, pp. 27, 77–79.

35. Khristov, *Agrarnite otnoshenie*, pp. 42–44, 52–53; Stanford J. Shaw, *Between Old and New: The Ottoman Empire under Sultan Selim III, 1789–1807* (Cambridge, Mass.: Harvard Univ. Press, 1971), pp. 236–46, 301–305; Fani Milkova, *Pozemlenata sobstvenost v Bulgarskiite zemi prez XIX vek* [Agricultural Property in Bulgaria during the 19th Century] (Sofia, 1969), p. 197.

36. Str. Dimitrov, "Kum istoriiata na chiflikchiistvo v Ruse" [Concerning the History of the *Chiflik* in Ruse], *Istoricheski pregled*, XIV, 4 (Sofia, 1958), pp. 90–98; Khristov, *Agrarnite otnoshenie*, p. 21; Boujour, pp. 27–33.

37. Boujour, p. 39; François Crouzet et al., *Histoire économique de la France, 1660–1789*, II (Paris, 1970), pp. 511–28.

38. Milkova, pp. 184, 224–32. On the primitive agricultural techniques

prevailing on even the most capitalistic sort of *chiflik*, see Dončo Zografski, *Razvitokot na kapitalicheskite elementi vo Makedonija* [Development of Capitalistic Elements in Macedonia] (Skopje, 1967), p. 67, and Khristov, *Agrarniat vupros*, pp. 126–28.

39. Khristov, *Agrarnite otnoshenie*, pp. 24–25; Todorov, pp. 170–74.

40. Khristo Gandev, *Zarazhdane na kapitalisticheskite otnosheniia v chiflishkoto stopanstvo na severnozapadna Bulgariia prez XVIII vek* [The Origin of Capitalist Relations in the Chiflik Economy of Northwest Bulgaria during the 18th Century] (Sofia, 1962), pp. 36–45.

41. Str. Dimitrov, "Kum vuprosa za otmeniavaneto na spahiiskata sistema v nashete zemi" [Concerning the Question of the End of the Sipahi System in our Lands], *Istoricheski pregled*, XII, 6 (Sofia, 1956), p. 34. The sum of more recent Bulgarian scholarship is reviewed in Thomas E. Meininger, "The Formation of a Nationalist Bulgarian Intelligentsia, 1835–1878" (Ph.D. dissertation, Univ. of Wisconsin, 1974), p. 17.

42. Halil Inalcik, "Common Traits of Economic and Social Development of Balkan and Southeast European Peoples under the Ottoman Empire," *Rapport* to the III. International Congress of Southeast European Studies, Bucharest, Sept. 3–7, 1974, pp. 24–32, provides description and appraisal of its importance.

43. See below on the role of the *maktu* system in the First Serbian Uprising, 1804–12.

44. Mellor, pp. 167–68; Cvijić, p. 170.

45. E.A. Hammel, "The Zadruga as Process," in Peter Laslett and Marilyn Clarke, eds., *Households in Past and Present* (Cambridge: Cambridge Univ. Press, 1972), pp. 338–40, 361–71. The role of the formally constituted *zadruga* as the basic economic unit of the Croatian Military Border is dealt with in Chapter 2.

46. Barkan, "Research," pp. 167–70, John R. Lampe, "Financial Structure and the Economic Development of Serbia, 1878–1912," (Ph.D. dissertation, Univ. of Wisconsin, 1971), pp. 68–75; Jack Tucker, "The Rumanian Peasant Revolt of 1907: Three Regional Studies," (Ph.D. dissertation, Univ. of Chicago, 1972), pp. 1–6; Zhak Natan et al., *Ikonomika na Bulgariia*, I (Sofia, 1969), pp. 197–207; Hariton Korisis, *Die politischen Parteien Griechenlands, 1821–1910* (Harsbruck/Nürnberg, 1966), pp. 112–21; Boujour, p. 85.

47. The principal economic effect of this transfer from rural cultivation to urban consumption was, not surprisingly, a 50 percent rise in the price of wheat marketed in Thessaloniki during the last half of the eighteenth century. Thus the profitability of wheat export declined and that of cotton export from nearby *chiflik*, considered further below, increased. Nicholas Svoronos, in his pioneering *Le commerce du Salonique au XVIIIme siècle* (Paris, 1956), p. 386, estimates that the price of wheat in Thessaloniki rose from 50 percent of the Marseilles price in 1739 to 80 percent by the 1780s. Transport costs and tariffs would absorb a majority of the profit from the later, smaller differential.

48. Ivan Sakazov, *Bulgarische Wirtschaftsgeschichte* (Berlin and Leipzig, 1929), p. 223. Concerning the connection of plague and cholera outbreaks with the passage of Ottoman troops, see A.P. Vakalopoulos, *A History of*

Thessaloniki (Thessaloniki, 1963), pp. 107–109, on northern Greece; Čubrilović, ed., pp. 760–761, on Belgrade; and Sergiu Columbeanu, *Grandes exploitations domaniales en Valachie au XVIIIme siècle* (Bucharest, 1974), pp. 41–44, on western Wallachian towns.

49. Records kept in the port by French consuls from 1718 and by the Marseilles Chamber of Commerce from 1722 generated the first usable trade figure for any Balkan area. Svoronos, pp. 107, 306–19, 387, has combined and corrected these estimates of export and import value, summarized in Tables 1.1 and 1.2. On population, see his pp. 7–11, 84–87, and also Vakalopoulos, p. 78, and Boujour, p. 85.

50. Their predominance dated back to privileges granted by Sultan Bayezid II to the Jewish community soon after they began pouring into Thessaloniki from Spain, Sicily, and Portugal in the 1490s. To make use of their European skills, the Sultan gave Jews the right to buy one quarter of all wool entering the town at a low, fixed price. They also received a monopoly on the manufacture of blue woolen cloth for Janissary uniforms. This manufacture reached its peak in the 1560s but then declined steadily under the weight of Western European competition. See E.M. Cousinery, *Voyage dans le Macedoine*, I (Paris, 1831), pp. 48–51, and Svoronos, pp. 57, 113, 220. On the continuing Jewish dominance of the port's import trade and money lending, see John MacGregor, *Commercial Statistics*, vol. 2 (London, 1850), p. 84.

51. Svoronos, pp. 193–96, 272–78; Leon, p. 30; Boujour, p. 80.

52. Traian Stoianovich, "The Conquering Balkan Orthodox Merchant," *Journal of Economic History*, XX, 2 (June, 1960), pp. 234–313, remains the most comprehensive study of merchant enterprise in the Ottoman Balkans. On the limits of Byzantine financial practice as applied to later Greek history, see A.A. Pepelasis, "The Legal System and Economic Development of Greece," *Journal of Economic History*, XIX, 2 (June, 1959), pp. 173–98.

53. Wood, pp. 159–60; Svoronos, pp. 39, 347.

54. The French textile industry was also able to undercut English competition in the Eastern Mediterranean with lower prices during most of the eighteenth century. Whatever the reason, France accounted for about 60 percent of the Levant's European trade in 1750, versus about 20 percent for England. These percentages held fairly constant until 1789. Davis, "English Imports from the Middle East," pp. 203–204; Wood, p. 143; Svoronos, pp. 262–63.

55. Svoronos, pp. 350–54. Also see Berrisav Arsitch, *La vie économique de la Serbie du Sud au XIX siècle* (Paris, 1936), pp. 118–19; Leon, pp. 32–34; Wood, pp. 186–92. Outside the scope of this chapter is what role subsequent economic reverses, which hit these Greek traders after the Napoleonic wars, might have played in spreading dissatisfaction with Ottoman rule and encouraging merchant support for the Greek War of Independence, 1821–29.

56. Stoianovich, "Land Tenure," pp. 403–404.

57. Paul Masson, *Histoire du commerce français dans le Levant au XVIIIme siècle* (Paris, 1896; New York: Bart Franklin, 1967), pp. 619–29; Boujour, pp. 45–50; Stoianovich, "Conquering Balkan Orthodox Merchant," pp. 274–75. For a more comprehensive treatment of the commerce of the

Peloponnesus at this time, see Vasilas Kremmydas, *To emporio teo Pelopon-nesa sto 18 aiona* [The Market of the Peloponnesus during the 18th Century] (Athens, 1972).

58. The northern thrust of Greek commercial activity and even migration after the 1718 treaty is detailed in A.P. Vacalopoulos, *History of Macedonia, 1354–1833* (Thessaloniki, 1973), pp. 288–307, 319–22, 410–12. Also see the map of emigration routes on pp. 380–81.

59. Ibid., pp. 49–50; Arsitch, p. 6; Svoronos, pp. 207–11.

60. Todorov, pp. 199–219.

61. Svoronos, pp. 197–99, 241–46.

62. Vlachs had first acquired their commercial connections in the course of moving their livestock seasonally back and forth between high and low ground. They were the main practitioners of transhumance in the Balkans, rivaled only by the Albanians, whose more isolated activity precluded much commercial activity. See Hammel, pp. 344–45, Cvijić, pp. 177–82; Braudel, pp. 86–100; Alan J.B. Wace and M.S. Thompson, *The Nomads of the Balkans* (New York, 1914; New York: Books for Libraries Press, 1971), pp. 214–16; Dušan Popović, *O cincarima* [Concerning the Tsintsars] (Belgrade, 1937), pp. 34–41.

63. Their control of money changing allowed the Tsintsars to adopt the use of bills of exchange and double-entry bookkeeping, both little-known tech-niques in the Ottoman lands. Popović, pp. 116–37; Čubrilović, ed., I, pp. 689–92.

64. Vera Mutafchieva and Al. Vianu, "Feodalnoto razmiritsi v severna Bul-gariia v nachalotot na XIX vek i tehnoto otrazhenie vuv Vlakhia" [Feudal Dissolution in Northern Bulgaria at the Start of the 19th Century and Its Repercussions in Wallachia] in D. Angelov, M. Berza et al., *Bulgarsko-rumunski vruski i otnoshenie prez vekove* [Bulgarian-Romanian Ties and Re-lations over the Centuries], I (Sofia, 1965), pp. 196–201; Shaw, *Between Old and New*, pp. 237–45.

65. D. Kosev, Vl. Diculescu, and V. Paskaleva, "Za polozhenieto i stopans-kata deinost na bulgarskata emigratsiia vuv Vlashko prez XIX v." [On the Position and Economic Activity of the Bulgarian Emigration to Wallachia in the 19th Century], *Bulgarsko-rumunski vruski*, pp. 285–91; C.C. Giurescu, *Contribuţiuni la studiul originilor şi dezvoltării burgheziei române pînă la 1848* [Contributions to the Study of the Origins and Development of the Romanian Bourgeoisie to 1848] (Bucharest, 1972), p. 57.

66. Slavko Gavrilović, *Prilog istorie trgovine i migracije Balkan-podunavlje, XVIII–XIX stoleća* [Introduction to the History of Trade and Migration in the Danubian Balkans, 18th–19th Centuries] (Belgrade, 1969), pp. 108, 132–33, 242–44. Also see Cvijić, p. 131. For details on the various Serbian migrations, see Aleksa Ivić, *Migracije Srba u Hrvatsku tokum 16, 17 i 18og stoleća* [Serbian Migrations to Croatia during the 16th, 17th and 18th Centuries] (Subotica, 1926).

67. Gavrilović, pp. 221–42; Čubrilović, ed., I, pp. 696, 757–61, 766–68, II, pp. 42–45. By 1800 the annual value of Serbian livestock exports (mainly pigs) to the Habsburg lands had risen to one third of that for Macedonian cotton and wool, according to Stoianovich, "Conquering Balkan Orthodox

Merchant," p. 283. On the Serbian *knezovi* and the First Uprising, see Tihomir Djordjević, *Iz Srbije Kneza Miloša* [From the Serbia of Knez Miloš] (Belgrade, 1924), pp. 220–31, and Michael B. Petrovich, *A History of Modern Serbia, 1804–1918*, I (New York: Harcourt Brace Jovanovich, 1976), pp. 23–33.

68. A recent and controversial overview of European economic history from 900 to 1700 that concentrates on changing transaction costs and contractual property rights, largely in response to population pressure, is Douglass C. North and Robert Paul Thomas, *The Rise of the Western World: A New Economic History* (Cambridge: Cambridge Univ. Press, 1973). Foreshadowing some of their conclusions is the reexamination of Fernand Braudel's hypothesis of Ottoman overpopulation after 1550 to be found in Cook, *Population Pressure in Rural Anatolia*, pp. 41–44. Cook concludes that for Anatolia the *çelali* uprisings against Ottoman authority toward 1600 were quite probably the result not only of rural population pressure but also of the local elite's lack of fiscal or other dependence on the central government.

2. The Economic Legacy of Habsburg Domination

1. Toussaint Hočevar, "Economic Determinants in the Development of the Slovene National System," Department of Economics and Finance, *Working Paper Series No. 8* (New Orleans: Louisiana State Univ., 1973), pp. 8–12, summarizes the early modern course of the Slovenian economy. On the medieval pattern of northern Italian urban commerce and its connection to rural agriculture through the colonate system of sharecropping, see C.T. Smith, *An Historical Geography of Europe to 1800* (New York: Praeger, 1968).

2. Frederick Lane, *Venice, A Maritime Republic* (Baltimore, Md.: Johns Hopkins Univ. Press, 1973).

3. Fernand Braudel, *The Mediterranean and the Mediterranean World*, vol. I (New York: Harper & Row, 1972), p. 127; Francis W. Carter, *Dubrovnik (Ragusa): A Classic City-State* (London: Seminar Press, 1972), pp. 134–46, 215, 257–62. Although less satisfactory as a comprehensive history, Carter's work is by far the best treatment in English of Dubrovnik's commercial evolution. Also see the English summary in Veselin Kostić, *Dubrovnik i Engleska, 1300–1650* [Dubrovnik and England, 1300–1650] (Belgrade, 1975), pp. 565–600.

4. Census data show Slavic names almost matching the number of Latin ones by the fourteenth century. Carter, pp. 20–25.

5. The importance of the Ottoman-Venetian wars may be seen in the two-to-tenfold wartime rise of customs revenue for imports, our best statistical index of the level of Ragusan trade. See Toma Popović, *Turska i Dubrovnik u XVI veku* [Turkey and Dubrovnik in the Sixteenth Century] (Belgrade, 1973) on the mechanics of this growing trade.

6. Braudel, pp. 195, 284–95; Carter, p. 392; Vuk Vinaver, "Dubrovačka trgovina u Srbiji i Bugarskoj krajem XVIII og veka, 1660–1700" [Dubrov-

nik's Trade with Serbia and Bulgaria at the End of the 17th Century, 1660–1700], *Istorijski časopis* (Belgrade), XII–XIII (1963), p. 231.

7. Carter, pp. 354, 392. For evidence of the English and Dutch price advantage by the seventeenth century, see Richard T. Rapp, "The Unmaking of the Mediterranean Trade Hegemony: International Trade Rivalry and the Commercial Revolution," *Journal of Economic History*, XXXV, 3 (Sept., 1975), pp. 449–525.

8. Mijo Mirković, *Ekonomska istorija Jugoslavije* (Zagreb, 1968), p. 147; Carter, *Dubrovnik*, pp. 18–24. As with the exaggerated estimates of the port's population, available evidence suggests that the actual population of the Republic's hinterland amounted to only another 5,000 to 7,000.

9. Vinaver, pp. 226–32; Vasa Čubrilović, ed., *Istorija Beograda*, I (Belgrade, 1974), pp. 444–50. Braudel, p. 111, finds Ragusan merchants even handling some of the Black Sea grain trade for Istanbul until the 1690s.

10. Carter, pp. 412–24; Čubrilović, I, pp. 371–74; Herbert Wilhelmy, *Hochbulgariens*, vol. II (Kiel, 1936), pp. 93–99.

11. Braudel, pp. 127–32; Carter, pp. 405–10, 423, 439.

12. Robert A. Kann, *A History of the Habsburg Empire, 1526–1918* (Berkeley: Univ. of California Press, 1972), pp. 123–24; Čubrilović, I, pp. 509–10.

13. Henry Marczali, *Hungary in the 18th Century* (Cambridge, Cambridge Univ. Press, 1910), pp. 77–89; Miroslavea Despot, *Pokušaji manufakture u gradjanskoj Hrvatskoj u 18. stoleću* [Attempts at Manufacturing in Civil Croatia in the 18th Century] (Zagreb, 1962), p. XIII; Mirković, pp. 165–67; Gustav Ostruba, *Die Wirtschaftspolitik Maria Theresas* (Vienna, 1963), pp. 127, 143.

14. Ostruba, pp. 129–30; Walter Markov, "Sporna pitanja oko Trshchanske Indiske Kompanije, 1775–1785" [The Stormy Question over the Trieste-India Company, 1775–1785], *Istorijski časopis*, VIII (Belgrade, 1958), pp. 69–81. Herbert Hassinger, "Der Aussenhandel der Habsburgermonarchie in der zweiten Hälfte des 18. Jahrhunderts," in Friedrich Lütge, ed., *Die wirtschaftliche Situation in Deutschland und Österreich um die Wende vom 18. zum 19. Jahrhundert* (Stuttgart, 1964), pp. 92–95; Ivan Erceg, *Trst i bivše habsburške zemlje u medjunarodnom prometu* [Trieste and the Former Habsburg Lands in International Trade] (Zagreb, 1970).

15. Kann, pp. 181–82; Marczali, pp. 40–43; Rudolf Bićanić, *Doba manufakture u Hrvatskoj i Slavoniji, 1750–1860* [The Era of Manufacturing in Croatia and Slavonia, 1750–1860] (Zagreb, 1951), pp. 199–201.

16. Ostruba, pp. 123–24, 143–51; C.A. Macartney, *The Habsburg Empire, 1790–1918* (New York: Macmillan, 1969), pp. 39–42; M. von Herzfeld, "Zur Orienthandelspolitik Österreichs unter Maria Theresa," *Archiv für österreichische Geschichte*, 108 (Vienna, 1919), p. 291.

17. Slavko Gavrilović, *Prilog istoriji trgovine i migracije Balkan-podunavlje, XVIII–XIX stoleća* [An Addition to the History of Trade and Migration in the Danubian Balkans, 18th–19th Centuries] (Belgrade, 1969), pp. 9–12; Čubrilović, I, pp. 533–34; Sonja Jordan, *Die Kaiserliche Wirtschaftspolitik im Banat in 18. Jahrhundert* (Munich, 1967), pp. 148–51; von Herzfeld, pp. 283, 296, 299–306.

18. F. Kaunitz, *Donau-Bulgarien und der Balkan* (Leipzig, 1883), vol. II, p. 214; Čubrilović, I, p. 511.

19. Čubrilović, I, pp. 511–14.

20. Ibid., pp. 681–84; Gavrilović, pp. 9, 24–27.

21. M.D. Popović, *Kragujevac i njegovo privredno prodručje* [Kragujevac and Its Economic Region] (Belgrade, 1956), pp. 32–42; Čubrilović, I, p. 534.

22. Robert Kann has convincingly suggested that the continuing threat of Ottoman invasion had delayed the integration of all the Eastern Crown Lands since 1526, pp. 60–61.

23. Gavrilović, pp. 15–46; Jordan, pp. 148–49.

24. Jordan, pp. 190–91; Marczali, *Hungary*, p. 92; Čubrilović, I, pp. 685–87.

25. In retaliation, the Serbs cut off livestock exports to the Habsburg lands. Čubrilović, II, pp. 42–50.

26. Charles Wilson, "Trade, Society and the State," in *Cambridge Economic History of Europe*, IV (Cambridge Univ. Press, 1966), pp. 487–576.

27. Kann, pp. 30–31, 60–61, 181. On recent interpretations of mercantilism and populationism, see D.C. Coleman, "Editor's Introduction," and Ingomar Bog, "Mercantilism in Germany," in D.C. Coleman, ed., *Revisions in Mercantilism* (London: Methuen, 1969), pp. 1–18, 162–89.

28. See Gunther E. Rothenberg, *The Austrian Military Border in Croatia, 1522–1747* (Urbana: Univ. of Illinois Press, 1960), pp. 28–30, 49–51, 90–97, for a brief account of the several Serbian migrations to the west and north between the fifteenth and seventeenth centuries. On the evolution of Serbian religious rights, into the eighteenth century, see idem, *The Military Border in Croatia, 1740–1881* (Chicago: Univ. of Chicago Press, 1966), pp. 5–27. By the 1786–87 Habsburg census, the Serbian population was reckoned to be half of the roughly 700,000 in the Military Border, excluding Transylvania. Macartney, p. 81.

29. The assorted limitations imposed on agriculture by the Border regime are described in Rothenberg, *Military Border in Croatia, 1740–1881*, pp. 49, 55–57, 132, 157, and Jozo Tomasevich, *Peasants, Politics, and Economic Change in Yugoslavia* (Palo Alto, Calif.: Stanford Univ. Press, 1955), pp. 79–81.

30. The population of Civil Slavonia totaled 235,000 in 1777 and 287,000 in 1805, with at least 100,000 Serbs and most of the rest Croats. Peasants with land on the estates of these few nobles were obliged to provide the 24 days of annual *robot* with a draft animal and 48 days without one, versus 52 and 104 days in Civil Croatia. Dušan Popović, *Velika seoba Srba* [The Great Serbian Migration] (Belgrade, 1954), p. 180. Slavko Gavrilović, *Agrarni pokreti u Sremu i Slavoniji na početkom XIX veka* [Agrarian Movements in Srem and Slavonia at the Start of the 19th Century], Srpska Akademija Nauke i Umetnosti, vol. 344, no. 37 (Belgrade, 1960), pp. 10–11; Josip Bösendorfer, *Agrarni odnosi u Slavoniji* [Agrarian Relations in Slavonia] (Zagreb, 1950), pp. 70–87.

31. Milan Meyer, *Die Landwirtschaft der Königreichen Kroatien und Slavonien* (Ph.D. dissertation, Univ. of Leipzig, 1908), p. 88; Mirković, p. 178; Marczali, pp. 52–57.

32. B. Jankulov, *Pregled kolonizacije Vojvodine u XIX, i XX.st.* [A Survey of the Colonization of the Vojvodina, 19th and 20th Centuries] (Novi Sad, 1961), pp. 9–25; Jordan, pp. 22–25; D. Popović, pp. 178, 217, 247.

33. Corn remained the major grain cultivated, despite official opposition. Peasants favored it over wheat because of its use for livestock feed and the lower taxes on its harvest. Jordan, pp. 29–36.

34. Ibid., pp. 83–92, 100–18; Jankulov, pp. 30–34.

35. Jankulov, pp. 33–49, 61–67.

36. Ostruba, p. 171; Mirković, p. 155; *Istoria Romîniei*, III (Bucharest, 1965), p. 421.

37. D. Popović, pp. 147–49, 180, 199–206, 218–31; Vl. Dedijer, I. Božić, S. Ćirković, M. Ekmečić, *History of Yugoslavia* (New York: McGraw-Hill, 1974), pp. 237–38.

38. For detailed evidence of this advance, see L. Katus, "Economic Growth in Hungary, 1867–1913," in E. Pamléyni, *Social-Economic Researches on the History of East-Central Europe* (Budapest, 1970), pp. 43–63, 106; and Scott M. Eddie, "Agricultural Production and Output per Worker in Hungary, 1870–1913," *Journal of Economic History*, XXVIII, 2 (June, 1968), pp. 197–222.

39. Jankulov, pp. 76–86, can offer only qualitative evidence of higher yields.

40. A majority of Slovak immigrants to the Bačka eventually moved to the Military Border area of the Srem to avoid feudal obligations to Hungarian nobles. Ibid., pp. 87–97.

41. Kalman Čehak, *Radnički pokret u Banatu, 1868–1890* [The Workers' Movement in the Banat, 1868–1890] (Novi Sad, 1971), pp. 14–18; Gavrilović, *Agrarni pokreti u Sremu i Slavoniji*, pp. 14–19.

42. Gavrilović, *Agrarni pokreti u Sremu i Slavoniji*, p. 80; Bela K. Kiraly, *Hungary in the Late Eighteenth Century* (New York: Columbia Univ. Press, 1969), p. 37, 52–53, 130–35. On the general movement of population from the northwest to the southeast of the Hungarian lands during the first half of the nineteenth century, see Marczali, pp. 32–33. By 1910, nearly 40 percent of the rural peasant population of the Vojvodina were reckoned to be landless. M. Erić, *Agrarna reforma u Jugoslaviji* (Sarajevo, 1958), p. 52.

43. Each settler's family was estimated to cost Habsburg authorities 500 florins in transport and initial costs. Serbian immigration had been reduced earlier, following the First Uprising in 1804–13. Jankulov, pp. 73–75.

44. Rothenberg, *Military Border in Croatia, 1740–1881*, pp. 122–33.

45. Ibid., p. 157; Tomasevich, pp. 87, 184–88. Philip Mosley, "The Peasant Family: The Zadruga in the Balkans," in Caroline E. Ware, ed., *The Cultural Approach to History* (New York: Columbia Univ. Press, 1940), pp. 95–108, reviews the historiography of the interwar Croatian debate on the nature of the *zadruga*. According to Gavrilović, *Agrarni pokreti u Sremu i Slavoniji*, p. 77, a survey in 1819 revealed that 62 percent of all land in the Croatian Military Border was distributed among the *zadruga*.

46. Igor Karaman, *Privreda i društvo Hrvatske u 19. stoleću* [The Economy and Society of Croatia in the 19th Century] (Zagreb, 1972), pp. 103–13; Rothenberg, *Military Border in Croatia, 1740–1881*, p. 169.

47. Jerome Blum, *Noble Landowners and Agriculture in Austria, 1815–1848* (Baltimore, Md.: Johns Hopkins Press, 1948), pp. 97–102. During the third quarter of the nineteenth century, rising grain prices and the spread of railway transport favored increased cultivation.

48. Ibid., pp. 39, 69; Rudolf Bićanić, "Osvobodjenje kmetova u Hrvatskoj g. 1848," *Djelo*, I (Zagreb, 1948), pp. 190–200. On the origins of the Hungarian gentry as vassals or lieutenants of the reconstituted Hungarian higher noble, or magnate, class during the early sixteenth century, as well as the subsequent evolution of both groups, see Kiraly, pp. 25–39.

49. Kiraly, pp. 131, 136–39; George Barany, *Stephen Szechenyi and the Awakening of Hungarian Nationalism, 1791–1841* (Princeton, N.J.: Princeton Univ, Press, 1968), pp. 194–99. A lower level of feudal obligations and greater intensiveness of cultivation for the Venetian-dominated part of the Istrian Peninsula is noted in Karaman, pp. 10–11.

50. Blum, pp. 115–24.

51. Karaman, pp. 17, 38. In order to enter the hereditary Austrian lands, Hungarian grain faced a tariff of about 25 percent ad valorem until the entire monarchy was united in a customs union in 1850. Bićanić, *Doba manufakture*, p. 236.

52. Blum, pp. 91–94. The noble reformer Szechenyi's most successful project was the negotiation of steamship transport on the Danube by the 1830s. Barany, *Stephen Szechenyi*, pp. 246–52.

53. Karaman, pp. 45–46.

54. See Nachum Gross, "The Hapsburg Monarchy, 1750–1914," in Carlo M. Cipolla, ed., *Fontana Economic History of Europe, The Emergence of Industrial Societies*, vol. 4, part 1 (London: Collins/Fontana, 1973), pp. 255–57; Karl Dinklage, "Die landwirtschaftliche Entwicklung," in Alois Brusatti, ed., *Die Habsburger Monarchie, 1848–1918*, I, *Die wirtschaftliche Entwicklung* (Vienna, 1973), pp. 403–27; Ivan T. Berend and Gyorgy Ranki, *Economic Development in East-Central Europe in the 19th and 20th Centuries* (New York: Columbia Univ. Press, 1974), pp. 30–33; and idem, *Hungary: A Century of Economic Development* (New York: Barnes & Noble, 1974), pp. 40–43.

55. Despot, pp. VIII–XI.

56. Karlovac had been so separated from the surrounding Military Border since 1778. There and elsewhere, only nineteen small flour mills existed in the Croatian lands by 1860. Karaman, pp. 48, 70; Bićanić, *Doba manufakture*, p. 217; Barany, p. 334.

57. Miroslava Despot, *Industrija gradjanske Hrvatske, 1860–1873* [Industrial Development of Croatia, 1860–1873] (Zagreb, 1970), pp. 10–13, 145–61; Igor Karaman, "Osnovna obilježja razvitke industrijske privrede u sjevernoj Hrvatskoj" [Basic Features in Industrial Development in Northern Croatia], *Acta historico-oeconomica iugoslaviae* I (Zagreb, 1974), pp. 41–45.

58. Karaman, "Osnovna obilježja," pp. 43–46, 50; Bićanić, *Doba manufakture*, p. 216, Karaman, *Privreda i društvo Hrvatske*, pp. 67–75.

59. Karaman, *Privreda i društvo Hrvatske*, pp. 81–83; Mirković, pp. 225–28.

60. See Franklin Mendels, "Proto-industrialization: The First Phase of the

Process of Industrialization," *Journal of Economic History*, XXXII, 1 (March, 1972), pp. 241–61; and Arnošt Klima, "Industrial Development in Bohemia, 1648–1771," *Past and Present*, no. 11 (April, 1957), pp. 87–99. On the limited development of Slovenian agriculture to 1848, see Toussaint Hočevar, *Structure of the Slovenian Economy, 1848–1963* (New York: Studia Slovenica, 1965), pp. 50–53. On the growing economic connection with Trieste, see Andreas Moritsch, "Das nahe Triester Hinterland," *Wiener Archiv für Geschichte des Sloventums und Osteuropa* (Vienna, 1969).

61. Hočevar, pp. 16–18.

62. Hočevar, pp. 32–34.

63. Alexander Gerschenkron, *Economic Backwardness in Historical Perspective* (New York: Praeger, 1965), pp. 119–51.

64. Hočevar, pp. 22–31.

65. *Istoria Romîniei*, III, p. 416; C.C. Kirițescu, *Sistemul bănesc al leului* [The Monetary System of the Leu], I (Bucharest, 1964), p. 124.

66. William H. McNeill, *Europe's Steppe Frontier, 1500–1800* (Chicago: Univ. of Chicago Press, 1964).

67. *Istoria Romîniei*, III, p. 420; Kiraly, pp. 442–44; Mathias Bernath, *Habsburg und die Anfänge der rumanische Nationsbildung* (Leiden: E.J. Brill, 1972), pp. 139–41.

68. For a summary of political developments, see Keith Hitchins, *The Rumanian National Movement in Transylvania, 1780–1849* (Cambridge, Mass.: Harvard Univ. Press, 1969), pp. 1–32.

69. Josif Kovacs, *Desființarea relațiilor feudale în Transilvania* [The Dissolution of Feudal Relations in Transylvania] (Cluj, 1973), p. 19; Barany, pp. 192, 406. By the late eighteenth century, the several available estimates place the Romanian proportion of Transylvania's population at two thirds. *Istoria Romîniei*, III, p. 405–406, 420.

70. Bernath, pp. 157, 162–63. Carl Göllner, *Die Siebenbürgische Militärgrenze* (Munich: R. Oldenbourg Verlag, 1974), pp. 90, 122–24. Once the Szekler regiments openly joined the Hungarian revolt against the Habsburg Monarchy in 1848–49, the days of the Transylvanian Military Border were numbered. All its regiments had been abolished by 1851.

71. Göllner, pp. 36–40, 47–50, 94–101.

72. Ibid., pp. 41, 51–53, 70–74; Bernath, p. 164; Ştefan Meteş, *Emigrări româneşte din Transilvania în secolele XIII-XX* [Romanian Migration from Transylvania, 13th–20th Centuries] (Bucharest, 1971), pp. 207–43.

73. *Istoria Romîniei*, III, pp. 413–417; C.C. Giurescu, *Transylvania in the History of Romania* (London: Garnstone Press, 1969), pp. 63–69; Jon I. Ghelase, *Mocanii: Importanța şi evoluția lor social-economică în România* (Bucharest, 1938), pp. 107–13.

74. Meteş, p. 234; I. Haseganu, *Mărginenii în viața economică a Transilvaniei* [Border People in the Economic Life of Transylvania] (Braşov, 1941), pp. 53, 64.

75. Giurescu, p. 67; *Istoria Romîniei*, III, p. 1017.

3. The Romanian Principalities
between Three Empires, 1711–1859

1. Impressive evidence of the evolution of this connection from the eighteenth century may be found in Vlad Georgescu, *Political Ideas and the Enlightenment in the Romanian Principalities, 1760–1831* (New York: Columbia Univ. Press, 1971).

2. For a discussion of the spread through early modern Northeastern Europe of *Gutsherrschaft,* or commercial cultivation of expanded estate reserves by resident noble owners, as opposed to the *Grundherrschaft* of absentee noble ownership and sharecropping in Western Europe, see Aldo de Maddalena, "Rural Europe, 1500–1700," in Carlo Cipolla, ed., *The Fontana Economic History of Europe–The 16th and 17th Centuries* (London: Collins/Fontana, 1974), pp. 287–95, and Jerzy Topolski, "Economic Decline in Poland from the 16th to the 18th Centuries," in Peter Earle, ed., *Essays in European Economic History, 1500–1800* (London: Oxford Univ. Press, 1974), pp. 127–42.

3. Jack Tucker, "The Romanian Peasant Revolt of 1907: Three Regional Studies" (Ph.D. dissertation, Univ. of Chicago, 1972), pp. 1–2; Sergiu Columbeanu, *Grandes exploitations domaniales en Valachie au XVIIIe siecle* (Bucharest, 1974), pp. 34–38. On the imprecise nature of these estimates for eighteenth century Romanian population, see Şt. Ştefanescu, "Istorie şi demografie," *Studii: Revista de istorie,* XX, 5 (Bucharest, 1967), pp. 933–46.

4. Florin Constantiniu, *Relaţille agrare din Ţara Românească în secolul al XVIII-lea* [Agrarian Relations in Wallachia in the 18th Century] (Bucharest, 1972), p. 190.

5. Tucker, pp. 5, 75.

6. Columbeanu, pp. 193–98.

7. Ibid., p. 53; V. Mihordea, *Relaţiile agrare din secolul al XVIII-lea în Moldova* [Agrarian Relations in the 18th Century in Moldavia] (Bucharest, 1968), pp. 42–48; Ştefan Ionescu, *Bucureştii în vremea fanarioţilor* [Bucharest in Phanariot Times] (Cluj, 1974), pp. 61–62; *Istoria Romîniei,* III (Bucharest, 1965), pp. 652–58.

8. Tucker, pp. 6, 17; Constantiniu, pp. 49–53; *Istoria Romîniei,* III, pp. 44, 625.

9. Columbeanu, pp. 11–13, 84–89; Mihordea, pp. 31, 53. Note the contrast to the Polish lands of the early modern period, where 44 percent of estate lands were held and cultivated as reserves by their noble owners. De Maddalena, "Rural Europe, 1500–1700," pp. 308–309.

10. Columbeanu, pp. 21, 90, 102, 121, 147, 172, 177; Constantiniu, pp. 172–73; Mihordea, p. 52.

11. The value of corn exported to Transylvania was reportedly over ten times that of wheat exported there during this period. *Istoria Romîniei,* III, pp. 660–67.

12. Tucker, pp. 9–15; Constantiniu, pp. 136–43, 190–91, 197.

13. Constantiniu, pp. 149–53; 181; Mihordea, p. 71; Columbeanu, p. 90.

14. Tucker, pp. 22–28; Constantiniu, pp. 157–59.

15. On the 1821 revolt, see *Istoria Romîniei*, III, pp. 850–917. On the dominance of *dijma*, see Tucker, pp. 19–21, and Mihordea, pp. 70–72.

16. David Turnock, "Bucharest: The Selection and Development of the Romanian Capital," *Scottish Geographic Magazine*, vol. 86 (1970), pp. 59–62.

17. Ibid., pp. 54–57; Roy E.H. Mellor, *Eastern Europe: A Geography of the Comecon Countries* (New York: Columbia Univ. Press, 1975), pp. 157–58.

18. *Istoria Romîniei*, III, pp. 67–69; C.C. Giurescu, *Istoria Bucureştilor* (Bucharest, 1966), pp. 77–78.

19. Giurescu, pp. 63–69; Turnock, p. 19.

20. Ionescu, p. 59; H.C. Barkley, *Bulgaria Before the War* (London, 1877), pp. 255–56; Giurescu, pp. 123–30.

21. Ionescu, pp. 14, 55–59. For a more detailed account, see Dan Berindei, *Oraşul Bucureşti, 1459–1862* [The Town of Bucharest, 1459–1862] (Bucharest, 1863), pp. 157–260.

22. Ionescu, pp. 51–53.

23. Giurescu, pp. 272–73; idem, *Contribuţiuni la studiul originelor şi dezvoltării burgheziei romane pînă la 1848* [Contributions to the Study of Romanian Bourgeois Origins and Development to 1848] (Bucharest, 1972), pp. 98–99.

24. Giurescu, *Contribuţiuni*, p. 59; idem, *Istoria*, pp. 271–72.

25. Giurescu, *Istoria*, pp. 269–71; idem, *Contribuţiuni*, pp. 91–96.

26. Giurescu, *Contribuţiuni*, pp. 149–50; *Istoria Romîniei*, IV, pp. 202, 218.

27. On Count Kiselev's unsuccessful efforts to reform conditions for the Russian state peasantry later in the 1830s, see Walter M. Pintner, *Russian Economic Policy under Nicholas I* (Ithaca, N.Y.: Cornell Univ. Press, 1967), pp. 154–83. The picture of Kiselev painted there shows no intent to free these serfs but rather to effect a scheme for state "guardianship" that would assure them land holdings of adequate size and fair fiscal and legal conditions.

28. Russian military campaigns had carried their troops into the Principalities in 1711, 1736–39, 1769–74, 1878–92 and 1806–12. The commanders had freely requisitioned Romanian grain and livestock, as well as demanding forced labor from the peasantry. Those demands reportedly reached the height of forcing peasants to pull Russian supply wagons. Marcel Emerit, *Les paysans roumains depuis le traité d'Adrianople* (Paris, 1937), pp. 49–50.

29. Ibid., pp. 55–57, 61–63, 66; *Istoria Romîniei*, III, pp. 936–37.

30. *Istoria Romîniei*, III, pp. 934, 942–44; Tucker, pp. 17, 34, 47.

31. Tucker, pp. 36–37; David Mitrany, *The Land and the Peasant in Rumania* (New Haven, Conn.: Yale Univ. Press, 1930), p. 32.

32. Only 173 of these 665 recorded lessees were themselves boyars. See Giurescu, *Contribuţiuni*, pp. 158–65. On the further growth of estate leasing to 1860, see Constantin Corbu, *Ţărănimea din România din perioada 1848–1864* [The Peasantry of Romania, 1848–1864] (Bucharest, 1973), pp. 52–54.

33. See Ilie Corfus' view of Romanian historiography on the question of

clacă days and the land tenure system during the Reglement period in the introduction to his *Agricultura Țării Românești în prima jumătate a secolului al XIX-lea* [The Agriculture of Wallachia in the First Half of the 19th Century] (Bucharest, 1969), pp. 5–9, 144–66. Also see Tucker, pp. 45–46, 109–119.

34. The less than satisfactory figures for Romanian grain acreage and production for 1829–64, indicative of trends but containing too many gaps and inconsistencies to be recorded here statistically, may be found in Corfus, pp. 302–79, for Wallachia, and in I. Adam and N. Marcu, *Studii despre dezvoltarea capitalismului în agricultura Rominiei* [Studies Concerning the Development of Capitalism in Romanian Agriculture], vol. I (Bucharest, 1956), pp. 9–11, summarized for Moldavia.

35. Daniel Chirot, *Social Change in a Peripheral Society—The Creation of a Balkan Colony* (New York: Academic Press, 1976), pp. 80–82, 100–101; E. Negruți-Munteanu, "Dezvoltarea agriculturii în Moldova între anii 1848 și 1864" [The Development of Agriculture in Moldavia from 1848 to 1864], in V. Popovici, ed., *Dezvoltarea economiei Moldovei* (Iași, 1963), p. 358; Corfus, pp. 276–93. On the widespread nineteenth-century presence of artisan and market activity in the upland areas of the Principalities, as opposed to the lowland, see G. Zane, *Industria din România în a doua jumatate a secolului al XIX-lea* [Industry in Romania in the Second Half of the 19th Century] (Bucharest, 1970), pp. 10–81.

36. For an exhaustive account and bibliography on the events of 1848 in the Principalities, emphasizing the economic aspects in Marxist perspective, see *Istoria Rominiei*, IV, pp. 13–179. On attitudes toward the agrarian question, see John C. Campbell, *French Influence and the Rise of Romanian Nationalism* (New York: Arno Press reprint, 1971), pp. 196–205; and Apostol Stan, *Le problème agraire pendant la révolution de 1848 en Valachie* (Bucharest, 1971), pp. 11–48, 93–121.

37. Ilie Corfus, *L'agriculture en Valachie depuis la Révolution de 1848 jusqu'à la Réforme de 1864* (Bucharest, 1976), pp. 71–74, 103–109, 200–206; Negruți-Munteanu, pp. 100–12. On the basis for estimating a rough increase of 2 percent a year in the Principalities' population from 1831 to 1859, with a 3 percent rise in the plains versus 1 percent in the uplands, see Chirot, pp. 100–101.

38. Corfus, *L'agriculture en Valachie*, pp. 111, 186–92; Tucker, pp. 47–53; N. Adăniloaie and Dan Berindei, *Reforma agrară din 1864* (Bucharest, 1967), pp. 47–53.

39. Georgeta Penela, *Les foires de la Valachie pendant la periode 1774–1848* (Bucharest, 1973), pp. 90–94; Vl. Diculescu, *Bresle, negustori și meseriași în Țara Româneasca, 1830–1848* [Guilds, Merchants and Artisans in Wallachia, 1830–1848] (Bucharest, 1973), pp. 13–37; Ionescu, pp. 61–62.

40. Emerit, pp. 65–66; *Istoria Rominiei*, III, pp. 976–77, 984.

41. Diculescu, pp. 37–42, 63–65, 77–80, 94–96, 108, 130–42.

42. Ibid., pp. 26–28; *Istoria Rominiei*, III, pp. 368–69, 645–50, 960–65.

43. G. Zane, *Economia de schimb in principatele romîne* [The Exchange Economy in the Romanian Principalities] (Bucharest, 1930), pp. 332, 334; Emerit, pp. 160–63, Diculescu, pp. 44–46.

44. Chirot, *Social Change*, pp. 104–109; F. Colson, "Merchants and Trade

after 1829" in Doreen Warriner, ed., *Contrasts in Emerging Societies* (Bloomington, In.: Indiana Univ. Press, 1965), pp. 170–71; Penela, pp. 118, 171–72.

45. Zane, pp. 268–70.

46. Ibid., pp. 281–92; Pintner, *Russian Economic Policy*, pp. 193–97, 257–61. This *agio* or premium for accepting the assignat in trade usually ran from 10 to 15 percent. On the behavior of specific exchange rates, see Mircea N. Popa, "Contribuţii privind circulaţia monetară în Ţara Românesca la începutual veacului al XIX-lea" [Contribution on the Monetary Circulation in Wallachia at the Start of the 19th Century], *Revista arhivelor*, XII, 2 (Bucharest, 1969), pp. 145–53.

47. Zane, pp. 225–26, has used 19 grain, livestock, and vegetable prices to compile the following index based on prices and exchange rates of 1800:

	Prices	Exchange rate for Ottoman Piastre
1800	100	100
1810	288	ca 200
1832	575	471
1849–50	973	528

48. Henry Hajnal, *The Danube* (The Hague, 1920), p. 65; John MacGregor, *Commercial Statistics*, vol. 2 (London, 1850), pp. 47–49. A railway line from Cernevoda on the Danube to Constanţa finally established the link in 1860. On the ill-fated canal project, see T. Mateescu, "Din geografia istorică a Dobrogei: Canalul Laman," *Revista arhivelor*, LII, 1 (1975), pp. 36–43.

49. I. Cartânâ and I. Şeftiuc, *Dunărea în istoria poporului rom*ân [The Danube in the History of the Romanian People] (Bucharest, 1972), pp. 32–33, 41.

50. Hajnal, pp. 149, 158–61; MacGregor, vol. II, pp. 55–56.

51. On the commercial development of Odessa from its founding in 1794 until 1861, see Patricia Herlihy, "Odessa: Staple Trade and Urbanization in Russia," *Jahrbücher für Geschichte Osteuropas*, vol. 21, no. 2 (1973), pp. 184–95, and Frederick W. Skinner, "Trends in Planning Practices: The Building of Odessa, 1794–1917," in Michael F. Hamm, ed., *The City in Russian History* (Lexington, Ky.: Univ. of Kentucky Press, 1976), pp. 139–59.

52. Hajnal, p. 65; Constantin Buşe, "Le commerce exterieur de la Moldavie par le port du Galaţi, 1837–1847," *Revue roumaine d'histoire*, XII, 2 (1973), pp. 301–306; N. Corivan and C. Turcu, "Comerţul Moldovei între anii 1848 si 1864," in V. Popovici, ed., *Dezvoltarea economiei Moldovei*, pp. 350–53.

53. Hajnal, pp. 62–63; Cartânâ and Şeftiuc, p. 35; Giurescu, *Contribuţiuni*, p. 114. The Crimean War began in 1853. Russia confronted Great Britain and France with no major European allies for three years before agreeing to terms at the Congress of Paris in 1856. As already noted, the treaty included joint Great Power control of Danubian navigation, at least at its mouth. On the subsequent history of this European Commission, see D.A. Sturdza, *Les Travaux de la Commission Européene des Bouches du Danube, 1859 & 1911* (Vienna, 1913).

54. Cartână and Şeftiuc, pp. 46–48; Hajnal, pp. 160–63.

55. According to the calculations of Simon Kuznets, in his *Modern Economic Growth* (New Haven: Yale Univ. Press, 1966), pp. 306–307, the value of world trade rose by 280 percent during 1850–70, almost half again the largest increase during any other twenty-year period between 1815 and 1914.

56. Buşe, pp. 304–307, and Corivan and Turcu, pp. 349–53. For Romanian grain exports before 1859, the Principalities' own statistics fail to show reexports beyond Istanbul. Hence three quarters of Romanian grain exports falsely appear directed only to Ottoman destinations. Figures collected from Mediterranean and Atlantic ports of arrival reveal the great predominance of Italian ports in these deliveries beyond Istanbul. For the exceptional year of 1846, 12.6 million lei of Romanian grain exports reached both France and Great Britain, together some 25 million of 45 million lei in total grain exports. On the scattered data of the 1850s, see B. Marinescu, "Economic Relations between the Romanian Principalities and Great Britain (1848-1859)," *Revue Roumaine d'Histoire*, VIII (1969), pp. 271–81.

57. Georgeta Penela, "Relaţiile economice dintre Ţara Românească şi Transilvania (1829–1848)," in N. Adăniloaie and Dan Berindei, eds., *Studii şi materiale de istorie modernă*, IV (Bucharest, 1973), pp. 18–19, 48–53.

58. Ibid., pp. 47, 53–54, 381; *Istoria Romîniei*, IV, p. 211. The surge of English and French imports into Moldavia during the Crimean War is deceiving. From 49 percent of total imports as late as 1857, the proportion dropped back to one third for 1858–64.

59. *Istoria Romîniei*, pp. 197–98; Penela, "Relaţiile economice," pp. 8–16; Barkley, pp. 248–50. On the general history of the Leipzig fairs and their ties to Southeastern Europe, see G. Netta, *Die Handelsbeziehungen zwischen Leipzig and Ost-und Südosteuropa* (Zurich, 1920), pp. 45–63, 81–89, 148–49.

60. Hajnal, pp. 115–17, 122–25, 141–44, 158–59.

61. Ibid., pp. 101–102, 148; MacGregor, vol. II, p. 55.

62. C.C. Kiriţescu, *Sistemul bănesc al leului şi precursorii lui* [The Monetary System of the Leu and its Predecessors] vol. I (Bucharest, 1964), pp. 264–67; Giurescu, *Contribuţiuni*, pp. 119–33, 171–85; *Istoria Romîniei*, IV, pp. 213–14.

63. See Chapter 6 and also John H. Jensen and Gerhard Rosegger, "British Railway Builders along the Lower Danube, 1856–1869," *Slavonic and East European Review*, XLVI (1968), pp. 105–28.

4. The Serbian National Economy and Habsburg Hegemony, 1815! 1878

1. A summary of the incomplete evidence on Serbian population growth during the period 1800–1850 may be found in Danica Milić, *Trgovina Srbije, 1815–1839* [The Commerce of Serbia, 1815–1839] (Belgrade, 1959), pp. 48–50.

2. Slavko Gavrilović, *Prilog istoriji trgovine i migracije Balkanpodunavlja XVIII–XIX stoleća* [A Contribution to the History of Trade and

Migration in the Danubian Balkans, 18th and 19th Centuries] (Belgrade, 1969), pp. 221–44.

3. Vasa Čubrilović, ed., *Istorija Beograda* [The History of Belgrade], II (Belgrade, 1974), pp. 44–47; Slavko Gavrilović, *Vojvodina i Srbija za vreme prvog ustanka* [Vojvodina and Serbia during the First Uprising] (Novi Sad, 1974), pp. 40–60.

4. Čubrilović, ed., *Istorija Beograda*, I (Belgrade, 1974), p. 766; II, pp. 42–49.

5. Milić, pp. 31–35.

6. The account in the following two paragraphs is drawn from the comprehensive survey by Michael B. Petrovich, *A History of Modern Serbia, 1804–1918*, I (New York: Harcourt Brace Jovanovich, 1976), pp. 82–128.

7. Milić, pp. 193–95, 197, 225–28; Čubrilović, ed., II, pp. 358–59. Table 4.2 below records the rough estimates of 4.8 million francs equivalent for average annual reports and 2.4 million for imports during 1835–38.

8. Milić, pp. 104–105, 246; D. Anáčijević, "Trgovački i zelenaški kapital u Srbiji u prvoj polovini devetnaestog veka" [Trade and Usury Capital in Serbia in the First Half of the 19th Century] (Ph.D. dissertation, Skopje Univ., 1956), pp. 136, 139.

9. Milić, p. 247; Anáčijević, pp. 107–108. These sources also cite evidence that leather hides were a distant second to pigs on the list of Serbian exports, then followed by wool and nuts.

10. Georges Castellan, *La vie quotidienne en Serbie, 1815–1839* (Paris, 1967), p. 203. The Serbian experience is a classic example of the layers of price differentials needed to set trade in motion throughout European economic history, in the fashion noted by Sir John Hicks, *A Theory of Economic History* (London: Oxford Univ. Press, 1969), pp. 43–44.

11. In addition to appointing a small highway patrol, Prince Miloš forced each village to pay damages for disorder in its area and to hunt down bandits, who were now deprived of Turkish oppression to justify their existence to the local population. Anáčijević, p. 102; Čubrilović, ed., II, pp. 379–80.

12. M. Glomazitch, *Histoire du credit en Serbie* (Nancy, 1926), p. 16; V. Stojančević, *Miloš Obrenović i njegovo doba* [Miloš Obrenović and His Era] (Belgrade, 1966), pp. 180–181; Milić, pp. 94–95.

13. The scattered evidence of total participants in Serbian trade at this time is summarized in Milić, p. 115.

14. On the generally consistent and relatively small size of the Serbian *zadruga* from the sixteenth until the nineteenth century, see E.A. Hammel, "The Zadruga as Process," in Peter Laslett and Marilyn Clarke, eds., *Households and Family in Past and Present* (Cambridge: Cambridge Univ. Press, 1972), pp. 365–66. See Jozo Tomasevich, *Peasants, Politics and Economic Change in Yugoslavia* (Palo Alto, Calif.: Stanford Univ. Press, 1955), pp. 178–89, for a discussion of the elements involved in this dissolution. Although surviving in some form until the present century, the *zadruga* had ceased to perform its traditional economic function for three quarters of Serbian peasant households by 1839, according to the most recent research on the matter in Stojančević, pp. 214–221.

15. Stojančević, pp. 161, 164, 167; Anáčijević, p. 105.

16. M.D. Popović, *Kragujevac i njegovo privredno područje* [Kragujevac and its Economic Area] (Belgrade, 1956), pp. 58–59.

17. Milić, p. 64; Glomazitch, pp. 12–13; Anaćijević, p. 98; Stojančević, p. 172.

18. Lamartine's "leafy ocean," seen in that year by the traveling French poet to cover almost all the Serbian countryside, in the fashion of the American wilderness, had been reduced by about one half by 1850. Popović, p. 61. The clearing of forests progressed so rapidly that by 1836 Prince Miloš felt his own acorn supply threatened, and pushed through legislation to slow the pace. Stojančević, p. 198.

19. Popović, p. 63; V. Dedijer, I. Božić, S. Ćerković, M. Ekmečić, *History of Yugoslavia* (New York: McGraw-Hill, 1972), p. 283. Milić, pp. 56–57, reckons that the wheat crop was sufficient to reduce if not end the import of Banat wheat before 1840 and that the corn crop rose with the demand for livestock feed. On cultivation techniques, see M. Stanojević, "Die Landwirtschaft Serbiens" (Ph.D dissertation, Univ. of Leipzig, 1912), pp. 191ff.

20. Castellan, p. 97.

21. Milić, pp. 53–56.

22. Stojančević, pp. 193–94. Tomasevich, pp. 42–45.

23. B. Milić-Krivodoljanin, *Zbornik radova o selu* [A Collection of Works on the Village] (Belgrade, 1970), pp. 9–10, 14–15, 47–50, 77–79; Petrovich, I, pp. 184–96; Milić, p. 50; Tihomir Djordjević, *Iz Srbije Kneza Miloša* [From the Serbia of Prince Miloš] (Belgrade, 1924), pp. 217–314.

24. Both of these towns, according to Ottoman records of the number of taxable houses, had populations exceeding 50,000 as late as 1700 but steadily lost ground during the wars and disorder of the eighteenth century. On the overwhelmingly Moslem population of Užice until the mid-nineteenth century, see St. Ignjić, *Užice i okolina, 1862–1914* [Užice and its Area, 1862–1914] (Titovo Užice, 1976). In total numbers Užice had continued to decline after 1830, along with Smederevo and Valjevo, while the northern border town of Šabac and the original capital of Kragujevac made the most rapid gains. Completing this limited urban sector were fewer than 40 small towns, or *varošice*. Their average population was only one thousand, but their location on the few rivers and roads in the interior made them trade and administrative centers. Branislav Kojić, *Varošice u Srbiji u XIX v.* [Small Towns in Serbia in the 19th Century] (Belgrade, 1970), pp. 7–16. N. Andrić, R. Antić, R. Veselinović, and D. Djurić-Zamolo, *Beograd u XIX veku* [Belgrade in the 19th Century], p. 68, and Castellan, p. 98.

25. Anaćijević, pp. 72, 79, 105; Castellan, p. 101; Ćubrilović, vol. II, pp. 525–29.

26. Dušan Popović, *O cincarima* [Concerning the Tsintsars] (Belgrade, 1937), pp. 165–68; Ćubrilović, ed., II, p. 372; Anaćijević, pp. 77, 128.

27. Castellan, pp. 94–97, 102–107; Ćubrilović, ed., II, pp. 387–88; D. Popović, *O cincarima*, pp. 169–71. On the changing composition and role of merchants from the Macedonian lands in Serbian trade, see K. Bitoski, "Kneževstvo Srbije kao pazar i tranzitna teritorija za makedonskite trgovci" [Serbia as a Market and Transit Territory for Macedonian Merchants], *Glasnik*, X, 2–3 (Skopje, 1966), pp. 113–33.

28. Only 21 rural shops were registered as operating with permits in 1839. The figures had increased to 74 by 1852. There were probably ten times that number operating without permits. Milić, pp. 121–28, 143–54; M.D. Popović, p. 47; Slobodan Jovanović, *Ustavobranitelji, 1838–1858* [The Defenders of the Constitution, 1838–1858] (Belgrade, 1912), p. 77; Anaćijević, pp. 128–29.

29. By 1843 there were 4,400 students in 143 Serbian primary schools, a majority of them opened since the departure of Prince Miloš. Both totals had roughly doubled by the end of the *Ustavobranitelji* era in 1858. Čubrilović, ed., II, pp. 569–71. The account of Serbian professional schools that follows is drawn from Milenko Karanović, "The Development of Education in Serbia, 1838–1858" (Ph.D. dissertation, Univ. of Wisconsin, 1974), pp. 215–55. Also see S. Čunković, *Prosveta, obrazovanje i vaspitanje u Srbije* [Aspects of Education in Serbia] (Belgrade, 1971), pp. 15–32.

30. Jovanović, pp. 77–78. Alex Dragnich, "King Peter I: Culmination of Serbia's Struggles for Parliamentary Government," *East European Quarterly*, vol. IV, no. 2 (June, 1970), pp. 170–72.

31. Jovanović, p. 80.

32. Anaćijević, p. 111.

33. Andrić et al., p. 64, provide a summary of the major Serbian imports and their points of origin during this period. Usable quantitative data for the composition of Serbian imports are not available before 1878. Slobodan Jovanović, *Druga vlada Miloša Mihaila* [The Second Reign of Miloš and Michael] (Belgrade, 1923), pp. 176–178, does describe the rise of the state's annual budget past the equivalent of 5 million francs by 1865, one third of which was given to military imports.

34. Andrić et al., p. 64.

35. Ibid., p. 62. The definitive work on the collapse of the traditional Serbian craft guilds during the period of autonomy is Nikola Vučo, *Raspadanje esnafa u Srbiji* [The Collapse of the Guilds in Serbia], 2 vols. (Belgrade, 1954–55).

36. Nikola Vučo, *Privredna istorija Srbije do prvog svetskog rata* [Economic History of Serbia to the First World War] (Belgrade, 1958), p. 239; Anaćijević, p. 242; Milić, pp. 259–60.

37. Anaćijević, p. 242; Glomazitch, pp. 25–26; Jovanović, *Ustavobranitelji, 1838–1858*, p. 75.

38. Jovanović, *Ustavobranitelji, 1838–1858*, pp. 75–80.

39. Ibid., pp. 80–81.

40. Anaćijević, pp. 242–43, cites these lawsuits as important evidence for his case that such loans were a major source of capital accumulation. On the early treatment of commercial disputes in Serbian courts, see Čubrilović, p. 391.

41. Jovanović, *Ustavobranitelji, 1838–1858*, pp. 80–83. The provisions on interest rates were a watered-down version of Prince Miloš's abortive 1859 law to allow peasant debtors to default on all interest payments that they would swear in church exceeded the maximum of 12 percent per year legally prescribed since 1836, idem, *Druga vlada Miloša i Mihaila*, p. 75. Whether Miloš's law was repealed for use or abuse is not clear.

42. Anaćijević, p. 233; Andrić et al., p. 66; Jovanović, *Ustavobranitelji, 1838–1858*, pp. 73–76; Milić, p. 265.

43. Anaćijević, pp. 182, 220, 230, 238–39; Milić, pp. 282–85.

44. Andrić et al., p. 67; Vučo, *Privredna istorija Srbije*, p. 234.

45. Miodrag Ugričić, *Novčani sistem Jugoslavije* [The Money System of Yugoslavia] (Belgrade, 1968), p. 48. M. Radosavljevich, *Die Entwicklung der Währung in Serbien* (Berlin and Munich, 1912), p. 2.

46. Castellan, p. 198; Ugričić, pp. 49–50.

47. Milić, pp. 251–52. From 1828 forward, for instance, the ferrymen whose boats carried goods across the Sava or Danube between Belgrade and Habsburg territory had refused to take any Ottoman coins for their services. Čubrilović, ed., II, pp. 366–67.

48. Anaćijević, pp. 256–57.

49. See *Srpske novine*, November 3 and 4, 1845, as cited in L. Cvijetić, "Pokusaji osnivanja prvih srpskih banaka" [Attempts to Found the First Serbian Banks], *Finansija* (Belgrade), 1–2 (1965), pp. 119–123.

50. Jovanović, *Ustavobranitelji, 1838–1858*, pp. 82–83.

51. Cvijetić, pp. 121–22.

52. Radosavljevich, p. 5.

53. Jovanović, *Ustavobranitelji, 1838–1858*, p. 76; Cvijetić, p. 122.

54. Momir Glomazić, *Istorija državne hipotekarne banke, 1862–1932* [History of the State Mortgage Bank, 1862–1932] (Belgrade, 1933), pp. 79–81; Stanislav Kukla, *Razvitak kreditne organizacije u Srbiji* [The Development of Credit Organization in Serbia] (Zagreb, 1924), pp. 64–68.

55. Cvijetić, p. 123.

56. Ugričić, p. 56.

57. The functions of the First Serbian Bank included accepting deposits, granting short or long-term credits, hiring an intermediary on the Vienna stock exchange, entering consortium partnerships, and conducting its own entrepreneurial ventures. See L. Cvijetić, "Prva Srpska Banka" [The First Serbian Bank] *Istorijski glasnik*, (Belgrade), 2–3 (1964), pp. 97–121.

58. Kukla, p. 70; Vučo, *Privredna istorija Srbije*, p. 240; Royaume de Belgique, *Receuil consulaire*, 1883, XV (Brussels), p. 265.

59. The policy of the Smederevo bank was to discount bills of exchange up to one half the value of the goods being sold. Royaume de Belgique, p. 266.

60. Probably the first Valjevo merchant to travel outside of Serbia, Radovan Lazić visited Pančevo, a town across the Danube from Belgrade on Habsburg territory, in 1869. When his hotel maid requested a tip, he reportedly asked to see others that she had received before giving her any money. She replied that the rest was earning her interest at the local savings bank, or *sparkasse*. The word was new to Lazić, as was her savings book. He thereupon visited the local bank to learn more and later wrote for a copy of its statutes. Lazić then used his influence in his town's commerce and local government to establish the Valjevska Štedionica, becoming its president until his death in 1884. M. Zarić, *Radovan Lazić* (Belgrade, 1888), pp. 31–34.

61. Royaume de Belgique, p. 267.

5. The Bulgarian Lands in a
Declining Ottoman Economy

1. Roderick Davidson, *Reform in the Ottoman Empire, 1856–1876* (Princeton, N.J.: Princeton Univ. Press, 1963).

2. The classic study of these growing economic difficulties may be found in Donald C. Blaisdell, *European Financial Control in the Ottoman Empire* (New York: Columbia Univ. Press, 1929).

3. Str. Dimitrov, "Chiflishkoto stopanstvo prez 50-70-te godina na XIX vek" [The Chiflik Economy during the 1850s–1870s], *Istoricheski pregled* XI, 2 (Sofia, 1955), pp. 8–16, 34, 56; Fani Milkova, *Pozemlenata sobstvenost v bulgarskite zemi prez XIX v.* [Landed Property in the Bulgarian Lands during the 19th Century] (Sofia, 1969), p. 236.

4. Khristo Khristov, "Agrarniat vupros i roliata na selianite v bulgarskata natsionalnata revoliutsiia" [The Agrarian Question and the Role of the Peasants in the Bulgarian National Revolution], *Aprilskoto vustanie, 1876–1886* [The April Uprising, 1876–1886] (Sofia, 1966), pp. 20–25. Also see William M. McGrew, "The Land Issue in the Greek War of Independence," in N.D. Diamandouros, ed., *Hellenism and the Greek War of Liberation*, Institute of Balkan Studies Monograph no. 156 (Thessaloniki, 1977), pp. 114–15.

5. Str. Dimitrov, "Kum vuprosa za otmeniavaneto na spahiiskata sistema v nasheta zemi" [Concerning the Question of the Breakup of the Sipahi System in Our Lands], *Istoricheski pregled*, XII, 6 (1956), p. 40.

6. Ibid., pp. 44–54; Z.Y. Hershlag, *Introduction to the Modern Economic History of the Middle East* (Leiden: E.J. Brill, 1964), p. 38.

7. Only 7 incomes from a list of 91 exceeded even 1,000 piastres a year. Dimitrov, "Chiflishkoto stopanstvo," pp. 25–52; Liuben Berov, *Ikonomicheskite razvitie na Bulgariia prez vekove* [The Economic Development of Bulgaria through the Ages] (Sofia, 1974), p. 72.

8. H.C. Barkley, *Bulgaria Before the War* (London, 1877), pp. 174–77; Thomas E. Meininger, "The Formation of a Nationalist Bulgarian Intelligentsia, 1835–1878" (Ph.D. dissertation, Univ. of Wisconsin, Madison, 1974), p. 16. The horse-drawn iron plow had been adopted throughout most of Western Europe in the medieval period. See B.H. Slicher von Bath, *The Agrarian History of Western Europe, A.D. 500–1850* (London: Edward Arnold, 1963), pp. 62–72.

9. J.A. Blanqui, *Voyage en Bulgarie pendant l'année 1841* (Paris, 1843), p. 225; Ami Boué, "Remarks on the Scenery, Antiques, Population, Agriculture and Commerce of Central European Turkey," *Edinburgh New Philosophical Journal* XXIV (1938), pp. 246–48 in N.V. Mikhov, *Contribution a l'histoire du commerce bulgare*, vol. II (Sofia, 1943), pp. 246–48; Ivan Sakazov, *Bulgarische Wirtschaftsgeschichte* (Berlin and Leipzig, 1929), p. 204.

10. N.G. Levintov, "Agrarnii perevorot v Bolgarii v 1877–79 gg." [The Agrarian Transition in Bulgaria, 1877–79] in *Osvobozhdenie Bolgarii ot turetskovo iga, 1878–1953* [The Liberation of Bulgaria from the Turkish Yoke, 1878–1953] (Moscow, 1953), pp. 164–65, 176–81.

11. Hershlag, pp. 39–41; Meininger, p. 18.

12. Khristo Khristov, *Agrarnite otnoshenie v Makenoniia prez XIX v. i v nachaloto XX v.* [Agrarian Relations in Macedonia during the 19th and at the Start of the 20th Century] (Sofia, 1964), pp. 102–13; Dimitrov, "Chiflishkoto stopanstvo," pp. 23–25. The railway from Thessaloniki to Skopje was completed by 1869.

13. Nicholas Svoronos, *Le commerce de Salonique en XVIIIme siècle* (Paris, 1956), p. 364; George B. Leon, "The Greek Merchant Marine, 1750–1850," in S.A. Papadapoulos, ed., *The Greek Merchant Marine, 1453–1850* (Athens: National Bank of Greece, 1972), p. 42; E.M. Cousinery, *Voyage dans le Macedoine*, I (Paris, 1831), pp. 49–51; John Macgregor, *Commercial Statistics*, vol. 2 (London, 1850), pp. 84–85.

14. I. Iurdanov, *Istoriia na bulgarskata turgoviia do Osvobozhdenieto: Kratuk ocherk* [A History of Bulgarian Trade until Liberation: A Short Survey] (Sofia, 1938), pp. 196, 222. The scattered evidence from European consular reports is summarized in Berov, pp. 67–69, and S. Damianov, *Frantsiia i bulgarskata natsionalna revolutsiia* [France and the Bulgarian National Revolution] (Sofia, 1968), pp. 23–26.

15. Damianov, p. 40; Zhak Natan et al., *Ikonomika na Bulgariia*, I (Sofia, 1969), pp. 259–60; F. Kanitz, *Donau-Bulgarien und der Balkan* III (Leipzig, 1883), p. 214.

16. V. Paskaleva, "Ikonomicheskite pronikvane na Austriia v bulgarskite zemi, 1857–1877" [Austrian Economic Penetration of the Bulgarian Lands, 1857–1877], *Izvestiia na institut na Bulgarskata istoriia*, 7 (Sofia, 1957), pp. 113–20; Kanitz, pp. 293–94. On French commercial limitations, see Damianov, p. 40.

17. Franklin F. Mendels, "Proto-industrialization: The First Phase of the Industrialization Process," *Journal of Economic History*, XXXII, 1 (March, 1972), pp. 241–61.

18. Meininger, pp. 5–8, 20–21; Sakazov, p. 223. See especially Nikolai Todorov, *Balkanskiiat grad, XV–XIX vek* [The Balkan Town, 15th–19th Centuries] (Sofia, 1972), pp. 295–321.

19. D. Kosev, Vl. Diculescu, and V. Paskaleva, "Za polozhenieto i stopanska deinost na Bulgarskata emigratsiia vuv Vlashko prez XIX v." [On the Position and Economic Activity of the Bulgarian Emigration to Wallachia in the 19th Century], in D. Angelou, M. Berza et al., *Bulgarsko-rumunski vruski i otnoshenie prez vekove* [Bulgarian-Romanian Ties and Relations over the Centuries], I (Sofia, 1965), pp. 304–17, 348; Meininger, pp. 8–13. On the Bulgarian colonies in Vienna, Istanbul, and Odessa, see Meininger pp. 34–37, and Natan et al., pp. 260–61.

20. C.C. Giurescu, *Istoria Bucureştilor* (Bucharest, 1960), p. 269, and idem, *Contribuţiuni la studiul şi dezvoltării originelor burgheziei române pîna la 1848* [Contributions to the Study of Romanian Bourgeois Origins and Development to 1848] (Bucharest, 1972), pp. 93–95.

21. Natan et al., I, pp. 255–56, 262, 274–75.

22. Petur Tsonchev, *Iz stopanskoto minalo na Gabrovo* [From the Economic Past of Gabrovo] (Sofia, 1929), pp. 457–61.

23. Sakazov, pp. 227, 233; Natan et al., p. 239.

24. Natan et al., pp. 228–32; Sakazov, pp. 231–33.

25. The following account is based on Tsonchev, pp. 610–21.

26. On the early modern Belgian experience, see Franklin F. Mendels, "Agriculture and Peasant Industry in Eighteenth-Century Flanders," in William N. Parker and Eric L. Jones, eds., *European Peasants and Their Markets* (Princeton, N.J.: Princeton Univ. Press, 1975), pp. 179–206.

27. Meininger, pp. 24–35; Natan et al., p. 234; Berov, pp. 75–81.

28. During the period 1878–1888, total Bulgarian artisans dropped sharply from 60 to 33 thousand. Berov, pp. 65, 87.

29. Todorov, pp. 378–89.

30. Looms per master only increased from two to three between 1836–45 and 1861–70. Ivan Undzhiev, *Karlovo: istoriia na grada do Osvobozhdenie* [Karlovo: A History of the Town until Liberation] (Sofia, 1968), pp. 41–75.

31. Todorov, pp. 256–60; Natan et al., p. 237.

32. Natan et al., p. 234; Berov, pp. 75–81; Sakazov, pp. 228, 234–35.

33. Konst. Kosev, *Za kapitalisticheskoto razvitie na bulgarskite zemi prez 60-te i 70-te godini na XIX vek* [On the Capitalist Development of the Bulgarian Lands in the 1860s and 1870s] (Sofia, 1968), pp. 34–39. Ostensibly the local Ottoman *bey* scuttled the project by withdrawing his approval on the grounds that the imported European workers were repeatedly stopping to look in his harem on the way to the smelter. Their offer to build the *bey* a new harem at a site of his choosing was, however, refused, giving credence to the Arie family's suspicion that rival Turkish ironmongers had prevailed on him to force out this new competition in any case.

34. Todorov, pp. 267–81; Natan et al., pp. 246–47.

35. The following account is drawn from Todorov, pp. 229–51, 283–91.

36. Khristo Khristov, "Kum vuprosa za klasite i klasovite otnosheniia v bulgarskoto obshtestvo prez Vuzrazhdaneto" [On the Question of Class and Class Relations in Bulgarian Society during the Renascence] *Izvestiia na institut istoriia*, XXI (1970), pp. 51–53. For a summary of the *chorbadzhii* debate in postwar Bulgarian historiography, see Meininger, pp. 40–44.

37. On the role of Father Paisii of Mt. Athos and the Orthodox monasteries in these first recorded stirrings of the Bulgarian cultural revival, see Marin V. Pundeff, "Bulgarian Nationalism," in Peter F. Sugar and Ivo J. Lederer, eds., *Nationalism in Eastern Europe* (Seattle, Wn.: Univ. of Washington Press, 1971), pp. 98–104.

38. Natan et al., p. 272; Meininger, pp. 7–11, 51–55.

39. Meininger, pp. 2–4, 17–25.

40. Ibid., pp. 47–55.

41. The Circassian experience contrasted sharply with that of the Tartars, who came somewhat earlier and in smaller numbers to the Dobrudja. Drawing on their own commercial traditions, they soon established a prominent place for themselves in the rural and urban economies. H.C. Barkley, pp. 74–79, 122–27, 285; Herbert Wilhelmy, *Hochbulgariens*, vol. I (Kiel, 1935), pp. 189–204. For a broader view of the migration of perhaps a million Circassians from the Crimean to the Ottoman Empire during the 1860s and a discussion of Ottoman military motives in concentrating a new Moslem settlement in the northern Bulgarian lands, see Kemal H. Karpat, "Population Movements in the Ottoman State and Modernization: The Bulgarian and

Circassian Migrations, 1857-1880," paper presented to the American Association for the Advancement of Slavic Studies Convention, Dallas, Texas, March 15-18, 1972.

42. Blaisdell, pp. 34-39, 47.

43. Following his father's career, Midhat Pasha had entered the Sultan's service as a secretary to the Grand Vezir in 1836, at the age of 14. By 1851, he had advanced to the high position of First Secretary to the Grand Council of the Porte. Twice during 1854 the Grand Vezir sent him on a special assignment to suppress banditry and restore public order in several northern Bulgarian districts. He came back from the first trip with a forerunner of the 1864 plan for provincial reform. Midhat returned again in 1857 on a little-known but significant mission to Turnovo, the medieval Bulgarian capital just north of the Balkan Mountains. There he faced boiling local resentment of the corrupt tax collection and arbitrary actions of the Bulgarian *chorbad-zhiia*. Midhat quickly convinced himself that these abuses were real and obtained a special edict from the Sultan. Its ten articles cut the terms of tax collectors to one year and imposed various requirements on their financial accountability and income. The edict was unfortunately not extended to other districts. For the period 1861-64, Midhat Pasha served as governor of the Niš district. Early conferences with elders of the mixed Bulgarian and Serbian population revealed two major grievances, an excess of banditry and a lack of decent roads for moving agricultural goods to market. His energy in attacking both problems was sufficient to reverse the flow of Serbian and even some Bulgarian emigration northward to autonomous Serbia. Midhat also set up two of the peasant savings banks that he would extend throughout the Danubian vilayet during his later tenure as its governor. *Encylopedie de l'Islam*, III (Leiden: E.J. Brill, 1936), p. 547; A.H. Midhat Bey, *The Life of Midhat Pasha* (London: John Murray, 1903), pp. 32-36; S.S. Bobchev, "Notes comparées sur les corbacis chez les peuples balkaniques et en particulier chez les Bulgars," *Revue internationale des études balkaniques*, 5-6 (1938), pp. 440-41; Davidson, pp. 144-46.

44. Davidson, pp. 151-71, summarizes this generally favorable appraisal of Midhat's policies in the so-called Tuna *vilayet*.

45. Zhak Natan, *Stopanska istoriia na Bulgariia* [An Economic History of Bulgaria] (Sofia, 1957), p. 138.

46. Natan et al., p. 221; Sakazov, p. 197; Dimitrov, "Chiflishkoto stopanstvo," pp. 16-18, 30.

47. Nearly 2,000 miles of new road was built but the great majority of this was unpaved and unpatrolled. Guards placed every 10 miles hindered trade with passport regulations as much as they deterred bandits. In fact, good macadam paving proceeded only a mile out of Ruse, giving way to 160 miles of unfinished road with scattered stones laid so as to make travel more arduous than before. Midhat instructed his troops to force travelers to use the roadway even though its roughness quickly destroyed the wheels of their carts. This only encouraged detours around the existing roadway. The English engineers brought in to supervise construction of the first Bulgarian railway, a line from Ruse to Varna completed in 1869, found themselves frustrated by Midhat's administration at every turn. The line was stopped at the

outskirts of Varna, well short of the new port facilities with which it was intended to link up. Midhat forced the British company to hire Turkish inspectors and locomotive engineers whose total lack of training made them a menace to the safe operation of the line. Barkley, pp. 61–70, 94–97, 153–64, 189–90; St. Chilingirov, *Midhat Pasha i Zemedelskite Kasi* [Midhat Pasha and the Agricultural Banks] (Sofia, 1942), p. 6.

48. Due these agricultural banks were one tenth of annual revenues from the land tax and two thirds of that from the silk and tobacco tax. Yet collections for the banks reportedly fell one third short of projected levels on a regular basis. Berrisav Arsitch, *La vie économique de la Serbie au sud au 19me siècle* (Paris, 1936), pp. 30–32; Kiril Popoff, *La Bulgaria économique, 1879–1911* (Paris, 1920), p. 452; Natan et al., pp. 275–76.

6. The Export Boom
and Peasant Agriculture

1. A recent reworking of Canadian data for the last prewar decade, with this present staple theory in mind, suggests that wheat exports accounted for a full fifth of the significant increase in per capita income. See R.E. Caves, "Export-led Growth and the New Economic History," in J.N. Bhagwati et al., eds., *Trade, Balance of Payments and Growth* (Amsterdam: North-Holland Publishing Co., 1971), pp. 417–19. For a critical appraisal of the current status of the staple theory in Canadian economic historiography, see Trevor O. Dick, "Frontiers in Canadian Economic History," *Journal of Economic History*, XXXVI, 1 (March, 1976), pp. 34–39.

2. A good review of these problems as seen by American development economists may be found in Lloyd G. Reynolds, ed., *Agriculture in Development Theory* (New Haven, Conn.: Yale Univ. Press, 1975), pp. 6–19.

3. Best estimates are reviewed in Richard L. Rudolph, *Banking and Industrialization in Austria-Hungary* (Cambridge: Cambridge Univ. Press, 1976), p. 18, and B.R. Mitchell, *European Historical Statistics, 1750-1970* (New York: Columbia Univ. Press, 1975), pp. 510–59.

4. Simon Kuznets, *Modern Economic Growth* (New Haven, Conn.: Yale Univ. Press, 1966), pp. 312–15.

5. Ibid., p. 305; B.R. Mitchell, "Statistical Appendix," in Carlo Cipolla, ed., *The Fontana Economic History of Europe, The Emergence of Industrial Societies*, 4(2) (London: Collins/Fontana Books, 1973), pp. 747–48, 795–810.

6. L. Katus, "Economic Growth in Hungary: A Quantitative Analysis," in E. Pamlenyi, *Social-Economic Researches in the History of East-Central Europe* (Budapest, 1971), p. 41; Mitchell, *European Historical Statistics*, pp. 19–25.

7. The Serbian experience of the 1860s, when grain cultivation became widespread for the first time, produced initial yields that surpassed those attained with more sophisticated methods and larger-scale cultivation in the Austrian lands. Michael R. Palairet, "The Influence of Commerce on the Changing Structure of Serbia's Peasant Economy, 1860–1912," (Ph.D. dissertation, Edinburgh Univ., 1976), pp. 23–27.

8. E.J. Tsouderos, *La relèvement économique de la Grèce* (Paris-Nancy, 1919), pp. 105–106, 130; Damianos Kyriazi, *Zur Entwicklung des Gewerbes im heutigen Griechenland* (Athens, 1916), p. 40; N.J.G. Pounds, *Eastern Europe* (Chicago: Aldine Publishing Co., 1969), p. 33.

9. Percy F. Martin, *Greece in the 20th Century* (London: Unwin, 1913), pp. 255–56; Kyriazi, pp. 39–40; Tsouderos, pp. 133, 210; M. Sivignon, "The Demographic and Economic Evolution of Thessaly, 1881–1940," in F.W. Carter, ed., *An Historical Geography of the Balkans* (New York: Academic Press, 1977), pp. 388–94.

10. *Spisanie na bulgarskoto ikonomichesko druzhestvo*, V, 2–3 (Sofia, 1901), pp. 116–17; Zhak Natan et al., *Ikonomika na Bulgariia* [The Economy of Bulgaria], I (Sofia, 1969), p. 340; Kiril Popoff, *La Bulgarie économique, 1879–1911* (Paris, 1920), pp. 163–404.

11. Popoff, pp. 159–68, 176, 179, 229–30.

12. Natan, I, p. 337; *Spisanie na bulgarskoto ikonomichesko druzhestvo*, V, 2–3 (Sofia, 1901), pp. 121–29. On the drop in Bulgarian exports for 1897–1900, see Table 6.2.

13. See Table 2 in John R. Lampe, "Varieties of Unsuccessful Industrialization: The Balkan States Before 1914," *Journal of Economic History*, XXV, 1 (March, 1975), p. 60.

14. Jack Tucker, "The Rumanian Peasant Revolt of 1907: Three Regional Studies," (Ph.D. dissertation, Univ. of Chicago, 1972), Table 6, p. 70; Table 13, p. 75.

15. Ibid., pp. 75, 77; Popoff, p. 176; Palairet, pp. 23, 215, 230.

16. Town sales of farm products were, of course, constrained by the small initial base of urban population, under 10 percent in 1862. Thus, it is not surprising that the increase to 17 percent by 1910 left urban sales at no more than 30 percent of total export value. Palairet, p. 45.

17. See Katus, pp. 44–52, and Scott M. Eddie, "Agricultural Production and Output per Worker in Hungary, 1870–1913," *Journal of Economic History*, XXVIII, 2 (June, 1968), pp. 197–222.

18. Palairet, pp. 161–63, 181–92. Only stall-feeding could have solved the pasturing problem. As we shall see below, such intensive techniques were beyond the means of the Serbian mass of smallholding peasants.

19. For a full statistical account of Habsburg hog production and a sketch of the rise of Hungarian protectionist sentiment, see ibid., pp. 87–105.

20. John R. Lampe, "Financial Structure and the Economic Development of Serbia, 1878–1912," (Ph.D. dissertation, Univ. of Wisconsin,1971), pp. 38, 214.

21. On the causes and course of the tariff war, see Wayne S. Vucinich, *Serbia Between East and West, 1903–1908* (Palo Alto, Calif.: Stanford Univ. Press, 1954) and the definitive Yugoslav work, Dimitrije Djordjević, *Carinski rat Austro-Ugarske i Srbije, 1906–1911* [The Tariff War between Austria-Hungary and Serbia, 1906–1911] (Belgrade, 1962).

22. Palairet, pp. 112–14, 242–53.

23. Ibid., pp. 390–94, 446–54, 464–67, 476–81.

24. Ibid., pp. 454–60, 477; Lampe, "Financial Structure," p. 37.

25. Tsouderos, pp. 134–35, 212–13. Olive oil, also hand pressed by village

labor, was exported only to Italy and never exceeded 5 percent of total export value. Tobacco accounted for less than 10 percent and wine less than 15 percent. Martin, pp. 255–58, 274–77.

26. In the absence of the separate monograph needed on this subject, see Great Britain, Diplomatic and Consular Reports, *Annual Series* (1906) no. 3785; William Miller, *Greek Life in Town and Country* (London, 1915), pp. 295–297; Martin, pp. 278–84.

27. Martin, p. 285.

28. British Parliamentary Papers, *Annual Series*, LXXVI (1903), no. 2357, and XC (1911), no. 4609.

29. Tsouderos, pp. 212–13.

30. British Parliamentary Papers, *Annual Series*, XCIV (1898), no. 2159, XCVIII (1898), no. 2357, CV (1902), no. 2827, LXXVI (1903), no. 2002.

31. The statistical basis for the argument is presented in Paul Bairoch, *The Economic Development of the Third World since 1900* (Berkeley, Calif.: Univ. of California Press, 1975), pp. 111–17. On the structure of Austro-Hungarian trade in particular see Rudolph, p. 230.

32. M. Avramović, *Naše seljačko gazdinstvo* [Our Peasant Economy] (Sarajevo, 1927), pp. 35, 39. Also see the commentary on the sources used to make this calculation and the attempt to use it as a basis for reckoning total agricultural income for 1911 in Palairet, pp. 40–44. The one Yugoslav sociological study of several pre- and post-1914 Serbian villages at the microeconomic level, B. Milić-Krivodoljanin, *Zbornik radova o selu* [Collection of Works on the Village] (Belgrade, 1970), pp. 57–58, finds little difference in the number of cattle owned by peasants with larger and smaller holdings.

33. Milić-Krivodoljanin, pp. 12, 79, 85, 110; M. Jovanovich, *Die serbische Landwirtschaft* (Munich, 1906), pp. 55–58; M.L. Stanojević, *Die Landwirtschaft in Serbien* (Ph.D. dissertation, Univ. of Halle, 1912), pp. 94–95; Dragoslav Janković, *O političkim strankama u Srbiji XIX veka* [On Political Parties in 19th-century Serbia] (Belgrade, 1951), p. 147.

34. Stanojević, pp. 57–58, 91–93. Table 6.6 indicates that Serbia still had only 5 horses per 100 persons in 1911, as compared with 6 for Greece, 12 for Bulgaria, and 13 for Romania.

35. Palairet, pp. 209–16, is able to show a 30 to 40-percent rise for both wheat and corn only by using 30-year-low yields of 1901–03 as a base figure.

36. *Spisanie na bulgarskoto ikonomichesko druzhestvo*, XXV, 1–2–3 (1926), p. 123; Popoff, pp. 163, 167–68; Natan, I, pp. 336–37.

37. British Parliamentary Papers, *Annual Series*, XCII (1893), no. 1300.

38. Two thirds of this land was seized from smallholding Turkish peasants, and not *chiflik* owners. Natan, pp. 307–19.

39. Ibid., pp. 328–33, 362, 367; Liuben Berov, *Ikonomicheski razvitie na Bulgariia prez vekove* [The Economic Development of Bulgaria over the Centuries] (Sofia, 1974), pp. 93–96; Popoff, p. 122.

40. U.S. Department of Agriculture, *Rumania. A Guide to Official Statistics of Agriculture and Food Supply*, Agricultural Economic Bibliography no. 49 (Washington, D.C.: U.S. Government Printing Office, 1930), pp. 108–109.

41. Great Britain, Diplomatic and Consular Reports, *Annual Series* (1907), no. 3785. Also see Sivignon, p. 398, and Tsouderos, pp. 117–18.

42. On the Lake Copäis Co., see Tsouderos, p. 132; Martin, p. 269.

43. Tucker, p. 75. Also see the best Romanian work on post-1864 agriculture, I. Adam and N. Marcu, *Studii despre dezvoltarea capitalismului în agricultura Rominiei* [Studies Concerning the Development of Capitalism in the Agriculture of Romania] vols. I and II (Bucharest, 1959).

44. The boyar estate owners not only received better land directly under the 1864 reform but also were owed higher redemption payments from the middle and larger peasant landholders, thus forcing some to sell out, and received the chance to buy state land. See Tucker, 60–65, 76, and Philip G. Eidelberg, *The Great Romanian Peasant Revolt of 1907, The First Modern Jacquerie* (Leiden: E.J. Brill, 1974), pp. 27–28. The definitive work from Romanian Marxist scholarship is N. Adăniloaie and Dan Berindei, *Reforma agrară de la 1864* [The Agrarian Reform of 1864] (Bucharest, 1967).

45. Tucker, pp. 48–53, 75–81. See Katus, pp. 90–96, for statistical evidence of the Hungarian advances.

46. Eidelberg, pp. 28–30.

47. By 1910, Romania had the lowest percentage in pastures, 10.6 percent, of any Balkan state. U.S. Department of Agriculture, *Rumania*, p. 119. Incomplete but persuasive evidence on peasant rents, earnings, consumption and disease is found in V. Liveanu, "On the Utilization of Mathematical Methods in History in Romania," *Revue Roumaine d'Histoire*, XII, 2 (1974), 329–33; Tucker, pp. 82–85; Eidelberg, p. 35; Adam and Marcu, II, p. 274.

48. U.S. Department of Agriculture, *Rumania*, pp. 108–109; Tucker, pp. 89–90; Eidelberg, pp. 55–59.

49. Tsouderos, p. 148; Stanojević, pp. 81–82.

50. C. Nicolae, *Organizarea și conținutul învățămîntului profesional și tehnic din România, 1864–1948* [Organization and Content of Professional and Technical Education in Romania, 1864–1948] (Bucharest, 1973), pp. 38–88.

51. Stanojević, pp. 93–94; Palairet, pp. 487–94.

52. Palairet, pp. 157–67, uses unpublished data from the Serbian state railways to assemble this calculation. His comparison of the cost of shipping grain to Belgrade by rail and Smederevo, also on the Danube, by road reveals an advantage to the latter.

53. Calculated from *Statisticheski godishnik na Bulgarskoto Tsarstvo, 1912* [Statistical Yearbook of the Bulgarian Kingdom, 1912] (Sofia, 1915), pp. 258, 312; *Anuarul statistic al României, 1915–1916* (Bucharest, 1919), pp. 130, 173; Adam and Marcu, pp. 247–50. The greater economic importance of the Romanian railways is confirmed by total freight of all kinds whose tonnage after 1900 was five times the Bulgarian and Serbian figures, or about three times both totals per kilometer of track, Mitchell, *European Historical Statistics*, pp. 591–94. Regional price data for goods and freight charges are far too fragmentary to permit the use of regression techniques to reckon the impact of rail transport, as attempted for Tsarist Russia by Jacob Metzer, "Railroad Development and Market Integration: The Case of Tsarist Russia," *Journal of Economic History*, XXXIV, 3 (Sept., 1974), pp. 529–50.

54. Palairet, pp. 46–56. On Bulgarian and Romanian tax structure, see Popoff, p. 428; *Anuarul statistic al României, 1915–1916*, p. 252.

55. Tucker, pp. 91–94, provides a good short summary. Eidelberg, pp. 23–64, has a longer one, plus reviewing Romanian historiography on the subject, pp. 4–10, and listing the major secondary works, pp. 249–52. The standard work in English, until it was superseded by the Tucker and Eidelberg contributions, was David Mitrany, *The Land and the Peasant in Romania* (New Haven, Conn.: Yale Univ. Press, 1931), pp. 42–92. The first and still most famous Romanian study is Radu Rossetti, *Pentru ce s'au răsculat țaranii* [Why the Peasants Revolted] (Bucharest, 1908). For the views of recent Romanian scholarship, see A. Oțetea et al., *Marea răscoală a țăranilor din 1907* [The Great Revolt of the Peasants in 1907] (Bucharest, 1968) and M. Iosa, "Răscoala țaranilor din 1907—premise și semnificații" [The Peasant Revolt of 1907—Theories and Facts], *Revista de istorie*, vol. 30, no. 2 (Feb., 1977), pp. 183–98.

56. Some 100,000 peasants bought a total of 500,000 hectares. A majority of Conservative delegates to the Chamber agreed to veto a government plan for selling 10 to 25-hectare plots that might have made a long-term dent in the land shortage. As it was, the inexorable subdivision for inheritance had started pushing the average size of peasants' smallholdings down again by the mid-1890s. Tucker, pp. 95–96; Eidelberg, pp. 29–30.

57. Over half of the Popular Bank loans were under 100 lei (or francs), when the peasants' annual needs for working capital alone were 300 lei. Eidelberg, pp. 73–108. On the origins of the Schulze-Delitzsch savings banks in the mid-nineteenth century, see J. Carroll Moody and Gilbert C. Fite, *The Credit Union* (Lincoln: University of Nebraska Press, 1970), pp. 1–25.

58. On the events of the revolt itself, see Eidelberg, pp. 190–228, and Tucker, pp. 112–40. On the subsequent land reform of 1918–1921, see Mitrany, pp. 95–566.

59. Over 90 percent of the bakers in Athens, for instance, were reckoned to be migrants from the northeast. Kyriazi, p. 143.

60. Over two thirds of this total left after 1905. Ibid., p. 43; and X. Zolotas, *Griechenland auf dem Weg zur Industrialisierung* (Athens, 1926), p. 30. For further information, especially on emigration to the U.S., see E. Vlachos, *An Annotated Bibliography on Greek Migration* (Athens: Social Sciences Center, 1966).

61. M.S. Eulambio, *The National Bank of Greece* (Athens, 1924), pp. 39–40; Great Britain, Diplomatic and Consular Reports, *Annual Series* (1907), no. 3818; (1909), no. 4208; and (1911), no. 4649.

62. The 11 percent of Serbian rural households found "landless" in the official survey of 1897 included rural artisans and other nonagricultural village residents, as well as a number of landowning peasants who lied to avoid anticipated taxes. Jelenka Petrović, *Prelaz seljaka u varoše i radnike* [The Transfer of the Peasants into Towns and Workers (*sic*)] (Belgrade, 1924), pp. 13–19. Palairet, pp. 520–22, finds no increase in the more likely total of 4–5 percent landless peasants by the more carefully cross-checked 1905 census.

63. Palairet, pp. 575–79.

64. Ibid., pp. 542–67; Petrović, p. 20; Berissav Orsitch, *La vie économique de la sud Serbie au XIXe siècle* (Paris, 1936), pp. 151–53.

65. Perhaps 20,000 emigrants left Bulgaria in 1907 from the northeastern and Macedonian areas for the United States. Afterwards, the smallholders' attachment to fertile grain land and the threat of government restrictions reduced annual emigration to the Serbian and non-Jewish Romanian totals of a few thousand annually. Trgovska Kamera na grad Ruse, *Skrateni protokoli za 1907* [Shortened Protocols for 1907] (Ruse, 1908), pp. 57–72; *Statisticheski godishnik na Bulgarskoto Tsarstvo* [Statistical Yearbook of the Bulgarian Empire] (Sofia, 1909), p. 164.

66. Berov, pp. 93–94.

67. From 1880 forward, "non-professional" moneylenders were allowed to extend credit, thereby bringing many merchants and smugglers into the practice. T. Girginov, *Istoricheski razvoi na suvremena Bulgariia* [The Historical Development of Contemporary Bulgaria] (Sofia, 1934), pp. 16–19; Palairet, *Spisanie na bulgarskoto ikonomichesko druzhestvo*, IV, 1 (1901), p. 50; Natan et al., pp. 354–55.

68. John W. Bell, *Peasants in Power: Alexander Stamboliiski and the Bulgarian Agrarian National Union, 1899–1912* (Princeton, N.J.: Princeton Univ. Press, 1977), pp. 55–84. For a Marxist critique of Stamboliiski's corporate ideas, see Zhak Natan et al., *Istoriia na ikonomicheski misul v Bulgariia* [The History of Economic Thought in Bulgaria], II (Sofia, 1973), pp. 76–82.

69. Frederick B. Chary, "The Bulgarian Agrarian Union's Parliamentary Program, 1902–1915," paper presented at the annual conference of the American Historical Association, Chicago, Illinois, Dec. 26–28, 1974.

70. Bell, pp. 22–54; Natan et al., pp. 369–72. On the limited role and minimal credit available from the several hundred prewar agricultural cooperatives in Serbia and Greece respectively, see Jovanović, pp. 84–94, and Tsouderos, pp. 124–27.

71. Natan, et al., p. 400. Also see Popoff, pp. 453–60; British Parliamentary Papers, *Annual Series*, 90 (1911), no. 4609; *Doklad do Ferdinand I ot Ministarski Savet, 1887–1912* [Report to Ferdinand from the Council of Ministers, 1887–1912] (Sofia, 1912), pp. 645–50.

7. Financial Consequences of Political Independence

1. The Balkan ratios are derived from Tables 6.4 and 7.5. The Western and Central European ratios, 46 percent for the less developed countries like Spain and Portugal and 138 percent for developed ones like France and Germany, may be found in Raymond Goldsmith, *Financial Structure and Development* (New Haven, Conn.: Yale Univ. Press, 1969), pp. 208–11. Table 7.4 suggests that Balkan bank density by 1911 approached .5 per 10,000 population, versus .48 for England and Wales in 1800, according to Rondo Cameron et al., *Banking in the Early Stages of Industrialization* (New York: Oxford Univ. Press, 1967), pp. 296–300.

2. See Rondo Cameron, ed., *Banking and Economic Development: The*

Lessons of History (New York: Oxford Univ. Press, 1972), especially the editor's introduction, pp. 3–25, for a concise review of Western economists' views on banking as a determinant of growth since Joseph Schumpeter's *The Theory of Economic Development* (Cambridge, Mass.: Harvard Univ. Press, 1933). For the closest thing to an explicit statement of the Gerschenkron hypothesis, see the Postscript to Alexander Gerschenkron, *Economic Backwardness in Historical Perspective* (Cambridge, Mass.: Harvard Univ. Press, 1962).

3. M.S. Eulambio, *The National Bank of Greece* (Athens, 1924), pp. 2–5; Dimitrios Tourpalis, *Die Bankwesen Griechenlands* (Würtzberg, 1933), pp. 27–34; Ep. K. Stinopolou, *Istoria tës Ethnekis Trapezis tës Ellados* [The History of the National Bank of Greece] (Athens, 1966).

4. This was the year in which the several European powers set up the Ottoman Public Debt Administration to collect revenues directly from the Ottoman state budget in order to repay outstanding obligations on schedule. For details and subsequent history, see Donald C. Blaisdell, *European Financial Control in the Ottoman Empire* (New York: Columbia Univ. Press, 1929).

5. Recent scholarship from Yugoslavia and Romania repeatedly displays awareness of the important symbolic overtones of any amount of national currency. See M. Ugričić, *Novčani sistem Jugoslavije* [The Monetary System of Yugoslavia] (Belgrade, 1968) and C. C. Kirițescu, *Sistemul bănesc al leului şi precursorii lui* [The Monetary System of the Lei and its Forerunners] I (Bucharest, 1964).

6. For a description of what one French observer of the 1860s aptly called "a terrible money anarchy," see Kirițescu, pp. 140–42, and John R. Lampe, "Serbia, 1878–1912," in Cameron, ed., *Banking and Economic Development*, pp. 135–36.

7. Kirițescu, pp. 155, 163–75, 191, 303; N. Razmiritza, *Essai d'économie roumaine moderne, 1831–1931* (Paris, 1931), pp. 135–39; Dickson H. Leavens, *Silver Money* (Bloomington, In.: Principia Press, 1939), p. 9.

8. Ugričić, pp. 58–62; Velimir Bajkitch, *Monnaies, banques et bourses en Serbie* (Paris, 1919), p. 48.

9. Kirițescu, pp. 198–99, 221–23, 294–95, 306–8.

10. For a summary of the rise and fall of Bontoux's financial empire see P.H. Emden, *The Money Powers of Europe in the Nineteenth and Twentieth Centuries* (New York: Appleton-Century, 1928), pp. 184–86. The definitive work on the subject is Jean Bouvier, *Le Krach de l'Union Générale* (Paris, 1960).

11. P. Cîncea, *Viața politica din România în primul deceniu al independenței de stat* [The Political Life of Romania in the First Decade of National Independence] (Bucharest, 1974), p. 30; Lazăr Ionescu, *Relațiile între Banca Națională a Rominiei şi stat, 1880–1935* [Relations between the Romanian National Bank and the State, 1880–1935] (Bucharest, 1935), pp. 89–93; Kirițescu, pp. 301, 314.

12. *Narodna Banka, 1884–1934* (Belgrade, 1935), pp. 20, 48.

13. Archives Nationales, F30, 346, July 3, 1881; *Narodna Banka*, pp. 19–23; M. Radosavljevich, *Die Entwicklung der Währung in Serbien* (Berlin

and Munich, 1912), p. 37; Lampe, "Serbia," in Cameron, ed., *Banking and Economic Development*, pp. 137–38, 142.

14. Bulgarian Ministry of Commerce and Agriculture, *Bulgaria of Today* (London, 1907), pp. 274–75; *Doklad do Ferdinand I ot Ministarski Savet, 1887–1912* [Report to Ferdinand I from the Council of Ministers, 1887–1912] (Sofia, 1912), pp. 278–79; *Iubileen sbornik na Bulgarskata Narodna Banka, 1879–1929* [Anniversary Yearbook of the Bulgarian National Bank, 1879–1929] (Sofia, 1929), pp. 14–15.

15. Zh. Natan et al., *Ikonomika na Bulgariia*, I (Sofia, 1969), pp. 356–57; Charles Jelavich, *Tsarist Russia and Balkan Nationalism, 1876–1886* (Berkeley, Calif.: Univ. of California Press, 1966), pp. 68–71, 96, 107.

16. *Bulgaria of Today*, p. 275; *Doklad do Ferdinand I*, pp. 282–84; *Iubileen sbornik*, pp. 18–22; John R. Lampe, "Finance and Pre-1914 Industrial Stirrings in Bulgaria and Serbia," *Southeastern Europe*, II, 1 (1975), pp. 39–40.

17. Eastern Rumelia, i.e., southern Bulgaria, had been reclaimed in 1885 from the Ottoman suzerainty imposed by the Western and Central European powers at the Congress of Berlin in 1878.

18. The recent questioning of the railways' indispensability had centered on the American experience. It began with Robert Fogel's *Railways and American Economic Growth: Essays in Econometric History* (Baltimore, Md.: Johns Hopkins Univ. Press, 1964) and has continued to be debated in subsequent issues of the *Journal of Economic History*. One isolated extension of this inquiry to Europe is Jacob Metzer, "Railroad Development of Market Integration: The Case of Tsarist Russia," *Journal of Economic History*, XXXIV, 3 (Sept., 1974), pp. 529–49. He finds their construction to be crucial in the rapid development of a national grain market (see Chapter 6 above for some brief consideration of the Balkan case and, on Russia, the note by William J. Kelly and Metzer's reply in *Journal of Economic History*, XXXVI, 4 (Dec., 1976), pp. 908–18.

19. Leo Pazvolsky, *Bulgaria's Economic Position* (Washington, D.C.: Brookings Institute, 1929), pp. 42–43; *Doklad do Ferdinand I*, p. 282.

20. J. H. Jensen and Gerhard Rosegger, "British Railway Builders along the Lower Danube, 1856–1869," *Slavonic and East European Review*, XLVI (1968), pp. 124–25.

21. Ibid., pp. 118–23. On the improvement of the Sulina channel through the Danube delta, see Chapter 3 above.

22. *Istoria Rômîniei*, IV (Bucharest, 1965), pp. 463–66, 473–75. On the cautious attitude of Bleichröder and the German chancellor Bismarck toward these Romanian loans, see Fritz Stern, *Gold and Iron* (New York: Alfred A. Knopf, 1977), pp. 351–93.

23. I. Tutuc, *Studiul valoarilor mobilare* [The Study of Movable Assets] (Bucharest, 1927), pp. 34–35.

24. Already in 1872, the country's entire tobacco production had been given over as a concession to the Pester Ungarische Komercialbank of Budapest in return for the bank's payment of 8 million lei a year into the Romanian budget. Chapter 8 will consider how the state tobacco monopolies in all the Balkan states that were imposed to help repay European debts restricted the development of an otherwise promising agricultural industry.

25. The grief to which this record and the availability of European credit brought all four governments received its first comprehensive treatment in Herbert Feis, *Europe: The World's Banker, 1870–1914* (New Haven, Conn.: Yale Univ. Press, 1930), pp. 258–92.

26. The Greek tragedy had its origins in unrepaid loans dating from the war of independence in the 1820s and a series of massive loans in the 1870s and 1880s to wipe away those debts and finance the several military mobilizations that promised, largely in vain, to expand the Greek state to its present borders from the southern core. No European loans were raised for railway construction until 1890. The funds were, in any case, diverted to the same noneconomic uses. (Ottoman intransigence prevented any railway connection across Ottoman-held northern Greece until it was annexed to the south after the First Balkan War in 1912). The best account of the Greek foreign debt's growth during the nineteenth century is William H. Wynne, *State Insolvency and Foreign Bondholders*, II (New Haven, Conn.: Yale Univ. Press, 1951), pp. 283–334.

27. The huge Karlsbad loan of 282 million francs in 1895 consolidated the existing long-term debt, but a projected 70 million franc loan the following year only realized 34 millions and left half of the floating short-term debt to burden future budgets with exorbitant interest rates. John R. Lampe, "Financial Structure and the Economic Development of Serbia, 1878–1912," (Ph.D. dissertation, Univ. of Wisconsin, 1971), pp. 145–49, 156–58.

28. The nadir of one half of the 1872 price was reached in 1893. Leavens, pp. 9, 28–33, 334.

29. Eduard März, *Österreichische Industrie- und Bankpolitik in der Zeit Franz Josephs I* (Vienna, 1968), pp. 249–60. Also see Leland B. Yeager, "Fluctuating Rates in the Nineteenth Century: The Experiences of Austria and Russia," in Robert A. Mundell and Alexander K. Swoboda, eds., *Monetary Problems in the International Economy* (Chicago: Univ. of Chicago Press, 1969), pp. 61–89.

30. Lampe, "Financial Structure of Serbia," Table III.6, p. 157.

31. Ibid., pp. 152–56.

32. Another 9-million-dinar credit to the state in 1898 boosted the total note issue of the Narodna Banka past 35 million dinars without adding anything to the money supply in general circulation. *Nardona Banka*, pp. 312, 325.

33. Lampe, "Financial Structure of Serbia," pp. 155–59; Radosavljevich, pp. 79–83.

34. Eulambio, pp. 9–14.

35. Tourpalis, pp. 27–51; Wynne, pp. 334–48.

36. Great Britain Diplomatic and Consular Reports, *Annual Series* (1911), no. 4825, pp. 20–27.

37. Kiril Nedelchev, *Parichnoto delo v Bulgariia, 1879–1940* [Monetary Affairs in Bulgaria, 1879–1940] (Sofia, 1940), pp, 11–13, 26–27; *Godishni otchet na Bulgarska Narodna Banka za 1894* [Annual Report of the Bulgarian National Bank for 1894] (Sofia, 1895), p. 18.

38. Lampe, "Industrial Stirrings in Bulgaria and Serbia," p. 40.

39. *Iubileen sbornik*, pp. 57–60; Nedelchev, p. 27; *Godishni otchet za 1894*, pp. 20–27.

40. See Chapter 6 on the disastrous harvests of 1897–1900. See below on the virtual denial of Bulgarian access to European capital markets between 1892 and 1902.

41. A.I. Popescu, *Variațiile sezonale ale leului* [Seasonal Variations in the Leu] (Bucharest, 1927), p. 7. Also see John R. Lampe, "Varieties of Unsuccessful Industrialization: The Balkan States Before 1914," *Journal of Economic History*, XXXV, i (April, 1975), pp. 75–76.

42. State debts to the central bank did not disappear by 1905 as in Serbia but were at least held at a constant 80 million lei, a figure which shrank from one half to one fifth of the bank's note issue during the last prewar decade. Ionescu, pp. 111–18.

43. Lampe, "Financial Structure of Serbia," pp. 191–93; *Narodna Banka*, pp. 37–38; Archives Nationales, F30, 346 (Rapport sur La Serbia), p. 140.

44. Lampe, "Financial Structure of Serbia," p. 182; Milorad Nedeljković, *Istorija srpskih državnih dugova* [The History of the Serbian State Debts] (Belgrade, 1909), pp. 259–60.

45. See Table VI.3 in Lampe, "Financial Structure of Serbia," for a rough estimate of the Serbian stock of money in 1895 and 1911. Note issue exceeded coin and bank deposits combined. For Bulgaria, Romania, and Greece, we lack sufficient data on bank deposits to estimate the total money supply. Their respective note issues by 1912 reached 164 million leva, 228 million drachma and 425 million lei, versus just 30–35 million leva, 50–55 million drachma and 90 million lei of coin in circulation. *Bulgaria Today*, p. 296; *Iubileen sbornik*, p. 194; *Statistikë epeteris tës Ellados, 1930* [Statistical Yearbook of Greece, 1930] (Athens, 1931), pp. 266–68; K. und K. Österreichische Handelsmuseum, *Rumänien: Landes und wirtschaftstatistchen Übersichten* (Vienna, 1917), p. 42.

46. Lampe, "Varieties of Unsuccessful Industrialization," pp. 74–75. Eulambio, pp. 22–29; Tourpalis, pp. 34, 54–56.

47. *Godishni otchet na Bulgarska Narodna Banka za 1907* (Sofia, 1908), p. 20; *za 1909*, pp. 12–13; *za 1910*, p. 14.

48. *Iubileen sbornik*, p. 32.

49. Ibid., pp. 108–12; *Godishni otchet na Bulgarska Narodna Banka za 1911* (Sofia, 1912), p. 12. The Romanian National Bank experienced the same halving of long-term loans from 37 to 18 percent for 1881–1913 and the Serbian National Bank a drop from 14 to 6 percent for 1885–1912. C.I. Băicoianu, *Istoria politici noastre monetare și Băncii Naționale* [The History of Our Monetary Policy and the National Bank] II (Bucharest, 1932), p. 526; *Narodna Banka*, p. 311. A similar, although unquantified reduction for the National Bank of Greece is described in Tourpalis, pp. 48–51.

50. *Iubileen sbornik*, p. 192; Eulambio, p. 28, shows the same sort of increase for Greece. Lampe, "Financial Structure of Serbia," p. 270, Table VI.3, indicates a larger Serbian addition, double the rise in note issue between 1905 and 1911.

51. *Nardno stopanstvo* VII, 6–7 (Sofia, 1911), pp. 2–4; *Iubileen sbornik*, pp. 300–301; Victor Slăvescu, *Istoricul Băncii Naționale a României, 1880–1924* [History of the National Bank of Romania, 1880–1924] (Bucharest, 1925), p. 186.

52. Lampe, "Financial Structure of Serbia," pp. 127–29, 289.

53. Ibid., pp. 167, 292–94; Momir Glomazić, *Istorija Državne Hipotekarne Banke, 1862–1932* [History of the State Mortgage Bank, 1862–1932] (Belgrade, 1932), pp. 70–71, 74–81, 87–92.

54. Tourpalis, pp. 45–53; Eulambio, p. 14.

55. See below for details on the European backing and Mediterranean activities of the Orientbank and the Bank of Athens.

56. Lampe, "Industrial Stirrings in Bulgaria and Serbia," p. 48.

57. This theme is reiterated in the bank's anniversary publication, *Banca Româneasca, 1911–1920* (Bucharest, 1920).

58. Kirițescu, p. 68. This dependent relationship was reinforced by the tendency of the smaller banks to hold as their principal asset shares in the large Bucharest ones. Victor Slăvescu, *Băncile comerciale mijlocii din România* [Middle-Sized Commercial Banks of Romania] (Bucharest, 1915), p. 48.

59. Lampe, "Financial Structure of Serbia," p. 275, Table VI.4; I. Iurdanov, *Bulgarska Narodna Banka, 1879–1908* (Sofia, 1909), p. 85.

60. Lampe, "Serbia," in Cameron, ed., *Banking and Economic Development*, pp. 139–49. The current account credit from these Belgrade banks rose fourfold for 1906–11, versus a doubling of their discounting, to account for 80 percent of such credit outside the central bank.

61. Austro-Hungarian and French consular reports reflect the growing reputation of the Serbian banks for reliability. As further testimony, the uninhibited Belgrade press could find only one case of embezzlement to report during the last prewar decade. Lampe, "Financial Structure of Serbia," pp. 278–84. On the easier transfer of financial as compared with industrial technology, see Goldsmith, p. 264.

62. See Rudolph Hilferding, *Finanz Kapitalismus* (Vienna, 1910), for the original hypothesis. The revisionist case against its extension to foreign policy is best summarized in D.K. Fieldhouse, *Economics and Empire, 1830–1914* (Ithaca, N.Y.: Cornell Univ. Press, 1973). For a summary of recent German scholarship on the contribution of their Great Banks to pre-1914 industrial growth and concentration, see Ranier Fremdling and Richard Tilly, "German Banks, German Growth and Econometric History," *Journal of Economic History*, XXXVI, 2 (June, 1976), pp. 416–24.

63. On Greece, see Tourpalis, p. 29. On the Romanian Principalities and the Bulgarian lands, see Jensen and Rosegger, pp. 105–28.

64. The run on Anatolian branch reserves followed a scandal over some forged banknotes in 1894 and the commercial chaos attending the Armenian massacres of 1895. Respectively, these problems reflected aspects of the economic and political weakness of the Ottoman Empire, capable at this late date of affecting only Bulgaria among the Balkan states. See Lampe, "Finance and Pre-1914 Industrial Stirrings," p. 47.

65. Ibid., p. 48. Only during the First World War did the bank's activities expand significantly and then to act as an agent for exploitative German procurement of military supplies. See Vera Katsarkova, "Ograbvaneto na Bulgaria ot germanskiia imperialism" [Exploitation of Bulgaria by German Imperialism], *Trudove na visshiia ikonomicheski Institut Karl Marx*, II (1969), pp. 164–223.

66. See Ulrich Trumpener, *Germany and the Ottoman Empire, 191* (Princeton, N.J.: Princeton Univ. Press, 1968), pp. 6–12; Karl Helferich, *Georg von Siemens* (Berlin, 1921); John G. Williamson, *Kurt Helferich, 1872–1924* (Princeton, N.J.: Princeton Univ. Press, 1971).

67. Lampe, "Finance and Pre-1914 Industrial Stirrings," pp. 36–37; Svetana Todorova, *Diplomaticheska istoriia na vunshnite zaemi na Bulgariia, 1878–1912* [A Diplomatic History of Bulgarian Foreign Loans, 1878–1912] (Sofia, 1971), pp. 175–77, 20–23, 242–56. Todorova's extensive archival research contradicts Alexander Gerschenkron's assertion that the Bulgarian government enjoyed ready access to cheap European capital around the turn of the century, in Gerschenkron, p. 231.

68. Tourpalis, pp. 87–89; Staatsarchiv (Vienna), *Administrative Registratur*, 28F23, Bulgarien 2, March 8, 1905.

69. See Richard L. Rudolph, *Banking and Industrialization in Austria-Hungary* (Cambridge: Cambridge Univ. Press, 1976), pp. 96–121.

70. V. Slăvescu, *Marile băncii comerciale din România* [The Large Commercial Banks of Romania] (Bucharest, 1915), p. 7; Lampe, "Finance and Pre-1914 Industrial Stirrings," pp. 48–49.

71. Lampe, "Financial Structure of Serbia," pp. 335–45.

72. See Feis, pp. 118–159; Henri Brunshwig, *Myths and Realities of French Colonialism, 1871–1914* (New York: Praeger, 1966); and Jean Bouvier, "Systèmes bancaires et enterprises industrielles dans la croissance européene au XIXe siècle," *Annales*, 27, no. 1–2 (Jan.–March, 1972), pp. 46–70.

73. Tourpalis, p. 77; H. Lefeuvre-Méaulle, *La Grèce économique et financière en 1915* (Paris, 1915), pp. 188–91.

74. Lampe, "Financial Structure of Serbia," pp. 351–61, and idem, "Serbia," in Cameron, ed., *Banking*, pp. 158–59.

75. Lampe, "Varieties of Unsuccessful Industrialization," pp. 76–77, and "Industrial Stirrings in Bulgaria and Serbia," pp. 37–38.

76. *Statisticheski godishnik na Bulgarskoto Tsarstvo 1911* [Statistical Yearbook of the Bulgarian Kingdom, 1911] (Sofia, 1912), p. 437; *Bulletin statistic al României*, III, 2–3 (Bucharest, 1909), pp. 66–68; Douglas Dakin, *The Unification of Greece, 1770–1923* (London: Ernest Benn, 1972), pp. 314–16; Rondo Cameron, "Profit, croissance et stagnation en France au XIXe siècle," *Économie appliquée*, 10, nos. 2–3 (April–Sept., 1957), p. 438.

8. Industrial Stirrings
and the Sources of Growth

1. Simon Kuznets has suggested to the satisfaction of most Western economists that 30 or 40 years of sustained growth is the minimum time for industrializing a pre-1914 economy. Kuznets, *Modern Economic Growth* (New Haven, Conn.: Yale Univ. Press, 1966), pp. 1–26. German growth from 1840 to 1880 is usually regarded as the classic case of a rapid transformation. The process took significantly longer in England and especially in France.

2. The Romanian questions were first posed and much of the present

answer provided in John R. Lampe, "Varieties of Unsuccessful Industrialization: The Balkan States before 1914," *Journal of Economic History*, XXXV, 1 (March, 1975), pp. 56–85. The Bulgarian problem has been considered separately in idem, "Finance and the Pre-1914 Industrial Stirrings in Bulgaria and Serbia," *Southeastern Europe*, II, I (1975), pp. 23–52.

3. *Rumänien, 1866–1906* (Bucharest, 1906), pp. 410–40; *Statistike spoljne trgovine Kr. Srbije* [Statistics of Foreign Trade for the Kingdom of Serbia], 1909 (Belgrade, 1910), pp. xxx–xxxiii and 1911 (Belgrade, 1912), pp. xviii–xxv.

4. "Finance and Pre-1914 Stirrings," pp. 71–72, and "Industrial Stirrings in Bulgaria and Serbia," p. 35.

5. Lampe, "Finance and Pre-1914 Stirrings," pp. 30–34; *Iubileena kniga na grad Sofiia, 1878–1928* [Jubilee Book of the City of Sofia, 1878–1828] (Sofia, 1928), p. 62. On the comparable role of Madrid, see David Ringrose, "The Impact of a New Capital City: Madrid, Toledo and New Castile, 1560–1660," *Journal of Economic History*, XXXIII, 4 (Dec., 1973), pp. 761–91.

6. *Spisanie na bulgarskoto ikonomichesko druzhestvo*, VIII, 4 (Sofia, 1904), p. 257; Zhak Natan et al., *Ikonomika na Bulgariia*, I (Sofia, 1969), p. 437.

7. Lampe, "Varieties of Unsuccessful Industrialization," p. 84, n. 55.

8. *Rumänien, 1866–1906*, pp. 410–40; John R. Lampe, "Financial Structure and the Economic Development of Serbia, 1878–1912" (Ph.D. dissertation, Univ. of Wisconsin, Madison, 1971), pp. 257–62.

9. This runs contrary to Arthur Lewis's scenario for developing economies still dominated by peasant agriculture. Arthur W. Lewis, "Economic Development with Unlimited Supplies of Labor," in A.N. Agarwala and S.P. Singh, *The Economics of Underdevelopment* (New York: Macmillan, 1963), pp. 400–49. A short summary and recent appraisal of the Lewis view may be found in Lloyd G. Reynolds, ed., *Agriculture in Development Theory* (New Haven, Conn.: Yale Univ. Press, 1975), pp. 11–15.

10. Lampe, "Financial Structure of Serbia," Appendix, pp. 400–14; Herbert Wilhelmy, *Hochbulgariens*, I (Kiel, 1935), p. 188.

11. Petur Tsonchev, *Iz stopanskoto minalo na Gabrovo* [From the Economic Past of Gabrovo] (Gabrovo, 1929), pp. 518–50. This detailed work is the best available source on the microeconomic operation of any branch of pre-1914 Balkan industry.

12. Natan et al., pp. 342–50.

13. I. Iurdanov, *Prinos kum promishlenata istoriia na grad Sofiia* [Contribution to the Industrial History of Sofia] (Sofia, 1928), pp. 48–54; Kiril Popoff, *La Bulgarie économique, 1879–1911* (Paris, 1920), p. 404.

14. Popoff, p. 353; Alexander Gerschenkron, "Some Aspects of Industrialization in Bulgaria, 1879–1911," in his *Economic Backwardness in Historical Perspective* (New York: Praeger, 1965), pp. 206–12; Great Britain, Diplomatic and Consular Reports, *Annual Series*, (1901), no. 2642.

15. This argument is persuasively presented in Michael R. Palairet, "The Influence of Commerce on the Changing Structure of Serbia's Peasant Economy, 1860–1912," (Ph.D. dissertation, Edinburgh Univ., 1976), pp. 36, 606.

Palairet has calculated that nearly 40 percent of Serbian nonagricultural consumption during the last prewar years came from the rural peasantry, and that a majority of these money purchases were textiles.

16. Percy F. Martin, *Greece of the 20th Century* (London: Unwin, 1913), pp. 263–69. On the Seres cotton center north of Thessaloniki, see Chapter 1.

17. Palairet, pp. 408–15, 418, 495–99; Lampe, "Financial Structure of Serbia," pp. 233–36.

18. Richard L. Rudolph, *Banking and Industrialization in Austria-Hungary* (Cambridge: Cambridge Univ. Press, 1976), pp. 22, 47–48, 56–57; William L. Blackwell, *The Beginnings of Russian Industrialization, 1800–1860* (Princeton, N.J.: Princeton Univ. Press, 1968), pp. 389, 423.

19. Martin, p. 254; Great Britain, Diplomatic and Consular Reports, *Annual Series*, (1904), no. 3302.

20. Palairet, pp. 343–49, 358–72; Iurdanov, p. 43; C.C. Giurescu, *Istoria Bucureştilor* [History of Bucharest] (Bucharest, 1967), pp. 155, 290.

21. I.I. Tatos and I. Ivănescu, *Industria morăritului în România* [The Milling Industry in Romania] (Bucharest, 1941), pp. 15–26; N.M. Ghiţescu, *Industria fainei* [The Flour Industry] (Bucharest, 1915), pp. 9–19. Stagnating output was all the more regrettable for food processing because it had the highest mechanical horsepower and output per worker of any branch of Romanian manufacturing. See Demetrius Leontieş, *Die Industrializierung Rumäniens bis zum zweiten Weltkrieg* (Munich, 1971), pp. 246–50.

22. *Anketa na nasurchavanata ot durzhavnata industriia prez 1909* [Report on the Encouragement of State Industry in 1909] (Sofia, 1910), V, pp. 100–11; Popoff, p. 366.

23. Palairet, pp. 295–97.

24. Palairet has calculated that the 13 million dinar loss in annual hog exports for 1906–10 was reduced only by a 4-million-dinar gain in corn exports that would otherwise have been hog feed. Ibid., pp. 307–21. Lampe, "Financial Structure of Serbia," pp. 230–32, 237–38, uses Austrian consular reports to piece together a history of Serbian meat-packing.

25. By 1910, these same Austrian reports spoke of a shortage building up in Vienna for the lower quality meats previously supplied by Serbia. On the Serbian interest in emulating Danish hog breeding, see Palairet, pp. 326–31.

26. Lampe, "Varieties of Unsuccessful Industrialization," pp. 72–73.

27. See George Ioaniţui and Nicolae Costache, *Industria cimentului în România* [The Cement Industry in Romania] (Bucharest, 1932), 36–45.

28. Lampe, "Financial Structure of Serbia," pp. 241–42.

29. Lampe, "Varieties of Unsuccessful Industrialization," pp. 79–80, n. 46. On the earlier connections of Braşov to the Wallachian economy, see Chapter 2.

30. Lampe, "Financial Structure of Serbia," pp. 231–32, 240–41, 258, 302. Sometimes these few technicians did not stretch far enough. Witness the Bulgarian project during the 1890s to found the country's first paper factory. It soon collapsed largely because of a Czech technical director whose training in engineering had brought him to the country to build a sugar refinery and whose time was largely spent on that project. Iurdanov, pp. 45–46.

31. Rudolph, pp. 189–93; Jean Bouvier, "Systèmes bancaires et

enterprises industrielles dans la croissance européene au XIXe siècle," *Les Annales*, 27, no. 1 (Jan.–Feb., 1972), pp. 46–70. On the more innovative mid-century behavior of major European banks, see Rondo Cameron, *France and the Economic Development of Europe, 1800–1914* (Princeton, N.J.: Princeton Univ. Press, 1962), pp. 105–203.

32. Victor Slăvescu, *Istoricul Băncii Naționale a Romîniei, 1880–1924* [History of the Romanian National Bank, 1880–1924] (Bucharest, 1925), pp. 111–206; Lampe, "Financial Structure of Serbia," pp. 274–78.

33. Lampe, "Finance and Pre-1914 Industrial Stirrings," pp. 40–42; *Anketa prez 1909*, V, pp. 49, 64–65, 71, 173, 224.

34. Lampe, "Financial Structure of Serbia," pp. 278–88.

35. These relatively low profits confirmed the judgment of a French consular report that modern manufacture remained a risky investment in a town the size of Ruse (less than 30,000 by this time) and that respectable profits would not come quickly. The ceramics factory of the Bulgarska Turgovska Banka was the most promising of the Ruse bank investments but could return an annual profit of only 7 percent on invested capital for the period 1908–11. See Lampe, "Finance and Pre-1914 Industrial Stirrings," pp. 45–46.

36. In Serbia, mortgage loans were left almost entirely to the Hipotekarna Banka, a semi-official institution whose conservative policy and dependence on European loans left little for industry or agriculture. See John R. Lampe, "Serbia, 1878–1912," in Rondo Cameron, ed., *Banking and Economic Development: Some Lessons of History* (New York: Oxford Univ. Press, 1972), pp. 141–43, and Momir Glomazić, *Istorija Državne Hipotekarne Banke, 1862–1932* [History of the State Mortgage Bank, 1862–1932] (Belgrade, 1932).

37. Lampe, "Financial Structure of Serbia," pp. 245–52, 306–13.

38. The Serbian central bank accepted no savings deposits. During these years, the savings deposits in the semiofficial mortgage bank, the Hipotekarna Banka, dropped from 20 to 10 percent of the total, given the rising amounts in private banks. The Bulgarian total remained unchanged, with the Serbian figure more than doubling for 1905–11 to fast approach it. The Bulgarian central and state agricultural banks held nearly 95 percent of total savings deposits throughout. Lampe, "Finance and Pre-1914 Industrial Stirrings," p. 44, Table III, and "Serbia," in Cameron, pp. 143–45.

39. Paraćin glass production of 500,000 dinars by 1911 approached total imports of 700,000 down 40 percent from the previous year. Lampe, "Financial Structure of Serbia," pp. 297–99. On the Johnson Affair, see Dimitrije Djordjević, *Carinski rat Austro-ugarskei Srbije, 1906–1911* [Tariff War between Austria-Hungary and Serbia, 1906–1911] (Belgrade, 1965), pp. 490–92.

40. Lampe, "Serbia," in Cameron, pp. 151–52, and "Financial Structure of Serbia," pp. 295–304.

41. For the most complete account in English of the industrial activities of any Balkan bank, see the house publication, *Banca Marmorosch–Blank, 1849–1923* (Bucharest, 1923).

42. Ibid., pp. 61–64; N.N. Constantinescu and V. Axenciuc, *Capitalismul*

monopolist în România [Monopoly Capitalism in Romania] (Bucharest, 1962), p. 148; *Anuarul Statistic al României, 1909* (Bucharest, 1910), pp. 826–87.

43. In 1913, 168 of about 550 industrial enterprises in Romania were joint-stock firms, versus 51 of 465 for Serbia and 80 of 345 for Bulgaria in 1911. The first Greek data on industrial activity counted only 26 of 282 firms as joint-stock in 1917. Lampe, "Varieties of Unsuccessful Industrialization," p. 78.

44. G.G. Caranfil and D.N. Jordan, *Études statistique sur les valeurs mobiliers en Roumanie de 1908 à 1930* (Paris, 1931), pp. 22–30; *Enciclopedia României* IV (Bucharest, 1940), pp. 520–21; Lampe, "Financial Structure of Serbia," pp. 243–44.

45. Lampe, "Financial Structure of Serbia," pp. 297–98, 313–19; Rudolph, pp. 91–121, 180–81; C.C. Kirițescu, *Sistemul bănesc al leului și precursorii lui* [Monetary System of the Leu and Its Forerunners], II (Bucharest, 1965), p. 77.

46. Simeon Damianov, *Frenskoto ikonomicheskoto pronikvane v Bulgariia, 1878–1914* [French Economic Penetration in Bulgaria, 1878–1914] (Sofia, 1971), pp. 202–204; Svetana Todorova, *Diplomaticheskata istoriia na vunshite zaemi na Bulgaria, 1878–1912* [Diplomatic History of Bulgaria's Foreign Loans, 1878–1912] (Sofia, 1973), pp. 302–17; Palairet, pp. 485–87; Lampe, "Financial Structure of Serbia," pp. 354–61, and idem, "Finance and Pre-1914 Stirrings," p. 50.

47. Kirițescu, pp. 63–64; V. Slăvescu, *Marile băncii commerciale din România* [Large Commercial Banks of Romania] (Bucharest, 1915), pp. 7, 42; Georges D. Cioriceanu, *La Roumanie économique, 1860–1915* (Paris, 1931), pp. 384–86.

48. Cioriceanu, pp. 384–86; Iurdanov, p. 44; Lampe, "Varieties of Unsuccessful Industrialization," pp. 78–80.

49. The consul specifically objected to the failure of the Srpska Kreditna Banka to accept an invitation for assistance from the Paraćin glass factory, leaving it to turn instead to the native Beogradska Trgovačka Banka. Lampe, "Financial Structure of Serbia," pp. 336–45.

50. On the Viennese Great Banks, see Rudolph, pp. 129–55, also Eduard März, *Österreichische Industrie und Bankpolitik in der Zeit Franz Josephs I* (Vienna, 1968), and Bernard Michel, *Banques et bancaires en Autriche au debut du 20ᵉ siècle* (Paris, 1976).

51. The classic statement of the Lenin-Hobson thesis is of course V.I. Lenin, *Imperialism: The Highest Stage of Capitalism* (Moscow, 1947). The case against the overall profitability of European penetration is most effectively marshalled in D.K. Fieldhouse, *Economics and Empire, 1830–1914* (Ithaca, N.Y.: Cornell Univ. Press, 1974).

52. On Serbia, see Lampe, "Financial Structure of Serbia," pp. 362–66. On Bulgaria, see Staatsarchiv (Vienna), *Administrative Registratur*, 64F23, Bulgarien 14, Reports of May 29 and June 21, 1911 and October 20, 1914.

53. Lampe, "Financial Structure of Serbia," pp. 346–57 and "Finance and Pre-1914 Industrial Stirrings," p. 48. Also Khristo Kosev, ed., *Bulgarsko-Germanskite otnoshenie i vruzki* [Bulgarian-German Relations and Ties]

(Sofia, 1969), pp. 161–64. On the reluctant role of the Deutsche Bank in pursuing the construction of the Berlin-Baghdad railway east from Istanbul, see Ulrich Trumpener, *Germany and the Ottoman Empire, 1914–1918* (Princeton, N.J.: Princeton Univ. Press, 1968), pp. 6–12.

54. Maurice Pearton, *Oil and the Romanian State, 1895–1948* (London: Oxford Univ. Press, 1971), pp. 7–121, provides a thorough description of the financial and especially the technical aspects of pre-1914 European and American investment in Romanian oil extraction, albeit one based almost exclusively on Western sources.

55. G.D. Creangă, *Raport asupra activității băncii generale române* [Report on the Activities of Romanian Commercial Banks] (Bucharest, 1919), pp. 1–4; *Anuarul statistic al României, 1909* (Bucharest, 1910), pp. 824–25.

56. Pearton, pp. 9, 33–55.

57. See Friedrich List, *The National System of Political Economy* (London: Longmans, 1928), pp. 247–52. On the German transition to protective tariffs, see Ivo N. Lambi, *Free Trade and Protection in Germany, 1868–1879* (Wiesbaden, 1963). A summary of the doubtful position of the infant industry argument in present Western economic theory may be found in Charles P. Kindleberger, *International Economics* (Homewood, Ill.: Richard D. Irwin, 1973), pp. 107–21, 168–69. Peter B. Kenen, ed., *International Trade and Finance* (Cambridge: Cambridge Univ. Press, 1975), Part I: Trade, Protection and Domestic Production, pp. 3–174, provides a longer account for readers familiar with economic literature.

58. *Stenografske dnevnitsi na Narodno Subranie* [Daily Minutes of the National Assembly], XIII, IIRS, no. V3, Oct. 27, 1904, pp. 77–91. On the general tariff of 1897, with a basic rate of 14 percent ad valorem with several higher specific rates, see Natan et al., pp. 394–95, and *Spisanie na bulgarskoto ikonomichesko druzhestvo*, VIII, 10 (1904), pp. 697–721. On the Serbian tariff of 1904–06, see Djordjević, pp. 106–292, and Horst M. Lorscheider, "The Commercial Treaty between Germany and Serbia of 1904," *Central European History*, IX, 2 (June, 1976), pp. 129–45.

59. Useful summaries of the Romanian tariffs from 1876 to 1914 may be found in Al. Hallunga, *Curs de economie și legislație industrială* [The Course of the Economy and Industrial Legislation] (Bucharest, n.d.), pp. 11–22, and St. Emilian, *L'industrie en Roumanie* (Bucharest, 1919), pp. 6–17. Overwhelming detail on trade and tariff policy is given in C.I. Băicoianu, *Istoria politicei noastre vamale și comerciale* [History of our Tariff and Commercial Policies], I and II (Bucharest, 1904).

Some representative estimates for ad valorem rates on individual products, calculated from "specific rates" or fixed money duties for a fixed quantity of the individual good, are as follows:

	1876–86	1886-91	1891
Wheat flour	exempt	30%	40%
Soap	18.5%	30%	33%
Tanned hides	5.7%	35%	19–23%
Footwear	5.3%	126%	–
Woolen fabric	8.6%	19%	66%

	1876–86	1886-91	1891
Ordinary paper	10.0%	30%	27%
Constr. lumber	exempt	–	6%
Furniture	3.0%	20%	22%

These calculations are based on C.I. Băicoianu, *Câteva cuvinte asupra politicei noastre vamale comerciale* [Some Words concerning Our Tariff and Commercial Policy] (Bucharest, 1901), pp. 13–14, and his *Istoria politicei noastre vamale şi comerciale*, I, Part 2, Annexes 5, 17, and 25.

60. *Anuarul statistic al României, 1915–16*, p. 256; Lampe, "Financial Structure of Serbia," pp. 44, 186; *Doklad do Ferdinand I ot Ministarski Savet, 1887–1912* (Sofia, 1912), p. 145.

61. H. Liepmann, *Tariff Levels and the Economic Unity of Europe* (New York: Macmillan Co., 1938), pp. 97–99, 159–71.

62. G. Ioaniţui and N. Costache, *Industria hârtiei în România* [The Paper Industry in Romania] (Bucharest, 1929), pp. 6, 67, 132; G. Ioaniţui and C. Calmuschi, *Industria zahărului în România* [The Sugar Industry in Romania] (Bucharest, 1936), pp. 34–35; C. Casassovici, *Trustul zahărului* [The Sugar Trust] (Bucharest, 1915), pp. 47, 159.

63. K. und K. Österreichische Handelsmuseum, *Rumänien: Landes- und wirtschaftsstatistischen Übersichten* (Vienna, 1917), pp. 11–21; Liepmann, pp. 159–71.

64. *Anuarul statistic al României, 1915–1916*, pp. 232, 238; *Spisanie na bulgarskoto ikonomichesko druzhestvo*, XVII, nos. 7–8 (1915), p. 431; Industrijska Komora Kr. Srbije, *Izveštaj* [Report] (Belgrade, 1911), Table 1; J. Tsouderos, *La relèvement économique de la Grèce*, (Paris/Nancy, 1919), p. 175. On special limitations of the Greek commercial code, borrowed from the Byzantine Empire with restrictions even on simple partnerships, see A.A. Pepelasis, "The Legal System and the Economic Development of Greece," *Journal of Economic History*, XIX (June, 1959), pp. 173–98.

65. P. Cîncia, *Viaţa politică din România în primul deceniu al indepedenţei de stat* [The Political Life of Romania in the First Decade of the State's Independence] (Bucharest, 1974), pp. 21, 247–51.

66. Four large foreign joint-stock sugar companies were founded from 1896 to 1900, the two largest of Belgian and Greek origin. The Banca Marmorosch-Blank reopened a refinery, closed since 1883, specifically because of the privileges' renewal. Cassassovici, pp. 47–51; Banca Marmorosch-Blank, p. 29. For a summary of the arguments for and against the effectiveness of the Hungarian program of industrial subsidies, with some additional evidence on the negative side, see Scott M. Eddie, "The Terms and Patterns of Hungarian Foreign Trade, 1882–1913," *Journal of Economic History*, XXXVII, 2 (June, 1977), pp. 338–340, 352–53.

67. N.I. Pianu, *Industria mare, 1866–1906* [Large Industry, 1866–1906] (Bucharest, 1906), pp. 110–12, 134–45; N.P. Arcadian, *Industrializarea României* (Bucharest, 1936), pp. 125–26; *Spisanie na bulgarskoto ikonomichesko druzhestvo*, X, 6 (1906), p. 437; Lampe, "Financial Structure of Serbia," pp. 324–29. Of the 76 Romanian firms that were newly privileged between 1904 and 1910 (none in sugar or paper and most presumably newly

founded enterprises), 32 reported no dividends and 23 less than the 8 percent net profit that was the minimum available in commerce and banking. C.
Hălăceanu, *Observaţiuni asupra proiectului de lege industrială* [Observa-
tions concerning the Industrial Law Project] (Bucharest, 1912), pp. 17–18.

68. Between 1887 and 1894, the number and proportion of privileged industrial enterprises in the Sofia area more than doubled to 54 of 266 firms,
more than in the Gabrovo, Ruse or Plovdiv areas. *Anketa prez 1909*, V, pp.
64–71; Wilhelmy, *Hochbulgariens*, II, pp. 181–88; Iurdanov, pp. 43–54;
Iubileena kniga na grad Sofiia, pp. 241–48.

69. The views of Romanian Liberals are summarized in Olga Constantinescu, *Critica teoriei "România-ţara eminamente agricolă"* [Critique of
the Theory "Romania—A Primarily Agricultural Country"] (Bucharest,
1973), pp. 66–78. For Bulgarian economists and political figures, see respectively, Zhak Natan et al., *Istoriia na ikonomicheski misul v Bulgariia* [A History of Economic Thought in Bulgaria], II (Sofia, 1973), pp. 61–71, 87–90,
156–71, and *Stenografske dnevnitsi na Narodno Subranie*, XIII, IIRS, no.
LXV3, Jan. 27, 1905, pp. 2460–67; XIV, IRS, no. XLIX3, Jan. 10, 1909, pp.
2154–68 and Jan. 27, 1909, pp. 3006–9, no. LXXIII3, Feb. 8, 1910, pp.
3436–53.

70. Leontieş, *Die Industrialisierung Rumäniens*, p. 95, and N.N. Constan-
tinescu, *Din istoricul formării şi dezvoltărei clasei muncitoare in România*
[On the History of the Formation and Development of the Working Class in
Romania] (Bucharest, 1959), p. 275. On artisans and the Bulgarian socialist
movement before 1914, see Joseph Rothschild, *The Communist Party of
Bulgaria* (New York: Columbia Univ. Press, 1959), pp. 26–27, 306–309, and
Iubileena kniga na grad Sofiia, pp. 229–31. On Serbia, see M. Vukmanović,
Radnička klasa Srbije u drugoj polovini XIX veka [The Working Class of
Serbia in the Second Half of the 19th Century] (Belgrade, 1972), pp. 61–66,
224–99, and S. Andrejević, *Ekonomski razvoj Niša od 1830 do 1946 g.* [The
Economic Development of Niš from 1830 to 1946] (Niš, 1970), pp. 37–68.

71. European investors, with Belgian firms in the majority, owned 94 percent of the stock in these Romanian refineries. Lampe, "Varieties of Unsuccessful Industrialization," pp. 80, 84. On the typically defensive and unin-
novative role of such horizontal cartels at this time, see Eric Maschke, "An
Outline of the History of German Cartels from 1875 to 1914," in François
Crouzet, W.H. Chaloner, and W.M. Stern, eds., *Essays in European Economic History, 1789–1914* (New York: St. Martin's Press, 1969), pp. 226–58,
and Rudolph, pp. 165–72.

72. Lampe, "Financial Structure of Serbia," pp. 216–17.

73. On the 1895 law, see Pearton, pp. 18–20. Note the stiffer terms, forbidding clear foreign control, in the Serbian mining law of 1900 that opened
the way to more modest European investment in the Bor copper mine.
Danica Milić, *Strani kapital u rudarstvu Srbije do 1918 g.* [Foreign Capital
in Serbian Mining Until 1918] (Belgrade, 1971), pp. 242–50, 289–95.

74. Palairet, pp. 485–87; Lampe, "Financial Structure of Serbia," p. 209;
Natan et al., pp. 385–86; B.R. Mitchell, *European Historical Statistics,
1750–1970* (New York: Columbia Univ. Press, 1975), pp. 285–86.

75. Royaume de Belgique, *Receuil Consulaire*, 155 (1912), p. 261; Popoff,
p. 338; Mitchell, pp. 362, 364, 409–11.

76. Gerschenkron, *Economic Backwardness*, pp. 119–51. A shortage of rolling stock plagued the Romanian economy as much as that of Serbia, the Balkan country with the smallest railway network, during the last prewar decade. Pearton, pp. 45–46, and Lampe, "Financial Structure of Serbia," pp. 206–11, 212.

77. Pianu, pp. 80–99; K und K. Handelsmuseum, *Rumänien*, pp. 14–18, 155–60, 171–72. A similar judgment on the industrial importance of the Hungarian railway network may be found in Eddie, pp. 353–54. On Bulgaria, see *Doklad do Ferdinand I*, p. 711; Iurdanov, pp. 35–36; Popoff, p. 346. On Serbia, see Andrejević, pp. 18–32; M. St. Djuričić, *Istorija Jugoslovenskog rečnog parabrodarstva do 1926* [A History of the Yugoslav River Steamship Co. to 1926] (Belgrade, 1926), pp. 42–54. The largest enterprise of any kind in Serbia, with over 2,000 employees by 1900, was the state arsenal at Kragujevac. Although producing only bullets, it trained more workers in metallurgy than the railway and ship repair facilities combined. Few were absorbed by the private metalworks in Belgrade, which grew in numbers but not size during the last prewar decade. See Ž. Spasić, *Kragujevačka vojna fabrika, 1853–1953* [The Kragujevac Military Factory] (Belgrade, 1973).

78. Lampe, "Varieties of Unsuccessful Industrialization," pp. 79–83.

79. See Ion Cojocaru, *Şcolile technice-profesionale şi de specialitate din statul român, 1864–1918* [Technical-Professional and Specialized Schools of the Romanian State, 1864–1918] (Bucharest, 1971), pp. 187–99, and the unpublished paper by John H. Jensen and Gerhard Rosegger, "Two Phases of River-Rail Competition in the Lower Danube Basin: 1856–1865 and 1896–1928."

80. By 1910, some 10.3 percent of the Bulgarian population were enrolled in primary schools, versus 9.3 percent for Greece, 8.4 percent for Romania, and just 5 percent for Serbia. The Bulgarian advantage was more striking for secondary schools, with 1.6 percent in attendance versus less than .4 percent for the other three Balkan states. Hence the superior literacy of Bulgarian army recruits for the Balkan War of 1912, 75 percent versus 70 percent for Greece, 59 percent for Romania, and 50 percent for Serbia. But for university and technical education, Romania led even Bulgaria. Its 5,425 university students and 6,127 in a variety of economic and technical schools in 1911 compared to 2,380 and 2,092 for Bulgaria, over half again as many on a per capita basis. Greece had 3,300 university students by 1910, but almost no technical schools. Serbia, still more reliant on its military academy than on public schools for technical training, trailed further behind. Mitchell, pp. 21–22, 753–75; *Statisticheski godishnik na Bulgarskoto Tsarstvo, 1912*, pp. 417–21, 438; *Anuarul statistic al României, 1915–16*, pp. 282–93; S. Ćunković, *Prosveta, obrazovanje i vaspitanje u Srbiji* [Higher, Secondary and Primary Education in Serbia] (Belgrade, 1971), pp. 16–32. Lampe, "Varieties of Unsuccessful Industrialization," p. 70; Douglas Dakin, *The Unification of Greece, 1770–1923* (London: Ernest Benn, 1972), p. 315. For details on the Bulgarian and Romanian educational systems, see T. Girginov, *Istoriia razvoi na suvremena Bulgariia* [A History of Contemporary Bulgaria] (Sofia, 1934), pp. 89–93. On Romania, see C. Nicolae, *Organizarea şi conţinutul învăţămîntului profesional şi tehnic in România* [Organization and Content of Professional and Technical Education in Romania] (Bucharest, 1973), pp.

16–29. On Greece, see G.M. Wilcox, *Education in Modern Greece* (Tiffin, 1933) and Th. Haralambidis, *Die Schulpolitik Griechenlands 1821–1935* (Berlin, 1935).

9. Economic Development in the Imperial Borderlands to 1914

1. The interwar statistical studies of national income in Austria-Hungary for the last prewar decade and the pro-Habsburg view they espouse are summarized in Frederick Hertz, *The Economic Problem of the Danubian States* (New York: Howard Fertig, 1970 ed.) and more recently appraised in Herbert Matis, *Österreichs Wirtschaft, 1848–1913* (Berlin, 1972), pp. 383–447. For examples of the critical attitude of Yugoslav and Romanian economic historians toward the last Habsburg decades, see Igor Karaman, *Privreda i društvo Hrvatske u 19om stoljeću* [Economy and Society of Croatia in the 19th Century] (Zagreb, 1972), pp. 302–48, and N.N. Constantinescu, *Din istoricul formării și dezvoltarea clasei muncitoara din Romînia* [On the History of the Formation and Development of the Working Class in Romania] (Bucharest, 1959), pp. 431–538.

2. For a brief survey of Albanian trade and agriculture, drawn from the minimal data available before the First World War, see K. und K. Österreichische Handelsmuseum, *Albanien, Wirtschaftliche Verhältnisse, 1914* (Vienna, 1915), pp. 6–21. An introduction to the more extensive material on the growing rural poverty, the limits on commercial development, and emigration from pre-1914 Montenegro may be found in Zharko Bulajić, *Agrarni odnosi u Crnoj Gori, 1878–1912* [Agrarian Relations in Montenegro, 1878–1912] (Titograd, 1959).

3. A.P. Vakolopoulos, *A History of Thessaloniki* (Thessaloniki, 1963), p. 114; M. Dimitrijević, *Privreda i trgovina u novoj Srbiji* [Economy and Trade in New Serbia] (Belgrade, 1913); B. Arsitch, *La vie économique de la Serbie du Sud au XIX siècle* (Paris, 1936), pp. 80–85.

4. Great Britain, Diplomatic and Consular Reports, *Annual Series*, 1898, no. 2111; 1900, no. 2468; 1909, no. 2730; 1903, no. 3100; 1907, no. 3867; 1911, nos. 4579 and 4797; 1913, no. 5234.

5. M. Erić, *Agrarna reforma u Jugoslaviji, 1918–1941* [The Agrarian Reform in Yugoslavia, 1918–1941] (Sarajevo, 1958), pp. 102–108.

6. Greek and Jewish merchants came to own a number, although not a majority, of *chiflik* estates in the area around Thessaloniki. A summary of the limited statistical data may be found in the comprehensive work of the Bulgarian scholar Khristo Khristov, *Agrarnite otnoshenie v Makedoniia prez XIX i v nachaloto na XX vek* [Agrarian Relations in Macedonia in the 19th and Early 20th Centuries] (Sofia, 1964), pp. 116–22.

7. Ibid., pp. 28–37, 90–100, 114–17, 122–38.

8. On increased Ottoman tax collections by the 1870s, see Traian Stoianovich, "Balkan Peasants and Landlords and the Ottoman State," paper given at the Conference on Balkan and Southeastern European Cities and the Industrial Revolution, Hamburg, March 22–26, 1976. The origins and

evolution of the *kmet* system are detailed in Jozo Tomasevich, *Peasants, Politics and Economic Development in Yugoslavia* (Palo Alto, Calif.: Stanford Univ. Press, 1955), pp. 91–107.

9. The transition to Austro-Hungarian occupation from 1878 is described in Peter Sugar, *The Industrialization of Bosnia-Hercegovina, 1878–1918* (Seattle: Univ. of Washington Press, 1964), pp. 6–39. Sugar, p. 13, notes that the 1907 reform in assessing harvest taxes was originally proposed by the last Ottoman pasha of the province. Also see Geoffrey Drage, *Austria-Hungary* (London, 1909), pp. 604–16, and H. Kapidžić, "Agrarno pitanje u Bosni i Hercegovini, 1878–1918" [The Agrarian Question in Bosnia and Hercegovina, 1878–1918], in Vasa Čubrilović, ed., *Jugoslovenski narodi pred prvi svetski rat* [The Yugoslav Peoples before the First World War] (Belgrade, 1967), pp. 93–117.

10. See the authoritative work by the head of the Austro-Hungarian statistical service in Sarajevo, Ferdinand Schmid, *Bosnien und die Herzegovenien* (Leipzig, 1914), pp. 312–15.

11. Ibid., pp. 549–52; N. Jarak, *Poljoprivredna politika u Bosni i Hercegovini i zemljoradničke zadruge* [Agricultural Policy in Bosnia-Hercegovina and Agricultural Cooperatives] (Sarajevo, 1956), pp. 23–27.

12. Schmid, pp. 412–14, records an average of 246 kilograms per capita, versus 378 for Serbia, 415 for Croatia/Slavonia, 596 for Bulgaria, 613 for Hungary proper and 741 for Romania. On the lack of rational economic incentives for the Bosniak landowners, their traditional and anticommercial mentality aside, to expand and improve their crop cultivation, see Ferdo Hauptmann, "Bosansko-hercegovački aga u procjepu izmedju privredne aktivnosti i rentierstva na početku XX stoleća" [Bosnia-Hercegovina's Agas Squeezed between Economic Initiative and Fixed Incomes at the Start of the 20th Century], *Godišnjak Bosne i Hercegovine*, XVII (Sarajevo, 1969), pp. 23–40.

13. Jarak, p. 49.

14. Schmid, pp. 396–404. See Chapter 6 on comparable efforts in Serbia. Of the 17 extension stations planned there in 1897, only 8 were operating by 1912.

15. These few thousand colonists were all that remained of up to 20,000 that first came during the 1880s. Ibid., pp. 351–59; Jarak, pp. 41, 214, and Ferdo Hauptmann, "Regulisanje zemlišnog posjeda u Bosni i Hercegovini i počeci naseljavanja stranih seljaka" [Regulation of Landholding in Bosnia-Hercegovina and the Initial Settlement of Foreign Peasants], *Godišnjak Bosne i Hercegovine*, XVI (Sarajevo, 1967), pp. 151–71.

16. H. Kapidžić, "Ekonomska emigracija iz Bosne i Hercegovine u SAD početkom XX vijeka" [Economic Emigration from Bosnia-Hercegovina to the U.S.A. at the Start of the 20th Century], *Glasnik ADA Bosne i Hercegovina*, VII (Sarajevo, 1967), pp. 191–220. On Princip's peasant origins and early life, see Vladimir Dedijer, *The Road to Sarajevo* (New York: Simon & Schuster, 1966), pp. 27–41, 175–217.

17. For evidence of the Hungarian Agricultural Revolution, see L. Katus, "Economic Growth in Hungary during the Age of Dualism, A Quantitative Analysis," in E. Pamlényi, ed., *Social-Economic Researches on the History*

of East Central Europe (Budapest, 1970), pp. 35–87, and Scott M. Eddie, "Agricultural Production and Output per Worker in Hungary, 1870–1913," *Journal of Economic History*, XXVIII, 2 (June, 1968), pp. 197–222.

18. Şt. Pascu, et al., *Die Agrarfrage in der österreichische-ungarische Monarchie* (Bucharest, 1965), p. 9; Erić, pp. 40, 51; L. Vajda, "Despre situaţia economicaă ,si social-politică în Transilvania în primele anii de sec. XX-lea" [Concerning the Economic and Sociopolitical Situation in Transylvania in the Early 20th Century], *Studii şi materiale de istorie moderne*, I (Bucharest, 1957), pp. 309–10.

19. Some 75 percent, versus 50–60 percent for Croatia/Slavonia, Transylvania, and the Vojvodina. Pascu et al., pp. 23–26; A. Csetii and I. Kovacs, "Repartizarea maşinilor agricole în Transilvania" [Distribution of Agricultural Machinery in Transylvania], *A M Napocensis*, IV (Cluj, 1967), p. 268.

20. Wheat accounted for 29 percent and corn just 21 percent of the 1911–13 crop acreage for Hungary proper. Katus, Table 16, p. 95.

21. Rudolph Signjar, *Statistički atlas Kr. Hrvatske i Slavonije, 1875–1915* [Statistical Atlas for Croatia/Slavonia, 1875–1915] (Zagreb, 1915), pp. 37, 48.

22. Ibid., pp. 16, 25; Katus, Tables 10, 11, and 13, pp. 92–93.

23. I. Kovacs, *Desfiinţarea relaţiilor feudale în Transilvania* [The Dissolution of Feudal Relations in Transylvania] (Cluj, 1973), pp. 162–68; Manuela Dobos, "The Croatian Peasant Uprising of 1883" (Ph.D. dissertation: Columbia Univ., 1974), pp. 51–62; Pascu et al., p. 19.

24. Rough calculations of average income for day laborers and *argaţii* are found in A. Egyed, "Geneza şi situaţia proletariatului agricol din Transilvania" [Origin and Situation of the Agrarian Proletariat in Transylvania], *Anuarul Institutului de Istorie din Cluj*, X (Cluj, 1967), pp. 202–13. A nonstatistical review of the conditions of hired agricultural labor in the Hungarian half of the monarchy is contained in Pascu et al., pp. 34–37.

25. Egyed, p. 200; Erić, p. 52; N. Gaćeša, *Agrarna reforma i kolonizacija u Sremu, 1918–1941* [Agrarian Reforms and Colonization in the Srem, 1918–1941] (Novi Sad, 1975), pp. 22–24. See Chapter 6 above on the landless number in the independent Balkan states.

26. Kovacs, pp. 161–80.

27. A. Egyed, "Emigrarea ţărănimii din Transilvania la începutul de sec. XX-lea" [The Emigration of Peasants from Transylvania at the Start of the 20th Century], *A M Napocensis*, VII (Cluj, 1970), pp. 369–73.

28. Toussaint Hočevar, *The Structure of the Slovenian Economy, 1848–1963* (New York: Studia Slovenica, 1965), pp. 80–92.

29. Dobos, pp. 62–67, 210–20; Milan Meyer, *Die Landwirtschaft der Königreichen Kroatien und Slavonien* (Leipzig, 1908), pp. 25–29; I. Kovačević, *Ekonomski položaj radničke klase u Hrvatskoj i Slavoniji, 1867–1914* [The Economic Position of the Working Class in Croatia and Slavonia, 1867–1914] (Zagreb, 1972), pp. 26–28, 31–32. The growth of peasant debt from the 1848 obligation to compensate noble estates for their formally private, or urbarial, land long occupied by the peasantry was abetted by rising state taxes and participation in a money economy even before the bulk of railway construction. See B. Stojsavljević, *Povijest sela Hrvatske, Slavonije i Dalmacije, 1848–1918* [History of the Village in Croatia, Slavonia

and Dalmatia, 1848–1918] (Zagreb, 1973), pp. 80–100, 200–11, and Dobos, p. 181. By the time most of the railway network had been completed in the 1890s, a majority of peasant smallholdings in western and southern Croatia were encumbered with debts that exceeded the value of the property. The loss of peasant vineyards under the terms of the 1848 emancipation had long ago deprived the Zagorje region of its major source of money income.

30. Meyer, pp. 61–69.

31. On the Transylvanian construction see L. Vajda, "Primele căi ferate din Transilvania" [The First Railroads in Transylvania], *A M Napocensis*, VII (Cluj, 1971), pp. 296–97. On the Rothschilds' struggle with the Périeres over the Südbahn, see Rondo Cameron, *France and the Economic Development of Europe, 1800–1914* (Princeton, N.J.: Princeton Univ. Press, 1961), pp. 213–47.

32. Karaman, pp. 144–46; Dobos, pp. 66–76.

33. Drage, pp. 394–400; Karaman, pp. 193–97. On Serbian railway freight rates, see Michael R. Palairet, "The Influence of Commerce on the Changing Structure of Serbia's Peasant Economy, 1860–1912" (Ph.D. dissertation, Edinburgh Univ., 1976), pp. 155–60.

34. That rivalry also served to deny the rest of the Dalmatian coast a rail link from Split to Zagreb, favored by the Hungarians. The Austrian side used their voice in the administration of Bosnia-Hercegovina, through which the line would have to pass to frustrate it. Vienna wanted instead a Sarajevo-Split-Trieste line, which Budapest in turn rejected. On the growth of a trade and industry in Rijeka and down the Dalmatian coast, see Karaman, pp. 148–51, 268–87. The gist of Croatian dissatisfactions with Habsburg economic policy may be gathered from R. Lovrenčić, "Ekonomska problematica u Supilovu 'Novom listu,' 1906–1914" [Economic Problems in Supilo's *Novi list*, 1906–1914], *Radovi Instituta hrvatske povijesti*, 6 (Zagreb, 1974), pp. 129–272.

35. Dobos, pp. 154–62; Drage, pp. 422–73; Karaman, pp. 183–86. On the size of the Serbian and other Balkan state revenues and the diminishing share contributed by peasant land taxes, see Chapter 6.

36. Signjar, pp. 57–61; Dobos, p. 156. On Serbian literacy rates, see Vl. Milenković, *Ekonomska istorija Beograda* (Belgrade, 1932), p. 76.

37. Sugar, pp. 71–86, 231–39; Schmid, pp. 582–91; Dž. Juzbašić, "Problemi austrougarske saobraćajne politike u Bosni i Hercegovini" [Problems of Austro-Hungarian Transport Policy in Bosnia-Hercegovina], *Godišnjak Društva istoričara Bosne i Hercegovine*, XIX (Sarajevo, 1973), pp. 96–138.

38. Krste Bitoski, ed., *Istorija na železnicite vo Makedonija, 1873–1973* [History of Railroads in Macedonia, 1873–1973] (Skopje, 1973), pp. 20–56.

39. Ibid., pp. 69–80.

40. See Richard L. Rudolph, *Banking and Industry in Austria-Hungary, 1867–1914* (Cambridge: Cambridge Univ. Press, 1976), pp. 96–121; Eduard März, *Österreichische Industrie-und Bank Politik in der Zeit Franz Josephs I* (Vienna, 1968), pp. 289–362; Bernard Michel, *Banques et banquiers en Autriche au debut de XXme siècle* (Paris, 1975), pp. 165–237.

41. On the Zagreb banks, see T. Timet, "Razvitak hipotekarnih i komunalnih zajmova . . . kod novčanih zavoda u Hrvatskoj i Slavoniji" [The

Development of Communal and Mortgage Loans . . . among the Banks of Croatia and Slavonia]. *Prilozi za ekonomsku povijest Hrvatske* [Contributions to the Economic History of Croatia] (Zagreb, 1967), pp. 143–262. On Slavonian banks, see Karaman, pp. 199–206. On the limited mortgage loans of Serbian banks amounting to one tenth of the total for Croatia/Slavonia, see Chapter 7.

42. John R. Lampe, "Serbia, 1878–1912," in Rondo Cameron, ed., *Banking and Economic Development: Some Lessons of History* (New York: Oxford Univ. Press, 1972), p. 161.

43. See J. Carroll Moody and Gilbert C. Fite, *The Credit Union Movement* (Lincoln: Univ. of Nebraska Press, 1970), pp. 1–25.

44. On education, see V. Schmidt, *Zgodvina šolstva in pedagogike na Slovenskem* [History of Educational Institutions and Pedagogy in Slovenia] (Ljubljana, 1966). The preceding account is drawn from the invaluable survey by Toussaint Hočevar, *The Structure of the Slovenian Economy, 1848– 1963* (New York: Studia Slovenica, 1965), pp. 52–74. More detailed study of Slovenian banks and cooperatives remains to be done.

45. Hočevar, pp. 77–78. Trieste's banking relations with Italy during the nineteenth century had been based on currency exchange, a practice doomed to decline with the Habsburg adoption of a stable gold standard by 1892, and on an intermediary role in Austro-Hungarian trade with Italy during the nineteenth century, services now assumed by Viennese and Italian banks. Michel, pp. 73–76, 241–42.

46. Michel, pp. 233–36, 298; Sugar, pp. 90–92, 108.

47. Jarak, pp. 38–40; Schmid, p. 627.

48. Schmid, pp. 363–67; Jarak, p. 225. Also see N. Ilijić, "Stav austrijske uprave prema zemljoradničkim zadrugama u Bosni i Hercegovini" [The Attitude of the Austrian Administration toward Agricultural Cooperatives in Bosnia-Hercegovina], in *Jugoslovenski narodi*, pp. 261–87.

49. Dimitrijević, pp. 123, 138; Michel, pp. 264–65.

50. Krste Bitoski, "Žakvarstvoto vo Makedonija vo ftorata polovina na XIX vek" [Usury in Macedonia in the Second Half of the 19th Century], *Glasnik*, XIV, 2–3 (Skopje, 1970), pp. 127; Arsitch, pp. 147–48.

51. L. Sokolov, *Industrijata na N R Makedonija* [Industry in the People's Republic of Macedonia] (Skopje, 1961), pp. 13–23.

52. Ferdo Hauptmann, "Bosanske financije i Kalleyeva industrijska politika" [Bosnian Finances and Kallay's Industrial Policy], *Glasnik arhiva Bosne i Hercegovine*, XII (Sarajevo, 1972), pp. 61–69; Sugar, pp. 49–64, 103–07, 151–59. The *Industrialization* in Sugar's title refers to "industrialization" only as desired by Kallay, rather than the rapid, sustained growth of industrial production, capital, and labor that development economists would regard as the agreed definition. The latter obviously did not occur in pre-1914 Bosnia-Hercegovina.

53. Sugar, pp. 130–41; Hauptmann, "Bosanske financije," pp. 70–76.

54. Schmid, pp. 538–43, 559–65; Jarak, pp. 18–20. On the inhibiting effect of the general Austrian tax on joint-stock companies, see Rudolph, pp. 159– 60.

55. This is an opportunity on which Tsarist Russian industry drew heavily

during the last prewar decades. Alexander Gerschenkron has tried, without great success, as noted in Chapter 8, to extend his Russian argument to Bulgaria and the opportunity it allegedly missed to expand heavy industry as a result of railway construction.

56. Hočevar, pp. 24–34, 44–47. Details on the practice of Slovenian coal mining may be found in J. Šorn, "Premogovniki in njihovi rudarji v obdobju 1848–1918" [Coal Miners and Their Mines in the Period 1848–1918], *Prispevki IZDG*, 8–9 (Ljubljana, 1969), pp. 3–102. The Slovenian total of 1.1 million metric tons by 1913 was almost four times the 300,000 tons of coal mined by Bulgaria, the largest Balkan producer. *Statisticheski godishnik na Bulgarskoto Tsarstvo, 1912* [Statistical Yearbook of Bulgaria, 1912] (Sofia, 1915), p. 200. On Slovenian supplies for the railroads, see Ivan Mohorić, *Zgodivina zeleznic na Slovenskem* [History of the Railroads in Slovenia] (Ljubljana, 1968).

57. The Siemens-Martin process was needed to make use of scrap iron and therefore compensate for the growing depletion of iron ore deposits in Slovenia. On the complex origins of investment in Slovenian industry, see J. Šorn, "Nacionalno poreklo velikega kapitala v industriji, rudarstvo in bancništva na slovenskim ozemlju" [National Origins of Big Capital in Industry, Mining, and Banking in the Slovenian Lands], *Jugoslovenski istorijski časopis*, VIII, 4 (Belgrade, 1969), pp. 136–41.

58. English and Belgian investment in Transylvanian mining was apparently minor. L. Vajda, "Capitalul străin în minerit-metalurgie a Transilvaniei, 1867–1900" [Foreign Capital in the Mining-Metallurgy of Transylvania, 1867–1900], *A M Napocensis*, IX (Cluj, 1972), pp. 243–53; Vajda, "Despre situația economică," pp. 292–97, 307. On the general scope of Credit Anstalt investments at this time, see März, pp. 71–79, 150–64.

59. An increase in the Romanian tariff virtually eliminated coal imports from Transylvania after 1902. Pig iron imported from Dualist Hungary, including Transylvania, into Romania amounted to less than 20 percent of total Romanian import value for 1901–1905 and fell under 15 percent by 1906–1910. Vajda, "Despre situația economics," pp. 289–97.

60. Ibid., pp. 295–97, 305–307; A. Egyed, "Unele characteristice ale dezvoltărei industrie in Transilvania, 1880–1900" [Some Characteristics of Industrial Development in Transylvania, 1880–1900], *A M Napocensis*, V (Cluj, 1968), p. 263. The technical development of Transylvanian mining and metallurgy to 1914 is summarized in D. Turnock, "The Industrial Development of Romania . . . ," Carter, ed., *Historical Geography of the Balkans*, pp. 331–32, 358–61.

61. On the evolution of the pre-1914 Swedish timber industry, see A.J. Youngson, *Possibilities of Economic Progress* (Cambridge: Cambridge Univ. Press, 1959), pp. 149–83, and Eli F. Hecksher, *An Economic History of Sweden* (Cambridge, Mass.: Harvard Univ. Press, 1954), pp. 225–28.

62. Egyed, "Unele characteristice," pp. 259–63; Vajda, "Despre situația economica," pp. 301–303.

63. Vajda, p. 292; Egyed, "Unele characteristike," pp. 252–59.

64. Hočevar, pp. 34–39, Table 6–2, p. 116.

65. I. Kovačević, *Ekonomiski polažaj radničke klase u Hrvatskoj i*

Slavoniji, 1867–1914 [Economic Position of the Working Class in Croatia and Slavonia, 1867–1914] (Zagreb, 1972), pp. 40–42; Karaman, *Privreda i društvo Hrvatske*, pp. 208–29, 245–49, 314; idem, "Osnovna obileža razvitke industrijske privrede u sjevernoj Hrvatskoj do provog svetskog rata" [General Outline of the Development of the Industrial Economy in Northern Croatia to the First World War], *Acta historica-oeconomica iugoslaviae*, I (Zagreb, 1974), pp. 39–58.

66. The idea of modernizing enclaves is introduced to the context of Habsburg economic history in the provocative survey of recent scholarship on Austro-Hungarian industrial growth by William Ashworth, "Typologies and Evidence: Has Nineteenth-Century Europe a Guide to Economic Growth?" *Economic History Review*, 2d ser., VII, 1 (March, 1977), pp. 153–57.

10. The Disruption of Prewar Patterns: Agriculture and Aggregate Growth

1. See for instance L.S. Stavrianos, *The Balkans since 1453* (New York: Holt, Rinehart & Winston, 1958), pp. 593–94; Hugh Seton-Watson, *Eastern Europe between the Wars, 1918–1941* (Cambridge: Cambridge Univ. Press, 1945; Hamden, Conn.: Archon Books, 1962), pp. 79–80; Nicholas Spulber, *The State and Economic Development in Eastern Europe* (New York: Random House, 1966), p. 28. On the importance of losing the Habsburg market, the classic work is Frederick Hertz, *The Economic Problem of the Danubian States* (New York: Howard Fertig, 1970 ed.). A recent restatement from the Hungarian Marxist viewpoint may be found in Ivan T. Berend and Gyorgy Ranki, *Economic Development in East-Central Europe in the 19th and 20th Centuries* (New York: Columbia Univ. Press, 1974), pp. 186–89.

2. League of Nations, *Agricultural Production in Continental Europe During the 1914–1918 War and the Recovery Period* (Geneva, 1943), pp. 11–15.

3. The most careful estimates of civilian and military losses both during the Balkan Wars and the First World War are summarized in the useful Soviet study by B. Urlanis, *Wars and Population* (Moscow, 1971), pp. 46, 63, 186, 209–68. The combined estimate for Serbia and Montenegro of 728,000, although less than the million dead cited in Yugoslav representations to the Paris Peace Conference, still leaves the smallest of the four prewar Balkan states with the heaviest losses, even in absolute numbers. Romania lost 680,000, Bulgaria 188,000, and Greece 176,000, according to Urlanis. Their death rates per thousand of 89, 40, and 36 were comparable to the high French and German rates (46 and 40), if well under the 148 deaths recorded by Serbia and Montenegro. Also see Marvin R. Jackson, "Comparing the Balkan Demographic Experience," *Faculty Working Papers in Economics*, 79–86 (Tempe, Ariz.: College of Business Administration, Arizona State Univ., 1979), Table B-3.

4. Greek rates of demographic change during the 1920s are subject to the uncertainty of a 1920 census that left perhaps 10 percent of the population

uncounted. Migration data is generally more reliable, but estimates of the influx from Asia Minor for 1921–39 range from 965,000 to 1,215,000. Perhaps 400,000 Turks left over the same period. More certainly, Greek emigration to the U.S., so large before the war, as noted in Table 6.15 above, showed a small net outflow for 1919–23 and then did not exceed a few thousand once the new U.S. law restricting immigration was passed. See Imre Ferenczi, *International Migrations*, vol. I (New York: National Bureau of Economic Research, 1929), pp. 388–93, 472–75.

5. Bulgaria's net reproduction rate appears to have fallen from 1900 to 1910. It rose slightly in 1920 and then fell continuously to 1956. See A.I. Totev, "Characteristic Demographic Features of Bulgaria," in Thomas Butler, ed., *Bulgaria Past and Present* (Columbus, Ohio: AAASS, 1976), p. 136.

6. *Statistikë epetëris tës Ellados* [Statistical Yearbook of Greece], *1935* (Athens, 1936), pp. 48–49.

7. Ivo Vinski, "Nacionalni dohodak i fiskni fondovi na području Jugoslavije 1909–1959" [National Income and Fixed Capital on Yugoslav Territory 1909–1959], *Ekonomski pregled*, X, 11–12 (Zagreb, 1959), 832–62; Ivo Vinski, "National Income, Product and Fixed Assets in the Territory of Yugoslavia 1909–1959," in International Association for Research in Income and Wealth, *Income and Wealth*, Series IX (London: Bowes & Bowes, 1961), pp. 206–52; St. Stajić, "Realni nacionalni dohodak Jugoslavije u periodima 1926–1939 i 1947–1956" [Real National Income of Yugoslavia in the Periods 1926–1939 and 1947–1956], *Ekonomski problemi-Zbornik radova* (Belgrade, 1957); St. Stajić, *Nacionalni dohodak Jugoslavije 1923–1939 u stalnim i tekućim cenama* [National Income of Yugoslavia 1923–1939 in Constant and Current Prices] (Belgrade, 1959); As. Chakalov, *Natsionalniiat dokhod i razkhod na Bulgariia 1924–1945* [National Income and Outlay of Bulgaria 1924–1945] (Sofia, 1946); Ch. Evelpidi, "To ethnikon eisodëma" [National Income], in *Agrotiken oikonomiken*, III, 4 (Athens, 1937); *Enciclopedia României*, vol. IV (Bucharest, 1943), 941–66. A review and comparison of these and other interwar estimates is contained in Marvin R. Jackson, "National Product and Income in Southeastern Europe before the Second World War," *ACES Bulletin*, 4 (Fall-Winter, 1982) in press.

8. World and European growth of foodstuffs, showing 1929 indices of 116 and 111, respectively, are calculated from League of Nations, *Memorandum on Production and Trade, 1913 and 1923–27* (Geneva, 1929), p. 78, and *World Production and Prices 1925–1933* (Geneva, 1934), p. 116; national production estimates from 1913 for the world's most developed countries are assembled in Angus Maddison, *Economic Growth in the West* (New York: Twentieth Century Fund, 1964), p. 201.

9. Together they totalled about 2 million tons of grain, perhaps two thirds of the large 1915 harvest, up 28 percent in volume over 1914. Glenn E. Torrey, "Rumania and the Belligerents, 1914–1916," *Journal of Contemporary History*, vol. 1, no. 3 (July, 1966), pp. 186–188; G. Ionescu-Siteşti, *L'agriculture de la Roumanie pendant la guerre* (New Haven, Conn.: Yale Univ. Press, 1929), pp. 20–28.

10. Ionescu-Siteşti, pp. 41–104.

11. Less than a third of the locomotives and about half the freight cars of

the Old Kingdom were in good repair by the beginning of 1920. In 1923, freight car capacity was less than 5 percent of that required for prewar exports. Rail connections inland were barely operational. Those to the Black Sea awaited repairs of the Cernavoda bridge in 1922. In the meantime, even desperately needed imports piled up at Constanţa. Accidents on poorly repaired bridges and lines delayed recovery. It would hardly have seemed necessary in these conditions to have created disincentives for agricultural freight, yet agriculture was the only sector paying full tariffs and exports were charged double rates. League of Nations, *Europe's Overseas Needs, 1919–1920, and How They Were Met* (Geneva, 1925), p. 8; Louis G. Michael, *Survey of Europe: The Danubian Basin—Part 2, Rumania, Bulgaria and Yugoslavia*, Technical Bulletin no. 126 (Washington, D.C.: U.S. Department of Agriculture, 1929), pp. 6, 65–68. Great Britain, Department of Overseas Trade, *The Economic Situation in Romania, April 1921*, p. 5, and its *The Economic Situation in Romania, March 1923*, p. 37; Ministère de l'industrie, *La Roumanie Économique, 1921* (Bucharest, 1921), pp. 101, xlii–xliii.

12. Great Britain, *Economic Situation in Romania, April, 1921*, pp. 9–10; Ionescu-Siteşti, p. 112; David Mitrany, *The Land and the Peasant in Rumania* (New Haven, Conn.: Yale Univ. Press, 1929), pp. 352–53, 437–39.

13. Mitrany, pp. 86–87; G. Danailov, *Les effets de la guerre en Bulgarie* (Paris, 1932). Given the Germans' right to use their own currency and send "military materials" across the frontier without customs inspection, it is hard to imagine how Bulgarian authorities could have controlled the situation successfully. Economic details of the German occupation, and best estimates of smuggled exports are found in Vera Katsarkova, "Ograbvaneto na Bulgariia ot germanskiia imperializum prez perioda na purvata svetvona voina" [Exploitation of Bulgaria by German Imperialism during the First World War], *Trudove na vishiia ikonomicheski institut "Karl Marx,"* v. II (Sofia, 1969), pp. 199–208.

14. T.S. Kapsalis, *La balance des comptes de la Grèce* (Lausanne, 1927), p. 74; *Statistikë epetëris tës Ellados, 1930*, 145–47.

15. *Statisticheski godishnik na Bulgarskoto Tsarstvo* [Statistical Yearbook of Bulgaria], *1913–22* (Sofia, 1923), pp. 75–76, 137, 168; *1940* (Sofia, 1941), p. 283.

16. N.V. Dolinski, "Dokhodnostuta na bulgarskoto zemedelie" [The Income of Bulgarian Agriculture], *Spisanie na bulgarskoto ikonomichesko druzhestvo*, XXVII, (Sofia, 1928), p. 168.

17. *Statistikë epetëris tës Ellados, 1930*, p. 201, and also *1935* (Athens, 1936), p. 408; Kapsalis, p. 64; Alex. J. Boyazoglu, *Contribution a l'étude de l'économie rurale de la Grèce d'apres la guerre* (Paris, 1931), pp. 142–47, 172–76, 209–11.

18. A. Tsankov, "Stopanskiiat zastoi v Bulgariia prez 1925–26" [The Economic Recession in Bulgaria during 1925–26], *Spisanie na bulgarskoto ikonomichesko druzhestvo*, XXVI (Sofia, 1928), p. 434; Katsarkova, pp. 199–200.

19. Great Britain Naval Intelligence Division, *Greece*, vol. II (London: H.M. Printing Office, 1944), pp. 209–11, 338–69; *Statistikë epetëris tës Ellados, 1930*, p. 298.

20. Danailov, pp. 516–22; Kapsalis, p. 67; Eliot G. Mears, *Greece Today: The Aftermath of the Refugee Impact* (Stanford, Calif.: Stanford Univ. Press, 1929), pp. 66–75.

21. D. Todorović, "Stopanski problemi na Makedonija so posebni osvrt na dejnosta na Trgovsko-Industrijskata Komora vo Skopje" [Economic Problems of Macedonia with Special Reference to the Activity of the Chamber of Commerce and Industry in Skopje], *Glasnik institut za natsionalna istorija*, vol. 18, no. 2 (Skopje, 1974), p. 31.

22. Ibid., pp. 22–43; D. Todorović, "Karakteristiki na stopanskite odnosi vo Makedonija od 1919 du 1922" [Characteristics of Economic Relations in Macedonia from 1919 to 1922], *Glasnik institut za natsionalna istorija*, vol. 18, no. 1 (Skopje, 1974), pp. 65–77; A. Apostolov, "Posledice velike ekonomske krize za makedonsku agrarnu privredu" [Consequences of the Great Depression for the Macedonian Agricultural Economy], *Jugoslovenski istorijski časopis*, 3–4 (Belgrade, 1973), pp. 181–88.

23. Kemal Hrelja, *Sarajevo u revoluciji* [Sarajevo in Revolution] (Sarajevo, 1976), pp. 75–76, 89–91, and his "Razvoj industrije u Bosni i Hercegovini do drugog svetskog rata" [The Development of Industry in Bosnia and Hercegovina to the Second World War], *Acta historico-oeconomica iugoslaviae*, I (Zagreb, 1974), pp. 29–31.

24. M. Kolar-Dimitrijević, *Radni slojevi Zagreba od 1918 do 1931* [The Working Classes of Zagreb from 1918 to 1931] (Zagreb, 1973), p. 299; Vasa Čubrilović, ed., *Istorija Beograda*, III (Belgrade, 1974), p. 200.

25. The best study of economic and political conditions in occupied Serbia is D. Djordjević, "Austro-ugarski okupacioni režim u Sibiji i njegov slom" [The Austro-Hungarian Occupation of Serbia and Its Fall] in Vasa Čubrilović et al., *Naučni skup u povodu 50-godišnjice raspada Austro-ugarske monarhije i stvaranje jugoslovenske države* [Scientific Gathering on the 50th Anniversary of the Fall of the Austro-Hungarian Monarchy and the Creation of the Yugoslav State] (Zagreb, 1969), pp. 206–23.

26. Dr. Janković, "Društveni i politički odnosi u Kr. SHS uoči stvaranja SRPJ (komunista)" [Social and Political Relations in the Kingdom of Serbs, Croats and Slovenes on the Eve of the Creation of the SWPY (Communists)], *Istorija XX veka*, I (Belgrade, 1969), pp. 28–30, 52–56; Kolar-Dimitrijević, pp. 300–304; Great Britain, Department of Overseas Trade, *Economic Conditions in Yugoslavia April, 1921*, pp. 18–29, *May, 1922*, pp. 5–21.

27. The Sava bridge did not reopen until October, 1920. The main line from Belgrade south to Niš did not resume operation until August, 1919. For details of railway damage, see M. Milenković, *Železničari Srbije, 1918–1920* [The Railway Workers of Serbia, 1918–1920] (Belgrade, 1971), pp. 14–15.

28. The late Rudolph Bićanić regarded separation from the ring of nearby commercial centers as a major economic trial facing the first Yugoslavia. See his "Ekonomske promene u Hrvatskoj izazvane stvaranjem Jugoslavije, 1918" [Economic Changes in Croatia Occasioned by the Creation of Yugoslavia, 1918], in *Prilozi za ekonomsku provijest Hvratske* [Contributions to the Economic History of Croatia] (Zagreb, 1967), pp. 83–87. On the food shortages in postwar Austria and Hungary, see Berend and Ranki, pp. 174–75.

29. Great Britain, Department of Overseas Trade, *Economic Conditions in Yugoslavia, May, 1928*, p. 8.

30. Peter Kilby and Bruce T. Johnston, "The Transferability of the Japanese Pattern of Modernizing Agriculture," in Erik Thorberke, ed., *The Role of Agriculture in Economic Development* (New York: NBER/Columbia Univ. Press, 1969), pp. 277–78.

31. In interwar Belgium, farms averaging twelve hectares also averaged 20–30 scattered parcels. Swiss farms in 1939 averaged 10 parcels. W.S. Woytinsky and E.W. Woytinsky, *World Population and Production* (New York: Twentieth Century Fund, 1953), pp. 493–94.

32. See especially Mitrany, pp. 284–365, and Jozo Tomasevich, *Peasants, Politics and Economic Change in Yugoslavia* (Stanford, Calif.: Stanford Univ. Press, 1955), pp. 344–82. The most noteworthy recent work in the area by a native scholar may be found in the several Yugoslav publications of Nikola Gaćeša. A good brief summary may be found in Michael, pp. 22–34 for Romania, pp. 88–90 for Bulgaria, and pp. 138–41 for Yugoslavia. For Greece, whose reform still awaits a detailed monograph, see G. Servakis and C. Pertountzi, "The Agricultural Policy of Greece" in O.S. Morgan, ed., *Agricultural Systems of Middle Europe* (New York: AMS Press, 1969, reprint from 1933), pp. 145–51.

33. Michael, pp. 21–33; Mitrany, pp. 416–21; *Enciclopedia României*, III, 305. A neglected sidelight is the state's initial use of village associations (*obştii săteşti*) to take over sizable shares of land redistributed by the reform. On the use of such cooperatives communes as holders and administrators of expropriated property, see Mitrany, p. 158; *Anuarul statistic al României, 1930* (Bucharest, 1932), p. 47. According to Mitrany 2,300 village associations were originally established, but in 1921 the idea was abandoned. At the end of that year, communes held 24 percent of Greater Romania's arable land. The share then fell sharply and reached zero in 1928.

34. Tomasevich, pp. 363, 368n, 423; Michael, pp. 138–41; Toma Milenković, "Stav radikalne stranke prema agrarnoj reformi, 1918–1929" [The Attitude of the Radical Party toward Agrarian Reform], *Istorija XX veka*, XI (Belgrade, 1970), pp. 116–17; *Statistički godišnjak Kr. Jugslavije* [Statistical Yearbook of the Kingdom of Yugoslavia], *1940* (Belgrade, 1941), pp. 514–15.

35. M.B. Simonide, "L'économie rurale et la crise de la guerre mondiale," in A. Andreades, *Les effets économiques et sociaux de la guerre en Grèce* (New Haven, Conn.: Yale Univ. Press, 1926), pp. 161–88; Servakis and Pertountzi, pp. 149–52; A. Varvaressos, "Land Ownership in Greece," *Foreign Agriculture* (August, 1950), pp. 180–83; Ch. Evelpidi, *La réforme agraire en Grèce* (Athens, 1926), pp. 1–39.

36. This more sympathetic view is presented in John G. Bell, *Peasants in Power: Alexander Stamboliski and the Bulgarian Agrarian National Union* (Princeton, N.J.: Princeton Univ. Press, 1977), pp. 162–67. The original negative view appears most persuasively in Danailov, pp. 566–72. He was a political contemporary and opponent of Stamboliski.

37. Two prominent Balkan historians made such assumptions. Stavrianos, p. 594, writes of "the thorough going manner in which land was . . . divided" and of the "drastic [re]distribution of land," without differentiating between changes in ownership and land use. Robert Lee Wolff, *The Balkans in Our*

Time (Cambridge, Mass.: Harvard Univ. Press, 1974), p. 163, concludes that "the result [of the Romanian reform] was to multiply the number of uneconomic smallholdings." His further comment that "a big estate could be worked with relatively few implements" applied only to the few prewar estates with consolidated holdings not operated through share cropping and money renting. The most careful treatment of land distribution statistics by any scholar is that by Henry L. Roberts, *Rumania: Political Problems of an Agrarian State* (New Haven, Conn.: Yale Univ. Press, 1951), pp. 362–76. The best explanation of the reform's impacts on farming practices is that by Doreen Warriner, *Economics of Peasant Farming* (New York: Barnes & Noble, 1963), pp. 153–54.

38. S.D. Zagoroff, Jeno Végh, and Alexander D. Bilimovich, *The Agricultural Economy of the Danubian Countries, 1935–45* (Stanford, Calif.: Stanford Univ. Press, 1955), p. 117; *Statisticheski godishnik na Bulgarskoto Tsarstvo, 1940*, pp. 246, 864; Tomasevich, p. 389.

39. Violations of Romanian restrictions are noted by Mitrany, pp. 223–24. Bulgarian acquisition data are from *Statisticheski godishnik na Bulgarskoto Tsarstvo, 1933* (Sofia, 1934), p. 11.

40. Woytinsky and Woytinsky, p. 497; *Statisticheski godishnik na Bulgarskoto Tsarstvo, 1933*, pp. 110–11 and for *1939* (Sofia, 1940), pp. 192–93; Gh. Ionescu-Siteşti, *Structure agraire et production agricole de la Roumaine* (Bucharest, 1924), p. 24; *Enciclopedia României*, IV, 892; Mitrany, pp. 244–48; Roberts, p. 369; *Statistički godišnjak kr. Jugoslavije, 1936* (Belgrade, 1937), pp. 84–90.

41. For this purpose we need net rental data which show, for farms of a given size, the difference between the amount of land rented out (like the Romanian data above) and the amount of land for use rented from others (the first Bulgarian and the Yugoslav data above). Bases for net rental calculations are available only for Bulgaria in 1934 and Romania in 1941. Perhaps the scarcity of data has led scholars to overlook instances where farms in a given size group might rent and rent out land at the same time. Such behavior could be rational even for one farmer whose properties were widely scattered.

42. *Statisticheski godishnik na Bulgarskoto Tsarstvo, 1939* (Sofia, 1940), pp. 192–93; Roberts, pp. 370–71.

43. *Statisticheksi godishnik na Bulgarskoto Tsarstvo, 1933*, pp. 124–25 and for *1940*, pp. 196–200; *Statisticki godišnjak kr Jugoslavije, 1937* (Belgrade, 1938), pp. 98–111.

44. V. Madgearu, *Evoluţia economiei româneşti după războiul mondial* [Evolution of the Romanian Economy after the World War] (Bucharest, 1940), p. 40; O. Parpală, *Aspecte din agricultura României, 1920–1939* (Bucharest, 1966), pp. 203–13.

45. *Statisticheski godishnik na Bulgarskoto Tsarstvo, 1939*, pp. 192–93, and for *1940*, pp. 196–200; *Statisticki godišnjak kr Jugoslavije, 1936*, pp. 89–90, for 1937, pp. 110–11; for evidence of intensive farming around Romanian cities, see Parpală, p. 129.

46. Tomasevich, p. 384; *Enciclopedia României*, IV, p. 893; Mitrany, pp. 246–47; Roberts, pp. 369, 371.

47. Woytinsky and Woytinsky, p. 488.

48. *Anuarul statistic al României, 1930* (Bucharest, 1931), p. 13.

49. Corn required about three times the man-hours of wheat, but its seed was about one tenth the cost of wheat by the 1920s. In return for more labor, corn also brought a more certain and a larger amount of human food and animal fodder per hectare of land. Data showing the greater shares on smaller farms of cultivated land in total land available and of vineyards, tree, vegetable and garden crops in total cultivated land can be calculated from the following sources: *Statisticheski godishnik na Bulgarskoto Tsarstvo, 1940*, pp. 184–86; A. Iu. Totev, *Sravnitelno izuchavane na bulgarskoto i iugoslavenskoto narodno stopanstvo* [A Comparative Inquiry on the Bulgarian and Yugoslav Economies] (Sofia, 1940), pp. 61–68, 87–90; Parpală, pp. 124–27; Roberts, p. 376.

50. Totev, p. 67; *Enciclopedia României*, III, p. 316; Tomasevich, pp. 434, 436.

51. Boyazoglu, pp. 46–72. This remains the best work in any language on Greek agriculture during the 1920s. Also see X. Zolotas, "Wirtschaftsstruktur Griechenlands," in Hermann Gross, ed., *Mittel und Südost Europa Wirtschaftsfragen* (Leipzig, 1931), pp. 123–28.

52. Gerald M. Meier, *Leading Issues in Economic Development*, 3rd ed. (New York: Oxford Univ. Press, 1976), p. 563. For the League's interwar data on disguised rural unemployment, see Wilbert E. Moore, *Economic Demography of Eastern and Southern Europe* (Geneva, 1945), pp. 55–77, 192–205, 237–57; for a more recent statement on its relative unimportance to rural savings and capital formation, see D.W. Jorgensen, "Surplus Agricultural Labour and the Development of a Dual Economy," *Oxford Economic Papers*, 19 (1967), pp. 288–312.

53. Totev, pp. 62, 104; Chakalov, pp. 25, 34, 50–59.

54. Tsankov, pp. 436–40.

55. On Bucharest, see *Enciclopedia României*, IV, p. 929; *Anuarul statistic al României, 1939* and *1940.* (Bucharest, 1940), pp. 499, 931. On Belgrade, see Great Britain, Overseas Trade Department, *Yugoslavia, Economic Survey, April, 1925*, p. 5, *May, 1928*, p. 42, and *Statistički godišnjak kr Jugoslavije, 1940*, p. 297.

56. Michael, pp. 38–39, 92–93, 145; Bell, pp. 169–70; Kh. Marinov, *Geografsko razpredelenie promishlenostta v Bulgariia mezhdu dvete svetovni voini* [Geographic Distribution of Industry in Bulgaria between the Two World Wars] (Sofia, 1965), pp. 19–29. On postwar trends in the world demand for wheat, see Wilfred Malenbaum, *The World Wheat Economy, 1885–1939* (Cambridge, Mass.: Harvard Univ. Press, 1953), pp. 78–88.

57. Leo Pasvolsky, *Bulgaria's Economic Position after the War* (Wash., D.C.: Brookings Institution, 1930), pp. 210–212; J.S. Moloff, "Bulgarian Agriculture," in Morgan, ed., *Agricultural Systems of Middle Europe*, pp. 58, 63–67, 76–78.

58. Cooperative credit was in turn one third of the bank's total assets. Moloff, pp. 69–75; Pasvolsky, p. 199; Bulgarska Narodna Banka, *Izvestiia na Bulgarska Narodna Banka*, 1 and 2, 1927 (Sofia), p. 36–37.

59. Tsankov, p. 439; V. Vasilev, "Za glavnite faktori na industrialniia podem (1925–1929)" [Concerning the Main Factors of the Industrial Boom (1925–1929)], *Izvestiia na instituta za istoriia*, XI (Sofia, 1962), pp. 86–88.

60. Dimitri Pentzopoulos, *The Balkan Exchange of Minorities and Its Impact on Greece* (Paris and The Hague, 1962), pp. 156–57.

61. Ibid., pp. 155, 160; Boyazoglu, pp. 50–53, 75–83; *Statistikë epetëris tës Ellados, 1930*, pp. 161, 272, 286.

62. Mears, pp. 75–77; Naval Intelligence Division, *Greece*, II, p. 63. The Bulgarian tax by contrast was 7 percent ad valorem. Kapsalis, p. 67.

63. Servakis and Pertountzi, pp. 166–169; Mears, pp. 66–68; Naval Intelligence Division, *Greece*, II, p. 71.

64. The First Rural Credit Society of Bucharest, not established until 1924, was the only significant source of Romanian mortgage credit during the 1920s and then dealt only with the few remaining properties over 100 hectares. Mitrany, pp. 424–26. On Croatia/Slavonia, see Chapter 9 and Tomasevich, pp. 657–60.

65. Tomasevich, pp. 461–64; Michael, pp. 22–23, 34–35.

11. The Disruption of Prewar Patterns:
Finance and Industry

1. G. Danailov, *Les effets de la guerre en Bulgarie* (Paris, 1932), p. 194.

2. Ibid., pp. 497–546; Leo Pasvolsky, *Bulgaria's Economic Position after the War* (Washington, D.C.: Brookings Institute, 1930), pp. 55–58.

3. From the end of 1923 to 1925, note issues increased only 14 percent, less from state financing of its debt than from the National Bank's purchase of foreign exchange in part provided by the Refugee Loan. In 1926, note circulation dropped 9 percent, mainly because of a forced loan by the Pangalos regime. The credit shortage would have been worse except for exchange controls evoked in mid-1926 which forced banks out of foreign exchange into domestic loans. In the meantime British war debts were settled and a commission was formed to recommend a new central bank and formal stabilization of the drachma. Note issue had grown only by an average of 4 percent a year from 1923 to 1928. Royal Institute of International Affairs, *The Balkan States, Economics*, vol. I (London: Oxford Univ. Press, 1936), 52; Eliot G. Mears, *Greece Today: The Aftermath of the Refugee Impact* (Stanford, Calif.: Stanford Univ. Press, 1929), pp. 206–208; Great Britain, Overseas Trade Department, *Economic Conditions in Greece in May, 1927*, pp. 7–11; *Statistikë epetëris tës Ellados* [Statistical Yearbook of Greece], *1930* (Athens, 1931), pp. 271–73, 381.

4. *Narodna Banka, 1884–1934* (Belgrade, 1935), pp. 93–100.

5. The first stamping of crowns in January, 1919, accounted for 5,322 million, of which 427 million were in Serbia and Montenegro. By October, 1919, some 344 million more were added and the total in Serbia and Montenegro had risen to 620 million. Besides the crowns, for which additional exchanges were made following the acquisition of Dalmatia in 1921, much smaller amounts of Bulgarian leva and Montenegrin perpers were also removed from circulation. Ibid., pp. 140–44; Dragoslow P. Mihailovitch, *Le problème monétaire en Yougoslavie* (Strasbourg, 1928), pp. 19–25; F.G. Steiner, "Vienna as an Exchange Market for the Succession States," *Manchester Guardian Commercial: Reconstruction in Europe* (April 20, 1922),

pp. 37–38. Also see John R. Lampe, "Unifying the Yugoslav Economy, 1918–1921; Misery and Misunderstandings," in Dimitrije Djordjević, ed., *The Creation of Yugoslavia 1914–1918*, (Santa Barbara, Calif.: ABC-Clio Press, 1980), pp. 139–56.

6. As in the case of Yugoslavia, evidence of internal purchasing power parities between the crown and the leu is rare. Beginning in June 1920, salaries of state functionaries in Transylvania were converted to lei at a rate of 3 crowns to one leu, while the railroad administration calculated freight rates at 3.3 crowns per leu. In spite of seemingly generous terms of the 2/1 exchange that attracted further crowns from Hungary, a money shortage soon appeared in Transylvania. The commercial banks, some desperate to protect themselves from the lost ties to Budapest and others already absorbed by Liberal interests from Bucharest, had apparently bought up vast amounts of crowns prior to the exchange. The lei notes of the Banca Generală were exchanged at 1/1 and both the Tsarist and Lvov ruble notes at sliding rates. The government loans that financed this issue drove the state's share of the National Bank's debt to 87 percent by 1922, comparable to the Yugoslav share that year of 90 percent and the Bulgarian of 98 percent. An account of the exchange by historical region is given in *Anuarul statistic al României* [Statistical Yearbook of Romania], *1922* (Bucharest, 1923), p. 284. Also see C.C. Kirițescu, *Sistemul bănesc al leului și precursorii lui* [The Money System of the Leu and Its Predecessors], II (Bucharest, 1967), 272–87. V. Slăvescu, *Istoricul Băncii Naționale României, 1880–1924* (Bucharest, 1925), pp. 238–68, 278–94, 316–21;Pasvolsky, pp.114–16; Royal Institute, *Balkan States*, p. 52.

7. Internal prices would be a technically preferred means for deflating note issues to comparable real prewar levels. The price indices shown in Table 11.1 and 11.3 have not been used because of their unknown quality. In any case, significant territorial changes were involved. Serbian note issues would be compared to those on the larger postwar Yugoslav territory just as Romanian Old Kingdom note issues would be compared with those for Greater Romania. What prewar money supplies might have been in equivalent prewar territories would be most difficult to estimate. Available price indices suggest that inflation was greater than exchange depreciation by 1920 in Bulgaria, Greece, and Yugoslavia. If the price indices are accepted as valid, then real per capita note issues were much lower in 1920 than indicated in the table. By 1926–30, there was a greater accord between exchange depreciation and price inflation in all four countries.

8. A good recent summary of postwar problems in the European capital markets is Derek H. Aldcroft, *From Versailles to Wall Street, 1918–1929* (Berkeley, Calif.: Univ. of California Press, 1977), pp. 78–156. The United States became the major source of international financial flows from 1921 to 1929. American funds moved mainly to Latin America or to Germany, now a debtor country. Britain directed larger portions of its diminished investments to the Empire. France was a heavy borrower until 1921 when it resumed its prewar role of an important creditor in Southeastern Europe. See Simon Kuznets, *Modern Economic Growth* (New Haven, Conn.: Yale Univ. Press, 1970), pp. 322–33.

9. These debts were a combination of damages done the oil fields in 1916, the Transylvanian share of Hapsburg obligations, and the 1921 liberation debt. Maurice Pearton, *Oil and the Romanian State, 1895–1948* (London: Oxford Univ. Press, 1970), p. 130; Rudolf Nötel, "International Capital Movements and Finance: 1919–1949," in Michael Kaser, ed., *The Economic History of Eastern Europe since 1919* (Oxford: Clarendon Press, forthcoming).

10. Kaser; Great Britain, Naval Intelligence Division, *Jugoslavia*, III (London, 1945), 253–59; L. Pejić, "Ekonomske ideje Dr. Milan Stojadinovića i balkanski privredni problemi" [The Economic Ideas of Dr. Milan Stojadinović and Balkan Economic Problems], *Balkanika*, VII (Belgrade, 1976), 254–58.

11. John A. Petropoulos, "The Compulsory Exchange of Populations: Greek-Turkish Peacemaking, 1922–1930," *Byzantine and Modern Greek Studies*, 2 (London, 1976), pp. 137–60; Dimitri Pentzopoulos, *Balkan Exchange of Minorities and Its Impact on Greece* (Paris and The Hague, 1962), pp. 145–49; William H. Wynne, *State Insolvency and Foreign Bondholders*, II (New Haven, Conn.: Yale Univ. Press, 1951), pp. 339–41, 349–50; H.G. Moulton and Leo Pasvolsky, *War Debts and World Prosperity* (Washington, D.C.: Brookings Institute, 1932), pp. 89–98, 115, 123–124.

12. Nötel, "International Capital Movements"; Wynne, pp. 552–560; Pasvolsky, pp. 66–81.

13. See the best available survey of the interwar Albanian economy, Hans-Joachim Pernack, *Probleme der wirtschaftliche Entwicklung Albaniens, Südosteuropa-Studien*, 18 (Munich, 1972), pp. 77–80.

14. Kirițescu, II, pp. 303–308. For other views on postwar monetary dynamics, see Mihail Manoilescu, *Politica producției naționale* [National Production Policy] (Bucharest, 1923), pp. 188–90; Great Britain, Overseas Trade Department, *Economic Conditions in Romania, March 1923*, p. 53; *Enciclopedia României*, IV (Bucharest, 1943), p. 688; Mihailovitch, pp. 110–14. The monetary estimates that follow have been calculated from the sources for Tables 10.6 and 11.1. On the workings of the postwar Gold Exchange Standard, see Aldcroft, pp. 168–88.

15. Slăvescu, pp. 316–21.

16. Liberal budgetary practices included charging commitments made in one budget year to following ones, deliberately delaying payments to private suppliers and simply not indicating that apparent surpluses had been spent. Of over 24 billion in ordinary budget "surpluses" from 1922–23 through 1928, about 40 percent was used to cover the deficits of the state railroad, and only 7.5 percent covered state debts. M. Maievschi, *Contribuții la istoria finanțelor publice* (Bucharest, 1957), pp. 99, 126–27, 132; Virgil Madgearu, *Drumul echilibrul financiar* [The Road to Financial Equilibrium] (Bucharest, 1935), p. 18; *Enciclopedia României*, IV, pp. 688, 777–78.

17. Kirițescu, II, p. 311; *Enciclopedia României*, IV, 721, 723; Maievschi, p. 124.

18. *Enciclopedia României*, IV; 688–91, 723; Kirițescu, 305–06; Maievschi, pp. 168–70.

19. Madgearu, pp. 14–19; Mihail Manoilescu, *De la leul hîrtie la leul aur*

[From the Paper Leu to the Gold Leu] (Bucharest, 1925), pp. 9–10; Maievschi, pp. 169–70.

20. Lampe, pp. 148–50.

21. S. Djurović, "Struktura aksionarskih društava a Beogradu izmedju 1918–1929g." [The Structure of Joint Stock Companies in Belgrade between 1918–1919]. *Acta historica-oeconomica iugoslaviae*, IV (Zagreb, 1977), pp. 147–48. For Bosnian and Macedonian complaints about the lack of National Bank credit, see respectively Kemal Hrelja, *Sarajevo u revoluciji* [Sarajevo in Revolution] (Sarajevo, 1976), p. 86, and D. Todorović, "Karakteristiki na stopanskite odnosi vo Makedonija od 1919 do 1922" [Characteristics of Economic Relations in Macedonia from 1919 to 1922], *Glasnik institut za natsionalna istorija*, vol. 18, no. 1 (Skopje, 1974), 80–82.

22. Great Britain, Overseas Trade Department, *Economic Conditions in Jugoslavia, April 1924*, p. 5. *April, 1925*, pp. 8–10, *May, 1928*, p. 8; Mihailović, pp. 57, 73–76, 85, 91–92, 105–107.

23. A.L. Georgiev, "Otrazhenie na vunshnite finansove dulgove na burzhoazna Bulgariia, 1918–1939" [The Development of Foreign Financial Debts in Bourgeois Bulgaria, 1918–1939], *Trudove na vishiia ikononomicheski institut "Karl Marx,"* II (Sofia, 1966), pp. 358–62; Pasvolsky, pp. 122–35.

24. A.S. Chakalov, "Stokoviiat i bankoviat kredit v Bulgariia" [Material and Bank Credit in Bulgaria], *Spisanie na bulgarskoto ikonomichesko druzhestvo*, 29 (Sofia, 1930), pp. 26–33; V. Vasilev, "Za glavnite faktori na industrialniia podem (1925–1929)" [Concerning the Main Factors of the Industrial Boom (1925–1929)], *Izvestiia na instituta za istoriia*, XI (Sofia, 1962), pp. 96–98.

25. In that year the big foreign banks held paid-in capital of 205 million leva versus 127 million in the four big private native banks. The five's combined short-term assets exceeded one billion leva and the four's were about half of that amount. Georgiev, p. 358; Chakalov, p. 27; Bulgarska Narodna Banka, *Izvestiia na Bulgarska Narodna Banka*, 2, 1929, p. 38; Great Britain, Department of Overseas Trade, *Economic Conditions in Bulgaria, March, 1926*, p. 9–10.

26. St. Bobchev, "Chuzhdi initsiativi i kapitali v Bulgaria" [Foreign Enterprises and Capital in Bulgaria] *Spisanie na bulgarsko ikonomichesko druzhestvo*, 23 (Sofia, 1924), pp. 140–49; Vasilev, pp. 96–97; L. Berov, *Ikonomicheski razvitie na Bulgariia prez vekove* [Economic Development of Bulgaria throughout the Ages] (Sofia, 1974), p. 109.

27. Mirko Lamer, "Wandlungen der ausländischen kapital auf der Balkan," *Weltwirtschaftliches Archiv*, vol. 48, no. 3 (1938), pp. 470–522.

28. Hrelja, pp. 85–86. On Serbia, see *Narodna Banka, 1884–1934*, p. 105, and Vasa Ćubrilović, ed., *Istorija Beograda*, III (Belgrade, 1974), pp. 201–11. On Macedonia, see Todorović, pp. 38–49.

29. Z. Simunčić, "Osnovne karaktaristike industrialnog razvitka na području Hrvatske u medjuratnom razdoblju" [Basic Characteristics of Industrial Development in Croatia during the Interwar Period], *Acta historica-oeconomiae iugoslaviae*, I (Zagreb, 1974), pp. 63–75; T. Timet, *Stanbena izgradnja Zagreba do 1954* [The Construction of Zagreb to 1954] (Zagreb, 1961), pp. 147–48; Djurović, pp. 140–46.

30. Great Britain, Overseas Trade Department, *Economic Conditions in Greece,1927*, pp. 9–12; Naval Intelligence Division, *Greece*, II (London, 1945), pp. 178–182. The calculation of total and individual bank assets for 1928 is based on data for 18 banks in *Statistikë epetëris tës Ellados, 1930*, pp. 272–77.

31. Great Britain, Department of Overseas Trade, *Economic Conditions in Roumania, April, 1921*, pp. 81–82, *May, 1923*, pp. 12, 53, *May, 1927*, pp. 4–6; *Enciclopedia României*, IV (Bucharest, 1943), pp. 267–68, 567–68; N.N. Constantinescu and V. Axenciuc, *Capitalismul monopolist în România* [Monopoly Capitalism in Romania] (Bucharest, 1962), pp. 139–40. On the Sofia banks' assets, *Statisticheski godishnik na Bulgarskoto Tsarstvo, 1934* [Statistical Yearbook of the Kingdom of Bulgaria], (Sofia, 1935), p. 290.

32. On petroleum, see Pearton, pp. 73–95; on other industrial sectors, N.N. Constantinescu, ed., *Situaţia clasei muncitoare din României, 1914–1944* [The Situation of the Working Class in Romania, 1914–1944] (Bucharest, 1968), pp. 88–89; M.A. Lupu, ed., *Istoria economie a României* (Bucharest, 1974), pp. 349–50.

33. *Statisticheski godishnik na Bulgarskoto Tsarstvo, 1923–1924* (Sofia, 1924), pp. B.65–89, *1933* (Sofia, 1934), pp. 188–92; *Izvestiia na Bulgarska Narodna Banka*, 9, *1927*, pp. 13–14, 3 and 4, *1927*, p. 50, 9, *1928*, p. 181; Pasvolsky, pp. 214–17; Berov, pp. 126–27.

34. S. Djurović, "Industrija Sibije na početku privrednog života Kr. Srba, Hrvata i Slovenaca" [The Industry of Serbia at the Start of the Economic Life of the Kingdom of Serbs, Croats, and Slovenes], *Istorija XX veka*, I (Belgrade, 1969), pp. 169–72, 204–205; idem, "Kriza uglja na territoriji Kr. Srba, Hrvata i Slovenaca 1919g." [The Coal Crisis in the Territory of the Kingdom of Serbs, Croats, and Slovenes, 1919], *Acta historico-oeconomica jugoislaviae*, II (Zagreb, 1975), pp. 74–81.

35. On the pattern of chemical production and export, see Ch. Evelpidi, *Les états balkaniques: Étude comparée politique, économique et financière* (Paris, 1930), pp. 283–85; *Statisticheski godishnik na Bulgarskoto Tsarstvo, 1931* (Sofia, 1931), pp. 274–75, 325; *Statistikë epetëris tës Ellados, 1930*, p. 161; Kenneth S. Patton, *The Kingdom of Serbs, Croats and Slovenes* (Washington, D.C.: U.S. Department of Commerce, 1928), pp. 209–15; O. Parpală, *Aspecte din agricultura României, 1920–1939* (Bucharest, 1966), pp. 149–50.

36. David Turnock, "The Industrial Development of Romania from the Unification of the Principalities to the Second World War," in Francis W. Carter, ed., *An Historical Geography of the Balkans* (New York: Academic Press, 1977), pp. 347–56; Norman L. Forter and D.B. Rostovsky, *The Roumanian Handbook*, (New York: Arno Press reprint, 1971), pp. 231–42.

37. From prewar totals of about 100,000, Sofia's and Belgrade's population had risen past 250,000 by 1928 and Athens' past 450,000. Piraeus accounted for another 250,000. See *Statistikë epetëris tës Ellados, 1930*, pp. 28–30; Naval Intelligence Division, *Greece*, II, pp. 104–105; Kh. Marinov, *Geografsko razpredelenie na promishlenostta v Bulgariia mezhdu dvete svetovne voini* [Geographic Distribution of Industry in Bulgaria between the Two World Wars] (Sofia, 1965), pp. 7, 14–15; *Iubileena kniga na grad Sofiia*

1878–1928 [Jubilee Book of the City of Sofia, 1878–1928] (Sofia, 1928), pp. 270–72.

38. *Statiskički godišnjak kr Jugoslavije* [Statistical Yearbook of Yugoslavia], *1930* (Belgrade, 1931), pp. 128–29; S. Kukoleća, *Industrija Jugoslavije, 1918–1939* (Belgrade, 1939), pp. 104–105; M. Kolar-Dimitrijević, *Radni slojevi Zagreba od 1918 do 1931* [The Working Classes of Zagreb from 1918 to 1931] (Zagreb, 1973), pp. 27–41.

39. Herman Gross, *Südosteuropa, Bau und Entwicklung der Wirtschaft* (Leipzig, 1937), p. 185; Pasvolsky, pp. 254–56. For evidence of how railway lines influenced industrial location, see Marinov, pp. 18–19, 28–29.

40. Vasilev, pp. 83–93; Berov, pp. 125–26.

41. Kukoleća, pp. 79–83.

42. Most of the Dalmatian cement production continued to be exported. Patton, pp. 193–94. On other areas, see Evelpidi, pp. 271–86; Simunčič, pp. 64–68; D. Todorović, "Stopanski problemi na Makedonija," [Economic Problems of Macedonia], *Glasnik institut za natsionalna istorija*, vol. 18, no. 2 (Skopje, 1974), pp. 43–46; Hrelja, p. 78.

43. Pentzopoulos, pp. 160–65; Naval Intelligence Division, *Greece*, II, pp. 120–30; X. Zolotas, "Wirtschaftstruktur Griechenlands," in Herman Gross, ed., *Mittel und Südosteuropa Wirtschaftsfragen* (Leipzig, 1931), pp. 188–92.

44. *Statistikë epetëris tës Ellados, 1930*, p. 287; A.A. Pepelasis, "The Legal System and the Economic Development of Greece," *Journal of Economic History*, XIX, 2 (June, 1959), pp. 173–98.

45. *Statisticheski godishnik na Bulgarskoto Tsarstvo, 1931*, (Sofia, 1932), pp. 240–45, *1940* (Sofia, 1940), pp. 380–94. The sugar and tobacco cartels were exceptional for their long duration. See *Izvestiia na Bulgarska Narodna Banka*, 1, *1930*, pp. 24–25; Marinov, pp. 12–14; *Iubileena kniga na grad Sofiia*, pp. 270–72; Berov, pp. 79–80.

46. For pre-1914 and post-1914 comparisons, see Frederick L. Pryor, *Property and Industrial Organization in Communist and Capitalist Countries* (Bloomington, Ind.: Indiana Univ. Press, 1973), pp. 148–62.

47. Only 3–4 percent of interwar Yugoslav industrial enterprises had their shares listed on the *berza*, VI. Rozenberg and J. Kostić, *Ko financira jugoslovensku privredu* [Who Finances the Yugoslav Economy] (Belgrade, 1940), pp. 44–45; Kolar-Dimitrijević, pp. 36–38.

48. Djurović, "Struktura aksionarskikh društava," pp. 150–51; Čubrilović, pp. 217–26; Hrelja, p. 81; Todorović, "Stopanski problemi na Makedonija," pp. 52–54.

49. Calculations on industrial incorporation and bank participation have been made from Institutul central de statistica, *Statistica societăților anonime dîn România* [Statistics of the Joint-Stock Corporations of Romania], v. XXII-1940 (Bucharest, 1942), pp. 2, 22–23, 56–57, and N.P. Arcadian, *Industrializarea României* (Bucharest, 1936), pp. 177–79, 248–49. An estimate of Jewish stock ownership may be found in D. Leontiaș, *Die Industrialisierung Rumänien bis zum zweiten Weltkrieg* (Munich, 1971), p. 156. On individual metallurgical enterprises, see Ion Păsărică, *Monografia uzinelor de fier și domeniilor din Reșița* [Monograph on the Iron Works and Domains of Reșița] (Bucharest, 1935), pp. 20–32; C. Murgescu et al., *Contribuții la*

istoria capitalului straăn în Romînia [Contributions to the History of Foreign Capital in Romania] (Bucharest, 1960), pp. 79–87; *Enciclopedia României*, III, pp. 848, 866–67. On the Rizescu partnership, see C. Filipescu and D.I. Gavriliu, *Textilele României* (Bucharest, 1938), pp. 210–13.

50. The Kanelopoulos bank was founded by the noted industrialist of the same name, mainly to support his other enterprises, which accounted for one third of Greek chemical production. Naval Intelligence Division, *Greece*, II, pp. 124–25, 174–77. On the structure of Greek commercial banking, see *Statistikë epetëris tës Ellados, 1930*, pp. 272–77 and Lamer, pp. 513–14.

51. Lamer, pp. 502–506; Bulgarksa Narodna Banka, *Les comptes rendus de la Banque Nationale Bulgare, 1925–1937* (Sofia, 1938), Table 7 for 1925–30; Berov, p. 74.

52. The Vračarska Banka backed the large Vajfert brewery and the Praška Kreditna Banka of Prague a small-machine works. Djurović, "Struktura aksionarskih drušatva," pp. 148–59. For the distribution of central bank credit, see *Narodna Banka, 1884–1934*, p. 319.

53. The Hungarian share was perhaps 10 percent. Kukoleća, p. 392; Timet, pp. 148–51; Rozenberg and Kostić, pp. 65–91.

54. Rozenberg and Kostić, pp. 32–68; Toussaint Hočevar, *Structure of the Slovenian Economy, 1848–1963* (New York: Studia Slovenica, 1965), pp. 162–66; Joze Šorn, "Razvoj industrije v Sloveniji med obem vojnama," [The Development of Industry in Slovenia between the Wars], *Kronika časopis za slovensko krajevno zgodovino*, 6–7 (Ljubljana, 1958–59), pp. 10–20.

55. Rozenberg and Kostić, pp. 82–91; Lamer, pp. 494–503.

56. N.G. Badea, *Das rumänische Bankwesen* (Frankfurt am Main, 1931), pp. 228–29; Constantinescu and Axenciuc, pp. 159–65.

57. The participation of the six largest Bucharest banks in industrial or related long-term investment peaked to 12 percent of their assets in 1927 and then fell off to 7 percent by 1928. Banque Nationale de la Roumanie, *Bulletin de l'information et de documentation*, 10 (Bucharest, 1930), pp. 784–85; Banca Marmorosch-Blank, *Les forces économique de la Roumanie 1927* (Bucharest, 1928), p. 115, *1928* (Bucharest, 1929), p. 132, *1929* (Bucharest, 1930), p. 132; C. Murgescu et al., pp. 56–57, 119. On industrial profits, see Arcadian, p. 274.

58. *Anuarul statistic al României, 1934* (Bucharest, 1935), pp. 160–65; *Enciclopedia României*, IV, pp. 565–66, 719–25.

59. Pearton, pp. 105–51, notes that Rockefeller interests failed to push the U.S. State Department into lifting the ban on American loans to the Romanian government pending the settlement of postwar claims and thus lacked the official leverage in resisting the Mining Law that students of Finance Capitalism might suspect. Pearton's thorough account, it should be noted, is based largely on data from the foreign oil companies and makes very limited use of Romanian sources.

12. Structural Change and the
State Sector during
the Depression

1. The best work on the early 1930s remains the contemporary study by the Royal Institute of International Affairs, *The Balkan States, I.: Economic* (London: Oxford Univ. Press, 1936). On Nazi penetration, the still useful standard study is Antonin Basch, *The Danubian Basin and the German Economic Sphere* (New York: Columbia Univ. Press, 1943). Attention to the state's role runs through the British studies collected and edited by Michael Kaser, *The Economic History of Eastern Europe since 1919* (Oxford: Clarendon Press, 1979), and dominates the recent Romanian work, Ioan V. Totu, ed., *Progresul economic în România, 1877–1977* (Bucharest, 1977).

2. Michael Kaser, "The Depression and the Genesis of Etatism," in Vasa Čubrilović, ed., *Svetska ekonomska kriza, 1929–1934g,* [The World Economic Crisis, 1929–1934], vol. 5, Balkanološki Institut (Belgrade, 1976), pp. 54–55.

3. United Nations, *Demographic Yearbook, 1965* (Geneva, 1966), pp. 611–16. One recent study has argued that more was involved in these high rural and agricultural shares than just low levels of economic development. Southeastern Europe's share of agricultural labor, it is argued, was 50 percent higher in 1940 and its urban share of population 50 percent less than would be expected from its place in the per capita rankings of national product for all European countries. Excessive historical dependence on agricultural exports is suggested as the reason for this discrepancy. See Gur Ofer, "Economizing on Urbanization in Socialist Countries: Historical Necessity or Socialist Strategy," in Alan A. Brown and Egon Neuberger, eds., *International Migration: A Comparative Perspective* (New York: Academic Press, 1977), pp. 281–82.

4. Herman Gross, *Südosteuropa, Bau und Entwicklung* (Leipzig, 1937), pp. 89–91; Great Britain, Overseas Trade Department, *Economic and Commercial Conditions in Greece, 1932–1934*, pp. 36–38. On prewar Greek agriculture, see Ch. 6.

5. Great Britain, Overseas Trade Department, *Economic and Commercial Conditions in Bulgaria, 1931*, pp. 30–32, *1932–34*, p. 29, *1935–36*, pp. 23–24, *1938*, p. 35; L. Berov, *Ikonomicheski razvitie na Bulgariia prez vekove* [Economic Development of Bulgaria across the Ages] (Sofia, 1974), pp. 116–18.

6. Great Britain, Overseas Trade Department, *Economic and Commercial Conditions in Romania, 1932*, p. 38, *1935*, p. 34, *1936*, p. 30; V. Bozga, *Criza agrară în România dintre cele două războaie mondiale* [The Agrarian Crisis in Romania between the Two World Wars] (Bucharest, 1975), pp. 100–107.

7. Most of the following account is drawn from Jozo Tomasevich, *Peasants, Politics and Economic Change in Yugoslavia* (Stanford, Calif.: Stanford Univ. Press, 1955), pp. 609–10, 640–44. This work provides extensive statistical data and description of Yugoslav agriculture during the 1930s. A more recent Yugoslav study is Nikola Vučo, *Agrarna kriza, 1930–1934* (Belgrade, 1968).

8. For an unquantified but persuasive account of this process in several villages, see William H. McNeill, *The Metamorphosis of Modern Greece since World War II* (Chicago: Univ. of Chicago Press, 1978), pp. 138–205.

9. A. Apostolov, "Posledice velike ekonomske krize za makedonske agrarne privede" [Consequences of the Great Economic Crisis for the Macedonian Agricultural Economy], *Jugoslovenski istoriski časopis*, XXII, 3–4 (Belgrade, 1973), pp. 181–88; Naval Intelligence Division, *Greece*, II (London, 1944), pp. 97–103.

10. Great Britain, Overseas Trade Department, *Economic Conditions in Greece, 1934*, p. 36; Gross, p. 91; X. Zolotas, "Wirtschaftsstruktur Griechenlands," in Herman Gross, ed., *Mittel und Südosteuropäische Wirtschaftsfragen* (Leipzig, 1931), pp. 142–44.

11. Tomasevich, pp. 604, 628–35, again provides the most detailed account.

12. Basch, pp. 100–102; Royal Institute, *Balkan States*, I, pp. 67–68.

13. Royal Institute, *Balkan States*, I, pp. 67–68.

14. Henry L. Roberts, *Rumania: Political Problems of an Agrarian State* (New Haven: Yale Univ. Press, 1951), p. 159; O. Parpală, *Aspecte din agricultura României, 1920–1939* (Bucharest, 1966), p. 163.

15. Bozga, pp. 108, 142–44, 186–91.

16. The central bank's reduction of agricultural credit coincides with the fall from power of the National Peasant Party, allowing traditional Liberal control of the bank to reassert itself. The brief Maniu government's revision of the Banca Națională statutes in 1929 had boosted agriculture's permissible proportion of commercial credit from 25 to 40 percent. But the party's own policies appear to have doomed the two other institutions to permanent weakness. Iliu Maniu and his economic advisors placed their faith in the market mechanism, freed from Liberal restrictions, to aid peasant agriculture. Measures in 1929 to decentralize the cooperatives' credit system, erected the year before, turned the restructured and renamed Banca Centrală Cooperativă into a private bank. Although half of its capital was furnished from state funds, its private character laid it open to all the commercial limitations that came with the Depression. In the same way and in the same year, the new Creditul Agricol Ipotecar had been established as an agricultural mortgage bank which the Maniu government expected to acquire most of its loanable funds through market sales of its own mortgage bonds (in the fashion of the prewar Croatian banks as described in Chapter 9). Such market operations proved so difficult during the 1930s that this highly touted Agricultural Bank had barely lent more by the end of the decade than the state had given it as a one-time grant for loans in 1929. Bozga, pp. 150–62; Great Britain, Overseas Trade Department, *Economic Conditions in Romania, 1933*, p. 20; *Enciclopedia României*, IV (Bucharest, 1943), pp. 599–602; Virgil Madgearu, *Evoluția economiei românești* (Bucharest, 1940), pp. 336–46, and his *Reorganizarea sistemul de credit* (Bucharest, 1934), p. 8.

17. A.J. Boyazoglu, *Contribution a l'étude l'économie rurale de la Grèce après la guerre* (Paris, 1931), pp. 75–83; Naval Intelligence Division, *Greece*, II, pp. 832–91; Great Britain, Overseas Trade Department, *Economic Conditions in Greece, 1934)*, p. 36.

18. League of Nations, Economic and Financial Department, *Commercial*

Banks, 1929–1934 (Geneva, 1935), p. 135; Tomasevich, pp. 614–20, 660–80; Toussaint Hočevar, *The Structure of the Slovenian Economy, 1848–1963* (New York: Studia Slovenica, 1965), p. 165.

19. S.G. Triantis, *Cyclical Changes in Trade Balances of Countries Exporting Primary Products, 1927–1933*, Canadian Studies in Economics, no. 20 (Toronto: Univ. of Toronto Press, 1967), p. 19; League of Nations, *Europe's Foreign Trade* (Geneva, 1944), p. 83.

20. See H.J. Schröder, "Deutsche Südosteuropapolitik, 1929–1936," *Geschichte und Gesellschaft*, 2 (1976), pp. 5–32.

21. The following paragraph is drawn mainly from Theodore I. Geshkoff, *Balkan Union* (New York: Columbia Univ. Press, 1940), pp. 145, 151–57, 161.

22. For instance, three quarters of Romanian imports for 1934–38 came in under quotas. *Enciclopedia Romîniei*, IV, p. 476. Also see Basch, pp. 78–86; Royal Institute, *Balkan States*, I, pp. 72–79, 124–27.

23. A good summary of recent scholarship on the dynamics of German economic policy during the mid-1930s is William Carr, *Arms, Autarky and Aggression, A Study in German Foreign Policy, 1933–1939* (New York: W.W. Norton, 1973), pp. 45–65, and the bibliographic note on pp. 127–28. On subsequent developments, see Dieter Petzina, *Autarkiepolitik im Dritten Reich: Der nationalsozialistische Vierjahresplan* (Stuttgart, 1968), and Alan S. Milward, *The German Economy at War* (London: Athlone Press, 1965).

24. Import surcharges were levied to provide revenue for the export premia. Great Britain, Overseas Trade Department, *Economic Conditions in Bulgaria, 1935*, p. 5; Royal Institute, *Balkan States*, I, pp. 95–99; Basch, 136–38.

25. Berov, pp. 135–37; Royal Institute, *Balkan States*, I, p. 77.

26. Phillipe Marguerat, *Le IIIe Reich et le petrole roumain, 1938–1940* (Leiden: A.W. Sijthoff, 1977), pp. 38, 71–73, 205–10; League of Nations, *Commercial Banks, 1929–1934*, p. xc; *Enciclopedia Romîniei*, IV, p. 494.

27. Maurice Pearton, *Oil and the Romanian State, 1895–1948* (London: Oxford Univ. Press, 1970), pp. 179–81, 194–99, 202; Marguerat, pp. 74–80; *Enciclopedia Romîniei*, IV, pp. 493–95.

28. League of Nations, *Commercial Banks, 1929–1934*, pp. LXI, LXII; Royal Institute, *Balkan States*, I, pp. 94, 127–28.

29. See Pejić, "Ekonomski ideje Dr. Milana Stojadinovića i balkanski privredni problemi" [The Economic Ideas of Dr. Milan Stojadinović and Balkan Economic Problems], *Balkanika*, VII (Belgrade, 1976), pp. 259–64. Stojadinović's own recollections of his policies in the 1930's may be found in Milan Stojadinović, *Ni rat ni pakt* [Neither War nor Treaty] (Belgrade, 1973).

30. Joachim Wünscht, *Jugoslawien und das Dritte Reich* (Stuttgart, 1969), pp. 93–94; Great Britain, Naval Intelligence Division, *Jugoslavia*, III (London, 1945), pp. 231–37; Tomasevich, pp. 627–28.

31. William H. Wynne, *State Insolvency and Foreign Bondholders*, II (New Haven: Yale Univ. Press, 1951), pp. 351–55; Basch, pp. 147–51. Great Britain, Overseas Trade Department, *Economic Conditions in Greece, 1934*, pp. 13–14.

32. Great Britain, Overseas Trade Department, *Economic Conditions in Greece*, pp. 40–44; Naval Intelligence Division, *Greece*, II, pp. 143–46. A

neglected aspect of this period is the Soviet effort to use clearing arrangements to sell agricultural machinery, in addition to the grain that they had been exporting since the mid-1920s, on an expanding Greek market. The effort failed probably because of poor quality control, leaving the increasing Soviet use of Greek shipping for its trade out from the Black Sea to build up a current account surplus for Greece. Great Britain, Overseas Trade Department, *Economic Conditions in Greece, 1937*, p. 20.

33. No one has yet undertaken an econometric study of the costs and benefits from these German clearing arrangements to states of Southeastern Europe, as has been done for Hungary in Philip Friedman, "The Welfare Costs of Bilateralism: German-Hungarian Trade, 1933–1938," *Explorations in Economic History*, vol. 13, no. 1 (January, 1976), pp. 113–25. At least the Bulgarian data might bear the weight of a similar inquiry.

34. The resulting reduction in note circulation was repaired by new state borrowing from the Bank of Greece. League of Nations, *Commercial Banks*, p. XXVII; League of Nations, *Money and Banking, 1936–37* (Geneva, 1937), p. 37; Great Britain, Overseas Trade Department, *Economic Conditions in Greece, 1934*, p. 21, *1937*, pp. 7–8. For greater detail see Bank of Greece, *Report for the Year, 1932–37* (Athens, 1933–38).

35. League of Nations, *Money and Banking, 1936-37*, pp. 58–59, 164–66; P.E.P. (Political and Economic Planning), *Economic Development in S.E. Europe* (London: Oxford Univ. Press, 1945), pp. 165–66.

36. Great Britain, Overseas Trade Department, *Economic Conditions in Bulgaria, 1932*, p. 13, *1935*, p. 5, *1937*, pp. 4, 23, *1939*, p. 6.

37. Ibid., *1932*, p. 18, *1937*, p. 5; League of Nations, *Commercial Banks, 1929–1934*, pp. 11–12; *Statisticheski godishnik na Bulgarskoto Tsarstvo, 1940* [Statistical Yearbook of the Kingdom of Bulgaria] (Sofia, 1941), pp. 578–79.

38. *Statisticheski godishnik na Bulgarskoto tsarstvo, 1940*, pp. 578–79. League of Nations, *Commercial Banks, 1929–1934*, pp. XVIII, LXXXVI, LXXXVII; Great Britain, Overseas Trade Department, *Economic Conditions in Bulgaria, 1939*, pp. 8–9.

39. *Narodna Banka, 1884–1934* (Belgrade, 1935), pp. 201–206, 221–36, 322–23; Great Britain, Overseas Trade Department, *Economic and Commercial Conditions in Jugoslavia, 1934*, p. 18, *1936*, pp. 5–7; League of Nations, *Commercial Banks, 1929–1934*, pp. 134–38, 306.

40. Naval Intelligence Division, *Jugoslavia*, III, pp. 262–68; Great Britain, Overseas Trade Department, *Economic Conditions in Jugoslavia, 1938*, p. 5.

41. Wünscht, pp. 90–96, emphasizes the role of this internal borrowing in Yugoslav rearmament. Also see Table 8 in Rudolf Nötel, "International Capital Movements and Finance: 1919–1949," in Kaser, ed., *Economic History of Eastern Europe*.

42. See n. 16 in Ch. 11 above.

43. N.N. Constantinescu and V. Axenciuc, *Capitalismul monopolist în România* (Bucharest, 1962), pp. 139–40; Great Britain, Overseas Trade Department, *Economic Conditions in Rumania, 1932*, pp. 18–22, *1936*, p. 12; League of Nations, *Commercial Banks, 1929–1934*, pp. 96–98; *Enciclopedia României*, IV, pp. 576–79.

44. The best available account of the demise of the Banca Marmorosch-

Blank is I.A. Adam, "Cu privire al activitatea şi falimentul Băncii Marmorosch-Blank" [Concerning the Activity and Failure of the Bank Marmorosch-Blank], *Studii şi cercetării,* 2 (Bucharest, 1974), pp. 165–71. Also see C. Murgescu et al., *Contribuţii la istoria capitalului străin în Romania* [Contributions to the History of Foreign Capital in Romania] (Bucharest, 1960), pp. 314–18. A separate monograph on the bank's long and influential history is badly needed.

45. Royal Institute, *Balkan States,* I, p. 115.

46. Annual indicators of industrial output are found in sources to Table 12.13. Comparative growth rates are calculated from Ingvar Svennilson, *Growth and Stagnation in the European Economy* (Geneva: UNECE, 1954), pp. 304–305.

47. Romanian rates for capacity utilization are from N.P. Arcadian, *Industrializarea României* (Bucharest, 1936), p. 233. Additional observations on capacity by Madgearu, with his general contention that Romanian industry, especially capital goods, was overdeveloped, are from his *Evoluţia economiei româneşti,* pp. 168–207.

48. T.S. Kapsalis, *La balance des comptes de la Grèce* (Lausanne, 1927), pp. 414–15; *Statistikë epetëris tës Ellados, 1930,* pp. 178–79, 191, *1935,* pp. 142–45, *1938,* pp. 135–38, 452; *Statisticheski godishnik na Bulgarskoto Tsarstvo, 1940,* pp. 379–81, 387–91; Arcadian, pp. 226–34; *Annuarul statistic al României, 1930* (Bucharest, 1930), pp. 189, 197, *1939–40,* pp. 468–69, 479, 489, 586–87, 593, 628–31; St. Kukoleća, *Industrija Jugoslavije, 1918–1939* (Belgrade, 1941), p. 403; *Statistički godišnjak kr Jugoslavije, 1940,* pp. 240–43, *1936,* pp. 233–36, *1932,* pp. 199–208.

49. Statisticheski godishnik na Bulgarskoto Tsarstvo, 1929–30 (Sofia, 1930), pp. 236–37, *1936,* pp. 284–85, *1940,* 220–21. On the acquisition of technology for shoe manufacture and other sophisticated leather processing in Romania and Greece, to the extent of successful exports in the latter, Ch. Evelpidi, *Les états balkaniques* (Paris, 1930), pp. 287–88; *Enciclopedia României,* III, pp. 981–95; *Anuarul statistic al României, 1939–40,* pp. 586–92; *Statistikë epetëris tës Ellados, 1930,* pp. 180, 208–209, 244–47, *1935,* pp. 143, 145, 163–64, *1938,* pp. 131, 153, *1939,* pp. 135, 138, 153–54. On the experience of the Czech Bata works in Yugoslavia, see Hugo von Haan, "Labour Conditions in a Rationalized Shoe Factory: The Bata Works at Borovo, Yugoslavia," *International Labor Review,* XXVI, 6 (Dec., 1937), pp. 780–811.

50. He argues that imported inputs had declined only because of extraordinary balance of payments measures and were still "a good deal more than 50 percent" in 1937. Alexander Gerschenkron, "Some Aspects of Industrialization in Bulgaria, 1878–1939," in his *Economic Backwardness in Historical Perspective* (New York: Praeger, 1965), p. 215. On the Greek experience, see *Statistikë epetëris tës Ellados, 1935,* p. 154.

51. Calculated from Svennilson, p. 279.

52. Madgearu, *Evoluţia economiei româneşti,* pp. 168–70. To explain the relatively better interwar performance of Romanian than Yugoslav metals and machinery requires some account of the precise mix of products. In 1929, Romania produced 73,000 tons of pig iron, 2.5 times more than Yugoslavia, and 161,000 tons of steel ingot, 1.6 times the Yugoslav output. These

figures reflect a Romanian recovery beyond the pre-1914 volume. Yugoslavia produced less than half its prewar amount. The Jesenice steel mill in Slovenia had no blast furnace for its own pig iron until the late 1930s. The Bosnian and Croatian blast furnaces used charcoal because of a lack of coke, and had no rolling capacity. Romania had the good fortune, on the other hand, to inherit fully integrated, coke-burning facilities at Reşiţa. The state-owned iron furnaces at Hunedoara and, from 1934, the Calan blast furnace, operated on charcoal. The latter was nonetheless fully integrated. By 1938, domestic production covered 90 percent or more of the consumption of pig iron and rolled metals. Domestic shares for equipment and machinery were much lower, with the exception of steel pipe (from 1938) and railway rolling stock. Domestic steel itself covered 76 percent of consumption by 1938. On Romanian metallurgy and machine production, see *Enciclopedia României*, III, pp. 852, 862–68, 871–77; Arcadian, pp. 213–15; *Anuarul statistic al României, 1939–40*, pp. 463–64, 579–85. On Yugoslav metallurgy and machine production, see Evelpidi, pp. 280–82; Balkanski Institut, *État économique des pays balkaniques, I: Yugoslavie* (Belgrade, 1938), pp. 66–67; Naval Intelligence Division, *Jugoslavia*, III, pp. 176, 187–99; Svennilson, pp. 259–63.

53. See for instance Zhak Natan et al., *Ikonomika na Bulgariia*, I (Sofia, 1969), pp. 579–87; M.F. Iovanelli, *Industria românească, 1934–38* (Bucharest, 1975), pp. 201–208.

54. On the rise of German cartels in the late nineteenth century in order to *prevent* concentration among a few large companies, see Erich Maschke, "Outline of the History of German Cartels from 1873 to 1914," in F. Crouzet, W.H. Chaloner, and W.M. Stern, eds., *Essays in European Economic History, 1780–1914* (New York: St. Martin's Press, 1969), pp. 226–58.

55. L. Berov, "Kum vuprosa za monopolisticheskite organizatsii v Bulgariia" [Concerning the Question of Monopolistic Organizations in Bulgaria], *Ikonomicheska misul*, 7 (Sofia, 1958), pp. 67–80. On Romanian cartels, see A. Vişa, *Monopoluri şi carteluri în România* (Bucharest, 1963), pp. 97–118, and on the Yugoslav, Kukoleća, pp. 426–48.

56. Great Britain, Overseas Trade Department, *Economic Conditions in Bulgaria, 1934*, pp. 36–41, *1937*, pp. 14–18; N.P. Arcadian, pp. 309–10.

57. Great Britain, Overseas Trade Department, *Economic Conditions in Greece, 1934*, pp. 29–33, *1937*, p. 17, *1939*, pp. 15–16; Naval Intelligence Division, *Greece*, II, pp. 107–11, 120–30.

58. Madgearu, *Evoluţia economiei româneşti*, p. 179. See pp. 232–35 on the greater impact of import quotas and failing prices than cartels on the level of industrial profits.

59. Ibid., p. 179. On the rising manufacture of cotton yarn, up from 2 to 17 firms for 1933–38, see Iovanelli, pp. 163–71. On the lack of success in growing cotton fiber, see *Enciclopedia României*, III, pp. 365–67.

60. David Turnock, "The Industrial Development of Romania from the Unification of the Principalities to the Second World War," in Francis W. Carter, ed., *An Historical Geography of the Balkans* (New York: Academic Press, 1977), pp. 362–66; *Enciclopedia României*, III, p. 862. On the Socomet metals cartel, see Vişa, pp. 128–38.

61. See Philippe C. Schmitter, "Reflections on Mihail Manoilescu and the

Political Consequences of Delayed-Dependent Development on the Periphery of Western Europe," in Kenneth Jowett, ed., *Social Change in Romania, 1860–1940* (Berkeley, Calif.: Institute of International Studies, 1977), pp. 117–23.

62. Vişa, pp. 121–25; Pearton, p. 215.

63. Barely 5 percent of textile output was cartellized, according to the survey of the industry in Kukoleća, pp. 422–53. For an accounting of state enterprises, see Jozo Tomasevich, "Postwar Foreign Economic Relations," in Robert J. Kerner, ed., *Yugoslavia* (Berkeley, Calif.: Univ. of California Press, 1949), p. 419.

64. Great Britain, Overseas Trade Department, *Economic Conditions in Jugoslavia, 1934*, pp. 12, 21, *1936*, pp. 24–28, *1938*, p. 4. Also see Naval Intelligence Division, *Jugoslavia*, III, pp. 218–20, and Vasa Čubrilović, ed., *Istorija Beograda*, III (Belgrade, 1974), pp. 232–33, 243, 251.

65. Lj. Dukanac, *Indeksi konjunkturnog razvoja Jugoslavije, 1918–1941* [Indexes of the Cyclical Development of Yugoslavia, 1918–1941] (Belgrade, 1946), pp. 23–24. These findings of relatively higher cartel prices through the 1930s are based only on a comparison with a list of different noncartellized products. No adjustment is made for regional differences in costs or taxes. On the shift of industry east from Zagreb, see Zh. Simunčić, "Osnovne karakteristike industrijskog razvitka Hrvatske, 1918–1941" [Basic Characteristics of the Industrial Development of Croatia, 1918–1941] *Acta historico-oeconomiae iugoslaviae*, vol. I (Zagreb, 1974), pp. 71–76.

66. Pejić, pp. 262–63. The decade's only legislation was a 1931 law that gave domestic firms priority in supplying state agencies. Arcadian, p. 109.

67. Madgearu, *Evoluția economiei românești*, pp. 351–53; Constantinescu and Axenciuc, p. 164; *Enciclopedia României*, IV, pp. 604–10; Institutul Central de Statistică, *Statistica societăților anonime din România*, XXII, *1940* (Bucharest, 1942), pp. 224–25. The two new institutes for industrial credit opened in 1937 fell far short of the more than 20 specialized industrial banks suggested the year before by Mihail Manoilescu in his *Un plan de organizarea creditului național* (Bucharest, 1936).

68. Jozo Tomasevich, "Foreign Economic Relations, 1918–1941," p. 179; Iovanelli, pp. 164–71; Marguerat, pp. 35, 53.

69. Belgrade's new state-owned sugar factory at Čukarica and the private Ilić textile mill, for instance, prospered on the basis of army orders from 1936 forward. Čubrilović, ed., *Istorija Beograda*, III, pp. 255–56.

70. Naval Intelligence Division, *Greece*, II, pp. 111–18, 131, 138–39.

71. Of 1,582 million leva in foreign industrial investment in 1936, cement production received 450 million, sugar refining 357 million, electric power 247 million, and textiles 203 million, together 80 percent of the total. Royal Institute for International Affairs, *Southeastern Europe* (London: Oxford University Press, 1939), pp. 173–74; Great Britain, Overseas Trade Department, *Economic Conditions in Bulgaria, 1937–38*, p. 73. On mining, see A.Iu. Totev, *Sravnitelno izuchavane na bulgarskoto i iugoslovenskoto narodno stopanstvo* [Comparative Research on the Bulgarian and Yugoslavian National Economies] (Sofia, 1940), pp. 129–32.

72. N. Živković, *Ratna šteta koju je Nemačka učinila Jugoslaviji u drugom*

svetskom ratu [War Damage Done by Germany to Yugoslavia during the Second World War] (Belgrade, 1975), pp. 34–44; Wünscht, pp. 95–97; Naval Intelligence Division, *Jugoslavia*, III, pp. 178–98.

73. Mirko Lamer, "Wandlungen der ausländischen Kapital auf der Balkan," *Weltwirtschaftliches Archiv*, vol. 43, no. 3 (1938), pp. 494–502.

74. Marguerat, pp. 29–33, 44–61; Turnock, pp. 364–66.

75. Most of the following account is drawn from Pearton, pp. 185–222. Full use of Romanian sources on the interwar evolution of the oil industry remains to be made.

76. Ibid., pp. 191–92, 201.

77. Ibid., p. 207.

78. Marguerat, pp. 29–32. According to Pearton, pp. 221–22, the British guarantee of Romanian sovereignty a week later was not on any expectations of holding onto Romanian oil supplies in case of a European war. The British hoped only to use it for their Asian commercial markets if war with Japan required the diversion of their Persian Gulf supplies to the Royal Navy.

13. The Economic Consequences of the Second World War

1. This reconciliation demands a separate and lengthy monograph to examine how the various statistical sources were collected and to integrate and manipulate prewar with postwar data as much as possible. For the wartime years and immediately afterwards, the lack of statistical yearbooks or comparable native publications forces us to rely on the relatively few foreign sources more than elsewhere in the book. Data on Albania are so scattered and questionable that its experience is omitted entirely.

2. Most of the preceding account is drawn from Karl Brandt, *Management of Agriculture and Food in the German-Occupied and Other Areas of Fortress Europe* (Stanford, Calif.: Stanford Univ. Press, 1953), pp. 215–31.

3. Ibid.; M.A. Lupu, ed., *Istoria economiei a României* (Bucharest, 1974), p. 552.

4. S.D. Zagoroff, Jenö Végh, and Alexander D. Bilimovich, *The Agricultural Economy of the Danubian Countries, 1935–1945* (Stanford, Calif.: Stanford Univ. Press, 1955), pp. 254–59; Henry L. Roberts, *Rumania: Political Problems of an Agrarian State* (New Haven, Conn.: Yale Univ. Press, 1951), pp. 238–39; Brandt, pp. 215–31.

5. This agency was used to collect the peasant's entire surplus production until the change to fixed deliveries and the formal establishment of a state trading organization in the second half of 1947. INCOOP crop collections for that year were 15 times the tonnage for 1945, admittedly a drought year. As late as 1948, however, almost 100,000 private traders still accounted for 65 percent of retail food sales. Institul de cercetare economice, *Dezvoltarea economiei RPR pe drumul socialismul, 1947–1957* [The Development of the RPR on the Road to Socialism, 1948–1957] (Bucharest, 1958), pp. 347–48; *Anuarul statistic al Romîniei, 1957* (Bucharest, 1958), pp. 163–66; M. Curteanu, *Sectorul de stat în România anilor 1944–47* [The State Sector in

Romania in the Years, 1944–1947] (Bucharest, 1974), pp. 91–92, 116; R. Georgescu-Roegen, *Modificare structurile venitul naționale al României in urma de al doilea război mondial* [Modifications in the Structure of the National Income of Romania as a Result of the Second World War] (Bucharest, 1947), p. 7, 10.

6. On rates of clearing exchange and Romanian export and import prices, see C.C. Kirițescu, *Sistemul bănesc al leului și precursorii lui* [The Monetary System of the Leu and Its Predecessors], II (Bucharest, 1967), pp. 505, 508, 518. On Romanian deliveries to the German war effort, see N.N. Constantinescu, "L'exploitation et le pillage de l'économie roumaine par l'Allemagne dans la periode, 1939–1944," *Revue roumaine d'istoire*, III, I (Bucharest, 1964), pp. 99–100.

7. I.V. Totu, ed., *Progresul economic în România, 1877–1977* (Bucharest, 1977), pp. 403–405; Nicholas Spulber, *The Economics of Communist Eastern Europe* (New York: John Wiley & Sons, 1957), pp. 237–40; Roberts, p. 237; Zagoroff, Végh, and Bilimovich, pp. 233–36, 265–76, 284.

8. Roberts, pp. 315–16.

9. Table 13.8; S.D. Zagoroff, *The Economy of Bulgaria* (Washington, D.C.: Council for Economic and Industry Research, 1955), p. 67; Zagoroff, Végh, and Bilimovich, p. 437.

10. Brandt, pp. 202–208.

11. Ibid., pp. 208–209; Zagoroff, Végh, and Bilimovich, pp. 391–94, 427–31, 443–47.

12. M. Minkov et al., *Poiava i razvitie na kooperativnoto zemedelie v Bulgariia pri usloviiata na kapitalizma* [The Appearance and Development of Cooperative Agriculture in Bulgaria under Conditions of Capitalism] (Sofia, 1969), pp. 164–73.

13. Exports to Germany were 88 percent of the reduced total value for 1944, according to Table 30 in Zagoroff, Végh, and Bilimovich, p, 432. For detailed evidence of Bulgaria's declining terms of trade with Germany, albeit to a lesser extent than Romania's, see L. Berov, "Kum vuprosa za vunshno-trgovskata orientatsiia na bulgarskiia fashizum, 1929–1945g." [On the Question of the Foreign Trade Orientation of Bulgarian Fascism, 1919–1945], *Trudove na visshiia ikonomicheski institut Karl Marx*, I (Sofia, 1954), p. 167.

14. Even domestic consumption of vegetables had held to 80 percent of the 1939 level for 1943 and 1944. The consumption of non-food items actually exceeded prewar levels, suggesting better deliveries of promised German imports than the Romanians received. On wartime production and consumption, see P. Kiranov, "Natsionalen dokhod na Bulgariia, 1939, 1944, 1945" [The National Income of Bulgaria], *Izvanredno izdanie na trimesechno spisanie na glavnata direktsiia na statistikata* [Special Edition, Quarterly Report of the Central Directorate for Statistics] (Sofia, 1946), p. 85.

15. Joint cooperative plantings of rice fields reaching 5,000 hectares, for instance, provided useful experience on how to go about collectivized farming. Minkov et al., pp. 315–18; Nikola Popov et al., *Ikonomika na Bulgariia*, II (Sofia, 1972), 241–68.

16. Calculated from Zagoroff, Végh, and Bilimovich, pp. 109–11. On the

fate of the United Tobacco Factory, see Natan et al., pp. 78–79, 103; Spulber, p. 162.

17. Naval Intelligence Divison, *Jugoslavia*, III (London, 1945), pp. 245–47; Zagoroff, Végh, and Bilimovich, *Agricultural Economy*, pp. 341, 439. On the role of the Reich Food Estate in German efforts for self-sufficiency, see Dieter Petzina, *Autarkiepolitik im Dritten Reich: Der nationalsozialistische Vierjahrsplan* (Stuttgart, 1968).

18. The best accounts in English remain Brandt, pp. 162–84, and Zagoroff, Végh, and Bilimovich, pp. 322–36. Also see Joachim Wünscht, *Jugoslawien und das Dritte Reich* (Stuttgart, 1969), pp. 206–16, for a West German view. For comparable data on the First World War, see Chapter 10.

19. Wünscht, p. 221; E.A. Radice, "Economic Developments in Eastern Europe under German Hegemony," in Martin M. McCauley, ed., *Communist Power in Europe, 1944–49* (New York: Barnes & Noble, 1977), Table 1.1 on p. 7.

20. Nikola Živković, *Ratna šteta koju je Nemačka učinala Jugoslaviji u drugom svetskom ratu* [War Damage Done by Germany to Yugoslavia during the Second World War] (Belgrade, 1975), pp. 280, 298; Brandt, pp. 157–61; Zagoroff, Végh, and Bilimovich, pp. 330, 336–41.

21. Zagoroff, Végh, and Bilimovich, pp. 124, 252, 344–55.

22. Ibid.; International Monetary Fund, *Balance of Payments Yearbook, 1948* (Washington, D.C., 1950), p. 427; Jozo Tomasevich, "Postwar Foreign Economic Relations," in Robert J. Kerner, ed., *Yugoslavia* (Berkeley, Calif.: Univ. of California Press, 1949), pp. 403, 407, 411.

23. Kerner, ed., p. 408; Spulber, pp. 140–41, 157, 238–40.

24. Brandt, pp. 235–47; Dimitrie Delivanis and William C. Cleveland, *Greek Monetary Developments, 1939–1948* (Bloomington, Ind.: Indiana Univ. Publications, 1949), pp. 65–66; Bank of Greece, *The Economic Situation in Greece and the Bank of Greece in 1946* (Reports for 1941, 1944–46) (Athens, 1948), pp. 63–69; Great Britain, Overseas Trade Department, *Economic and Commercial Conditions in Greece, 1949*; pp. 7–17.

25. Great Britain, Overseas Trade Development, *Economic and Commercial Conditions in Greece, 1949*, p. 22; International Monetary Fund, *Balance of Payments Yearbook, 1948*, p. 213; Delivanis and Cleveland, pp. 71–72, 159–60; Beckham Sweet-Escott, *Greece, A Political and Economic Survey, 1939–1953* (London: Royal Institute of International Affairs, 1954), pp. 147–49; Table 13.6. One instance where a wartime effort had been made to improve agricultural techniques occurred on the Lake Copäis estate. Its new Italian administration brought in German agronomists and equipment in order to increase provisions for the needy Athens area. After the war the estate's original English owners sold the property to the Greek government rather than resume operations. On postwar prospects for Greek tobacco production and export, see K. Varvaressos, *Report on Greek Economic Problems* (Washington, D.C.: IBRD mimeograph, February 12, 1952), pp. 164–77.

26. See for instance George Macesich, *Yugoslavia: The Theory and Practice of Development Planning* (Charlottesville, Va.: Univ. Press of Virginia, 1964), pp. 93–153, and Wray O. Candilis, *The Economy of Greece, 1944–1966* (New York: Praeger, 1968), pp. 89–151.

27. These funds covered all sterling expenses outside of Greece and up to

£5 million in the country. Candilis, pp. 11–13; Great Britain, Overseas Trade Department, *Economic Conditions in Greece, 1949*, pp. 17–18; Delivanis and Cleveland, pp. 23–57.

28. Delivanis and Cleveland, pp. 55–99; Candilis, pp. 14–19.

29. Candilis, pp. 14–19.

30. Ibid., pp. 23–48; Delivanis and Cleveland, pp. 109–68.

31. Sweet-Escott, pp. 153–61; Candilis, pp. 48–85. Also see William H. McNeill, *Greece: American Aid in Action, 1947–56* (New York: Twentieth Century Fund, 1957).

32. Of the Bank's direct credit, 67 percent went to agriculture, 17 percent to tobacco alone. Of its loans to other banks, 27 percent, the largest single share, was directed to restoring tobacco cultivation. Bank of Greece, *Economic Situation*, pp. 98–99, 103–105.

33. League of Nations, *Money and Banking, 1942–44* (Geneva, 1944), p. 220, Wünscht, pp. 203–204; Naval Intelligence Division, *Jugoslavia*, III, pp. 176–79.

34. Radice, Table 1.2, p. 9, records costs of $375 per capita for Serbia, $67 for Croatia, and $50 for Bulgaria and Romania. Also see Živković, pp. 393–401, 448–75, and Wünscht, pp. 218–19.

35. M. Ugričić, *Novčani sistem Jugoslavije* [The Monetary System of Yugoslavia] (Belgrade, 1967), pp. 139–51; Spulber, pp. 104–109.

36. Spulber, pp. 95–96; M. Golijanin, *Bankarstvo Jugoslavije* (Belgrade, 1977), pp. 39–42. A brief account of subsequent evolution is J.J. Hauvonen, "Postwar Developments in Money and Banking in Yugoslavia," *International Monetary Fund Staff Papers*, XVII, 3 (November, 1970), 563–601.

37. Note the virtual absence of references to the banking system in the two leading American works on Bulgarian and Romanian economic development since 1950, George R. Feiwel, *Growth and Reforms in Centrally Planned Economies: The Lessons of the Bulgarian Experience* (New York: Praeger, 1977), and John Michael Montias, *Economic Development in Communist Rumania* (Cambridge, Mass.: M.I.T. Press, 1967).

38. Natan et al., 132–36; P. Petkov, "Restriction and Abolition of Capitalist Ownership in Bulgaria," in M. Isusov, ed., *Problems of the Transition from Capitalism to Socialism in Bulgaria* (Sofia, 1975), pp. 154–56; Spulber, pp. 100–17.

39. Kiranov, p. 43; Natan et al., *Ikonomika na Bulgariia*, I (Sofia, 1969), p. 625; M. Maevschi, *Contribuţii la istoria finanţelor publice ale Romîniei* (Bucharest, 1957), Annex IX; C.C. Kiriţescu, *Sistemul bănesc al leului şi precursorii lui* [The Monetary System of the Leu and its Predecessors], II (Bucharest, 1967), pp. 503–26.

40. Maurice Pearton, *Oil and the Romanian State, 1895–1948* (London: Oxford Univ. Press, 1970), pp. 287–89; Kiriţescu, II, pp. 505–31; III (Bucharest, 1971), pp. 16–23.

41. United Nations, *Economic Survey of Europe in 1948* (Geneva, 1950), Table XIV; United Nations, *UN Statistical Yearbook, 1951* (Geneva, 1952), pp. 374–75; Kiriţescu, III, p. 40; Institutul de cercetare economică, *Dezvoltarea economiei RPR*, p. 390.

42. G. Sonia, *Naţionalizarea principalelor mijloace de producţie în România* [The Nationalization of the Principal Means of Production in

Romania] (Bucharest, 1968), pp. 38–40; Curteanu, pp. 135–37; Kirițescu, III, pp. 81–87, 93–98. The most comprehensive survey of Romanian finance immediately after the war is in Kirițescu, III, pp. 11–139.

43. The best available work is Joachim Pernack, *Probleme der wirtschaftliche Entwicklung Albaniens,* Südosteuropa Studien, 18 (Munich, 1972).

44. On Greece see William H. McNeill, *The Metamorphosis of Greece since World War II* (Chicago: Univ. of Chicago Press, 1978), pp. 138–205. For a study of how postwar urbanization in Yugoslavia, Bulgaria, and Romania have been more successful in raising shares of industrial than service employment to the European average, see Ger Ofer, "Economizing on Urbanization in Socialist Countries: Historical Necessity or Socialist Strategy," in Alan A. Brown and Egon Neuberger, eds., *International Migration: A Comparative Perspective* (New York: Academic Press, 1977), pp. 281–312.

45. On subsequent Romanian growth, see Montias, and Marvin R. Jackson, "Industrialization, Trade and Mobilization in Romania's Drive for Economic Independence," Joint Economic Committee of the U.S. Congress, *East European Economies Post-Helsinki* (Washington, D.C.: U.S. Government Printing Office, 1977), pp. 886–940.

46. L. Berov, "Kapitalobrazuvaneto v Bulgariia prez godinite na ftorata svetovna voina" [Capital Accumulation in Bulgaria during the Second World War], *Trudove na vishiia ikonomicheski institut Karl Marx,* II (Sofia, 1971), 17–40.

47. The latter was formed largely on the basis of a wartime German project. Radice, p. 16.

48. Petkov, pp. 153–68; Natan et al., 93–126.

49. Kirițescu, II, pp. 469, 491; David Turnock, "Industrial Development of Romania from the Unification of the Principalities to the Second World War," in Francis W. Carter, ed., *An Historical Geography of the Balkans* (New York: Academic Press, 1977), pp. 362–64. Altogether, German investment held a controlling interest in about 200 Romanian enterprises, with about 11 billion 1938 lei in commerce and banking as well as industry by 1942, pp. 316–18.

50. Totu, pp. 312–15. Pearton, pp. 240–63.

51. Pearton, pp. 291–96, 315–321.

52. Ibid., pp. 208–14; Sonia, pp. 21, 38–40, 96–99, 108; Curteanu, pp. 96, 106–15, 172; Spulber, pp. 77–80, 172–76, 180.

53. See R.V. Burks, *The Dynamics of Communism in Eastern Europe* (Princeton, N.J.: Princeton Univ. Press, 1961), pp. 118–30.

54. Živković, pp. 286–96. On the lack of wartime statistics, see B. Petranović, "O promenama u društveno-ekonomskoj strukturi Jugoslavije u toku NOB (1941–1945)" [On Changes in the Socioeconomic Structure of Yugoslavia during the National Liberation War, 1941–45], *Prilozi za istorije socializma,* 6 (Belgrade, 1969), 158–59.

55. Živković, pp. 314–25; Wünscht, pp. 206–16; Radice, pp. 7, 12.

56. Živković, pp. 279–80, 296–99. On Macedonia under Bulgarian occupation, see L. Sokolov, *Industrija na NR Makedonija* (Skopje, 1961), pp. 123–26.

57. B. Petranović, *Politička i ekonomska osnova narodne vlasti u Jugo-*

slaviji za vreme obnova [Political and Economic Foundation of the People's Power in Yugoslavia during the Rebirth] (Belgrade, 1969), pp. 231–55. The state's share of industrial capital totalled just 10 percent in 1938, according to S. Kukoleća, *Industrija Jugoslavije, 1918–1939* (Belgrade, 1941), p. 385.

58. For contrasting Western views on Yugoslav industrial growth from the end of the war into the 1950s, see the critical Joseph Bombelles, *The Economic Development of Communist Yugoslavia, 1947–1964* (Stanford, Calif.: Hoover Institute, 1968), pp. 12–47, and the favorable F.E.I. Hamilton, *Yugoslavia: Patterns of Economic Activity* (New York: Praeger, 1968), pp. 53–153. A good overview of the record since then is Egon Neuberger, "Industry and Handicrafts," in Klaus-Detlev Grothusen, ed., *Jugoslawien*, Südosteuropa-Handbuch, I (Göttingen, 1975), pp. 235–73. For a bibliographic survey of the numerous works in English since 1966 on the economies of Yugoslavia, Bulgaria, Romania, and Albania, see John R. Lampe, "The Study of Southeast European Economies, 1966–1977," *Balkanistica*, IV (1977–78), pp. 63–88.

59. Delivanis and Cleveland, p. 23.

60. Bank of Greece, *Economic Situation*, pp. 75–82, 94, 99; United Nations, *Economic Survey of Europe, 1953* (Geneva, 1953), pp. 98, 110–112; Jackson, p. 903.

61. Candilis, pp. 48–51, 65–66.

62. Ibid., pp. 180–93. Also see the annual economic surveys on Greece published by the Organization for Economic Cooperation and Development since 1960.

Conclusion: Postwar Industrialization
in Historical Perspective

1. The only comprehensive survey of postwar Albanian economic development in English is Michael Kaser and Adi Schnytzer, "Albania: A Uniquely Socialist Economy" in Joint Economic Committee, U.S. Congress (hereafter JEC), *East European Economies Post Helskinki* (Washington, D.C.: U.S. Gov. Printing Office, 1977), pp. 567–646.

2. See the chapter on socialist growth in Lloyd G. Reynolds, *Image and Reality in Economic Development* (New Haven, Conn.: Yale Univ. Press, 1977), pp. 397–428, especially pp. 398–401. For a specific description of price distortion, see Marvin R. Jackson, "Prices and Efficiency in Romanian Foreign Trade," in Josef C. Brada, ed., *Quantitative and Analytical Studies in East-West Economic Relations*, Studies in Eastern European and Soviet Planning, Development and Trade No. 24 (Bloomington, Ind.: International Development Research Center, 1976), pp. 117–33.

3. On the limitations of official Yugoslav statistics, see Vinod Dubey, et al., *Yugoslavia: Development with Decentralization* (Baltimore, Md.: Johns Hopkins Univ. Press, 1975), Appendix A, pp. 310–318. On the more serious problems with postwar Bulgarian and especially Romanian data, see Marvin R. Jackson, "Bulgaria's Economy in the 1970s: Adjusting Productivity to Structure," pp. 571–617, and idem, "Romania's Economy at the End of the 1970s: Turning the Corner on Intensive Development," in JEC, *East Euro-*

pean Country Studies 1980 (Washington, D.C.: U.S. Gov. Printing Office, 1981), pp. 231–97.

4. Mark Allen, "The Bulgarian Economy in the 1970s," in JEC, *East European Economies,* pp. 675, 671–91; Paul Bairoch, *The Economic Development of the Third World since 1900* (Berkeley, Calif.: Univ. of California Press, 1977), p. 19.

5. Gur Ofer, "Growth Strategy, Specialization in Agriculture and Trade: Bulgaria and Eastern Europe," in Paul Marer and John Michael Montias, eds., *East European Integration and East-West Trade* (Bloomington, Ind.: Indiana Univ. Press, 1981), pp. 283–312.

6. Jackson, "Bulgaria's Economy," pp. 571–617.

7. Marvin R. Jackson, "Industrialization, Trade, and Mobilization in Romania's Drive for Economic Independence," in JEC, *East European Economies,* pp. 926–36. Also see the calculations in Gregor Lazarchik, *Bulgarian Agricultural Production, Output, Expenses, Gross and Net Product, and Productivity, at 1968 Prices, for 1939 and 1948–1970* (New York: Riverside Research Institute, 1973); and Gregor Lazarchik and George Pall, *Romania: Agricultural Production, Output, Expenses, Gross and Net Product, and Productivity, 1938, 1948, 1950–71* (New York: Riverside Research Institute, 1973). The best account of Romanian agriculture from 1950 to 1965 is John Michael Montias, *Economic Development in Communist Romania* (Cambridge, Mass.: M.I.T. Press, 1967), pp. 23–32, 87–134.

8. Jackson, "Industrialization, Trade and Mobilization," pp. 900, 918, and Ofer, pp. 283–312. Also see Andreas C. Tsantis and Roy Pepper, *Romania: The Industrialization of an Economy under Socialist Planning* (Washington, D.C.: World Bank, 1979), p. 258.

9. Dubey et al., pp. 272–76. Also see Branko Horvat, *The Postwar Evolution of Yugoslav Agricultural Organization* (New York: IASP, 1974), and Yugoslav FAO Committee, *The Development of Agriculture in Socialist Yugoslavia* (Belgrade, 1979).

10. Yugoslav FAO Committee, pp. 154–60.

11. OECD Economic Surveys, *Greece, 1978* (Paris: OECD, 1978), pp. 20–28, 69; Wray O. Candilis, *The Economy of Greece, 1944–1966* (New York: Praeger, 1968), pp. 125–31.

12. By 1975 agriculture received just 14 percent of short-term bank credit but fully half of long-term credit. See D.J. Halikias, *Money and Credit in a Developing Economy: The Greek Case* (New York: New York Univ. Press, 1978), pp. 135, 235–49, and E.G. Panas, "Greece," in Organization for Economic Cooperation and Development, *Utilization of Savings* (Paris: OECD, 1968), pp. 222–44.

13. Charles Wilson, *England's Apprenticeship, 1603–1763* (London: Longman's, 1965).

14. On Southeast Asia, see Stephen A. Resnick, "The Decline of Rural Industry Under Export Expansion: A Comparison among Burma, Phillipines and Thailand, 1870–1938," *Journal of Economic History,* XXX, 1 (March, 1970), pp. 33–50.

15. Bairoch, p. 162, notes that the average extractive sector in the Third World of 1970 employed less than one percent of the national labor force.

16. Montias, pp. 16–19. On the generally neglected question of Soviet

economic relations with Romania and Bulgaria in the early 1950s, see Janos Horvat, "Grant Elements in Intra-Bloc Aid Programs," *ASTE Bulletin*, vol. 8, no. 30 (Fall, 1971), pp. 1–17, and Paul Marer, "Soviet Economic Policy in Eastern Europe," in JEC, *Reorientation and Commercial Relations in the Economies of Eastern Europe* (Washington, D.C.: U.S. Government Printing Office, 1974), pp. 135–63.

17. Montias, pp. 205–206; Edward A. Hewitt, *Foreign Trade Prices in the Council for Mutual Economic Assistance* (London: Cambridge Univ. Press, 1974), pp. 70–71, 97–98; Marshall I. Goldman, *Soviet Foreign Aid* (New York: Praeger, 1967), pp. 27–28.

18. The Bulgarian ratios of 2.83 in 1970 and 2.78 in 1930 contrast with 1.89 versus 3.94 for Romania and 2.94 versus 4.86 for Greece. Yugoslavia also shows little change in 1970 over 1930, recording 1.79 and 1.69 ratios. Calculated from sources in Table 11.3.

19. Frederick Levcik and Jan Stankowski, *Industrial Cooperation between East and West* (White Plains, N.Y.: M.E. Sharp, 1979), p. 14, shows Bulgaria with the highest share of specialized exports under CMEA agreements (19.3 percent of total exports) and Romania with the lowest (3.5 percent). Also see Jackson, "Romania's Economy at the End of the 1970s."

20. For the 1950s, see George W. Hoffman, *Regional Development Strategy in Southeastern Europe* (New York: Praeger, 1972), pp. 95–99, and Montias, pp. 15–16, 39–48. For the 1960s, even the Alton growth rates for Gross National Product, lower than official rates for Net Material Product which exclude services, calculate industrial rates that exceed 10 percent. See George Staller, *Bulgaria: A New Industrial Production Index, 1963–1972* (New York: L.W. International Research, 1975), and Thad P. Alton, "Economic Growth and Resource Allocation in Eastern Europe," in JEC, *Reorientation and Commercial Relations*, pp. 274–75. On the problems undermining calculations of capital investment, see Jackson, "Bulgaria's Economy" and his "Romania's Economy," in *East European Country Studies 1980*, pp. 571–617 and 231–97.

21. George Feiwel, *Growth and Reforms in Centrally Planned Economies: The Lessons of the Bulgarian Experience* (New York: Praeger, 1977), pp. 30–48; Montias, pp. 38–39, 53–71. Also see Alexander Bajt, "Investment Cycles in European Socialist Economies: A Review Article," *Journal of Economic Literature*, XI:1 (March, 1971), pp. 53–63. For recent Western argument that suppressed inflation and disguised unemployment have accompanied this irregular pattern of industrial growth, see Josef C. Brada, "Inflationary Pressures and the Optimal Tautness of Plans in a Centrally Planned Economy," *Journal of Comparative Economics* (in press); Frederick L. Pryor, "Some Costs and Benefits of Markets: An Empirical Study," *Quarterly Journal of Economics*, XCI:1 (Feb., 1977), pp. 81–102; and Morris Bornstein, "Unemployment in Capitalist Regulated Market Economies and Socialist Centrally Planned Economies," *American Economic Review* (May, 1978), pp. 38–43.

22. In addition to the volumes on Eastern Europe published in 1969, 1974, 1977, and 1980 by the Joint Economic Committee of the U.S. Congress, see recent articles in *Soviet Studies. ACES Bulletin, Osteuropa-Wirtschaft* and

Jahrbuch der Wirtschaft Osteuropas, the Studies in East European and Soviet Planning, Development and Trade published by the International Development Research Center in Bloomington, Indiana, and Hans Hermann Hohmann, Michael Kaser, Karl C. Thalheim, eds., *The New Economic System of Eastern Europe* (Berkeley, Calif.: Univ. of California Press, 1975).

23. See note 19 above. Also see Dubey et al., pp. 289–95; OECD, *Greece, July 1978*, pp. 27–35.

24. Candilis, pp. 152–58; OECD, *Greece, 1978*, p. 32; Dubey et al., pp. 80–84.

25. On developments during the 1960s, see Laura D'Andrea Tyson, *The Yugoslav Banking System and Monetary Control-Trade Credit and Illiquidity Crises in the Yugoslav Economy* (Geneva: ILO, 1975) and Dimitrije Dimitrijević and George Macesich, *Money and Finance in Contemporary Yugoslavia* (New York: Praeger, 1973).

26. Dubey et al., 34, 222, 229, 263–64.

27. Candilis, pp. 117–19, 187. Of 227 Greek enterprises receiving foreign capital in 1964, only 50 acquired any in the form of joint-stock equity treatment.

28. Dimetrios A. Germidis and Maria Negreponti-Delivanis, *Industrialization, Employment and Income Distribution in Greece* (Paris: OECD, 1975), pp. 20–34, 40–43, 82–84; Halikias, pp. 129–62.

29. On regional imbalances, see Dubey et al., p. 191; M.I. Logan, "Regional Economic Development in Yugoslavia, 1953–1964." *Tydschrift voor Economische en Sociale Geographic*, 59 (1968), pp. 42–52; and Germidis and Negreponti-Delivanis, pp. 81–93.

30. See Stephen R. Sacks, *Entry of New Competitors in Yugoslav Market Socialism* (Berkeley, Calif.: Institute of International Studies, 1973). On the pressures of a small internal market, see E.A.G. Robinson, ed., *The Economic Consequences of the Size of Nations* (New York: St. Martin's Press, 1960) and Meir Merhav, *Technological Dependence, Monopoly and Growth* (Oxford: Pergamon Press, 1969), pp. 114–36.

31. On socialist problems of selling industrial exports on present world markets, see Josef C. Brada and Marvin R. Jackson, "The Organization of Foreign Trade under Capitalism and Socialism," *Journal of Comparative Economics*, vol. 2, no. 4 (Dec., 1978), pp. 293–320; Marvin R. Jackson, "The CPE Export System as a Marketing Organization," in Josef C. Brada and V.S. Somanath, eds., *East-West Trade: Theory and Evidence*, Studies in East European and Soviet Planning, Development and Trade No. 27 (Bloomington, Ind.: International Development Research Institute, 1978), pp. 3–27; and Brada, ed., *East-West Economic Relations*.

32. See Paul Marer, "East Europe Economies: Achievements, Problems, Prospects," in Teresa Rakowska-Harmstone and Andrew Gyorgy, eds., *Communism in Eastern Europe* (Bloomington, Ind.: Indiana Univ. Press, 1979), pp. 244–89, and Marvin R. Jackson, "Perspectives on Romanian Economic Development in the 1980s," in Daniel N. Nelson, ed., *Romania in the 1980s* (Boulder, Colo.: Westview Press, 1981), pp. 254–305. Also see Jackson, "Bulgaria's Economy" and "Romania's Economy," in *East European Country Studies 1980*, pp. 571–617 and 231–97.

Selected
Bibliography

As in the notes, self-evident titles, e.g., *Istoria Romîniei*, have not been translated. The bibliography includes a number of works profitably consulted but not specifically footnoted. In the interest of relevance or brevity, a number of footnoted works are omitted here.

I. Primary and Statistical Sources

Statistical Yearbooks

Ancheta industrialǎ din 1901–1902. 2 vols. Bucharest, 1904.

Annuaire statistique Hongroise, 1910. Budapest, 1912.

Anuarul statistic al României, 1904, 1909–16, 1922–40. Bucharest, 1905, 1910–19, 1923–41.

Institutul Central de Statistica. *Recensamântul general al populaţiei României din 29 decemvrie 1930.* [General Census of the Romanian Population of 29 December 1930]. Vols. I–X. Bucharest, 1930.

Ministarstvo na turgoviata, promishlenostta i truda. *Enquete sur l'industrie encouragée Bulgare, 1909.* Sofia, 1912.

Institutul Central de Statisticǎ, *Statistica societaţilor anonime din România.* [Statistics of the Joint-Stock Corporations of Romania]. *1919–40.* Bucharest, 1920–42.

Statistikë epetëris tës Ellados. [Statistical Yearbook of Greece]. *1930–39.* Athens, 1931–40.

Statistikë toy emporioy tes Ellados meta ton xenon epikration [Statistics of Foreign Trade for Greece] *1930–1938.* Athens, 1933–40.

Statisticheski godishnik na Bulgarskoto Tsarstvo. [Statistical Yearbook of the Bulgarian Kingdom]. *1909–42*. Sofia, 1910–43.

Signjar, Rudolph. *Statistički atlas Kr. Hrvatske i Slavonije, 1875–1915* [Statistical Atlas for Croatia/ Slavonia, 1875–1915]. Zagreb, 1915.

Statistički godišnjak Hrvatske–Slavonije [Statistical Yearbook of Croatia–Slavonia]. *1905–1914*. Zagreb, 1905–14.

Statistički godišnjak Kr. Jugoslavije [Statistical Yearbook of the Kingdom of Yugoslavia]. *1929–40*. Belgrade, 1930–41.

Statistički godišnjak Kr. Srbije [Statistical Yearbook of the Kingdom of Serbia]. *1893–1908*. Belgrade, 1895–1913.

Statistike spoljne trgovine Kr. Srbije [Statistics of Foreign Trade for the Kingdom of Serbia]. *1909–11*. Belgrade, 1910–12.

Official Publications and State Archives

a. Southeastern Europe

Bulgarian Ministry of Commerce and Agriculture. *Bulgaria of Today*. London, 1907.

Industrijska Komora Kr. Srbije. *Izveštaj* [Report]. Belgrade, 1911.

Institutul Central de Statistică. *Înterprinderile particulare industriale, comerciale şi de transport* [Private industrial, trade, and transport enterprises]. Bucharest, 1947.

Ministarski savet na tsarstvo Bulgariia. *Doklad do Ferdinand I ot Ministarski Savet, 1887–1912* [Report to Ferdinand from the Council of Ministers, 1887–1912]. Sofia, 1912.

Ministère de l'industrie et du commerce. *La Roumanie économique, 1921*. Bucharest, 1921.

Rumänien, 1866–1906. Bucharest, 1906.

Trgovska-industriska kamara, Sofia. *Godishnik* [Yearbook]. *1923–38*. Sofia, 1924–41.

Union des chambres de commerce et d'industrie de Roumanie. *La roumanie économique en 1926*. Bucharest, n.d.

b. Western Europe and the United States

Archives Nationales (Paris). F30.

Great Britain, Diplomatic and Consular Reports. *Annual Series*.

Great Britain, Overseas Trade Department. *Economic Conditions in Bulgaria*. Annual, 1921–39.

———. *Economic Conditions in Greece*. Annual, 1921–39.

———. *Economic Conditions in Jugoslavia*. Annual, 1921–39.

———. *The Economic Situation in Rumania*. Annual, 1921–39.

Great Britain, Parliamentary Papers. *Annual Series*.

K. und K. Österreichische Handelsmuseum, *Albanien, Wirtschaftsverhältnisse, 1914*. Vienna, 1915.

———. *Bulgarien: Wirtschaftsverhältnisse, 1909–1916*. 4 vols. Vienna, 1910–18.

———. *Griechenland: Wirtschaftsverhältnisse, 1909–14*. 2 vols. Vienna, 1912, 1915.

———. *Rumänien: Wirtschaftsverhältnisse, 1909–14*. 2 vols. Vienna, 1912, 1915.

―――. *Rumänien: Landes und wirtschaftstatistischen Übersichten.* Vienna, 1917.

―――. *Serbien: Wirtschaftsverhältnisse, 1909–11.* Vienna, 1912.

Royaume de Belgique. *Receuil consulaire.* Vols. XLV–155 (Brussels, 1883–1912).

Staatsarchiv (Vienna). *Administrative Registratur.*

U.S. Department of Agriculture. *Rumania. A Guide to Official Statistics of Agriculture and Food Supply.* Agricultural Economic Bibliography no. 49. Washington, D.C.: U.S. Government Printing Office, 1930.

―――. *Agricultural Survey of Europe: The Danube Basin—Part 2, Romania, Bulgaria, and Yugoslavia* (by Louis G. Michael). Technical Bulletin No. 126. Washington, D.C.: U.S. Government Printing Office, October, 1929.

U.S. Department of Commerce. Bureau of Foreign and Domestic Commerce. *Kingdom of Serbs, Croats and Slovenes (Yugoslavia): A Commercial and Industrial Handbook* (by Kenneth S. Patton). Trade Promotion Series No. 61. Washington, D.C.: U.S. Government Printing Office, 1928.

―――. *Roumania, an Economic Handbook.* Special Agents Series No. 222. Washington, D.C.: U.S. Government Printing Office, 1924.

c. League of Nations

League of Nations. *Balance of Payments, 1928–39.* Geneva, 1933–39. *1928–39.* Geneva, 1929–39.

League of Nations, Economic and Financial Department. *Commercial Banks, 1929–1934.* Geneva, 1935.

―――. *International Trade Statistics. 1931–38.* Geneva, 1933–38.

―――. *Memorandum on Balance of Payments and Foreign Trade Balances 1911–1925.* Geneva, 1926. League of Nations.

―――. *Memorandum on International Trade and Balance of Payments 1913–1927.* Geneva, 1928.

―――. *Memorandum on Currency and Central Banks, 1913–25.* Geneva, 1926.

―――. *Money and Banking. 1936–42.* Geneva, 1937–42.

―――. *Statistical Yearbook. 1928–39.* Geneva, 1929–39.

―――. *World Production and Prices 1936/37.* Geneva, 1937.

United Nations, *International Capital Movements during the Interwar Period.* Lake Success, N.Y., 1949.

Bank Publications

Banca Marmarosch-Blanc. *Banca Marmorosch-Blank, 1849–1923.* Bucharest, 1923.

―――. *Les forces économiques de la Roumanie 1927.* Bucharest, 1928. *1928.* Bucharest, 1929. *1929.* Bucharest, 1930.

Bank of Greece. *Report for the Year 1932–37.* Athens, 1933–38.

―――. *The Economic Situation in Greece and the Bank of Greece in 1946* (Reports for 1941, 1944–46). Athens, 1948.

Banque Nationale de Bulgarie. *Comptes rendus de la B.N.B. 1925–40.* Sofia, 1941.

Banque Nationale de la Roumanie. *Bulletin de l'information et de documentation*. Monthly, Bucharest, 1929–46.

Bulgarska Narodna Banka. *Izvestiia na Bulgarska Narodna Banka*. Sofia, 1924–40.

———. *Godishni otchet na Bulgarska Narodna Banka* [Annual Report of the Bulgarian National Bank]. *1894–1912*. Sofia, 1985–1913.

———. *Iubileen sbornik na Bulgarskata Narodna Banka, 1897–1929* [Anniversary Yearbook of the Bulgarian National Bank, 1879–1929]. Sofia, 1929.

Narodna Banka Kr. Jugoslavije. *Narodna Banka, 1884–1934*. Belgrade, 1935.

———. *Razvoj narodne privrede u Jugoslavije* [The Development of the National Economy of Yugoslavia]. 12 vols. Belgrade, 1929–40.

Other Statistical Sources and Publications

Avramović, M. *Naše seljačko gazdinstvo* [Our Peasant Economy]. Sarajevo, 1927.

Bobchev, S. *Bulgarski aktsii i obligatsii* [Bulgarian Stocks and Bonds]. Sofia, 1910.

Caranfil, G.G., and Jordan, D.N. *Études statistique sur les valeurs mobiliers en Roumanie de 1908 a 1930*. Paris, 1931.

Chakalov, As. *Natsionalniiat dokhod i razkhod na Bulgariia 1924–1945* [National Income and Outlay of Bulgaria 1924–1945]. Sofia, 1946.

Direcţia Centrală de Statistică. *Din istoria statisticii româneşti: culegere de articole* [From the History of Romanian Statistics: A Collection of Articles]. Bucharest, 1969.

Djuričić, V.M., et al. *Naša narodna privrede i nacionalni prihod* [Our National Economy and National Income]. Sarajevo, 1927.

Dukanac, Lj. *Indeksi konjunkturnog razvoja Jugoslavije, 1918–1941* [Indexes of the Cyclical Development of Yugoslavia, 1918–1941]. Belgrade, 1946.

Evelpidi, Ch. "Le revenu national de pays balkaniques." *Metron* 14 (Rome, June 1940). 159–69.

———. "To ethnikon eisodëma" [National Income]. *Agrotiken oikonomiken*, vol. 4, no. 3 (Athens, 1937). 383–424.

Fellner, Friedrich. "Die Verteilung des Volksvermögens und Volkseinkommens der Länder des Ungarischen Heiligen Krone zwischen dem heutigen Ungarn und den Successions-Staaten." *Metron* 3 (Rome, 1928): 226–307.

Ferenczi, Imre. *International Migrations*, vol. I. New York: National Bureau of Economic Research, 1929.

Georgescu-Roegen, R. *Modificare structurile venitul naţionale al României în urma de la doila razboi mondial* [Modifications in the Structure of the National Income of Romania as a Result of the Second World War]. Bucharest, 1947.

Jackson, Marvin R. "Agricultural Output in Southeastern Europe, 1910–1938." *ACES Bulletin* 14 (Summer, 1982), in press.

———. "Comparing the Balkan Demographic Experience, 1860–1950."

Faculty Working Papers in Economics. Nos. 79–86. Tempe, Arizona: College of Business Administration, Arizona State University, 1979.

————. "National Product and Income in Southeastern Europe before the Second World War." *ACES Bulletin* 14 (Fall-Winter, 1982), in press.

Jackson, Marvin R. and John R. Lampe. "Survey of Evidence of Industrialization in Southeastern Europe, 1900–1950." *East European Quarterly* XVI (1982), in press.

Kapsalis, T.S. *La balance des comptes de la Grèce.* Lausanne, 1927.

Kiranov, P. "Natsionaleṅ dokhod na Bulgariia, 1939, 1944, 1945" [The National Income of Bulgaria]. *Izvanredno izdanie na trimesechno spisanie na glavnata direktsiia na statistikata.* Sofia, 1946.

Kukoléca, S. *Industrija Jugoslavije, 1918–1939.* Belgrade, 1941.

Liepmann, H. *Tariff Levels and the Economic Unity of Europe.* New York: Macmillan Co., 1938.

Lupu, Marin. "Studii privind dezvoltarea economiei României în perioada capitalismului" [Studies concerning the development of the economy of Romania in the period of capitalism]. *Studii şi cercetări economice* (Bucharest, 1967): 245–372.

MacGregor, John. *Commercial Statistics.* 2 vols. London, 1850.

Manescu, Manea and Ionescu, Constantin, eds. *Istoria statisticii din România: contribuţii* [The History of Statistics in Romania: Contributions]. Bucharest, 1969.

Milošević, S.B. *Spoljna trgovina Srbije, 1843–1875* [Foreign Trade of Serbia, 1843–1875]. Belgrade, 1902.

Mitchell, B.R. *European Historical Statistics, 1750–1970.* New York: Columbia Univ. Press, 1975.

Mollev, I. and Totev, A.U. *Tseni na zemedelskite produkti u nas, 1881–1934* [Prices of Our Agricultural Products, 1881–1934]. Sofia, 1935.

Moore, Wilbert E. *Economic Demography of Eastern and Southern Europe.* Geneva, 1945.

Pianu, N.I. *Industria mare, 1866–1906* [Large Industry, 1866–1906]. Bucharest, 1906.

Popoff, Kiril. *La Bulgarie économique, 1879–1911.* Paris, 1920.

Popović, N. and Mišić, P. *Naša domaća privreda* [Our Domestic Economy]. Belgrade, 1929.

Rozenberg, Vl. and Kostić, J. *Ko financira jugoslovensku privredu* [Who Finances the Yugoslav Economy]. Belgrade, 1940.

Şerbulescu, Al. "Venitul naţional şi fiscalitatea în perioada 1929–1936" [National Income and the Fiscal Burden in 1929–1936]. *Independenţa economică* 1 (Bucharest, 1938): 34–45.

Stajić, St. *Nacionalni dohodak Jugoslavije 1923–39 u stalnim i tekućim cenama* [National Income of Yugoslavia 1923–1939 in Constant and Current Prices]. Belgrade, 1959.

Stipetić, Vladimir. *Kretanje i tendencije u razvitku poljoprivredne proizvodneje na području NR Hrvatske* [Growth and Trends in the Development of Agricultural Trends on the Territory of the PR Croatia]. Zagreb, 1959.

Svennilson, Ingvar. *Growth and Stagnation in the European Economy.* Geneva, 1954.

Totev, A.Iu. *Sravnitelno izuchavane na bulgarskoto i iugoslavenskoto narodno stopanstvo* [A Comparative Inquiry on the Bulgarian and Yugoslav Economies]. Sofia, 1940.

Tutuc, I. *Studiul valoarilor mobilare* [The Study of Movable Assets]. Bucharest, 1927.

Vinski, Ivo. "Nacionalni dohodak i fiskni fondovi na području Jugoslavije 1909–1959" [National Income and Fixed Capital on Yugoslav Territory 1909–1959]. *Ekonomski pregled* X (Zagreb, 1959): 832–62.

―――. *Klasna podjela stanovništva i nacionalnog dohotka Jugoslavije* [The Class Distribution of the Population and National Income of Yugoslavia in 1938]. Zagreb, 1970.

Vurkhovna stopanska kamara. *Natsionalniiat dokhod na Bulgariia, 1936–1945* [The National Income of Bulgaria, 1936–1945]. Sofia, 1947.

Woytinsky, W.S. and Woytinsky, E.S. *World Population and Production.* New York: Twentieth Century Fund, 1953.

II. Secondary Sources

Economic History and Development

Ashworth, William. "Typologies and Evidence: Has Nineteenth-Century Europe a Guide to Economic Growth?" *Economic History Review* 2d ser., VII (1977):153–57.

Bairoch, Paul. *The Economic Development of the Third World since 1900.* Berkeley, Calif.: Univ. of California Press, 1975.

Black, Cyril E. *The Dynamics of Modernization.* New York: Harper Torchbooks, 1966.

Brada, Joseph C. and Jackson, Marvin R. "The Organization of Foreign Trade under Capitalism and Socialism." *Journal of Comparative Economics* 2 (Dec. 1978):293–320.

Cameron, Rondo, ed. *Banking and Economic Development: The Lessons of History.* New York: Oxford Univ. Press, 1972.

Denison, John H. *Why Growth Rates Differ.* Washington, D.C.: Brookings Institution, 1967.

Dobb, Maurice. *Studies in the Development of Capitalism.* New York: International Publishers, 1962.

Fieldhouse, D.K. *Economics and Empire, 1830–1914.* Ithaca, N.Y.: Cornell Univ. Press, 1974.

Gerschenkron, Alexander. *Economic Backwardness in Historical Perspective.* New York: Praeger, 1965.

Goldsmith, Raymond. *Financial Structure and Development.* New Haven, Conn.: Yale Univ. Press, 1969.

Gould, J.D. *Economic Growth in History.* London: Metheun, 1972.

Hicks, Sir John. *A Theory of Economic History.* London: Oxford Univ. Press, 1969.

Johnston, Bruce F. and Kilby, Peter. *Agricultural and Structural Transformation-Economic Strategies in Late-Developing Countries.* New York: Oxford Univ. Press, 1975.

Jorgensen, D.W. "Surplus Agricultural Labour and the Development of a Dual Economy." *Oxford Economic Papers* 19 (1967):288–312.

Kenen, Peter B., ed. *International Trade and Finance.* Cambridge: Cambridge Univ. Press, 1975.

Kuznets, Simon. *Modern Economic Growth.* New Haven, Conn.: Yale Univ. Press, 1966.

Lewis, Arthur W. "Economic Development with Unlimited Supplies of Labor." *Manchester School of Economic and Social Studies* XXII (May 1954):139–91.

————. *The Theory of Economic Growth.* London: Allen & Unwin, 1955.

List, Friedrich. *The National System of Political Economy.* London: Longmans, 1928.

McClelland, Peter D. *Causal Explanation and Model Building in History, Economics and the New Economic History.* Ithaca, N.Y.: Cornell Univ. Press, 1975.

Mendels, Franklin. "Proto-industrialization: The First Phase of the Process of Industrialization." *Journal of Economic History* XXXII (1972):241–61.

Merhav, Meir. *Technological Dependence, Monopoly and Growth.* Oxford: Pergamon Press, 1969.

Ofer, Gur. "Economizing on Urbanization in Socialist Countries: Historical Necessity or Socialist Strategy." In *Internal Migration: A Comparative Perspective,* ed. Alan A. Brown and Egon Neuberger. New York: Academic Press, 1977.

Pryor, Frederick L. *Property and Industrial Organization in Communist and Capitalist Countries.* Bloomington, Ind.: Indiana Univ. Press, 1973.

Reynolds, Lloyd G., ed. *Agriculture in Development Theory.* New Haven, Conn.: Yale University Press, 1975.

————. *Image and Reality in Economic Development.* New Haven, Conn.: Yale Univ. Press, 1977.

Robinson, E.A.G., ed. *The Economic Consequences of the Size of Nations.* New York: St. Martin's Press, 1960.

Thorberke, Erik, ed. *The Role of Agriculture in Economic Development.* New York: NBER/Columbia Univ. Press, 1969.

Tilly, Charles et al. *The Formation of National States in Western Europe.* Princeton, N.J.: Princeton Univ. Press, 1968.

Tuma, Elias H. *Economic History and the Social Sciences: Problems of Methodology.* Berkeley: Univ. of California Press, 1971.

Wallerstein, Immanuel. *The Modern World System: Capitalist Agriculture and the Origins of the European World Economy in the Sixteenth Century.* New York: Academic Press, 1974.

Warriner, Doreen. *Economics of Peasant Farming.* New York: Barnes & Noble, 1963.

Southeastern Europe

a. 1550–1850

Aumard, Marcel. *Venise, Raguse et le commerce du blé dans la seconde moitié du XVI siècle.* Paris, 1966.

Berov, Liuben. *Dvizhenieto na tsenite na Balkanite prez XVI–XIX v. i evropeisakata revolutsiia na tsenite* [The Movement of Prices in the Balkans During the 16–19th Centuries and the European Price Revolution]. Sofia, 1976.

Blum, Jerome. *Noble Landowners and Agriculture in Austria, 1815–1848.* Baltimore, Md.: Johns Hopkins Press, 1948.

Braudel, Ferdinand. *The Mediterranean and the Mediterranean World in the Age of Philip II.* 2 vols. New York: Harper & Row, 1972.

Carter, Francis W. *Dubrovnik (Ragusa) A Classic City-State.* London: Seminar Press, 1972.

Carter, Francis W., ed. *An Historical Geography of the Balkans.* New York: Academic Press, 1977.

Cook, M.A., ed. *Studies in the Economic History of the Middle East.* London: Oxford Univ. Press, 1970.

Cousinery, E.M. *Voyage dans le Macedoine,* vol. I. Paris, 1831.

Cvijić, Jovan. *La Peninsule balkanique.* Paris, 1918.

Gibb, H.A.R. and Bowen, Harold. *Islamic Society and the West.* 2 vols. London: Oxford Univ. Press, 1957.

Gross, Nachum. "The Habsburg Monarchy, 1750–1914." In *Fontana Economic History of Europe, The Emergency of Industrial Societies,* vol. 4, part 1, ed. Carlo Cipolla. London: Collins/Fontana, 1973.

Hassinger, Herbert. "Der Aussenhandel der Habsburgermonarchie in der zweiten Hälfte des 18. Jahrhunderts." In *Die wirtschaftliche Situation in Deutschland und Österreich um die Wende vom 18 zum 19. Jahrhundert,* ed. Friedrich Lütge. Stuttgart, 1964.

Inalcik, Halil. "Land Problems in Turkey." *Muslim World* 45 (1955):221–28.

———. *The Ottoman Empire, The Classical Age, 1300–1600.* New York: Praeger, 1973.

Karpat, Kemal H. *Social Change and Politics in Turkey.* Leiden: E.J. Brill, 1973.

Kiraly, Bela K. *Hungary in the Late Eighteenth Century.* New York: Columbia Univ. Press, 1969.

Kostić, Veselin. *Dubrovnik i Engleska, 1300–1650* [Dubrovnik and England, 1300–1650]. Belgrade, 1975.

Laiou-Thomadakis, Angliki. *Byzantine Peasant Society.* Princeton, N.J.: Princeton Univ. Press, 1977.

Mantran, Robert. *Istanbul dans la second moitié du XVIIe siècle.* Paris, 1962.

Marczali, Henry. *Hungary in the 18th Century.* Cambridge Univ. Press, 1910.

McNeill, William H. *Europe's Steppe Frontier, 1500–1800.* Chicago: Univ. of Chicago Press, 1964.

Mosley, Philip. "The Peasant Family: The Zadruga in the Balkans." In *The Cultural Approach to History,* ed. Caroline E. Ware. New York: Columbia Univ. Press, 1940.

Ostruba, Gustav. *Die Wirtschaftspolitik Maria Theresas.* Vienna, 1963.

Popović, Toma. *Turska i Dubrovnik u XVI veku* [Turkey and Dubrovnik in the Sixteenth Century]. Belgrade, 1973.

Rothenberg, Gunther E. *The Austrian Military Border in Croatia, 1522–1747.* Urbana, Ill.: Univ. of Illinois Press, 1960.

――――. *The Military Border in Croatia, 1740–1881.* Chicago: Univ. of Chicago Press, 1966.

Sadat, Deena R. "Rumeli Ayanlari: The Eighteenth Century." *Journal of Modern History* 44 (1972):346–63.

Stoianovich, Traian. "Land Tenure and Related Sectors of the Ottoman Economy." *Journal of Economic History* XIII (1953):398–411.

――――. "The Conquering Balkan Orthodox Merchant." *Journal of Economic History* XX (1960):234–313.

Sugar, Peter. *Southeastern Europe under Ottoman Rule, 1354–1804.* Seattle: Univ. of Washington Press, 1977.

Vinaver, Vuk. "Dubrovačka trgovina u Srbiji i Bugarskoj krajem XVII og veka 1660–1700" [Dubrovnik's Trade in Serbia and Bulgaria at the End of the 17th Century, 1660–1700]. *Istorijski časopis* XII–XIII (Belgrade, 1963):189–225.

Wood, A.G. *A History of the Levant Company.* London: Barnes & Noble, 1964.

b. 1850–1950

Balkanski Institut, *État économique des pays balkaniques,* vols. I and II. Belgrade, 1938.

Basch, Antonin. *The Danubian Basin and the German Economic Sphere.* New York: Columbia Univ. Press, 1943.

Berend, Ivan T. and Ranki, Gyorgy. *Economic Development in East-Central Europe in the 19th and 20th Centuries.* New York: Columbia Univ. Press, 1974.

Blaisdell, Donald C. *European Financial Control in the Ottoman Empire.* New York: Columbia Univ. Press, 1929.

Brandt, Karl. *Management of Agriculture and Food in the German-Occupied and Other Areas of Fortress Europe.* Stanford, Calif.: Stanford Univ. Press, 1953.

Brusatti, Alois, ed. *Die Habsburger Monarchie, 1848–1918, vol. I. Die wirtschaftliche Entwicklung.* Vienna, 1973.

Čubrilović, Vasa, ed., *Svetska ekonomska kriza, 1929–1934g* [The World Economic Crisis, 1929–1934]. Vol. 5. Balkanološki Institut. Belgrade, 1976.

Eddie, Scott J. "Agricultural Production and Output per Worker in Hungary, 1870–1913." *Journal of Economic History* XXVIII (1968):197–222.

Evelpidi, Ch. *Les états balkaniques.* Paris, 1930.

Geshkoff, Theodore I. *Balkan Union.* New York: Columbia Univ. Press, 1940.

Gross, Herman. *Südosteuropa, Bau and Entwicklung.* Leipzig, 1937.

Hertz, Frederick. *The Economic Problem of the Danubian States.* New York: Howard Fertig, 1970.

Hoffman, George W. *Eastern Europe: Essays in Geographic Problems.* London: Metheun, 1971.

Jensen, J.H. and Rosegger, Gerhard. "British Railway Builders along the Lower Danube, 1856–1869." *Slavonic and East European Review* XLVI (1968):105–28.

Kaser, Michael, ed., *The Economic History of Eastern Europe since 1919.* Oxford: Clarendon Press, forthcoming.

Katus, L. "Economic Growth in Hungary, 1867–1913." In *Social-Economic Researches on the History of East-Central Europe,* ed. E. Pamlényi. Budapest, 1970.

Lamer, Mirko. "Wandlungen der ausländischen Kapital auf der Balkan." *Weltwirtschaftliches Archiv* 48 (1938):470–522.

Lampe, John R. and Jackson, Marvin R. "An Appraisal of Recent Balkan Economic Historiography." *East European Quarterly* IX (1975):199–240.

Manchester Guardian Commercial: Reconstruction in Europe. Weekly, Manchester, 1919–24.

März, Eduard. *Österreichische Industrie- und Bankpolitik in der Zeit Franz Josephs I.* Vienna, 1968.

Mellor, Roy E.H. *A Geography of the Comecon Countries.* New York: Columbia Univ. Press, 1975.

Michel, Bernard. *Banques et bancaires en Autriche au debut du 20e siècle.* Paris, 1976.

Roglić, Joseph L. "Die Gebirge als die Wiege des geschichtlichen Geschehens in Südosteuropa," *Colloquium geographicum, Argumenta geographica,* 12 (Bonn, 1970):225–30.

Royal Institute of International Affairs. *The Balkan States, Economics,* vol. I. London: Oxford Univ. Press, 1936.

Rudolph, Richard L. *Banking and Industrialization in Austria-Hungary.* Cambridge: Cambridge Univ. Press, 1976.

Spulber, Nicholas. *The State and Economic Development in Eastern Europe.* New York: Random House, 1966.

———. *The Economics of Communist Eastern Europe.* New York: Praeger, 1957.

Zagoroff, S.D., Vegh, J., and Bilimovich, A.D. *The Agrarian Economy of the Danubian Countries, 1933–1945.* Palo Alto: Stanford Univ. Press, 1955.

Albania

Great Britain, Ministry of Economic Warfare. *Albania, Basic Handbook.* London, 1943.

Marmullaku, Ramodan. *Albania and the Albanians.* Hamden, Conn.: Archon Books, 1975.

Milona, Ferdinando. *L'Albania economica.* Padova, 1941.

Pascu, Dimitrie P. *Banca națională a Albaniei* [The National Bank of Albania]. Bucharest, 1936.

Pernack, Hans-Joachim. *Probleme der Wirtschaftliche Entwicklung Albaniens.* Vol. 18, Südosteuropa-Studien. Munich, 1972.

Polaccio, F. "Organization of Agricultural Statistics in Albania." *International Review of Agriculture* XXXI (Rome, Feb. 1940):1615–45.

Ronart, Otto. "L'evolution économique de l'Albanie." *Revue économique internationale* 4 (Dec. 1936):581–97.

Skendi, Stavro, ed. *Albania.* London: Atlantic Press, 1957.

Bulgaria

Barkley, H.C. *Bulgaria before the War*. London, 1877.

Bell, John W. *Peasants in Power: Alexander Stamboliski and the Bulgarian Agrarian National Union, 1899–1923*. Princeton, N.J.: Princeton Univ. Press, 1977.

Berov, Liuben. *Ikonomicheskite razvitie na Bulgariia prez vekova* [The Economic Development of Bulgaria through the Ages]. Sofia, 1974.

————. "Kapital obrazuvaneto v Bulgariia prez godinite na ftorata svetovna voina" [Capital Accumulation in Bulgaria during the Years of the Second World War]. *Trudove na V.I.I. Karl Marx*, no. 11 (Sofia, 1971):17–40.

————. "Kum vuprosa za monopolisticheskite organizatsii v Bulgariia" [Concerning the Question of Monopolistic Organizations in Bulgaria]. *Ikonomicheska misul* 7 (Sofia, 1958):67–80.

————. "Kum vuprosa za vunshnoturgovskata orientatsiia na Bulgariskiia fashizum 1929–1944" [The foreign trade orientation of Bulgarian fascism 1929–1944]. *Trudove na V.I.I. Karl Marx* 2 (Sofia, 1954):121–222.

Bobchev, S.S. "Notes comparées sur les corbacis chez les peuples balkaniques et en particulier chez les Bulgares." *Revue internationales des etudes balkaniques* III (1937–38):428–45.

Browning, Robert. *Byzantium and Bulgaria*. Berkeley, Calif.: Univ. of California Press, 1975.

Chakalov, As. *Formi, razmer i deinost na chuzhdiia kapital v Bulgariia 1878–1944* [The form, extent, and activity of foreign capital in Bulgaria 1878–1944]. Sofia, 1962.

Chilingirov, St. *Midhat Pasha i zemedelskite kasi* [Midhat Pasha and the Agricultural Banks]. Sofia, 1942.

Damianov, S. *Frantsiia i bulgarskata natsionalna revolutsiia* [France and the Bulgarian National Revolution]. Sofia, 1968.

Danailov, G. *Les effets de la guerre en Bulgarie*. Paris, 1932.

Dellin, L.A.D., ed. *Bulgaria*. New York: Praeger, 1957.

Dimitrov, Str. "Chiflishkoto stopanstvo prez 50–70-te godina na XIX vek" [The Chiflik Economy during the 1850s – 1870s]. *Istoricheski pregled* XI (Sofia, 1955):3–34.

————. "Kum istoriiata na chiflikchiistvo v Ruse" [Concerning the History of the Chiflik in Ruse] *Istoricheski pregled* XIV (Sofia, 1958):90–98.

————. "Kum vuprosa za otmeniavaneto na spahiiskata sistema v nashete zemi" [Concerning the Question of the End of the Sipahi System in our Lands] *Istoricheski pregled* XII (Sofia, 1956):27–58.

Gandev, Khristo. *Zarazhdane na kapitalisticheskite otnosheniia v chiflishkoto stopanstvo na severnozapadna Bulgariia prez XVIII vek* [Origin of Capitalist Relations in the Chiflik Economy of Northwest Bulgaria during the 18th Century]. Sofia, 1962.

Isuov, M., ed. *Problems of the Transition from Capitalism to Socialism in Bulgaria*. Sofia, 1975.

Iubileena kniga na grad Sofiia, 1878–1928 [Jubilee Book of the City of Sofia, 1878–1928]. Sofia, 1928.

Iurdanov, I. *Bulgarska Narodna Banka, 1879–1908*. Sofia, 1909.

————. *Istoriia na bulgarskata turgoviia do Osvobozhdenieto: Kratuk ochert* [A History of Bulgarian Trade until Liberation: A Short Survey]. Sofia, 1938.

————. *Prinos kum promishlenata istoriia na grad Sofiia* [Contribution to the Industrial History of Sofia]. Sofia, 1928.

Katsarkova, Vera. "Ograbvaneto na Bulgaria ot germanskiia imperializm" [The Exploitation of Bulgaria by German Imperialism]. *Trudove na V.I.I. Karl Marx* II (Sofia, 1969):164–223.

Kaunitz, F. *Donau-Bulgarien und der Balkan.* 3 vols. Leipzig, 1883.

Khristov, Khr. *Agrarnite otnoshenie v Makedoniia prez XIX i v nachaloto na XX vek* [Agrarian Relations in Macedonia in the 19th and Early 20th Centuries]. Sofia, 1964.

————. *Agrarniat vupros v Bulgarskata natsionalna revolutsiia* [The Agrarian Question in the Bulgarian National Revolution]. Sofia, 1967.

————. "Kum vuprosa za klasite i klasovite otnosheniia v bulgarskoto obshtestvo prez Vuzrazhdaneto" [On the Question of Class and Class Relations in Bulgarian Society During the Renascence]. *Izvestiia na institut istoriia* XXI (Sofia, 1970):51–85.

Kosev, D., Diculescu, Vl., and Paskaleva, V., "Za polozhenieto i stopanskata deinost na bulgarskata emigratsiia vuv Vlashko prez XIX v." [On the Position and Economic Activity of the Bulgarian Emigration to Wallachia in the 19th Century]. In *Bulgarsko-rumunski vruski i otnosheniia prez vekovete* [Bulgarian-Romanian Ties and Relations over the Centuries], ed. D. Angelov, M. Berza et al., vol. I. Sofia, 1965.

Kosev, Konst. *Za kapitalisticheskoto razvitie na bulgarskite zemi prez 60-to i 70-to godini na XIX-vek* [On the Capitalist Development of the Bulgarian Lands in the 1860s and 1870s]. Sofia, 1968.

Kozul, J.P. *La restauration financière de la Bulgarie (1922–1931).* Paris, 1932.

Lampe, John R. "Finance and Pre-1914 Industrial Stirrings in Bulgaria and Serbia." *Southeastern Europe* II (1975):23–52.

Levintov, N.G. "Agrarnyi perevorot v Bolgarii v 1877–79 gg." [The Agrarian Transition in Bulgaria, 1877–79]. In *Osvobozhdenie Bolgarii ot turetskovo iga, 1878–1953* [The Liberation of Bulgaria from the Turkish Yoke], pp. 139–221. Moscow, 1953.

Marinov, Kh. *Geografsko razpredelenie promishlenostta v Bulgariia mezhdu dvete svetovni voini* [The Geographic Distribution of Industry in Bulgaria between the Two World Wars]. Sofia, 1965.

Meininger, Thomas E. "The Formation of a Nationalist Bulgarian Intelligentsia, 1835–1878." Ph.D. Dissertation, Univ. of Wisconsin, Madison, 1974.

Milkova, Fani. *Pozemlenata sobstvenost v Bulgarskiite zemi prez XIX vek* [Agricultural Property in Bulgaria during the 19th Century]. Sofia, 1969.

Minkov, M., et al. *Poiava i razvitie na kooperativnoto zemedelie v Bulgariia pri usloviiata na kapitalizma* [Appearance and Development of Cooperative Agriculture in Bulgaria under Conditions of Capitalism]. Sofia, 1968.

Moloff, J.S., "Bulgarian Agriculture." In *Agricultural Systems of Middle Europe,* ed. O.S. Morgan. 1933. Reprint, New York: AMS Press, 1969.

Natan, Zhak, et al. *Istoriia na ikonomicheski misul v Bulgariia* [A History of Economic Thought in Bulgaria]. 2 vols. Sofia, 1973.

———. *Ikonomika na Bulgariia, Vol. I, Ikonomika no Bulgariia do sotsialisticheska revolutsiia.* Sofia, 1969.

Nedelchev, Kiril. *Parichnoto delo v Bulgariia, 1879–1940* [Monetary Affairs in Bulgaria, 1879–1940]. Sofia, 1940.

Paskaleva, V. "Ikonomicheskite pronikvane na Avstriia v bulgarskite zemi, 1857–1877" [The Austrian Economic Penetration of the Bulgarian Lands, 1857–1877]. *Isvestiia na institut na Bulgarskata istoriia* 7 (Sofia, 1957):113–62.

Pasvolsky, Leo. *Bulgaria's Economic Position after the War.* Washington, D.C.: Brookings Institution, 1930.

Popov, Nikola, et al. *Ikonomika na Bulgariia.* Vol. II. *Ikonomika na Bulgaria prez prekhodniia period ot kapitalizma do sotsializma* [The Economy of Bulgaria during the Transition Period from Capitalism to Socialism]. Sofia, 1972.

Sakazov, Ivan. *Bulgarische Wirtschaftsgeschichte.* Berlin and Leipzig, 1929.

Spisanie na bulgarskoto ikonomichesko druzhestvo. Vols. I–XXXVIII. Bimonthly, Sofia, 1896–1940.

Todorov, Nikolai. *Balkanskiiat grad, XV–XIX vek* [The Balkan Town, 15th–19th centuries]. Sofia, 1972.

Todorova, Svetana. *Diplomaticheska istoriia na vunshnite zaemi na Bulgariia, 1878–1912* [A Diplomatic History of Bulgarian Foreign Loans, 1878–1912]. Sofia, 1971.

Tsonchev, Petur. *Iz stopansko minalo na Gabrovo* [From the Economic Past of Gabrovo]. Sofia, 1929.

Vasiliev, V. "Za glavnite faktori na industrialniia podem (1925–1929)" [Concerning the Main Factors of the Industrial Boom (1925–1929)]. *Izvestiia na instituta za istoriia* XI (Sofia, 1962):83–100.

Weiss-Bartenstein, W.K. *Bulgariens Volkswirtschaft und ihre Entwicklungsmoglichkeiten.* Berlin, 1918.

Wilhelmy, Herbert. *Hochbulgariens.* 2 vols. Kiel, 1935.

Zagoroff, S.D. *The Economy of Bulgaria.* Washington, D.C.: Council for Economic and Industry Research, 1955.

Greece

Alexander, A.P. *Greek Industrialists: An Economic and Social Analysis.* Athens, 1966.

Andreades, A. *Les effets économiques et sociaux de la guerre en Grèce.* New Haven, Conn.: Yale Univ. Press, 1926.

Boujour, Felix. *A View of the Commerce of Greece 1787–1797.* Translated by Thomas H. Howe. London, 1800.

Boyazoglu, Alex. J. *Contribution a l'étude de l'économie rurale de la Grèce d'apres la guerre.* Paris, 1931.

Candilis, Wray O. *The Economy of Greece, 1944–1966.* New York: Praeger, 1968.

Coutsoumaris, George. *The Morphology of Greek Industry.* Athens, 1963.

Dakin, Douglas. *The Unification of Greece, 1770–1923.* London: Ernest Benn, 1972.

Delivanis, Dimitrie, and Cleveland, William C. *Greek Monetary Developments, 1939–1948.* Bloomington, Ind.: Indiana Univ. Publications, 1949.

Eulambio, M.S. *The National Bank of Greece.* Athens, 1924.

Evelpidi, Ch. *La reforme agraire en Grèce.* Athens, 1926.

———. *E georgia tës Ellados* [The Agriculture of Greece]. Athens, 1944.

———. *Theoria kai praxis agrotikës politikës kai oikonomias* [Theory and Practice of Agricultural Policy and Economics], vol. A. Athens, 1939.

Great Britain, Naval Intelligence Division, *Greece.* 2 vols. London: H.M. Printing Office, 1944.

Kremmydas, Vasilas. *To emporio teo Peleponnesa sto 18 aiono* [The Market of the Peloponnesus during the 18th Century]. Athens, 1972.

Kyriazi, Damianos. *Zur Entwicklung des Gewerbes im heutigen Griechenland.* Athens, 1916.

Lefevre-Meaulle, H. *La Grèce économique et financière en 1915.* Paris, 1915.

Leon, George B. "The Greek Merchant Marine, 1750–1850." In *The Greek Merchant Marine, 1453–1850,* ed. S.A. Papadapoulos. Athens: National Bank of Greece, 1972.

Martin, Percy F. *Greece in the 20th Century.* London: Unwin, 1913.

McGrew, William M. "The Land Issue in the Greek War of Independence." In *Hellenism and the Greek War of Liberation,* ed. N.D. Diamandouros. Institute of Balkan Studies Monograph no. 156. Thessaloniki, 1977.

Mears, Eliot G. *Greece Today: The Aftermath of the Refugee Impact.* Stanford, Calif.: Stanford Univ. Press, 1929.

Miller, William. *Greek Life in Town and Country.* London, 1915.

Pentzopoulos, Dimitri. *The Balkan Exchange of Minorities and Its Impact on Greece.* Paris and The Hague, 1962.

Pepelasis, A.A. "Greece," in Pepelasis, A.A. et al., *Economic Development: Analysis and Case Studies,* pp. 500–22. New York: Harper, 1966.

———. "The Legal System and the Economic Development of Greece." *Journal of Economic History* XIX (June, 1959):173–98.

Petropoulos, John A. "The Compulsory Exchange of Populations: Greek-Turkish Peacemaking, 1922–1930." *Byzantine and Modern Greek Studies* 2 (1976):137–60.

Servakis, G. and Pertountzi, C. "The Agricultural Policy of Greece." In *Agricultural Systems of Middle Europe,* ed. O.S. Morgan, pp. 137–200. 1933. Reprint New York: AMS Press, 1969.

Sivignon, M. "The Demographic and Economic Evolution of Thessaly 1881–1940." In *An Historical Geography of the Balkans,* ed. F.W. Carter, pp. 379–408. New York: Academic Press, 1977.

Stinopolou, Ep. K. *Istoria tës Ethnekis Trapezis tës Ellados* [History of the National Bank of Greece]. Athens, 1966.

Svoronos, Nicholas. *Le commerce de Salonique en XVIIIme siècle.* Paris, 1956.

Sweet-Escott, Beckham. *Greece, A Political and Economic Survey, 1939–1953.* London: Royal Institute of International Affairs, 1954.

Thompson, Kenneth. *Farm Fragmentation in Greece: The Problem and Its Setting.* Athens, 1963.

Tourpalis, Dimitrios. *Die Bankwesen Griechenlands.* Wurtzberg, 1933.

Tsamis, Demetre. *L'evolution monetaire en Grèce 1928–1938.* Nancy, 1939.

Tsouderos, *La relevement économique de la Grèce.* Paris-Nancy, 1919.

Vakolopoulos, A.P. *A History of Thessaloniki.* Thessaloniki, 1963.

————. *History of Macedonia, 1354–1883.* Thessaloniki, 1973.

Varvaressos, K. *Report on Greek Economic Problems.* Washington, D.C.: IBRD mimeograph, 1952.

Vlachos, E. *An Annotated Bibliography on Greek Migration.* Athens: Social Sciences Center, 1966.

Vouras, Paul P. *The Changing Economy of Northern Greece since World War II.* Thessaloniki, 1962.

Wilcox, G.M. *Education in Modern Greece.* Tiffin, Ohio: Commercial Printing Co., 1933.

Wynne, William H. *State Insolvency and Foreign Bondholders,* vol. II. New Haven, Conn.: Yale Univ. Press, 1951.

Zolotas, Xenophon. *Griechenland auf dem Weg zur Industrialisierung.* Athens, 1926.

————. "Wirtschaftstruktur Griechenlands." In *Mittel und Südosteuropa Wirtschaftsfragen,* ed. Herman Gross. Leipzig, 1933.

Romania

Adam, I. and Marcu, N. *Studii despre dezvoltarea capitalismului în agricultura Rominiei* [Studies Concerning the Development of Capitalism in the Agriculture of Romania]. 2 vols. Bucharest, 1959.

Adăniloaie, N. and Berindei, Dan. *Reforma agrară de la 1864* [The Agrarian Reform of 1864]. Bucharest, 1967.

Arcadian, N.P. *Industrializarea României.* Bucharest, 1936.

————. *Legislaţia industrială a României din ultimii douăzeci de ani (1916-1936)* [Industrial Legislation of Romania during the Last Twenty Years (1916–1936)]. Bucharest, 1937.

Băicoianu, C. Fl. *Istoria politicei noastre monetare şi a Băncii Naţionale, 1880–1914* [The History of Our Monetary Policy and the National Bank]. 2 vols. Bucharest, 1932.

————. *Istoria politicei noastre vamale şi comerciale* [The History of our Tariff and Commercial Policies]. 2 vols. Bucharest, 1904.

Bozga, V. *Criza agrară in România dintre cel două războaie mondiale* [The Agrarian Crisis in Romania between the Two World Wars]. Bucharest, 1975.

Berindei, Dan. *Oraşul Bucureşti, 1459–1862* [The Town of Bucharest, 1459–1862]. Bucharest, 1963.

Bernath, Mathias. *Habsburg und die Anfänge der Rumänischen Nationbildung.* Leiden: E.J. Brill, 1972.

Buşe Constantin. "Le commerce exterieur de la Moldavie par le port du Galaţi, 1837–1847." *Revue roumaine d'histoire* XII (1973):301–307.

Cârtâna, I. and Seftiuc, I. *Dunărea în istoria poporului român* [The Danube in the History of the Romanian People]. Bucharest, 1972.

Chirot, Daniel. *Social Change in a Peripheral Society: The Creation of a Balkan Colony*. New York: Academic Press, 1976.

Cojocaru, Ion. *Şcolile technice-professionale şi de specialitate din statul român, 1864–1918* [Technical-Professional and Specialized Schools of the Romanian State, 1864–1918]. Bucharest, 1971.

Columbeanu, Sergiu. *Grandes exploitations domaniales en Valachie au XVIII siècle*. Bucharest, 1974.

Constantinescu, N.N. *Din istoricul formării şi dezvoltărei clasei muncitoare în România* [On the History of the Formation and Development of the Working Class in Romania]. Bucharest, 1959.

———. *Situaţia clasei muncitoare din România, 1914–1944* [The Situation of the Working Class in Romania, 1914–1944]. Bucharest, 1968.

Constantinescu, N.M. and Axenciuc, V. *Capitalismul monopolist în România* [Monopoly Capitalism in Romania]. Bucharest, 1962.

Constantiniu, Florin. *Relaţiile agrare din ţara Românească în secolul al XVIII-lea* [Agrarian Relations in Wallachia in the 18th Century]. Bucharest, 1972.

Corbu, Constantin. *Ţărănimea din Romania din perioada 1848–1864* [The Peasantry of Romania, 1848–1864]. Bucharest, 1973.

Corfus, Ilie. *L'agriculture en Valachie durant la premiere moitié du XIX siècle*. Bucharest, 1969.

Diculescu, Vl. *Bresle, negustori şi meseriaşi în Tara Românească, 1830–1848* [Guilds, Merchants and Artisans in Wallachia, 1830–1848]. Bucharest, 1973.

Dobrovici, Gh. M. *Istoricul datoriei publice a România* [The History of Public Debt in Romania]. Bucharest, 1913.

Dragomirescu, Gheorge. *Controlul întreprinderilor publice economice* [The Control of Public Enterprises]. Bucharest, 1939.

Egyed, A. "Geneza şi situaţia proletariatului agaricol din Transilvania" [Origin and Situation of the Agrarian Proletariat in Transylvania]. *Anuarul Institutului de Istorie din Cluj*, X (Cluj, 1967):202–13.

Eidelberg, Philip G. *The Great Romanian Peasant Revolt of 1907, The First Modern Jacquerie*. Leiden: E.J. Brill, 1974.

Emerit, Marcel. *Les Paysans roumains depuis le traite d'Adrianople*. Paris, 1937.

Enciclopedia României, vols. I–IV. Bucharest, 1938–43.

Ghelase, Jon I. *Mocanii: Importanţa şi evoluţia lor social-economică în România* [Mocanii: Their Socioeconomic Importance and Evolution in Romania]. Bucharest, 1938.

Giurescu, C.C. *Contribuţiuni la studiul originelor şi dezvoltării burgheziei române pînă la 1848* [Contributions to the Study of Romanian Bourgeois Origins and Development to 1848]. Bucharest, 1972.

———. *Istoria Bucureştilor*. Bucharest, 1966.

Göllner, Carl. *Die Siebenbürgische Militärgrenze*. Munich: R. Oldenbourg Verlag, 1974.

Hajnal, Henry. *The Danube*. The Hague, 1920.

Haseganu, I. *Mărginenii în viaţa economică a Transilvaniei* [Border People in the Economic Life of Transylvania]. Brasov, 1941.

Ionescu, Stefan. *Bucureşti în vremea fanarioţilor* [Bucharest in Phanariot Times]. Cluj, 1974.

Ioaniţui, G. and Calmuschi, C. *Industria zahărului în România* [The Sugar Industry in Romania]. Bucharest, 1936.

Ioaniţui, G. and Costache, N. *Industria cimentului în România* [The Cement Industry in Romania]. Bucharest, 1932.

———. *Industria hârtiei în România* [The Paper Industry in Romania]. Bucharest, 1929.

Ionescu, Lazar. *Relaţiile între Banca Naţională a Romîniei şi stat, 1880–1935* [Relations between the Romanian Bank and the State, 1880–1935]. Bucharest, 1935.

Ionescu-Siteşti, G. *L'agriculture de la Roumanie pendant la guerre.* New Haven, Conn.: Yale Univ. Press, 1929.

Iosa, M. "Rascoală ţăranilor din 1907—premise şi semnificaţii" [The Peasant Revolt of 1907—Theories and Facts]. *Revista de istorie* 30 (Bucharest, 1977):183–98.

Iovanelli, M.F. *Industria românească, 1934–38.* Bucharest, 1975.

Istoria Romîniei, vols. III and IV. Bucharest, 1964 and 1965.

Kovacs, Josif. *Desfiinţarea relaţiilor feudale în Transilvania* [The Dissolution of Feudal Relations in Transylvania]. Cluj, 1973.

Kiriţescu, C.C. *Sistemul bănesc al leului şi precursorii lui* [The Monetary System of the Leu and its Predecessors]. 3 vols. Bucharest, 1964, 1967, 1971.

Lampe, John R. "Varieties of Unsuccessful Industrialization: The Balkan States before 1914," *Journal of Economic History* XXV (1975):56–85.

Leontieş, Demetrius. *Die Industrialisierung Rumäniens bis zum zweiten Weltkrieg.* Munich, 1971.

Lupu, M.A. ed. *Istoria economiei a României.* Bucharest, 1974.

Madgearu, V. *Evoluţia economiei romaneşti după războiul mondial* [Evolution of the Romanian Economy after the World War]. Bucharest, 1940.

Manoilescu, Mihail. *Politica producţiei naţionale* [National Production Policy]. Bucharest, 1923.

Marguerat, Phillipe. *Le III Reich et le petrole roumain, 1938–1940.* Leiden: A.W. Sijthoff, 1977.

Marinescu, B. "Economic Relations between the Romanian Principalities and Great Britain." *Revue roumaine d'histoire* VIII (Bucharest, 1969):271–81.

Meteş, Stephan. *Emigrări româneşti din Transilvania în secolele XIII-XX* [Romanian Migration from Transylvania, 13th–20th Centuries]. Bucharest, 1971.

Mihordea, V. *Relaţiile agrare din secolul al XVIII-lea în Moldava* [Agrarian Relations in the 18th Century in Moldavia]. Bucharest, 1968.

Mitrany, David. *The Land and the Peasant in Romania.* New Haven, Conn.: Yale Univ. Press, 1931.

Murgesu, Costin. *Casa regală şi afacerile cu devize, 1935–1940* [The "Casa Regala" and Foreign Currency Manipulation, 1935–1940]. Bucharest, 1970.

Murgesu, Costin, Constantinescu, N.N., et al. *Contribuţii la istoria capitalului straăn în Romînia* [Contributions to the History of Foreign Capital in Romania]. Bucharest, 1960.

Netta, G. *Die Handelsbeziehungen zwischen Leipzig and Ost- und Südost-europa.* Zurich, 1920.

Nicolae, C. *Organizarea și conținutul învățămîntului profesional și tehnic din România, 1864–1948* [Organization and Content of Professional and Technical Education in Romania, 1864–1948]. Bucharest, 1973.

Oțetea, A. et al., *Marea răscoală a țaranilor din 1907* [The Great Revolt of the Peasants in 1907]. Bucharest, 1967.

Parpală, O. *Aspecte din agricultura României, 1920–1939.* Bucharest, 1966.

Pascu, Şt., et al. *Die Agrarfrage in der österreichische-ungarische Monarchie.* Bucharest, 1965.

Pearton, Maurice. *Oil and the Romanian State, 1895–1948.* London: Oxford Univ. Press, 1971.

Penela, Georgeta. *Les foires de la Valachia pendant la periode 1774–1848,* Bucharest, 1973.

———. "Relații economice dintre Țara Românească și Transilvania în epoca regulamentara" [Economic Relations between Wallachia and Transylvania in the Reglement Epoch, 1829–1848]. In *Studii și Materiale de istoria modernă,* vol. IV, ed. N. Adăniloaie and Dan Berendei. Bucharest, 1973.

Popovici, V., ed. *Dezvoltarea economiei Moldovei, 1848–1864* [The Development of the Economy of Moldavia, 1848–1864]. Bucharest, 1963.

Razmiritza, N. *Essai d'économie roumaine moderne, 1831–1931.* Paris, 1931.

Roberts, Henry L. *Rumania: Political Problems of an Agrarian State.* New Haven: Yale Univ. Press, 1951.

Roman, Louis. "Demographie historique de la Roumaine, 1972–1978: Bibliographie analytique." *Revue roumaine d'histoire* XIX (Bucharest, 1980):85–127.

Rossetti, Radu. *Pentru ce s'au rasculat țaranii* [Why the Peasants Revolted]. Bucharest, 1908.

Sitescu, P.M. *Die Kreditbanken Rumänien.* Bucharest, 1915.

Slăvescu, Victor. *Băncile comerciale mijlocii din România* [Middle-Sized Commercial Banks of Romania]. Bucharest, 1915.

———. *Istoricul Băncii Naționale a României, 1880–1924* [History of the National Bank of Romania, 1880–1924]. Bucharest, 1925.

———. *Marile băncii comerciale din România* [The Large Commercial Banks of Romania]. Bucharest, 1915.

Sonia, G. *Naționalizarea principalelor mijloace de producție în România* [The Nationalization of the Principal Means of Production in Romania]. Bucharest, 1968.

Stan, Apostol. *Le problème agraire pendant la revolution de 1848 en Valachie.* Bucharest, 1971.

Ştefanescu Şt. "Istorie și demografie." *Studii: Revista de istorie* XX (Bucharest, 1967):933–46.

Sturdza, D.A. *Les Travaux de la Commission Européene des Bouches du Danube, 1859 and 1911.* Vienna, 1913.

Tardeanu, Lucien I. *Avuția publică în România* [Public Wealth in Romania]. Bucharest, 1941.

Tatos, I.I. and Ivănescu, I. *Industria morăritului în România* [The Milling Industry in Romania]. Bucharest, 1941.

Torrey, Glenn E. "Rumania and the Belligerents, 1914–1916." *Journal of Contemporary History* 1 (July, 1966):171–91.

Tucker, Jack. "The Romanian Peasant Revolt of 1907: Three Regional Studies." Ph.D. Dissertation, Univ. of Chicago, 1972.

Turnock, David. "Bucharest: The Selection and Development of the Romanian Capital." *Scottish Geographic Magazine* 86 (1970):53–68.

———. "The Industrial Development of Romania from the Unification of the Principalities to the Second World War." In *An Historical Geography of the Balkans,* ed. New York: Academic Press, 1977.

Vajda, L. "Capitalul strain în minerit-metalurgie a Transilvaniei, 1867–1900" [Foreign Capital in the Mining-Metallurgy of Transylvania, 1867–1900]. *A M Napocensis* IX (Cluj, 1972):243–53.

———. "Despre situatia economică şi social-politică în Transilvania în primele anii de sec. XX-lea" [Concerning the Economic and Sociopolitical Situation in Transylvania in the Early 20th Century]. *Studii şi materiale de istorie moderne* I (Bucharest, 1957):285–350.

Vişa, A. *Monopoluri şi carteluri în România.* Bucharest, 1963.

Xenopol, Nicholas. *La Richesse de la Roumaine.* Bucharest, 1916.

Zane, G. *Economia de schimb în Principatele Române* [The Exchange Economy in the Romanian Principalities]. Bucharest, 1930.

———. *Industria din România în a doua jumătate a secolului al XIX-lea* [Industry in Romania in the Second Half of the 19th Century]. Bucharest, 1970.

Yugoslavia and Its Predecessors

Acta historico-oeconomica iugoslaviae. Vol. I– , Zagreb, 1974– .

Aleksić-Pejković, L. *Odnosi Srbije ca Francuskom i Engleskom, 1903–1914* [Relations of Serbia with France and England, 1903–1914]. Belgrade, 1965.

Anaćijević, D. "Trgovački i zelenaški kapital u Srbiji u prvoj polovini devetnaestog veka" [Trade and Usury Capital in Serbia in the First Half of the 19th Century]. Ph.D. dissertation, Skopje Univ., 1956.

Andrejević, S. *Ekonomski razvoj Niša od 1830 do 1946 g.* [The Economic Development of Nis from 1830 to 1946]. Nis, 1970.

Apostolov, A. "Posledice velike ekonomske krize za makedonske agrarne privede" [Consequences of the Great Economic Crisis for the Macedonian Agricultural Economy]. *Jugoslovenski istoriski časopis* XXII (Belgrade, 1973):181–88.

Arsitch, Berrisav. *La vie économique de la Serbie au sud au 19me siècle.* Paris, 1936.

Bajkitch, V. *Monnaies, banques et bourses en Serbie.* Nancy, 1926.

Bibliographia historico-oeconomica iugoslaviae. Zagreb, 1978.

Bićanić, Rudolf. "Ekonomske promene u Hrvatskoj izazvane stvaranjem Jugoslavije, 1918" [Economic Changes in Croatia Occasioned by the Creation of Yugoslavia, 1918]. In *Prilozi za ekonomsku provijest Hvratske*

[Contributions to the Economic History of Croatia], pp. 82–112. Zagreb, 1967.

———. *Doba manufakture u Hrvatskoj i Slavoniji, 1750–1860* [The Era of Manufacturing in Croatia and Slavonia, 1750–1860]. Zagreb, 1951.

Bitoski, Krste, ed. *Istorija na železnicite vo Makedonija, 1873–1973* [The History of Railroads in Macedonia, 1873–1973]. Skopje, 1973.

———. "Kneževstvo Srbije kao pazar i tranzitna teritorija za makedonskite trgovci" [Serbia as a Market and Transit Territory for Macedonian Merchants]. *Glasnik* X (Skopje, 1966):113–33.

Blagojević, Miloš. *Zemljoradnje u srednovekovnoj Srbiji* [Agriculture in Medieval Serbia]. Belgrade, 1973.

Bojanovski, Dime, Tsonev, Kiril, and Penovska, Ana. *Razvitokot na zemedelstvoto vo Makedonije* [Development of Agriculture in Macedonia]. Skopje, 1955.

Bösendorfer, Josip. *Agrarni odnosi u Slavoniji* [Agrarian Relations in Slavonia]. Zagreb, 1950.

Bulajić, Žharko. *Agrarni odnosi u Crnoj Gori, 1878–1912* [Agrarian Relations in Montenegro, 1878–1912]. Titograd, 1959.

Castellan, Georges. *La vie quotidienne en Serbie, 1815–1839*. Paris, 1967.

Čehak, Kalman. *Radnički pokret u Banatu, 1868–1890* [The Workers' Movement in the Banat]. Novi Sad, 1971.

Čubrilović, Vasa, ed. *Istorija Beograda*, 3 vols. Belgrade, 1974.

Ćunković, S. *Prosveta, obrazovanje i vaspitanje u Srbiji* [Higher, Secondary, and Primary Education in Serbia]. Belgrade, 1971.

Cvijetić, L. "Prva Srpska Banka" [The First Serbian Bank]. *Istorijski glasnik* 2–3 (Belgrade, 1964):97–121.

Despot, Miroslava. *Industrija gradjanske Hrvatske, 1860–1873* [The Industry of Civil Croatia, 1860–1873]. Zagreb, 1970.

———. *Pokušaji manufakture u gradjanskoj Hrvatskoj u 18om stoleću* [Attempts at Manufacturing in Civil Croatia in the 18th Century]. Zagreb, 1962.

Djordjević, D. "Austro-ugarski okupacioni režim u Srbiji i njegov slom" [The Austro-Hungarian Occupation of Serbia and Its Fall]. In *Naučni skup u povodu 50-godišnice raspada Austro-ugarske monarhije i stvaranje jugoslovenske države* [Scientific Gathering on the 50th Anniversary of the Fall of the Austro-Hungarian Monarchy and the Creation of the Yugoslav State], ed. Vasa Čubrilović. Zagreb, 1969.

———. *Carinski rat Austro-Ugarske i Srbije, 1906–1911* [The Tariff War between Austria-Hungary and Serbia, 1906–1911]. Belgrade, 1962.

Djordjević, Tihomir. *Iz Srbije Kneza Miloša* [From the Serbia of Prince Miloš]. Belgrade, 1924.

Djurović, S. "Struktura aksionarskih društava u Beogradu izmedju 1918–1929g." [The Structure of Joint Stock Companies in Belgrade between 1918–1929]. *Acta historica-oeconomica iugoslaviae* IV (Zagreb, 1977):139–60.

Dobos, Manuela. "The Croatian Peasant Uprising of 1883." Ph.D. dissertation, Columbia Univ., 1974.

Erceg, Ivan. *Trst i bivše habsburške zemlje u medjunarodnom prometu*

[Trieste and the Former Habsburg Lands in International Trade]. Zagreb, 1970.

Erić, M. *Agrarna reforma u Jugoslaviji, 1918–1941* [The Agrarian Reform in Yugoslavia, 1918–1941]. Sarajevo, 1958.

Gaćeša, N. *Agrarna reforma i kolonizacija u Sremu, 1918–1941* [Agrarian Reforms and Colonization in the Srem, 1918–1941]. Novi Sad, 1975.

Gavrilović, Slavko. *Agrarni pokreti u Sremu i Slavoniji na početkom XIX veka* [Agrarian Movements in the Srem and Slavonia at the Start of the 19th Century]. Belgrade, 1960.

―――. *Prilog istoriji trgovine i migracije Balkan-podunavlje, XVIII-XIX* [Contribution to the History of Trade and Migration in the Danubian Balkans, 18th–19th centuries]. Belgrade, 1969.

Glomzaitch, M. *Histoire du credit en Serbie*. Nancy, 1926.

Glomazić, Momir. *Istorija državne hipotekarne banke, 1862–1932* [History of the State Mortgage Bank, 1862–1932]. Belgrade, 1933.

Great Britain, Naval Intelligence Division. *Jugoslavia*. 4 vols. London, 1945.

Von Haan, Hugo. "Labour Conditions in a Rationalized Shoe Factory: The Bata Works at Borovo, Yugoslavia," *International Labor Review* XXVI (1937):780–811.

Hammel, E.A. "The Zadruga as Process." In *Households in Past and Present*, ed. Peter Laslett and Marilyn Clarke. Cambridge: Cambridge Univ. Press, 1972.

Hauptmann, Ferdo. "Bosanske financije i Kalleyeva industrijska politika" [Bosnian Finances and Kallay's Industrial Policy]. *Glasnik arhiva Bosne i Hercegovine* XII (Sarajevo, 1972):61–69.

―――. "Regulisanje zemlišnog posjeda u Bosni i Hercegovini i počeci naseljavanja stranih seljaka" [The Regulation of Land Holding in Bosnia-Hercegovina and the Initial Settlement of Foreign Peasants]. *Godišnjak Bosne i Hercegovine* XVI (Sarajevo, 1967):151–71.

Hočevar, Toussaint. *Structure of the Slovenian Economy, 1848–1963*. New York: Studia Slovenica, 1965.

Hrelja, Kemal. *Sarajevo u revoluciji* [Sarajevo in Revolution]. Sarajevo, 1976.

Institut za savremenu istoriju. *The Third Reich and Yugoslavia, 1933–1945*. Belgrade, 1977.

Ivić, Aleksa. *Migracije Srba u Hrvatsku tokum 16, 17, u 18og stoleća* [Serbian Migrations to Croatia during the 16th, 17th, and 18th Centuries]. Subotica, 1926.

Jankulov, B. *Pregled kolonizacije Vojvodine u XIX i XX st.* [A Survey of the Colonization of the Vojvodina in the 19th and 20th Centuries]. Novi Sad, 1961.

Jarak, N. *Poljoprivredna politika u Bosni i Hercegovini i zemljoradnicke zadruge* [Agricultural Policy in Bosnia-Hercegovina and Agricultural Cooperatives]. Sarajevo, 1956.

Jordan, Sonja. *Die Kaiserliche Wirtschaftspolitik im Banat in 18. Jahrhundert*. Munich, 1967.

Jovanović, Slobodan. *Ustavobranitelji, 1838–1858* [The Defenders of the Constitution, 1838–1858]. Belgrade, 1912.

Jovanovich, M. *Die serbische Landwirtschaft*. Munich, 1906.

Juzbašić, Dz. "Problemi austrougarske saobraćajne politike u Bosni i Hercegovini" [Problems of Austro-Hungarian Transport Policy in Bosnia-Hercegovina]. *Godišnjak društva istoričara Bosne i Hercegovine* XIX (Sarajevo, 1973):96–138.

Kapidžić, H. "Agrarno pitanje u Bosni i Hercegovini, 1878–1918" [The Agrarian Question in Bosnia and Hercegovina, 1878–1918]. In *Jugoslovenski narodi pred prvi svetski rat* [The Yugoslav Peoples before the First World War], ed. Vasa Čubrilović, pp. 93–117. Belgrade, 1967.

———. "Ekonomska emigracija iz Bosne i Hercegovine u SAD početkom XX vijeka" [Economic Emigration from Bosnia-Hercegovina to the U.S.A. at the Start of the 20th Century]. *Glasnik ADA Bosne i Hercegovina* VII (Sarajevo, 1967):191–220.

Karaman, Igor. *Privreda i društvo Hrvatske u 19om stoljeću* [The Economy and Society of Croatia in the 19th Century]. Zagreb, 1972.

———. "Osnova oblilježja razvitke industrijske privrede u sjevernoj Hrvatskoj" [Basic Features in Industrial Development in Northern Croatia]. *Acta historico-oeconomica iugoslaviae* I (Zagreb, 1974):37–60.

Kojić, Branislav. *Varošice u Srbiji u XIX v.* [Small Towns in Serbia in the 19th Century]. Belgrade, 1970.

Kolar-Dimitrijević, M. *Radni slojevi Zagreba od 1918 do 1931* [The Working Classes of Zagreb from 1918 to 1931]. Zagreb, 1973.

Kovačević, I. *Ekonomiski polažaj radničke klase u Hrvatskoj i Slavoniji, 1867–1914* [The Economic Position of the Working Class in Croatia and Slavonia, 1867–1914]. Zagreb, 1972.

Kresevljanović, Hamdja. *Gradska privreda i esnafi u Bosni i Hercegovini* [The Urban Economy and Guilds in Bosnia and Hercegovina], vol. I. Sarajevo, 1949.

Kukla, Stanislav. *Razvitak kreditne organizacije u Srbiji.* [Development of Credit Organization in Serbia]. Zagreb, 1924.

Lampe, John R. "Financial Structure and the Economic Development of Serbia, 1878–1912." Ph.D. dissertation, Univ. of Wisconsin, 1971.

———. "Serbia, 1878–1912." In *Banking and Economic Development: Some Lessons of History,* ed. Rondo Cameron. New York: Oxford Univ. Press, 1972.

———. "Unifying the Yugoslav Economy, 1918–1921: Misery and Misunderstandings." In *The Creation of Yugoslavia, 1914–1918,* ed. Dimitrije Djordjević. Santa Barbara, Calif.: ABC-Clio Press, 1980.

Meyer, Milan. *Die Landwirtschaft der Königreichen Kroatien und Slavonien.* Univ. of Leipzig, 1908.

Milenković, Vl. *Ekonomska istorija Beograda.* Belgrade, 1932.

Milić, Danica. *Strani kapital u rudarstvu Srbije do 1918 g.* [Foreign Capital in Serbian Mining until 1918]. Belgrade, 1971.

———. *Trgovina Srbije, 1815–1939* [The Commerce of Serbia, 1815–1839]. Belgrade, 1959.

Milić-Krivodoljanin, B. *Zbornik radova o selu* [Collection of Works on the Village]. Belgrade, 1970.

Mirković, Mijo. *Ekonomska istorija Jugoslavije.* Zagreb, 1968.

Mohorić, Ivan. *Zgodivina železnic na Slovenskem* [A History of the Railroads in Slovenia]. Ljubljana, 1968.

Narodno blagostanje [National Wealth]. Monthly, Belgrade, 1929–40.

Obradović, S.D. *La politique commerciale de la Yougoslavie*. Belgrade, 1939.

Palairet, Michael R. "The Influence of Commerce on the Changing Structure of Serbia's Peasant Economy, 1860–1912." Ph.D. dissertation, Edinburgh Univ., 1976.

Pejić, L. "Ekonomske ideje Dr. Milan Stojadinovića i balkanski privredni problemi" [The Economic Ideas of Dr. Milan Stojadinović and Balkan Economic Problems]. *Balkanika* VII (Belgrade, 1976):241–68.

Petranović, B. *Politička i ekonomska osnova narodne vlasti u Jugoslaviji za vreme obnova* [The Political and Economic Foundation of the People's Power in Yugoslavia during the Rebirth]. Belgrade, 1969.

Petrovich, Michael B. *A History of Modern Serbia, 1804–1918*. 2 vols. New York: Harcourt Brace Jovanovich, 1976.

Popović, Dušan. *O cincarima* [Concerning the Tsintsars]. Belgrade, 1937.

Popović, M.D. *Kragujevac i njegovo privredno područje* [Kragujevac and its Economic Area]. Belgrade, 1956.

Radosavljevich, M. *Die Entwicklung der Währung in Serbien*. Berlin and Munich, 1912.

Schmid, Ferdinand. *Bosnien und die Herzegovenien*. Leipzig, 1914.

Simunčić, Z. "Osnovne karaktaristike industrialnog razvitka na području Hrvatske u medjuratnom razdoblju" [Basic Characteristics of Industrial Development in Croatia during the Interwar Period]. *Acta historica oeconomiae iugoslaviae* I (Zagreb, 1974):63–75.

Sokolov, L. *Bibliografije za stopanskata istorija na Makedonija* [Bibliography of the Economic History of Macedonia], vol. I (to 1945). Skopje, 1955.

———. *Industrijata na N R Makedonija* [Industry in the People's Republic of Macedonia]. Skopje, 1961.

Šorn, "Razvoj industrije v Sloveniji med obem vojnama" [Development of Industry in Slovenia between the Wars]. *Kronika časopis za slovensko krajevno zgodovino* 6–7 (Ljubljana, 1958–59):10–20.

Spasić, Z. *Kragujevačka vojna fabrike, 1853–1953* [The Kragujevac Military Factory, 1853–1953]. Belgrade, 1973.

Stojančević, B. *Miloš Obrenević i njegovo doba* [Miloš Obrenović and His Era]. Belgrade, 1966.

Stanojević, M.L. "Die Landwirtschaft in Serbien." Ph.D. dissertation, Univ. of Halle, 1912.

Stojsavljević, B. *Povijest sela Hrvatske, Slavonije i Dalmacije, 1848–1918* [The History of the Village in Croatia, Slavonia, and Dalmatia, 1848–1918]. Zagreb, 1973.

———. *Seljaštvo Jugoslavije 1918–1941* [Agriculture of Yugoslavia]. Zagreb, 1952.

Sugar, Peter. *The Industrialization of Bosnia-Hercegovina, 1878–1918*. Seattle: Univ. of Washington Press, 1964.

Timet, T. "Razvitak hipotekarnih i komunalnih zajmova . . . kod novčanih zavoda u Hrvatskoj i Slavoniji [The Development of Communal and Mortgage Loans . . . Among the Banks of Croatia and Slavonia]. *Prilozi za ekonomsku povijest Hrvatske* [Contributions to the Economic History of Croatia], pp. 143–62. Zagreb, 1967.

————. *Stanbena izgradnja Zagreba do 1954* [The Construction of Zagreb to 1954]. Zagreb, 1961.

Todorović, D. "Karakteristiki na stopanskite odnosi vo Makedonija od 1919 do 1922" [Characteristics of Economic Relations in Macedonia From 1919 to 1922]. *Glasnik institut za natsionalna istorija* 18, (Skopje, 1974):65–77.

Tomasevich, Jozo. *Peasants, Politics and Economic Development in Yugoslavia*. Palo Alto, Calif.: Stanford Univ. Press, 1955.

————. "Postwar Foreign Economic Relations." In *Yugoslavia*, ed. Robert J. Kerner. Berkeley, Calif.: Univ. of California Press, 1949.

Ugričić, Miodrag. *Novčani sistem Jugoslavije* [The Money System of Yugoslavia]. Belgrade, 1968.

Vučo, Nikola. *Agrarna kriza, 1930–1934*. Belgrade, 1968.

————. *Raspadanje esnafa u Srbiji*, [The Collapse of the Guilds in Serbia]. 2 vols. Belgrade, 1954–55.

Vukmanović, M. *Radnička klasa Srbije u drugoj polovini XIX veka* [The Working Class of Serbia in the Second Half of the 19th Century]. Belgrade, 1972.

Wünscht, Joachim. *Jugoslawien und das Dritte Reich*. Stuttgart, 1969.

Živković, N. *Ratna šteta koju je Nemačka učinila Jugoslaviji u drugom svetskom ratu* [War Damage Done by Germany to Yugoslavia during the Second World War]. Belgrade, 1975.

Zografski, Dončo. *Razvitokot na kapitalicheskite elementi vo Makedonija* [The Development of Capitalist Elements in Macedonia]. Skopje, 1967.

National Economic Development, 1950–1980*

Allen, Mark, "The Bulgarian Economy in the 1970's." In *East European Economies Post-Helsinki*, Joint Economic Committee of the U.S. Congress, pp. 647–97. Washington, D.C.: U.S. Government Printing Office, 1977.

Alton, Thad P., et al. *Official and Alternative Consumer Price Indexes in Eastern Europe, Selected Years, 1960–1979*. Occasional Papers of the Research Project on National Income in East Central Europe, OP-60. New York: L.W. International Financial Research, Inc., 1980.

Bajt, Alexander. "Investment Cycles in European Socialist Economies: A Review Article." *Journal of Economic Literature*, IX (March, 1971):53–63.

Bombelles, Joseph. *The Economic Development of Communist Yugoslavia, 1947–1964*. Stanford, Calif.: Hoover Institute, 1968.

Bornstein, Morris. "Unemployment in Capitalist Regulated Market Economies and Socialist Centrally Planned Economies." *American Economic Review* 68 (May, 1978):38–43.

Botsas, E.N. "The Trade Stability of Balkan Economies, 1956–1970." *Weltwirtschaftliches Archiv* 111 (1975):573–84.

Brada, Josef C., ed. *Quantitative and Analytical Studies in East-West Economic Relations*. Studies in East European and Soviet Planning, Devel-

*No sources in Southeastern European languages have been cited for the period 1950–1980.

opment and Trade No. 24. Bloomington, Ind.: International Development Research Center, 1976.

Brada, Josef C., and Jackson, Marvin R. "Strategy and Structure in the Organization of Romanian Foreign Trade." In *East European Economies Post-Helsinki*, Joint Economic Committee of the U.S. Congress, pp. 1260–1276.

Dimitrijević, Dimitije and Macesich, George. *Money and Finance in Contemporary Yugoslavia*. New York: Praeger, 1973.

Dubey, Vinod, et al. *Yugoslavia: Development with Decentralization*. Baltimore, Md.: Johns Hopkins Univ. Press, 1975.

Feiwell, George R. *Growth and Reforms in Centrally Planned Economies: The Lessons of the Bulgarian Experience*. New York: Praeger, 1977.

Germidis, Dimitrios A. and Negreponti-Delivanis, Maria. *Industrialization, Employment and Income Distribution in Greece*. Paris: OECD, 1975.

Granick, David. *Enterprise Guidance in Eastern Europe*. Princeton Univ. Press, 1975.

Grossman, Gregory, ed. *Money and Plan: Financial Aspects of East European Economic Reforms*. Berkeley: Univ. of California Press, 1968.

Grothusen, Klaus-Detlev, ed. *Jugoslawien. Südosteuropa-Handbuch*. vol. I. Göttingen, 1975.

———. *Rumänien. Südosteuropa-Handbuch*, vol. II. Göttingen, 1977.

Halikias, D.J. *Money and Credit in a Developing Economy: The Greek Case*. New York: New York Univ. Press, 1978.

Hamilton, F.E.I. *Yugoslavia: Patterns of Economic Activity*. New York: Praeger, 1968.

Hočevar, Toussaint. "Economic Determinants in the Development of the Slovene National System." *Working Paper Series No. 8*. New Orleans, La.: Department of Economics and Finance, Louisiana State Univ., 1973.

Hoffman, George W. *Regional Development Strategy in Southeastern Europe*. New York: Praeger, 1972.

Höhmann, Hans Hermann, Kaser, Michael, and Thalheim, Karl C., eds. *The New Economic Systems of Eastern Europe*. Berkeley, Calif.: Univ. of California Press, 1975.

Horvat, Branko. *The Postwar Evolution of Yugoslav Agricultural Organization*. New York: IASP, 1974.

———. *The Yugoslav Economic System*. New York: IASP, 1976.

Jackson, Marvin R. "Bulgaria's Economy in the 1970's: Adjusting Productivity to Structure," and "Romania's Economy at the End of the 1970's: Turning the Corner on Intensive Development." In *East European Country Studies 1980*, Joint Economic Committee of the U.S. Congress, pp. 571–617 and 231–97. Washington, D.C.: U.S. Government Printing Office, 1980.

———. "Industrialization, Trade and Mobilization in Romania's Drive for Economic Independence." In *East European Economies Post-Helsinki*, Joint Economic Committee of the U.S. Congress, pp. 886–940.

———. "Perspectives on Romania's Economic Development in the 1980's." In *Romania in the 1980's*, ed. Daniel N. Nelson. Boulder, Colo.: Westview Press, 1981.

———. "Prices and Efficiency in Romanian Foreign Trade." In *Quantitative and Analytical Studies in East-West Economic Relations,* ed. Joseph C. Brada.

Kaser, Michael, and Schnytzer, Adi. "Albania: A Uniquely Socialist Economy." In *East European Economies Post-Helsinki,* Joint Economic Committee of the U.S. Congress, pp. 567–646.

Lampe, John R. "The Study of Southeastern European Economies, 1966–1977." *Balkanistica,* IV (1977-78):63–88.

Lazarchik, Gregor. *Bulgarian Agricultural Production, Output, Expenses, Gross and Net Product, and Productivity, at 1968 Prices, for 1939 and 1948–1970.* New York: Riverside Research Institute, 1973.

Lazarchik, Gregor, and Pall, George. *Roumania: Agricultural Production, Output, Expenses, Gross and Net Product, and Productivity, 1938, 1948, 1950–71.* New York: Riverside Research Institute, 1973.

Logan, M.I. "Regional Economic Development in Yugoslavia, 1953–1964." *Tydschrift voor Economische en Sociale Geographie* 59 (1968):42–52.

Maddison, Angus, Stavrianopoulos, Alexander, and Higgins, Benjamin. *Foreign Skills and Technical Assistance in Greek Development.* Paris: OECD, 1966.

McNeill, William H. *The Metamorphosis of Modern Greece since World War II.* Chicago: Univ. of Chicago Press, 1978.

Montias, John Michael. *Economic Development in Communist Rumania.* Cambridge, Mass.: M.I.T. Press, 1967.

Ofer, Gur. "Specialization in Agriculture and Trade: Bulgaria and Eastern Europe." In *East European Integration and East-West Trade,* ed. Paul Marer and John Michael Montias. Bloomington, Ind.: Indiana Univ. Press, 1980.

Organization for Economic Cooperation and Development. *Agricultural Policy in Yugoslavia.* Paris: OECD, 1973.

———. *Agricultural Policy in Greece.* Paris: OECD, 1973.

———. *Economic Surveys, Yugoslavia.* Annual, Paris, 1961– .

———. *Economic Surveys, Greece.* Annual, Paris, 1961– .

Panas, E.G. "Greece." In Organization for Economic Cooperation and Development. *Utilization of Savings,* pp. 224–44, Paris: OECD, 1968.

Pryor, Frederic L. "Some Costs and Benefits of Markets: An Empirical Study." *Quarterly Journal of Economics* XCI (Feb. 1977):81–102.

Sacks, Stephen R. *Entry of New Competitors in Yugoslav Market Socialism.* Berkeley, Calif.: Institute of International Studies, 1973.

Shaw, Lawrence H. *Postwar Growth in Greek Agricultural Production.* Athens, 1969.

Staller, George. *Bulgaria: A New Industrial Production Index, 1963–1972.* New York: L.W. International Research, 1975.

Tsantis, Andreas C., and Pepper, Roy. *Romania: The Industrialization of an Economy under Socialist Planning.* Washington, D.C.: World Bank, 1979.

Tyson, Laura D'Andrea. *The Yugoslav Banking System and Monetary Control—Trade Credit and Illiquidity Crises in the Yugoslav Economy.* Geneva: ILO, 1975.

———. "The Yugoslav Economy in the 1970's: A Survey of Recent Developments and Future Prospects." In *East European Economies Post-Helsinki*, Joint Economic Committee of the U.S. Congress.

Tyson, Laura D'Andrea and Eichler, Gabriel. "Continuity and Change in the Yugoslav Economy in the 1970s and 1980s." In *East European Country Studies 1980*, Joint Economic Committee of the U.S. Congress.

United Nations, Economic Commission for Europe. *A Survey of The Economic Situation and Prospects of Europe*. Geneva, 1948.

————. *Economic Survey of Europe 1948–* . Geneva, 1949– .

————. *Economic Bulletin for Europe*. Vol. I– (April, 1948–). Geneva, 1948– .

Index